THE CAMBRIDGE HISTORY OF CHINA

General Editors
DENIS TWITCHETT and JOHN K. FAIRBANK

Volume 13
Republican China 1912–1949, Part 2

THE CAMBRIDGE HISTORY OF CHINA

Volume 13
Republican China 1912–1949, Part 2

edited by
JOHN K. FAIRBANK

and

ALBERT FEUERWERKER

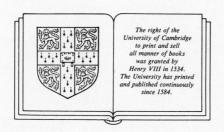

*The right of the
University of Cambridge
to print and sell
all manner of books
was granted by
Henry VIII in 1534.
The University has printed
and published continuously
since 1584.*

CAMBRIDGE UNIVERSITY PRESS

CAMBRIDGE

LONDON   NEW YORK   NEW ROCHELLE
MELBOURNE   SYDNEY

Published by the Press Syndicate of the University of Cambridge
The Pitt Building, Trumpington Street, Cambridge CB2 1RP
32 East 57th Street, New York, NY 10022, USA
10 Stamford Road, Oakleigh, Melbourne 3166, Australia

First published 1986

Printed in Great Britain by the
University Press, Cambridge

British Library cataloguing in publication data

The Cambridge history of China.
Vol. 13, Republican China 1912–1949, Part 2.
1. China – History
I. Twitchett, Denis   II. Fairbank, John King
III. Feuerwerker, Albert
951   DS735

Library of Congress cataloguing in publication data

(Revised for volume 13)
Main entry under title:
The Cambridge history of China.
Vol. 13 edited by John K. Fairbank and
Albert Feuerwerker.
Includes bibliographies and indexes.
Contents: – v. 3. Sui and T'ang China,
589–906, pt. 1. – v. 10. Late Ch'ing, 1800–
1911, pt. 1. – v. 13. Republican China, 1912–1949, pt. 2.
1. China – History.   I. Twitchett, Denis Crispin.
II. Fairbank, John King, 1907–   . III. Feuerwerker, Albert.
DS735.C3145   951'.03   76-29852

ISBN 0 521 24338 6

GENERAL EDITORS' PREFACE

As the modern world grows more interconnected, historical understanding of it becomes ever more necessary and the historian's task ever more complex. Fact and theory affect each other even as sources proliferate and knowledge increases. Merely to summarize what is known becomes an awesome task, yet a factual basis of knowledge is increasingly essential for historical thinking.

Since the beginning of the century, the Cambridge histories have set a pattern in the English-reading world for multi-volume series containing chapters written by specialists under the guidance of volume editors. *The Cambridge Modern History*, planned by Lord Acton, appeared in sixteen volumes between 1902 and 1912. It was followed by *The Cambridge Ancient History*, *The Cambridge Medieval History*, *The Cambridge History of English Literature*, and Cambridge Histories of India, of Poland, and of the British Empire. The original *Modern History* has now been replaced by *The New Cambridge Modern History* in twelve volumes, and *The Cambridge Economic History of Europe* is now being completed. Other Cambridge Histories include a history of Islam, of Arabic literature, of Iran, of Judaism, of Africa, and of China.

In the case of China, Western historians face a special problem. The history of Chinese civilization is more extensive and complex than that of any single Western nation, and only slightly less ramified than the history of European civilization as a whole. The Chinese historical record is immensely detailed and extensive, and Chinese historical scholarship has been highly developed and sophisticated for many centuries. Yet until recent decades the study of China in the West, despite the important pioneer work of European sinologists, had hardly progressed beyond the translation of some few classical historical texts, and the outline history of the major dynasties and their institutions.

Recently Western scholars have drawn more fully upon the rich traditions of historical scholarship in China and also in Japan, and greatly advanced both our detailed knowledge of past events and institutions, and also our critical understanding of traditional historiography. In addition, the present generation of Western historians of China can also draw upon the new outlooks and techniques of modern Western historical scholarship, and upon recent developments in the social sciences, while continuing to build upon the solid foundations of rapidly progressing European, Japanese and Chinese sinological studies. Recent historical events, too, have given prominence to new problems, while throwing into question many older conceptions. Under these multiple impacts the Western revolution in Chinese studies is steadily gathering momentum.

When *The Cambridge History of China* was first planned in 1966, the aim was to provide a substantial account of the history of China as a bench mark for the Western history-reading public: an account of the current state of knowledge in six volumes. Since then the out-pouring of current research, the application of new methods, and the extension of scholarship into new fields, have further stimulated Chinese historical studies. This growth is indicated by the fact that the History has now become a planned fifteen volumes, but will still leave out such topics as the history of art and of literature, many aspects of economics and technology, and all the riches of local history.

The striking advances in our knowledge of China's past over the last decade will continue and accelerate. Western historians of this great and complex subject are justified in their efforts by the needs of their own peoples for greater and deeper understanding of China. Chinese history belongs to the world, not only as a right and necessity, but also as a subject of compelling interest.

JOHN K. FAIRBANK
DENIS TWITCHETT

CONTENTS

MAPS

TABLES

PREFACE TO VOLUME 13

The titanic drama of the Chinese revolution is hardly known, as yet, to the English-reading public, though in the twenty-first century it will be seen in retrospect as a major event of modern times. The fifteen authors of this volume are pioneers in its exploration and analysis. Their work, like all historical writing, may both help the understanding of the current generation and serve researchers now and later. The bibliography, bibliographical essays and glossary are designed to aid researchers. The text and index are aimed at non-specialist readers.

After a preliminary overview stressing economic and social history, chapters 2, 3 and 4 present a narrative of events in China's foreign relations to 1931 and in the political history of the Nationalist government and its Communist opponents from 1927 to 1937. The middle chapters from 5 to 9 then analyse key facets of Chinese society – economic, social, governmental, educational and literary – offering critical appraisals of the major achievements and problems in each of these areas. Chapters 10 to 14 concern the climactic impact of Japan's invasion, China's war of resistance, the civil war to 1949, and the portentous development of the thought of Mao Tse-tung up to his coming to power.

In the production of this volume of *The Cambridge history of China*, as with volumes 10, 11 and 12 that preceded it, the editors are chiefly indebted to the contributors. Some of them participated in a research conference in 1976. Their admirable patience has been exceeded only by their good sense in recognizing that a pluralistic symposium may possibly wrap up more wisdom than monographs can do separately. For the overview of 1800 to 1949 offered in chapter 1, her co-authors are especially indebted to the leadership of Mary B. Rankin. As before, we wish to thank Chiang Yung-chen for skilled bibliographical assistance, Joan Hill for indefatigable administrative and editorial assistance, and Katherine Frost Bruner for sapient indexing. We are indebted for space to Harvard University and for support of editorial costs to the Ford Foundation, the Mellon Foundation, and the National Endowment for the Humanities through the American Council of Learned Societies. Most basically we wish to thank the Cambridge University Press for its vision of history as the underpinning of civilization – a Chinese idea from ancient times. Our bibliography and essays at the back in fact testify to the achievements of generations of Chinese and also Japanese and other scholars of many lands who have laid the foundation on which this kind of book can be set up, as a stepping stone to further work.

JOHN K. FAIRBANK
ALBERT FEUERWERKER

On romanization

For purely technical reasons we continue, as in preceding volumes, to use the Wade-Giles system for transcription of Chinese sounds into alphabetic writing. The technical reasons are first, that our library catalogues and reference works have generally accumulated over the years in the Wade-Giles system, and a change would therefore handicap researchers who use this volume; second, the references to persons and places in the source materials on modern China in English, such as newspaper and correspondence files, both official and unofficial, are also generally embalmed in Wade-Giles forms so that a change would confuse some readers. At the same time we note that names and terms in publications today, both from the People's Republic and from around the world, are using the official *pinyin* romanization, based on the incontrovertible assumption that a nation has the right to decide how it wishes its writing system to be romanized abroad. To meet this situation we have inserted a conversion table at the back of the book and in the Glossary-Index have also inserted cross-references from major *pinyin* forms to Wade-Giles forms.

To avoid enslavement by the arbitrary nature of any romanization system, we have consciously tolerated deviations, especially in personal names. Thus the reader will sometimes find chow instead of chou, yi instead of i, hwa for hua, teh for te. (Such deviations need not be called to our attention.) We also take no responsibility for the name Chen, which should often be Ch'en.

CHAPTER 1

INTRODUCTION: PERSPECTIVES ON MODERN CHINA'S HISTORY

Words are blunt and slippery tools for carving up and dissecting the past. The history of modern China cannot be characterized in a few words, however well chosen. The much used term 'revolution' is sometimes less useful than 'revival', while the term 'modern transformation' signifies little more than 'change through recent time' and leaves us still ignorant of what 'time' is. At a less simplistic level, however, each of the twenty-eight authors writing in volumes 10 to 13 of this series has offered generalizations about events and trends in China within the century and a half from 1800 to 1949. Making more inclusive generalizations about less inclusive ones is no doubt the historian's chief activity, yet most of the writers in these four volumes would accept the notion that the broader a generalization is, the farther it is likely to be removed from the concrete reality of events. In this view the postulating of all-inclusive processes (such as progress or modernization) or of inevitable stages (such as feudalism, capitalism, and socialism) generally belongs to metahistory, the realm of faith. While we need not deny such terms to those who enjoy them, we can still identify them as matters of belief, beyond reason.[1]

At a less general level, however, social science concepts help us to explain historical events. Though history is not itself a social science, its task is to narrate past happenings and to synthesize and integrate our present-day understanding of them. For this purpose, metaphor has long been a principal literary device of narrative history. Cities fall, wars come to an end, hopes soar, but conditions ripen for an uprising and prospects for progress grow gloomy – on and on, we describe social events largely in metaphoric terms derived from the senses. Social scientists, too, having to use words, write of structures, levels, downswings, acceleration or equilibria. Increasingly, however, mid-level concepts derived from social science analyses are used to explain how events occurred, relating one to another. Chapter 1 of volume 12 suggested, for example, that the concept of 'Maritime China', as an area of different ecology, economy, politics

[1] For helpful comments on this chapter we are indebted to Marianne Bastid-Bruguière, Paul A. Cohen, Michael Gasster, Philip A. Kuhn and Ramon Myers, among others.

and culture from 'Continental China', might be used to describe the channels by which foreign influences came into Chinese society. In this framework, the present chapter is concerned primarily with Continental China. Moreover, since volumes 10, 11 and 12 dealt mainly with political, economic and intellectual history, the present chapter seeks to take account of recent work in the rapidly developing area of social history.

The reader will note at once that the customary attempt to treat 'China' as a unitary entity is becoming attenuated by the great diversity of circumstances disclosed by closer study. The old notion of 'China's cultural differentness' from the outside world, though it still strikes the traveller, is becoming fragmented by the variety of sub-cultures to be found within China. 'Chinese culture' as an identifiable style of configuration (created by the interplay of China's distinctive economy, polity, social structure, thought and values) becomes less distinctive and identifiable as modern international contact proceeds. As our knowledge grows, generalization becomes harder, not easier.

Nevertheless we venture to begin at a high level of generality by asserting that the Chinese revolution of the twentieth century has differed from all other national revolutions in two respects – the greater size of the population and the greater comprehensiveness of the changes it has confronted. China's size has tended to slow down the revolution, while its comprehensiveness has also tended to prolong it.

Consider first the flow of events: China underwent in the nineteenth century a series of *rebellions* (White Lotus, 1796–1804; Taiping, 1850–64; Nien, 1853–68; Muslim, 1855–73) and a series of *foreign wars* (British, 1839–42; Anglo-French, 1856–60; French, 1883–5, Japanese, 1894–5; and the Boxer international war of 1900). There followed in the twentieth century a series of *revolutions*: the Republican Revolution of 1911 that ended the ancient monarchy, the Nationalist Revolution of 1923–8 that established the Kuomintang party dictatorship, the Communist Revolution that set up the People's Republic in 1949, and Mao Tse-tung's Cultural Revolution of 1966–76.

These milestones suggest that China's old order under the Ch'ing dynasty of the Manchus was so strongly structured and so skilled in self-maintenance that it could survive a century of popular rebellions and foreign attacks. Yet its very strength undid it. It was so slow to adapt itself to modern movements of industrialism and nationalism, science and democracy, that it ensured its eventual demise.

Sheer size contributed to this slowness. Before the building of telegraph lines in the 1880s, for instance, communication between Peking and the provincial capitals at Foochow and Canton by the official horse post required at least a fortnight in each direction. The empire could not react quickly. The imperialist wars of the nineteenth century were largely decided by foreign naval power on the periphery of Chinese life. For example, the 50 million people of Szechwan (now 100 million) were never invaded even by the Japanese in 1937–45. China's '400 million' (now 1,000 million) remained until recently unintegrated by widespread literacy, a daily press, telecommunications or ease of travel by steamship, rail or bus. Change could come only slowly to peasant life on the land.

The comprehensiveness of change in modern China is a matter of dispute between two schools of interpretation which posit linear and cyclical patterns. The linear view stresses the influence of modern growth not only in population and economy but especially in technology of production, political nationalism and scientific thinking, which all contribute to what some envision as 'modernization' and others are content to call an overall revolution. The cyclical view sees a repetition of phases: decline of central power, civil war and foreign invasion, widespread disruption and impoverishment, military revival of central power, resumption of livelihood and growth. We incline to see these patterns overlapping in various combinations. Innovation and revival are not incompatible: modern China has borrowed from abroad but even more from its own past.

From 1800 to 1949 China's cultural differentness strongly persisted even though it was diminishing. Cocooned within the Chinese writing system (which Japan, Korea and Vietnam broke out of by adding to it their own phonetic systems), the bearers of China's great tradition preserved its distinctive cultural identity as stubbornly and skilfully as the Ch'ing dynasty preserved its power to rule. In fact, the symbiosis of China's old state and culture was one secret of their longevity together.

If we look for a moment at the realm of thought and ideology, the tenets of Confucianism had legitimized both imperial rule at Peking and family patriarchy in the village. The dynastic monarchy collapsed only after Confucianism had been disrupted by the tenets of evolution and Social Darwinism.[2] The idea of the survival of the fittest among nations implied that the Manchu rulers and indeed imperial Confucianism lacked the capacity to lead the Chinese nation. It was as if the French Revolution, instead of building upon ideas of the Enlightenment, had had to go further back and begin by renouncing Plato, Aristotle and Descartes, as well as the Virgin Mary. As one political scientist has remarked, 'Total revolutions, such as the one in France that began in 1789 or the one that

---

[2] See James Reeve Pusey, *China and Charles Darwin*; also *The Cambridge history of China* (*CHOC*) 12, ch. 7 (Charlotte Furth).

has transformed China during this century, aim at supplanting the entire
structure of values and at recasting the entire division of labor. In France
between 1789 and 1797 the people employed violence to change the
systems of landholding, taxation, choice of occupation, education,
prestige symbols, military organization, and virtually every other characteristic of the social system.'[3]

For China, this statement might go even further. The comprehensiveness
of the Chinese revolution was evident in its reappraisal of the whole
Chinese past. The fact that modern science and technology, leading on
into industrialization and modern armament, came from abroad, in fact
from the imperialist West, put China's revolutionary generation in a
greater dilemma than European revolutionaries (to say nothing of
Americans) had ever faced. America's political leaders could quote British
authorities in support of their revolutionary actions. French revolutionaries could find support in their own European heritage. For the
Chinese leadership of the early twentieth century, in contrast, the
intellectual authorities legitimizing their revolution were largely from
outside the country – and this in a land famous for being self-sufficient
in all things! A revolution in such terms, whether those of Rousseau,
Locke, Mill, Marx or Kropotkin, was subversive of the old China in the
most complete sense. While realizing the claims of nationalism, it
questioned the worth of China's historical achievements. These intellectual
demands of the revolution were hard for many patriots to accept. In fact,
the twin claims of science and democracy had implications too radical even
for many of Sun Yat-sen's generation. The displacement from tradition
was too great. This made it easier for patriots nostalgic for China's wealth
and power to speak of revival, putting their new wine in old bottles,
as has happened in the later phases of other revolutions.

Our historical thinking today about China's revolution is inevitably
multi-track, using analytic concepts from economics, sociology, anthropology, politics, literature and so on. We find useful many mid-level concepts
in the respective disciplines, but patterns of analysis that seem supportable
on one track may have no exact counterparts on other tracks. Incon-
sistencies may even appear among them. Since each line of analysis is
marked by phases, we begin with periodization.

CHANGE AND CONTINUITY: PERIODIZATION

Despite much continuity, China from 1800 to 1949 underwent tremendous
changes. The political system, especially the relationship between state

[3] Chalmers Johnson, *Revolutionary change*, 2nd ed., 126.

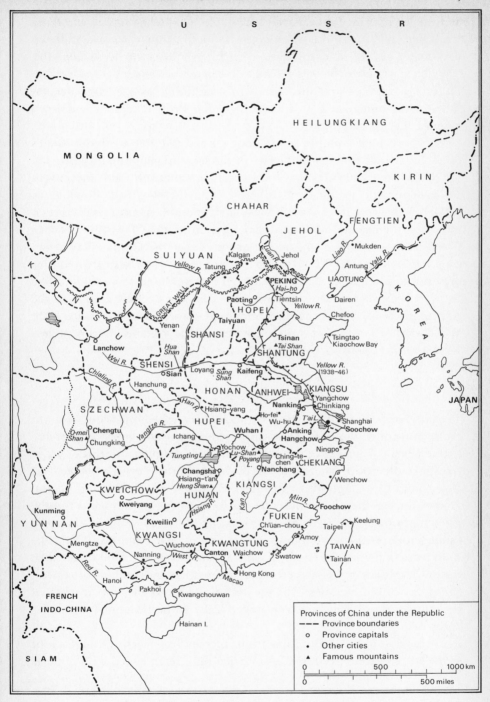

MAP 2. Provinces of China under the Republic

and society, changed decisively. The old Confucian social structure weakened; new social classes emerged. Parts of the economy were drawn into world trade; industrialization began in cities. Intellectual inquiry broadened in scope; it was refocused through selection and adaptation of foreign ideas. Rural life, although continuing in the same general mould, was punctuated by natural disasters, riots, rebellions and wars, culminating in revolution.

Efforts to find a simple progression or a single key to the dynamics of all this change founder in the face of the size and geographical diversity of the country, differences of local social organization, and unevenness of development in different spheres. Nonetheless, it is possible to subdivide this century and a half into shorter periods so as to reveal certain trends or themes and also important discontinuities. To begin modern Chinese history from 1840, on the grounds that the Opium War began a period of decisive Western impact, would overemphasize foreign as opposed to internal causes of change. We prefer 1800 as a dividing line between the prosperous, expansive, self-confident Chinese empire of the eighteenth century and the disruption and disorders of the nineteenth. We discern four periods, each covered by a volume in this series: 1800–1864, 1865–1911, 1912–1930, 1931–1949.

1800–1864

The first period, until the major mid-century rebellions were brought under control in the mid-1860s, displayed many phenomena interpreted as traditional symptoms of dynastic decline: for example, systems of water transport and control began to break down, partly through neglect but also ironically through over-expansion. Excessive dike building in central Hunan during the eighteenth century to create more farmland for the growing population restricted waterways and blocked drainage channels, leading to a protracted flooding in this rich agricultural area. Along the Yangtze, conflicting interests of officials and local elites inhibited dike repair. Water control elsewhere suffered from similar conflicts of interest and decay of old facilities. The greatest disaster was the shift in 1853 of the course of the Yellow River, never really to be brought back under control.[4]

Corruption in the metropolitan bureaucracy had reached a high point in the late eighteenth century. The Ch'ien-lung reign ended with popular

---

[4] See Pierre-Étienne Will, *Bureaucratie et famine en Chine au 18ᵉ siècle*; and review article by R. B. Wong and P. C. Perdue, 'Famine's foes in Ch'ing China', *Harvard Journal of Asiatic Studies* (*HJAS*), 43.1 (June 1983) 291–332.

unrest: riots, protests against taxes and rent, and rebellions inspired by both heterodox millenarian sects and socio-economic dislocation. Invasion of the imperial palace during an otherwise minor sectarian rising in 1813 shocked the court and metropolitan officials.[5] By the late 1850s rebellions were seriously threatening to bring down the dynasty. Minority peoples on the borders took advantage of disorder in the central provinces to launch their own rebellions.[6] Pirates operated along the coast, and Western nations began to attack the seaboard cities and exact political and economic concessions.

In the face of these problems the government appeared weak. Its armies were unable to suppress rebels, its taxes inadequate to pay the cost of doing so. Difficulties in grain transport along the Grand Canal threatened Peking's food supply. The nineteenth-century emperors appeared timid and incompetent in comparison with their brilliant and forceful predecessors. Official corruption and negligence seemed widespread. Suppression of the major rebellions by newly organized, regionally based armies suggested a decentralization of power was under way, while deflation contributed to governmental fiscal problems and more general economic retrenchment.

However, the traditional downswing of the dynastic cycle did not cover two major aspects of this period. First, the population grew to truly unprecedented levels. Whereas there were 200–250 million people in China in 1750, there were 410–430 million in 1850.[7] The economic, social, political, and administrative repercussions of this growth could not be simply cyclical in character. Second, the imperialist West, powered by the industrial technology and economic expansiveness of Western capitalism, posed a more fundamental challenge than China's previous nomadic invaders. These two factors alone meant that changes would transcend cyclical patterns. The wave of rebellions threatening the old order in the mid-nineteenth century failed. Reorganized government armies with superior fire power would limit the scope of popular upheaval for the rest of the century. Impetus for change was not thereby cut off, but reappeared in other channels.

1865–1911

In the second period growth and innovation became more prominent than decline and decay. The latter did not, of course, disappear. For example,

---

[5] Susan Naquin, *Millenarian rebellion in China: the Eight Trigrams uprising of 1813.*

[6] See S. M. Jones and P. A. Kuhn, 'Dynastic decline and the roots of rebellion', *CHOC* 10, especially 132–44.

[7] Dwight Perkins, *Agricultural development in China 1368–1969*, 207–14.

famines were caused by floods on the North China plain in the late 1870s and in the Yangtze and Huai River valleys in the 1900s. Rural unrest, which had diminished after the end of the mid-century rebellions, increased again after 1890, along with the growth of anti-dynastic secret societies.

Such manifestations of decline were, however, accompanied by new developments that would continue into the twentieth century. The startling military threat of imperialism roused an effort at self-defence through Western-style industralization and modern army building. New types of official-entrepreneurs and educated army officers emerged. Foreign trade and industry in treaty ports produced compradors, merchant-capitalists, professional people and factory workers. While these new urban social classes were coming into being, a genuine public opinion, roused by patriotism and spread through the treaty-port press, became a political factor in the 1880s. Activist political organization among the scholar elite began in the reform movement of the 1890s. Various elite elements then clashed with and became alienated from the existing political authority. Some turned to foreign examples and ideas for ways both to strengthen the country and to further political or personal goals. The result was a vast expansion in the range and nature of intellectual inquiry, which brought into question the fundamental tenets of the Confucian world view and social order.[8]

Major rebellions of the mid-nineteenth century had originated in peripheral or impoverished areas: the Kwangsi hills populated by Hakka, the flood-plagued plains of Huai-pei, the homelands of the Miao tribes in south-west China and the Muslim areas of the south-west and north-west. In the late nineteenth and early twentieth centuries, however, major political activity arose in the wealthy economic cores: the Canton delta, the urbanized Lower Yangtze, the middle Yangtze with its rich agricultural lands and emerging industrial centres. The major actors, too, now included the new social groups within the fragmented elite.

During the last decade of the Ch'ing, the competition between bureaucratic leaders of the central government and a variety of provincially based social elites attained a new height in Chinese politics. Reform and change were in the air, accepted on both sides. The issue was whether the new and greater political and economic potential of the state should continue, like the old, to be centralized in the bureaucratic monarchy, or should be diffused so that policies could reflect initiatives of elite groups outside the government. This question forecast a significant shift in the relationship of the state to the society. It ensured that the 1911 Revolution would not be just another dynastic change.

[8] See M. Bastid-Bruguière, 'Currents of social change', *CHOC* 11.535–602.

1912–1930

Many claim that the 1911 Revolution did little to alter rural social relationships; some even question whether it was a revolution at all. There were indeed many continuities running through 1911. Industrial growth continued in urban centres – for example, around Tientsin and in southern Manchuria as well as in the mid- and Lower Yangtze and the southern coast. Despite the disintegration of central power and military competition between warlords, some provinces like Chekiang were relatively stable and free of war. Even in places like Kwangsi, where there was considerable fighting, it often avoided disrupting the agricultural schedule. Political activity and organization remained centred in the cities.

As the new trends continued, however, differences in degree became differences in kind. The modern economic sector developed more rapidly than the rural sector. The new social classes, aided by the emancipation of youth and women, continued to reshape the old social structure. Meanwhile vernacular literature and the popular press, intellectual debate and the idea of mass mobilization, became increasingly significant. The disappearance of the emperor and the old political structure changed the sources of legitimacy and profoundly altered the nature of politics. Han Chinese nationalism, an overt concern for China, replaced loyalty to an imperial dynasty.

Second, in the absence of the imperial institution, military power became a more important political factor than it had been since the end of the Taiping Rebellion, and operated with a freedom from civil control impossible under the Ch'ing. But since military power was too fragmented to win control of the country, a third major change of this period was the effort by out-of-power urban elites to mobilize the lower classes in politics. This extension of participation was attempted by new, more-than-factional party organizations that tried to encourage and control such mobilization. It was accompanied by new political ideologies of Marxism-Leninism and Sun Yat-sen's Three People's Principles.

The goals of revolution and the nature of radicalism changed. The 1911 Revolution had been largely an elite rebellion against the centralized bureaucratic monarchy. Political radicalism began by espousing national-istic and racial themes against the Ch'ing political structure. A social radicalism also arose against the authoritarian Confucian familial bonds. This strain culminated in the individualism, demands for further liberation of youth and women, and enthusiasm for science and democracy of the New Culture movement. Subsequently during the May Fourth movement radicalism was redefined in class terms to further the needs of workers and peasants against warlords, capitalists and landlords. Revolution now meant both national liberation from 'imperialism' and class struggle against 'feudalism' – goals which radicals sought to combine, while conservatives sought to keep them apart.

In the mid-1920s the revolution expanded by combining military and party organization with anti-imperialist patriotism and a mobilization of workers and peasants under the leadership of urban intellectuals. The Communist-Nationalist alliance and Northern Expedition were logical culminations of this period. The break in 1927 between the Chinese Communist Party (CCP) plus their left-wing Kuomintang (KMT) allies and the right-wing of the KMT revealed the contradiction in aims that had been temporarily obscured by shared nationalism and opposition to warlords. Establishment of the Nanking government, controlling at the outset only about two provinces, left undecided the question whether changes would be brought about by a new bureaucratic modernizing state or by continued efforts to mobilize broader participation on a more egalitarian and less centralized basis.[9]

1931–1949

Three events at the beginning of the 1930s decade profoundly affected the course of Chinese history. First, in 1931 the world economic depression hit China. Abandonment of the gold standard by Britain and Japan forced a dramatic devaluation of the Chinese silver-based currency, while US government purchases drained silver from China. Foreign markets for silk and other exports collapsed, and Japanese dumping damaged the staggering cotton textile industry. Agricultural prices in commercialized core areas dropped faster than prices generally, to about half their 1929–31 levels, hurting both farmers and landlords.[10] Capital was scarce, interest rates were up, urban workers unemployed, governments had problems collecting revenues. Severe floods in the Yangtze basin in 1931 and an equally disastrous drought in 1934 made matters worse for the Nationalists. Despite some evidence of recovery in 1936, economic improvement was forestalled by the Japanese attack. In the 1940s run-away inflation wrecked the livelihood of the urban middle classes, and played havoc with Nationalist government finances. Rural areas tended to economic autarky.

Second, the Japanese seized Mukden in September 1931, conquered Manchuria, established a puppet government, took control of Hopei and

---

[9] See C. M. Wilbur, 'The Nationalist Revolution: from Canton to Nanking, 1923–28', *CHOC* 12.527–720.
[10] See *CHOC* 12.71–2.

in 1937 began a full-scale war against all China. Japan's occupation of the most developed areas near the coast, but not the entire country, completely altered the terms of the Nationalist-Communist political competition. The question became who could best mobilize the populace and build up military strength in the more rural and less modernized parts of the country. War shifted the balance away from bureaucratic modernization towards social revolution.

Third, the CCP established its Kiangsi soviet government in early 1931 and after escaping on the Long March to Shensi built up a new regime at Yenan under Mao Tse-tung. Despite a long history of policy fluctuations and intra-party power struggles, the CCP built a revolutionary movement based in rural areas. During the Japanese War peasants in a number of bases were brought into a revolutionary process to restructure the rural social order, reorganize government, and bring the state further into society. This revolution finally emerged from the countryside in 1949.

GROWTH AND CHANGE IN THE CHINESE ECONOMY

The question of what happened to the Chinese economy in the nineteenth and twentieth centuries has been a major focus of discussion. Such problems are complicated because the economy during this time reflected the external impact of Western trade and imperialism, as well as short-term instabilities that had many different causes, and slowly progressing internal changes that did not represent a complete break with the past. Discussions of the nineteenth-century economy have a way of slipping back a few hundred years to consider processes of commercialization, urbanization, and monetization or changes in rural social relationships and land tenure, traceable to at least the Ming dynasty during the sixteenth and seventeenth centuries.[11] While some historians even still debate whether or not the structural outlines of the late imperial economy and society were fixed during the Sung, others focus on nineteenth-century Western intrusion.

[11] For a survey of the literature see Ramon Myers, 'Transformation and continuity in Chinese economic and social history', *Journal of Asian Studies* (*JAS*), 33.2 (Feb. 1974) 265–77. Interpretative trends in the People's Republic of China during the early 1980s are summarized in William Rowe, 'Review article: recent writing in the People's Republic on early Ch'ing economic history', *Ch'ing-shih wen-t'i* (*CSWT*), 4.7 (June 1982) 73–90. See also Mark Elvin, *The pattern of the Chinese past*; Mi Chu Wiens, 'Lord and peasant; the sixteenth to the eighteenth century', *Modern China* 6.1 (Jan. 1980) 3–40; Robert Marks, 'Peasant society and peasant uprisings in South China: social change in Haifeng County, 1630–1930' (University of Wisconsin, Ph.D. dissertation, 1978), ch. 6; Arif Dirlik, 'Chinese historians and the Marxist concept of capitalism: a critical examination', *Modern China*, 8.1 (Jan. 1982) 105–32. Summaries of both Chinese and American recent scholarship on China's early modern economy and society are in Albert Feuerwerker, ed., *Chinese social and economic history from the Song to 1900: report of the American delegation to a Sino-American symposium*.

Paucity of pre-twentieth-century data and the incompleteness and unreliability of more recent figures have handicapped analysis. Regional diversity and the lack of an integrated national market mean that aggregate figures can hide important regional variations, whereas local studies risk describing atypical situations. In these circumstances historians have reached no consensus. We do, however, need to consider debates over such questions as the nature of the Chinese economy of the late imperial period, the impact of imperialism, where and how the economy grew in the twentieth century, and whether and in what way rural standards of living were worsening. Answers given to such broad economic questions have also affected interpretations of social and political history. These economic issues, therefore, form a logical starting point.

Pre-capitalist commercialization in late imperial China

Commercialization permeated the agrarian economy during the Ch'ing. The overwhelming majority of the populace who farmed were free to move about and congregate in small villages linked to one another and to larger trading centres through marketing structures. Peasants were likely to produce a cash crop as well as basic foods, to supplement their income by handicrafts, and to purchase some household necessities. Local commerce was supplemented by long-distance inter-regional trade in basic commodities. By the eighteenth century, for instance, Kiangsu and Chekiang no longer produced enough rice to feed their large city populations, which were supplied from the rich agricultural basins of the middle Yangtze.[12] Long before the opening of the treaty ports there was a large inter-regional coastal and Yangtze valley trade. In the Shanghai and Ningpo areas the number of market towns increased in the Ch'ing, particularly from the second half of the eighteenth century. These gradually filled up the landscape, indicating progressive integration of village economies with a metropolitan centre.[13]

Commercialization and related urbanization did not, of course, occur evenly throughout the country. Population density and city growth were by far the highest in the Lower Yantze. Some estimates suggest this area kept its lead despite the enormous number of deaths during the Taiping Rebellion, and that disparities between the most and least urbanized

---

[12] Han-sheng Chuan and Richard Kraus, *Mid-Ch'ing rice markets and trade: an essay in price history*, 59–65; Ho Ping-ti, *Studies on the population of China, 1368–1953*, 289–91.

[13] Shiba Yoshinobu, 'Ningpo and its hinterland', in G. William Skinner, ed. *The city in late imperial China*, 397–405; Mark Elvin, 'Market towns and waterways: the county of Shang-hai from 1480 to 1910', in *ibid.* 470–1.

regions widened during the nineteenth century.[14] The persistent economic centrality of the Lower Yangtze shows it was a core area of development, importing grain first from other parts of the country, and later from abroad, and radiating its own goods to markets in other regions.

Commercial growth stimulated supportive structures, which by the nineteenth century had become complex and sophisticated. Specialized firms and brokers handled different phases of commodity production. Networks of guilds and native place associations regulated business practices and provided support for merchants. Banking institutions grew up to meet different ranges of need. One of the first was the network developed by Shansi merchants to finance their inter-regional transactions by bank drafts. During the nineteenth century another system of credit extension through 'native banks', or *ch'ien-chuang*, developed to finance the growing coastal trade. These essential facilities continued to function throughout the Republican period alongside larger Western-style banks (*yin-hang*). Still smaller transactions could be financed through pawnshops and little moneylending shops. Meanwhile a considerable body of commercial customary law was built up to regularize business practices.[15]

The size of the total output of agriculture and handicrafts grew significantly during most of the eighteenth century. It was encouraged by population growth, the availability of arable land, the diffusion of the 'best' agricultural practices from more advanced to less advanced regions, and the general absence of personal restrictions on the labour force. China's Marxist historians have further raised the question whether the late-Ming and early-Ch'ing economy was beginning a qualitative reorganization that pointed toward indigenous development of 'capitalism' before the introduction of modern industry from abroad in the nineteenth century. Their studies have emphasized changes in the 'relations of production'. Evidence of the separation of ownership of the means of production from labour power has been adduced from mercantile investment and the use of wage labour in mining, from the development

[14] Tables in Skinner, *The city*, 213, 226, 229 indicate that although population density declined more in the Lower Yangtze after the Taiping Rebellion than in any other macro-region, urban population as a percentage of total population increased relative to less urbanized regions between 1843 and 1893. Population density in North China increased markedly during the Republican period, but still had not reached Lower Yangtze levels by 1953. For China's macro-regions, see *ibid.* 214–15. On Taiping depopulation see Ho Ping-ti, *Population*, 236–47; Perkins, *Agricultural development*, 210–11.

[15] On *ch'ien-chuang* see *Shang-hai ch'ien-chuang shih-liao* (Historical materials on Shanghai native banks); Andrea McElderry, *Shanghai old-style banks (ch'ien-chuang), 1800–1935*; Susan Mann Jones, 'Finance in Ningpo: the "ch'ien-chuang", 1750–1880', in W. E. Willmott, ed. *Economic organization in Chinese society*. On smaller moneylending shops see Shiba, 415. Examples of customary law are translated in Fu-mei Chang Chen and Ramon H. Myers, 'Customary law and the economic growth of China during the Ch'ing period', *CSWT* 3.5 (Nov. 1976) 1–32; 3.10 (Dec. 1978) 4–27.

of managerial farming by landlords and rich peasants using hired workers in North China and parts of the Lower Yangtze, and from analogies to the proto-capitalist European putting-out system in the organization of silk weaving.[16]

Such evidences, however, fit into a typical pattern of 'pre-modern' economic growth, where population and total output both increase but without any sustained increase in per capita output. We cannot say that the production of grain and handicraft textiles or the extent of trade and markets increased any faster than population. 'Capitalism' – or, better, 'modern economic growth' characterized by increments to per capita as well as to total output – did not appear in early modern Europe (or in Meiji Japan two centuries later) because of changes in the forms of property ownership alone. Equally essential were developments in science and technology, including the 'technology' of finance, investment and management, that is, in Marxist terms, changes in the 'forces of production'. It was on the foundation of the continuous application of new methods of investment and reinvestment that Europe entered the capitalist epoch. And a strong case can be made – both for Europe and for Japan – that the critical starting point of modern economic growth was an 'agricultural revolution', a breakthrough in technology and organization that severed the age-old link between population size and food production.

Indigenous science and technology in eighteenth-century China in most important respects were elaborations of Sung discoveries.[17] Where there were significant departures, they were apparently not widely diffused or applied. The limitations of China's pre-modern science, it would seem, were as salient as its considerable achievements. The explanation of this vital matter is probably beyond our present competence. But even had the improved technology existed to produce, for example, large increases in grain output, it is likely that the population–land ratio in early Ch'ing China was already too high to permit easy increases in per capita production. This was precisely the case in the Low Countries of Europe in the seventeenth century, where the new technology that fostered England's agricultural revolution among a sparse population could not be profitably applied because of the density of the population. It appears

[16] *Ming Ch'ing tzu-pen chu-i meng-ya yen-chiu lun-wen chi* (Collected research essays on capitalist sprouts in the Ming and Ch'ing dynasties) and *Chung-kuo tzu-pen chu-i meng-ya wen-t'i lun-wen chi* (Essays on capitalist sprouts in China) contain the best recent work by China's economic historians on this topic.

[17] This is evident in the all-important sector of agricultural technology, studied in much detail in Amano Motonosuke, *Chūgoku nōgyō shi kenkyū* (A study of the history of Chinese agriculture); see, for example, 687–918 on agricultural implements and machinery, and 389–423 on rice technology.

doubtful that the instances of 'capitalist sprouts' in agriculture and handicrafts discovered by Chinese historians were either quantitatively important in the country as a whole or that they were on the verge of triggering a major socio-economic reorganization along capitalist lines. The nineteenth-century economy can better be described as a considerably commercialized agricultural economy which, within the limits of its pre-modern technology, was highly 'developed'. The changes it was undergoing were limited, but nonetheless capable of modifying social and political structures within their existing frameworks.

Economic stagnation

Because the Chinese economy did not of itself undergo a major institutional reorganization or technological breakthrough leading to a period of sustained per capita economic growth comparable to modern Europe and Japan, attention has been focused on factors inhibiting such change. The numerous explanations are usually grouped into two categories: technological and distributionist. The latter concerns the use of the surplus product among the populace and gives greater weight to a variety of political, cultural and historical impediments.[18]

Both distributionist and technological theorists recognize the importance of population growth, although they assess its effects differently. It seems evident that growth of output in the seventeenth and eighteenth centuries was accompanied by a substantial rise in agricultural productivity per unit of land resulting from improved seed strains and better farming methods, as well as by an increase in the area of cultivated and cropped land (this last as a consequence of the spread of double-cropping). But eventually there were fewer possibilities for increasing production by traditional means, and at some point in time (widely estimated as between the late eighteenth and early twentieth centuries) agricultural production per unit of land began to stagnate and fall behind population growth.[19]

[18] Some issues under debate are brought out in Victor Lippit *et al.* 'Symposium on China's economic history', *Modern China*, 4.3 (July 1978) and W. E. Willmott, '"Review" of *The development of underdevelopment in China*', *JAS* 41.1 (Nov. 1981) 113–15. Both views are represented in Dwight Perkins, ed. *China's modern economy in historical perspective*, with the article by Carl Riskin most strongly representing distributionist perspectives, and those by Mark Elvin, Thomas Rawski, and Robert Dernberger falling on the technological side. Related issues are discussed in Susan Mann Jones, 'Misunderstanding the Chinese economy – a review article', *JAS* 40.3 (May 1981) 539–58. Distributionists in general agree that economic growth was inhibited by socio-economic inequalities and maldistribution, socio-political structure and foreign imperialism, whereas technologists stress technological levels, demography, and barriers to private capital investment and accumulation. Marxist economic analysis in terms of relations of production predates this dichotomy, but has been drawn upon by distributionist historians. In reality the two categories need not be mutually exclusive, and comprehensive explanations combine aspects of both.
[19] Elvin, *Pattern*, 308; Perkins, *Agricultural development*, 188.

This stagnation was caused partly by heavy population pressure, which might undermine ecological balances (as in Hunan where excessive dike building paradoxically caused flooding)[20] or lead to uneconomic fragmentation of landholdings, lowering of peasant living standards, and creation of an itinerant, socially marginal stratum of rural poor. The abundance of cheap labour also lessened incentives to invent and spend money on technological improvements.

The most sophisticated technological explanation for stagnation has been formulated as a 'high-level equilibrium trap'.[21] This argument posits that the impressively high levels of agricultural and water transport technology combined with population growth and disappearance of unused land to reduce the amount of surplus product that might become available above the minimum needed for subsistence. Even though the surplus never disappeared entirely, its fall per capita reduced demand. Production and consumption entered into a circular flow that merely maintained subsistence with little left over for investment. At the same time, the sophistication of existing technology mainly based on manpower made it difficult to achieve the dramatic advances needed to reduce costs with mechanical power and greatly raise productivity per capita. This 'trap', therefore, produced stagnation at high levels of pre-modern production technology.

Critics of this theory assert that there was, in fact, considerable surplus within the Chinese economy in the nineteenth and twentieth centuries.[22] They point not only to conspicuous consumption, but also to commercial investment, expenditures on local overheads and similar indications that the problem was not lack of money but the failure to mobilize it for development. Those accepting this view have looked beyond technological problems for social, political and cultural factors that impeded development. Marxist historians, led by the Japanese, have devoted a great deal of research to the nature of rural class structure and landholding, topics of field research in the 1920s and 1930s.[23] Though this work perhaps produced contradictory evidence – in fact supporting both the distributionist view by elaborating a model of a prevalent 'landlord society', and

[20] Peter Perdue, 'Official goals and local interests: water control in the Dongting Lake region during the Ming and Qing periods', *JAS* 51.4 (Aug. 1982) 745–7.

[21] Elvin, *Pattern*, 298–318; Elvin, 'Comment' in Lippit *et al.* 329–30.

[22] Carl Riskin, 'Surplus and stagnation in modern China', in Perkins, ed. *China's modern economy*, 64–81; Riskin, 'Discussion and comments', in Lippit *et al.* 359–75.

[23] An excellent survey of Japanese research is Linda Grove and Joseph Esherick, 'From feudalism to capitalism: Japanese scholarship on the transformation of Chinese rural society', *Modern China*, 6.4 (Oct. 1980) 397–438. Republican studies include J. L. Buck, *Land utilization in China*; Ch'en Cheng-mo, *Ko-sheng nung-kung ku-yung hsi-kuan chi hsu-kung chuang-k'uang* (Hiring practices in agriculture and industry and the supply and demand for labour in various provinces). See below, ch. 5 (Myers).

the technological analysis by documenting the lack of sustained investment – for the twentieth century at least it still provides the best empirical data available to scholars outside China. The use made of the surplus was important because successful industrialization has historically been associated with either prior modernization of agriculture or concurrent milking of it, and regardless of the size, or existence, of a surplus, the economic growth experienced by China after 1949 would come primarily from extractions from the agricultural sector.

Tenant-landlord relations were invariably complex, so that simple allegations of exploitation as an explanation for why surplus was not invested in ways that fostered economic development must usually be qualified. Tenants in Central and South China (where tenancy rates were highest) had gained various kinds of permanent-use rights that afforded them an important degree of security. Tenancy *per se* was indeed not a good measure of rural prosperity. Land ownership was more likely to be equally distributed in economically peripheral areas where agriculture was too unprofitable to attract investment in land. Alternatively some tenants in core areas such as Szechwan or the Lower Yangtze might be wealthy men who leased and then sublet or managed large tracts of land.[24]

Rents varied but averaged about 50 per cent of the crop, though it is uncertain how much of the rent was actually collected. Urban landlords around Soochow in Kiangsu established professional rent-collection bursaries in the mid-nineteenth century and received official help in making collections. However, some bursary managers evidently were careful not to violate notions of fairness in collections. After the Taiping Rebellion sharply reduced the population in the Lower and Middle Yangtze provinces, landlords were for a time relatively weak and had difficulty making collections.[25]

Some twentieth-century observers suggested that tenancy was disappearing, but land continued to be a profitable investment in the Lower Yangtze until the 1920s or later. Despite regional variations (particularly substantially lower tenancy rates in the north), approximately 40 per cent of agricultural land in the country was rented. Moreover, ownership was

---

[24] Grove and Esherick, 408, 412–13; Chen and Myers, 16–20; Marks, 'Peasant society', 76–90; Elizabeth Perry, *Rebels and revolutionaries in north China, 1845–1945*, 25–33.

[25] On bursaries see Yūji Muramatsu, 'A documentary study of Chinese landlordism in late Ch'ing and early Republican Kiangnan', *Bulletin of the School of Oriental and African Studies*, 29.3 (Oct. 1966) 566–99; and Frank Lojewski, 'The Soochow bursaries: rent management during the late Ch'ing', *CSWT* 4.3 (June 1980) 43–65. On rent forgiveness and reduced collections see Lojewski, 53–5; Marks, 'Peasant society', 338, 362–3; Kang Chao, 'New data on land ownership patterns in Ming-Ch'ing China – a research note', *JAS* 40.4 (Aug. 1981) 733. On the effect of the Taiping Rebellion see Grove and Esherick, 417–18, and contemporary reports, e.g. *Shen-pao*, 5 Mar. 1878, 3.

unevenly distributed: about 10 per cent of the populace were classified as landlords or rich peasants owning over 50 per cent of the land.[26] Detailed studies of several areas suggest that during the Republican period landlords received more governmental help in collecting rents, and tenancy contracts gave tenants less security. Rents were often burdensome, but it is difficult to say that tenancy had any one kind of economic impact.

More persuasive is the general argument that during most of the Ch'ing and Republican periods the rural economy was dominated by an interlocking elite of landlords (often gentry degree-holders in the Ch'ing), merchants, and moneylenders.[27] This stratum absorbed any peasant surplus through rent, interest and pricing mechanisms. At the same time it partially financed peasant livelihood through loans and land purchases and linked peasant households to the market by purchasing commercial crops and by selling materials to and purchasing products from domestic handicraft industries. This circular economic relationship, though flexible, may well have discouraged development of a new class of rich peasants or others who would have both capital and incentive to introduce technological change. Fragmentation of holdings owing to population pressure and to the social practice of distributing land equally among heirs further inhibited concentration of agricultural wealth. In general, rural people sought stable arrangements, in which all sides could protect rather than expand their interests. These patterns could not easily be disrupted. At the urban end of the marketing structure were analogous patterns of circular organization.

Chinese merchants were capable of entrepreneurial behaviour when incentives existed. The Fang, Li and Yeh families of Ningpo pioneered in the coastal trade and were in on the beginnings of foreign trade in Shanghai. The silk merchants of Kiangnan were quick to take advantage of opportunities created by expanding exports. An outstanding example of aggressive marketing behaviour in the late nineteenth century was the unsuccessful challenge to the foreign merchants' control over silk export prices by the Hangchow financier Hu Kuang-yung, who went bankrupt after buying up much of the northern Chekiang silk crop for two years to hold it off the export market. Merchants were quite capable of reinvesting profits and, like the Fang family, maintaining business interests for several generations. The Shanghai merchant, Ch'in Tsu-tse, portrayed by the Japanese sociologist Negishi Tadashi, showed rectitude,

---

[26] On land distribution and tenancy estimates see Joseph Esherick, 'Number games, a note on land distribution in prerevolutionary China', *Modern China*, 7.4 (Oct. 1981) 387–411.

[27] Jūzō Kawashi's rendition of this theory is summarized in Grove and Esherick, 422–4.

frugality and devotion to duty worthy of the most dedicated samurai or ethical Protestant.[28]

Nonetheless, brokerage remained the dominant pattern of commercial activity in the Ch'ing, and continued so into the Republic. Merchants preferred to divide up markets and phases of marketing, to scatter their assets among several enterprises and more than one line of business, and to pursue profits in urban centres away from their family homes. Profits not reinvested in business or used to maintain high living standards were invested in land, education of family members, lineage facilities, and the public overhead of their home areas. Such expenditures represented gentry values as well as productive and profitable diversification of economic interests. Nonetheless, the diffusion of risk and responsibility inherent in this kind of economic behaviour militated against concentration of pools of wealth and inhibited widespread capitalist entrepreneurship.[29] Public or private institutions for mobilizing wealth, like the European joint stock companies, corporations and stock markets or a funded national debt were lacking.

In these circumstances of circular and self-perpetuating economic and social organization, what was the role of the state? Much economic development seems to have occurred outside state control. The state extracted a relatively small amount of the surplus. The land tax during the Ch'ing was light compared, for instance, with that of Meiji Japan.[30] Likin and other commercial taxes in late Ch'ing did not fundamentally change this picture. The Ch'ing state sought to regulate important monopolies, maintained the grain transport to feed the capital, and supervised grain markets because of its interest in price stabilization. However, the official granary system broke down to some degree after the eighteenth century.[31] The monopolies were also functioning poorly and most of the growing

---

[28] On the Fang, Yeh, and Li families see *Chen-hai hsien-chih* (Gazetteer of Chen-hai county), 26:31b–32b; 27:12b–15a, 40a–41a; *Shanghai ch'ien-chuang*, 730–4, 743–4; Susan Mann Jones, 'The Ningpo *pang* and financial power at Shanghai', in Mark Elvin and G. William Skinner, eds. *The Chinese city between two worlds*, 84–5; Negishi Tadashi, *Shanhai no girudo* (The guilds of Shanghai), 142–6. On Hu Kuang-yung see Robert Eng, 'Imperialism and the Chinese economy: the Canton and Shanghai silk industry, 1861–1932' (University of California, Ph.D. dissertation, 1978), 112. On Ch'in Tsu-tse, see Negishi Tadashi, 118–19.

[29] Investments of the Yeh and Li families illustrate business diversification. On the silk industry see Lillian Li, *China's silk trade: traditional industry in the modern world, 1842–1937*, 61. On mercantile sojourning see G. William Skinner, 'Mobility strategies in late imperial China', in Carol Smith, ed. *Regional analysis*, vol. 1, *Economic systems*, 343–8.

[30] Yeh-chien Wang, *Land taxation in imperial China, 1750–1911*, 128; ch. 6 *passim*. The land tax burden fluctuated, being relatively high in the mid-nineteenth century, and decreasing with inflation in the late nineteenth and early twentieth centuries.

[31] Will, *Bureaucratie et famine*, 97–100. Lillian Li, 'Introduction' to 'Food, famine and the Chinese state – a symposium', *JAS* 41.4 (Aug. 1982) 694–9.

numbers of markets and burgeoning commercial organizations were outside of, or only very loosely under, official Ch'ing control. In the Republican period, both the numerous warlord governments and the Nationalists extorted money from merchants, and there were constant complaints about high and frequent taxation. But these governments did not exercise comprehensive control over the economy. One estimate suggests that all the government expenditures in 1931 were still below the level of those of the Meiji government in 1880.[32]

When merchants did come into contact with the government they were subject to exactions in both the late imperial and Republican eras. But they were not oppressed by the Ch'ing or they would never have developed the wealth and status they enjoyed by the nineteenth century. Detailed studies show Ch'ing officials willing to provide strong incentives to obtain merchant cooperation in monopolies like salt.[33] Merchants who met official requests for contributions or services often profited by receiving contracts, bank deposits, or other indirect rewards to their private business ventures.

Relations between bureaucrats and merchants could be worked out to mutual advantage in stable situations of slow growth. On the whole, however, government policies did not favour long-term, productive investment. Lack of legal protection was one reason why merchants preferred to disperse their assets. Moreover, high interest rates diverted capital into short-term consumption oriented loans, in part because members of the court and high officials who profited from money lending did not enforce laws against usury.[34] Problems arose, however, when the state tried to play a more active or developmental role. Bureaucratic desires for control might then conflict with merchant interests in autonomy and profit-making. Corrupt practices from both sides might interact to undermine enterprises. The self-strengthening companies founded by officials in the late nineteenth century showed how uneconomic political and social behaviour might inhibit business growth. Merchants soon learned to avoid involvement. After 1904 similar problems hampered cooperation between the new ministries and business leaders. During the last Ch'ing decades the government lacked the financial strength to

---

[32] Thomas Rawski, *China's republican economy: an introduction*; Thomas Metzger, 'On the historical roots of economic modernization in China: the increasing differentiation of the economy from the polity during late Ming and early Ch'ing times', in Chi-ming Hou and Tzong-shien Yu, eds. *Modern Chinese economic history*, 3–14.

[33] Thomas Metzger, 'The organizational capabilities of the Ch'ing state in the field of commerce: the Liang-Huai salt monopoly, 1740–1840', in Willmott, ed. 23–7.

[34] Wei Ch'ing-yuan and Wu Ch'i-yen, 'Ch'ing-tai chu-ming huang-shang Fan-shih ti hsing-shuai' (The rise and fall of the Fan: a famous Ch'ing imperial merchant family), *Li-shih yen-chiu*, 3 (1981) 127–44.

provide capital necessary for modern industry. It tended to smother merchants and gentry whom it took into partnership, and failed to create financial and other conditions favourable to economic growth.[35] Similar inadequacies appeared in the 'bureaucratic capitalism' practised under the Nanking government in the 1920s and 1930s and plagued even disinterested efforts at reform. Attempts to improve silkworm strains and silk-production methods, for instance, were hampered because the government had neither the means to enforce its policies nor the confidence of the local populace.

In sum, the technological and distributive factors seem to have reinforced one another so as to keep economic change within moderate limits, unable to break through the existing equilibria. Change was occurring, but in the absence of a major revamping of the rural sector – of an 'agricultural revolution' Chinese style – it appears unlikely that continuing commercialization, further concentration of capital in the Lower Yangtze, or growth of the considerable, if technically illegal, trade with South-East Asia would have soon led to a radical reorganization of the economy. As it was, the major impetus came from abroad.

External factors: foreign trade and imperialism

Virtually all historians assume that Western imperialism had an effect on Chinese economic growth, but they differ over the weight and timing of its effect and whether it had a negative or positive influence. One line of analysis suggests that foreign activity played a crucial role in fostering sustained industrial development in the late nineteenth and twentieth centuries. Foreign industry in the treaty ports provided capital equipment and stimulated Chinese enterprise. Loans provided capital to modernize transportation and communications and establish heavy industry. Foreigners were the source of new technical knowledge. In short, an exogenous shock was needed to overcome the inertia of the Chinese economy and concentrate necessary resources.[36]

Chinese Marxist-Leninist and other historians, on the contrary, have argued that from the time of the Opium War imperialism inhibited internal forces favouring growth and capitalism: imports destroyed Chinese handicrafts, thus impoverishing peasants and restricting the

---

[35] See W. K. K. Chan, *CHOC* 11.460–2; Wang Hsi, 'Lun wan-Ch'ing ti kuan-tu shang-pan' (On the system of official supervision and merchant management during the late Ch'ing), *Li-shih hsueh* (Historical study), 1 (1979) 95–124. A much more positive assessment of the Ch'ing state's economic role appears in Ramon Myers, *The Chinese economy: past and present*.

[36] For this view see Robert Dernberger, 'The role of the foreigner in China's economic development, 1840–1949', in Perkins, ed. *China's modern economy*, 19–48.

domestic market. Chinese merchants were drawn into peripheral and dependent relations with foreign firms; unequal competition hampered growth of Chinese industry. Foreign loans and investments drained profits abroad and led to administrative interference in government finance. Although China was never ruled by Western foreigners, except in the treaty ports, Chinese governments were discouraged from promoting modern industry by fear of foreign seizure by military power. Most obviously, foreign control of Chinese tariffs prevented their protecting Chinese industry by excluding foreign competition.[37] A major variant of this approach argues that expansive capitalist states in search of markets and resources forced weaker unindustrialized countries into relationships of dependency, in order to secure the export of their resources for use by industries of the capitalist states. This perpetuated the economic underdevelopment of the weaker states, increased inequality both between social classes and between regions of the world, and to some degree impoverished peasants in the underdeveloped countries.[38]

All these theories, particularly the last, seem to underestimate the previous level of indigenous commercial development in China. They do not explain how external factors could be so decisive when the foreign trade was so small in comparison with the total Chinese economy. Mooveover, even in the twentieth century, the national market was still imperfectly integrated and many rural economies still produced mainly for consumption within a limited geographical area, although linked to markets elsewhere. The common-sense conclusion is that internal and external factors interacted and their relative importance varied with time, place, and circumstance. Foreign interests both inhibited and encouraged Chinese industry, sometimes, as in the case of tobacco, encouraging some aspects while retarding others. The largely foreign-financed railroad construction in late Ch'ing and Republican China did benefit the Chinese economy despite the context of imperialism within which these railways were built.[39] In areas where agricultural production remained locally

---

[37] Hu Sheng, *Imperialism and Chinese politics, 1840–1925* is one of many examples of this range of views.

[38] For general theory of underdevelopment see C. K. Wilber, ed. *The political economy of development and underdevelopment.* A generalized theory emerges from Wallerstein's concept of a capitalist dominated world economic system (Immanuel Wallerstein, *The modern world-system: capitalist agriculture and the origins of the European world-economy in the sixteenth century* and subsequent studies). Brief suggestions on how this theory might apply to China appear in Angus McDonald, Jr. 'Wallerstein's world economy: how seriously should we take it?' *JAS* 38.3 (May 1979) 535–40. There is substantial evidence for world impact on sectors of the Chinese economy since the sixteenth century (e.g. William Atwell, 'Notes on silver, foreign trade, and the late Ming economy', *CSWT* 3.8 (Dec. 1977) 1–33), but thus far few detailed studies.

[39] Sherman Cochran, *Big business in China: Sino-foreign rivalry in the cigarette industry, 1890–1930,* 202–20. Ralph William Hueneman, *The dragon and the iron horse: the economics of railroads in China 1876–1937* systematically examines the question of the economic consequences of the railways.

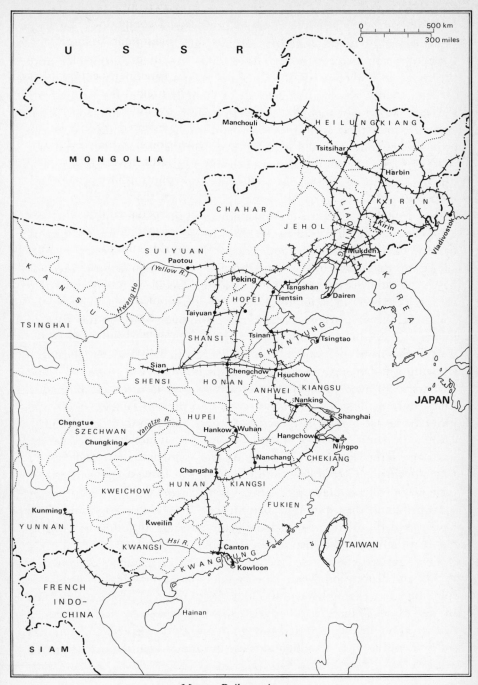

MAP 3. Railways in 1949

consumed, foreign trade had little impact. However, it is not necessary to postulate general economic dependency to recognize that growing involvement in world trade could have important repercussions. The stimulus to commerce in the Han River valley caused by export trade from the 1870s to the 1910s or the brief boom in sugar-cane production in Haifeng county, Kwangtung, because of a temporary world shortage from the late 1880s to mid-1900s,[40] showed that effects were not limited to major cities. As industrialization proceeded and foreign trade increased, world economic conditions had a growing effect on the economy in important parts of China. The ambivalence of this impact of trade and imperialism can be seen in the relatively well-studied cotton textile and raw silk industries.

The decline of domestic cotton-spinning in the nineteenth century has been cited repeatedly to illustrate the adverse impact of imperialism on nascent Chinese capitalism and peasant livelihood. However, blanket allegations that textile imports and subsequently foreign factories in China destroyed rural handicrafts do not hold up. Detailed studies show that although household spinning largely disappeared it was replaced by handicraft weaving using foreign yarn. Moreover, yarn for the warp of looms was still produced by peasant spinners after imports supplied the weft; in fact hand spinning declined at different times in different localities, allowing a rather long period for peasant households to adjust.[41] Hand weaving continued to compete successfully with factories established in China during the twentieth century because peasant families could still profit from using their surplus labour even when prices had declined. Moreover, hand weaving spread to new areas – for instance, central Chekiang at the end of the Ch'ing, and parts of north-western and western China during the Republic – indicating a spread of domestic demand and penetration of manufactured yarns. On balance weaving was probably more profitable than spinning, so in the long run the changeover may well have raised the living standards of many peasants although it probably lowered the household incomes of even more.

This aggregate, long-term picture obscures local instances of short-run decline and dislocation. Textile imports initially hurt the highly developed spinning and weaving handicraft industries of the urbanized Canton delta. In the 1830s Chinese handwoven exports (Nankeens) declined and a market grew up for imported foreign yarns. Both weavers and spinners suffered, and in 1831 a sudden increase in foreign yarn imports triggered

[40] Liu Ts'ui-jung, *Trade on the Han River and its impact on economic development, 1800–1911*; Marks, 'Peasant society', 205–26.
[41] Kang Chao, *The development of cotton textile production in China*, 174–86; Bruce Reynolds, 'Weft: the technological sanctuary of Chinese handspun yarn', *CSWT* 3.2 (Dec. 1974) 4–13.

a boycott led by spinners. Eventually the textile workers shifted from spinning to weaving, but the unemployment fostered hostility to foreigners and the social disruption contributed to the Taiping Rebellion.[42] Handicraft spinning in Haifeng county, further north along the Canton coast, persisted until the end of the Ch'ing. After it died out between 1890 and 1910, weaving continued under a putting-out system. But modern mills in Haifeng after 1918 replaced household weaving. Local textile production overall probably expanded, but the conversion of peasant family producers into factory wage labourers had unsettling socio-political consequences.[43] Even where domestic weaving flourished most strongly in the twentieth century, it was not a stable occupation. Weaving in North China tended to concentrate in centres that competed with one another and went through phases of boom and retrenchment from the 1910s to the 1930s. Fluctuation was caused more by this local competition and by domestic market conditions than by direct foreign factors until the world depression of the 1930s. Japanese occupation of Manchuria later restricted markets and hastened the decline of the North China centres.[44] Expansion of the textile industry thus led to different kinds of economic fluctuations resulting from growth, competition, and international market movements. Such changes might disrupt village communal patterns and make handicraft production a less predictable source of income for peasant families who had to supplement their income from farming.[45]

The history of silk production in the Lower Yangtze during the last seventy years of the Ch'ing shows a more unambiguously expansive impact of foreign trade.[46] In the late 1840s raw silk exports shifted from Canton to Shanghai where they expanded rapidly in the 1850s during the Taiping Rebellion. Cutting off of domestic markets as well as declining production of the imperial silk factories probably made silk more available for export. In the early 1860s the rebellion devastated Lower Yangtze silk-producing areas, causing a sharp drop of exports in 1863–4 and rather slow recovery during the rest of the decade. For the rest of the century

[42] Kang Chao, *Textile production*, 82, 87–8; Ming-kou Chan, 'Labor and empire: the Chinese labor movement in the Canton Delta, 1895–1927' (Stanford University, Ph.D. dissertation, 1975), 11–12, 367.

[43] Marks, 'Peasant society', 231–41. See below, ch. 6 (Bianco).

[44] Kang Chao, *Textile production*, 188–9, 192–201.

[45] Linda Grove, 'Creating a northern soviet', *Modern China*, 1.3 (July 1975) 259; Myers, *The Chinese economy*, sees market fluctuations due to external causes as leading to unemployment, violence and economic crisis.

[46] The major English-language work on the silk trade is Li, *China's silk trade*. See also Eng, 'Imperialism and the Chinese economy' and E-tu Zen Sun, 'Sericulture and silk production in Ch'ing China', in Willmott, ed., 79–108. On the relative expansiveness of silk production, see David Faure, 'The rural economy of Kiangsu province, 1870–1911', *Journal of the Institute of Chinese Studies*, Chinese University of Hong Kong, 9.2 (1978) 380–426.

the foreign economic impact on the Kiangnan economy reflected this conjunction of Taiping destruction with strong foreign demand for silk. By about 1870 mulberry trees had been replanted and production recovered. But old silk-weaving centres were not fully reconstructed because production was so strongly oriented to foreign trade. This trade caused silk production to increase more rapidly than that of other agricultural products, and mainly accounted for the area's rapid recovery from the Taiping Rebellion and prosperity during the rest of the dynasty. It restructured the raw silk industry, brought new areas into silk production, and helped market town centres of silk collection recover more rapidly than the large depopulated cities. Though efforts were made to improve handicraft reeling so as to meet foreign demands for uniformity, the major technical change came with steam filatures, mainly in Shanghai. These became significant in the late 1890s, and thereafter outstripped hand-reeled production. By 1911 filatures had secured peasant specialization in cocoon production and a new set of brokers to move cocoons quickly from farms to factories.

The silk trade helped the rise of new vigorous merchant-gentry families and commercial organizations. How much peasant producers benefited has not been determined. The record of silk in the Republican period was to be much more ambiguous, but in the late nineteenth century it seems that this foreign trade caused expansion of silk production, encouraged modern industry, and had important socio-political ramifications within elite society. The trade would have been still more profitable if Chinese had been able to control export prices, and it would have survived better in the long run if the government had made a concerted effort to improve production methods, but for the time being it was the key to the prosperity of Kiangnan.

Continuity after 1911

In the Republican era the substance of China's economic problems remained essentially that of the late empire. First, a highly intensive, traditional agricultural sector was barely able in 'normal' times to feed an immense population. It was therefore usually incapable of providing farm products for possible consumption by a large urban work-force, or as raw materials for developing industry, or as exports to finance the importation of critically needed capital and technology. Neither Yuan Shih-k'ai nor the Peking mandarins who succeeded him, neither Sun Yat-sen nor Chiang Kai-shek's Nanking and Chungking regimes, certainly not the Japanese aggressors (except in Manchuria to a degree), not even Mao Tse-tung in Kiangsi or Yenan – no one significantly affected and improved the performance of China's agriculture in the first half of the twentieth century.

Second, from the beginning of the third decade of the century the times were rarely 'normal'. Civil wars and Japanese aggression and then civil war again filled most of the next thirty years. The physical and especially the human destruction inflicted upon China beggars any description. Yet people survived, however scantily, and the economy before the very last years of this grievous turmoil was not shattered. Indeed it showed a remarkable resiliency during the infrequent periods of relative peace. This we take as a sure sign of its low level of 'modern' development, of the overwhelming persistence of traditional technology and localized organization, not susceptible of being destroyed by invaders as a more developed economy might have been.

Third, in much the same manner the modern sector of China's economy was by far the less important in fact. Though China was much buffeted by the world – the treaty powers and others – China's economy in the first half of the twentieth century was still only very incompletely linked to the world economy. The dualistic model of distinct treaty-port and hinterland sectors may be too crude to describe the actual complexity of Shanghai's economic role, or Canton's or Wuhan's. However, excessive attention to bullion flows, to Maritime Customs statistical series, to the terms of trade, or to foreign loans and investments can only be misleading. There was simply no effective programme for the essential technical and organizational (redistributive) changes in agriculture, without which no genuine modern economic growth could ensue. Enlarged international trade had fostered commercialized agriculture in some places during the twentieth century. In parts of North China this process had in turn enhanced economic and social differentiation in the villages, leading in some circumstances to the 'semiproletarianization' of the poorer peasants.[47] But this was neither a token that capitalist agriculture was emerging in modern China nor is it much evidence of foreign economic iniquities.

A fourth observation concerns the sometimes neglected power of compound growth. The tiny modern industry initiated in the late nineteenth century became a genuine and growing modern industrial sector. The estimated rate of growth of these modern industrial enterprises in the first five decades of the twentieth century was probably of the order of 7 or 8 per cent per annum.[48] This annual rate is approximately what

[47] Philip C. C. Huang, *The peasant economy and social change in North China* is a major study of changes in the dominant small-peasant economy.
[48] John K. Chang, *Industrial development in pre-Communist China: a quantitative analysis*, 70–103. And

the People's Republic of China has achieved since 1949. Of course the base from which this development began was infinitesimal at the start and real annual increments to productive capacity were similarly tiny. But over the decades, as growth was compounded, the structure of China's economy began to change, at first slowly and then more rapidly, until in the 1970s nearly 50 per cent of China's gross domestic product was attributable to industry (factories and handicrafts), mining, utilities, and transportation – not all 'modern' to be sure, but clearly differentiated from agriculture, whose share had declined from perhaps two-thirds at the beginning of the century to one-third in 1971.

Nevertheless, the Kuomintang's Nanking government and its predecessors in Peking contributed little to this surprisingly vigorous, if still sectorally and geographically limited, modern economic development. Pre-modern growth – the increase of both total population and total output but without sustained per capita increments – such as occurred in the eighteenth century might not require a substantial state role; indeed it probably benefited from its absence. But for a late effort to achieve modern economic growth, larger political inputs are likely to be needed. The Kuomintang government was not politically strong enough, or sufficiently adaptable intellectually, to harness and develop the potential of the private Chinese economy while at the same time ensuring an acceptable minimum of personal and regional equality.[49]

As a result, the small pre-1949 modern industrial sector, in the eighteen province of China within the Great Wall and in Manchuria, provided the PRC with managers, technicians, and skilled workers – the cadre that could train the vastly expanded numbers who would staff the many new factories that went into production in the 1950s. It was of course largely unintended, but even if the foreign presence in China before 1949 had sometimes inhibited independent development, its most efficacious legacy appears to have been the initial transfer of technology that made possible China's early industrialization.

Thus the Republic was more than a holding period in which the economy everywhere remained stagnant while the political system disintegrated. On the contrary, aggregate growth in the modern urban sector

see Albert Feuerwerker, 'Lun erh-shih shih-chi ch'u-nien Chung-kuo she-hui wei-chi' (On the social crisis in early twentieth-century China), in Ts'ai Shang-ssu, ed. *Lun Ch'ing-mo Min-ch'u Chung-kuo she-hui* (Chinese society in the late Ch'ing and early Republic), 129–33.

49 Susan Mann Jones, 'Misunderstanding the Chinese economy' skilfully reviews some of these issues with references to the literature. For a revisionist Soviet view of the Kuomintang's economic policies, which describes a combination of economic accomplishment and political failure, see A. V. Meliksetov, *Sotsial'no-ekonomicheskaia politika Gomin'dana v Kitae. 1927–1949* (Kuomintang social-economic policy in China, 1927–1949). The relations of the Nationalist regime to the Shanghai merchant community are examined in Joseph Fewsmith, *Party, state, and local elites in Republican China.*

prepared the way for further advances after 1949. At the same time, however, most rural areas were not achieving the same growth as the cities. Imbalances, instabilities, local disasters, warfare and at times inflation all dragged down levels of production, inhibited commerce and discouraged rural investment. Such troubles, though most shattering in the 1930s and 1940s, were present in varying degrees in different places throughout the late Ch'ing and Republican eras. The social consequences were unsettling.

CHANGES IN SOCIAL STRUCTURE AND BEHAVIOUR

As a baseline from which to judge modern trends we posit first China's high degree of socio-cultural homogeneity. The Han Chinese in different regions and at different class levels had a common sense of identity and historical continuity. Values were widely shared. Until recent times the elite sought to maintain a rural base close to nature. In the villages a little tradition did not set them sharply apart from a great tradition of the city elite. Instead the two strata shared a common folklore and cosmology, including respect for ancestors, learning, property, and legitimized authority.

Footbinding evidenced the cultural homogeneity under elite leadership. The practice began at the T'ang court. It was backed by philosophers of the Sung and pervaded the peasantry during the Ming and Ch'ing. The crippling of women's feet, that had begun as an upper-class male sexual fetish and continued as an ostentatious display of urban affluence, spread to the villages and seriously impaired the working capacity of half the farming people. To ape their betters by such uneconomic mutilation of females showed a high degree of peasant subservience to elite norms. Similarly, village pantheons that integrated family stove gods, agricultural spirits, and city deities into hierarchies reminiscent of the imperial bureaucracy suggested a common acceptance of the authority structure that the elite dominated.

Certain features of this homogeneous culture were slow to change – such as respect for superiors and elders, sexual inequality, preservation of the paternal line and equal inheritance among brothers. Local modifications did not destroy such general practices even though the philosophical or ideological expressions concerning them might change.[50] Although

50 Arthur Wolf, 'Gods, ghosts and ancestors', in Arthur Wolf, ed. *Religion and ritual in Chinese society*, 133–45. Stevan Harrell, *Ploughshare village: culture and context in Taiwan*, 9–15 discusses interaction between general cultural principles, variations in customary behaviour expressing such principles, and the socio-economic contexts (including such factors as class, geography, and technology) in which such behaviour occurs. See also, Maurice Freedman, 'On the sociological study of Chinese religion', in Arthur Wolf, ed. *Religion*, 19–42.

Confucianism was bitterly attacked in the twentieth century, its modes of behaviour and underlying assumptions still persisted.

Horizontal and vertical social structures

The horizontal class structure of late imperial China was theoretically divided by the Classics into the four occupational classes: scholar-gentry, peasants, artisans, and merchants. In reality it more closely approached a flexible two-tier structure: a small, educated, wealthy elite stratum or ruling class (about 5 per cent of the population) and the vast majority, who mainly did manual labour either on the land or in the cities. This two-tier division left room for upward and downward mobility and for borderline positions bridging elite and non-elite status: such as poor teachers and other underemployed lower-degree holders, or wealthy peasants, or shop keepers. Dividing lines were flexible and there was considerable variation in criteria determining elite status. Military prowess or leadership of local organizations including illegal groups might be more important than education in determining elite status in some areas.

At the bottom were two strata below the respectable non-elite categories. One was a permanently disadvantaged substratum of personal slaves and mean people who were excluded from most respectable activities. The second consisted of drifters, beggars, bandits, smugglers, and others operating outside the organizing structures of society. These were mainly (but not entirely) drawn from the very poor, but like those on the borderline of elite status their social position was somewhat flexible, for if they had not severed kinship or local ties they might move back into the lower levels of respectability. There is no good measurement of the size of this diverse stratum, but we believe it was growing during the nineteenth and twentieth centuries, enlarged by disorders and natural disasters. Moreover, it had a preponderance of males over females, increased by waves of female infanticide that occurred during rebellions or natural disasters.

This horizontal class structure, with its extreme differences of wealth, was overlapped by vertical organizing principles based on kinship and locality. Especially in Central and South China, extended family lineages were a major form of social organization. They enhanced the security and continuity of elite families and provided services and opportunities for poorer lineage members. One's position in society might depend as much upon what lineage one belonged to as on one's economic and occupational status. Between rich and poor, lineage ties were often stronger than class antagonism. Where lineages did not develop, simpler kinship organization might have similar effect.[51]

Local loyalties had much the same influence. Lineage and village ties often reinforced each other, and villagers had common interests in self-protection and in maintaining community resources. Inter-village cooperation or conflict was likely to follow both marketing relations and kinship networks. Lower-class families might be pulled into protective-dependent patron-client relationships with richer and stronger families. Exclusion from the protection of these kinship, community and patronage structures produced socially marginal outcasts more than poverty *per se*.

Interaction of locality and kinship was illustrated by marriage practices of the Teng lineage of the Hong Kong New Territories during the first half of the twentieth century.[52] In this cohesive lineage rich and poor followed the same marriage rituals, but wealthy members selected wives to enhance business and political contacts useful in maintaining upper-class status. Such alliances were sought over a fairly wide geographical area. Brides came with dowries, providing some financial independence, and the two families continued to interact. Peasant men, on the contrary, married women from villages close to home, paid a bride price, and thereafter had little contact with their wives' families. Their isolation from other communities reinforced their dependency as tenants of the wealthy Tengs who controlled most of the village land. Such examples suggest that although upward mobility was not impossible, most of the poor could not expect to change their class status.

Unequal vertical relationships proved useful to both parties in part because, as in other Chinese hierarchies, they incorporated principles of mutuality and reciprocity. It appears to have been a standard practice, for instance, for landlords in the nineteenth century to forgive rent in bad years, sometimes repeatedly accepting partial payments, just as the government granted tax remissions. Confucian teachings fostered a 'moral economy' in which upper-class consumption and profit-making should be restrained while peasants should accept social inequalities and obligations to landlords and the state. Within this value system peasants

---

[51] Literature on lineages is surveyed and the term lineage defined in James Watson, 'Chinese kinship reconsidered: anthropological perspectives on historical research', *China Quarterly (CQ)*, 92 (Dec. 1982) 589–627. See also Jack Potter, 'Land and lineage in traditional China', in Maurice Freedman, ed. *Family and kinship in Chinese society*. On other strong kin ties in North China villages see Perry, *Rebels*, 60, 75–8, 80 and for evidence of lineages in Hopei and Shantung see Prasenjit Duara, 'Power in rural society: North China villages, 1900–1940' (Harvard University, Ph.D. dissertation, 1983) ch. 2. On Shaohsing lineages see James Cole, 'Shaohsing: studies in Ch'ing social history' (Stanford University, Ph.D. dissertation, 1975), ch. 3.

[52] Rubie Watson, 'Class differences and affinal relations in South China', *Man*, 16.4 (Dec. 1981) 593–615.

would accept arrangements that seemed to embody 'justice'. The popular perception of injustice therefore became important.[53]

The increase of social instability

In the changes that hit China from inside and outside between 1800 and 1949 we discern certain general features. Most striking is the increase of militarism, organized violence, among the common people, beginning especially in poor peripheral areas where recent immigration had outdistanced government services and controls. Examples included continual inter-village feuding in central and eastern Kwangtung and chronic banditry in areas of the North China plain.[54] In the Kiangsi highlands, for instance, poor migrants to hills lived at odds with the more prosperous, lineage-dominated rice-growers in the valleys.[55] Illegal societies flourished and rebellion sprang up in such under-governed peripheral areas, some of which in the 1930s and 1940s became Communist bases.

Local and provincial militarization against mid-century rebels increased troop levels and created insoluble problems of how to disband out-of-date armies. The end of Ch'ing military domination after 1911 saw a proliferation of local security forces. Soon the warlords' civil wars damaged cities and trade routes even when they did not disrupt agriculture.[56]

Another feature of instability was population movements. Early and mid-Ch'ing had seen migration into provinces like Szechwan, which had been depopulated by late-Ming rebellion, and into border areas including illegal entry into Manchuria. These outlets (except Manchuria) were becoming filled up by the late eighteenth century. Surplus males from Fukien and Kwangtung were emigrating to South-East Asia and by 1850 to the Americas as contract labour. After the Taiping Rebellion the depopulated Lower Yangtze was a temporary focus of migration. By the twentieth century, however, Manchuria was the only remaining region with large amounts of attractive uncultivated land. The net result of these

---

53 On 'moral economy' see n. 73 below.
54 On Kwangtung: Harry Lamley, 'Hsieh-tou: the pathology of violence in southeastern China', *CSWT* 3.7 (Nov. 1977) 1–40; Marks, 'Peasant society', 135–51. On the North China plain see Perry, *Rebels*, 59–94. Interpretations of the social effects of banditry and warlordism in North China during the Republic are in Philip Billingsley, 'Bandits, bosses, and bare sticks: beneath the surface of local control in early Republican China', *Modern China*, 7.3 (July 1981) 235–88; and R. G. Tiedman, 'The persistence of banditry: incidents in border districts of the North China Plain', *Modern China*, 8.4 (Oct. 1982) 395–433.
55 This hill society is analysed in Stephen Averill, 'The shed people and the opening of the Yangzi Highlands', *Modern China*, 9.1 (Jan. 1983) 84–126.
56 James Sheridan, *CHOC* 10.317–19. On the growth of militarism see also below, p. 65.

migrations was a growth of population outside the Yangtze valley to the north, west, and south-west.

Superimposed upon these permanent migrations were two kinds of temporary movements: travel to employment and flights from war, famine and poverty. Urban tradesmen, businessman and workers, even when settled permanently where they worked, often remained 'sojourners' organized by native place, who hoped eventually to return to their original homes. A large flow of people occurred on an annual basis. Thus workers at the traditional iron-foundries of the town of Ch'ing in northern Chekiang, or tinbeaters in Hangchow, worked at their trades most of the year, but returned to Wusih, Kiangsu, and to parts of Ningpo prefecture respectively in the summer to help their families with harvesting. Impoverished peripheral regions set up migration patterns of their own. For example, poor people from Huai-pei sought seasonal jobs in Shanghai as labourers, porters and rickshaw pullers, but often ended up begging because of lack of jobs. Begging in a richer urban locality became an accepted off-season means of subsistence, just as itinerant begging was a way to survive when natural disaster struck one's home area. Banditry and smuggling, as more aggressive, illegal ways to earn a living, were sometimes pursued on a seasonal basis, often to extract money from outside areas. If one adds the travel of porters, boatmen, traders and peddlars along trade routes, the amount of occupational movement in the late Ch'ing was very considerable.[57]

In addition, natural disasters, rebellions and wars created waves of refugees. Bands of 'distressed people' inspired fear in the towns they passed through, where small family groups or individuals were highly vulnerable.

These kinds of popular mobility cannot be measured, but undoubtedly increased during the nineteenth and twentieth centuries. The growth of foreign trade, urban jobs, and transport improvements fostered new patterns of temporary migration. In 1882, for example, 70,000 Chinese travelled by steamer from Ningpo to Shanghai and 73,000 booked a passage from Shanghai to Ningpo. Twenty years later these figures had approximately doubled, and by 1910 467,000 Ningpo passengers travelled to and 470,000 travelled from Shanghai. Even allowing for a shift from

---

[57] A general theory of sojourning is in Skinner, 'Mobility strategies'. For Ch'ing town ironworkers: Mary Rankin, 'Rural-urban continuities: leading families of two Chekiang market towns', *CSWT* 3.7 (Nov. 1977) 67–104. Hangchow tin-beaters: *Shen-pao*, 17 Sept. 1874, 3. On banditry as a seasonal sojourning occupation, see Perry, *Rebels*, 55, 60–70; also Cole, *Shaohsing*, 167. Impact of permanent migration to Yunnan on urbanization and agriculture is analysed in James Lee, 'Food supply and population growth in Southwest China, 1250–1850', *JAS* 41.4 (Aug. 1982) 711–46.

junk to steamer travel, these escalating figures indicated more people were travelling.[58]

These population movements were, first of all, beyond the ability of governments to control, and, secondly, they affected all parts of China. Isolated villages were growing rarer. The search for urban jobs was not necessarily channelled through marketing structures in an ascending hierarchy of towns and cities. Surplus rural labour moved directly into urban centres, creating new channels of contact, while city merchants became more involved in the villages – putting out materials for rural handicrafts, purchasing agricultural produce, and like other wealthy city dwellers buying agricultural land.

Third, these movements affected the social structure. Urban wage earners, both male and female, acquired new importance in the village families whose incomes they augmented. Meanwhile flights from rural poverty meant unanticipated uprooting, broken families, sale of wives and children, and individual powerlessness. We cannot trace a simple process of immiseration. But in some areas of high tenancy, rental agreements became less favourable to tenants. In eastern Kwangtung, for instance, in the 1890s, peasants were required to assume more risk and had less right to rent reduction in a bad year. By the 1920s some peasants were operating under one-year oral agreements that provided no security whatever. In the Lower Yangtze rent-pressing bureaus had spread after 1911, rent deposits became more common, and short-term rentals increased. Inconsistent government policies could add to tensions, as in Chekiang where a rent-reduction law was passed in 1927 and then vitiated.[59] Meantime the increase of violence and popular motility both weakened the protection formerly afforded by patron-client relationships and community networks.

Instability does not lend itself to quantitative comparisons. We note, however, that the social disorders of the mid-nineteenth century came at a time of mounting population, deflation, and decay of major government-supported systems of water transport, control and famine prevention. During the last Ch'ing decade and the early Republic social instabilities were further induced by economic expansion and reforms. During the

[58] Imperial Maritime Customs, Inspectorate General of Customs, *Trade reports* 1882, 270; 1900, 374; 1910, 525.

[59] On Kwangtung, see Marks, 'Peasant society', 338. On the Lower Yangtze see Bradley Giesert, 'Power and society: the Kuomintang and local elites in Kiangsu province, China, 1924–1937' (University of Virginia, Ph.D. dissertation, 1979) 94–5, 101, 189–93, 213–15. On Chekiang land reform see Noel Miner, 'Chekiang: the Nationalists' effort in agrarian reform and construction, 1927–1937'. For the view that peasant living standards did not fall except under abnormal wartime conditions see Ramon Myers, *The Chinese peasant economy: agricultural development in Hopei and Shantung, 1890–1949* 292–5 and *passim*; and below, ch. 5 (Myers).

second half of the Republican era instability was more and more often produced by economic adversity and war. Life became less secure for everyone.

Fusion and fragmentation of traditional elites

Elite society began to change when commercialization led to the final breakdown of formal distinctions between merchants and gentry degree-holders. The fusion of these two groups was indicated by the sale of degrees during the late imperial period. Wealthy Canton hong merchants, Kiangsu and Chihli salt merchants, and Shansi bankers had bought degrees and enjoyed high status in the eighteenth century. In the nineteenth century, many merchants in any given city were likely to be non-natives and, therefore, distinct from the native gentry, but the two groups merged in their home areas. Trade never acquired the prestige of first-class scholarship or high office, but it was at least as good a way to make money. The evidence for the assimilation of merchants into the ruling class is overwhelming.

Members of large extended families had normally pursued diverse routes to success, different brothers specializing in scholarship, trade and estate management. Lineage ties obscured merchant-gentry distinctions, as did their cooperation in managerial activities. This coalescence meant more than merchants purchasing degrees or officials investing in business. By the mid-nineteenth century individuals began to display both merchant and gentry characteristics, combining scholarship and trade, high degree-holding with active business management, and a willingness to leave stagnating official careers in favour of broader opportunities in industry. In regions of economic growth like the silk-producing areas of Chekiang and Kiangsu, scholars could not resist being drawn into production or trade.[60] This convergence of merchant and gentry was made final and unavoidable by the end of the examination system in 1905, which left education more open to those who could pay for schooling. This change created a more broadly defined and open elite, ready to welcome social mobility but well able to maintain itself as a class because it could draw on diversified sources of income and status.

This broadening of the elite social category was accompanied by an

---

[60] On the fusion of elites in general see Bastid-Bruguière, 'Social change'. Comment in the Shih-men (Chekiang) gazetteer is cited in Li, *China's silk trade*, 106. The case for fusion of merchant and gentry has been repeatedly made: e.g. Keith Schoppa, 'The composition and functions of the local elite in Szechuan', *CSWT* 2.10 (Nov. 1973) 11 and *passim*; and Rankin, 'Rural-urban', 83–4. Continuing differences are stressed in Edward Rhoads, *China's Republican revolution: the case of Kwangtung, 1895–1913*, 82, 93, 174.

increase in elite-directed social organizations. The most obvious were guilds and native-place associations (*hui-kuan*). Although the history of such groups goes back several centuries, they developed strongly during the latter part of the Ch'ing to meet the needs of sizeable groups of merchants, workers and artisans living away from home.[61] Money derived from trade often supported other kinds of societal organizations. Newly wealthy families continued into the twentieth century to set up charitable estates. Elites took charge of dike repair, burial, and other community associations. Public associations run by gentry, merchants, and temples increased markedly in the second half of the nineteenth century. During rebellions or in peripheral areas of chronic unrest, militia and defence associations overshadowed elite-run civil organizations. These multi-faceted organizational capacities helped the local elite preserve its position not only in agrarian society, but also vis-à-vis the bureaucratic state.[62]

While merchants and gentry were coalescing into a broader single elite, signs appeared of fracturing along different lines that would eventually produce a new class structure. During the eighteenth and early nineteenth centuries more and more scholar-gentry had been diverted into career paths outside the bureaucracy. The spread of education accelerated this process during the last decades of the Ch'ing. There were simply too many qualified men to be absorbed into government posts. Some wealthy young men turned to idleness and dilettantish literary pursuits. Less affluent lower-degree holders might find a living locally in collusion with corrupt elements in the yamen sub-bureaucracy. But there were also serious, respectable alternatives to bureaucratic careers. An early example was the academic community that grew up in the Lower Yangtze in the eighteenth century – men who specialized in precise scholarship, research and academy teaching supported by salaries from private patrons or provincial officials. Establishment of new, high-level scholarly oriented academies gave them a solid institutional base. Appointments were made by governors or governors-general. Such positions were highly prized and keenly sought by ambitious scholars. Bibliophiles enlarging their libraries furthered book-printing, and so helped the printing profession. This academic substratum had a life of its own not oriented to the official examinations or pursuit of office.[63]

In the nineteenth century, particularly the latter half, gentry management

---

[61] See Ho Ping-ti, *Chung-kuo hui-kuan shih-lun*.

[62] For more on this trend see below, ch. 7, 'The role of elites in local government'.

[63] Benjamin Elman, 'The unravelling of Neo-Confucianism: the Lower Yangtze academic community in late imperial China' (University of Pennsylvania, Ph.D. dissertation, 1980), 166–261; also his *From philosophy to philology: intellectual and social aspects of change in late Imperial China*.

also became a major career alternative. Managerial activities were frequently generalist, like those of a magistrate, but some specialized in functions like water control. Management of lineage property became another respectable use of administrative ability. Wealthy merchants or investors often hired managers to run individual firms.

Specialization appeared within the bureaucratic sphere as some men trained to be clerks and others to become legal or financial secretaries (*mu-yu*, 'tent friends') in the entourage of high officials. Li Hung-chang, for example, kept scores of supernumerary specialists on his staff. These specializations often had local bases. Thus scholars from Shaohsing, Chekiang, were particularly noted for their skills as legal secretaries and their success in obtaining clerical positions in the capital.[64] Some Shaohsing families also made fortunes managing banks owned by Ningpo merchants.

More fundamental changes of role began in the treaty ports, where foreign affairs experts, compradores, treaty-port entrepreneurs, and Western-style professional men formed a small urban bourgeoisie; educated army officers appeared as forerunners of militarists of the Republican period; both missionary and modern Chinese schools began to produce an urban intelligentsia outside the Confucian framework. This fragmentation and redefinition of old elites continued during the Republic. Whereas late Ch'ing elites had never been homogeneous, they were now more divided, not only by region but by occupation. New differences gradually emerged between elites of core and peripheral areas as much as between city elites and rural 'gentry'. Armed force often became a more important buttress of elite status in the countryside. Indeed in some militarized rural areas local elites were almost defined by control of defence forces,[65] whereas in core regions wealth was still likely to be divorced from arms. There was no longer a more or less uniform elite stratum definable by simple criteria of degree-holding or wealth.

This fracturing of elites was accompanied by organizational diversification. As China had more contact with the modern international world, her urban life saw the growth of elite-managed institutions comparable to those abroad – steam and/or electrical-powered manufacturing, transport and communication; more open markets for the mobilization of capital, labour, and ideas; institutions of social overhead (education, public health, police, disaster control, the administration of justice); and even political activity. Chinese urban elites assimilated Western ways that they

[64] Kenneth E. Folsom, *Friends, guests, and colleagues*; and James Cole, 'The Shaoxing connection: a vertical administrative clique in late Qing China', *Modern China*, 6.3 (July 1980) 317–26.

[65] See Guy Alitto, 'Rural elites in transition: China's cultural crisis and the problems of legitimacy', in *Select papers from the Center for Far Eastern Studies*, 3 (1978–9) 218–75.

found useful so as to update and strengthen Chinese counterpart institutions that might already have had a long history in China.

These trends lay behind the attack on Confucian social values in the first decade of the twentieth century. The assault was led by urban intellectuals as part of a broad challenge to family authoritarianism, beginning with the emancipation of women and youth.

Women had been slowly securing a higher status and a considerably broader range of activities than permitted by orthodox Confucian moralists. The number of educated women in elite families had been rising since the sixteenth century. Nineteenth- and twentieth-century Chekiang gazetteers record public donations by women; some biographies indicate their vigorous role in local as well as familial affairs. Women of poorer families played a more crucial economic role and were more active outside the family than were elite women. Women fought on and sometimes commanded pirate ships in the early nineteenth century. They took leading positions in heterodox sects, and participated in riots. Economically independent women weavers in the Canton delta established their own organizations and even eschewed marriage.

By the late nineteenth century restrictions were slowly relaxing even among the wealthy, but the convention that women properly pursued their activities within, not outside, the household remained an impassable barrier to their assuming public roles. One impetus for breaking this barrier came from abroad. Missionaries argued in favour of schools for girls and against footbinding. Foreign ideas and examples provided a new image of women's place in society; ideals of nationalism and freedom furnished a rationale. Liang Ch'i-ch'ao in 1896 wrote one of the first denunciations of the stifling of Chinese women. The anti-footbinding movement became widespread and vigorous, although its history has hardly been studied. In the 1900s and 1910s advocacy of women's liberation was a hallmark of radicalism and opposition to footbinding a basic ingredient of social progressiveness. Some women easily moved outside the household, others faced a difficult and painful struggle.[66]

It was easier, though never simple, for male youths to declare independence from family ties. Students became part of the new political

---

[66] A good starting point for information on women in the late Ch'ing and Republic is Margery Wolf and Roxane Witke, eds. *Women in Chinese society*. On their part in the May Fourth movement, see Roxane Witke, 'Transformation of attitudes toward women during the May Fourth era of modern China' (University of California, Berkeley, Ph.D. dissertation, 1970). For an example of a woman active in local as well as family affairs, see Cole, *Shaohsing*, 94–6. For an example of female rioters: Roxanne Prazniak, 'Community and protest in rural China: tax resistance and county-village politics on the eve of the 1911 revolution' (University of California, Davis, Ph.D. dissertation, 1981), 127–31, 142–9. On women pirates: Dian Murray, 'Mid-Ch'ing piracy: an analysis of organizational attributes', *CSWT* 4.8 (Dec. 1982) 7. See also 'women' in indexes of *CHOC* 10, 11 and 12.

landscape as soon as they began to study abroad or in new schools. Abolition of the traditional examination system made education less time-consuming. Young men spearheaded the demands for political and social change. The assertion that the young were independent of their elders and should quickly assume positions of responsibility was a radical step. Students and intellectuals formed the backbone of revolutionary parties before 1911 and would continue to be leaders of radical parties in the Republic.[67]

Rural organizations and popular movements

Associational groups among the peasantry ranged from legitimate institutions, such as lineages and village associations led by respectable elites, through borderline institutions like village protection associations and militia (which could be founded with government approval but potentially could challenge official control), to distinctly illegal (but sometimes tolerated) groups like sects, secret societies, or smuggling, bandit and pirate bands. Even the illegal sects, gangs and secret societies were imbedded in local social and commercial structures. Many were continuous organizations that helped members make a legal or illegal living and offered them protection, companionship, and (in the case of sects) religion. In effect they complemented the official and high-level elite organizations, but they were not perceived primarily in terms of social class. A variety of lower elites or partially educated men could be found among sectarian and secret society leaders, and the members appear to have shared the values that permeated respectable society. These organizations cannot, therefore, be looked upon as embodiments of a separate peasant little tradition with its own separate values. The distinction was more between those included in or excluded from orthodox and officially sanctioned institutions. Illegal organizations therefore had a competitive capacity vis-à-vis the state and upper-class society, insofar as they were formed by people who felt unfairly excluded or inadequately provided for.[68] This tension, underlined by the fact of illegality, surfaced periodically in rebellions or in official repressions of still peaceful groups.

Was there an expansion of illegal or borderline organizations in the late Ch'ing comparable to the increase in autonomous elite-run organizations? All that can now be said with certainty of religious sects is that they were numerous, that a considerable number of risings in the late eighteenth and early nineteenth centuries indicated a surge of activity, and that sects

[67] The rebellion of Chinese youth against the family system is addressed in literature more than in academic scholarship. See Leo Lee, 'Romanticism and emancipation', *CHOC* 12.476–80.

[68] This competitive aspect within a framework of shared values is pointed out in Susan Naquin, *Shantung rebellion: the Wang Lun uprising of 1774*, 161.

continued to be active into the Republic.[69] Somewhat better evidence exists about secret societies. Triads, first established in the early Ch'ing, extended their activities into the interior of the south and south-west in connection with the opium trade and other smuggling during the early nineteenth century. They further spread among settled communities in the Canton delta during the Opium War. The Elder Brother Society probably emerged in the 1850s or 1860s to become the dominant society in the Yangtze valley. A handful of new societies was established in Chekiang in the latter half of the nineteenth century.[70] Local studies also show that natural disasters and disorders had produced a large number of societies/sects/gangs/defence associations north of the Huai River by the late Republic.

It seems probable, therefore, that population growth and commercialization stimulated organization within lower as well as upper levels of society. Disorder acted as a catalyst to produce new organizations. This proliferation was important because, although riots and protests might arise spontaneously, disorders were likely to be more frequent and prolonged when pre-existing organizations were involved. While increasing the possibility of disorder, the involvement of either societies or sects might also serve to keep it within bounds, for they both supplemented and existed in tension with the state and its adherents. In situations of instability, the internal logic of their practices and often illegal activities tended to push them from their marginal positions into rebellion against, rather than coexistence with, authority. Yet their members had, or aspired to, too many ties with the existing order and shared too many of its values to reject it completely or leave if for long.

Thus we believe that rural unrest was multi-faceted, and until the 1930s and 1940s seldom aimed at a revolutionary restructuring of government and society. Theories put forth to explain popular movements have stressed a variety of different aspects.[71] Dominant Chinese Marxist his-

[69] A list of sectarian risings in the late eighteenth and early nineteenth centuries is in *ibid.* 154–7. Perry, *Rebels*, 96–152, shows how sects became integrated with local social structures in North China during the late Ch'ing and Republic, whereas members of earlier sects were recruited as individuals (Susan Naquin, 'Connections between rebellions: sect family networks in Qing China', *Modern China*, 8.3 (July 1982) 340–9).

[70] On the Elder Brother Society, see Charlton Lewis, 'Some notes on the Ko-lao Hui in late Ch'ing China', in Jean Chesneaux, ed. *Popular movements and secret societies in China, 1840–1950.* On late nineteenth-century Chekiang societies see Mary Rankin, *Early Chinese revolutionaries: radical intellectuals in Shanghai and Chekiang, 1902–1911*, 128–39; see also Wang Ssu-chih, 'Tsung-tsu chih-tu ch'ien-lun' (A brief discussion of the lineage system), in *Ch'ing-shih lun-ts'ung, ti ssu chi* (Essays on Ch'ing history, fourth collection), 152–78.

[71] For a survey of the literature see Frederic Wakeman, Jr. 'Rebellion and revolution: the study of popular movements in Chinese history', *JAS* 36.2 (Feb. 1977) 201–38. Some major aspects of rebellions are set forth in Joseph Esherick, 'Symposium on peasant rebellions: some introductory comments', *Modern China*, 9.3 (July 1983) 275–84.

toriography from the 1950s to the late 1970s stressed the class consciousness of peasant rebels and pointed to poverty, economic inequities and social oppression as the causes of revolt. Straightforward economic explanations may account for a range of anti-rent and anti-tax revolts, such as those associated with the 'Tao-kuang deflation' of the 1840s, the riots in towns and villages touched off by inflation and new taxes at the end of the Ch'ing, or the tax protests during the 1930s depression. A focus on class-consciousness and oppression, however, ignores contrary evidence and the complexities of rural unrest. In the late 1970s and early 1980s Chinese historians offered broader interpretations.[72]

Another line of explanation looks at primitive (but often organized) agrarian social protest against landlords, officials and urban capitalists. Peasants objected to specific injustices and aimed to right specific wrongs, not to overturn the old social order in favour of a new one. This perspective, first elaborated as 'social banditry' in southern Europe, was broadened through study of food riots and the early English labour movement, and adapted to analyse peasant reactions when subsistence village economics were disrupted by imperialist capitalism. While specifics from other countries cannot necessarily be transferred to Chinese contexts, the general concept of non-revolutionary, morally-infused protest fits a range of Chinese rural unrest.[73]

[72] Two major bibliographic studies of Chinese Marxist historiography are James Harrison, *The Communists and Chinese peasant rebellions: a study in the rewriting of Chinese history*; and Liu Kwang-Ching, 'World view and peasant rebellion: reflections on post-Mao historiography', *JAS* 40.2 (Feb. 1981) 295–306. A theory of a class-conscious, revolutionary peasant counter-culture in Ralph Thaxton, *China turned rightside up: revolutionary legitimacy in the peasant world* (chs. 1, 8) requires substantiation. Convincing evidence of correlation between late Ch'ing disturbances, rice prices and copper devaluation appears in David Faure, 'Local political disturbances in Kiangsu province, China, 1870–1911' (Princeton University, Ph.D. dissertation, 1976), 270–392. On this whole question see below, ch. 6 (Bianco).

[73] The concept of social banditry derives from Eric Hobsbawm, *Primitive rebels*. Although criticized on the ground that all bandits are not socially conscious and many ally themselves with power holders, not the poor (Anton Blok, 'The peasant and brigand: social banditry reconsidered', *Comparative Studies in Society and History*, 14.4 (Sept. 1972) 495–504), Hobsbawm's general assertion of localized, specific, morally infused rural protest appears to hold up. The phrase 'moral economy' originated in E. P. Thompson, 'The moral economy of the English crowd in the eighteenth century', *Past and Present*, 50 (Feb. 1971) 76–136. Eric Wolf, *Peasant wars of the twentieth century*, and James Scott, *The moral economy of the peasant*, have applied the concept to peasant societies of Latin America and Indo-China, seeing a basis for union between villagers and Communist revolutionaries in peasant desire to recapture security and social cohesion lost when closed villages were invaded by capitalist market forces. Samuel Popkin, *The rational peasant: the political economy of rural society in Vietnam*, suggests that power and interest, not morality, determined rural relationships. Scott's and Wolf's ideas cannot be applied directly to China where villages were already commercialized, the direct impact of international capitalism geographically limited, and traditional rural societies sometimes fragmented and competitive. However, the general notions of standards of justice and protest of violations can be applied. Some issues are brought out in 'Peasant strategies in Asian societies: moral and rational economic approaches – a symposium', *JAS* 52.4 (Aug. 1983) 753–868.

The idea of social banditry can be seen in the Chinese tradition of bandit heroes sympathetic to the downtrodden as well as in popular perceptions of some actual bandit-rebels like White Wolf in the 1910s.[74] How local riots and risings could begin when peasants decided that officials or the rich would do nothing to help them is illustrated by a report in the *Hong Kong Telegraph* of the confession of a leader of a rising in eastern Kwangtung in 1907. 'The cause of this rebellion was that rice was very dear and scarce in that part and had been so for about a year. The authorities knew this the whole time and would not take any steps to make rice cheaper. They knew well the laws and duties cast upon them in cases of this kind. They simply ignored the people and let them starve.'[75]

A variant of the peasant demand for simple 'justice' was sale of rice at low 'fair' prices forced by urban mobs or rural bands, including appropriation of stores accumulated for temple-sponsored festivals. One such incident was the invasion of a market town in Kiangsi by out-of-work tea-pickers organized into a society led by 'Taoist Immortals'. When forewarned town leaders called off the fair, the tea-pickers forced a rich merchant known to be hoarding grain to 'sell' them supplies from the town charitable granary. They then repaired to a temple to hold their own drunken festival banquet, becoming so satiated that they were still there several days later when militia finally arrived and cut them down.[76]

The importance of religion in sectarian rebellions has contributed to the identification of a common, free-floating popular religion with its own scriptures and doctrines. These originated in Mahayana Buddhism and by the late imperial era combined aspects of Buddhism, Taoism and Confucianism in millenarian cults revolving about the Venerable Mother and Maitreya Buddha.[77] This sectarian faith, in different guises and divorced from any specific organizational base, played a role in three major risings: the White Lotus, the Taiping, and the Boxers, as well as numerous minor ones. The role of this religion was twofold. Its sects offered individuals hope in the midst of life's difficulties and maintained, over long periods, usually peaceful alternatives to the elite and state-dominated systems of belief and ritual.[78] But in appropriate circumstances

[74] For this interpretation of White Wolf see Edward Friedman, *Backward toward revolution: the Chinese Revolutionary Party*, 124–5, ch. 6, and Elizabeth Perry, 'Social banditry revisited: the case of Bai Lang, a Chinese brigand', *Modern China*, 9.3 (July 1983) 355–82.

[75] Marks, 'Peasant society', 186, analyses and quotes from *Hong Kong Telegraph*, 14 Sept. 1907. For a general discussion of food riots see Bin Wong, 'Food riots in the Qing dynasty', *JAS* 41.4 (Aug. 1982) 767–88.

[76] James Polachek, 'The moral economy of the Kiangsi Soviet (1928–1934)', *JAS* 42.4 (Aug. 1983).

[77] Daniel Overmyer, *Folk Buddhist religion: dissenting sects in late traditional China*, chs. 5, 7; Susan Naquin, *Millenarian rebellion*, 9–31.

this religion, with its belief in the coming of a new just age, emphasis on personal salvation, and absorption of folk martial practices, might help rebellions to break out from their local roots – to mobilize a following quickly from other social and marketing structures as did the Eight Trigrams in 1813, or to spread rapidly from an original geographical base as did the Taipings and Boxers.[79]

A study of rebellions in the poor, flood-plagued sections of Kiangsu, Anhwei, and Honan north of the Huai River found that rebellions emerged from either predatory or protective strategies devised by kinship and community networks to enable their members to survive in the particularly unpromising areas in which they lived. Predatory strategies utilized banditry, beggary, smuggling and feuds; protective ones set up militia and defence associations and created fortified villages. These two strategies interacted, both involved creation of military force, and both could expand into rebellion if the existing local balance was upset.[80] This perspective emphasizes continuities in rural unrest and its non-revolutionary character, and could be applied to situations of endemic unrest, like lineage feuding in Kwangtung.

These various aspects of illegal social organization and different causes of unrest might at times be compounded into movements that transcended their origins, as illustrated in the nineteenth century by the Taiping and Boxer Rebellions. Such major events raise most clearly the questions of the revolutionary potential and the limitations of traditional millenarian ideology and economic protest.

The causes of the Taiping Rebellion, which some have called an aborted revolution, included poverty and social disruption, an adverse foreign economic impact, patriotic anger at invasion, and contempt for a militarily weak government – causes that sound much like those put forth to explain revolution in the twentieth century. The millenarian message and utopian vision adapted from Christianity inspired the rapid march of a zealous army and presented a strong challenge to Confucian ethical and religious

---

[78] On long-lived peaceful sects see David Kelley, 'Temples and tribute fleets: the Luo sect and boatmen's associations in the eighteenth century', *Modern China*, 8.3 (July 1982) 361–91; and Richard Shek, 'Millenarianism without rebellion: the Hungtian Dao in North China', *Modern China*, 83. (July 1982) 305–37. Kenneth Lieberthal, *Revolution and tradition in Tientsin, 1949–1952*, 14–15, points to many peaceful sects in Tientsin in 1950.

[79] Daniel Overmyer, 'Alternatives: popular religious sects in Chinese society', *Modern China*, 7.2 (April 1981) 159–61, 167–8: Stevan Harrell and Elizabeth Perry, 'Syncretic sects in Chinese society: an introduction', *Modern China*, 8.3 (July 1982) 288–93. On millenarian aspects of Taiping Christianity see Philip Kuhn, 'Origins of the Taiping vision: cross-cultural dimensions of a Chinese rebellion', *Comparative Studies in Society and History*, 19.3 (July 1977) 350–66; and Rudolph Wagner, *Reenacting the Heavenly vision*.

[80] Perry, *Rebels*, ch. 3.

norms. The social egalitarianism and programmes for land redistribution spoke to peasant complaints, and the response revealed hostility to landlords that in the twentieth century would attract peasants to communist programmes. The idealistic social-political structure designed by Taiping leaders would have fundamentally altered the existing system of government. Whereas some of the claims made for the transcendental universalism of the Taiping message seem a bit overblown, and it was not solely a peasant revolution, it was indeed the most massive attempt to address rural grievances before the middle of the twentieth century.[81]

However, the Taipings failed because of internal weaknesses in leadership and organization and the strength of the elite-led opposition. They foundered on the persistent localism of Chinese society. Once they had abandoned their original base in Kwangsi, they failed to penetrate communities in the Yangtze valley where they set up their government. Peasants were not thoroughly mobilized, elites were not enlisted, and secret societies retained independent identities. At the end the Taipings came to the Lower Yangtze not as revolutionaries but as invaders, bringing death to poor and rich alike.[82] Having failed to transform the social order, the rebellion's main historical legacy was to help set in motion other social and political forces that would bring down the dynasty fifty years later.

The Boxers were in no way a revolutionary group, but their brief rising also combined numerous aspects of rural unrest and set in motion events that had nothing to do with the beginnings of the incident.[83] Evidence for direct organizational connection with White Lotus sects is scattered and fairly weak. However, Boxers did practise sectarian rituals and absorbed some sectarian beliefs that put them in competition with Catholic communities in western Shantung. Their local groups developed in two distinct ways. In the relatively prosperous south-west part of the province where landlords were strong and tenancy rates high, Boxers began as elite-led local defence societies which protected property from bandits. In the poorer north-west, where the land was not productive enough to attract landlord investment, there was relatively little tenancy. Here, Spirit Boxers led by ordinary villagers practised an egalitarian ritual through which anyone could be deified by being possessed by spirits. The Shantung governor encouraged those Boxers organized for village defence and failed to recognize that the north-west groups were fundamentally

[81] See Philip A. Kuhn, 'The Taiping Rebellion', CHOC 10, ch. 6.

[82] James Cole, The people versus the Taipings: Bao Lisheng's 'Righteous Army of Dongan', 7–21.

[83] This account follows Joseph Esherick, 'Lun I-ho ch'uan yun-tung ti she-hui ch'eng-yin' (On the social causes of the Boxer movement), Wen shih che (Literature, history, and philosophy), 1 (1981) 22–31.

different. It was these Spirit Boxers, unrestrained by weak elites, that expanded aggressively into eastern Chihli, threatening to turn against officials but directing most of their hostility against Christians and foreigners.

Once the movement began to expand out of control it became disastrously mixed up with court politics. Conservatives in the court tried to use the Boxers to strengthen their position while ridding the country of foreigners. Such high-level support allowed further rapid development of a movement that the government would have normally sought to suppress. It soon inspired foreign intervention. Different phases of the movement thus involved different constellations of social forces. Eventual political ramifications, including further alienation of southern elites from the government and resentment of tax surcharges to pay the Boxer indemnity, were far removed from any outcome predictable when the incident began.

Both these rebellions showed an extremist potential that nonetheless stopped short of changing the existing social structure. They failed not only because opposing forces were stronger, but also because leaders had no clear plan of a new order and followers had even less. The political possibilities of violent rural discontent remained to be realized under a different kind of leadership.

The labour movement and its rural ties

Industrialization began to create a distinct urban proletariat in the twentieth century, but city workers were neither a new phenomenon nor very far removed from their peasant origins. Artisans and labourers had long been part of the urban scene. Frequently they were migrants from specific rural areas who resided only temporarily in the cities. Their organization in gangs, secret societies, native-place associations and guilds was not sharply separate from rural social organization. Indeed in the highly commercialized Canton delta, guilds in the nineteenth century might span continuums of urban workshops in towns, and household producers in villages, interacting with local lineage and religious institutions.[84]

Introduction of factories using steam power started to change this situation by bringing together larger numbers of workers in distinctly urban settings where operations were largely governed by impersonal

---

[84] Winston Hsieh, 'Guild capitalism in village China: the legacy of rural entrepreneurship in the Canton delta, 1875–1925' (paper presented at the Columbia University Seminar on Modern China, Nov. 1982), 1–4.

market forces. However, there was no sharp break with the past. On the one hand, many small workshops with power-driven machinery were intermediate between older handicraft establishments and larger factories. On the other, rising demand for factory labour accelerated rural migration. Cities in the Republican period were constantly absorbing peasants from the countryside, who brought old patterns of behaviour with them.[85]

These workers often came from specific localities and did not sever connections with home. Thus women cotton-mill workers in Shanghai came mainly from parts of southern Kiangsu, particularly Wusih and Changchow, or from areas in the north of the province. Hiring reflected personal connections and workshops were usually composed of girls from the same villages. Apprentice ironworkers in Tientsin were similarly recruited from specific counties in Hopei with ironworking traditions, and were likely to be connected to the owner by ties of kinship, locality or other personal relationships originating in the countryside.[86]

Such patterns, typical of early industrialization in other countries, meant that from one perspective the proletariat was an urban projection of a highly mobile rural populace. Workers did not necessarily remain long in the city. Girls returned home to marry. Older workers often left their families in the villages, and there is some evidence that people who lost jobs in Lower Yangtze cities during the 1930s depression returned to the countryside. Wages also supplemented peasant family incomes. Part of children's factory earnings might be sent directly to their parents. Earnings of urban workers might be used to increase the landholdings of the more successful families or to maintain the livelihood of poorer ones.[87] The urban worker's social perspectives were likely to depend upon whether he or she was part of a rurally based family supplementing its agricultural income, or whether (usually) he came from a marginal rural stratum unsupported by kinship networks.

Within the city, the recent rural origin of the work-force was likely to interfere with labour solidarity. Hostility between relatively well-off

[85] Irene Taeuber, 'Migrants and cities in Japan, Taiwan, and Northeast China', in Mark Elvin and G. William Skinner, eds. *The Chinese city between two worlds*, 374; Gilbert Rozman, *Urban networks in Ch'ing China and Tokugawa Japan*, 78.

[86] Information on Shanghai women textile workers is from Emily Honig, 'Women cotton mill workers in Shanghai, 1912–1949' (Stanford University, Ph.D. dissertation, 1982); that on Tientsin iron-workers is from Gail Hershatter, 'Flying hammers, walking chisels: the workers of Santiaoshi', *Modern China*, 9.4 (Oct. 1983) 387–420. For the contract labour system, see Honig, 'The contract labor system and women workers: pre-liberation cotton mills of Shanghai', *Modern China*, 9.4 (Oct. 1983) 421–54.

[87] Aspects of rural-urban labour interchange are described in Randall Stross, 'A hard row to hoe: the political economy of Chinese agriculture in Western Jiangsu, 1911–1937' (Stanford University, Ph.D. dissertation, 1982), 44–50.

and cultivated cotton-mill workers from Kiangnan, and the poorer cruder women from north Kiangsu, who got the dirtiest jobs with least chance for advancement, obscured resentment against mill-owners. Even major incidents like the Peking tramway workers' strike of 1929 might have more in common with traditional riots than with the class-based economic protest that appeared in later stages of capitalist industrialization in Europe.[88]

In addition, the bargaining position of many urban workers was exceedingly poor. Early modern industry was in effect subsidized by the surplus of agricultural labour. Workers who left their families behind could be paid very low wages, and the young girls and boys who were a major part of the labour force in some industries had even less control over their situations than did adult workers. Long established methods of recruitment and training could become warped in these transitional circumstances. Contract recruitment systems, for instance, reflected locally based patterns of work-related migration, but control by gangs in Shanghai exposed women millworkers to kidnappings and rape and depressed their living conditions, because labour bosses paid for and controlled their dormitories. Similarly, the apprentice system of the Tientsin iron factories provided owners with a rotating supply of inefficient but exceedingly cheap unpaid apprentices, who were often dismissed to look for jobs elsewhere when their three years of service were over.[89]

Despite these weaknesses, labourers did begin to organize in the 1920s in cities where there were substantial numbers of factory workers. Old style guilds provided one foundation for mobilization in places like Canton where they were already highly developed, but the new organizations followed the model of Western trade unions. The leading wedge was provided by relatively skilled and vigorous adult male workers, such as mechanics and seamen, while organizational impetus came mainly from new intellectuals.

In the Canton area unions rapidly replaced craft and trade guilds after the May Fourth movement. The first wave of formation in 1920–2 during the postwar boom reflected the workers' own appreciation of their growing numerical strength during a period of economic expansion when labour was in demand. Strikes in these years advanced spontaneous demands for higher wages and better working conditions. A two-year

---

[88] David Strand and Richard Weiner, 'Social movements and political discourse in 1920s Peking: analysis of the tramway riot of October 22, 1929', in *Select papers from the Center for Far Eastern Studies*, 3 (1978–9) 137–80.

[89] Ming-kou Chan, 'Labor', 140–1, 150, makes points similar to those made by Honig about Shanghai and by Hershatter about Tientsin.

hiatus coincided with both economic recession and the nationwide political retreat of the labour movement following the bloody suppression of the Peking–Hankow railway workers early in 1923. Erosion of earlier gains by renewed inflation was partly responsible for a second strike wave in 1925–7, but in these years the labour movement was much more closely involved in political and nationalistic issues – as exemplified by the Canton–Hong Kong general strike and boycott. The merger of the Nationalist and Communist parties fostered radicalism, and the new Nationalist government at Canton encouraged mass organization. By 1927 there were 200 unions in Hong Kong, 300 in Canton, and an estimated 700–750 thousand members in the delta as a whole.

The labour movement never became a strong political force, however. Intellectual agitators, especially Communists, had limited rapport with union rank and file, who remained primarily interested in improving their own economic situations. Workers saw political struggles against imperialists and warlords as a means to this end, whereas left-wing intellectuals promoted worker economic struggles as a step toward revolution. As unions became mixed up in politics they became more dependent on government tolerance. Their political role in Canton ended with participation in the unsuccessful Communist insurrection late in 1927. Surviving unions were still allowed by more conservative governments to advance limited economic demands but no longer participated in larger movements.[90]

Details and timing of the labour movement varied from place to place, but a similar evolution can be seen in the other two centres of activity, Shanghai and Hunan.[91] The urban workers were still too few, too weak, and too beset by their own difficulties to be an independent political force. The proletariat probably did not number more than a few million in the 1920s, even including people in workshops and service jobs as well as in modern factories. It was concentrated in a few places where there was a substantial amount of modern industry or mining: Shanghai, Canton, Hunan/Hupei, eastern Shantung, north-east Hopei around Tientsin, and southern Manchuria. These pools of urban workers grew when economic conditions favoured industrial expansion, as they did from the late 1910s through much of the 1920s. Political conditions in Central and South

[90] Ming-kou Chan, 'Labor', 163–6, 208–28, and *passim*; Lynda Shaffer, *Mao and the workers: the Hunan labor movement, 1920–1923*, 109–12.

[91] On Shanghai see Jean Chesneaux, *The Chinese labor movement, 1919–1927*. For somewhat contrasting views on the dynamics in Hunan see Angus McDonald, Jr. *The urban origins of rural revolution*, 142–206, 241–50; and Shaffer, *Mao and the workers*. Chesneaux (407–12) maintains that the labour movement was the leading revolutionary force of the 1920s. For additional bibliography see Ming K. Chan, *Historiography of the Chinese labor movement, 1895–1949*.

China permitted, and in some places favoured, organization until 1927. However, once brought into politics, workers were pushed into confrontations with stronger adversaries at a very early stage of union development. There was very little time for growth and organization. Some Nationalist officials and some capitalists recognized that workers' living conditions needed improvement, but world depression and war in the 1930s and 1940s created very unfavourable conditions for any enlargement of an urban working class and were even less conducive to a labour movement.

STATE AND SOCIETY IN THE REVOLUTIONARY PROCESS

Society and state are whole and part, comparable perhaps to cell and nucleus. China had inherited from politically creative eras – like Ch'in plus early Han and Sui plus early T'ang – a remarkably powerful state based on time-tested structures, practices and ideas. Not least of its strengths was a capacity for coalition politics and decentralized administration that the outside world is only beginning to study.

Political history of the late Ch'ing and the Republic has usually been summed up in one of three ways: in cyclical terms, seeing a late dynastic decline, a period of disorder and military competition, and the re-establishment of a centralized state; in terms of a slow, uneven expansion of state power into the society as government sought to extend its administrative apparatus to the village level; and in terms of a revolutionary process through which old political myths and social structures were destroyed, new classes brought into politics, and a new state created on a radically different ideological and social base.[92] All these approaches provide insights. There was a decline, interregnum and reconsolidation. Governments did indeed try to extend their authority, centralize control, and restructure finances and administration. But on balance we believe the history of these 150 years is more adequately defined as a revolutionary

[92] Theories of ninteenth-century cyclical dynastic decline, expressed either in terms of loss of control and consequent rise in corruption and disorder, or in terms of decentralization accompanied by the rise of regional armies, appear in Franz Michael, 'Regionalism in nineteenth-century China', introduction to Stanley Spector, *Li Hung-chang and the Huai army*; and in Hsiao Kung-chuan, *Rural China: imperial control in the nineteenth century*, 501–18. An interpretation of twentieth-century Chinese politics in terms of traditional disintegration and modern reintegration appears in James Sheridan, *China in disintegration: the republican era in Chinese history, 1912–1949*, ch. 1. A similar framework, drawing upon theories of political culture, is advanced in Lloyd Eastman, *The abortive revolution: China under Nationalist rule, 1927–1937*, vii–xiv, 283–313 (see also ch. 3 below). Twin theories of elite invasion of local government powers in the mid-nineteenth century and twentieth-century governmental efforts to extend administrative control downwards to the village level appear in Kuhn, *Rebellion and its enemies in late imperial China: militarization and social structure, 1796–1864*; and ch. 7 below.

movement of society out from under the old state control, the emergence of new social classes, the redefinition of political relationships, and the creation of a new state structure and ideology. It was an uneven, spasmodic, and often bloody process.

Compared with younger and smaller countries, this modern transformation of the Chinese state was slow and tortuous. As the government began to bulk larger within the society, the cognate phenomena of penetration and participation, of state-building and popular mobilization, formed two sides of the same coin, but both were slow to develop. In China, as elsewhere in the nineteenth century, modern firearms, steam transport and telegraphic communication became available, but the Ch'ing government's use of them to penetrate the society down to the level of village and household was tardy and halting. A similar slowness in the spread of literacy, a daily press and postal service inhibited the growth of popular participation in politics. No doubt this record of non-performance, of potentialities realized only gradually and grudgingly, reflects the innate strength of China's late imperial polity. It did not change easily. Despite an appearance of metamorphosis between 1800 and 1949, basic features of elitism and authoritarianism strongly persisted.

Disequilibrium in the Ch'ing establishment

Basic relations between the Manchu-ruled Ch'ing state and Chinese society were mapped out in the seventeenth and early eighteenth centuries. Once the conquest was achieved, precedents for alien rule were so well established that anti-Manchu sentiment found expression mainly in Confucian-style loyalty to the Ming dynasty, not in a Chinese nationalism. Fundamentally, the examination system inherited from the Ming tied the interests of the upper class to the monarchy, created bridges between localities and the capital, and helped to maintain the orthodox ideology.[93] Several other basic arrangements further defined state-societal relations.

First, at the time of the conquest, the upper-class elites for the most part accepted Manchu rule as a reasonable price to pay for a return to order and stability. In return they were allowed to retain a substantial portion of their local position and interests.[94] Second, the government

---

[93] See Barrington Moore, Jr. *Social origins of dictatorship and democracy: land and peasant in the making of the modern world*; Philip A. Kuhn and Susan Mann Jones in *Select papers from the Center for Far Eastern Studies*, 3 (1978–79) xiv, 'Introduction', discusses 'the relationship between the central government bureaucracy (the state) and local administrative systems (society)'.

[94] Hilary J. Beattie, 'The alternative to resistance: the case of T'ung-ch'eng, Anhwei', in Jonathan D. Spence and John E. Wills, Jr., eds. *From Ming to Ch'ing: conquest, region, and continuity in seventeenth-century China*, 242–3, 256; I Songgyu, 'Shantung in the Shun-chih reign: the establishment of local control and the gentry response', *CSWT* 4.4 (Dec. 1980) 19–27; 4.5 (June 1981) 13–23.

subsequently followed tax and other policies that encouraged the break-up of large manors in North China and curbed landlord power in the south. The unplanned results of these two policies were that the government was willing to allow elites considerable latitude because they did not control large concentrations of economic (and potentially military) power, elites were willing to support a government generally favourable to their interests, and the tensions between rich and poor that had been building up during the late Ming were defused.[95]

Third, the early Manchu rulers kept taxes low and maintained a rather small, underfinanced bureaucracy that did not penetrate below the county level. This policy, inherited from the Ming, was supported by Confucian ministers both on ideological grounds and because it was in the interest of their landholding families. In the early Ch'ing the smallness of the bureaucracy was partly offset by an efficient system of official post routes and bureaucratic reporting supplemented by a personal information-gathering network centring on the emperor.[96]

But these devices circumvented rather than squarely addressed the growing problem of administrative superficiality. The Yung-cheng Emperor in the early eighteenth century made a serious attempt to provide adequate financing for local government and official salaries but had to move very slowly in the face of considerable opposition.[97] By the late eighteenth century demography was playing havoc with the balance between the bureaucratic apparatus and society. Population growth, commercial and urban expansion outran the ability of the bureaucracy to supervise the populace or provide necessary services. Breakdown of the granary system was one symptom. In these circumstances the bureaucracy could not remain static. The number of regular civil officials remained fairly stable, at about 20,000, half of whom served in the capital, but they were supplemented by a far larger body of low-prestige clerks, runners, and personal servants with official functions and by more prestigious private secretaries. The number of clerks varied with the size of the county.[98] Government efforts to control the numbers and activities of this sub-bureaucracy and of the secretaries were ineffectual, because population

---

[95] See Marks, 'Peasant society', ch. 2, and the theories of Jūzō Kawachi set forth in Grove and Esherick, 412. Other authors variously emphasize peasant revolts or see little balance between state, gentry, and peasant interests. See additional citations in Grove and Esherick (404–12) on landholding and tax reform.

[96] Fairbank and Teng, *Ch'ing administration: three studies*, 23–8, 44–8: Jonathan Spence, *Ts'ao Yin and the K'ang-hsi Emperor: bondservant and master*, ch. 6; Silas H. L. Wu, *Communication and imperial control in China. Evolution of the palace memorial system, 1693–1735.*

[97] Madeline Zelin, '*Huo-hao kuei-kung*: rationalizing fiscal reform and its limitations in eighteenth-century China' (University of California, Berkeley, Ph.D. dissertation, 1979), 90–132, 348–467.

[98] Chang Chung-li, *The Chinese gentry*, 110; Ch'ü T'ung-tsu, *Local government in China under the Ch'ing*, 39, 59–60.

increase required larger numbers of low-level functionaries to carry out necessary business. Throughout the nineteenth century the sale of examination degree status added to the ranks of nominal degree holders. In the latter part of the century the civil bureaucracy was expanded still further by the addition of officials specializing in foreign, commercial, industrial or military affairs, by the frequent employment of deputies (*wei-yuan*) to conduct official business, and by the addition of new specialized bureaus. The rate of this expansion was, of course, dramatically increased by the reform policies of the first decade of the twentieth century.

Particularly in the last half of the nineteenth century, an effort was made to restructure government finances by raising land-tax surcharges, and there was a marked increase in the percentage of revenue derived from commercial taxes including customs duties on foreign trade. One estimate is that government revenues in current taels approximately quadrupled between 1753 and 1908 (or doubled in real terms if one adjusts for price changes).[99] This was not enough, however. The Ch'ing state simply failed to extract an adequate share of the increased national product resulting from the growth of the economy. Serious attempts at reform were undertaken only after the military costs of suppressing rebellions had badly strained finances in the middle of the nineteenth century. Thereafter the central government appears never to have brought its fiscal situation under control. Local government remained equally underfinanced. At the end of the dynasty, large indemnities severely strained a financially straitened government that was suddenly attempting to expand its functions. Increases in surcharges and new forms of taxation to finance local reform expenditures after 1900 contributed more to political and social unrest than to financial stability.

Aside from the structural problems besetting Ch'ing fiscal policy, there is a large body of literature suggesting that the bureaucracy was undermined by corruption, and the monarchy by the degeneration of the emperors in the nineteenth century. Allowing for some exaggeration, it nonetheless appears that the corruption inherent in tax-farming, with officials living on their take, had become so embedded in tax-collection and many other aspects of local government that it could not be eradicated short of the most drastic restructuring. On the higher level, however, corruption did not seriously threaten to engulf the entire bureaucracy except during the late Ch'ien-lung period. Administrative checks and regulations stifled initiative but kept the machinery functioning. During the eighteenth century the Grand Council had gradually changed from

99 Wang Yeh-chien, *Land taxation*, 80, 131.

an informal means by which the emperor could circumvent the regular bureaucracy to a major policy-making institution in its own right, capable of keeping government going even when emperors weakened at the end of the dynasty.[100] Reorganization of the Grand Secretariat at the beginning of the nineteenth century by officials determined to prevent a recurrence of massive corruption at the court actually improved the flow of documents and gave high officials more leverage vis-à-vis the court. Moreover, during much of the nineteenth century, the throne was able to enlist the services of some remarkably able officials ranging from Juan Yuan to Chang Chih-tung. This success was due more to the seriousness of crises in the nineteenth century than to the abilities of the emperors whom they served. Even so, the nineteenth-century Manchu rulers were not pernicious, and other elements in the court appear to have exercised a really disastrous influence on policy only during the last two or three decades of Manchu rule.

The Ch'ing government structure was riddled with flaws, but collapse came not so much from internal bureaucratic inadequacy or court degeneracy as from failure to adjust to societal developments. Massive mid-century rebellions demonstrated the existence of problems, but failed to overturn the political and social structures. To understand the end of the imperial system one must look at the political challenges that came from the elite layer of society.

The rise of elite activism

This movement stemmed naturally from the fusion and fragmentation of traditional elites, noted above. By the beginning of the nineteenth century expanding societal initiatives were evident in a growth of non-official economic, social, and managerial activities, but an autocratic government blocked any corresponding growth of political expression or redistribution of political power. This situation was exacerbated throughout the nineteenth century by further expansion of societal organizations, while the number of lower-level bureaucratic functionaries also increased. The demands for redistribution of power did not follow European patterns. In the integrated and centralized Chinese state, no militarily powerful group comparable to feudal barons, no peripheral but economically essential class like European burghers, could demand concessions from the state. The Manchu court remained extremely sensitive to the danger

[100] Beatrice S. Bartlett, 'The vermillion brush: the Grand Council communications system and central government decision-making in mid Ch'ing China' (Yale University, Ph.D. dissertation, 1980), 296–308.

of internal military challenge. Despite the deterioration of the old military forces, it was able to maintain control over commanders of the new regional/provincial armies built up to suppress mid-nineteenth-century rebellions. Initial challenges did not arise through direct political confrontations. They came rather through exercise of initiative and expression of opinion by men in peripheral positions, who accepted the existing system, but were assuming more active roles to meet recurrent crises. Tensions developed between political insiders and outsiders in three areas within the existing state structure: extra-bureaucratic scholarly-managerial (or 'gentry') circles, lower levels of the metropolitan bureaucracy, and the treaty ports. They pressed for redistribution of power outward from government to societal leaders and downward within the administrative structure. In the 1890s and 1900s this slowly maturing opposition merged and mounted a frontal attack on the existing authority.

Gentry management of public services arose because the bureaucracy was unable to provide necessary services in such fields as water control, order, and welfare at the local level. Dike administration, for instance, had been a service obligation during the Ming dynasty, but after the collapse of the *li-chia* system a new system had to be devised.[101] Management by yamen underlings was fraught with problems, arising both from corruption and from inadequate financing. Elite management and contributions offered an alternative solution. There are isolated references to gentry participation in public works management in such areas as Shanghai and Ningpo during the seventeenth century. During the second half of the eighteenth century, local elites appear to have participated more frequently in public management, and by the early nineteenth century one begins to find specific references to 'gentry managers' (*shen-tung, tung-shih*).[102] 'Gentry management' grew up at different speeds in different places, depending upon local needs and the vigour and wealth of local elites, but by the mid-nineteenth century it appears to have been a widespread phenomenon. Merchants, as well as gentry, managed public institutions. Guilds in cities like Hankow expanded the services rendered their members to the community at large.[103]

Autonomous management grew rapidly in three phases during the second half of the nineteenth century. The first impetus came during the

[101] Elvin, 'Market towns', 457.
[102] *Ibid.* 462–3, 472; Shiba, 'Ningpo', 442.
[103] For an example involving riot-suppression, see William T. Rowe, 'Rebellion and its enemies in a late Ch'ing city: the Hankow plot of 1883', *Select papers from the Center for Far Eastern Studies*, 4 (1979) 71–111. More broadly: William T. Rowe, *Hankow: commerce and society in a Chinese city, 1746–1889*.

mid-century rebellions, when local elites organized militia and assumed taxing and other local powers usually reserved to officials. The second arose from the need for reconstruction after rebellion. Local men, who assumed the chief responsibility for relief and rebuilding, expanded their activities in education and welfare to the point where extra-bureaucratic management was an essential part of the local civil government structure. These activities were financed mainly by endowments, by elite and business contributions, and by commercial taxes over which officials did not have complete control. The final phase of expansion began in the mid-1890s as degree holders and gentry managers began to engage in self-strengthening activities in education and industry. After 1902 gentry managerial functions were formalized in associations, chambers of commerce, and bureaus mandated by the Ch'ing government as part of its reform policies.[104]

The nineteenth-century managerial explosion upset the balance between the local elite and the bureaucratic state. Gentry have often been pictured as brokers between officials (particularly magistrates) and local society, sharing some interests with both, combining sometimes with one side and sometimes with the other, and sometimes mediating between them.[105] The new managerial elites did not forsake this role in the nineteenth century, but they increasingly supplanted the bureaucracy in local government at a time when magistrates were becoming less effectual.[106] Although elites were given a formally defined role in local government only with the establishment of elective councils and assemblies in 1909, managers selected by elite community consensus had actually been an essential part of some local administrations for the previous fifty years.

This phenomenon has been seen as related both to local militarization and the decentralization and localization of power. There was, however, no simple trend as long as the Ch'ing dynasty existed. Some areas continued to be militarized after the rebellions, with guns spread about the countryside in an active competition between militia and bandits. But some officials were firm and successful in trying to disband militia and control gentry assumptions of police or military power. Meanwhile

---

[104] On the Taiping period see Kuhn, *Rebellion*. For the second and third phases see Mary Rankin, 'Elite activism and political transformation in China: Zhejiang province, 1865–1911'. For an analogous process in the Middle Yangtze, see Rowe, *Hankow*.

[105] Edwin O. Reischauer and John K. Fairbank, *East Asia, the great tradition*, 311–13. For data on local gentry-official relationships, that stress disruptive and self-seeking gentry behaviour, see Msiao Kung-chuan, *Rural China*. A summary of components in the gentry's local political/social roles is in Frederic Wakeman, Jr. *The fall of imperial China*, 27–34. On Chinese views of the local control and autonomy problem, see P. A. Kuhn, 'Local self-government under the Republic', in Frederic Wakeman, Jr. and Carolyn Grant, eds. *Conflict and control in late imperial China*, 257–98.

[106] Faure, 'Local political disturbances', 251–9, ch. 7; Robert Weiss, 'Flexibility in provincial government on the eve of the Taiping rebellion', *CSWT* 4.3 (June 1980) 17.

significant new accretions of local elite power came in civil pursuits related to scholarly, business and community interests.

This tendency arose most strongly in core economic and cultural areas, epitomized by the Lower Yangtze. In that area rural unrest did not simply result in movement of elites to cities, it also inspired managerial activities, aiming not only at local police control but at alleviating some of the causes of trouble. This was neither an exclusively rural nor urban movement, because wealthy, educated 'rural' elites had business interests in the cities and high-level bureaucratic ties. They conceived of an upward flow of civilian initiative that would modify national policies and bring them into public service outside their native areas. This evolution had several features.

First, rivalry with officialdom. Elites became convinced of the superiority of their own autonomous management over bureaucrat-run activities. Their chief animosity was directed against the sub-bureaucracy. Most higher officials approved of managerial activities that contributed to public organization and order, but disagreements could erupt when vigorous, reform-minded officials came into contact with equally vigorous, publicly active gentry managers who were convinced that they were the best judges of local needs. A governor like Ting Jih-ch'ang, who sought to curb local elites and strengthen magistrates as part of administrative reform, inevitably was suspicious of initiatives outside the bureaucracy. Tensions with officials might be aggravated when merchants opposed likin taxation, for instance, or when landlord gentry sought to take over supervision of land-tax collection from yamen clerks and runners.[107]

Second, patriotism. Many managers viewed their activities as a statecraft response to the needs of the age, related to broader problems. Men who had been shaken by the experience of rebellion and whose education (and often careers) had been aimed toward public responsibilities, were quite capable of seeing their activities in a national framework. This generalizing tendency was reinforced in the late nineteenth century by patriotic response to the foreign danger.

Third, social cohesion. Elite managers belonged to informal scholarly-mercantile, managerial-official social networks that cut across marketing

---

[107] On this process see Rankin, 'Elite activism', chs. 2–6. On Ting Jih-ch'ang see Jonathan Ocko, *Bureaucratic reform in provincial China: Ting Jih-ch'ang in Restoration Kiangsu, 1867–1870*, 143–4. Ocko suggests a competition between elite and official reformism at the local level during the T'ung-chih restoration. For examples of gentry invasion of tax-collection and conflicts over tax-collection see James Polachek, 'Gentry hegemony: Soochow in the T'ung-chih Restoration', in Wakeman and Grant, eds., 244–5; Tsung Yuan-han, *I-ch'ing kuan wen-kuo chi* (Illustrious collection from the I-ch'ing Hall), 3.6b–11a; *T'ung-hsiang hsien-chih* (Gazetteer of T'ung-hsiang district), ch. 6.

structures and regional boundaries. In the Lower Yangtze surviving members of the badly fractured old academic community, like Ting Ping, redirected their energies into management, officials retired to devote themselves to the problems of their home areas, and wealthy merchants managed local institutions as well as funding them. Elite-managed institutions were established at various levels of the urban hierarchy, down to the market town level, but often with high-level official connections. In short, local management did not develop in isolation.[108]

Fourth, proliferation. Managerial activities tended to be expansive and not restricted by locality or level of urban hierarchy. Some individuals managed autonomous institutions in different places at different stages of their business or academic careers. Other managers in county capitals travelled about the county supervising subsidiary institutions in towns and villages. Managerial skills acquired in one place could be used elsewhere, and local institutions could be used as bases for activities in other areas.

These features were impressively illustrated in the mobilization of Lower Yangtze welfare institutions to provide relief to victims of serious floods and the great famine in North China in the late 1870s. Relief committees, inspired by the foreign example, were established by gentry and merchants in Shanghai and three other major cities of Chekiang and Kiangsu. Welfare institutions and publicly active individuals collecting in smaller cities and towns forwarded money to these centres. The proceeds were then sent to representatives of the committees, who dispersed relief in the famine area. A rough accounting of income and expenditures and reports of relief activity were published in the Shanghai newspaper *Shen-pao*. In this effort local institutions raised funds for autonomous activities that took place in an entirely different region of the country, in response to a crisis that Lower Yangtze managers considered to be of nationwide importance. Organization was entirely outside the bureaucratic structure (although there was close cooperation), and these elite-run organizations were considerably more successful than officials in raising funds. Finally, the press played a crucial part in promoting public awareness of the magnitude of the famine, in encouraging contributions by such devices as printing names of individual donors, and by providing a forum for the committees. Participants were well

---

[108] E.g. *Nan-hsun chih* (Gazetteer of Nan-hsun), 21.10b–11a, 18a–20a, 22b; 34.2b, 4b, 8b, 10b, and chs. 21 and 24, *passim; T'ung-hsiang hsien-chih*, 4: *shu-yuan*, 1b; *shan-t'ang*, 1b–2b, 5a, 13a; *Wu-Ch'ing chen-chih* (Gazetteer of Wu and Ch'ing towns), 29.25a–b; Ching Yuan-shan, *Chü-i ch'u-chi* (First collection while dwelling quietly), 2.41a–42a, 48a–63b; 3.66a–69b and *Shang-yü hsien-chih* (Gazetteer of Shang-yü district), 35.18a.

aware of the autonomous character of their activities, which were described by *Shen-pao* as 'popular contribution and popular management' – a phrase also used for local managerial activities.[109]

This kind of apolitical participation in public affairs, as elites assumed more responsibilities and believed their views should be consulted, eventually fostered political demands. However, by 1900 there were still no mechanisms other than personal contacts and patronage networks to convey public demands to the government.

Alienation and demands for wider participation in decision-making also spread within the bureaucracy in the last decades of the nineteenth century, but the origins go back to the late eighteenth. Although the Chia-ch'ing Emperor managed to regain the loyalty of officials disillusioned by the corruption of the late Ch'ien-lung period, constant crises in the nineteenth century kept alive doubts about the vitality of the system, and fuelled demands for broader consultation to seek solutions to problems. Such demands were inherent in the flow of suggestions and criticisms from the lower levels of the metropolitan bureaucracy, where underemployed officials lacked effective ways to make their views known to influence policy. Even in the early nineteenth century it was impossible to rebuild consensus over how government should work, and by the 1830s patriotism was encouraging divisive activism, as groups of officials called for the end of the opium trade and criticized leaders who could not defeat the British.[110]

After Chinese provincial leaders loyal to the throne had saved the dynasty from the mid-century rebellions, the central power over the provinces had to be rebuilt on a less autocratic basis. The Ch'ing banner forces having been eclipsed by the new regional armies, the Ch'ing monarchy faced again, as it had in the mid-seventeenth century, the necessity of securing collaboration from high provincial officials in a marriage of convenience.[111] Weakness of the court made it easier for the foreign policy discussions culminating in the Ili crisis with Russia and the Sino-French and Sino-Japanese Wars to break out of the bonds previously circumscribing opinion-expression within the bureaucracy. The 'pure criticism' (*ch'ing-i*) voiced in these crises marked the beginning of oppositional public opinion within the government. However unfair some of the criticisms and ill-judged some of the attacks, their legacy was a growing conviction that some major officials could not be trusted, that

109 See *Shen-pao*, 1878–9, *passim*, e.g. 8 June 1878, 4; 20 July 1878 1; 4 Dec. 1878, 3; 21 Feb. 1879, 3; 10 Aug. 1879, 3; 14 Aug. 1879, 3.
110 James Polachek, *The inner opium war*, ch. 2.
111 On regional armies see Kwang-Ching Liu, 'The Restoration in perspective', CHOC 10.477–90; and Liu and R. J. Smith, 'Ch'ing armies of the post-Taiping era', CHOC 11.202–11.

the Ch'ing dynasty could not protect the country, and that the solution lay in broadening political participation, so that upper-class public opinion could be heard. Militant patriotism in the capital was thus wed to concepts of elite-led social mobilization and institutional reform.[112]

The third major contribution to an oppositional public opinion and broader political participation came from men who lived in the treaty-port cities, together with a smaller number who travelled abroad. They were among the first to introduce Western methods, ideas and values into China. Treaty ports attracted not only socially marginal compradors but also scholars and merchants, who flourished in these urban centres without cutting ties with kin and native place. Such men provided money, organizational impetus, and sometimes direct leadership for autonomous local management. They also led the way in questioning arbitrary government practices, from which the foreign-run concessions gave them some freedom.[113] Their alienation and the confrontation between the state and elite society were hastened, and in part defined, by the treaty-port press after the mid-1870s. Wang T'ao, who had been impressed by foreign newspapers, began publishing in Hong Kong at this time. Equally significant was the establishment of the first successful daily newspaper in Shanghai, *Shen-pao*. Henceforth the press provided news of and rationales for autonomous managerial activities. It was a source of knowledge about foreign alternatives, a forum for criticizing officials, and a powerful catalyst of patriotic sentiment, nourishing distrust of Ch'ing officials and welding together opposition arising from different quarters by expressing attitudes common to all.

Reform and revolution at the end of the Ch'ing

The 1898 Reform Movement was the first climax of this growth of public opinion and political demands. Politically oriented study societies and other associations that sprang up after the Sino-Japanese War were a genuinely new departure, heralding the end of the Ch'ing ban on overt public policy activity. Certain aspects of the Reform Movement have received particular attention, notably the One Hundred Days of 1898 when

[112] On the political significance of *ch'ing-i* see Mary Rankin, '"Public opinion" and political power: *qingyi* in late nineteenth-century China', *JAS* 51.3 (May 1982) 463–77. Effects of *ch'ing-i* on policy-making are suggested in Lloyd Eastman, '*Ch'ing-i* and Chinese policy formation during the nineteenth century', *JAS* 24.4 (Aug. 1965) 609–11.

[113] On establishment of the treaty ports and the men involved see John K. Fairbank, *Trade and diplomacy on the China coast: the opening of the treaty ports, 1842–1854, passim,* 394–8; Paul Cohen, *Between tradition and modernity: Wang T'ao and reform in late Ch'ing China*; also Jung-fang Tsai, 'The predicament of the compradore ideologists: He Qi (Ho Kai, 1859–1914) and Hu Liyuan (1874–1916)', *Modern China* 7.2 (April 1981) 191–225.

the reform party controlled policy in the capital, the reform movement in Hunan, and the ideas and activities of a group centring about K'ang Yu-wei and Liang Ch'i-ch'ao. In reality the movement was more widespread and had a broader elite constituency. Gazetteer and press accounts show considerable pressure from gentry and merchant circles in Chekiang, for instance, although it is not usually included among centres of a significant reform effort. In provinces like Chekiang, where reform leaders emerged from the top of local elite society, there was little ideological resistance to reform. At the outset the issue was not reform *per se*, but the kinds of reforms to be pursued, and whether the bureaucratic monarchy could accept new political initiatives from outside its structure. Where the most extreme reformers achieved prominence – mainly in the capital and Hunan – they alienated moderates by pushing for very rapid change and by attacking basic Confucian family principles. The government at the centre waited for moderates to become doubtful and then refused to broaden access to political power. The entrenched leaders in the bureaucracy and court were too strong to eliminate without military force. The 1898 anti-reform coup in Peking was engineered by men who were not only conservative, but also predominantly Manchu or dynasty oriented, concerned to preserve both their own positions and autocratic control over society. They rejected, as it turned out, their last chance to accommodate societal initiatives within the existing political structure.[114] The anti-reform coup sent shock waves through the publicly active segment of elite society, increasing distrust of and alienation from the dynasty. At first it was not clear how far arrests were going to go – and where elites had been broadly engaged in reform activities, as in the Lower Yangtze, many had reason to be uneasy. Further antagonism was aroused by a policy of replacing high Chinese provincial officials with Manchus. Soon thereafter, court support for the Boxers, executions of officials who protested it, and the disastrous international consequences of irrational racism in 1900 alienated still wider circles of elites who were extremely sensitive to the danger of encouraging social disorder and disgusted with a government that had provoked still another foreign invasion.

At the turn of the century metropolitan officials were resigning and returning home in disillusionment, scholars outside were confirmed in the belief that they could not serve the Ch'ing government. Anti-Manchuism, which had been a latent, elusive attitude throughout the century, now became overtly political, joined with hostility to autocratic oppression.

[114] On the 1898 Reform Movement see Chang Hao, *CHOC* 11.274–338; T'ang Chih-chun, *Wu-hsu pien-fa shih lun-ts'ung* (Collected essays on the 1898 Reform Movement). This interpretation is from Rankin, 'Public opinion', 470–2.

Perhaps the first openly published attack on Manchu rule appeared in *Shen-pao* in the summer of 1900.[115] Some have held that once the government embarked on a course of reform after 1901 it could have succeeded if only it had been able to maintain control for a little longer. Such arguments underestimate the problem of change in so large a country, but rightly point to the vigour of the official Ch'ing reform movement and the rapid progress it made in a few years. The flaw in this argument lies in its underestimating the political gap that had opened between the bureaucratic state and elite society.

Participation and control, not reform, remained at the heart of the clashes that occurred in the last ten years of the dynasty. The way in which the Peking government combined reform with aims of centralizing power and extending bureaucratic control provoked opposition.[116] One of the most persistently reformist governors-general, Chang Chih-tung, clashed with elites over who would control railway development despite their shared commitments to national strengthening and industrial modernization. Had leading elites been offered what they considered a meaningful role they might have joined or cooperated with the government, but they withheld support when officials repeatedly sought to limit outside initiatives.

The opposition that produced the 1911 Revolution was shaped by the basic conflict with the bureaucratic state.[117] It grew from a number of elite social groups that had different interests and various ideas about government and society. They did not, however, function as interest groups in the liberal democratic sense. Chinese society was too corporate, distinctions within the elite class too weak, and socio-political concepts too holistic for politics to suddenly adopt Western European or, particularly, American patterns. Members of different elite strata, old and new, remained interconnected by kinship, geographical and other ties. Members of the opposition also shared some basic views: they were nationalistic, believed in some degree of popular mobilization, desired redistribution of political power to provide greater societal participation in government, and were prone to feel betrayed by and ready to distrust the Ch'ing officials. Major political movements of the 1900s, like the anti-American boycott of 1905, the provincial railway agitations, and the constitutional movement broadly defined, mobilized combinations of opposition groups and inextricably intertwined nationalistic sentiments with their demands for representational government.[118] Fierce competition

115 *I-ho t'uan* (The Boxers), 4.171–2.
116 On the Ch'ing official reform programme, see C. Ichiko, *CHOC* 11.375–415.
117 On the 1911 Revolution, see M. Gasster, *CHOC* 11.463–534.
118 Basic works on the constitutionalist movement are Chang P'eng-yuan, *Li-hsien p'ai yü Hsin-hai*

developed abroad, in an émigré situation, between the Revolutionary Alliance and the constitutional monarchists led by K'ang Yu-wei, but their struggles in Toyko, South-East Asia, and the United States were not duplicated within China.

At home the divisions between different elements in the opposition were not as great as the gap between all of them and the centralizing bureaucratic state. Their roles were complementary rather than competitive. The revolutionary parties put forth a republican alternative that was eventually accepted as preferable to a vitiated, Manchu-defined constitutionalism that sought to control rather than enlarge the scope for outside, non-governmental, initiatives. Radical intellectuals provided visions of a stronger nation based on a freer, more equitable society and won public sympathy through occasional heroism. Their violent tactics helped to illegitimize a resistant government. The revolutionary infiltrated New Army units furnished the military strength that unreliable secret society allies failed to supply. Merchants and gentry, business and professional elites provided a measure of social support without which the 1911 Revolution would not have succeeded.

In the mid-nineteenth century, elites supported the Ch'ing government against rebellion to preserve their positions. In 1911 they defended their interests by supporting revolution against a political system from which they had became estranged. Chambers of commerce, educational associations, and provincial assemblies all served as vehicles for upper-level social mobilization, furthering the opposition. Economic strains of course increased the turmoil of the last Ch'ing decade. Inflation, copper devaluation, land-tax surcharges, renewed flooding in the Yangtze and

ko-ming (The constitutionalists and the 1911 Revolution) and Chang Yu-fa, Ch'ing-chi ti li-hsien t'uan-t'i (Constitutionalist groups of the late Ch'ing period). See also Chang P'eng-yuan, 'Provincial assemblies: the emergence of political participation 1909–1914', Bulletin of the Institute of Modern History, Academia Sinica, 12 (June 1983) 273–99. Interpretations of elite roles in the last Ch'ing decade include Esherick's theory of an 'urban reformist elite' (Joseph Esherick, Reform and revolution in China: the 1911 Revolution in Hunan and Hubei, ch. 3) and Fincher's picture of a substantial movement for self-government and democracy, expressed through the assemblies, that rested on older socio-economic changes but was triggered by the Ch'ing official reforms (John Fincher, Chinese democracy: the self-government movement in local, provincial and national politics, 1905–1914). MacKinnon has suggested a less competitive picture of expanding political power at national, provincial and county levels, providing room for both officials and elites to expand their political roles (Stephen MacKinnon, Power and politics in late imperial China, 10–11, conclusion); whereas, C. Ichiko sees gentry adjusting to initiatives by the government or revolutionaries in a conservative way, simply to maintain their power (Chūzō Ichiko, 'The role of the gentry: an hypothesis', in Mary C. Wright, ed. China in revolution: the first phase, 1900–1913, 308). Proliferation of elite organizations in inner-core areas of Chekiang as an index of socio-political development is detailed in Keith Schoppa, Chinese elites and political change: Zhejiang province in the early twentieth century, 59–74. For a basic historical perspective on the Chinese approach to local government in general, see Kuhn, 'Local self-government', pp. 257–98 in Wakeman and Grant, eds.; also Kuhn, 'Late Ch'ing views of the polity', Select papers from the Center for Far Eastern Studies, 4 (1979–80) 1–18.

Huai River valleys, and, above all, new miscellaneous taxes to finance the New Policies on the local level contributed to anti-government social unrest. In some places these strains brought lower classes into conflict with dominant elites. In the violence-prone rural society of Honan, for instance, the Revolutionary Alliance found allies among bandit forces competing with militia or with gentry-led village-protection forces with government backing.[119] In 1911 village-based peasant armies, from regions hit by a drop in the silk market and by the competition from rice imports after the opening of the Canton-Kowloon railway, converged on Canton and occupied the city for several weeks.[120] Urban mobs also took part in the revolution in Canton, Shanghai and other major cities.

On balance, however, in 1911 the Revolution emerged from economic growth in core areas, from involvement of China in world trade, and from social organization on the upper, not the lower, levels of society. It was not narrowly bourgeois and not entirely urban, but it did centre in areas experiencing economic growth and was led by groups created or strengthened by this growth. It successfully forestalled the inherently doomed effort of an outmoded bureaucratic monarchy to convert itself into a modern authoritarian state. It did not solve the problem of how locally rooted popular movements without strong military forces could create a new national government.

Trends in Republican politics

Because the main features of China's late imperial polity were as deeply rooted as those of the economy and society, the first half of the twentieth century saw an often bewildering fluctuation between new and old, innovation and reaction. Modern-minded patriots, hoping for China's regeneration, canvassed and discussed contemporary political thought from the outside world in great abundance, often with precocious insight.[121] Despite the range and fecundity of their ideas, however, the main trends of Chinese politics grew out of situations already being defined at the end of the Ch'ing.

First of all, the cluster of doctrinal beliefs and institutional practices by which the imperial Confucian monarchy had controlled China since the T'ang continued to disintegrate.[122] It would not be easy to reassemble

[119] Billingsley, 'Bandits', 261.
[120] Winston Hsieh, 'Peasant insurrection and the marketing hierarchy in the Canton delta, 1911', in Elvin and Skinner, eds., 138–41.
[121] The breadth and variety of avant-garde political discussion is exhibited in Robert A. Scalapino and George Yu, *Modern China and its revolutionary process*, vol. 1: *Recurrent challenges to the traditional order, 1850–1920*.
[122] For analysis of Chinese despotism and 'officialism' (scholar-official domination of the society) see

such a cluster because all the components were in flux, rapidly changing. In the end, a consensual belief system and world view, official examinations to select self-indoctrinated bureaucrats, an autocratic and self-perpetuating central leadership and its monopoly of justice, education, surveillance and military power – all these ingredients of the old Chinese state would not be brought fully to function together again until after 1949. But by that time both their content and their overall configuration would be quite different.

Within four years of the 1911 Revolution it was clear that there would be no simple progression to follow either the proto-liberal democratic mobilization or the statist modernization at the end of the Ch'ing. In 1912–13, when the newly organized Nationalist Party (KMT) won China's first and only parliamentary elections, it was continuing the trend toward urban elite participation in government. But both it and the rival Progressive Party were hardly more than 'elite alliances', whose con-stituency was thin and scattered even in the restricted electorate of some 40 million.[123] Although Sung Chiao-jen hoped his followers among the gentry-merchant elite could control the new Republican government, multi-party government was distrusted as divisive by party leaders like Sun Yat-sen.[124] In 1913 Yuan Shih-k'ai ended China's experiment in parliamentary democracy by suppressing revolutionaries, disbanding parliament and provincial assemblies, and ending the thousands of local assemblies that had flourished in the first year of the republic.[125] Yuan's build-up of his dictatorship included revived examinations and a strengthening of civil bureaucracy over the military, together with censorship, surveillance and terror against the vanquished revolutionaries. He succeeded in eradicating the still immature institutional sprouts of broader participation in local government, but not in winning the loyalties of elites who had briefly moved into the new positions. Yuan's career ended in his destructive effort to revive the monarchy and his death in

Étienne Balazs, *Chinese civilization and bureaucracy: variations on a theme*, 6; also Arthur Wright's introduction. For late Ch'ing the classic study is by Kung-chuan Hsiao, *Rural China*; see also Ping-ti Ho, 'Salient aspects of China's heritage', in Ping-ti Ho and Tang Tsou, eds. *China's heritage and the Communist political system*, 1–37, especially 15–25. For a long-term perspective, see H. G. Creel, *The origins of statecraft in China*, vol. 1, *The Western Chou empire*.

123 P'eng-yuan Chang, 'Political participation and political elites in early Republican China: the parliament of 1913–1914', *JAS* 37.2 (Feb. 1978) 293–313; see p. 301. The trend toward more representative institutions is more hopefully appraised by Fincher, *Chinese democracy*. Lest 'local self-government' be erroneously assumed to be representative of the common people in town-meeting style, we should remember that it consisted rather of official devolution upon the local gentry elite of administrative functions they had long been performing informally. See Kuhn, *Rebellion*, 216–19.

124 Friedman, *Backward toward revolution*, ch. 2, on the late 1912 'attempts to build an inclusive single party' (p. 30).

125 Ernest Young in *CHOC* 12.242.

1916, further discrediting central authority by identifying it with a return to imperial control.

The ensuing warlordism was remarkable less for the breakdown of the already considerably rationalized central administrative institutions (as in dynastic interregnums of the past) than for this general 'disintegration of political authority'.[126] This trend was highlighted by three aspects of republican politics: militarism, an intellectual ferment in the search for legitimacy, and the rise of party dictatorship.

Military power had started to grow and change character in the nineteenth century. The personally organized armies of mid-nineteenth-century governor-generals began the transformation, but they still exemplified Confucian principles of moral leadership and reciprocal loyalty of troops to officers.[127] However, in the latter half of the century military growth became linked to industrial change. Armament manufacture, exemplified by the Kiangnan arsenal at Shanghai and the gunboat industry of the Foochow dockyard, became central to the self-strengthening movement.[128] Yuan Shih-k'ai's career under the Ch'ing exemplified how by the end of the century a builder of a modern army could become a power within the bureaucracy.

With the fall of the Ch'ing there was no longer a long-established, legitimized government to absorb military leaders. Yuan Shih-k'ai and his subordinate commanders in the Peiyang army who became warlords after his death faced a military with new status and orientations, under conditions in which military power was integral to modern government.[129] First, the imported technology of modern industrialized warfare created military specialities like artillery, engineering and communications. The necessary training required military schools, whose students became men of military learning, part of the new student body of the country. Second, like other students, the new military men might be moved by patriotism rather than teacher-pupil loyalties. Military patriots like Huang Hsing and Chiang Kai-shek appeared in their respective generations. Nationalism, in short, ennobled the soldier as its necessary front-line leader. It also demanded that he follow a new style of dedication, not simply order and

---

[126] Wang Gungwu as quoted in Diana Lary, 'Warlord studies', *Modern China*, 6.4 (Oct. 1980) 439–70; see p. 448.

[127] M. Bastid, 'The new military', *CHOC* 11.539–47. Cp. Kuhn, *Rebellion*, 147–8, 183–5.

[128] Thomas Kennedy, *Arms of Kiangnan: modernization of the Chinese ordnance industry 1860–1895*. The theme of the gunboat as the means of progress is illustrated in Robert Hart's long-continued promotion of Ch'ing naval power. See J. K. Fairbank, K. F. Bruner and E. M. Matheson, eds. *The I.G. in Peking: letters of Robert Hart 1868–1907, passim.*

[129] Stephen MacKinnon, 'The Peiyang Army, Yuan Shih-k'ai, and the origins of modern Chinese warlordism', *JAS* 32 (May 1972) 405–23; also *ibid. Power and politics*; Edmund S. K. Fung, *The military dimension of the Chinese revolution*; and Edward A. McCord, 'Recent progress in warlord studies in the People's Republic of China', *Republican China*, 9.2 (Feb. 1984) 40–7.

obedience. The new technology made an officers' corps as essential to government as constitutions, parties or bankers. On one level, militarism, arising from the ashes of Confucianism, altered both the structure and the ideology of the state. Sun Yat-sen re-entered the warlord fray at Canton as a 'generalissimo', and his eventual successor actually was one.[130] In another sense, militarism made it more difficult for governments to retain control. Subordinates with their own forces betrayed their commanders; more or less evenly matched warlord armies carried on their private wars; and the destruction and disruption turned city elites not only against warlords but also against those governments that could not control them. The new military would henceforth be part of the state structure, but they alone were not able to beat their rivals and reconstruct a central state unless they were part of a government that also attracted non-military support. The Ch'ing dynasty had been recognized as legitimate by Confucian-educated elites until the very last years of its rule. Its successor would have to win similar acceptance on new grounds.

Intellectual turmoil was heightened by nationalistic sentiment as patriotism continued to spread among the urban populace, primarily in response to Japanese encroachment (the Twenty-one Demands, 1915; Versailles, 1919; Tsinan, 1928; the North-east, 1931).[131] Meanwhile the fragmentation of government authority opened a temporary window for intellectual freedom and academic autonomy. Thus the stage was set for China's experience of liberal education under Anglo-American–French influences. The new belief in 'science' as the key to modernity, plus study abroad, professional specialization, and university independence made possible the rise of an academic community of the sort essential for national success in the modern world.[132] At the same time intellectuals were attracted to countless liberal, romantic, neo-traditional and other theories; they formed associations and published journals to set forth their views.

Parallel with this fragile growth of liberal pluralism, especially in higher education, was a trend to accept the revolutionary ideology of Marxism-Leninism, a universal 'science of society'.[133] From the beginning, Chinese revolutionaries had tended to see in Russia 'a paradigm of universal revolutionary progress'. The heritage of imperial Confucianism, with its faith in 'ethocracy', reinforced the concern aroused by the many social problems one could observe in China.[134] Simple nationalism was morally

---

130 C. Martin Wilbur, *Sun Yat-sen: frustrated patriot.*
131 See ch. 2 below.
132 See ch. 8 below.
133 *CHOC* 12.446–50 (Schwartz), 505–14 (Jerome Ch'en).
134 Don C. Price, *Russia and the roots of the Chinese Revolution 1896–1911.* 'Ethocracy' (as opposed to theocracy) is suggested by W. T. De Bary, in J. K. Fairbank, ed. *Chinese thought and institutions,* 131.

inadequate. Theories were not pursued only in the abstract, for both international and domestic crises continued to turn elite and urban attention to politics. Governments were not going to be accorded real legitimacy by volatile, independent urban groups unless they appeared to fulfil complex, sometimes contradictory, aspirations for economic progress, national strength, fairness and representation.

Behind this situation lay a basic change in the myth of the state that legitimized its power. Under imperial Confucianism the emperor's rule had been sanctioned by virtue of his right conduct in maintaining the social order, functioning at the central point in a cosmos that embraced both nature and humankind in an organic whole. The principles of form (*li*) were innately imbedded in this organismic cosmos, so that the imperial rule was immanent in the nature of things, not imposed from outside the human scene by a transcended deity or law as in the West.[135] By maintaining unity at home the Chinese ruler more easily asserted his universal superiority over rulers in contact abroad. But during the nineteenth century, imperialist expansion on China's periphery destroyed her suzerain-tributary relations with adjoining states and with it the Son of Heaven's claim to universal superiority.[136] Ch'ing weakness internationally, together with the influx of Western learning, destroyed the validity of imperial Confucianism.

It was replaced in the twentieth century by the nationalistic myth that ultimate state power resided with the Han people. The classical dictum that 'Heaven decides as the people decide' could be reinterpreted as a Chinese form of popular sovereignty. This Western idea gained adherents early. Liang Ch'i-ch'ao was one of the first popularizers. It was also picked up by Sun Yat-sen and enshrined in his Three People's Principles (*San-min chu-i*) as early as 1905. This myth of popular sovereignty represented the growth of political consciousness, participation, and mobilization, but it said little about how popular politics could be tied to the state power-structure.

The political party was to be the vehicle for actual exercise of popular sovereignty under the new republican system. The major innovation in political institutions was the party dictatorship that began to emerge within a decade after 1912 as a successor to monarchial government. This appearance of the single party as a vehicle for mobilization, indoctrination

---

[135] The Chinese 'have regarded the world and man as uncreated, as ... the central features of a spontaneously self-generating cosmos having no creator, god, ultimate cause or will external to itself'. F. W. Mote, *Intellectual foundations of China*, 18. Heaven's mandate, 'the cornerstone of the Chinese Empire' (Creel, *Origins of statecraft*, 93), must be viewed as operating within this impersonal, immanent framework; also discussed with European comparisons by Kuhn, 'Late Ch'ing views', 5–9.

[136] See J. K. Fairbank, ed. *The Chinese world order*.

and control signified the failure in China of the party as a pluralistic, representational institution, along with the failure of parliamentary government – a phenomenon widely met with in late-developing industrial states of the twentieth century.

After the Revolutionary Alliance (T'ung-meng hui) expanded in 1912 to form a parliamentary party, the Kuomintang, its functioning in a multi-party government was aborted by Yuan Shih-k'ai's dictatorship. However, the idea of the elite party as a public organization, more principled than a faction, more open than a conspiracy, had taken hold. What had not been established was a theory of separation of powers between legislative and executive that would be a prerequisite for the practical politics of a Western-style loyal opposition. Instead, old-style loyalty to persons continued to produce factionalism and, in the absence of legitimized government, disunity. Sun Yat-sen, rather than adopt a separation of powers among the legislative–executive–judicial triad as in Western democracies, had added examination and control powers to create the five-power constitution adopted by the Nationalist government of the Kuomintang. This Chinese pentagon worked even less well than the Western triad. When Chiang Kai-shek became the Nationalist leader he based his power on a tripod of party, army and government, each headed by himself.[137] Similarly, law, although developed to meet commercial needs, remained little more than a tool of administration, and constitutions were changed almost as readily as American party platforms.

In circumstances so unfavourable to a multi-party system, the party in Republican China developed along two intersecting lines – as an instrument of indoctrination and control and as a vehicle of revolutionary mobilization. Sun Yat-sen early developed the concept of tutelage, seeing a party mission to instruct the people in their political conduct while mobilizing them in politics. Behind this idea lay a long history of Confucian-Mencian faith in the power of ethical teaching and example to induce virtue and orderly conduct. With the rise of nationalism, reformers and revolutionaries had agreed that China's leaders had to train the hitherto politically inert populace to participate actively as citizens in a new form of national politics. By 1914 the task of tutelage in Sun Yat-sen's view had to be undertaken by a party with dictatorial powers.[138] Thus the ground was prepared for a Leninist party dictatorship even before it came into being in Russia and was transplanted to China.

This claim of the party to monopolies in indoctrination and mobilization,

[137] Robert E. Bedeski, *State-building in modern China: the Kuomintang in the prewar period*; also Ch'ien Tuan-sheng, *The government and politics of China*.
[138] Friedman, *Backward toward revolution*; also George T. Yu, *Party politics in Republican China: the Kuomintang, 1912–1924*.

if combined with government power, had an unprecedented potentiality for control. If officials were unchecked except by the usual considerations of expediency and loyalty, the combination of modern techniques of transport, communications and fire power with those of indoctrination, manipulation and control opened up the possibility of a twentieth-century interventionist state penetrating the society with little restraint. Under dynastic rule the Confucian myth of benevolent despotism as well as practical limitations of technology had kept a balance between imperial prestige and state coercion. Public order and proper administration were maintained not only by surveillance and coercion, but also by widespread and persistent indoctrination in Confucian principles of hierarchy and reciprocity. The examination system meant that upward mobility was for men who thought right. Confucian homilies of graded duties and responsibilities were dispensed in the villages and permeated the family system. Government was by moral authority almost as much as by coercion.

After the disappearance of the emperor ended his moral authority, Yuan Shih-k'ai and the warlord governments, lacking legitimacy, had to rely more on force. In the 1920s when two parties, the KMT and the CCP, were organized in the Leninist mould, they advanced new claims to legitimacy based on their differing mixes of nationalism and social justice. Each, however, soon denied the moral legitimacy of the other and sought to annihilate it.

The second role of the Leninist party – and the reason for its appearance in twentieth-century China – was as an agent of revolution. The attractiveness of the revolutionary party was many-sided: the urgent egalitarian concern for the common people; a world view claiming the prestige of science and suggesting strategy and tactics for action; patriotic and humane social ideals; a daring conspiracy that could satisfy the most insistent conscience while providing an exclusive comradeship. Loyalty to the party as the ongoing embodiment of China's salvation was a way forward.[139]

During the Republican era such attractions were, however, predicated upon the party continuing to act as an instrument of political and social change. Both the Kuomintang and the Communists originated as revolutionary parties. These common origins, plus nationalism and mutual opposition to warlordism, made their early collaboration possible. But there was certainly no consensus in favour of revolution among the elites from whom these parties had to draw support. The Leninist reorganization of the Kuomintang in 1923–4 was, moreover, a late

[139] See Jerome Ch'en, 'Conversion to the doctrine', *CHOC* 12.505–14.

addition to a congeries of provincial and personal factions that traced their roots back to before the amalgamation of the Revolutionary Alliance in 1905. In 1927–8 bitter ideological divisions between leftists, who favoured violent social revolution, and rightists, who favoured either non-violent change or the status quo, were superimposed on the older factionalism. The Central Executive Committee and Politburo where power was concentrated were soon dominated by the military leader, Chiang Kai-shek. The purge of left-wing party members weakened morale and, as the Kuomintang became more the party of the status quo, the ideology of Dr Sun was most prominent at the level of slogans and did not attract many intellectuals. The KMT, despite its weekly small-group meetings and centralist control of lower by higher levels, continued to be severely faction-ridden.

The Communists were more effective in maintaining party solidarity, combining Soviet and Chinese practices. To survive, they had to adjust flexibly as they were pushed underground in the cities and into peripheral rural areas where the Kuomintang or warlords were weak. They remained more clearly devoted to their original revolutionary cause.

Later chapters of this volume will appraise China's problem of government at different times and from various angles. In general, the governments of the Republican period were not as effective as the Ch'ing had been within the less ambitious sphere in which it had exercised power. Partly this was because the interventionist ambitions of state officials outran their capacities when they were unwilling to share power with those urban elites who might otherwise have supported and participated in their regimes. The burden on state bureaucracies consequently increased, especially as their very legitimacy depended upon unifying China. Much can be said for the thesis that the Nationalist government's claims to encompass, at least potentially, all aspects of society and all areas of China created a problem of control so great that the state's energies became largely absorbed in self-maintenance. As a counterpart to the 'high-level equilibrium trap' in the economy, this may be called a 'security maintenance syndrome' in the polity. Revenues had to be channelled to fighting competitors. Officials were unreliable, particularly at lower levels.[140] Bureaucrats watched each other and the ever-suspect public to such a degree that flexibility and innovation became difficult, especially after the KMT-CCP split of 1927 increased political tensions.

---

[140] Duara, pp. 327–36, argues that although the bureaucracy was extended down to the ward in Hopei province, the new sub-district officials were not effectively controlled by higher levels. Geisert, 'Power and society', 260–1 concludes that in Kiangsu the Nanking government bureaucracy was superimposed upon existing elite-controlled structures without liquidating the power of local elites.

Another part of the difficulty in reconsolidating state power lay in the activism and politicization of the elite populace that had begun in the nineteenth century. Would-be governments during the Republic had to expand their power in the face of elites who had already organized to advance their own interests or had their own agenda for national policy. Entrenched rural elites, city businessmen and professionals, and intellectuals all provided some support for the Nationalist government, but many were never fully committed.[141] Repression of dissidence, by alienating more and more observers, created precisely the distrust and opposition that was feared. Intent upon expanding and protecting its own power, the Nationalist state of the KMT still did not effectively control local affairs and became incapable of devising institutions that might have broadened popular participation in government. Cycles of violence and counter-violence fed upon one another, and those who neither condoned the government nor wished to risk opposing it withdrew to private pursuits or local activities.

There were at least three spheres of politics. First, a limited circle in which factions within governments or parties competed for power, and people on the outside acceptable to the regime established contacts with officials to protect or further their interests.[142] Second, urban oppositional politics, encompassing mass demonstrations and other expressions of dissent through organization and the press. These sometimes violent mobilizations of elites (and some allies in the labour movement) shaded off into the clandestine organizations of Communists and other leftists in the cities. The third sphere was the politics of the countryside, which included such diverse elements as the struggles of local military leaders with autonomous ambitions, efforts of governments to collect taxes and

---

[141] Theories of the relations between the Kuomintang and social elites fall into three categories. Marxist historians and a variety of contemporary writers have called the Kuomintang the party of the urban bourgeoisie and rural landlords (e.g. Harold Isaacs, *The tragedy of the Chinese revolution*, 31, 182). Other authors have stressed the personal dictatorship of Chiang Kai-shek (Ch'ien Tuan-sheng, *Government and politics of China*, 123, 132, 137); or suggested that the Nanking government was a dictatorial regime, which pursued its own interests unresponsive to any social class (Eastman, *Abortive revolution*, 240, 286); or characterized it as an authoritarian military regime, which ruled by controlling, suppressing, and arbitrating between weak social forces (Parks Coble, Jr. *The Shanghai capitalists and the Nationalist government, 1927–1937*, 341–2). A more complex picture is suggested by historians who argue that neither the Kuomintang nor the elites were monolithic. Through complicated, shifting political interactions, elements in the party and government and various rural and urban elites sought to advance their power and interests. The Kuomintang was thus more pre-authoritarian than authoritarian, for it was too militarily and financially over-extended to effectively control social groups. See Bradley Geisert, 'Toward a pluralistic model of KMT rule', *Chinese Republican Studies Newsletter*, 7.2 (Feb. 1982) 1–10; Geisert, 'Power and society', 1–10 and *passim*; Richard Bush, 'Industry and politics in Kuomintang China: the Nationalist regime and Lower Yangtze Chinese cotton mill owners, 1927–1937', 18–24, 307–8, 332–4.

[142] Bush, 'Industry and politics', 308–13.

of taxpayers to avoid them, and landlord suppression of apolitical peasant social protest. Political relationships followed patterns of patronage and brokerage, and violence was common when these mechanisms broke down.[143]

Pushed out of the cities controlled by the KMT, the Communist Party advanced its revolutionary programme and competed with local power holders in remote rural base areas under wartime conditions.[144] As yet unburdened with many of the administrative problems weighing down the Nationalist government, CCP members devised flexible policies to advance their cause by appealing to the most pressing social grievances in any area where they were trying to establish a base. In Shantung and Hopei, for instance, 'class struggle' to politicize peasant discontent was directed at 'local bullies' and tax-collectors, whom peasants considered more oppressive than landlords.[145] The moderate redistributive policies and inclusive assemblies promising non-party elites some political voice facilitated the goal of bringing a broader spectrum of villagers into local governments under party control. By giving political direction to social discontent the Communists began a process of building power from the bottom up.[146] The full potential for expanding state power would not be realized until after 1949.

These twentieth-century changes raised again the issue of the relationship of the individual to the state. Throughout history Chinese writers have generally stressed the duties and obligations of individuals to rulers, peasants, or others with little regard for any doctrine of human rights.[147] On the other hand, conceptions of justice and concern over injustice were always present in China. More specific concern over the rule of law and civil liberties inspired nineteenth-century Westerners to insist upon

---

[143] See below, ch. 6 (Bianco).

[144] See below, ch. 12 (Van Slyke) and ch. 13 (Pepper). Detailed historical studies of Communist base areas written during the 1970s and early 1980s provide information on Communist organizational efforts, relations with local power holders, and the leadership they gave to 'spontaneous' peasant demands. See David Paulson, 'Leadership and spontaneity: recent approaches to communist base area studies', *Chinese Republican Studies Newsletter*, 7.1 (Oct. 1981) 13–18. Major base area studies include Stephen C. Averill, 'Revolution in the highlands: the rise of the Communist movement in Jiangxi province'; Kathleen Hartford, 'Step-by-step: reform, resistance and revolution in the Chin-Ch'a-Chi border region'; David Paulson, 'War and revolution in North China: the Shandong base area, 1937–1945'; Linda Grove, 'Rural society in revolution: the Gaoyang district, 1910–1947'. Ch'en Yung-fa, 'The making of a revolution: the Communist movement in eastern and central China, 1937–1945' is the most comprehensive study of Communist Party strategies.

[145] Suzanne Pepper, *Civil war in China: the political struggle 1945–1949*, 282, 286–9; Ch'en Yung-fa, 243 and ch. 3 *passim*.

[146] Perry, *Rebels*, chs. 6–7 contrasts Communist social-political restructuring with rebel violence that did not rearrange local society. On the representational aspects of Communist base area policy, the realigned community consensus in base areas during wartime, and the potential of Communist policies for building state power and control, see Ch'en Yung-fa, 351–3, 412–14, 541, 795–803.

[147] See Donald J. Munro, *The concept of man in early China*, and *The concept of man in contemporary China*.

extraterritoriality (foreign consular jurisdiction over foreigners), which lay at the heart of the unequal treaty system and impaired the sovereignty of the Chinese state from 1842 to 1943. Thus human rights, as they are now called, were part and parcel of imperialism. In recent times there has been persistent questioning as to the prospects for the rule of law and civil liberties within the new state framework of China.

How far to give primacy to the individual citizen and how far to give it to the collectivity to which the individual belongs has been a choice resting on a recognized cultural difference between Chinese and Western value systems. It may be seen as a crucial matter of emphasis, yet it still lies within the larger question of the role of the people, elites and commoners of all sorts, in Chinese political life. Put in such broad terms, the question of 'democracy', however defined, was a key issue on the agenda of the Chinese Revolution. Cognate trends toward state penetration of society and social mobilization in political activity were inherited from the late Ch'ing. The Chinese Republic confronted a vexed relationship between rebuilding a strong state and broadening popular participation in it.[148] This tension was increased by the young republic's international environment.

[148] This issue may be viewed as part of a modernization process. Thus developments in material technology – roads, radio, aircraft, guns and books – brought Chinese governmental influence to bear in the remotest village. Yet the non-quantifiable influence of immaterial beliefs, customs and values often determined the balance between national and local interests, between official autocracy and non-official activism, between dictatorship and democracy. Granted that processes subsumed under the term modernization were plainly occurring, we find the concept lacking in capacity to evaluate and discriminate among the various results. For a stimulating application of the concept, see Gilbert Rozman, ed. *The modernization of China*; also the review by Susan Mann in *JAS* 42.1 (Nov. 1982) 146–53.

CHAPTER 2

CHINA'S INTERNATIONAL
RELATIONS 1911–1931

Modern China's fate has been intricately intertwined with the foreign policies of the powers, in particular Japan. Although historians nowadays may shun the detailed chronicling of wars and treaties relating to China (as in H. B. Morse's *International relations of the Chinese Empire*), this aspect of Chinese history is becoming more important in retrospect. After all, as Mary Wright pointed out in *China in revolution*, the presence of foreigners and their various activities on Chinese soil provided part of the milieu in which Chinese politics evolved in the twentieth century. Moreover, not only the maritime and 'foreign presence' described in volume 12 of this series, but also the contradictions and conflicts among the foreign powers, affected developments within Republican China. This chapter, and chapter 10 below, therefore look at the external context of twentieth-century Chinese history, beginning naturally with the collapse of the old order.[1]

CONTEXT: DECLINE AND FALL OF THE CH'ING EMPIRE AS AN
EAST ASIAN REGIONAL ORDER

The Ch'ing emperors' great achievement had been to assert their central power over the arid peripheral regions of Manchuria, Mongolia, Sinkiang and Tibet as well as over the heartland so densely populated by the Han Chinese. Military force, feudalism, religion and trade had all served the Ch'ing politics of empire, in mixtures that varied for each region and people. In all these regions of Inner Asia, Ch'ing rule had been set up by warfare and was maintained by garrisons. In Manchuria and Mongolia the emperor made the tribal chieftains his personal vassals. In Tibet and Mongolia he patronized the heads of the Lamaist church. In Kashgaria (southern Sinkiang) he appointed as rulers the local Islamic officials ('begs') and also accepted the Muslim law and the Islamic religious establishment. This use of Lamaist Buddhism and of Islam in governing

---

[1] The author is gratefully indebted to Douglas Reynolds, Marius Jansen and Akira Iriye for assistance in completing the English version of this chapter.

parts of Inner Asia, like the Manchus' use of Confucianism in governing China, showed a high order of skill.[2]

Foreign trade was similarly subordinated to imperial needs. Peking failed to protect the Mongol princes and monasteries from becoming disastrously indebted to Chinese local merchants. But trade with Japan via Liu-ch'iu, with Russia at Kiakhta, with Central Asia (Kokand) at Kashgar, and with the British, Americans and Europeans at Canton was successfully restricted and controlled. Only the trade from South-East Asia to Canton and Amoy was left outside the tribute system, for the simple reason that by the nineteenth century this trade was in Chinese, not foreign, hands.

The Ch'ing empire, like Ch'ing rule over China, was sustained by an intricate and sophisticated system of checks and balances between, for example, the local chieftains, ecclesiastics and tribal princes on the one hand and the central government generals and administrators on the other, between religious and civil elites within the local scene, between the military and civilian officials of the Ch'ing central government, and between local trade revenues and military expenditures. The empire began to fall apart only when international trade, backed by foreign military power, increased on the frontiers. The commercial, political and military advance of the tsarist Russian empire on China's north and west, and of the French and British empires on China's south and south-east is one of the best-known sagas of imperialism in the nineteenth century.[3] Soon Japan encroached upon the east and north-east.

Certain patterns of Ch'ing response to encroachment may be seen all around the periphery of the empire. First, the Ch'ing subordinated frontier trade to strategic interests because historically the central government's control of the Inner Asian periphery had been essential to the security of the Chinese core area. As long as possible the foreign powers' traders were confined to emporia on the frontier. Thus the Russians were ejected from Manchuria in the 1690s and confined to the Kiakhta trade after 1727, with occasional caravans allowed at Peking.[4] Meanwhile, as the British Canton trade increased in the early nineteenth century, the Ch'ing dealt with it along lines that they had found effective a bit earlier in Central Asia. The trade at Kashgar of the foreign state of Kokand had given rise to foreign traders' demands and a holy war led by rebel religious leaders. The upshot was that after suppressing the Kokandian invasion of Kashgar, the Ch'ing sought stability; they paid an indemnity to the foreign merchants and accepted a kind of extraterritorial jurisdiction on

[2] See Joseph Fletcher, 'Ch'ing Inner Asia c. 1800', CHOC 10.35–106.

[3] The classic survey is still W. L. Langer, The diplomacy of imperialism: 1890–1902.

[4] Mark Mancall, Russia and China: their diplomatic relations to 1728.

the part of Kokand's representatives, who superintended the activity of their merchants in Kashgar, whereupon the trade continued on a stable basis. The similarity of this settlement in Central Asia in 1835 to the eventual settlement at Canton in the 1840s is too striking to be a pure coincidence.[5]

Second, as the Ch'ing dynasty's structure of power began to crumble around its periphery both in Inner Asia and along the eastern sea-coast, the dynasty found its defensive military capacity quite inadequate and so the foreigners had to be appeased by concessions of residence and further trade. This again was reminiscent of the well-developed methods for barbarian-taming. After the Opium War the Ch'ing followed the early Ming policy of being ready, first, to admit all foreign states to contact with China and, second, to treat all such foreign states impartially.[6] Egalitarian foreign relations had indeed been customary in times of weak central power in China.[7] This long-time policy lay behind Peking's acceptance of the most-favoured-nation clause in the British Supplementary Treaty of 1843. The emperor's claim to ritual supremacy, i.e. the tribute system, was left unresolved; as the emperor was a minor after 1860 the issue of foreign envoys performing the kotow before him could be deferred until 1873.

This was of course not the first time that Chinese foreign policy had had to be conducted from a position of weakness. The inveterate strategy in such a situation had been the playing off of one invader against another. Almost before the geographical whereabouts of the United States and France were clearly ascertained, the barbarian-managers at Canton sought their help to check the British aggression. Subsequently Li Hung-chang, for example, made repeated efforts to secure American mediation and diplomatic help in his various efforts to check Japanese, Russian and French encroachments. After Britain failed to help against Japan in 1894, Li turned to Russia. 'Using barbarians to control barbarians' (*i-i chih-i*) was a principal strategy throughout the modern era.[8] Although Chinese thinking had to give up Sinocentrism, the idea of using one foreign power against another easily continued. It fitted rather neatly the Western concept of the balance of power.

During this transition Sino-foreign relations after 1860 were briefly characterized by the age-old device of synarchy – a non-Chinese dynasty's

[5] See *CHOC* 10.360–95 (Joseph Fletcher).
[6] Wang Gungwu, 'Early Ming relations with Southeast Asia', in John K. Fairbank, ed. *The Chinese world order: traditional China's foreign relations*, 50–60.
[7] Morris Rossabi, ed. *China among equals: the Middle Kingdom and its neighbors 10th–14th centuries.*
[8] Michael H. Hunt, *The making of a special relationship: the United States and China to 1914*; see ch. 4, 'The United States in Li Hung-chang's foreign policy, 1879–1895'.

use of other non-Chinese in joint administration over China. Synarchy in the late Ch'ing was first exemplified by the Chinese use of foreign-officered gun corps to defend Shanghai and Ningpo, and then by the growth of the Imperial Maritime Customs Service under Robert Hart, but Hart was only the most prominent of many foreign employees and advisers after mid-century. After all, the borrowing of foreign technology naturally brought foreign experts along with it. All this was achieved by taking Britain into a sort of entente. But the tendency to achieve stability by adding the British to the Mongols in the synarchic Ch'ing power structure at Peking and in the treaty ports was feasible only under sinocentrism. Like the Mongols, the Manchus' skill at using Westerners to help govern China prolonged their alien rule; but it proved unavailing as soon as China began in the 1890s to see herself as a nation among nations.[9]

The fact that Manchu rulers could not lead a movement of Han Chinese nationalism was one principal impediment postponing China's adjustment to the international world. The Sinocentric empire of East Asia under the Ch'ing had institutionalized the relations between China's pre-ponderant central culture and material power and the lesser peoples around her landward periphery. But when the republic succeeded the empire it confronted a profound dilemma. The emperor's former suzerainty over local rulers among the Inner Asian peoples could hardly be claimed by the president of a republic founded on the principle of nationalism. The concepts of nation and empire were compatible only if one accepted the Western type of colonial imperialism, against which Chinese patriots were most incensed. The traditional imperative that a new regime must unify the Chinese realm put the Chinese Republic under the burden of maintaining its central authority over the diverse peoples and sprawling terrain that had formerly comprised the Ch'ing empire. Yet the ideology of national liberation from imperialism provided little sanction for it. In fact, by the time the extinction of the Ch'ing monarchy in February 1912 shattered the multi-ethnic and supra-national empire that it had created, the new principle of nationalism had already undermined it.

Nationalism, in short, was among the 'maritime' influences that were eclipsing the old continental order.[10] The late Ch'ing regime had presided uneasily over the continuing expansion of the Han Chinese economy. Increasingly the Mongol princes and lamasaries had become debtors in the grip of Chinese merchants. Chinese settlers also had pressed into Inner

[9] Richard J. Smith, *Mercenaries and mandarins; the Ever-Victorious Army in nineteenth century China*; J. K. Fairbank, 'Synarchy under the treaties' in *ibid.*, ed. *The Chinese world order*.
[10] See *CHOC* 12, ch. 1.

Mongolia and eastern Tibet as well as into Manchuria. This penetration into Inner Asia of a Chinese 'secondary imperialism', to use Lattimore's phrase,[11] had its counterpart in the commercial inroads and ambitions emanating from Russia into Mongolia and Central Asia and from British India into Tibet. The outlying non-Han parts of the Ch'ing empire thus found themselves caught in the middle between the expanding continental empires of Russia and Britain and the growth of the Chinese Han nation. As a result the Inner Asian peoples began to look two ways and nurture their own national identities while playing off Europeans against the Chinese. In the decade before 1911 anti-Ch'ing movements for independence had arisen in both Mongolia and Tibet, provoked by late Ch'ing reformist policies there.[12]

In Mongolia, the encroachment of an expanding China had ended the Ch'ing policy of abstention and indirect rule through the tribal princes and Lamaist prelates. As the pastoral economy was drawn into trade, both the ruling classes and the common people became impoverished and indebted to Chinese moneylenders, while Ch'ing subsidies were diminished and taxes increased.[13] The New Policies (or New Administration: *hsin-cheng*) of the last Ch'ing decade (1901–11) opened Mongolia to Chinese colonization and agricultural settlement, permitted intermarriage and Mongol use of the Chinese language, and so threatened to sinify the Mongols' previously preserved homeland. Projects for provincial governments, military conscription, railways and other reforms increased the Ch'ing demand for taxes, alienated the Mongol elites and roused a sentiment of nationalism. By July 1911 a group of leaders decided to seek independence and sent a delegation to Russia seeking help.

Tsarist Russia's aim for Mongolia, which bordered Siberia for 1,700 miles, had been worked out during the mid-nineteenth century: Russia secured from Peking more and more trading privileges and aspired to a dominant influence, as over a protectorate, but for this purpose St Petersburg favoured Mongolian autonomy under continued Ch'ing suzerainty, not independence. The reason was simple: independence would open Mongolia to contact with all the other powers, whose prospective trading rights would compete with those Russia already enjoyed; an independent country could not be taken over as a protectorate without diplomatic conflict with other powers such as Japan, whereas actual Russian predominance could be achieved under the cloak of the nominal suzerainty of China, whose nationalists loudly claimed Mongolia as part

[11] See Owen Lattimore, *Inner Asian frontiers of China*, 143–5.
[12] On these trends see Morris Rossabi, *China and Inner Asia: from 1368 to the present day*.
[13] On this process see Joseph Fletcher, 'Mongolia's nomadic society in decline', *CHOC* 10.352–60.

of China. By 1911 Russian trade was less than Chinese, and there were only about 800 Russians in the area. Russia therefore assumed a dual posture – against independence but for autonomy – and sent two squadrons of cossacks to reinforce its consular guard in Urga.

The outbreak of the Chinese Revolution in October 1911 quickly inspired an Outer Mongolian declaration of independence. On 29 December the Living Buddha at Urga, the Jebtsundamba Khutughtu, was enthroned in a rather Chinese style as theocratic ruler of a new state, and debts to China were repudiated. However, instead of recognizing Outer Mongolia as a sovereign state open to international relations, Russia continued to recognize Chinese suzerainty. While beginning to arm and train the Mongol army, Russia in January 1912 issued a disclaimer of any territorial ambitions while urging Peking to give up direct rule, colonization or stationing of troops. By 3 November 1912 a Russo-Mongolian treaty recognized Outer Mongolia's autonomy and confirmed Russia's trade privileges. But Russia refused to recognize Mongolian independence or Urga's leadership of a pan-Mongol movement including the western tribes that were still under Chinese rule. It only remained for a Russo-Chinese treaty of 5 November 1913 to acknowledge the formula of Mongolian autonomy under Chinese suzerainty; and after long and acrimonious negotiations at Kiakhta, a tripartite Chinese-Russian-Mongolian agreement of 7 June 1915 reconfirmed this formula as well as Russia's economic rights. In effect Russia had set up an informal protectorate which the Chinese Republic was powerless to oppose.

The new government of the Living Buddha (or Bogdo Khan) at Urga, however, upset the balance that the Ch'ing had maintained between the lay princes of the Mongol tribes and the Lamaist church. Once in power, the church 'came increasingly to compete with the lay princes for people, livestock, and pastures' and began to divert resources to purely religious purposes. The conservatism of this theocracy was matched at Peking, where the Chinese Republic tried to preserve the appearances of the ancient tribute system and uphold at least on paper the interests of the Mongol princes. But within a decade the Mongolian People's Revolutionary Party, under Soviet inspiration and the leadership in succession of Sukebator and Choibalsang, set up a new government in 1921, and after the Living Buddha died in 1924 declared it to be a republic no longer under Chinese suzerainty.[14]

---

[14] Thomas E. Ewing, *Between the hammer and the anvil? Chinese and Russian policies in Outer Mongolia 1911–1921*, 39 and *passim*. See the full account in Peter S. Tang, *Russian and Soviet policy in Manchuria and Outer Mongolia 1911–1921*, chs. 7–13; also the more recent survey by Rossabi, *China and Inner Asia*, ch. 9. Events from 1917 are covered in an official *History of the Mongolian People's Republic*, vol. 3, *The contemporary period*, ed. B. Shirendev and M. Sanjdorj.

A comparable process occurred in Tibet but with a different ending. British India's concern for the trade and strategic security of the hill states of Ladakh, Nepal, Sikkim, Bhutan and Assam on the southern slope of the Himalayas created a British resolve to keep Russian influence out of Tibet, to which the hill states were culturally and sometimes politically tributary. Ch'ing suzerainty over Tibet and also Nepal had been established by arms in the eighteenth century and as late as 1886 Britain acknowledged it in a Sino-British 'Burma-Tibet convention'. By 1904, however, Britain felt obliged to forestall Russian influence by sending the Younghusband expedition to fight its way to Lhasa and negotiate a British protectorate over Tibet. London, however, backed away from this commitment on the inaccessible roof of the world; in 1906 Britain, in an Anglo-Chinese agreement, once again acknowledged Peking's suzerainty over Tibet as the best way to safeguard British interests there. The British, aiming to keep Russian influence out of Tibet, disregarded the Tibetans' interest in establishing their independence from China.

This set the stage for a vigorous Ch'ing reassertion of control over eastern Tibet in 1908; eventually in 1910 modern-armed Chinese troops entered Lhasa, where a Chinese administration attempted to rule. This ruptured the ancient patron-client relationship between the rulers in Peking and Lhasa. The Dalai Lama, traditional ruler of the theocratic state, fled to India. Soon the Revolution of 1911 and collapse of the Ch'ing led to the expulsion of Chinese troops and officials. The young Chinese Republic could not reassert control, and in January 1913 the Dalai Lama declared the independence of Tibet and is said to have made a treaty with the Living Buddha at Urga (number three in the Lamaist hierarchy) which mutually recognized their independences. This led to prolonged Anglo-Chinese-Tibetan negotiations in 1914 at Simla, where British India tried to recognize Tibet's independence but China refused to do so. A British protectorate or suzerainty was never asserted, though trade and cultural relations with India were carried on independently. The Chinese Republic maintained its claim to Tibet as part of China, while the British settled for the formula of Chinese suzerainty (not sovereignty) and Tibetan autonomy (not independence). This meant no direct Chinese control over Tibet, and a growth of British Indian-Tibetan relations, but only as long as the British stayed in India and China remained weak and non-assertive.[15]

Sinkiang, like Tibet, lacking railway access to the outside world, also remained on the periphery of international politics during the early

[15] H. E. Richardson, *A short history of Tibet*, ch. 7, 'The Simla convention, 1914'; Clive Christie, 'Great Britain, China and the status of Tibet, 1914–21', *Modern Asian Studies*, 10.4 (Oct. 1976) 481–508; Alastair Lamb, *The China-India border: the origins of the disputed boundaries*.

Republic. Yang Tseng-hsin, a metropolitan graduate of 1890 who had served during two decades in Kansu and Sinkiang and since 1908 as circuit intendant at Aksu, was confirmed by Peking as governor of Sinkiang in 1912, and retained the post until his death in 1928. He placated Chinese revolutionaries, Muslim Uighur proto-nationalists, and Kazakh tribesmen by carrot-and-stick, divide-and-rule methods, suppressing official corruption and encouraging trade. By making Sinkiang virtually semi-autonomous, he was remarkably successful at insulating it from the disruptive affects of both the Chinese and the Russian upheavals. Yang's 1924 commercial agreement with the Soviet Union provided for reopening consulates and for relations as equals that respected the laws and judicial authority of each other's territory. Trade between Sinkiang and the Soviet Union increased dramatically in the wake of this commercial agreement. From a value of 3.4 million roubles in 1923-4, it jumped to 22.0 million roubles in 1926-7. No nationalist movement had gained power in politically fragmented, multi-ethnic Sinkiang, and Governor Yang managed to maintain a unified regime, trade with the Soviet Union, and yet ward off its political intervention.[16]

In these various fashions Outer Mongolia, Tibet and Sinkiang fell out of Peking's control but remained of only marginal importance to the Chinese Republic. Manchuria was quite a different matter, because there the Republic directly confronted an imperialist power in a Han Chinese area, and China's national sovereignty was at stake.

Japan's encroachment raised the whole question of China's position in the international system. How could China, having had to abandon her traditional claim to ritual superiority over outsiders, get out of the humiliating status of semi-colony imposed by the unequal treaties? For this purpose how could she substitute, for the old image of a unitary world order centred at Peking, a new image of an international order of equally sovereign nations? In this context, how did wars taking place in and around China – whether or not the Chinese state was directly involved – affect its politics and economy? What were Chinese criteria for peace and order in East Asia? When conflicts arose with another country – Japan, in most instances – how did Chinese leaders and public opinion envisage the struggle? In short, how did they see their new position in the world? Efforts to answer these questions were an educational process through

---

[16] Irie Keishirō, *Shina henkyō to Ei-Ro no kakuchiku* (Chinese frontiers and the Anglo-Russian power struggle); and Rossabi, *China and Inner Asia*, 220–9. Also *Biographical dictionary of Republican China*, 4.11–13. Yang's preservation of Chinese dominance in Sinkiang was continued by Sheng Shih-ts'ai, a Japan-trained officer under Chiang Kai-shek who seized power in 1933, executed many opponents, and dealt with the Russians until Nationalist control was reasserted in 1943. For a recent appraisal see F. Gilbert Chan, 'Sheng Shih-ts'ai's reform programs in Sinkiang: idealism or opportunism?'.

which modern Chinese came to define their conceptions of themselves and of the modern international world.

JAPAN'S RISE TO POWER IN MANCHURIA

China's international position on the eve of the Republican revolution was affected profoundly by the rise of Japan to a position of power and a relative decline in the role of Western powers in East Asia.[17] After 1901 the Western powers had increasingly confined themselves to maintenance of the status quo and to the pursuit of their own established economic interests – Russia and Germany excepted. Russia proceeded with her penetration of Mongolia and North Manchuria, even after relinquishing her unequal treaty rights in China proper following her 1917 Revolution; and Germany, in the aftermath of the First World War, disappeared altogether from the East Asian theatre until her resurgence in the 1930s. Japan by contrast not only pursued her expanding economic interests but flexed her political muscle in diplomacy and military action. The primary focus of her activity, after the absorption of Korea, was Manchuria.

The homeland of the Manchu tribes (now known as China's North-east) was the most attractive of all the thinly populated regions around China. The old Chinese pale below Mukden (Shenyang), known as Liaotung, had been a settled part of China since the Han. Northern Manchuria, however, had remained tribal, and after the Manchu conquest of China the Ch'ing dynasty reserved the area as a racial preserve and governed it as a military frontier. By the mid-nineteenth century, immigration of Chinese could no longer be kept out, and Peking realized that it must even be encouraged lest Russia expand southward from the Amur to fill a vacuum. Yet the further opening of Kirin and Heilungkiang to immigration led to economic exploitation, especially of opium and ginseng root, accompanied by smuggling and banditry, which created problems of control and taxation more rapidly than the thinly spread Ch'ing military administration could cope with them. The Mongols in Manchuria, susceptible like those in Mongolia to Chinese merchants' exploitation, also posed a problem of loyalty.

By the 1890s the Ch'ing in self-defence had begun a programme of railway-building northward from the Great Wall to counter the threat of Russia's projected trans-Siberian line, but Chinese efforts were too late and too little. Japan's victory over China in 1895 led directly to the Sino-Russian alliance of 1896 and Russian building of the Chinese Eastern

[17] Hence Richard Storry's choice of title for his 1979 book *Japan and the decline of the West in Asia 1894–1943*. For the general context of this section see Marius B. Jansen, *Japan and China: from war to peace 1894–1972*; also Joshua A. Fogel, *Politics and sinology: the case of Naitō Konan (1866–1934)*.

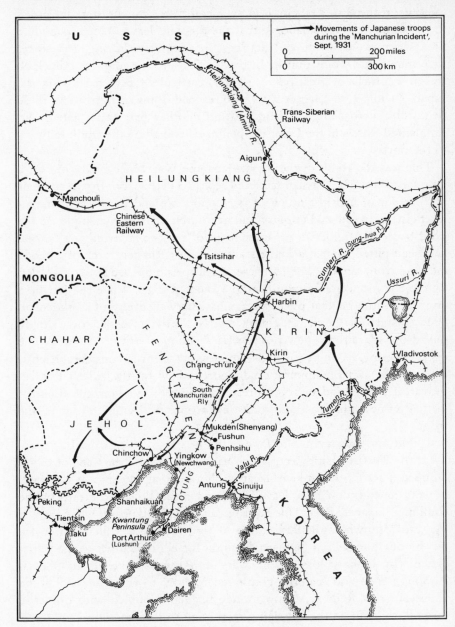

MAP 4. Manchuria (the 'Three Eastern Provinces')

Railway across Manchuria. Russian military occupation of Manchuria at the time of the Boxer rebellion in 1900 completed the disaster. Japan led the other powers in demanding that the Russians leave Manchuria, while the tsarist government did its best to pressure Peking for secret agreements that would suit its interests. The onetime Manchu homeland was now a focus of great power rivalry, particularly between Russia and Japan.[18] Unlike the other powers who reached China mainly by sea, these two were encroaching by land. Within another five years, Japan had supplanted Russia in the Liaotung peninsula and along the trunk railways to the north.

This was the result of the Russo-Japanese War which broke out on 8 February 1904. The Russians suffered repeated defeats, but by the summer of 1905 Japan had lost much of her confidence and means to carry on the fight. Between 23 February and 10 March 1905, for example, at the great battle of Mukden, a Japanese force of 240,000 men and 992 cannon had been pitted against a numerically superior Russian force of 370,000 men and 1,219 cannon. The Japanese, not surprisingly, had been outshelled by 540,000 rounds of ammunition to 350,000 rounds. When the Japanese army began its general offensive against the walled city of Mukden on 9 March and took the city the following day, the main Russian force simply pulled out by rail to a new position at Tiehling, north of Mukden. The Japanese army, having surrounded the Russian army at considerable cost, could not for lack of ammunition do more than watch the orderly Russian retreat. Their second reserves already mobilized, the Japanese found it virtually impossible to send additional troops and ammunition to the front.

Conditions thus seemed to favour the Russians, at least until 27 May, when the Russian Baltic fleet, which had sailed around the Cape of Good Hope and across the Indian Ocean with a final supply stop at Camranh Bay in French Indo-China, was annihilated in the Tsushima Straits by the combined Japanese fleet. This put Russia in a difficult position to continue the war. Meanwhile, the Revolution of 1905 in Russia, which had begun on 'Bloody Sunday', 22 January, brought further difficulties to the tsarist system. In June, sailors of the warship *Potemkin* rebelled at Odessa. Although men and materiel continued to flow to the front along the Trans-Siberian Railway, troop morale flagged. Coupled with domestic turmoil, this caused the Russian government to lose its will to fight.

On 31 May, the Japanese secretly asked President Theodore Roosevelt

---

[18] See Joseph Fletcher, *CHOC* 10. 332–50, 'The loss of North-east Manchuria'. Also Robert H. G. Lee, *The Manchurian frontier in Ch'ing history*, and other sources cited in Michael H. Hunt, *Frontier defense and the Open Door*, ch. 1.

to act as mediator in arranging the peace conference, which convened at Portsmouth, New Hampshire in August. Prior to doing so Roosevelt sought assurances about Japanese intentions, and accepted Tokyo's response that Japan adhered to the Open Door in Manchuria and intended to restore it to China. As the negotiations progressed the Russian plenipotentiary, Count Sergei Witte, refused to admit defeat, concealed Russia's domestic situation, and intimated Russia's intent to fight on. Pressed by this hard Russian line, the Japanese government, realizing its inability to continue the war, gave up its demand for a financial indemnity, saw that it would not succeed in asking for all of Sakhalin, and settled for the southern half. Russian rights and interests in the Liaotung peninsula were transferred to Japan, as was the South Manchurian Railway between a point near Changchun and Port Arthur.

Foreign Minister Komura Jutarō, who knew Japan's real war situation, conducted the tortuous negotiations with Count Witte, and was blamed by many for what seemed a diplomatic setback. The Japanese public, not knowing the true situation, was angered by the treaty terms. Newspapers denounced the government, and anti-government disturbances, centring around Hibiya Park in central Tokyo, took three days to quell.[19] The government leaders, however, knowing that the Portsmouth treaty offered the best settlement they could get, tried to gain the approval of China and the powers for the treaty in order to further East Asian stability and reduce the possibility of a Russian war of revenge.

They first approached China. Komura, who had returned from his exhausting negotiations with Count Witte in September, departed in November for Peking. Negotiating with Prince Ch'ing (I-k'uang) and Yuan Shih-k'ai, he obtained Peking's recognition of those rights and interests ceded Japan by Russia. The Japanese also negotiated with the Chinese a secret protocol that strengthened Japanese economic gains and included a Chinese promise not to build any railway lines that would impair the interests of the South Manchurian Railway Company. The Sino-Japanese Treaty of Peking was signed on 12 December 1905.[20] Within two years, however, discussions for American and British participation in Manchurian communications found the Chinese disputing this arrangement.

[19] On the Anglo-Japanese alliance and Russo-Japanese War see Ian H. Nish, *The Anglo-Japanese alliance: the diplomacy of two island empires, 1894–1907*; Shumpei Okamoto, *The Japanese oligarchy and the Russo-Japanese War*; John A. White, *The diplomacy of the Russo-Japanese War*; and Morinosuke Kajima, *The diplomacy of Japan 1894–1922*, vol. 2, *Anglo-Japanese alliance and Russo-Japanese War*.

[20] The secret protocol is included in John von A. MacMurray, ed. and comp. *Treaties and agreements with and concerning China, 1894–1919*, 1.554, and is discussed by White, *Diplomacy*, 341. Hunt, *Frontier defense*, 159–61, however, casts doubt on its validity.

Japan simultaneously sought to strengthen its alliance with Great Britain. As initially concluded in 1902, the Anglo-Japanese alliance applied only to China and Korea, but as the confrontation between Britain and Russia during the Russo-Japanese War had spread across the entire Eurasian continent, Britain wanted to strengthen the alliance, while Japan wanted a stronger bond to help deter Russia from a war of revenge. Accordingly the Anglo-Japanese alliance was revised on 12 August 1905, with its scope extended to India. After Anglo-Russian relations took a sudden turn for the better in 1907, in response to the swift rise of German power, the character of the Anglo-Japanese alliance changed once more. By 1911, in a third revision that ran for ten years, its focus was on Germany as well as Russia. An exclusion of countries with whom either power had a treaty of arbitration (such as that between Britain and the US) relieved English fears of conflict with the United States.[21]

France meanwhile felt it necessary to secure additional guarantees for its position in Asia. In 1907 Japan reached agreement with France in a compact which began with affirmations of respect for Chinese sovereignty and equal opportunity, and went on to forswear interference with each other's special interests and spheres. Buttressed with additional unpublished provisions, the agreement indicated France's desire to come to terms with the new continental position of Japan, and its desire to stabilize East Asian politics so that Russia might once again be free to exercise a larger role in the developing European alliance against Germany. As part of this new cordiality France permitted Japan to float a 300 million franc bond issued in Paris that same year. Japan now had English and French support for its increased Manchurian role as well as for its economic primacy in Fukien province.

To reduce the danger of a Russian war of revenge, Foreign Minister Hayashi Tadasu also prepared for negotiations with Russia about outstanding problems. The Russians seemed at first unwilling to come to terms, but as Russian prospects for German support grew worse, St Petersburg was forced to seek accommodation in Asia. Russian relations with England improved, and her French allies urged stabilizing relations with Japan. Russia was shifting its foreign policy focus toward Eastern Europe. Negotiations culminated in the first Russo-Japanese agreement, signed on 30 July 1907. The agreement once again promised respect for China's independence and territorial integrity and the principle of equal opportunity in China, but in secret clauses Japan and Russia recognized

---

[21] See Ian H. Nish, *Alliance in decline: a study in Anglo-Japanese relations 1908–1923*, 70, for ambiguities in the treaty's focus and wording, and Nish's conclusion that 'The 1911 treaty was largely negative'.

each other's spheres of influence in northern and southern Manchuria, respectively; more, Russia acknowledged Japan's primacy in Korea; and Japan, Russia's special interests in Outer Mongolia.[22] By 1909, when American Secretary of State Philander C. Knox put forward a proposal to neutralize the South Manchurian Railway, Japan's and Russia's common opposition brought them even closer together. A second Russo-Japanese agreement, in July 1910, recognized the right of both states to take all necessary measures to defend their respective special spheres in Manchuria. When the United States, Great Britain, France and Germany formed a consortium to provide loans to the Ch'ing government in April 1911, Japan and Russia jointly protested their exclusion. As a result, it was made a six-nation consortium. Relations between the two became even more intimate. A third Russo-Japanese agreement, which divided Inner Mongolia into two parts, and recognized Japanese and Russian special interests in east and west respectively, was concluded on 8 July 1912. Thus England, France, Russia and Japan reached mutual agreements, essentially at the expense of China, whose protection and support they solemnly pledged.

Japan's relations with the United States meanwhile were strained over the anti-Japanese exclusion movement on the west coast. The American closing of California's Open Door for Chinese immigrant labourers had been achieved between 1882 and 1895 by dint of racist agitation, led by American labour organizers.[23] Thereafter the same racism focused on the Japanese. In 1906 California tightened its regulations governing Japanese immigration and excluding Japanese children from public schools.

Although China's first big patriotic boycott in 1905 was of American goods, in protest against the treatment of Chinese in the United States, the makers of Ch'ing foreign policy saw a chance to profit from the American-Japanese antagonism. The opportunity was seized principally by Yuan Shih-k'ai, who was in Li Hung-chang's old post at Tientsin from 1901 to 1907 and then dominant in Peking until his fall from power in 1909. Yuan and his group of reform-minded servitors of the empress dowager managed the late Ch'ing development of railways, telegraphs, mines, new armies and police forces, including relations with the imperialist powers.[24] Their strategy in Manchuria echoed that of Li Hung-chang in Korea twenty years before – to open the area to foreign trade and so give the trading powers a vested interest in preserving China's

---

[22] Japan, *Gaimushō, Nihon gaikō nempyō narabi ni shuyō bunsho*, 1. 280–1.
[23] Hunt, *Special relationship*, ch. 3, 'The politics and diplomacy of exclusion, 1879–1895'.
[24] Stephen R. MacKinnon, *Power and politics in late imperial China: Yuan Shih-kai in Beijing and Tianjin, 1901–1908*.

paramount position, or at least opposing Japan's or Russia's encroachment – an Open Door strategy.

Unfortunately the commerce of the trading powers did not keep up with Russo-Japanese military-economic penetration of Manchuria, and so Yuan had to fall back on a strategy of competition by promoting railways and other developments there under Chinese auspices. For this he hoped to get American financial aid. Many schemes were in the air. In 1905 the American railway magnate E. H. Harriman had approached Prime Minister Katsura in Tokyo proposing a unified transportation system encircling the globe that would include joint Japanese-American administration of the South Manchurian Railway, but on his return from Portsmouth, Foreign Minister Komura opposed the plan, and it was shelved. Meantime the governor-general of the three Manchurian provinces, Hsu Shih-ch'ang, began to develop a reformed civil administration. He and his subordinate, the American-educated T'ang Shao-i, governor of Liaotung, approached Harriman to finance railways that would compete with the Russian-built South Manchurian Railway that Japan had taken over. To finance this they proposed to imitate the imperialists by setting up a development bank to secure American and/or British loans. Their schemes found a ready response among young State Department officers suspicious of Japan's intentions toward China and toward American trade. In 1907–8 Chinese officials actively pushed the idea of a Sino-American alliance, an arbitration treaty was actually negotiated, and T'ang Shao-i started for Washington to settle a deal for American financing of China's development plans in Manchuria. By the time he reached Washington on 30 November 1908, however, his hopes had been undone by *realpolitik*.

President Theodore Roosevelt, conscious of China's weakness, dealt realistically with Japan. In return for a 'gentleman's agreement' whereby Japan restricted immigration to the United States, the Root-Takahira agreement of 30 November 1908 attempted to reduce tensions between America and Japan. Both countries subscribed to the status quo in the Pacific area, agreed to respect each other's territorial possessions there, to uphold the Open Door in China, and to support by peaceful means the 'independence and integrity of China'. In the event that any of these were threatened, both countries promised to exchange views. In informing Peking of this agreement, Tokyo made plain that it rounded out the agreements Japan had already made with Britain, France and Russia.[25]

[25] The accounts in Herbert Croly, *Willard Straight*, and Paul S. Reinsch, *An American diplomat in China*, have been superseded by Hunt, *Frontier defense*. See also Raymond Esthus, *Theodore Roosevelt and Japan*; Charles E. Neu, *An uncertain friendship*; Akira Iriye, *Pacific estrangement*. Text in Japan, Gaimushō, *Nihon gaikō nempyō narabi ni shuyō bunsho*, 1.312–13, and *FRUS 1908*, 511–12.

Although President Roosevelt took a realistic view of Japanese strength, and the American fleet was greeted warmly on its visit to Japan in 1908, American misgivings about Japanese expansion in Manchuria did not end, and each country's naval leaders regarded the other's fleet as a possible future enemy. The Japanese navy's 1907 national defence plan focused on the United States as Japan's hypothetical enemy.[26]

Japan attained a new level of effectiveness in penetration of China by establishing the South Manchurian Railway Company (SMR) in 1906, to operate the railway lines transferred by Russia in the Portsmouth treaty. The company's first director-general, Gotō Shimpei, had earlier served as civil administrator on Taiwan, and had ambitious plans for the SMR. He saw it as the centre of an economic plan that would include the development and operation of mines, agriculture and industry, and the administration of land adjoining the railway tracks. In this way, Gotō thought, Japan would be able to coordinate its efforts to colonize Manchuria and offset the Chinese development efforts organized by Hsu Shih-ch'ang and T'ang Shao-i. The SMR was set up as a joint-stock company under Japan's commercial law, with 50 per cent of the stock held by the government. The remainder was to be offered to Japanese and Chinese investors, but by the closing deadline on 5 October 1906 no Chinese had purchased any stock. The company thus became, by default, entirely Japanese owned. The Chinese government protested after the fact, but it was too late.[27]

The administration of the Kwantung leased territory, that area on the southern tip of the Liaotung peninsula transferred to Japan following the Russo-Japanese War, was based in the small town of Lushun. Lushun's Port Arthur had been developed as an impressive naval base under the Russians, and its seige by General Nogi's armies had been the most costly episode of the war. Its harbour was shallow, however, and the Japanese navy maintained only limited facilities there. The authority of the governor-general of the Kwantung leased territory extended only to this limited area. Until 1919 that individual commanded the army forces there; when the post became civilian, troop control passed to the commanding general of the Kwantung Army.

The South Manchurian Railway Company was based at Dairen. The Dairen harbour was deep, and under SMR administration the city quickly developed into one of East Asia's leading commercial ports, the gateway to Manchuria. From that base, the company functioned almost like an

[26] Tsunoda Jun, *Manshū mondai to kokubō hōshin*, 705ff.
[27] Japan, Gaimushō, *Nihon gaikō bunsho*, 39, pt. 1, 650ff.; and Tsurumi Yūsuke, *Gotō Shimpei*, 2.732–809, for Gotō's position papers and ten-year plan. Administration of the area brought sharp clashes between the Japanese army and civilian leaders for primacy.

independent government. Its primary mandate of railway administration soon expanded. The broad-gauge tracks of the Russian period were replaced by standard gauge, and an ambitious programme of development was set in motion; up-to-date railway technology, and even railway ties, were imported from the United States. As relations with Russia improved, travel on the SMR through Harbin and on the Trans-Siberian Railway through Irkutsk became the shortest route linking East Asia and Europe. Taxes collected by the SMR from its lands were added to its operating profits, and large sums were devoted to everything from city planning and the construction of roads and water and gas lines, to education and research activities. The facilities of the SMR elementary and middle schools were frequently superior to those within Japan, and the SMR's Manchuria Medical College became one of the most advanced in the whole of China. SMR research on China was another outstanding achievement; it concentrated on current conditions when few scholars were doing so, and thereby laid a factual basis for the later flood of Japanese work on modern China's economy and society.[28]

To protect its rights and privileges in the Kwantung leased territory and the South Manchurian Railway Company, the Japanese government, as noted above, established the Kwantung Army. Headquartered in Lushun, its detachments were stationed outside the leased territory. Under the Portsmouth treaty, up to fifteen soldiers were permitted for every kilometre of railway line. This allowed Japan to have one full army division in Manchuria in peacetime. These units quickly became the vanguard of Japanese penetration into China.

It was inevitable that this range of activities would produce numerous sources of friction for which the language of the Portsmouth treaty contained no solution. Relations between Japan and China had been fairly amicable prior to the Russo-Japanese War, but after the Japanese victory and settlement those relations quickly deteriorated as conflict centred around four major issues.

First, the Chientao area: this border area had formed the traditional, unmarked boundary between China and Korea. By November 1905, as Japan set up a protectorate over Korea, it sent troops into the Chientao area, claiming territorial sovereignty. However, Japan later yielded the area to China, and the rights of the area's Korean residents were recognized by the September 1909 Sino-Japanese treaty regarding Chientao. But as the colonization of Korea by Japan proceeded, many Koreans who opposed Japanese rule moved to Chentao, and the area became the base for a Korean anti-Japanese movement.

[28] John Young, The research activities of the South Manchurian Railway Company, 1907–1945: a history and bibliography.

Second, the Antung-Mukden railway question: during the Russo-Japanese War, Japan had built a narrow-gauge railway from Antung on the Yalu River to Mukden, as an auxiliary route to the northern front. Administration of this railway was entrusted to Japan by the 1905 Sino-Japanese treaty of Peking. Linkage of this railway with the Pusan-Sinuiju railway would make it the fastest route between Japan and Europe, as well as a military supply route from Korea into Manchuria. For these reasons, the SMR Company sought to convert the railway to standard gauge. China protested vehemently, on grounds that no such conversion was provided for under the treaty. Japan finally had its way in the summer of 1909, but not before an ultimatum had forced Peking to yield.

Third, coal mines: Russia had begun the development of mines near its railway lines in south Manchuria. Japan continued the development of the rich open-pit Fushun mines 40 km east of Mukden. Japan also operated the high-quality anthracite Yentai mines north of Anshan. Since all these mines were far removed from the railway zone mentioned in the treaty, they were worked without a treaty basis or Chinese permission; eventually the Chinese government recognized this state of affairs as a fait accompli.

Fourth, the Yingkow-Tashihchiao railway: Russia had originally been granted permission to construct this line as a temporary measure, to transport materials from the port of Yingkow for the construction of the Chinese Eastern Railway on the promise that it be dismantled upon the latter's completion. China therefore demanded that Japan dismantle the railway. The real Chinese objective was to take the line over, but Japan ignored the Chinese demands and retained the line as a branch of the South Manchurian Railway.

All of these conflicts irritated Sino-Japanese relations, and Japan's rise in national power stimulated the growth of nationalism in China. Chinese students in Tokyo learned from the example of Japan's progress in the modernization of her national life, while reform-minded officials of the Ch'ing government were roused to counter Japan's expansion.[29] This in turn brought a hardening of Japan's drive toward empire. At the same time that efforts to reach a modus vivendi with the United States were leading toward the Root-Takahira agreement of November 1908, a foreign policy plan the Katsura cabinet adopted on 25 September 1908 revealed Japan's determination to hold on to its rights in Manchuria, and formalized the resolve to make the Kwantung leased territory Japan's permanent possession.[30]

[29] Marius Jansen, 'Japan and the Chinese Revolution of 1911', CHOC 11, ch. 6.
[30] Japan, Gaimushō, Nempyō, 1.305–9. The same statement stressed the importance of directing future Japanese immigration to the continent in order to strengthen the Japanese presence there.

JAPAN'S TWENTY-ONE DEMANDS

When the Chinese Revolution broke out in October 1911, the Japanese government's major concern was the preservation of rights and interests in Manchuria obtained after the victory over Russia in 1905. Since agreements had been worked out with the Ch'ing government and the revolutionaries were an unknown element, both Foreign Minister Uchida Yasuya and Minister to Peking Ijūin Hikokichi leaned toward providing assistance to the Ch'ing government. They persisted in this advice even after the revolution spread south of the Yangtze, arguing, as did many conservative Japanese, that even a divided China, with the Ch'ing ruling the north, was preferable to Republican rule of a united China. A republican system throughout China would be a negative example for Japan's monarchical system as well as a threat to Japanese interests.[31] So the Japanese government proposed to the British government a joint military expedition. It also agreed to meet a Ch'ing government request for the purchase of arms. England rejected the Japanese proposal. The greater part of British interests lay in territory under revolutionary army control, and would be endangered by aid to the Ch'ing. London therefore replied that though it favoured a constitutional monarchy in China, it did not consider outside intervention desirable. When Yuan Shih-k'ai finally returned to Peking on 13 November, the British were already acting as secret intermediaries between him and the revolutionaries. Thus even while Yuan was declaring his support of a constitutional monarchy to Japanese Minister Ijūin, he had begun peace talks with the revolutionaries. Even T'ang Shao-i, Peking's negotiator with the revolutionaries, favoured a republic. The situation developed steadily in the direction of a republican system with Yuan as president. Thus Yuan's skilful political manoeuvres profited from British support. Japan felt that its stake in China was the greatest of any power's, but without the support of its British ally it could not send in troops and expect to maintain the Ch'ing as a constitutional monarchy. Intervention having failed, the Japanese government fell in line with Britain and switched to non-intervention.

Not a few Japanese outside of government firmly supported Sun Yat-sen's revolutionary movement. Over 600 Japanese are said to have gone to China to take part in the revolution. Some had been active in the people's rights movement in Japan, and considered the Chinese Revolution to be in the interest of China's democratization. Most believed that a strong China was essential to the liberation of Asia from Western

[31] Japan, Gaimushō, *Bunsho*, special volume on 'Shinkoku jiken' (The China incident), 382ff. See also Marius B. Jansen, *The Japanese and Sun Yat-sen*; and Masaru Ikei, 'Japan's response to the Chinese Revolution of 1911', *JAS* 25.2 (Feb. 1966), 213–27.

dominance. Many others, however, went to China as 'revolutionaries' with their own interests uppermost. Initially these Japanese were warmly welcomed by the Chinese revolutionaries, but before long they were being shunted aside as troublesome meddlers. Prominent Japanese like the influential rightist Tōyama Mitsuru travelled to Shanghai to try to control the activities and behaviour of the adventurers.[32]

China's revolutionary forces ended up compromising with Yuan Shih-k'ai partly for financial reasons. Immediately upon reaching Shanghai, for example, Sun had contacted the Shanghai office of Mitsui & Co. to request arms. Its head agreed and granted several large loans; the Japanese aim was to bring the Hanyehping Co. under joint Sino-Japanese management.[33] Soon after Yuan took office in Peking as provisional president on 10 March 1912, Japan, the United States, Great Britain, Germany, France and Russia formed a six-nation consortium to underwrite foreign loans to China.

Having adopted a policy of non-intervention, the Japanese foreign ministry tried to stabilize Sino-Japanese relations through negotiations at Peking. This effort was undercut by the kind of independent military action that was to hamper Japan's China policy in future decades. Military men in the field were more aggressive than the Foreign Office representatives, and the popular reception of their unauthorized acts by jingoist elements in Japan encouraged them. The first challenge to government policy by Japanese outside government was the Manchu-Mongol independence movement. An activist named Kawashima Naniwa, who had been involved in the Ch'ing programme of police reform, had developed intimate personal ties with members of the Manchu nobility. During the 1911 Revolution, Kawashima and a group of Japanese military men plotted to make Manchuria and Mongolia independent, and persuaded the Manchu Prince Su (Shan-ch'i) to head the effort. According to plan, Prince Su left Peking for Port Arthur in the Kwantung leased territory, arriving there on 2 February 1912. But as the Japanese foreign ministry protested repeatedly to the army, Prince Su was forced to dissociate himself from the movement and go into retirement in Lushun. (His daughter, who married Kawashima, was executed as a Japanese collaborator after the Second World War.)

The Kawashima group succeeded in obtaining a large quantity of arms

32 Kokuryūkai, ed. *Tōa senkaku shishi kiden* (Biographical sketches of pioneer patriots in East Asia), 2.467. See also Jansen, *The Japanese*; and for the account of Sun's close collaborator, Miyazaki Tōten, *My thirty-three years dream*.

33 Nakajima Masao, ed. *Zoku Taishi kaiko roku* (Memoirs concerning China, supplement), 2.153ff. Sun had first, however, travelled to England to urge against Japanese government proposals to help the Ch'ing. For discussion of this and other loan proposals see Jansen, *The Japanese*, 146; Albert A. Altman and Harold Z. Schiffrin, 'Sun Yat-sen and the Japanese: 1914-16', *Modern Asian Studies*, 6.4 (Oct. 1972) 385-400; and C. Martin Wilbur, *Sun Yat-sen: frustrated patriot*, 78ff.

and munitions from the Japanese army. Strong feelings of animosity against Han Chinese were prevalent among the Mongols, and few welcomed the thought of coming under the rule of Yuan and his regime. Two Mongol princes took the Kawashima bait and joined the Manchu-Mongol independence movement. Arms were then sent into Inner Mongolia under Japanese escort, westward by horsecart from the Kungchuling station of the South Manchurian Railway. This convoy was attacked by Chinese government troops, however, and thirteen Japanese guards and nine Mongols died, thus ending this particular attempt. Until the Manchurian incident of 1931, however, Japanese were continually involved in movements for an independent Manchuria and Mongolia.[34]

At another extreme of unofficial intervention were the Japanese who opposed Yuan by assisting the revolutionaries. When the anti-Yuan movement known as the Second Revolution broke out in July 1913 it was suppressed within seven weeks, and Sun Yat-sen, Huang Hsing, and the military leader Li Lieh-chün had to flee for their lives. Yuan Shih-kai's government asked Britain and Japan not to admit Chinese political refugees to their territories. Despite the foreign ministry's best efforts, Japanese outside of government as well as military officers helped the revolutionary leaders escape. Huang Hsing was given passage on the Japanese warship *Tatsuta* from Nanking to Shanghai. From there he fled to Hong Kong on a private Japanese steamer, before transferring to another Japanese steamer bound for Moji, Japan. Sun Yat-sen fled from Shanghai to Foochow, where he was met by the Japanese steamer *Bunjun-maru* which took him to Kobe by way of Taiwan. Li Lieh-chün, after his defeat in battle, was granted asylum at the Japanese consulate in Changsha on 1 September 1913 and then put on a Japanese steamer for Hankow, whence he escaped on the warship *Fushimi*.[35]

The Second Revolution was marred by three incidents that influenced Japanese opinion against their government's cautious policy: the detention of a Japanese army captain, the arrest of an army second lieutenant, and acts of violence by Yuan's troops as they entered Nanking which resulted in the deaths of three Japanese. The Tokyo foreign ministry sought to resolve these matters by quiet diplomacy, but the Japanese army, outraged by these 'insults', demanded the punishment of those responsible. As tensions mounted, Abe Moritarō, head of the Political Affairs Bureau of the foreign ministry, was murdered by a jingoist youth. Several thousand

---

[34] Kurihara ed. and comp. *Tai-Man-Mō seisakushi no ichimen, Nichi-Ro sengo yori Taishōki ni itaru,* 139ff. See also Sadako N. Ogata, *Defiance in Manchuria: the making of Japanese foreign policy, 1931–1932.*

[35] See, for the Second Revolution, Chün-tu Hsueh, *Huang Hsing and the Chinese Revolution,* 159ff.; and Jansen, *The Japanese,* 154ff.

indignant Tokyo residents demonstrated to show their opposition to the foreign ministry's policies. These pressures constrained the foreign ministry in its dealings with the Yuan government.[36] Ultimately the Tokyo government prevailed, but in the process Chinese intellectuals, including revolutionaries, developed broadly anti-Japanese suspicions and animosities.

When the First World War broke out in Europe on 28 July 1914, China quickly issued a 24-point declaration proclaiming itself a non-belligerent. The thrust of the statement was that belligerents were not to occupy or conduct warfare on Chinese soil or in Chinese territorial waters; and Chinese territory was not to be used as a staging area for attacks. Troops and arms of belligerents were liable to detention or confiscation if they passed through Chinese territory.

For Japan, the First World War provided the opportunity to stabilize its imperialist interests. The Manchurian interests Japan had taken over from Russia had only a short time to run, and the affront Germany had organized in the Triple Intervention of 1895 could now be countered. Britain tried to discourage military action against Germany on the part of Japan, however, and the dominions of Australia, New Zealand and Canada were even more averse to Japanese involvement. Consequently the British tried to limit Japan's participation to naval action in the form of protection for British merchant shipping from German privateers in the Pacific. Japan was unwilling to accept such a limited role, however, and on 15 August delivered an ultimatum to Germany demanding that Germany hand over, not later than 15 September 'to the Imperial Japanese Authorities, without condition or compensation, the entire leased territory of Kiaochow with a view to eventual restoration of the same to China'.[37] Foreign Minister Katō Takaaki's idea was that the Kiaochow territory, if obtained without compensation, could be turned back to China in due course; if it was obtained at a high cost in blood and money, on the other hand, Japan would not give it up as easily.

As Germany did not respond to the ultimatum, Japan declared war and blockaded Tsingtao in the German leased territory. To minimize losses, the Japanese army decided to attack German fortifications from the rear, but to do so it would have to pass through Chinese territory and violate China's neutrality. Tokyo applied great pressure on Peking to get it to exclude the province of Shantung from its neutral zones, but Foreign Minister Sun Pao-ch'i steadfastly refused. Instead, China concentrated large numbers of troops in Shantung. Peking finally yielded, however,

[36] Kurihara, 87ff.
[37] Japan, Gaimushō, *Nempyō*, 1.381.

despite its doubts that Japan would abide by its promise to return Kiaochow to China after taking it by force.

Japanese troops landed on the north side of the Shantung peninsula on 2 September 1914. Instead of concentrating on attacking the German fortifications at Kiaochow Bay, however, part of the army occupied Weihsien and then headed westward, occupying the Shantung railway line all the way to Tsinan. The army then attacked and occupied Tsingtao. Even after the German surrender, however, the Japanese maintained troops along the entire railway line.

Throughout all of this, China stood alone. Britain, France and Germany were totally preoccupied with the war in Europe, and had no time or resources for Asian concerns. England also felt that the concentration of Japanese interests in North China might help stabilize British interests in Central and South China. Since, moreover, the Allies were hard pressed in Europe, Britain increasingly began to feel the need for Japanese assistance, and so tacitly approved Japan's pressures upon China. Russia, too, which was plotting its own penetration of China, had no objection to Japan's actions. Only the United States, which was not yet involved in the European war, offered China any sympathy. Yet even America, its primary concern concentrated on the war in Europe, had no wish for a confrontation with Japan over China. Unable to expect outside help, consequently, Vice Foreign Minister Ts'ao Ju-lin conveyed to the Japanese Yuan Shih-kai's willingness to negotiate Japanese economic demands; it was hoped that Japan, in return, would strictly control the Chinese revolutionaries in Japan.

The war years thus offered an excellent opportunity for Japan to stabilize its relations with China. Since the Shantung holdings, which had been taken by force, had to be renegotiated, it seemed a logical time to renegotiate the Manchurian concessions which did not have as long to run. Europe was unlikely to interfere. Numerous Japanese groups agitated for an overall settlement with China; the senior statesmen thought it important to have a meeting of minds in view of Europe's suicidal struggle, while pressure groups of many kinds presented arguments for overthrowing the Chinese regime altogether. Even Sun Yat-sen, a refugee in Japan once more, thought he saw the opportunity for help against Yuan Shih-k'ai. Needless to say, army leaders were particularly insistent.

In time the foreign ministry drew up a list of fourteen demands, arranged in four groups, and seven 'wishes' (Group V) which the Ōkuma government adopted at a cabinet meeting on 11 November. On 18 January 1915, Minister Hioki in Peking presented these directly to

President Yuan and proceeded to explain them in an overbearing manner; should they be accepted, he assured Yuan, Japan would control Chinese revolutionaries and students in Japan.

Hioki asked Yuan to keep the content of the demands and the process of negotiation secret, but the Peking government, through the young diplomat V. K. Wellington Koo, soon leaked the demands to American Minister Paul Reinsch. Sun Pao-ch'i resigned as foreign minister, to be replaced by Lu Cheng-hsiang. Then began a leisurely process of negotiations in which Yuan wore out the patience of the Japanese. Twenty-five formal and twenty informal negotiating sessions over an 84-day period resulted in many revisions.[38] In the course of the negotiations, the American government became increasingly disturbed both by Japan's demands and by its negotiating manner, and American public opinion turned against Japan. Secretary of State William Jennings Bryan was initially prepared to accept Japanese assurances that there was no substance to talk of a 'Group V', but when it became clear that the Japanese had not been candid with him, and as Minister Reinsch from Peking, in response to Chinese warnings, sent urgent predictions of a Japanese conquest, President Wilson took over direction of the American response.[39] Ultimately Tokyo abandoned Group V, and issued an ultimatum on 7 May 1915. The Chinese then gave in. On 9 May, at one o'clock in the morning, the new foreign minister, Lu Cheng-hsiang, and Vice Foreign Minister Ts'ao Ju-lin went to the Japanese legation and accepted the demands in their final revised form. The differences between the original and the final demands, including their long-term outcome, can be summarized as in the accompanying chart.

Considered in the light of imperialist precedents, the Twenty-one Demands contained little that was new; nor, with the exception of the extension of the Manchurian leases, did they mean a great deal to the Japanese position in China. They fitted into the sequence of special rights secured by the powers in China, and they did not directly threaten American economic interests or counter directly the general principles of the Open Door for trade.[40] The Japanese saw the 'wishes' of Group V as giving their nationals the sort of rights that Western missionaries already enjoyed; Japanese advisers and arms were already sought by most factions

[38] Madeline Chi, *China diplomacy, 1914–1918*; *ibid*. 'Ts'ao Ju-lin', in Akira Iriye, ed. *The Chinese and the Japanese: essays in political and cultural interactions*; Horikawa Takeo, *Kyokutō kokusai seijishi josetsu*; Pao-chin Chu, *V. K. Wellington Koo: a case study of China's diplomat and diplomacy of nationalism, 1912–1966*, 10; and Jansen, *Japan and China*, 209–23.

[39] Paul S. Reinsch's account is *An American diplomat in China*; the Washington response receives authoritative treatment in Arthur S. Link, *Wilson*, vol. 3, *The struggle for neutrality, 1914–1915*.

[40] James Reed, *The missionary mind and American East Asia policy, 1911–1915*, ch. 5.

The Twenty-one Demands

Synopsis of original demands	Final disposition
Group I Shantung	
1 China to assent fully to any agreements between Japan and Germany regarding former German rights and interests in the province of Shantung	Included in the 25 May 1915 treaty between China and Japan; annulled in 1922
2 No part of Shantung to be ceded or leased to any third power	Provided for in the 25 May 1915 exchange of notes
3 Japan permitted to construct a railway connecting Chefoo or Lungkow with the Kiaochow–Tsinan railway	Included in the 1915 treaty; invalidated in 1922
4 China to open to foreign residence and commerce additional Shantung cities and towns, to be named in separate agreements	Included in the 1915 treaty; invalidated in 1922
Group II South Manchuria and eastern Inner Mongolia	
1 Leases of Port Arthur and Dairen (the Kwantung leased territory) and of the South Manchurian Railway and the Antung–Mukden railway to be extended to 99 years	Included in the 1915 treaty; in effect up to Japan's defeat in 1945
2 Japanese subjects to be permitted to lease or own land in south Manchuria and eastern Inner Mongolia for commercial, industrial and agricultural use	Granted for south Manchuria only
3 Freedom of Japanese subjects to reside and travel in south Manchuria and eastern Inner Mongolia, and to engage in business and manufacturing of all kinds	Granted for south Manchuria only
4 Japanese subjects to have the right to open and operate mines in south Manchuria and eastern Inner Mongolia, the mine sites to be determined by separate agreement	Permitted for specified mining areas of south Manchuria only, in the exchange of notes
5 China to obtain prior Japanese consent before granting railway concessions in south Manchuria and eastern Inner Mongolia to a third power, or before securing any foreign loans against the taxes of said areas	China to seek foreign capital from Japanese capitalists first with regard to both matters, according to the exchange of notes
6 China to consult with the Japanese government before engaging any foreign political, financial, or military advisers or instructors in south Manchuria and eastern Inner Mongolia	Japanese granted priority in employment for south Manchuria only
7 Japan to control and administer the Kirin–Changchun railway for 99 years	Left to later negotiations
Group III The Hanyehping coal and iron complex of the mid-Yangtze valley area	
1 The Hanyehping complex to be placed under joint Sino-Japanese management, before which time no right or property to be disposed of without prior Japanese consent	Included in the exchange of notes
2 No mining to be undertaken by other operators in the vicinity of Hanyehping without prior consent of the Hanyehping Company	Deleted

Synopsis of original demands	Final disposition
Group IV Non-alienation of China's coastal area	
1 No harbour or bay or island along the China coast to be ceded or leased to any third power	Deleted. Identical statement issued separately by the Chinese president
Group V Japanese involvement in China's internal administration, and other rights	
1 Japanese to be engaged by the Chinese government as political, financial and military advisers	Tabled for future negotiations; given up by the Japanese government in 1922
2 Japanese hospitals, temples and schools in China's interior to be permitted to own land	
3 Localities in China with a history of Sino-Japanese conflict and police disputes to establish police departments jointly administered or staffed with Japanese	
4 Japan to supply China with 50 per cent or more of China's munitions, or to establish a jointly managed arsenal utilizing experts and materials from Japan	
5 Japan to be granted the right to construct a railway connecting Wuchang with the Kiukiang–Nanchang railway, and to construct railways between Nanchang and Hangchow and between Nanchang and Chaochow	
6 Japan to be consulted first when foreign capital is needed for railways, mines, and harbour works in the province of Fukien, due to its proximity and relationship to the Japanese colony of Taiwan (Formosa)	
7 Japanese subjects to be granted the right to preach in China	

in China. What was distinctive about the demands was the insensitivity and clumsiness of Japanese diplomacy. The world, and especially America, saw a crafty Japan taking advantage of its weaker neighbour at a time when the Western powers were preoccupied elsewhere. Japanese diplomats, by requesting secrecy, enabled Chinese statesmen to build up alarm and distrust by leaking the contents of supposedly non-existent demands. The final ultimatum served on Yuan Shih-k'ai in May 1915 completed the picture of Japanese insensitivity. It gained Japan little the Chinese had not already agreed to, and provided the symbolism for what became, each 25 May, a Day of National Humiliation. Japan's attempt to forestall republican nationalism in China to guarantee its own position thus ended by advancing that nationalism and focusing it against Japan. What made the Twenty-one Demands so inflammatory to Chinese and also to the American public, was their anachronism. They were made in the spirit of the imperialist scramble of the 1890s but twenty years later, after the rise of the Republic of China and the progressive movement in the United States. It was, in every sense, a Pyrrhic victory for Japan.

JAPANESE INFLUENCE AND CHINA'S PARTICIPATION IN THE FIRST WORLD WAR

From the outset of the World War, the British had hoped for China's entry on the allied side. The Japanese government did not favour this, believing that Chinese participation would enhance China's voice in international affairs and thereby reduce Japan's role as a leader and spokesman for China. After consultations with the Japanese, Great Britain decided not to negotiate for China's participation without prior Japanese consent.

Japan's coercion of China into signing the Twenty-one Demands was subsequent to this understanding, and the Japanese government continued to deal in bad faith with the Yuan government. Non-government Japanese, meanwhile, continued to plot to detach Manchuria from China by exploiting the anti-Chinese sentiments of the Manchu and Mongol minorities, while other Japanese continued to be openly sympathetic to the anti-Yuan southern revolutionary forces around Sun Yat-sen. Thus, when Yuan Shih-k'ai in late 1915 attempted to create a new imperial dynasty with himself as monarch, Japanese government and non-government elements alike vehemently objected. Japan sought the support of Great Britain and then of the United States, Russia and France, to press for postponement of Yuan's monarchical plans. All but the United States agreed.

After an anti-Yuan movement sprang up in southern China in December 1915 and grew in force, the Japanese government decided in March 1916 to grant the southern revolutionary forces recognition as a belligerent body equal to the north and to give its tacit support to those Japanese activists aiding it. In North China, meanwhile, Japanese activists, with secret supplies of arms from elements of the Japanese army, were again plotting a Manchu-Mongol independence movement around the person of Prince Su, then retired in Lushun. The Japanese foreign ministry itself gave these efforts its tacit support, to put pressure on the Yuan government. But in June 1916 Yuan Shih-k'ai died. The Japanese army decided that the movement had little chance of success, and withdrew its support. The independence army collapsed, bringing an end to the second Manchu-Mongol independence movement.

Following Yuan's death, Prime Minister Tuan Ch'i-jui, who controlled the army, moved swiftly to strengthen the executive power of the cabinet, but came into conflict not only with President Li Yuan-hung but also with the national assembly on almost every issue. To increase his political leverage and consolidate his personal power base, Tuan planned to cultivate closer ties with Japan, where the political landscape was also in flux. In October 1916, Ōkuma Shigenobu was replaced as prime minister by Terauchi Masatake, and Katō Takaaki as foreign minister by Motono Ichirō. Terauchi planned to approach the Tuan cabinet through Nishihara Kamezō, a close friend from Terauchi's days as governor-general of Korea.

Throughout this period relations between the United States and Germany continued to deteriorate. After the United States protested in April 1916 against German submarine attacks, Germany promised to restrict them. She reversed herself on 31 January 1917, however, with notification of her intention to resume unlimited submarine warfare. When President Wilson immediately severed diplomatic relations with Germany, the United States on 3 February called upon China and other neutral nations to do likewise. The Peking government demanded an American loan as a quid pro quo.

As the war dragged on, the European Allies faced a labour shortage in France and recruited 140,000 labourers from China. In February 1917 a French ship carrying 900 Chinese labourers was sunk by a German submarine in the Mediterranean, killing 542 Chinese. To counter such German submarine activity, the Allies turned to the Japanese navy. Great Britain in the previous month had already asked Japan to send destroyers into the Mediterranean and Japan had seized this opportunity to ask that the British support Japanese claims to former German rights and privileges in Shantung and to German Pacific territories north of the equator. The Japanese government made identical requests to Russia, France and Italy. All four countries secretly pledged to support Japanese claims at any future peace conference. Moreover, the Tuan government in China was now intent upon improving its Japan ties, and the war had suddenly strengthened Japanese economic power, precisely as it had caused the sudden weakening of European – particularly British and French – power in East Asia. For these new reasons, the Japanese government now shifted to a policy of acceding to China's entry into the war.[41]

In January 1917, Nishihara had arranged a five-million yen gold loan to the Tuan government. Thus began the 'Nishihara loans'. After returning briefly to Japan, Nishihara arrived back in Peking in February and informed the Chinese government it could expect substantially greater

[41] Usui Katsumi, *Nihon to Chūgoku: Taishō jidai* (Japan and China: the Taishō era), 104ff.

aid if it declared war on Germany. Nishihara met repeatedly with Prime Minister Tuan, strongly urging him to enter the war. Tuan finally concurred, against the objections of Vice-President Feng Kuo-chang and the even stronger objections of President Li, and on 14 August 1917 the Tuan government declared war on Germany and Austria-Hungary. Feng eventually aligned himself with Tuan on this issue, but Li Yuan-hung persisted in his firm opposition, precipitating an intense internal power struggle. In exchange for China's entry into the war, Tuan hoped for financial assistance from the powers both to strengthen his own leading position within China and to enhance the stature of China within the international community. Tuan's policies enjoyed the support of three elements within China: first, the Anhwei faction of the Peiyang military clique under Tuan's personal leadership; second, the group around Ts'ao Ju-lin, the main funnel of the Nishihara loans; and lastly, the group of conservative republicans in the national assembly, around the person of Liang Ch'i-ch'ao. The latter opposed the Revolutionary Party or Kuomintang of Sun Yat-sen. Actively opposed to China's entry into the war were those with business interests, who hoped for continued prosperity from neutrality, and the Kuomintang which feared that participation would strengthen the Tuan regime.

At the urging of Hayashi Gonsuke, Japan's minister to Peking, the Japanese government decided to aid Tuan exclusively, primarily through more Nishihara loans, and to ban all loans, arms and non-government assistance to the Kuomintang in the south. The confrontation between Tuan and the southern revolutionaries intensified until, in late August 1917, 134 anti-Tuan national assemblymen met at Canton and elected Sun Yat-sen generalissimo (*ta-yuan-shuai*) of a new military government.

Japanese aid to Tuan increased enormously following his government's declaration of war. During the two years 1917 and 1918, eight Nishihara loans were extended to the Tuan regime for a total of some 145 million yen, or about US $72·5 m (of which a mere five million yen was ever repaid). These loans were violently attacked by anti-Tuan elements centred around the Kuomintang as promoting internal discord and propping up a reactionary regime. They thus served as a catalyst for the growth of the Chinese nationalist movement.[42]

Collusion between the Tuan and Terauchi governments did not end there. When the Bolshevik Revolution occurred in November 1917, and the new Soviet government suspended hostilities with Germany and Austria-Hungary through the treaty of Brest-Litovsk, Japan was suspicious of a Soviet-German alliance. Dreading Marxism-Leninism, she sought to

[42] See Suzuki Takeo, ed. *Nishihara shakkan shiryō kenkyū* (Studies of materials on the Nishihara loans).

stem the flood tide of Bolshevism in Siberia, and to that end proposed a military alliance with the Tuan regime. On 25 March 1918 in Tokyo, Japanese Foreign Minister Motono and Chinese Minister to Japan Chang Tsung-hsiang agreed to cooperate to counter the growth of hostile forces in Russia. On 16 May, the two countries signed a secret mutual military assistance agreement, followed by a series of separate agreements detailing army and navy cooperation. The terms of these agreements were kept secret by both China and Japan, who merely announced that negotiations were in progress. This secrecy heightened fears among Chinese intellectuals that Chinese troops were essentially being brought under Japanese army control, and that these agreements were but another manifestation of Japanese penetration. Anti-agreement demonstrations broke out around China, while large numbers of Chinese students in Japan returned home in protest.[43]

The active pro-Tuan stance of the Japanese government did in fact strengthen the Tuan regime financially and militarily, and adversely affected the anti-Tuan, Kuomintang-centred forces of South China. The peace conference at Shanghai between North and South China, convened on 20 February 1919, thus faced insurmountable odds at the outset, and came to nought. In any event, the military agreements concluded between Japan and the Tuan regime lost all effect following the overthrow of the Tuan regime in mid-1920. They were collectively abrogated by Chinese notification to Japan on 28 January 1921.

Almost concurrent with the north-south peace conference at Shanghai was the Versailles peace conference at Paris. When it rejected the Chinese demands that German rights in Shantung be returned to China, the Chinese delegation walked out and the 4 May 1919 demonstration erupted in Peking. The impact of foreign affairs on domestic politics was never more clearly demonstrated.[44]

THE WASHINGTON CONFERENCE AND CHINA

Great Britain, France and the Netherlands, although exhausted by the war, desired nevertheless to maintain their interests in the Pacific and the Far East. But to do so would require the cooperation of both the United States and Japan, which not only had not suffered from the European war but had benefited economically from it. Canada, Australia and New Zealand were wary of Japan's recent expansion and Britain felt it essential to gain the goodwill of the United States to contain Japan. Yet, at the same time,

[43] Usui, *Nihon*, 127ff.
[44] See *CHOC* 12.407 (B. Schwartz).

Britain needed the friendship of its ally Japan to protect its own China interests. For all these reasons, the British desired a large-scale conference to adjust with one stroke their relations with the dominions, with the United States, and with Japan.[45]

Ever since the Russo-Japanese War, the United States and Japan had frequently been at odds over China. Moreover, despite the best efforts of both governments, the immigration question had raised tensions further. These two countries, whose economies had flourished while war had sapped the European economies, rushed into a heated naval race in the Pacific. Japan, though lacking the natural resources, capital accumulation and productive capacity of the United States, nevertheless adopted an arms expansion programme to counter the United States naval build-up, imposing an enormous burden upon its people. For 1920, military expenditure constituted 48 per cent of total Japanese government expenditures and for 1921, 49 per cent. To reduce this burden, the reduction of tensions with the United States was absolutely essential.

The United States also felt the economic burden of the naval race. More than that, she saw a need to respond somehow to the sudden advance of Japan into China during the First World War. Secretary of State Robert Lansing had attempted to maintain an Open Door in China by granting recognition to certain special rights of Japan in the exchange of notes known as the Lansing-Ishii Agreement of 2 November 1917. This culmination of several rounds of negotiations in Washington between Lansing and the Japanese ambassador, Ishii Kikujirō, had two essential points. First, recognition of the existence of a special relationship between countries having contiguous boundaries. On this basis, Japan was recognized as having special interests in China. Second, the guarantee of China's independence and territorial integrity and the upholding of the Open Door principle of equal opportunity in commerce and industry. Once the war had ended, however, the United States revised its conciliatory position, and began to feel out alternatives, believing that the old diplomacy of imperialism should now be superseded by a new international order in East Asia. In 1918 the United States had proposed that a consortium of American, British, French and Japanese banks should be set up to make loans to China. In 1920 Washington also urged the abrogation of the Anglo-Japanese alliance as the device that had protected Japan's encroachment on China.

As part of this process, the Washington Conference met from November 1921 to February 1922. Armaments and Far Eastern relations were taken

[45] See Roger Dingman, *Power in the Pacific*; Thomas Buckley, *The United States and the Washington Conference*; Akira Iriye, *After imperialism: the search for a new order in the Far East, 1921–1931*.

up in parallel sessions. The Chinese plenipotentiary, Alfred Sao-ke Sze (Shih Chao-chi), made an effort to chip away at the unequal treaty system. He confirmed the Open Door for equal commercial-industrial opportunity of the treaty powers in China but demanded that all agreements concerning China must be openly declared, made only with Chinese participation, have stated time limits, and be strictly construed in favour of the grantor.[46]

At this time Japan was herself experiencing a flurry of democratizing activity (universal male suffrage, for example, became law in 1925) while suffering under the burden of her anti-communist intervention since 1918 in Siberia. She thus desired harmonious relations with the United States and Britain, and sought to keep in step with their China policies. She took a cooperative attitude on the eventual revival of full Chinese sovereignty and, along with advocating an unreserved, unconditional Open Door and equal opportunity in China, agreed to future negotiations to abolish extraterritoriality.

In the end, two treaties and nine resolutions on China came out of deliberations on sixteen separate items such as tariffs, spheres of influence, the Open Door, and a ban on military supplies to China. The Anglo-Japanese alliance was ended and a four-power treaty (Britain, France, Japan and the United States) took its place but without any military provisions, merely promises to consult. A naval limitation treaty agreed to a 5–5–3 ratio for the British, American and Japanese fleets, which would leave Japan secure in her home waters. Concerning China, it was agreed that the power would subsequently convene a separate conference aimed at the abolition of extraterritoriality. On tariff matters, since the Chinese government was in severe financial straits, a major objective was to increase Chinese government revenues. A treaty provided for revision of tariff rates at the same time that it called for a future conference to revise the entire tariff structure. Most important was the nine-power treaty of 6 February 1922 on China, which incorporated strict and concrete stipulations regarding the Open Door and equal opportunity, and against unfair discrimination on railways in China. Japan and China settled the Shantung question through direct negotiations from 1 November to 4 February 1922, when they signed a treaty returning the former German leased territory of Kiaochow to China. Japan withdrew all troops from Shantung. The Tsingtao custom-house was integrated into the Chinese Maritime Customs Service, and the Kiaochow-Tsinan railway and all its properties were transferred to China.

[46] *Conference on the Limitation of Armament, Washington*, 866–8; and Tamura Kōsaku, *Daitōa gaikōshi kenkyū* (Study of diplomatic history of Greater East Asia), vol. 2.

The Washington Conference formulated high ideals but provided no way to enforce them. It left China's sovereignty still impaired by the unequal treaty system, partly because China in 1922, split between regimes in Peking and Canton, had no single government capable of exercising sovereignty. At the same time the Soviet Union and Germany were left out of the new system. At first glance the chief practical result was a negative one, that Japan's expansion during the First World War had been cut back to the boundaries of 1905. Great power expansion had been forsworn, but only by the nine-power signatories and only on paper.

Some historians, on the other hand, have argued that the 'Washington powers' – notably, the United States, Britain and Japan – successfully put an end to years of rivalry and mutual suspicion, and were at last taking seriously the idea of cooperative action in the Far East to minimize instability. In this regard, Anglo-American–Japanese diplomacy may be seen paralleling postwar developments in Europe in which recent historians have detected a pattern of internationalist cooperation underneath surface animosities. The term 'informal entente', which has been applied to the postwar pattern of Anglo-American relations in the Middle East, might be applied also to East Asian affairs after the Washington Conference. True, there was no rigid mechanism for enforcing collective behaviour; but the three countries opted for entente instead of hostility, and for cooperative competition instead of unilateral or particularistic action.[47]

One's interpretation of the Washington Conference period may ultimately hinge on one's view of the 1920s either as a decade of short-sightedness and failures that prepared for the tragedies of the following decade, or as a time of serious efforts to restructure the international order, efforts that have continued to this day. In this latter perspective, the conference represented a search for a new order in the Far East, paralleling similar searches in Europe, the Middle East and Latin America. The story of Chinese foreign affairs, then, takes on significance as a chapter in the struggle to define a global structure that would ensure international security and domestic stability.

The Washington Conference system was to have been one such structure. Unfortunately, it could never be solidified. For one thing, China's political and financial instability threatened it. Even as the conference closed, in 1922, Westerners and Japanese were proclaiming that China was on the verge of political collapse; the Peking government

[47] See Akira Iriye, *After imperialism*, ch. 1; Jon Jacobson, 'A new international history of the 1920s?' *American Historical Review*, 88.3 (June 1983) 617–45; Michael Hogan, *Informal entente*; Ian Nish, ed. *Anglo-Japanese alienation 1919–1952*.

no longer able to pay full salaries to its officials; teacher salaries unpaid for several months; classes not held; and market conditions in Peking in sharp decline. Government finances seemed beyond repair, and the cabinet changed hands five different times.

Then on 6 May 1923, the Blue Express of the Tientsin-Pukow railway was attacked at Lincheng by more than a thousand bandits.[48] The bandits killed a number of Chinese travellers and carried off over a hundred others, including some sixteen foreigners, among whom was a woman of the Rockefeller family. The Peking government in a panic ordered the release of the foreign hostages. Their release finally came on the 12th, but not without reminding everyone of the impotence of the Peking government. The debate over a joint foreign government administration of China revived in earnest.

If a government existed as the central government in anything more than name, it was because the powers chose to recognize it as such. For the powers required a central government to pay China's debts, negotiate new foreign privileges and deal with various matters under international law. Without one main conduit through which to channel their interests, the powers would have had to negotiate individually with numerous territorial warlords. Thus, the Peking government was a mockery as a central government – no more, really, than a fiction – but it was kept in being by the powers. Despite political instability, they went ahead with a special tariff conference, convened in 1925, to discuss tariff revision in accordance with the Washington Conference agreement. Ironically, the convening of such meetings coincided with the launching of a nationalist revolution led by the Kuomintang and its Communist allies, who denounced the Washington Conference as imperialist collusion and demanded the unconditional return of full sovereignty to China. Meantime warlord dealings with foreign countries surged ahead, as exemplified by the ties of Chang Tso-lin and Tuan Ch'i-jui to Japan, of Wu P'ei-fu and Ch'en Chiung-ming to the British, and of Feng Yü-hsiang and the Kuomintang to the Soviet Union.

MOSCOW'S DUAL APPROACH TO CHINA

Where the Washington Conference powers had aimed at gradual reforms to abolish the treaty system at some future time, the Soviet Revolution had a far more active approach to China's problems both domestic and foreign. V. I. Lenin, from early on, had formulated the notion that backward countries might serve as the reinforcements of the proletarian

[48] Lau Kit-ching Chan, 'The Lincheng incident', *Journal of Oriental Studies*, 10.2 (July 1972).

revolution. The 18 May 1913 issue of *Pravda* carried a short essay entitled 'Backward Europe and advanced Asia'. Lenin's main points may be summarized as follows. (1) In Europe the bourgeois class, its life nearly exhausted, still controls things through its governments. And, likewise, the bourgeoisie in Europe is the enemy of the proletariat, the sole advanced class. (2) These bourgeois governments rule their colonies in Asia by joining hands with the medieval, reactionary controlling forces of Asia. It followed that the democratic movement in these colonies in Asia was propelled forward by the combined anti-colonial movement of the colonial bourgeoisie and the proletariat. And so, the bourgeois democratic movement of Asia was progressive, whereas the bourgeoisie that controlled Europe was regressive.

Lenin accordingly believed in the possibility of an alliance between the proletariat of Europe and the bourgeois democratic movements of Asia. A similar concept inspired Joseph Stalin to write 'Don't forget the East' in 1918. The idea was taken up concretely at the second congress of the Comintern in Moscow in 1920. The national bourgeoisie of backward colonies were thus granted revolutionary status. That is, they were seen as the standard bearers of nationalism. But, at a certain stage, the colonial bourgeoisie would go beyond this to become oppressors of the proletariat. The congress agreed that the proletarian movements of backward colonies could support national liberation movements of the bourgeoisie only to the extent that the bourgeoisie was truly revolutionary. Moscow ruled the nationalist movement of Kemal Pasha of Turkey to be a bourgeoisie national liberation movement, and supported it actively. Next came China. Lenin had decided at about the time of the 1911 Revolution that Sun Yat-sen's political involvements constituted bourgeois nationalism. Moscow's principal China policy thus came to be for China's proletariat and its revolutionary bourgeoisie to work together in an alliance, with Moscow aiding in that effort. It fell upon the Comintern to carry out the plan.

A second Moscow plan was to work directly with the Peking government and with various warlord regimes.[49] The original principle of revolutionary work was to minimize the number of one's enemies and maximize the number of allies and friends. Lenin explained his thoughts on exploiting all the cracks and conflicts of interest within enemy ranks, and all the possibilities of alliance with the masses, in his 1920 essay, '"Left-wing"

---

[49] On the Soviet approach to central and local governments, consult Wang I-chün, *Chung-Su wai-chiao ti hsu-mu* (Prelude to Sino-Soviet foreign relations); and Sow-Theng Leong, *Sino-Soviet diplomatic relations, 1917–1926*.

Communism – an infantile disorder'. (Stalin was to make a similar argument in his 1924 work *Foundations of Leninism*.) And so, after the Bolsheviks came to power in November 1917, though their power base was still shaky and troubled by anti-revolutionary forces within and intervention from without, it became incumbent to somehow make allies of neighbouring countries or, barring that, at least to establish friendly relations by having those countries sever relations with Moscow's enemies, namely the anti-revolutionary Russian troops, Japan, Great Britain and other intervening countries. On top of that, even China's Peking government and warlords could play an auxiliary role to the extent that their sense of nationalism pitted them against the imperialism of Japan and Great Britain. In terms of minimizing the number of one's enemies, the idea of improving relations with the Peking government seemed promising indeed. The Soviet government itself assumed responsibility for this.

Moscow, in short, attempted to support and enlarge the forces of socialism in China by a policy of double dealing: giving aid to Chinese revolutionary forces through the Comintern, while promoting friendly relations with the domestic enemies of those same forces (like the Peking government and the warlords) through the Soviet government.

The initiative toward the Peking government came very early with the call for the restoration of diplomatic relations immediately after the October Revolution. Then in July 1919, Soviet Russia, through Assistant Foreign Commissar Leo M. Karakhan, boldly announced its termination of Boxer indemnity claims and its readiness to relinquish all the other old tsarist rights and privileges in China. This was followed in September 1920 with a more concrete set of proposals. The two declarations taken together are known as the Karakhan manifesto. Coming in the immediate post-May Fourth period, when the rights recovery movement in China was near its height, the Karakhan manifesto created a considerable stir throughout China, in and out of government. However, it left unresolved the major question of the Chinese Eastern Railway, which the Soviet Union simply refused to give up. A high-ranking Soviet diplomat, Adolf Joffe, began to discuss restoration of diplomatic relations in Peking in 1922. (While there he received an invitation from Gotō Shimpei to visit Japan, where he played a major role in the restoration of Soviet diplomatic relations with Japan. He was later accused of being a Trotskyite and committed suicide in 1937.) Next, Karakhan's lengthy negotiations in Peking in 1923-4 primarily with Chinese Foreign Minister V. K. Wellington Koo finally resulted in a 1924 agreement to restore diplomatic relations, based on three guidelines: (1) abrogation of the unequal treaties; (2) the suzerainty of China over Outer Mongolia; (3) the joint management of the Chinese Eastern Railway by China and the Soviet Union.

In tandem with the efforts of the Soviet government were the Comintern efforts toward the Kuomintang and Chinese socialists, considered to constitute China's revolutionary force.[50] In the spring of 1920, Gregory Voitinsky, who bore the title of head of the Far East department of the Comintern, turned up in Peking and met with Li Ta-chao. With Li's enthusiastic recommendation, Voitinsky proceeded to Shanghai to meet with Ch'en Tu-hsiu. There, in July 1921, the first national congress of the Chinese Communist Party was secretly convened in the French concession, and the party formally founded. In the Comintern analysis of the situation, the Kuomintang was a revolutionary bourgeois political party. To the extent that it was revolutionary, the Communist Party as the representative of the Chinese proletariat must cooperate with it. The question was what form that cooperation should take. This was discussed at the central committee meeting of the Chinese Communist Party at Hangchow, in August 1922. Maring (Hendricus Sneevliet),[51] the Comintern representative in China, argued that cooperation should take place within the Kuomintang, with Communist Party members entering the Kuomintang as individuals (the 'bloc-within' strategy). Opposed to this was Ch'en Tu-hsiu, who argued for cooperation with the Kuomintang from outside the party. After a heated debate, Maring declared that the party should properly observe Comintern directives and his view prevailed.[52]

Next, Joffe visited the hapless Sun Yat-sen, then a refugee in Shanghai from the warlord Ch'en Chiung-ming. This resulted in the Sun-Joffe joint statement of 26 January 1923. The clause declaring that the Communist system was not suited to Chinese conditions represented a major concession from Joffe. Sun was reinvited to Canton in February to head a new government whose exchanges with Moscow became surprisingly active. In August, Chiang Kai-shek and Chang T'ai-lei were sent for several months to the Soviet Union to study Soviet military organization and her political representative system. Starting around November, the political adviser Mikhail M. Borodin arrived at Canton and was followed in 1924 by the military adviser General Vasilii K. Blyukher (known in

---

[50] For details of the Comintern approach to the Chinese revolutionaries, see C. M. Wilbur and Julie Lien-ying How, eds. *Documents on communism, nationalism, and Soviet advisers in China, 1918–1927*; Richard C. Thornton, *The Comintern and the Chinese Communists, 1928–1931*; Allen S. Whiting, *Soviet policies in China, 1917–1924*; and Robert C. North, *Moscow and Chinese communists.*

[51] Dov Bing, 'Sneevliet and the early years of the CCP', *CQ* 48 (Oct. – Dec. 1971), 677–97.

[52] These developments are treated more fully in *CHOC* 12.514–18 (J. Ch'en); and 531–40 (C. M. Wilbur).

China as Galen). Aid and arms flowed in with them. Against this background the Kuomintang held its first national congress in January 1924. Under the rubric of the new basic Kuomintang policy of *lien-O jung-kung* (ally with the Soviets, admit the Communists), Li Ta-chao and two other CCP members were elected to regular membership in the 24-member central executive committee of the KMT. Mao Tse-tung's name appears on the list of its seventeen alternate members.

The subsequent vicissitudes of the Comintern-Kuomintang alliance were to be deeply imbedded in the great drama of China's Nationalist Revolution from 1923 to 1927. This Russo-Chinese cooperation in making revolution has been recounted in its socio-political context in volume 12 of this series. Here we can note that it saw the start of a Soviet influence on the Chinese Revolution which continued in one form or another for a whole generation. It also set up an alternative structure of international order based on the premise that Moscow's brand of communism would inevitably sweep over the world. As the Nationalist Revolution marched north from Canton, the Washington Conference powers were put on the defensive and made various accommodations.

CHINA'S NATIONALIST REVOLUTION AND THE POWERS

The National Revolutionary Army of the Kuomintang under Chiang Kai-shek's command headed north through Hunan in July 1926 with the aim of unifying the country. Changsha fell on 12 August, Yochow on the 18th, Hanyang on 6 September, Hankow on the 7th, Wuchang on 10 October, Kiukiang on 4 December, and Nanchang on 7 December. Lurking in the background of this invincible military sweep was the growing discord between the Kuomintang left wing and the new anti-Communist right wing around Chiang Kai-shek. The Comintern judged the time ripe to seize the leadership of the Chinese Revolution, so it issued directives to pursue a radical revolutionary course.

Britain, who until then had taken a hard line against Chinese nationalism, made an about-face in December 1926 and announced a moderate new China policy. Her hopes for moderation were dashed, however, as the tide of nationalism picked up greater force. Massed demonstrators broke into the British concession areas of Hankow and Kiukiang on 4 and 9 January 1927 respectively. Unable to send in relief forces, the British ultimately gave up these concession areas through a restoration agreement.[53]

[53] For these developments in detail see C. M. Wilbur, 'The Nationalist Revolution: from Canton to Nanking, 1923–28', *CHOC* 12.527–720.

When Nanking fell on 24 March, six foreigners were killed in acts of violence by revolutionary army elements. British and American gunboats on the Yangtze shelled the city from the river to help their nationals get away. Japanese who had assembled at their Nanking consulate were raided by officers and troops of the revolutionary army. Some were manhandled and others pistol-whipped. Property was damaged. But at no point was any resistance offered. The naval officers and men who happened to be at the consulate to establish communication links dismantled their machine-guns and stored their weapons in a back room at the request of Japanese civilians, lest their weapons excite the Chinese soldiers. As a result, and despite the violence, not one life was lost, and all were rescued without incident.

In the aftermath of this Nanking incident, Britain reinforced her Shanghai defences, and pressed Japan and the United States to do likewise. The United States sent reinforcements, but tried to avoid exciting Chinese nationalist feeling. Japanese Foreign Minister Shidehara Kijūrō held fast to his principle of non-intervention in China. Criticism of the moderate Shidehara foreign policy, led by the opposition Seiyūkai party, had been growing in strength for some time. Both the army ministry and the army general staff, moreover, supported joint military action with the British, arguing that the British dilemma of today could well be the Japanese dilemma of tomorrow.

Shidehara's thinking was different. He felt, first, that Japan's real China interests lay not in territory but in markets. Secondly, if indeed, as seemed likely, the Nationalist government should bring all China under its control, it behoved Japan to avoid friction. Thirdly, signs of a split were emerging, as the confrontation between pro- and anti-Communist elements within the Nationalist government intensified. And lastly, what if China failed to respond to a Japanese ultimatum, and rejected Japanese demands? To give Chiang Kai-shek foreign support might make him seem like a traitor. There was no real alternative to letting Chiang clean the CCP out of the Nationalist government on his own. This is of course what he did in the bloody coup of April 1927 and in the subsequent effort to exterminate the CCP.

With Chiang's anti-radical coup, it might have been expected that the Washington Conference system would finally be in place. After all, there was a central government in China with a promise of stability, standing against the Soviet Union, the one power that had remained outside the Washington framework. Despite their differences, the Washington powers had not entirely given up the principle of mutual consultation and cooperation in China. Unfortunately, the years after 1927 were to demonstrate how difficult it was to create a stable international order in the Far East, in a period of domestic turmoil which was to engulf not only China but Japan and the Western nations as well.

The story of this progressive destabilization is treated in a subsequent chapter. Here, a bare outline of Chinese-Japanese relations after 1927 should suffice to illustrate the extreme difficulties in working out a pattern of international order that would be acceptable to and sustained by domestic forces.

In the same month that Chiang Kai-shek made his move against the Communists, opening up the possibility of the foreign treaty powers dealing with him and his new Nanking government, the Japanese cabinet changed hands. Japan's new prime minister and concurrent foreign minister was retired army general Tanaka Giichi. As head of the opposition party, Tanaka had never missed an opportunity to criticize his predecessor, Shidehara, for the weakness of his China policy. Now suddenly Tanaka was in the position of having to adopt a strong China policy of his own.[54]

In May, as revolutionary army troops approached the province of Shantung in the 1927 phase of the Northern Expedition, Tanaka despatched troops to Shantung on the pretext of protecting Japanese lives. Chinese troops drew back south of Shantung, and a clash was avoided. The Northern Expedition was resumed in April 1928, whereupon Tanaka again sent troops into Shantung. Chinese troops who had taken possession of Tsinan earlier encountered the Japanese there, and the two sides clashed on 3 May after some minor incidents. Driven by anti-imperialist passions, some Chinese soldiers went out and massacred eleven Japanese civilians. The Japanese army initiated a large-scale operation against the Chinese army, and drove them out of the Tsinan vicinity. Chinese forces evaded the Japanese and marched north toward Peking. Though there were no further clashes with Japanese troops, the fighting at Tsinan nurtured deep anti-Japanese feelings even among Chiang's politically moderate troops.

Marshal Chang Tso-lin, defeated by these Chinese forces, left Peking by special train on 3 June, headed for his Mukden (Shenyang) base. A large explosion just this side of Mukden killed him early the following morning. His assassination had been plotted by a small group of Japanese army officers. Their thinking was that the death of Chang Tso-lin would deprive Manchuria of its leader and plunge it into chaos. The Japanese army would then step in to restore order, and occupy Manchuria.[55] But, on the contrary, Manchuria was not plunged into chaos. Chang Hsueh-

[54] William F. Morton, *Tanaka Giichi and Japan's China policy*.
[55] Gavan McCormick, *Chang Tso-lin in Northeast China, 1911–1928*; and Nobuya Bamba, *Japanese diplomacy in a dilemma: new light on Japan's China policy*.

liang, then in Peking, rushed back to Mukden where his father's death was kept a secret until 21 June, when young Chang assumed his father's mantle. The assassination was soon confirmed to be the work of the Kwantung army but, realizing that to make an issue of it might put him at the mercy of Japan, Chang Hsueh-liang held his peace.

While taking care not to upset Japan, this new ruler of Manchuria also found himself drawn to the rights recovery element of Chinese nationalism. First he grasped the hand of his father's old enemy, the Kuomintang, and then he hoisted the Kuomintang 'blue sky and white sun' flag over Manchuria. The flag went up on 29 December 1928, at the end of secret negotiations with the Nanking government. Chang joined the Kuomintang, and was designated commander-in-chief of the north-east frontier defence army. Thereafter, Chang gradually adopted an anti-Japanese policy and the Chinese anti-Japanese movement in Manchuria came into the open. Japanese businessmen suffered, and even the giant South Manchurian Railway Company fell into the red. Then came the great depression of late 1929.

The deteriorating situation in Manchuria was marked by a series of incidents. Korean farmers in Manchuria, who at one point were said to have numbered two million, were engaged chiefly in rice culture. But in 1931 the Chinese anti-Japanese movement became far more widely organized, and farmers from Korea, Japanese subjects since 1910, living in remote areas out of easy reach of Japanese authority, bore the brunt of countless incidents. The Korean population of Manchuria fell to about 800,000.

In 1931, about 400 Korean farmers rented land in Wanpaoshan, north of Changchun, from some Chinese, and began the hard work of converting it to rice lands. However, Chinese authorities forbade them to settle, and ordered them out. The order was temporarily rescinded at the protest of the Japanese consul. But on 1 July, about 800 Chinese farmers stormed the land and started smashing the new irrigation ditches. Skirmishes broke out between the interlopers and the Japanese police who rushed to the scene from nearby Changchun. This made the front page of Japanese newspapers, and for some time Koreans in various parts of Korea took violent revenge on local overseas Chinese.

The number one hypothetical enemy of the Japanese army at this time was the Soviet Union. During the period of the Wanpaoshan incident, the Japanese army had sent general staff officer Captain Nakamura Shintarō into western Manchuria to survey its geography, in the event of a war with Russia. Rabidly anti-Japanese soldiers of Chang Hsueh-liang caught and shot him. The alleged murderer was finally brought to Mukden on 18 September 1931, and the Japanese consul notified.

But it was too late, for 18 September was the night of the Mukden incident. A small group of Kwantung army officers blew up a part of the South Manchurian Railway and, using that as a pretext, launched an attack on Chinese troops. In less than half a year, the whole of Manchuria had fallen to the Japanese army and been severed from China. Japan had become the primary concern of Chinese foreign policy. Within less than a generation, a mere two decades, the East Asian regional order of the Ch'ing dynasty, the international legal order envisaged by the Washington Conference treaty powers, and the world revolutionary order dreamed of in Moscow, had all proved unavailing as an international matrix for the Chinese Republic.

CHAPTER 3

NATIONALIST CHINA DURING THE NANKING DECADE 1927–1937

The Nanking regime was born of factional strife and bloodshed. In the early morning of 12 April 1927, gangs of thugs belonging to the Mafia-like Green Gang plunged through the streets of Shanghai, seized Communists and suspected Communists, and executed them on the spot with pistols or broadswords. Several thousand were massacred then and during the ensuing month. Chiang Kai-shek had split with the Communists; the first united front was ended. Six days later, on 18 April, the Nationalist government was inaugurated at Nanking.

The challenge confronting the new government was awesome – nothing less than to turn back the tide of national disintegration that, for a century and more, had been washing over the Chinese nation. A central, national government had virtually ceased to exist. Political power had devolved into the hands of regional militarists, 'warlords', who too often were unconcerned for the popular welfare and sought only to enhance their wealth and power by reliance on military force. The sense of moral community – the broad and pervasive consensus regarding the values and proper relationships of cultural and social life, which had so richly contributed to the stability of traditional China – had disintegrated, and in its place were confusion and contention. Even the economic foundations of the traditional political system had eroded.

THE INITIAL CONSOLIDATION OF POWER

Because the Chinese were profoundly sensitive to the abject condition of their nation, to the ravages of warlord struggles, and to the humiliations of imperialist aggression, the Nationalist revolutionary armies had been greeted exultantly as their Northern Expedition moved from Canton in the south (beginning in July 1926) to Peking in the north (occupied in June 1928) (see volume 12). To many Chinese, Nationalist rule marked the beginning of a new era, when China would again be unified and strong, when there would be economic plenty for all, and when they would no longer feel shame at being Chinese. As early as 1929, however, these extravagant expectations turned ashen. For the Nationalists, before turning their attention to the constructive tasks of the new era, had first to resolve who among them was to wield the power of the new government.

Since the death of Sun Yat-sen in March 1925, there had been a bitter, even bloody, struggle for leadership of the Nationalist movement. These power rivalries had been papered over during the Northern Expedition. Early in 1927, however, with the prize of national power within reach, the intraparty struggles resumed with a new and unprecedented ferocity. When the Nanking decade dawned, therefore, the Nationalist movement was in utter disarray. Indeed, in the spring of 1927, there existed two Nationalist governments (that of Chiang Kai-shek and the 'Centrists' in Nanking, and that of the Left-Kuomintang, still allied with the Communists, in Hankow) and three headquarters claiming leadership of the Kuomintang (besides those in Hankow and Nanking, the extreme right-wing Western Hills faction claimed sole legitimacy for its Central Executive Committee in Shanghai). Complicating the situation was that each of these power centres was backed by the armed forces of one or more provincial militarists. These had only recently declared allegiance to the revolution; they had little or no commitment to the ideological goals of the movement; and they were now simply indulging in political manoeuvres which, they hoped, would result in the preservation, if not the enhancement, of their personal and regional power.

Early in these struggles, Chiang Kai-shek was nearly eliminated from the competition. Only three months after establishing the government in Nanking, his troops were defeated by the warlord army of Sun Ch'uan-fang while he was attempting to push the Northern Expedition toward Peking. The result was a rout, during which Sun Ch'uan-fang's army threatened even to occupy Nanking. Chiang Kai-shek's prestige was badly tarnished as a consequence, and a new coalition within the Nanking government, headed by the Kwangsi faction of Li Tsung-jen and Pai Ch'ung-hsi, forced him from power in August 1927.

The Left-Kuomintang at Hankow, headed by Wang Ching-wei, had meanwhile followed Chiang's example and purged the Communists from their own ranks. With Chiang Kai-shek in retirement and with the Communists eliminated, the two chief causes of intraparty altercations had been removed, and the way lay open to a reconciliation of the warring factions. In September 1927, representatives of the Nanking and Hankow governments and of the Western Hills faction formed a 'Central Special Committee' which established a new, supposedly unified, Nationalist government at Nanking.

This new government was no more stable than its predecessors. The two most powerful leaders in the Nationalist movement, Chiang Kai-shek and Wang Ching-wei, had been excluded from it. And it never became financially viable. By January 1928, therefore, the government of the Special Committee had crumbled. Chiang Kai-shek, after five months in retirement (during which time he married the comely Soong Mei-ling), returned to office more powerful than before. In February he was named chairman of the Central Executive Committee of the Kuomintang and commander-in-chief of the army. In October, he also assumed the office of chairman of the State Council (and thus was the formal head of state). He now controlled all three legs of the Nationalists' triad of power – the party, government and military.

Under Chiang's aegis, the Nationalist government in Nanking was transformed into a military dictatorship. Prior to his rise to leadership, the Nationalist movement (whether in the form of the Kuomintang or one of its organizational antecedents) had never been a cohesive, ideologically unified, or tightly disciplined political party. Since Sun Yat-sen first formed the Hsing-Chung-hui (Revive China Society) in 1894, his following had comprised persons of widely diverse orientations and motivations. Indeed, he seems never to have refused membership in his party to anyone who applied. In at least one instance he even enrolled the entire army of the warlord Ch'en Chiung-ming into the Kuomintang. As a consequence, wrote T'ang Leang-Li, who was a member of the party, the Kuomintang before the 1924 reorganization was not a political party but simply 'an agglomeration of different individual politicians, the majority of whom, caring little for the principles Sun Yat-sen stood for, were merely out to exploit his great reputation and prestige among the population for their own ends'.[1] The agglutinative tendencies of the Kuomintang had worsened as the movement approached the threshold of national power. For then careerists and opportunists of every political stripe leapt onto the victorious bandwagon; membership in the party grew from only 150,000 in 1926 to 630,000 in 1929. The party organization, never tightly controlled, admitted the new applicants with utter disregard for their backgrounds, character, or commitment to the goals of the revolution. 'Party headquarters at all levels,' complained Ho Ying-ch'in, chief-of-staff of Chiang Kai-shek's army, in January 1928, 'are concerned only about the quantity, and pay no attention to the quality [of the new members]. The spirit of the party therefore becomes more rotten by the day'.[2] The Kuomintang membership by 1927 had therefore become

[1] T'ang Leang-Li, *The inner history of the Chinese Revolution*, 330.
[2] *Ch'en-pao* (Morning post), 11 Jan. 1928, in Hatano Ken'ichi, comp., *Gendai Shina no kiroku* (Records of contemporary China), Jan. 1928, 110.

intolerably disparate, and Chiang Kai-shek accordingly began to screen out many of the members that to him appeared to be undesirables. In the process, he fundamentally altered the character of the Nationalist movement.

The first to be purged from the movement were the Communists. Never, in all probability, could the Nationalists have gained national power had it not been for the united front that Sun Yat-sen formed with the Chinese Communists and the Soviet Union in 1923–4. With the advice, material aid and organizational skills of the Communists, the Kuomintang had been reorganized on the model of the Russian Communist Party; a party-led and politically indoctrinated army had been created; and young revolutionary cadres had gone among the peasants and workers in the warlord-held areas, stirring up and organizing support for the revolution. Significantly, those who had engaged in the difficult and dangerous work of organizing the masses were more closely identified with the Communists than with the Kuomintang. 'Kuomintang members were unwilling to do the real and lower-level work,' Ho Ying-ch'in admitted, and consequently 'the Communists naturally took on this work to split our party from the peasants and workers'.[3] Those less committed to the revolution avoided working among the masses and thus avoided the taint of communism. The purge of the Communists therefore had a filtering effect, leaving the self-servers untouched, but removing from the revolutionary movement many of those who had infused a degree of vigour, discipline and commitment into the Kuomintang during the period of revolutionary success.

Even after the purge of the Communists, however, there remained a broad stratum of Kuomintang members who advocated more radical solutions to the nation's problems than those favoured by Chiang Kai-shek. This was the left wing of the party, which during 1928 and 1929 was Chiang's most formidable political rival and which he successfully suppressed only after nearly two years of bitter struggle. These leftists loudly denounced the 'one-man military dictatorship' that Chiang was creating, and they demanded that the Kuomintang revive the policies and spirit that had energized the movement during the period of Sun Yat-sen's revolutionary leadership in 1924. The party, they contended, and not the army, should control and provide direction to the regime. The leftists, in contrast to the Communists, rejected the concept and policies of class struggle, but they believed that the party must maintain and strengthen its relations with the masses by means of peasant, worker, and other mass organizations. Only with such a mass base, they insisted, could they

[3] Ho Ying-ch'in, 'Chin-hou chih Chung-kuo Kuo-min-tang' (The Chinese Kuomintang from now on), *Chung-yang pan yueh-k'an* (Central semi-monthly), 2 (Oct. 1927) 102.

prevent the revolution from becoming a plaything of bureaucrats and militarists.[4]

Many Kuomintang members, perhaps a majority, supported these radical views. But the estimate of T'ang Leang-Li, himself a member of the left, that 80 per cent of the party members in this period belonged to the left wing was surely an exaggeration.[5] Still, it is clear that many of the low-ranking and young members of the party (one-third of the Kuomintang members in 1929 were under twenty-five years of age) were sympathetic with the views of the left wing.

Wang Ching-wei was the recognized leader of the left, but he was sojourning in Europe during 1928 and 1929, and formally at least dissociated himself from the movement opposing Chiang Kai-shek. Moving spirit behind the left-wing organization, therefore, was Wang's loyal associate, Ch'en Kung-po, a one-time Communist, who in May 1928 began publishing the weekly *Ko-ming p'ing-lun* (Revolutionary critic) as a mouthpiece for the left wing. Although this journal never exceeded a circulation of 15,000 copies, it enjoyed such popularity and influence that the Nanking government suppressed it in September after an existence of only $4\frac{1}{2}$ months.

Facing the prospect of government suppression, Ch'en Kung-po decided that the left wing, hitherto an amorphous body of Wang Ching-wei supporters, should organize. Although Wang himself was ambivalent about the plan, viewing himself as a leader of the entire Kuomintang rather than merely a factional leader, Ch'en in late 1928 organized the Chinese Kuomintang Reorganizationist Comrades Association (Chung-kuo kuo-min-tang kai-tsu t'ung-chih hui) – the name symbolizing the group's advocacy of the revolutionary principles that the Kuomintang had adopted at the time of the 1924 reorganization. The Reorganization clique, as it was called, was a formal organization with a written constitution, a party headquarters in Shanghai, and branches throughout much of the country. During 1928, too, Ch'en organized the Ta-lu University in Shanghai, the purpose of which was to indoctrinate youth with the political views of the left and to train cadres for the faction.

The leftists, although they all recognized Wang Ching-wei as their leader, were not unified. Ku Meng-yü led a faction within the Reorganization clique that was notably less radical than the faction led by Ch'en

---

[4] Ssu-ma Hsien-tao, *Pei-fa hou chih ko-p'ai ssu-ch'ao* (The doctrines of the various cliques after the Northern Expedition), 133–99; T'ang Leang-Li, *Inner history*, 331–3; Arif Dirlik, 'Mass movements and the left Kuomintang', *Modern China*, 1.1 (Jan. 1975) 57–9.

[5] T'ang Leang-Li, *Inner history*, 334. Actual membership in the leading left-wing organization (the Reorganization clique) at this time was perhaps 10,000. See Chiang Shang-ch'ing, *Cheng-hai mi-wen* (Secrets of the political world), 72.

Kung-po. Ku, whose views were publicized in his own journal, *Ch'ien-chin* (Forward), disapproved of Ch'en's emphasis upon peasants, workers and petty bourgeoisie as the core of the Nationalist Revolution. Ku also expressed greater mistrust of the mass movement. Other leftists, like Ho Ping-hsien, disliked Ch'en Kung-po and held aloof from the Reorganization clique, although they remained loyal to Wang Ching-wei. Thus, the left wing of the Kuomintang suffered much the same kind of internal fragmentation that plagued the right wing led by Chiang Kai-shek.[6]

Left-wing opposition to Chiang and the authorities in Nanking was not limited to ideological theorizing and propaganda, for the radicals, often dominant in the local and provincial party branches, worked strenuously to bring the revolution to fruition. In Chekiang, for example, leftists organized boycotts of foreign goods and led popular demonstrations against foreign churches and hospitals. They organized special tribunals to judge and punish counter-revolutionaries. They also began a programme of rent-reduction, which stirred the enmity of the landlord class and consequently damaged Nanking's efforts to raise money from that group. In Kiangsu, similarly, the radicals provoked Nanking's displeasure by organizing the masses and by confiscating temples which were then converted into welfare centres for the local people.[7]

The activities of the radicals, and the implicit political challenge of Wang Ching-wei, deeply disturbed the right wing of the party. Immediately following Chiang's return to power in January 1928, therefore, there began an intensive, albeit generally bloodless, suppression of the left wing. At the fourth plenum of the Kuomintang's Central Executive Committee in February, for example, all provincial party organizations 'not creditable to the party' were ordered dissolved. A re-registration of the party membership was ordered; and all party members were ordered to conduct themselves in the 'spirit' of the party leadership. The move to re-register the members was patently designed to weed out those who had displayed radical tendencies, and to guarantee a membership that would complaisantly accept the dictates of leaders then ensconced in power. Mass movements were also, for all intents and purposes, suspended. Henceforth, the mass organizations would serve as Nanking's instruments of control, not as organs for the expression of popular opinions or initiatives. In Chekiang, where landlord opposition to the land redistribution policy was

[6] Chiang Shang-ch'ing, 68–73; Ssu-ma Hsien-tao, 140–52; Ch'en Kung-po, *The communist movement in China*, 178–90.
[7] Noel Ray Miner, 'Chekiang: the Nationalists' effort in agrarian reform and construction, 1927–1937', 64–79; Patrick Cavendish, 'The "New China" of the Kuomintang', in Jack Gray, ed. *Modern China's Search for a political form*, 158–9; Bradley Kent Geisert, 'Power and society: the Kuomintang and local elites in Kiangsu province, China, 1924–1937', 96–131.

fierce, at least one leftist leader was assassinated, and others were beaten and stabbed. Landlords may have been responsible for this violence. But the Chekiang provincial government, under Chiang Kai-shek's intimate supporter Chang Jen-chieh (Chang Ching-chiang), sided with the landlords by arresting recalcitrant leftists and suspending the provincial party newspaper *Min-kuo jih-pao* (Republic daily), which had been dominated by the leftists.[8]

Youth, who were most susceptible to the idealism and radicalism of the left, were unequivocally instructed to get out of politics. 'The most deplorable fact,' read the manifesto of the fourth plenum (February 1928) 'is the participation by immature students today in our political and social strifes. To permit these young boys and girls, not yet [having] attained maturity, and without sufficient knowledge and experience, to participate freely in the affairs of the nation is not only to sacrifice the life of our race in the future, but also to allow them to treat the entire nation and human society as playthings'.[9]

The paramountcy of the right wing was finally and formally established at the Third Party Congress in March 1929. Recognizing that the lower ranks of the party were permeated by adherents of the left, Chiang Kai-shek's faction took special measures to guarantee its control of the congress. On the grounds that re-registration of party members had not been completed and that the organization of the party at the local level was still in disarray, only one-fourth of the delegates to the congress were elected by the party members. The remaining delegates were appointed by the central-party headquarters.[10] The leftists vehemently denounced this violation of democratic principles within the party, and declared that the Third Party Congress was illegal. The denunciations were in vain, however, for Chiang Kai-shek had now placed his own supporters in control of the Kuomintang, and imposed his own conception of the revolution upon the party and the government. Leaders of the left wing were disciplined: Ch'en Kung-po and Kan Nai-kuang were 'expelled forever' from the party; Ku Meng-yü's party membership was suspended for three years; and Wang Ching-wei was reprimanded for his error of 'straddling parties'.[11] Thereafter, the leftists' contention that the govern-

8 Hsiao Cheng, *T'u-ti kai-ko wu-shih-nien: Hsiao Cheng hui-i-lu* (Fifty years of land reform: the memoirs of Hsiao Cheng), 27–9; *China year book* (hereafter *CYB*), *1929–30*, ed. H. G. W. Woodhead, 1163–73; Miner, 'Chekiang', 64–79; Cavendish, 158–9; Geisert, 'Power and society', 144–66.

9 *CYB*, *1929–30*, 1170.

10 Jürgen Domes, *Vertagte Revolution: die Politik der Kuomintang in China, 1923–1937*, 325. Most of the elected delegates were Overseas Chinese. In actual fact, therefore, only a tenth of the elected delegates represented party branches within China. See *CYB*, *1929–30*, 1202.

11 *I-shih-pao* (Social welfare post), 21 Mar. 1929, in Hatano Ken'ichi, *Gendai Shina no kiroku* (Records of contemporary China), Mar. 1929, 276–8; *Fan-Chiang yun-tung shih* (History of the anti-Chiang movement), 46–7.

ment ought to be simply the administrative arm of the party and that the party should be the superior organ during the period of revolutionary construction was conclusively rejected. Instead, during 1929–31, the party was stripped of most of its power, and it ceased to play a significant role either in policy formation or as a supervisory organ. Somewhat earlier, Chiang had also dismantled the system of party commissars in the army.[12] Ineluctably, the left wing was repressed, and the status of the party was correspondingly reduced.

Even as he purged Communists and Kuomintang leftists from the movement, Chiang Kai-shek relied increasingly upon old-style bureaucrats and the army. As soon as the revolution gave evidence of success, large numbers of former bureaucrats in the various warlord regimes had descended on Nanking seeking new and remunerative employment. And Chiang, confronted with the challenge of administering a national government, welcomed them into his camp. By 1929, at least four of the ten ministries were headed by these new converts to the revolutionary cause. They filled so many other bureaucratic posts that Quo Tai-chi (Kuo T'ai-ch'i), a long-time member of the Kuomintang, angrily resigned his vice-ministership of foreign affairs, charging that 'the Party is nearly usurped by the old mandarin influence even as it was usurped last year by the Communists'.[13] The effects of this mandarin influence on the new regime were far-reaching. These groups brought with them the same outlooks, the same lust for power cum disregard for the public weal, that they had displayed in their former jobs. The bureaucracy became routinized; bureaucrats wrote innumerable documents and shuffled papers, but paid minimal heed to the actual implementation of policy; and corruption quickly seeped through the administration. Thus, the values, attitudes and practices of the old warlord regimes had been injected into the new government. Even eighteen years later, in 1946, would-be Kuomintang reformers surveyed the corruption of their government and attributed it to the political opportunists and bureaucrats who in this period had swarmed into the Nationalist ranks.[14]

Perhaps even more decisive in determining the future course of the Nationalist movement was the pervasive influence of the military. During Sun Yat-sen's lifetime, the military had been a relatively disparaged

---

[12] The system of political commissars was reinstituted beginning in 1932. See Joseph H. Heinlein, Jr. 'Political warfare: the Chinese Nationalist model', 268–330.

[13] *North China Herald*, 14 Apr. 1928, 48.

[14] See e.g. Ch'eng Yuan-chen, 'Ko-hsin yun-tung chih-hsu ch'eng-kung pu-hsu shih-pai' (The renovation movement can only succeed and must not fail), in *Ko-hsin chou-k'an* (Renovation weekly), 1.5 (24 Aug. 1946) 3–5; and Li Ta, 'Ko-hsin yun-tung ti ta ching-shen' (The great spirit of the renovation movement), in *Ko-hsin chou-k'an*, 1.6 (31 Aug. 1946) 5.

element in the movement. Under Chiang, however, Sun's relative ranking of these groups – first the party, then the government, and lastly the army – was turned upside-down, and the army now became the preponderant element. Some indication of this is found in the fact that, in 1929, more than half the members of the Kuomintang in China were soldiers, not civilians. Of the party leaders – members of the Central Executive Committee – 43 per cent in 1935 were military officers. Twenty-five of the thirty-three chairmen of provinces controlled by the Nationalists between 1927 and 1937 were generals.[15] And about two-thirds of the government's expenditure during the decade was allocated for the military and payments on debts (most of which had been contracted to pay military outlays).[16] The true measure of the dominance of the military is provided less by these statistics, however, than by the overshadowing presence of a single soldier, Chiang Kai-shek – a presence that would grow in importance as the Nanking decade advanced.

THE STRUGGLE IN THE PROVINCES

With his victory over the left wing, Chiang Kai-shek's power within the councils of the Nanking government was secured. Then, however, the main arena of internecine struggle shifted to the provinces.

By 1929, the flag of the National government flew over the whole of China proper and Manchuria. Peking had been occupied by Nationalist forces in June 1928, at which time the city's name was changed from Peking (Northern capital) to Peiping (Northern peace). And on 29 December 1928, Chang Hsueh-liang, warlord of the four provinces of Manchuria, proclaimed his loyalty to the Nationalist government. With the nation now nominally unified for the first time since 1916, the authorities in Nanking could look ahead to the tasks of peaceful national reconstruction.

A major obstacle, however, remained. The military phase of the revolution had been successful in large part because many of the provincial militarists had not been defeated on the field of battle but instead had been coopted into the revolutionary movement. Although these warlords had gained membership in the Kuomintang and accepted prestigious posts in the Nanking hierarchy, they distrusted Chiang Kai-shek, were jealous of his growing power, and were largely indifferent to the ideology of the Nationalist movement. During the Northern Expedition, Chiang and the

[15] Robert C. North, *Kuomintang and Chinese Communist elites*, 53; Domes, 572; Hung-mao Tien, *Government and politics in Kuomintang China, 1927–1937*, 140.
[16] Arthur N. Young, *China's nation-building effort, 1927–1937: the financial and economic record*, 75, 147.

authorities in Nanking, who were committed to the unification of the nation and to the centralization of authority, had necessarily tolerated the independent power of the provincial militarists. They had, in fact, even institutionalized the position of the provincial militarists by creating a number of branch political councils. These councils, established in 1928, were nominally subordinate to the Central Political Council in Nanking. In fact, however, they were autonomous administrative organs that, momentarily at least, legitimized the regional dominance of the major warlord groupings. Thus, Feng Yü-hsiang, who controlled Kansu, Shensi and Honan, headed the branch political council at Kaifeng; Yen Hsi-shan's administration of Shansi was legitimized by the branch political council at Taiyuan; and the so-called Kwangsi clique dominated the councils at Hankow, Peiping and Canton, which were headed respectively by Li Tsung-jen, Pai Ch'ung-hsi and Li Chi-shen. A sixth branch political council was established at Mukden after Chang Hsüeh-liang's capitulation in Manchuria.[17]

Chiang Kai-shek regarded the branch political councils as temporary expedients, for he aspired to centralize all power, administrative and military, under the Nanking government. Soon, therefore, he challenged the autonomous power of the provincial militarists. First, in late 1928, Nanking announced that the branch political councils would be abolished in March 1929. Then, in January 1929, a National Reorganization and Demobilization Conference convened in Nanking, at which the central government authorities presented a plan for the reduction of China's armed forces.

The desirability of military demobilization was generally recognized. Armies in China had swollen prodigiously since the fall of the Ch'ing dynasty, and in 1929 probably numbered about two million men (as compared with about 400,000 under the dynasty, and about 1,200,000 in 1922). Now that the military phase of the revolution was concluded, these huge forces were no longer needed and were, moreover, an insupportable burden on the nation's financial resources. In 1928, for example, Nanking's own army, which totalled roughly 240,000 men, cost approximately Y360 million a year (Y = *yuan*, Chinese dollars), although Nanking's revenue (after payments on debts) amounted to only Y300 million a year.[18] Furthermore, while the armies of the provincial militarists did not constitute a direct financial burden upon Nanking, they did absorb revenue that might otherwise have been channelled to the central government. It was therefore argued that, unless the armies were reduced,

---

[17] Diana Lary, *Region and nation: the Kwangsi clique in Chinese politics, 1925–1937*, 117.
[18] Young, *Nation-building*, 15.

the government would have no means with which to undertake the social and economic reconstruction of the nation.

At the demobilization conference, the nation's leading militarists – Chiang Kai-shek, Feng Yü-hsiang, Yen Hsi-shan, Li Tsung-jen and others – agreed to trim the nation's armies to 800,000 men, to limit military expenditures to 41 per cent of the government's revenues, and to establish a unified command structure. The conference was a failure, however, because the militarists' suspicions of Chiang Kai-shek were exacerbated during the meetings. Using the principle that the less efficient armies should be demobilized first, and because his own Whampoa-led troops tended in fact to be the best-trained and best-led units in China, Chiang Kai-shek was asking greater sacrifices of the provincial militarists than of himself. Because their armies were their principal source of political power, the provincial militarists felt that Chiang was merely using the issue of military disbandment to establish a political advantage over them. However dedicated they might have been to the national interests – and that was debatable – the provincial militarists were disinclined to abandon their own ambitions so that Chiang might enhance his power. For they did not perceive that he had any greater claim to national power and leadership than did they. They therefore left the conference in late January 1929 applauding the principle of military disbandment, but determined to maintain their military and political positions against Chiang. Chiang, on his part, was equally determined to establish the dominance of the central government over the provinces. The result was a long and costly series of civil wars.

The first of the civil wars erupted in March 1929, only two months after the demobilization conference, when the Kwangsi clique – as a result of a crisis seemingly provoked by Chiang Kai-shek – revolted against Nanking. This was a formidable challenge, for the Kwangsi leaders were skilled tacticians and commanded about 230,000 troops. There was also the possibility that Feng Yü-hsiang, commanding 220,000 men and perhaps Chiang Kai-shek's most ardent military rival, would join forces with the rebels. This challenge might have doomed a lesser man, but it was tailored to Chiang Kai-shek's talents. For Chiang bought off Feng Yü-hsiang, reportedly with Y2 million and a promise of control over Shantung province. Then, with his superior troops, he defeated the Kwangsi armies in less than two months. The empire of Li Tsung-jen and Pai Ch'ung-hsi in Hopei and Hunan-Hupei thereupon collapsed. They hastily retreated to their home province of Kwangsi to nurse their humiliation and to plan for another day.

Only one month later, in May 1929, Chiang provoked Feng Yü-hsiang into rebellion by reneging on his pledge to hand Shantung over to Feng's control. In this confrontation, half of Feng's army – fully 100,000 of his best troops – suddenly defected to the central government, a shift of loyalties precipitated again by massive bribes. During this struggle, Yen Hsi-shan in nearby Shansi watched passively as Feng's remaining forces were pushed out of Shantung and Honan.

With Feng Yü-hsiang's army now badly mauled by the central government forces, the balance of power in North China had clearly shifted in Nanking's favour. Yen Hsi-shan therefore felt threatened, and in February and March 1930 he, together with the now much weakened Feng Yü-hsiang, formed a new anti-Chiang movement. This Northern Coalition, as it was called, posed the most serious challenge yet to Chiang's power. For Yen and Feng had now formed a broad alliance of anti-Chiang forces. Li Tsung-jen and Pai Ch'ung-hsi of the Kwangsi clique promised to coordinate their attack from South China. Many of Chiang's civilian opponents – including such diverse groups as Wang Ching-wei and his Reorganizationist clique, and the extreme right wing Western Hills faction – provided administrative and ideological muscle to the movement. Soon these disparate elements began creating the institutional structures of a separate and permanent regime. An 'Enlarged Conference of the Kuomintang', functionally equivalent to a Central Executive Committee of the party, convened in Peiping in July. And in September a new National government was instituted, with Yen Hsi-shan as chairman of the State Council. By promulgating a provisional constitution (*yueh-fa*), which contained articles guaranteeing personal freedoms, the new regime also attracted much popular support, especially from the nation's intellectuals, who had begun to feel the sting of Nanking's political repression.

As early as July, however, Chiang ordered his troops against the Northern Coalition. The fighting in this civil war fitted none of the stereotypes of warlord battles. Nanking and the northerners fought furiously. Physical devastation was enormous; in four months of fighting, the two sides incurred some 250,000 casualties. By September, just when the Northern Coalition announced the formation of a new government, Nanking was gaining the upper hand in the war, and the rebel government fled from Peiping to Yen's provincial capital of Taiyuan. To the very end, however, the leaders of the Northern Coalition and of Nanking realized that Chang Hsueh-liang, warlord of Manchuria, could tip the scales of battle either way. Both sides therefore wooed him. Finally, apparently won over by Nanking's bribe of 10 million *yuan* and by the promise that he might administer all of China north of the Yellow River, Chang in mid-September issued a public declaration in support of the central government. The Northern Coalition was thereby doomed. Still, Nanking gained little from its victory. For Chang Hsueh-liang quickly led 100,000 of his own troops into the Peiping-Tientsin area, and took control of the major railroads and of the rich revenues from the Tientsin customs. North China, therefore, still lay outside the administrative sway of Nanking.

The concatenation of revolts was still not ended. The next one actually succeeded – for six weeks – in forcing Chiang Kai-shek from power. The basic causes of the revolt were identical to those of the preceding ones: jealousy of Chiang Kai-shek's growing power and fear of Nanking's centralizing pretensions. As always, however, there were secondary issues that provided the rebels with a facade of moral justification. In this case, the catalysing event was Chiang Kai-shek's arrest of Hu Han-min. Stung by the Northern Coalition's popularity as a result of proclaiming a provisional constitution, Chiang Kai-shek in February 1931 declared his determination to promulgate a similar document. 'Without a Provisional Constitution,' he insisted, 'there could be no security for the lives and property of the people...without guarantees to person and property there could be no real unification of the country and an end of civil wars.'[19]

Hu Han-min, however, heatedly rejected this proposal. He publicly avowed that the proclamation of a provisional constitution would be contrary to the intention of Sun Yat-sen – although the actual cause of his objection may well have been the fear that Chiang meant to enhance his power by having himself named president under a new constitution. In protest against Chiang's unilateral decision to promulgate the provisional constitution, Hu resigned his position as head of the Legislative Yuan. Chiang Kai-shek thereupon arrested Hu, because – as Chiang explained – 'It is only in this way that his glorious past may be preserved intact.'[20]

Ostensibly in protest against Hu Han-min's arrest, the provincial militarists of Kwangtung and Kwangsi, and a mixed assortment of Chiang Kai-shek's civilian rivals (such as Wang Ching-wei, the Western Hills partisans, and Sun Yat-sen's son, Sun Fo) established a new separatist regime in Canton in May 1931. An 'Extraordinary Conference' of the Kuomintang's Central Executive Committee was formed, and this in turn created a new National government on 1 June.[21] Real power rested with the provincial militarists, most notably Ch'en Chi-t'ang, chairman of Kwangtung province.

Mutual denunciations and impeachments emanated from the new Canton regime and from the Nanking government. Canton asserted that

---

[19] CYB, 1931–32, 529.
[20] Ibid. 530; Lei Hsiao-ts'en, San-shih-nien tung-luan Chung-kuo (Thirty years of China in turmoil), 205.
[21] Domes, 439–44.

it would abandon its opposition only if the dictator Chiang Kai-shek relinquished his positions in Nanking.

Had not the Japanese invaded Manchuria on 18 September 1931, this conflict, like its predecessors, would presumably have been fought on the battlefield. As a result of an impassioned anti-Japanese reaction from the Chinese people, especially the students, pressures to terminate the intraparty squabbling and to form a united government to oppose the foreign aggressor became irresistible. After extraordinarily arcane negotiations and complex conferences, including two Fourth Party Congresses held separately in Nanking and Canton and a joint peace conference in Shanghai, an agreement between the rival regimes was worked out. On 15 December, Chiang Kai-shek resigned his posts of chairman of the National government, president of the Executive Yuan, and commander-in-chief of the army. Retaining only his membership on the standing committee of the Kuomintang's Central Executive Committee, Chiang 'retired' to his native village of Hsi-k'ou in Chekiang.

A new government was thereupon formed in Nanking. Lin Sen, a venerable but ineffectual old revolutionary, was named chairman of the National government. Sun Fo assumed the presidency of the Executive Yuan and became effective head of the new administration.

The Sun Fo government, which took office on 1 January 1932, survived only twenty-five days. All three of the Kuomintang's leading personalities – Wang Ching-wei, Hu Han-min and Chiang Kai-shek – were excluded from or refused to associate with the new government. The regime failed to win the support of the Shanghai financial classes, and consequently could not meet its financial responsibilities. The central army remained loyal to Chiang. And the leaders of the new government were overwhelmed by the problems of the crisis confronting them – even as early as 2 January entreating (unsuccessfully) Chiang Kai-shek and Wang Ching-wei to return to Nanking so that the government might benefit from their advice.

The plight of the Sun Fo government worsened with each passing day, and Chiang Kai-shek discerned in that plight an opportunity to regain power. So virulent had the opposition to his 'dictatorship' been, however, that he knew he could not simply reassume the offices that he had held prior to his retirement. The solution to this predicament was thrashed out at Hangchow in three days of intense negotiations between Chiang, Wang Ching-wei, and Sun Fo. On 21 January 1932, the three men together returned to Nanking. Soon the outlines of those negotiations became clear. On 25 January, Sun Fo and his cabinet resigned. Three days later Wang Ching-wei was sworn in as president of the Executive Yuan, and on 29 January Chiang Kai-shek became head of the newly created Military Affairs Commission. Wang, as 'prime minister', was formally the chief administrative officer of the civilian branch of the regime. Progressively it became apparent, however, that real power rested in the hands of Chiang Kai-shek, and from 1932 until 1949 he was the overwhelmingly dominant leader of the Nationalist regime.

FACTORS CONTRIBUTING TO CHIANG KAI-SHEK'S POLITICAL DOMINANCE

Assessments of Chiang Kai-shek have varied greatly over the course of his long career. Some Chinese revered him as a flawless national leader; others reviled him as a feudalistic militarist. Some foreigners lauded him as a Christian and defender of democracy; others denounced him as an outmoded Confucian and ruthless dictator. Whether friend or foe, however, all recognized that Chiang was no ordinary man.

Chiang Kai-shek's succession to the mantle of Sun Yat-sen could not have been predicted in, say, 1925 at the time of Sun's death. At that time, leadership of the Kuomintang seemed destined for Wang Ching-wei, Hu Han-min, or perhaps Liao Chung-k'ai, each of whom had a much richer revolutionary background and more intimate ties with Sun than did Chiang. Yet Chiang held three advantages over his rivals, and to these his rise to power was largely attributable. First, he was a soldier, and military force had become the primary political coinage of the time. The most important step in his rise to power was his appointment by Sun Yat-sen in 1923 to command the party's military academy at Whampoa. As commandant of the academy, Chiang oversaw the training of thousands of cadets (during 1924–6, 5,000 graduated in just the first four classes), and with many of these he formed what in China was the powerful bond between teacher and student. After graduation, these young officers assumed commands in the party army, which was generally better trained and equipped than were the armies of the warlords. This army became a loyal and powerful instrument that Chiang effectively employed in his subsequent political career. After he was forced into retirement in August 1927, for example, he retained the loyalty of, and hence effective control over, the party army. Without Chiang's cooperation, therefore, the Central Special Committee was virtually impotent to resume the Northern Expedition against North China. On 20 December 1927, moreover, eighteen of the army's leading commanders, including Ho Ying-ch'in, sent a wire to the Special Committee demanding that Chiang be renamed supreme military commander.[22] Using this military backing – together with the support of various political and financial elements – Chiang

[22] *Ko-ming wen-hsien* (Documents of the revolution), comp. Lo Chia-lun, 18.10–11; Domes, 295; Ch'ien Tuan-sheng, *The government and politics of China*, 96.

forced the resignation of the Special Committee, and in January 1928 resumed the dominant positions in the army, party and government.

Chiang also in 1928 began employing Germans, such as Colonel Max Bauer, as military advisers and instructors. The military training and knowledge that Bauer and others imparted to Chiang's army (although still generally rudimentary by Western standards), together with that army's bonds of loyalty to Chiang, made it far-and-away more effective militarily and dependable politically than were those of any of his rivals. Wang Ching-wei in the summer of 1927, for example, headed the rival Nationalist government at Wuhan, and his most powerful military supporter was the warlord of Hunan, T'ang Sheng-chih. T'ang, however, had political aspirations of his own. As a result, Wang in September 1927 was suddenly stripped of power and forced to seek a coalition with his archrival, Chiang Kai-shek. Similarly, Hu Han-min after 1932 cast his fortunes with the militarist of Kwangtung, Ch'en Chi-t'ang. Ch'en found Hu useful, because Hu, the leading Kuomintang ideologue, lent an aura of legitimacy to Ch'en's otherwise purely warlord administration. Never, however, was Hu able to impose his will upon Ch'en Chi-t'ang or significantly influence Cantonese policies.

A second advantage that Chiang enjoyed in his political struggles was a superior financial base. During the Northern Expedition, some revolutionary leaders had counselled Chiang to by-pass Shanghai, which was then heavily defended, in order to occupy North China. Shanghai would then drop, it was argued, into the hands of the revolutionaries without a fight. Chiang, however, like Sun Yat-sen after 1913, regarded the great city on the Yangtze as his primary military target.

More than most other Nationalist leaders, Chiang recognized the financial importance of Shanghai, and knew that control of its revenues would be worth more than the command of many army divisions. Between 1912 and 1922, he had spent much time in the city. He had close ties there with leaders of the financial community and, allegedly, with bosses of the Green Gang (Ch'ing-pang), a secret society that controlled the city's underworld. The financial resources of Shanghai, of course, had to be tapped. This initially would not be difficult, for the city's capitalists were panic-stricken now in the spring of 1927 by the approaching spectre of communism, and they appealed to Chiang to prevent the outbreak of revolutionary excesses in the city. This precisely suited Chiang's wishes. Although he had in the past sometimes voiced the radical rhetoric of the left, he too was disturbed by the growing radicalism of the Communists. He was disturbed even more, perhaps, by the political threat to his leadership being mounted in Wuhan by Borodin and the Chinese leftists.

Chiang and the capitalists therefore needed each other. The capitalists of Shanghai agreed in late March to provide him with an initial advance of Y3 million. In return, he promised to put an end to the labour disturbances in the city and to eliminate Communist influences from the revolutionary movement. In the predawn hours of 12 April 1927, Chiang faithfully fulfilled his part of the bargain by launching a massacre of the Communist-led labour unions in the city. Hundreds, perhaps several thousands of Communists and workers were murdered in this bloody purge. But the capitalists had attained their wish; the Communists no longer posed a threat to Shanghai.

The Shanghai businessmen and bankers, however, still had to pay Chiang for his service. On 25 April, they gave him an additional Y7 million. But this merely whetted Chiang's financial appetite, for his military expenses were running at about Y20 million every month. His agents went from shop to shop and factory to factory demanding contributions. The Nanyang Tobacco Company, for instance, was ordered to give Y500,000; the Nantao Electric and Gas Works, Y300,000; and the Sincere Company Department Store Y250,000. When the capitalists balked, Chiang's agents threatened, blackmailed, and even kidnapped. 'Wealthy Chinese would be arrested in their homes or mysteriously disappear from the streets... Millionaires were arrested as "Communists"', reported Owen Chapman. 'Under no previous regime in modern times had Shanghai known such a reign of terror'.[23] Chiang's minister of finance, T. V. Soong, even admitted publicly after the Northern Expedition that 'in time of war, we have perhaps been forced to resort to extraordinary means to raise funds'.[24]

Although the Nationalists ceased to employ such tactics after mid-1928, Shanghai and its environs continued to serve as the government's primary source of revenue. During the Nanking decade, it derived approximately 85 per cent of its tax revenue from the trade and manufacturing sectors of the economy – much of which was centred in the Shanghai area. The government was also heavily dependent for its fiscal survival on loans. Here again, it was the Shanghai capitalists who subscribed to most of the government loans. Able to tap the wealth of China's largest and most modern city, Chiang enjoyed an enviable advantage over his rivals. Feng Yü-hsiang, for example, complained bitterly that he could not compete with Chiang, because the Nationalist armies were invariably better paid, fed, and armed than his own. Chiang also, he claimed, was sufficiently wealthy that he could cripple his opponents by purchasing defections from the rival armies.[25]

[23] H. Owen Chapman, *The Chinese revolution, 1926–1927*, 232.   [24] *CYB, 1929–30*, 629.
[25] Feng Yü-hsiang, *Wo so-jen-shih-ti Chiang Chieh-shih* (The Chiang Kai-shek I know), 17–18.

The third ingredient that contributed to Chiang's ascendancy in the Nationalist movement was his mastery of the techniques of factional and warlord politics. He seldom committed himself irreversibly to an ideological position or factional policy. He easily accommodated himself to – without becoming a part of – any faction if it was politically advantageous to do so. In late 1927 and early 1928, for instance, he associated himself with the Left Kuomintang and the *yüan-lao* (genrō in Japanese; a group of former anarchists and elder statesmen represented by Chang Jen-chieh, Wu Chih-hui, Ts'ai Yuan-p'ei, and Li Shih-tseng); by August 1928, he was allied with the *yüan-lao* and the right against the left; and by March 1929, he had allied with the right against both the *yüan-lao* and the left. Within a year and a half, therefore, he had associated himself with groups at most points of the Kuomintang's political spectrum. He also had a talent for holding the loyalties of factions that were bitterly antagonistic to each other. In the mid-1930s, for example, the CC clique and the Blue Shirts were ready to fight each other – yet each revered him as their leader. And both the CC clique and the Blue Shirts despised the Political Study clique – yet many of Chiang's most intimate advisers and trusted officials were members of the Political Study clique.

This skill in political manipulation was discernible also in Chiang's relations with the provincial militarists. These quondam warlords were jealous and distrustful of Chiang, and, at one time or another, nearly all of them raised the flag of revolt against him. Invariably, the rebelling militarists expected other provincial militarists to join forces with them, and it is certain that, if Chiang's enemies had acted in concert, he could have been crushed. Yet he isolated his opponents and eliminated them one by one. He, more than any of the other militarists, was a master of the use of 'silver bullets', bribes used to induce defections from opposing armies. And, when not employing silver bullets, he cajoled, promised, and threatened in order to gain the support, or at least the neutrality, of his provincial rivals – until he was ready to turn on them.

Although Chiang's ideology was flexible, his drive for power was unswerving. But his ambition for power was fuelled not solely by the desire for personal gratification, for he was deeply committed to the welfare of the Chinese nation. He was, however, so deeply convinced of his selflessness and moral rectitude that he perceived his power interests as being identical to those of the nation. What was beneficial to Chiang, therefore, was beneficial to the nation. And – in Chiang's view – one who opposed him was thereby acting against the best interests of the nation. Such persons, he claimed, were 'perverse', 'opportunistic', and lacked 'innate goodness'.[26] There was no room in Chiang's world for a loyal opposition; if they opposed him they were, ipso facto, disloyal to the nation. This self-righteousness was one of Chiang's great strengths; it gave him determination in the face of criticism and adversity. It was also, however, the tragic element in his character, for it pushed him ineluctably to his defeat in 1949.

IDEOLOGY, STRUCTURE AND FUNCTIONING OF THE NANKING REGIME

The regime that took shape in Chiang Kai-shek's hands after 1927 was neither totalitarian nor democratic, but lay uncertainly between those points on the political spectrum. Its structure, which was preserved in its essential features even after 1949 on Taiwan, had been erected in a governmental reorganization of October 1928. The blueprint for the new government had been drafted by Sun Yat-sen in his lectures on the Three People's Principles and in his *Fundamentals of national reconstruction*. Underlying the whole structure of government was Sun's concept of political tutelage. Sun Yat-sen was committed to the goal of popular sovereignty but he was also convinced that the Chinese people were unprepared for the responsibilities of self-rule. He had therefore predicated three stages of the Nationalist Revolution. First was the stage of military rule, during which the revolutionaries would rely on military force to consolidate their power. Following the capture of Peiping in June 1928, the Nationalist government declared that this initial stage of the revolution was completed, and that it had now progressed to the second stage, that of political tutelage. During this phase, the revolutionary party, the Kuomintang, was to exercise the sovereignty of the nation on behalf of the people. At the same time, the party was to train the people at the local level in the exercise of self-government. Through elections of *hsien* (county) magistrates, the convening of hsien representative assemblies, and the making of laws so that the hsien could become fully self-governing, the people would be educated in preparation for the third stage of the revolution, that of democratic, constitutional rule.

Political tutelage ostensibly meant that the Kuomintang was to exercise 'party rule' (*tang-chih*) on behalf of the people. Party rule was expressed institutionally in the authority invested in the party organs, the Central Executive Committee and the Central Political Council. The former was

---

[26] 'Tzu-shu yen-chiu ko-ming che-hsueh ching-kuo te chieh-tuan' (Stages traversed in studying revolutionary philosophy), *Chiang tsung-t'ung yen-lun hui-pien*, 10.50.

the supreme organ of party power (except during the brief sessions of the National Party Congress, only three of which were convened during the Nanking decade). It and especially its Standing Committee were charged with the formulation of the guiding principles of party rule and with the overall direction of party administration.

The Central Political Council was a bridge between the party and the governmental structure. Although it was merely a subcommittee of the Central Executive Committee, it was, formally at least, the supreme authority over the National government, combining both legislative and executive functions. As a legislative body, it could initiate legislation or transmit decisions of the Central Executive Committee to the government. As an executive body, it was empowered to provide general direction to and supervision of the government. Theoretically, then, the Political Council wielded virtually unlimited powers over the civilian branch of the government. In practice, too, the Political Council was the locus of authority in the government, for the head of the council was Chiang Kai-shek.[27]

Under the Political Council, in accordance with Sun Yat-sen's specific prescription, was established the five-*yuan* (or five-branch) system of government. This was similar to Montesquieu's threefold division between the executive, legislative and judicial branches of government. In addition to these three branches of government, however, Sun had added two branches that were derived explicitly from traditional institutions. These were the Examination Yuan (for determining the qualifications of government employees by means of civil-service examinations) and the Control Yuan (an ombudsman of government, similar to the imperial system of censors who supervised the policies and morals of officials). Of these five branches, the Executive Yuan was preponderant. The president of the Executive Yuan served as prime minister, directing the work of the subordinate ministries of foreign affairs, finance, education, commerce and so on.

It would be a mistake, however, to devote exclusive attention to the structure of the Nationalist government or to the formal relationship between, say, the Executive Yuan and the Legislative Yuan. For, regardless of the formal positions that Chiang Kai-shek held in the party, government or army, he wielded ultimate authority over the regime as

---

[27] Ch'ien Tuan-sheng, *Government and politics of China*, 139–145. Because the government was formally subordinate to the Kuomintang, and because the actual locus of authority frequently lay in an indeterminate relationship between the party, government and military, it is frequently appropriate in this chapter to employ the term Nationalist regime rather than Nationalist government. No pejorative connotation is intended by use of the term regime.

a whole. He exercised that authority with minimal concern for formal chains of command. 'The real authority of the government,' recalled Franklin Ho, one-time adviser to Chiang, 'went wherever the Generalissimo went. In terms of authority, he was the head of everything.'[28] Or, as an American foreign service officer observed in 1934, 'The shadow of Chiang Kai-shek extends over this whole scene. [Before coming to Nanking,] I would have been unwilling to believe that he dominated the Government set-up here to the extent that is now so apparent. Where his interest touches, there you will find a certain governmental activity; elsewhere, if not paralysis, at least a policy of drift.'[29]

As a result of Chiang's overriding dominance of the regime and of his predilection for ignoring formal chains of command, the government, as a policy-formulating and administrative organization, languished. The bureaucracy did formulate numerous plans for social and economic reconstruction, and the Legislative Yuan assiduously drafted new laws and a draft constitution. Much of this governmental activity, however, had little relation to political realities. For the civilian apparatus had neither the money to finance its various projects nor the power to enforce its decisions. Only 8 to 13 per cent of the total budget during the 1930s, for example, was allocated for the operations and maintenance of the civil bureaucracy – as contrasted with the much larger expenditures of the army.[30] T. V. Soong, minister of finance until 1933, endeavoured strenuously to restrain Chiang's military spending so that the government could proceed with the tasks of peacetime reconstruction, but Chiang ignored him. The civil government thus always remained subordinate to the interests of Chiang and the military, and it never generated a momentum of its own.

The party, the Kuomintang, atrophied even more than did the governmental administration as a result of Chiang Kai-shek's transformation of the revolutionary movement into a military-authoritarian regime. Where Sun Yat-sen had regarded the party as the ultimate locus of authority and as the trustee of the people's sovereignty during the pre-constitutional phases of the revolution, Chiang Kai-shek emasculated the party. After 1929, with the suppression of the left wing of the party, the Kuomintang performed no independent role. It became merely the propagandist, journalist and historian for the regime.

This emasculation of the party, together with the rise to prominence in the regime of old-style bureaucrats and warlords, had a deadening effect

[28] Franklin L. Ho, 'The reminiscences of Ho Lien (Franklin L. Ho)', 160.
[29] United States, State Dept. doc. 893.00/12842, Gauss to Johnson, 16 Sept. 1934, p. 1.
[30] Lloyd E. Eastman, *The abortive revolution: China under Nationalist rule, 1927–1937*, 221.

on the morale of formerly idealistic party members. A former Kuomintang member recalled that he 'like many...schoolmates, originally joined the Kuomintang in the belief that it was the only agency in China capable of destroying the powers so long held by provincial warlords'. As a result of Chiang Kai-shek's deradicalization of the movement, however, he and many like him 'were understandably disillusioned with the Kuomintang and many of us virtually withdrew'.[31] Party membership continued to be a prerequisite for government employment, but during the 1930s the party became a hollow shell, its role – as Arthur N. Young remarked – becoming 'almost nominal'.[32]

The Kuomintang continued in existence, however, because its committees and congresses provided a stamp of legitimacy for decisions already made by Chiang Kai-shek. The party therefore provided some substance, however transparent, to the regime's claim that it was not a military and personal dictatorship but rather – in accordance with Sun Yat-sen's instructions – a one-party dictatorship on behalf of the people until they were prepared to undertake the responsibility of ruling themselves.

The Nationalist regime was ambivalent in nature: at times it was despotic and arbitrary; at other times it was compliant and feeble. In its authoritarian guise, its power was derived largely from control of a superior military force. Consequently, individuals or groups that challenged its power or criticized its policies were, if within the reach of the Nationalists' army or police, often forcibly suppressed. Labour unions, for example, had become powerful, well organized, and highly politicized during the mid-1920s. After 1927, the leadership of these unions was removed and replaced by agents of the regime. The guiding principle of the unions now was not class conflict but cooperation with the employers and with the government. Independent union activities were proscribed, and the unions became weak, complaisant instruments of the regime.

The student movement, which since the May Fourth Movement (1919) had been a potent factor in national politics, was also suppressed – albeit less effectively and permanently than were the unions.[33] In 1930, for example, the Kuomintang's Ministry of Training proscribed all non-academic student organizations except those that were stringently regulated by the party. Students were simultaneously directed to concen-

[31] Wang Cheng, 'The Kuomintang: a sociological study of demoralization' (Stanford University, Ph.D. dissertation, 1953), 150.
[32] Young, *Nation-building*, 424.
[33] John Israel, *Student nationalism in China, 1927–1937*.

trate upon their studies and to avoid political activities. The students were, however, among the most passionately nationalistic groups in the country. And in 1931–2, and again in 1935–6, when Japanese imperialist pressures mounted and the Nanking authorities seemingly took refuge behind a policy of appeasement, the students' patriotism erupted into demonstrations, boycotts, and even physical attacks on government officials. To these student protests the regime invariably responded, ultimately, with force. Distrustful of any political movement that it had not initiated and did not control, and immoderately sensitive to the fact that a few Communists were among the student agitators, Nanking threw at least one thousand, and perhaps several thousand, students into prison. Students were terrorized by the presence of government informers in their classes, surprise searches of their rooms, and sudden disappearance of fellow students. The regime was thus largely successful in controlling the student movement as a political force. In accomplishing this, however, it alienated the students and pushed them politically leftward, many of them eventually becoming members of the Communist Party.

Political repression became a primary instrument of Nationalist rule. As early as 1929 and 1930, by which time the corruption, factionalism, and maladministration could no longer be varnished over, the regime was no longer sustained by popular support. 'Contrasted with the enthusiasm of less than eighteen months ago,' wrote the *North China Herald* in May 1930, 'the sense of hopelessness...among all Chinese today is perhaps the worst feature of all.'[34] Three years later, the much respected *Kuo-wen chou-pao* (National news weekly) observed that 'the masses unconcealedly dislike and detest the Kuomintang'.[35]

Determined to quash this rising tide of discontent, the regime tightened controls over its critics. Political opponents were assassinated; captious newsmen were arrested; newspapers and journals were censored. Because the territorial control of the government was still limited, its critics could find refuge and relative safety in the foreign-administered treaty-port concessions or in the provinces controlled by Chiang Kai-shek's opponents, such as in Hupei province under Chang Hsueh-liang or in Kwangtung under Ch'en Chi-t'ang. During the Nanking decade, therefore, China enjoyed a considerable intellectual and political vitality. In the areas of Central China controlled by Nanking, however, opposition to Chiang Kai-shek's policies was muted. Organizations and groups that might have imposed restrictions on the regime's power or policies were either

---

[34] *North China Herald*, 20 May 1930, 297.
[35] Liu Chen-tung, 'Chung-kuo ch'u-lu wen-t'i' (The question of China's way out), *Kuo-wen chou-pao* (National news weekly), 10.24 (19 June 1933), 2.

dissolved or rendered harmless through the imposition of controls by the regime.

Like the relationship between *yin* and *yang*, however, the authoritarian character of the regime was balanced by its essential weakness. Factionalism and corruption eroded the movement's early revolutionary commitment, and rampant bureaucratism stifled its policy initiatives. Even within itself, therefore, the regime lacked the drive, dedication and efficiency that might have enabled it to realize the programmatic goals of Sun Yat-sen. But the regime was also weak, because it lacked a firm footing in society. A characteristic of strong, modern nation-states is that significant segments of the population are mobilized in support of those governments' political goals. But the Nationalists, placing a premium on political control and social order, distrusted mass movements and private initiative; they therefore failed to create the kinds of broadly based popular support that, in the twentieth century, generate true political power.

As a result of these inherent weaknesses, the regime had to accommodate itself, at times grudgingly, to the leaders of the existing social order, most notably the landlords and capitalists. Indeed, this accommodation has caused many – perhaps most – non-Kuomintang writers to infer that the Nationalist regime was a class instrument of those classes.[36] And, in fact, the interests of the capitalists and landlords did sometimes correspond closely to the interests of the ruling regime. Nanking avoided, for example, implementing even a moderate rent-reduction law as a result of landlord opposition, and the Nanking leaders sometimes went to extraordinary lengths to maintain the landlord system. It was customary, for example, for the Nationalists, after recovering areas where the Communists had carried out their policy of land redistribution, to dispossess the tillers and restore the lands to the original landlords. This policy was sometimes exceedingly difficult to implement, because the Communists had in some areas held these lands for over six years and the boundary-markers and deeds of ownership had in many cases been destroyed.

The regime also formed an intimate relationship with the nation's more powerful bankers. Having surrendered collection of the important land tax to the provinces, the central government never contrived a means of supporting itself financially from taxes or state-operated enterprises. It consequently borrowed, approximately one-fifth of the government's revenues being derived through the sale of government bonds or through

---

[36] See, e.g. Ho Kan-chih, *Chung-kuo hsien-tai ko-ming shih* (History of the modern Chinese revolution), vol. 1, 119–23; Barrington Moore, Jr. *Social origins of dictatorship and democracy: land and peasant in the making of the modern world*, 187–201.

bank loans and overdrafts. For a time, therefore, the regime was heavily dependent on the banks and bankers. The banks, for their part, profited hugely from the relationship, especially because the government customarily sold its bonds to them at less than – often only 60–75 per cent of – face value. The banks in this way could often realize an effective annual return on their loans to the government of 12–25 per cent.[37] Many contemporaries, as a result, concluded that the regime represented capitalist class interests.

Assuredly, the interests of the capitalist and landlord classes did overlap with those of the regime. Each was opposed to social revolution; each feared the Communists; each was distrustful of the mobilization of the peasants and workers. But sometimes their interests conflicted. The capitalists had first been apprised of this truth in 1927–8 when the regime resorted to threats, blackmail and kidnapping to finance the last phase of the Northern Expedition. In 1935, too, the government broke whatever political power the bankers had wielded. By simply issuing new government bonds, and forcing the privately owned Bank of China and the Bank of Communications to accept these bonds as capital, H. H. Kung with a single blow made the government the banks' major stockholder. Using similar tactics, Kung quickly gained control of several lesser private banking corporations, and by 1937 the Nanking government controlled about 70 per cent of the nation's total banking assets.[38] These banking coups effectively ended the bankers' role as a political pressure group, and demonstrated beyond doubt that it was the regime that controlled the capitalists rather than vice versa.

The long-term interests of landlords were also frequently in conflict with those of the regime. These landlords generally wished to maintain, or even increase, their dominance of their local areas. They organized militia, operated schools, managed construction and other local programmes. They also collected taxes, ostensibly to support these projects, although indeterminately large portions of these revenues were siphoned into the pockets of the local elite. The regime, by contrast, endeavoured to maximize its control, constantly pushing its administrative, fiscal and military authority downward into the villages. Proposed reforms of the tax system, for instance, threatened to restore to the tax rolls landlord-held lands that for years and decades had escaped the tax-collectors' grasp. The government's attempts to install its own cadres in local government posts

[37] Young, *Nation-building*, 98, 507–8.
[38] Parks M. Coble, Jr. *The Shanghai capitalists and the Nationalist government, 1927–1937*, 161–207. A recent study shows in detail that cotton-mill-owners in the Shanghai area were by no means powerless vis-à-vis the National government, but neither did they control the government. See Richard Bush III, 'Industry and politics in Kuomintang China: the Nationalist regime and Lower Yangtze Chinese cotton mill owners, 1927–1937'.

likewise threatened to oust members of the local elite from positions that assured them power, preferment, and wealth.[39] There were, as a result, fundamental contradictions between the interests and goals of the regime and of these landlords.

During the Nanking decade, however, the conflicts generated by those contradictions were usually muted and localized, because the regime's attention was then focused much more on the Communist and Japanese problems than on questions of local administration. The relationship between the government and the local elites during this decade might therefore be described as mutual toleration and limited cooperation. But to baldly ascribe a class character to the Nationalist regime, without noting its important differences with the landlords and capitalists, conceals its fundamental nature. For the regime was dependent, first of all, on the support of the military. From that fact, all else followed. It was not in any basic way accountable to this or that social-economic class or indeed to any forces outside itself. It was, in many respects, its own constituency. This is a basic reason why the regime's modernizing and developmental impulses were so weak; why the Nationalist bureaucracy could be sustained so long despite its corruption and administrative lethargy; and why the regime could perpetuate itself with so few new faces or new ideas for over two decades. Some members of the regime were, of course, enlightened, dedicated, and competent. Too many, however, took advantage of the institutional character of the regime to maximize their own power, prestige and wealth rather than to strive for the national good.

KUOMINTANG FACTIONS

In this kind of regime, which was customarily free of the constraints of public opinion and which tolerated no meaningful political activity that it did not control, the competition for political power was conducted not in society at large but within the councils of the regime itself. And, because the distribution of political authority was determined less by formal chains-of-command than by the personal decisions of Chiang Kai-shek or one of his favoured aides, allocation of power was determined inordinately by personal influence. It was a common practice, for example, for a new minister or bureau chief to dismiss the previous employees in that office and to replace them with his cronies and supporters. The key to political success, therefore, lay less in the possession of technical

[39] Geisert, 'Power and society', 167–242; Philip A. Kuhn, 'Local self-government under the Republic: problems of control, autonomy, and mobilization', in Frederic Wakeman, Jr. and Carolyn Grant, eds. *Conflict and control in late imperial China*, 284–98.

expertise than in the maintenance of personal relationships with leaders of the regime. Factionalism, in other words, was the principal medium for political struggle.

Factions proliferated. There were, for example, the factions of Wang Ching-wei, T. V. Soong, H. H. Kung, Ho Ying-ch'in, Chu Chia-hua, Sun Fo – the list goes on and on. The largest factions, however, and those which were generally the most influential in the policy-making process, were the CC clique, the Political Study clique, and the Whampoa clique.

The CC clique coalesced around the brothers Ch'en Kuo-fu and Ch'en Li-fu. Bound to Chiang Kai-shek by extraordinarily close personal and emotional ties – they were nephews of Ch'en Ch'i-mei, who, until his assassination by Yuan Shih-k'ai in 1916, had been Chiang's mentor and father-figure – the two Ch'en brothers after 1926 directed the organizational operations of the Chiang-dominated Kuomintang. In June 1927, they first created the secret organization that became known as the CC clique (CC-hsi) – a term that was thought to represent either 'Central Club' or the 'two Ch'ens'. The actual name of the organization may, instead, have been the Ch'ing-pai-she (lit. Blue-white society) or the Kuo-min-tang chung-shih t'ung-chih-hui (Kuomintang loyal-and-faithful comrades' association), although details of the clique's names, structure, and operations remain obscure.[40]

Using the Organization Department of the Kuomintang as their institutional base, the Ch'en brothers placed adherents throughout the party and governmental apparatus, particularly in the middle and lower strata of those organizations. In this way, the CC clique became a dominating influence in the civilian branches of the regime, controlling much of the bureaucratic administration, educational agencies, youth organizations and labour unions. The clique also controlled various publications, such as the *Shih-shih yueh-pao* (Times monthly) and *Wen-hua chien-she* (Cultural reconstruction), and operated the Kuomintang's Central Bureau of Investigation and Statistics (Chung-yang tiao-ch'a t'ung-chi chü) which was one of Chiang Kai-shek's two principal secret police organizations.

By contrast with the civilian oriented CC clique, the Whampoa clique (Huang-p'u hsi) was formed preponderantly of military officers, but it too had broad political concerns that potentially at least touched all aspects of national life. Loosely defined, the Whampoa clique denoted the former

---

[40] Ch'en Tun-cheng, *Tung-luan ti hui-i* (Memoirs of upheaval), 29; Ch'en Shao-hsiao, *Hei-wang-lu* (Records of the black net), 290–1. Ch'en Li-fu, however, denied the existence of such an organization. See Shu-wen, 'Ch'en Li-fu t'an CC' (Ch'en Li-fu chats about the CC), *Hsin-wen t'ien-ti* (News world), 20 (1 Feb. 1937) 13.

faculty and students of the Whampoa Military Academy, who maintained strong bonds of loyalty to Chiang Kai-shek. The faction thus defined had, however, no organization, and some of the members – such as Ho Ying-ch'in, Ch'en Ch'eng and the younger officers – were bitterly antagonistic one to the other. The operative nucleus of the Whampoa clique, therefore, at least during the period 1932–8, was a tightly disciplined, clandestine organization known popularly as the Blue Shirts (Lan-i she).

The Blue Shirts were organized in early 1932 by a small group of young military officers, former students of Chiang Kai-shek in the Whampoa Military Academy, who were alarmed by the condition of the nation and of the Kuomintang movement. The Japanese were invading Chinese territory; the Communists survived in the interior despite repeated annihilation campaigns against them; and, perhaps most alarming, members of the Nationalist movement had become corrupt and were more concerned about enhancing their power than they were about attaining the goals of the revolution. That is, in the Blue Shirts' view, the revolution had failed and the nation lay in peril.

With Chiang Kai-shek's consent, financial support, and at least formal leadership, these young officers – represented, for example, by Ho Chung-han, Tai Li, Teng Wen-i and K'ang Tse – created a pyramidal organization comprising three basic levels. At the top, the dominant leadership constituted the Li-hsing she (Vigorously-carry-out society); the middle echelon was named the Ko-ming ch'ing-nien t'ung-chih hui (Revolutionary youth comrades association); and the foot-soldiers of the movement, drawn from lower levels of the army, from students and from governmental agencies, were organized into the Chung-hua Fu-hsing she (Chinese revival society). In reaction against the disarray and poor discipline of the Kuomintang, the Blue Shirts stressed the need for absolute, unquestioning obedience to the leaders of the organization. Frugality, incorruptibility and secrecy were also emphasized.

Progressively, as a result of the growing power of Mussolini's Italy and Hitler's Germany, fascist doctrines became attractive to the Blue Shirt leaders. Chiang Kai-shek, too, made extensive efforts to learn about Nazi methods of organization and operation and in about 1935 he reportedly declared to a gathering of Blue Shirts, 'Fascism...is a stimulant for a declining society.' 'Can Fascism save China? We answer: yes. Fascism is what China now most needs.'[41] As a result of this fascination with the apparent successes of fascism in Europe, the Blue Shirts likewise

[41] 'Ranisha no soshiki to hanman kōnichi katsudō no jitsurei' (The organization of the Blue Shirts and examples of anti-Manchukuo, anti-Japanese activities), in Ranisha ni kansuru Shiryō (Materials on the Blue Shirts), 11.

propounded ultra-nationalism, the cult of the Leader, elimination of liberalism and individualism, and the 'militarization' of society.

The Blue Shirts became highly influential during the 1930s. They dominated political training within the army, thus helping to assure Chiang Kai-shek of the continuing support of that ultimate source of political power. The Blue Shirts also became involved in various civilian activities, such as the schools, the Boy Scouts and the police. They provided many, perhaps most, of the cadres of the New Life movement. And they also operated the much feared Military Bureau of Investigation and Statistics (Chün-shih tiao-ch'a t'ung-chi chü) under Chiang Kai-shek's Military Affairs Commission. This secret police organization, headed by Tai Li, conducted intelligence operations against Chiang Kai-shek's putative enemies (who ranged from the Japanese and the Communists to corrupt officials and even political rivals within the Kuomintang). It was involved in press censorship. It was also responsible for many of the most notorious assassinations during the decade, such as that in 1934 of Shih Liang-ts'ai, editor of Shanghai's leading newspaper, *Shen-pao*.

In contrast to the CC and Whampoa cliques, the Political Study clique (Cheng-hsueh-hsi) was all head and no tail; its members were each men of prominence, but it had no following among the rank-and-file of the regime. It had no organization or clear-cut leadership, but consisted informally of a group of friends, or friends-of-friends, who shared generally similar political views. Two of the clique's foremost representatives, Huang Fu and Chang Ch'ün, were sworn-brothers of Chiang Kai-shek, a relationship which in China signified the closest possible tie of loyalty outside the family. Probably in large part through this relationship, the Political Study clique became enormously influential in Chiang Kai-shek's coterie of advisers and leading administrators. On the recommendation of Huang Fu and Chang Ch'ün, for example, Chiang Kai-shek in 1932 appointed Yang Yung-t'ai as his secretary-general in the headquarters of the Military Affairs Commission. From that position, Yang – until he was assassinated in 1936 – was one of the two or three most powerful political figures in the nation. Other members of the clique included Wang Ch'ung-hui, Hsiung Shih-hui, Wu Ting-ch'ang, Chang Kia-ngau, Weng Wen-hao and Huang Shao-hung. To name these and other members is to list many of the leading figures in the nation and in the regime. Significantly, however, the relationship of these clique members to the Kuomintang was, at best, tenuous. Huang Fu, for example, steadfastly refused even to become a member of the party. They were less politicians than they were specialists – economists, industrialists, bankers, publishers, intellectuals – who adhered to no ideological doctrine but stood instead for technical expertise and bureaucratic professionalism.

The relations among these several factions were complex. Each of them publicly expounded the doctrines of Sun Yat-sen; each supported Chiang Kai-shek as the leader of the regime. At the same time, their dealings with each other were sometimes exceedingly strained, because they were the principal vehicles in the intra-party struggle for power. Ch'en Kuo-fu and Ch'en Li-fu, for example, were extremely jealous of the Political Study clique's position in the civilian apparatus and competed with them for bureaucratic office. The Blue Shirts viewed the others as corrupt civilian politicians, and were particularly hostile to the CC clique, because the political, educational and intelligence operations of the two factions overlapped, thereby generating intense frictions.

Ideological and policy differences, significantly, were not the main cause of these frictions. Although the differences between the factions would frequently be expressed in terms of policy orientations, the fundamental issue was power and position. The Blue Shirts and the CC clique expressed differences, for example, on how to implement Sun Yat-sen's Principle of Economic Livelihood. A former Blue Shirt leader admitted, however, that 'any [factional] struggle is not a struggle resulting from differences of policy, but is a struggle for the rice bowl'.[42]

Chiang Kai-shek knew of these intra-party conflicts, but unless they threatened to erupt into violence – as one did in 1934 between the Blue Shirts and the CC clique – he did not intervene. Indeed, he appears actually to have fostered the competition among the factions. For the struggle among factions prevented any one of them from becoming overly powerful. Chiang thus assured his supremacy over all of them.

Nationalist rule has customarily been labelled 'conservative'. This is misleading, however, for leaders of the regime were in fact intensely dissatisfied with the status quo, and they envisioned drastic, even 'radical', departures from China's existing condition of national decrepitude. They admired, for example, the scientific and industrial progress of the West, and they aspired to employ Western technology to improve the economic well-being of the Chinese people. They wished also to restructure the Chinese socio-political order. The model for Chiang Kai-shek's ideal society lay not in the Chinese past, but in the specifically militaristic aspects of Japan, Italy and Germany. He recalled his student days in a Japanese military academy, and declared that the rigorous barracks discipline there represented precisely his ideal for Chinese society as a whole.[43] He thought that fascist Italy and Germany fulfilled that ideal. 'In fascism,' he declared

---

[42] Interview with Liu Chien-ch'un, Taipei, 27 May 1969.
[43] Chiang Kai-shek, 'Hsin-sheng-huo yun-tung chih yao-i' (Essentials of the New Life movement), *Chiang tsung-t'ung ssu-hsiang yen-lun chi* (Collection of President Chiang's thoughts and speeches), 12.110.

admiringly, 'the organization, the spirit, and the activities must all be militarized...In the home, the factory, and the government office, everyone's activities must be the same as in the army... In other words, there must be obedience, sacrifice, strictness, cleanliness, accuracy, diligence, secrecy... And everyone together must firmly and bravely sacrifice for the group and for the nation.'[44]

It was precisely this image of a militarized society, strictly disciplined and unconditionally obedient to the Leader's will, that Chiang aspired to re-create in China. These were the goals of his vaunted New Life movement, inaugurated in 1934, which he regarded as providing the basic cure for China's ills. 'What is the New Life Movement that I now propose?' Chiang asked. 'Stated simply, it is to militarize thoroughly the lives of the citizens of the entire nation so that they can cultivate courage and swiftness, the endurance of suffering and a tolerance for hard work, and especially the habit and ability of unified action, so that they will at any time sacrifice for the nation.'[45] Patently, his image of fascism had been translated virtually intact into the New Life movement.

Chiang Kai-shek and the Nationalist leaders also, however, paid obeisance to the ethics of Confucianism, and it was this that convinced many observers that the Nationalist regime was actually a conservative, even reactionary, force. Customarily, for example, Chiang declared that the goals of the New Life movement were the Confucian virtues of *li*, *i*, *lien* and *ch'ih*, loosely translated as social propriety, justice, integrity, and sense of self-respect. He greatly admired the great conservative, Confucian officials of the late Ch'ing dynasty, Tseng Kuo-fan and Hu Lin-i. And, under his aegis, the official worship of Confucius was restored; Confucius's birthday was proclaimed a national holiday; and study of the Confucian classics by students and military officers was encouraged.

This traditionalism of the Nationalist regime was comparable to the classicism promoted in fascist Italy and Nazi Germany. Confucianism, that is, was not propounded as a goal in itself, but as a moral ingredient that would contribute to the cohesiveness of the Chinese people as they moved forward to a new society. It provided, as a member of the CC clique asserted, a 'central belief', without which the Chinese people became politically anarchic and morally confused.[46] Thus, Chiang Kai-shek frequently spoke in the idiom of Chinese tradition. Indeed many of his

[44] [Iwai Eiichi], *Ranisha ni kansuru chōsa* (An investigation of the Blue Shirts), 37–8.
[45] Chiang Kai-shek, *Chiang tsung-t'ung ssu-hsiang yen-lun chi*, 12.111. On the New Life movement, see Arif Dirlik, 'The ideological foundations of the New Life movement: a study in counterrevolution', *JAS* 34.4 (Aug. 1975) 945–80; Eastman, *Abortive revolution*, 66–70.
[46] Fang Chih, 'Min-tsu wen-hua yü min-tsu ssu-hsiang' (National culture and national thought), *Wen-hua chien-she* (Cultural reconstruction), 1.2 (10 Nov. 1934) 20.

methods and outlooks – such as his stress on traditional morality, his conception of the political utility of education, and his elitism – did reveal that his vision of the modern world was limited. But his political goal, that of a thoroughly regimented society, bore no resemblance to China's Confucian past. He was a would-be totalitarian, aspiring to extend the controls of his regime down to the local level, and to subordinate the individual and all of society to the regime to a degree that emperors of the Ch'ing dynasty had not even dreamed of. This was not a conservative ideal, for it differed fundamentally from either the ideals or realities of the past.

ACHIEVEMENTS OF THE NATIONALIST REGIME

There exists no consensus regarding Nationalist achievements during the Nanking decade. Some historians have concluded that the Nationalists established a fundamentally sound system of rule and laid the foundations upon which a strong, democratic and prosperous nation could be constructed – although this promising beginning was aborted by the onslaught of the war with Japan in 1937. Others contend that the government established by the Nationalists was corrupt and inefficient, that the Nationalist leaders did not comprehend the problems confronting them, and that they were ignorant of alternative political and economic strategies available to them. Accordingly, in this view, the regime was doomed to failure even if the Japanese had not launched their war of aggression.[47]

These issues are passionately debated. They are perhaps irresolvable, because what would have occurred had the Japanese not attacked is, by its very nature, unprovable. Two facts, however, are clear. First, the task confronting the Nationalists – namely, reversing the tide of national disintegration – was gargantuan. Second, the circumstances under which they attempted the task were extraordinarily uncongenial to successful or rapid solutions. Economic depression, foreign invasion and civil strife – conditions that were largely beyond the control of the Nationalists – militated against the implementation of meaningful reforms. They were, moreover, allotted only about six years in which to accomplish those reforms, because the first four years of the Nanking decade had been devoted chiefly to securing the regime in power.

The outstanding achievement of the Nationalists was to reverse the trend toward territorial disintegration. When they seized power in 1927,

---

[47] Studies that are generally favourable to the Nationalists are Domes and Young; less favourable are Hung-mao Tien and Eastman, all cited above.

they controlled only Kiangsu, Chekiang, and part of Anhwei. As a result of the civil wars in 1929–31, the central government forces cowed the provincial militarists, thus guaranteeing the existence of the Nanking government, but the writ of the central government in 1931 was still restricted to a constellation of provinces, or parts of provinces, in central China (most notably in varying degree in Chekiang, Kiangsu, Anhwei, Honan, Kiangsi, Hupei and Fukien).[48]

Nanking's effective authority expanded rapidly, however, after Chiang Kai-shek's fifth annihilation campaign against the Communists. A central premise in Chiang Kai-shek's strategic thinking was that, before China could repulse the Japanese aggressors, it must be unified internally. 'The Japanese,' he liked to say, 'are like a disease of the skin, but the Communists are like a disease of the heart.' To cure this disease of the heart, Chiang, in October 1930, immediately after his victory over the Yen Hsi-shan Feng Yü-hsiang rebellion, had launched his first annihilation campaign against the Communists in Kiangsi. The Communists, however, employing the mobile tactics of guerrilla warfare, repulsed the Nationalist attackers by 1 January 1931. Other annihilation campaigns followed. But not until the fifth annihilation campaign of 1933–4 – in which Chiang employed about 800,000 troops, was advised by German and Japanese advisers, and augmented his military offensive with a stringent economic blockade of the Communist areas – did he gain a nearly decisive victory over the Communists. The Communists, defeated militarily and suffering incredibly from shortages of food and especially salt, summoned their last reserves of strength and courage, broke out of the Nationalist encirclement, and in October 1934 commenced what was to become the Long March.

The Long March, which has become a legend in the history of the Communist Revolution, provided Chiang Kai-shek with an unprecedented opportunity to inject his military forces and political power into the provinces of South and West China. Pursuing the retreating Communists, Chiang's well-equipped armies entered Hunan, Kweichow, Yunnan and Szechwan. The provincial militarists, feeling endangered by the presence of the Communists, welcomed the Nationalist armies – not whole-heartedly, because these too threatened their provincial autonomy, but as the lesser of two evils. Chiang Kai-shek fully exploited the opportunity. For, once Chiang's bandit-suppression army had entered a province, his agents began imposing 'reforms' designed to break down that province's isolation. In Szechwan, for example, the garrison areas (*fang-ch'ü*), which had been the military and economic bases of operations of the several Szechwanese warlords, were abolished, and a more centralized system of

48 Domes, 486.

provincial administration was instituted. A massive road-construction programme, designed to integrate the province politically and militarily with the rest of the nation, was launched. Szechwan was also drawn into Nanking's economic orbit as a result of the widespread use of Nationalist currency (*fa-pi*) in place of the several currencies that had been issued by various banks in the province.[49] Prior to the war with Japan, such reforms as these had attenuated, without breaking, the south-west provinces' accustomed independence, and the local authorities continued to strain against the tightening tentacles of the central government. In the spring of 1937, for example, relations between Chiang and Liu Hsiang, the dominant warlord in Szechwan, became so tense that a renewed outbreak of civil war was narrowly avoided. As a result of Chiang's anti-Communist campaigns of 1934–5, however, the autonomy and political manoeuvrability of the provincial militarists in Hunan, Yunnan, Kweichow and Szechwan had been sharply reduced. And the power and prestige of the Nanking government had been commensurately enhanced.

The ultimate fruit of the anti-Communist campaign did not ripen until 1936 when Kwangtung was finally and completely brought under the control of the central government. Although Kwangtung had been the revolutionary base of the Kuomintang prior to the Northern Expedition, it had never been effectively incorporated into the political and financial system of the Nanking government. Especially since 1931, when the militarist Ch'en Chi-t'ang became provincial chairman, Kwangtung had conducted its affairs virtually without reference to the central government. Ch'en, together with Li Tsung-jen and Pai Ch'ung-hsi, leaders of the Kwangsi faction, in late 1931 had established the South-west Political Council and the South-west Headquarters of the Kuomintang Central Executive Committee. These governmental and party organs formed the basis of a formidable regional coalition against Nanking, uniting the rich economic resources of Kwangtung with the military expertise and fighting qualities of Kwangsi. The political challenge of this coalition against Nanking was enormously enhanced by the participation of Hu Han-min, the party's leading theoretician and venerated elder (albeit only fifty-two years old in 1932), who imparted to the so-called South-west separatist movement a legitimacy that other anti-Chiang movements had lacked. For some five years, Chiang Kai-shek had endured the taunts and criticisms of Kwangtung and Kwangsi, because they were a formidable political and military power and more especially because they lay protected behind a buffer formed by the semi-autonomous provinces of Fukien, Hunan and

[49] Robert A. Kapp, *Szechwan and the Chinese Republic: provincial militarism and central power, 1911–1938*, 99–120.

Kweichow. As a result of his pursuit of the Long March, however, Chiang by late 1935 had eliminated that buffer. Chiang was also assembling troops near the Kwangtung-Kwangsi borders, constructing airfields in neighbouring Hunan, and rushing the Hankow-Canton railway to completion.

In May 1936, Hu Han-min suddenly died, and Chiang seized the occasion of Hu's funeral to throw down the gauntlet to the Kwangtung-Kwangsi leaders, demanding that they now submit to the central government. The ultimatum was rejected, and the South-west authorities in early June began moving their troops northward into Hunan province. Their purpose was avowedly to fight the Japanese aggressors in North China. Chiang inferred, however, probably correctly, that Ch'en Chi-t'ang and the Kwangsi leaders were planning to attack, in an attempt to overthrow the Nanking government.

Chiang Kai-shek's genius for political manipulation shone at its brightest in this kind of situation. On the one hand, he bribed the Cantonese air force, causing it in July to defect *en masse* to the central government. Then, with a combination of military threats and offers of alternative official posts to the rebel leaders, Chiang brought about the collapse of the rebellion in September. As a consequence, Kwangtung, for the first time in the Nanking period, was brought under the effective administration of the central government. Kwangsi, which retained some vestiges of its former autonomy, was subdued, no longer in a position to challenge Nanking.

By late 1936, therefore, Chiang Kai-shek had consolidated political control over the greater part of the nation – only seven of the eighteen provinces in China proper continued to be essentially autonomous – and he had thus laid the foundation for a viable political system. Yet he had attained his control at enormous cost. Not only had his strong reliance upon armed force cost the nation heavily in terms of the destruction of life and property, but it had diverted the regime's attention from the exigent demands of social, economic and political reform. Chiang's advisers sometimes warned him against relying excessively on force to attain political ends. In introspective moments he even admitted this failing. He was, however, a soldier, and alternative strategies of attaining national unity seem never to have engaged his interest. He might, for example, have contented himself with merely the nominal allegiance of the various provincial militarists, and then have endeavoured to create a model of political, economic and social reform in the areas that he did control. Doing this he might have avoided the bloody and costly civil wars, established economic and fiscal stability, and developed the administrative and technical expertise that would serve him when other provinces were gradually drawn into the economic and political orbit of the Nanking government. Perhaps this scheme of creating a model area in the Lower Yangtze provinces – which was in fact envisioned at the time by Nanking's economic adviser, Arthur N. Young[50] – betrays the naïvety of the intellectual rather than the realism of the man of action. The history of the decade suggests, however, that it could not have been less successful than were the policies pursued by Chiang. For Chiang attempted to control too much, with the result that nothing was controlled well. Nowhere was this more evident than in the economy.

The Chinese economy was overwhelmingly agrarian and traditional. In 1933, for example, the modern sector of manufacturing, mining, and utilities accounted for only about 3·4 per cent of the net domestic product. Four out of every five Chinese, on the other hand, were employed in agriculture, and produced about 65 per cent of the net domestic product. The farmers lived in appalling poverty, a year of sickness or poor weather plunging them over the edge of subsistence. Destitution is not easily measured, but some rough indication of the misery of the Chinese masses is the fact that in 1930 China's death rate was about the highest in the world, two and a half times higher than that of the United States and markedly higher even than that of India.[51]

Many contemporary observers, both Chinese and Westerners, believed that the basic cause of this rural poverty was the unequal distribution of land. They contended that a small number of landlords owned a disproportionate number of the farms, and rented these to tenants at extortionate rates. As the League of Nations' leading agricultural specialist in China, Ludwig Rajchman, remarked in 1934, 'Of the economic and social factors [contributing to the rural crisis], perhaps the system of tenancy is the most disquieting'.[52]

The Legislative Yuan, under the leadership of Hu Han-min, had attacked this problem by drawing up a Land Law. This law, promulgated in 1930, imposed a maximum on rents (37·5 per cent of the harvest). It also held out the prospect of eliminating landlordism by authorizing tenants of an absentee owner to purchase their farms if they had farmed the land for more than ten years. The 1930 Land Law remained nothing more than an admirable expression of intent, for it was never implemented by the Nanking authorities. Rents, 50-70 per cent of the main crop,

50 Young, Nation-building, 425.
51 T. C. Liu and K. C. Yeh, The economy of the Chinese mainland: national income and economic development, 1933–1959, 66 and 89; John Lossing Buck, Land utilization in China, 387.
52 League of Nations, Council Committee on Technical Cooperation between the League of Nations and China, Report of the technical agent of the Council on his mission in China from the date of his appointment until April 1st 1934, 18.

continued to be exacted, and approximately half the Chinese farmers continued to rent all or part of their land. The Nationalists feared to tamper with the social-economic relations in the villages. They may have had, as Arthur Young suggests, an empathy for the landlord class, and they therefore wished not to dispossess or alienate the landlords by redistributing the land.[53] Or, as has been suggested alternatively, they feared that an attack on the system of tenancy would provoke a social revolution, the outcome of which they could neither control nor predict.[54] Whatever the reasons, tenancy rates remained virtually unchanged during the Nanking decade.

The system of tenancy was, however, only a proximate cause of the social and political inequities in China's villages. The fundamental cause of rural impoverishment was the unfavourable ratio between population and food production, and this was the problem that the Nationalists primarily attacked.

Largely through the National Economic Council, which was assisted by prominent League of Nations' specialists such as Rajchman and Sir Arthur Salter, and the agriculture-related bureaus of the Ministry of Industries, the Nanking government undertook a broad programme to increase the farmers' productivity. It sponsored research on new seed varieties, pesticides and fertilizers. To prevent floods, the Yangtze, Yellow, and Hwai Rivers were dredged and the dikes were strengthened. Irrigation systems were constructed, and efforts were made to revitalize the production of silk, cotton and tea through the introduction of disease-resistant plants, and improved marketing techniques.

These reform projects had slight impact on the rural areas. Less than 4 per cent of the government's total expenditures for the years 1934–6, for example, was devoted to economic development.[55] And much of even this minuscule amount was dissipated in bureaucratic boondoggling that resulted in little positive achievement. As a Nationalist partisan wrote in 1937, 'The year before last, the work was to survey such-and-such an area; last year the work was also to survey such-and-such an area; this year the work is still simply to survey, gather statistics, draw maps, and hold conferences. Because the appropriations have been expended, however, the actual engineering work cannot be carried out.'[56]

There is some indication that Nanking's agricultural specialists did

[53] Young, Nation-building, 389.
[54] Eastman, Abortive revolution, 217.
[55] Computed from figures in Young, Nation-building, 437 and 439. ('Reconstruction' was the term used for economic development. See Young, 77.)
[56] Kao T'ing-tzu, Chung-kuo ching-chi chien-she (Chinese economic reconstruction), 122–3.

achieve some progress in the realm of research, but results of that research were not brought effectively to the farmers. 'In agricultural extension,' wrote Franklin Ho, 'nothing went beyond the planning stage at the national level during the period from 1927 to 1937.'[57] The irrigation projects were also utterly insignificant relative to China's needs, bringing water to an area that totalled only about 6,000 square miles. A government apologist in 1936 summed up the ineffectuality of the Nationalists' rural reconstruction policies and the regime's fear of provoking social revolution, when he admitted that 'The direct benefits to the people [from the government's reconstruction measures] were very small,' because 'the Government was not seeking to give immediate and direct help to the people by drastic changes, but preferred to follow a slow and gradual policy that would avoid too great a disturbance in the country.'[58]

The Nationalists thus did little to ameliorate rural impoverishment during the Nanking decade. The problems were, however, so great, and the time allotted to the regime so short, that it would be absurd to expect that prior to 1937 the agricultural sector could have been transformed. A combination of economic and climatic factors, moreover, plunged China's farmers into even more straitened circumstances during the years 1932–5. A major reason for the crisis was a deflationary trend that hit China in the wake of the world economic depression. Farm prices consequently fell precipitously, and in 1934 struck a low that was 58 per cent below the 1931 level. This deflation caused especial hardship for peasants, who had to pay cash for debts, taxes or rents. During this same period, also, large parts of the country suffered the worst weather within memory. Particularly during 1934–5, when the monetary depression was at its depth, drought, floods, winds and hail wreaked widespread devastation. According to a highly respected agricultural specialist at the Academia Sinica, the rice harvest in 1934 was 34 per cent below that of 1931; soy-beans were down nearly 36 per cent, and wheat was down 7 per cent. Cotton was the only major crop that year to exceed the 1931 level.[59] The value added by agriculture to the gross national product dropped from Y24·43 billion in 1931 to Y13·07 billion (in current prices) in 1934.[60] Such data are not wholly reliable in detail, but eyewitness

57 Franklin L. Ho, 'First attempts to transform Chinese agriculture, 1927–1937: comments', in Paul Sih, ed. The strenuous decade: China's nation-building efforts, 1927–1937, 235.
58 W. L. Holland and Kate L. Mitchell, eds. Problems of the Pacific, 1936: aims and results of social and economic policies in Pacific countries, 166.
59 Chang P'ei-kang, 'Min-kuo erh-shih-san nien ti Chung-kuo nung-yeh ching-chi' (China's agricultural economy in 1934), Tung-fang tsa-chih, 32.13 (1 July 1935): 134.
60 Liu Ta-chung, China's national income, 1931–36: an exploratory study, 10, 35–40.

accounts at the time confirm that the villages suffered severe destitution, especially during 1934 and 1935.[61]

Governmental policies and actions, whether by the central or various local governments, had not been the cause of this agricultural crisis. They had, however, in many cases exacerbated the peasants' plight by imposing new burdens. Because the Nationalists endeavoured to extend their control down to the villages, the size of the bureaucracy at the hsien, or district, level grew. More administrators and tax-collectors were appointed, and the size of the police and militia expanded. These new local authorities provided few palpable services that benefited the peasants, but they had to be paid. The rural tax burden thus increased at the very time that the countryside was in a depression. Surtaxes were added to the main land tax. *T'an-p'ai*, or special assessments, were levied in increasing amounts. There were also indirect taxes – on salt, tobacco, wine and matches; on sales of pig bristles and animal hides; on slaughtering of pigs and chickens; on stamps for receipts and legal agreements – that assailed the villagers in bewildering variety. Some of these taxes were not new. And it is impossible to generalize how much the farmers' tax burden increased during the 1930s, because the variations between localities were often great. Chiang Kai-shek's assessment in 1935 did, however, reflect the general situation:

Government expenditures grow steadily higher. Whenever a programme is begun, new taxes arise. Surtax charges are often attached to the regular taxes as needed, and miscellaneous taxes are also created. Occasionally, [the local authorities] collect unspecified taxes from house to house according to their own wishes. As a result tax items are numerous. The people have suffered immensely under this heavy tax burden.[62]

Peasants were subjected not only to the increased demands of the tax collectors; they were also faced with onerous and unpredictable demands of the government and army for labour, supplies and land. Nanking's armies, for example, especially while on the march or engaged in a campaign, frequently suffered from supply shortages, and they therefore requisitioned food from local sources. These troops were often like a plague upon the landscape, seizing homes, food, carts and manpower. Such requisitions, declared one writer (perhaps with forgivable hyperbole), cost the peasant 'forty times more than the regular taxes'.[63]

[61] Eastman, *Abortive revolution*, 190–4.
[62] Hung-mao Tien, 168.
[63] Ch'en Chen-han, 'Cheng-fu yin-hang hsueh-shu chi-kuan fu-hsing nung-ts'un' (Government, banks, academic institutions, and revival of the villages), *Kuo-wen chou-pao*, 10.46 (20 Nov. 1933) articles, 4.

Any attempt to draw up a balance-sheet of the Nationalist record in the rural sector is fraught with difficulties. The nation was so large, local conditions so varied, and the available data so skimpy and imprecise that definitive conclusions are elusive. During 1936 and 1937, moreover, the agrarian crisis ended. Clement weather in those years resulted in the best crops (except in Kwangtung and Szechwan) that China had known in almost twenty years. Farm prices were simultaneously high, largely as a result of an inflationary trend that began in late 1935. As a result of this adventitious set of circumstances, China's farmers generally enjoyed a prosperity they had not known for a decade. The basic character of the political, economic and social system that ensnared the peasants had not changed, however, and the relative prosperity of 1936–7 proved, therefore, to be a transient phenomenon.

Leaders in Nanking were largely uninterested in the problems of the peasants. To the extent that they concerned themselves with economic problems, they were oriented primarily to the modern sectors of the economy. They aspired to create a significant industrial base, and they produced numerous plans and issued innumerable directives to realize that aspiration. It is a signal fact that industry grew at an impressive rate during the Nanking decade. According to one reliable estimate, industry in China (exclusive of Manchuria) grew at an annual rate of 6·7 per cent from 1931 to 1936. Other indicators of economic development generally support this estimate. The output of electric power, for example, doubled during the decade, increasing at an annual average of 9·4 per cent; cotton cloth, 16·5 per cent; bank deposits (at 1928 prices), 15·9 per cent; and so on. These indicators compared favourably with those of most other countries in the world. In Germany, for example, production in 1936 was only 6 per cent above the 1929 level, while in the United States and France production in 1936 was still, respectively, 12 per cent, and 21 per cent *below* the 1929 levels.[64]

To assess the significance of these figures, however, it is necessary to note that the base upon which production increases were calculated was exceedingly small. China's electric-power output in 1928, for instance, was a mere 0.88 million megawatt-hours – compared to 5 million in Russia the same year and 88 million in the United States.[65] Relative increases therefore appeared large, whereas absolute increases remained minuscule by comparison with the more advanced industrial nations and with China's real needs. Still, in view of the adversities afflicting the Chinese

[64] Young, *Nation-building*, 310 and 396–9.
[65] John K. Chang, *Industrial development in pre-Communist China: a quantitative analysis*, 119; Abram Bergson, *The economics of Soviet planning*, 84; *Statistical abstract of the United States, 1929*, 367.

economy during the 1930s – the effects of the world depression, civil war and Japanese aggression – it is remarkable that the Nanking decade witnessed any industrial growth at all.

The impact of the National government upon China's industrial development during the 1930s has been the topic of intense debate. The economist John K. Chang has contended, for example, that the increases were the result of the 'growth-inducing measures' of the government.[66] Douglas Paauw, by contrast, remarked that the Chinese economy remained stagnant during the Nanking decade and that 'the government had less capacity to promote economic development in 1937 than a decade earlier'.[67]

Paauw's contention that the industrial sector of the economy remained stagnant is no longer sustainable, but Chang's conclusion that the growth of industry resulted from government policies is also suspect. The government, it is true, did undertake a number of reforms that helped lay a groundwork for a unified and modern economic system. In 1929, for example, it threw off the restraints on tariffs that the foreign powers had imposed under the unequal treaties. In 1931, it abolished the likin (transit tax) that since the mid-nineteenth century had impeded the development of inter-regional trade. It began to impose some order on the monetary system – described by the Kemmerer Commission in 1928 as 'unquestionably the worst currency to be found in any important country'[68] – by banning use of the tael and in 1935 proclaiming *fa-pi* to be the sole legal currency. The government proscribed taxes on inter-port trade and proclaimed a uniform system of weights and measures. It also markedly improved the nation's communications network, expanding the postal and telegraphic services, instituting regular airline routes, and constructing some 2,300 miles of railway track – an increase of 47 per cent over the 1927 trackage.[69]

Unfortunately, some of these reforms were only partially effective, because – as in other areas of Nationalist administration – there frequently existed a broad gap between the formulation and the implementation of policy. The likin, for instance, was abolished, but provincial governments often replaced it with a 'special consumption tax' or some other euphemistic substitute. Uniform weights and measures were enforced only in the official bureaus. And the banks of the various provinces, such as

[66] John K. Chang, 'Industrial development of Mainland China, 1912–1949', *Journal of Economic History*, 27.1 (Mar. 1967) 73-81.

[67] Douglas S. Paauw, 'The Kuomintang and economic stagnation, 1928–1937', *JAS* 16.2 (Feb. 1957) 220.

[68] Young, *Nation-building*, 163.

[69] *Ibid.* 317.

those in Yunnan, Kwangtung and Shansi, continued to issue their own paper notes.

Some measures of the government, moreover, appear to have run counter to the requirements of industrial growth. The government was heavily dependent upon borrowing, for example, and, by providing high returns on bonds and loans to the government, fully 70 per cent of the country's investment capital was channelled to the government and, therefore, away from industrial and commercial enterprises. To obtain loans in competition with the government, private industries had to pay interest rates of 18–20 per cent annually. These were rates, Frank M. Tamagna observed, that 'most Chinese industries were unable to pay; as a result, industrial activity was turned into speculative ventures'.[70]

Taxation also inflicted hardships upon the industries. Because the central government had surrendered the revenues of the land tax to the provincial governments in 1928, it became almost wholly dependent upon the manufacturing and trade sectors for its tax revenues. The full impact of Nanking's tax policies remains to be studied, but it is clear that such exactions as the consolidated taxes (excise taxes levied on rolled tobacco, cotton yarn, flour, matches, etc.) and the business tax (a levy on the assets of commercial enterprises, instituted as a partial replacement for likin) created grave difficulties for entrepreneurs in the Nationalist-controlled area. Fully two-thirds of the 182 Chinese-owned cigarette companies in Shanghai in 1927, for example, closed down by 1930 – and the owners generally agreed that the chief reason was Nanking's taxation. Cotton-textile manufacturers, too, felt heavily burdened by the consolidated tax on cotton yarn, and in 1934 they repeatedly appealed for a reduction in the tax rate. The tax burden on these cotton-texile manufacturers is not known, but in 1936 taxes took fully 38·7 per cent of the Nanyang Brothers Tobacco Company's total income – a burden that the family owners could not sustain. Besides the legal exactions, companies were also subject to occasional demands for payoffs or 'gifts' to the government or to individual officials.[71]

All these facts raise substantial doubts regarding the reputed efficacy of Nanking's 'growth-inducing measures'. That Nanking's policies may not have significantly contributed to the growth of industry is also suggested by the fact that industrial production grew at a generally constant rate throughout the period from 1912 to 1936.[72] This demon-

[70] Frank M. Tamagna, *Banking and finance in China*, 211–12.
[71] Sherman Cochran, *Big business in China: Sino-foreign rivalry in the cigarette industry, 1890–1930*, 188–190; Bush, 'Industry and politics', 250; Coble, 155.
[72] John K. Chang, 'Industrial development', 66–7.

strates that fundamental social and economic forces were working toward industrial development regardless of political regimes or governmental policies.

During the Nanking decade, the Nationalist government assumed an increasingly direct role in the management of economic enterprises. The economic consequences of this trend are unclear, but the political implications are patent. Initially, after 1927, government participation in economic enterprises had been slight. After the banking coup of 1935, however, the government quickly became involved in other areas of the economy, acquiring ownership of at least 12 per cent of the Chinese-owned industries in the country by the end of 1936. It was even more extensively involved in commercial enterprises, and its share of the modern sector of the economy was growing rapidly in the months before the war with Japan.

A prime instrument of government participation in the industrial economy was the China Development Finance Corporation. This was a private-stock corporation, organized in 1933 by T. V. Soong for the purpose of mobilizing Chinese and foreign investments in support of economic development in China. The corporation initially floundered, because it was unable to attract sizeable amounts of capital. After the banking coup, however, the government-controlled banks invested heavily in the corporation. Its assets leaped from Y12·6 million in late 1934 to Y115 million in June 1936, the government-controlled banks providing nearly Y90 million of the added assets.[73] With this capital, the corporation extended loans to and undertook joint management of various electrical, mining, water-control, and other enterprises. Because the bulk of the corporation's capital was obtained from the government, and because most of the leading stockholders of the corporation were either government officials (like H. H. Kung) or officers in government-controlled banks (like T. V. Soong), the government had thereby become directly and actively involved in the economy.

Other prominent instruments of government participation in industry and commerce were the Bank of China and the Ministry of Industries. The Bank of China was now headed by T. V. Soong, and after the 1935 banking coup was a leading component of the government-controlled banking group. When the war broke out in 1937, the Bank of China was operating fifteen spinning mills, which comprised 13 per cent of all the spindles in Chinese-owned mills. It also held investments in, inter alia, flour, meat-packing, telephone, paper, and vegetable-oil companies.

73 Coble, 220.

Sun Yat-sen, in his lectures on economic development, had instructed that only heavy industry, transportation and communications should be nationalized. But Sun's prescription was honoured more in the breach than in the practice, for most of this direct and indirect governmental involvement in the economy was either in light industry or in marketing and speculation. The China Cotton Company, for example, which was headed by T. V. Soong and indirectly controlled by the government, was in 1936 and 1937 one of the largest commodity trading firms in China. The Ministry of Industries, too, established the Central Fish Market in Shanghai. This joint government-private undertaking instituted a virtual monopoly on the fish trade in Central China, reaping big profits for both the ministry and the selected private individuals who were permitted to invest in the venture. The ministry also traded in vegetable oils, paper, tea, and miscellaneous 'national products'.[74]

The Nanking government's quest for revenues – combined with individual officials' efforts to enrich themselves – was clearly the primary reason for these ventures into the fields of light industry and commerce. Among the government's many economic undertakings, only Chiang Kai-shek's National Resources Commission appears both to have accorded with Sun Yat-sen's economic model in its emphasis on heavy industry, and to have been motivated strictly by concerns for the nation's economic development. This commission, created in 1935, was an agency of Chiang's Military Affairs Commission, and its purpose was to create an industrial base that would support the nation's armed forces. To accomplish this goal, the National Resources Commission in 1936 drafted a five-year plan of industrialization, with a planned capitalization of Y270 million. Central to the commission's work was the creation of an industrial zone in the interior, safely removed, supposedly, from the coastal centres which were vulnerable to enemy attack. During the two years prior to the war, the National Resources Commission's most ambitious projects were located in Hunan, where work was begun on factories to produce steel, heavy machinery, and radio and electrical equipment. Coal, iron, zinc, tin and copper mines were also planned in Hunan, Hupei, Kiangsi and Szechwan.

From the beginning, however, the commission suffered from financial shortages; it received only Y30 million of the projected Y270 million. As a result of the paucity of funds, the commission succeeded in completing only three new factories; fifteen of its projects remained in the planning stages. Significantly, the commission's most measurable growth was

[74] *Ibid.* 245–6.

attributable to the several previously existing private enterprises – coal mines, a copper mine, an oil field, and an electrical company – that had simply been taken over, in part through confiscation, and then operated by the commission. Otherwise, the work of the commission was still largely on paper when the war broke out.[75]

Participation by the National government in these economic enterprises was by no means unprecedented in Chinese history. Throughout much of the dynastic period, merchants had been relegated to secondary status, often subject to the domination and intimidation of the emperor's officials. During the self-strengthening movement of the late nineteenth century, officials had become deeply involved in the operations of the several Western-inspired economic ventures, even those that were ostensibly privately owned and managed. In these enterprises, the interests and money of the government were inextricably mixed up with the private interests and money of leading officials. During the warlord period, however, this intimate bond between the government and the economy had loosened; as the governments weakened, the private entrepreneurs achieved an unaccustomed freedom from official intervention and control. But when the Nationalists at least partially restored the power of government, the government again began participating in the economy. Officials such as T. V. Soong and H. H. Kung became involved in economic ventures, both officially and privately, much as had Li Hung-chang in the 1890s. The growing entrepreneurial role of the National government was actually, therefore, a reassertion of a traditional mode of political behaviour.[76]

CHINA'S NEW MOOD, 1936–7

Beginning in the autumn of 1936, a new sense of optimism and national unity suffused the nation. The turning-point was marked by Nanking's suppression of the revolt of Kwangtung and Kwangsi in June–September of that year. These were the last provinces that had blatantly proclaimed their opposition to Nanking rule, and with their defeat China for the first time since 1916 appeared to be unified. The suppression of the revolt, moreover, had been largely peaceful, convincing many Chinese – now profoundly weary of civil strife – that the Nanking authorities were not mere militarists and that Chiang Kai-shek was a wise and able statesman.

---

[75] *Ibid.* 235–40. On the secret origin of the National Resources Commission (under the geologist Weng Wen-hao) and the Nationalist programme to use German military and industrial support, see the thorough study by William C. Kirby, *Germany and Republican China.*

[76] Coble, 259–60.

A second reason for the new mood of the nation was that Chiang Kai-shek now appeared to have aligned himself with the prevailing anti-Japanese sentiment. Hitherto, he had consistently stressed that China was too weak and divided to resist imperialist aggression, and he had used all the resources at his command, including secret police and censors, to repress the critics of his policy of appeasement. The anti-Japanese stance of the Kwangtung-Kwangsi rebels had, however, forced Chiang on 13 July 1936 to declare that China, rather than agree to further territorial concessions to the Japanese, was prepared to make 'the ultimate sacrifice' of an all-out war of resistance. Although Chiang had doubtless timed this declaration so that it would defuse potential popular support for the rebels, the declaration may in fact have resulted from a hardening of his determination to resist further Japanese encroachments. When in November 1936 the Japanese attempted to establish a satellite state in Suiyuan province, for example, a Nationalist army under General Fu Tso-i strongly and successfully resisted. In November and December, too, the Chinese foreign minister, Chang Ch'ün, unflinchingly rejected a set of Japanese demands, displaying thereby a defiance of the Japanese that the Nationalists had not shown throughout their entire tenure in Nanking. No doubt Chiang Kai-shek still hoped to postpone what was felt to be the inevitable war with Japan. Strong nationalistic sentiment, both among the people and perhaps especially within his army, however, persuaded him now to assume an unprecedentedly firm stance against the Japanese.

A third factor contributing to China's new national mood was its emergence from the economic depression that had gripped the country since the winter of 1931–2. In November 1935, with silver flooding out of the country to foreign buyers – thereby badly eroding public confidence in *fa-pi* – Nanking abandoned the silver standard and switched to a managed currency. This enabled Nanking to meet its financial needs by increasing the volume of note issues, and in just a year and a half the volume of *fa-pi* in circulation more than tripled. The effect was to stimulate an inflationary trend that by mid-1937 had restored agricultural prices to their 1931 level. Farm credit now also became more readily available and interest rates fell. Thus, although the inflationary effects of the currency reform had been unanticipated and actually unwanted by Nanking's fiscal experts, that reform started the entire economy on the road to recovery.

Coinciding in 1936 and 1937 with the rising agricultural prices were bumper harvests, the best in nearly twenty years. As a consequence of this happy juxtaposition of excellent crops and high prices, the value of China's harvest in 1936 was 45 per cent higher than the average for the years 1933–5. With relative prosperity in the villages, peasants began buying the industrial commodities that they had denied themselves since 1931. The result was a fresh stimulus also to the urban economy.

The upturn of the economy in the autumn of 1936, together with the enhanced unity of the nation and the government's new-found determination to resist the Japanese, had an extraordinary effect on the national spirit. 'At the moment,' reported Columbia University professor Nathaniel Peffer in October 1936, 'Chinese are inclined to a mood of confidence and impassioned patriotism.'[77] Likewise an editorial in China's leading independent newspaper, the *Ta-kung-pao* ('L'Impartial'), declared in December, 'In the period of the last few months, the people's confidence seems as though it were revived from the dead.'[78]

Chiang Kai-shek was the principal political beneficiary of this new national mood. Earlier in the decade, he had been widely viewed as an ill-educated militarist striving only for personal power. Now, however, he was praised as a far-seeing leader who, so long as the nation had been torn by internal struggles, had wisely avoided a confrontation with the Japanese. Chiang for the first time had become a popular and seemingly inexpendable leader.

At the crest of this new popularity, however, the Nanking regime was suddenly plunged into a brief but unprecedented crisis when Chiang Kai-shek was kidnapped at Sian. Despite his expressed determination to resist further Japanese encroachments, Chiang's *bête noire* was still the Communists. And he was convinced that, with just one further campaign, the Communists – located since the completion of the Long March in northern Shensi, and reduced to about 30,000 armed men – could be finally annihilated. But the North-west Bandit-Suppression Force that Chiang assigned to this operation had not responded to his marching orders. This army, commanded by Chang Hsueh-liang and composed largely of natives of Manchuria, felt little zeal for the anti-Communist campaign. They were convinced that the real enemy was not the Communists, whom they had learned to respect as true patriots, but the Japanese, who had invaded their homes.

Unable to enforce his orders from Nanking, Chiang Kai-shek flew to the army headquarters in Sian on 4 December, where he exhorted Chang to commence the attack. The Manchurians were adamant, however, that they should, in concert with the Communists, fight the Japanese. And, when their entreaties failed, they overpowered Chiang Kai-shek's bodyguard in the pre-dawn hours of 12 December and placed their commander-in-chief under arrest.

For two weeks, Chiang Kai-shek was held prisoner in Sian. Radical young Manchurian officers demanded that he be put to death. But the calmer voice of Chang Hsueh-liang, who sought not to kill Chiang but only to change his policy, prevailed. That Chang Hsueh-liang succeeded in this purpose has never been officially admitted, although it is now clear that Chiang Kai-shek did make a verbal promise to cease attacking the Communists and to resist the Japanese. Finally, on 25 December, with the concurrence of Communist representatives who were in constant consultation with the mutineers, Chiang was released and flew back to Nanking.[79]

The Sian incident had been a traumatic episode for the Chinese. Public response – marked by profound agony and concern during his captivity, and by unrestrained relief and joy upon his release – confirmed Chiang's widespread popularity and buttressed his increasingly autocratic powers within the regime. Despite his asseverations that he had made no concessions to his captors, there were no further attacks against the Communists. Indeed, negotiations between Nanking and the Communists, leading to the formation of a united front, were soon under way. For the first time in a decade, the Chinese seemed to be putting aside their domestic quarrels in order to resist the foreign aggressor.

AN ASSESSMENT OF NATIONALIST RULE DURING THE NANKING DECADE

The Nationalists were granted only ten years from the establishment of their government in Nanking until the nation was engulfed in a long and devastating war. Ten years was too brief a time to establish a completely new national administration and to turn back the tide of political disintegration and national humiliation that for a century and a half had assailed the nation. Even if conditions had been ideal, the new government could have done little more than initiate political, social and economic reforms.

Despite the adverse conditions afflicting the nation, there had been progress during the decade. By mid-1937, the central government was seemingly ensconced in power, so that there was greater political stability than at any time since 1915. The economy was on the upturn; the

---

[79] Tien-wei Wu, *The Sian Incident: a pivotal point in modern Chinese history*, 142–8 and *passim*.

government was pushing ahead with various transportation and industrial schemes; the currency was more unified than ever before. Many observers, both Chinese and foreign, believed that the Nationalists had in just ten years reversed the tide of disintegration. The American ambassador, Nelson T. Johnson, for example, wrote in April 1937 that 'An observer... cannot but be impressed by the energy with which the Chinese government is pushing its program of economic reconstruction on all fronts, agricultural, industrial and communications.'[80] The British commercial counsellor at about the same time noted 'the increasing, justified confidence which the Chinese themselves as well as the world at large have in the future of this country, a confidence based on the remarkable growth of stability achieved in recent years and the improved political, financial and economic conduct of affairs – government and private'.[81]

The conditions that had generated this swelling optimism, however, were of such recent vintage – appearing less than a year before the war began – that it would be folly for a historian to insist dogmatically that those conditions necessarily portended long-term success and stability for the regime. The improved economic situation, for example, was directly related to the vagaries of China's weather and to the uncertainties inherent in the inflationary trend set off by the creation of a managed currency. The political and military unity of the nation was also extremely fragile, as would become grievously apparent later in the war years. And the popularity of Chiang Kai-shek was attributable to his avowed determination to resist the Japanese rather than to any fundamental reforms in the regime itself.

The new mood of the nation, in other words, had been generated largely by superficial and possibly transient phenomena. Peering beneath those surface features, one discerns that the regime continued to be, even at the end of the Nanking decade, a clumsy and uncertain instrument of national renewal. The civil bureaucracy remained inefficient and corrupt. Government offices were filled with nepotistic appointees who had few if any qualifications for office, but filled the government bureaus with superfluous and self-serving personnel. Wages of these employees were low, and corruption was consequently rife in the administration. As late as September 1936, Chiang Kai-shek bemoaned the ineptitude of the bureaucracy, asserting that 'If we do not weed the present body of corruption, bribery, perfunctoriness, and ignorance, and establish instead a clean and efficient administration, the day will soon come when the revolution will be started against us as we did against the Manchus.'[82]

---

[80] Quoted in Young, *Nation-building*, 419.   [81] Quoted in *ibid.* 420.
[82] *North China Herald*, 16 Sept. 1936, 482.

Some of the civilian leaders in the bureaucracy were educated, modern-minded men. Since 1935, in particular, Chiang Kai-shek had brought into government service a number of respected bankers, journalists and intellectuals, such as Chang Kai-ngau, Weng Wen-hao, Wu Ting-ch'ang and Tsiang T'ing-fu, who were generally highly capable and relatively progressive. These new men, however, exerted minimal influence on basic government policy. The men who in fact controlled the regime seldom comprehended how to cope with the tasks of social and economic regeneration. Franklin Ho, who became a close political and economic adviser to Chiang Kai-shek in 1936, recalled that 'One can only be surprised to know just how unaware people at the top were of what was going on, how little they knew of actual conditions in the country, and how they were even less aware of the theoretical basis of those conditions.'[83] Some of these people at the top were skilled technicians, but they tended to be almost exclusively oriented to the urban, modernized sectors of society. They therefore had little understanding of the problems or of the potentialities of the rural areas, which constituted the soul of the nation. T. V. Soong and H. H. Kung, for example, were skilled financiers and budget managers, but they never confronted the problem of how to mobilize the resources of the agricultural sector – which provided two-thirds of the national product – if China were to develop any momentum in its programmes of transport and industrial development.

The military continued to hold ultimate power in the Nationalist regime and to establish the regime's priorities. However enlightened the civilian administrators might have been, therefore, they were little more than tools of the military. And the military men tended to be considerably less worldly than the civilians, and were much less oriented to the problems of social and economic reconstruction. They found solutions to the national problems chiefly in authoritarianism and political repression. 'All too often,' remarked Arthur Young, these militarists 'were incompetent, reactionary, and/or corrupt.'[84] With this kind of men dominant in the upper reaches of the regime, the prospects of the government responding creatively to the nation's exigent problems were exceedingly unpromising.

One of the problems for which the Nationalist leadership provided no solutions, for example, was that, as Arthur Young put it, 'The government failed to identify with the people, but rather stood above them.'[85] The regime was a dictatorship built on and maintained by military power. Its leaders were jealous of their power, disinclined to share that power and

[83] Franklin L. Ho, 'The reminiscences of Ho Lien', 144.
[84] Young, *Nation-building*, 423.   [85] *Ibid.* 423.

its perquisites with others, and repressive of political rivals and critics. In a modernizing and increasingly nationalistic polity, where the citizens are inevitably becoming more politically alert, this kind of exclusivist wielding of power is generally self-destructive. Certainly this is not to suggest that China needed to adopt Anglo-American institutions of democracy, for assuredly those were not suitable to China at the time. The Nationalists should, however, have allowed and even encouraged the politically mobilized elements to become involved in the processes of government. It might, for example, have permitted trade unions, student and professional associations, and local self-government assemblies to become vehicles of political mobilization. Or it might have injected life into the Kuomintang by making it an instrument for the supervision of government rather than being an atrophied limb of the regime.

During periods of extreme political crisis, the regime did go through the motions of expanding political participation. In 1932, for instance, when public opinion had turned strongly against the regime for its unmilitant response to the Japanese attacks on Manchuria and Shanghai, the government convoked a National Emergency Conference designed to allow prominent persons outside the regime to advise the authorities. Whenever such crises passed, however, the regime returned to its accustomedly authoritarian and exclusivist methods of rule. In some regimes, such as Franco's Spain or Salazar's Portugal, such authoritarian solutions have been remarkably stable. China, however, was many times larger and therefore incomparably more difficult to control than were those European states.

Exacerbating the inherent instability of the Nationalist regime were the unresolved problems in China's villages. Scholars are currently debating whether the peasants' standard of living was declining during the Republican period or remaining at about the same level. There is little dispute, however, that the life of the peasants generally was impoverished and occasionally even brutish. As a consequence, peasant rebellions, banditry, and other forms of social pathology had become endemic in the rural areas. These dissident activities had, however, lacked the political awareness and the organization needed to transform them into politically revolutionary movements. By the 1930s, however, both the aspirations and the organization were being brought to the peasants. As a result of the increasingly rapid process of modernization in China, the peasants were learning of ways of life different from their own mundane existence. Largely through the flow of commerce, they learned of worlds beyond their villages, and commerce had expanded dramatically by the 1930s. In 1935, for instance, about 54 per cent of China's families bought kerosene;

cigarettes and cigarette advertising penetrated even to the farthest provinces. Rural youths, moreover, who were being recruited to work in urban factories, vastly broadened their intellectual horizons by exposure to the cities and to workers from other provinces – and, returning home periodically, they communicated what they had learned to their fellow villagers.[86] Radio and newspapers were also making inroads into the hinterlands, conveying information about alternative modes of existence. 'Nothing,' Samuel Huntington has observed, 'is more revolutionary than this awareness.'[87] Although little research has yet been attempted on this question of changing peasant attitudes and outlooks in modern China, the probability that peasants were becoming aware not only that they were suffering, but that those sufferings were not inevitable, suggests the presence of a potentially powerful destabilizing factor in the countryside.

The Communists, moreover, had begun providing the organization that could transmute peasant discontents into political power. The Nationalists might, in the absence of a Japanese invasion, have continued employing repressive measures against the Communists. But the facts that the Nationalists assigned such a low priority to the elimination of the socio-economic causes of peasant discontent, and that the Communists had already demonstrated their tenacious capacity to survive, also suggest that the rural areas of Nationalist China were destined to remain a tinder-box even if there had been no war with Japan.

These several factors – the ineffectual administration of the Nationalists, their incomprehension of the tasks of national reconstruction, their failure to accommodate into the political process the broadening strata of the population that were becoming politically alert, and the persistence of the rural problem – did not mean that the Nationalist regime was fated to be overthrown. They did, however, portend continuing instability.

[86] Dwight H. Perkins, *Agricultural development in China, 1368–1968*, 111–12, 126–7; Jean Chesneaux, *The Chinese labor movement, 1919–1927*, 48–9, 66–70; Cochran, 18–22; Albert Feuerwerker, 'The foreign presence in China', *CHOC* 12.196; Martin M. C. Yang, *Chinese social structure: a historical study*, 339.

[87] Samuel P. Huntington, *Political order in changing societies*, 298.

CHAPTER 4

THE COMMUNIST
MOVEMENT 1927–1937

The decade between the first and second united fronts, from the KMT-CCP break-up in mid-1927 to mid-1937, was a time of disaster, trial and tribulation for the Communist movement that brought it close to extinction. Yet from this period emerged an experienced and tested leadership with a capacity not only to survive but to win power. The severity of the problems met and surmounted by the CCP in these years can be best understood by looking first at its crisis of membership and organization.

RECONSTITUTION AND LEADERSHIP OF THE PARTY

In brief, the CCP from its Second Congress in 1922 had been a branch of the Communist International (CI) which, in spite of differing views occasionally expressed by Chinese leaders, had its way throughout the period of the first united front of 1923–7. After 1927, however, the prestige of the CI plummeted and vigorous efforts were needed to restore it. This meant the deposition and criticism of Ch'en Tu-hsiu, the recall and rebuke of Ch'ü Ch'iu-pai, the trial of Li Li-san; more significantly, this also meant the convocation of the Sixth Congress in Moscow and the reconstruction of the party presided over by Pavel Mif. From the autumn of 1927 to January 1931 the CI's interference in the affairs of the CCP virtually reduced the Chinese party to the status of a 'colony'. After the fourth plenum of January 1931, however, the CI's influence over the CCP declined, due to complex factors, including Stalin's increasing preoccupation with Russian and European affairs, the destruction of the liaison organization in Shanghai by the KMT police in the summer of 1934, and Stalin's bloody purges that by 1937 had rendered the CI an unreliable vehicle for transmitting his policies.

Meanwhile, Ch'en Tu-hsiu's leadership of the CCP had ended in mid-1927. His successors were younger men – Ch'ü Ch'iu-pai in the second half of 1927, Li Li-san from summer 1928 to summer 1930, and the International Faction (or the 28 Bolsheviks, *erh-shih-pa shu*) from

January 1931 to January 1935. Under the guidance of the CI they undertook to rebuild the shattered party and develop a new, feasible revolutionary strategy. The membership of the party dropped from its peak of nearly 60,000 in April 1927 to probably less than 10,000 by the end of the year. It was perhaps to Ch'en's credit that the CCP had not been entirely destroyed in the debacle of 1927. Some attribute this resilience to the inculcation of 'a common state of mind', or, in other words, the strength of the ideology that had been disseminated through the party organs, chiefly *The Guide Weekly* and the theoretical journal, *New Youth*.[1] As the intellectuals were the people in whose minds the ideology had taken firmest root, it was they who remained firm in the face of the anti-Communist upsurge, to carry on the torch of revolution. In the words of one such survivor of the persecution of 1927, 'to lose contact with the party or the [Communist Youth] Corps was like losing one's loving mother'.[2] It was this sentiment that turned the politically alienated to brotherly comradeship with each other and gave them a ruthless determination against their foes within and without the party.

When the storm broke in 1927, the attention of the party had shifted to a young man, only twenty-eight years of age, perhaps not nearly as resolute in action as Ch'en, but certainly more Leninist and adventurist and with considerable theoretical sophistication. Ch'ü Ch'iu-pai had been opposing Ch'en's leadership on several issues for some time before Ch'en's retirement from his commanding position. A prolific polemicist in the party organs he edited, he was fluent in Russian and thus gained access to Lenin's writings on party organization and strategy, such as *What is to be done?* and *Two tactics*. Upon taking over the secretaryship in July–August 1927, Ch'ü proceeded to bolshevize the CCP. Then, as later in 1928, he regarded the party as an elite organization clearly different from any mass organization under its leadership. Its vanguard status came from its capability of exposing and learning from its own mistakes through intra-party struggles.[3] Here he echoed not only Lenin but also Stalin's 1925 definition of bolshevization.[4] Putsches attempted at Swatow in

---

[1] This chapter is a continuation of the same author's 'The Chinese Communist movement to 1927' in *CHOC* 12.505–26. See also *ibid.* 430–3, 'Introduction of Marxism-Leninism' (B. Schwartz); and 566–73, 'The Russian role by early 1926' (C. M. Wilbur). For a survey narrative, see James P. Harrison, *The long march to power: a history of the Chinese Communist Party, 1921–72*. The other major account is Jacques Guillermaz, *A history of the Chinese Communist Party 1921–1949*.

[2] *Hung-ch'i p'iao-p'iao* (Red flags flying), hereafter *HCPP*, 6.15.

[3] Previously no intra-party differences had reached this dimension. See 'Letter to all the members', *Hung-se wen-hsien* (Red documents), 96. On Ch'ü Ch'iu-pai's background and literary interests see Jonathan Spence, *The Gate of Heavenly Peace: the Chinese and their revolution 1895–1980*, 145–8 and *passim*; Tsi-an Hsia, *The gate of darkness: Studies on the leftist literary movement in China*, 3–54; and ch. 9 below.

[4] Published in *Pravda*, 3 February 1925 and included in Boyd Compton, *Mao's China: party reform documents, 1942–44*, 269–71.

September and at Canton (the 'Canton commune') in December 1927 both failed. The CCP leadership was decimated. At a time when the existing structure of the party was fractured by blows from without and rent by factionalism within, Ch'ü could do only as much as the circumstances allowed. His attempt to introduce the democratic process of consultation at least at the top level, when often a quorum of the Politburo was scarcely possible, only aggravated the sectarian wrangles.[5] However, through Ch'ü's emphasis on the land revolution, the party branched out from the urban underground to the embryonic rural base areas, some fifteen of which were now taking shape.

Class composition

After a series of disastrous adventures known as the Autumn Harvest uprisings, in April 1928 Ch'ü vacated the party secretaryship in favour of Hsiang Chung-fa, a colourless proletarian. Under persecution and in war conditions, along with the omnipresent concern with safety and defections, the party centre faced a host of organizational problems. First, the class composition of the membership had changed from urban workers and intellectuals to a rural predominance.[6] The change threatened to transform the class base, the style of work and the policies of the party. Therefore both the resolutions of the Sixth Congress of July 1928 and the letter to the CCP from the ECCI (Executive Committee of the Communist International) on 8 February 1929 urged an increase in urban membership. Second, in order to consolidate the proletarian base of the party, the centre had to re-establish contact with those members who had lost touch with their party cell. It had to find jobs for and to plant back among the non-party masses those activists who had exposed themselves during the period of open work before June 1927 but were now living on the slender resources of the party. Above all it had to unify its control over radical labour unions which were in the hands of the 'real work' group under such union leaders as Ho Meng-hsiung and Lo Chang-lung. Third, the rural branches were for a long period of time completely cut off from any connection with their provincial committees and the centre. The Ching-kang-shan Front Committee in the mountain fastness far

---

[5] Mao Tse-tung, *Hsuan-chi* (Selected works), hereafter Mao, *HC* 3.980 and Harrison, *Long march*, 124.

[6] None of the sets of figures of the CCP membership can be taken without question. I am using the official statistics as a rough guide. See for example, Mao Tse-tung, *Selected works*, hereafter Mao, *SW* 4.270. It is generally held that the size of urban membership in all these reports is exaggerated. But, on the other hand, the exodus of members of the CCP to the countryside may have also inflated the size of the rural membership. Many of the people working in the rural soviets were obviously of urban origins.

south-east of Changsha between Kiangsi and Hunan, for instance, took five months to re-establish its communication with the Hunan provincial committee. A letter from the centre to Mao, then the secretary of the Front Committee, sent on 4 June 1928, reached him six months later. Ho Lung in west Hunan and Hupei knew the resolutions of the Sixth Congress only in the spring of 1929! Fourth, within the central leadership factionalism, especially Ch'en Tu-hsiu's 'rightist' influence, persisted. As the situation worsened after the repeated failures in the second half of 1927, it appeared to dim the hopes for consolidating the party organization.[7]

The Sixth CCP Congress held outside Moscow in June and July 1928 charged the new leadership (principally Li Li-san from Hunan, who had been in France and Russia) with rehabilitating the party along the following lines. The party had to be proletarianized by bringing more workers into its organization and leadership. This should not be done at the expense of ideological and organizational unity, which would happen if localism and factionalism were allowed to continue. To curb localism and factionalism it would be necessary to intensify the education and training of members of the party and at the same time to practise true democratic centralism without, however, endangering the safety of the party and its members. In the widely scattered rural base areas all efforts should be made to arouse the broad masses in the land revolution and soviet movement led by the party. The response of the masses was to be a major criterion of correctness of policy and style; putschism and commandism, which were likely to lose mass support, were deemed erroneous. In the base areas, the Communists should act only as ideological leaders, not as administrators of the soviets themselves, so as to give the masses the power to supervise their own governments, although not to supervise the party itself.[8]

Following these resolutions, Li Li-san took immediate steps to strengthen the central leadership. Although the Sixth Congress showed a distrust of the intellectuals and Li himself noticed a barrier between the workers and intellectuals in the party, he does not seem to have developed an anti-intellectual stand. One can hardly describe Li Wei-han, Teng Chung-hsia, and the cultural workers in Honan, all staunch supporters of Li, as anything but intellectuals.[9] Initially the main threat to the security

[7] ECCI to CCP, 8 February 1929; Mao's report, 25 November 1928, *Mao Tse-tung chi* (Collected writings of Mao Tse-tung), ed. Takeuchi Minoru, hereafter *MTTC*, 2.25, 28; *Hsing-huo liao-yuan* (A single spark can start a prairie fire), hereafter *HHLY*, 1, pt. 2, 603–14. After vol. 1 citations are by volume and page.

[8] Resolutions of the Sixth Congress in *Hung-se wen-hsien*, 169–91.

[9] Wang Ming, Postscript to 'Liang-t'iao lu-hsien' (The two lines), in his *Hsuan-chi* (Selected works), 3.140–1.

of Li's leadership came from the labour union leaders and it would have been unwise for him to alienate his intellectual colleagues.[10]

In the first few months of Li Li-san's leadership, when the small rural soviets were still struggling for their existence, the major problems of party unity and consolidation did not lie in the rural bases. It was the remnants of party-led labour unions and their leaders whom Li condemned for excessive democratization, egalitarianism, bureaucratism and unprincipled factionalism.[11] His endeavour to curb intra-party democracy in order to safeguard the party under the 'white terror' may have ended in too much centralization of power. The complaint was that he, like Ch'en Tu-hsiu, became a patriarch.[12] Essentially a man of action rather than of intellectual power, Li relied chiefly on the reinforcement of discipline to achieve unity. Now that the CCP's status as a branch of the CI had been reaffirmed at the Sixth Congress, Li had the backing of the CI's authority to help him pursue this line of action. Often he resorted to dismissal to eliminate the opposition. Occasionally he even dissolved an entire provincial committee for the same purpose.[13] Not until September 1930, after the collapse of the Li Li-san line, did he try to lay down some rules on the rampant intra-party struggles.[14] Even then the emphasis was evidently on discipline in a crude and authoritarian manner. Li's attempt to unify the party included the use of party organs. The *Bolshevik* (*Pu-erh-sai-wei-k'e*), created by Ch'ü Ch'iu-pai in October 1927, was continued and Li launched the weekly *Red Flag* (*Hung-ch'i*) in November 1928, which was published twice weekly from October 1929 to July 1930. And finally he formed the General Action Committee, combining the heads of the party, youth corps, and labour unions into one body.[15]

The much discussed differences between Li and Mao related more to their assessment of the revolutionary situation and their corresponding strategies than to party organization. The widely shared anxiety over the increase in peasant membership, hence the possible permeation of peasant mentality in the party, appeared to Mao to be an unwarranted fear. Operating in remote rural areas, Mao and other soviet leaders could

---

[10] Richard C. Thornton, *The Comintern and the Chinese Communists, 1928–1931*, 34.

[11] Conrad Brandt *et al. A documentary history of Chinese communism*, 172–3.

[12] Ilpyong J. Kim, *The politics of Chinese Communism: Kiangsi under Soviet rule*, 183–4.

[13] 'Resolutions of the second plenum' (June 1929), in Kuo Hua-lun (Warren Kuo), *Chung-kung shih-lun* (An analytical history of the CCP); hereafter Warren Kuo, *History*, 2.43–4. This trend culminated in the dismissals of Ch'en Tu-hsiu, P'eng Shu-chih and many others in November 1929. See Wang Fan-hsi, *Chinese revolutionary: memoirs 1919–1949*, translated and with an introduction by Gregor Benton.

[14] Hsiao Tso-liang, *Power relations within the Chinese communist movement, 1930–1934*, 55–6.

[15] All things considered, the tribute paid to Li's organizational achievement by the ECCI expressed a general optimism rather than a description of reality. The ECCI resolution, often dated 23 July 1930 (see *Hung-se wen-hsien*, 354), was drafted in April-May and adopted in June.

depend only to a limited degree on developing small-scale industries in order to increase the proletarian component of the soviet party. Mao in particular had to resort to political education for the proletarianization of the peasants, who were the only masses under the party's influence and the only important source of party recruitment. The anxiety remained unrelieved – all that Li could do was to develop the party's work among the workers. In the context of 1928-30, Li's effort in that respect did not get very far.

Unity of a party so widely scattered and so badly mauled as the CCP under Li was more a matter of ideology than of organization. Yet he was anything but a mighty ideologue. With Moscow divided first between Stalin and Trotsky and then between Stalin and Bukharin, Li had either to evolve his own line or to vacillate as the CI did. Whatever direction he followed, he had to persuade his followers. When persuasion failed, the unconvinced left for Moscow or left the party altogether. But Hsiang Chung-fa, Li Wei-han, Ho Ch'ang, Teng Chung-hsia, and several others supported him to form a caucus powerful enough to control the centre effectively.[16]

In spite of Wang Ming's acrimony against Li's organization line,[17] Li was removed by the CI not on that ground, but because of his strategic blunders to be noted below. After a short interval of confusion, the centre passed into the hands of the '28 Bolsheviks', of whom Wang Ming was the leader, through the authority of the CI. A situation thus arose in the centre where the CI's authority was pitched against the 'real work' group of union leaders who, persistently opposed to Li Li-san, found their power base much eroded by Chiang Kai-shek's persecution.[18] In the countryside it was pitched against the soviet leaders whose power in terms of territory and men had grown enormously since the Sixth Congress.

Of all the crucial intra-party struggles, the issues that triggered the dispute between the 28 Bolsheviks and the 'real work' group led by Ho Meng-hsiung and Lo Chang-lung are perhaps most obscure; so obscure that they defy intelligent speculation. By the time the dispute broke out, the old contention between Ho and Li Li-san had been settled. The only link between the two disputes seems to have been the ways by which the party should be reconstructed and who should be the people to do it. The single intelligible point to emerge from examining the existing docu-

---

[16] Wang Ming, 'The two lines', in his *Hsuan-chi*, 3.70, 100, 108, 140-1, and 143-4; Warren Kuo, *History*, 2.334. I give these names to correct an impression that Li had almost no supporters at all in 1929-30.

[17] Wang Ming, *ibid.* 3.68-71.

[18] HHLY 1, pt. 1, 16; Pei-p'ing she-hui tiao-ch'a so (Peiping Social Survey Institute), *Ti-erh-tz'u Chung-kuo lao-tung nien-chien* (Second yearbook of Chinese labour), preface, 2.

ments, mostly biased against the 'real work' group, was the emergency conference proposed by Ho, Lo, and their supporters with a wider representation than the fourth plenum of the Central Committee proposed by the 28 Bolsheviks and their mentor, Pavel Mif. The emergency conference proposal envisaged a reconstruction of the party from below, whereas the fourth plenum of the Sixth Central Executive Committee – as actually convened in January 1931 – consisted of a narrow representation which preferred to do so from above. As far as the 'real work' group could see, the latter course would have most dire consequences for the party as well as for the revolutionary movement as a whole.[19] Personal factors, for example rivalry for leadership positions and distrust of the inexperienced and young 'Bolsheviks', certainly entered into the dispute; nonetheless they may not have been the deciding factors. When the issues were joined, it turned out that both Ho and Lo had grossly overestimated the strength and unity of the labour union opposition – a miscalculation that ended in their total defeat at the fourth plenum in January 1931. Ho and 22 others, including five young leftist writers, were evidently betrayed to the police and were then shot on 7 February 1931.

Having seized the central leadership, the 28 Bolsheviks might have attempted to 'bolshevize' the party organization – on the one hand by insisting on absolute fidelity to the political line of the CI; on the other by practising 'democratic centralism'.[20] As they were sharp debaters,[21] it is reasonable to assume that they would have preferred committee discussions rather than patriarchal commandism or a system of penalties they seem to have disliked. In fact, however, when the cloak-and-dagger struggles between the secret service men of the KMT and CCP were exacerbated in 1931 immediately after the fourth plenum, and the work of the party in the 'white area' suffered disastrous reverses, it is highly doubtful that committee meetings and democratic centralism could have been attained.[22]

---

19 'Centre's resolution concerning the question of Comrade Ho Meng-hsiung' (16 December 1930) in *Tang ti kai-tsao* (Reconstruction of the party), no. 1 (25 January 1931). See Hsiao Tso-liang, *Power relations*, 95. Also 'Resolution concerning the removal of Lo Chang-lung as a member of the central committee and the party' (20 January 1931) in *Tang ti kai-tsao*, 3 (15 February 1931). Full text reproduced in Warren Kuo, *History*, 2.218–21. See also Hsiao Tso-liang, *Power relations*, 135.

20 Wang Ming, 'Chung-kuo hsien-chuang yü Chung-kung jen-wu' (The present situation of China and the tasks of the CCP), speeches at the 13th plenum of the ECCI, Moscow, 1934, 78. On centralism, see the end of his famous pamphlet, 'The two lines', in *Hsuan-chi*, 3.111.

21 In 1939 I had a chance to listen to Wang Ming's public speech given in the tennis court of the YMCA, Chengtu, when Wang Yü-chang and Lin Tsu-han were on their way back to Yenan after a session of the People's Political Council. I have not heard any Chinese speaker, before or since, more eloquent than Wang.

22 Warren Kuo, *History*, 2.250-9.

The 28 Bolsheviks, however, achieved a greater measure of centralized control over the fifteen or so rural soviets than had Li Li-san. Soon after the fourth plenum, the 'front committees' which had governed the soviets, were replaced by a central bureau of the soviet areas directly under the Politburo, with six soviet areas under its jurisdiction. At least four of these six soviets each had a branch bureau – the central soviet in eastern Kiangsi on the border of Fukien (to which Mao and Chu Teh had removed from Ching-kang-shan at the end of 1928), the O-Yü-Wan (Hupei-Honan-Anhwei) soviet, Hsiang-o-hsi (West Hupei and Hunan), and Hsiang-kan (Hunan-Kiangsi).[23] The other two may have been directed by a special committee.[24] The new institution may have weakened the growing power of Mao Tse-tung in the central soviet; it was certainly possible for the 28 Bolsheviks to use it to eradicate Li Li-san's residual influence in the O-Yü-Wan soviet when Ch'en Chang-hao, Shen Tse-min, and Chang Kuo-t'ao superseded Hsü Chi-shen and Tseng Chung-sheng, while in the Hsiang-o-hsi soviet Hsia Hsi replaced Teng Chung-hsia.[25]

As the 'white area' activities became almost unfeasible, the party centre took steps to remove itself to the central soviet, accompanied by a migration of party members. The transfer of the centre was completed early in 1933, leaving only a skeletal liaison staff in Shanghai, who were soon arrested by the KMT police. The transfer not only exacerbated the struggle over issues and for power, but introduced many urban party members to day-to-day administration in the open countryside that was vastly different from clandestine work in cities. Their old styles of life, work and writing had to undergo appropriate modifications as they were now in close touch with a massive peasantry. Though facing similar difficulties, they differed from the old imperial officials, who under the principle of avoidance had to come in as outsiders, because they did not want to cultivate bureaucratism purposely. Yet they also differed from the old cadre in the soviet areas in the sense that the newcomers had neither participated in the creation of the base areas nor acquired the styles of peasant life and some understanding of local dialects, including Hakka. And they did not eliminate their disdain of the peasants, or prevent the growth of bureaucratism once they had gripped the helm of governmental power.[26]

[23] Hsiao Tso-liang, *Power relations*, 151; *She-hui hsin-wen*, 6.19–20 (27 February 1934), 264; Warren Kuo, *History*, 2.183–4.

[24] Wang Chien-min, *Chung-kuo kung-ch'an-tang shih-kao* (A draft history of the CCP), hereafter Wang Chien-min, *Draft history*, 2.503.

[25] *Hung-ch'i* (Red flag), no. 29 (25 January 1932); Warren Kuo, *History*, 2.335 and 367–8.

[26] Ts'ao Po-i, *Chiang-hsi su-wei-ai chih chien-li chi ch'i peng-k'uei* (The establishment and collape of the Kiangsi soviet), hereafter Ts'ao Po-i, *Soviet*, 464.

The mass line

Guerrilla fighters everywhere from Algeria to Cuba have depended upon the support of the masses for whom they fight. But the practice of winning popular support through propaganda and action does not necessarily imply a conceptualized 'mass line'. To be sure, both the party centre and the soviet leaders since the Sixth Congress of the CCP accorded high priority to the mobilization of the masses. In fact the political resolution of the Sixth Congress went as far as to say that in the soviet areas the party should expand itself into a mass organization,[27] while Mao in his *Hunan report* of 1927 commented, 'To talk about "arousing the masses of the people" day in and day out and then be scared to death when the masses do rise...'[28] Mass mobilization had become an urgent matter when the CCP in its first wave of migration to the countryside in 1927 encountered the people of rural China. At that time the members of the party had to define: Who were the peasants? How active were they in giving support to the revolution? Or how timid if they lost the protection of the Red Army, thus exposing themselves to reprisal by the reactionaries? How could they be more efficiently mobilized – through organization and technique or through policy and propaganda?

The views of the 28 Bolsheviks also began to change once they came in close touch with the peasant masses. They in no sense formed a monolithic bloc within the party now; nor did they all migrate into the central soviet. But none of them had fully accepted the mass line with all its connotations, as Mao advocated. Although the centre's directive of 1 September 1931 urged the central soviet to do its utmost in mass mobilization so as to consolidate the base area,[29] its tenor was clearly on mobilizing the masses through intensified class struggle. Its criticism of the vaguely phrased army slogan against 'rascals' instead of specifically against landlords, rich peasants and merchants, its insistence that rich peasants be given only poor land, and its dissatisfaction with the neglected anti-imperialist work, all illustrated this point. In the view of the centre, only by sharpening class distinctions and class struggle could the soviet arouse a broader mass of the oppressed. Its criticisms and suggestions were reflected in the resolutions of the first party representatives' conference, the First All-China Soviet Congress, which proclaimed the Chinese Soviet Republic at Juichin, Kiangsi, in November 1931, with Mao Tse-tung as president.[30] There were no indications in these early directives

27 *Hung-se wen-hsien*, 194.
28 Mao, *SW* 1.56.
29 Warren Kuo, *History*, 2.312.
30 Hsiao Tso-liang, *Power relations*, 165; Warren Kuo, *History*, 2.306.

that the campaigns could be a way of mobilization, no reference to caring for and cherishing the people, and no allowance for the people to supervise and criticize the work of the government and party.

Even in the fifth plenum, held in January 1934 at the height of the line of the 28 Bolsheviks, and before the decisive battles in 1934, the resolution on the present situation and the tasks of the party stated: 'the victory of the revolution depends upon the party, its Bolshevik political line and work, its unity of thought and action, its discipline and ability to lead the masses, and its opposition to any deviation from or distortion of the line of the International and the Chinese party.'[31] Only after the first serious military reverses in that year did dissensions and uncertainties appear in the statements and acts of even the leading 28 Bolsheviks. For example, Chang Wen-t'ien, generally regarded as one of the 28 who drew closest to Mao just before the Long March, said on the one hand

we must always follow the line of mobilizing the masses, working through them and relying on them, regardless whether we arrest and kill counter-revolutionary landlords and rich peasants, organize them into forced-labour corps, or confiscate and requisition their food-stuff. For the problem here is not simply to arrest and kill a few people or to confiscate and requisition some belongings of the landlords and rich peasants. *The problem is how to promote the activism of the masses, raise the degree of their consciousness, and rally and organize them round the soviet regime, when we carry out our clear and definite class line.*[32]

On the other hand, he tightened the 'red terror'. 'Red terror ought to be our reply to these counter-revolutionaries. We must, especially in the war zones and the border areas, deal immediately, swiftly with every kind of counter-revolutionary activity.'[33]

Mao's views on the same set of problems and his solutions to them, which admittedly were still in the process of development, showed a breadth of difference. As a founder of his base area, he had worked, fought and lived with the masses longer than any of the 28 Bolsheviks. Although he may not yet have conceptualized his experiences into a line of policy, the Ku-t'ien resolutions of December 1929 emphasized two essential points – the masses had the right to criticize the mistakes of the Red Army, helping it rectify its mistakes, and the party's resolutions were to be implemented through the masses.[34] To be sure, the Red Army was then dominated by the party commissars.[35] To criticize the army's errors was synonymous with criticizing the party. Mao defined the sources of the

[31] *Tou-cheng* (Struggle), 47 (16 February 1930).
[32] *Hung-se Chung-hua*, hereafter Red China, 28 June 1934. My italics.
[33] *Ibid.* 25 May 1934.
[34] MTTC 2.82.
[35] Party centre's directive to the soviet areas, 1 September 1931, in Warren Kuo, *History*, 2.302–4.

party's wisdom and ability to lead correctly in an unambiguous fashion: 'The upper-level organizations must clearly understand the conditions in the lower-level organizations and the living conditions of the masses. This will become the social origins of a correct leadership.'[36] This train of thought led in 1932 to the following conclusion: 'All the methods [of political and economic work] which are detached from the masses are bureaucratic.'[37]

To combat bureaucratism (that is, peremptoriness and pretentious infallibility) was, and still is, the most important single component of Mao's mass line. The required attitude was to be the willing pupils of the masses, not just their leaders, and not to regard the masses as clumsy and stupid country bumpkins but as people who deserved trust and must be involved in administration and political campaigns. Only in this way could the masses be aroused without doing damage to their voluntarism. In Mao's fairly developed conceptualization of the mass line (*ch'un-chung lu-hsien*) of 1933, no one – neither the vanguard nor the class – was presupposed to be perfect, hence the need of education for everyone. Through education for everyone, both the cadre and masses, bad habits and styles could be eliminated so that correct and reliable information might be transmitted from the grass roots to become the basis of correct policy decisions and so that the decisions might be carried out as intended.

In practical terms, this meant every possible care for livelihood and social justice among the people under soviet rule, once that rule was established by the army. The army itself undertook to propagandize and organize the people in preparation for setting up a regime, while land and other property were redistributed, counter-revolutionaries and reactionaries were punished, and relief was provided.[38] When the regime became firm, its economic and financial measures should be aimed at increasing production, facilitating trade, and sharing the tax burden fairly. In some cases, this might entail changes in the economic structure, for instance, cooperativization and mutual aid teams.[39] It might also entail the use of production drives and 'model workers'. Sometimes even the red soldiers took part in farming.[40] To mobilize women, the Soviet Republic introduced and adopted the Marriage Law of December 1931, while women's activities branched out from the hearth to the fields and battlefields.[41] The evacuation of the Red Army from Central China in 1934

[36] *MTTC* 2.82.   [37] *Ibid.* 3.168.
[38] 'The Ku-t'ien resolutions', *MTTC* 2.123.
[39] Information given by Wang Kuan-lan to Edgar Snow, *Random notes on Red China*, 38; *Red China*, 26 July 1934; Ts'ao Po-i, *Soviet*, 345–50; Edgar Snow, *Red star over China*, 183 and 253.
[40] *Red China*, 30 June 1934; Ts'ao Po-i, *Soviet*, 152–4; *HHLY* 2.100; *HCPP* 13.65.
[41] Mao, *SW* 1.142; Ch'ien T'ang, *Ko-ming ti nü-hsing* (Revolutionary women), 13–5; *HCPP* 11.166, 171 and 210.

enhanced the role of women in the remaining guerrilla areas. Less feared by the KMT soldiers and militia, the female activists gathered information, transported food and other necessities to the guerrillas, nursed the wounded, and fought.[42]

In the administration of the law, the masses must be clearly differentiated from their enemy and the laws made understandable to them. The Marriage Law and Labour Laws were obviously designed to protect them, while the laws and acts controlling the activities of counter-revolutionaries were to safeguard the soviet regime.[43] In the application of the mass line the regime became less concerned that justice be done than that justice be seen to be done. The hearings were therefore public under mass supervision, educating and warning the public at the same time.[44] However defective it may have been, the soviet judicial system impressed none other than the leading opponent of the CCP, General Ch'en Ch'eng: 'Its strength lies in its judicial consideration to the exclusion of personal feelings. Its beneficial consequence is shown in the scarcity of cases of embezzlement and corruption.'[45]

If one assumes that the mass line as defined by Mao had won the approval of the party leaders, it follows that the other soviets would have accepted it together with all its organizations and apparatus. It is true that the basic pattern of mass mobilization in the Hupei-Honan-Anhwei (O-Yü-Wan) soviet was similar, with perhaps less attention to economic work but more to the liberation of women than in the central soviet.[46] But the leader there, Chang Kuo-t'ao, had less confidence in the efficacy of land redistribution as a means to arouse people than in the strength of the Red Army to protect the mass work. Therefore he probably relied more on coercion than careful persuasion; and so military reverses often ended in the collapse of his mass work.[47] Conceptualized in this way, Chang's mass line differed from Mao's. Judging from extremely scanty information, the West Hupei and Hunan (Hsiang-o-hsi) soviet under the rough and tough Ho Lung seems to have developed a more elaborate network of mass organization in 1930-1. His soviet tackled problems of production and social welfare by launching production and land reclamation drives and campaigns against superstition, opium addiction and gambling. But Hsia Hsi, one of the 28 Bolsheviks, seems to have

---

[42] HCPP 1.74; 7.79–108; 9.176–8; 11.151, 200–8; HHLY 4.266–8.

[43] The soviet code was promulgated on 15 October 1933. See Ch'en Ch'eng Documents, roll. 16; Trygve Lötveit, Chinese communism, 1931–1934: experience in civil government, ch. 5, section B; Ts'ao Po-i, Soviet, 404–6.

[44] Ts'ao Po-i, Soviet, 413–14.

[45] Wang Chien-min, Draft history, 2.353.

[46] HHLY 2.462 and 6.379–80; Wang Chien-min, Draft history, 2.192.

[47] Chiao-fei chan-shih (History of the war to suppress the bandits), 4.685.

reversed this approach.[48] As to the other, smaller soviets, information is even scarcer. What is known is no more than that the Japanese discrimination against Chinese women in the factories in the north-east of China drove them to the arms of the guerrillas. And on Hainan island in the early 1930s there was a red detachment of 120 women commanded by Feng Tseng-min[49] – a heroic episode later adapted as the plot of one of the revolutionary operas.

Factionalism and defection

The history of the CCP has witnessed many factional fights, struggles for power in an attempt to control the course of the revolution.[50] Right at the beginning, the party was formed on clientelist ties mainly of the master-disciple type, with Li Ta-chao and Ch'en Tu-hsiu as the two revered figures. The lack of cooperation between them, though not yet carefully documented and analysed, was obvious and may have been attributable to doctrinal differences and personal disagreements. Both Li and Ch'en, being firmly committed Marxists, worked under conditions of intensifying persecution, but did not simply drop out like some of the other early party members. From 1927 onward, the whole revolutionary situation took a sharp turn. Outlawed, the dissidents could defect from the party only by going through a humiliating and agonizing process of confession to the KMT police or secret police, often entailing the betrayal of one's erstwhile comrades with no assurance of one's own safety. Refusal to do so could jeopardize one's life. Under such conditions, members of the party who held opposing views tended to indulge in factional struggles short of separatism or defection.

But to say that it was fear of reprisal that bound the party together in spite of factionalism is to underestimate the strength of the ideology. Whatever divergent opinions these factionalists possessed, they were still Communists fighting for a common goal. Ruptures among them were concerned essentially with organization and political lines; personal traits and power-seeking were secondary factors. In addition to ideology, there was also the 'iron discipline' of the party. It is true that a Communist throve on class hatred and was combative in character. This was, however, only one aspect of his personality; the other was a comradely love

---

[48] *HHLY* 2.100–2; Ho Lung's article in *HHLY* 1, pt. 2, 617.

[49] Ch'en Hsueh-chao, *Man-tsou chieh-fang-ch'ü* (Wanderings in the liberated areas), 94–5; *HHLY* 2.510–22.

[50] For a theoretical treatment, see Andrew J. Nathan, 'A factionalism model for CCP politics', *China Quarterly*, hereafter *CQ*, 53 (Jan.–Mar. 1973) 59; also Harrison, *Long March*, 149–51.

transcending the clientelist ties. The view that brutalization caused factionalism within the CCP must be taken with a large pinch of salt.[51]

Extreme factionalism was usually the precursor of either separatism or defection, both of which implied an ideological reorientation. A separatist might transfer from the predominant ideology of the party to another – Trotskyism in the case of Ch'en Tu-hsiu and P'eng Shu-chih – while a defector perceived a discord between belief and reality – for example, Li Ang, Kung Ch'u and Chang Kuo-t'ao. Dismissed from the party, Ch'en organized the Trotskyist opposition because in the later 1920s and early 1930s he felt that the 1927 debacle was chiefly the responsibility of the CI and he accepted Trotsky's criticism of it.[52] In the spring of 1929, P'eng Shu-chih received two articles by Trotsky – 'The past and future of the Chinese revolution' and 'The Chinese revolution after the Sixth Congress' – which he agreed with implicitly. This, together with his earlier opposition to Ch'ü Ch'iu-pai's putschism, led both him and Ch'en to Trotskyism and opposition to the CCP.[53] Their transfer of faith required a considerable measure of intellectual integrity.[54] Li Ang was quite different. He justified his defection in incredibly naive terms – he wanted to be on the side of the truth forever and he wanted to expose the dark aspects and the conspiracy of the Communist movement. He vehemently opposed the 'dictatorship of Mao Tse-tung', appraising it as 'more despotic than Hitler',[55] Kung Ch'u, an early leader in Kwangsi, left the party when its fortunes were at a nadir. His personal dissatisfaction apart, the main reasons for his action were that the CCP for eleven years had not worked for the independence, democracy and glory of the nation. On the contrary, the party had caused untold suffering to the people and deviated far from the goals of the revolution. It was no more than 'the claws and fangs' of the Soviet Union, 'a big lie'. In 1971, in another series of articles in the Hong Kong monthly Ming-pao, Kung repeated the same reasons for his defection.[56]

51 Harrison, Long march, 149; Ezra Vogel, 'From friendship to comradeship', CQ 21 (Jan.–Mar. 1965) 46–59.

52 Ch'en Tu-hsiu, 'Kao ch'uan-tang t'ung-chih-shu' (Letter to all the comrades of the party), 10 December 1929, 7b–8a. For the other reasons for Ch'en's separatism, see Lin Chin's article in She-hui hsin-wen, 9.8 (11 December 1934) 296–300; and Thomas C. Kuo, Ch'en Tu-hsiu (1879–1942) and the Chinese Communist movement, ch. 8.

53 P'eng Shu-chih, 'Jang li-shih ti wen-chien tso-cheng' (Let historical documents be my witness), Ming-pao yueh-k'an (Ming Pao monthly), hereafter Ming-pao, 30.18–19.

54 It is because of this that Chinese separatist literature should be treated differently from Chinese defector literature. In this respect, students of the CCP do not share the fortune of their colleagues in the Russian field, where a large body of good and reliable defector literature is available.

55 Li Ang, Hung-se wu-t'ai (The red stage), 189 and 192. Li even claims to have been a participant of the First Congress of the CCP: ibid.75–6. Li's book is probably one of the least reliable of its genre.

56 Kung Ch'u, Wo yü hung-chün (The Red Army and I), 2–10, 445.

The process of separatism and defection, not necessarily a protracted one, usually started from differences over issues. When these differences grew in intensity, the actor's belief system itself disintegrated, resulting in his increasing estrangement from the formerly accepted ideology, while he himself went through a period of negativeness and alienation from his comrades. At this stage, a separatist needed an alternative ideology to believe in, whereas a defector had to find an opportunity to survive. If the transfer was from a logically more coherent to a less rigorous ideology (as from communism to Sun Yat-sen's Three Principles of the People), the rationale for the transfer might strike a false note, suggesting opportunism and sheer perfidy. Kung Ch'u's case illustrates this process well. He seems to have had some difficulty in convincing the KMT of his good faith and so he was ordered by the KMT to destroy some red guerrilla bands on the Kiangsi-Kwangtung border and even to attempt to seek out Hsiang Ying and Ch'en I in south Kiangsi.[57] Other defectors, such as Ku Shun-chang, K'ung Ho-ch'ung *et al.*, were either captured by or surrendered to the KMT with almost no ideological concern.

Chang Ku-t'ao was both a separatist and a defector (as to his separatism, see below, p. 211). Arriving at Yenan on 2 December 1936, ten days before the detention of Chiang Kai-shek in Sian, when the policy line he had presented at the Mao-erh-kai Conference in 1935 had completely failed, Chang felt alienated and sank into a negative mood. Then there came the public humiliation of the struggles against him (the 'trials of Chang Kuo-t'ao') in February and November 1937, at which he was accused of all kinds of hideous crimes against the party. Before the return of Wang Ming from Moscow, he had a faint hope of a possible alliance with Wang in opposition to Mao Tse-tung. When Wang came and accused him of 'being a tool of the Trotskyists', his disappointment in the Communist cause in China was complete. It was not the party he had helped found; nor was it the party he wanted.

Earlier he had doubted the viability of the rural soviet movement. Without a proletarian base, only petty bourgeois in nature, he thought the soviets were merely a disguise for power and territorial occupation which had nothing to do with the welfare of the nation.[58] Leaping from one ideology to another, Chang found nationalism and Chiang Kai-shek. He agreed with Mao's Ten Point Programme for the anti-Japanese united front, but blamed Mao for betraying his own principles for the seizure of power and territory. He regarded Mao as no more than 'a traitor in

[57] *HHLY* 4.117–18; *HCPP* 3.229–33.
[58] *Ming-pao*, 57.95; 60.88–90; 61.83–4. See Chang's message to the nation (20 May 1938) in *Ming-pao*, 62; an earlier version appeared in Chang Kuo-t'ao, Liu Ning *et al.*, *I-ko kung-jen ti kung-chuang chi ch'i-t'a* (A working man's confession and other essays), 4.

communist skin', whereas Chiang's effort in the anti-Japanese war should be supported unreservedly since it was anti-imperialist, and Chiang's work in unifying China should be supported also, since it was anti-feudal. As his 'leftist day-dreams' were rudely awakened and Chiang fitted perfectly into the formula of an anti-feudal and anti-imperialist bourgeois national revolution, Chang felt no qualms in his reorientation. Legally speaking one could leave the party voluntarily; therefore Chang thought that there was no question of either betrayal or treachery. Beneath his personal alienation and ideological considerations, his rivalry with Mao cannot be denied. A full generation after his departure from the CCP, he still described his old rival with blazing emotion – 'dictatorial', 'unreasonable to the extent of being barbaric', 'narrow-minded', 'selfish', 'short-sighted', 'ruthless', 'scheming', 'hypocritical', and even 'aspiring to become an emperor of China'.[59]

CREATION OF RURAL SOVIETS

Since the collapse of the first united front in July 1927, the major preoccupation of the CCP had been to create sanctuaries in rural China wherein lay a possibility to continue the revolution and a hope to bring it to final victory. There seemed to be no other feasible choice for that outlawed and persecuted party. These sanctuaries were in fact *imperia in imperio*. Their creation required an army and that was why the Fifth Congress of the CCP at Hankow in April 1927 toyed with three ideas – to push eastward from Central China to defeat Chiang Kai-shek; to march southward to take Canton; or to strengthen the revolutionary forces in Hupei and Hunan. In the absence of any armed force none of these aims could be accomplished.[60] Belatedly, by the end of May 1927, the ECCI advised the CCP to agitate for army mutiny and organize workers' and peasants' troops in order to give teeth to the revolution.[61] This train of thought developed into the CI's call for revolt in July.

The insurrections of 1927

For the rest of the year, in response to this call, the CCP staged a series of insurrections – in Nanchang, Kiangsi on 1 August, the Autumn

---

[59] *Ming-pao*, 56.86 and 93; 58.89; 59.85–6, 60.85; 61.93–4; 62.85–8. See also Chang's preface to Kung Ch'u, *Wo yü hung-chün*, iii–iv.

[60] Harrison, *Long march*, 105.

[61] Jane Degras, *The Communist International 1919–1943: documents*, 2.390. For the description of the Nanchang uprising, I rely chiefly on C. Martin Wilbur, 'The ashes of defeat', *CQ* 18 (April–June 1964) 3–54.

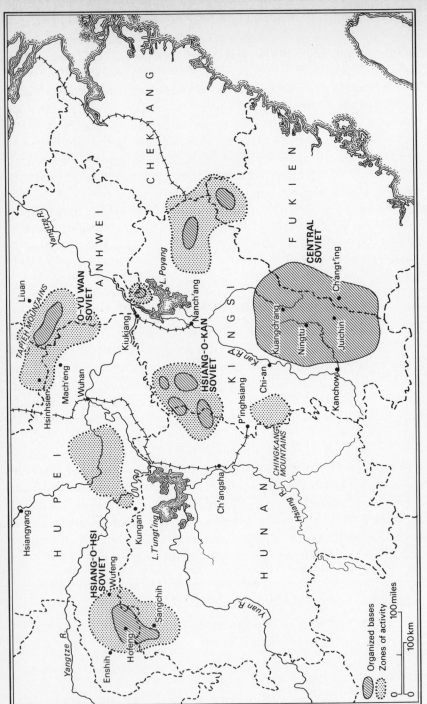

MAP 5. Chinese Communist areas, early 1930s

Harvest uprisings, chiefly in Hupei and Hunan from August to October, and the Canton commune in December. In a sense they were the continuation of the three ideas broached at the Fifth Congress under the assumptions that the city must lead the countryside, that the decisive struggle must be waged in the cities, and that the tide of revolution was rising.

Why Nanchang of all places? The superiority of the Communist and pro-Communist military strength (especially that of the leftist Chang Fa-k'uei) explains the choice of the location of the first armed uprising organized by the CCP. It may have been hoped that by taking this important city, which lay between the quarrelling Nanking and Wuhan, the Communists would be able to turn the whole situation to their favour.[62] Not an industrial city of great importance, Nanchang provided no proletarian base. There was no peasant participation either. Under the command of Chou En-lai, most of the people who took part in the uprising were KMT troops under Communist influence and the revolutionary youth of Hupei and Hunan.[63]

In spite of accusations that poor training and organization of the army units and a lack of coordination and mass support had caused the uprising to fail, the retreating armies from Nanchang under Yeh T'ing, Ho Lung and Chu Teh showed, however, the first of the signs that were to characterize the Red Army later. Chu's 25th Army, which had a large number of revolutionary youths as its low-ranking officers, dispersed into companies and platoons for political propaganda and land confiscation.[64] Yeh and Ho launched their land programme of confiscating landlords' and communal land for redistribution among poor peasants and reducing rent to a maximum of 30 per cent in Ch'ao-chow and Swatow in Kwangtung.[65] Even at this early stage, these units were already different from other troops in China.

After the defeat at Nanchang, the CCP called its historic emergency conference on 7 August 1927 – the type of conference that the 'real work' group demanded later in January 1931. It is not certain whether the party was doctrinally under the persuasion of the CI representatives B. Lominadze and his successor, H. Neumann, who held that Chinese society was less feudal than it was Asiatic with small, fragmented units

[62] Jerome Ch'en, *Mao and the Chinese revolution*, 129; cf. Guillermaz, *A history*, ch. 12.
[63] Su Yü in *HHLY* 1, pt. 1, 19; Chin Fan, *Tsai Hung-chün ch'ang-cheng ti tao-lu shang* (On the route of the Red Army's Long March), 10–11; 'Nan-ch'ang ta-shih chi' (Important events at Nanchang), in *Chin-tai-shih tzu-liao* (Materials of modern history), 4 (1957) 130. Most of these young people were members of either the CCP or the Youth Corps.
[64] Yang Ch'eng-wu in *HHLY* 1, pt. 1, 101.
[65] *Hua-tzu jih-pao* (The Chinese mail), 28 and 30 September 1927.

of production as its chief characteristic. Its bourgeoisie (represented by the KMT) therefore was also weak and disunited, quite unable to lead the bourgeois democratic revolution to completion, which thus stood a good chance of being propelled straight into a socialist stage without interruption, if it was assisted by a foreign proletariat.[66] The 'letter to the comrades' issued after the emergency conference[67] refused, on the one hand, to recognize the land revolution as an anti-feudal revolt but on the other asserted the bourgeois democratic nature of the Chinese revolution. The transition from its present stage to the next was conceived as possibly an uninterrupted one. The conference also stressed the interrelation between the national and social revolutions; the anti-imperialist and anti-feudal struggles were interlocked to make the peasants' participation in them absolutely necessary. Seen from this perspective, the Autumn Harvest uprisings of 1927, that unleashed an attack from the countryside on the cities without planned urban insurrections to give it support, were vastly different from the endeavour a week earlier at Nanchang and provided the only feasible counteraction to the KMT repression.[68]

The Autumn Harvest uprisings, 'tak[ing] advantage of the harvesting period of this year to intensify the class struggle', were directed at the overthrow of the Wuhan government of the left KMT, to create a state within a state so that the CCP could survive to carry on the revolution. It was planned to cover the Hunan-Kiangsi border, south Hupei, the Hupei-Hunan border, south Kiangsi, north-west Kiangsi, and other places from Hainan to Shantung.[69] The three components of the strategy were: to use assorted armed forces as a shield to protect and arm the peasants, to seize local power either to transfer it into peasant committees or restructure it into soviets, and to redistribute land. The key to the success of the strategy was the expectation that the peasants could become an effective combat force so that the gains of the uprisings could be preserved and enlarged to win victory in one or more provinces. As this assumption was proved invalid, the uprisings were doomed.

However, this is not to say that the peasants, especially those in the hills, were unready for insurrection. If they were unready, the rest of the land revolution cannot be explained, except by an unconvincing conspiracy theory. Nor was the failure due to the leaders' conscious neglect of the peasants. Both the party centre and Mao, for example, regarded workers

---

[66] Thornton, *Comintern*, 5 and 15–16.
[67] *Hung-se wen-hsien*, 93–135.
[68] Brandt *et al. Documentary history*, 118. Hsiang Chung-fa did start an abortive strike in Wuhan in support of the uprisings. See *Hua-tzu jih-pao*, 5 August 1927.
[69] Brandt *et al. Documentary history*, 122. For this geographic plan, consult Roy Hofheinz, 'The Autumn Harvest insurrection', *CQ* 32 (Oct.–Dec. 1967) 37–87.

and peasants as the main force of the uprisings.[70] Strategic errors abounded. The party conceived the attack on cities from countryside as being a short process; starting from county towns the armies were to capture large cities and then to overthrow the Wuhan government in a matter of months or weeks. When the party found that even the county towns were either too well defended or too hotly disputed to be taken by the motley troops under Mao and the other leaders of the uprisings, it then scaled down its ambitions to a more cautious and protracted guerrilla warfare in remote rural areas like Ching-kang-shan.[71] From the ashes of defeat, Mao reorganized his troops in one regiment (enormous compared with what his comrades in the Hupei-Honan border region and West Hunan could muster) and made a new start. Not until the summer of 1928 did he have a relatively stable base area incorporating one or two county towns, but still relying on mountainous terrain for safety. The future O-Yü-Wan base took and held its first county town, Shang-ch'eng, only in the winter of 1929 and the base area was formally created as late as the eve of Li Li-san's adventures.[72] Ho Lung arrived back in his home county towards the end of 1927 with only eight rifles and twenty members of the party, and did not rally enough following to capture two county towns till May 1929. Although the November conference of the Politburo recognized these strategic mistakes, it did not share the feeling of loneliness and ebbing tide of revolution that hit the guerrilla leaders fighting in the mountains and hills. At this stage of the revolution, as Mao put it in one of his reports, 'You [the party centre] desire us not to be concerned with the military but at the same time want a mass armed force.'[73] There seems to have been both a lack of experience in military operations and costly hesitation, to bear out what Mao said in 1938: 'war had not been made the centre of gravity in the party's work'.[74]

In mass work, too, experience was lacking. Discussion of when and how the soviet form of government should be introduced seems to have hung on such criteria as whether China in 1927 was comparable to Russia in 1905 (that is, ready for a bourgeois revolution) or in 1917 (a socialist revolution). Li-ling in Hunan saw its first soviet at the beginning of the

---

[70] Brandt *et al. Documentary history*, 122; *Chung-yang t'ung-hsin* (Central newsletter), 6 (20 September 1927), in *MTTC* 2.13.

[71] Even a county town like Huang-an in Hupei was under too strong an attack for the Communists to hold it for any length of time. See Hsu Hsiang-ch'ien and Cheng Wei-san in *HHLY* 2.363–77 and 1, pt. 2, 734–55 respectively. See also Lo Jung-huan, in *HHLY* 1, pt. 1, 139–40 and Huang Yung-sheng in *HCPP* 13.7.

[72] Hsu Hsiang-ch'ien, *ibid.*; Ch'en Po-lu in *HHLY* 1, pt. 2, 795–9.

[73] Ho Lung in *HHLY* 1, pt. 2, 603–14; Hsiao Tso-liang, *Chinese communism in 1927: city vs. countryside*, 110; *Chung-yang t'ung-hsin*, 5 (30 August 1927), in *MTTC* 2.13.

[74] Mao, *SW* 2.236.

Autumn Harvest uprisings.[75] This and later soviets were formed largely by utilizing old social ties centred on the gentry, for example the clan associations, rural schools and militia units. Sometimes even secret societies were useful. The radicalized and educated young people returned to their native villages from the suppressed cities to infiltrate these organizations both for sanctuary and for agitation. From these organizations they obtained men, arms and money for the creation of soviet base areas. They made their mistakes and paid for them dearly. But by the end of 1927 there appeared clearly two streams of communism in China – the rural soviets and the urban leadership; the former had to be led by the latter, else the whole movement might have sunk into the traditional pattern of Chinese peasant rebellions. As the rural soviets were still weak and unstable, the establishment of the central authority was not particularly arduous.

Continuing to regard the tide of revolution as rising, Ch'ü Ch'iu-pai and the urban leadership went on with their insurrections in I-hsing and Wusih in Kiangsu, Wuhan in Hupei, Nan-k'ou and Tientsin in Hopei – all miserable failures.[76] Then occurred the Canton commune of 11 December 1927. In the background was Stalin's desire, expressed through the CI, for a victory of China to justify his policy there in the face of Trotsky's criticisms. As Yeh Chien-ying recalled, 'A revolutionary must find a direction for him to go forward.' After the Nanchang uprising Canton seemed the only hope of proving that the CCP could not be bullied by its enemies and that a victory in one province was still feasible.[77] The decision to stage such an uprising was indeed taken at the November conference of the party centre, but the operation was directed by the people on the spot who, once again, cherished a forlorn hope of Chang Fa-k'uei's cooperation.[78] When it failed, any attempt to capture a major city was shelved till Li Li-san's actions in the summer of 1930. The revolution was decidedly at a low ebb; no major action could be contemplated.

The need for bases

Small actions towards the end of 1927 included the establishment of base areas in almost inaccessible places – Ching-kang-shan, the Tapieh Mountains, the Hung Lake region, north Szechwan, and the Left and

---

[75] HHLY 1, pt. 1, 164. On the role of the radical, educated people, see J. M. Polachek, 'The moral economy of the Kiangsi soviet (1928–1934)', JAS 42.4 (Aug. 1983) 805–29.

[76] Ch'ü Ch'iu-pai, 'Chung-kuo hsien-chuang yü Kung-ch'an-tang ti jen-wu' (The present situation in China and the tasks of the CCP), report at the November conference, in Hu Hua, 200–22.

[77] Yeh in HHLY 1, pt. 1, 196–7.

[78] Hsiao Tso-liang, Power relations, 147–8.

Right Rivers of Kwangsi – where the rebels had security and could carry on the struggle.[79] But the revolutionaries had to ask: was it necessary to have a base area? Could they win peasants' support? What would be the future of the revolution from the purview of the mountain fastness?

At the beginning of the Ching-kang-shan soviet, Mao told his soldiers:

> While working for the revolution, we cannot simply run here and there. We must have a home; otherwise we will get into all sorts of difficulties. The base area is our home from which we carry on revolutionary struggles against the enemy. If he does not come, we train soldiers and mobilize the masses here; if he comes, we fight him from our home. We chew up or drive away our enemies bit by bit and our days will gradually improve.[80]

The truth is that the red soldiers and their party, engaged in building a base area, needed men and money which could be procured only by confiscating the property of the rich and distributing some of it to the poor. Afraid of reprisals, the poor peasants would not take part in land and property confiscation and redistribution, unless the shield of the Red Army was strong enough to protect them and give the new property system a measure of permanency. Once the new system became settled, the red regime could legitimately recruit soldiers and tax the people. In a sense this was similar to a warlord's satrapy, except that the warlord protected the gentry instead of the poor peasants. By having a sufficiently strong army to defend the new property system and the red regime, the party hoped to introduce social and economic changes with the effect of arousing the loyalty of the poor and oppressed. Mao and a few others like Fang Chih-min had faith in this strategy, while Chang Kuo-t'ao believed that the peasants, opportunistic and concerned only with their own survival, gave support to the Red Army only when the army was winning. In Chang's view, peasant mobilization hinged entirely on the CCP's military strength; it had nothing to do with the land policy.[81]

That the peasants were active and responsive enough to give their allegiance to the CCP as a result of land redistribution appears from another source of information and assessment – the missionaries and foreign journalists who had first-hand knowledge of the Communists in

---

[79] About the 'ecology' of the Chinese Communist success, see Roy Hofheinz's essay under that title in *Chinese Communist politics in action*, ed. A. Doak Barnett. In Hofheinz's essay quoted here and his earlier article on the Autumn Harvest uprisings (*CQ* 32), he overlooks the existence of peasant associations at Ching-kang-shan. In his report dated 25 November 1928 (*MTTC* 2.61), Mao referred to basic work of the party among the masses in Ching-kang-shan more than a year before his arrival there. About the foundation of the Ching-kang-shan base area, see the detailed discussion with the staff of the museum there on 7 and 8 July 1980, reported by Jerome Ch'en under the title 'Ideology and history' (xeroxed for circulation).

[80] Speech recorded by Huang Yung-shen in *HCPP* 13.8. See Mao's report on 25 November 1928 in *MTTC* 2.28 and 47–8.

[81] Chang in *Ming-pao*, 46.99.

Central China. As early as 1931 an article in the *Chinese Recorder* (a leading missionary journal) admitted that 'god-less as they were', the Communists had the 'support of millions of peasants and workers'.[82] Popular periodicals like the *China Weekly Review* (an American journal published in Shanghai) reported peasants' support of the Communists throughout 1933 and 1934.[83] When the Communists left for the Long March, Hallett Abend and A. J. Billingham inspected the areas formerly under Communist occupation, where they discovered that the peasants preferred the CCP to the KMT.[84] It was this support that enabled the red regimes to survive before the Long March and enabled the guerrilla areas to continue after it. It is curious that in discussing this problem scholars generally ignore the reports by foreign missionaries from Hunan, Kiangsi, Fukien and other provinces affected by the soviet movement.

As soon as the groundwork of the base area was laid, the revolutionaries had to choose between two long-range strategies. The first would be to give up the small base area in the mountains, whose economic resources were inadequate for a large-scale operation, and instead roam about the countryside fighting guerrilla warfare. This strategy would spread the political influence of the party through propaganda and economic dislocation until guerrillas were ready and able to seize power in a nation-wide insurrection. The second strategy would be to hold on to and expand the base area, while organizing and arming the masses, wave after wave outwardly. This would aim at enhancing the influence of the red regime in an orderly manner, benefiting the peasants at the same time, and hastening the arrival of a revolutionary upsurge.[85]

Following a pattern similar to that of Ching-kang-shan, the O-Yü-Wan, Hsiang-o-hsi, and a few other soviets emerged along the foothill regions of China between her highlands to the south and west and the plains to the north and east. The existence of soviets in this region and the unusually frequent civil wars, hence the concentration of troops there, suggest a correlation between the establishment of soviets and peasant misery, which deserves careful and systematic research. The civil wars and concentration of troops in this region in the 1910s and 1920s may have created a social and economic dislocation more severe than, say, on the plains of China. To study the plains, rather than this region, and to come to the conclusion that peasant misery had only marginal relevance to rebellion is like tasting chalk and rating it as cheese. By 1930 the thirteen

[82] *Chinese Recorder* 13 (June 1931) 468.
[83] See for instance, *China Weekly Review*, 22 July 1933, 18 November 1933 and 13 January 1934.
[84] Hallett Abend *et al. Can China survive?*, 238–9.
[85] Mao's letter to Lin Piao, 5 January 1930, in *MTTC* 2.128–9.

or so soviets probably had 300 counties under various degrees of Communist control or influence. The guerrilla bands that did not create soviets, such as those led by K'uang Chi-hsun in Szechwan between July and October 1929, vanished into oblivion.[86]

The rich peasant problem

The soviets set out to confiscate land and mobilize the poor peasants, a task usually allocated to revolutionary committees or village and district soviets, which were initially dominated by immigrant intellectuals from cities and towns.[87] This fact implied that a passive role was played by the politically inexperienced peasants and that party cells tended to overshadow the administrative organizations.[88] A period of six months was normally needed for the peasants to break through their passivity and scepticism, and thus involve themselves first in economic problems such as grain scarcity and taxation and then political matters such as the class struggle.[89] Once the wall of passivity was pulled down, the land revolution helped release the long pent-up hatred of the poor against the rich and inspired them to participate more actively in military and political work. To reach through to this peasant activism was the very essence of the land revolution. It is nonetheless an irony that the intellectual thinking of the CCP at that time paid scant attention to this process of politicization and activization of the poor peasants. All the while the party's attention and eulogies went to the urban proletariat, which was bogged down in economic struggles for more money and better working conditions, both issues of limited political significance.

The land policy of the CCP fell victim to the wrangling for power between Stalin and Bukharin. Based on Lenin's attitude towards the kulaks and the Russian experience that the kulaks exploited the masses even more cruelly and savagely than had the landlords, the CI instructed the CCP on 20 June 1929 to radicalize its policy toward rich peasants. Consequently, the Kiangsi soviet in February 1930 adopted a land law that stipulated the confiscation of all communal, landlords' and rich peasants' land; and the conference of the soviet areas held in May 1930 (without Mao Tse-tung)

[86] Hu Hua, *Chung-kuo hsin-min-chu chu-i ko-ming-shih ts'an-k'ao tzu-liao* (Historical materials on the Chinese new democratic revolution); hereafter *Materials*, 230. Estimates of the size, population and strength of the red armies vary widely. Indeed, even the concept of 'Communist occupation' requires stringent definition, as Hofheinz has pointed out (n. 79 above). Although K'uang lost his Szechwan soviet, his guerrilla activities continued in the border region between Szechwan, Hupei and Hunan, as frequently reported in the *Shih-pao* (The eastern times) of Shanghai.

[87] About the structure and functions of the soviet governments, see Lötveit, *Communism* and Kim, *Politics*.

[88] Mao's report of 25 November 1929 in *MTTC* 2.51–2.

[89] Po-ku (Ch'in Pang-hsien) related this experience to Snow, *Random notes*, 19.

advocated the confiscation of that part of rich peasants' land which was rented out to others to farm.[90]

Down at the soviet level the rich peasants presented a tough practical problem. When their vital interests were threatened, they obstructed the work of land redistribution. Trade between the base areas and the nearby towns was in their hands and they could stop this with dire consequences to the Communists. This experience was reflected in the Ching-kang-shan land law of December 1928.[91] Later the land law of Hsing-kuo, April 1929, adopted a milder attitude toward rich peasants.[92] Probably due to the same considerations, the rich peasants of the O-Yü-Wan soviet retained their land up to 1931. Neither the Hsiang-o-hsi nor Hsiang-kan soviet pursued a rigorous policy towards rich peasants.[93]

When the 28 Bolsheviks took power at the party centre, the rich peasant issue sharpened. Mao's way of curbing the influence of the rich peasants by taking away their 'surplus land' (ch'ou-to pu-shao) in the first land redistribution and by taking away their 'good land' (ch'ou-fei pu-shou) in the second redistribution,[94] without violating the principle of equality, came under fire at the fourth plenum in January 1931.[95] He was directed to change his policy by the centre's letter dated 1 September 1931. To be sure, the rich peasant question formed an important link in the centre's class line which was deemed essential to mobilizing the poor masses. What the centre wanted was to give only poor land to the rich peasants while no compensation was to be considered for the landlords. Theoretically, Mao did not regard all rich peasants as exploiters. They could be semi-landlords or semi-capitalists, but they could also be merely potential exploiters.[96] The 28 Bolsheviks, on the other hand, defined rich peasants as those who 'before the revolution, rented a part of their land, loaned money at usurious rates of interest, and usually hired labour'. They were

[90] On the CI directive, see *Hung-se wen-hsien*, 324–7 and Thornton, *Comintern*, 87–91. This and other directives of the CI, contrary to Thornton's impression, are couched in vague terms. The kulak problem, this particular instruction says, could be relegated to a secondary position when the war against imperialists and reactionaries became embittered. It was probably on this qualification that Li Li-san reversed his land policy in the summer of 1930. For texts of these laws see Wang Chien-min, *Draft history*, 2.357–61. But it would be wrong to say that Li Li-san's land law of May 1930 represented a sharp turn towards a radical policy against the rich peasants. As it did not insist upon the liquidation of the kulaks, it stood to the right of the CI instructions.

[91] *MTTC* 2.67–9 and also 47 and 56.

[92] *Ibid.* 2.73–5 and 179–84.

[93] Wang Chien-min, *Draft history*, 2.191–2 and 245–8; *HHLY* 2.99–100.

[94] Ho Kan-chih, *Chung-kuo hsien-tai ko-ming shih* (History of the modern Chinese revolution), 1.143. The Chinese edition of this book is far superior to its English translation published in 1960.

[95] *Hung-se wen-hsien*, 236.

[96] Resolution no. 2 adopted by the Joint Meeting of the Front Committee and the Western Fukien Special Committee, June 1930 in Hsiao Tso-liang, *The land revolution in China, 1930–1934: a study of documents*, 153–5.

thus plainly exploiters.[97] To treat them leniently was to blur the class line or to abandon class struggle altogether.[98]

The difference between taking away a part of the 'good land' of a rich peasant and giving him only 'poor land' might seem trivial. Certain facts, however, should be borne in mind. First, the expansion of soviet areas to include cities and towns and the growth of a trading system under the soviet government or in the form of cooperatives drastically reduced the mercantile function of the rich peasants, whose interests could be impaired for the sake of mobilizing the masses. Second, the rich peasants, making use of clan associations to conceal their actual land holdings, prevented the land revolution from being carried out thoroughly. This became evident during the land investigation campaign of 1933. Third, they leased land from the orphaned or the widowed, the aged or the young, because they had more able-bodied men in their families, more farming animals, more tools, and more liquid capital. Fourth, by falsifying their class category, they could infiltrate and take control of the poor peasants' corps, cooperatives and other mass organizations to make the land revolution and mass mobilization in some places a farce.[99] Therefore from 1931 onward, the land laws of the newly established Soviet Republic of China accepted the class line of the 28 Bolsheviks by distributing only poor land to rich peasants while confiscating their surplus tools, livestock and houses.[100] To what extent this new anti-kulak line was implemented cannot be ascertained. In O-Yü-Wan, Chang Kuo-t'ao accepted this line and seems to have pushed the policy of the First Congress of the Soviet Republic (held in November 1931) with vigour.[101] After the transfer of his soviet to north Szechwan in 1933, Chang and his comrades intensified their drive against rich peasants. Elsewhere, the new line was carried out only half-heartedly.[102] It was to accelerate the struggle against rich peasants that the land investigation campaign was launched.

---

[97] Centre's letter, 10 January 1932 in Wang Chien-min, *Draft history*, 2.508.

[98] Hsiao Tso-liang, *Land revolution*, 49.

[99] *MTTC* 2.166–7; Wang Chien-min, *Draft history*, 2.508.

[100] *MTTC* 2.259–62; Ts'ao Po-i, *Soviet*, 192–3 and 495; Hsiao Tso-liang, *Land revolution*, 53. Land transactions, however, were allowed in Wang Ming's 'Two lines' (*Hsuan-chi*, 3.61). According to the land policy of the First Congress of the Soviet Republic, landlords and rich peasants were not permitted to purchase land. Slightly later, notice no. 2 issued by the Central Revolutionary Military Commission gave rich peasants the right to buy or sell land but they were not allowed to do it in a monopolistic fashion. The questions are: who was actually buying and selling land in the soviet areas and who had the money to buy? See *MTTC* 2.262.

[101] *Ming-pao* 40.98; Wang Chien-min, *Draft history*, 2.245.

[102] For experiences in Hsiang-o-hsi and Hsiang-kan, see Wang Chien-min, *Draft history*, 2.245 and 249–51; *HHLY* 2.99.

The land investigation

Precisely who was responsible for launching this campaign is not easy to say. For a work of this magnitude and importance it is inconceivable that the party centre had no part in the decision, and without involving the entire structure of the soviet government it is doubtful that the decision could be implemented. The party centre in 1933 was firmly in the hands of the 28 Bolsheviks, and yet no one is sure to what extent the influence of the centre reached down to the grass roots. On the other hand, before 1934 Mao was still the dominant figure in the government with his prestige riding high among the masses. In all probability, the campaign began as a joint effort using the authority of the party and the prestige of Mao, a combination of the class line and mass line.[103] In the first phase of the campaign, between June and September 1933, it was obvious that Mao was responsible. Then in October the party centre stepped in to announce its new policy, which interrupted, and for a time suspended the movement till the convocation of the Second Congress of the Soviet Republic held in January-February 1934. Thereafter Chang Wen-t'ien, as the chairman of the People's Commissariat, took it over.[104]

The military situation at the end of the fourth KMT encirclement, when the campaign began, was favourable to the CCP, although food had become a serious problem. Since March 1933 a series of measures had been taken to counteract the KMT blockade – such as setting up a Food Board (Liang-shih t'iao-chieh chü), investigating the supply of foodstuff in the counties, and the prohibition of cornering grain by merchants.[105] Because they were otherwise preoccupied, the soviet government also encouraged the masses to help officials and cadres farm their shares of land.[106] Finally, the land investigation campaign was decreed.[107] Its main purpose was not to redistribute land again, unless the masses demanded it; rather it was to investigate the class background of as many people as possible without affecting production.[108] It was hoped that in this way the hidden counter-revolutionaries and feudal elements could be ferreted out and at the same time the enthusiasm of the masses could be heightened in order to consolidate the defence of the soviet area against the forthcoming fifth encirclement. Take the poor peasants' corps, for instance. In some places

103 Warren Kuo, *History*, 2.409–12; Ts'ao Po-i, *Soviet*, 203–5; Lötveit, 154–84.
104 For instance, all the directives on the land investigation were now issued by Chang Wen-t'ien.
105 Directive of the Central People's Commissariat, 4 March 1933 in *MTTC* 3.195–6 and 3.195–6.
106 Directive of the Central Executive Committee, 14 April 1933, *MTTC* 3.207–8.
107 Directive of the Central People's Commissariat, 1 June 1933, *MTTC* 3.223ff.
108 *MTTC* 3.254.

they existed in name only and in other places they had not even been organized until after the campaign was in progress.[109]

Class categorization was obviously a vital but complex problem, especially when it came to deciding who were the kulaks and who were the rich middle peasants. According to Mao's definition, given on 29 June 1933,

The rich peasant as a rule owns land. But some rich peasants own only part of their land and rent the remainder. Others have no land of their own at all and rent all their land. The rich peasant generally has rather more and better instruments of production and more liquid capital than the average and is engaged in labour himself, but always relies on exploitation for part or even the major part of his income. His main form of exploitation is the hiring of labour (long-term labourers). In addition, he may lease part of his land and practise exploitation through land rent, or may lend money or engage in industry and commerce. Most rich peasants also engage in the administration of communal land. A person who owns a fair amount of good land, farms some of it himself without hiring labour, but exploits other peasants by means of land rent, loan interest or in other ways, shall also be treated as a rich peasant. Rich peasants regularly practise exploitation and may derive most of their income from this source.[110]

One can imagine that such a complex definition was difficult to apply. Indeed, the second resolution of the party centre on 8 August 1933 noted the confusion caused by this definition.[111] Subsequently the People's Commissariat took it upon itself to discuss some of the problems arising from the land struggle. A rich peasant was redefined as one whose exploitative income amounted to more than 15 per cent of the total. With this new definition there was the need for a reinvestigation and re-categorization. In Sheng-li county alone, 1,512 households out of 3,125 were changed from landlords or rich peasants to middle or poor peasants; the investigation of class background thus dwindled into a calculation of class background. The situation became an unholy chaos.[112]

If Mao's statistics are to be trusted, the campaign up to September 1933 had succeeded in recovering 307,539 piculs of land (land was measured by its yield in some parts of Kiangsi) and confiscated property worth Y606,916. He also reported that in some counties production had increased by 15-20 per cent from 1932 to 1933.[113] To put these figures in their proper perspective, note that the soviet government floated a public loan of Y3 million in July 1933, issued Y10 million of currency in 1933-34,

---

[109] *MTTC* 3.223 and 257; *Tou-cheng*, 24 May 1934; Wang Kuan-lan in *HHLY* 2.211.
[110] Mao, *SW* 1.138.
[111] Ts'ao Po-i, *Soviet*, 211-12.
[112] *Tou-cheng*, 26 May 1934; Chang Wen-t'ien's directive in *Red China*, 15 March 1934.
[113] *Red China*, Second Soviet Congress Supplement, 26 January 1934.

and borrowed 600,000 piculs of grain from the people in July 1933.[114] As an economic measure, the land investigation campaign cannot be described as a seminal success.

When it was resumed in January 1934, the aims of the campaign were no longer principally economic, not even for the food supply to the Red Army, but political. It became a campaign against counter-revolutionaries, a red terror against landlords and rich peasants.[115] As such, it was pursued till the collapse of the central soviet.

The Red Army

The struggle in the border area, as Mao put it, 'is exclusively military'.[116] But since the failure of the Autumn Harvest uprisings followed by the reorganization of his troops at San-wan on his way to Ching-kang-shan, Mao, like the other creators of border areas, had under his command former KMT officers and men who had radical intellectuals as their political officers. At Ching-kang-shan these mercenaries were joined with riff-raff (or the lumpen-proletariat, *yu-min fen-tzu*), who were excellent fighters but totally unruly and unaware of the political purposes of the revolution. The poor peasants looked on, reluctant to take part in whatever they were doing.[117]

In April 1928, Chu Teh and his followers came; they too were former KMT troops. In fact, mutinies of KMT armies seem to have been an important source of recruitment for the Red Army in 1928 and 1929. In the first place, the KMT armies were poorly paid and inhumanly treated by their officers and, second, the jealousies and rivalries among KMT officers could often be exploited by the Communists.[118] In July 1928 two KMT officers, P'eng Te-huai and Huang Kung-lueh, brought their troops over to Mao and a year later there were the mutinies of Lo Ping-hui's army in Kian and K'uang Chi-hsun's in Szechwan.[119] By 1930, however, the peasants showed their readiness to join and some of them were even promoted to officers.[120] This was probably why among the middle-ranking officers of the Fourth Front Army very few could read and write.[121] In

[114] Ts'ao Po-i, *Soviet*, 360 and 368; *Red China*, 26 July 1934.
[115] Chang Wen-t'ien's article in *Red China*, 25 June 1934; Hsiao Tso-liang, *Land revolution*, 285.
[116] Mao, *SW* 1.80.
[117] Mao's report, 25 October 1928 in *MTTC* 2.37; Lo Jung-huan in *HHLY* 1, pt. 1, 139–40; *HCPP* 1.57–9.
[118] *HHLY* 1, pt. 2, 465–70.
[119] Fang Ch'iang in *HHLY* 1, pt. 2, 431–6: *HCPP* 10.186: Snow, *Red star*, 273; Agnes Smedley, *The great road: the life and times of Chu Teh*, 270.
[120] *HCPP* 1.57–9.
[121] Ch'en Hsi-lien in *HCPP* 3.90.

the spring of 1934 the class composition of the First Front Army showed 30 per cent workers and 68 per cent peasants, the majority of whom (no less than 77 per cent) came from the central soviet itself, while KMT deserters and mutineers accounted for no more than 4 per cent.[122]

To make the Red Armies different from those of warlords and the KMT, political training had first priority. Many of the erroneous tendencies listed in the Ku-t'ien resolutions of December 1929 drafted by Mao can be summed up as a lack of discipline, an unawareness of the political goals of the revolution, and an ignorance of the tasks of the Red Army – combat, financing itself, and mass mobilization. Political training required that the Red Army set up a dual system of organization to take charge of strategic command and political work. By a curious coincidence, at the very time when the Red Army introduced its soldiers' committees (shih-ping wei-yuan-hui), Chiang Kai-shek abolished political commissars in his army. The soldiers' committees ensured a measure of democracy in the Red Army so that the men would not be treated like animals by their superiors.[123] There were also political officers whose duties were not clearly defined; hence their functions were not firmly delineated till the Ku-t'ien conference. Their main job was to help the Red Army mobilize the masses and set up new regimes.[124] In addition to these, the party representatives (tang tai-piao) organized a cell in each squad and a branch in each company, for at Mao's insistence the optimum ratio between party and non-party members in the army had to be one to three. In fact, the ratio in 1934 was 28 per cent to 72.[125] The command and political systems were separate, with independent revenues and a similar ranking system; they had well-developed channels of communication between them. Within the political system, the General Political Department, established in February 1931, controlled both the political officers and the party representatives (now called political delegates, cheng-chih wei-yuan) of various ranks, but a party representative of a given rank always took precedence over a political officer of the same rank.[126] In neither of the two systems were salary differences instituted. Everyone in the army, regardless of his rank, received the same pay and shared the same style of life.[127] In battle and in keeping law and order, the army was assisted by the Red Guards and peasant self-defence forces.[128] An army so trained naturally differed considerably from the other troops in China of the same

---

[122] Ti-erh-tz'u kuo-nei ko-ming chan-cheng shih-ch'i shih-shih lun-ts'ung (Discourses on the history of the second revolutionary war period), 63–4.
[123] Lo Jung-huan in HHLY 1, pt. 1, 139–40.
[124] The Ku-t'ien resolutions in MTTC 2.123–4.
[125] Lo Jung-huan, ibid. 140.   [126] MTTC 2.124 and 253–4.
[127] Mao, SW 1.81.   [128] Ibid. 85–6.

period. Apart from the Fu-t'ien incident of December 1930, when a Red Army unit mutinied and was suppressed with many hundreds of executions, the Red Army had not fought an internecine battle; seldom did it feel the need to quell peasant hostility towards it. With the party wielding all the ideological authority and political officers holding the purse strings, the Red Army was always dominated by the party. It was a politicized army supported by the masses.

The mass line permeated the Red Army, which was repeatedly reminded of the three disciplines and the eight points of attention worked out by Mao and his colleagues, so that soldiers would not alienate the masses for whom they fought. They propagandized and protected the people, and also helped in productive work. Cementing their relations with the people this way, they could be sure of reliable information on enemy movements, and in defeat they could depend on the people to hide them in safety. This mutual dependence became more important after the evacuation of the First Front Army on the Long March in October 1934 when only small guerrilla bands were left behind to harass the KMT armies.[129]

According to various estimates, the Red Army became better organized under Li Li-san's leadership, and had some 50,000 men in 1930. This was to grow to over 100,000 in 1931, 200,000 in 1932, and 500,000 in 1933. The two most significant reorganizations came before and after Li Li-san's adventure in 1930. Before the summer of that year, the army was reorganized into army corps and, after that, the front armies came into existence. In spite of regrouping in July-August 1935, the front armies continued in this way till their reorganization into the Eight Route Army of three divisions of 1937 and the New Fourth Army in 1938.[130]

THE SEARCH FOR A STRATEGY

Created at the low ebb of the revolution in 1927, the Red Army was considered an important instrument for the CCP's seizing power, even for hastening the arrival of the revolutionary 'high tide' expected in the near future. But nowhere in the political resolutions of the Sixth Congress of 1928 was it stated that military struggle had now become the central form of struggle and the army the deciding factor of victory. The next upsurge was believed to depend on a host of external and internal factors, perhaps even more important than the army.

[129] HHLY 1, pt. 1, 309-10 and 2.145-8; Smedley, Great road, 237.
[130] Tang Leang-li, Suppressing communist bandits in China, 99-100; Hollington Tong, Chiang Tsung-t'ung chuan (A biography of President Chiang), 1.203.

Stalin's coinage of 'the revolutionary tide', vague as it was, had a leftist bias built into it. To admit the ebbing of the tide without in the same breath asserting it would rise again, in the context of a strong prejudice against right opportunism, would be tantamount to 'liquidationism'. In the spirit of the resolutions of the Sixth Congress, the tide would rise next when the labour movement increased its scope and intensity, the imperialists threatened to disturb the peace of the Pacific, the ruling cliques in China engaged themselves in more ferocious fighting, and the guerrilla war conducted by the Red Army spread further.[131] The resolutions repeatedly stressed the unevenness of the revolutionary situation in China, which would condition the tide to rise unevenly in different areas and different sectors of society. As long as it remained uneven, a nationwide revolutionary situation did not exist. As to when the tide would rise and the upsurge inundate a part or the entirety of the country, no one could tell with precision.

The Li Li-san line

In the second half of 1929 frequent civil wars, worsened intra-party feuds in the KMT, and the Wall Street crash gave the CI reasons for describing the Chinese national crisis as 'deepening' and to blame the CCP for 'lagging behind the growth of mass discontent'.[132] It may be a mistake to interpret this as the CI's call to action;[133] nonetheless it did encourage Li Li-san to shake off his earlier pessimism and to assess the situation with over-optimism. He went on to design his military strategy, which formed the kernel of the so-called Li Li-san line. By early summer 1930, the CI adjudged the high tide in China 'an undeniable fact', though still uneven: 'The direction of recent events is such that if the revolutionary situation cannot embrace the entire territory of China, at least it will cover several important provinces in the very near future.' Under such circumstances the CCP should prepare for the imminence of a war of liberation and the most deadly error would be a right-opportunist tendency.[134]

Thus radicalized by the ambiguous directives of the CI, Li began to exploit the deteriorating economic depression abroad and military disorder at home. Heartened, Li Li-san went even as far as to assert that the outcome of a revolution was not decided by the political forces involved in it but by the tasks to be accomplished. Therefore the bourgeois

---

[131] *Hung-se wen-hsien*, 152–3 and 166.
[132] ECCI to CCP, either 26 October 1929 (*Hung-se wen-hsien*, 334 and 340) or alternatively late December 1929.
[133] Brandt *et al. Documentary history*, 180.
[134] ECCI to CCP, 23 July 1930 (or in June 1930), *Hung-se wen-hsien*, 346–55.

revolution in China could be led by the proletariat. As soon as the proletariat took power and introduced its leadership, the transition to the socialist stage of the revolution could begin. 'There is no need to wait for the conquest of the whole country before the transition. To do so is to commit rightist deviation.'[135] In the vitally important resolution on the new revolutionary high tide and preliminary victory in one or more provinces adopted by the CCP Politburo in 11 June 1930, the call for a preliminary victory did not mean a prolonged war to defend the CCP's occupation of one or more provinces. To seize power in one or more 'important provinces', including key administrative or industrial cities, except in the north-east and south-west, would inevitably threaten the security of the central government and trigger a death duel between the government and the rebellion till one of the belligerents was destroyed.[136] Hence a durable local regime was unlikely; hence the unevenness of the situation would be quickly made even. This is then not a question of Li Li-san's denial of the unevenness; to him the question was how soon the unevenness could be transmuted into evenness. After all, the CI's letter of June or July 1930 did refer to a decisive war in the nearest future and a swifter transition from the bourgeois to socialist revolution in China than had occurred in Russia.[137] The vagueness of the CI's assessment of the situation and its policy proposals on the one hand reflected a lack of clear thinking on the part of the CI and on the other allowed Li Li-san ample room for his own interpretation.[138]

To be sure, Li had refrained from giving military instructions to the soviet leaders for several months after his assumption of power in the summer of 1928.[139] This was perhaps because at the beginning of his leadership he was touched by a streak of pessimism about the future of the revolution. He did not begin to develop his military strategy until the second half of 1929.[140] Insisting on urban leadership and dismissing the idea of depending on the Red Army alone for victory as 'a serious error',[141] Li thought that the key to a preliminary victory in one or more provinces (a goal agreed upon at the Sixth Congress) lay in the workers'

[135] Li Li-san, *Fan-t'o* (Anti-Trotsky), 9; see also Mao's comment on this in *HC* 3.982.
[136] Wang Chien-min, *Draft history*, 2.42–51; Hsiao Tso-liang, *Power relations*, 22ff.
[137] *Hung-se wen-hsien*, 355 and 358. The date of this letter is given vaguely as June 1930 (see A. M. Grigoriev's article in L. P. Deliusin, ed. *Komintern i vostok*, 334–5). These different dates do not help to decide whether the letter was a response to the CCP's strategic plan before or after the momentous Politburo meeting on 11 June 1930.
[138] See for instance, Kuusinen's report at the 10th plenum of ECCI, and L. Magyar's article in *International Press Correspondence*, 5.40 (20 August 1929) and 10.18 (10 April 1930), respectively.
[139] Kiangsu Provincial Committee's comments on the centre's work in *Chung-kung ti cheng-chih kung-tso*, 1.166–7.
[140] Mao, *SW* 3.998.
[141] *Hung-ch'i* (Red flag), 29 March 1930; *Chung-yang t'ung-hsin*, 15 (8 November 1928).

struggles in the big cities with the support of the Red Army, peasants' uprisings, and mutinies of KMT troops. The ripening of the revolutionary situation would be signalled by an outburst of workers' struggles. In other words, in February 1930 Li visualized that the workers would start their strikes and armed insurrections, while the Red Army marched on the cities to give them support.[142] Once a preliminary victory was won in one or more provinces, the uneven situation would soon become even enough for the CCP to seize national power. At this stage of Li's strategic plan the target city was Wuhan, and the plan was translated into a letter to the secretary of the Front Committee of the Fourth Red Army on 3 April 1930, directing the army to march along the Kan River towards the riverine city, Kiukiang, and take it.[143]

The army's supporting role was to be fulfilled not by waging guerrilla warfare but by attacking large cities and disrupting the transport lines of the KMT armies. According to the Politburo resolution on 11 June 1930, the army was to capture such administrative centres and medium-sized cities as Changsha, Nanchang, Kiukiang, Shashih and Huang-p'i before its final assault on Wuhan.[144]

The CI, on the other hand, had never spelt out a strategic plan of its own, let alone a programme for action, in its directives to the CCP in February, June, and October or December 1929. Even its directive or letter of June or July 1930 to the Chinese party, perhaps prompted by an uneasy feeling over Li's writings and the Politburo's resolutions in the spring, said no more than that 'Attention must be focused on the organization and strengthening of a Red Army so that one or more industrial and administrative *key cities* can be occupied according to the political and military circumstances *in the future*'.[145] Insofar as the capture of the key cities was concerned, the CI and Li did not differ; as to how such cities could be taken, the CI suggested no strategy; as to the ripening of the revolutionary circumstances, the CI was vague; the meaning of 'the future' was anyone's guess. The uncertainties had presumably to be ascertained by the leaders on the spot, the commanders in the field. This was precisely what Li did when he worked out his programme for action once the uncertainties were made certain. This was why CI's official organ, the *International Press Correspondence*, in its issue on 7 August 1930, could rejoice and praise Li's ephemeral success in capturing Changsha.

From the perspective of a leader of the party centre, urban struggles

---

[142] *Chung-yang t'ung-hsin*, 70 (26 February 1930).
[143] Hsiao Tso-liang, *Power relations*, 15.
[144] *Hung-ch'i* (Red flag), 16 August 1930.
[145] Benjamin I. Schwartz, *Chinese communism and the rise of Mao*, 143. My italics.

and the capture of cities doctrinally and practically looked larger and more decisive than the guerrilla activities in the widely scattered mountain fastnesses. But from the perspective of the guerrilla leaders, the preservation of their base areas was a life-and-death concern. Even before the collapse of the first united front, Mao had already come to the conclusion that the peasant question was the central issue of the Chinese revolution.[146] The progress around the Ching-kang-shan base that he and his comrades had made in 1928 renewed their confidence in the future of the revolution. Mao had no fear of the peasants' struggle outstripping the workers' struggles.[147] Nonetheless he realized that the struggle was arduous and protracted, for the rule of the landlords and warlords, unlike that of a handful of capitalists of a few key cities, permeated the vastness of rural China.[148] The struggle was directed at the heart and brain, not merely the limbs, of that 'feudal' regime. Based on his gains in 1928 and early 1929, Mao could optimistically forecast at the Juichin Conference on 18 May 1929 that within a year it would be possible for the Red Army under his command to occupy the province of Kiangsi.

At the beginning of 1930, when he wrote his famous letter to Lin Piao,[149] Mao not only corrected his earlier hastiness but also defined his strategy of concentrating armed forces to capture counties, expand red areas in order to spread the political influence of the party and army, and speed up the arrival of the high tide. Kiangsi remained his goal, and that was what he understood by a preliminary victory in one or more provinces which would give the CCP a solid local regime as the basis for future expansion. As to urban struggles, it was time for rallying the masses around the party, not time yet for armed insurrection. In his analysis of the situation, Mao paid almost no attention to either the world economic depression or the larger conflicts among China's military cliques. In any case he was against the dispersal of his troops and their dispatch to take distant cities like Changsha.[150]

Reluctantly Mao accepted Li Li-san's orders to be a part of Li's plan. He tried to take Nanchang at the end of July 1930 when P'eng Te-huai's Third Army Corps occupied Changsha, but was repulsed by the garrison of the city. In less than ten days P'eng had to evacuate the capital of Hunan. Then came the second assault on Changsha, with the combined forces of Mao and P'eng, from 1 September to the 13th. Seeing it as a hopeless struggle, Mao persuaded his comrades to retreat and direct their resources

---

[146] *MTTC* 1.175.   [147] *Ibid.* 2.133.

[148] *Ibid.* 2.59 and 128.   [149] *Ibid.* 2.135 and 139.

[150] Mao, *SW* 1.54 and 61.

to the rebuilding and expansion of soviet base areas.[151] In Mao's view Li's strategic directives in the summer of 1930 read like fiction.[152]

Wang Ming's 'two lines'

The defeat of the Li Li-san line was to be followed by a series of encirclement campaigns by Chiang Kai-shek against the soviet areas. But CCP thinking was on an entirely different course. The theoretical framework of the CCP's strategy in this period was laid out in Wang Ming's famous pamphlet, *The two lines* (*Liang-t'iao lu-hsien*), of July 1931 which made much of the crisis of postwar capitalism in its third stage of development, when the contradictions among imperialist powers became increasingly acute.[153] As if to give support to this thesis, the Japanese Kwantung army seized Manchuria after 18 September 1931. Suddenly the anti-imperialist struggle took precedence over the anti-feudal struggle. The Japanese invasion of Shanghai in January 1932 inevitably involved the proletariat there, though to an unascertainable extent, giving the 28 Bolsheviks a gleam of hope of taking the revolution back to the cities. The anti-imperialist thesis and the strategy of urban revolution were to remain the consistent policies of the 28 Bolsheviks throughout the first half of the 1930s, up to the formation of the second united front in 1937.

Under their leadership the strategy still aimed at winning a preliminary victory in one or more provinces, with the Red Army of the rural soviets now their sole weapon. The first stage of this strategy was to consolidate and coordinate the existing and new soviet areas. Only when this was accomplished would the CCP fight for national power in the second stage.[154] The anti-Japanese high tide after September 1931 gave the 28 Bolsheviks fresh hopes, and their strategic plan, the 'Resolution on winning a preliminary victory in one or more provinces' of 9 January 1932, once again contemplated the possibility of capturing key cities. 'What used to be the correct strategy of refusing to take big cities does not hold true any more.'[155] South of the Yangtze all the soviet areas should try to link up with the central soviet, while north of the river they should do likewise, with the O-Yü-Wan soviet as the centre. By this consolidation and coordination the Red Army could in the near future march on Nanchang, Foochow and Kian, while the army north of the Yangtze

---

[151] Mao, *SW* 3.1020, no. 4; Smedley, *Great road*, 278–9; Jerome Ch'en, *Mao*, 156–9. The second attack on Changsha was not ordered by the CI. See Harrison's article on Li Li-san, *CQ* 14.187 and Wang Ming, *Hsuan-chi*, 3.75. [152] Wang Ming, *Hsuan-chi*, 3.56.
[153] *Ibid.* 246–69. [154] *Ibid.* 50 and 74.
[155] *Shih-hua* (Honest words), 3 (20 April 1932).

would threaten the security of Wuhan, the Peking-Hankow railway, and transport on the Yangtze. To do this the Red Army could not just wait for the enemy to attack, lure him into the soviet area, and then destroy him. Such a tactic was criticized as designed by 'a country scholar', not by a Marxist revolutionary.[156] Chou En-lai himself showed an intense distrust of it in his well-known Shao-shan report of 1931. The party's directive to the soviet leaders dated 1 September 1931 also regarded guerrilla tactics as of only secondary, supplementary importance. The Red Army must be trained differently under a unified political and military leadership and made fit for positional warfare, so that victories in one or more provinces could be won.[157]

A new strategy required a new army leadership. At the Ningtu Conference of the central bureau of the soviet areas in August 1932 Chou En-lai replaced Mao as the political commissar of the First Front Army and later was made the political commissar of the Red Army as a whole.[158]

DESTRUCTION OF THE SOVIETS

Chiang Kai-shek's first three encirclement campaigns (in late 1931 and 1932) were fought while Mao was still firmly in the military saddle. Grossly belittling the strength and skill of the Red Army and unaware of the importance of mass political work, Chiang tried to kill two birds with one stone by pitching a motley of warlord troops against the Communists in a war of attrition. These 'expatriate' armies, unfamiliar with local conditions, were easily enticed into the soviet area and defeated.[159] The Red Army, on the other hand, relied on the speed of their movement and mass support, 'usually moving at night' and 'appearing suddenly and disappearing quickly', in a situation best described by the KMT's official history of the 'suppression of the bandits':

When the National Armies advanced into an area, they found very few people there. The old and sick left behind were controlled by the bandits' underground

---

[156] Liu Po-ch'eng in *Ko-ming yü chan-cheng* (Revolution and war), 1 (1 August 1932).
[157] Chou En-lai in *Hung-hsing* (Red star), 4 (27 August 1933); Wang Ming, *Hsuan-chi*, 3.74.
[158] Warren Kuo, *History*, 2.345–8. In place of the generally held view that Mao and the 28 Bolsheviks with Chou En-lai's support waged a power struggle between them, I. J. Kim (*Politics*) advances the theory of 'division of labour' with Mao concentrating on the government, Ch'in Pang-hsien on the party, and Chou on the army work, to form a collective leadership. Kim's basic hypothesis is that the 28 Bolsheviks, having no real power base, only theoretical articulation, did not dare to challenge the military leaders, including Mao. With almost no documentary evidence to support it, Kim's thesis seems unacceptable. See the analysis of personnel and their roles in Lötveit, *Communism*, 86–97.
[159] *Chiao-fei chan-shih* admits this point of inadequacy, 1.93–4; T'ang Sheng-chih and Sun Fo also criticized this intention of Chiang's: see Sun Fo *et al. T'ao Chiang yen-lun-chi* (Anti-Chiang messages), 41 and 133. See also Tang Leang-li, *Bandits*, 42.

organization and therefore would not dare to talk with the government troops. Sometimes they even helped the bandits by hindering the advance of the troops... The National Armies had very little knowledge of the conditions of the bandits.[160]

A similar pattern occurred in the second encirclement campaign (May-June 1932) during which the Communists' mass work showed a remarkable progress. The KMT's official history complained that 'the bandits carried away both men and grain with them'; that people destroyed bridges behind the government troops, denied information to them, and even ambushed them; that the people harassed the supply lines of the government troops to such a degree as to require a full regiment to protect government messengers and quartermasters.[161]

Chiang realized now that he was dealing with a tough enemy. He set up his headquarters in Nanchang and deployed his own crack troops, thus relegating the 'miscellaneous' forces to a supporting role in the third campaign (July-October 1932). Under the able command of General Ch'en Ch'eng, whose quality even Mao admitted,[162] to the chagrin of the Communists, the government troops penetrated deeply into the soviet area. At the same time Chiang became aware of the non-existence of a civil government structure below the county level, so that he had no way of collecting reliable intelligence about the Communists. He also made a beginning in his type of mass work by forbidding the press-ganging of porters and orderlies.[163] But the crisis in relations with Japan, intensifying after the 'Mukden incident' on 18 September 1931, eventually forced Chiang to wind up the third campaign quite abruptly. In the respite, the CCP reviewed the war situation and questioned Mao's strategy of luring the enemy deep into the soviet area before destroying him. As a result, in the summer of 1932, after Ho Lung's soviet in the Hung Lake area was overrun by the KMT troops, Chou En-lai replaced Mao.[164]

When the national crisis with Japan subsided, Chiang resumed his efforts to 'achieve internal peace before dealing with the foreign foe' by launching in 1933 the fourth encirclement campaign. But the Red Armies continued to be elusive, with a speed that 'tired the government troops out in chasing them'. Their mass work had now reached a point that government troops 'had no one to use, thus making us both blind and deaf'.[165] This was the war situation around the central soviet. In O-Yü-Wan

[160] *Chiao-fei chan-shih*, 1.107–14.
[161] *Ibid.* 1.128–44.
[162] Mao, *SW* 1.222.
[163] *Chiao-fei chan-shih*, 1.154–67.
[164] Ho Lung attributed the loss to Hsia Hsi's 'mountain top-ism'; see Miao Ch'u-huang, *Chung-kuo Kung-ch'an-tang chien-yao li-shih* (A brief history of the CCP), 90.
[165] *Chiao-fei chan-shih*, 2.170 and 239; Ts'ai T'ing-k'ai remarked in his *Tzu-chuan* (Autobiography), 1.375 that having been converted to communism, the people became united and happy.

the mass work, though well done, tended to become inert and disappear whenever the Fourth Front Army had suffered a reverse and retreated.[166] With Chiang in personal command of the campaign since May 1932, the O-Yü-Wan soviet was destroyed in September, forcing Chang Kuo-t'ao and Hsu Hsiang-ch'ien to go on what might be described as their first long march to north Szechwan. There the fighting between the 24th and 29th Armies of the province gave the Fourth Front Army a chance to set up a new soviet.[167]

Chiang's fifth campaign

Thus at the beginning of the fifth campaign in late 1933 the central soviet had lost the support of both O-Yü-Wan and Hsiang-o-hsi, although Ho Lung was creating another soviet in the north-west of Hunan and there were still the smaller and weaker soviets of Fang Chih-min on the Hunan-Kiangsi border and Hsiao K'o at the old Ching-kang-shan base. Chiang, taking a leaf from his enemy's book, now ascribed greater importance to political work and altered his strategy. In the political sphere he prepared the ground by organizing an officers' training course in the summer of 1933; some 7,000 army cadres took the course. Then he militarized the administration, economy, and social and educational work around the central soviet area, so that the KMT government, party and army cooperated in an all-out effort to defeat the Communists. At the grass roots he gave help to the spring sowing of 1934 and revived the collective security system known as *pao-chia*.[168] People living around the soviet were forced to move into what were prototype 'strategic hamlets' and put under the *pao-chia* so as to create a ring of no-man's-land, intended to blockade and starve the Communists.[169] A road-building programme was initiated, employing 20,000 workers to construct 700 miles of motor roads in order to increase the mobility of Chiang's armies, while wireless apparatus, telephones and aeroplanes were extensively used to achieve better coordination among his army units. While all this was being done Chiang's troops advanced steadily and slowly, lining their routes of penetration with blockhouses. In other words, this was a strategic offensive coupled with tactically defensive warfare, which rendered Mao's

[166] On the mass work of the Fourth Front Army, see *Chiao-fei chan-shih*, 3.467 and 4.683–5.
[167] For the creation of a new soviet by the Fourth Front Army, see *ibid.*, 4.519 and Wang Chien-min, *Draft history*, 2.207–11.
[168] Much of the information used here comes from *Chiao-fei chan-shih*, 2 and 3 *passim* and Tang Leang-li, *Bandits, passim*.
[169] Liu Pei-shan in *Chung-kuo Kung-ch'an-tang tsai Chiang-hsi ti-ch'ü ling-tao ko-ming tou-cheng ti li-shih tzu-liao* (Historical material concerning the revolutionary struggles led by the CCP in Kiangsi), 1.188.

old strategy of luring the enemy into the soviet area obsolete. 'There was no need to seek out the main force of the bandits. We only have to occupy strategic places where the bandits must come out and fight.' This was Chiang's directive on 17 October 1933. In this way the Red Army was forced from offensive mobile warfare to defensive positional warfare. Ironically, Chiang described his strategy as that of the foolish old man who removed the mountains. To be sure, the Red Army did not want to fight a purely defensive war, although Mao was to make that charge against the military leadership at the Tsun-yi Conference in January 1935. But, according to Chou En-lai, a defensive positional war became inevitable.

This [blockhouse warfare, positional warfare and night battles] was unavoidable and this is why we are doing it. But of course our main form of war remains mobile warfare. In the present [February 1934] circumstances, we often see a rencontre of mobile war quickly turn into positional war.[170]

The KMT's blockhouse tactic went through two important stages. At the beginning there were only a few blockhouses, each of which was guarded by a company or a platoon of regular soldiers. In November 1933 more were built with a distance of only two-thirds of a mile between them and guarded usually by a squad or at most a platoon. In this way the blockhouses formed a supporting network and a regiment of troops could defend a line thirteen or fourteen miles long. The second change came early in 1934 when militia units were ordered to guard the blockhouses while regular troops were transferred to offensive duties. At this stage the Red Army's fire-power had been so weakened that the KMT armies could afford to build more earthen blockhouses than brick ones.

As the lines of blockhouses tightened, the Red Army changed its positional warfare to what was known as 'short, swift thrusts' (*tuan ts'u t'u-chi*), a tactic whose invention was attributed to Lin Piao.[171] They depended on the building of 'supporting points' (*chin-ch'eng tien*) – the Communist version of blockhouses, which could help the Red Army move within a few miles of the KMT troops. Making use of its speed and good organization, the Red Army hoped to attack while the enemy was building

---

[170] *Hung-hsing* (Red star), 29 (18 February 1934).
[171] The official history of the war (*Chiao-fei chan-shih*) published by the KMT government speaks of 'the steadily tightening rings' (2.266) and Wang Chien-min's draft history of the CCP supports this description. In accordance with the general strategic plan of the fifth campaign, roads protected by blockhouses were constructed to penetrate the soviet area. On Otto Braun's tactic see Chi-hsi Hu's article in *CQ* 43.34. Snow's attribution of this tactic to Lin Piao was recently vindicated by an article in *Hung-ch'i* (Red flag), 1 (1975). See also Otto Braun, *A Comintern agent in China 1932–1939*, 68. I myself saw a copy of Lin's pamphlet on this subject in the War Museum, Peking, in 1980.

his blockhouses. The coordination of the units fighting around a supporting point needed telephones of which the Red Army had hardly any; the supporting point itself could scarcely withstand the bombardment of the KMT's heavy artillery pieces. In any case, such a tactical move was no answer to the Red Army's strategic needs. After the decisive battle of Kuang-ch'ang in April 1934, guerrilla warfare, the last resort it seemed, was brought back to the centre of the party's and the army's attention.[172] But the revival of guerrilla warfare at this stage of the struggle was chiefly for diversionary purposes. It was intended to gain time for the eventual evacuation of the central soviet and to mobilize the masses again so that guerrilla bases could be re-established after the evacuation. Writing in the army's organ, *Red Star (Hung-hsing)* on 20 August 1934, Chou En-lai pointed out that the weakest link in the Communist strategy lay in the lack of guerrilla warfare deep behind enemy lines; writing two years after the evacuation, Mao remarked:

but where it is evident that the campaign cannot be terminated on our interior lines, we should employ the main Red Army force to break through the enemy's encirclement and switch to our exterior lines (that is, the enemy's interior lines) in order to defeat him there. Now that the enemy has developed his blockhouse warfare to a high degree, this will become our usual method of operation.[173]

Probably because of this consideration, Fang Chih-min's 10th Army Corps was ordered in July 1934 to move from east Kiangsi to west Chekiang and south Anhwei, ostensibly to engage the Japanese in war but in fact to divert Chiang's attention from the central soviet.[174] In August, Hsiao K'e's 6th Army Corps was ordered to break through the encirclement to join forces with Ho Lung in north-west Hunan.[175] Finally, the central soviet, by now much reduced in size, was abandoned in October 1934, leaving behind Hsiang Ying, Ch'en I, Su Yü and others to spend lonely years fighting in scattered guerrilla enclaves till the formation of the New Fourth Army in 1938. In Central China there remained only the small soviet under Ho Lung and Jen Pi-shih. Further north were Chang Kuo-t'ao's soviet in north Szechwan and Liu Chih-tan's and Kao Kang's soviet in north Shensi. The state so arduously created since 1927 was now destroyed under Chiang Kai-shek's overwhelming might as the First Front Army started on its Long March.

[172] *Hung-hsing* (Red star), 55 (25 July 1934).
[173] Mao, *SW* 1.247.
[174] Wang Chien-min, *Draft history*, 2.258–9; Miao Ch'u-huang, *Brief history*, 92–3; Sheng Li-yü, *Chung-kuo jen-min chieh-fang-chün san-shih-nien shih-hua* (An informal history of the 30 years of the People's Liberation Army of China), 16–18.
[175] Hsiao K'e in Nym Wales, *Red dust*, 139; Wang Chen in *ibid.* 101; Miao Ch'u-huang, *Brief history*, 93.

The Long March

This epic hegira covered some 6,000 miles on foot, across a dozen or more big mountain ranges and two dozen rivers in about a year. History offers few comparable triumphs of will-power over circumstance, nor a better example of constant improvisation. There is hardly any doubt that the first destination of the Long March was a junction with the Second Front Army commanded by Ho Lung – an intention which did not escape Chiang's calculation.[176] Chiang seems to have been aware of the incomplete ring of encirclement in the south-west corner of the soviet area which might afford a chance for the First Front Army to slip through to north Kwangtung and Kwangsi. As it was too late to close the ring, Chiang hoped to use the new situation of the Communist invasion to solve to his own advantage the thorny problems of the South-west Political Council under the military dissidents there.[177] But the Kwangtung and Kwangsi leaders let the Red Army pass through without much fighting; they only scorched the earth to create difficulties for the oncoming red soldiers. Therefore they had no need for Chiang's military aid to induce their submission to him.[178] Assured now of the intention of the First Front Army, Chiang laid four lines of defence between the First Front Army and Ho Lung,[179] making it absolutely impossible for the two red forces to unite. Having crossed the Hsiang River and lost nearly two-thirds of the 100,000 combatants and non-combatants of the First Front Army, the leaders of the Politburo held their first meeting on the Long March at Li-p'ing near the Kweichow border (now in Kweichow); the plan to join the Second Front Army was abandoned and the decision to invade Kweichow was taken.[180] This was in December 1934. Chang Kuo-t'ao and Hsu Hsiang-ch'ien of the Fourth Front Army in north Szechwan were informed of the decision and of the plan to join forces with them somewhere in north-west Szechwan.[181] The projected route would cross the Yangtze at I-pin (Sui-fu).

On reaching Tsun-yi in January 1935, the Red Armies suddenly appeared to threaten the security of Szechwan from the north, south and

[176] Li T'ien-yu in *HHLY*, Hong Kong, 19; Liu Po-ch'eng, *ibid.* 4; Miao Ch'u-huang, 'Chung-kuo kung-nung hung-chün ch'ang-cheng kai-shu' (A brief account of the Long March of the Workers' and Peasants' Red Army of China), *Li-shih yen-chiu*, 2 (1954), 88. Details of the Long March are in Dick Wilson, *The Long March, 1935*.

[177] Ho Kuo-kuang's statement in Wang Chien-min, *Draft history*, 624. Ho was then the director of Chiang's field headquarters.

[178] Chang Kuo-p'ing, *Pai Ch'ung-hsi chiang-chün chuan* (A biography of General Pai Ch'ung-hsi), 62–4; *Ch'un-ch'iu* (Spring and autumn), 99.14.

[179] Chin Fan, *Tsai Hung-chün ch'ang-cheng ti tao-lu shang*, 45.

[180] Liu Po-ch'eng in *HHLY*, Hong Kong, 4.5.

[181] *Ming-pao*, 48.85.

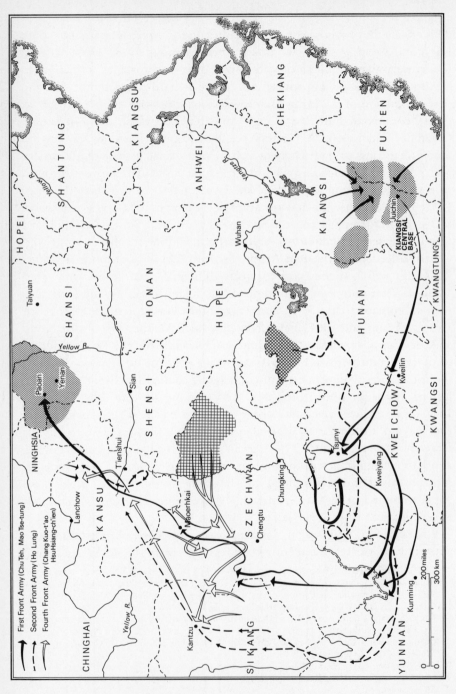

MAP 6. The Long March to Shensi

east.[182] This panic situation gave Chiang an opportunity to insert his military and political influence into that province, while the First Front Army gained its first respite since October. It took Tsun-yi on 7 January 1935 and left that small city on the 19th,[183] during which time the army was reorganized while the party leaders sat through the historic conference of the Politburo. The Tsun-yi Conference decided on joining forces with the Fourth Front Army by way of T'ung-tzu, Sung-k'an and Ch'ih-shui, and to enter Szechwan and cross the Yangtze at I-pin as previously planned. When this plan was frustrated by reinforced enemy defences, the First Front Army had to choose another route. According to Teng Fa, the chief of political security, the purpose of going north to join the Fourth Front Army was to be close to the Japanese and engage them in a war of national liberation without Chiang and his allies. Another purpose may have been to find 'the possibility of contact with Russia, the certainty of not being surrounded [again]'.[184]

Strategically the Tsun-yi Conference marked the beginning of a new stage. Before this the First Front Army had had to fight enemies both in front and behind, thus suffering tremendous casualties and desertions.[185] After the eleven days of respite and reorganization, the main anxiety of the army was not the unworthy Kweichow troops ahead but the dogged Nationalist troops behind. The reorganization and abandonment of heavy equipment enabled the army to return to mobile warfare, and use high speed and feints to disengage the pursuing armies under Generals Hsueh Yueh and Chou Hung-yuan.[186]

Chang Kuo-t'ao's separation

At this time Chang Kuo-t'ao gave up his soviet, though not under unusually heavy military pressure from the central and local forces. His own explanation of this move was to enable him to meet the oncoming First Front Army, whereas the Maoist historians have accused him of 'flightism'.[187] The route Chang took led his troops across the Chialing River, through Nan-t'ung, Chien-men, Chien-ko, Tzu-t'ung, then across the Fu River through Chiang-yu, and finally across the Min River to Li-fan and Mou-kung.[188] Chang had an alternative choice of going north to join

---

[182] *Chiao-fei chan-shih*, 5.883; Hsueh Yueh, *Chiao-fei chi-shih* (A factual account of the campaigns against the bandits), pt. 3, 13-4.

[183] Liu Po-ch'eng in *HHLY*, Hong Kong, 5; Hsueh Yueh, *ibid.*, pt. 3, 7-9.

[184] *HHLY*, Hong Kong, 48 and 50; Hsiao Hua in *HCPP* 13.87; André Malraux, *Anti-memoirs*, 533.

[185] Liu Po-ch'eng in *HHLY*, Hong Kong, 4.4.

[186] *Ibid.* 6; *HCPP* 14.102-3.

[187] *Ming-pao*, 49.78; Liu Po-ch'eng, *HHLY*, Hong Kong, 9.

[188] Hsu Hsiang-ch'ien in Wales, *Red dust*, 161.

forces with Liu Chih-tan and Kao Kang. Had he done so and abandoned Mao and Ho Lung to their fate in the south, the entire Communist movement might have been reduced to political insignificance. What Chang actually did had the effect of enfeebling the First Front Army while preserving it, but it gave him a military edge which might lead to his political supremacy in the party. Later events were to prove that Chang's apparently astute calculations in February 1935 turned out to be the first major mistake he made on the Long March. Either choice, however, implied that he must give up his soviet.

From what is known, the Tsun-yi Conference avoided political polemics, concentrating on criticism of the military line which had led to the losses of the soviets and the disastrous defeats in the initial stages of the Long March. The 'pure defence' tactics, the unwillingness to exploit the disunity among Chiang Kai-shek's ranks during the Fukien rebellion in the winter of 1933–4, the refusal to make a strategic retreat and transfer the main forces behind the enemy's lines of blockhouses in order to crush the encirclement, and the poor preparation for the Long March, all came under Mao's merciless attack in the resolutions he drafted.[189] With Wang Chia-hsiang gravely wounded, Chou En-lai having admitted his mistakes, Chang Wen-t'ien drawing close to Mao, and the German adviser Otto Braun in disgrace, the leadership of the party was in awful disarray. In an atmosphere reminiscent of the 7 August conference of 1927, the enlarged conference at Tsun-yi, including representatives of the military who were unhappy with the leadership, elected Mao to be the first of the three-man commanding team, including Chou En-lai and Wang Chia-hsiang, to act in place of the military commission of the party while the soviet government's military affairs committee was still headed by Chu Teh. In addition Mao regained his seat on the Polituro and probably a secretaryship in the central secretariat headed by Chang Wen-t'ien.[190]

Two major points were to be the bone of contention when the First and Fourth Front Armies met in Mou-kung on 12 June 1935 – the first

[189] Jerome Ch'en, 'Resolutions of the Tsunyi Conference', *CQ* 40. In Fukien the 19th Route Army commanded by Ts'ai T'ing-k'ai, which had distinguished itself in the defence of Shanghai in January 1932, having entered into an agreement with the Communists on 26 October 1933 (see Hsiao Tso-liang, *Power relations*, 49), set up a 'People's Revolutionary Government' in Foochow in November 1933. This seriously weakened Chiang's encirclement in its north-eastern corner. Complicated by many political issues, the situation did not result in any form of cooperation between the 19th Route Army and the CCP, and the Foochow government was soon defeated by Chiang.

[190] Dieter Heinzig's article in *CQ* 46.287. Mao's new position as 'the first' (*ti-i-pa-shou*) of the three-man commanding team (*san-jen chün-shih hsiao-tsu*) is now held to be his true position in the party's military hierarchy by the curatorial staff of all the important museums in China and by such authorities as Professor Hu Hua at the People's University, Peking. See Hu's *Chung-kuo ko-ming-shih chiang-i* (Lectures on the history of the Chinese Revolution), 1.363.

was the legality of the Tsun-yi Conference, as by then several members of the Politburo were not even members of the Central Committee elected at the Sixth Congress in 1928. They included Ch'in Pang-hsien, Chang Wen-t'ien, Wang Chia-hsiang and Chu Teh. The second and more important point which had been avoided at Tsun-yi concerned the future of the soviet movement in China. In Mou-kung the situation was different; Chang Kuo-t'ao wanted to challenge the legality of the new leadership, including Mao, and to change the course of the revolution.

It is generally agreed that at the time the two armies made their junction, the Fourth Front Army was numerically stronger and better equipped, though less well disciplined, than Mao's worn-out First Front Army. Chang Kuo-t'ao knew perfectly well that the CCP lacked a democratic tradition for settling intra-party disputes through committee discussion, and yet he agreed to the convocation of the Liang-ho-k'ou Conference of 24 June 1935. Perhaps he hoped that, with his military preponderance and firm belief that the soviet movement was doomed to fail, he could carry the majority of the party leadership with him, as they and they alone were in a position to legitimize his policy proposals. He was still working with the party; he was not yet a separatist. His close colleague, Ch'en Ch'ang-hao, asked him a crucial question: 'If you come out clear and criticize the mistakes of the centre to hasten the bankruptcy of the leadership, what will be the result?'[191] Chang did not record his reply; nor did he criticize the leadership. Instead, he preferred to argue at the conference over whether the soviet movement had or had not been a success and to discuss what the future would be if all of them marched northward to join forces with Kao Kang and Liu Chih-tan.[192] In other words, what he presented to the conference was not his maximum demand for an overhaul of the central leadership, but his minimum demand, the thin end of the wedge, of replacing the soviet government with a north-west autonomous government based on a coalition of the minority nationalities to be decided at a high cadres' conference. Presumably the high cadres' conference would contain a greater representation of the Fourth Front Army. If his autonomous government proposal was adopted, this would give Chang the supreme leadership of the party which he so coveted.

But Chang's proposal would have obliterated the class base of a government led by the CCP. In spite of its mild social programme, which included land redistribution and the abolition of extortionate taxes, it would not be a socialist government.[193] His policy proposal therefore was tantamount to a transformation of the CCP into a party of minority races.

---

[191] *Ming-pao*, 51.82.   [192] Liu Ning, *I-ko kung-jen ti kung-chuang*, 12.
[193] *Ming-pao*, 49.80.

It was no surprise that Mao won the day. But as a compromise for the sake of unity, the military commission was reorganized with Mao continuing to serve as its chairman and Chang and Chu Teh as its deputy chairmen. This compromise Chang willingly accepted.[194]

To patch up still other differences, the Mao-erh-kai Conference was convened on 5 August. At this point no one there knew the whereabouts of Hsu Hai-tung's 25th Army Corps or had any inkling of a new united front strategy being formulated in Moscow. The conference did not consider Chang's proposal of a new government again; it concentrated on the question of the march northward. Chang's suggestion to hold a high cadres' conference was rejected on the ground that matters concerning the party should not be treated by the representatives of only two front armies, whose proper jurisdiction was over military affairs such as the command system and the northward march itself.[195] As to the command system, Chu Teh nominated himself as the commander-in-chief with Chang as the general political commissar. All strategic problems were to be determined by the commander-in-chief's headquarters with the final approval of the party's three-man commanding team headed by Mao.[196] Therefore Mao, as the chairman of the commission holding the powers of final decision, was above both Chu and Chang. There was no question of Mao's disobedience of Chang, only Chang's defiance of Mao.

This defiance was exhibited by Chang's different interpretation of the 'northward' march. Mao's destination was the north Shensi soviet, but Chang argued at the conference that the armies should go only as far as to Min-hsien and Kan-nan in Kansu before the next step of the march was decided.[197] Much to Chang's chagrin, Mao began his march with the east column, an act that Chang interpreted as Mao's contempt for his authority. In Mao's view, Chang's demand that he should return to A-pa was sheer disobedience.[198] Behind this disagreement lay the issue of the future of the soviet movement. If the movement was assessed as a success and there was a future in continuing it, there was every reason to go to north Shensi; if it was adjudged a failure, it would be better to heed Chang's advice, to coop up in the remote Sikang-Kansu mountains and wait for another day. At a personal level, to accept Chang's judgment and proposal would result in accepting Chang's leadership and all that that implied. This Mao could not do.

With Mao's refusal to return south, the CCP split. Soon after that, Chang called his cherished high cadres' conference in Cho-k'e-chi to

[194] *Ibid.* 50.88.
[196] *Ibid.* 51-79 and footnote 191.
[198] Liu Po-ch'eng, *HHLY*, Hong Kong, 10.
[195] *Ibid.* 51.81-2.
[197] *Ibid.* 52.83.

inaugurate a provisional party centre with Chang as its secretary. The army was to be commanded by the provisional centre.[199] Three months later fortune turned against Chang's west column – the cold weather set in and Liu Hsiang, the Szechwan warlord, repeatedly defeated Chang's troops, forcing them to retreat deep into Sikang and Chinghai.[200] Meanwhile Ch'en Ch'ang-hao's attempt to advance to south Kansu was thwarted by Chiang's troops.[201] To add more gloom to his future, Chang made an overture to Yang Hu-ch'eng, a warlord in north-west China, for a non-aggression pact, which was cold-shouldered.[202]

In the meantime the Second Front Army under Ho Lung started its Long March on 12 November 1935. But for the strong KMT defence to the north-west of Hunan, Ho Lung might have gone straight north to join forces with Mao without tramping through half of China.[203] On the other hand, the turmoil in Kwangtung and Kwangsi gave Ho a chance to penetrate south.[204] He followed roughly the footsteps of the First Front Army to reach Chang Kuo-t'ao in Sikang at a time when the frustrated Chang was under pressure to reunite with Mao's centre. Lin Yü-ying, Lin Piao's uncle, had brought back from Moscow a compromise formula for reunification. Exploiting this opportunity, the newly arrived leaders, Jen Pi-shih, Kuan Hsiang-ying and Ho Lung joined with Chu Teh and Liu Po-ch'eng in urging Chang to march north.[205] To explain his long delay in resuming the march, Chang gave the reason that he was training his troops so that they could deal with the cavalry of the Muslim generals in the Kansu corridor.[206] Of course, he had done no such thing. He did not embark upon a programme of training in preparation for crossing the Yellow River to fight the Muslim cavalry until he was persuaded to march again.[207] But now his destination was not north Shensi as his persuaders intended, but somewhere in the Kansu corridor to the north of the Yellow River. This shrewd plan was to regard Mao's north Shensi base as his front line against Japan while using Sinkiang or the USSR as his rear. If the projected united front was formed and the war against Japan broke out, Mao's military strength would be spent in the fighting, while Chang, retaining his own troops behind Mao and with Russian backing, would be the only strong man in the Communist movement of

[199] *Ming-pao*, 52.96.
[200] Liu Po-ch'eng, *HHLY* 10.
[201] *Ming-pao*, 54.88.
[202] *Ibid.* 48.85.
[203] *HHLY* 4.264.
[204] *Chiao-fei chan-shih*, 6.997.
[205] *Ming-pao*, 53.91 and 54.88. As to the formula, according to uncorroborated information, Lin Yü-ying suggested that Mao's centre be transformed into a north-west bureau and Chang's into a south-west bureau with Lin himself as the mediator between the two to bring about a reunification. See *Ming-pao*, 53.89.
[206] *Ibid.* 50.86.
[207] *Ming-pao*, 54.88.

China. The crossing of the Yellow River was necessary for the western column on another account. It must not remain south of the river if it was to avoid tough fighting against Chiang's troops and run the risk of being driven back to Mao-erh-kai and an impasse. What happened after the crossing was unexpected by Chang. The western column was annihilated by the Muslim cavalry of the KMT. With it went Chang's hope of challenging Mao's leadership. Politically he ceased to be a man of any weight. With his separatism bankrupted, his defection began.[208]

UNDERGROUND WORK IN THE 'WHITE AREA'

Since the creation of the rural soviets, tension as well as cooperation had developed between the 'white area' work and the land revolution. The former was doctrinally blessed to lead the latter, while the latter was all the time outgrowing the former in strength and importance. Still, as summed up in the 'Resolution of some questions in the history of our party' in 1945,[209] the party centre stubbornly refused to subordinate 'white area' work to rural work. It continued to insist on a mechanical interpretation of proletarian hegemony, quite oblivious to the fact that neither the proletarian theory nor the proletarian party was the domain of the proletariat.

It is undeniable that in both the Ch'ü Ch'iu-pai and Li Li-san periods the urban labour movement had become narrowly economic while the peasants, especially the armed peasants, were waging political and social battles to destroy the bastions of what they called 'feudal China'. In the arts and literature, through which many young people were radicalized, the CCP had a greater influence. The creative arts and literature of China began their own radicalization after the May Thirtieth movement of 1925, a tendency clearly shown, for instance, in the writings of Lu Hsun and the transformation of such literary organizations as the Creation Society

---

[208] There are only fragments of information on the provisioning of the Red Army on the Long March. It seems safe to assume that requisitioning from landlords and rich peasants was the usual source (*HHLY* 4.179–80), a pattern similar to the provisioning of the guerrillas after the Autumn Harvest uprisings.

The well-known story of Liu Po-ch'eng swearing brotherhood with a Lolo chieftain (Wales, *Red dust*, 71) is not typical. When the Red Army stayed in the Miao area in Lung-p'ing-chen in Kwangsi for some ten days, fires broke out near the army camps every night (*HCPP* 9.32). On the grassland, Ho Lung and Lo Ping-hui, who had fought the rearguard action almost all the way, were harassed by the Tibetans (Wales, *Red dust*, 130). Whenever there was a tribal feud, the Red Army made skilled use of it in order to obtain supplies (*HHLY* 4.128–30). Naturally they exploited the misgovernment of the KMT to help the poor and the imprisoned, who could not pay taxes and rent, in order to ingratiate themselves with the Yi and other tribes (*HHLY* 4.118–21).

[209] Mao, *HC* 3.978.

(Ch'uang-tsao she). In March 1930 the different strands of the general development of left-wing literature were gathered together in the founding of the Left-wing Writers' League. The magazines under its infuence challenged the academic critics, the proponents of 'art for art's sake', and the Nationalist writers. The league also influenced, to a remarkable degree, the film industry in Shanghai to turn its attention from costumed sword-fighting dramas to contemporary social problems. In both literature and film, this was the most celebrated period before the resistance war. Artists and writers produced praiseworthy works under severe persecution. Many of their writings were proscribed by KMT censorship and many writers were themselves either arrested and executed or driven to the soviet areas.[210] (See below, chapter 9.)

Curiously enough, the CI's July 1931 instruction on 'white area' work paid almost no attention to art and literature, hardly any to the student movement, but a great deal to labour unions and anti-imperialism. One result of this instruction was the party's effort to organize Shanghai workers during the Japanese invasion of January 1932, to agitate among the soldiers, and to try to carry the war into the foreign settlements. This all came to nothing.[211] The sectarianism of the CCP's urban work led the party to fight against the KMT Reorganizationists led by Wang Ching-wei, the Third Party led by Teng Yen-ta, and the Trotskyists led by Ch'en Tu-hsiu. With the 'yellow' labour unions, the CCP consciously or unconsciously found little in common for cooperation.[212]

The migration of party members to the soviet areas in 1931–3 further weakened 'white area' work. A conscious endeavour was initiated to reverse the flow and to give a semblance of equilibrium between town and country. On record some 150 cadres were sent back to the cities. But on the whole Liu Shao-ch'i's charge of the failure of the 'leftists' (the 28 Bolsheviks) to develop urban work was fully justified.[213]

One obstacle to expanding the CCP's urban work was, of course, the KMT's counter-espionage. To deal with this the CCP set up its own special security branch soon after the Sixth Congress. It was headed by Hsiang Chung-fa, Chou En-lai and Ku Shun-chang. In the underground war between these clandestine agents, the CCP centre in Shanghai was discovered and destroyed no less than fourteen times. The terror that the

[210] See Ch'eng Chi-hua *et al.*, *Chung-kuo tien-ying fa-chan-shih* (A history of the development of Chinese cinema); Jay Leyda, *Dianying, an account of films and the film audience in China*; Liu Shou-sung, *Chung-kuo hsin wen-hsueh shih ch'u-kao* (A preliminary draft history of modern Chinese literature). See also Wang Chien-min, *Draft history*, 2.137; T. A. Hsia, *Gate of darkness*.
[211] *Hung-se wen-hsien*, 386–92; Snow, *Random notes*, 17; Warren Kuo, *History*, 2.326.
[212] Wang Ming, *Hsuan-chi*, 3.51–2.
[213] *Ming-pao*, 58.87.

KMT's Investigation Department brought against the Communist provincial organizations, Youth Corps, Shanghai General Labour Union, the Workers' Mutual Aid Association (Kung-chi hui), anti-imperialist societies and cultural organizations caused their activities to decline or discontinue. With the arrests of Ku Shun-chang and Hsiang Chung-fa in April and June 1931, the party centre could hardly exist and function in Shanghai, hence its removal to the central soviet. In all, no less than 24,000 members of the CCP were either arrested or killed and 30,000 others had to go through the process of confession to the KMT police.[214] Nonetheless it was not impossible to buy one's way out of difficulty, the KMT special agents being so inefficient and corruptible. Sixty *yuan* was all that was needed for Liu Ning, for example, to have a chest of documents destroyed and himself released from prison.[215]

Around the soviet areas, K'ang Tse organized his Special Activities Corps (Pieh-tung-tui) of five columns, consisting of some 24,000 men to collect red deserters, blockade trade, inspect travellers and mail, and train and organize the masses.[216] The CCP, on its part, tightened the political security system in the soviets. They had anti-counter-revolution committees to ferret out hidden reactionaries and rescue arrested comrades, give aid to the families of the arrested, gather intelligence, set up an intelligence network from Kiangsi to Shanghai and Hong Kong, and take retaliatory action against KMT agents.[217]

Liu Shao-ch'i

Late in 1934 or early in 1935 Liu Shao-ch'i's task of picking up the shattered pieces of 'white area' work was far from easy. Apart from his rich experience in the labour movement, Liu was the man who had tidied up the shambles of urban work after Ch'ü Ch'iu-pai's putschism and replaced Lo Chang-lung as head of the Shanghai General Labour Union before his own exodus to the central soviet. In 1935–6 Liu now focused his attention on students, youth, and writers instead of the inactive labour unions. Because of the weakness of the party branches in the cities and the reluctance of left-wing sympathizers to accept extreme radicalism, Liu was critical of the adventurism manifested in the December Ninth

---

[214] Warren Kuo, *History*, 2.228–61; Ts'ao Po-i, *Soviet*, 408–14.

[215] Liu Ning, *I-ko kung-jen ti kung-chuang*, 66.

[216] Hollington Tong, *Chiang*, 1.208–9; Lloyd Eastman, 'Fascism in Kuomintang China: the Blue Shirts', *CQ* 49 (Jan.–March 1972), 1–31.

[217] Warren Kuo, *History*, 2.228–38; Ts'ao Po-i, *Soviet*, 408–14. The information given here is uncorroborated and should be accepted only with great care. I have deliberately left out whatever information there is in Kung Ch'u and Li Ang, for it is my view that whenever possible these two authors should be avoided.

movement, an anti-Japanese demonstration organized by Peking students on that date in 1935 (see p. 411). The first step he took was to distinguish clearly between secret and open work and to moderate political slogans in order to improve relations between the party and its front organization and the masses. It was hoped that party members could work in legally recognized organizations and thus be in closer contact with the masses without actually committing the sin of legal Marxism.[218] Liu's style was strictly that of the united front – organizing students' study groups and art circles, establishing students' national salvation associations, and supporting the 29th Army stationed in the Peking area. The village propaganda teams (Nan-hsia hsuan-ch'uan-t'uan) of 400–500 students organized after the December Ninth movement seemed to him too radical, as they only helped expose the hard core of the left-wing youth movement. Instead, Liu encouraged the organization of the semi-open National Salvation Vanguard (Min-hsien) – a small beginning of 300 members in February 1936 which was to grow to 1,300 in July.[219] In the student unions the left-wing played an increasingly important role, with P'eng Chen, Ch'en Po-ta and Huang Ch'eng working behind the scenes. Huang even managed to have himself elected president of the Tsing Hua Union.[220] In this way Liu Shao-ch'i preserved his precious cadres and brought students and the armies stationed in Hopei under their influence. This group – to be known as the December Ninth cadre – who after the outbreak of war migrated to the rural areas of Hopei and Shansi to work among the peasants, helped the 8th Route Army set up base areas. The experience of 1927 was thus re-enacted. In both his urban underground and rural open work, Liu laid a solid foundation for future development. With such attainments, his return to Yenan in 1937 was triumphal, with enough prestige for him to criticize the 28 Bolsheviks and to secure for himself a seat on the Politburo. It was probably then that the alliance between Liu and Mao was forged. However, working in 'white areas' Liu had no administrative routine to deal with, no bureaucratism to tackle. His theoretical aspirations were given vent in his study of a moral philosophy such as was needed for clandestine work. He was the first Communist of any importance to have trodden that forbidden philosophical territory which other Marxist angels feared to tread.

[218] Liu Shao-ch'i, 'Lun kung-k'ai kung-tso yü mi-mi kung-tso' (On open and secret work), in *Kung-ch'an-tang-jen* (The Communist), 1. A handwritten copy of this is in the Hoover Institution.
[219] Li Ch'ang, 'Hui-i min-hsien tui' (Reminiscences of the National Salvation Vanguard), in *I-erh-chiu hui-i-lu* (Memoirs of December 9), 16.
[220] *Ibid.* 187–9.

PREPARATION FOR THE SECOND UNITED FRONT

In September 1935, when Hsu Hai-tung's army eventually reached the north Shensi base area, the reconstructed soviet there was only two years old. Claiming some six counties, with its capital at Wa-yao-pao, this soviet had once been destroyed by Chiang, thanks largely to the motorways built by the China International Famine Relief Commission. This had also prevented it from joining with Chang Kuo-t'ao's soviet in north Szechwan.[221] When Mao and his east column arrived in October, they added to the strength of the soviet and gave it a chance to expand. Its capital was moved to Pao-an in mid-1936 and then to Yenan in January 1937. By the time the second united front came into being it had some 35,000 square miles and 1,500,000 people under its control.[222] Coincidentally, Chang Hsueh-liang's Manchurian army was transferred to Sian to fight the Communists, also in October 1935. The 8,000 strong Red Army was then opposed by seventeen KMT divisions in what was planned to be the final campaign of annihilation.[223]

Largely through their own mistakes and clumsy manoeuvres, the Long March saw the decline of the 28 Bolsheviks and Chang Kuo-t'ao, thus giving the party at long last a measure of unity unknown since the end of Ch'en Tu-hsiu's leadership. The CCP's time in the wilderness was drawing to a close. On the opposing side Chiang, using the suppression of 'bandits' as his reason, managed to penetrate into the south-west with his army, political apparatus, and economic institutions to give him a measure of national unity unknown since the death of Yuan Shih-k'ai in 1916. In the process of consolidating the situation in the south-west the various local forces had to make a choice in national politics – either to parley with the CCP so as to ward off Chiang's influence, or to succumb to Chiang's pressure in order to keep the Communists out of their territory. This consolidating process was in a sense beneficial to China, and probably helped her to withstand the strains and stresses of eight years of resistance against Japan.

After September 1931, the intensified aggressiveness of Japanese militant nationalism had produced its first reaction from the CCP, a call for a united front, published in October 1932. In this resolution, the party envisioned that Chiang's regime might disintegrate under the pressure of Japan and therefore there was no thought of an alliance with Chiang.

[221] *K'ang-jih chan-cheng shih-ch'i chieh-fang-ch'ü kai-k'uang* (The liberated areas during the anti-Japanese war), 6; *HCPP* 3.168–80.
[222] Wales, *Red dust*, 75; US War Department, Military Intelligence Division, 'The Chinese Communist movement', 2355.
[223] *HHLY*, Hong Kong, 10–11; *China year book, 1936*, 425–6.

However, this call attracted little attention outside the soviet areas and was interpreted by the country at large mainly as a move to protect the socialist fatherland rather than China. In no sense did the call succeed in gaining the CCP a share in the KMT's leadership of the struggle for national independence. The CCP was still considered by many as a mere instrument of Russia.

The CCP's proposal for a united front acquired a new meaning after the fall of Kuang-ch'ang during Chiang's final encirclement in April 1934; it became an attempt to reverse the worsening civil war situation and to rescue the CCP from its predicament. The central committee's letter to the nation on 10 April 1934 left the role of the KMT in the united front purposely vague. The KMT was not explicitly left out of the alliance; nor was the aim of overthrowing it renounced.[224] The deteriorating war situation moderated the CCP's attitude to the KMT, as shown in Chou En-lai's Six Point Programme of 20 July 1934,[225] which suggested a united front including all anti-Japanese forces, even Chiang Kai-shek's. Pragmatic as the new proposal indeed was, it was not completely opportunistic. In embryonic form it contained a new theoretical formulation to direct the revolution from the withering soviets onto a more hopeful course. Lenin's old theses of a national united front were obviously worth reviving. In Lenin's conception a nation may have no ultimate value; but in a China under the pressure of Japanese aggression, the existence of the Chinese nation was a matter of cardinal importance. In other words, the struggle for national liberation (anti-imperialist) was gradually overshadowing the struggle for social liberation (anti-feudal). In reviving this idea, the CCP had on its mind the bad experiences of the first united front of 1923-7, especially the 'betrayal' by the bourgeoisie and big landlords thought to be represented by Chiang Kai-shek. If the CCP was to mitigate its land revolution for the sake of a united anti-imperialist struggle, the questions that must be answered were (in the language of the day): was it to be a united front on a national-political level with all the anti-Japanese forces who had been at variance with Chiang? Or was it to be a united front of a social revolutionary sort based on the mobilization of the workers, peasants and soldiers with sufficient political consciousness to supervise their leaders so as to ensure its solidarity and success? The contradiction between these two approaches was explicit. Then tactically should the CCP forge a united front before mobilizing and arming the masses or vice versa? The failure of the first united front was to a large measure due to the absence of an independent Communist armed force. In 1935-6, the CCP

<hr>

[224] Hsiao Tso-liang, *Power relations*, 226.
[225] *Hung-hsing* (Red star) (20 July 1934), 1.

did have an army and an occupied territory. For the sake of unity against Japan, should the party give them up or should the resistance war be left to cement national unity without either of the major parties sacrificing its autonomy? Closely related to this last question was that of the temporary or permanent nature of the united front. If it was merely temporary, it followed that the two opposing parties entered into an alliance for national preservation without at the same time abandoning their long-range goals, whose fulfilment required both to continue their military and territorial expansion. If it was permanent, China must undergo a basic political change in order to permit the parties to contend for their long-term goals by peaceful means. The change would entail the nationalization of all armed forces, the creation of a democratic assembly, the guarantee of the basic freedoms, and so on. Above all, the most difficult question in 1935–6 was: could a united front with Chiang be meaningful and effective in view of Chiang's enmity and fickleness? These questions received serious consideration at the Seventh Congress of the CI in the summer of 1935, when the International called for a general anti-imperialist united front to curb the growth of fascism in the West and Japanese aggression in the East. In the spirit of this call, the August First Declaration was issued in the name of the Central Committee of the CCP by Wang Ming in Moscow.[226]

The scope of the united front envisaged in the declaration was broad enough to embrace all anti-Japanese forces. However, it still attacked Chiang as the enemy of the nation who should be excluded from the alliance. But there was a change in priority – Japan had replaced Chiang as the most feared enemy.[227] The exclusion of Chiang from both the proposed national defence government and the anti-Japanese allied armies provoked further questions: would Chiang stand aside and watch the allied armies fight Japan without taking any action? Would he continue to fight the CCP and other opponents while the anti-Japanese war was in progress? What justification could he have for either his action or inaction? Was he to declare neutrality in the Japanese war or to play the role of an ally of Japan? The illogicality of the declaration was soon realized and remedied by Wang Ming in his speech at the Seventh Congress of the CI on 7 August 1935. 'The path is left open for the Kuomintang if Chiang Kai-shek is to call off his anti-Communist

[226] Hu Hua, *Materials*, 263–9. At the Mao-erh-kai Conference no one even mentioned the possibility of an anti-Japanese united front; no one knew of the publication of the August First Declaration. Chang Kuo-t'ao, *Ming-pao*, 50.85.

[227] For discussions on the various aspects of the second united front, see L. P. Van Slyke, *Enemies and friends*; and Tetsuya Kataoka, *Resistance and revolution in China: the Communists and the second united front*.

campaign and join in the fight against Japan.' Still later, in his essay 'New situation and new strategy', Wang Ming addressed Chiang as 'Mr Chiang', saying, 'If Mr Chiang is willing to change his attitude, the Chinese Communist Party can cooperate with him'. In Wang's view, the national contradiction so outweighed the class contradiction that 'apart from the people's interests the Chinese Communist Party had no other interest in mind'.[228]

The thinking in north Shensi, where the real power of the party resided, if not the real authority, seems to have been different. The Red Army's anti-Japanese manifesto of 13 November 1935 was decidedly against both Japan and Chiang.[229] Two days later Mao drafted his Ten Point Programme, which was discussed and adopted without much revision by the Wa-yao-pao Conference of the Politburo on 25 December. Mao described Chiang as a 'running dog' of Japan, to be opposed by the CCP.[230]

The Wa-yao-pao Conference envisaged a broad alliance of all revolutionary classes against Japanese imperialism and the traitorous group led by Chiang. In order to arouse and mobilize these classes of people, it was necessary to satisfy the peasants' demand for land and workers', soldiers' and intellectuals' demands for improvement in their livelihood. Only in that way could their revolutionary zeal be sustained. It followed that the property of traitors, including Chiang, should be confiscated and redistributed; extortionate taxes should end; wages and salaries should be increased; and relief work should be organized. As to the strategy of this national war, the Red Army and the red territories should under no circumstances be abolished. Instead, in the Japanese and KMT occupied areas, revolutionary bases should be founded, and a two-front struggle against internal oppressors and foreign foes should be carried on from these bases. As conceived at Wa-yao-pao, the war of resistance was to be simultaneously a war of social revolution. Otherwise it could never become the mass war needed to ensure victory. Organizationally the first step was to set up an anti-Japanese government, similar to Wang Ming's national defence government. But organizational development would not stop there. In the base areas, revolutionary committees would serve as a transitional form of government leading to the creation of soviets. A prerequisite for the creation of the base areas was the expansion of all anti-Japanese armed forces and guerrillas. If the situation evolved in this

[228] Wang Ming, *Hsuan-chi*, 1.9–10, 11–13, 25 and 53; Van Slyke, *Enemies and friends*, 53–4; Kataoka Tetsuya, 23ff.
[229] Ho Kan-chih, *Modern revolution*, 1.187.
[230] *MTTC* 5.10 and 13–14.

manner, Chiang's China would be subject to external pressure from Japan and internal pressure from his opponents; it would grow weak and disintegrate. The CCP would then make fresh allies with the dissidents from Chiang's clique.[231]

Two points emerged clearly from the Wa-yao-pao resolutions – north Shensi had as yet no appetite for parleying with Chiang; and the peasant war remained the leading form of struggle, with the proletarian struggle in the cities its closest ally. The strategy of encircling the cities from the countryside would continue with little revision. But the application of such a strategy in a national war begged a theoretical and a pragmatic question: how could peasants be aroused to anti-imperialist struggle? Was a united anti-Japanese front without Chiang feasible?

In the nation at large there existed a widespread belief that the Communist movement was at the end of its tether and its grandiose plans did not deserve serious attention. To put teeth in its proposals the CCP launched in February–April 1936 its 'eastern expedition' across the Yellow River into Shansi, ostensibly to engage the Japanese in Hopei and Jehol. As Liu Chih-tan's army pushed towards Taiyuan, Yen Hsi-shan, the perennial governor there, sent a call for help to Chiang Kai-shek. The subsequent death of Liu in action and the withdrawal of the Red Army did not mean that the venture was a total failure. In addition to demonstrating the CCP's determination to fight the Japanese, it recruited 8,000 fresh troops and broke the back of Chiang's encirclement campaign which had been manned by a motley of 'miscellaneous' troops.[232] (See below, chapter 12.)

Another significant result of the 'eastern expedition' was that local military leaders in north-west China, including Chang Hsueh-liang, were now convinced of the CCP's patriotic commitment; consequently they lost their interest in fighting the Red Army. Relations between Chang and the CCP began to improve.[233] It was at this juncture that Lin Yü-ying came back from Moscow with the CI's new policy proposal. On 14 March 1936, Mao could therefore declare to the KMT that if the government troops stopped attacking the soviet area, the Red Army was prepared to conclude a truce with them.[234] The party's policy thus underwent a sharp change from the idea of a two-front struggle against both Japan and Chiang to that of forcing Chiang to join the united front. The way to

---

[231] The text of the Wa-yao-pao resolutions in *MTTC* 5 *passim*.
[232] Mark Selden, *The Yenan way in revolutionary China*, 103; Kataoka Tetsuya, 35–7.
[233] Snow, *Red star*, 370–8.
[234] Van Slyke, *Enemies and friends*, 60.

force him was to provoke a fight with Japan, to struggle first in order to achieve unity later. It was perfectly Maoist.[235]

Now there was at least a basis for bargaining between the two major parties. They could jockey for the most advantageous terms to ensure victory against Japan, and also for hegemony to rule and shape China after the conclusion of the resistance. When Chiang replied by assaulting the soviet area in April 1936, Mao and Chu loosed a tirade of violent language against him; when Chiang's assault was called off, the military commission of the Red Army proposed that the civil war be stopped for the sake of unity.[236] Meanwhile Chou En-lai and other CCP representatives were in Shanghai making contact with KMT leaders, such as Chang Ch'ün and Ch'en Li-fu, over the terms of cooperation.[237]

From the end of 1935, when Japan's East Hopei Anti-Communist Special Regime was established,[238] Chiang's efforts to reach a detente with Japan came to an impasse. The negotiations between Chang Ch'ün and Kawagoe, the Japanese ambassador to China, deadlocked while the Kwantung army instigated Mongolian troops to invade Suiyuan. Students in Peking, leading intellectuals in Shanghai, and military leaders in Kwangtung and Kwangsi criticized Chiang's accommodating attitude to Japan in harsher and more strident tones. Unable to contain Japanese militant nationalism or to destroy the CCP, Chiang's frustration led him to prepare for an eventual showdown with the foreign aggressor. That eventuality required moral and material aid from the USSR, the only major power willing to assist China. According to Chiang himself,[239] he sent an emissary to Vienna to sound out Russia's intention to help and these negotiations for a non-aggression pact and military aid between the two governments went on throughout 1936. It was in the context of popular sentiment against Japanese aggression, of deteriorating Sino-Japanese relations, of improving Sino-Russian feelings, and of a softer attitude of the CCP to Chiang, that the epochal Sian incident took place on 12 December 1936.[240]

[235] Ho Kan-chih, *Modern revolution*, 1.302.
[236] *Ibid.* 1.194; *Red China*, 26 May 1936.
[237] Chiang Kai-shek, *Soviet Russia in China: a summing-up at seventy*, 72–3.
[238] Hollington Tong, *Chiang*, 2.225.
[239] *Ibid.* 245.
[240] Charles McLane, *Soviet policy and the Chinese communists, 1931–1946*, 79–91. Prof. T. F. Tsiang visited Moscow at Chiang's request in late 1934; see Charles Lilley, 'Tsiang T'ing-fu: between two worlds 1895–1935'.

The Sian incident

The plot to arrest Chiang in Sian was hatched in great secrecy. When it occurred it shocked the world, the nation, and the CCP. Understandably, the CCP's initial reaction, based on imperfect information, showed signs of panic. From the point of view of all the anti-Japanese forces concerned – the USSR, the CCP and Chiang's captors – Chiang's death at any stage of the incident would have defeated their purpose of forming a united front. Chiang was narrowly preserved from death during the initial hours of his capture (in the chaos and confusion on the morning of the 12 December), and after that his safety was secured for the duration of his detention in Sian. Since Chang Hsueh-liang, Chiang's captor, gave no orders to kill Chiang, it is safe to assume that he had never entertained the thought of assassinating him. Moscow's directive to the CCP was clearly for Chiang's preservation. Among the rank and file of Chang Hsueh-liang's and Yang Hu-ch'eng's troops and the CCP there may have been a strong enough hatred to demand Chiang's blood, but this hardly reflected the wisdom of the leaders. True, Mao is reported to have gone into a rage when the Moscow directive arrived;[241] even this may have been a way to pacify his followers or an expression of his indignation against Moscow's interference in the CCP's internal affairs. With Chiang captured, the united front was definitely in the offing. The problems to be negotiated concerned the strategies, organizations, and ideologies that in the long term would affect the future of both Chiang's and the Communists' revolutions. (See pp. 162–3 above.)

In Nanking the pro-Japanese wing, represented by General Ho Ying-ch'in, advocated a tough reaction to the Sian incident by starting a punitive expedition against the rebels and the reds, while Wang Ching-wei was to be invited back to strengthen the possibility of a rapprochement with Japan.[242] But the influential press like the *Ta-kung-pao* demanded the release of Chiang and a settlement of the differences between Nanking and the rebels by peaceful means.[243] At the scene of the incident, Chou En-lai, Yeh Chien-ying and others held talks with Chiang, insistently arguing for a united front.[244] On both sides, the toughest problems lay in the reconciliation between erstwhile enmity and future friendship, unity and struggle, revolution and counter-revolution.

[241] Snow, *Random notes*, 1ff.
[242] Shigemitsu Mamoru, *Japan and her destiny*, 222–3.
[243] Editorial of *Ta-kung-pao*, 14 December 1936 in Chang Ch'ih-chang, *Chi-luan wen-ts'un* (Taipei ed., 1962), 222–3.
[244] J. M. Bertram, *Crisis in China: the story of the Sian mutiny* (also titled *First act in China*), 170; Kataoka Tetsuya, 46.

Up to this time Chiang's method of resolving these contradictions had been to eliminate the class struggle as represented by the CCP before facing up to the tension between China and Japan – a solution in line with Prince Kung's and Tseng Kuo-fan's policy of the 1860s toward the Taiping rebels. Wang Ming's method was to subordinate class struggle to national struggle so as to achieve national unity, for without unity China could not resist Japan. Mao, however, believed that unity was to be obtained only through struggle, as unity could not be bought cheaply. If it came cheaply, the unity would not be durable enough for a mass war against Japan. The Sian incident made Chiang give up his method. Thereafter a debate was to develop in the CCP between Wang Ming's broad cooperation to achieve unity *for* struggle and Mao's limited cooperation to achieve unity *through* struggle.

With his more orthodox view on the lack of political consciousness of the peasants, Wang was anxious to take the national revolution back to the cities where the KMT dominated. His original plan for a national defence government and anti-Japanese allied armies did not imply an overhaul of the government in Nanking, only its reform to include representatives of the other parties and popular bodies. Later he went even further to advocate unity of command, discipline, supply, equipment, and planning of the anti-Japanese allied forces.[245] According to him, unity without sincere cooperation could not ensure a successful resistance to Japan.[246] For him, therefore, everything must be for the resistance war and for unity. To be sure, he still had a considerable following in his party and the backing of the authority of the CI and the USSR. China's need for Russian aid tended to enhance his status in the CCP. Furthermore, in Central and South China there were guerrilla bands soon to be grouped together to form the New Fourth Army under Hsiang Ying, a follower of Wang Ming. Wang's personal prestige in the ECCI, his eloquence, and his real power made him a considerable figure capable of challenging Mao's leadership.

Mao, on the other hand, had scarcely any trust in Chiang as an ally. The war could be localized; it could be settled peacefully and quickly be transformed into a Japanese-Chiang joint campaign against the CCP. In that eventuality, to give up the Red Army and soviet territory would be sheer folly. To prepare against such an eventuality the CCP must not only preserve its autonomy and its ability to defend itself. It must also promote what Mao called democracy and progress for the improvement of people's livelihood and mass participation in the war, turning it into a true people's war. The struggle for democracy and progress was in itself a guarantee

[245] Wang Ming, *Hsuan-chi*, 1.168–9.   [246] *Ming-pao*, 61.91.

of the solidarity of the nation. In a mass war, even if the grande bourgeoisie and big landlords turned away from fighting Japan, the CCP could still stand alone without repeating the sorrowful history of 1927.

The crux of mass mobilization for a mass war lay in an appropriate land policy and economic reform. Once again the focus of the party was on the rich peasants. Wang Ming in his 'New situation and new strategy' of 1935 came out with a land policy even more moderate than Mao's before 1931: only landlords' land was to be confiscated while rich peasants could retain their farming tools and receive an equal share of land, not just poor land.[247] To be sure, Wang at this stage was disheartened by the failure of the land revolution, regarding it as merely an armed struggle with little social and political meaning.[248] At the Wa-yao-pao Conference this more lenient land policy was accepted. The rich, middle and poor peasants were to receive an equal share of the same land while the rich peasants' investments in commerce and industry were to remain intact. Their livestock, movable property and farm tools were not to be redistributed.[249] By the summer of 1936 the CCP tempered its land policy still further to draw it closer to Wang Ming's views, in order to facilitate cooperation between the two major parties.[250]

There were pragmatic reasons for the mitigation of CCP land policy. The fundamental agrarian problems of north Shensi, for that matter of North China in general, were not high tenancy rates and a hunger for land, but a shortage of labour and how to organize labour efficiently in order to achieve high productivity. Earlier, an ultra-left land policy implemented there had proved to be detrimental to agricultural production.[251] The change in land policy in December 1935, to one of confiscating only the rich peasants' land for rent, eliminated extreme inequality in land distribution and released the middle and poor peasants' enthusiasm for mass work. Their activism was to put an end to the monopoly of local power by landlords and rich peasants. The emphasis then was not on redistribution of land, but on a fairer distribution of grain.[252]

Mao's alternative strategy was never as crude as the 'defeat both Japan and Chiang' policy described by Chang Kuo-t'ao.[253] Its essence was how to keep Chiang in the war of resistance and if Chiang made peace with Japan, how to fight on independently and win the revolution. With

[247] Wang Ming, *Hsuan-chi*, 1.97-8.   [248] *Ibid*. 81.
[249] Ho Kan-chih, *Modern revolution*, 1.191; Central Executive Committee's directive on 15 December 1935 in *MTTC* 5.13.   [250] *MTTC* 5.63-5.
[251] Mao Tse-tung, *Ching-chi wen-t'i yü ts'ai-cheng wen-t'i* (Economic and financial problems), 8-9 and 12.
[252] *Ibid*. 12-15.   [253] *Ming-pao*, 60.88.

inferior military strength, victory could be assured only by mass mobilization to set up, defend and enlarge base areas, and thus to hasten the arrival of a nationwide revolutionary situation. The overall strategy in the war of resistance, as in the civil war before it, had to be the encirclement of cities from the countryside, thus cutting the ground under the feet of the cities and thereby taking the revolution to the cities. Meanwhile a social revolution in the countryside was in progress that was protected by the party's army and guided by its mass line. Early in 1937, as in the summer of 1936, when Mao engaged Edgar Snow in systematic conversation, his strategy may not yet have developed in its full form. But the main points were all there. Many of Mao's comrades, particularly Wang Ming, disagreed with him and the debate within the party continued. Meanwhile fast-moving events on the national front compelled the two major parties to enter a formal alliance in April 1937, less than three months before the outbreak of the war against Japan.

CHAPTER 5

THE AGRARIAN SYSTEM

The narratives in preceding chapters have concerned China's international relations to 1931 and the fortunes of the Nationalist government in power at Nanking and its Chinese Communist opponents down to 1937. Yet, as earlier volumes in this series have made plain, China's modern history can hardly be grasped through narrative alone; too many specific (though often little known) situations affected the course of events – institutional practices, economic and social conditions, the ideas and aspirations of leaders and followers. The next chapters therefore deal with the agrarian economy, peasant movements, local government, higher education and literary trends – contextual elements that influenced the dramatic events from 1937 to 1949. We begin with an appraisal of the livelihood of the common people on the land.

By the end of the *ancien régime* in 1912 Chinese agriculture supported a huge farming population, which worked hard and diligently but had to use ingenious methods to make a living from the inadequate amount of land available. Since aggregative statistics are lacking, this chapter presents a qualitative account in order to describe a situation quite unfamiliar to most people in Europe and the Americas.

While travelling to Nanking in January 1869 Ferdinand von Richthofen noted the following scene:

That honeybee-like diligence to cultivate the land is the special quality of the Chinese. I know of a most astonishing example.... At the rear of a mine workmen had thrust large coal slabs into the ground .... Nearby villagers had built a staircase to the top of these slabs and carried soil and fertilizer on their backs .... In this way small parcels of land were farmed above the land. These areas were several square meters in size. From below, one could see only jagged coal slabs jutting upward, but from above, one only saw green fields laid out in a complex pattern. In the winter the peasants planted wheat, in the summer rice.[1]

Chinese farmers had mastered the secrets of replenishing the soil's nutrients even while obtaining two crops a year in some regions and three

---

[1] Ferdinand Paul Wilhelm von Richthofen, *Tagebücher aus China*; tr. Eihara Masao as *Shina ryokō nikki* (Diary of travel in China), 1.139.

crops every two years in others. Their skill at multiple cropping, in the words of the American agronomist King in 1909, made possible 'the fullest possible utilization of every minute of the growing season and of the time of the family in caring for the crops'.[2]

But farming skill and diligence were not sufficient to enable all families to feed and clothe themselves. Some households – what fraction they were of the farming population remains unknown – found life difficult and even intolerable. The following report describes the plight of some farmers in Kiangsu and Chekiang provinces during the 1870s:

Formerly the men farmed and the women wove cloth. A hundred *mou* (6.6 hectares) of land could be worked with one farm labourer. A household of eight never suffered from hunger. In a family with five *mou* (0.3 hectares) one woman tended the silkworms; a seventy-year-old woman could easily support herself from these earnings. Today's farmers and weavers are unable to support themselves and their children on an equivalent amount of land with the same size household as in former times. Formerly widows, widowers, orphans, the childless, being without the support of a family might suddenly die at any time. But today even those having parents are on the verge of death. Moreover, they have no means to live. Are not these conditions different from those of yesterday?[3]

Our raconteur provides no information whether crop yields declined, taxes increased, or the prices of goods and services sold declined relative to those received. Conditions of rural poverty and prosperity varied between districts, perhaps even regions, and fluctuated according to the state of the harvest.

Taken together, however, the writings of foreign observers and even native experts on rural conditions in the final years of the Ch'ing dynasty convey neither a sense of production decline nor a singular state of foodgrain or fibre shortage. Japanese visitors were probably the most severe critics of agriculture, which they were constantly comparing with their own. The following comment by Masuko Teisuke, who travelled in central and south-east China in 1911, is typical:

Of China's various industries, agriculture produces 50 per cent of the country's wealth and employs about 70 per cent of the population. Further, the various farming techniques have already been developed for a very long time. Yet, in spite of the widespread knowledge on such matters many areas between hills remain uncultivated, and a great deal of barren land remains unfarmed. These possibilities of improvement simply have been ignored. The peasantry cannot escape from their bare subsistence level as they cannot accumulate any savings. And if there is one bad harvest, they are reduced to starvation.[4]

[2] F. H. King, *Farmers of forty centuries: or, permanent agriculture in China, Korea, and Japan*, 233–4.
[3] Li Wen-chih, comp. *Chung-kuo chin-tai nung-yeh-shih tzu-liao* (Historical materials on modern China's agriculture), 1.910.
[4] Masuko Teisuke, *Chūbu Shina* (Central China), 29.

Why peasants could not save and escape their precarious fate of depending only on the harvest is never explained. Whether this difficulty originated from poor soils, overcrowding, or the farmers' inability to narrow the gap between the potential and actual output is never clear from the descriptions of agriculture of this period.

What does seem clear, however, is that some Chinese began to sense that they were suffering more and more losses in the form of opportunities foregone to modernize agriculture, that is to say, to increase the productivity of land and labour by adopting available modern technology. Ko Ching-chung, writing in 1921 for the fiftieth anniversary of Shanghai's major newspaper, *Shen-pao*, assessed his country's foodgrain situation over the previous half century and found the performance poor.

Rice, wheat, and five other miscellaneous cereals are the outstanding basic products of our country's agriculture. Yet because of the steady growth of population, the absence of any expansion of cultivated land, and the lack of improvement in farming techniques, harvests have not been bountiful. There exists barren land that people do not know how to reclaim. There are rivers that we do not know how to control. During some years the production of foodgrain has not been sufficient to supply the needs of the country. These were the years of floods and droughts when we were without the resources to do anything. The reader will note that the Maritime Customs statistics reporting foodgrain imports and exports show that exports have barely attained one-third the volume of imports. I can only say that these last fifty years of agricultural history have been years of great disappointment.[5]

The failure of agriculture to modernize was not absolute. After the advent of the railway and new treaty-port urban centres, agriculture gradually became more commercialized. This process was more rapid in the north than in the south. Agrarian conditions would change after the First World War when in many regions the rural market systems were disturbed from outside by sharp shifts in supply and demand. In heavily populated areas these changes in supply or demand required reallocation of resources in order to avoid large-scale unemployment and a fall in rural income. Because of the failure of state and local administration to maintain law and order or provide economic assistance, such market readjustments had very high social costs. But before describing these conditions of agrarian crisis it is necessary to outline and clarify the agrarian system of this period.

[5] Ko Ching-chung, 'Wu-shih-nien lai Chung-kuo nung-yeh shih' (The last fifty years of Chinese agriculture), in Liang Ch'i-ch'ao *et al. Wan-ch'ing wu-shih-nien lai chih Chung-kuo* (China during the last fifty years), 210.

ASPECTS OF THE AGRARIAN SYSTEM

By 1887 roughly 87 per cent of China's land was privately owned. The rest belonged to the Manchu court, Manchu banner units, schools and military organizations, or consisted of village common fields.[6] On this privately owned land the typical rural family did not exclusively farm; its members repaired structures and tools, spun thread and wove cloth, made decorative or useful objects from braided straw, carted goods, or hawked wares. Rural surveys of the 1930s suggest that probably only six out of every ten households, often less, obtained 50 per cent or more of their income from farming. By this definition – the one I shall use – only three out of four households could be called farms in, for example, Lao-wa-chuang village in T'ai-an county (Shantung).[7] Likewise, in Sung village of P'eng-te county (Honan), six out of ten households were farms.[8] In South China the number of bona fide farms was even less. What kind of an agrarian system operated to make possible this variety of rural households?

Product markets and factor markets

Let us begin by visualizing rural families or households as carrying out economic activities in markets of two distinct kinds, the product market and the factor market. Product markets were formal or informal market-places where households sold their goods for cash or exchanged them for other goods. Their location ranged along a continuum from large cities, through small towns, to villages or points along well-travelled routes. The overwhelming proportion of goods marketed from villages entered the periodic markets, or standard marketing-places, which typically served between 20 and 30 villages.[9] Exceptions existed, but this pattern was widespread by the late nineteenth century as urban population became concentrated less in a few large centres and more in places with periodic markets.[10]

Most households were within a half-day's travel of some periodic market, where a legion of merchants, brokers and peddlers circulated at prescribed times during the lunar month. The large number of buyers

[6] Li Wen-chih, comp. *Chung-kuo chin-tai nung-yeh-shih tzu-liao*, 1.22

[7] South Manchurian Railway Company, henceforth SMR, Chōsabu (Research Section), *Hoku-shi nōson gaikyō chōsa hōkoku* (Research report on village conditions in North China), 2.68.

[8] *Ibid.* 3.22.

[9] G. William Skinner, 'Marketing and social structure in rural China, Part II', *JAS* 26.2 (Feb. 1965); see pp. 18–19.

[10] Gilbert Rozman, *Urban networks in Ch'ing China and Tokugawa Japan*, 103–4.

and sellers that haggled over prices suggests that price competition was intense. One foreign observer remarked that 'in no other country are the free play of competition and the law of supply and demand still so completely relied upon for the regulation of prices'.[11] Powerful merchant guilds might exercise some restraint of trade in some markets, but 'to avoid uncertainty and reduce risk, most merchants delegated their buying and selling to brokers' who had to compete with each other in the market.[12]

Equally important, there were so many merchants competing within each county that no single buyer could corner the market. For instance, in Chien-te county in Chekiang, located on the Tung River, 100 km south of Hangchow, there were some 190 large merchant establishments in 1930; all used brokers and 'kept their affairs quite secret, so that we know very little about them'.[13] Finally, consider the following conditions of rice marketing in Hankow in 1913–14:

Rice exchange in Hankow is no different than in Shanghai, where it is handled through rice brokerage firms. In Hankow the main rice market is in the harbour at Ch'en-chia-tsui. There are 20 rice brokerage firms connected to the same rice merchant guild, which controls the profits from rice marketing in Hankow. However, there is no case where these firms buy large quantities of rice at a fixed time, or send agents to the rice producing areas to corner the rice supply. Nor are there any examples where they resort to cunning means to collude with various shops which buy rice. We can say that these practices simply do not exist on a yearly basis, and for Chinese merchants this is one of their noteworthy characteristics.[14]

In general, these competitive product markets seem to have allowed rural families to obtain fair prices, because buyers and sellers never held sufficient economic power to fix prices for very long. Further, these competitive markets encouraged the participation of every family in some kind of market activity.

The term 'factor market' refers to those informal and formal arrangements between rural households by which labour, land and loanable funds were exchanged on some negotiated, contractual basis, with payment either in money or in kind. Families seeking to lease or rent land used middlemen to find a customer. Households wanting to hire labour visited

[11] Albert C. Muhse, 'Trade organization and trade control in China', *American Economic Review*, 6.2 (June 1916) 309–23, see p. 309.
[12] Tōa dōbun kai hensan kyoku, *Shina keizai zensho* (A compendium on the Chinese economy), 7.225.
[13] Tiao-ch'a Che-chiang ching-chi so t'ung-chi-k'o, *Che-chiang Chien-te hsien ching-chi tiao-ch'a* (Survey of the economy of Chien-te county, Chekiang), 1.6.
[14] Higashi Norimasa, comp. *Chūbu Shina keizai chōsa* (Research on the economy of Central China), 1.1, 361.

special areas in market towns where young and old men congregated at early hours to hire out for a day's work. Families in need of credit visited shops, found merchants, or approached kin or friends to negotiate a loan. A family needing cash used its land to borrow. It might pledge some land as security for a small loan, repayable with interest within a few months. For a larger loan, to be repaid without interest in a year or so, it might actually transfer the property right to the creditor. In this case, the creditor would either use the land or lease it, to the borrower or another family, and collect rent. When the loan was repaid, the property right reverted to its original owner.

Together, these product and factor markets linked villages to towns and households to households through exchange transactions that represented incomes to some families and expenditures to others. When farmers harvested and sold some of their crops, those families with storage facilities and less need for cash stocked to sell later. The farmers who sold first received cash to repay debts and purchase goods. Therefore, during the harvest season a flow of cash was already returning to the towns, and some cash was circulating between village families. In later months, rising farm prices encouraged some farmers to relinquish their stocks. Other farmers began to sow for the next crop, and households short of cash borrowed. Meanwhile, the cash flow to villages continued as farm stocks were reduced, and borrowing between rural families continued.

All cash flowing to the market passed through brokers and merchants to become income for urban households and suppliers. This was because the brokers and merchants selling to farmers used part of their income to stock goods, which they obtained from urban producers and importers. Those of the urban producers who used agricultural raw materials had already paid the brokers and merchants who purchased directly from the farmers, and such expenditure finally became the cash farmers received when they marketed their goods. In this way the product market linked villages to market towns and so completed one link in the circular cash flow.

For many households, either wage income or credit was an indispensable means of survival until they could harvest their crops. The formal and informal contracts that linked households in exchange relationships made it possible for farmers to share scarce resources and, to some extent, minimize the risks and uncertainties of economic activities. These transactions between households in the factor market completed the final link in the circular flow.

Land and labour

Farming in all parts of China was characterized by a definite sequence and rhythm of work. In the north-east, north and north-west the farmers lightly ploughed and raked the fields during late February and March.[15] Beginning in April and May, until late autumn, they sowed, irrigated, weeded, and harvested their crops. A study of 24 farms around Yung-loh-tien, a town in Chin-yang county in central Shensi, in 1926 reported that 'according to the yearly distribution [of labour], May to September are the busiest months'.[16] Another study, this one of farms in Wei county (Shantung) in 1924, concluded that 'the farm work on crops begins late in March and is finished by December first'.[17] In central, south-east, and south-west China, climate and soil favoured a cycle of two crops a year instead of the three crops every two years that were raised in the north. Rice was planted in April and harvested in late July and August.[18] Farmers then sowed wheat, barley, and green manure crops (broad beans, etc.) in late autumn and harvested them in late spring, as was common in the fertile Kiangsu delta area around Shanghai in 1939:

The farmers in this vicinity produce two crops, mainly of cotton and rice. For the summer crop they grow cotton, rice, soy-beans and vegetables between late April and late summer. For the winter crop they grow wheat, barley, and broad beans between late autumn and early spring. They consume all their rice, barley, and soy-beans; and wheat and vegetables are sold to brokers and other buyers.[19]

In the south-east, farmers harvested two rice crops from the same plot, sowing the first crop in late spring and the second in late autumn.

A certain fixed amount of family labour was required to produce each crop. In Wei-hsien, W. Y. Swen found that the annual man-labour hours per *mou* of land varied greatly with the crop: 28.2 hours per *mou* for yellow beans; 36.6 for wheat; 72.5 for sorghum; 79.0 for millet; 91.6 for sweet potatoes; and 241.1 for tobacco.[20] Moreover, labour requirements depended greatly upon the amount of irrigation. Japanese researchers in Sung village of P'eng-te county reported the following conditions in 1940:

[15] Ramon H. Myers, *The Chinese peasant economy: agricultural development in Hopei and Shantung, 1890–1949*, 177–8.

[16] Wu Hwa-pao, 'Agricultural economy of Yung-loh Tien in Shenshi province', *Nankai Social and Economic Quarterly*, 9.1 (April 1936) 171.

[17] W. Y. Swen, 'Types of farming, costs of production, and annual labor distribution in Weihsien County, Shantung, China', *Chinese Economic Journal*, 3.2 (Aug. 1928) 653.

[18] *Chinese Economic Journal* (Nov. 1927) 921; *Shina keizai zensho* 8.31–2; *Chinese Economic Monthly* (July 1926) 295–9.

[19] SMR, Shanghai Research Section, *Chū-shi ni okeru nōson no shakai jijō* (Social conditions in villages of Central China), 2.

[20] Swen, 'Types of farming', 667.

Even farming in this county depended upon human labour power to an extraordinary degree. In areas of well-irrigated farming, this tendency was still more marked. In Sung village different amounts of labour power were required for cultivating the major crops, and if irrigation existed, the labour requirements were even higher... One-third of the total labour input for cultivating cotton went for irrigation alone, and for millet, it was one-quarter the total labour input.[21]

When households farmed more land, the inputs they used per unit of land declined beyond a certain farm size as did the value and yield per unit of land. In Manchuria the Japanese found in 1933 that, for 10,047 households in 230 villages, the number of labour animals used per unit of land began to decline after the farm reached 150 *mou*, and the amount of labour declined after 1,000 *mou*.[22] John Buck also reported that the man-equivalent units of labour per farm rose as farm size enlarged, but that in many cases both crop yield and labour input per hectare declined after a certain farm size had been reached.[23] The same inverse relationship between labour input and farm size was found in Central China by a Japanese survey of four villages in Sung-Kiang county of Kiangsu in 1939:

We observed that 50.4 persons per *mou* were used for farms of less than 4.9 *mou*; 31.5 persons per *mou* for farms between 15 and 19.9 *mou*; and no more than 21.1 persons per *mou* for farms larger than 20 *mou*. Therefore, as the farm size enlarged, there was a tendency for the amount of labour used per unit of land to decline. The smallest farms applied more than the necessary amount of household and hired labour even though they had less labour power than did the large farms. This is an extremely significant point.[24]

The Japanese never explained why this inverse relationship was significant, but it is one that characterizes pre-modern agriculture, even modern agriculture, and in recent years has become the object of considerable study and theorizing.

This agrarian system possessed defined limits. Agricultural production was characterized by sequential activities that required a fixed relationship of land to labour. Any deviation from this relationship, as when labour was withdrawn from soil preparation, irrigating, or weeding, invariably reduced the level of output. This important fact was noted by von Richthofen in 1868, while he was travelling near Hangchow in Chekiang province.

---

[21] SMR, *Hoku-shi nōson gaikyō chōsa hōkoku*, 118.
[22] Jitsugyōbu, *Nōgyō keiei zokuhen* (A supplementary study of agriculture management), 88–9.
[23] J. L. Buck, *Land utilization in China*, 293–4, 291, 306, 297, 295.
[24] SMR: Mantetsu Shanhai jimusho chōsashitsu, *Kōsoshō shōkōken nōson jittai chōsa hōkokusho* (Research report of village conditions in Sung-chiang county, Kiangsu), 158.

This area, which has been allowed to go fallow [after the Taiping Rebellion], once supported a very large population and contained really rich land; even now most of it is not being cultivated. The reason for this seems to be that the method of land use in China depends upon the available population being of a certain size, which, if too small, cannot even farm a small area of land. Moreover, the limited labour supply of the Chinese and their undeveloped tools seem to be the principal reasons for that tightly knit organization of labour which works so hard. The scale of cultivated land in this country seems to be in fixed relationship with the quantity of fertilizer that a certain number of people can produce. If any of these people are lost due to sickness or war, the production of fertilizer declines. Then that potential farming land diminishes in size. So if half of your population dies, half of the land will never be farmed.[25]

This, then, was the land and labour relationship that made it possible for family farms to feed China's large population.

Village and household

Rural families, whose number might consist of as few as four to six persons or as many as thirty, lived in villages of varying size. In the harsh climate of the north-east, favoured with abundant fertile land, new villages rapidly emerged after the 1880s. Numbering between twenty and fifty households, these new communities received migrants from the northern provinces and offered them a chance to farm the soy-bean and foodgrains. Southward in the hilly country and coarse, sandy soil of south Manchuria and the Liaotung peninsula, villages were more numerous, some being only half a mile from each other. They were also larger, sometimes containing as many as a hundred households, and had been founded more than a century earlier. A traveller moving southward across the North China plain – a vast, fertile area despite its bitter winters and hot, frequently drought-ridden summers – encountered a veritable sea of villages. In the 1890s the American missionary Arthur H. Smith estimated that the typical village of this region had eighty households. But then in a three-mile area in Hopei he found 'sixty-four villages, the smallest having thirty families and the largest more than 1,000 while the average [was] 188 families'.[26] Decades later, Chinese scholars studying Ting-hsien south of Peking on the Hankow-Peking railway line found the average number of families per village to be 150, with around 70,000 persons residing in 453 villages.[27]

In east-central China, the rice-wheat region, climate becomes warmer,

[25] von Richthofen, *Tagebücher*, tr. Eihara, 2.79–80.
[26] Arthur H. Smith, *Village life in China: a study in sociology*, 18–19.
[27] Sidney D. Gamble, *Ting Hsien: a North China rural community*, 22.

rainfall less variable, and the soil slightly acidic – conditions favourable for higher crop yields. By 1933–4, many thousands of villages could be found there, nestled in coves or perched on high ground off small creeks and waterways. Villages were smaller in size than north of the Huai River: in four Kiangsu counties, twenty-seven villages averaged 31 households per village, and in four Chekiang counties, thirty-one villages averaged 39 families per village.[28] In the foremost south-east province of Kwangtung, a tropical environment enabled peasants to grow fruit, engage in fish-farming, and cultivate a great variety of crops with rice, which could be double-cropped in many districts. In fairly remote areas, such as the islands south of the New Territories adjacent to present-day Hong Kong, there were villages with only twenty to forty households; the majority contained less than 20 families.[29] In more densely populated districts such as Kao-yao, an early 1930s survey cited many villages as having over 200 households. Yet the range of household numbers was extremely great: a sample of 5,000 villages included communities with as few as 22 families, whereas the largest embraced 927 households, a range matched by communities on the North China plain.[30] Similar diversity and irregularity in village size existed in the provinces of Kiangsi, Hunan, Szechwan and Yunnan. In newly settled areas of central and south-west China, villages appeared to be small in size compared to the older and larger communities in the heartland of the country's traditional farming areas: the Pearl River delta region; the river basin of the Min in Fukien; the Yangtze delta region; and the North China plain. Where communities had been settled for over a century, most villages were very small and virtually a stone's throw away from each other, in spite of their different sizes. Most communities were compact, with households clustered close together; only in parts of Szechwan were households located some distance from each other.

Rural elites

Every village had its elite of wealthy families who owned land and played the leading role in village affairs. In some villages virtually all the land might belong to one or two such families. The Wang and Chou families of Hsiao-ying village in Mi-yun county (Hopei) owned 83 per cent of the

---

[28] Hsing-cheng-yuan nung-ts'un fu-hsing wei-yuan-hui (Executive Yuan Rural Reconstruction Commission), comp. *Chung-kuo nung-ts'un tiao-ch'a tzu-liao wu-chung: Chiang-su sheng nung-ts'un tiao-ch'a*, see App. in vols. 1 and 2.

[29] James W. Hayes, 'Old ways of life in Kowloon: the Cheng Sha Wan villages', *Journal of Oriental Studies*, 8.1 (Jan. 1970) 154–88, see pp. 154, 157.

[30] Negishi Benji, *Minami Shina nōgyō keizai ron* (Essays on South China's agricultural economy), 196–7.

land. The Wei family in Kao-wei-chuan of Ts'ao county (Shantung) owned 5,700 out of 6,000 village *mou*. The Ma family owned 90 per cent of the land in Yang-chia-kou village in Mi-chih county (Shensi). Chang-an village in Hsiao county (Kiangsu) was made up of six hamlets; in one of them, a single family controlled all the land.[31]

In other villages most of the land might be owned by landlord bursaries (*tsu-chan*) or by a wealthy family living in another village or, more typically, in the market town. A good example of such absentee ownership was reported by a Chinese academic travelling in Anhwei province in 1935.

One village several kilometers from the county seat (Fou-yang) contained mostly tenant farmers with their rice fields finely divided into small plots. If one travelled further on, the number of owner-cultivator farmers increased in number. According to these tenants, the land nearest the county seat belonged to the merchants who lived there, and each owned several hundred *mou* of land. When we investigated further, we saw a great wall along the Chuan River. We learned the land around the wall belonged to a great landlord who owned 700 *mou*, leased 670 *mou*, and farmed the rest. He was also a wine merchant. Stretching far from these walls were other villages with embankments belonging to the Chou, Liu, T'ang, and Chang families of Ho-fei-hsi village.[32]

This mixture, running from part farmer-managed to purely tenant-managed farms, with most households owning their land, defies simple categorization because of complex regional variation.[33] In the mid-1930s rural statistics gathered by the Nationalist government suggest that as many as 46 per cent of rural households owned their land and supported themselves by farming; another 24 per cent were part-tenants and owner-cultivators who supplemented farming income with other income sources; the final 30 per cent were labouring-tenant households who depended on wage income to supplement farm income earned from rented land.[34]

Large landowners formed the backbone of local elite power in villages or market towns. Yet they were not a permanent caste-like group; their large, extended families rarely maintained their position in the community

[31] Amano Motonosuke, *Shina nōgyō keizai ron* (An essay on the Chinese farm economy), 1.28–31.

[32] Abe Yoshinori, 'Anki tochi chōsa nikki' (A diary of land investigation in Anhwei), *Mantetsu chōsa geppo*, 19.1 (Jan. 1939) Part 2, 129.

[33] The best study of this complex land tenure system in North China is Tōa kenkyūjo, *Keizai ni kansuru Shina kankō chōsa hōkokusho: toku ni Hoku-Shi ni okeru kosaku seido* (An investigative report of old customs in China concerning the economy: the tenant system in North China). For Central China see Sun Wen-yu, Ch'iao Ch'i-ming, Ying Lien-keng, Lo Wen-shu and Wang Yung-hsin, comps. *Yu-O-Wan-Kan ssu-sheng chih tsu-tien chih-tu* (The tenant system in the four provinces of Honan, Hupei, Anhwei and Kiangsi). For Szechwan see Meng Kuang-yu and Kuo Han-ming, *Szu-ch'uan tsu-tien wen-t'i* (The tenant problem in Szechwan).

[34] Yen Chung-p'ing *et al. Chung-kuo chin-tai ching-chi-shih t'ung-chi tzu-liao hsuan-chi* (Selected statistical materials on the economic history of modern China), 262.

for more than a generation or two before being replaced by other families. Even in the single lineage dominated villages of south-east China, wealthy households of a given surname were eventually replaced by other families with the same surname. Evidence to support this assertion of a revolving elite is scanty, but it does exist. For example, when 37 Manchurian villages are ranked by period of settlement, and the households within each of these ranks are compared in terms of their social and land tenure status at the time of their arrival in the village and then in 1934–6, the results are as follows: for the oldest villages the data clearly show that by 1934–6, the total percentage of landlords had declined, that of owner-cultivators had risen, and that of tenants had declined.[35]

Only a few families residing in rural communities ever accumulated considerable land; the remainder either rented land from them or worked their lands as hired labourers. Eventually, of course, land changed hands, new families accumulated land, but the same renting and labouring, only by different households, continued. How was it possible for some families to accumulate land, only to lose it later?

A large family – ten to twelve persons – could reclaim land and farm a large tract of 40 to 60 *mou* (nearly 3–4 hectares). But landholdings exceeding several hundred *mou* (about 15 ha.) or even larger, could only be acquired by families of great wealth. The few facts available about these families indicate that most became wealthy originally through trade, moneylending, or as officials. They then purchased land, developed new lands, or acquired land from families who had pledged or mortgaged it to acquire credit. The records of 135 former landlords in Shantung during the nineteenth century, collected and analysed by two Marxist Chinese historians, show that nearly 60 per cent of this sample had formerly been officials or urban merchants.[36] These landlord households, located in the main commercial centres near the Grand Canal, accumulated their wealth in the cities and then purchased rural land. Some of it they leased to families of the same village; the remainder they farmed with teams of hired labour from surrounding households. This example is probably representative of other provinces during the same period.

Wealthy urban families also purchased tracts of land, hired labourers to develop it, and then invited families to settle and farm it as tenants. In Mi-chih county of northern Shensi, 8 km south-east of the county seat and 16 km south of Sui-te county, six hamlets of 271 households were

[35] Ramon H. Myers, 'Socioeconomic change in villages of Manchuria during the Ch'ing and Republican periods: some preliminary findings', *Modern Asian Studies*, 10.4 (1976) 591–620, see pp. 614–15.

[36] Ching Su and Lo Lun, *Ch'ing-tai Shan-tung ching-ying ti-chu ti she-hui hsing-chih* (Landlord and labour in late Imperial China: case studies from Shantung), see Appendix.

located on the Yang-chia-kou Canal, which flowed off the Wu-ting River. Fifty-one of these families leased land and belonged to the Ma lineage. They resided together behind large walls near a mountain.[37] The lineage founder, Ma Chia-lo, first managed a shop in Sui-te county seat in the late 1820s. Ma saved his money and opened his own shop in 1833 in Mi-chih county seat. His four sons helped him, and a fifth son became an official and remitted his money home. Ma used these savings to lend, buy land, and speculate in the grain market. He finally invested a large sum to buy land near Yang-chia-kou, hired workers to clear it, and invited families to settle and farm the land as tenants. The Ma lineage then sold its shops and moved to live in Yang-chia-kou. For the next seventy years, the third and fourth generation sons of the Ma lineage loaned money, collected rents from their land, and speculated in the grain market. From the account books of Ma Wei-hsin, a fourth-generation landlord, we know that the Ma households collected grain rents and loan repayments that annually far exceeded the grain used for their households. They stored surplus grain and later sold it when market prices had reached their zenith. After 1910, the landholdings of the lineage remained stable in size until the late 1930s when many households began to sell their land in fear it would be expropriated.

In other instances, wealthy individuals joined together to develop land. Near Hsiang-yin, a city south of Lake Tung-ting in Hunan, ten persons in 1917 formed a company, hired 8,000 workers to build dikes, and invited families to rent the land and farm.[38] An even more common procedure was for city people to acquire land through moneylending and then lease the land, preferring to remain absentee landlords. Farmers were introduced to wealthy families from which they borrowed by pledging or mortgaging their land. If they were unable to repay, their land became the property of their creditors. Yuan Shih-k'ai, to judge from the following account by Japanese researchers, practised this type of moneylending on a large scale in 1909–11 to become one of Honan's largest landlords.

Yuan Shih-k'ai acquired his land during the period when he retired to Honan after his fall from power. The method he used to acquire large tracts of cultivated land was not to purchase it from various sellers at a fair price but to take land offered as collateral for securing a loan (*ju-tien*). In the tenth section of P'eng-te county he amassed most of his land that way. His relatives and agents, too, are known to have acquired land by the same methods. The land mortgaged to Yuan (*ch'u-tien*) represented the receipt of both immediate cash and a signed contract

[37] Kawachi Jūzō, 'Chūgoku no jinushi keizai' (The landlord economy of China), *Keizai nempō*, 18 (1965) 48–124.
[38] Hsin Hu-nan pao, *Hu-nan nung-ts'un ch'ing-k'uang tiao-ch'a* (A survey of village conditions in Hunan), 48.

by peasants who had encountered troubles and needed money. The period of time for which land was mortgaged to Yuan was three years, which was later extended to eight years. During the eight-year period, many areas suffered floods and droughts, and as a result few peasants could repay their loan and recoup their mortgaged land. When relatives and agents of Yuan Shih-k'ai accepted mortgages the warlord-landlord Yuan used cash loans and contracts as bait. He then allowed postponement of the loan until expiration of the agreed period of land mortgage, when the borrower usually could not repay. By acquiring those mortgaged lands, he amassed huge tracts of cultivated land.[39]

In order to keep their lands intact and collect a dependable land rent from them, wealthy families, especially within lineages, would often form an association and place some of their land at its disposal for lease. The association would then use the revenue to organize a village school, a temple, or other public facility. Sometimes these landlord-type associations held more land in an area than did any individual landlord, as this report from 1933–4 testifies:

In Kwangtung the power of private landlords is simply not as great as that of the landlord associations. If we exclude the public property owned by the many county offices and the numerous philanthropic agencies, the land area owned by the landlord associations occupies a very great share of the cultivated land of Kwangtung province. These associations' land consists of schools (*hsüeh-tien*), temples (*miao-tien*), various private associations (*hui-tien*), and lineages (*ta-kung-tien*).[40]

In other areas, urban families that had acquired considerable land through moneylending or other activities assigned the management of their land to bursaries. These in turn leased the land to families of different villages, collected rents, paid taxes to the state, remitted part of the rental income to the urban landlords, and retained a fee for their services.[41]

Partible inheritance

This powerful landlord class, the dominant influence in so many rural communities, rarely kept its land intact for more than one or two generations unless the land was assigned to a lineage association. The reason for this was the custom of partible inheritance, which divided the land and household property among the sons, while providing some

[39] SMR, Research Section, *Hoku-shi nōson gaikyō chōsa hōkoku: Keimin ken dai-ichiku, Waheikyō, Sonkabyō* (Research report on village conditions in North China: Sun-chia-miao village, Ho-p'ing township, in district one of Hui-min county), 62–3.

[40] Ch'en Han-seng, 'Kantō nōson no seisan kankei to seisanryoku' (Production relationships and production power in Kwangtung villages), *Mantetsu chōsa geppō*, 15.6 (June 1935) 175.

[41] Muramatsu Yūji, *Kindai Kōnan no sosan* (Bursaries in the Lower Yangtze area in modern times); see ch. 5.

security for the aged parents. This custom was practised by all households, large or small, wealthy or poor, located either north or south.[42] It guaranteed the ultimate demise of the large, extended family of great wealth, and the creation in its place of new households with the same surname but weaker kinship ties. A Japanese scholar who analysed village studies of North China for information about partible inheritance had this to say about it:

the Chinese household (*chia*) economically, socially, and even spiritually rests upon weak foundations – foundations that seem gradually to be disintegrating. Here the underlying reason appears to be the numerous cases of family disharmony and the impoverished living conditions that typically cause household partition (*fen-chia*). Yet ... family disharmony and impoverished living conditions are actually used as opportunities to partition the household....the principle of equal household division is so powerful that it can promote and create disagreement between brothers and sisters-in-law, which then causes household partition.[43]

If farmers and landlords firmly believed in the principle of equal property division, together with other values emphasizing ancestor worship and filial piety, what then? Obviously, as this quotation suggests, the sanctioned right or norm justifying the partition of household wealth must have provided many family members with a rationale for creating family cleavages. And these must invariably have brought about household partition. But even if partible inheritance provided a rationale for conflict within families, why so much conflict to start with? Although this issue has not received the scholarly attention it deserves, one of several possible explanations, based upon a recent illuminating study of rural women in Taiwan, points to a powerful source of conflict. The author, Margery Wolf, argues that Taiwan girls, when they enter the household of their husband, are driven by emotional need to establish their own uterine family. In essence, this uterine family will be 'her own children and grandchildren'. Cut off as she is from those she loves and feels most attached to, the young bride must struggle for survival in a new family that is frequently dominated and even controlled by a new mother-in-law. Wolf further asserts: 'In most cases, by the time she, the young bride, adds grandchildren, the uterine family and the household will almost completely overlap, and there will be another daughter-in-law struggling with loneliness and beginning a new uterine family'.[44]

As the young bride struggles to establish her position in a household dominated by the mother-in-law, her only effective weapon is to rely upon

[42] SMR, *Chū-shi ni okeru nōson no shakai jijō*, 17–21.
[43] Uchida Tomoo, *Chūgoku nōson no bunke seido* (The system of family division in rural China), 413–14.
[44] Margery Wolf, *Women and the family in rural Taiwan*, 36.

her husband to establish a closely knit family of her own. In families of two or more brothers, the efforts by their wives to establish their respective uterine families within the large, patrilineal household will invariably lead to conflict between brothers. Ultimately, one or more of the brothers will insist upon division of land and property.

Whatever the reasons for *fen-chia*, this widespread, long-practised custom served to fragment large and even small landholdings. Some examples will show why downward social mobility was always occurring and eventually overcame the rich. In 1930, a wealthy rural family in Sui-hua county in Manchuria divided its 1,000 odd *shang* (667 hectares) estate between eleven sons.[45] Seven years later, these eleven families had already sold 45 *shang*, which meant a 5 per cent reduction in the land transferred from parents to their male children. In Hsu-hsiu county of Hopei, a landowner with 210 *mou* (15 ha.) in 1882 divided it among his three sons, who in turn divided their property among their progeny.[46] In 1940, a total of fifteen new families farmed 324 *mou* (about 21 ha.) between them, whereas sixty years before a single household had farmed 210 *mou* (14 ha.).

The *chia* and its income

Below the landowning elite were other households of varying size and wealth in which the members also lived together and shared everything in common.[47] The household, or *chia*, was the smallest, most cohesive social unit anywhere in rural, or for that matter, urban China. Fei Hsiao-t'ung has described it vividly:

The basic social group in the village is the *chia*, an expanded family. The members of this group possess a common property, keep a common budget and cooperate together to pursue a common living through division of labour. It is also in this group that children are born and brought up and material objects, knowledge, and social positions are inherited.[48]

The *chia* functioned as a corporate unit. Its members performed the tasks assigned to them, handed over their earnings to the household head (*chia-chang*), and shared equally in the disposition of rewards. Major decisions were made only after discussion between the *chia-chang* and other members. In the following interview, farmers in Sha-ching village of Hopei describe the functioning of such a household.

[45] Iwase Suteichi, 'Hoku-Man nōson ni okeru daikazoku bunke no ichi jirei' (An example of equal division of property in a large family farm of a north Manchurian village), *Mantetsu chōsa geppō*, 20.12 (Dec. 1940) 66–95.

[46] Kumashiro Yukio, 'Kahoku ni okeru nōka no bunke to tochi no udoki' (Peasant household division of land and land transfer in North China), in *Nōken hōkoku chōhen*, 167–266.

[47] Makino Tatsumi, *Shina kazoku kenkyū* (Studies of the Chinese family), 10–11.

[48] Fei Hsiao-t'ung, *Peasant life in China*, 27.

What is the main activity of the family?

Farming.

Is the division of labour different for household head, his wife, the eldest son, and the next son?

No, they cooperate.

What is the duty of the household head?

He manages the work of the family members. Men farm, and women do housework and embroider.

Do all household members perform field work?

No. For the most part only men do this, but if hands are scarce, women help.

At such times will the household head also work?

He works like everyone else in the family.

How is the daily work programme decided?

The household head assembles everyone, and they discuss it at breakfast.[49]

Every *chia* was linked to other *chia* before it in an endless chain maintained by ancestor worship and ceremonial display.[50] Although this chain sometimes broke when a family line ended, parents raised their children to worship certain *chia* ancestors and taught them to work hard, save, venerate the aged, and assume ancestral obligations. They also encouraged their children to identify with their parents' and ancestors' goals, and strive 'for more wealth, for larger family honour, for more advantageous graveyards, for bigger clan temples, for costlier ceremonials, and for a host of other measures which [were] calculated to increase the welfare and prestige of the living and of the dead'.[51] When the *chia-chang* transferred property to his sons, they were obliged to honour him and his ancestors with appropriate rites. The accumulation of wealth, especially property, ensured that these rites could be performed. It also guaranteed that they, too, would be venerated by their children after they had passed property on to them.

In many ways, then, this corporate unit, the *chia*, was strongly motivated to accumulate wealth. It is not surprising that good household management, hard work, frugality and diligence were attributes all farming families tried to acquire. Every *chia* and its *chia-chang* aspired to become wealthy and achieve extended family form, though few in fact ever realized

---

[49] Chūgoku nōson kankō chōsa kankōkai, comp. *Chūgoku nōson kankō chōsa* (A survey of traditional customs in Chinese villages), 1.236.

[50] Francis L. K. Hsu, *Under the ancestors' shadow: kinship, personality and social mobility in village China*, see chs. 9–10.

[51] *Ibid.* 249.

these goals. These values, held by all farmers, were the bedrock upon which this rural society was founded. The similarity between rural families, regardless of size and wealth, has been emphasized – not without irony – by Niida Noboru:

To sum up, the conditions which have given rise to the small family in China have existed from earliest times ... In recent years, people who have travelled in China, especially in areas where the small family predominated, have observed that most rural families in China are small, and the large family which people had presumed to exist was very rare. For some time there have been attempts to explain the decline of the large family system in China. But such theories have ignored the continued existence of the small family and have failed to note that both small and large families have essentially the same characteristics. Thus, if we can say that today's small family is the result of the decline of a family system of long ago, we can say that the Chinese family system has been on the decline for over two thousand years.[52]

For this corporate unit to earn income the *chia* used its resources in many different ways, and farming was only one of many possibilities.

There were many different combinations of income-earning sources for the *chia*. At one end of the continuum were day-labouring jobs of low status, performed away from the family and even the village, dirty and inconvenient. Next came peddling, clerking, and brokerage tasks that required some skill, carried higher status, and were cleaner to perform. They were often scarcely more profitable than work as a labourer, but their higher social status made them more desirable. At the middle of this continuum came farming, either working one's own land or renting from another. Toward the other end of the continuum were managing land, lending money, operating a shop, becoming an official, or serving as a military officer. Each *chia-chang* had to choose among the different sources of income when he allocated household resources. Although some tasks produced more income than others, the social costs of each task – distance to and from work, status, cleanliness, extent of drudgery or risk – also had to be carefully considered.

By the second quarter of the twentieth century, farm families seem to have had a clear order of preference in choosing occupations for their children. At the top were official and even military careers; next were entrepreneurial pursuits; then farming, followed by labouring tasks that ranged from monthly or day-by-day farm work to working as a household servant. Fei Hsiao-t'ung reports that the *chia-chang* usually tried to educate at least one son to become an official or military officer.[53] Lin Yueh-hwa's study of two Fukienese families recounts how Huang Tung-lin wanted

---

[52] Niida Noboru, *Chūgoku no nōson kazoku* (The Chinese rural family), 151.
[53] Fei Hsiao-t'ung, *China's gentry: essays on rural-urban relations*; see chs. 4–5.

to cooperate with his brother-in-law to start a store rather than help on the farm. The store eventually prospered, so that he was able to build a new home for his family.[54] After families had accumulated considerable land, they began to lease part of it, lend money, and engage in commercial activities.[55] If we rank rural families according to their assets, we find that the poorer, smaller families invariably earned a high percentage of their income from low-prestige, high-risk, and low-return income sources that were either wholly outside farming or supplemented their very small farm earnings.[56] Families with more than enough land to support themselves devoted more of their resources to farming, while the very wealthy frequently engaged in mercantile activities instead of farming their land.[57]

Only if it could acquire certain scarce resources from another household could the individual household allocate its resources as it wished. This required inter-family arrangements, usually on a kinship basis. We have already seen how such arrangements were concluded by means of informal or formal agreements, written as contracts or orally understood, that pertained to leasing and renting land and farm capital, lending and borrowing money, and hiring or supplying labour for different periods of time. On first consideration, the contracts between families in Taiwan and those used on the mainland to pledge and mortgage land, lease and rent land during the late Ch'ing and early Republican periods appear to be quite similar.[58] Families were constantly breaking old contracts and making new ones with different families. In short, private contractual agreements between rural families were the preferred way of obtaining a scarce resource.

Forms of *chia* cooperation

The rural families struggling to make a living in their villages did not depend solely upon contracts; they also cooperated with each other. Such cooperation was referred to by various terms, and was prevalent in some communities but not in others. It took two different forms.[59] The first

[54] Lin Yueh-hwa, *The golden wing: a sociological study of Chinese familism*, 25–35.

[55] Fei Hsiao-t'ung and Chang Chih-I, *Earthbound China: a study of rural economy in Yunnan*; see ch. 27.

[56] Myers, *Peasant economy*, 153–8; see below, ch. 5.

[57] Chang Yu-i, comp. *Chung-kuo chin-tai nung-yeh shih tzu-liao* (Historical materials on modern China's agriculture), 2.319–32, 333–6, 343–67.

[58] Fu-mei Chang Chen and Ramon H. Myers, 'Customary law and the economic growth of China during the Ch'ing period', *CSWT* 3.5 (Nov. 1976) 1–32.

[59] Ramon H. Myers, 'Cooperation in traditional agriculture and its implications for team farming in the People's Republic of China', in Dwight Perkins, ed. *China's modern economy in historical perspective*, 261–78.

involved only a few households, which shared their land, labour, or farm capital for short periods when seasonal demand was greatest. This form of cooperation occurred among friends or kin, lasted for short periods, and was terminated by mutual agreement; it existed everywhere in the countryside. The second form involved many households in a village – sometimes, in several villages – grouped together and bearing the costs of undertaking a certain enterprise. Some examples would be crop-watching, widespread in North China, or forming a village defence corps, an activity common to all villages when law and order broke down. There was also cooperative processing of crops, such as sugar-cane, especially in Kwangtung and southern Taiwan. But the most important activity requiring large-scale cooperation was probably water control to counter drought, including water storage to prevent flooding and irrigation.

Village organizations for water control were of two types. Some of them were integrated into large-scale systems; they were managed by the public officials who maintained dikes along large rivers. The second type consisted of one or more village organizations that serviced only the households in their own communities. The two types of organization had some common features. Their participants were landowning households; their rules for allocating costs and benefits were based on the amount of land each household owned (families with less land contributed and received less); and they were run by a hierarchy of water-control managers consisting of experienced farmers who rotated the discharge of their duties.[60] Morita Akira, in his definitive study of water control during the Ch'ing period, summarizes the experiences of more than half a dozen provinces which carried over into the Republican period as well.

In Hsing-t'ai county of Hopei there were two organizations for water control established in areas to utilize rivers. These organizations designated the watergate (*cha*) as the standard unit for water control. The personnel for each watergate were peasant households who owned land; they were called *lien-hu*. Because these households paid for the repairs of the watergates and the canals furnishing water, made tax payments, and provided cost-free labour, they participated in water control management and also acquired the benefits of water use. Even in Suiyuan and Shansi there were water control organizations made up of owners of irrigated land, and these households, like those mentioned above, were also landowners. These landowning households supplied the labour required for construction and repair of water control facilities. The amount of water they used to irrigate their fields was apportioned according to the different amount of land owned by each household (*an-ti-mou chiao-shui*). The basic principles governing these water control organizations, such as the personnel being landowning households who

---

[60] Ramon H. Myers, 'Economic organization and cooperation in modern China: irrigation management in Hsing-t'ai county, Hopei province', in the late Professor Yūji Muramatsu commemoration volume, *The polity and economy of China*, 189–212.

shared costs and received benefits according to the amount of land they owned, were the same for water control organizations in Central and South China.[61]

Of course, before farmers could be induced to commit their resources to such undertakings, they had to perceive that the benefits would exceed the costs. Outsiders might evaluate the potential benefits from village cooperation quite differently from the inhabitants, who habitually disregarded certain costs. But in any case, cooperation played a very important role in village life because it permitted households to share scarce resources. In this respect, it performed the same function as private contracts between families, namely, it enabled them to earn a higher income with their resources than they would have earned otherwise.

COMMERCIALIZATION OF AGRICULTURE

By the early 1900s railways were built and the city-ports expanded. These developments meant new opportunities for farmers. But in the early 1920s, just as a new supply of farm capital (American cotton-seed, chemical fertilizer, etc.), was being generated, and farmer beliefs were beginning to alter, agriculture encountered its first major crisis. As a result, these new inputs, still weak and scarcely perceptible in the hinterland, never really affected the majority of villages.

Nevertheless, the growth of trade and crop specialization were responsible for a rise in the marketed surplus from agriculture during this brief period. Both were made possible by the dramatic improvement in transportation. Between 1894 and 1911, there was a 26-fold increase in railway track. In contrast, the increase between 1911 and 1927 was a mere 35 per cent.[62] Railways speeded up long-distance deliveries, encroached upon traffic moving on waterways and roads, and in certain locales eliminated many periodic markets.[63] Not only did they redirect trade from traditional transportation routes to the city-ports; they also brought new goods into the hinterland and collected agricultural products for shipment.

The first new demand for a marketed surplus from agriculture came from foreign trade. Exports of farm products expanded more rapidly between the 1890s and 1910 than at any other time. Between 1876 and 1890 the value of food and industrial crops exported increased respectively by only 26 and 38 per cent.[64] But for the 1890–1905 period, the corresponding

---

[61] Morita Akira, *Shindai suirishi kenkyū* (Studies in the history of water management during the Ch'ing period), 399.

[62] Yen Chung-p'ing *et al.* 190.

[63] Skinner, 'Marketing and social structure in rural China, Part II', 211–28.

[64] Huang Yen-p'ei and P'ang Sung, comps. *Chung-kuo shang-chang shih-pai shih* (The history of China's

figures were 300 and 600 per cent. By 1911–15, the annual growth rate was 12 per cent for food-crop exports and 11 per cent for industrial-crop exports. Between the First World War and 1930, however, the growth rate of all exports in value terms was only 4.8 per cent per annum.[65]

The second new demand came from the expansion of medium and large cities. Most large cities at the turn of the century were still below a quarter of a million people. Between 1900 and 1938, the urban population living in cities of over 100,000 persons expanded at a rate of nearly 2 per cent a year, and for medium-sized and small cities the rate was faster.[66] Except for the cities that served as provincial capitals in the 1930s and 1940s, urban centres grew more rapidly in their initial expansionary phase between 1895 and the late 1910s than at any other time. During this initial phase, recent arrivals in the city were largely peasants, especially males between 18 and 45 years of age, who were looking for work.[67] Since the food-consumption patterns of these families were still similar to when they lived in villages, the urban demand for foodgrains during this period continued very high.[68]

Increased specialization of resources

If new sources of demand fostered by railways and foreign trade made it profitable for more farmers to market their crops, what developments on the supply side made possible this increase in the marketed rural surplus? The answer lies in increased specialization of peasant resources, and the associated increased returns to labour. The following hypothetical example will serve to illustrate these developments. Imagine an economy, primarily rural and without foreign trade, in which urban and village population grow at the same rate, and a certain combination of food and industrial crops is marketed by villages to cities. This economy resembles China before her railway revolution. Imagine further that transportation improves and foreign trade develops. These new market demands force the prices of certain crops to rise. But the villages cannot increase their cultivated area as all the good land is already farmed, and reclaiming poor land is extremely costly. Accordingly, farmers begin to specialize in certain

commercial struggles and failures), republished as *Chung-kuo ssu-shih-nien hai-kuan shang-wu t'ung-chi t'u-piao: 1876–1915* (Statistical tables of China's 40 years of Maritime customs and commercial affairs).

[65] Cheng Yu-Kwei, *Foreign trade and industrial development of China: an historical and integrated analysis through 1948*, 258–9.

[66] Dwight H. Perkins, *Agricultural development in China 1368–1968*, 155.

[67] Lin Sung-ho, 'T'ung-chi shu-tzu hsia ti Pei-p'ing' (Peking: a statistical survey), *She-hui k'o-hsueh tsa-chih*, 2.3 (Sept. 1931) 385.

[68] For a similar observation of urban composition patterns in the postwar Philippines see Allen C. Kelley, 'Demand patterns, demographic changes and economic growth', *The Quarterly Journal of Economics*, 83.1 (Feb. 1969) 110–26.

crops that bring higher income, while improved transportation and marketing make available certain goods they require, at prices they can afford to pay. Some areas specialize in food, others in industrial crops. Under this increasing specialization, farmers obtain an increasing amount of product for their labour. The economy exports industrial crops, raw or processed. Urban population begins to increase faster than village population because new employment opportunities attract villagers to the cities. Urban demand for food rises, but when the countryside fails to supply sufficient food, it can be imported in small quantities from abroad. Under these conditions family farms have increased their total production while also increasing the proportion of their marketed surplus. These developments are still possible even under the assumption of a constant return for labour in food production.[69]

These are the conditions that existed in China between the 1870s and late 1910s. After 1920, however, the process was continually being disrupted. What is the evidence for crop specialization after the 1870s? The soy-bean advanced rapidly across central Manchuria; farmers grew more tobacco along the Tsinan-Tsingtao railway; farmers planted peanuts in north-west Shantung, southern Hopei, northern Honan, Kiangsu, and Anhwei.[70] Between 1900 and 1937, rapeseed cultivation expanded roughly fivefold, especially in Szechwan, Anhwei and Honan. There was more tung oil from central and southern provinces, and more sesame in Honan, Anhwei, Kiangsu, Hupei, Hopei, Shantung and Kiangsi.[71] Cotton cultivation also expanded through North China, especially in Shantung, Hopei and Shansi.

The new market demands made it profitable for farmers in many areas to switch to new crops. Friederich Otte observed these rural developments in the 1910s:

The Chinese farmer is fairly quick to notice his own advantage provided he is left alone and is sure that the fruits of his own labour become his. One need only point to the tremendous increase in the cultivation of groundnuts in the neighbourhood of the Tsinan-Tsingtao railway, or of soy-bean and wheat along all the Manchurian railway, or to the transformation of agriculture around Shanghai: wheat and cotton instead of rice, in order to realize that the passiveness even of the northern Chinese farmer is by no means due to dullness of perception.[72]

---

[69] R. T. Shand, 'The development of trade and specialization in a primitive economy', *The Economic Record*, 41 (June 1965) 193–206; p. 200.

[70] Amano Motonosuke, *Chūgoku nōgyō no sho mondai* (Problems of Chinese agriculture), 1.103.

[71] SMR, *Chū-Shi ni okeru nōson no shakai jijō*, 2.

[72] Friederich Otte, 'Correlation of harvests with importation of cereals in China', *Chinese Economic Journal*, 15.4 (Oct. 1934), 338–414.

Yet in some areas farmers had not seemed to respond to the new market signals, and very little change in land use had taken place. A Japanese investigation of three villages outside Mukden, undertaken in 1939 but covering a period of more than a quarter century, found that a few villages ignored the new commercial influences, even when located near cities that had enjoyed tremendous growth.

In comparing village change between the early Republican period and 1939 under the impact of rapid urban growth, our study examined landownership relationships and the attendant conditions of off-farm labour and farm work. There had occurred considerable transport, commercial, and industrial development in recent years [around Mukden] as compared to the early Republican period.

But on the other hand, we can say that in agriculture nothing had changed: the same farming technology used by the uneducated farmers continued in use down to the present. The villages surveyed near the town of Su-chia-t'un were located within a very short distance from the city of Mukden, and the farmers could have developed much better farm management. Unfortunately, the clay soil was very unsuitable for growing vegetables. At the present time these farmers purchase their vegetables. If the farmers instead had supplied vegetables to Su-chia-t'un and to Mukden, we know they would have been able to increase their farm income greatly. But they made the effort neither to improve the quality of their land nor to raise the yields of crops other than vegetables.

Fortunately, only a few kilometers away there is a river, and during the slack farming season the river boats haul sand. Would it not have been possible for the farmers to have obtained some topsoil by this means to add to their clay soil, and so improve their land? But the farmers say they could not have done this. 'Where would the money have come from? We did not have enough labour.'

This is a situation where no one had any plan for community improvement. In this single example, were there not opportunities for gradually improving cultivation methods? Instead, the farmers continued to rely upon traditional farming methods, and they did not make any positive efforts to advance. There is no hope for agricultural progress under these kinds of conditions.[73]

Many farmers, like the villagers outside Mukden, never responded to the new market expansion because their perception of the costs and benefits of producing more marketed surplus as opposed to using their resources in other ways differed completely from that of outsiders such as these Japanese researchers. Some farmers, like those outside Mukden, must have preferred to work in the city rather than cooperate to grow vegetables. Their remuneration would have been higher in the city, and they would have encountered greater social opportunities there. In general, differing farmer perceptions meant that some areas derived great benefit from the new market demand for food and special crops while other areas did not. Still others experienced decline because the new urban growth and railway

[73] SMR, Hsingking Branch Office, Research Division, *Toshi no bōchō ni tomonau ichi nōson no ugoki* (Change in a village under the influence of urban growth), 44–5.

development by-passed them altogether or disrupted their traditional market outlets.

The new market development also influenced rural handicraft production, employment and income. For example, imports of machine-spun yarn of high count from Japan, India and England increased only during the period from 1870 to the First World War, after which they declined.[74] What happened was that imported yarn, which had greater tensile strength than the domestic yarn spun in villagers' homes, became cheaper. Villagers began substituting more foreign yarn for native yarn, particularly for the woof, in their weaving of cloth (*t'u-pu*).[75] Many merchants began to supply foreign yarn and cash to peasant weavers in villages and market towns in exchange for their cloth. This new rural putting-out system evolved for the first time in such counties as Wei-hsien (Shantung), Kao-yang (Hopei), Yü-lin (Kwangsi), Hsin-ning (Kwangtung) and Chang-chow (Kiangsu). A complex reallocation of rural resources took place after the 1870s: in some areas, household yarn-spinning declined, whereas in others household weaving increased.[76] Events in the tea, silk, and ceramic producing areas followed a similar course, as expanding trade and new commodities forced a gradual restructuring of handicraft production. The net effect of these changes upon all types of rural handicraft between the 1870s and 1910s was extremely complex. The general impression, and it is only that, is one of more expansion than contraction, but the subject still requires more study.

The emerging rural economy

In spite of great variation among villages in the amount of agricultural surplus that they supplied to the market, rural surveys during the 1920s and 1930s reported that families, on the average, marketed a very high percentage of what they produced. Thus a survey in northern Manchuria (1922-4) found that the farmers sold 48 per cent of their farm output.[77] Similarly, John L. Buck, who collected data for farms in northern and east-central China between 1921 and 1925, found that roughly 50 per cent of family income came from marketed sales, irrespective of whether the family rented, owned part, or owned all of the land farmed.[78]

---

[74] Ramon H. Myers 'Cotton textile handicraft and the development of the cotton textile industry in modern China', *Economic History Review*, 18.3 (1965) 614–32; see p.619.

[75] Bruce L. Reynolds, 'Weft: the technological sanctuary of Chinese hand-spun yarn', *CSWT* 3.2 (Dec. 1974) 1–19; see p. 1.

[76] Myers, 'Cotton textile handicraft', 621–4.

[77] SMR, Mantetsu taiheiyō mondai chōsa jumbikai, *Nōka no keiei narabi ni keizai jōtai yori mitaru Manshū nōka to Chūbu Shina nōka no taishō* (A comparison of Manchurian and central China farms as seen from the economic and managerial aspects of the family farm), 60.

[78] John L. Buck, *Chinese farm economy*, 65–80.

However, when families are grouped and compared according to farm size and wealth, it becomes apparent that large farms earned between two and five times as much as small farms, and that their earnings from marketed sales were considerably greater as well. In fact, some rural surveys for a typical North China village in Fen-jun county (Hopei) show that wealthy farmers even earned a much smaller share of their total income from non-farm income sources.[79] After deducting all farm costs, including consumption expenditures, taxes, depreciation and opportunity costs, from total farm income, the top wealthy households were left with a residue far exceeding that for all other households. Although these same farms supplied the largest share of the village's marketed surplus, they also invested fewer inputs per unit of crop output than did part-owner and tenant farms. This pattern, whereby a small group of wealthy households supplied as much as one-half or more of the entire surplus marketed by the village, was by no means uncommon.[80]

Several other peculiar marketing characteristics were associated with farm size. Farm survey data showed that small farms allocated a higher percentage of their land and labour to crops for market, and that such specialization – specialization in industrial crops or special foodgrains – required them to use more labour input.[81] Large farms, on the other hand, allocated a smaller percentage of their land and labour for marketed crops than did small farms. It appears that during this period, as the number of households multiplied, the average farm size continued to decline. At the same time, more of the smaller family farms began to specialize in production to take advantage of the rise in farm prices. The increased returns to labour enabled small farms to purchase from the market food that, because of their small size, they could not produce on their own land. Both small and large family farms mobilized more labour per unit of land during the year than formerly because of increased specialization and exchange. But these developments merely allowed the small farms to hold their own, just to tread water, so to speak. If there should be a poor harvest, or unanticipated debts, or an unfavourable price exchange in the market, their living immediately became wretched and uncertain.

In sum, the rapid commercialization of agriculture that occurred from the 1870s to the First World War, especially after the coming of the railway, enabled most villagers to feed more people and support the gradual expansion of a small urban sector. This agrarian system made

[79] SMR, Hoku-shi keizai chōsajo, *Shōwa jūninendo nōka keizai chōsa hōkoku: Hojunken Sensochin Beishoson* (An investigation report of the farm economy for 1937: Mi-ch'ang village, Hsuan-chuang-chen, Feng-jun county) see Appendix.

[80] Ramon H. Myers, 'The commercialization of agriculture in modern China', in W. E. Willmott, ed. *Economic organization in Chinese society*, 173–91; see p. 186.

[81] *Ibid.* 184–5.

many adjustments to new market forces without rural unemployment becoming serious, without importing large quantities of food from abroad, and without creating serious inflation. However, this was a fragile, complex, and very interdependent rural economy that, when exposed to severe shocks from outside, transmitted the reverberations rapidly throughout its whole extent, thereby falling prey to serious dislocations of production and exchange.

THE AGRARIAN CRISIS

Before 1920 few observers of the rural scene reported any alarm about an impending disaster to agriculture. Whether one refers to the unofficial impressions of the Chinese literati or to the official reports of the commissioners of Maritime Customs, who zealously recorded local conditions in the areas around their posts each year, the situation was one of gradual agricultural advance, sometimes slowed by poor harvests. Even at the local level, for which on occasion there exist unique records of long-term rural conditions, there is no indication of any major decline in farm production or income on a sustained basis. The land records for bursaries in Kiangsu, an area reputed for widespread tenancy, heavy rents and frequent violent conflicts between tenants and landlords, show wild fluctuations for rent collections and land-tax payments only after 1920, but reveal relative constancy for the years 1890 to 1920.[82]

After 1920, however, the written record universally shows real difficulties besetting agriculture. Customs officials persistently mentioned the breakdown of law and order, the disruption of transportation and marketing, and widespread, uncontrolled flooding and drought throughout the country. W. R. Myers, reporting from Kiaochow in Shantung in 1931, stated that 'during the decade under review [the 1920s], the province of Shantung had undergone a series of natural and political calamities; most of the gentry fled to the cities to find a temporary refuge, while the poorer class emigrated to Manchuria'.[83] By 1931, the agrarian situation had become grave. A study of the foodgrain problem in fourteen provinces containing about 280 million people and covering the principal farming regions of the country reported that supply fell short of demand by 5 per cent.[84]

---

[82] Muramatsu Yūji, *Kindai Kōnan no sosan*, 723, 725–7, 732, 734–7.
[83] Inspectorate General of Customs, *Decennial Reports, 1922–1931*, 442.
[84] Chang Hsin-i, *Chung-kuo liang-shih wen-t'i* (China's foodgrain problem), 33.

The crisis defined and described

This was not just a temporary crisis of subsistence for rural people but a series of dislocating effects taking place on a sustained basis, producing two new phenomena. On the one hand, there occurred the periodic economic separation of city and villages, whereby the city became more dependent upon foreign trade when denied food and fibre from the villages. On the other hand, rural misery increased by leaps and bounds, evidenced in mass migrations from one province to another; famine; farmers fleeing to towns to beg; the degradation of women; parents forced to sell their children; huge rural unemployment; widespread rural debt and forced sale of land. Such events became as familiar as they had previously been rare. To be sure, a breakdown in the supply of foodgrain and fibres and its distribution to markets and in turn to cities and other regions had often occurred in imperial times, but not on the sustained basis that was the case between 1920 and 1949. Despite the paucity of statistics, let us present what we have.

First, China became more dependent upon foreign sources of foodgrain between 1921 and 1941. In fact, an unprecedented import of foodgrain occurred in these decades, because of the disruption of production and distribution in rural markets which caused foodgrain prices in large cities to rise relative to other prices, thus making foreign grain for the first time cheaper to buy. Table 1 shows that net imports of foodgrain ranged between 200,000 and 350,000 metric tons a year between 1886 and 1920. The increase in the 1906–10 years can be traced to a very high import of over 800,000 metric tons in 1907. Prior to 1880, these imports fluctuated but remained low, probably below 25,000 metric tons a year. Their sudden rise after 1886 was due to the burgeoning growth of the treaty-port cities and the construction of new cities in the interior along railway lines in North China. Foodgrain was gradually purchased from abroad until villagers could reallocate more resources to specialize in its production. Their import shot upward after 1920 when annual imports during that decade approached one million metric tons and then jumped to two million between 1931–5. They leapt again after war began with Japan, but declined after 1941 when China was sealed off from international trade, and domestic resources were shifted from fibre and special crops to foodgrain production. During the war-torn 1940s, the country barely fed itself. In sum, our foreign trade statistics show that after 1920 China became more dependent upon foreign sources for grain than at any time in its prior history.

Although exports from China increased at a more rapid rate between

TABLE I

China's average annual foodgrain imports and exports (metric tons),
1867–1949[a]

Period	Imports	Exports	Net imports	Net exports
1867–70	19,375	—	19,375	—
1871–5	21,540	—	21,540	—
1876–80	22,030	—	22,030	—
1881–5	11,530	—	11,530	—
1886–90	214,340	—	214,530	—
1891–5	346,450	—	346,450	—
1896–1900	297,360	—	297,360	—
1901–5	251,750	—	251,750	—
1906–10	465,010	—	465,010	—
1911–15	390,770	139,590	251,180	—
1916–20	328,670	355,560	—	26,890
1921–5	1,070,170	262,830	807,340	—
1926–30	1,295,560	356,730	938,830	—
1931–5	2,142,205	133,040	2,009,165	—
1936–40	628,581	70,220	558,361	—
1941	1,147,300	10,800	1,136,500	—
1946–8	109,833	500	109,283	—
1949	—	—	—	—

[a] Foodgrain imports included rice, wheat, and wheat flour; foodgrain exports included sorghum, millet, wheat and wheat flour. Data between 1867 and 1949 were in units of picul and converted to metric tons at a ratio of 20 piculs = 1 metric ton.
Source: data for 1867–1949 obtained from Hsiao Liang-lin, *China's foreign trade statistics 1864–1949*, 32–3, 83.

1920 and 1930 than between 1890 and 1920, this was not the case for agricultural exports. The value share of agricultural goods and handicraft products mainly made from agricultural raw materials in total exports was lower and declined respectively for the years 1920, 1925, and 1930 compared with 1913.[85] And the quantity of both handicraft goods and food and fibres in the export trade stagnated and declined in the late 1920s compared to the two decades before.

The price structure also began to change during the 1920s as compared with the previous decade. The Nankai price index for 44 foodgrain commodities rose between 1913 and 1920 but at the same rate as the overall price index for the same period. Further, relative prices between food and fibre, metals, fuels, and construction material goods did not change. Between 1925 and 1930, however, food prices rose more rapidly than the overall price index.[86] Similar changes in relative prices are

[85] P'eng Tse-i, comp. *Chung-kuo chin-tai shou-kung-yeh shih tzu-liao, 1840–1949* (Source materials on the history of handicraft industry in modern China, 1840–1949), 3.63.

[86] Nan-k'ai ta-hsueh ching-chi yen-chiu-so, comp. *Nan-k'ai chih-su hui-pien* (Collected Nankai indices), 14–15.

observable for Shanghai and Canton during the 1920s.[87] These price trends strongly suggest that food scarcity in the principal cities during the 1920s became more severe than in prior decades and this confirms the declining export of food and fibres from the villages to large cities during that decade.

Pre-1949 crop statistics are notoriously unreliable, because the crop-sown area was grossly under-reported and yield observations were obtained from very small samples, probably not at all representative for the country. Given the agricultural production and handicraft output trends in export trade during the 1920s, it is conceivable that overall farm production of food and fibre fluctuated around a constant trend line for that decade, but confirming evidence beyond that of trade trends is non-existent. For the 1929–37 period, it is, however, clearer that foodgrain and fibre production did stagnate, merely fluctuating around a constant growth trend line.[88] Between 1937 and 1949 total farm production, including livestock and special crops, fell, but foodgrain production may very well have remained fairly constant over the period.[89] The reason for this was that farmers shifted their resources from producing special products and livestock to the maintenance of foodgrain output which was essential for their livelihood.

Fragmentary as our data are, there seems to be a definite trend after 1920 of less food and fibre being exported for trade and to the large cities than had been the case before 1920. Further, food production after 1929 definitely stagnated. There is a great quantity of descriptive evidence that rural economic conditions generally worsened for long periods, briefly recovered, only to worsen again so that the overall pattern was presumably one of socio-economic decline in welfare for the majority of people. The specific causes of greater rural market instability during these three decades were of four principal kinds.

First, a rapid and often irreversible change in the structure of demand, either domestic or foreign, could force economic organizations to allocate resources of land and labour to alternative uses. If resource owners failed to employ these as fully as before demand changed, household income fell, land and labour became idle, and capital funds moved out of agriculture.

[87] Chung-kuo k'o-hsueh yuan Shang-hai ching-chi yen-chiu so, comp. *Shang-hai chieh-fang ch'ien-hou wu-chia tzu-liao hui-pien: 1921–1957* (Collected materials on prices before and after the liberation of Shanghai, 1921–1957), 126, 184.
[88] Chang Yu-i, 3.922–2. I have compiled an output index from production data here cited and used price weights for 1935–7 to value foodgrain output to confirm this assertion.
[89] These trends are evident in the crop reports for nine provinces cited in Kuo-min cheng-fu chu-chi-ch'u t'ung-chi-chü, comp. *Chung-hua min-kuo t'ung-chi t'i-yao* (Statistical abstract for the Republic of China), 15–16.

Second, farm resources or income were taken either without compensation or at prices below current exchange values, so that farmers had to reduce their spending and savings, thereby affecting the next cycle of farm production and exchange. This occurred when the state or warlord armies levied new taxes, confiscated farmers' resources, or mobilized their labour for non-farm activities.

The third cause was when total market demand for the products of rural economic organizations suddenly collapsed. Such a decline in aggregate market demand might originate from an export of silver and the resulting decline in money supply. This was usually accompanied quickly by a decline in the velocity of money, which then adversely affected spending for all goods and services. Market demand declined also because of the loss of important markets or the disruption of trade and transport through military activities. Economic organizations were then forced to incur debt or sell their assets in order to cover their costs of production. The liquidation of assets often brought about a redistribution of claims to wealth, which in turn made the pattern of income and land ownership distribution more unequal.

The final cause was the disruption to market activities because of natural disasters when economic organizations were not forewarned or had not the means to protect themselves. Floods and drought forced farmers to market less, reduced their seed for the next harvest, drove many to seek work elsewhere, and even produced famine. The consequent decline in marketed surplus from one region sorely affected exchange with normal trading regions so that farm prices and food and fibre distribution were adversely influenced.

These four sources for market instability occurred at different times after 1920 and with varying intensity. What makes their impact so different from that of previous decades is that the state and private economic organizations had neither the capacity nor ample time to gain relief from one outbreak of market instabilities before they were overwhelmed by another. It was the increased frequency of these rural market instabilities which plagued farmers for these three decades as never before. We now turn to a brief examination of these causes of market instabilities and their results by referring to the historical record of the period.

The 1920s

At least seven principal handicraft products that were exported began to decline in quantity and value after 1924; another six showed neither growth nor decline.[90] The most important handicraft industries, sericulture

90 P'eng Tse-i, 3.64–5, trade statistics derived from customs reports.

and cotton-cloth weaving, declined during this decade, and the rural industries of embroidery, carpet making, straw braiding, fancy lace work, oil pressing, paper making, and the production of tea and sugar also declined or stagnated. The changes in demand affecting the first two of these deserves some comment. First, synthetic fibres began to replace the Chinese silk that had so long been used in garments produced and sold in major Western markets. Between 1923 and 1930, Chinese silk prices in New York declined by 67 per cent.[91] This substitution rapidly reduced the demand for silk thread and cloth on the part of foreign export firms in Chekiang, Fukien and Kwangtung.[92] Moreover, the synthetic fibres imported into China increased in volume to the point at which they gradually expelled domestic silk from such markets as Hangchow.[93] Nishida Hakutarō, a Japanese observer of the silk industry, pointed out in the late 1920s that increased exports of synthetic fibre to China had 'very recently' dealt the depressed Chinese silk industry still another serious setback. In his opinion, this had made Japan the world's leading silk producer.[94]

Nor did the Chinese cotton industry escape hard times. Rising prices for cotton cloth during the First World War had brought prosperity to the new rural weaving centres, and merchants supplied more looms and yarn to expand cloth production. After 1920, however, foreign cotton articles again began competing with handicraft cloth (t'u-pu).[95] Japanese spinning mills in Tientsin and Tsingtao had previously sold most of their yarn to the Chinese merchants who supplied weaving centres. But between 1920 and 1924, the number of mechanized looms in these mills increased more than threefold. By 1924–5 they had begun producing machine-made cloth that was superior to the native t'u-pu. While the Japanese mills in the city-ports expanded production, the Chinese mills barely stayed in business, plagued as they were by labour strikes, managerial difficulties, and scarcity of working capital. A few weaving centres, like those of Wei county (Shantung), managed to obtain machine-spun yarn cheaply enough to weave cloth by hand and still remain in business. But this was at the expense of other centres, such as Kao-yang (Hopei), which they undersold.[96] In 1926, Kao-yang produced only 544,125 p'i of cloth compared to over one million p'i in 1921.[97] Other cloth-weaving centres were affected in the same way.[98]

Probably the chief source of market instability in this period was civil

[91] Ibid. 3. 4.
[92] Ibid. 3.7; Tōa kenkyūjo, Shina seishi no sekai teki chii (The world status of Chinese silk-reeling), 63.
[93] P'eng Tse-i, 3.5.
[94] Ibid.
[95] Ibid. 3.17.
[96] Ibid. 3.18.
[97] Ibid.
[98] Ibid. 3.19–25.

war. The years 1924–7 brought terrible violence and suffering to millions of villagers. Competing warlords imposed a variety of new taxes and levies upon farmers – a burden aggravated by the decline in sales due to railway stoppages and loss of storage facilities.[99] Even in 1916, intermittent warfare had broken out in 9 of the 22 provinces, but the violence appears to have heavily affected some 15 provinces between 1925 and 1928.[100] Shantung was especially hard hit, and each year hundreds of thousands of villagers, fearing for their lives, fled from it to other provinces. A Japanese study of military campaigns and farmer self-defence units during this period paints a picture of stark terror and misery endured by all classes.

Not only have arson, theft, and rape occurred everywhere, as if wild beasts were on the prowl, but murders and kidnappings are performed in broad daylight. Further, after the food mobilized for the military has been seized by bandit groups, more food is forcibly taken by various warlord armies. In this fashion, peasants in the same locale are pillaged two and three times by outsiders. Bandits and warlord factions abscond with their chickens and dogs. The people are without houses, without food, and their plight has become extremely miserable. They now are abandoning their villages; the old, the young, and the women flee to Manchuria and the south. These waves of migrations are like an endless tide; no matter how much time elapses, the same conditions continue to persist.[101]

A spate of natural disasters, unusual in their severity and frequency even for China, struck various provinces. In 1918, a great drought swept six northern provinces, killing 500,000 people and severely injuring crops in 317 counties. In February of the same year, a great earthquake ripped Shensi and Kansu. In 1921, six provinces suffered great floods.[102] The following year, a typhoon struck Swatow, and in the year after that, twelve provinces experienced both drought and floods. By 1924 and 1925, the scope and impact of such natural disasters worsened because so much labour had been diverted to warfare and could not be mobilized to provide proper relief. Yunnan suffered a tremendous earthquake and then great floods. Six more provinces experienced crop pests, and floods churned over the Yellow River region.[103]

These calamities, together with the outbreak of violence and warfare, produced the greatest movement of refugees in over a century. Millions fled the northern provinces for Manchuria.[104] Farmland in many parts of the country became wasteland. The beneficiaries of these disasters were

[99] Chang Yu-i, 2.559–89.   [100] Ibid. 2.609.
[101] SMR: Kozawa Shigeichi, *Shina no dōran to Santō nōson* (Shantung villages and the upheaval in China),
    3.   [102] Chang Yu-i, 2.619.
[103] Walter H. Mallory, *China: land of famine*, chs. 1, 2.
[104] Chang Yu-i, 2.659–60.

the warlord armies, as their ranks swelled with the very young and the aged. Rabble bands of these armies and outlaws swarmed like hordes of locusts across the countryside, destroying everything in their path: Hunan, one of the country's major rice bowls, actually 'ceased shipping grain to cities on the lower Yangtze.[105]

All these developments contributed to widespread rural unemployment. There was a sudden increase in food imports to feed the large city-ports. The government employment statistics, notoriously unreliable though they are, provide some indication of the catastrophe. For 1925, unemployment was reported at over 168 million persons, of whom 87 million were supposed to be farmers and rural labourers.[106] Imports of rice, wheat, flour, tobacco and raw cotton had increased but slowly since the 1870s. After 1921, however, they jumped to unprecedented levels. Rice imports doubled once in volume between 1921 and 1922, and nearly once again between 1925 and 1926. Even more spectacularly, wheat imports doubled between 1923 and 1924, and rose seven times between 1925 and 1926. Similar jumps occurred for flour and raw cotton imports.[107]

The Nanking decade

Just as it began to seem that there was no end to agrarian crises, the Kuomintang and its armies defeated the northern warlords. Peace came to most of the country in 1928. At the same time the weather improved, bringing good harvests. But new difficulties lay just ahead. Although sporadic warfare continued in some provinces and farmers paid higher taxes, these were not as troublesome for the farming population as the events between 1932 and 1934. From 1921 to 1931, while Western countries were reeling under the shock of worldwide economic depression, China benefited from the devaluation of her silver currency, which boosted her exports in both quantity and value.[108] The first blow came with the loss of the Manchurian market in 1932. The second followed in 1933–4, as a large quantity of silver flowed out of the country in response to rising silver prices in the United States. Exports declined; the money-supply contracted violently; commodity price levels took a nose-dive. The result for the rural economy was massive deflation.

The silk and cotton handicraft industries, already deep in trouble, were especially hard hit between 1932 and 1935. 'The loss of the north-east

[105] *Ibid.* 2.632.   [106] P'eng Tse-i, 3.66.
[107] Chang Yu-i, 2.674.
[108] Wu Ta-yeh, 'Shih-chieh ching-chi shuai-lo chung chih Chung-kuo' (China during world economic collapse), in Fang Hsien-t'ing, ed. *Chung-kuo ching-chi yen-chiu* (Studies of the Chinese economy), 1.45–56.

greatly influenced silk sales from Chao-hsing (Chekiang): production in 1931 was 156,000 *p'i*, each *p'i* priced at 32 *yuan*, for a total of 5,075,200 *yuan*. When compared to 1929 this was a decline of more than 43,000 *p'i* valued at a loss of more than two million *yuan*.'[109] After the Japanese occupied Manchuria, they raised import duties – an action that, according to the same source, 'effectively blocked silk imports from Yen-t'ai (Shantung)'.[110] Importers of cotton cloth in Dairen and throughout south Manchuria ceased buying from the China market. In Lao-yang, Ting, Yu-tien, and Ch'ing-shou counties of Hopei, and in T'ung-chou and Ch'ang-te counties of Kiangsu, the consequences were serious enough to have an adverse effect on the entire cotton textile industry.[111] Villagers' demand for yarn from spinning mills greatly declined.

In 1931 and 1932, as world trade began contracting, so did Chinese handicraft exports of silk, special silk products, cotton cloth, straw braid, paper, porcelain, bamboo, oilseed products, and hemp cloth, which together made up roughly 50 per cent of total exports. Farm labour greatly contributed to their supply, and the decline in handicraft income forced rural households to alter expenditures. By 1936–7, these handicraft exports were still far below the all-time high of 1930–1, in both quantity and value. In fact, their prices fell more rapidly than foodgrain prices.[112] For tea, tobacco, beverages, livestock, grain, cotton goods and oilseed products, the price indices in Tientsin and Shanghai show a steady decline during the years 1931 to 1934. Soon domestic prices fell as well, and farmers quickly found that the lower sale price could not even cover their unit production costs. Chen Han-seng reported in 1934 that the farmers in Kwangtung took mulberry fields out of production so that 'the area of mulberry land declined by more than 30 per cent'.[113] A study of the tea industry reported a similar decline in crop area.[114] The economic conditions for cotton production had equally gloomy indications for the farming population.

Recently, [around 1932] the collapse of the world economy has become more pervasive and has caused the prices of farm products to fall. The major cotton markets in China were hard hit by world cotton market conditions, so that in every cotton market throughout our country production costs could not be covered, as buying in the market had declined.[115]

The same source goes on to describe how, in Shensi, production costs of cotton exceeded its market price by three times. The downward plunge

109 P'eng Tse-i, 3.392.   110 Ibid. 3.393.
111 Ibid. 3.396.   112 Chang Yu-i, 3.615.
113 Ibid. 3.627.   114 Ibid. 3.629–30.
115 Ibid. 3.632.

in cotton prices in Hupei and Chekiang also squeezed the peasantry in a vice-like grip of high fixed costs and falling marketed sales.

But it was not just the contraction of world trade that ruined the rural economy. The great outflow of silver from the hinterland to coastal cities that began in 1932 was an unprecedented movement of financial capital out of agriculture, sparked by rising silver prices in the United States. It occurred at precisely the time when the rural economy urgently needed credit. A sharp fall in the rate of return for investing in agriculture accompanied the outflow of silver. Bank deposits in Shanghai more than doubled between 1932 and 1933.[116]

Farmers had yet another blow to endure. In time past, when China periodically suffered crop failures in different areas because of drought or flood, local officials had responded by distributing grain or by purchasing it from other provinces. During this period, however, the weakening of administrative capability prevented these measures from working as successfully as in the past. Some areas even began to suffer famine. A Chinese rural investigation team that visited Shensi in 1933 described the misery in the countryside in the team diary.

July 14 [1933]. We investigated the Shih-chia-mo village. Shih-chia-mo has irrigated land; the water comes from a small river. When drought occurs, the stream dries up, and the irrigated land becomes dry land. Opium is cultivated on this irrigated land, and the county administration taxes this land. In March of this year the peasants had to eat grass and bark. Since May they have eaten scarcely anything except grass. They still eat the leftovers from oilseed bearing plants, bran, etc. Now that wheat is being harvested, they will have flour again. This flour is mixed with straw, and water is added to make a soup called *p'an-t'ang* [literally, 'a bowl of soup']. A person eats no more than two flour cakes at meal time. There are days when a person eats only one meal a day. Death from starvation, death from sickness, flight, selling oneself into bondage are common occurrences...

July 15. Hsiao-t'ang village is much poorer than other villages. The peasants in this village starved to death in the autumn of 1928. The price of wheat in the county is eight or nine *yuan* per *tou*, and only those with money can afford to buy it. The gates of the county seat are closed to prevent the peasants from entering. The townspeople are afraid that once they are inside, they will steal everything.[117]

Such conditions were commonplace in many rural areas during the early 1930s. How different from the countryside described by Richthofen and King!

[116] *Ibid.* 3.678.
[117] Hsing-cheng-yuan nung-ts'un fu-hsing wei-yuan-hui, comp. *Shan-hsi sheng nung-ts'un tiao-ch'a* (A survey of villages in Shensi province), 164.

Between 1931 and 1933, rich and poor alike had to sell their land. The resulting redistribution of land ownership was very complex; many households abandoned the ranks of the wealthy to others. In 1933, the Committee for Village Reconstruction in the Executive Yuan of the Nationalist government examined a sample of 155,000 households in seventeen districts of Shensi, Kiangsu, Chekiang, Yunnan and Kwangsi. The period covered by the sample was from 1928 to 1933. The committee found that in eight districts the number of landlord households increased, in four districts their number declined, and in five it remained unchanged.[118] It also found that wealthy households declined in fourteen districts and increased in only three districts. The number of middle-range households owning some land, yet obtaining income from wages, fell in thirteen districts, increased in three districts, and remained unchanged in another. The number of poor households – that is, households whose income was mainly from wages – increased in fourteen of the seventeen districts. Many wealthy families lost both land and economic status. Closer inspection of land acquisition also shows that in Kiangsu, many middle-level families enlarged their holdings even as the total number of families at this level was declining.[119] How unequal land distribution became between 1928 and 1933 may never be known for certain. The basic cause of these developments, however, was clearly the market instability that engulfed the countryside, not control of the village economy by an entrenched landlord elite.

The war years

In 1937, Japan invaded China. For the next eight years the Chinese were engaged in mortal combat with a powerful adversary. After that they had to endure four years of fratricidal civil war before peace came at last. A country at war not only loses many of the goods and services it normally produces; it also risks losing the capital stock upon which its future productive capacity depends. The longer the period of warfare, the greater the sacrifice required of the people to replace the capital lost or worn out. The breakdown of production and economic organization is accompanied by social changes that gradually make themselves felt as a disregard for morals and convention, and a tendency for the strong to abuse the weak. The Japanese invasion of North China in 1937 badly frightened the

---

[118] Furushima Kazuo, 'Kyū Chūgoku ni okeru tochi shoyū to sono seikaku' (Land ownership and its characteristics in traditional China), in Yamamoto Hideo and Noma Kiyoshi, *Chūgoku nōson kakumei no tenkai* (The development of the Chinese agrarian revolution), 41.

[119] Hsing-cheng-yuan nung-ts'un fu-hsing wei-yuan-hui, comp. *Chung-kuo*, 1.25, 28, 30.

merchants and moneylenders. They closed their shops and fled. The movement of so many troops along major roads and railways – the Chinese fleeing and the Japanese advancing – quickly led to the conscription of rural labour and the confiscation of their carts and draft animals. Aside from several large battles in the next few years, conditions in North China soon stabilized. But after 1941 Chinese guerrilla warfare intensified, and the Japanese retaliated with search-and-destroy operations. The overall effect of the war upon the North China countryside is very hard to determine because comprehensive surveys of damage were never undertaken. On the basis of local surveys made between 1938 and 1943, one Chinese scholar attempted a general assessment of how extensively war had affected agricultural production.

As for changes in crop area, we can say that there was a shift from commercial crops to major food crops. The area under cotton cultivation fell most of all, and the cultivated area for millet, potato, etc., rose. Sorghum was a major foodgrain for farm families, and the Japanese military prevented large-scale planting of the crop in order to eliminate the fields as protective covering for guerrillas. Therefore, its cultivated area declined. The total cultivated area, however, declined very little.[120]

The 1939 harvest was especially poor, mainly because of poor weather. By 1941–2, however, output and yields had recovered to their 1937 levels. Then, from 1942 onwards, farm production appears to have declined severely.

In 1943, and thereafter, the Japanese intensified their fighting, conscripted more people for their campaigns, and destroyed considerable life and property. The time lost by not farming, the shortage of labour animals and manpower, and the great shift toward more self-sufficiency by farmers caused a deterioration in the quality of farming and reduced output to a lower level. It is possible that the three-year period from 1940 to 1942 was the most stable and best period for agriculture in the north during the entire war.[121]

Changing land-use patterns and growing shortages of labour and draft animals also occurred in other parts of the country. In 1938 and 1939, the Nationalist government retreated to Szechwan and Yunnan. As a result, cities such as Chungking more than tripled their size overnight. The new city-dwellers, mostly of middle-class origin, preferred a diet of pork, chicken, eggs, flour, vegetables and fruit. The surrounding region could not produce a sufficient quantity to satisfy demand. Prices rose, and

---

[120] Ma Li-yuan, 'Chan-shih Hua-pei nung-tso-wu sheng-ch'an chi ti-wei tui liang-shih chih lieh-to' (Agricultural production and pillaging of foodstuffs by the Japanese and their puppets in North China during the war), She-hui k'o-hsueh tsa-chih, 10.1 (June 1948) 65.
[121] Ibid. 71–2.

farmers responded by reallocating much of their land and labour to these products instead of foodgrains, which consequently fell into short supply.[122] By 1941–2, the price of rice, wheat, and other foodgrains began to rise against those of special farm products. Farmers accordingly began to shift more of their land into the production of these foodgrains. Meanwhile, the wartime demand for labour had diverted many young men away from farming to work in factories and transportation, not to mention service on the front lines. By 1943, there were many indications that the south-west farm economy had been extended to its limits. Farm production was declining, albeit gradually. There was drought, but the main reason was the scarcity of farm labour.[123]

During peaceful, stable times, farm production might fall briefly but quickly recover. But under wartime conditions, when labour was withdrawn from planting, soil care, or harvesting, production declined on a sustained basis. Labour-intensive crops were, of course, the hardest hit. There were major regional variations in types of crops and the frequency with which they were planted, so that a withdrawal of the same amount of labour in the north or south affected production quite differently.

The farms that supplied the largest share of marketed surplus usually employed part-time labour. Although the demand for farm crops pulled farm prices upward, the cost of hiring farm labour during peak farming periods rose more rapidly than many crop prices. We know that this situation was very serious in Szechwan after 1941.[124] Presumably the same was true in other parts of the country. By 1943–4, many farms were caught in a severe price and cost squeeze, and had to cut back on the amount of land they could sow. The large, well-to-do farms still had sufficient land to feed themselves. Nevertheless, the cutbacks caused total production to decline and land use patterns to change. As a result, the marketed surplus of industrial crops declined most of all. Even the sale of foodgrains to the cities fell.

The burdens of war still fell mainly upon the rural people. Graham Peck, who travelled extensively in southern Shensi and northern Honan in 1941, reported that troops everywhere conscripted farmers' carts and even members of farm families. Wherever he went, 'the one problem of crises which really interested the farmers was the Kuomintang conscription of carts'.[125] Without carts the autumn harvest could not be moved; without

---

[122] Tung Shih-chin, 'K'ang-chan i-lai Ssu-ch'uan chih nung-yeh' (Agriculture in Szechwan since the beginning of the war of resistance), *Ssu-ch'uan ching-chi chi-k'an*, 1.1 (15 Feb. 1943) 48.

[123] *Ibid.* 51.

[124] Wang Yin-yuan, 'Ssu-ch'uan chan-shih nung-kung wen-t'i' (The problem of farm labour during wartime in Szechwan), *Ssu-ch'uan ching-chi chi-k'an*, 2.3 (1943–4), 107–8.

[125] Graham Peck, *Two kinds of time*, 260.

carts fields could not be fertilized that winter; without carts farmers could not ship their grain to market and buy what they needed. Another onerous burden was the periodic grain levies, payable in kind of a fixed amount by the entire village. Hardly a village was exempt. Although cities like Chengchow and Loyang were occupied by the Japanese, life there seems not to have been as harsh as it was for the farmers. Peck describes the grim, rural conditions widespread in north-central China in the early 1940s.

Taxes and requisitions had become so heavy, the average farmer knew that if the weather should get a little worse, or if this plough would break, this ox should die, he would be in serious trouble. So many of the able-bodied young men had been taken away as conscripts – nearly three-quarters of them in some villages – that most families could get along only if the old people, children and pregnant women worked regularly in the fields.[126]

In 1949 and 1950, Communist teams visited villages in the north to make spot checks on the progress of land reform. They reported that, in every village they visited, a great decline in the supply of livestock, tools, cultivated area and crop yields had taken place between 1937 and 1949. In P'ing-yuan county (Hopei), crop yields in 1949 were still below those of 1937.[127] A survey of 49 villages in Shantung found that the cultivated area per household in 1949–50 was below the 1931–6 average. The supply of tools had also declined, and crop yields were lower.[128]

The bleak picture of rural poverty that emerges from the historical record for these years has been interpreted – contrary to our own views set forth earlier in this chapter – by many commentators as evidence that conditions had never been different, and that the countryside had never experienced better times. Clearly, rural China paid a huge price for the political and military disasters of these three decades.

[126] *Ibid.* 312–13.
[127] Chung-yang nung-yeh-pu chi-hua ssu, comp. *Liang-nien-lai ti Chung-kuo nung-ts'un ching-chi tiao-ch'a hui-pien* (A collection of surveys on the Chinese farm economy in the past two years), 149–50, 160–1.
[128] *Ibid.* 224–36.

CHAPTER 6

PEASANT MOVEMENTS

The Chinese revolution is often considered the greatest peasant revolution in history, even the very archetype of peasant revolution. Certainly the Chinese Communists could not have won power without the peasant armies and the support of so many villagers. Yet without the Communists the peasants would, quite simply, never have conceived the idea of a revolution.

To support this proposition the present chapter deals first with peasant unrest that was spontaneous, contemporary with and yet independent of the Communist movement, and provoked by those three major drains on peasant income, namely rent, interest and taxes.[1] A second section sketches a typology of rural disturbances in Republican China, after briefly describing those which were not provoked by rent, usury or taxation. Both the disturbances that are analysed in the first section and those alluded to in the second section were eminently traditional flare-ups of peasant anger, as ephemeral as they were sudden, and seldom a threat to the established order. In short, a huge distance lay between what the peasants could do spontaneously and what the Communists made it possible for them to do under Communist leadership. The third section therefore examines some of the difficulties that the Communists faced and the methods they used to overcome them. To forge victory for the revolution, using the basic peasant material, was such an opportunity but also such a challenge! Faithful to Lenin's teaching and example (never mind if the peasantry rather than the workers constituted the basic material), the Chinese apostles of the revolution, who became specialists in the conquest of power, took up that challenge and overcame the difficulties by dint of a mixture of abnegation and cunning that aroused not only enthusiasm but also resentment.

A preliminary warning must be given about statistics on the relative frequencies of the various categories of rural disturbances and riots. Statistical tables and percentages would provide only an illusory guarantee

---

[1] See the chart in Joel S. Migdal, *Peasants, politics and revolution: pressures toward political and social changes in the Third World*, 89.

of accuracy on account of the heterogeneity of the sources and the extreme variability of the details that they contain. For example, during the Nanking decade, of close to a thousand incidents recorded or simply mentioned, barely one hundred can be described in accurate detail on the basis of the information available, which varies from a few lines to a few pages or at most a few dozen pages. The rest of these 1,000 incidents are known to us all too cursorily from no more than one or two lines in a summary[2] or, worse still, in the majority of cases from general references that provide no details at all.[3] Moreover, some incidents recorded separately in one or another record may be connected with the same affair. This would seem to be true for most of the twenty instances of resistance to tax-collection recorded in Soochow prefecture (Kiangsu) during the first half of 1936. Should each be considered separately?[4] Again, at what point (duration, numbers involved, level of violence) can an expression of peasant anger be considered to be a riot? And when does a riot become an uprising? In other words, we must recognize the uneven levels of importance of the incidents recorded.

For these reasons, the credibility of any statistical assessment would in any event be compromised by the disparate nature of the information

[2] Cf. Chang Yu-i, comp. *Chung-kuo chin-tai nung-yeh shih tzu-liao, ti-san chi, 1927-1937* (Materials on China's modern agricultural history, third collection, 1927–1937), sometimes cited under the name of Li Wen-chih, the compiler of the first volume, which covers the period 1840–1911, hereafter *NYTL*, 3: 26 cases of resistance to land tax or to rent (3.1021–3), 24 disturbances connected with the salt tax or committed by salt producers (*ibid.* 1023–5), 21 disputes relating to water and to waterworks (*ibid.* 1026–8), 6 relating to the land (*ibid.* 1026) and, finally, 27 cases of looting (*ibid.* 1031–2). Cf. also 43 disturbances relating to salt, all of which took place in the single year of 1934 (*Chung-hua jih-pao*, 4 April 1935) and more than 100 incidents relating to six other categories that took place in that same year (*Chung-hua jih-pao*, 27 February; 6, 13, 20, 27 March; 18 and 25 April 1935). Another drawback to these tables is that the information that they contain, sparse though it is, sometimes suggests that one should distrust or even reject the classification of a particular incident or riot.

[3] E.g. 25 cases of looting in Wu-hsi hsien, Kiangsu, between 11 May and 10 June 1932; and 40-odd cases within two weeks (between 25 July and 8 August 1934) in the *chen* of Wang-tien alone (in Chia-hsing hsien, in north-east Chekiang). See respectively, Feng Ho-fa, ed. *Chung-kuo nung-ts'un ching-chi tzu-liao* (Materials on the Chinese rural economy), hereafter *NTCC*, 1.423; United States, State Department Archives, hereafter USDS, 893.00B/1070, enclosure 5; also 70 fiscal riots in the province of Shensi alone during the summer of 1932 (*NTCC* 2.413); 197 incidents involving tenant-farmers, mostly in Kiangsu and Chekiang between 1923 and 1932, that is to say, spanning the Nanking decade and the preceding decade: Ts'ai Shu-pang, 'Chin shih-nien lai Chung-kuo tien-nung feng-ch'ao ti yen-chiu' (Research on tenant riots in China during the past ten years), *Tung-fang tsa-chih*, hereafter *TFTC*, 30.10 (16 May 1933) 26–38. Account should also be taken of looting and other incidents of minor importance, the frequency of which is almost impossible to gauge since the sources do no more than indicate that they are 'very numerous' or even 'almost daily events' in particular periods and localities, for example in the silkworm-producing zone of Chekiang and Kiangsu in May and June 1932 (*NYTL* 3.1030). The 40 cases in Wang-tien and the 25 in Wu-hsi mentioned above confirm their 'almost daily' nature; and the latter represent only a minority of the cases of looting in the hsien between 11 May and 10 June 1932; the vast majority of cases were not reported in the newspapers and were therefore not recorded (*NTCC* 1.423).

[4] *NYTL* 3.1021–2. On this Soochow case, see below, pp. 273–5.

provided by the sources, while a statistical assessment which drew comparisons between things not comparable (disturbances of widely varying kinds, duration or importance) might well prove to be lacking in any significance at all.

One last point of methodology: the sample of rural disturbances known to us is not very representative of the frequency of such disturbances over a longer period of time and not at all representative of their spatial distribution. Should we, for example, attribute the increase in the number of anti-fiscal riots, recorded from the twenties to the thirties, to the increase in land tax coupled with the decrease in agricultural prices (and hence also in the income of those taxed) or should we attribute it rather to a greater interest in the condition of the peasantry shown by witnesses (journalists and other intellectuals)? (Perhaps the answer is both, but then in what proportion?) As many of these witnesses were writing in Shanghai newspapers, the overwhelming majority of the incidents known to us took place in Kiangnan (south of Kiangsu) and northern Chekiang.[5] Provinces of the interior, particularly those in the west, are under-reported; and in those provinces, prefectures and hsien most distant from the provincial capital, even more so.

A statistical analysis has been drawn up by C. K. Yang, not for the Republican period but for the nineteenth century (1796–1911).[6] For that relatively long period of time, his study has a much wider scope (not only rural disturbances but also the much more numerous urban riots and clashes, acts of banditry, and collective donations made to help the government meet its military expenses, not to mention 1,600 incidents connected with the rebellions of the Taiping and the Nien). For historians of the Republican period, to put together annual totals comparable to the 6,643 incidents and mass actions (that is, 58 per year) analysed by C. K. Yang would not be impossible. It would, however, be desirable to reach less uncertain and in some cases less tautological conclusions. There is a striking contrast between the modest and controversial results of his ambitious project[7] on the one hand, and the very valuable findings of his classic works on the family, the village and religion, on the other.[8] Equally eloquent is the contrast between the disappointing results of the

---

5 One compiler remarks, quite justifiably, that the record number of cases of looting in these two provinces reputed to be 'the paradise' (*t'ien-t'ang*) of China indicates no more than the superiority of the press of Kiangsu and Chekiang over the press in other provinces (*NYTL* 3.1032).

6 C. K. Yang, 'Some preliminary statistical patterns of mass actions in nineteenth-century China', in Frederic Wakeman, Jr. and Carolyn Grant, eds. *Conflict and Control in late imperial China*, 174–210.

7 'It attempts to use computer-processed historical data as a heuristic tool to discern the magnitudes and configurations of mass action incidents ...', Yang, 'Statistical patterns', 174 and n.1.

8 C. K. Yang, *The Chinese family in the Communist revolution; A Chinese village in early Communist transition; Religion in Chinese Society.*

'ecological' study made by Roy Hofheinz and the massive store of information provided by that historian from his more traditional research.[9] Of course, the qualitative methods favoured in the present chapter are themselves open to obvious hazards such as subjectivism, but they at least do not present an appearance of scientifically established truth which may be quite misleading.

SPONTANEOUS RESISTANCE TO RENTS AND TAXES

Conflicts between tenants and landlords

K'ang-tsu (resistance to land rents) is a privileged category among the non-Communist peasant actions recorded in the People's Republic of China, because it best represents the struggle of the exploited against the exploiters. Sometimes alone, sometimes preceding the more fully documented but socially less pure category of *k'ang-shui* (movements of resistance to taxes), it figures fairly prominently in archives and compilations, a fact which can lead to exaggeration of the insubordination of tenant-farmers. This insubordination increased in the Republican period but remained confined to a minority and caused disputes and confrontations more than real riots.

Among the real riots it is worth noting the one that disturbed the countryside round Soochow during the winter and spring of 1935–6. The numerous absentee landlords there, some of whom did not even know where their fields lay, and also some resident landlords, had acquired the habit of entrusting the collection of rents to middlemen, the *ts'ui-chia* (rent-collectors), who were detested both for their corruption and for their exactions.[10] However, the institution of the *ts'ui-chia*, which was already old, was not the only cause of the revolt. The agitation followed two consecutive bad harvests. For reasons of economy, the landlords decided in 1935 not to send to the scene 'calamity inspectors' entrusted with the task of judging the size of the disaster, particularly as the tenant-farmers had fought with those they had sent the previous year. The hsien

---

[9] Roy Hofheinz, Jr. 'The ecology of Chinese Communist success: rural influence patterns, 1923–1945' in A. D. Barnett, ed. *Chinese Communist politics in action*, 3–77; *The broken wave: The Chinese Communist peasant movement, 1922–1928*; 'Peasant movement and rural revolution: Chinese Communists in the countryside, 1923–1927' (Harvard University, Ph.D. dissertation, 1966).

[10] On the *ts'ui-chia* of Soochow, see Yūji Muramatsu, 'A documentary study of Chinese landlordism in late Ch'ing and early Republican Kiangnan', *Bulletin of the School of Oriental and African Studies*, 29.3 (Oct. 1966) 569, 587–9; and Frank A. Lojewski, 'The Soochow bursaries: rent management during the late Ch'ing', *CSWT*, 4.3 (June 1980) 44–5. Note, however, that the incidents of extortion for which the *ts'ui-chia* are blamed by the farmers of Soochow during the Nanking decade appear to have been more frequent than those at the end of the Ch'ing; and furthermore, the *ts'ui-chia* studied by Muramatsu and later by Lojewski were employees of the *tsu-chan* (landlord bursaries), which was not necessarily the case during the Nanking decade.

government had therefore asked all tenants to make 'declarations of calamity', but the landlords suspected they were exaggerated, and so they automatically reduced the totals of losses declared in their calculation of the rent reductions to be permitted. There was a second reason for tenant discontent, connected with the payment in kind of a rent expressed in terms of money: just before the rents were fixed, the price of a picul of rice in Soochow dropped from 8 *yuan* to 7.5 *yuan*, with the result that tenants were obliged to hand over an extra sixteenth of rice for a rent that remained nominally unchanged. A third reason for their anger was an alteration in the weights and measures (the old picul now equalled 1.6 new piculs), which was misunderstood by the tenants, who wrongly interpreted it as an increase in rent.

The trouble started in November 1935, in the villages and districts where the harvest had been poorest, when the officials started trying to collect rents and to arrest defaulting tenants. After the failure of a petition requesting a rent reduction, several thousand peasants demanded the liberation of the arrested tenants, besieged and destroyed the local police station (the police opened fire and wounded a few demonstrators) and set fire to the houses of the *ts'ui-chia*. Clashes and incidents (none of which lasted more than two days) occurred again during the first few months of 1936 in several districts (*ch'ü*) of Wu-hsien (the hsien of Soochow). The most serious of these took place at the end of April, a few days after the officials had tried to seize seeds in lieu of unpaid rents. As a result of these incidents, which caused deaths on both sides, the hsien magistrate tried to restore calm by belated and limited concessions: a reduction of 20 per cent in rents in districts where the harvest had been poorest, cancellation of the fines imposed on tenants who had not paid their rent on time, and so on. But clashes between peasants and police continued through May and June.[11]

The first characteristic of these Soochow riots was their lack of preparation. The rebels do not appear to have had a strategy nor is there any discernible progression in the forms taken by the resistance (protests, petitions and propaganda alternated with violent clashes at the end of the period just as at the beginning). What we have here, rather, is a series of explosions which spread by contagion and with a markedly seasonal character (at the time of rent-collection, then of sowing). Second, these

---

[11] See Hung Shui-chien, 'Su-chou k'ang-tsu feng-ch'ao ti ch'ien-yin hou-kuo' (Causes and results of the tenant riots in Soochow), *Ti-cheng yueh-k'an* (Land administration monthly), 4.10 (October 1936) 1547–62; 'Su-chou ti nung-ch'ao' (The peasant riots in Soochow), *Chung-kuo nung-ts'un*, hereafter *CKNT*, 2.6 (June 1936) 6–8; *Ch'en-pao*, 29, December 1935, quoted in *NYTL* 3.1020. On the October 1934 disturbances, during which tenants had set fire to more than 40 houses belonging to *ts'ui-chia*, see Wu Ta-k'un, 'Tsui-chin Su-chou ti nung-min nao-huang feng-ch'ao' (The recent disturbances among Soochow peasants due to poor harvests), *TFTC* 32.2 (16 Jan. 1935) 83–4.

explosions of fury were provoked by particular causes, even accidents: 'calamities' (a bad harvest) or the refusal of landlords to accept without question the declarations of calamity, a local drop in the price of rice, a change in the system of weights and measures. There was no fundamental questioning of the principle of tenancy, simply a protest against sudden changes in the status quo. Third and finally, in this conflict between tenants and landlords, just as in anti-fiscal riots, as we shall see, people attacked officials or underlings and public buildings. Heads of villages or of *pao-chia* and the local offices of the public security forces were, like the *ts'ui-chia*, the most frequent targets for violence – much more frequent than the landlords themselves, who were not all absentees. The tenants were angry that the soldiery should come right into the villages to collect unpaid rents. The troops intervened as a result of appeals for help, complaints and sometimes disguised threats ('if we do not receive the rents, we shall be unable to pay our taxes') from the landlords. But the anger aroused in the tenants by the collusion between the exploiters and the authorities turned almost exclusively against the latter. Thus the anti-rent disturbances, which are deemed social rebellions *par excellence*, were aimed less at the rich than at the authorities.

In at least one province, Chekiang, the solidarity between the authorities and the landlords faltered momentarily. For a short period during the first years of the Nationalist regime in Chekiang, the local representatives of the KMT tried to defend the interests of the tenant farmers, a policy which produced a multiplication of the conflicts between the latter and their landlords. Thanks to this unfortunate episode (the failure of agrarian reform in the only province where the authorities tried to apply it), we have a considerable body of evidence to illustrate a second point concerning the tenants' affairs: although riots and revolts were rare, the same was not true of disputes and lawsuits. Though they seldom degenerated into violence, they cast a glaring light on the nature of the relations between landlords and tenants. With rare exceptions, the landlords alone express their views but from their often prolix recriminations we can try to grasp the subjects of disagreement between the two sides.

The government decision to reduce land rents by 25 per cent provoked numerous complaints and petitions from the landlords, who are usually reluctant to identify themselves as such and often sign themselves 'citizens' (*kung-min*), or even bluntly 'farmers' (*yeh-nung*) or 'delegates of the peasants in the canton' (*hsiang nung-min tai-piao*).[12] Some petitions claim

---

[12] For the paragraphs that follow, cf. three files in the Second Historical Archives, Nanking: no. 1–2–1001 and 1–2–1002, entitled 'Che-chiang ko-ti nung-min k'ang-tsu tou-cheng' (Peasant resistance to rents in various localities in Chekiang) (1927–1930); no. 2–2–1129, 'Che-chiang

to have several hundred signatures, among which there must certainly be those of landlords' agents, relatives and clients, since the number of landlords in the district was likely to be lower than the number of petitioners. Others, on the other hand, bear only the signatures of the usual spokesmen of the local elite (head and sub-head of the district, commander of the militia, etc.). But what varies hardly at all is the content of the petitions; identical arguments expressed in the same terms and using the same clichés, as if models had been passed around (just as they were for the fabrication of the *'cahiers de doléances'* or lists of grievances before the meeting of the States General in France in the spring of 1789). We are obviously dealing here with a concerted offensive, or rather counter-offensive.

In their complaints, the Chekiang landowners are careful not to call into question the principle of a 25 per cent rent reduction. They simply claim that this measure is responsible for the deterioration in relations between landlords and tenants; the worst elements among the latter – 'swindler-tenants' (*chien-tien*) and 'bad peasants' (*o-nung*) – are taking advantage of the law and applying a reduction of much more than 25 per cent, or even quite simply refusing to pay up at all. Bad tenants are often manipulated by hoodlums (*p'i-t'u*) or vagabonds (*wu-yeh yu-min*, 'vagabonds without regular occupation') and supported by traditional or (more often) newly established leaders and organizational bodies: the village heads and village committees, the peasant unions and the local sections of the Kuomintang.

The landlords particularly resent the arbitration committees (*tien-yeh chung ts'ai-hui*) which are responsible for settling the litigations that stem from the application of the law: they accuse them of systematic partiality in favour of the tenants and of brutality and intimidation towards the landlords. They suggest that these arbitration committees (also known as 'conciliation committees') are inciting the tenants to refuse to accept harvest inspections and instead to submit their own evaluations or even to use for the excellent year of 1930 grain harvests figures which were those of the poor harvests in 1929 and 1928; the committees are encouraging the tenant farmers to use smaller measuring units when they pay rent in grain; and not to pay their rent until the landlord has drawn up a new lease for them, etc. Deprived in this way of their legitimate

ko-hsien ch'eng-ch'ing ch'ü-hsiao shih-hsing er-wu chien-tsu i-mien chiu-fen' (Petitions from various hsiens of Chekiang requesting that the 25 per cent rent reduction be no longer applied in order to avoid conflicts) (Nov. 1931 – June 1934); and Noel R. Miner, 'Agrarian reform in Nationalist China: the case of rent reduction in Chekiang, 1927–1937', in F. Gilbert Chan, ed. *China at the crossroads: Nationalists and Communists, 1927–1949*, 69–89. I am grateful for the help extended to me by Mr Sun Xiufu and the staff of the Second Historical Archives.

profits, the landowners of a province once prosperous but now ruined can no longer acquit their fiscal obligations: it is often with a veiled threat of this kind aimed in the direction of the authorities that they conclude their litany of complaints and lamentations.

Some of the official documents preserved in the Nanking archives, originating in local sections of the Kuomintang or even the provincial government, refute the allegations contained in a number of these landlords' petitions, point by point. However, their recriminations are not all totally unfounded. Quite a few tenants, who did not fully understand the stipulations of the new law, and others, who were quite simply making the most of a favourable political situation, took the course of not paying any rent at all. Some landlords were threatened or robbed or beaten, a few were killed. But these acts generally seem aimed against landlords who refuse to apply the rent reduction or who reassume possession of the land so as to cultivate it themselves or else rent it to a more submissive tenant (a course sanctioned by local custom only in cases where the tenant farmer has been a serious defaulter). Indeed the obstructive tactics of many landlords originally prompted the directives concerning the introduction of new leases: the old leases were declared null and void, the only valid ones now to be those that observed the 25 per cent rent reduction. Complaints about measuring units that were 'too small' were matched by just as many, on the part of tenant farmers or the administration, about landlords using measures that were 'too big'. It was, precisely, to prevent fraudulent practices that the conciliation committees were driven to impose their own measuring units. In a similar fashion they also forbade tenants to dampen the rice used to pay rent in kind, in order to make it heavier.

Two lessons can be learned from the resurgence of friction and conflict provoked by rent reduction. The first is that the resistance of the privileged class proved successful. The threat of a tax strike prompted the provincial government, which needed the money and cooperation of the landowners so as to be able to cary though its other projects, to give up its programme of agrarian reform. The second lesson to be learned from the agitation provoked by rent reform in Chekiang is that it released frustrations that had been accumulating over a long period. The tenants did not take the initiative in calling into question the contracts that bound them to their landlords, but once the authorities introduced a new measure, it was a catalyst.

Most of the subjects of dispute between tenants and landlords in Chekiang are also naturally to be found in the rest of the country. The most frequent conflicts are connected with the amount of rents or rent deposits, which the landlord either increases (for example, because his own taxes have risen) or refuses to lower (or lower as much as the tenant wants him to) when the harvest is poor. But there are so many other conflicts of interest that it is impossible to list them all: farmers being evicted, disputes over calculating the size of the harvests or over the measures employed, excessive strictness or brutality on the part of the rent-collectors, etc. Tenants sometimes accuse the agent of an absentee landlord of demanding a 'little deposit' for himself on top of the big one that is required for the landlord. They also reproach the agent with charging a commission or a bribe for recommending a candidate for a tenancy when a vacancy occurs. As for the landlords, their complaints concern first and foremost delay in payments or refusals to pay (in reality usually inability to pay), but also, sometimes, the illicit use of some source of water or the secret felling of bamboos.[13]

Many altercations are caused by a third party: the heavens. Most of the requests for rent reductions are presented in years of poor harvest. An inquiry concerning the hinterland of Shanghai cites 220 causes of incidents connected with rent. Apart from 15 refusals to reduce the rent in years of poor harvests, there were 39 incidents caused by meteorological vagaries (flooding: 24 cases; destruction caused by high winds: 8 cases; drought: 7 cases) and 23 caused by devastation by locusts.[14] Here we may stress two points: (1) the role played by factors that are 'accidental' (even if recurrent) in provoking incidents connected with rents; (2) the general predominance in these conflicts of disputes over particular points. The principle of paying rent is almost never called into question.

During the twenties and thirties these conflicts do seem to become slightly more frequent and intense. The inquiry mentioned above records for the decade 1922–31 from two Shanghai newspapers (the *Shen-pao* and the *Hsin-wen-pao*) a total of 197 incidents connected with rent.[15] During the first three years (1922–4), the number of recorded incidents varies between 9 and 11 each year. During the next three years, the troubled years of 1925–7, the number swings between 17 and 19 each year. From 1928 on, it never went below 20. Thus there appears to be a slight intensification of agitation. Moreover the proportion of violent acts (such as invading the home of the landowner and killing and eating his pigs) and of riots and revolts tends to rise: from 33 per cent of the incidents recorded over the first five years (1922–6) to 39 per cent of those recorded over the last five years (1927–31).

[13] Hsiao Hsin-i, 'Économie et société rurale du Sichuan (Szechwan) de 1927 à 1945' (École Pratique des Hautes Études, Paris, Ph.D. dissertation, 1972) 96–7.

[14] Ts'ai Shu-pang, 'Chin shih-nien lai Chung-kuo tien-nung feng-ch'ao ti yen-chiu', 36.

[15] *Ibid.* 26–38. The compilation noted only 197 incidents for 220 causes of incidents since some incidents resulted from several causes at once.

All the same, that is not a spectacular change! Considerably more significant are the annual fluctuations that occur: 46 (23.35 per cent) of the total number of incidents occur in 1929, a catastrophic year (with a plague of locusts and drought at the beginning of the season and flooding later on), as against no more than 20 during the excellent year of 1930. Taking the riots alone, the correlation between climatic accidents and agitation is even clearer: 18 riots in 1929 (out of a total of 73 for the whole decade, i.e. almost one quarter) and only 4 in 1930. As for the incidents that are not riots, many continue to take traditional forms: demonstrations, petitions, lawsuits and cases where tenants have run away so as to avoid paying rent account for more than half the cases recorded. All in all, the traditional character of the incidents connected with rent and an equally traditional link between poor harvests and agitation seem more significant than the slight increase in the frequency of incidents. At all events, revolts remain extremely rare.

The norm in China under the Kuomintang remained submission to landlords.[16] They were treated with deference and continued to practise reciprocity (*kan-ch'ing*) in an atmosphere strongly tinged with Confucian paternalism. Class consciousness and solidarity among exploited tenants are less common and less passionate than competitiveness among candidates for tenancies. The scarcity of land and demographic growth play into the hands of the landowners. For farmers the best course is to acquire the reputation of a tenant who makes no trouble, so as not to risk being evicted from one's tenancy. Even when the tenants do revolt, the targets of their destructive acts are, as we have seen, more often public offices and buildings than the houses of the 'lords', and their fury is more often unleashed against the police who come along to support the rent-collectors than against the landlords who have requested them to do so.

The local moneylender appears to benefit from the same circumstance for he too is on the whole spared by the debtors upon whom he exerts pressure. He certainly runs the risk of being massacred once the people have risen up *for other reasons* but, outside militant literature, one hardly ever comes across concerted movements directed specifically against a grasping moneylender.[17] Rather, the infrequent riots usually take place when employees or other creditors come to a village to claim their dues:[18]

[16] Note the interesting evidence of the Japanese widow of a large landowner in Szechwan: Vincent S. P. Brandt, 'Landlord-tenant relations in Republican China', *Papers on China*, 17 (1963) 225–6.

[17] E.g., with the complicity of his debtors, bandits rob a moneylender, burn the IOUs and distribute his wealth to the poor: *Wen-chi yueh-k'an*, 2.1 (1 Dec. 1936), cited in Chang Jyh-er, 'La vie des paysans à travers la littérature chinoise contemporaine' (École des Hautes Etudes en Sciences Sociales, Paris, Ph.D. dissertation, 1976).

[18] As in Shansi in 1934. See Donald Gillin, *Warlord: Yen Hsi-shan in Shansi province, 1911–1949*, 158.

riots in this category are comparable to those provoked by the collection of rents or taxes. But as a general rule, the situation is one of a simple bilateral relationship between two individuals or two families, that is to say, between a single debtor, on his own, and his creditor, a creditor to whom, even if he is a moneylender practising usury, it will surely be necessary to turn again at some future date. The point is that the necessity of borrowing overrides every other consideration. There are hardly any revolts against intractable creditors whereas there are some instances where neighbours with reserves of funds but who refuse to lend them, in times of penury or when pre-harvest loans are needed, are attacked or even killed.[19] More often it is a matter of compelling the wealthy to advance two or three piculs of rice to tide one over until the harvest.[20] The necessity of borrowing, which sometimes leads to violence, at the same time makes it imperative to deal circumspectly with the lender. There is one act that symbolizes the dependence felt with regard to this figure (and also the quasi non-existence of any movement of debtors or, *a fortiori*, of any revolt by the insolvent): one of the most popular ways to take revenge upon a pitiless creditor is to commit suicide before his door. Shylock loses face, his censor his life.

Anti-fiscal agitation

'By far the most fertile and important source of riots was official extortion in connection with tax collection.'[21] That characteristic of traditional peasant agitation in late Ch'ing China, as well as in seventeenth-century France,[22] was still true during the Nanking decade of Republican China.

As examples, let us cite two anti-fiscal riots which took place during the same month (October 1932) and in the same region, although it is not possible to establish the slightest contagion between them. A fiscal investigation (*ch'ing-ch'a t'ien-fu*) ordered by the Department of Finance of the Kiangsu provincial government provoked serious disturbances in the western cantons (*hsiang*) of Chiang-tu hsien in the neighbourhood of the town of Yang-chou. This inquiry disclosed that the area of many agricultural plots was greater than declared on the title-deeds. The administration gave the farmers concerned the option of either buying

---

[19] This is what happened to a peasant of Ching-an, Kiangsi, who was killed by members of his clan (*Shen-pao*, 26 May 1930, cited in *NYTL* 3.1029).

[20] This is the enforced loan (*ying-chieh*) described in Feng Ho-fa, *NTCC* 1.427.

[21] Kung-chuan Hsiao, *Rural China: imperial control in the nineteenth century*, 441.

[22] This feature is stressed by all students of peasant revolts in France during the seventeenth century, as we are reminded by Jean Jacquart: 'Les paysanneries à l'épreuve', in Pierre Deyon and Jean Jacquart, eds. *Les hésitations de la croissance 1580–1730*, vol. 2 of *Histoire économique et sociale du monde*, 489.

up the excess areas at a relatively low price or else giving it to the state. Indignant at having to buy up or else see confiscated these lands they already considered their own, the peasants set fire to the surveyors' tents and destroyed their tools; they then took to the streets of Yang-chou to demonstrate (19 October 1932). The arrest of fifty or so of the demonstrators (on 21 October) set off a riot. The following day several thousand peasants came into the town, invaded the hsien government offices and then seized fiscal and cadastral documents which they burned or carried off. They set up traffic blocks across the roads and canals, just as wine-producers of Languedoc do these days in France. Troops dispersed the angry peasants and proceeded to make two hundred further arrests. In order to free the demonstrators arrested in the course of the last two days, several tens of thousands of armed peasants (some with rifles but most with sticks and agricultural implements) returned to lay siege to the town on 23 October. According to the official report of two investigators appointed by the provincial government, they hit at least a dozen of the garrison's officers and soldiers after seizing from them weapons less rudimentary than their own. The same report states the troops only fired into the air to disperse the peasants but that is belied by the losses among the rioters: eight dead and at least as many wounded.

After the bloody incidents of 23 October, agitation continued for a few more days: there were gatherings of armed peasants and looting; and houses belonging to peasants who had refused to join the movement, or to village and small-town heads, or to rich landlords (*ta-hu*) were set on fire. The execution of six of the supposed leaders (at dawn, on 29 October) put an end to the movement. In accordance with well-tried methods, the pitiless punishment meted out to the leaders (or those charged as such) was offset by the pardoning of the rank and file (the 250 demonstrators who had been arrested were released on 24 October) and the granting of concessions: to wit, the suspension of the survey programme and also of the fiscal investigation.[23] Surveys or revision of cadastral surveys were frequently the cause of riots, especially if the surveyors found a discordance between cadastral registers and the farming plots involved.[24]

[23] On the Yang-chou riot, see 'Chiang-su Chiang-tu hsien nung-min fan-tui ch'ing-ch'a t'ien-fu yun-tung' (The movement of opposition to fiscal inquiry by the peasants of Chiang-tu hsien, Kiangsu), Second Historical Archives, Nanking, file no. 2/2/973. This file is composed of four documents: the last (no. 16712) is by far the most detailed but is not very objective. Also USDS 893.00/12198 (Peck, consul general in Nanking), 25 October 1932; 893.00 PR Nanking/57 (5 November 1932) and /58 (21 December 1932), monthly reports by the same. Lastly, NTCC 1, 534–5 and *Chung-yang jih-pao*, 23, 24, 25 October 1932.

[24] E.g., in the spring of 1935, the villagers of Ho-hsien, in eastern Anhwei, resisted the surveying and registration of their land. Like the peasants of Yang-chou, they were afraid that the disparity between units of measurement (their local *mou* was bigger than elsewhere) would cause an increase in land tax. (*Chung-kuo jih-pao* (15 April 1935) 7).

The Yang-chou peasants, rightly or wrongly, attributed the discordance to the fact that the surveyors were using smaller units of measurement.

A riot in Yang-chung (a hsien several dozen kilometres south-east of Yang-chou) was provoked by another frequent cause of unrest: an increase in taxation and, in particular, in the surcharges on the land tax. In this riot furthermore it is possible to have a less crude idea of the social class of the leaders. The movement of resistance to taxation in Yang-chung was initially organized by two notables (*ti-fang shih-shen*, 'local gentlemen'), who were delegates for two of the five districts (*ch'ü*) that made up the hsien. Having already campaigned in vain for the unification of the little hsien of Yang-chung with a neighbouring hsien, in hope of reducing administrative expenses from the fusion and so reducing taxation, these two notables during the summer of 1932 opposed a further increase in the surcharges decided upon by the hsien magistrate. A hsien government official, who had been sent to visit the two recalcitrant districts in order to calm down the delegates and also the members of the local gentry, took fright at the sight of the crowd awaiting him and fled, disguised as an old woman. Seeing the failure of their petitions for fusion of the two hsien, but the success of the gathering which intimidated the hsien representative (and at the same time prompted the magistrate to retire), the local taxpayers decided to resist. The two notables assumed the leadership of this movement up to the point where it became radicalized under the influence of leaders who emerged from the peasantry. The latter led ten thousand or more peasants in an attack against the hsien yamen (on 4 October 1932) but did not succeed in setting fire to it; on the contrary, the principal leader was arrested and one peasant was killed. However, they had already destroyed the houses of the director of the tax-collection office, the local representative of the KMT, the captain of the militia, the largest landowner in the hsien, and so on. The fact that the victims included this rich landowner who had no official responsibilities gives this riot a social colouring. Written up a quarter of a century after the event, when the Communists had taken power, the account of it may have been somewhat embroidered.[25] The replacement of the gentry leaders by authentic peasants who display much more resolution is an edifying feature but not a common one. Ordinarily, the peasants constitute the rank and file troops in movements of resistance to taxation, and these movements are often led by the local elite.

Such is the case, in particular, where the resistance is led by the Red Spears (*Hung-ch'iang-hui*), a secret society active in the provinces of

[25] Tai Wen, *Chiang-chou huo an* (The case of the Chiang-chou fire).

Shantung and Honan during the 1920s.[26] In their revolts against the tax-collection, the notables who control the Red Spears or, *a fortiori*, legal organizations such as the 'Village Federations' (*lien-chuang-hui*) in no way aim to overthrow or even to challenge the state. For one thing, the adversary they are fighting is much closer at hand: the hsien administration or a quasi-autonomous warlord or even local collectors who are rapacious and corrupt. Above all, their first preoccupation is defence of their own possessions and persons. They have become over the years accustomed to protecting one another against aggressions on the part of bandits or soldiery, since the public authorities, split into more or less legitimate groups of rival powers,[27] have seldom been capable of ensuring order. So they quite naturally extend this protection, on behalf of the community of which they are influential and prosperous members, to the preservation of patrimonies threatened by taxation.

Thus, these anti-fiscal riots, which are so much more numerous than other categories of rural rioting, do not express the claims of the most underprivileged layers in the rural population. They are not inspired by a deliberately offensive desire to redistribute wealth within the village. Their favourite targets are not the rich villagers as such but rather the civil servants and especially the local government's subordinate agents, the tax-collectors or their henchmen responsible for speeding up the collection of taxes. The anti-fiscal riots are not directed towards bringing the established order, or even traditional forms of taxation, into question. Rather, they seek to preserve them by defending the established rights or even privileges of individuals or local communities. These could vary from the 'right' recognized by custom not to pay a slaughtering tax on pigs killed for the New Year festival[28] to tax exemption for 'black land' (*hei t'ien*) on which no tax has been paid for generations.

Sometimes the wrongs against which the taxpayers rise up are purely

---

[26] Elizabeth J. Perry, *Rebels and revolutionaries in North China, 1845–1945*, 163, 166, 205 and *passim*. Roman Slawinski, *La Société des Piques Rouges et la mouvement paysan en Chine en 1926–1927*, 92–3, 99, 142.

[27] Guy S. Alitto, 'Rural elites in transition: China's cultural crisis and the problem of legitimacy', *Select papers from the Center for Far Eastern Studies*, 3 (1978–9) 218–75.

[28] *NYTL* 3.1020–1. On a quite different scale in seventeenth-century Europe, the revolt in Catalonia (1640) was aimed at preserving fiscal and military privileges that were under threat from Castilian centralism. As in the Lustucru war in the Boulonnais in 1662, many peasant revolts in France (notwithstanding the important social aspects that they exhibited more and more frequently between 1660 and 1675) were directed against the violation of fiscal immunities and privileges by Louis XIV and Colbert. See Pierre Vilar, *La Catalogne dans l'Espagne moderne: recherches sur les fondements économiques des structures nationales*, 1.627, 629–32; P. Heliot, 'La guerre dite de Lustucru et les privilèges du Boulonnais', *Revue du Nord* (Lille), 21 (1935) 265–318; Léon Bernard, 'French society and popular uprisings under Louis XIV', *French Historical Studies*, 3.4 (1964) 457–9.

imaginary. They suspect any project of fiscal reform *a priori*, even when its intentions are of the very best. In the rare cases where revisions of the cadastral survey (or the unpopular registration of properties, *tu-t'i ch'en-pao*) are carried through, they may considerably diminish the fiscal burden of most taxpayers while at the same time bringing more money into government coffers; the only losers are the owners of large expanses of 'black land' hitherto exempted from taxation.[29] So we find the administration cursing the 'stupid' peasants (*yü-min*), who allow themselves to be incited into a revolt, which is harmful to their own interests, by a handful of large landowners practising tax-evasion on a large scale.

The continual worsening of the tax burden, right up to the end of 1933, is the essential feature of this period.[30] But it was the individual innovations (the details, in short, of this general tendency) that provoked the taxpayers' indignation. They did not revolt against the tendency as a whole but against the imposition of a new surtax in particular, or a refusal to grant the customary tax reduction after a poor harvest, or the umpteenth new tax exacted in the course of a single year, an illegal extortion, a particularly glaring fraud or abuse, etc. In short, they reacted against new measures deemed to be intolerable without, however, calling into question the principle of taxation itself.

Such sporadic reactions were easily crushed, although not inevitably doomed to complete failure. For every rebellion that managed to last for several months there occurred plenty of riots put down the same day or within a week. There was very seldom any coordination between one and another. Nearly all were badly – if at all – prepared, badly organized and badly conducted: even if the primitive weapons of the rioters and their lack of training and discipline were not enough to doom their enterprises, defeat might be caused by the improvised nature of their initiatives.[31] The rapid crushing of a riot was in most cases followed up by equally swift

---

[29] See three conclusive examples carried out in Tang-tu hsien (Anhwei), Hsiao hsien and Chiang-tu hsien (Kiangsu): Ts'ai-cheng-pu cheng-li ti-fang chüan-shui wei-yuan-hui (Committee for the reorganisation of local taxes of the Ministry of Finance), *T'u-ti ch'en-pao tiao-ch'a pao-kao chih i: An-hui sheng Tang-t'u hsien t'u-ti ch'en-pao kai-lueh* (First report on the inquiry into land registration: summary of the registration of land in Tang-t'uhsien, Anhwei); *Chiang-susheng Hsiao-hsient'u-ti ch'en-pao kai-lueh* (Second Report: summary of the registration of land in Hsiao hsien, Kiangsu); *Chiang-su sheng Chiang-tu hsien t'u-ti ch'en-pao kai-lueh* (Third Report: summary of the registration of land in Chiang-tu hsien, Kiangsu). Chiang-tu county was the seat of the Yangchow riot referred to above. Land registration provoked a quickly suppressed riot in Hsiao county.

[30] This worsening was to resume and gather momentum during the 1940s: see Lloyd E. Eastman, 'Peasants, taxes, and Nationalist rule, 1937–1945', 6–16.

[31] In October 1932 in Yang-chung demonstrators attacked the hsien yamen only after they had spent ten hours setting fire to private houses (seven in all) situated well apart from one another; the authorities had had ample time to take precautions (Tai Wen, 22). In Yang-chou, similarly, the insurgents gave the authorities ample time to bring in reinforcements and close the town gates before the decisive confrontation of 23 October.

repression. As at Yang-chou, it would usually be pitiless but selective; the leaders (or, if these could not be identified, those declared to be leaders) would be executed, all the rest released. Quite often the county magistrate (*hsien-chang*) would be transferred and the measure that caused the flare-up would be abrogated. In such cases, defeat did not mean failure.

Resistance to the opium tax

The land tax and above all the surcharges to the land tax were at the root of most anti-fiscal riots but not of all of them: levies on alcohol, on the slaughtering of animals, on salt and on opium, etc. also provoked resistance. Let us limit ourselves to a discussion of the last mentioned tax. The extremely high rate of the opium tax was not the only cause of disturbances involved. The fact that poppy cultivation was made compulsory at times and prohibited at other times provoked numerous clashes with the police or the army.

Poppy cultivation was not only exposed to reversals of government policy and the threat of repression. It was also affected by meteorological risks,[32] which made it a much more delicate crop than cereals, as well as by market risks of over-production and falling prices. However, the cultivation of poppies could prove extremely profitable: four to six times as profitable as a field of wheat in Kweichow at the beginning of the Sino-Japanese War; while in Yunnan a few years earlier a harvest of poppies would bring in one quarter of the value of the field in which they grew.[33]

Taxation was proportionate. Officially, the exorbitant rates aimed to discourage the cultivation of poppies, or even to impose sanctions against it, as can be seen from the most common name of the tax: *mou-fa*, 'the per *mou* fine'. Sometimes the continual increases in a tax that was severe in the first place did deter peasants from planting poppies, as happened in many places during the season of 1925–6. The authorities concerned (military, as it happened) then hurriedly reduced the opium land taxes in order to stimulate production.[34] For the rest of the time, though, the 'prohibitive' taxation of opium certainly achieved its true end (the reverse of those officially proclaimed), namely, the extension of poppy cultivation. No other crop brought in enough to make such high taxation viable and in many regions the tax was collected whether peasants grew poppies or

[32] 'Rain or moisture in the air at the time of harvest could easily ruin the crop', J. C. S. Hall, *The Yunnan provincial faction, 1927–1937*, 109.

[33] *Ibid.* 105; Institute of Pacific Relations, comp. *Agrarian China*, 119.

[34] H. G. W. Woodhead, ed. *The China year book*, hereafter *CYB*, *1928*, 524.

not.[35] Szechwan was particularly suited, thanks to its fertile, well-irrigated land and its abundant rivers, to the production and transport of opium, and a 'lazy tax' was imposed upon those cultivators who refused to plant poppies. Although it was supposed to equal the sum that poppy cultivators were supposed to pay, it was in fact sometimes as much as double.[36]

Before they were incited if not forced by the exigencies of taxation to cultivate increasing quantities of poppies to the detriment of grain harvests (which caused a number of local famines), many peasants had been obliged to plant poppies in the first place by militarists, also for fiscal reasons.[37] These same peasants were then forced to pull up their poppy plants when the Nationalist government, faithful to the wishes of Sun Yat-sen and anxious financially to weaken and control the semi-independent regimes of the south-west (the principal opium-producing region), at last managed, after several unsuccessful campaigns, to impose a prohibition. The production and consumption of opium did not disappear overnight, but there was a slight fall in both from 1934 onward, despite the efforts of provincial or local authorities to avoid giving up the revenue. Opium enabled rival militarists of Szechwan to finance their armies and was the highest source of income in the provincial budgets of Yunnan and Kweichow. Even Kwangsi, which was almost devoid of poppies, taxed opium from Yunnan as it passed through the region bound for the Yangtze. Similarly Shansi province under Yen Hsi-shan forbade poppy cultivation but profited from illicit taxation of opium smuggled in from Shensi across the Yellow River.

The prohibition of opium had the immediate effect of impoverishing, sometimes ruining, the poppy producers, the value of whose land fell overnight. If they tried to continue to produce this crop secretly, and it was a difficult one to conceal, they at the very least risked incurring a heavy fine and sometimes much more. In the extreme north of Kiangsu at the end of 1932, the official inspections of poppy fields were accompanied by threats of death to those who did not uproot their plants within two weeks.[38] So the reversal of policies did nothing to alter an

---

[35] Examples in Kansu (*CYB, 1925*, 579), Yunnan (*CYB, 1926*, 642), Kweichow (*ibid.* 637) and Fukien (*ibid.* 627).

[36] *CYB, 1926*, 620 and *1925*, 586.

[37] There are examples of direct constraint in seven different provinces (Shensi, Kansu, Szechwan, Yunnan, Honan, Hupei, Fukien) in *CYB, 1921–1922*, 791; *1925*, 575, 578, 583; *1926*, 626, 641–2; *1928*, 531; *1931*, 591, 599–600.

[38] USDS 893.00 PR Nanking/59 (14 January 1933) 21. In regions under direct Nationalist control, the anti-opium campaign had been effective as early as 1932. Though poppy cultivation had gradually spread over most provinces of China, it remained most intensive in the western opium belt which included, as well as the south-west already mentioned, the north-west (Shensi, Kansu, Ninghsia, Suiyuan).

essential continuity, that peasants were threatened with death, first if they did not, and then if they did, plant poppy.[39]

Faced with policies that varied in time and space (poppy cultivation might be obligatory in the western provinces and Fukien just when it was prohibited in the other coastal provinces), the peasants reacted in their usual fashion: usually without violence but with sudden explosions of anger or despair when they could no longer endure the intolerable abuses. In 1925 in Wan-hsien, Szechwan, where poppies had not been cultivated since 1909, the headman of every *chia* refused to comply when the military ordered them to return to planting poppies.[40] That same year at Fu-ling, a little further up the Yangtze, the whole population, led by the gentry and merchants, gathered to lend more solemnity to its protest against an increase of 600,000 *yuan* in opium taxes.[41] And there were the other customary non-violent reactions, including petitions requesting the hsien government to authorize restrictions on the production of opium, the flight of those owing taxes when the tax-collectors were due to arrive, and the definitive desertion of land too highly taxed.[42]

In Fukien, a province which produced very little opium, the army and navy organized the smuggling on a large scale. Exploitation of the producers was entrusted to individuals or companies that could count upon military protection so as to conclude their tax-collection successfully. This occasioned repeated clashes and conflicts between soldiers and Fukien peasants.[43] In Fukien and elsewhere, the conflicts were as a rule as ephemeral as they were chronic. One exception was the long, and in one instance victorious, resistance to the army and the authorities collecting opium taxes put up in February and during the summer of 1932 by the peasants in the four northern hsien of Anhwei and in one hsien of northern Kiangsu.[44]

[39] Cf. *CYB, 1926*, 620 and *1928*, 534. But during this first period, before the prohibition decreed by the Kuomintang, it sometimes also happened that peasants were executed for having planted opium (*CYB, 1925*, 575); it all depended on the local authorities.

[40] *CYB, 1926*, 641. There were similar refusals in four hsien in the south-west of the province (*CYB, 1931*, 600) and other places outside Szechwan (*CYB, 1926*, 626; *1928*, 524 and 531).

[41] *CYB, 1926*, 641.

[42] *CYB, 1926*, 626 and 628; *Agrarian China*, 129–30.

[43] For example in 1925 (*CYB, 1925*, 571 and 574), 1928 (USDS 893.00 PR Foochow/4, 4 April 1928, 6–7), 1931 (*ibid.* PR Foochow/37, Feb. 1931) and 1932 (*ibid.* PR Foochow/51, 4 April, 1932, 14). These clashes caused deaths chiefly among the peasants, but occasionally the latter would kill a soldier, a tax-collector or even a hsien magistrate, as they did at Hui-an in the spring of 1934 (*ibid.* 893.00 PR Amoy/80, 8 May, 1934, 8–9).

[44] Perry, *Rebels*, 181; *Chung-kuo ching-chi* 1.1 (April 1933) 16–17, cited in *NYTL* 3.1016.

SPONTANEOUS PEASANT AGITATION: TYPOLOGY AND CHARACTERISTICS

Our first, apparently paradoxical, conclusion thus emerges: land rent, however onerous, and usury, however dramatic its consequences, provoke less impassioned resistance and agitation and do so less frequently than land tax, which is relatively light, albeit increasing. We have also noticed that agitation against land tax is accompanied by agitation against other taxes (like that on opium), accentuating still further the predominance of anti-fiscal agitation.

Disturbances not related to rent and tax, and typology

We shall now briefly consider other kinds of disturbances and sketch a general typology covering both these disturbances and those dealt with at more length in the preceding section.

What the disturbances we shall consider first have in common is the fact that they are aimed against the local representatives of public authority (civil or military) and, with few exceptions, not against the rich as such. They are thus closer to the traditional forms of anti-fiscal agitation than to the social struggle (against landlords and moneylenders) that was postulated and encouraged by the Communists but was on the whole not very widespread – until, that is, they themselves took things in hand.

Resistance to administration, compulsory labour and the army – Some of the riots aimed against the administration were provoked by various abuses (arbitrariness, brutality or corruption on the part of the local officials), others by initiatives which were well-intentioned but misunderstood (and frequently badly explained). At Tungpei in northern Kwangtung, in 1930, a measure aimed at getting the solar calendar adopted in local market transactions provoked a riot which claimed five dead. The rioters thought that the *yang* character which appeared in the expression 'solar calendar' was the *yang* meaning 'foreigner'.[45] Three years later, in Yunnan, the peasants became restive, laying the blame for the persistent drought on the propaganda against superstitions which, they believed, had offended the rain-dispensing dragon.[46] Sometimes the reform that aroused the anger of the peasants was one intended to improve their lot. Ten thousand (or twenty thousand, according to a different source) silk-worm cultivators in Yü-hang hsien in northern Chekiang, in April 1933 took part in a revolt

---

[45] USDS 893.00/10916, Jenkins despatch (Canton, 14 May 1930).
[46] *Ibid.* 893.00 PR Yunnan/54 (monthly report of the vice-consul, Charles S. Reed), 3 April 1933.

because the provincial office of rural reconstruction wanted to make them buy a particular type of silk-worm so as to fight Japanese competition. One official from the provincial office was bitten, another killed and the equipment and tents of the agents for rural reconstruction were set alight; cocooneries were destroyed as were a number of administrative buildings. It should be added that the order to buy these cocoons favoured by the administration (which were more expensive than the others) was accompanied by no explanation whatsoever. When the provincial office at last decided to send a section head to the district to parley with the peasants, they fell on their knees before him after the fashion of the Tsar's subjects in St Petersburg during the January 1905 Bloody Sunday. The alarmed section head is then said to have driven his vehicle straight at them, injuring a number of kneeling peasants, and that apparently set the situation alight.[47]

The example of Yü-hang underlines how very alien to the peasants' mental world were the distinctions made above between peasant actions intended as revenge for notorious abuses on the part of the administration and misguided responses to attempted efforts at modernization. The clumsiness and in some instances arrogance of the officials imposing a particular reform may well have exceeded the patience of peasants already bothered by the said reform which would anyway in the long run be unlikely to serve the interests of more than a tiny fraction of their number (those with the means to invest in the cocoons or, in other instances, in seed or more expensive equipment). Such flare-ups of anger against innovation and progress may be described as reactionary but that does not necessarily mean they were irrational. Faced with the eruption of the agents of modernization who sought to impose their innovations from above, the peasants had *a priori* no reason to react in any way differently than they reacted to the all too familiar corruption (also on the part of those set above them).[48]

Nothing better illustrates the clash between the world of the peasants and modernization conducted in an authoritarian (although not always efficient) fashion than the institution of compulsory labour. A directive from Chiang Kai-shek to the provincial governments published on 3

[47] On the Yü-hang incident, cf. three sources which are sometimes at variance: 'Che-chiang erh-wan nung-min pao-tung' (The uprising of twenty thousand peasants in Chekiang); USDS 893.00 PR Shanghai/57 (monthly report, April 1933) and 893.00/12371 (Cunningham despatch, 20 May 1933); Noel R. Miner, 'Chekiang: the Nationalists' effort in agrarian reform and construction, 1927–1937' (Stanford University, Ph.D. dissertation, 1973, 221–8).

[48] In the same year of 1933 the agitation of small landowners in K'un-yang (Yunnan) followed a plan to build a road across their fields. The initial route had not affected their land but the other landowners whose fields were supposed to be cut through by the road bribed responsible officials. Chow Yung-teh, *Social mobility in China*, 151.

December 1934 authorized them to use compulsory labour to complete works in the public interest: digging irrigation canals, consolidating river dikes, land clearance, afforestation, road-construction, and so on, all of which the directive claimed to be operations from which the labourers (recruited from amongst the local villagers) would directly benefit. But that did not prevent compulsory labour from being extremely unpopular among those upon whom it was imposed. They did not, in general, coincide with the principal beneficiaries: namely, the rich landowners, who would make greater use of the modern road and have more fields to irrigate and preserve from flooding and who slipped bribes to the officials so as not to have to serve in the labour gangs, where – that is – they were not automatically exempted in the first place. Only the poorest peasants took part in the construction of a road linking south-east Szechwan and north-western Hunan (the work lasted from November 1935 to January 1937, but the labourers drafted into the gangs only worked on the section of the road nearest to their homes). Poorly treated, poorly fed and poorly – if at all – paid, the labourers eventually revolted (at least a minority of them did, in two of the seven hsien through which the road passed: Ch'ien-chiang and Fu-ling).[49]

Sometimes the mere process of drawing lots to select the peasants to be drafted was enough to provoke a riot: at Pi-yang, Honan, in 1935, a thousand old women destroyed the *pao-chia* registers containing the names of all able-bodied adults (their husbands and sons) and wounded an officer.[50] More often, however, as at Ch'ien-chiang and Fu-ling, the agitation was caused by the poor treatment meted out to the labourers or by a deterioration in their living and working conditions (as a result of regulations not being properly observed) or by the corruption of the officials set over them. It was quite exceptional for the labourers to be neither paid nor fed; many received a basic or minimum wage and almost all were fed, albeit usually inadequately. But, for example, it sometimes happened that they were refused upkeep on days when it rained (since they were not working), despite the fact that it was impossible for them to return to their homes; or a corrupt *pao-chia* chief would extort a few coppers from each man – to cover 'the cost of calling the roll'; or else overseers would speed up the work or would beat and injure (or even kill) the labourers, quite without justification. As a general rule it was abuses of this kind that provoked 'resistance to compulsory labour' (*k'ang li-i*). The resistance might be non-violent (a strike) or, on the contrary, bloody, as when ten or twenty thousand labourers set upon the escort

49 *CKNT* 3.7 (July 1937) 72–4.
50 *NYTL* 3.1025.

party (*lu-tui*) responsible for preventing their escape, attacking them with their picks. In either case the trump card of the labourers was clearly their number: albeit unwillingly, they represented a huge concentration of workers who would normally have been much more widely dispersed. But, in the first case, these peasants transformed into labourers would be trying out a form of resistance with which they were unfamiliar (agricultural workers themselves would hardly ever go on strike). In the second case, in contrast, they would quite simply be anticipating (or reproducing) the habitual pattern of battles between peasants and soldiers (or 'bandit-soldiers').[51]

During the spring of 1926, the Red Spears of western Honan (a secret society identified as a movement of protection for the rural inhabitants) are said to have massacred as many as fifty thousand, meaning a great many, defeated soldiers.[52] Peasant self-defence against the soldiery had been especially necessary and widespread in the warlord era. During the Nanking decade, it continued to be so both in outlying provinces fought over by quasi-autonomous warlords and also against units of 'bandit-soldiers': bandits who, it had been believed, could be domesticated if they were enrolled in the regular forces but for whom the temptation to return to their old ways was all the stronger given that their pay was hardly ever forthcoming at the appointed time.[53]

The Lung-t'ien incident (27–28 December 1931) illustrates just such a case. Because the exactions and brutality of the troops stationed in the Lung-t'ien peninsula, Fu-ch'ing hsien, Fukien, had exceeded normal levels, several tens of thousands of peasants attacked 2,500 soldiers, all – including their commanding officer – former bandits. These soldiers had kidnapped villagers for ransom, auctioned off looted goods and tortured peasants who resisted them. Finally, when a soldier had attempted to cut off the finger of a woman who had not been quick enough at removing the ring that he wanted and the incident had been followed by collective rape, the peasants armed themselves better than usual (with the inevitable clubs, daggers and pikes but with pistols and rifles as well) and exterminated the soldiers. More than half the 2,500 men are said to have perished. The peasants also suffered heavy losses but remained masters of the field. They would agree to stop the fighting only when given an official promise that the troops (or what was left of them) would be transferred elsewhere. And, on 17 January 1932, reinforcements

---

[51] Many cases of resistance to compulsory labour are recorded in *NYTL* 3.1025–8.
[52] Tai Hsuan-chih, *Hung-ch'iang-hui* (The Red Spear Society), 192. On the Red Spears, cf. Elizabeth Perry, *Rebels*, ch. 4.
[53] Lucien Bianco, 'La mauvaise administration provinciale en Chine (Anhui, 1931)', *Revue d'histoire moderne et contemporaine*, 16 (April–June 1969) 306–7.

brought up from Foochow did indeed overcome the obstinacy of the head of the vanquished troops (who had been holding out for a bribe in return for agreeing to a transfer).[54]

The exactions in which the regular army indulged from time to time, although less frequent than those of former bandits integrated into the army, were equally feared, sometimes even more than those of the bandits whom the army was sent in to crush. These expeditions against bandits (to whom the army would sometimes be selling arms and ammunition) were seldom effective. Some resulted in even more farms and villages being burned down and more peasants being massacred than in the course of the raids by the bandits themselves.[55] Judging 'the remedy to be worse than the original evil', the inhabitants of one zone of Fukien, which was infested by banditry in 1932, sent off one petition after another requesting (in vain) that the forces of order be recalled 'so that they would be left with only the bandits to fight'.[56]

During the Sino-Japanese War, not only the provinces over which the Kuomintang control was weak but also the very ones in which it was entrenched, starting with Szechwan, became the scene of confrontations between the peasantry and a predatory army. Thus, the peasants in the Hsü-fu region (at the confluence of the Yangtze and the Min Rivers) appealed to the Big Sword Society (*Ta-tao-hui*) which, one fine summer morning in 1943, lost no time in dealing with a group of soldiers from the 76th Army who were pilfering marrow. A ten-day battle ensued from 16 to 27 July (dubbed 'the Marrow war'). The outcome was that the 76th Army, which had received reinforcements, put the Big Swords to flight – and went on to loot more than ever on the pretext of looking for Big Sword members.[57]

Theft and extortion provoked fewer revolts than abuses in the conscription system and the requisitioning of men for the army. In a famous memorandum to Chiang Kai-shek, General Wedemeyer reminded him of the scandalous trafficking and the terror inspired by conscription: 'conscription comes to the Chinese peasant like famine or flood, only more regularly – every year twice – and claims more victims'.[58] On top of the

---

[54] On the Lung-t'ien incident, cf. the official correspondence of the American consul at Foochow (Burke) in USDS 893.00/11815 (25 January 1932); 893.00/11837 (12 February 1932); 893.00 PR Foochow/48 (13 January 1932) and /49 (10 February 1932).

[55] One example (among dozens of others) concerning the region to the east of P'ing-tu (Shantung) is described in USDS 893.00/8841, Webber (Chefoo), 2 April 1927.

[56] *Ibid.* 893.00 PR Foochow/57, 4 October 1932.

[57] *Ibid.* 893.00/15141 (G. E. Gauss, Chungking, 29 September 1943).

[58] Cited in Charles F. Romanus and Riley Sunderland, *Stilwell's mission to China*, 369. On the suffering of the peasants conscripted as soldiers and inflicted by them on the civilian population, see, among others, Joseph W. Esherick, ed. *Lost chance in China: the World War II despatches of John S. Service*, 35–7; Theodore H. White and Annalee Jacoby, *Thunder out of China*, 132–40, 143–4;

iniquities of a conscription system that hit only the poorest, there was the periodic requisitioning of thousands and thousands of coolie labourers who were herded about like cattle. The high mortality rate among conscripts as well as coolies (often ill-treated and always ill-cared for) and the brutalities and harassment inflicted upon civilians by the army over eight years of the war, all exacerbated the peasants' traditional hatred of the army. By the early 1940s, the iniquities of conscription and the exactions of the army had become comparable even to taxation as a factor leading to peasant agitation. For a while, it seemed that a combination of the two types of factors was prevalent: quite a few revolts were provoked both by resentment at collection of land tax in kind and by hatred of recruiting sergeants, a euphemism for the gangs who would swoop down upon the cultivators in their fields and promptly tie their hands behind their backs. Within less than a year (between autumn 1942 and summer 1943), peasant revolts of varying size and duration (some involved fifty thousand men and lasted for several months) affected virtually every province of China.[59] They were followed by another wave in 1944, when Chinese soldiers fleeing before the new Japanese offensive in Honan sustained numerous attacks from the survivors of the serious famine of 1942–3.[60] The worst would befall soldiers who were isolated, left behind or wounded. It was mainly in fiction that the peasants would end up feeling pity for the plight of the soldiers (who were, after all, peasants like themselves). Their initial instinct was to mete out to them a slow and painful death.[61]

A schematic chart (table 2) sets out the various types of spontaneous peasant disturbances. The affairs classified separately (in the bottom part of the table) comprise on the one hand a very small number of complex movements, lasting longer than the average disturbances; on the other hand, a very large number of elementary movements as short-lived as they were frequent. From the point of view of our first criterion (the target), complex movements were, by definition, mixed. Even when not aimed from the start against several different targets, they tended, as a consequence of their very duration, to acquire new ones as time passed. Nevertheless, they were more closely related to the first category of

---

and Lucien Bianco, *Origins of the Chinese Revolution, 1915–1949*, 155–7. For a later period, see Suzanne Pepper, *Civil war in China: the political struggle 1945–1949*, 163–8.

[59] And in particular: the east and west of Kweichow (USDS 893.00/14991; 15095), north Szechwan (*ibid*. 893.00/14997; 15022; 15026; 15055), and above all the Lin-t'ao region in southern Kansu (*ibid*. 893.00/15009; 15033; 15047; 15074; 15107; 15112, published in Esherick, *Lost chance*, 20–2).

[60] USDS 893.00/6.1044 (Gauss, Chungking, 10 June 1944), 13 and n. 26.

[61] Chang T'ien-i, *Ch'ou-hen* (Hatred).

TABLE 2

Typology of peasant disturbances

	Directed against the public authorities		Directed against a fraction of the rural population	
Disturbances classified according to their targets	A *Anti-fiscal riots*		A *The poor against the rich*	
	Land tax	+ +	Tenants	=
	Opium tax	+	Debtors	—
	Salt tax[a]	+ +	Agricultural workers[a]	—
	Others[a] (dues on alcohol, pig-slaughtering, etc.)	—		
	B *Others*		B *Vertical movements*	
	Against initiatives and abuses on the part of the administration	+	One community against another	+
	Resistance to compulsory labour	+		
	Resistance to the army	=		
Disturbances classified separately because either too major or too minor	Major: Complex movements	—	Minor: Elementary movements (looting)	+ +

[a] Items not discussed in this chapter, for lack of space.
Frequency (a subjective estimation):
    — extremely rare
    – rare
    = average frequency or, in the case of the army, variable
    + quite frequent
    + + very frequent

disturbances, that is to say, those that were directed against the public authorities (hence their position in the table). The elementary movements (simple incidents of looting with or without violence of limited proportions) are placed in the right-hand column of the table: the hungry went to loot or eat grain where they knew they would find it, that is to say, in general, in the homes of the rich or the stores of grain-merchants.

Among the disturbances classified according to their targets, we know that those directed against the public authorities were by far the most frequent. Not only were disturbances placed in the right-hand column of the chart less frequent, but furthermore the social significance of the two sub-categories that we have distinguished are quite different. With 'A' disturbances (the only ones we have so far examined), the poor are opposed to the rich. 'B' disturbances (vertical movements) set in opposition socially heterogeneous communities, each of which is composed of a majority of poor and a minority of rich who either protect or manipulate the poor and at all events organize them.

Vertical movements. As under the Ch'ing, these vertical social conflicts (feuds, vendettas) would set in opposition two clans, two villages or two groups of villages over some issue – such as the use of water (or the prevention of flooding), an area of cleared land, the exploitation of forests, burial grounds, or control over a local market.[62] On the northern boundary of Anhwei and Kiangsu, a region prone to frequent flooding was within four years the scene of four conflicts relating to the control of the water. In June 1932, the drainage operations and the work of dredging two rivers undertaken by the inhabitants of Hsiao-hsien (Kiangsu, but now Anhwei) were threatening to cause flooding in the fields of Su-hsien (in Anhwei). Over two thousand armed men from Su-hsien accordingly set out to fill in the ditches that had recently been dug. A conflict in which cannon were used resulted in the destruction of several villages of Hsiao-hsien (1 July 1932). The following year only the intervention of the army prevented the peasants of Feng-hsien and P'ei-hsien (Kiangsu) from breaching river dikes in order to direct the threatening flood towards the neighbouring hsiens. The March 1935 disturbance followed the 1932 pattern: the dredging of a tributary of the Huai by villagers of Hsiao-hsien was brutally interrupted by the inhabitants of Su-hsien and fighting ensued, claiming many dead. In May 1936, another conflict brought the same antagonists, of Hsiao-hsien and Su-hsien, into confrontation yet again.[63]

Repeated conflicts between neighbouring communities created a tradition of hostility and strife. A clash of interests would keep such a tradition alive but it would also be fuelled by a thirst for vengeance to such a degree that the most unexceptional incidents would serve to renew hostilities. To protect themselves and defend the interests of the community, the villagers when necessary would resort to secret societies or organize themselves into rival societies such as the Red Flags and the Black Flags of Haifeng and Lufeng in Kwangtung (see below, pp. 296–7, 313–14). One instance of a secret society revived by a threatened community was the Small Swords Society (*Hsiao-tao-hui*) in four hsien close to Chen-chiang (Chinkiang, Kiangsu), in 1927–8. The members of the Small Swords were all immigrants from north of the river. Meanwhile the natives formed a rival society, the Big Swords (*Ta-tao-hui*). In September 1928, two thousand peasant members of the Small Swords massacred two hundred

---

[62] Hsiao Kung-chuan, *Rural China*, 361–9 and 419–26; Harry J. Lamley, 'Hsieh-tou: the pathology of violence in southeastern China', *CSWT* 3.7 (Nov. 1977) 1–39; Robert B. Marks, 'Social change in Haifeng county on the eve of the Haifeng peasant movement, 1870–1920', 17–29.

[63] *Ta-wan-pao*, 22 June 1932 and *Shih-shih hsin-pao*, 5 July 1935, cited in *NTCC* 1.535; USDS PR Nanking/68 (Oct. 11, 1933) 9 and PR Nanking/86 (April 8, 1935) 11; *NYTL* 3.1027.

people and burned down six villages in Tan-t'u hsien, which had been guilty of setting up local sections of the Big Swords.[64]

The antagonism between the Small Swords and the Big Swords divided each village down the middle, whereas the Red Flags and the Black Flags of eastern Kwangtung represented veritable village alliances, formed in the nineteenth century when new market towns had been established. The new villages founded in the no man's land between two marketing systems, and the weaker lineages that were situated on the periphery of a market system and were seeking to escape from the domination of a lineage solidly entrenched in the market town, tended to federate themselves with the organization that was the rival of the one to which their over-powerful neighbours belonged: namely, the Black Flags if the closest market town was controlled by the Red Flags, and vice versa. Thus, by the end of the nineteenth century, Haifeng and Lufeng counties were covered by a veritable (black and red) chequer-board of rival organizations polarized into two great antagonistic camps. These organizations, somewhat similar to Brecht's Round Heads and Long Heads, were still very active during the 1920s.[65]

The Red Flags and the Black Flags of eastern Kwangtung were thus organized on a much larger scale and were potentially more destructive than the sections of the Small Swords revived by the communities under threat in Kiangnan. But this difference in scale should not mask the identical nature of the vertical conflicts in which these various organizations engaged. Although the demarcation line between Small Swords and Big Swords divided each village, it did not separate the well-off or wealthy homes from the poor ones. The real division, symbolized by the opposition between the two secret societies, was between local folk and the colonizers from elsewhere (a few leagues to the north) and their children born locally but from families too recently arrived to be integrated as yet; a body of foreigners which still, after one or two generations, had not become assimilated.[66] Similarly, the conflicts which had become endemic in eastern Kwangtung in the late nineteenth and early twentieth centuries did not divide wealthy landlords from their tenants or other landless peasants, but instead set in opposition rival communities each with its own habitual cross-section of rich and poor. The leader of the Red Flags or of the Black Flags was usually a wealthy man, who could

---

[64] L. Bianco, 'Secret societies and peasant self-defence, 1921–1933', in J. Chesneaux, ed. *Popular movements and secret societies in China, 1840–1950*, 221–2.

[65] Marks, 'Social Change in Haifeng', 18–19 and 24–9.

[66] Some immigrants really were foreigners: at Wan-pao-shan, eastern Liaoning, in July 1931, 500 Chinese peasants destroyed a dam and irrigation canal built by Korean immigrants. The Japanese made a diplomatic incident out of it, two months before the Mukden coup.

use his fortune and influence to bribe or intimidate the officials and protect his followers against taxation as well as against the enemy Flags. It was, in effect, this protection that guaranteed the peasants' loyalty to their particular Flag – protection which was even more necessary here than in the rest of the Chinese countryside, on account of the insecurity fostered by the activities of the rival Flags.

While conflicts between tenants and landlords may legitimately be termed social, vertical conflicts only expressed local parochialism: the adversary was not the rich but 'the others'. On occasion, the alien was the worker (who was also a peasant) who had come from elsewhere; in that case, the competition was not over land or water but over employment. In 1921, the China International Famine Relief Commission made the mistake of employing on the construction of the Peking-Tientsin road (destined, among other things, to make it possible to transport food to areas in need) 2,800 workers recruited in Shantung. On the morning when work started, the peasants of Hopei, helped by hooligans, attacked these intruders and put them to flight, following which several hundreds of local men demanded to be taken on in place of those they had dispersed.[67] In early nineteenth-century France, artisan and worker corporations used to inflame provincial and professional rivalries. They put a brake on the development of class consciousness and undermined the beginnings of a modern social movement. The struggles between the Red and the Black Flags and the Big and the Small Swords, etc., a century later, were to some extent a (Chinese and rural) replica of those French confrontations between the *Gavots* and the *Dévorants*.

Complex movements: the example of Ch'ang-le. From the outset, the revolt that erupted in November 1931 in Ch'ang-le (to the south of Foochow, Fukien) was a double resistance: against both the army and taxation. In January–February 1932, this movement targeted against the public authorities was amplified by a vertical conflict, which precipitated the eventual collapse of the movement. At the source of the disturbances was a surtax on land imposed in the *hsiang* of Hu-ching (in Ch'ang-le county). The purpose of this surtax was to help finance a plan for hydraulic improvements undertaken by a naval detachment who were deeply loathed by the villagers (they forced the latter to sow poppy seeds with the sole aim of taxing the opium smokers). When the Hu-ching villagers refused to pay the surtax, two naval battalions were rushed to the spot to make them pay up. But the result was quite the opposite: the naval battalions arrived on 4 November; on the 5th, the peasants declared war on them.

[67] John Earl Baker, 'Fighting China's famines' (unpublished manuscript, 1943), 147.

This movement was not just complex; it was also better organized than most peasant riots and revolts (which probably explains how it lasted so long). The villagers of Hu-ching, who since 1922 had been compelled to serve in the local militia, were better – or at least less poorly – trained and armed than their peers elsewhere. The leader of the revolt, Lin Ku-ju, was none other than the commander of the militia of Hu-ching *hsiang*. Lin hired several graduates from the Pao-ting military academy to complete the training of the militiamen and also a number of bandits to whom he paid two months' salary in advance in return for their commitment to serve right in the front line. During the night of 21 December, prepared and reinforced in this fashion and with a ten to one superiority in numbers, the peasants of Hu-ching attacked the hsien yamen of Ch'ang-le. The navy troops responsible for protecting it rapidly took to their heels, abandoning arms and ammunition and the hsien magistrate too.

This initial success made the rebels over-confident. They destroyed two pumping stations installed by the navy and demanded that the latter depart forthwith. Liu Ku-ju declared local autonomy and, without further ado, took over the administration of the whole of Ch'ang-le county. He seized all the revenues so as to cover his military expenses, retained and collected the opium tax that he had been denouncing two months earlier and lifted restrictions on the opening of opium dens and gambling houses. The inhabitants of the other cantons (*hsiang*) of Ch'ang-le county, who had not been subject to the surtax in the first place, were discontented at being obliged to finance a struggle that was no concern of theirs. Furthermore, the bandits who had been hired as mercenaries liberated common-law prisoners and held up and robbed those fleeing on the roads. Clashes ensued and soon turned into an inter-*hsiang* war at the very moment when the authorities were sending in reinforcements. In February 1932, an enemy *hsiang*, Hao-shang, captured Lin Ku-ju and handed him over to the authorities, who executed him. On the 28th the navy attacked Hu-ching and lent strong support to the inhabitants of Hao-shang when they came to burn down the Hu-ching villages. By the time calm was restored, at the end of March, forty villages had been razed to the ground and more than seven thousand people were without shelter. During the agricultural season of 1932, there was a wide band of uncultivated land between Hu-ching and Hao-shang; but nobody dared venture into it to farm the fields situated alongside enemy territory.

The Ch'ang-le revolt was exceptional in its complexity and organization but in the end it foundered by reason of weaknesses that were not exceptional at all: namely, the failure to maintain control over the bandits whose help had initially been so valuable; the unpopular devices used to raise fresh tax money in order to face the authorities' counter-attack (although that counter-attack was very slow in coming); and finally – and above all – the absence of solidarity between neighbouring villages whose divergent interests set them in opposition to one another at the very moment when repression fell upon them.[68]

Elementary movements. In contrast to complex movements, elementary movements were directed against one fraction (the most wealthy) of the rural population. But, except in a few cases, the looters were not after the rich men in person, but only their possessions, in particular their grain. Often enough, they did no more than go to quell their pangs of hunger in the houses of the rich, in times of famine. Expressions such as *ch'ih-ta-hu* (to eat in the houses of the rich) or *hsiang fu-min tso-ch'ih* (to go and sit at the tables of the rich) recur time and again in the inquiries and reports concerning virtually every province, from Chekiang and Kiangnan, both of which were affected by the crisis in silk-worm production, to poorer provinces like Anhwei and Honan.

A few very incomplete data give some idea of the extraordinary frequency of incidents of looting (*ch'iang-mi feng-ch'ao*, seizing stocks of rice). An agency for economic information notes 64 cases of looting for the year 1934 as follows: Chekiang, 28 cases; Kiangsu, 19 cases; Szechwan, 5 cases; Anhwei, 4 cases; Honan, 3 cases; Shensi, 3 cases; Kwangtung, 2 cases.[69] Almost three quarters (47 out of 64) of these cases took place in the reputedly rich provinces of Chekiang and Kiangsu, since the inquiry was based, essentially, upon information provided in the newspapers of Shanghai and Nanking. In another report that mentions 26 cases of looting for the summer of 1934 alone (between 1 July and 11 September),[70] only four provinces are represented (Chekiang, 14 cases; Kiangsu, 5; Anhui, 4; Honan, 3), all of which are quite accessible to the reporting newspaper in Nanking. A single hsien close to Shanghai (Chia-hsing, Chekiang) is the scene of 6 of the 26 incidents recorded. One final example illustrates not only the non-representative nature of the statistics at our disposal but also the extreme frequency of looting incidents: twenty-five cases are recorded in Wu-hsi hsien (Kiangsu) alone, within the space of a month (from 11 May to 10 June 1932) and furthermore the compiler points out that the local newspapers on which

[68] The Ch'ang-le incident is described in detail in USDS 893.00 PR Foochow/47 (4 December 1931); /48 (13 January 1932); /49 (10 February 1932); /50 (7 March 1932); /51 (4 April 1932); /52 (4 May 1932). In contrast, the moneylenders' practices in Ch'ang-le denounced four years later gave rise to no agitation: *TFTC* 33.10 (16 May 1936) 111–12.

[69] *NYTL* 3.1032.

[70] *Chung-hua jih-pao*, 12 September 1934, cited in *NYTL* 3.1031–2.

his information is based only mention two or three out of every ten cases of looting that actually took place.[71]

Another type of relatively serious and less ephemeral incident was itinerant looting. Groups of as many as several hundred or even a thousand hungry men, each equipped with a sack, would go from village to village, seizing provisions.[72] Sometimes they would band themselves into associations of the needy; the 'association of the poor people' (ch'iung kuang-tan hui), 'the company of starving people' (ch'i-min-t'uan) or 'the company of those who eat together' (kung-ch'ih t'uan).[73]

But, for the most part, rice looting and rioting are typically elementary movements, of limited scope and duration. In the spring, at the bridging time between the harvests, a few hundred or even just a few dozen men (and sometimes bands composed solely of women, old people and children) would sally forth to make sure of a few days' provisions by robbing a landowner, a shop, a depot or a junk. When the police or authorities did intervene, it was sometimes to distribute provisions to the looters, to get them to disperse more quickly.[74] Occasionally, the forces of order would open fire but that was not the usual pattern. It was, in principle, only when the starving peasants were forced to 'set out along the dangerous road' (become bandits in order to survive) that repression was unleashed.[75]

These occasional looters were at pains to distinguish themselves from professional bandits. Sometimes they petitioned the hsien magistrate to be allowed to go looting, by reason of the exceptionally difficult circumstances; or they would fall on their knees before the landowner they were robbing, begging him to forgive them for the excesses to which they were momentarily driven. Many of these looters took care to limit their thefts to items of food and some were anxious to leave behind food in sufficient quantities for the landowner and his family not, in their turn, to go hungry.[76]

---

[71] NTCC 1.423.

[72] Examples relating to Honan and Hunan in NYTL 3.1030.

[73] Examples relating to Honan, Hupei, Anhwei and Kiangsu in NYTL 3.1033; to Szechwan, ibid. 3.1029.

[74] The same procedure was followed during the 'expensive bread riots' in France under Louis XIV: cf. Yves-Marie Bercé, Histoire des Croquants: étude des soulèvements populaires au XVIIème siècle dans le sud-ouest de la France, 548.

[75] For an example in eastern Szechwan, see NYTL 3.1029–30 (troops of warlord Yang Sen sent against starving peasants turned bandits).

[76] Cf. an example in Wu-hsi in June 1932 (Hsin-ch'uang-tsao (New creation) 2.1–2, July 1932, cited in NTCC 1.428).

Characteristics

The spontaneous peasant movements analysed above show three main characteristics.[77] The first is the weakness of class consciousness among the peasantry, a weakness illustrated by the comparative rarity and traditional nature of the social movements directed against the wealthy. Tenants usually acted alone vis-à-vis their landlords, and in fact might do so in competition with one another. Quite apart from the fact that the landlord who has remained in the village can be relied on for small services, the tenant-farmers depend upon him for their land. The competition between them to obtain or retain the plot which will enable their family to subsist seems to be more keenly felt than any sentiment of solidarity among the exploited. Refusals to pay land rent were seldom the result of a collective decision taken together by the tenants of one or several landlords. More often, they were individual actions dictated by necessity. In cases where landlords or the administration denounced such refusals, it would usually be more accurate to speak of an inability to pay the rent – an inability illustrated by the many instances of tenants taking to flight at the approach of the date when the rent fell due.[78] Seven of the 197 cases involving tenants recorded by two Shanghai newspapers between 1922 and 1931 (above, p. 278) consisted of tenants committing suicide in desperation at not being able to pay the rent.[79] Some of those seven suicides, like the suicides of debtors at the doors of their creditors, may have been motivated by a desire to make a pitiless landlord or agent lose face. But the fact remains that it was, to put it mildly, a roundabout way of expressing aggression towards the exploiter.

Of the representatives of the elite, it was the official, not the landlord, who was the most common target. The spontaneous orientation of peasant anger suggests that the peasants of Republican China were more conscious of state oppression than of class exploitation. In this respect they were, perhaps, simply continuing a tradition that dated from the imperial age[80] further reinforced by the abuses perpetrated by the warlords. The state

---

[77] I retain three of the six characteristics I have distinguished in a former study: 'Les paysans et la révolution: Chine 1919–1949', *Politique étrangère*, 2 (1968) 124–9.

[78] A special prison for tenant-farmers, visited by Ch'iao Ch'i-ming in about 1925, held fifteen prisoners, five of whom were women who had been arrested in place of their husbands who had fled. Each prisoner owed on average rather less than 30 *yuan* in rent: Ch'iao Ch'i-ming, *Chiang-su K'un-shan Nan-t'ung An-hui Su-hsien nung-tien chih-tu chih pi-chiao i-chi kai-liang nung-tien wen-t'i chih chien-i* (A comparison of the farm tenancy system of K'un-shan and Nan-t'ung in Kiangsu and Su-hsien in Anhwei, and a proposal on the question of the reform of farm tenancy), cited in *NTCC* I.109.

[79] Ts'ai Shu-pang, 'Tien-nung feng-ch'ao', 31.

[80] Cf. Kwang-Ching Liu, 'World view and peasant rebellion: reflections on post-Mao historiography', *JAS* 40.2 (Feb. 1981) 311.

embodies the world outside the village, a world that the villagers have the impression of supporting in return for nothing – which is not at all that far from the truth.

The second main characteristic of spontaneous peasant movements is their parochialism. In default of class consciousness, there was a sense of belonging to a local community, which overrode distinctions of class. It was this socially heterogeneous community that villagers sought to protect against attacks and threats from outside. The parochialism of peasant actions is, needless to say, attested by the frequent incidence of vertical movements. By reason of the quasi-unanimity of local hostility displayed against neighbours or strangers, these movements resemble wars between different peoples rather than social warfare. As in a national war (as opposed to a civil war), the natural enemy is not the privileged member in one's community but the foreigner, in other words the member of a different community – or, indeed, that community as a whole.

Even when there is no vertical movement, the peasants only take up arms to defend strictly local interests. The quickest way to pacify a canton that has risen up against heavily repressive troops is to transfer the soldiers to a neighbouring canton, where they can pursue their abusive ways to the detriment of other villagers. The same sacred egoism dictates the attitude of a village which, in time of famine, has managed to preserve adequate stocks of rice but refuses to sell any to the neighbouring village whose inhabitants are dying of hunger.[81] In the refugee camps set up following the great flooding of the Yangtse in 1931, the peasants angrily took issue with the charitable souls who were determined to feed people already too weak to survive: why waste precious grain?

The need to limit themselves to survival strategies, which dictated these attitudes, also explains the third characteristic of peasant agitation, namely its almost invariably defensive nature. The transition to illegality is simply the last resort. During the famine of the spring of 1937 an official, who expressed surprise that a Szechwan peasant had become a bandit instead of continuing to cultivate his field, was told by that peasant: 'You will find the explanation in my stomach.' And, sure enough, the autopsy carried out after his execution revealed a stomach full of nothing but grass.[82] Others would limit themselves to committing petty larcenies in the hope of being arrested and fed while in prison.[83] Elsewhere, and for the same reason, the police who come to arrest those owing taxes are implored by the neighbours to take them to prison too.[84] Even more

---

[81] *Hsin Wu-hsi* (The new Wu-hsi), 4 June 1932, cited in *NTCC* 1.425.
[82] Fan Ch'ang-chiang, 'Chi-o-hsien shang ti jen' (People on the line of hunger), *Han-hsueh yueh-k'an* (Sweat and blood monthly) 9.4 (July 1937) 125.
[83] *Ibid.* 131.   [84] *NTCC* 1.426.

numerous (as in the case of forty to fifty peasants in two or three villages of Lo-t'ien hsien, Hupei, in the spring of 1931) are those who beg district officials to confiscate their land so that they will be delivered from the obligation to pay a tax that is beyond their means.[85]

The peasants may react vigorously to a new situation or an attack from outside, but they never take the initiative. They are, so to speak, at the disposal of their adversary. The external assailant may, at one time or another or simultaneously, be represented by the authorities (increased taxation, unpopular administrative measures), the landlord (insisting on a pledge deposit or payment of rent following a bad harvest), the heavens (a bad harvest or some other natural disaster), one's neighbour (vertical movements), bandits – or the soldiers who come to repress the bandits. The essential point is that the peasants themselves hardly ever take up arms offensively with a view to improving their lot or, *a fortiori*, putting an end to their exploitation. It is only when a situation has deteriorated[86] or when they feel threatened by some new measure (even if it is, in reality, a reform) that the peasants rise up, with the sole aim of re-establishing the former situation.

At the origin of every peasant riot or revolt there was nearly always one particular innovation that was deemed intolerable. Far from attacking the established order, of which the peasants were themselves the principal victims, they would rise up in arms only to re-establish it, to right some wrong or return to the pre-existing norm, which they were prone to idealize. Unlike those who took part in large rebellions like those of the Taipings or the 'masters' of certain secret societies, the peasants and the leaders who organized the general run of revolts and riots in Republican China (with the exception of the Communist Revolution, that is) do not appear to have been inspired by any overall vision of society nor to have questioned the bases of its organization.

The parochial and self-defensive nature of peasant disturbances are complementary. To defend a local group (whose composition is more often heterogeneous than homogeneous) and safeguard its precarious existence are the aims of most peasant riots or revolts. In principle, such defence

---

[85] Ch'en Teng-yuan, *Chung-kuo t'ien-fu shih* (A history of land tax in China), 17 and *TFTC* 31.14 (16 July 1934) 110.

[86] To mention only two examples, remember the coincidence (noted on p. 279) between poor harvests (which themselves reflect the meteorological situation) and heavy periods of agitation amongst the tenant-farmers; exactly like the coincidence between agricultural crises and peasant movements in New Spain in the eighteenth century (cf. Pierre Vilar, 'Mouvements paysans en Amérique latine', in XIIIème Congrès international des Sciences Historiques: *Enquête sur les mouvements paysans dans le monde contemporain, rapport général, 82–3*). Second example: the frequency of revolts against the army, which is much greater during the Sino-Japanese War than before 1937 (*supra*, p. 293). It is the problem or scourge of the moment (not the desire or hope for progress) that provokes the agitation.

was no different from protecting the harvests against marauders or defending oneself against raids by bandits. To stand up to the latter, the villagers (or, to be more precise, the village landlords) were, given the frequent inefficiency of the authorities, inevitably obliged to set up self-defensive militia (*tzu-wei t'uan*) or, when they were faced with larger bands, veritable village leagues (*lien-chuang hui, lien-ts'un hui*). The link between self-defence and agitation, also discernible in the case of the Red and Black Flags of eastern Kwangtung (*supra*, p. 297) is even more evident when it is a matter of 'revolts of insecurity',[87] where resistance to bandits precedes (and grows into) a riot or insurrection. As a general rule, the insurrection is organized by the same men (landowners or village notables) who had earlier organized the self-defence.

This leads to three negative observations in conclusion:

1. It is not the peasants themselves who organize the majority of 'peasant revolts'. Despite their diversity, most of these movements are inspired and organized by the notables of the village, the canton (*hsiang*) or even the district (*ch'ü*). What are generally referred to as peasant disturbances should, strictly speaking, be called rural disturbances: they often involve the rural community as a whole, not just the peasants. The peasants who are involved provide most of the 'troops', in other words, the masses to be manoeuvred by the organizers who, for their part, seldom work the land with their own hands. Like the Fourth Estate in France in 1789, the peasant rioters of Republican China are dragged along in the wake of a different class.

2. Whether 'peasant' or 'rural', these disturbances did not constitute a movement. All that can be said is that a series of non-coordinated and for the most part badly organized and ill-prepared local actions took place, sudden flare-ups of anger or instances of 'fury', to borrow a term used in connection with an earlier period.[88] These presented little threat to the authorities. While the behaviour and weapons of the Chinese peasants of the twentieth century remained close to those of their ancestors of the seventeenth century, the central government had at its disposal the arms and means of transport and communication of the twentieth century. The rebellious peasants and the forces of order were to say the least unevenly matched. The local riots so swiftly repressed do not represent the

---

[87] I borrow the expression from the French historian Yves-Marie Bercé, who analyses a similar process in seventeenth-century France: 'the duty of the people of the low-land to unite in the face of enemies, looting soldiers or bandits can easily change into a riot against the soldiers of the king' (*Croquants et nu-pieds*), 84–5. In relation to China, cf. Bianco, 'Peasant self-defence', 215–18 (and 222–4 for the implications of the defence of the group), and above all chapter 5 in Elizabeth Perry's *Rebels*, which is entitled, precisely, 'Protectors turn rebels'.

[88] Roland Mousnier, *Fureurs paysannes: les paysans dans les révoltes du XVIIème siècle* (*France, Russie, Chine*).

equivalent of a 'peasant movement', then. Their multiplicity and their recurrence suggest a discontent both widespread and persistent that is often postulated but for which there is hardly any written evidence. It was a discontent that the Communists were to express and exploit in their own fashion.

3. Finally, the typology that we have suggested with regard to the targets of these peasant struggles would not have made much sense to those who took part in them. Whether the peasants came to grips with bandits, soldiers, or even tax-collectors, they felt that they were defending themselves against an assailant, a foreign element that preyed as a parasite upon the social body of the village. As we have noticed, the state often symbolized such a parasite. If the Chinese peasantry did harbour a certain revolutionary potential at the time when the Communists set about leading it into the revolution, this potential consisted almost entirely in the fact that the rural population was alienated from the state (and from the society at large that was ruled by the towns). It lay in the confused but deeply rooted and tenacious feeling that the state was alien to the villagers, that what it embodied was, precisely, the external world which exploited and oppressed the closed world of the village.[89] The Communists achieved the *tour de force* of turning this potential (just one possibility among many others) into action, in the process overcoming difficulties that at first sight appeared insurmountable.

The difficulties were proportionate to the vast distance that separated the way the peasants behaved (and, left to themselves, would have continued to behave) from what the Communists in the end made them achieve. Or, to put it another way: the distance between local self-defence and revolutionary action, which implies an overall ambition and an offensive strategy. To tell the truth, the Communists did not need to get their peasant troops to cover the whole of that distance. The strategy continued to be their concern alone. They used this peasant material to create the rank and file of the revolution: no more, no less; but that was in itself a considerable achievement.

PEASANTS AND COMMUNISTS: THE UNEQUAL ALLIANCE

'An utter fantasy' is one scholar's verdict on the famous *Report on the peasant movement in Hunan* which Mao wrote after carrying out an inquiry in his native province during the winter of 1926–7.[90] At the moment when

---

[89] Migdal has produced an excellent analysis of this feeling in connection with traditional peasantries in general: *Peasants*, 47.

[90] Hofheinz, *Broken wave*, 35.

the CCP were preparing to tackle the rural reconversion of their movement, Mao's wishful thinking predisposed him to a dynamic view of the agitation that was provoked by the arrival in Hunan of the armies of the Northern Expedition. His description of reality is inseparable from his creator's vision of what a skilful revolutionary leader might make of the peasant material. The fact remains that, in effect, the action of the peasantry of Hunan in 1926–7 (or, to be more precise, the various and divergent activities of a minority of peasants, some of whom continued to be manipulated by their traditional masters) justified neither the enthusiasm that Mao expressed in his *Report*, after the event, nor the hopes he had entertained before it. The graduates of the Canton Peasant Movement Training Institute that were sent into Hunan were not successful in stirring up the masses before the arrival of the Northern Expedition. On the contrary, the increase in numbers, membership and activity of the peasant associations were a direct result of the progress and victories of the military forces. Although duly lauded by Chinese Communist historiography, the rare cases of effective peasant participation in the fighting were, with very few exceptions, of no strategic importance at all: 'these fights were peripheral to the main war'.[91] Subsequently, the lamentable failure of the Autumn Harvest uprising in September 1927 confirmed the unprepared state and uncombativeness of the peasant armies.[92] In March 1928, over 200,000 rebellious peasants were incapable of seizing the town of P'ing-chiang in eastern Hunan.[93] Still later (August 1928), Mao suffered a defeat in Ching-kang-shan, after the 29th regiment of the 4th Red Army had completely disintegrated in the course of a battle. The peasants who made up the regiment were homesick and decided to return to their native I-chang in southern Hunan.[94] These few examples suggest that on the eve and in the early days of their agrarian saga, the Chinese Communists could place very little reliance upon the peasant soldiers, thanks to whom, twenty years later, they were to conquer the whole of China.

[91] Angus W. McDonald Jr. *The urban origins of rural revolution*, 268. See also 269–70 and more generally pages 264–80; Hofheinz, 'Peasant movement', ch. 6; and Donald A. Jordan, *The Northern Expedition* 194–8, 203, 227–8.

[92] Roy Hofheinz, 'The Autumn Harvest insurrection', *CQ* 32 (Oct.–Dec. 1967) 37–87; 'Peasant movement', ch. 7.

[93] *Hsing-huo liao-yuan*, 1.431–43, cited by Hu Chi-hsi, *L'Armée rouge et l'ascension de Mao*, 126, n. 16.

[94] Hu Chi-hsi, *L'Armée rouge*, 12.

P'eng P'ai and the peasants of Hai-Lu-feng (1922–8)

The first encounter between professional revolutionaries and villagers was led by the pioneer of the Communist peasant movement, P'eng P'ai, in two counties of eastern Kwangtung.[95] His initial success was remarkable. The peasant associations that he founded as early as 1922 developed vigorously. A few years later he maintained soviet rule over the two densely populated counties of Hai-feng and Lu-feng (together known as Hai-Lu-feng) for a period of several months (November 1927 – February 1928), at a time when Mao Tse-tung was still trying to establish himself in the sparsely populated Chingkang mountains. But the difficulties that faced the Communists in the mobilization of the Hai-Lu-feng peasants prefigured those they continued to come up against later on. And the methods to which they resorted prefigured the methods that they continued to refine later on from Kiangsi to north Shensi. To link the test case of Hai-Lu-feng with the two decades of 'peasant' revolution that followed, let us now summarize this first experiment, distinguishing (in Chinese fashion) ten features of it.

1. *Initial suspicion.* P'eng P'ai's first attempts were discouraging, revealing the abyss that separated the villagers from a revolutionary whom they quite rightly regarded as a member of the elite.[96] Doors were shut in his face, dogs barked at the intruder and the villagers turned away in alarm. They suspected this well-dressed gentleman of having come from the town to collect taxes or to insist on the repayment of debts. When P'eng replied that it was up to the landlords to repay the tenant-farmers whom they were exploiting, he elicited at first incredulity ('not to owe anything to anyone would be good enough in itself; how could anyone possibly owe *me* anything?') and then alarm from his questioners, who excused themselves hurriedly and made off. Fear and suspicion of the stranger was the initial reaction of the villagers, who had learned from long experience. The fact that this stranger was urging them to free themselves from their

---

[95] P'eng P'ai had probably not yet joined the CCP when he launched the Hai-feng peasant movement and created the first peasant associations; nevertheless, he was an intellectual revolutionary at grips with the problem of mobilizing the peasant masses. Furthermore, he was a member of the parent organization, the Socialist Youth Corps, long before he joined the CCP. On the date of P'eng P'ai's membership of the CCP, see Fernando Galbiati, 'P'eng P'ai, the leader of the first soviet: Hai-lu-feng, Kwangtung, China (1896–1929)' (Oxford University, Ph.D. dissertation, 1981), 203–4. This monumental thesis is the most reliable and by far the most detailed of the many that are devoted to P'eng P'ai.

[96] P'eng P'ai, 'Hai-feng nung-min yun-tung' (The peasant movement of Hai-feng), reprinted in *Ti-i-tz'u kuo-nei ko-ming chan-cheng shih-ch'i ti nung-min yun-tung* (The peasant movement during the first revolutionary civil war period), 52–5. English translation by Donald Holoch, *Seeds of peasant revolution: report on the Haifeng peasant movement by P'eng P'ai*, 20–3.

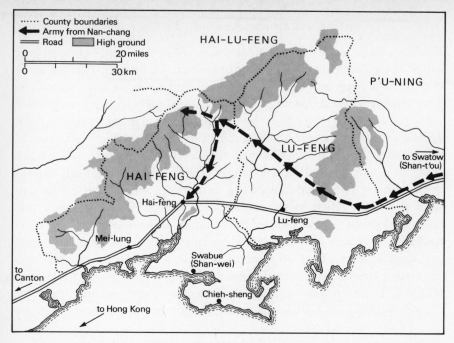

MAP 7. The Hai-Lu-feng region

chains made no difference at all – as if fate had not once and for all fixed
who should cultivate the land and who receive the rent! If P'eng was
suggesting the impossible, he must be out of his mind, as indeed the
rumour put about by his family had it and as many of the villagers were
inclined to believe.

2. *Adaptation and practical benefits.* P'eng very quickly adapted to the
situation.[97] He changed his clothes and his way of speaking, had himself
introduced by one of the villagers, waited until the evening (when work
in the fields was over) before starting to harangue the peasants, and took
care not to attack their gods. He enticed and entertained them as a
conjuror and magician, taught the children a song of his own composition,
had them listen to a gramophone he had brought along, and put on a
puppet show.[98] The adults too began to enjoy the entertainment and, at
the same time, swallowed the political potion P'eng P'ai had prepared.
Setting up a peasant association proved difficult in the early stages. But
once the initial step was taken, members flocked to benefit from the

[97] P'eng P'ai in *Ti-i-tz'u*, 56–69. Holoch, 25–40.
[98] Compare the prestige of the 'magician' gipsy Melquiades in Macondo (Gabriel García Márquez,
One hundred years of solitude), 9–16 (of the French edition).

services the association offered: free medical treatment, practical instruction, and arbitration to settle their quarrels. A pharmacy and a little clinic managed by the association soon became so popular that it proved necessary to check the membership cards, which were circulating from hand to hand. The peasants learned how to write the names of their tools and agricultural products and to check out the simple calculations hitherto carried out unsupervised by the landlords and grain merchants. Not content simply to settle disagreements relating to marriages, debts and land ownership, the association also offered its members personal protection, as a secret society would. The accidental drowning of a child-fiancée living according to custom in the home of her future father-in-law who was a member of the association, strengthened its authority. P'eng and other members succeeded in intimidating and turning back thirty or more assailants (relatives of the dead girl), who had come to avenge the drowning.

To sum up this second phase: the revolutionary wins partisans to his organization if not his cause by adapting himself to the world of the peasants, sometimes at the cost of concessions, such as displaying tact with regard to their superstitious beliefs, and by conferring upon a privileged group (the members of the association) certain practical benefits which answer their daily needs and preoccupations. A symbol of the practical interest motivating the adhesion of the majority of those who allow themselves to be won over could be the three dollars (*yuan*) which P'eng P'ai lent to two of his earliest followers and which they then chinked in the ears of their parents, who had been infuriated to see them leave their work in the fields to follow a man of fine speeches.

3. *Fomenting class struggle.* The sight of those three dollars mollified and even delighted the mother of one of the earliest militants. But the fact is that he and a handful of others followed P'eng P'ai because they believed in him, not out of personal interest. It was the interest of their class (rather than simply the interest of an individual or a group) that they wanted to defend and promote by uniting around P'eng P'ai. He, for his part, recognized this and forthwith addressed these first converts for social reasons as 'comrades'. As for the mass of others, P'eng P'ai strove to mobilize them with objectives that they would not spontaneously have envisaged for themselves, and so drew the peasants into a veritable social revolution.

The peasant association started by challenging the control of the notables over commercial transactions; in the domain of practical benefits referred to above, it set up its own scales in the public market-place in order to prevent the merchants from cheating when they weighed the harvest. The association also won acquittal in a court of law for a tenant who had refused to pay a rent increase and for five other farmers who had declared solidarity with him. This solidarity, the first marker on the way towards class consciousness, was actively encouraged, not to say provoked by the association, which ended up by forbidding its members to rent any field from which a tenant had been evicted by his landlord. It was a disciplinary measure that reversed the normal situation of competition between candidates for the tenancy of a field.

This solidarity and union were above all a means of pursuing an offensive strategy with the aim of involving the peasants in new conflicts. To this end the real state of class relations was deliberately blackened. The association put about a simplistic chart which exaggerated the landlords' exploitation of the peasants.[99] The slightest conflict was seized upon and deliberately exacerbated to bring into confrontation a minority of exploiters and a mass of exploited peasants. The poverty and sufferings of the peasants were described in apocalyptic terms. The devastation occasioned by a typhoon in July 1923 was magnified so as to claim a 70 per cent reduction in land rents. Most of the tenant-farmers would have been content to accept the traditional procedure: a rent reduction proportionate to the damage suffered and the extent to which the harvest had failed. Some landlords were equally prepared to negotiate, but the tiny minority of intellectuals and peasants who controlled the peasant association deliberately sought a confrontation.[100] A hard core of landlords had also concluded that the exorbitant claims of the peasant association could no longer be tolerated. P'eng P'ai could congratulate himself upon having divided the entire population of Hai-feng county into two classes: on one side the peasants, on the other the landlords.

After the defeat of the peasant association, the changing fortunes of war, punctuated by the two East River Expeditions in February and October 1925, maintained the tension and eventually turned these two classes into two enemy camps. Every swing of the pendulum brought executions and sometimes a massacre that would subsequently have to be avenged. In 1927 alone, two insurrections in April and September prepared the way for the establishment of a soviet government in November. Under this government, in effect a dictatorship, the question of the peasants' commitment to the Communist cause was clearly no longer in the same terms. Even if we allow for the element of constraint,

---

[99] P'eng P'ai in *Ti-i-tz'u*, 93–4. Holoch, 70.

[100] Of the several opposed factions within the association, one at least favoured more flexible tactics. The affair of the typhoon (see Galbiati, 311–14 and Hofheinz, *Broken wave*, 161–4) illustrates the tactic of exploiting any circumstances to reach a new stage in the mobilization of the masses.

for the flight to Hong Kong, Swatow and Canton of more than 50,000 inhabitants from two hsien (and not all of them wealthy people, far from it) and also for the participation of many peasants in revolts in truth provoked mainly by parochial considerations,[101] the fact remains that a large number of peasants did support the regime that cancelled their debts and abolished their land rents (although the gradations in the intensity of their support ranged from enthusiasm to passive fellow-travelling). Even if they had not consciously sought the revolution upon which they found themselves embarked and were no more partisans of collectivization than of a return to the old order, most of them had profited sufficiently from the change to fear any restoration of landlord domination.

4. *Polarization by terror.* There was also a more pressing reason to fear any restoration: the reprisals that many could have had no hope of evading, since they had been involved in looting, arson and murder, in short, in exercising the 'red terror'.[102] The soviet authorities had resorted systematically to terror – as usual with a view to mobilizing the peasants. The latter had both to be encouraged to shake off their psychological bonds of submissiveness (by becoming convinced that the old order had been destroyed never to return) and also to be made to participate in acts of destruction and massacre so that it would be impossible for them to pull back or defect. The plan, in short, was to banish all neutrality and all abstention from Hai-Lu-feng: 'Whoever is not with us is against us.' Hence the public, even theatrical nature of the executions of counter-revolutionaries, in the midst of a vast crowd invited to applaud and give advice: 'Should these prisoners be killed?'; and even to take an active part in the massacre. Hence too, the custom of organizing 'meetings of heads' which prefigured (usually it is the other way around) the 'banquet of heads' described by the poet Prévert.[103] But in Hai-feng there was no banquet; the recently severed heads were simply strung on a line above the rostrum, providing an appropriate décor for the impassioned words of the orator.

Actually though, there *were* banquets in Hai-Lu-feng. Sometimes (at Chieh-sheng, for example) it even happened that those who refused to consume the heart and liver of the victims were denounced as 'false brothers'. But it was the peasants themselves, not the soviet authorities, who initiated this convivial cannibalism. The deliberate terrorism of P'eng P'ai (there can be no question of one giving way to pity and pardoning,

---

[101] Like that of the White Flags in Lu-feng in early January, 1928 (Galbiati, 779).
[102] On the terror in Hai-Lu-feng, see Galbiati, 704–84 *passim* and 825–49.
[103] Jacques Prévert, *Paroles*, 7–18.

for that would imply indifference and cruelty towards the revolutionaries) is reminiscent of the icy reasoning of a Saint-Just,[104] but it has nothing to do with the sadistic festivity, exuberance and refinements of peasant terrorism. Public executions? They were better than a spectacle; they were a festival not to be missed which many peasants attended, making themselves hoarse with shouts of 'kill, kill, kill'. As for the (more numerous) executions that were not an occasion for a public spectacle, by the time a fortnight had passed the soviet government had no need to pay their executioners: Red Guards (most of them young peasants) were only too happy to be honoured with the enviable task. For a counter-revolutionary, it became a privilege to be killed without being tortured. Those who got off with having a limb cut off, cooked and eaten before their very eyes before being killed were lucky. Some were quartered, others (for instance a local magistrate of the Chieh-sheng district) were shut in a crate and sawn into pieces with skilful slowness, the executioners from time to time taking a tea-break so as to prolong the agony. The peasants who tortured their victims felt they were taking their revenge. The Chieh-sheng magistrate had had over a hundred peasants executed and had forced the father and the brother of the chairman of the Chieh-sheng Peasant Association to be present at his execution. Not to do things by halves, brother was sometimes forced to execute brother, and brother and son were occasionally made to eat a piece of the father's flesh with the victim, not yet dead, looking on.

5. *Parochial motivations.* The avengers thus gave as good as they got to the officials and landlords, paying them back in their own coin. The action provoked by P'eng P'ai and his Communist comrades undeniably succeeded in inflaming class hatred. But, as practised in Hai-Lu-feng during the winter of 1927–8, the vengeance exacted smacks less of the revenge of an oppressed class than of the clan or village vendettas of a still recent past. It perpetuated the tradition of rivalry and reprisals that had inspired the conflicts between the Red and the Black Flags. In a similar fashion, the refinements of torture and cannibalism simply repeat the practices to which the chronicle of those conflicts so often testifies.[105] It is a chronicle that is in no way interrupted by the 'modern' peasant movement; quite the contrary. Lineage and community heads reacted to the arrival of the Communists by reactivating their traditional organizations. They even took the opportunity to settle old scores with rival or

---

[104] P'eng P'ai: 'class justice is not concerned with the individual being judged; it is a necessary measure in the civil war'. Saint-Just addressing the members of the Convention: 'You are not here to pass a sentence upon an individual (Louis XVI), simply a measure of national emergency.'
[105] On Flags, clans and localism, see Galbiati, 518–21, 777–83, 827–8, 848 and *passim*.

hated neighbours. But these conscious reactions and deliberate calculations are of less significance than the spontaneous appraisal of the Communist struggle as just a new episode in the only conflict that was familiar (or the one that was the most familiar) to them: the local wars between the Flags. When, in January 1928, the revolutionary army marching from Hai-feng with its red flags flying passed through some villages of Lu-feng hsien, it was welcomed with open arms by all and sundry, landlords included. These villages, which belonged to the Red Flags, fêted the ally who, they were convinced, had come to help them against the rival villages dependent upon the Black Flags.

What becomes of social warfare in such circumstances? Sometimes, to be sure, local conflicts and secular rivalries between neighbouring communities did in effect mask a social antagonism. Consider the battle which, in January 1926 in P'u-ning in eastern Kwangtung, set in opposition on the one hand the powerful Fang lineage and, on the other, the peasants of the neighbouring villages. The motivation of parochialism was powerful in both camps but the Fang, who alone accounted for half of the twenty thousand inhabitants of the chief town of the hsien, controlled most of the economic activities of the hsien as a whole.[106] When parochialism brings the town into opposition to the countryside (as also in the case of Chieh-sheng, mentioned above) it naturally takes on a social colouring. The same is not true when entire villages, rich and poor alike, are opposed to other villages. The persistence of local parochialism, which virtually banished the Communist-peasant movement from certain villages in Lu-feng hsien that were traditionally controlled by the Black Flags, could not but be reinforced by the parochialism of peasant associations and local activists, who claimed to be acting in the name of the soviet regime even when they were in truth satisfying local hatreds. Two powerful clans (the Ho in Chieh-sheng and the Lin in Mei-lung) were particularly detested by the peasants whom they exploited and mistreated. There was nothing selective about the revenge taken upon them: however lowly his or her social status, whoever went by the name of Ho in the one locality or Lin in the other was doomed to butchery. Chinese Christians concentrated in certain localities and martyred at Christmas in 1927 were also the victims of parochialism, or – to put it another way – of a rejection of 'otherness', as were the lepers shot like rabbits as they fled, or burned alive in their lazarets when they made no attempt to escape.

[106] P'u-ning hsien, neighbouring but independent from the two hsiens of Hai-feng and Lu-feng, also attracted P'eng P'ai's attention because of his overall responsibilities in the (Kuomintang) peasant movement for the province as a whole. P'eng P'ai had founded the Peasant Association of P'u-ning upon which the rebel peasants centred to defend their cause against the Fang faction of the chief local town.

On the whole, the cruelty of the peasants favoured, rather than upset, the plans of the revolutionary intellectuals. On the other hand there were excellent reasons for the latter to fear the demobilizing effects of local solidarities or rivalries. It was not for nothing that P'eng P'ai had chosen a red and black flag as the emblem of the first peasant association of Hai-feng: it symbolized the idea that the social struggle upon which the association was engaged transcended the 'vertical conflicts' between the Red and the Black Flags. Later on, at the time of the soviet government, whoever protected a counter-revolutionary became liable to the death penalty. This measure was principally aimed against peasant families which were concealing the possessions of richer members of their clans, whom they might well have attacked a few weeks earlier from within the body of the peasant association.

6. *Peasant worship.* In the eyes of the Communists, local parochialism and clan power were survivals from feudalism, as were the religious beliefs and superstitious customs of the peasants. If, during the heroic days of his initial overtures towards the peasants, P'eng P'ai had been careful to accommodate the village gods, such precautions were no longer in order by the time the soviet dictatorship was installed. But it is difficult to assess how far P'eng P'ai was personally responsible for the attacks against the 'feudal' ideology and practices which stemmed, naturally enough, from the first measures adopted in the euphoria of victory. The names of towns were changed (most of them becoming 'red': *ch'ih* or *hung*) as were street names (Hai-feng now had streets named after Marx, Lenin, Rosa Luxemburg or Karl Liebknecht); the Temple of Confucius was renamed the Red Palace (and Hai-feng also boasted a Red Square, a Red Bridge and a Red Flag). From there it was but a short step to attacking the idols. It was a step soon taken by the Red Guards, the Pioneers and detachments of the Communist Youth Corps, who carried through a mini-cultural revolution forty years before the major one, destroying temple statues, burning down religious buildings and attacking all those – diviners, sorcerers or geomancers – who lived off the credulity of the peasants.[107] The Red Guards were themselves young peasants, but their elders desperately resisted the destruction of their idols which they had taken care to daub with red paint to indicate that they were well-disposed towards the soviet. They painted the landlords' Buddhas white to show that these did deserve to be punished and destroyed, but they strove to preserve the centres of popular religion that most of the Taoist and

---

[107] On the traditional mentality of the peasants and the facts mentioned in this and the following paragraphs, see Galbiati 319, 521, 675, 732, 737–8, 767, 781–3, 789 and Appendix, 204 (no. 32).

Buddhist temples represented. They were even worshipping a new god, almost as much revered and obeyed as Buddha himself, to wit P'eng P'ai, whom heaven had chosen to found a new order and make it possible for peace to reign once he became emperor. For them, taking part in the revolution consisted primarily in blindly following a leader (as they used to follow Ch'en Chiung-ming, who held a mandate before P'eng); which did not, of course, prevent them from calling upon the gods (the other gods) to protect the cause of their divine leader. At one critical moment when the Kuomintang army, the militia and the police were on the point of crushing the second of the revolts that preceded the establishment of the Hai-feng soviet (on 25 September, 1927), a procession of peasants bearing offerings went off to the temple to pray for the speedy arrival of reinforcements which might, indeed, have represented a last hope, namely the army of Yeh T'ing and Ho Lung which had reached Swatow after a mini-Long March (another prefiguration of another saga) of the Red Army remnants from Nanchang.

7. *Dependence on military power.* When a party of these fugitives at last reached the mountains of Hai-Lu-feng, a full three weeks after the second insurrection had been crushed, they had to change their tune: in the launching of a new offensive, it would certainly be impossible to count upon these fugitives exhausted and discouraged by their series of defeats and also by the lack of cooperation forthcoming from a peasantry their leaders had described as being ready to rise up in arms.[108] And yet, less than two weeks later, Hai-feng was once more in the hands of the Communists (1 November, 1927); it remained so for four months. This easy occupation, less ephemeral than earlier ones, owed much to the rivalry between two generals (Li Chi-shen and Chang Fa-k'uei), who could quite easily have prevented or crushed the revolt. It would not even have been necessary for the two rivals to unite forces to put the red troops to flight: it would have been quite enough for either one or the other to grant the same strategic importance to districts as distant from Canton as Hai-feng and Lu-feng as they did to the central areas of the province. In short, they both deferred settling the score of the soviet until such time as they would no longer be engaged in more serious matters. When that moment came, the soviet collapsed like a house of cards (29 February 1928).[109]

[108] C. Martin Wilbur, 'The ashes of defeat', *CQ* 18 (April–June 1964) 20.
[109] Galbiati, 697, 701, 703–4, 744–5, 902, 905–6. The ephemeral nature of the Canton commune, which lasted fewer days (11–13 December 1927) than the months that Hai-Lu-feng survived, provides an *a contrario* confirmation. In Canton, the authorities could not afford to tolerate the challenge.

The birth, survival and fall of the soviet thus illustrate the decisive importance of the relationships among those who controlled power (or the military forces) in the local and provincial context. In general, the Communist-peasant movement only succeeded in implanting itself and surviving thanks to either the rivalries (and in 1927–8 in Kwangtung there were many others apart from the struggle between Li and Chang) or the complex manoeuvring between the powerful (such as that which prompted Ch'en Chiung-ming to tolerate the activities of the Peasant Association of Hai-feng for so long, before 1924). In a complementary fashion, as soon as those who held the greater power on a local and provincial level decided that the threat had become too serious to be tolerated any longer, or that it was playing into the hands of their rivals,[110] the fact that the forces were so unevenly matched sealed the fate of the revolutionaries in advance.

The activities of P'eng P'ai in the rest of Kwangtung province during the period between the official dissolution of the Hai-feng Peasant Association, in March 1924, and the founding of the soviet in November 1927 do more than simply confirm the precarious nature of the first 'peasant' enterprises of the CCP (and the KMT), and the crucial importance of the regional or local political situation. They also illustrate what has been called the 'politics of dependency', the lack of autonomy inherent in many of the enterprises which were time and time again saved from failure by the providential intervention of the provincial authorities. In this instance, as in Kwangning (in the north-west of the province) in 1924, it was the secular authorities who came forward as allies, or even protectors. And the interceder here was none other than P'eng P'ai, secretary of the peasant section of the Kuomintang currently in power in Canton. It was he who persuaded the governor of the province to dismiss the hsien magistrate of Kwangning who was hostile to the peasant movement, even before a later governor, Liao Chung-k'ai, who was even more cooperative, sent a brigade of shock troops to help the peasant adventure of the revolutionary apprentices of Kwangning.[111]

This dependence upon external support naturally rendered the peasant movement extremely vulnerable; the Kwangning movement did not survive for long after the departure of the revolutionary armies of Kwangtung on the Northern Expedition.

---

[110] In March 1924, Ch'en Chiung-ming eventually authorized the dissolution of the Peasant Association of Hai-Lu-feng, apparently after allowing the local notables to convince him that it was hand-in-glove with his adversaries (both Communist and Kuomintang) in Canton (Galbiati, 339–40; Hofheinz, *Broken wave*, 177).

[111] Hofheinz, *Broken wave*, ch. 8 (in particular pp. 189 and 197).

8. *Non-peasant leadership*. The promoters of the peasant movement of Kwangning were natives of Kwangning who had received their secondary education in Canton;[112] in short, modest replicas of the 'returned student' P'eng P'ai, who belonged to one of the richest families of Hai-feng. Whatever their standing in the intellectual and social hierarchy, those who launched and organized the Kuomintang peasant movement (an official label that in most cases masked a Communist takeover) from the east to the west of the province shared in common their membership in the elite, an elite by definition separate from the peasantry. While this may have rendered the first contacts with the peasants more delicate, it greatly facilitated their penetration of the local political game.

The landlords of Hai-feng, who without doubt would promptly have repressed a purely peasant movement, waited for a long time before riposting to the increasingly audacious initiatives of the peasant association under P'eng P'ai's direction, no doubt because they were aware that they could not count upon firm support from the regional power embodied by Ch'en Chiung-ming, but also quite simply because P'eng P'ai and his associates came from the best families in the locality and were educated. One could not treat P'eng P'ai, the former director (at the age of 26!) of the Education Office of Hai-feng hsien, as one would a vulgar peasant leader. The relations between the leader of the Hai-feng Peasant Association and Ch'en Chiung-ming, whom P'eng visited in his head-quarters to plead the cause of the association, would have been altogether inconceivable if P'eng had not been one of the elite. To be sure, Ch'en, himself a former revolutionary (from the First Revolution of 1911) who retained a number of reformatory inclinations, was no ordinary warlord. But even where the local holders of power came from a more traditional mould and the revolutionaries came from a lower intellectual level than P'eng did, the latter still benefited from a network of relations (*kuan-hsi*) among the families of influence (and from friendships or complicities among the educated scions of those families) which opened to them doors that were closed to the peasants and assured them, initially at least, of a relative impunity.

Sometimes it was the school holidays or the return of students to their homes which sparked the peasant movements that urbanized intellectuals operating from outside had been preparing.[113] However sincere and deep the commitment of the latter towards the peasant masses, it almost always followed and derived from a more global revolt. The review launched

112 Hofheinz, *Broken wave*, 181–3. Galbiati, 414.
113 For Kwangtung, see Conrad Brandt, *Stalin's failure in China, 1924–1927*, 48.

by P'eng P'ai and the young radical intelligentsia of Hai-feng in the autumn of 1921 did not differ significantly in its title (*Hsin Hai-feng*) (New Haifeng), or its content, from what was being written or the claims being made by their peers elsewhere. Their writing was perhaps more impassioned, their tone more inflamed and their sense of urgency and their rejection of half-measures more absolute. But the links of filiation with *Hsin ch'ing-nien* and of kinship with the radical posterity of 4 May are undeniable.[114] The revolutionary vocation of P'eng P'ai and his friends was fuelled from the same sources (national and ideological rather than social or specifically peasant) as those of the rest of the revolutionaries of their generation who, like them, almost all came from the most favoured social classes. In a very classic fashion, the Chinese revolution began by setting in opposition among themselves the members (or in some cases generations) of an elite in a state of crisis. The secession of family heirs who were traitors to their class preceded their adoption of the strategy of mobilizing the peasant masses.

9. *Organization*. That mobilization was in effect no more than a means to an end. This fact was squarely recognized by Lo Ch'i-yuan, who, together with P'eng P'ai, was one of the pioneers of the Communist-peasant movement and one of P'eng's principal Cantonese associates. Lo speaks quite forthrightly of 'using them [the peasants] as the basic force' and so of offering them something in exchange to persuade them to rally.[115] During the 1920s an alliance was forged in Hai-feng and the rest of Kwangtung that was to prove most fruitful for the Communist movement, but it was an ambiguous and unequal alliance to which the peasants rallied with a view to obtaining satisfaction for specific claims of an economic nature without, however, any clear idea of how far their guides were to lead them.

These guides who came from outside the peasantry brought it the efficient organization without which peasant agitation was doomed to failure. But, by virtue of that very organization, they assured themselves of the direction of the movement. It is a point that should be emphasized: the organization provided by the Communists conferred upon the peasant movement an effectiveness which it had hitherto lacked but which undermined its independence. The peasant movement thus became subordinated to the interests and overall strategies of the revolutionary movement (Kuomintang before 1927, Communist thereafter).

[114] Galbiati, 205–12.
[115] Gerald W. Berkley, 'Peasant mobilisation in China, 1924–1926' (unpublished paper, Washington and Southeast Regional Seminar on China, March 1979) 17.

In Hai-Lu-feng, P'eng P'ai concentrated in his hands the powers of a dictator. But he exercised them officially in his capacity as secretary of an organ which coordinated the activities of all the other institutions: namely, the special committee of the CCP for the East River Region (the part of Kwangtung that included Hai-feng and Lu-feng). The peasants were incapable of distinguishing between their government (the 'People's government of the Hai-feng soviet', officially created only in February 1928, the last month of the soviet's existence) and the real power which had penetrated their own little world with the abridged title of the 'East Special' Committee. During the few months of soviet dictatorship, the peasants of Hai-feng (and to a lesser degree those of Lu-feng) flocked to join the CCP *en masse*. They are said eventually to have made up 85 per cent of the local party membership. But that 85 per cent had fewer powers of decision than the 2.5 per cent of intellectuals – who, for their part, were strictly controlled by the directives of the 'East Special'.[116]

10. *Local predispositions?* The last item is more of a question than affirmation; but it cannot be avoided for it raises an important problem: did the Hai-Lu-feng area (or the East River region or even Kwangtung province as a whole) possess some particular quality that predisposed these regions to the pioneer role that they played in the history of the Communist-peasant movement? Or did the adventure that has earned Hai-feng the names of 'Little Moscow' stem from fortuitous historical circumstances? Could it have taken place *anywhere* in China?

The coastal hsien of Hai-feng can hardly be called representative of interior China; and yet in many respects it is a faithful reflection of it; a traditional China in miniature. Hai-feng and its port of Swabue (Shan-wei) were more open to external influences than the average hsien of a province of the interior. The proximity of Hong Kong (where many émigrés from Hai-feng the name of 'Little Moscow' stem from fortuitous historical missionary settlements in the hsien multiplied the opportunities for contacts with foreigners. The same goes for the province of Kwangtung as a whole, which was more outward-directed than the rest of China. Throughout the century that preceded the first Provincial Congress of Peasant Associations (1925), history had underlined and reinforced the originality of this province that had never been quite the same as the rest. The combination of the outlying location of Kwangtung and its particular historical traditions may have been favourable to the development of a revolutionary peasant movement in this region where the T'ung-meng hui had also found a preferred terrain for its subversive activities.

[116] Galbiati, 738, 787 and Appendix 217, n. 87.

Kwangtung's 'predisposition' to its destiny of pioneering the Communist-peasant movement was thus strongly dependent upon its connections (and therefore heritage); it owed much to the revolutionary successors of one of its native sons, Sun Yat-sen, born in a southern district where the appeal and influence of the outside world were more keenly felt than elsewhere. The first peasant unions of Hai-feng themselves owed nothing to the implantation of the Kuomintang in Canton but, in the absence of any revolutionary legacy, it is always possible to point to the martial traditions of the natives which had been kept alive by incessant feuds and private wars. The inhabitants of Hai-feng had the reputation of enjoying battles; they set more store by courage in combat than most other Chinese and they had for many years had at their disposal an instrument of conflict: the para-military organizations of the Red and the Black Flags that chequered the entire region. The violent parochialism that had often prompted them to attack their neighbours could, on occasion, cause them to rise up against the authorities and their agents who arrived from elsewhere; in Hai-feng the Cultural Revolution was to take on the aspect of a struggle between local inhabitants and strangers and it was to prove particularly bloody.[117]

In short, it is easy enough to record the local antecedents and aptitudes of the inhabitants that would favour P'eng P'ai's enterprise; easy enough, too, to point out that a mountain barrier isolated Hai-feng, in the west, from the rest of the province and lent the hsien a strategic advantage (not simply an added encouragement to parochialism). It is also easy enough to underline the particular customs and character of the Hakkas and Hoklos (originally natives of Fukien), and so on. But all this is convincing only up to a point. From the strategic point of view, it is equally easy to object that the mountains of Hai-feng did not provide a refuge in any way comparable to either the Ching-kang-shan or the more northern ranges that provided sanctuary for the Communist forces during the Sino-Japanese War. Parochialism and outward-looking attitudes are to a certain extent contradictions in terms: if external influences had deeply affected and transformed Hai-feng, they would certainly have blunted the local parochialism. Above all, none of the points we have made affected the economic and social conditions of the masses whom P'eng P'ai was going to attempt to rouse.

There was much in those conditions to provoke indignation and revolt. But they did not differ radically from the conditions that prevailed in the

[117] Galbiati, 1004 and 1000–14 *passim*. For the rest of the paragraph and the next one (Hai-feng four or five decades before the Cultural Revolution), see Galbiati, vi, xi, 1, 8–9, 35–6, 39, 50, 56–66, 96–104, 144, 275, 789 and *passim*.

rest of the country. Where they did differ (in, for instance, a greater diffusion of clan-owned land, with slightly lower land rents) the poor did not necessarily suffer by it. Other atypical elements (such as a high proportion of fishermen and salt producers among the inhabitants of the two hsien) may have favoured the mobilization of the masses, but there is no particular evidence to prove it. More important is the fact that among those who devoted their entire time to farming, a lower proportion than in the rest of China (although not lower than in the rest of Kwangtung or in the rest of the East River Region) owned the land that they farmed. In 1923 Hai-feng comprised about 20 per cent owners (*tzu-keng-nung*) as against 25 per cent part-owners and 55 per cent tenants. The average rent for privately owned land was neither higher nor lower than in the rest of China; the shortage of land was as acute as it was in most densely populated regions of eastern and south-eastern China. All in all, the differences are less impressive than the similarities between the living conditions of the peasants and fishermen of the Hai-Lu-feng in the early 1920s and those of the majority of peasants in the rest of the country during the same period.[118] More to the point, the particular characteristics of these two coastal hsiens on the south-eastern border of the country do not provide an explanation for the fact that the modern peasant movement was born there rather than elsewhere. Other things being equal, the actions of P'eng P'ai from 1922 onward seem to have been just as much the determining factor as the actions of Lenin (or, to be even more provocative, his early 1917 return from Switzerland in a sealed railway carriage) in bringing about the victory of the October Revolution.

Nevertheless, Lenin would not have failed to diagnose in P'eng P'ai's creative efforts the stamp of communism's 'infantile sickness'. In more prosaic terms, P'eng has been criticized for 'adventurism', especially in relation to the orientation he gave to the Hai-Lu-feng soviet. That orientation was altogether in harmony with the official line of the CCP (dominated at the time by Ch'ü Ch'iu-pai) that was reaffirmed during the enlarged plenary session of the Political Bureau in November 1927 and illustrated the following month by the Canton commune. One might conclude that that harmony simply confirms the extent to which every development in the Communist-peasant movement depended upon the

---

[118] I take responsibility for asserting 'Hai-Lu-feng was more or less like the rest of rural China', despite the contradictory information in the first part ('The world of Hai-Lu-feng') of the thesis by Fernando Galbiati (Galbiati, 1–146), where Hai-feng is presented at times as atypical, and at other times as altogether typical. My own feeling that Hai-feng is after all a microcosm of rural China is also based upon a brief visit to Hai-feng, almost 60 years after P'eng P'ai came back from Japan to his native home.

overall strategy as defined by the leadership of the CCP. But P'eng P'ai was in no need of encouragement from the party centre to pursue in Hai-Lu-feng extremist policies of which the terrorism mentioned above was simply the most spectacular manifestation. Those policies made the Soviet many enemies from far beyond the ranks of the landlords: they ranged from the bourgeoisie to retailers whose firms and shops were confiscated and to artisans who were deprived of their erstwhile clientèle. Not content with making more internal enemies than necessary, the soviet greatly underestimated the military strength of the external enemy. Its superstitious faith in the numbers and the might of the people (mostly peasants, whose revolutionary enthusiasm was much overestimated) meant that indispensable military preparations were neglected. The suddenness with which defeat came took the leaders (P'eng P'ai first and foremost) by surprise. In the heat of battle they learned to their cost how difficult it was to repulse machine-guns and cannon with no more than the spears and local guns at their disposal.[119]

The excessive optimism and 'adventurism' of P'eng P'ai symbolize the infancy of the Communist-peasant movement. Experience was gradually to banish the Communists' illusions and incite (or constrain) them to improve their target-selection, where necessary to accommodate one or another social class (even to the point of making it a temporary ally), to establish less summary and better founded distinctions between the various strata of the peasantry, and eventually to perfect the techniques of their famous 'mass line'. In short, the party was to learn and make improvements in the light of the problems that had virtually all emerged in the course of the early pioneer experiment in Hai-Lu-feng.

Elsewhere and later

We will not repeat here what can be read elsewhere in this volume about Communist-peasant mobilization during the two decades that followed the liquidation of the Hai-Lu-feng soviet.[120] In general, the experience of the 1930s and 1940s duplicated the Hai-Lu-feng matrix, in spite of obvious differences in circumstances and in scale. Let us now look at some of these continuities and differences.

One such difference is the role of nationalism. The most decisive advances in Communist-peasant mobilization were achieved during the Sino-Japanese War and as a consequence of it.[121] But the fact that the

[119] Galbiati, 793 and 904.   [120] See chs. 4, 12 and 13 by J. Ch'en, L. Van Slyke and S. Pepper.
[121] Chalmers A. Johnson, *Peasant nationalism and Communist power: the emergence of revolutionary China, 1937–1945*. While disagreeing, as this paragraph makes clear, with Johnson's unilateral emphasis on the nationalist (as opposed to social) factors of Communist-peasant mobilization, I hail *Peasant nationalism* as one of the most stimulating works which have ever appeared in our field.

Communists seized upon the providential chance represented by the foreign invasion does not alter the essential continuity between the three periods of rural soviets, Sino-Japanese War and civil war. During both war and peace, the Communists paid attention to local problems and tried to satisfy the peasants' most pressing claims. During the late thirties, when Chinese peasants rallied to the banner of leaders in the anti-Japanese resistance (who happened to be Communists), they were seeking not so much the liberation of the country *per se* as protection against local insecurity. This demand had become their most pressing need in the conditions that prevailed at the beginning of the war. Even then, insecurity was far from general: extensive areas of rural China remained unaffected by it and in those areas the peasants could not have cared less about resistance. However, in areas that came into direct contact with the invader, a feeling of urgency and panic predisposed the local population to flock to the support of the first champion that came along, provided he was resolute. And the Communists were undeniably resolute. They furthermore continued throughout the war to defend the social interests of the rural poor, using the same pragmatic approach of identifying concrete grievances and targets.[122]

If protecting the peasants against local exploiters or Japanese invaders was a first step in the process of mobilization, that step was itself subordinated to the more basic precondition of military control. One of the earliest peasant unions, which was set up at Yueh-pei (Hengshan county, Hunan) in 1923, was initially able to grow, like that of Hai-feng a year before, 'in the interstices of control and power'. It did not last long; when a local war between competing warlords ended with the victory of the one who was more hostile to the peasant movement, 'the interstices disappeared – and so did the Union'.[123] Some ten years later, 'the fortunes of the Northern Szechwan soviet ... rose and fell with the fluctuations of the Szechwanese military politics'.[124] The Communists deliberately entered the game of warlord politics, a game that anyone aspiring to power was bound to play. They quite rightly considered military force a prerequisite to political power and to the application of a programme of reform.[125] Upon arriving in any region, Communist leaders had to rely on brute force in order to install and entrench themselves. No wonder, then, that in the main the Communist-peasant movement survived and

---

[122] See Suzanne Pepper, 'The growth of Communist power', pp. 751–8 below.

[123] McDonald, *Urban origins*, 218–23.

[124] Robert A. Kapp, *Szechwan and the Chinese Republic: provincial militarism and central power, 1911–1938*, 88. See also 90–2 and 103–4.

[125] Tetsuya Kataoka, *Resistance and revolution in China: the Communists and the second united front*, 265ff. Also Pepper, *Civil war*, 329 and Lyman Van Slyke, 'The New Fourth Army incident', pp. 665–71 below.

grew not in the areas where exploitation was the most rife and social tension the most strained but in places where political or strategic conditions were favourable.[126] To be sure, most of these places (like the Ching-kang mountains or northern Shensi) were also especially poor. However, mountainous or remote or peripheral areas (in short, areas which are not easy to reach) are likely to be more poverty-stricken than centrally located or densely populated plains. One can absolutely not postulate that the peasants living in the Communist bases of northern and north-western China, most of whom owned the land they farmed, were more prone to revolution than, say, tenant-farmers in the fertile Red Basin of Szechwan. The land rent, as well as the tenancy rate, was much higher in Szechwan, and the landowning minority suffered a much more abusive taxation than in the north. Strategy prevailed over this web of social factors – namely, the single obvious fact that the Red Basin was the least likely place to develop and maintain a red peasant base as long as the Nationalist government's wartime capital was located in nearby Chungking.

Not only were Kiangsi and later northern or north-western Chinese peasants not more suited to Communist mobilization than other Chinese peasants, but also within any particular soviet area or wartime base, poor peasants do not appear to have been the first to rally. In the early days when the Kiangsi peasants (both poor and middle) were reluctant to commit themselves and to join the Red Army, the latter was made up of a large proportion of mercenaries, mutineers (such as those whom P'eng Te-huai had led after the P'ing-hsiang uprising), prisoners who had come over from enemy armies and *déclassé* elements who had no links at all with the land.[127] The peasants also tended to keep away from the civil organs of the soviet which, to judge by the example of Yung-feng district (Hsing-kuo county, Kiangsi), were at first mainly composed of rural outcasts (salt smugglers, professional gamblers, secret societies' members) who were feared or despised by other villagers. These marginal figures, together with the urban or urbanized intellectuals, who were only too glad to recruit them for want of other, 'better' supporters, were a strange and motley crowd with which to get a peasant movement started.[128] Once it had got going, thanks to the launching of agrarian reform, the Communists were able to start recruiting authentic peasants. Later on, they

[126] Van Slyke, *ibid.* also Lucien Bianco, 'Peasants and revolution: the case of China', *The Journal of Peasant Studies*, 2.3 (April 1975) 332.

[127] Chi-hsi Hu, *L'armée rouge*, 13, 20–4.

[128] Philip C. C. Huang, 'Intellectuals, Lumpenproletarians, workers, and peasants in the Communist movement: the case of Xingguo county, 1927–1934', in Philip C. C. Huang *et al. Chinese Communists and rural society, 1927–1934*, 7–13.

expelled from their ranks those outcasts who could not overcome their predatory outlaw habits. Once they had become sufficiently strong, the Communists also purged many local cadres and party members with rich-peasant and small-landlord backgrounds.[129] They systematically recruited new activists from amongst the middle or preferably poor peasants and agricultural workers. The Communists had good reasons for preventing rich peasants and landlords from resuming their longstanding domination by penetrating the new power apparatus, whose policies they might attempt to influence or sabotage. They also had good reasons to mobilize the poor by setting them in opposition to the rich. One should not, however, regard the behaviour of the various strata of the rural population, after they were modified by the deliberate policies of the Communist elite, as the simple expression of previous cleavages.

Once mobilized peasants took their part in the Communist Revolution, they also found themselves part and parcel of an administrative machine. There is only one really important difference between the short-lived Hai-Lu-feng matrix and later developments: the Maoist construction did last and therefore could reach the new stage of fully-fledged statehood. Mao succeeded in organizing and maintaining a dissident regime. The celebrated mass line illustrates the problems facing a revolutionary elite transformed into a governing elite, an elite that must at once build a state and make a revolution. This dilemma arose as soon as the first government constraints were felt during the Kiangsi period. Like post-1949 rural cadres in the PRC, the Kiangsi peasants who had become local Communist leaders in the Chinese Soviet Republic were caught between two fires. They had to implement some unpopular directives although, later on, they would be reproached for authoritarian excesses in trying, for instance, to make their reluctant fellow-villagers purchase an inordinate quantity of treasury bonds or even 'voluntarily' give back, without reimbursement, the bonds they had already bought.[130] Fifteen years later, towards the end of the Sino-Japanese War and during the civil war, new deviations of local cadres (this time, 'rightist' rather than 'leftist' ones) were held responsible for the weaknesses of the agrarian reform and the delays in mass-mobilization. So much for the cadres, but the continuity between Communist revolutionary mobilization before 1949 and Communist control after that date holds also for the behaviour of the rural masses. As soon as a recruitment campaign for the Red Army was announced on the Honan-Shantung border in 1946, local peasants 'sent their young men

[129] Hsiao Tso-liang, *The land revolution in China, 1930–1934: a study of documents*, 169.
[130] Hsu King-i, 'Agrarian policies of the Chinese Soviet Republic, 1931–1934' (Indiana University, Ph.D. dissertation, 1971), 449–50.

off to visit relatives'.[131] (One third of a century later, it would be the young women who were sent to visit relatives in other villages; at that point, during the 1979 intensification of the birth-control campaign, it was not a matter of escaping 'voluntary' conscription, but of evading compulsory abortion.)

To sum up, we have not bridged, but rather deepened the chasm that separates spontaneous peasant agitation from the Communist-peasant movement. The one is not a continuation of the other. Spontaneous peasant agitation has features in common with the instances of 'peasant fury' in classical Europe. For many of the incidents described above we could adopt the diagnosis of a French historian of the *Nu-pieds* (Barefooted) insurrection in Normandy in the France of Louis XIII: 'This accidental coincidence of particular feelings of discontent in no way resembled the concerted preparation of an uprising with a view to obtaining a common result.'[132] Even less did it resemble the preparation of a revolution of the Leninist type, a planned conquest of power. Even when side-tracked by strategic or organizational problems, the Leninist revolutionary never lost sight of his ultimate objective. Peasant agitation, in contrast, did not aim to seize power. The only aim common to the various disparate initiatives we have grouped together under the title of 'spontaneous agitation' has been described by Eric Wolf as: 'the peasant fights to remain traditional'.[133] Nostalgia for a past whose good aspects alone were remembered or, in default of that past's return, the preservation of an established order that the peasants had every reason to complain about but whose great merit was that it was familiar – this aspiration was implicit in many apparently incoherent defensive reactions and rejections: for example, self-defence against external aggression but also suspicion and rejection of anything unknown, anything new, in short of virtually anything, deliberate or accidental, that struck at the status quo. Such aspirations cannot be considered aberrations. Indeed, they are very understandable if one accepts, with Migdal, that innovations that threatened or undermined the stability traditionally preserved in 'inward-oriented villages' brought in their wake stress and crisis, if not despair, to the village in question.[134]

A tiny minority of intellectuals succeeded in mobilizing for revolution

[131] Pepper, *Civil war*, 294.

[132] D. Caillard in Caillard, Duval and Guillet, Gricourt: *À travers la Normandie des XVIIème et XVIIIème siècles*, 55.

[133] Wolf more exactly wrote about the middle peasant: his 'very attempt...to remain traditional... makes him revolutionary' (*Peasant wars of the twentieth century*, 292). I would myself use the term 'rebel' instead of 'revolutionary'.   [134] Migdal, *Peasants*, ch. 5.

those peasants bogged down in a yearning for the past or in parochialism. The mechanisms of mobilization do not, however, represent the whole picture. Antecedent were more general conditions. There would have been no revolution in China without the poverty and exploitation suffered by the peasantry. This chapter on the peasant movement could usefully be balanced by one devoted to the peasant condition and its evolution.[135] One does not have to take the view shared by many contemporary observers and latter-day historians that conditions generally deteriorated under the republic to agree that any local or passing deterioration was invariably tragic and sometimes a provocation to revolt for a larger proportion of the peasantry, which only just managed to keep its head above water even in a normal year.[136] Even without any deterioration, the peasant condition throughout the length and breadth of the land urgently called for radical change. Our refusal to regard the inhabitants of the future 'liberated areas' as the victims of exploitation worse than elsewhere has aimed to refute a simplistic socio-geographic determinism. But it should be clear that there was everywhere in China enough poverty and oppression, discontent and alienation for the Communist organizers to be assured from the outset of finding many peasants who would be receptive to their propaganda (even if not to the extent of taking the risk of supporting them, which was a very different matter).

In the end, there *were* many peasants who took risks and even made the ultimate sacrifice, knowing full well what they were about. Many priceless heroic gestures were made in the service of the revolution by the peasants whose egoism, rather than altruism, this chapter has chiefly noted. Of course, they were not necessarily the same peasants although, given the right circumstances, the seed of heroism can flower anywhere, even among villagers reputed to be absorbed in their down-to-earth calculations and petty squabbles. It is not simply by chance that not only the propaganda of the Communists but also their policies and example encouraged a minority (but that is already saying a lot) of peasants to surpass and sacrifice themselves. A very special kind of link gradually *was* forged between the Communists and the peasants. Between the Nationalists and the peasants nothing of the kind took place.

A serious ambiguity, however, stems from the fact that, though sincere in its concern for the plight of the peasantry and in its will to better it, the Communist elite used the mobilization of the peasants and the promise of liberation as a means to serve an end which held much less interest

---

[135] For want of a whole chapter, see illuminating information and conflicting interpretations by Albert Feuerwerker (*CHOC* 12, 71–90) and Ramon Myers, pp. 256–69 above.
[136] In R. H. Tawney's words: 'up to the neck in water' (*Land and labour in China*, 77).

for those peasants: the independence, power and might of the nation. Once power had been won, the Communist elite continued to use the tool that the peasantry represented for it, in a new form: the huge reservoir of discontent that it had been successful in mobilizing for the purpose of overthrowing the *ancien régime* subsequently became a huge reservoir of manpower which it tried, much less successfully, to mobilize for the industrialization of a rural country. If relations between those who worked the land and the revolutionaries in power became far from harmonious, that was, among other things, because the liberation of the peasantry was not, and never had been, the fundamental aim of the Chinese revolution.

CHAPTER 7

THE DEVELOPMENT OF
LOCAL GOVERNMENT

From earliest times, the quality of China's political system as a whole was thought to be no better than the quality of government at the lowest levels. Late Ch'ing political theory was heir to a longstanding debate about the merits and defects of the existing bureaucratic system as it affected local communities. What would be the costs and benefits if counties were administered by natives rather than by centrally chosen outsiders? To what degree could the bureaucratic state risk the participation of local persons? After 1860 the needs of the modernizing state posed these old questions in acute form. If national strength required the mobilization of popular energies, through what local channels could such energies best be enlisted? If the state required more money, through what local institutions might it best be acquired? In the twentieth century, military modernization, the expanded and Westernized school systems, modern-style police forces – all required that the state find ways to control local society better and extract more resources from it.

Even as the state was impelled to penetrate local society in new and more effective ways, attention was also directed to local government by the ideologies of popular movements. Nationalism was a great mobilizer: as the fate of China was increasingly seen to be everybody's business, new groups clamoured for access to politics. These were predominantly the commercial classes and new-style school graduates of the modernizing cities, but also included some landlords and old-style examination graduates in the hinterland. Constitutional government would require a bottom-upwards model of political development: a legitimate national parliament had to be preceded by surveying and certifying an electorate. Building institutions through which local elites could participate regularly in politics marked a definite departure from the old Ch'ing system, in which elite participation was, while powerful, typically informal.

Thus the demand from below was added to pressure from above to reshape China's local political system. Much of the texture of China's modern politics would result from the interaction of these two forces. Which would ultimately prevail? Would China's local politics become more participatory as a result, or would the bureaucratic state succeed in imposing a finer and more stringent control upon Chinese communities than ever before?

THE ROLE OF ELITES IN LOCAL GOVERNMENT

Late Ch'ing elite activism grew from internal social and economic conditions long before the modern sector became important in the late nineteenth century. Maladministration in the government grain tribute system had led to resistance among the lower gentry by the 1820s in the form of ad hoc leagues, complete with written rules, officers and non-official financing, formed to submit judicial appeals to Peking. These never acquired official sanction, and their members were subject to prosecution. The local elite became involved in analogous organizations during the Taiping Rebellion, but this time in the form of officially patronized local defence associations (*t'uan-lien*). Typical of these traditional forms of elite activism, these associations were not strictly specialized in their functions. The same local leadership could employ them for various purposes such as education and charitable relief, much as a lineage organization might use its resources for varied needs. The government's dependence on local elite leadership during the years of rebellion established a pattern by which elite initiative in organization and funding would acquire official patronage and legitimation.

Management of waterways had become a significant arena for local managerial talent by the late eighteenth century. In Shanghai county, for example, local elites took charge of dredging canals and levied funds from landowners and merchants. This went beyond ad hoc community voluntarism: managers had quasi-official titles such as 'gentry manager' (*shen-tung*) to signify their place on the margin of the bureaucracy. This was known as 'official supervision and elite management' (*kuan-tu shen-pan*), a hybrid institution that made up for the thinness of bureaucratic rule on the county level.[1]

The nexus between elite activism and official patronage can also be seen in charitable relief. For example, the system of sub-county administration in Chia-ting, Kiangsu, grew out of a network of relief-depots. Thirty-one such soup kitchens were originally established in 1805 to cope with a famine. During the course of the nineteenth century their managers (*tung-shih*) became more or less permanent functionaries charged with

[1] Mark Elvin, 'Market towns and waterways: the county of Shang-hai from 1480 to 1910', in G. William Skinner, ed. *The city in late imperial China*, 441–73. On the rise of elite activism, see above, ch. 1, pp. 53–9.

helping the magistrate in local administration. Serving under them by rotation were headmen on the village level. As the network of market towns ramified and market areas fissioned, the map of local administration changed accordingly. Here was a formalization of the political function of marketing communities, with local elites serving as quasi-bureaucratic managers. In such rich, commercialized areas, local elite management was already moving beyond the informal mediation and ad hoc community services usually associated with our concept of 'gentry society'.[2]

City gentry and merchants, too, found themselves acquiring new generalized administrative roles as urbanization outdated the old rudimentary city services. Gentry-run charity halls and merchant guilds were assuming general responsibility for urban services by the late nineteenth century. These were traditional institutions being put to new uses. By the late nineteenth century, that is, before the advent of modern-style chambers of commerce, traditional urban associations were empowered by local bureaucrats to take on some of the functions of city government. Again, the pattern was of generalized responsibility growing out of specialized, rather than the reverse: fire-fighting societies took on charitable and militia work; charity-halls took on militia and fire-fighting, street-cleaning, and road-maintenance. All this was done, of course, in the interest of creating a profitable and secure arena for business and for gentry residence, very much in the spirit of old-style gentry services. The quasi-governmental powers of such bodies included the levying of taxes on commerce. As these institutions evolved in the first decade of the new century, their powers multiplied. The Shanghai City Council was founded in 1905, partly inspired by the success of the municipal council in the International Settlement. Under direct official sponsorship, local gentry and merchants were authorized to choose directors to manage urban services such as roads, electric lighting and police. Further marks of a city government were the council's taxing and judicial authority.[3]

The financial underpinnings of new elite-managed public enterprises had to be outside the boundaries of the regular land tax. The imperial government had done its best to keep local elites out of the regular land tax system, though by the nineteenth century certain surtaxes on the land were being collected by gentry-staffed bureaus. Generally, however, it was trade taxes (*tsa-chüan*) which afforded local elites a legitimate channel into the local fiscal system. Like the more famous likin, these trade excises were

[2] *Chia-ting hsien hsu-chih* (Chia-ting county gazetteer, rev. edn.), 1.4b–5.

[3] Mark Elvin, 'The administration of Shanghai, 1905–1914', in Mark Elvin and G. William Skinner, eds. *The Chinese city between two worlds*, 240–50. Shirley S. Garrett, 'The chambers of commerce and the YMCA', in *ibid*. 218. Imahori Seiji, *Pepin shimin no jichi kōsei* (The self-government organizations of Peiping burghers), 23–4.

readily expansible to new sources of revenue and hard for the bureaucracy
to keep track of. The 'local self-government' activities of the first decade
of the twentieth century, including new-style schools and police forces,
drew upon these revenues. Collections were largely managed by local
elites, who were eager to keep these new revenue sources out of the hands
of the county clerks.

An institutional change that emerged from these local activities was
the official definition of a sphere of explicitly 'local' taxation. Previously,
county governments had only the legally 'retained' amounts from the
regular tax revenues, in addition to the irregular 'customary fees' which
supplemented the inadequate salaries of the magistrate and his sub-
bureaucracy. It was not until 1908 that a local tax base was established
to delimit the kinds of revenue that county elites might use to finance
the new enterprises of local government. In the 1908 regulations for
self-government of county seats, market towns and rural townships, it
was stipulated that special excise taxes and surtaxes on land be considered
the legitimate revenue of these new units.

In 1909, the spheres of national, provincial and local finance were laid
out in detail in a series of massive publications commissioned by the
newly-formed Ministry of Finance (Tu-chih-pu).[4] These showed how
deeply local elites were already involved in collecting and disbursing local
revenues. Miscellaneous excises were being levied on local commerce and
services, and receipts spent on the newly organized county police forces
and modern-style schools. Elite participation was particularly important
in the new educational system, which urgently demanded new sources
of revenue. Modernized schools increased rapidly in number (in Shantung,
for instance, from 140 in 1903 to 3,424 in 1907), an inviting arena for elite
involvement. Much of the local take from commercial excises was kept
out of the county office, 'managed by gentry and not passed through
official hands'.[5]

Managerial work by local elites was accompanied by an outpouring of
theoretical writing. The focus in local government had been an important
part of the 'Restoration' in the 1860s, when China was faced with
widespread chaos and devastation in the wake of the mid-century
rebellions.[6] The effort by provincial authorities was to firm up the bases

---

[4] *Ts'ai-cheng shuo-ming shu* (Explanatory accounts of fiscal administration), 20 vols. Liu Shan-shu,
Tzu-chih ts'ai-cheng lun (On local self-government finance), 25. Philip A. Kuhn, 'Local taxation
and finance in Republican China', *Select papers from the Center for Far Eastern Studies*, 3 (1978–79)
100–36.

[5] Chang Yü-fa, *Chung-kuo hsien-tai-hua ti ch'ü-yü yen-chiu: Shan-tung sheng, 1860–1916* (Modernization
in China, 1860–1916: a regional study of social, political and economic change in Shantung
province), 458–9. On elite involvement in local taxes, see Kuhn, 'Local taxation'.

[6] See *CHOC* 10.435–56, 'Post-war problems in the Lower Yangtze', by K. C. Liu.

of local taxation and order by strengthening traditional agencies of control and indoctrination: cleaning up county administration, reviving Confucian education, rebuilding the local economy. At the same time, some called for new approaches: a recognition that only if a new way were found to harness the energies of local elites could the imperial system survive. It was argued (most notably by Feng Kuei-fen) that the old informal power of local elites was not a suitable basis for imperial control, and that a firmer administration was needed at the county level and below. By the late decades of the Ch'ing, a substantial body of thought held that a rejuvenation of the Chinese polity would depend on a new approach to local government. How was this to be accomplished? The issue was whether elite energies were to be harnessed to state purposes by coopting them into a system of local self-government institutions; or whether a more bureaucratic control system, extended down to the village level, was more appropriate to China's political traditions.

The crisis precipitated by the international pressures on China during the late 1890s gave the question new urgency. Elite outrage against China's oppressors (and covertly against the Manchu-dominated regime which had failed to defend the nation) led to pressure for broadened involvement in politics. The reform movement of 1898 contained a significant stream of local activism, which envisaged the harnessing of local elite energies as the only way a strong nation could be built. Reformers such as Huang Tsun-hsien clearly had the Japanese example in mind when they called for local self-government as the basis of a strong state. Official control, he asserted, simply led to dependency and passivity, exactly the opposite qualities of a successfully aroused populace.[7]

The failure of the 1898 reform movement, along with the disaster of the Boxer uprising, heightened the clamour for constitutionalism, a substantial part of which was considered to require reforms in local politics. K'ang Yu-wei wrote in 1902 that local self-government was essential to national revival. The key was the mobilization of popular energies, particularly those of the local elite. Only long cultivation in the arts of running their own local communities would make the Chinese fit to survive in a competitive world. Here K'ang drew upon the old 'feudalistic' (*feng-chien*) ideas that Ku Yen-wu had espoused in the seventeenth century, which asserted that the concern of local people for their community's welfare far exceeded that of a bureaucratic official

---

[7] Huang Tsun-hsien, 'Speech to the Southern Study Society', in *Hsiang-pao lei-tsuan*, 307ff. Criticism of local administration harked back to the early Ch'ing writings of Ku Yen-wu and Huang Tsung-hsi that were studied in late nineteenth-century Japan as well as China. See Joshua A. Fogel, *Politics and sinology: the case of Naitō Konan (1866–1934)*, 182–90.

posted from elsewhere according to the rule of avoidance. That Western nations had been able to mobilize popular energies was entirely due, thought K'ang, to their long practice of local self-government. Economic development and national strength would inevitably follow the mobilization of local political energies. These energies were to be harnessed to national purposes through a constitutional system; in no sense was localism to detract from national cohesion. Rather, the two were deeply connected in K'ang's thinking.[8]

Among the constitutionalists, K'ang's disciple Liang Ch'i-ch'ao was the foremost promoter of new ideas about local self-government. He believed that the main beneficiary of self-government would be China's public morale. Far from being a formula for parcelling out power, self-government was a way of imbuing the entire body politic with a heightened internal discipline. With no officials to rule them from 'outside', as it were, the people would eventually become animated by a body of social rules which would move them toward shared goals: national unity and strength. Like K'ang, he believed in the transformative effects of self-government upon the individual character, and therefore ultimately upon the group. Constitutionalism's leading rival, Chang Ping-lin, led the attack against the 'feudalistic' idea as spokesman for the T'ung-meng hui. Unlike the Western nations, to say nothing of Japan, China was thousands of years removed from her feudal age. It was absurd, he thought, to assume that China was an appropriate home for representative government of the Western variety, which would only produce self-seeking and contention among politicians and anarchy in local communities. What was needed (presumably as the aftermath of revolution) was a bureaucracy purged of corruption and disciplined to the needs of the unitary nation-state.[9]

The official Ch'ing view of local self-government was in large measure shaped by the activities and proposals of Yuan Shih-k'ai. As governor-general of Chihli province, he set about constructing a modernized police and educational system in Tientsin shortly after his appointment in 1902. Tientsin was seen by the Powers as an essential link in their access route to the capital, and an efficient urban administration was considered necessary to avoid repeated outbreaks of Sino-foreign conflict after the Boxer affair. Yuan's programme involved not only modern police and

[8] Min Tu-ki, 'Ch'ŏngdae ponggŏllon ŭi kŭndaejŏk pyŏnmo' (The modern transformation of traditional political feudalism in the Ch'ing period), in *Chungguk kŭndaesa yŏn'gu*, 228–73. Philip A. Kuhn, 'Local self-government under the Republic: problems of control, autonomy, and mobilization', in Frederic Wakeman, Jr. and Carolyn Grant, eds. *Conflict and control in late imperial China*, 272–6.

[9] Philip A. Kuhn, 'Late Ch'ing views of the polity', *Select papers from the Center for Far Eastern Studies*, 4 (1979–80) 10–16.

schools, but also a mechanism for coopting and utilizing the local elite. This was to be done through a system of representative assemblies in the counties of Tientsin prefecture. Beginning with Tientsin county as a pilot project, the new police bureaus were to conduct a complete census of inhabitants as the basis of an electoral list. The Tientsin County Assembly (*i-shih-hui*), elected in 1907, became the prototype of the Ch'ing government's efforts to set up elite representative bodies which would adhere to an essentially conservative view of the prerogatives of local self-government. Along with this step toward an elite-based constitutionalism, Yuan set about extending his new police system to other areas in Chihli, thus strengthening the hand of the county magistrates by bringing the local security system firmly under bureaucratic control.[10]

The Yuan Shih-k'ai experiment in elite-based democracy linked with bureaucratic control can be seen as a reaction to the anarchic North China situation which Yuan inherited after the post-Boxer withdrawal of the Powers. Under Japanese influence, a tighter government control was to be established with the cooperation of local elites.

This outlook was embodied in the Ch'ing court's own view of local administration, which was revealed on the occasion (1908) of the decree authorizing the step-by-step installation of local assemblies as the basis for a national constitutional system. The court viewed local self-government as a mere extension of the traditional gentry-bureaucracy relationship, in which local elites would do those jobs which county government was unable to perform: essentially in the old gentry realm of education, public relief and public works. Closely supervised by the bureaucracy, self-government bodies were to play a purely supplementary role in local government. Certainly, there was nothing here of the vibrant calls for popular mobilization that we have seen in the writings of the reformers. Between these two conceptions – the quest for mobilization and the quest for control – Chinese local governmental reform was to oscillate for the next three decades.

Assemblies and 'new administration' (hsin-cheng)

For all its limitations, government-sponsored constitutionalism had a huge impact on local politics. It is an indication of the overwhelming prestige of state agencies that the innate activism of the local elite only began to flourish in a big way once the Ch'ing court itself became

[10] Stephen R. MacKinnon, *Power and politics in late imperial China: Yuan Shih-kai in Beijing and Tianjin, 1901–1908*, 137–79. John H. Fincher, *Chinese democracy: the self-government movement in local, provincial and national politics, 1905–1914*, 30–42.

committed to limited institutional reform and created legitimate bodies to carry it out. The shock of the Boxer humiliation in 1900 led to court-sponsored measures that had the effect of creating a number of channels through which local elites could participate in administration. Chief among these were the educational reforms of 1901–5, which first mandated a new school structure modelled on the Japanese, with the introduction of Western-style curricula. When the traditional examination system was abolished in 1905 and the new-style schools became the standard channels for social mobility, there followed a vast expansion of elite involvement in the administration of the new system. The shortage of both funds and personnel in local government ensured that the new school system would be primarily a local elite enterprise. The 'Education Promotion Offices' (*ch'üan-hsueh so*) set up in all counties by imperial order in 1906 typically installed local elites as directors, who quickly became involved in countywide fund-raising and management.[11] What education was for the local literati, the new officially mandated chambers of commerce were for the merchants and manufacturers. Like the new school system, the chambers were an unofficially sponsored system through which elite activists could play a role in public affairs.[12]

Local self-government, however, in the form of municipal councils and county assemblies, was the most important channel for the county elite's move into politics. Its institutional prestige was invitingly close to officialdom, and its capacity to intervene in governmental affairs seemed to address certain longstanding sore points on the agenda of local elites. Chief among these was some measure of control of public finance, which was seen as a source of extortionate profits for clerks and local officials, with little benefit for the community. Having been a rallying cry for reformers since the late 1890s, local self-government now emerged as an official component of the new constitutional programme announced by the court in 1908. Shortly after the promulgation of rules for electing delegates to provincial assemblies, it was announced (27 August 1908) that self-government regulations for administrative cities (*ch'eng*), non-administrative market towns (*chen*) and rural townships (*hsiang*) were to be drawn up. These regulations were forthcoming from Peking on 18 January 1909.[13] Self-government for administrative units followed that

---

[11] Local gazetteers are full of information on this move by local elites into county educational systems. See for example *Wan-hsien (Hopei) hsin-chih*, 1933 edn., 3.8–9, 4.37ff. Also see Edward Rhoads, *China's Republican Revolution: the case of Kwangtung, 1895–1913*, esp. ch. 4. For Chihli, see Richard A. Orb, 'Chihli academies and other schools in the late Ch'ing: an institutional survey', in Paul A. Cohen and John E. Schrecker, eds. *Reform in nineteenth-century China*, 231–40.

[12] See *CHOC* 11.563 by M. Bastid-Bruguière; and 12.721–825 by M. C. Bergère.

[13] Fincher, *Chinese democracy*, 104. The operative memorial from the Constitution Drafting Office regarding local self-government is reproduced in *Ta-Ch'ing Kuang-hsu hsin fa-ling* (New laws of

traditional mechanisms of elite power were inadequate to an increasingly complex social and economic system. (In more backward areas, it was evidently less useful to have new, public institutions: traditional kinship and economic ties were all local elites needed.)

A second trend was the gradual reimposition of bureaucratic authority. Faced with an obstreperous local assembly movement, Yuan Shih-k'ai decreed the abolition of local self-government and substituted a format more congenial to official control. Yuan's system retained a unit on the sub-county scale: the ward (*ch'ü*), a territory so large that there were but four to six per county, and whose headman was in reality to be a functionary of the county government, not a community-chosen representative.[17] After the death of Yuan and the failure of his imperial project, local assemblies enjoyed a brief second flowering from 1921 to 1927; but the context had changed. Specialized administrative agencies had emerged to handle such functions as education, so assemblies were now called upon merely to fund such bodies, not manage them. Furthermore, magistrates gained back a large measure of control over county affairs through executive boards (*ts'an-shih-hui*), of whose members only a minority were chosen by the assemblies. Thus Yuan's attack on the assembly system can be seen as but an extreme example of a general trend toward the reimposition of bureaucratic control: the fledgling local elite political institutions were no match for it.[18]

Nor was the elite-led assembly movement popular among the peasantry. It was clear from the outset that local self-government was not likely to build a constituency among the masses at the county level. On the contrary, sporadic popular violence broke out in many areas in reaction to what was perceived as merely another kind of elite profiteering. In particular, mass anger was vented against the modern schools. These cost considerably more than schools of the traditional sort; money for them had to be raised from the commoners in the form of excises on daily trade commodities and surtaxes on the land. Since the modern schools were less accessible to the peasantry than the traditional schools and taught subjects less useful to them, they were reasonably seen as taxing the people for purposes not to their benefit. Another object of popular ire was the local self-government office itself; projects such as a local census for election rolls were feared as the prelude to a head tax. The widespread practice of taking over local temples for use as schools or self-government offices offended popular religiosity. The early years of self-government brought a rash of riots leading to burnings of modern schools and houses

---

[17] Cp. *CHOC* 12.237–46 on Yuan's dictatorship, by E. Young.
[18] Schoppa, *Chinese elites*, 31–4, 186–90, and *passim*.

of self-government leaders. The local elite had got themselves into a situation where the most progressive-seeming reform and development programmes were seen as exploitative as well as culturally offensive.[19] Self-government was tending to drive reformist elite and conservative peasantry further apart, rather than to create a vigorous local politics with an elite leadership and a popular constituency. With allies neither above nor below, county-level elites were not likely to transform China's political system from the ground up, nor to compete successfully with a resurgent bureaucratic state.[20]

REGIONAL REGIMES

Out of the confused mêlée of proposals, regulations, and local power-competition that made up the constitutional movement, there emerged some concrete efforts to reorganize local government. It should not be surprising that as the central government lost its capacity to enforce its will locally, these efforts first took root under provincial auspices. They began with the programme of Yen Hsi-shan, warlord leader of Shansi province, to establish better control over his territory by placing new emphasis on village-level organization. Undertaken as they were by military power-holders, provincial initiatives of this sort were not likely to place much store by popular mobilization or participation. Although no such scheme was without 'self-government' rhetoric, the practical emphasis was in quite another direction.

The Shansi programme

The 'village system' (*ts'un-chih*) of Shansi, inaugurated by Governor Yen Hsi-shan in 1917, is an example of the process by which bureaucratic solutions grew out of voluntarist and populist programmes, and eventually came to dominate the local government of the republic. Yen's system was an outgrowth of two trends, both conservative in intent: first, the abolition of county and province self-government by Yuan Shih-k'ai (1913–14) was followed by an 'experimental' system of local administration by wards (*ch'ü*), a sub-county unit roughly on the scale of the traditional *hsiang* district. These districts were, in Yuan's plan of 1914, to be managed by appointed headmen, essentially as adjuncts of county government. The

---

[19] Cp. ch. 6 (Bianco).

[20] Wang Shu-huai, 319–27. Amy Fei-man Ma, 'Local self-government and the local populace in Chuan-sha, 1911', *Select papers from the Center for Far Eastern Studies*, 1 (1975–76) 47–84. Roxanne Prazniak, 'Community and protest in rural China: tax resistance and county-village politics on the eve of the 1911 revolution' (University of California, Davis, Ph.D. dissertation, 1981).

ward system was adopted by Yen Hsi-shan as a bridge between county and village; the three to six wards per county functioned primarily as police and taxation authorities. Second, Yen drew upon a tradition of gentry activism that sought village revitalization through education and the transformation of public morals.

The origins of the Shansi system have been traced to a gentry-led model town in Hopei, the Chai-ch'eng experiment which later became famous as the basis of the Ting-hsien project in the late 1920s and 1930s (see below, pp. 353–5). The Mi family of Chai-ch'eng had been so successful with local education and self-government activism that the county magistrate, Sun Ch'un-chai, had the town declared a model and subsequently the county itself. Sun had become magistrate of Ting-hsien in 1914. Two years later he was chosen by Yen Hsi-shan to be chief administrator of the Shansi provincial government (*sheng-chang*). Whether or not his elevation stemmed from his unique experience with village-level administration, he seized the opportunity to urge upon his patron his approach to revitalizing local government. Sun lost his post in less than a year, but the new administrative system remained as Yen Hsi-shan's basic strategy for local control.[21]

As it developed, Yen's new system was quite compatible with the local self-government regulations issued by Yuan Shih-kai's administration in 1914. These had been aimed at taming the vigorous county and provincial politics of the republic's early years, in which local elites competed with the bureaucracy for control of local resources. Yuan's abolition of provincial and county assemblies aimed at a more bureaucratic tone in local government: the basic unit, the ward (*ch'ü*), was an administrative territory too large to conform to any natural sub-county unit (too large, for instance, to conform to a standard marketing community). The implication was clear: sub-county self-government, when it finally emerged after a series of prescribed stages, was to be more responsive to the supervision of officials than to the political organizations of local communities.[22] What the new 'village' system added was the *ts'un* unit: this was similar to the old 'administrative village' (*pien ts'un*) of the Ch'ing, in that small communities were generally linked under a headman. As the system developed in Shansi, it became a sub-bureaucratic framework for transmitting government directives. The village heads, generally illiterate and dependent on county authorities for appointment, could take little

21 Yin Chung-ts'ai, ed. *Chai-ch'eng ts'un chih* (Gazetteer of Chai-ch'eng ts'un, 1925; Taipei reprint, 1968) 211. Guy S. Alitto, *The last Confucian: Liang Shu-ming and the Chinese dilemma of modernity*, 146.
22 On Yuan's regulations see Ch'en Po-hsin, *Chung-kuo ti ti-fang chih-tu chi ch'i kai-ko* (China's local system and its reform), 58ff.

independent initiative. A 1922 inspector's report found them ineffective even for channelling official orders. The ward heads were men of larger capacities. Though all were from Shansi, they were not appointed within their own counties, which amounted to extending the old Ch'ing 'rule of avoidance' to the sub-county level. As petty administrators, they were not likely instigators of vigorous local politics of the 'self-government' variety. However, their direct appointment by the provincial government gave them a higher status in the bureaucratic order.

The bureaucratic flavour of the Shansi system was enhanced by a campaign to fix the boundaries of the administrative villages. This was substituting known administrative jurisdictions for customary inter-personal ties. More important was its usefulness for the land-tax administration. The administrative village (*ts'un*) functioned as the descendant of the old *li-chia* tax-collection areas of the Ch'ing, now furnished with more accurately drawn boundaries based on cadastral surveys undertaken during Yen's early administration.[23]

In terms of administrative history, Yen Hsi-shan's highly touted 'village system' amounted to little more than a voluntarist self-government façade for what was essentially an old imperial tax-administration system, onto which was attached a version of the old *pao-chia* surveillance system of decimal population units.

In this respect, Yen's system is an example of the twentieth-century practice of fixing tax responsibilities upon villages as a whole and thereby strengthening the village as a political-administrative unit. The particular taxes in question were known as 'special assessments' (*t'an-k'uan*), extraordinary levies upon local communities to meet the expanding needs of government. The special assessments were initially a way of meeting the immense Boxer indemnity payments, but later became a common method for financing the modern needs, particularly the military needs, of provincial and local governments. Yen Hsi-shan's success in building armies owed much to his effective taxation of local communities through the village-run special assessments. This was obviously a calculated result of his 'village system', however prettily that system was dressed up with reformist programmes.

Reformist programmes, nevertheless, did achieve a nationwide reputation for Shansi. The old *pao-chia* and *li-chia* formats were used to promote anti-footbinding, anti-opium, public security and literacy campaigns, with impressive results. Liang Shu-ming, who was highly critical of Yen's

---

[23] The evolution of *li-chia* units and their connection with administrative villages may be found in *Lu-ch'eng hsien-chih*, 2.7b–10b. Also see *Hsiang-ning hsien-chih*, 5, 7b; *T'ai-ku hsien-chih*, ch. 3. Also see Hsiao Kung-ch'uan, *Rural China: imperial control in the nineteenth century*.

programme for its bureaucratic tone, found much to commend it for in social reform. Overall, the Shansi programme can be evaluated as a determined effort by an activist provincial government to project its bureaucratic power downward to the village level. Its debt to the Chai-ch'eng experiment of the Mi family was mostly rhetorical, yet there was a shared conviction that close attention to sub-county government was high on the twentieth-century agenda.[24]

Shansi was not the only province to undertake local government reforms. Another notable effort was that of the 'Kwangsi clique' to tighten local government through a province-wide militia system. By training village and township leaders and enrolling them as cadres of the local militia, it was hoped to infuse them with a spirit of military discipline, so that orders from provincial authorities would be effectively passed on to lower levels. These headmen would also serve as teachers in a system of 'basic schools' (*chi-ch'u hsueh-hsiao*) to foster literacy, public spirit, and economic self-sufficiency. From a strictly military standpoint. the militia served as the basis of a province-wide conscription system. The ideal was the old 'union of soldiers and people' (*ping-min ho-i*) which was designed not only to build an immense military pool, but also to infuse the whole populace with a heightened sense of discipline. The system was begun in 1933, but was unable to repel the Japanese invasion six years later. Like the Shansi system, the Kwangsi format aimed at local control and development by strengthening the power of the provincial bureaucracy to penetrate village society.[25] It was also believed that provincial organization of the Kwangsi militia would shoulder aside the indigenous local militia corps that were under the control of powerful 'local bully' elites.

Provincial initiatives like these tended to reflect the interests and temperaments of their warlord patrons. The Shansi system emphasized conservative social goals and moral uplift; Kwangsi emphasized a militant nationalism along with its community-building rhetoric. Both touted local self-government, but their essence was bureaucratic control. Noteworthy in both cases was the determination to make such control effective on the lowest level of organization, in effect to extend bureaucracy below its late

---

[24] The Chai-ch'eng local boosters were of course eager to show how influential their initiative had been around the country. See *Chai-ch'eng ts'un-chih*, 165–231. A general treatment of the Shansi system is Chou Ch'eng, *Shan-hsi ti-fang tzu-chih kang-yao* (An outline of Shansi local self-government), in *Ti-fang tzu-chih chiang-i* (Lectures on local self-government). On *t'an-k'uan* and its effects, see Prasenjit Duara, 'Power in rural society: North China villages, 1900–1940' (Harvard University, Ph.D. dissertation, 1983), 326–36.

[25] Ch'iu Ch'ang-wei, *Kuang-hsi hsien-cheng* (County government in Kwangsi), 222–41. *Kuang-hsi min-t'uan kai-yao* (A general view of the Kwangsi militia). Diana Lary, *Region and nation: the Kwangsi clique in Chinese politics, 1925–1937*, 170–93.

imperial level, the county. The Shansi system was particularly important in this regard because it influenced the local system of the Nanking government after 1928.

EARLY POLICIES OF NANKING ON LOCAL ADMINISTRATION

As a movement pledged to social transformation as well as national unification, the Nationalists of the 1920s came to power committed to carrying out Sun Yat-sen's vision of a democratic China. This vision, embodied in the *Fundamentals of national reconstruction (Chien-kuo ta-kang,* Sun's blueprint for what we would now call 'nation-building'), represented his mature views on constitutional questions. Issued in 1924, at a time when the Kuomintang's alliance with the Soviet Union was in full swing, it is remarkable how little it reflects the views of the Kuomintang left. Actually it was a restatement and culmination of views long held by Sun about how popular sovereignty should be instituted.

Sun believed that a nation unaccustomed to the forms and ideas of constitutional government and political participation had to build from the ground up: from county, to province, to centre. Under the supervision of the Kuomintang, citizens were to be tutored in the form and practice of 'self-government' on a county format. In this 'tutelage' stage of political development, party guidance was to aim at making all the counties in a province 'self-governing', and then the province itself. When a majority of provinces became self-governing in this manner, the National People's Congress was to promulgate a constitution based on the five-part division of powers.

This bottom-up model of political development Sun had derived from none other than the 'self-government' theories made popular in the first decade of the century by K'ang Yu-wei, Liang Ch'i-ch'ao, and their followers. Sun was clearly committed to the local self-government ideas as early as 1912. It was, he thought, the natural foundation of a strong, unified state. His rationale was hardly different, in either tone or substance, from that of Liang Ch'i-ch'ao which we have already discussed. By 1916, Sun had linked local self-government to his vague but deeply felt populism; to avoid the old round-robin of one despotic regime replacing another (which had characterized most of Chinese history and was now being replayed under the republic), it was necessary to make the people the basis of government. To do this, the institutions of government must be rebuilt from the ground up. The culminating national structure would be as a roof-beam to the foundations of a house.

The essence of Sun's vision of national political development cannot, however, be understood on the basis of populist self-government alone. Although he was impressed by contemporary American progressive measures such as initiative, referendum and recall, he was also convinced that elite leadership was needed to train the Chinese people to use such powers. 'Those who have foresight', the most enlightened elements of the modernized elite, were to lead the people to democracy. The Chinese people were by nature tractable and trainable, and therefore were particularly apt objects of this kind of elite tutelage.[26] This amalgam of genuine hope for a democratic China, and a conviction that firm guidance was needed on the way to it, infused Sun's political thinking from the beginning. It was to prove a conundrum to Kuomintang administrators in later years, who found the two elements quite incompatible in the process of consolidating their power after 1928. At the time the new Nationalist government adopted Sun's *Fundamentals of national reconstruction* as its guiding text, it had virtually no experience in local administration. It is not surprising that the confused historical roots of the theory, added to the vagueness of its presentation, did not readily produce a viable form of constitutional democracy in China's local communities.

Bureaucratization of local government

The evolution of the Nationalist government's policy toward local administration embodied a general trend away from Sun's conception of local self-government and toward a more rigorous system of bureaucratic control. In the process, the vestiges of local elite participation in the management of community affairs were the targets of repeated attacks. Much of this work took place in the context of a resurgence of conservative thinking within the Kuomintang, as well as the frantic quest for internal security which characterized its approach to civil administration during the 1930s.

In September 1928, the Nanking government issued the first version of its County Organization Law (Hsien tsu-chih-fa), which attempted to define both the administrative structure and the representative democratic functions of local government. The county administration itself was divided between those functional offices directly under the magistrate (*k'o*, or sections), and those specialized bureaus (*chü*) which were controlled by the analogous departments (*t'ing*) of the provincial government. For instance, the financial section (*ts'ai-cheng-k'o*) of the county government was paralleled by the financial bureau (*ts'ai-cheng-chü*), which was controlled by the provincial Financial Department. This curious division

[26] Sun Yat-sen, *Fundamentals of national reconstruction*, 126–49.

of authority was actually designed to separate purely local functions (entrusted to the bureaus) from those of the province and nation (handled by the sections of the county administration). The fact that the magistrate did not control the appointment of the heads of bureaus meant that a substantial part of local administration (and the funds that financed it) remained outside his control. Local education, for example, would be managed by the education bureau, whose head would be appointed directly by the provincial Department of Education.[27]

The County Organizational Law also sought to define the units of government below the county level and their role in representative government. Following the example of Shansi province (whose governor, Yen Hsi-shan, was named minister of interior under the new Nanking government), a multi-layered system of units was established. Directly under the county was the ward (*ch'ü*), an important administrative subdivision since the early republic. Its extent was left vaguely specified, from ten to fifty townships according to local conditions. Like its Shansi exemplar, however, it was clearly a much larger unit than could be defined by any natural community, suitable for bureaucratic administration or electoral districting, but not for local home rule.[28] Below the ward were the natural communities: rural villages of 100 families or more (*ts'un*), or urban neighbourhoods of the same size (*li*). Beneath these were a kind of mutual-surveillance and local-responsibility unit familiar to students of Chinese history as *pao-chia*, but termed here *lü* and *lin* (25- and 5-family groupings). Besides the wards, each of the natural communities was eventually to have an elected headman and a council. Until local elections were held, however, the heads were to be appointed by the county magistrate.

Whatever the prospects for actually putting them into effect, the provisions for local democracy in the original County Organization Law were the least that could be expected, given the prescriptions of Sun's *Fundamentals of national reconstruction*, to which the Nationalist government was explicitly committed. The county was to be both an administrative and a self-government unit: the magistrate, at the head of an executive council (*hsien-cheng hui-i*) composed of section and bureau heads, was to be paralleled by an elected county assembly (*hsien ts'an-i-hui*) with broad powers to review budgets and executive performance. Below the county level, all units were seen as totally 'self-government' bodies, with elected

---

[27] Hsieh Chen-min, *Chung-hua min-kuo li-fa shih* (History of legislation in the Republic of China), 826.

[28] Chao Ju-heng, *Ti-fang tzu-chih chih li-lun yü shih-chi* (Theory and practice of local self-government), 77.

ward chiefs and elected assemblies at lower levels. Of course, until such time as the election procedures could be worked out and the people educated to the practice of self-government, personnel at these levels were still to be appointed by the magistrate.[29]

The environment in which such a plan for local democratization was to be carried out, however, was likely to bring about a desire for greater control, rather than greater local self-government. Beset by recurrent civil war and foreign aggression, as well as by the social effects of the worldwide depression, the government saw internal security as the order of the day. The result was to strengthen those elements within the Kuomintang who were more impressed by bureaucratic and military effectiveness than by popular participation. Beginning in late 1928, Nanking worked out revisions of the County Organization Law that had the effect of strengthening bureaucratic administration and, at the same time, putting off the date for implementing local self-government. A conference of representatives from the civil administration departments (*min-chen-t'ing*) of the provinces under Nanking's control suggested that the county organization law had been too hasty in promoting county assemblies, for which the people were unready. Such assemblies were now to be put off until the time when ward heads were popularly elected. This was subsequently defined as taking place no later than 1933.[30] (The hesitation to convene county assemblies is reminiscent of Yuan Shih-k'ai's suspicion of such bodies a generation earlier, at which time the local self-government movement was virtually destroyed.) In the spirit of the conference, the Legislative Yuan passed a law (11 May 1929) which affirmed the 'tutelage' role of the county magistrate in all matters relating to local self-government. It also strengthened the role of the provincial government in local administration by placing the appointment of ward heads directly within the power of the provincial Department of Civil Affairs. The magistrate was given greater power to control the special-function bureaus within his county by being made responsible for nominating their heads to the provincial government for appointment.[31]

At the same time, the original model of sub-county administration was found to be unsuitable for general application. The 'administrative village' system of Shansi (as adapted by Nanking) had been close to the old *pao-chia* principle of numerical aggregates: an administrative village was to include approximately a hundred households, linking several small natural villages under government appointed headmen. Nanking now

[29] Hsieh Chen-min, *Li-fa-shih*, 825–9.
[30] Ch'ien Tuan-sheng, *Min-kuo cheng-chih shih* (History of the Republican political system), 553.
[31] Hsieh Chen-min, *Li-fa-shih*, 829–32.

found this too discordant with natural settlement units and decreed that the more conventional 'township' (*hsiang*) and 'market town' (*chen*) designations of the early Republic be restored.[32] It was also a move away from a single, national system of local administration and an admission that Nanking's ability to control provincial governments outside east-central China was limited.

The objectives of the County Organization Law, in respect to both self-government and administrative reform, were found increasingly impractical by provincial administrators. Two conferences of provincial civil officials sponsored by the Ministry of Interior produced resolutions aimed at diluting its original purposes. The first of these 'civil administration conferences' (*nei-cheng hui-i*), in 1931, resolved to loosen the rigid numerical limits on the sizes of local units: to limit townships and market towns to administrative aggregates of no more than 1,000 households was impractical for densely populated areas, since it would result in a finer network of local control than could be financed or staffed. Further, it was found impractical to limit the office of ward head to trained local government personnel, since there were insufficient facilities to produce the numbers needed. And finally, the requirement that the County Organization Law be fully implemented by the end of 1929 was found impractical under the variety of provincial conditions.

The second conference, convened in December 1932, went further in its attacks in the County Organization Law. No longer was a unified national system thought feasible, given the variety of local traditions and social conditions. Henceforth neither the sizes of local sub-county units, nor their principles of organization, nor their nomenclature was to be dictated by the Ministry of Interior in Nanking. More significant was the attack on self-government as a principle of local organization: sub-county units, from the ward downward, had been designated by the County Organization Law as purely self-government bodies; now local home rule formed only part of their function – they were to serve also as lower-level administrative units under county officials. The county itself was now primarily administrative and only secondarily a home-rule unit. On all levels, the functions of self-government were more closely circumscribed: police, for example, were to be solely the business of national administrative organs, not agents of any self-government body. Procedures were recommended which would give the county magistrate greater supervisory power over the budgets and activities of self-government bodies, including a virtual veto over any resolutions passed by self-government assemblies. These recommendations of the civil administrators were

---

[32] *Ibid.* 830–1; Chao Ju-heng, *Ti-fang tzu-chih*, 350ff.

directed at a supervising and controlling self-government bodies, and even turning them into auxiliary branches of county administration. At the same time, they were a recognition that the powers of the Nanking government to enforce its writ in the form of a standardized and reorganized local administrative system were very limited.[33]

Another important change recommended by the second civil administration conference was the abolition of the specialized bureaus (*chü*) in county administration and the subsuming of their functions under the analogous sections of the county government. The significance of this idea went beyond mere simplification. It had the effect of returning county administration to a more conventional format by strengthening the authority of the magistrate over all sectors of public life. However, this enhancement of the magistrate's authority may have been based less in traditional practice than in the effort by the 'CC clique' to extend its influence by inserting modern-trained graduates of its Central Political Institute into county magistracies in KMT-controlled provinces. If so, then the erosion of the magistrate's power since the Ch'ing was indeed a serious problem. Chiang Kai-shek complained in 1932, for example, that the proliferation of specialized bureaus had taken much power from the magistrate; in practice, he said, it was the analogous departments (*t'ing*) of the provincial government that had the power to appoint and supervise bureau heads in the counties.[34]

Losers under the new policy were the specialists at the provincial level, as well as local elites who had participated in the work of the bureaus since the early republic. Neither group would now have much control over county resources. Just how deep was the involvement of local elites in the county bureaus by the 1930s is a question awaiting research. It seems likely that it had diminished somewhat from the days of the early republic, when local literati had considerable control over bureaus such as education and economic development. If so, then the abolition of bureaus and their amalgamation into the sections of county government (*ts'ai-chü kai-k'o*), which became a watchword of governmental reform during the mid 1930s, was the final step in a process of bringing county government back to a more conventional bureaucratic format. Reducing local participation of this sort was analogous to the virtual scuttling of plans for local self-government which occurred during the early years of Nationalist rule.[35]

These policies, which were largely adopted by 1937, were close to the

---

[33] *Nei-cheng nien-chien* (Ministry of Interior year book), 1936, B. 639–42.
[34] Ch'eng Fang, *Chung-kuo hsien-cheng kai-lun* (An introduction to county government in China), 39.
[35] Ch'ien Tuan-sheng, *Min-kuo cheng-chih shih*, 551ff.

spirit of the 'bandit suppression' (anti-Communist) campaigns then being commanded from Chiang Kai-shek's military headquarters at Nanchang. Until we have access to operational documents from the archives, we shall have to rely on inference to determine where the bureaucratization drive originated. But the evidence suggests clearly that Chiang and his close advisers promoted them.

For example, the programme of abolishing bureaus seems to have originated in Hupei in 1932-3 as part of a campaign to reduce administrative expenses, possibly under the sponsorship of Chiang's protégé, Chang Ch'ün. Taken up by the 'bandit-suppression' of Communist bases in Hupei, Honan and Anhwei, the programme became official policy at the county level. In March 1934, Chiang Kai-shek convened a conference of provincial administrators at his Nanchang headquarters to devise new measures of civil administration to complement his military suppression campaigns in Kiangsi and other 'bandit-suppression provinces'. The 'bureaus into sections' idea was announced as general policy in the report by Chiang's administrative secretary, Yang Yung-t'ai. Formal regulations were promulgated in December 1934 for all bandit-suppression provinces.[36] Whether or not this reform achieved its purpose of strengthening the authority of the county magistrate, it must be conceded that the system it supplanted was wasteful and confusing. To have documents passing between specialized county bureaus and their counterparts in the provincial capitals, without ever crossing the desk of the magistrate, was a recipe for weakening county government and injecting yet another patronage system into local politics.

Another bureaucratic advance of the mid-thirties was the reestablishment of the ward (ch'ü) as a sub-county public security unit. It will be recalled that the ward was originally borrowed from the Shansi example, and eventually was to take on self-governing powers. It was then temporarily abandoned in favour of the three-tier system of natural units from the early republic. But the anti-Communist campaigns of the 1930s brought the ward back into prominence. Originating with the Hupei-Honan-Anhwei bandit-suppression headquarters (like the effort to eliminate bureaus), this measure took shape in 1932 as a way of introducing a public security office that could supervise the reinstituted pao-chia system. This measure, too, was endorsed by Chiang Kai-shek at the 1934

---

[36] Ko-sheng kao-chi hsing-cheng jen-yuan feng-chao Nanchang chi-hui chi-lu (Record of the meeting of high provincial administrators held at Nanchang) issued by the Headquarters of the Chairman of the National Government Military Commission, Nanchang, June 1934. On county government see 'Work critiques' on pp. 52–5. Also see Ch'eng Mao-hsing, Chiao-fei ti-fang hsing-cheng chih-tu (Governmental system of the bandit-suppression areas); Ch'ien Tuan-sheng, Min-kuo cheng-chih shih, 556–7; Ch'en Chih-mai, Chung-kuo cheng-fu (The Chinese government), 3.83–7.

Nanchang Conference. The problem was that strengthening government at the county level was not enough. Below the ward level, complained Yang Yung-t'ai, was still a world of the 'corrupt local bullies and evil gentry'. These were presumably more likely to incite rebellion than to pacify it.[37] In any event, such local elites were not seen as effective tools of a reformed county administration. Instead, the five bandit-suppression provinces (Honan, Hupei, Anhwei, Kiangsi and Fukien) were now ordered (December 1934) to establish between three and six wards in every county, their headmen to be appointed by the provincial governments on recommendation by county magistrates. A bureaucratic touch borrowed from the Shansi system was that ward headmen might not serve within their home counties: the rule of avoidance, traditionally the bridle of the regular bureaucracy, was now to control personnel at the sub-county level.[38]

Between county and province, the tightening of bureaucratic control also left its mark. Although the Nanking government had abolished the intermediate level of circuit (tao), which the early republic had inherited from the Ch'ing, the peculiar difficulties of local administration in the 1930s induced a number of provincial governments to reinstitute this scale of supervision. The officials known as administrative supervisors (hsing-cheng tu-ch'a chuan-yuan) were appointed first in the bandit-suppression provinces in 1932 but were gradually instituted more widely. Internal security, especially the anti-Communist campaigns, was their chief concern. The new institution arose out of such organizations as the 'branch government/party committees' set up for anti-Communist work in Kiangsi. The promulgation of the system did not proceed initially through the regular procedures of the central government, but rather (like the county-level measures just discussed) through the military Communist-suppression headquarters. Because of their dubious legitimacy in the constitutional scheme (which officially held to a two-level system of province/county), the administrative supervisors were considered a 'temporary' measure in the Executive Yuan directives that finally emerged. In practice, the appointment of circuit-level supervisors (often serving magistrates holding the office concurrently) involved a confused mixture of civil and military regulations emanating from Nanking and from the bandit-suppression headquarters.[39] This piling-up of supervisory layers was contrary to the spirit of the Kuomintang's theoretical inheritance, which stressed popular mobilization over bureaucratic machinery. The impressive persistence of this middle-layer unit in local

[37] Ko-sheng kao-chi hsing-cheng jen-yuan...(Report of the Nanchang Conference, 1934) Work critiques, 56.
[38] Ch'eng Mao-hsing, 111-28.
[39] Ch'ien Tuan-sheng, Min-kuo cheng-chih shih, 526ff.

administration also suggests the persisting weakness of the province-county link in a country with poor communications and cumbersome administrative routines.

It may well be wondered whether the Kuomintang party itself had anything to offer the development of new relationships between local government and society. Although the party was envisaged by Sun as a supervisor of political 'tutelage', in practice the county-level Kuomintang branches found themselves virtually helpless to influence the conduct of the local bureaucracy. Dependent on government for their funding, inferior to the bureaucracy in prestige (and in access to high provincial officials), county branches were at best an awkward inconvenience to county administrators and were hardly likely to serve as the nuclei of greater popular participation in local government. Here, as in other respects, the weight of the bureaucratic state lay heavily upon the political system as a whole.[40]

It was during the exile at Chungking that the Nationalist government attempted to redress the balance between bureaucracy and participation, and in the process to reinvigorate local government. This was the highly touted 'New County System' (*hsin-hsien-chih*), first outlined by Chiang Kai-shek in June 1939. The new system, which unfortunately remained largely a paper plan save in areas near the wartime capital, envisaged a county government with a secure local tax base and a mechanism for self-government. County revenues were to include designated fractions of the land tax and certain miscellaneous excises, all of which were to be collected by the county government itself, not by provincial or central agencies. Higher levels of government could no longer force counties to raise funds locally for provincial or national projects. With this strengthened tax base, the county would supposedly be able to implement a genuine local self-government system, with some real funds for the county assembly to appropriate. The assembly was to be built up of representatives from towns (*chen*) and townships (*hsiang*), which themselves drew representatives from none other than the *pao-chia* units, which were now declared to be for both 'self-defence and self-government'. Though there was no hope of adequately testing this system during wartime, it does suggest that Chiang was well aware of the declining effectiveness of local government and of its failure to elicit mass support.[41]

[40] David Tsai, 'Party government relations in Kiangsu Province, 1927–1932', *Select papers from the Center for Far Eastern Studies*, 1 (1975–6) 85–118.
[41] Ch'ien Tuan-sheng, *Min-kuo cheng-chih shih*, 176ff.

THE RURAL RECONSTRUCTION MOVEMENT

While governments attempted to control rural China, making what use they could of twentieth-century ideologies, some Chinese intellectuals did rural work in a different way. The vogue of the 'peasant problem' (*nung-min wen-t'i*) in 1927 was, in one sense, nothing new: rural uplift formed one focus of reformists' concern in late imperial times. What was new was the fascination of some urban intellectuals with problems of rural development, intellectuals who had in many cases been educated in Western fashion and who had little personal experience with the rural sector of Chinese life. Their approaches to rural problems involved some political experiments, but more typically aimed at educational work in the villages. In this sense 'rural reconstruction' shared the liberal conviction that political-institutional change was meaningless unless based on a change of consciousness. Rural reconstructionists also tended to believe that the political forms of rural life would never be sound until peasants learned to cope with their terrible economic problems.

Rural reconstruction (*hsiang-ts'un chien-she*) was associated with several key conceptions. 'Reconstruction' (*chien-she*) seems actually closer to our idea of 'development', and may be considered a modernized extension of the old 'public works' rubric in traditional Chinese government. Associated with it were the ideas of 'investigation' and 'experiment', the first describing the increasingly popular exercise whereby concerned urban intellectuals got in touch with rural conditions through on-the-spot surveys (the whole August 1927 issue of the *Eastern Miscellany* (*Tung-fang tsa-chih*) was devoted to such reports). The second involved field projects in education and rural extension work, some of which became quite famous both at home and abroad; 'demonstration' would be a more appropriate way to describe them, since they were designed as models for nationwide imitation.

The continuity of elite concern for rural problems is seen in the history of Ting county, Hopei, which was the site of one of the best known of these demonstrations. Amid the enthusiasm of the post-1900 'new policies' (*hsin-cheng*) reforms, a prominent elite family in the market town of Chai-ch'eng sought to transform local society through education – hardly a new activity for rural elites, but animated now by nationalism and by a radical scepticism about conventional neo-Confucian views. Mi Chien-san, the founder of reform in Chai-ch'eng, believed that Confucian teachings had been perverted by undue stress on self-cultivation and not enough on practical government. Restating some early Ch'ing critiques, he saw hidden Buddhist influence in Chu Hsi's classical commentaries, the canons of the civil service examinations. Having failed the provincial examination himself, he forbade his son, Ti-kang, to take it. Instead, the family were to devote themselves to practical service (*ching-shih*) in their home town.[42]

In 1902–3, Mi Chien-san was asked by the magistrate to create a system of modern-style schools in Ting county. Mi's system extended beyond the standard school format to stress popular literacy and citizen education. As the local self-government movement was being promulgated after 1908, the Mi family naturally took a leading role. Chai-ch'eng soon became an active model of local reformism, with the emphasis on education, public mores (anti-opium, anti-footbinding), and local security. Chien-san's Japanese returned son, Mi Ti-kang, saw the strengthening of the village format as the basis of a nationwide revival. Village-level communal institutions (especially in compulsory education and farm credit) would form a new basis for rural society.[43] Beginning in 1924, Mi Ti-kang collaborated with the Shantungese reformer Wang Hung-i to found an informal association in Peking to promote their ideas. This 'village government group' (*ts'un-chih p'ai*) eventually attracted the attention of Liang Shu-ming, who went on to become the most influential of the Confucian-oriented rural reconstructionists. (As we have seen, the ideas of the Mi family had already been taken over as the rationale for a 'village government system' in Shansi.)[44]

Given more than two decades of success in Ting county, it was appropriate that Yen Yang-ch'u (Jimmy Yen) should have chosen the county as the locus of his Mass Education Association's principal rural site. Yen, American-educated and a Christian, had been active since 1922 in urban mass education. In 1926 Ting county was selected by his Mass Education Association (Chung-hua p'ing-min chiao-yü ts'u-chin hui) as the centre of its national efforts, and in 1930 Yen himself moved there from Peking. The association's vigorous work in basic literacy, along with Yen's international connections, made Chai-ch'eng and Ting county a magnet for Chinese and foreign research workers in rural society. Work in Ting county was mainly in an 'experimental area', comprising some 60 villages and market towns. The number of 'people's schools' (*p'ing-min hsueh-hsiao*) directly managed by the association numbered only 20, out

---

[42] *Chai-ch'eng ts'un-chih*, 44–7. Sidney D. Gamble, *Ting Hsien: a North China rural community*, 146–65. Charles Hayford, 'Rural reconstruction in China: Y. C. James Yen and the Mass Education Movement' (Harvard University, Ph.D. dissertation, 1973).

[43] Mi Ti-kang, 'Yü chih Chung-kuo she-hui kai-liang chu-i' (My proposals for reforming Chinese society) reprinted in *Chai-ch'eng ts'un-chih*, 314–28.

[44] Alitto, *The last Confucian*, 145–7, has the authoritative account of the village government group.

of 440 being operated in the county by the year 1932 (the others being the product of county government or of purely local initiative).[45]

Yen's vision for rural China centred on developing its human potential rather than remaking its institutions. Illiteracy was a hopeless disadvantage in the international power-struggle, for 'how can a blind man compete with a normal seer?' Education would go beyond literacy to remedy China's four great ills: ignorance, poverty, physical weakness, and lack of public spirit. The programme of the people's schools therefore combined practical training with social morality and civics. Although concrete problems of social injustice were not attacked directly, the tone of the association's rhetoric was populist: most civilized nations run education for the elite, to train the sons of the propertied class (*tzu-ch'an chieh-chi*); the association's aim is to educate for the 'abolition of class education'. The implication was that national strength, along with democracy and economic progress, rested on the transformation of public consciousness; a task which could only be approached through education, and from the bottom of society upwards. Thus Yen's programme was not incompatible with the spirit of the original gentry-style efforts in Ting county; and, like the Mi family, Yen operated under the patronage and protection of the regular bureaucratic system.[46]

This melding of populism and patronage was also to be seen in the work of the mass educator T'ao Hsing-chih, who became involved in rural work as a born-again disciple of John Dewey. T'ao's fascination with Deweyan educational theory, which he studied at Columbia Teachers College between 1915 and 1917, fitted right into his existing belief in Wang Yang-ming's 'unity of knowledge and action' (*chih-hsing ho-i*). Dewey's distaste for a 'spectator' theory of knowledge, and Wang's insistence that right thinking and right action emerged simultaneously rather than one from the other, lent joint impetus to T'ao's activist nature. In the early twenties, T'ao became convinced that not only would a school-bounded education fail to reach China's masses, but also that the Western mode of education was basically unsuited to solving China's rural problems. Having been active in the city-based Mass Education Association, T'ao broke out of his urban and Western orientations simultaneously in 1927 when he opened a teacher-training school in a village outside Nanking. This school at Hsiao-chuang sought to remake young teacher-trainees by immersing them in the life of the peasantry. Only thus could they become

[45] K'ung Hsueh-hsiung, *Chung-kuo chin-jih chih nung-ts'un yun-tung* (The rural movement in contemporary China), 112.
[46] *Ibid.* 67–9. Yen's principal foreign support was from the Rockefeller Foundation.

effective village schoolmasters. T'ao's view of the school as a motive force in rural society was not too alien to the ideas of the gentry-reformers of Chai-ch'eng: teacher trainees operated as activists in various spheres of life, including the reform of morals, the improvement of agriculture, and the organization of local security. A self-defence corps was organized among 240 local villages and the peasants instructed in rudimentary military skills. T'ao, unlike Yen, was unabashedly nativist: the West was neither a likely source of inspiration for China's reform, nor a particularly attractive one.

T'ao's relationship to political authorities was ambivalent, and in the end his rural experiment was unable to secure the effective protection of anyone in power. A mysterious relationship existed between T'ao and Feng Yü-hsiang, the 'Christian general', a rival of Chiang Kai-shek who admired and probably aided the operation of the Hsiao-chuang school. Chiang himself took a brief interest in the progress of Hsiao-chuang, but in 1930 ordered it closed, probably because of what he considered its socially radical potential.[47]

Liang Shu-ming's rural reconstruction experiment in Shantung achieved at least a temporary protection by political authorities, and relied on a radically nativist Confucian reformism. Under a considerable grant of authority from Governor Han Fu-ch'ü (a general formerly in Feng Yü-hsiang's organization), the Shantung Rural Reconstruction Institute was opened in the county of Tsou-p'ing in 1931. Not only were numerous counties eventually designated as experimental reconstruction districts under the institute's guidance (more than 70 by 1937), but two counties were practically turned over to the institute's administrative control. Such an extraordinary delegation of powers was legitimized in 1933 by the Nationalist government itself, which was apparently seeking both to control and to profit from the various rural reconstruction projects then being undertaken. The guiding genius of the Shantung project, Liang Shu-ming, was the most explicitly nativist and socially radical of the rural reconstruction group. His radicalism was self-consciously anti-Western and based on Confucian premises. China had to blaze her own path toward modernity. That path could have nothing to do with the individualistic and selfish attitudes fostered by Western cultural contact, but instead must utilize the supposedly collectivist and unselfish spirit inherent to Chinese civilization.

Like T'ao Hsing-chih's school at Hsiao-chuang (which Liang admired), Liang's institute sought to train a special type of rural cadre: the educated

---

[47] See the recently published *T'ao Hsing-chih chiao-yü wen-hsuan* (Selected essays on education by T'ao Hsing-chih); also the 320 letters published in T'ao Hsing-chih, *Hsing-chih shu-hsin chi.*

youth who would be taught to endure the privations of the peasantry and communicate easily with them. The style was distinct from that of the Western-educated Jimmy Yen, whose Ting-hsien centre was decidedly not worshipful of Chinese traditional ways. Liang's cadre-students were mainly from rich peasant or landlord families, and therefore presumably already had a certain adaptability to rural ways. Confucian influence was prominent in the style of moral indoctrination and personal self-cultivation which characterized the routine of the school.

Local organization in Tsou-p'ing was also made to accord with Liang's neo-traditional bent. Sub-county divisions were redrawn to conform with supposedly 'natural' pre-existing areas, with the natural village (ts'un) and apparently the market areas (hsiang) as the format. Abandoned were the larger, more artificial wards and townships of the Nanking code. Administrative bodies on township and village levels were called 'schools', in accord with their educational and motivational approach to the peasantry. To what extent Tsou-p'ing's system furthered popular participation in local politics remains unclear. But the nativist emphasis assumed, at least, that rural ways were slow to change, and that forcing exotic new systems or coercive bureaucratic forms upon village society would lead nowhere. Building from below, thought Liang, required that government work slowly and unobtrusively through education and motivation of the peasantry. 'Too many restrictions, too much "helpful" initiative,' he thought, damage society without really improving matters. The weight of a busy, pushy government apparatus can only be an extra burden if there is no corresponding activism among the people.[48]

Quite a different spirit animated the local organization in western Honan run by P'eng Yü-t'ing, a former secretary of Feng Yü-hsiang. Where Liang stressed a return to native values and a utopian communalism, P'eng built his organization on the longstanding self-defence needs of village society. His was essentially a militia network transformed into a local government. P'eng may have absorbed some of his rural reconstruction ideas at Feng's headquarters, for Feng himself had apparently developed a lively interest in the subject (it will be remembered that he was a close friend of T'ao Hsing-chih). P'eng's approach to rural organization, however, built upon a more traditional base: the vigorous and ancient local defence tradition

---

[48] Liang Shu-ming, 'Pei-yu so chien chi-lueh' (An account of what I observed on my northward journey), in *Chung-kuo min-tsu tzu-chiu yun-tung chih tsui-hou chueh-wu* (The final realization about the Chinese people's self-help movement), 287–8. Kuo-min cheng-fu chün-shih wei-yuan-hui wei-yuan-chang hsing-ying, Hupeh ti-fang cheng-wu yen-chiu-hui tiao-ch'a-t'uan (Field HQ of the chairman of the National Government Military Commission, Hupeh local government study association), comp. *Tiao-ch'a hsiang-ts'un chien-she chi-yao* (Record of rural reconstruction investigations), 75–6. The foregoing account of Tsou-p'ing is indebted to Alitto, *The last Confucian*, esp. 238–78.

of the North China countryside. Linking villages in local defence compacts, led by lower gentry, was a natural response to regional banditry, and had characteristically displayed either pro- or anti-government spirit, depending on the situation. For all its localism, however, P'eng's organization in Chen-p'ing county had modern and patriotic dimensions. P'eng was linked to the village government group through Feng Yü-hsiang, who brought him together with Wang Hung-i (Liang Shu-ming's Shantungese reformer friend) and Liang Shu-ming himself in 1929, to found a Honan Village Government Academy. Ideologically, P'eng's local regime in Chen-p'ing had a nationalistic flavour derived (in P'eng's own words) explicitly from Sun Yat-sen's conception of bottom-up constitution building. It was unfortunate for P'eng that the direction of his movement was, by force of circumstance, anti-government. The only way to participate in China's national revolution, he declared, was to foster 'local revolution' – a necessary precursor to 'local self-government' in that area because of society's need to protect itself against rapacious government troops ('bandit soldiers') and greedy local officials. In the end, P'eng found himself taking over local government in Chen-p'ing (with associates doing the same in neighbouring counties). After Chiang Kai-shek's followers assumed power in Honan in 1930, P'eng's consistent refusal to comply with government tax demands made him a marked man. He was assassinated by 'bandits' in 1933. An enterprise such as P'eng's could hardly survive the Nanking government's determination to bureaucratize local society and wipe out all vestiges of 'local self-government'.[49]

Predictably, the Nanking authorities became involved in rural reconstruction too. 'Experimental counties' were established, under the sponsorship of the Nanking authorities, at Lan-hsi (Chekiang) and Chiang-ning (Kiangsu), operating as explicit models of bureaucratic local reform. Chiang-ning, right outside Nanking, was designed as a model administrative system under the aegis of the Kiangsu provincial government. Staffed by faculty and students of the Central Political Institute (Chung-yang cheng-chih hsueh-hsiao – a CC clique institution), it was an avowedly top-down reform project, and also a showplace for visitors. A county governing committee supervised the work of the magistrate's office, and itself reported directly to the provincial government. The tax system was administered by a trained, salaried staff (a reform measure that had been proposed since early in the century). All tax revenues were retained and disbursed within the county – hardly a demonstration of practical reality.

[49] *Chen p'ing hsien tzu-chih kai-k'uang* (Local self-government in Chen-p'ing county); Guy S. Alitto, 'Rural elites in transition: China's cultural crisis and the problem of legitimacy', in *Select papers from the Center for Far Eastern Studies*, 3 (1978–9) 218–86.

Lower-level unit boundaries were redrawn to conform to natural villages and market streets. The townships and market towns (*hsiang* and *chen*) were supposed to be self-governing after a suitable period of tutelage. Unfortunately, little seems to have been accomplished. By the testimony of Ch'en Kuo-fu, former governor of Kiangsu, the experiment was more name than reality. It foundered on poor leadership at the magistrate's level and little or no tutelage of the local communities. By 1936 it was acknowledged to be a failure, and the county's 'experimental' status was abolished.[50]

Rural reconstruction thus involved a broad range of types: Western-influenced and nativist, educational and military, populist and bureaucratic. Common to all was a strong political relevance. To revitalize the countryside through educational and economic reforms meant working out relationships of patronage and protection with political authorities. This was surely because any attempt to work with the peasantry in an organized project inevitably raised questions of political orientation and legitimacy, whether or not the project had any explicitly political aims or activities. From their earliest days, the Ting-hsien and Tsou-p'ing projects secured the blessings or acquiescence of provincial authorities. The Nanking-administered experiments, it could be said, had such heavy bureaucratic input that they were unable to generate more than a pallid local response. The independent projects of T'ao Hsing-chih and P'eng Yü-t'ing were not only without sufficient political patronage, but also aroused the suspicion and antagonism of state power: T'ao, because of his populist leanings and independent style; P'eng, because of his open resistance to corrupt and predatory state agents. Both these unorthodox experiments were crushed. The rural reconstruction experiments as a whole fared no better in the end; the Japanese invasion wiped them all out. What remained was a legacy of widespread interest in basing China's nation-building effort in rural society; and, by implication, a recognition that rural reform could not survive in a hostile political environment. The base-areas concept, developed by the Communists, was an attempt to encase a new rural system in its own political and military protection.

Participation and bureaucracy: the historical process

From the material presented here, it appears that the dichotomy suggested at the beginning of the chapter may not represent a true contradiction

---

[50] Ch'en Kuo-fu, *Su-cheng hui-i* (Memories of governing Kiangsu), 14. Hsu Ying-lien *et al. Ch'üan-kuo hsiang-ts'un chien-she yun-tung kai-k'uang* (General account of the nation-wide rural reconstruction movement), 530–648.

at all. The development of local government has not, in fact, been a series of choices between more participatory or more bureaucratic alternatives. Rather, development has proceeded as an alternation, with popular demands for access to local politics providing the framework in which bureaucracy could make further inroads. The determination of the Ch'ing court to move ahead with a constitution was conceived from a mind-set in which participation would end in the strengthening of bureaucratic prerogatives. The history of county assemblies indicates a beginning full of enthusiasm and with broad involvement by the local elite, ending with cooptation of assembly leadership by the magistrate's executive council and the ultimate strengthening of his administrative power.

Patterns of sub-county division that originated in gentry activism and communitarian élan (the Chai-ch'eng 'model') lent impetus to a heavily bureaucratic and authoritarian system of local management (Yen Hsi-shan's 'village system'). Sun Yat-sen's bottom-upwards model of political development, with its vibrant populist tone and 'self-government' prescriptions, did indeed produce some initial plans which might have led to greater participation in local politics. Yet the way these plans were modified by the Nanking regime during the thirties meant that the very units which were supposed to be vehicles for self-government became units for deeper bureaucratic penetration of local society.

Participation and bureaucracy have been, it seems, interrelated in a close historical nexus; the eagerness of elites (and, to some degree, the broader citizenry) for access to politics did indeed produce strong surges of institutional reform. But riding the crest were the agencies of the bureaucratic state. These were what remained when the waves receded.

CHAPTER 8

THE GROWTH OF THE
ACADEMIC COMMUNITY 1912–1949

Institutions of learning not only educate oncoming generations but also create, import and disseminate culture and technology. By performing such vital functions, a modern nation's schools and colleges, libraries and laboratories become of central importance to the state as well as to the society in general. In the Chinese case, moreover, education had from early times been a principal concern of government, and so it would become, eventually, a central focus of the Chinese revolution after 1949. Meanwhile during the first half of the twentieth century, education proliferated in China in the most varied forms and with many kinds of foreign influence and participation. The voluminous record is widely scattered and just beginning to be studied.[1] For example, new work suggests that functional literacy among the common people was more widespread than was formerly assumed. Many important aspects of twentieth-century education need attention – the inheritance of social style and pedagogic method from the thousands of academies (*shu-yuan*) that had functioned in late imperial China, the growth of a modern school system and of urban public education through the press, the formal education of women, the rise of publishing houses like the Commercial Press (Shang-wu yin-shu-kuan, founded at Shanghai in 1896, a great publisher of journals as well as textbooks), and the founding of educational associations and new schools as seedbeds of reform and revolution.[2]

[1] For helpful comments on this chapter we are indebted to Chiang Yung-chen, Paul A. Cohen, Merle Goldman, Jerome Grieder, William J. Haas, John Israel and Suzanne Pepper, among others. Education is a subject peculiarly rich in documentation. The principal early compilations of documents by Shu Hsin-ch'eng (4 vols. 1928; 3 vols. 1962) and the most recent by Taga Akigorō (3 vols. 1976) are noted in the bibliographical essay below.

[2] On literacy see Evelyn S. Rawski, *Education and popular literacy in Ch'ing China.* On *shu-yuan* see Tilemann Grimm, 'Academies and urban systems in Kwangtung', in G. William Skinner, ed. *The city in late imperial China,* 475–98. On the new school system to 1911, Sally Borthwick, *Education and social change in China: the beginnings of the modern era.* On the Commercial Press's work in education see Wang Yun-wu, *Shang-wu yin-shu-kuan yü hsin chiao-yü nien-p'u* (A chronology of the Commercial Press and the New Education), covering events, publications, reports, etc. 1897–1972. On the vicissitudes of education in one province (Shantung) see David D. Buck, 'Educational modernization in Tsinan, 1899–1937', in Mark Elvin and G. William Skinner, eds. *The Chinese city between two worlds,* 171–212. The overall problems of education in modern China will be discussed by Suzanne Pepper in *CHOC* 14, ch. 4.

Within this broad terrain, the focus of this chapter is limited to higher education. This fact in itself testifies to the scholarly neglect thus far of the vital story of elementary and secondary education in Republican China. It also reflects the greater visibility of efforts made by China's revolutionary educators to create elite institutions capable of producing new upper- class leaders.

After 1911 the Chinese government's prolonged weakness opened an unusual window of opportunity for China's revolutionary educators. Fervently patriotic and still endowed as a class with the prestige of scholarship, they had an opportunity to lead the way in creating the academic institutions needed for modernity. Their new role had both intellectual and institutional aspects. Intellectually they confronted the necessity of reconciling the Chinese and Western Cultural traditions – a task more awesome in its dimensions than most human minds have ever faced. The vast proportions of this intellectual problem and how it was approached have been appraised in other volumes in this series.[3] The present chapter therefore focuses on the academic community and its institutional achievements in the first half of the twentieth century.

We confront here a tremendously complex but largely unexplored story with three main facets. First, China's intellectual history has outpaced her institutional history, and we know more about the late Ch'ing schools of Neo-Confucian thought – the Sung and Han learning, New Text and Old Text scholarship, even the T'ung-ch'eng school – than we do about the network of academies, libraries, printing shops and patrons that sustained Confucian scholarship. Second, in China's relations with Japan, politics has thus far eclipsed the academic story. Most of the thousands of Chinese students who went to Tokyo returned to careers of service in their homeland; not all by any means became revolutionaries. Many no doubt taught in the new schools of law and government (*fa-cheng hsueh-t'ang*) that proliferated in the late Ch'ing, but the content and reach of their teaching, like other aspects of Japanese influence in Republican China, remain still largely unknown. Third, the educational influences streaming into China from Europe and America constitute a vast terrain of unimaginable variety and unexplored proportions. Nearly all the nations and all the disciplines were involved in this largest of all cultural migrations. For example, Catholic and Protestant missions in all their diversity lay behind the Christian colleges in the Chinese Republic, yet they were but threads in a tapestry. The modern West was in flux and China herself was embarked on many transformations. Methods, curricula, textbooks and systems of instructions from Japan, Europe and America

---

[3] See *CHOC* 11, ch. 5 and *CHOC* 12, chs. 7 and 8. For a more recent fresh account see Jerome B. Grieder, *Intellectuals and the state in modern China: a narrative history.*

all added their stimuli to the educational maelstrom in which the deeply imbedded values and social roles of the old Chinese literati underwent a gradual adaptation to modern needs. Given this preponderance of the yet-to-be-discovered over the known, this chapter attempts only to block out major areas and aspects of a new field.

One feature, however, is clear – in the face of Japanese expansion the institutional structure of the unequal treaty system including extraterritoriality persisted; and foreign, especially American, influence on Chinese higher education reached a high point despite the rapid rise of Chinese nationalism. The 1920s in particular were a period of vigorous Sino-American collaboration in science and higher education.

THE EMERGENCE OF MODERN INSTITUTIONS 1898–1928

For analytic purposes we look in succession at the training of personnel, the formation of certain major institutions, and aspects of research and financial support. In each case our reconnaissance tries to offer representative examples drawn from a terrain which is still imperfectly surveyed. Provincial, municipal and technical/vocational institutions are largely beyond our purview.[4]

Personnel: an elite trained abroad

The leaders in the building-up of higher education were a truly extraordinary group of people who responded to the needs of an extraordinary time. When China's modern transformation required the creation of a system of higher education comparable to the new systems arising in other countries, this meant in human terms the training of a new scholar class versed in Western as well as Chinese learning – a truly revolutionary departure from long-established tradition. So revolutionary was this very idea – that Chinese could and indeed must learn from foreigners – that efforts in this direction after 1860 had been comparatively few and ineffective in comparison, for example, with Japan and India. The Ch'ing government's inability to provide modern learning within China and to control those Chinese students it sent to study in Tokyo had in fact proved to be a major cause of its downfall. The new educational elite thus grew to maturity in an age of revolutionary change. In setting up new institutions they felt themselves to be creators of a new world, not by any means the defenders of an establishment already in being. One can

---

[4] In 1922 a survey by the National Association for the Advancement of Education reported the existence of 1,553 vocational schools in China. By 1925 the National Association for Vocational Education was composed of more than 100 educational bodies. *China year book*, hereafter *CYB*, *1926*, 423.

only imagine the adventurous and determined spirit of those Chinese women who came into higher education at a time when footbinding was still being widely practised as the ancient Chinese way of keeping women in subjection.

Several things characterized these educators. First of all, they were generally men and women educated abroad. The generation of Liang Ch'i-ch'ao (1873–1929) had sought foreign learning in Japan, that of Hu Shih (1891–1962) sought it in Western Europe and the United States. The size of this student migration is imperfectly known because, for example, many more Chinese enrolled in Japanese schools and colleges than ever graduated. One estimate of enrollees during 1900–37 is 136,000, while the best figure for Chinese graduates from Japanese institutions during 1901–39 is 12,000.[5] The political contribution made by these returned students from Japan stands out in the annals of the Revolution of 1911; their academic contribution has been generally lost to sight. After 1915 the growing antagonism engendered by Japanese expansion and China's rising nationalism all but eclipsed the Chinese academic debt to Japan; no doubt future studies will exhume and appraise it.[6]

The Sino-Japanese antagonism helped to turn Republican China's scholars toward Western Europe and America. Chinese students making the longer journey to the West required more financing and so were more carefully chosen, more specifically committed, and more likely to complete their studies. One estimate is that during the century 1854–1953, 21,000 Chinese studied in American institutions.[7]

However these figures may be further refined and analysed, it is evident that the 20,000 or so Chinese who returned from the West in the twentieth century were a remarkably small but potent group. In numbers, among a population of some 400 million, they were as few in proportion as had been the metropolitan graduates (*chin-shih*) under the old regime. But where their predecessors in the triennial examinations at Peking had customarily accepted a personal bond of loyalty to the emperor who nominally conducted the palace examinations, these scholars from the Chinese Republic found that their foreign experience confirmed their patriotic devotion to the Chinese nation. This new 'returned-student' elite were more than ever mindful of the Sung reformer Fan Chung-yen's

---

[5] See M. Jansen, *CHOC* 11.351, citing Sanetō Keishū, *Chūgokujin Nihon ryūgaku shi*, the major work of the top Japanese specialist on Sino-Japanese educational relations.

[6] The principal survey by Y. C. Wang, *Chinese intellectuals and the West 1872–1949*, actually includes the late Ch'ing efforts to learn from Japan as well as extensive data on many later aspects of this subject. Aspects of Sino-Japanese intellectual relations are explored in Akira Iriye, ed. *The Chinese and the Japanese: essays in political and cultural interactions.*

[7] How many graduated is uncertain. See Y. C. Wang, 119–20, 167, 185, citing data from the China Institute in America.

dictum, 'a scholar should be the first to become concerned with the world's troubles and the last to rejoice at its happiness'.[8] While the proportions of returned students who went into government, industry, the professions, the arts and education is still unknown, it seems plain that they enjoyed a special status derived from old custom as well as from modern revolution. They functioned in a widespread network of interpersonal relations or *kuan-hsi*. Those who elected to embark upon the task of creating a system of higher education clung firmly to the classical tradition that the scholar is not a mere technical expert but must think like a statesman on behalf of the whole society, rulers and people alike. This sense of a responsibility helped the new leaders returned from Europe and America to begin building the academic institutions of the early republic – the colleges, universities, libraries, laboratories and research institutions needed in a twentieth-century nation.

Yet their extraordinary status as a selected (or self-elected) few who had achieved the top level of scholarship was not an unmixed blessing. Their experience abroad, usually a period of several years necessary to secure a Ph.D. degree, led these liberal intellectuals into a cosmopolitan stance of unavoidable ambivalence.[9] Like all who study abroad, they became to some degree bicultural, at home both in China's elite culture and in that of the outer world. Added to their elite status as scholars, this acquisition of foreign ways made them all the more alienated from village China. The fact that they forged common bonds with the Western liberal arts tradition ensured that the New Culture movement in education would foster more than the mere transfer of technology, but it raised acutely the problems of making their foreign training effective and relevant to China's problems, both in fact and (equally important) in the eyes of China's political and military elite who were called upon to give the educators continuing support. At the same time, some feel that their foreign orientation threatened these scholars with deracination, a loss of the sense of community with their homeland, in short, anomie and alienation. Bicultural experience can confuse one's identity. The proportions of this problem are as yet unknown. It may have been all the greater for those many individuals of the May Fourth generation who had, in fact, a threefold educational background: Chinese (traditional and early modern), Japanese, and American-European.[10]

Thus the task of importing foreign learning (in both technology and

[8] See James T. C. Liu, 'An early Sung reformer: Fan Chung-yen', in John K. Fairbank, ed. *Chinese thought and institutions*, 111.

[9] The paradoxes of this ambivalence were explained in particular by Joseph Levenson. His last work was *Revolution and cosmopolitanism: the Western stage and the Chinese stages*.

[10] To get an impression of the type of training received by educators of the Republican revolutionary

values) was complicated both inside and out. Within himself, the foreign-trained educator had to work out his self-image of how best to make his contribution. In his environment, meanwhile, he might confront quite different expectations of how he should behave. One new feature of modern education was the burden of administration. Residential and, soon, coeducational colleges were a new phenomenon with an infinite capacity to generate student opinion and organization, leading to strikes and political movements. The new students of the Republic shared their teachers' concern and sense of responsibility for the fate of the nation. Often they demanded political action. Note 11 offers an impression of the activities to which the educational elite applied themselves. Only a small minority were able to pursue pure scholarship. Keeping their institutions running was a constant problem.[11]

generation, we surveyed the experience of 75 persons as follows:

Educational background	Number	% of total
1. Passed traditional examinations at various levels	16 (minimum)	20
2. In Chinese modern-style schools		
a. as students	54	72
b. as teacher or staff	30	40
3. Studied abroad in		
a. Japan	21	28
b. Europe and/or US	24	35

The information is based on a representative selection of leading individuals, the *Biographical dictionary of Republican China*, hereafter *BDRC*, ed. Howard L. Boorman and Richard C. Howard; and *Hsin-hai ko-ming hui-i lu* (Recollections of the 1911 Revolution), 5 vols. There are inevitable overlappings between the categories. A further look into the social background of all those who took part in various liberal-reformist movements among the biographies in *BDRC* shows that over one-third had come from the scholar-official class: Virginia E. Reynolds, 'Social movements: an analysis of leadership in China 1895–1927' (Pennsylvania State University, Ph.D. dissertation, 1983), Part VB: Quantitative summary.

[11] To get an impression of the career activities of leading members of the academic community 1912–49, we totalled up the types of work pursued by 173 individuals. Roughly a third pursued more than one type of activity.

Type of work	Number of activities (not of individuals)	% of total
Academic teaching and research only	37	21.3
Teaching and educational administration	73	42.4
Teaching and research-institution administration	25	14.4
Teaching and government service outside education	36	20.8
Teaching and voluntary services	24	13.8
Teaching combined with other professional work (e.g. library, journalism, publishing, writing)	38	21.9

This list is based on the biographies of 173 individuals in *BDRC* whose professional activities ranged

Sooner or later the educators also faced as a group the problem of their relationship to political authority. Labouring in the shadow of the 1200-year-old government examination system that was abolished only in 1905, the Western-trained educators inherited the values and issues that had concerned preceding generations of Chinese scholars at the same time that they embraced new values and models met abroad. They succeeded in creating by the 1930s a more autonomous and diverse system of higher education, less directly under the thumb of the government and of an official orthodoxy. Yet this was a temporary situation, due to the lack of both a central government and an orthodoxy during the warlord era. Education in China, because of the tradition of scholar-government, remained intertwined with politics. Higher education had always been for the ruling stratum, not for the individual commoner. To divorce it from the ideological orthodoxy of the state would not be easy. Small wonder that the growth of a more independent type of education separate from politics was fitful and halting.

Moreover, in the early republic education was facilitated not only by the weakness of central power but also by the pluralistic influence of the imperialist powers. The interest of foreigners in China included the fostering of modern education both through Christian missionary schools and colleges and through the setting up of autonomous educational foundations, both protected by extraterritoriality. China's academic development in 1912–49 may be seen as part of the worldwide growth of modern learning in which North and South Americans, Russians, Japanese and Indians all at one time or another turned to Western Europe for enlightenment. Yet one side-effect of the Chinese educated elite's participation in the international world was its vulnerability to the xenophobic charge of being foreign-oriented. This bicultural, bilingual elite educated in the outside world paid the price of sometimes feeling or appearing as strangers in their homeland, even as persons in foreign pay.

The psychological and intellectual pressures of their experience in China and abroad would move some of the politically minded wing of the returned-student generation toward Marxism. The academically inclined wing was also in need of a new system of belief, new verities to steer by. Many educators adopted a fervent belief in the efficacy of science. Indeed the talisman for China's catching up with the outside world became the universal truth of 'science', which had figured in reformist thinking of the 1890s as well as the New Culture movement. China's educators sought

from partial affiliation (such as teaching at college level for a short period only) to life-long involvement with various aspects of higher educational and research institutions. The group is admittedly selective, but it embraces those persons who most actively influenced the growth of the modern academic community.

her salvation through the applications of the 'scientific method', not only in the natural and social sciences but in the humanistic sciences and Chinese historical studies as well. For some it was a tenet of faith which took on almost religious proportions. Wang Feng-chieh, a professor of education, expressed the prevalent attitudes of the 1920s when he declared that

The old educational system and old national customs have been destroyed. New education – an education based on science – has begun... We must realize that an educational system cannot be obtained through imitation, but must be achieved through deliberation and experience. Western ways of education cannot be transplanted in their entirety to China; we must consider the conditions in China and make appropriate choices. Therefore my conclusion is the new education must be guided by science: theories should be based on scientific data and proof, practice should follow scientific methods, and the results should be counted up scientifically.[12]

Here were the main themes underlying educational modernization in the early republic: that the old order had been irrevocably disabled with the collapse of the imperial system, that China must work to establish a new system of education of its own, and – following the rise of the New Culture movement – that 'science' and scientific methods would prove to be the firmest foundation upon which the new system could be built.[13]

Universities: the creation of institutions

Bringing young men and also women into residential communities presided over by faculty members was as much an innovation as the rise of the factory system in industry. Similarly it had its forebears in China's long educational history, though the connections have hardly been explored as yet. The conscious aim of those who built up higher education was usually to imitate foreign models. But which ones? The choice might well be influenced by the foreign model's resonance with Chinese needs or traditions. Unfortunately, while biographical materials are abundant, institutional histories are still few. Below we look first at Peking University, then at private, technical and Christian institutions, and finally at the role played by foreign funding.

Peking University. In 1912 the new republic inherited from the fallen Ch'ing dynasty, among other things, a small and rather uncertain institution named Ching-shih ta-hsueh-t'ang or 'Metropolitan University'.

---

[12] Wang Feng-chieh, *Chung-kuo chiao-yü-shih ta-kang* (An outline history of Chinese education), 5. Wang was at Ch'en-kuang University in Changsha.

[13] On the various views of 'Science' in the New Culture movement, see B. I. Schwartz's summary in *CHOC* 12.424–8, 440; also D. W. Y. Kwok, *Scientism in Chinese thought 1900–1950*.

Founded during the reforms of 1898, it drew heavily on the modernized Japanese model while attempting to meet what its founders perceived to be an urgent Chinese need: to retrain some of the Ch'ing scholar-officials so they would be reasonably knowledgeable about affairs and conditions of the modern world. Surviving the empress dowager's *coup d'état* of 1898, this institution was reorganized in 1902 to add a teacher-training division, and at the same time absorb the Interpreters' College or T'ung-wen kuan, thus adding five foreign language programmes as well as basic sciences to the existing curriculum.[14]

The students in Peking University at the turn of the century were mainly officials who enrolled to be taught a minimum of modern subjects, but even before the 1911 Revolution the assessment of their accomplishments were extremely low.[15] The quality of the students was uneven. Some, their minds still firmly imbedded in the old civil examination system, treated their experience at the new academy as a step toward another qualifying degree, thereby giving the institution a reputation for decadence. Others, however, more progressive and venturesome in outlook, in spite of an environment of frivolity and indolence, were genuinely concerned with current issues, and engaged in lively discussions on campus.[16] At the government level, however, there was still lacking a consensus on higher educational policy, so there was no progress in developing a coordinated structure for all levels of the educational system.

After Ts'ai Yuan-p'ei was appointed minister of education in 1912, he convened a National Provisional Educational Conference to serve as 'the starting point of the nation's educational reforms'. Meeting in Peking in July, the delegates from all the provinces charted new policies and regulations in response to these needs.[17] They concluded that Chinese

[14] Ch'iu Yü-lin, 'Ching-shih ta-hsueh-t'ang yen-ko lueh' (A brief history of Peking University), in *Ch'ing-tai i-wen* (Informal records of the Ch'ing period) 5.1-2; Yü Ch'ang-lin, 'Ching-shih ta-hsueh-t'ang yen-ko lueh', in Shu Hsin-ch'eng, *Chung-kuo chin-tai chiao-yü-shih tzu-liao* (Source materials on modern Chinese education), 159-60. On the Interpreters' College see Knight Biggerstaff, *The earliest modern government schools in China*. After the Boxer Protocol of 1901 attempts were made to establish universities at the provincial level, as in Shansi under the leadership of Ku Ju-yung: see Chou Pang-tao, *Chin-tai chiao-yü hsien-chin chuan-lueh* (Biographical sketches of leaders of modern Chinese education), first part, 295. However, Brunnert and Hagelstrom recorded in 1910 in their *Present day political organization of China* that there was only one university, the new one in Peking (p. 223). In the 1920s, year books listed half a dozen provincial institutions devoted to agriculture or engineering, e.g. H. G. W. Woodhead, ed. *CYB, 1926*, lists them for Chekiang, Fukien, Hunan, Kiangsi, Kiangsu and Shantung (434b).

[15] Ch'iu Yü-lin, 2; Yü Ch'ang-lin, 160.

[16] Yü T'ung-kuei, 'Ssu-shih nien ch'ien wo k'ao-chin mu-hsiao ti ching-yen' (How I matriculated in my Alma Mater [Peking University] forty years ago), in T'ao Ying-hui, 'Ts'ai Yuan-p'ei yü Pei-ching ta-hsueh 1917–1923', hereafter T'ao Ying-hui, 'Ts'ai/Peita', *Bulletin of the Institute of Modern History*, 5 (1976) 268.

[17] Wo I, 'Lin-shih chiao-yü-hui jih-chi' (Diary of the Provisional Educational Conference), in Shu Hsin-ch'eng, 296–7.

education was wanting in three aspects: it needed to be built into a well-articulated system, extended to reach all parts of the country, and brought up to modern standards. Higher education for the first time took its place, at least on paper, as part of an integrated national system.

Within the next two decades there would generally emerge in China a number of colleges and universities of diverse types – national, provincial, or private in origin, with varied objectives. Their unfolding story would reveal, however, that these institutions shared certain characteristics. The general philosophy was that higher education constituted an indispensable component of the larger task of national reconstruction, since it would be the training ground for future leaders; at the same time, those who took an active part in developing higher education were young intellectuals who had studied in late-Ch'ing modern schools and become associated with political movements. As a group they generally shared a common origin as sons of scholar-class families. Many had worked in the cause of the Republican revolution. They came to regard each other not only as fellow-students of that period, but comrades as well in pursuit of national goals. Thus no one objected to Article I of the laws governing colleges and universities officially announced in 1912: 'The objectives of colleges and universities are to instruct [students] in advanced learning, to train knowledgeable experts, and to meet the needs of the nation.'[18]

Under the laws of 1912, higher education in universities was to be conducted by a Faculty of Letters and a Faculty of Science, plus such professional discipline as business, law, medicine, agriculture and engineering. To achieve the standing of a university an institution must have both the Faculties of Letters and of Science, or a combination of Letters and Law and/or Business, or Science and/or Medicine, Agriculture, or Engineering. Peking University, renamed National Peking University during the chancellorship of Yen Fu, was the sole national university, that is, under the direct jurisdiction of the Ministry of Education, from 1912 till the end of 1916.[19]

All was not smooth sailing for National Peking University – or 'Peita' for short – in its new status; in fact, for five years it was rocked by student protests, frequent changes of chancellor, and general uncertainty of institutional life,[20] all of which reflected the unsettled political condition

18 *Ta-hsueh ling* (Ordinance on colleges and universities), promulgated by the Ministry of Education in October 1912: see Shu Hsin-ch'eng, *Chung-kuo chin-tai chiao-yü-shih tzu-liao* (Source materials on modern Chinese education), 647. The 1917 revision of the 'Objectives' in this ordinance removed a comma in the statement, so that the new version read 'to train knowledgeable experts for meeting the needs of the nation'. *Ibid.* 671.

19 *Ibid.* 647; T'ao Ying-hui, 'Ts'ai/Peita', 271.

20 T'ao Ying-hui, 'Ts'ai/Peita', 270–1. A CCP view of Peita history is presented in Hsiao Ch'ao-jan *et al. Pei-ching ta-hsueh-hsiao-shih, 1898–1949* (A history of Peking University, 1898–1949).

of the country as a whole. The turning point came with the appointment of Ts'ai Yuan-p'ei as chancellor. A *chin-shih* degree holder and a member of the Hanlin Academy under the Ch'ing who, out of conviction, threw in his lot with the revolutionaries at the turn of the century, Ts'ai was widely respected for his knowledge of both Chinese and Western learning, and for his firm dedication to liberal ideals. Called back from his studies in France in late 1916, Ts'ai assumed his duties in January 1917.[21] At the age of fifty he could now put into practice what he had worked out in his own mind during the preceding years of European study and revolutionary activity.

Once at the helm, Ts'ai worked vigorously to revamp Peita, aided by the support of the minister of education, Fan Yuan-lien, an old friend and fellow-revolutionary, plus the fact that a university president enjoyed great administrative authority at that time. First, he improved the quality of the teaching faculty by hiring on the basis of academic competence alone without regard to a person's political opinion or intellectual bias; as a result, most of the young faculty members of the Ts'ai era became well-known personalities in scholarly and professional circles in subsequent years while raising the academic standard of Peita.[22]

Ts'ai next tackled the problems of the attitudes and life-styles of the students. In his inaugural speech he urged them to embrace 'new views of the world and of life'. While attending the university they should 'take it as their unavoidable responsibility to devote themselves to learning, not to use the institution as a stepping-stone for official advancement and the gaining of wealth'.[23] He also encouraged recreational and study societies and campus journals as desirable forms of extracurricular activity. Third, the structure of Peita was rationalized, so that by 1923 the institution was completely free of the 'preparatory school' atmosphere inherited from the previous era. Its three main divisions now were Science, Social Science, and Language and Literature. The use of elective courses was begun in 1919 and approved in 1922 by the Ministry of Education

---

21 T'ao Ying-hui, *Ts'ai Yuan-p'ei nien-p'u* (A chronological biography of Ts'ai Yuan-p'ei), 1.473–4. In taking the post, contrary to the advice of some friends, Ts'ai cited the history of the unification of Germany. He gave credit to the 'effective higher education' of Prussia which trained good primary school teachers who, in turn, taught their pupils the qualities that made them patriotic modern citizens, eventually leading to the victory over France in the Franco-Prussian War. Sun Yat-sen was said to be among those who urged Ts'ai to accept the appointment; see Lo Chia-lun, 'Ts'ai Yuan-p'ei hsien-sheng yü Pei-ching ta-hsueh', in *Shih-che ju-ssu chi* (Recollections of those who are gone), 55.

22 T'ao Ying-hui, 'Ts'ai/Peita', 276–9. In 1920 Peita became the first Chinese university to appoint a woman to a professorship when Ch'en Heng-che (Sophia H. Chen Zen) joined the history faculty. Among the famous scholars at Peita at that time were Hu Shih and Shen Yin-mo in philosophy, Ch'ien Hsuan-t'ung in philology, Ku Hung-ming in English literature, and Ma Yin-ch'u in economics. Wang Ch'ung-hui taught constitutional law, and Yü T'ung-kuei chemistry.   23 *Ibid.* 280.

for nationwide adoption. Peita also led the way in 1920 in admitting women students to a previously all-male campus.[24] Government primary schools had admitted females in 1911 and by 1920 a national tide was running. By 1922 China's national universities reported 405 women in a total student body of 10,535.[25]

Other innovations included plans drawn up in 1918 to establish programmes in graduate study in the humanities, science, social science and law. Ts'ai had to adapt these new programmes to available resources. In setting up the Department of Law, for example, at a time when China's own judicial system was undergoing revision and qualified instructors were scarce, Ts'ai decided to use 'comparative law' as a starting point. The first two lecturers hired, Wang Liang-ch'ou and Lo Wen-kan, were both on the staff of the Ministry of Justice, which precluded their being appointed full-time professors. As Ts'ai related later, all these factors made it extremely difficult to construct a course of law studies; it was only years later when legal scholars like Wang Shih-chieh and Chou Keng-sheng came on the scene that a proper Department of Law could be organized.[26] In his attention to postgraduate studies and research, Ts'ai was strongly influenced by his experience in Germany, where he became inspired by Berlin University and its founder Wilhelm von Humboldt. At Peita his efforts met with enthusiastic support, partly because of the high quality of the new faculty, and partly on account of a tradition of faculty-student discussion on scholarly topics that dated back to the Peking University era when most of the students were mature men with some learning.[27]

The leading role played by Peita in the May Fourth movement seemed to reaffirm the link between young academics and the fate of the nation. As an institution the National Peking University had, by the early 1920s, come to represent the general direction in which higher education was to develop in China: a curriculum organized along the disciplinary lines common in modern Western practice, and a faculty that embodied both Chinese and foreign studies backgrounds, with the possibility of continued learning and research beyond the undergraduate course of studies. The relevance of higher education to nation-building was visibly symbolized by Peita's status as the first of the national universities. The growth of other leading institutions, such as National South-eastern (later Central) University at Nanking, when more fully studied, should offer enlightening comparisons and contrasts.

Private institutions: Nankai. Not all leading universities were government-related. Private colleges of diverse types and qualities began

[24] *Ibid.* 291–6, 297–8.   [25] Jessie Gregory Lutz, *China and the Christian colleges, 1850–1950*, 136–7.
[26] T'ao Ying-hui, 'Ts'ai/Peita', 296–7, and Ts'ai's own account of his years in Peita in *ibid.* 276.
[27] Lo Chia-lun, *Shih-che ju-ssu chi*, 57, 64–5.

to multiply, especially in Peking and Shanghai and some provincial cities. The best-known example of educational entrepreneurship was Nankai, the secondary school and higher education complex that grew up in Tientsin under the leadership of Chang Po-ling (1876–1951). In contrast to many late Ch'ing pioneers of modern education, Chang was no classical scholar, but a star graduate of the Peiyang Naval Academy, a modern school, at the age of eighteen. He ended his naval career abruptly, however, in 1898, after witnessing the lowering of the Chinese flag and the raising of the British one at Weihaiwei, the Chinese naval base acquired by the British as a leased territory in that year. That excruciating humiliation had a traumatic impact on Chang. Leaving the navy, he vowed to devote his life to education, 'the road to self-strengthening'.[28] As Chang related in his *Reminiscences*, 'The Nankai Schools were born from China's calamity. Therefore their object was to reform old habits of life and to train youth for the salvation of the country.' The task of educators was to aim this training at the elimination of the five aspects of China's weakness: physical weakness and poor health, superstition and lack of scientific knowledge, economic poverty, disunity as shown by the lack of a group life and activity, and selfishness. The comprehensive educational programme Chang later developed in the Nankai system was designed to meet China's needs in these five areas.[29]

Chang's educational odyssey had begun modestly as family tutor to the children of Yen Hsiu, a prominent Tientsin gentryman who, like Ts'ai Yuan-p'ei, was a progressive-minded Hanlin scholar. On the basis of this connection and that of another tutorship in the home of a second well-known Tientsin gentryman, Wang I-sun, Chang Po-ling was to build the first of his schools. In 1904 Yen and Wang jointly financed the establishment of a middle school and a normal school. The first normal school class graduated in 1906, and the first middle school class in 1908. Although the local gentry were heavily represented in the first group of students – family names such as Han, Yen, T'ao, Pien and Cheng figured prominently in the initial rosters – the new curriculum of the school attracted a rapidly increasing enrolment. In 1908, through the generous donation of land by a third local benefactor, Cheng Chü-ju, and further financing by Yen Hsiu, the school was able to move into its first permanent buildings at a location called Nan-k'ai Hollow, from which the school took its name.[30]

Despite the political upheavals at the end of the Ch'ing, Chang Po-ling

[28] Chang Po-ling, 'Ssu-shih-nien Nan-k'ai hsueh-hsiao chih hui-ku' (Retrospect of Nankai after forty years, 1944), in Wang Wen-t'ien *et al. Chang Po-ling yü Nan-ka'i* (Chang Po-ling and Nankai), hereafter Wang Wen-t'ien, *Chang/Nankai*, 83. BDRC 1.101.
[29] Hu Shih, 'Chang Po-ling, educator', in J. L. Buck, *et al. There is another China*, 10.
[30] Wang Wen-t'ien, *Chang/Nankai*, 7–9. The Nankai Normal School closed in 1906, therefore only

was too single-minded to allow himself or his school to become entangled in revolutionary activities. He concentrated on plans for further development. After studying for a year at Teachers College at Columbia University in 1917–18, Chang enlisted the support of Yen Hsiu and Fan Yuan-lien in his plan for a university. By mobilizing his connections with the Tientsin upper class (for example, the Yen and Cheng families) and the national intelligentsia (Fan Yuan-lien was ex-minister of education and a close associate of Ts'ai Yuan-p'ei), and also with the international educational community (Chang had become a Christian in 1909 and established ties with the YMCA), he raised enough funds for the construction of the first building of Nankai University. The first freshman class of over forty students entered in the autumn of 1919.[31] Nankai University opened with three divisions: Letters, Science and Business. As soon as the first class graduated in 1923 the university was able to move into its more spacious campus at Pa-li-t'ai, where it remains today. A new science building was opened when Nankai moved to this suburban campus, another gift from a private donor.[32]

Chang made several trips to the United States to observe the system of higher education and raise funds. After returning from one such journey in 1928–9 he reorganized Nankai University into three colleges: the College of Letters, consisting of the Departments of Political Science, History and Economics; the College of Science, with the Departments of Mathematics, Physics, Chemistry and Biology under it; and the College of Business, comprising the Departments of Financial Administration, Banking, Statistics and Business.[33]

Chang Po-ling's bicultural achievement was to integrate support from the Tientsin upper class, the national intelligentsia of returned-student educators and the international (especially Anglo-American) educational community. Achievements of other educational entrepreneurs, though less well known, are of comparable nature. For example, another private institution, Fu-tan University in Shanghai, grew out of an academy founded in 1905 by students who withdrew from the Catholic academy that became Chen-tan (Aurora) University. A moving spirit in these developments was the Catholic layman, Ma Liang (Ma Hsiang-po, 1840–1939, see below). Still another private institution, Amoy (Hsia-men) University, was founded in 1921 by the Overseas Chinese entrepreneur and philanthropist, Tan Kah Kee (Ch'en Chia-keng), who had become

one class graduated from it. Among this class of ten graduates, however, were several who later figured prominently in the academic community, among them T'ao Meng-ho and Mei I-ch'i.

[31] *Ibid.* 8–9, 10, 13–14.

[32] *Ibid.* 14–15. The importance of private financial support to Nankai stood in sharp contrast to other leading universities of the time.   [33] *Ibid.* 17.

a Singapore millionaire in the rubber, pineapple and shipping industries. Amoy University was developed from 1921 to 1937 by its first president, Lim Boon Keng (Lin Wen-ch'ing), a gifted Singapore doctor who took his medical degree at Edinburgh and became also a classical scholar and journalist.[34] The long historical tradition of Chinese private philanthropy in education plainly calls for further study, to say nothing of the Overseas Chinese influence in recent times. Amoy had of course been a major entrepôt in Chinese trade with South-East Asia, a focal point in the 'Maritime China' discussed in volume 12.

Technical schools. As the curricula of the early universities indicate, education in applied science and engineering was developing only slowly. Practical skills like railway building, no matter how spectactular, could not quickly acquire the prestige of the book learning that had for so long distinguished the examination graduate. However, some exclusively technical and professional schools did come into existence, starting with the campaign for modern education in the final years of the Ch'ing, and many of these institutions evolved until they reached college or university level. A few examples will illustrate the diversity of origins of some of the best-known technical institutions in modern China. In 1895 Sheng Hsuan-huai sponsored the founding of Hsi-hsueh hsueh-t'ang (School of Western Learning) in Tientsin with a curriculum emphasizing specialities in the fields of electrical, mining, and mechanical engineering; eight years later, when the educational system of the country was undergoing reappraisal, this school was reorganized as the Peiyang College of Engineering, and moved to its new campus outside the city of Tientsin.[35] Another school established under Sheng's aegis, the Nan-yang kung-hsueh in Shanghai, began with an emphasis on political science, but eventually developed into the highly regarded Chiao-t'ung University,[36] considered the southern counterpart in engineering education to Peiyang College in Tientsin.

Aside from officially sponsored technical schools, advocates of modern education on occasion were able to establish such institutions with private funding. The industrial and community developer Chang Chien, in response to the trend of the times, founded in 1906 Nan-t'ung College in Kiangsu, which tried to combine classroom instruction with practical experience. The college offered a curriculum in agriculture, textile

[34] See *Lin Wen-ch'ing chuan* (Life of Lim Boon Keng); also Wang Tseng-ping and Yǔ Kang, *Ch'en Chia-keng hsing-hsueh chi* (Tan Kah Kee's promotion of learning).

[35] Ts'ai Yuan-p'ei *et al. Wan-Ch'ing san-shih-wu-nien lai chih Chung-kuo chiao-yü (1897–1931)* (Chinese education in the 35 years since late Ch'ing), hereafter *Wan-Ch'ing*, 66–7. Ting Chih-p'in, *Chung-kuo chin ch'i-shih-nien lai chiao-yü chi-shih* (Chronology of Chinese education in the past seventy years), hereafter Ting Chih-p'in, *Seventy years.* Cp. *CHOC* 11.330–1, 377–83.

[36] *Wan-Ch'ing*, 68.

technology, engineering and medicine, and was linked to a textile factory, a hospital, and 16,000 *mou* of land for agricultural experiments.[37] Another source of funding for technical schools was foreign business interests that operated within the modern industrial sector of China: in 1909 a British firm, the Foo Chung Company in Honan province, opened Lu Kung College at Chiao-tso, the location of a growing modern coal industry. Briefly closed in the political upheavals of 1912, the school reopened in 1914 as the Fu Chung College of Mining. Under the Nationalist government after 1928 it was reconstituted as the Chiao-tso College of Engineering,[38] a school with a rising reputation until Chinese academic progress was once again disrupted by war in 1937. The foregoing instances were part of an accelerating trend toward education in technology and engineering, which would receive further emphasis during the Nationalist period.

The Christian colleges. When they began in most cases at the secondary level, the original objective of these institutions was to help spread the Christian religion. In time, however, they made a major contribution in the liberal arts. The earliest Christian school on record within China dated back to 1845. Several more emerged in the 1860s and 1870s, in the early years of the self-strengthening movement. Inevitably the disintegration of the old order in late nineteenth-century China gave the mission schools a chance to take the initiative in several areas of non-traditional instruction, such as science and foreign language training. By so doing, these schools demonstrated the new types of learning. After 1900, as the demand for modern education grew, some Christian schools evolved by stages through a complex process of expanded offerings and amalgamations into college-level institutions. In 1906 Protestant missionaries had over 2,000 primary schools and almost 400 intermediate-level schools, from which by the 1920s a dozen (and eventually 16) colleges or universities had gradually emerged.[39] Nevertheless, spreading and deepening the Christian religious cause in China usually remained high among their priorities. President Francis L. H. Pott of St John's University in Shanghai, for example, held that the university should be kept small, not only to maintain the quality of faculty-student contact, but also because 'too large an element of non-Christian students will have the effect of chilling the Christian atmosphere of the institution'. He also made

---

[37] See Samuel C. Chu, *Reformer in modern China: Chang Chien, 1853–1926.*

[38] Anthony C. Li, *The history of privately controlled higher education in the republic of China,* 10, 11–12.

[39] Lutz, *Christian colleges,* 531–3, sequential chart of the evolution of 16 Christian colleges and universities from the mid-nineteenth century to after the First World War. For a further summary see *CHOC* 10.576–7 (P. A. Cohen) and 12.174–7 (A. Feuerwerker); also William Purviance Fenn, *Christian higher education in changing China 1880–1950;* and an illuminating study, Jane Hunter, *The gospel of gentility.*

religious courses and services compulsory, justifying them on the ground that if a student did not want to be introduced to the Christian religion, he need not come to this college.[40]

Catholic higher education could build on the foundation of Jesuit scholarship established particularly at Zicawei (Hsu-chia-hui, the ancestral home of the great convert of the late Ming, Hsu Kuang-ch'i) outside Shanghai. A vigorous and omnicompetent personality, Ma Liang, in the course of a long career as Jesuit priest, Ch'ing official and reformer, founded in 1903 Chen-tan (Aurora) Academy, which later became a Catholic university. In 1905 he set up Fu-tan Academy, which became a private university as noted above.[41]

The academic quality of the Christian institutions was uneven.[42] Some were outstanding universities in instruction, innovative programmes and the professional attainments of their faculty members, some of whom were nationally or internationally known. Yenching University in Peking, for example, had a Department of Journalism that drew students from all parts of China, while its faculty included such well-known figures as Hung Yeh (William Hung) in Chinese history, Ku Chieh-kang (folklore), Hsu Shu-hsi (political science), Wu Wen-tsao (sociology), Hsu Ti-shan, Hsieh Wan-ying (Ping Hsin) and Hsiung Fu-hsi in literature and Chao Tzu-ch'en in religion. Yenching had high visibility due to its location at Peking. Meanwhile there were of course many solid achievements at other Christian institutions like Nanking (Ginling) University and Lingnan (formerly Canton Christian College).

Yet regardless of where they stood in the scale of academic attainment, the Christian colleges found themselves ambivalent. Although the original missionary purpose had been evangelistic, some missionaries had very early found it desirable to spread secular learning also. The movement toward modernization in China carried their educational institutions past the boundaries of proselytizing, and caused them to be gradually absorbed into the general secular programme of national development. For the majority of the students enrolled in the Christian colleges, they were simply centres of modern higher education. The students did not to any appreciable extent become Christian converts,[43] nor did they divorce

---

[40] Mary Lamberton, *St. John's University, Shanghai, 1879–1951*, 65.

[41] See Chang Jo-ku, *Ma Hsiang-po hsien-sheng nien-p'u* (Chronological biography of Ma Hsiang-po [Ma Liang]).

[42] For example, a Japanese report translated and published in the official Chinese *Chiao-yü kung-pao* (Educational gazette), 8.1–2 (Jan.–Feb. 1921) rated Aurora (Chen-tan) University in Shanghai very low in academic quality; see Shu Hsin-ch'eng (1962), 1103.

[43] Clarence Burton Day, *Hangchow University: a brief history*, reports that a 1930 survey revealed that there existed little interest among the students in religious meetings or courses, and only about 25% of the university's students were professing Christians.

TABLE 3

Major colleges and universities in China and their distribution, 1922

Institution	No. in category	Peking	Shanghai	Tientsin	Canton	Nanking	Wuhan	Foochow	Other
I. National universities	5								
National Peking		×	.	.	.	.	.	.	
Chiao-t'ung (three campuses)		×	×	.	.	.	.	.	Tang-shan
Peyang College of Engr.		.	.	×	.	.	.	.	
South-eastern (later Nat. Cent.)		.	.	.	.	×	.	.	
Shanghai College of Commerce		.	×	.	.	.	.	.	
II. Provincial universities	2								
Shansi		.	.	.	.	.	.	.	Taiyuan
O-chou, preparatory division		.	.	.	.	.	×	.	
III. Private universities	13								
Min-kuo		×	.	.	.	.	.	.	
Chung-kuo		×	.	.	.	.	.	.	
Ch'ao-yang		×	.	.	.	.	.	.	
P'ing-min		×	.	.	.	.	.	.	
Nankai		.	.	×	.	.	.	.	
Ho-pei		.	.	.	.	.	.	.	Ch'ing-yuan
Fu-tan		.	×	.	.	.	.	.	
Ta-t'ung		.	×	.	.	.	.	.	
Nan-t'ung Agricultural College		.	.	.	.	.	.	.	Nan-t'ung
Ts'ung-sheng min-chih		.	×	.	.	.	.	.	Kiangsu
Hsia-men		.	.	.	.	.	.	.	Amoy
Chung-hua		.	.	.	.	.	×	.	

Institution									Location
Yenching		×‌							
Cheloo									Tsinan
St John's			×						
Tung-wu (Soochow) – main campus			×						Soochow
– Law School									
Ginling (Nanking)									
Ginling College for Women									
Chen-tan (Aurora)			×			×			
Hu-chiang (Shanghai)			×			×			
Fu-chien hsieh-ho (Fukien Christian)				×					
Chih-chiang (Hangchow)									Hangchow
Hua-nan College for Women				×					
Wen-hua (Boone)							×		
Ya-li (Yale-in-China)									Changsha
Hua-hsi hsieh-ho (West China Union)									Chengtu
Lingnan					×				
Hsia-k'e Medical College					×				
TOTAL	37	7	10	2	2	3	4	2	10

Note: 37 institutions had forty individual campuses.

Sources: adapted from Wan-Ch'ing, 99–100; Lutz, Christian colleges, 531–3, 'List of Chinese Christian colleges'.

themselves from the 'new-tides' sweeping over the country as a whole. In fact, some of them, particularly those in Peking and Shanghai,[44] were often in the forefront of student activism.[45]

By the early 1920s the Christian colleges and universities had reached their peak of growth. As table 3 shows, they constituted nearly one-half of the major institutions of higher education in 1922. This was the period when the New Culture movement was running high, therefore even as their numbers increased the Christian colleges were having to face new challenges from Chinese society. The May Fourth movement brought Chinese intellectuals into conflict with Christian proselytism. A meeting in Peking of the World Christian Student Federation in 1922 touched off an anti-religious and anti-Christian movement among student youths all over China. As Hu Shih pointed out in a talk at Yenching in 1925, Christian education in China faced three new difficulties. First was the new nationalistic spirit of the Chinese since the First World War, 'fear [of the foreign powers] has diminished, while self-awareness has gradually increased', hence the movement for the recovery of lost sovereign rights and, among other things, the belief that 'the methods the imperialist powers used in cultural aggression were the dissemination of religion and the opening of schools'. Second, the 'new enlightened rationalism' of the younger intelligentsia would challenge the Christian credo itself by demanding, 'give us proof!'[46] Lastly, Hu saw the entire missionary enterprise as shot through with inherent weakness. (Chinese patriots noted that in their historical development the colleges had begun with faculty members who were sometimes more religious than academic in their primary qualifications.) Hu Shih therefore urged missionary educators to arrive at a prescription for themselves in answer to two questions: could they not concentrate their resources and energies in developing a few truly excellent, high-quality institutions rather than large numbers of mediocre

---

44 Among the most notable centres of student movements of the early 1930s were Yenching Unversity, Shanghai University, and Hangchow Christian College (later renamed Hangchow University); see Lutz, *Christian colleges*, 330–3.

45 For a vivid first-hand account of Yenching student activism in 1935 see Hubert Freyn, an American student at Yenching who took part in the demonstrations and propaganda against Japanese aggression, *Prelude to war: the Chinese student rebellion of 1935–1936*; see also John Israel, *Student nationalism in China, 1927–1937*.

46 Hu Shih, 'Chin-jih chiao-hui chiao-yü ti nan-kuan' (Difficulties facing Christian education today), a talk he gave at Yenching University in 1925, in *Hu Shih wen-ts'un* (Collected writings of Hu Shih), 3rd series, 4.728–33; for a useful survey, see Jessie G. Lutz, 'Chinese nationalism and the anti-Christian campaigns of the 1920s'. *Modern Asian Studies*, 10.3 (July 1976) 395–416; also Yamamoto Sumiko, *Chūgoku Kirisuto kyōshi kenkyū* (Studies on the history of Christianity in China); and for a detailed account, Ka-che Yip, *Religion, nationalism and Chinese students: the anti-Christian movement of 1922–1927*. On the tie-in between the anti-Christian movement and educational 'rights recovery', see Jessie Gregory Lutz, 'Nationalism, Chinese politics, and Christian missions' (unpubl. MS, 1984).

or poor schools? He cited the Peking Union Medical College as an example of excellence. And could the Christian schools give up evangelism and devote all their attention to education? Hu Shih held that you could not serve both religion and education well.[47]

In speaking out against conventional missionary education, Hu Shih and other academics like him were troubled by what they saw as a dangerous lack of rationality in religious propagation. In this they were at one with the Western rationalist attack on revealed religion in the name of science, and also with the Confucian scholastic tradition of agnosticism. Simultaneously, however, Chinese who accepted a faith in Marxism as a new 'science of society' joined in the patriotic anti-Christian movement as part of the anti-imperialist effort in general. By 1924 an increase in 'anti-foreign and anti-Christian' sentiment was attributed in some missionary circles to Sun Yat-sen and his 'hot-bed of radical elements' in Kwangtung.[48]

Early initiatives in science and research

The institutional development of modern science in all its multiplicity worldwide made great strides during the same decades before and after 1900 that saw the onset of rapid change in China. The Chinese and foreigners who joined in developing higher education in China thus participated in a tremendously complex process that needs to be compared with other areas of the world. One landmark certainly was the setting up of the Geological Survey of China in 1916 (see below). Another was the nascent stress on scientific learning. In December 1918 Ts'ai Yuan-p'ei declared: 'What we call a "university" is not just a place where classes are given on schedule resulting in the production of college graduates; it is in reality a place for conducting research in areas of knowledge of common interest and...thus creating new knowledge to offer to scholars here and abroad.'[49]

New knowledge, it was generally agreed, was to be achieved through the scientific method. By the 1920s this had become a faith that viewed the scientific outlook as an instrument for dismantling the traditional order and opening the way for China's attainment of modern nationhood. Young intellectuals concerned over China's lack of success in the international world became convinced the key to the problem was science,

[47] Hu Shih, 'Chin-jih'.
[48] During the Northern Expedition of 1927 young officers told a Western teacher at Hangchow that, once the fighting was over, the Chinese would 'give attention to taking back our educational authority'. Day, Hangchow, 56, 59–60; cp. Lutz, Christian colleges, 225.
[49] Shu Hsin-ch'eng (1962), 1049, Ts'ai's foreword to the first issue of the Peking University Monthly, December 1918.

a conviction so deep and widespread that decades later they continued to say in all sincerity: 'Science is the wellspring of Western civilization'.[50] 'If we truly wish to develop a new culture, then we ought to pay special attention to the development of science'.[51]

The level of science education was generally held to be low in the early republic, largely, it was thought, because of the inadequate training many teachers had received in Japan, and with a few exceptions this overall condition did not improve until the early 1920s.[52] From the mid-twenties several factors led to greater progress: universities such as Nankai, Tsing-hua and Chiao-t'ung set up more solid science programmes taught by returned students from Europe and the United States; other types of organizations also promoted science, and brought about the establishment of institutions for advanced research.

Of the many organizations that emerged among Chinese students abroad in the era of the First World War, few were more active or influential than the Science Society, launched in 1914 by a small group of Chinese students at Cornell.[53] The society's full English name was 'Chinese Association for the Advancement of Science', echoing its American counterpart, but in Chinese it was Chung-kuo k'o-hsueh she. A *she* was a voluntary association, the type of activist, elite-led organization that gentry had commonly formed to organize local schools or irrigation projects, or recruit militia against the Taiping rebels or British invaders at Canton, or later to undertake projects in 'self-government'. The Science Society aimed not only to 'promote science, encourage industry, authorize [translation of] terminologies, and spread knowledge', but with a crusading zeal it wished eventually to regenerate China's entire society and culture through science.[54] Beginning with 55 members in the United States, the Science Society moved to Shanghai in 1918, following the return to China of its key founders, and by 1930 membership had risen to more than one thousand. These included returned students from Europe, the US and Japan, and a national membership of younger scientists trained in China. The activities of the Science Society also expanded in scope: in addition to its journal, *Science* (*K'o-hsueh*), first published in 1915, the society also held meetings for the presentation of

[50] Jen Hung-chün (H. C. Zen), 'Wu-shih tzu-shu' (Autobiography at fifty) (unpubl. MS, 1938).

[51] Ts'ai Yuan-p'ei, 'San-shih-wu-nien lai Chung-kuo chih hsin-wen-hua' (New Culture in China during the past 35 years), in *Wan-Ch'ing*, 297, article dated 1931.

[52] Roger S. Greene, 'Aspects of science education', in J. L. Buck, *et al. Another China*, 101.

[53] Four of the nine founders, including Hu Shih, had begun their studies in the College of Agriculture. The nine included Jen Hung-chün (H. C. Zen, who had joined the T'ung-meng hui in Tokyo in 1908 and assisted Sun Yat-sen in Nanking in 1912 before studying chemistry in the United States) and Yang Ch'uan (who had been Hu Shih's student in 1909 in a Shanghai modern school, and then also a secretary to Sun in 1912 before studying engineering in the United States).   [54] Peter Buck, *American science and modern China 1876–1936*, 94–5, 169.

research papers, published translated works on science, and established a science library; in 1931 the library was moved from Nanking, its first location, to Shanghai, where it remained a major resource. Meanwhile in 1922 the society had established its biology laboratory in Nanking.

Promoting science in China was a two-front struggle: both to replicate and augment knowledge gained abroad and to fit it into the Chinese scene. Inevitably, China's young scientists were dependent on the international world of learning, to which they tried to contribute. Simultaneously they faced the task of bringing scientific thought and practice into the life of the Chinese people so as to reduce China's backwardness. Both dependence and backwardness could later be stigmatized as symptoms of a colonial status.[55]

Funding and American influence: Tsing-hua

In view of the ancient Chinese stress on advanced education for state service, it is ironic that a major influence on Chinese higher education during the warlord era, 1916–28, came from the United States, where the federal government as yet played little part in education (beyond agronomy, which had been subsidized by land grants to state agricultural colleges). American higher education was still led by private more than by state universities, and the denominational colleges of New England and the Middle West had actually been the prototypes of the Christian colleges sponsored by missionaries in China. But the American influence, through an unusual conjuncture of events, went far beyond the Christian effort.

The American claim of US $25 million as the United States' share of the Boxer indemnity exacted from the Ch'ing government in 1901 was privately regarded by the responsible American officials at the time as excessive, probably double what could be justified. It was, however, only a tiny part of the $330 million total indemnity, an exorbitant sum that crippled the Chinese government and from almost any point of view can be stigmatized as a high point of imperialistic exploitation.[56] In 1908 the United States Congress remitted to China that part of the indemnity which was in excess of certified claims for actual losses, amounting to a sum of $11,961,121.76. This sum was to be used for educating Chinese in the United States, and it created a potent mechanism for support of Chinese higher education. The Chinese government sent a first group of 47 Boxer indemnity students to the United States in 1909 and 70 in 1910. By 1929 the total was 1,268.[57] The roster of Boxer scholars included many young men of talent.

[55] Ibid. 216–26.
[56] Michael H. Hunt, 'The American remission of the Boxer indemnity: a reappraisal', JAS 31.3 (May 1972) 539–59. [57] See data in Grieder, Intellectuals, 210–12.

Meanwhile the government also set up a training programme to prepare young students for study in the United States. In 1909 a foreign-staffed college preparatory school was started, entrance examinations were held in 1910, and what later became Tsing-hua College opened in 1911 as Tsing-hua School.[58] One secret of its success was that its annual budget was assured at a time when other institutions were precariously dependent on warlord regimes. Also, until 1929 it stressed specific preparation for study in American universities. A pupil who passed the entrance examination between eleven and thirteen years of age had to take five years of junior division courses and three years of the senior division, after which he or she would be sent abroad to study in an American college. The first group, entering in 1912, graduated in 1920 after eight years of study in the standard modern middle-school subjects such as English, French, German, history, geography, physiology, physics, chemistry, as well as some music, art, and physical education.[59] The preparatory-school status of Tsing-hua came to an end in 1926, when it was reorganized as Tsing-hua College with a four-year programme leading to the bachelor's degree.

By that time a high point of American influence on Chinese education had been reached in large part through the channels of Teachers College at Columbia University. A number of able Chinese Ph.D. candidates had worked with Professor John Dewey and others there. The two years that Dewey spent lecturing in China (May 1919 – July 1921) coincided with the visit of the British mathematical philosopher and socialist Bertrand Russell (October 1920 – July 1921). Dewey gave some 70 lectures in eleven provinces, with Hu Shih translating, but his advocacy of experimentalism contained no political panacea for ardent Chinese patriots. Later his colleague Professor Paul Monroe visited China and the heads of major institutions – Chiang Monlin at Peita, Kuo Ping-wen at National South-eastern (later to be Central) University – counted themselves Dewey's disciples. Yet his typically American message of individual fulfilment through education offered little that could be of immediate use in the search for a Chinese way in education. From 1919 to 1924 an educational reform movement was led by American-returned scholars, both through major journals like *New Education* (*Hsin chiao-yü*) first edited by Chiang Monlin and through the Chinese National Association for the Advancement of Education; but its plans and hopes were soon eclipsed

58 Y. C. Wang, 79, 111–14. For a comprehensive 500-page account to 1949 see Ch'ing-hua ta-hsueh hsiao-shih pien-hsieh-tsu, comp. *Ch'ing-hua ta-hsueh-hsiao shih-kao* (Draft history of Tsing-hua University).

59 Liu Shih-shun, 'I-chiu-erh-ling chi tsai-hsiao shih-tai chih Ch'ing-hua' (Tsing-hua in the days of the class of 1920), 3–4.

in political turmoil. Caught between a nationalistic surge of anti-Deweyan conservatives and the KMT vs. warlord struggle in Kiangsu, Kuo Ping-wen was forced to resign in January 1925. An autonomous higher education independent of the political power holders was not in prospect. During the warlord era, higher education functioned at the mercy of local militarists.[60]

In the case of Tsing-hua, however, the American transplant took firm root. After the successful conclusion of the Northern Expedition in 1928, the Nationalist government designated it National Tsing-hua University,[61] and Lo Chia-lun, a Peita alumnus and returned-student from Britain and the United States, was appointed its first president. In his inaugural address in September 1928, Lo hailed the attainment of national university status as an effort by the Nationalist government 'to establish a new cultural force in North China'.[62] He moved toward adding a College of Engineering to the three Colleges of Letters, Sciences and Law, and stressed graduate studies and advanced research. He also proposed to invite accomplished scholars from abroad to be residential faculty for relatively long periods, 'not to stir consciousness, but to teach'; it should not be 'like several years ago when famous foreign scholars [an obvious reference to Dewey and Russell] were invited to lecture for a few months or a year', because that time had passed.[63] Under the administration of Lo and his successor, Mei I-ch'i (Y. C. Mei), Tsing-hua grew steadily in scope and substance, and was one of the outstanding institutions of higher education in the following decade.

Another phase of American influence opened with the appearance on the scene of the China Foundation for the Promotion of Education and Culture (or China Foundation) in 1925, an historic event. In 1924 the US

[60] Barry Keenan, *The Dewey experiment in China*, ch. 5, indicates the extreme complexity of factionalism among educators and between them and military authorities. On 3 June 1921, after Peking's teachers in eight institutions of higher education had gone unpaid for several months, a demonstration by students and teachers marching to petition at the presidential palace was dispersed by gunfire with many casualties. *Chiao-yü tsa-chih* (Chinese educational review) 13.7 (20 July 1921) 2–4 reports this incident.

The difficulties in the way of applying American liberal ideals to revolutionary China may be examined in a notable series of biographical studies: W. J. Duiker, *Ts'ai Yuan-p'ei*; Laurence A. Schneider, *Ku-Chieh-kang and China's new history*; J. B. Grieder, *Hu Shih and the Chinese renaissance*; Charlotte Furth, *Ting Wen-chiang: science and China's new culture*; Guy S. Alitto, *The last Confucian: Liang Shu-ming and the Chinese dilemma of modernity*; Stephen Hay, *Asian ideas of east and west: Tagore and his critics*; see also R. W. Clopton and T. C. Ou, *John Dewey: lectures in China, 1919–1920*, and Paul Monroe, *China: a nation in evolution*.

[61] Ch'en Chih-mai, 'Ch'iu-hsueh yü chih-hsueh' (Study and research [of Tsiang T'ing-fu]), in *Chiang T'ing-fu ti chih-shih yü sheng-p'ing* (The life and deeds of Tsiang T'ing-fu), 19.

[62] Lo Chia-lun, 'Hsueh-shu tu-li yü hsin Ch'ing-hua' (The independence of scholarship and the new Tsing-hua), speech delivered in September 1928 on Lo's assumption of the presidency, in *Shih-che ju-ssu chi*, 7.

[63] *Ibid.* 9–10, 11, 12.

Congress, by a joint resolution, returned the remaining portion of the Boxer indemnity for use in China. The understanding then reached between the governments of the two countries was that the money, amounting to approximately US $12,545,000, should be administered by a foundation and used for educational and cultural purposes in China. Within a few months the Chinese government appointed the first board of trustees consisting of ten Chinese and five Americans, and the China Foundation came into being in June 1925.[64] Of the ten Chinese board members, three were first-rank diplomats (W. W. Yen, V. K. Wellington Koo, and Alfred Sao-ke Sze), and the others well-known scientists and/or names familiar in modern educational work: Fan Yuan-lien (Fan Ching-sheng), Huang Yen-p'ei (a leader in education in Kiangsu province), Chiang Monlin (president of Peita), Chang Po-ling (of Nankai), Y. T. Tsur (Chou I-ch'un, president of Tsing-hua) and Ting Wen-chiang (of the Chinese Geological Survey). The five Americans were known for their work in connection with education in China: John Dewey, Paul Monroe (both of Columbia), Roger S. Greene (director of the Rockefeller-funded Peking Union Medical College), John Earl Baker (of the China International Famine Relief Commission), and C. R. Bennett (of the National City Bank).[65] The board appointed Fan Yuan-lien to be the first director of the foundation, and he invited Jen Hung-chün (H. C. Zen), an ardent advocate of science in China, to become the administrative secretary.[66]

The China Foundation was to administer not only the Boxer funds returned in 1924 but also those returned in 1908 as endowment for scholarships and for Tsing-hua University. It was also empowered to handle those of Fan Memorial Institute of Biology, as well as other professional endowments. Its major tasks were first, to subsidize institutions in qualified activities including, for example, the Vocational Education Association led by Huang Yen-p'ei; second, to support governmental and private institutions in new projects as cooperative ventures; and third, to launch new projects on the foundation's own initiative.[67] In the modern

---

[64] Jen Hung-chün (H. C. Zen), *A summary report of the activities of the China Foundation for the Promotion of Education and Culture, 1925–1945*, hereafter *Summary report*, 1–2.

[65] *Ibid.* Later additions to the board of trustees included names equally well known in the development of modern Chinese education and culture, among them Y. R. Chao, Fu Ssu-nien, Hu Shih, J. Leighton Stuart, T. F. Tsiang and Weng Wen-hao.

[66] Jen recalled later that, ever since his return from the US in 1918, 'I had persisted in bending my fellow-countrymen's ears about the importance of science.... Now here is this well-endowed organization with an annual budget of some one million dollars towards the promotion of scientific enterprise!... So I gladly accepted...' Jen, 'Wu-shih tzu-shu', under '1925'. He became director of the China foundation in 1929.

[67] *Summary report*, 4. Margo S. Gewurtz, 'Social reality and educational reform: the case of the Chinese Vocational Education Association 1917–1927', *Modern China*, 4.2 (April 1978) 168.

style all project proposals must receive approval from the board of trustees
or its special committees.[68] Fan and Jen, conscious of the innovative role
of the China Foundation, agreed that it should not operate merely as a
fund management office, but also as a strong promoter of modern
scientific scholarship.[69] Located in a former princely mansion in Peking,
the China Foundation in 1926–7 granted research subsidies to thirteen
universities and colleges, three research institutes, five cultural and
educational organizations, and one unclassified recipient, for a total of
Ch. $419,906.[70] When the foundation was taken to task for dispensing
large sums of money at the discretion of a small group of individuals
instead of through official national authorities, Jen replied that such was
precisely the China Foundation's strength: it was set up to prevent the
government from misusing these funds for fighting civil war.[71] In time,
when the educational activities in China of Japan, Britain, Canada, France,
Germany and other Western nations have been more fully studied, it may
be possible to evaluate the American influence in a broader context,[72]
which will include the Rockefeller Foundation support of medical and
other sciences in China. Returned British, French and Italian Boxer funds
were used in part for educational purposes.

HIGHER EDUCATION AND NATION-BUILDING DURING THE NANKING DECADE

All this non-governmental growth had taken place under the impetus of
the New Culture movement and in spite of the crises of the Nationalist
Revolution of the 1920s. The degree of foreign activity in funding and
advising China's new educational development was denounced by
Marxists as cultural imperialism and was inevitably a source of concern
to all patriots eager to build a fully sovereign nation. As the Nationalist
government came into being in 1928, the country experienced a rare
interlude of relative peace. Nominal peace and unity under Nanking gave
greater scope to young intellectuals who had started their careers as the
cutting edge of the New Culture and had now reached professional
maturity. Many found the Nationalist government's stand on policy

---

[68] Personal communication from Leong-ts'ai Yip, 15 August 1981. Yip served the China Foundation
as financial secretary 1932–78, assistant treasurer 1935–78, and trustee 1962–78.

[69] Jen Hung-chün, 'Wu-shih tzu-shu, 1925'.

[70] *Summary report*, 5.

[71] *BDRC* 2.221.

[72] For example, the German biologist-philosopher Hans Driesch lectured on metaphysics in
Nanking and Peking during 1922–3 and his sponsor, Chang Chün-mai, precipitated the scholarly
polemic on 'Science and philosophy of life', See Furth, *Ting Wen-chiang*, 94–135; Kwok, *Scientism*,
135–60; and Peter Buck, 190–6.

matters largely acceptable, and from the mid-thirties on a process of cooptation was clearly in evidence, with academic people going into government posts. These intellectuals maintained close contact through the years. In all their fields of endeavour – be it promotion of science and modern medicine, social reform, research on the Chinese economy, or developing new thought and new literature – they felt that the threshold of genuine national development had now been reached at last. In their minds the end of the warlord era might be considered a positive outcome of a larger historical process in which they themselves, to varying extent, had played a part.

Central government leadership

The work of the Ministry of Education at Nanking has not yet been evaluated. It was of course concerned with literacy, schools, teacher training and a multitude of problems other than higher education. One immediate aim at Nanking from 1928 was to express China's newly ascendant nationalism and carry out an 'educational rights recovery' campaign, which required that all foreign-founded Christian colleges and universities register with the Ministry of Education, and that the heads of such schools or colleges must be Chinese nationals. One result was to assert the state's authority against compulsory religious instruction in Christian colleges – an aim that expressed both scientific rationalism as in the liberal West and the jealous nationalism of the KMT party dictatorship now in power. This secular challenge to the Christian colleges was first put forward in 1925. The policy was continued and more strictly enforced after 1927. It touched upon not only the political issue of foreign vs. Chinese control, but more deeply on the question of which should dominate, secular or religious-evangelical values. The more perceptive leaders among Western educators in China, such as those at Yenching University, were able to see the practical issues involved, for

If the University did not register with the government, when it became possible to do so, the door of public service would be closed to its graduates, and they would not be permitted to teach in registered schools or colleges. There was therefore the danger that both faculty and students would be isolated from the educational life of the country and have no influence thereon.[73]

Consequently, Yenching was among the first to comply with the registration requirement, doing so in February 1927. One of the government rules for Christian institutions was the prohibition of including religious courses among required subjects, and Yenching made all its religious

[73] Dwight W. Edwards, *Yenching University*, 129, also 130, 149–51, 155. See also Philip West, *Yenching University and Sino-Western relations, 1916–1952*, ch. 3.

courses elective. The place of religious instruction was not as smoothly resolved in other places, however. St John's in Shanghai, for example, regarded the Nationalist government's demand that religious courses be 'voluntary' electives as a major obstacle to registration, and the university's leaders strongly resisted the prospect of government or KMT party activities on campus. St John's took a waiting attitude – a course of action no doubt easier to follow in Shanghai, where foreign interests dominated, than it would be in Peking or other places, where institutions were more closely attuned to the Chinese environment. Soochow University was, for instance, pressed to register with the Ministry of Education by its Chinese alumni. By 1933 all the major Christian universities and colleges had completed registration with the Nationalist government.[74] Soon Kuomintang political education in Dr Sun's Three Principles of the People entered the scene and required courses and exercises of its own.

The other Nationalist requirement, that Christian colleges have predominantly Chinese boards of trustees and Chinese presidents, led at Yenching to a dual system by which the American trustees in New York handled the main part of the budget and the foreign faculty under President J. Leighton Stuart, while a board of managers in China, with a Chinese majority after 1928, took charge of other policy matters under a Chinese chancellor: Wu Lei-ch'uan assumed the latter post in 1929, but resigned in 1934 owing to policy differences, and after 1934 the chancellorship was held principally by Lu Chih-wei.[75] Thus, in spite of local problems, the evangelical intentions of the schools were de-emphasized, while these institutions were brought into the formal structure of China's educational system.

Another policy was the strengthening or creating of national universities across the country, where they would be under the direct administrative supervision of the Ministry of Education in Nanking. After Tsing-hua was designated a national university in 1928, for example, President Lo Chia-lun immediately launched major reorganization and reforms, such as terminating Tsing-hua's function as a preparatory school for US colleges and transforming it into a coeducational university that offered a regular four-year college curriculum. He also removed Tsing-hua from the joint

[74] Lamberton, 106–9; see also the following United Board for Christian Colleges in China histories: Roderick Scott, *Fukien Christian University*; W. B. Nance, *Soochow University*; Mrs Lawrence Thurston and Ruth M. Chester, *Ginling College*; L. Ethel Wallace, *Hua-nan College: the women's college of South China*; Lewis C. Walmsley, *West China Union University*.

[75] West, 91–109, 129–35; Edwards, 130, 209, 120–211: As further evidence of the advance of the secular state power in 'making Yenching Chinese', Yenching had to dissolve the Department of Religion in 1930, the Ministry of Education asserting that such courses as the philosophy of religion and history of religion could be taught in the Departments of Philosophy and of History respectively.

supervision of the Ministries of Education and of Foreign Affairs, placing it under the sole jurisdiction of the Ministry of Education; a new building programme was also initiated.[76]

Higher education was one channel for the extension of central government authority. This was illustrated in the amalgamation in 1931 of the University of Chengtu, Szechwan University, and Chengtu Normal College into the National Szechwan University; the Nationalist government further ordered that the salt revenues of the province should be appropriated for the university.[77] These measures were taken five weeks after the Japanese invasion of Manchuria, and appeared to be one of the multifarious steps taken in the long-range plan known as 'reconstruction of the Great Hinterland', that in a few years' time was to combine the government's nation-building function with the activities required by total war. A president for National Szechwan University would have to be not only professionally qualified, influential among academic people, and able to work with the new intelligentsia; he should also understand his additional role as a bridge between the Nanking government and the provincial militarists. In 1935 the government asked Jen Hung-chün (then director of the China Foundation) to become president of Szechwan University.[78] Reflecting that in the underdeveloped regions of the south-west cultural and educational growth was most urgently needed, Jen accepted the appointment and, by attacking several issues at once, in two years was able to bring about these reforms: the curriculum was reorganized and brought up to date; a building programme was begun with an allocation of Ch. $3 million; the professional attitudes of faculty and students were improved; and, most important of all, well-known scholars and writers from other parts of the country were gathered to improve the quality of academic instruction at the university.[79] Although Jen's presidency was short, the reorganization and reforms he initiated with support from the central government laid the foundation for the future development of National Szechwan University in a part of the country that was to be crucial in the war years to come. What happened at this university symbolized the twofold process then taking place in the hinterland: the improvement of higher education as an aspect of national regeneration, and the extension of central authority into the interior in the continuing effort to achieve national unity. This effort included a campaign to propagate a standard North China (essentially Pekingese) pronunciation of Chinese as the 'national language' (*kuo-yü*). The

---

[76] BDRC 2.430.   [77] Ting Chih-p'in, *Seventy years*, 254.

[78] Nanking's appointees to assume authority in a previously semi-autonomous province such as Szechwan were covertly resented and referred to as *chung-yang jen*, 'central men'.

[79] Jen Hung-chün, 'Wu-shih tzu-shu', section on '1935–1937'.

government also promoted a national system of romanization for writing Chinese in the Latin alphabet. Meanwhile a national commission on compilation and translation had for some years been working out standard Chinese equivalents for foreign technical terms in order to facilitate the absorption of modern technology.

One main educational objective of the Nationalist government was to standardize programmes of study in the universities. Beginning in 1933, ordinances were issued to govern such matters as required courses, electives, and procedures for college entrance examinations. In the last, limits were placed on the number of candidates for the liberal arts disciplines, so as to encourage more enrolment in the natural sciences and technology.[80] Although the restructuring of academic programmes had not yet been completed by the time war broke out in 1937, the government's efforts were beginning to bear fruit: according to Ministry of Education statistics, in 1930 a total of 17,000 students graduated in liberal arts programmes as compared with a little over 8,000 in the areas of agriculture, engineering, medicine and the natural sciences combined,[81] but by 1937 the figures were 15,227 for the liberal arts, and 15,200 for science and technical disciplines.[82]

For learning beyond the bachelor's degree, the Ministry of Education in 1933 promulgated provisional regulations for the organization and operation of postgraduate schools to be established within existing universities with a capacity to award the master's degree. To be eligible for registration with the Ministry of Education as a duly constituted postgraduate school (yen-chiu yuan), the institution must comprise at least three disciplinary departments from among the fields of letters, science, law, agriculture, education, engineering, medicine, or business, each with its own head, all to be placed under a director of the postgraduate school, a position that might be filled by the president of the university concurrently.[83] In actual fact, however, postgraduate training in Chinese universities remained relatively undeveloped.

Chinese critics of the 1930s were aware of the shortcomings in the country's higher education both in quantity and quality. Common criticisms of college education were that it had not developed to meet the needs of the nation, that there had been an imbalance in college programmes with a 'disproportionate' growth in such subjects as literature

[80] K'o Shu-p'ing, 'Wang Hsueh-t'ing hsien-sheng tsai chiao-chang jen-nei chih chiao-yü ts'o-shih' (Educational measures taken by Wang Shih-chieh as minister of education), Chuan-chi wen-hsueh (Biographical literature), 239 (April 1982) 125.
[81] Wang Yen-chun and Sun Pin, eds. Chu Chia-hua hsien-sheng yen-lun chi (Dissertations of Dr Chu Chia-hua), hereafter Chu Chia-hua, 139.
[82] K'o Shu-p'ing, 126.   [83] Ibid. 125.

and law while science and technical subjects lagged behind, and that funding for higher education in general was far from sufficient.[84] In fact, financing the colleges and universities from a variety of sources remained difficult throughout the Nanking period. In the early 1920s the national universities depended on the central government budget for 90 per cent of their operating funds, with tuition and other fees and donations making up less than 10 per cent. While the central government budget of 1934 stipulated that 15 per cent of its annual expenditures should be assigned to the support of education and cultural activities, that was a goal never achieved in actuality; in 1936, for example, the total amount budgeted for education and culture stood at a high point of 4·5 per cent, while military appropriations received 32·5 per cent and public debt service 24·1 per cent in the same year.[85]

Compounding the problem for the national universities was the fact that the central government, following the custom of earlier imperial regimes, often assigned certain parts of a province's tax revenues for the support of a national university located in that province; should the provincial finances fall into disarray for any reason, payment of the allotted funds to the university would become highly undependable.[86] Added to this was the early lack of a uniform standard on which funding was to be based, so that within the meagre total amount of the education budget the government's fairness might be called into question. Witness this petition from the universities in Peking in 1929: 'Chung-shan University in Canton and Central University in Nanking each has a student body of 1,000 to 2,000, and each receives a monthly appropriation of Ch. $150,000 to Ch. $160,000; at Peiping University there are seven colleges and an enrolment of 3,500 students, yet the monthly appropriation is only some Ch. $90,000....'[87]

Universities and colleges at the provincial level encountered still other obstacles in getting public funding. The Nationalist government's effort to centralize the national finances after 1929 was a long-drawn-out process. In the collection and disbursement of tax monies, the procedures and the bureaucratic interrelationships had to be worked out between Nanking

[84] *Chu Chia-hua*, 125, 138; Ho Ping-sung, 'San-shih-wu-nien lai Chung-kuo chih ta-hsueh chiao-yü' (Chinese higher education in the past 35 years), in *Wan-Ch'ing*, 130; Huang Chien-chung, 'Shih-nien lai ti Chung-kuo kao-teng chiao-yü' (Chinese higher education in the past ten years), in *K'ang-chan ch'ien shih-nien chih Chung-kuo* (China in the decade before the war), 503.

[85] Ch'en Neng-chih, 'Chan-ch'ien shih-nien Chung-kuo ta-hsueh chiao-yü ching-fei wen-t'i' (Problems of financing higher education in China in the decade before the war), *Li-shih hsueh-pao*, 11 (June 1983) 173–6.

[86] *Ibid.* 175–7. Examples of this condition can be seen in the cases of the National Chung-shan, Wuhan, Chekiang, and Szechwan Universities from 1928 to the early 1930s.

[87] *Ibid.* 179.

and the provincial authorities. This led to the need for stop-gap funding in several provinces, while local contingencies such as natural disasters adversely affected provincial tax revenues.[88]

Private institutions (including the Christian colleges and universities) depended on a wide range of sources for support, running from central government appropriations to private donations and tuition and other fees, the latter being most important. Those depending on government support shared the problems that beset the public universities, while those that relied primarily on private sources would be affected by economic conditions in China and abroad.[89] Thus, financial insecurity constituted a continuing challenge to the academic community.

Students, restless in the midst of endemic financial crises, and also charged with 'being too interested in political issues', often vented their frustration by staging riots and strikes, causing campus administrative crises in turn.[90] This 'interest in political issues' reflected the basic sense of malaise in Chinese society as a whole, at a time when Japan's invasion of Manchuria in 1931 was followed by the Shanghai undeclared war of 1932, while KMT-CCP relations deteriorated into the long anti-CCP military campaigns of the early 1930s. Fuelled by patriotic fervour, this unrest was to find expression in the student movement of 1935 and 1936.[91]

The distribution and types of institutions of higher education in 1934–5 (table 4) shows the extensive growth since 1922 (table 3), but also its limitations. Most striking was the growth of the national government sector after 1928 from 5 institutions to 23; second in the rate of growth were provincial colleges, universities and technical institutions, along with specialized private schools. Yet most of this expansion took place in just a few locations, concentrated in eastern cities and coastal provinces: by 1934 Shanghai had 24 of the 110 institutions of higher education (or 21 per cent) in the entire country, while Peking followed with 17 (15·5 per cent). Among the provinces, Hopei had the largest number of provincial institutions, leading that category with 9 (8·2 per cent), and Kwangtung was second with 8 (7·2 per cent). At the other end of the geographical distribution were peripheral provinces like Sinkiang, Shensi, Kansu and Yunnan that each had only one institution of higher education of any kind in 1934, usually a provincial university or technical institute, while

[88] *Ibid.* 183–90.   [89] *Ibid.* 191–201.

[90] As one example among many: on 27 June 1932 the students at National Tsing-tao University struck against final examinations, which led to the resignation of the university's president, Yang Chen-sheng; Ting Chih-p'in, *Seventy years,* 263.

[91] See Israel, *Student nationalism,* ch. 5; John Israel and Donald Klein, *Rebels and bureaucrats: China's December 9ers*; on the social background see also Ka-che Yip, 'Nationalism and revolution: the nature and causes of student activism in the 1920s', in Gilbert Chan and Thomas H. Etzold, eds. *China in the 1920s,* 94–70.

TABLE 4[92]

Distribution of colleges and universities in China, 1934–5

Location	(No. of institutions)	National	Public-technical	Provincial	Municipal	Private
Shanghai†	(24)	7	2	—	—	15
Peking†	(17)	6	1	1	1	8
Hopei	(9)	1	—	6	—	2
Kwangtung	(8)	2	—	1	—	5
Hupei	(6)	1	—	1	—	4
Kiangsu	(6)	—	—	1	—	5
Nanking†	(5)	1	2	—	—	2
Shansi	(5)	—	—	4	—	1
Chekiang	(4)	2	—	1	—	1
Fukien	(4)	—	—	—	—	4
Szechwan	(4)	1	—	2	—	1
Honan	(3)	—	—	2	—	1
Shantung	(3)	1	—	1	—	1
Kiangsi	(3)	—	—	3	—	—
Hunan	(2)	—	—	1	—	1
Kwangsi	(2)	—	—	2	—	—
Anhwei	(1)	—	—	1	—	—
Yunnan	(1)	—	—	1	—	—
Kansu	(1)	—	—	1	—	—
Shensi	(1)	1	—	—	—	—
Sinkiang	(1)	—	—	1	—	—
Total	110	23	5	30	1	51

† Municipalities under the direct administration of the central government.
Sources: based on graphs in fig. 1, and on statistical table 9, in Ministry of Education, Office of Statistics, *Erh-shih-san nien-tu ch'üan-kuo kao-teng chiao-yü t'ung-chi* (Statistics on higher education in China for the academic year 1934–5).

Kweichow had none at all. Clearly, these regions had only just begun to build higher education programmes. But it is surprising to see the low showing of Anhwei, a Lower Yangtze province generally active in progressive movements. Its backwardness shows us some of the problems of higher education in many parts of China in the early 1930s. First, the province lacked resources. Quite different from the Lake T'ai region further east, which had been one of the most productive areas of China

[92] Note: (1) The 'private' category includes Christian colleges and universities; (2) the figures show only those institutions of higher education that had been registered with, and duly recognized by, the Ministry of Education; (3) data from the North-east (Manchuria), then under Japanese occupation, are missing from the official figures. (4) A slightly different set of figures is given by Huang Chien-chung, 'Shih-nien-lai ti kao-teng chiao-yü', 504–14. In Huang's list the total number of institutions comes to 108, no precise year given; the relative size of the categories, however, is the same as the Ministry of Education's figures for 1934–5, thus: national, 24; public-technical, 2; provincial, 28; municipal, 2; private 52. These totals may be compared with an official list of 86 institutions in 1928–31 comprising 59 universities of which 15 were national, 17 provincial, and 27 private; and 27 technical schools of which 21 were public and 6 private. See Chiao-yü pu kao-teng chiao-yü ssu, comp. *Ch'üan-kuo kao-teng chiao-yü t'ung-chi* (Statistics of national higher education, Aug. 1928 to July 1931), table 1.

for many centuries, Anhwei was the poor sister of the Lower Yangtze region with its hilly terrain traversed by the Huai River, cause of many natural calamities. Anhwei's marginal economy precluded any rapid development of higher education. A second factor was political instability due to the struggle for power between provincial factions on one level, and between the Nationalist authorities and local groups on another. In Anhwei volatile provincial politics created extreme instability: six changes of governor between 1929 and 1930, with an extra bonus of a military uprising, led to personnel turnovers at the provincial university; moreover, the university received only about half its budgeted funds, since higher education ranked low at the provincial capital.[93] Meanwhile, to make the situation more complex, the central government, attempting to achieve real authority in Anhwei, began to integrate the provincial Anhwei University with the national power structure through the KMT party apparatus and a political education programme.

A further factor that could help explain Anhwei's poor showing in higher education was the considerable geographic mobility of the young intelligentsia. Students everywhere move about, the more ambitious tending to enter the better-known universities in other places if their local institutions were deemed inadequate. Areas less well endowed would often see their young students leaving for the larger centres. A less than complete tabulation of the native provinces of Chinese college and university students for 1934 reveals that of the 945 Anhwei students registered nationwide, 44 per cent were attending national universities outside the province, with another large segment scattered among private and Christian colleges.[94] Finally there was also faculty mobility on a national scale. Wen I-to, for example, moved from place to place among well-known institutions in Shanghai, Nanking, Wuchang and Tsingtao in 1926–30, eventually settling at Tsing-hua University in 1931. The reasons for his peripatetic existence were primarily the budgetary difficulties of the colleges, and student unrest.[95]

Chinese education was still a small show after a quarter century of the republic. The national figure for student enrolment in colleges and universities stood at 42,710 in 1932–3, and increased to 46,758 in 1933–4.[96]

---

[93] Yang Liang-kung, *Tsao-ch'i san-shih-nien ti chiao-hseuh sheng-huo* (My life as an educator: the first 30 years), 73–5. Yang was president of the Provincial Anhwei University (1929–31), where the student enrolment was about 400.

[94] Ministry of Education, Office of Statistics, *Erh-shih-san nien-tu ch'üan-kuo kao-teng chiao-yü t'ung-chi* (Statistics on higher education in China for the academic year 1934–5), 100–1, table 60. Unfortunately no separate figure is shown for the student enrolment at the Provincial Anhwei University alone.

[95] Liang Shih-ch'iu, *T'an Wen I-to* (About Wen I-to), 73–101.

[96] K'o Shu-p'ing, 'Wang Hsueh-t'ing (Wang Shih-chieh)', 4.

College graduates totalled 7,311 in 1933 and 7,552 in 1934, hardly enough to keep pace with the growth of government. These results were too small when projected against the size of the country. In a comparative summary of higher education in twenty-six countries compiled by the Ministry of Education in 1935, China ranked last, showing 0·88 college-level student for every 10,000 population in 1934. Turkey, ranked 25 just above China, had in 1928 (five years into the regime of Ataturk) three college students per 10,000 population.[97] In short, college-educated persons at this high point of Republican China still constituted a thin top segment of the modern elite, hardly more numerous than the upper degree holders of the scholar-gentry class had been in the traditional era. Meantime the detailed substance of modern higher education, the content of the curriculum and how well it was taught, remain still obscure. The institutional record comes almost entirely from professors and administrators rather than from students. We have as yet little idea of the instruction that was actually made available, its appropriateness to meet China's current needs, or even the numbers it reached.

Advanced research

With the advent of the Nationalist government the scholarly community was encouraged in its hopes by the creation of a central research academy, the Academia Sinica. Plans for the founding of a national research institute had been discussed in 1927, initially by Ts'ai Yuan-p'ei, Chang Jen-chieh (Chang Ching-chiang), and Li Shih-tseng, all veteran KMT members with years of service in modern education. Their common goal was to create in China the type of government-financed research at advanced levels that had so strongly impressed Ts'ai years before in Germany. Later on younger scientists and scholars, including Hu Kuang-fu, Wang Chin, Wang Shih-chieh, and Chou Lan (Chou Keng-sheng), were asked to join in the planning. Academia Sinica's formal founding was announced in Shanghai on 9 June 1928, with Ts'ai Yuan-p'ei as its government-appointed president.[98] Placed directly under the supervision of the central government, the academy was to have three divisions: Research, comprising the individual research institutes; Administration, headed by a secretary-general; and an advisory organ called the National Science Council that

---

97 Ministry of Education, *Statistics 1934–5*, section 2, 'Tables', 2–3, table 1, 'Higher education in China and major nations in the world'. The years included in the table range from 1928 to 1934; in contrast to China and Turkey, the US (1932) ranked first with 73 college students per 10,000 population, but Japan ranked twenty-second with 9 per 10,000.

98 T'ao Ying-hui, 'Ts'ai Yuan-p'ei yü Chung-yang yen-chiu-yuan 1927–1940' (Ts'ai Yuan-p'ei and the Academia Sinica, 1927–1940), in *Bulletin of the Institute of Modern History*, 7 (1978) 6.

consisted of both charter members and members by special invitation.[99] Inspired by a vision of China clothed in modernity and contributing to the fund of world knowledge, the scholars and scientists began their research projects as soon as the institutes were organized. Two features stood out: the majority of the research institutes were in the natural sciences, and a substantial portion of the leaders of Academia Sinica had been active in the work of the Science Society as well as in the emerging professional associations.[100]

Academia Sinica, however, had no monopoly on the top scientists and scholars. As differences of view widened between Ts'ai Yuan-p'ei and Li Shih-tseng (Li Yü-ying, who had received advanced training in France) over the proper structure of higher education and research, Li left the original Academia Sinica group, and in 1929 founded the National Peiping Research Academy, a separate entity under which for the next two decades half a dozen scientific institutes carried out advanced research and publication. Li Shu-hua later joined this institute as its deputy director.[101]

In both science and social science, one important new development was the young returned-scholars' insistence that field investigation be given equal attention with laboratory analysis and library research. But field research, using the methods of modern science, had to demonstrate its value to Chinese classical scholars trained to literary research only. This demonstration began when Chinese palaeographers versed in the ancient writing on prehistoric bronzes became aware in the 1890s that 'oracle bones' from the Anyang area bore inscriptions in prehistoric Chinese. Collecting thousands of inscribed oracle bones from dealers, these scholars began to decipher the prehistoric characters and were prepared to dig for more. Another stimulus for field work came from the Geological Survey of China set up in 1916 under the Ministry of Industry and Commerce, to map the country and survey its natural resources. Under the energetic leadership of Ting Wen-chiang (V. K. Ting), Weng Wen-hao, Li Ssu-kuang (J. S. Lee) and others, mainly trained in Britain, the survey's mapping and explorations set new standards. It also sponsored work in palaeontology that culminated in the discovery of Peking Man. Set up in the Peking Union Medical College was a Cainozoic Laboratory which in the 1920s demonstrated how explorers and scientists from New York State (A. W. Grabau, palaeontological adviser to the Geological Survey), Canada (Davidson Black), Sweden (J. G. Andersson), Germany

(J. F. Weidenreich), and France (P. Teilhard de Chardin) could help train a new generation of Chinese archaeologists including P'ei Wen-chung, who led the excavations that in 1929 discovered Peking Man at Chou-k'ou-tien, south-west of Peking.[102]

The most famous discovery after Peking Man was the unearthing of the formerly-only-legendary Shang dynasty capital at Anyang, Honan. In 1928 the Academia Sinica's Institute of History and Philology under the direction of Fu Ssu-nien, who had been a student leader of the May Fourth movement at Peita, added archaeology to its historical and linguistic work. Fu invited Li Chi, who had taken his Ph.D. in 1923 in anthropology at Harvard, to direct the Anyang project. The excavations pursued there from 1928 to 1937 have been described in Li's remarkable book, *Anyang*. It recounts an heroic saga, how the field work, laboratory analyses and scientific study of the results were carried to completion over decades of warfare and dislocations – a great achievement of scholarship.[103]

In medical education the highest standards were set by the Peking Union Medical College which, following a century of medical efforts by missionaries, was supported from 1915 to 1947 by the Rockefeller Foundation to be a research and training hospital. Its 300 or more graduates after 1924 helped staff the national public health service while its faculty's researches contributed especially in parasitology and in dealing with communicable diseases like schistosomiasis, hookworm and kala-azar.[104]

Universities also helped to extend the frontiers of learning. The first had been the Institute of Chinese Studies founded by Peita in 1921 under the directorship of Shen Yin-mo. Although its plans at Peita included publication of research results and a drive to recruit corresponding research fellows, this institute as it came into being was actually more like a Western postgraduate school, with *yen-chiu-sheng* (postgraduate students or 'research students') working independently with individual professors in pursuit of given topics.[105] Admission to the institute was determined at first not by the possession of a college degree but by submission of previous professional publications.

[102] Jen Hung-chün, 'Wu-shih-nien lai ti k'o-hsueh' (Science in the past 50 years), in P'an Kung-chan, ed. *Wu-shih-nien lai ti Chung-kuo* (China in the past 50 years), hereafter cited as Jen, 'Wu-shih-nien', 190; *BDRC* 3.67; and Li Chi, *Anyang*, 34–48.
[103] Li Chi, *Anyang*; Kwang-chih Chang, *The archaeology of ancient China*, 3rd edn., 1977, 3–18 summarizes the growth of archaeological research on China.
[104] See Mary Brown Bullock, *An American transplant*; Mary E. Ferguson, *China Medical Board and Peking Union Medical College*; and John Z. Bowers, *Western medicine in a Chinese palace*. The files in the Rockefeller Foundation archives indicate that in addition to its broad medical concerns, the foundation assisted work in mass education, agricultural research, librarianship and other areas, especially in the 1930s.
[105] T'ao Ying-hui, 'Ts'ai/Peita', 397.

Ideals, enthusiasm, and expert planning aside, the work of the academic community in the 1920s still encountered a frequent obstacle, inadequate financial support. More than one contemporary record refers to this in a matter-of-fact tone: 'China being in the midst of civil war, government colleges and universities suffered from arrears in receipt of budgeted revenues...'[106] In order to make ends meet some professors had to teach at two or more institutions simultaneously. In such circumstances, getting allocations for research would be difficult, and so assistance from friends and from outside sources could be crucial.

The sociology of knowledge may be expected to benefit from detailed studies of the personnel configurations, groups, factions and cliques that advanced modern learning in Republican China. To begin with, the small elite of students abroad followed tradition by forming student fraternities or associations (*hui*) for mutual support among themselves. Quite different in aim and style from the secret society lodge (*tongs*) among Chinatown merchants, these student fraternities selected and counselled junior members, convened summer retreats, and formed personal bonds of trust and friendship that could be of use later on in China. Best known of these several groups was CCH (abbreviated from Ch'eng-chih hui, an 'association for the achievement of one's life goals', also known as 'Cross and Sword').[107]

On their return to China the young Ph.D.s became professors committed, like all professors, to reproducing themselves; a fortunate few in university institutes for advanced research were able to pursue their specialities, while younger students who assisted them received training. Peita, Tsing-hua, and Yenching in the Peking area, and Chung-shan University and Lingnan in Canton, for example, set up specialized research institutes and the results, generally of high quality, were published in their own academic journals.

Among the outstanding institutes of this type was the Nankai Institute of Economics, established in 1931 under the leadership of Franklin Ho (Ho Lien), who as professor of public finance and statistics at Nankai University was also pioneering Nankai's systematic studies of North China industries. This charted a new direction in the teaching of economics in China; instead of using Western experience and examples, the study of Chinese economic life was not based on data gathered from within the

[106] H. D. Fong, *Reminiscences of a Chinese economist at 70*, 31.
[107] Now no longer secret, CCH published a history and directory. Its membership included Chi Ch'ao-ting, Chiang T'ing-fu (T. F. Tsiang), Chiang Meng-lin (Monlin), Fang Hsien-t'ing (H. D. Fong), Ho Lien (Franklin Ho), K'ung Hsiang-hsi (H. H. Kung), Kuo Ping-wen, Meng Chih (Paul Meng), Tsou Ping-wen, Weng Wan-ko (Wango Weng), Yen Yang-ch'u (Y. C. James Yen). Personal communication from Wango Weng, August 1979.

country. Ho used personal contacts he had made as a graduate student in the United States, including membership in CCH (of which Chang Po-ling was also a member), and was able to attract other young and well-trained economists. H. D. Fong (Fang Hsien-t'ing), for example, a Yale Ph.D. of 1928, joined the Nankai faculty in 1929, and became a member of the Committee on Social and Economic Research that evolved into the Institute of Economics.[108] Ho and Fong were soon joined by Wu Ta-yeh, Li Cho-min (Choh-min Li), Lin T'ung-chi, and Leonard G. Ting, all of whom became well-known economic researchers.

While Nankai as a private university had the advantage of financial independence and administrative stability, still its resources were inadequate for the ambitious design of the institute, which Ho modelled on the London School of Economics. To bring the institute into being, Ho had contributed a personal gift of Ch. $500 as well as his own library, and in 1929 a grant of Ch. $2,000 from the Institute of Pacific Relations assured the institute of its existence. This also marked the beginning of the Nankai Institute Library that later became famous for its comprehensive collection on the Chinese economy.[109] At this juncture Professor R. H. Tawney of London arrived at Nankai University for research and to give lectures during the winter of 1929–30.[110] The international visibility thus gained, and evidence of the high level of scholarship among the Chinese economists, led to a five-year grant in 1932 from the Rockefeller Foundation. Thus aided, the institute published some twenty well-researched monographs (including massive field data) before war erupted in 1937 and the Nankai campus was devastated.[111]

Research on land use as pioneered at Cornell was undertaken at Nanking University in the 1920s by J. L. Buck and others, whose sample data on the Chinese farm economy opened up the whole field of agronomic technology. From 1934 this was pursued by Shen Tsung-han and others at the Chinese National Agricultural Research Bureau.[112]

Sociology as it developed at Yenching University began with social

108 Fong, *Reminiscences*, 36, 39–40. Fong points to the many able faculty members Chang Po-ling was recruiting for Nankai, 'especially from among members of his own fraternity Chen [sic] Chih Hui'. *Ibid.* 38.

109 *Ibid.* 41, 42, 45.

110 *Ibid.* 45. Tawney's research resulted in the book *Land and labour in China* (1932). He also contributed to a League of Nations report along with C. H. Becker (Berlin), M. Falski (Poland), and P. Langevin (Paris), *The reorganization of education in China*, which questioned many things including the appropriateness for China of the American educational model.

111 Fong, *Reminiscences*, 45–7. The grant enabled the Nankai Institute to add half a dozen faculty members recently returned from the US, including Wu Ta-yeh, Li Choh-min, Lin T'ung-chi and Leonard G. Ting.

112 See John Lossing Buck, *Land utilization in China*; also T. H. Shen, *Shen Tsung-han tzu-shu* (Shen Tsung-han's memoirs), by a Cornell-trained leader in the field.

surveys originally inspired by a YMCA secretary, who in 1912 formed the Peking Students Social Service Club in order to bring the members more into contact with the facts of Chinese life. By 1915 this group had conducted a pioneer study of 320 Peking rickshaw-pullers, an eye-opening look at the human condition later immortalized by the novelist Lao She (see ch. 9). The 'social survey wing' of the Yenching Sociology Department set up in 1928 a rural research station in the village of Ch'ing-ho, three miles north of the new Yenching campus north-west of Peking.[113] Building on this beginning in social survey work, Western-trained Chinese sociologists at Yenching then proceeded to lay the foundations of this science in China. This growth at Yenching was led by Wu Wen-tsao, who arrived in 1929 from Columbia where he had met J. S. Burgess and studied sociology. Wu Wen-tsao's leadership and planning, sending his students abroad, produced a group who played a dominant role in developing their field. Its growth was stimulated when leading American and British sociologists visited and lectured at Yenching.[114]

Social research, as always, required a basis of historical and institutional knowledge. By 1928 L. K. T'ao (T'ao Meng-ho) who had finished his London B.A. in 1912, was head of the Peiping Institute of Social Research supported by the China Foundation. Its researchers among other things began to explore the newly opened Ch'ing archives for purposes of social and economic institutional history.[115] In 1934 it merged with the Academia Sinica Institute of Social Research.

Field work was also pursued by the Institute for Research in Chinese Architecture. It had been founded by a prominent ex-official (Chu Chi-ch'ien) in 1928 but pursued mainly library research until after 1930, when its field explorations to discover ancient monuments – temples, pagodas, bridges – were led by two architects trained at the University of Pennsylvania, Liang Ssu-ch'eng and his wife Lin Hui-yin, and a Japan-trained colleague, Liu Tun-chen. Here again, a new scientific interest, aided by imported methods, led to historic discoveries.[116]

113 In this development J. S. Burgess, who had represented Princeton-in-Peking, worked with Hsu Shih-lien (Leonard Hsu). Burgess and Sidney Gamble published in 1921 *Peking: a social survey*. See Yung-chen Chiang, 'The Yenching Sociology Department: from social service to social engineering 1919–1945' (unpublished paper, 1984, cited with author's permission). See also David Arkush, *Fei Xiaotong (Fei Hsiao-t'ung) and sociology in revolutionary China*.

114 His students included Fei Hsiao-t'ung (*Peasant life in China*), Lin Yueh-hua (*The golden wing: a sociological study of Chinese familism*) and C. K. Yang (Yang Ch'ing-k'un) (*Religion in Chinese society*); see also Francis L. K. Hsu, *Under the ancestor's shadow: Chinese culture and personality*.

115 See the files of *Chung-kuo chin-tai ching-chi shih yen-chiu chi-k'an* (Studies in modern economic history of China).

116 See introduction by Wilma Fairbank to Liang Ssu-ch'eng, *A pictorial history of Chinese architecture: a study of the development of its structural system and the evolution of its types*.

TABLE 5

Leadership in the Academia Sinica 1928–40 during Ts'ai Yuan-p'ei's presidency

	Years	Highest earned degree	Other professional affiliations
I. Secretary-general			
Yang Ch'üan	1928–33	Harvard MBA (following Cornell B.Sc. in Mech. Engr.)	Bd. of Directors, Science Society; prof. engr., South-east U.; in Ministry of Education
Ting Wen-chiang (V. K. Ting)	1934–6	Glasgow B.Sc. Zool. & Geol.	Prof. geol. Peking U.; director Geol. Survey of China
Chu Chia-hua	1936–8	Berlin U. Ph.D. Geology	Chairman geol. dep., Peking U.; president, Chung-shan U., Nat. Central U.; Minister of Education
Jen Hung-chün (H. C. Zen)	1939–42	Columbia M.Sc. Chemistry	President, Science Society, prof. Peking U.; director, China Foundation; president Nat. Szechwan U.
II. Institute directors			
Physics			
Ting Hsi-lin	1928–47	Birmingham M.Sc.	Prof. physics, Nat. Peking U. and Nat. Central U.
Chemistry			
Wang Chin	1928–34	Lehigh U. B.Sc.	Chm. chem. dept., Nat. South-east U. and Nat. Central U.; Bd of Directors, Science Society
Chuang Ch'ang-kung	1934–8	Chicago Ph.D.	Prof. & chm. chem. dept., Nat. North-east U.; dean, Coll. of Science Nat. Central U.
Jen Hung-chün	1939–42	(see above)	
Engineering			
Chou Jen	1929–49	Cornell M.Sc. in Mech. Engr.	Bd. of Directors, Science Society; chief engr. Szechwan Iron & Steel Works; dean, Coll. of Engr., Nat. Central U.
Geology			
Li Ssu-kuang	1928–49	Birmingham D.Sc.	Prof. & chm. geology dept., Nat. Peking U., chm. & Bd of directors, Chinese Geol. Assoc.
Astronomy			
Kao Lu	1927–9	Peking U., B.Sc., studied at Brussels	Director, Central Meteorol. Station, Peking; head of Chinese Coll. of Meteorology
Yu Sung-ch'ing	1929–47	U. California Ph.D.	Chm. astronomy Dept., U. of Amoy; director, Purple Mountain Meteorol. Station, Nanking
Meteorology			
Chu K'o-chen (Koching Chu)	1928–46	Harvard Ph.D.	Prof. Nat. South-east U.; pres., Chekiang U.; president, Science Society; president, Chinese Meterol. Assoc.

TABLE 5 *(cont.)*

	Years	Highest earned degree	Other professional affiliations
History & Philology			
Fu Ssu-nien	1928–50	Studied at London U. and Berlin U. following Peking U., B.A.	Prof. & dean, Nat. Central U.; prof. Nat. Peking U.; (later) Secretary-general, Ac. Sin.
Psychology			
T'ang Yueh	1929–33	Harvard Ph.D.	Prof. Nat. Peking U.; chm. psychology dept., Tsing-hua U.
Wang Ching-hsi	1934–47	Hopkins, Ph.D.	Prof. Nat. Chung-shan U.; prof. & chm. zoology dept., Nat. Peking U.
Social Sciences			
Yang Tuan-liu	1928–9 (1929–34 various acting directors)	Studied at London U.	Chief of Accounting, Ac. Sin.; prof. econ., Nat. Wuhan U.
T'ao Meng-ho	1934–49	London U., B.A.	Prof. Nat. Peking U.; director, Inst. of Social Research of the China Foundation to 1934
Zoology & Botany			
Wang Chia-chi	1934–44	U. of Penn. Ph.D.	Prof. biology, Nat. Central U.; Bd. of Directors, Science Society

Adapted from T'ao Ying-hui, 'Ts'ai/Ac. Sin.', 33–6.

Research support

During the early 1930s research and publication expanded apace. Leaders of the Academia Sinica's ten research institutes (table 5), who were of the May Fourth generation of intellectuals, took their responsibilities with a great deal of seriousness. Scientific journals and other publications (table 6), sponsored by diverse research and professional organizations, increased manyfold; among the major periodicals there were nine in geology and palaeontology, six in biological sciences, two in meteorology, two in chemistry and chemical engineering, and one in physics.[117] The ultimate vision of these scientists was to place Chinese science on an equal footing with that of other modern countries and so contribute creatively to the world of science. At the same time in fields of advanced work such as geology, organic and inorganic chemistry and nutrition, progress was inspired by the immediate objective of industrialization. Under the direction of Fu Ssu-nien, the *Bulletin of the Institute of History and Philology* of Academia Sinica, along with its special publications, set a high standard for scholarly research in Chinese history and culture.

It is not possible here to appraise the very extensive efforts of the

[117] Jen, 'Wu-shih-nien', 191–8.

TABLE 6

Major research institutions and professional journals, 1916–44

Founding date	Institution	Major publications
1916	Geological Survey of China	*Bulletin of Chinese palaeontology*; *Geological Review*; *Geol. Journal*; *Chinese Mining Industries*; *Journal of Seismology*; *Journal of Energy Resources*; *Journal of Agronomy*
1922	Chinese Geological Society	*CGS Review: Geological Critic*
	Huang-hai (Yellow Sea) Laboratory of Chemical Industries	
	Inst. for Biological Research (Science Society organ)	IBR *Bulletin*
1926	Chinese Meteorological Soc.	*Meteor. Rev.*
1927	Fan Memorial Biological Inst.	FMBI *Review*
1928	Academia Sinica: *research insts. established in succeeding years*:	
	Institute of:	
	Physics	
	Chemistry	*Bulletin* of the Ch. Chem. Soc.; *Chemical Engineering* (Ch. Soc. Chem. Engr.)
	Astronomy	
	Meteorology	*Bulletin* of Inst. of Meteorol.
	Geology	
	Engineering	
	History and Philology	*Bulletin* of IHP and special series
	Social Sciences	
1929	Zoology and Botany	*Bulletin* of IZB; *Journal of Experimental Biology*
	Psychology	
1929	Peiping Research Academy	
	Physics	
	Chemistry	
	Zoology	
	Botany	
1930	Radiology	
1932	Pharmacology	
1931	Central Industrial Experimental Institute	
	Nankai Institute of Economics	*Bulletin* of NIE and monographs
1932	Central Agricultural Exper. Institute	
1934	Research labs of universities	Various disciplines, e.g., *J. of Forestry and Botany*, Chung-shan U. (Canton)
1940	Chinese Geographical Institute	
1943	Institute of Physiological Psychology	*Chinese Journal of Physiology*

Sources: based on Jen Hung-chün, 'Wu-shih-nien', 188–9; T'ao Ying-hui, 'Ts'ai Yuan-pei yü Chung-yang yen-chiu-yuan', 7.

Ministry of Education in Nanking, where Wang Shih-chieh, former president of Wuhan University, served as Minister of Education from 1933 to 1937. The ministry was charged with promotion of the national school system, campaigns for literacy, and the setting of standards for middle-school graduation and admission to college. Quite separate from the ministry and under the protection of the unequal treaty system, which assured a steady flow of funds from the central government, the China Foundation bore a special responsibility for aiding advanced training and research. While developing separately, the expanding activities of the China Foundation interpenetrated those of the universities and the Academia Sinica, for the funding programmes of the foundation touched a wide range of scholarship. A summary of the grants awarded by the China Foundation in the two decades 1926–45 shows that 96 institutions – including universities and colleges, research institutions, and cultural and educational organizations – were assisted by grants that reached a total of Ch. $24,250,893 plus US $392,795.[118]

The projects launched or financially assisted by the foundation fell into several categories.[119] (1) A direct cooperation from 1931 to 1937 with the National Peking University, whereby each contributed Ch. $200,000 annually to subsidize faculty salaries and to support released time for research. The aid from the China Foundation drastically reduced the number of professors holding concurrent teaching positions in other institutions; and now that professors could have more time for their own scholarly pursuits with improved salaries, the morale at Peita was greatly improved, to the point where several distinguished scholars were attracted to the faculty. (2) The establishment of science professorships in six leading normal colleges chosen with geographical diversity in view: Mukden, Nanking, Wuchang, Canton, and Chengtu. (3) Grants of research fellowships to senior scientists for the furtherance of their research; these (table 7) were long-term grants awarded to a limited number of individuals whose professional work already had gained wide recognition. (4) Scientific research fellowships for younger scholars in the natural and social sciences for advanced training either in China or abroad. Of the 732 fellowships and 3 special prizes given out between 1928 and 1945 (table 8), 327 fellows did their advanced study and research in China; among those who went abroad, 208 went to the United States, 64 to France, 56 to Germany, and 39 to Britain. Their specializations ranged broadly from agriculture and archaeology, through botany, chemistry, and dozens of other fields to zoology. It was notable that soil

[118] *Summary report,* 5.
[119] The present account is based on *ibid.* 6–16, and Peter Buck, 221–4.

TABLE 7

China Foundation Scientific Research Fellowships, 1930–45

Name	Field	Institutional affiliation
Chen Huan-yung	Botany	Botanical Institute, Chung-shan University
Chuang Ch'ang-kung	Chemistry	Sometime Director, Institute of Chemistry, Ac.Sin.
A. W. Grabau	Palaeontology	National Peking University
Hu Hsien-hsiao	Botany	Director, Fan Memorial Biological Institute
Li Chi	Archaeology	Institute of History and Philology, Ac.Sin.
Ping Chih	Zoology	Director, Biological Laboratory, Science Society
Weng Wen-hao	Geology	Director, National Geological Survey of China

Source: based on *Summary report*, 8.

TABLE 8

Distribution of China Foundation Fellowships by field of specialization, 1928–45

	28	29	30	31	32	33	34	35	36	37	38	39	40	41	42	43	44	45	Total
Zoology	5	13	12	10	11	13	9	12	12	6	7	8	10	6	6	3	3	1	147
Chemistry	5	8	7	9	13	11	11	9	7	9	14	10	11	5	5	4	2	6	145
Physics	2	4	7	9	4	6	5	6	8	8	6	2	1	3	1	2	2	3	79
Botany	3	1	6	8	6	6	10	9	5	7	2	—	1	—	1	2	2	6	75
Geology	2	3	3	1	2	3	4	7	4	4	2	4	4	2	3	4	2	2	55
Physiology	4	5	1	—	2	2	4	3	5	7	4	2	2	2	—	—	—	6	49
Mathematics	—	—	1	—	—	2	5	4	3	4	2	—	—	—	—	2	1	6	32
Engineering	—	—	—	—	—	—	—	—	—	—	2	6	7	5	5	4	1	1	31
Agriculture	—	—	3	—	—	1	—	—	—	—	1	1	—	3	7	4	2	4	25
Medicine	—	—	1	—	—	—	—	—	—	—	—	—	1	1	8	3	1	2	17
Soil technology	—	—	2	—	—	—	—	2	1	—	2	1	1	1	2	1	1	1	15
Meteorology	—	—	1	2	—	1	2	1	1	1	1	—	—	—	—	1	1	2	14
History	—	—	—	—	—	—	—	—	—	5	1	—	—	—	1	1	1	—	9
Anthropology	—	1	1	—	1	—	—	—	1	1	—	1	1	1	—	1	1	—	9
Economics	—	—	—	—	—	—	—	—	—	3	2	—	—	—	2	—	—	—	7
Psychology	—	1	—	—	1	2	—	—	—	—	—	—	—	—	—	1	1	—	6
Sociology	—	—	—	—	—	—	—	—	—	2	2	—	—	—	—	2	—	—	6
Astronomy	1	—	—	1	1	—	—	1	—	—	—	—	—	—	—	—	—	—	4
Palaeontology	1	—	1	1	—	—	—	—	—	—	—	—	—	—	—	—	—	—	3
Geography	—	—	—	—	—	—	—	—	—	—	—	—	—	—	—	1	1	—	2
Philology	—	—	—	—	—	—	—	—	—	—	—	—	—	—	1	—	—	—	1
Education	—	—	—	—	—	—	—	—	—	—	—	—	—	—	—	—	1		1
Total	23	36	46	41	43	47	50	53	48	57	48	35	39	28	42	37	21	41	735

Source: table 1 in *Summary report*, 10.

technology, a relatively new speciality in China, received fifteen fellowships over the period, while no area in the humanities and social sciences had more than ten. Engineering definitely made its appearance as a rewarding field after the start of the war. (5) Establishment of institutions or organizations under the auspices of the China Foundation, including several that evolved into major institutions in the world of science and culture, such as the Fan Memorial Institute of Biology founded in 1928 in honour of the China Foundation's first director, Fan Yuan-lien, the Peiping Institute of Social Research that merged into an institute of Academia Sinica in 1934, and the China Institute in America that administered the Boxer fellowships there.

While faculty members of the Christian colleges and universities shared in the China Foundation's support on a merit basis, another foundation, the Harvard-Yenching Institute, supported sinological studies among the Christian colleges in particular. Set up in 1928 through the initiative of the heads of Yenching University (J. Leighton Stuart) and of the Harvard Business School (Wallace B. Donham), this Harvard-based agency supported scholarly training and research programmes in Chinese classical studies and history under William Hung (Hung Yeh) at Yenching. The aim was to promote studies in China with modern standards and equipment (such as indexes) on the lines developed by European sinology. Grants were made to help Chinese studies in other Christian colleges; fellowships brought Chinese scholars for training at Harvard.

One institution that began as a special project of the China Foundation and subsequently grew into a major Chinese cultural resource was the National Library of Peiping, as it was officially known between 1931 and 1949.[120] In 1928 the China Foundation funded the establishment of the Metropolitan Library, with temporary quarters in Pei-hai Park, as the first step toward a national library, and appointed Yuan T'ung-li (T. L. Yuan, New York State BLS 1923) as its director. Three years later the foundation appropriated Ch. $1,374,000 for the construction of a spacious new library building, at the same time that the Ministry of Education proposed the merging of the Metropolitan Library with the old National Library; the latter organ, established in 1909, contained a valuable collection of books transferred from the former imperial Hanlin Academy and the Grand Secretariat depository. Thus, by the time the new buildings were completed in 1931, the National Library of Peiping also came into being.[121] T. L. Yuan made it into the centre of library activities in China,

[120] By 1926 the largest library in China was reported to be that of National Peking University (176,000 volumes) with Tsing-hua second (87,000), Canton Christian (Lingnan) third (68,000), Nanking University fourth (61,000), followed by Chiao-t'ung, Nankai and others. *CYB, 1926,* 430.

[121] *Summary report,* 12–13. Ch'eng Yuan, ed. *T. L. Yuan: a tribute,* hereafter *T. L. Yuan,* 53–4.

leading the way in introducing new techniques such as the compilation of union catalogues, a union list of serials, inter-library loans, a photostat service, exchange of materials with institutions in other countries, and the exchange of librarians.[122] In addition, the National Library of Peiping initiated the publication of research tools, among them the highly regarded *T'u-shu chi-k'an* (*Quarterly bulletin of Chinese bibliography*), documentary collections, and indexes in the areas of sinology, literature and historical geography. After helping to found the Library Association of China in 1925 Yuan was instrumental in publishing two periodicals on library science.[123] As a segment in the effort to modernize China, Yuan and the other forward-looking librarians of the 1930s found their role integral to the growth of science and modern education. In 1933 the Nationalist government established the National Central Library, which eventually became the official repository of materials received by exchange from other governments.

In 1936 a 'last and largest' science convention was held. Sponsored by the Science Society in conjunction with the Chinese Mathematical, Zoological, Physical, Chemical, and Botanical Societies, 250 papers were presented at the sessions, and of these some 60 per cent 'reflected work done at institutions that had received financial aid from the China Foundation'.[124]

Up to 1937, by strenuous efforts and with mutual support, the leaders of the academic community were able to influence educational policy to a large extent, and bring about important progress in developing modern institutions. Judging by appearances, China would seem to have arrived at the take-off point, with a new generation of intellectuals busily engaged in study and research in an expanding number of universities and institutions and extending their activities into new territories of inquiry. The great majority of the leaders of the mid-thirties were heavily influenced by Western models. Being liberals – a term full of multi-faceted implications – they firmly believed in the possibility of progress. Being also educated Chinese who still retained, consciously or unconsciously, the Confucian social ethic, they were equally convinced of their own obligation to shoulder a share of the responsibility for national reconstruction. To establish in China academic institutions comparable to leading schools in Western nations was a vision shared by most of these academic leaders. Hu Shih, for example, held to a lifelong ideal formed during his student years at Cornell, that in developing into a modern nation China should establish such indispensable institutions as great national universities at the levels of Harvard, Oxford, Cambridge and the Sorbonne, as well

[122] T. L. Yuan, 55.   [123] Ibid. 56–7.
[124] Ibid. 234.

as public libraries at local, provincial and national levels, the last to be comparable to the Library of Congress, the Bibliothèque Nationale, and the British Museum. Lo Chia-lun confessed that in 1927, when he was in charge of the Central Political Institute, he envisioned changing the school into a four-year institution that would combine the characteristics of the London School of Economics and L'École des Sciences Politiques.[125] For a few years, the first generation of modern intellectuals believed themselves to be reasonably successful in their design for a modern China.

The negative side of this well-articulated and close-knit world of academic leaders, however, was a reality that could not be ignored, for the entire academic structure was built upon a paradoxical situation. While the scientists and scholars bent their efforts to institution-building, the opportunity for translating their aims into actuality was predicated on their ability to sway the political establishment which, after 1928, meant the Kuomintang. Many academic leaders had participated in the republican revolution under Sun Yat-sen, and could rely on that linkage to help their educational work; nationalism, the common language and overriding sentiment prevailing in all segments of society, also served to mitigate potentially destructive confrontations between the liberal individual and government authority. Yet the contradictions were never far below the surface, as for example in the case of the low-grade but continuing tension regarding control of the foundation's funds between the Nationalist government and the executives of the China Foundation.[126]

In 1933 the precariousness of liberalism in China was suddenly demonstrated. The rise of fascism in Italy and Germany was inspiring imitators in China (see chapter 3), authoritarian doctrines were coming to the fore, and the academic wing of the May Fourth movement, though they eschewed revolutionary politics, could never be entirely unaware of former colleagues who had chosen the path of Marxist revolution. The continuing rivalry of the two party-dictatorships strengthened the forces of KMT mobilization and repression. It happened that Ts'ai Yuan-p'ei's right-hand man was Yang Ch'üan (Yang Chien, Yang Hsing-fo, 1898–1933), a one-time secretary of Sun Yat-sen, graduate of Cornell and Harvard, secretary of the Science Society 1919–22, who had served as the first secretary-general or chief executive officer of Academia Sinica since 1928. Among his many activities Yang worked with Mme Sun Yat-sen (Soong Ch'ing-ling) in humanitarian causes and also had helped set up the short-lived China League for Civil Rights, which had a liberal and also

---

[125] Hu Shih, *Hu Shih liu-hsueh jih-chi* (Diaries of Hu Shih as a student abroad), 3.583. Lo Chia-lun, 'Wo so jen-shih ti Tai Chi-t'ao hsien-sheng' (The Tai Chi-t'ao I knew), in 'Recollections', 146.
[126] Peter Buck, 223–4.

leftist backing. Yang Ch'üan was spectacularly assassinated outside his Academia Sinica office in June 1933 by gunmen who were then quickly killed by the Nanking police. Unlike the assassination of Sung Chiao-jen in 1913, the instigators of this deed were never traced. Ts'ai Yuan-p'ei, though he continued as president of the Academia Sinica until his death in 1940, chose to keep a low public profile after 1933.[127] After the murder of Yang Ch'üan came the final Nationalist campaign to exterminate the CCP in Kiangsi and the eventual Chinese resistance to Japan's aggression in 1937, when the KMT's chief party organizer, Ch'en Li-fu, took over as minister of education.

In short, the successes of liberal educators in Republican China were achieved during an interlude when violence from abroad and from within were not yet in the ascendant. The relative success of the academic leaders, working among largely like-minded colleagues, could well have fostered a sense of confidence that, in the larger context, was not supported by reality. Yet this sense of confidence and community placed a screen between these leaders and the world far beyond their circle of friends. With the exception of a few specialists, the life and problems of the mass of the population of China remained untouched by academic work. Huang Yen-p'ei, erstwhile disciple of Chang Chien, struggled to establish vocational education (*chih-yeh chiao-yü*) as one of the options open to those who needed vocational training; the impact of this movement, however, was confined largely to segments of the urban population, as links to the rural communities were not effectively forged, and after 1928 vocational schools became increasingly like general schools.[128] And in the mid-thirties the rural reconstruction movement was just getting started under leaders like T'ao Hsing-chih, Yen Yang-ch'u at Ting-hsien, Hopei, Liang Shu-ming at Tsou-p'ing, Shantung, and in an experimental county near Nanking.[129] As T. F. Tsiang, an academic pioneer in the history of China's foreign relations at Tsing-hua, put it to a London audience in 1935, 'We have sinned in living apart from the people...we cannot make ourselves understood to a village crowd in China, far less make ourselves accepted as leaders of the peasants.'[130]

[127] See John King Fairbank, *Chinabound: A fifty-year memoir*, 71–6. The enmity between Ts'ai and Ch'en Kuo-fu is touched upon in Allen B. Linden, 'Politics and education in Nationalist China: the case of the University Council, 1927–1928', *JAS* 27.4 (Aug. 1968) 763–76.

[128] Gewurtz, 157–74.

[129] See the discussion of the rural reconstruction movement by P. A. Kuhn in ch. 7 above; also Wu Hsiang-hsiang, *Yen Yang-ch'u chuan* (Biography of Yen Yang-ch'u), chs. 3, 5, 6; and Charles Hayford, 'Rural reconstruction in China: Y. C. James Yen and the Mass Education Movement' (Harvard University, Ph.D. dissertation, 1973).

[130] T. F. Tsiang, 'The present situation in China', *International Affairs* (14 July 1935); on T. F. Tsiang's development at Tsing-hua of research specialists on the history of modern China's foreign relations see Charles R. Lilley, 'Tsiang T'ing-fu: between two worlds, 1895–1935' (University of Maryland, Ph.D. dissertation, 1979), chs. 8–9.

For the leaders of the academic community the modernization of China's ancient culture at the level of higher education had been an all-absorbing task of intellectual innovation and institution building. They followed tradition in believing that scholars have a responsibility to advise on public policy. Notable among several journals of opinion in the 1930s was the *Independent Critic* (*Tu-li p'ing-lun*). This weekly review was edited by a group of liberal intellectuals in Peking that included many names familiar from the academic and research world, among them Ting Wen-chiang (V. K. Ting), Hu Shih, Hu Hsien-hsiao, T'ao Meng-ho, Jen Hung-chün (H. C. Zen), Ch'en Heng-che (Sophia H. Chen Zen), Chiang Monlin, Chiang T'ing-fu (T. F. Tsiang), and Ch'en Chih-mai. Editorial board meetings were held monthly by rotation in the home of a board member, and the discussions could last well into the night. Disagreements among the editors over current public policy, or the appropriate developmental model for China, only enhanced the role of the *Independent Critic* as spokesman for the Chinese liberal-reformist viewpoint of the early 1930s.[131]

The threat of war with Japan produced a patriotic closing of ranks. Intellectuals who previously had avoided service under the party-based KMT regime at Nanking now accepted posts under Chiang Kai-shek. Weng Wen-hao and T. F. Tsiang became executive secretaries of the Nationalist government cabinet (as Chiang Monlin also was to do after the war). Hu Shih served as wartime ambassador in Washington while others served in Chungking.

Meanwhile students in the Peking-Tientsin area took the lead to rouse the country against Japanese aggression. In 1935 the 9 December and 16 December demonstrations against the formation of the Japan-inspired Hopei-Chahar Autonomous Council again pitched the students of Tsing-hua, Peita, Yenching, and other universities and secondary schools of Peking against the police and gendarmerie.[132] Perceiving the students, and the colleges and universities that nurtured them, as the cause of anti-Japanese sentiment, the Japanese summoned Chiang Monlin, president of Peita, to the Japanese barracks in the Legation Quarter and charged him with carrying on 'an extensive propaganda' against Japan. Chiang pointed out that anti-Japanese sentiment would naturally recede if Japan stopped its aggression; pressed for his personal opinion, Chiang answered, 'I am a friend of the Japanese people, but an enemy to Japanese militarism...'[133] The effort at intimidation failed but it presaged Japan's

[131] Trends of opinion in the *Independent Critic* are analysed in Eugene Lubot, *Liberalism in an illiberal age: New Culture liberals in Republican China, 1919–1937*.

[132] Freyn, *Prelude, passim*; Israel and Klein, *Rebels and bureaucrats*.

[133] Chiang Monlin (Meng-lin), *Tides from the West*, 204. The episode is also recounted in Lo Chia-lun,

savage destruction of Chinese college campuses after war broke out in July 1937.

WAR AND POSTWAR CHANGES 1937–1949

Higher education and research in wartime

War forced a debate over whether higher education should give way to military work or should continue to pursue its academic goals. But by 1938 the academic community had accepted the continuity of its educational task as essential for China's future. In the midst of major military upheavals and population dislocation, the leading uiniversities and colleges chose the strategy of moving to safer locations in the interior. The migration of dozens of institutions of higher education – involving the various stages of planning the move, negotiating for quarters in the target locations, the financing and logistics of physically moving faculty, students, staff, books and equipment, and the preparations necessary for the travellers en route – was a stirring saga in itself. Its execution demanded determination, organizational skill, coordination and adaptability. The academic community accomplished it within the first year of the war and in the process brought modern education into the less-developed hinterland.

The migration routes from the eastern provinces were diverse, but all pointed west, north-west, or south-west. A few years previously Chang Po-ling had acquired a site in Chungking in order to establish a second middle school in the Nankai system; and so the Nankai Middle School in Tientsin had no difficulty moving to its new Chungking home. Nankai University, on the other hand, was ordered by the Ministry of Education to join the National Peking and Tsing-hua Universities to form, first, the Temporary University at Changsha, Hunan, then from late 1938 onward the National South-west Associated University in Kunming, Yunnan. Other northern universities, including Peiyang College of Engineering, travelled north-westward and combined to form the National North-west Associated University at Sian for the duration of the war. The campus of West China Union University in Chengtu became home to seven other Christian colleges. Still other schools moved singly, each re-establishing itself in a new, totally unfamiliar locale: for example, National Chekiang University maintained itself in the mountain town of Tsun-i, Kweichow, and National Central University in a Chungking suburb.[134]

'Chiang Meng-lin hsien-sheng chuan-lueh' (Brief biography of Chiang Meng-lin), in 'Recollections', 98–102.
134 Chuang Tse-hsuan, 'K'ang-chan shih-nien-lai Chung-kuo hsüeh-hsiao chiao-yü tsung-chien-t'ao' (General assessment of Chinese formal education in the ten years since the [beginning of the]

TABLE 9
Wartime damage to educational institutions

Universities and colleges	Number	Loss (in Chinese $)
National	23	37,003,467
Provincial	16	8,045,919
Private (incl. Christian colleges)	38	44,171,005
Total reported damages and losses		89,220,391

Not all students were able to trek with their universities, however, nor all faculty members, and the violence of war made 1937–8 a year of setbacks and losses. Total student enrolment in 1938 was less than that of 1936 by some 20,000 persons, while the number of college faculty dropped by about 2,000 nationwide, decreases of nearly 50 and 30 per cent respectively, as the number of institutions of higher education was reduced to 91.[135] Even more devastating, both materially and psychologically, was the loss of campus property damaged or destroyed not through the random chance of war but largely by deliberate efforts of the Japanese military. The targeted bombing of Nankai University at the start of the war, which left it in ruins, was a widely-known instance of such destruction, but nearly all other institutions also suffered property losses either through bombing or through destructive use during Japanese occupation. The losses of the higher education institutions in physical structures and equipment up to the end of 1940, as compiled by the Ministry of Education, are shown in table 9.[136] In comparison the officially reported national revenue from direct taxes in 1940 amounted to only Ch. $92,441,020.[137] Yet the institutions survived and strove for continued development in the face of such destruction. Harsh wartime conditions led to an inevitable decline in the quality of scholarly endeavours even as quantitative growth took place. From a low point of 91 institutions in 1937–8 the total began to rise past the 1936–7 level

war of resistance), in *Chung-hua chiao-yü-chieh* (Chinese education), 3; see also *Chiao-yü tsa-chih* (The journal of education), 31.1 (10 Jan. 1941), special issue on higher education since the beginning of the war of resistance.

135 Chuang Tse-hsuan, 3. Ch'en Li-fu, *Four years of Chinese education (1937–1941)*, 3. Ch'en adds that part of the reason for reduced student enrolment was that some had joined the armed forces or other war-related work; see p. 29.

136 Ch'en Li-fu, 22–6. The list was not a complete one, as data were not available from ten institutions, and some figures reported only loss of equipment.

137 *China handbook 1937–1945*, comp. Chinese Ministry of Information, 189. By another computation, the total cost of higher education in 1936 nationwide was Ch. $39,275,386, or less than half of the estimated loss; see Ou Yuan-huai, 'K'ang-chan shih-nien lai ti Chung-kuo ta-hsüeh chiao-yü' (Chinese higher education in the ten years since the beginning of the war of resistance), in *Chung-hua chiao-yü-chieh*, N.S., 1.1 (15 Jan. 1947) 7.

and reached 113 in 1940. By the end of the war in 1945 the number of higher education institutions had increased to 145, and student enrolment that year grew to 73,669,[138] more than half as many again as in the peak years just before the war.

To see how the migrant universities functioned during the eight years of war, let us look at the most famous of them, the National South-west Associated University (Lienta). The tenacity of the whole academic community was a key factor in sustaining wartime education. Lienta's classroom instruction was resumed even as warfare spread to more parts of the country in the autumn of 1937: the Temporary University at Changsha opened its classes on 1 November, with the combined students and faculty of Peita, Tsing-hua, and Nankai Universities. The campus consisted partly of borrowed quarters, and partly of the planned future campus of Tsing-hua University's College of Agriculture, acquired shortly before the war just outside Changsha. At the end of the autumn term, however, with the Japanese pressing ever closer to the Central Yangtze region, the decision was made to move the university to the south-western frontier province of Yunnan. No one questioned the propriety of expending human energy and material resources in such long-distance, large-scale moving: clearly the institutions of higher education were a most valuable national resource and therefore, as a matter of course, must be saved and reconstructed so far as circumstances permitted.

In the autumn of 1938 the faculty members and students reassembled in Kunming, Yunnan (for lack of sufficient space the College of Arts and Letters and the College of Law were at first lodged in the town of Meng-tzu for several months). Some 300 students, accompanied by a few professors, had marched overland in two months from Changsha, a distance of about 1,000 miles, while a much larger contingent arrived by ship and rail through Hong Kong and the Yunnan–Indo-China Railway. When the reunion took place the university known as Lienta was born.[139] Meanwhile, college entrance examinations had been conducted, and a new freshman class was admitted to swell the existing student body from North China.

The faculty of Lienta included some of the best-known academic people in China. Student enrolment grew by 1940 to more than 3,000. The enlarged enrolment prompted Lienta to set up a branch campus for freshmen at Hsü-yung, Szechwan, beginning in 1940. The over-taxed Kunming facilities included both old buildings borrowed from local

---

[138] Ch'en Li-fu, 3. Chu Chia-hua, 'K'ang-chan ti-pa-nien chih chiao-yü' (Chinese education in the eighth year of the war), in *Chu Chia-hua*, 172.
[139] See John Israel's MS. history of Lienta.

schools and a 'New Campus' hastily and inexpensively constructed in 1938–9. The scope of the curriculum was expanded when a Teachers College was added to the four original Colleges of Arts and Letters, Science, Law and Business, and Engineering.[140] Chiang Monlin, Mei I-ch'i and Chang Po-ling, the prewar presidents of Peita, Tsing-hua and Nankai respectively, showed a statesmanlike ability to cooperate by dividing their responsibilities. Chiang and Chang spent most of their time in Chungking looking after Lienta's interests by maintaining constant communications with the government, while Mei took charge of the daily administration of the institution in Kunming. The faculty members exerted themselves to teach while adapting their own scholarly work to the vastly different geographical and intellectual environment. The sociologist Fei Hsiao-t'ung, for example, having relocated at the Provincial University of Yunnan, though sometimes invited to teach courses at Lienta, shifted his research from Lower Yangtze villages to a study of the ethnic minorities of south-western China; the Nankai Institute of Economics, cut off from its North China base, delved into the economy of the undeveloped hinterland.

Serious practical difficulties intensified as the war continued. A perennial problem was how to obtain books and equipment. What was saved and brought to Yunnan was far from enough, and new supplies were difficult to get, especially after the Indo-Chinese Railway was cut in 1940. In 1939-40 the Nationalist government appropriated US $1,000,000 for the purchase of books and equipment for Chinese universities, but by 1945 'not all had arrived'. The government decreed that science classes in secondary schools should use only domestic products for experiments so as to conserve the imports for college laboratories, but such measures were far from adequate.[141] Material deprivation of this sort caused a decline in the quality of course work in scientific and technical subjects. At the same time, a dearth of library books made the majority of undergraduate courses heavily dependent on lecture notes and basic textbooks, and consequently both teaching and learning took place under severe constraints.

Another problem was the steady decline in the living standard of students and faculty members. As inflation worsened, a professor's creative energies were often diverted to making ends meet. The government authorized educational and public office workers to buy a stated amount of rice each month at a fixed low price.[142] Many college students were

---

[140] Chang Ch'i-chun, 'Hsi-nan lien-ta chi-yao' (Record of the South-west Associated University), in *Kuo-li Hsi-nan lien-ho ta-hsueh*, a volume in the *Hsueh-fu chi-wen* series, 25–39.

[141] *Chu Chia-hua*, 173.

[142] An outstanding example was Wen I-to, poet and professor of literature at Lienta, who was

in worse plight. Early in the war the government began granting loans to the truly impecunious students who had been cut off from their homes, and by 1941 more than 16,000 students had received such aid.[143] The stipends kept the recipients on a bare subsistence level, without a healthy diet or enough clothing through the year, let alone books and other necessities. By early 1941 the saying at Lienta was that you pawned your winter clothes to buy spring term books, then pawned your books in the autumn to redeem the winter clothes.

A third problem, less immediately visible, posed the most fundamental difficulty of all, the relationship between organized authority and the liberal intellectual, who perceived himself as one of the builders of a modern China. The fact that the nation-building endeavour now had to be carried out with scarce resources in wartime intensified the differences in aim between the liberal intellectuals and the KMT party dictatorship. As minister of education, Ch'en Li-fu aspired to expand Free China's student body and organize its ideological adherence to Sun Yat-sen's Three Principles of the People, hoping thereby to prevent disaffected youths turning toward the CCP. The resultant KMT policing of students' and faculty members' thought led to a sharp struggle at Lienta. Since Kunming's inflated prices were higher than elsewhere, Lienta's government rations were even less adequate. Lienta professors opposing KMT authoritarianism found support from the local warlord, Governor Lung Yun of Yunnan, who checked the efforts of central government agents to police the university community's political thinking. In this situation differences over seemingly pragmatic issues could lead to polarization of views. For example, dissatisfaction with the government's heavy emphasis on the utilitarian parts of the university curriculum at the expense of the liberal arts was voiced in 1940 by Ch'ien Tuan-sheng, professor of political science: 'The basic goal of the university is the quest for knowledge, it is not utility. If university education is able, at the same time, to produce something useful, that is an ancillary function and not its original goal.'[144] This statement was symptomatic of the dualism inherent in the New Culture movement: which was more important, to develop the individual mind through the pursuit of knowledge, or to apply useful knowledge for a collective national purpose?

compelled to teach additional classes in the local middle school as well as to carve and sell seals in order to barely support his family. See Liang Shih-ch'iu, *T'an Wen I-to* 109, quoting from 'Mourning my friend Wen I-to' by Wu Han, a professor of history at Lienta. For a perceptive account that has captured the living conditions and physical exhaustion of the majority of the academic community in wartime China, see Fairbank, *Chinabound*.

143 Ch'en Li-fu, 30.
144 Ch'ien was professor of political science at Lienta; quoted from John Israel's manuscript. Ch'ien's subsequent study, *The government and politics of China*, analyses the growth of KMT militarism.

The difficulties of advanced research paralleled those of higher education. The research institutes of Academia Sinica were relocated in several places, including Kunming, Chungking, and other localities in Szechwan, where scientists and scholars carried out research as best they could. Chinese astronomers organized an expedition to the north-west in September 1941 to observe the total solar eclipse. Certain new fields of technology were developed in response to war needs, such as industrial chemistry and the use of wood-oil fuel for transportation.[145] But in general wartime academic and scientific work was a holding action.

Postwar changes

Warfare had long since brought China's higher education out of its foreign-tinted ivory tower. The postwar years pulled it down into the chaos of revolution. When the Kunming students led in anti-civil war demonstrations in November 1945, the political climate in Yunnan was already changing: governor Lung Yun, though he cooperated with the central government during the war, had defended the academic community. As soon as the war ended a contest for provincial power ensued. Lung was bested and the Chungking government replaced him with Lu Han, who was agreeable to the central government's exercising more power in Yunnan. The students' anti-civil war movement, therefore, brought them face to face with the KMT authorities, who moved quickly to put an end to any expression of dissidence. The Democratic League, with its strong representation of academic and professional circles, took a strong stand in support of the students, and demanded the establishment of a coalition government. By late November the lines were sharply drawn. Led by Lienta students, a large meeting on 25 November protested against the renewal of the KMT-CCP civil war, but it was dispersed by armed troops. In Chungking the government, while still engaged in negotiations with the CCP leaders, now categorically labelled the anti-war sentiment as Communist-instigated. The students persisted, however, and nearly all college and secondary school students in Kunming were involved in planning a grand demonstration, when on 1 December armed groups, some in military uniforms, invaded several campuses. Fighting broke out, rocks against guns and grenades. When it ended three students and one music teacher had been killed and about a dozen other students wounded.[146]

Had the government set out deliberately to alienate the intellectuals,

[145] Jen, 'Wu-shih-nien', 197, 198.
[146] Suzanne Pepper, Civil war in China: the political struggle 1945-1949, 44-50. See also ch. 13 below.

it could not have had greater success than on 1 December 1945. Alienation emerged as an open fact, and in less than a year after the Allied victory Kunming was turning into 'a world of terror' for the intellectuals: first, a 'hit list' was rumoured to have been drawn up by the government, then came the dual assassination of two professors, Li Kung-p'u on 11 July 1946, and Wen I-to on 15 July after he had delivered an emotional speech at a public memorial service for Li.[147] Ten other leading members of the Democratic League, including Professors P'an Kuang-tan (dean of Tsing-hua), Fei Hsiao-t'ung (anthropologist, Yunnan University), and Chang Hsi-jo (political scientist, Lienta) immediately took refuge in the US Consulate in Kunming, until their safety was assured by a special envoy sent from Chungking.[148]

In this context of uncertainty, apprehension and rising disenchantment with the existing power structure, the major task of the academic community was to pack up the migrant universities and return to their original campuses. The job was done with considerable dispatch. Nankai University, for example, reopened at its Pa-li-t'ai campus outside Tientsin in the autumn term of 1946. The student body of over 800 resumed their studies at the original site, where 70 per cent of the buildings had been destroyed, but after one year approximately 30 per cent of the restoration was completed, leaving the administrators with still a long road ahead to rebuild the institution. Continuing its policy of unification and understanding, the government now conferred national status on all leading universities, including Nankai. Additions and reorganizations were undertaken. For example, Peiyang College of Engineering returned from Shensi after the war, and was renamed the National Peiyang University in 1946, with its faculty set up in two divisions, a College of Science and a College of Engineering. Following their return from Szechwan several Christian colleges combined to form East China University, located at the old St John's University campus in Shanghai.[149]

In 1944 the total amount appropriated for higher education had reached Ch. $18,000 million (as compared with Ch. $30 million in 1937), but its real purchasing power was equal to only Ch. $1,800,000 in 1937 terms. The larger enrolments and more numerous institutions therefore meant, in the late 1940s, a drastic reduction in quality.[150] On the whole, the quantitative growth during the war years did not bring a commensurate advance in quality, although in some institutions specific areas of under-

---

[147] Kuan-ch'a (The observer), 1.1 (1 Sept. 1946) 22–4.
[148] Ibid. 24. On this whole subject see Yeh Wen-hsing, 'The alienated academy: higher education in Republican China'.
[149] Chung-hua chiao-yü chieh, N.S., 1.1 (15 Jan. 1947) 108.
[150] Ou Yuan-huai, in ibid.

graduate instruction did manage to retain a high level by world standards. Beginning in 1941–2, also, the policy of the Ministry of Education for individual, official registration and accreditation of college faculty members created a controversial issue.[151]

The publication of a new weekly journal, *Kuan-ch'a* (The observer), in September 1946 might be seen as the last stand of Chinese liberals at mid-century. Ch'u An-p'ing, the chief editor, received active support from intellectuals like those who a dozen years before had contributed to the *Independent Critic*. The list of those writing for the initial issue of *Kuan-ch'a* was a partial roll-call of leaders in higher education and the modern professions: Wang Yun-sheng, editor-in-chief of *Ta-kung-pao* ('L'Impartial'), then the most highly regarded and widely circulated daily newspaper; Wu Ch'i-yuan, professor of economics, Tsing-hua; Ts'ai Wei-fan, professor of history, Nankai; Feng Yu-lan, professor of philosophy and dean of the College of Arts and Letters, Tsing-hua; Chang Tung-sun, professor of political science at Yenching University; Ch'en Chih-mai, a political scientist who was then consul in the Chinese embassy in Washington; and Pien Chih-lin, poet and professor of literature at Nankai.[152]

Ch'u An-p'ing declared that *Kuan-ch'a*'s task was to 'express political opinion but not to act as a tool of political contention', and that the journal would 'generally speak as the voice of the liberals and in behalf of the great masses of the common people; we have no behind-the-scenes organizations for support'. Ch'u presented a fourfold credo which might be taken as the epitaph of Chinese liberalism: first, to promote democracy in China. 'The people must be permitted to discuss national policies, to determine the accession or dismissal from power of the government, and all administrative measures must be responsible to the people.' Second, to support all basic human rights and the equality of all persons before the law. Third, to foster in China political democracy, industrialization, and the growth of the scientific spirit and a modern mentality. Lastly, to promote rationality in the resolution of all types of conflict, eschewing emotional attitudes and the use of force. 'The war has been won, but the national situation is becoming ever more chaotic. Political instability and

---

[151] On the state of Chinese education two years after the war, see *ibid*. 12–13; also the special issues of *Chung-hua chiao-yü chieh*, N.S. 2.1 (15 Jan. 1948) and 2.2 (15 Feb. 1948). For details of the institutional losses, personnel, current conditions and remedies in prospect in 1947, see Wilma Fairbank, 'Chinese educational needs and programs of US-located agencies to meet them: a report to UNESCO'. The same author's *America's cultural experiment in China, 1942–1949* is the official State Department history of the Cultural Relations programme during the 1940s, of which Roger S. Greene as a consultant to the State Department was one of the architects.

[152] *Kuan-ch'a*, 3. The 68 intellectuals whose names appeared on the title page of this initial issue of *Kuan-ch'a* as 'contributors' included some of the best-known people in the academic world.

economic depression have brought the entire society to the brink of collapse; the entire population has sunk into a morass of frustration and fear...'[153] In this adverse environment, the academic community in the postwar years could but try to preserve what had survived the military, political and economic upheavals of the past decade. By 1949 the future of a liberal or autonomous higher education in China seemed woefully obscure. The relationship of scholars to political authority, long a subject of debate and struggle under the republic, would henceforth not be loose or haphazard. Yet building a new China, including the rebuilding of state authority, did not diminish the need for academic creativity.

[153] *Ibid.* 3, 4.

CHAPTER 9

LITERARY TRENDS: THE ROAD TO REVOLUTION 1927–1949

In its broadest connotation, the term 'May Fourth literature' (*Wu-ssu wen-hsueh*) encompasses at least two decades – the 1920s and 1930s. Most Western scholars have adopted this vague definition and equated, in fact, the May Fourth era with the modern phase of Chinese literature, to be followed by the Yenan (1942–9) and Communist (since 1949) phases. This facile division, while clearly juxtaposing the basic differences between the individualistic thrust of May Fourth literature and the collective orientation of Communist literature, seems to gloss over other areas. Most Chinese and Japanese scholars agree that the literary euphoria of the May Fourth period had gradually dissipated itself by the late 1920s, to be replaced by a more 'mature' phase of literary creativity in the early 1930s. The term 'literature of the thirties' (*san-shih nien-tai wen-hsueh*) thus refers essentially to works produced in the decade from 1927 to 1937.

In this perspective, the thirties represented a crucial phase in the history of modern Chinese literature. Inheriting the May Fourth legacy, writers of the thirties were able to attain a depth of vision and a sophisticated technique which the early May Fourth practitioners of New Literature failed to achieve (the major exception being, of course, Lu Hsun). This artistic depth was accompanied by a sharpened consciousness of the deepening social and political crisis as the spectre of Japanese invasion loomed large in the north and the Communist Revolution gathered new momentum in its rural headquarters in Kiangsi. It was in this momentous decade, therefore, that art became inextricably enmeshed with politics and the romantic temper of the early twenties gave way to some sombre reassessments of the writer's social conscience. By the early 1930s, a new leftist orientation was already taking shape in the literary scene.

From literary revolution to revolutionary literature

The impact of the May Thirtieth incident on the political sensibilities of modern Chinese writers was immense.[1] It triggered a shock of recognition among many of them and opened their eyes to the 'imperialistic' presence of the Western powers and to the plight of workers who lived with it, side by side, in the commercial metropolis of Shanghai. A process of politicization was set in motion as most writers' sympathies gradually drifted toward the left. Most literary historians agree that the May Thirtieth incident marked a crucial turning point: modern Chinese literature moved, in the memorable phrase of Ch'eng Fang-wu, from 'literary revolution' to 'revolutionary literature'.

For years before the incident occurred, a few groping attempts to relate literature to politics and revolution had been made. In 1923, some members of the newly founded Chinese Communist Party, notably Teng Chung-hsia and Yun Tai-ying in their journal *Chung-kuo ch'ing-nien* (Chinese youth), argued that literature should be used as a weapon to arouse people's revolutionary consciousness.[2] In 1924 and 1925, Chiang Kuang-tz'u, a young Communist writer who had just returned from Russia, published two articles: 'Proletarian revolution and culture' and 'Contemporary Chinese society and revolutionary literature'. Both Kuo Mo-jo and Yü Ta-fu used terms such as 'proletarian spirit' and 'class struggle' in their articles published in 1923. In 1925 Lu Hsun sponsored the publication of a translated text called *Literary debates in Soviet Russia* (*Su-e wen-i lun-chan*) by the Unnamed Society (Wei-ming she) in Peking, and thereafter avidly followed the rapid shifts of Soviet literary policy.

These isolated efforts, however, did not create much stir until the impact of the May Thirtieth incident brought the issue of literature and revolution to the fore. The leftist trend was again set by members of the Creation Society, particularly Kuo Mo-jo. Kuo claimed to have been converted to Marxism in 1924 after having read a book by the Japanese Marxist Kawakami Hajime. In 1926, he wrote what is now regarded as the manifesto of the revolutionary literature movement: a tendentious, badly argued, emotional essay titled, 'Revolution and literature' (*Ko-ming yü wen-hsueh*). Kuo broadly defined revolution as the revolt of the oppressed classes against the oppressors in different historical eras. He came to the presumptuous conclusion that: 'Everything that is new is

[1] On the incident see *CHOC* 12.548–9.
[2] Chang Pi-lai, 'I-chiu-erh-san nien "Chung-kuo ch'ing-nien" chi-ko tso-che ti wen-hsueh chu-chang' (The literary views of some authors from *Chinese Youth* in 1923), in Li Ho-lin *et al.* *Chung-kuo hsin wen-hsueh shih yen-chiu* (Studies of the history of new Chinese literature), 36–49.

good, everything that is revolutionary fulfils the need of mankind and constitutes the keynote of social organization.' Thus, he argued that good literature ought to be revolutionary, that genuine literature consisted only of revolutionary literature, and that 'the content of literature follows the changes of revolution'. Kuo believed that revolution brought out the strongest human emotions and that its failure resulted in noble tragedies, both on the individual and on the collective level. Therefore, a revolutionary period was bound to be 'a golden age of literature'. Literature and revolution never stood in opposition; rather, they always converged. Literature could, in fact, be 'the vanguard of revolution'.[3]

Kuo wrote his essay in Canton, the 'revolutionary' headquarters of the KMT-CCP united front, where the Northern Expedition was about to be launched. Kuo was to be a participant, marking the first involvement of a literary man in political action. The hyperbolic language of the article was a clear indication of Kuo's effusive mood. Instead of referring to Marxist theory, Kuo seemed eager to justify his new role as a literary intellectual turned revolutionary. Kuo's ebullience was shared by his fellow Creationists. Ch'eng Fang-wu, for instance, in his celebrated article, 'From literary revolution to revolutionary literature', echoed Kuo's emotionalism and further argued, with a flourish of his newly acquired jargon, that even the early romanticism of the Creationists represented the temper of this 'revolutionary intelligentsia' of the petty-bourgeois against the 'bourgeois class'. But times had changed, Ch'eng hastened to add, and their class was about to be 'aufheben' (ao-fu-he-pien), their 'ideology' (i-te-wo-lo-chi) no longer useful. Ch'eng concluded: 'If we wish to shoulder the responsibilities of revolutionary "intelligentsia", we must negate ourselves once more (negating the negation). We must strive to acquire class consciousness. We must make our [literary] medium close to the idiom of the masses. We must treat the masses of peasants and workers as our subjects.'[4] Ch'eng's showy slogans were probably utterly incomprehensible to his colleagues, not to mention other writers and the masses. But in his laboriously pretentious way, Ch'eng managed to hit upon some of the central issues of the leftist polemics which would soon ensue.

In 1927, this type of slogan-shouting could only enrage Lu Hsun, whose realistic assessment of the situation in Canton convinced him that the revolutionary optimism of these former romantics was premature. Compared to Russia, China was not in the throes of a revolution, Lu Hsun

[3] *Chung-kuo hsien-tai wen-hsueh shih ts'an-k'ao tzu-liao* (Research materials on the history of modern Chinese literature), hereafter *Ts'an-k'ao tzu-liao*, 1.214–16.

[4] *Ibid.* 222–4.

commented; moreover, borrowing from Trotsky, he argued that there would be no literature in a truly revolutionary period. What was urgently needed was 'revolutionary men' rather than 'revolutionary literature' – the power of the gun rather than the impotence of the pen. But in April 1927 Lu Hsun was disillusioned by the 'revolutionary men' of the Kuomintang, whose massacre of Communists and other sympathizers in Shanghai and Canton shattered whatever residual hope he might have entertained for a possible 'revolution'.

From 1928 to 1930, Lu Hsun was embroiled in several heated debates with a younger group of revolutionary writers of the Creation and Sun Societies, who had replaced the veteran Creationists as leading theoreticians on the left. He first defended the intrinsic value of literature against the mere propaganda of his opponents: 'Great works of literature,' he remarked in 1927, 'have never obeyed any orders or concerned themselves with utilitarian motives. They must naturally spring from the heart. If a topic is hoisted in advance for writers to write on, how does it differ from composing eight-legged essays?'[5] Upon arriving in Shanghai, he remarked cynically on the empty 'advertisements' of his leftist opponents in the 'revolutionary coffee houses'. His charge of amorphous terminology – that they were so drunk with their own revolutionary slogans as to have 'blurred vision' – was matched by a counter-charge from his opponents that his criticism was itself 'blurred', that he was like an aged Don Quixote awkwardly fighting a windmill. His young opponents thus labelled him 'Don Lu Hsun' in addition to calling him an old man of 'leisure, leisure and leisure' (a reference to the title of one of his essay collections).

This welter of nasty metaphors and name-calling created sound and fury in debates which also touched on more substantive issues. The basic tenets of the revolutionary writers may be summarized as follows: (1) all literature is based on and determined by class; (2) all literature is a weapon for propaganda (an aphorism quoted *ad nauseam* from Upton Sinclair); (3) literary criticism must be derived from materialism (it must be interpreted from the point of view of Marxist economics); (4) revolutionary literature should be proletarian literature; that is, it should be written for and by the working class. For the time being, however, it could only be written by the petty-bourgeois intellectuals. The crucial determinant was the 'standpoint' or 'outlook': if a writer adopted the class standpoint and outlook of the proletariat, he could, in fact, still produce proletarian literature.[6]

5 Lu Hsun, *Lu Hsun ch'üan-chi* (Complete works of Lu Hsun), 3.403.
6 Lu Ho-lin, *Chung-kuo hsin wen-hsueh shih yen-chiu*, 61–2; Amitendranath Tagore, *Literary debates in Modern China, 1918–1937*, 86–94.

These injunctions, as Chinese Communist historians later admitted, were no more than doctrinaire formulas. In spite of their crudity and simplicity, these tenets represented the impetuous radicalism of a younger generation of self-styled Marxists such as Ch'ien Hsing-ts'un (A Ying), Li Ch'u-li and Chu Ching-wo, and their desire to edge out the domination of older writers on the literary scene. In their attempts to set a new literary trend they also wanted to give a political reorientation to May Fourth literature and to provide a theoretical framework which would henceforth guide and shape literary creation. This imposition of a radical orthodoxy was understandably unbearable to Lu Hsun, a man of indomitable spirit and himself a leader of youth.

Lu Hsun's rebuttals revolved around the recurring theme of his opponent's self-delusion: instead of boldly attacking the realities of the KMT reaction after 1927, he argued, these revolutionary writers were still complacently enveloped in their hollow 'revolutionary' theories. Their pose of self-righteousness presented merely a 'fierce and ugly appearance of extreme leftism' which veiled their ignorance of Chinese society. Lu Hsun first criticized the simplicity of their formulas. Turning Sinclair's phrase around, he argued in 1928 that although all literature is propaganda, not all propaganda, and certainly not the works of these revolutionary writers, is literature. Lu Hsun did not deny the class nature of literature, but he strongly doubted his opponent's claim to act as spokesman for the proletariat. The 'proletarian literature' created by a few armchair philosophers sitting in a café in Shanghai, he held, certainly did not reflect working-class demands. Lu Hsun indulged in a bit of satire:

This year, the literary ranks of Shanghai are supposed to welcome the representatives of the proletariat. Their arrival is announced in all pomp and circumstance. But one asks the rickshaw driver, and he says that he never pulls any representatives... So one searches for them inside the big mansions, the restaurants, the houses of foreigners, in bookstores and coffee houses...[7]

Lu Hsun's views are clear: the urban intellectual in his sheltered bourgeois existence had no contact with working-class life and it would be ridiculous for him to try to adopt the standpoint of the proletariat.

This view was shared by Mao Tun, whose trilogy, *Eclipse*, was criticized by the radical leftists for presenting a 'sick' portrait of the wrong class from the wrong standpoint. Mao Tun described the petty-bourgeois intellectuals' quest for idealism, their consequent vacillation and their final disillusionment during 'revolutionary' experiences on the Northern Expedition. In his essay, 'On Reading *Ni Huan-chih*', Mao Tun defended this realistic novel by Yeh Shao-chun and his own fictional work, arguing

7 *Lu Hsun ch'üan-chi*, 4.70–1.

that a literary work reflecting the darker aspects in the lives of the 'backward' elements of the petty-bourgeoisie could still render a positive contribution to the leftist cause. 'In terms of moving or educating [the readers], this kind of dark portraiture,' Mao Tun added, 'may be more profound than those unrealistic, utopian, and optimistic descriptions!'[8]

The issue implicit in Lu Hsun's arguments but explicitly stated by Mao Tun was the crucial one of audience: who were the readers of New Literature? In his long essay written in 1928, 'From Kuling to Tokyo', Mao Tun acknowledged that modern Chinese literature in the past six or seven years had provided reading material only for educated youth, and noted that the readership of the recent 'revolutionary literature' was even narrower. As for the labouring masses, they would never understand it, nor would they be willing to listen even if it were fed to them. Rather than championing the proletariat, Mao Tun wanted to enlarge the scope of the petty-bourgeoisie both as readers and as subject matter:

Now for the future of 'New Literature' – or even more boldly, the future of 'revolutionary literature' – the first task is to move it out of youth and students and into the petty-bourgeois masses, where it will then take root. In order to achieve this, we must first of all redirect our subject-matter to the lives of such people as small merchants, middle and small peasants. We should not use too many new terms or Europeanized sentence structures. We should not merely do didactic propaganda of new ideas but should faithfully and forcefully depict the essence of petty-bourgeois life.[9]

Mao Tun did in fact carry out this injunction in the early thirties in his novel *Midnight* and his trilogy of stories – 'Spring silkworms', 'Autumn harvest', and 'Winter ruin'. His fictional canvas was peopled by a variety of petty-bourgeois characters in cities and the countryside. The revolutionary writers, on the contrary, offered only a meagre and slipshod corpus of 'proletarian literature', mainly by Chiang Kuang-tz'u.

Mao Tun and Lu Hsun succeeded in exposing the superficiality of the young radicals' arguments. Mao Tun's fiction and Lu Hsun's *tsa-wen* demonstrated the vitality of critical realism. But they did not offer an alternative theory that was diametrically opposed to the radicals' canon of revolutionary literature. Mao Tun was already a party member who differed with his fellow Communists only in his more sombre assessment of the revolution's prospects. Lu Hsun's experiences in Canton had made him disillusioned with the revolutionary potential of the Kuomintang. Circumstances under the new Nanking government further solidified his

---

[8] Li Ho-lin, *Chung-kuo wen-i lun-chan* (Literary debates in China), 412.

[9] *Ibid.* 379. An English translation by Yu-shih Ch'en of this article appeared in John Berninghausen and Ted Huters, eds. *Revolutionary literature in China: an anthology*, 37–44. The editors have also supplied a perceptive introductory essay.

opposition, especially after five young leftist writers, including his disciple Jou Shih, were executed as part of a group of 22 CCP leaders shot at Lung Hua outside Shanghai on 7 February 1931 (see above, p. 174). Lu Hsun was so stricken by the tragedy that, more than ever, he felt persecuted under the 'white terror'. Political urgency thus thrust him on to a common ground with his leftist rivals.

Moreover, in order to pinpoint the weaknesses of the radicals' arguments, Lu Hsun was compelled to delve into the foundations of Marxist aesthetics. From 1928 to 1930, he began to read and translate the works of Plekhanov and Lunacharsky. His self-education resulted in a gradual reversal of his previous notion of literature's essential irrelevance to politics. A literature of discontent against the status quo, he now believed, could serve to undermine the existing political authority and could, indeed, be termed 'revolutionary'.[10]

By 1930 Lu Hsun had virtually accepted the basic tenets of the young radicals, albeit in his own refined formulation. He concluded that revolutionary literature had to be produced precisely because of the setbacks of the revolution; the writers and the workers were united in their common 'passion' of suffering. This shared experience under oppression forged a common bond which made this literature 'belong to the broad masses of revolutionary toilers' and hence, proletarian.[11] Lu Hsun's reconciliation with his radical critics did not necessarily signify that he was won over in argument, for a man with his intractable character and seasoned insight would never have bowed to anyone. Rather, he must have sensed that for all their trendiness, the revolutionary writers had captured the changed mood of the urban intelligentsia.

After a brief spell of political optimism in 1926–7 when the Northern Expedition offered the prospect of genuine revolution, most of the young Chinese intellectuals became alienated again from the state. Rather than make an appeal to these literary intellectuals through accommodation or persuasion, the new Nanking government under Chiang Kai-shek demonstrated only distrust, followed in the early thirties by censorship and oppression. As Chiang Monlin, a liberal sympathetic with the KMT, later observed, the government had 'lost touch with the broad masses; it had no deep or clear understanding of the mood of societal discontent'.[12] The CCP, on the other hand, capitalized on this increasingly pervasive

[10] For an analysis of Lu Hsun's changing conceptions of literature and revolution, see Leo Ou-fan Lee, 'Literature on the eve of revolution: reflections on Lu Xun's leftist years, 1927–1936', *Modern China*, 2.3 (July 1976) 277–91.
[11] Gladys Yang, ed. *Silent China: selected writings of Lu Xun*, 176.
[12] Liu Hsin-huang, *Hsien-tai Chung-kuo wen-hsueh shih-hua* (Discourse on the history of modern Chinese literature), 485.

sentiment and, with organizational acumen, made a concerted effort to rally the restless urban writers to its objectives. The stage was set for a leftist united front that was to dominate the literary scene in the 1930s.

THE LEAGUE OF LEFT-WING WRITERS AND THE POLEMICS ON LITERATURE

On 2 March 1930, about forty writers (out of an initial membership of more than fifty) gathered in Shanghai to found the League of Left-wing Writers. On 16 February, two weeks before this momentous gathering, preliminary discussions had been held at the invitation of Lu Hsun and Hsia Yen (Shen Tuan-hsien) to form a planning committee for the founding of the league. While Lu Hsun has been credited with a leading role, the real initiative came probably from the Chinese Communist Party through its agent Hsia Yen, who was specifically assigned to this task.[13] Under the Li Li-san leadership, the CCP had embarked upon a general programme in late 1929 and early 1930 to create in urban centres a series of cultural 'front organizations' in order to attract sympathetic fellow travellers like Lu Hsun.[14] Aside from the League of Left-wing Writers, several similar organizations – ranging from fields of drama, film, art and poetry to social science, education, journalism and Esperanto – were created. These front organizations fell under the general umbrella of the 'Left-wing Cultural Coalition' (Tso-i wen-hua tsung t'ung-meng), although the centre of activities was the League of Left-wing Writers.[15]

The leadership of the league consisted nominally of an executive committee of seven standing members: Hsia Yen, Hung Ling-fei (both party members in charge of cultural work), Feng Nai-ch'ao, Ch'ien Hsing-ts'un (Lu Hsun's former critic from the Sun Society), T'ien Han (a leading dramatist), Cheng Po-ch'i (one of the founding members of the Creation Society) and Lu Hsun. While Lu Hsun had the honour of giving the inaugural address, he was clearly isolated in the league's power structure both by his erstwhile opponents and by party activists. The position of the league's secretary was held by three party members

---

[13] According to an official source, as early as late 1928 the Kiangsu party committee of the CCP had dispatched Hsia Yen, Li Ch'u-li and Feng Nai-ch'ao to contact Lu Hsun to plan a united front. See *Tso-lien shih-ch'i wu-ch'an chieh-chi ko-ming wen-hsueh* (Proletarian revolutionary literature in the period of the Left-wing League), 353. A list of the inaugural membership is included in *Chung-kuo hsien-tai wen-i tzu-liao ts'ung-k'an ti-i chi* (Sources of modern Chinese literature, first series), 155–7.

[14] Harriet C. Mills, 'Lu Hsun: 1927–1936, the years on the left', 139.

[15] Ting I, 'Chung-kuo tso-i tso-chia lien-meng ti ch'eng-li chi ch'i ho fan-tung cheng-chih ti tou-cheng'(The founding of the League of Left-wing Writers and its struggle against reactionary political forces), in Chang Ching-lu, ed. *Chung-kuo hsien-tai ch'u-pan shih-liao* (Historical materials on contemporary Chinese publications), 2.42.

consecutively: Feng Nai-ch'ao, Yang Han-sheng and Chou Yang. (The last two, together with Hsia Yen and T''ien Han, later became the vicious gang of 'four heavies', whom Lu Hsun singled out for special attack in the battle of 'two slogans' in 1936.) It can be surmised that after an initial period of euphoria, Lu Hsun served merely as a figurehead who enjoyed neither power nor friendly relations with the party activists.

The league's two official documents – the 'Theoretical guideline of literature' adopted in the inaugural meeting, and a lengthier position paper drafted by the league's executive committee titled 'The new mission of the revolutionary literature of the Chinese proletariat' – were, like Lu Hsun's vague inaugural speech, unfocused. The 'Guideline' called upon league members to 'stand on the battle line of the proletariat's struggle for emancipation' and to 'assist and engage in the birth of proletarian art'. But it failed to define either the meaning or scope of proletarian literature. Three injunctions on writing were given in the position paper: first, the league writers must 'pay attention to the large number of subjects from the realities of Chinese social life', especially those related directly to revolutionary objectives; second, the league writers must 'observe and describe from the proletarian standpoint and outlook'; and third, the form of their literature 'must be simple and understandable to the workers and peasants. When necessary, dialects can be used.'[16] Again, except for the third injunction, the document did not define proletarian or revolutionary literature exclusively in the framework of workers, peasants and soldiers, as Mao later did in his Yenan talks. It called for the 'popularization' of literature – a reflection probably of Ch'ü Ch'iu-p'ai's ideas – but the issues were confined to language. As the Communist scholar Liu Shou-sung has pointed out, the two documents failed to give a genuine proletarian thrust to leftist literature.[17] The documents defined the league's standpoint, organization and mission as primarily a literary vanguard and a propaganda machine. The promotion of a genuine kind of proletarian literature was secondary in importance. Thus in the league's numerous publications, banned repeatedly by the government, there appeared a plethora of doctrinal criticism, but a paucity of good creative writing.

In its emphasis on ideological correctness, organizational discipline, but not literary creativity, the league resembled the RAPP organization in Soviet Russia: it attempted to define a 'we' group that was pitted against the 'they' of all other ideological persuasions.[18] And like RAPP, to which

---

[16] *Ts'an-k'ao tzu-liao*, 1.290–1.
[17] Liu Shou-sung, *Chung-kuo hsin wen-hsueh shih ch'u-kao* (A preliminary draft history of modern Chinese literature) 1.214–15.
[18] For the exclusivist position of RAPP (Russian Association of Proletarian Writers), see Edward J. Brown, *Russian literature since the revolution*, 112–13.

some of the league members owed a direct intellectual debt, the league
was most active, not so much in promoting new proletarian talents, but
in provoking ideological polemics. The seven-year record of the league
was one of continuous debates against all kinds of 'enemies': beginning
with Lu Hsun's polemic with the liberal Crescent Moon Society, the league
combated successively the conservative proponents of 'nationalist
literature', the left-leaning 'third category' writers, and finally some of
its own members in the debate on 'mass language' and in the famous battle
of the 'two slogans' connected with the league's sudden dissolution in
1936.

Prelude: Lu Hsun vs. the Crescent Moon

The most formidable enemies of the Left-wing League did not come
initially from the right – the KMT government had never concentrated
its efforts in the field of literature – but from the centre. Even before the
league was formed, the Japanese-educated men of letters who comprised
the majority in the Creation and Sun Societies could never get along with
the Anglo-American group around the Crescent Moon (Hsin yueh). Since
some of the Crescent Moon members had close associations with Ch'en
Yuan and the *Contemporary Review* group who clashed with Lu Hsun in
the early twenties, these 'gentlemen' scholars and writers were viewed
with animosity even before Liang Shih-ch'iu, the theoretician of the
Crescent Moon group, fired his first shot against proletarian literature.
Personalities and personal backgrounds thus added the necessary fuel to
the burning fire of crucial ideological differences.

When the *Crescent Moon* magazine was first published in March 1928,
it featured an eight-page manifesto, supposedly written by Hsu Chih-mo,
which set forth two guiding principles of the journal: 'health' and
'dignity'. With these two amorphous slogans, Hsu in his ebullient style
declared war on all the 'bacteria' on the literary scene, which he divided
into no less than 13 categories: sentimentalism, decadentism, aestheticism,
utilitarianism, didacticism, detracticism, extremism, fragilism, eroticism,
fanaticism, venalism, sloganism and 'ism-ism'. Apparently some of these
'isms' were aimed, explicitly or implicitly, at the revolutionary writers
of the Creation and Sun Societies, who immediately rose to the occasion
by calling Hsu Chih-mo a 'clown', Hu Shih a 'compromising idealist'
and the Crescent Moon group a hypocritical bunch of compradorial
'gentlemen' in the service of the capitalist class.[19]

The substantive issue which divided the two camps lay deeper than mere
name-calling. From its inception, the *Crescent Moon* posed the threat of

[19] The various polemical articles are included in *Ts'an-k'ao tzu-liao*, 1.359–412.

an alternative theory of literature. As voiced by its chief spokesman, Liang Shih-ch'iu (though Liang later claimed that he had no backing from his colleagues),[20] this theory offered the familiar Anglo-American notion of the autonomy of literature – that literature depicts 'eternal and universal human nature', that creative writing has always been the product of individuals (the 'aristocratic elite', in Liang's words), and that it must be judged by its own intrinsic values without considerations of historical age, environment or class. Moreover, Liang Shih-ch'iu clearly modelled himself after his most admired 'teacher' of Western literature – Irving Babbitt, with whom Liang had studied at Harvard. From Babbitt he had learned to distrust Rousseau, and to disdain chaos in favour of reason and discipline, an idea which Liang traced to Matthew Arnold. In a period in which the Chinese literary scene was fraught with chaos, what was most urgently needed, in Liang's view, was a commitment to catholic tastes and high standards. It is clear from Liang's various articles published at this time that his own ambition was to become a Chinese Dr Samuel Johnson – an arbiter of literary taste and a critic in the Arnoldian sense. The practice of literary criticism as a scholarly discipline was, of course, non-existent in modern China, and any attempts to emulate the likes of F. R. Leavis or Edmund Wilson (roughly Liang's contemporaries) were doomed to failure.

Liang Shih-ch'iu also proved to be an especially prickly thorn in the eyes of Lu Hsun, possibly because this doyen of the Shanghai literary scene felt the challenge of Liang's ambition and, to some extent, a certain envy of Liang's knowledge of Western literature. Before the league was formed, Lu Hsun was already involved in a few skirmishes in print with Liang. The incentive had been provided by two timely articles Liang published in *Crescent Moon* in 1929: 'Is literature conditioned by class?' and 'On Mr Lu Hsun's hard translation'. In these Liang elaborated on his ideas presented in a previous article, 'Literature and revolution' (1928), and maintained that neither revolution nor class – both extrinsic to literature – could serve as a criterion for literary criticism. Concerning the problem of proletarian literature, Liang asserted that since literature had always been the creation of a minority of talented minds, the term 'literature of the masses' was itself a contradiction. True literature, Liang argued, was above class; its right domain was the 'fundamental human nature' – love, hate, pity, terror, death – that could not be confined to any class. Liang Shih-ch'iu further found fault with Lu Hsun's translations of Plekhanov and Lunacharsky. Lu Hsun translated the 'hard' way, being conscientiously

---

[20] Hou Chien, *Ts'ung wen-hsueh ko-ming tao ko-ming wen-hsueh* (From literary revolution to revolutionary literature), 162.

literal and following the Japanese re-translation, and Liang found it difficult to understand. Finally, Liang opined that whatever effort Lu Hsun put into his translations, literary ideologies were still secondary to the quality of creative work: 'we do not want advertisements, we want goods'.[21]

Lu Hsun's rebuttal, titled 'Hard translation and the class nature of literature', was one of the longest essays he ever wrote. Obviously, Liang had hit where it hurt most, for to be affronted for his painstaking introduction of the Soviet canons of Marxist aesthetics was something Lu Hsun could hardly swallow. The tone of this long article was generally quite reasonable and, in several passages, touched with humane passion. He disagreed with Liang's classless view of literature not only on the basis of his recently acquired theory from Plekhanov, but also out of a sense of empathy for the lower classes. Liang was not aware, Lu Hsun argued, that his very position of literary autonomy was itself a reflection of his bourgeois background. As regards 'human nature' depicted in literature, would a poor starving peasant have enough leisure time to plant flowers simply for their beauty? 'How could an oil magnate understand the sorrow and suffering of an old Peking woman who picked charcoal for a living?' To appreciate literature was a privilege, but the physical conditions and the illiteracy of the poor made it impossible for them to enjoy such a privilege. Lu Hsun also conceded that, regrettably, thus far there had not been many 'goods' of quality in proletarian literature. But it was an act of 'bourgeois maliciousness' to demand immediate products from the proletariat.

While Lu Hsun may have revealed an unsure grasp of Marxist aesthetics (his defence of class remained elementary – an act of faith rather than erudite argument), he more than made up for this weakness by his honesty and humanity. This is especially true of his apologia for translation. He explained that he did it the 'hard' way because of his own language deficiencies, and because he had to be honest with himself and his readers. Moreover, since the task of translating Plekhanov and Lunacharsky served as a test for his leftist critics and himself to see whether or not they had erred in theory, Lu Hsun was compelled to remain faithful to the texts. 'When it hit upon the wounds of those critics I did not admire, I smiled; when it hit upon my own wounds, I bore with it but never wanted to alter [the text]. This was a reason for my persistent effort at "hard translation".'[22]

Lu Hsun's essay was written in early 1930 (probably shortly before the formation of the league) when he was well on his way to closing ranks

---

[21] Ibid. 167–8. [22] Ts'an-k'ao tzu-liao, 1.394.

with his leftist opponents. The essay showed Lu Hsun in a spirit that was less caustic than either before or after its composition. It was also considerably less dogmatic than his writings in 1931 and 1932, for he agreed with Liang that propaganda was not literature and that leftist slogans in the past did not constitute true proletarian literature. But the essay nevertheless revealed the emotional commitment of a true convert to the leftist cause. His debate with Liang Shih-ch'iu and the Crescent Moon group did not represent an undisputed triumph of Marxist over liberal theories of literature. He did, however, win on other accounts. In a period of crisis and commitment, clarion-calls for the neutrality of literature could be seen, especially in leftist eyes, as both untimely and 'ivory-towerish'. In Communist literary history, therefore, the Crescent Moon group are viewed as arch-villains, whose 'defeat' by Lu Hsun is considered a major victory of the league.

The case of 'nationalist literature'

Compared to the liberal critics of the Crescent Moon Society, the proponents of the so-called 'nationalist literature' (*min-tsu chu-i wen-hsueh*), which emerged in June 1930, only three months after the founding of the Left-wing League, were weaker in ideological and organizational strength. Obviously, this was designed as a counter-league measure by a group of literary men – Wang P'ing-ling, Huang Chen-hsia and others – who had close associations with the Kuomintang. But their slogan, which smacked of Taine's theory of 'nationality, environment and time', was very vague, since it called for a literature that reflected a 'nationalistic spirit and consciousness' to replace the leftist view of class. As scholars from Taiwan have admitted, the group's criticism of the left consisted mainly of personal attacks, and none of its members commanded prestige or respect within the literary scene.[23] Their creative output was even less than that of the leftists. But the group's major liability lay in the fact that their pro-Kuomintang stance ran counter to the critical temper of the literary intelligentsia. It was almost unimaginable to the early thirties for a conscientious man of letters to be a mouthpiece of the government. The advocates of 'nationalist literature' were thus doomed to failure from its very inception. But this minor debate served, coincidentally, as a catalyst for a most intriguing polemical episode in modern Chinese literary history – the controversy over the 'free men' (*tzu-yu jen*) or 'the third category of men' (*ti-san-chung jen*) in literature.

[23] Liu Hsin-huang, 513–15. See also Li Mu, *San-shih nien-tai wen-i lun* (On the literature and arts of the 1930s), 61.

The case of 'free men' and the 'third category' of writers

In September 1931, Hu Ch'iu-yuan, a young scholar, published an essay attacking 'nationalist literature'. One of his central arguments was that literature should never be denigrated as a 'gramophone' of politics. Hu's assertion touched the very core of the leftist stance and was immediately taken as an attack on the league. A series of debates ensued between Hu and the league's major theoreticians.

Hu Ch'iu-yuan had been educated in Japan, where he acquired considerable knowledge of Marxism and wrote a lengthy book on Plekhanov and his theory of art, which was published in 1932. The league writers were probably unaware of Hu's background and treated his views as another variation of Crescent Moon liberalism. To their surprise, Hu proved himself to be a liberal Marxist whose command of Marxist scholarship was superior to that of his league critics. From his reading of Plekhanov, Trotsky, Voronsky and other Soviet theoreticians, Hu argued that although literature has a class basis, literary creation should not be subjected to the same laws as can be found in Marxist economic or political treatises. Literature, in Hu's view, reflected life aesthetically by showing its complexities and ambiguities. Reacting strongly against the mechanistic views of his leftist opponents, particularly Ch'ien Hsing-ts'un and other members of the Sun Society, Hu Ch'iu-yuan cited a battery of sources from the Marxist canon to show that the function of literary criticism was to understand literature 'objectively' rather than to dictate its creation. Literature, in other words, had its own values which could be beneficial to revolution, especially in the case of good literature. (Thus Hu admitted the possibility of good proletarian literature.) But he felt that literary creation should never be treated as something 'below' politics. In Hu's sense, being a 'free man' did not necessarily mean being anti-Marxist or apolitical as Liang Shih-ch'iu believed; it merely referred to 'an attitude' of a somewhat pedantic scholar who embraced Marxist theory with all seriousness but who opposed the tendency 'to judge everything in accordance with the current practical policies or urgent needs of the party leadership'.[24]

Hu's challenge to the league's monopoly of leftist literature was echoed in 1932 by Su Wen (Tai K'e-ch'ung) who, by no means unsympathetic to the leftist cause, voiced a similar concern over the excessive 'invasion' of literature by political necessities. The 'third category' of men, in Su's original meaning, referred to those writers who were caught between, or

[24] Su Wen, ed. *Wen-i tzu-yu lun-pien chi* (Debate on the freedom of literature and art), 20. For Hu's own recapitulation of the debate, see Liu Hsin-huang, 539–64.

left behind, the two types of Marxist advocates – Hu Ch'iu-yuan's 'free man' and the 'unfree, party-dominated' league. However sympathetic, a good writer simply could not write according to the dictates of the league's theoreticians. Literature, in Su's view, was more than a political weapon, although he admitted a need for such. 'I am not opposed to the political purpose of literature,' Su Wen stated, 'but I am against sacrificing reality because of this political purpose.' A writer had to be honest in depicting life as he saw it. 'We demand a truthful literature more than a utilitarian literature that serves a certain current political purpose.'[25] Thus, between the Kuomintang's oppression and the league's dictation of literature, the majority of writers, Su Wen argued, fell almost involuntarily into the 'third category'.

In the league's rebuttals, the most cogent argument was put forth by Ch'ü Ch'iu-pai. In a long essay, Ch'ü (using the pseudonym I-chia) criticized Hu and Su for their failure to recognize the fundamental Marxist tenet of the class basis of literature. In Ch'ü's judgment, Hu Ch'iu-yuan had overemphasized the function of literature as an aesthetic exploration of images and as a passive reflection of life. He attributed Hu's weaknesses to Plekhanov, who had himself been criticized in the Soviet Union for his 'idealistic' tendencies. Literary creation, in Ch'ü's view, could never be divorced from the socio-economic background of its author and had to serve its political function. For the Chinese proletariat who were engaged in a life-and-death struggle, literature had to be a weapon against the oppressors. 'When the proletariat demands openly that literature be a weapon of struggle,' Ch'ü asserted, 'whoever cries out against the "invasion of literature" is unconsciously becoming the "gramophone" of the bourgeois hypocrites and their theory of art above everything.'[26] In the period of class struggle, there could be no 'middle ground'.

While affirming class determinism and the need for commitment, neither Lu Hsun nor Ch'ü Ch'iu-pai was prepared to defend the league's infallibility. They freely acknowledged the folly of infantile leftism and mechanistic interpretations among a few of its members, particularly Ch'ien Hsing-ts'un. But Ch'ü argued that despite their weaknesses, these eager members were sincerely groping toward a revolutionary theory and practice, whereas Hu and Su, on the contrary, ignored political reality and did mere fence-sitting.

When compared with the vehement counter-attacks directed against other enemies, this was a mild response. How does one account for this 'soft' stance? The clue may be found behind the often verbose exchanges of theoretical differences. The arguments of Hu Ch'iu-yuan and Su

25 Su Wen, 189–91.   26 Su Wen, 85.

Wen – two individuals who were apparently not affiliated with any literary or political group – raised two important issues unprecedented in leftist literature in China (though Hu was clearly familiar with their Soviet precedents): the principle of *partiinost* ('party spirit') or party direction of literature, and the problem of the 'fellow travellers', those writers who were sympathetic to the leftist cause but did not choose to join the league or the party. The two problems were compounded by the league's own definition of its functions.

On the one hand, the formation of the league was meant to provide a unified direction to revolutionary literature. Since its leadership consisted mainly of party members, the way was paved for party domination and control of literature. However, the CCP in the early thirties was organizationally weak and beset with factional strife; it was in no position to enforce a consistent *partiinost*. The league was created, on the other hand, to provide a broad front for leftist writers as well as their sympathizers. Thus, from the party's operational standpoint, the league was a front organization to attract 'fellow travellers', those 'third category' writers who were followers of neither KMT nor CCP but who nevertheless harboured more sympathies for 'proletarian literature' than for 'nationalist literature'. Both Hu Ch'iu-yuan and Su Wen, like Lu Hsun before them, could be enlisted as fellow travellers. And according to Hu, some attempts to lure him into the leftist camp were actually made.[27]

It is interesting to see how the two issues were resolved by Ch'ü Chiu-pai and Feng Hsueh-feng (under the pen names Lo Yang and Ho Tan-lin) in their summary articles of the debate, which apparently represented the majority opinion of the league. In Ch'ü's article, the principle of *partiinost* was mentioned as being first laid down by Lenin in 'Party organization and party literature'. Lenin wrote that *partiinost* 'should naturally be applied to the creation of revolutionary and proletarian literature, particularly to criticism'. But Ch'ü made an important qualification: he felt that the issue lay in whether *partiinost* could be applied 'correctly or incorrectly'. Ch'ü added that even when it was applied to league writers, it was not to be 'coerced, but rather to be discussed, studied, and learned'. As for non-league writers, they were asked merely to 'recognize' the principle. Ch'ü further defended creative freedom within the league by explaining that its 'Guidelines' provided only some 'general directions' and did not constitute 'orders'.[28] In fact, throughout the league's history, the correct form and content of proletarian literature was repeatedly discussed and debated, but never enforced.

[27] Liu Hsin-huang, 550.
[28] Li Ho-lin, *Chin erh-shih-nien Chung-kuo wen-i ssu-ch'ao lun* (Chinese literary trends in the recent twenty years), 333–4.

With regard to the policy toward fellow travellers, Ch'ü dismissed the radical view ('if you don't follow us, you are an anti-revolutionary') as dogmatic and sensationalist – an indirect reference perhaps to radical young leftists and Chou Yang. But it was Feng Hsueh-feng who made the final conciliatory statement. At the end of his long article Feng made the following redefinition, couched in highly tendentious language, of the 'third category':

If the third category of literature is 'opposed to the old ages and old society', it is certainly not anti-revolutionary literature, although it does not take a proletarian point of view. In that case, this type of literature is already beneficial to revolution, it is no longer neutral, and therefore it does not need the title of third category literature.[29]

Feng Hsueh-feng's conciliatory statement, at the end of a polite polemical rebuttal, apparently satisfied the two challengers, who later considered their battle a success, in the sense that the league was forced to admit certain errors and subdue its strident ideological tone.[30] But the 'third category' men were clearly no match for the league in terms of power and influence: neither Hu nor Su was a creative writer, and they faded from the literary scene shortly afterwards.

After 1932, there was no major challenge to the league's ideological domination. A considerable number of literary men revolved around Lin Yutang's three popular magazines – *Lun-yü* (Analects), *Jen-chien-shih* (Human world) and *Yü-chou feng* (Cosmic wind) – and remained purposefully 'apolitical' in their emphasis on humour and gentle satire, but they certainly posed no threat to the league's ideological authority. Lu Hsun's attacks against them were subdued, perhaps due to some soft spots in his heart for Chou Tso-jen, his 'separated brother', and even for Lin Yutang, his former friend and erstwhile employer. Other non-league writers, such as the *Hsien-tai* (Contemporary) magazine group, maintained a neutral stance, though still open to contributions or overtures from the left. The debates which ensued on 'mass language' and 'national defence' literature sprang essentially from within the leftist front and, in the latter case, all but terminated its ideological unity.

The debate on '*mass language*' and '*Latinization*'

The issue of 'mass language' (*ta-chung hua* or *ta-chung yü*) was first raised in 1932 by Ch'ü Ch'iu-pai, the most brilliant leftist theoretician of the 1930s.[31] Ch'ü's concern with language was inseparable from his Marxist

[29] Su Wen, 287.
[30] Liu Hsin-huang, 549.
[31] For a detailed study of this issue, see Paul Pickowicz, 'Ch'ü Ch'iu-pai and the Chinese Marxist

literary convictions: since proletarian literature was a literature for the masses, Ch'ü logically argued that it must be understood by the masses. The May Fourth *pai-hua*, as used in New Literature, had become in Ch'ü's opinion a new elitist idiom characterized by saturation with foreign terms, Europeanized syntax, Japanese phrases, and *wen-yen* remnants. It was, in short, a language monopolized by a small minority of urban intellectuals who were alienated from the masses. Ch'ü therefore called for a new 'literary revolution', this time led by the rising proletarian class against three targets: the residual *wen-yen*, the May Fourth *pai-hua* (which Ch'ü termed a new *wen-yen*), as well as the old *pai-hua* of the traditional vernacular novels. What emerged from this second revolution was to be a new mass language that reflected the living tongues of the populace. With his Marxist predilections, Ch'ü naturally envisioned the prototype of this new popular language to be a collection of 'common idioms' (*p'u-t'ung-hua*), much like the language spoken by the metropolitan workers who came from all over China and managed to communicate with one another in modern factories.[32]

In a critical article in response to Ch'ü's ideas, Mao Tun showed that the language of the urban workers was by no means uniform: in Shanghai, for instance, the popular tongues were naturally based on the Shanghai dialect, while in other cities the 'common idioms' varied greatly from region to region. There was no such thing, in Mao Tun's view, as a national 'common idiom'. Mao Tun further defended the May Fourth *pai-hua* as still viable, though needing to be simplified and de-Europeanized. The urgent task for Mao Tun was to reform the modern *pai-hua* and to enrich it with local dialects.[33] Thus, between Mao Tun's realistic defence of modern *pai-hua* and Ch'ü Ch'iu-pai's radical vision of *p'u-t'ung hua*, the leftist camp was divided, as the debate was renewed in 1934, into two different, but not mutually exclusive, positions on the basis of Ch'ü's general premise. Some argued that in order to establish a new common language of the masses, the elitist *pai-hua* had to be rejected in toto; others favoured the popular language but still wished to salvage *pai-hua*. After reaching a compromise solution to reject the bad and assimilate the good elements in *pai-hua*, the debate soon shifted to a discussion of the need for Latinization.

Conceding that the common idiom he had envisioned was still in the process of formation, Ch'ü Ch'iu-pai nevertheless maintained that it was definitely not to be encased in a written form. Chinese characters were

conception of revolutionary popular literature and art', *CQ* 70 (June 1977) 296–314. See also his book *Marxist literary thought in China: the influence of Ch'ü Ch'iu-pai*, ch. 9.
[32] Li Ho-lin, *Chung-kuo wen-i ssu-ch'ao lun*, 360–1.
[33] *Ibid.* 362–3.

too complicated to learn and also inadequate to register the living vitality of the popular language with its variegated spoken expressions. Other critics pointed out that the written *pai-hua* was a vehicle of the Peking dialect, as were the previous systems of romanization (the so-called *Kuo-yü lo-ma tzu*). The new phonetic scheme, according to Lu Hsun and others, should be simpler and without the four tonal indicators. This new system of Latinized Chinese ('Latinxua'), which presumably had been tried out by two Russian Sinologist-linguists on the Chinese residents in the Far Eastern Maritime province of the Soviet Union, would be the alphabetic script of the *p'u-t'ung hua* which would replace entirely the centuries-old written ideographs.[34] While allowing for regional variations, both Ch'ü and Lu Hsun were confident that the phonetic system would still be much easier to master than the written characters.

This naive utopian theory of language was clearly impracticable in the 1930s, and was never put into successful practice. The Latinized script has become, at best, a phonetic aid to reading Chinese characters, not their replacement. But the other parts of this language debate proved to be most useful to Mao Tse-tung. In his radical critique of May Fourth literature, Ch'ü Ch'iu-pai had laid the groundwork for Mao's Yenan Talks. Both Ch'ü and Mao agreed that the language of proletarian literature must be close to the idiom of the masses. The 'popularization' of literature was thus to become a hallmark of Mao's policy in 1942, and the second 'literary revolution', begun by Ch'ü with little success, was launched again in Yenan with spectacular results.

The battle of the 'two slogans'

With the departure from Shanghai in late 1933 of Ch'ü Ch'iu-pai and Feng Hsueh-feng for Juichin, the league lost two of its most influential leaders and entered a phase of uncertainty. From 1934 to 1936, the league's ties with the central organs of the CCP were tenuous at best, and the party's underground headquarters were decimated by arrests and executions. An internal split developed between the league's new organizational leadership, particularly Chou Yang, and Lu Hsun, his disciples and other veteran writers.[35] In 1934, Hu Feng arrived in Shanghai from Japan and in 1935, with Lu Hsun's support, twice challenged Chou Yang's ideological authority on matters of interpretation concerning models and typical characters in literature. But the crowning event, which brought

---

[34] Tagore, 160.
[35] For a brilliant analysis of this entire episode, see Tsi-an Hsia, 'Lu Hsun and the dissolution of the League of Leftist Writers', in his *The gate of darkness: studies on the leftist literary movement in China*, 101–45.

these internecine bickerings into the open, was the sudden dissolution of the league in the spring of 1936 in response to the CCP's declaration for a national united front against Japanese invasion. On this important move Lu Hsun was not even consulted.

It remains unclear, for lack of adequate documentation, how the decision to dissolve the league was made. But it can be surmised that the decision was carried out by the Chou Yang group, who wished to replace the league by forming a broader coalition: the Association of Chinese Writers and Artists (Chung-kuo wen-i chia hsieh-hui). This group was formally inaugurated on 7 June 1936, at least two or three months after the league was dissolved. This apparent delay, in a time in which patriotic organizations were springing up spontaneously and rapidly, indicated that factors other than simple confusion among leftist writers were involved. Lu Hsun, Pa Chin, Hu Feng, Huang Yuan and others were invited to join the new association, but the invitation was either refused or ignored. Shortly afterwards, on 1 July, Lu Hsun and others signed a 'Declaration of Chinese literary workers' (Chung-kuo wen-i kung-tso che hsuan-yen) without forming a formal organization. The rivalry between the two camps on the left was thus further demarcated.

Toward the end of 1935, articles had begun to appear in which slogans reflecting the new political situation were bandied about. The term, 'national defence literature' (*kuo-fang wen-hsueh*), was mentioned together with other terms like 'national self-defence literature' (*min-tsu tzu-wei wen-hsueh*) and 'national revolutionary literary movement' (*min-tsu ko-ming wen-hsueh yun-tung*). The decision to adopt 'national defence literature' as the formal literary slogan of the United Front policy and the guiding principle of the association was probably made by the Chou Yang group (with or without the tacit consent of the CCP leadership).[36] Its appropriateness was presumably justified by its Soviet origins and by the fact that Mao Tse-tung had called for the establishment of a 'national defence' government. But the vague implications of the term received instant criticism from the various writers of the left.

Recognizing the need to clarify definitions and to silence the 'Trotskyite' opposition, Chou Yang made his first public statement on behalf of 'national defence literature' in June 1936, after preparations for founding the association were completed. He berated his ultra-leftist opponents for their narrow-minded abstractionism and their refusal to recognize the new political situation created by the Japanese invasion. While still considering urban revolutionary literature to be the main force since 1927, he nevertheless argued that a vast readership of 'middle

[36] Liu Hsin-huang, 463.

ground' writers did exist and should be attracted to the common cause. This was essentially a faithful parroting of the CCP's new stance and a far cry from his earlier position against the 'third category' of writers. But in his eagerness to champion his slogan as 'literature', Chou Yang had probably gone beyond the primarily political purpose of the party: 'to crystallize a strong body of united intellectual opinion which would force the Nationalist Government to come to some sort of coalition with the Communists and thus fight the Japanese'.[37] For he proceeded to dictate the theme and method of 'national defence literature': he asserted that national defence should become the central theme in the works of *all* writers except traitors, and that since 'questions of theme are inseparable from questions of method, the creation of national defence literature must adopt the creative method of progressive realism'. In a subsequent article, he even argued (presaging his 1958 statements on 'revolutionary romanticism') that national defence literature 'should not only depict the present state of national revolutionary struggles but at the same time sketch out the future vistas of national progress ... national defence literature, therefore, should concurrently use romanticism as part of its creative method.'[38]

Chou Yang's 'dictatorial' tendencies met with immediate opposition from veteran writers including Lu Hsun. Writing from Japan and sensing the political connection of the slogan, Kuo Mo-jo tried to defend it while modifying Chou's literary pretensions. 'National defence literature,' he stated, 'ought to be a standard of relations among writers and not a principle of creative writing.' Mao Tun agreed with this understanding but further warned that to apply the slogan to creative writing faced the dangers of 'closed-door sectarianism' – a direct reference to Chou Yang's injunction. Against Chou Yang's desire to control literature and 'to regulate others through the use of a slogan', Mao Tun insisted on the writer's prerogative of creative freedom within the context of his political commitment.[39]

Mao Tun's resentment of Chou Yang was shared, even more intensely, by Lu Hsun. As the late T. A. Hsia has pointed out in his vivid recapitulation of Lu Hsun's last years, the dissolution of the league had 'triggered a crisis, the last one, alas, in his life. Not only had he to redefine his own position, but Marxism, the sustenance of his spiritual life for so many years, was at stake.'[40] The league's demise put a sudden end to seven years of hard struggle against forces of the right and the

<hr/>

[37] Tagore, 114.

[38] Chou Yang, 'Kuan-yü kuo-fang wen-hsueh' (Concerning national defence literature), in Lin Ts'ung, ed. *Hsien chieh-tuan ti wen-hsueh lun-chan* (Current literary debates), 36–7, 81.

[39] Lin Ts'ung, 311–12.　　　　　　　　[40] T. A. Hsia, 129.

centre: Lu Hsun was now forced to ally himself with his erstwhile enemies. Moreover, the slogan of 'national defence literature', which was thrust upon him with all its compromise and authoritarian weight, represented both a rebuff of his Marxist convictions and an affront to his personal stature. Simmering in silence, he would not give in but worked on a new counter slogan 'which would not suggest the termination of leftist literature but rather an extension of it, and which would incorporate the new policy of the Communist Party into the tradition of the proletariat'.[41] The slogan finally decided upon, after he consulted Mao Tun and others, was 'mass literature of national revolutionary war' (*min-tsu ko-ming chan-cheng ti ta-chung wen-hsueh*).

In May 1936 the new slogan was used by Hu Feng, obviously under Lu Hsun's direction, in an article titled: 'What do the masses demand of literature?' The battle of the 'two slogans' was thus launched. For Hu Feng and Lu Hsun the slogan 'mass literature of national revolutionary war' clearly defined the 'common interest' which linked the proletarian revolutionary movement with the national struggle against Japan. In both, the common denominator was anti-imperialism. The slogan also served notice that the masses were the major force in the anti-Japanese war. For Chou Yang and Hsu Mou-yung, however, Hu Feng's article had pointedly ignored 'national defence literature' in favour of a long-winded, hard-to-remember phrase, whose intended function was to limit and de-emphasize the importance of the united front. The revolutionary writers, according to Chou Yang, should 'not only create pointed revolutionary works, but at the same time unite with those who originally stood at some distance from us in thought and art ... and extend the influence of the national united front to those readers exposed to revolutionary literature'.[42]

These statements from both sides seemed to give the impression that, in matters of literary policy, the dictatorial Chou Yang argued for more liberality whereas the anti-authoritarian opposition opted for more rigidity. But in matters of literary practice the situation was just the reverse: Lu Hsun and Mao Tun insisted on creative freedom for the revolutionary writer while Chou Yang considered it 'a dangerous illusion'. Veiled in their conflicting slogans was therefore a basic difference in outlook between the literary commissar and the creative writer. For Chou Yang, the literary commissar *par excellence*, the party policy of the united front took precedence over everything else, including artistic creation. As writers, Lu Hsun and Mao Tun placed more value on creative writing for the goals of the revolution: they were obstinate in their belief

[41] *Ibid.*   [42] Lin Ts'ung, 74.

that conscientious artists should never compromise their personal integrity or lose their creative prerogatives. They strongly resented the imposition of this new *partiinost* by a self-appointed party spokesman. For Lu Hsun, Chou Yang's action was especially distasteful because, instead of further consolidating the league, Chou Yang dissolved it and ordered the committed leftist writers to turn to the right!

Lu Hsun was finally angered to action by a letter from Hsu Mou-yung in which Hsu politely reminded Lu Hsun of the 'treachery' and 'flattery' of his two disciples, Hu Feng and Huang Yuan. Hsu also flatly dismissed Lu Hsun's painstaking effort to introduce a left-wing slogan into the united front as 'a mistake and harmful to the cause'. To be reprimanded by a young writer and former disciple who questioned the soundness of his judgment on human character and the current political situation was too great an insult to Lu Hsun's ego. In his long reply, written almost immediately after he received Hsu Mou-yung's letter, Lu Hsun vented his pent-up feelings in a passionate outpouring of unmitigated and undisguised wrath. He frankly exposed the 'treachery' of his opponents: the sectarianism of the Association of Chinese Writers and Artists, the slyness of Hsu Mou-yung, and above all the machinations of Chou Yang, T'ien Han, Hsia Yen, and Yang Han-sheng – the sinister gang of 'four heavies' (*ssu-t'iao han-tzu*) who were really behind Hsu Mou-yung's accusatory letter.[43]

Obviously Lu Hsun's anger was directed against Chou Yang's 'monopoly' in literature and his 'gang style' behaviour. The slogan 'national defence literature' was criticized more for its 'sectarian' implications (especially in Chou Yang's authoritarian interpretation) than for its theoretical errors. Lu Hsun acknowledged that he never regarded the two slogans as in opposition to each other; rather he considered the term 'mass literature of national revolutionary war' to be 'clearer and deeper in meaning and more substantive in content'. It could supplement and correct the obscurities of the 'national defence literature' slogan. In an interview he announced that 'mass literature of national revolutionary war' could serve as a 'general slogan' under which other strategic slogans such as 'national defence literature' could also be allowed to exist. Paraphrasing Lu Hsun's statement but giving it a more balanced focus, Mao Tun explained that 'mass literature of national revolutionary war' should be the slogan for creative writing among left-wing writers, whereas 'national defence literature' could be a banner to characterize relations among all writers.[44]

Lu Hsun's new slogan was certainly not what the party leaders had

[43] *Ibid.* 334–49.   [44] *Ibid.* 315, 342.

anticipated. But the sheer eloquence of such an eminent 'fellow traveller' had to be respected, for otherwise more denunciation would have been tantamount to an open admission of the failure of the united front. This was apparently the conclusion which party leaders other than Chou Yang had reached. Earlier in April 1936, Feng Hsueh-feng had come back to Shanghai as the party's liaison man from Yenan. Instead of joining up with Chou Yang, Feng became persuaded by the arguments of his old master and chose Lu Hsun's side. Shortly after Lu Hsun published his long rejoinder to Hsu Mou-yung, Feng wrote a most devastating critique of Chou Yang, in which he reiterated the charge, first raised by Mao Tun and Lu Hsun, that Chou Yang's high-handed monopolistic tendencies had led to a harmful sectarianism which 'closed the door' on other writers. Chou had made a gross error, Feng charged, by imposing a pre-emptive dichotomy between 'national defence literature' and 'traitor literature', in the same way that he had mechanically dismissed all 'non-proletarian literature' as 'capitalist literature' in the debate on 'third category men' three years before. Chou's most serious fault, in Feng's judgment, was his refusal to heed the demands for 'creative freedom'. 'Three years ago ... we did not positively unite all groups to fight for creative freedom; we did not acknowledge with maximum flexibility the principle of creative freedom in our criticism. This was certainly a mistake, which we must admit even three years later.' At a time when the mobilization of all writers was urgently needed for the anti-Japanese struggle, Feng concluded, Chou Yang's imposition of regulatory 'conditions' had 'greatly narrowed the anti-Japanese front' and his insensitivity to the issue of creative freedom was a clear indicator that he had accustomed himself to the role of a 'local emperor'.[45]

Feng Hsueh-feng's personal animosity revealed in this most blatant charge against Chou Yang did not, however, reflect well on his discretion as a party representative. According to T. A. Hsia, Feng's mismanagement in Shanghai caused him to be censured by the party. (He was eventually purged in 1957 by his old rival Chou Yang.) But one of the party leaders, Ch'en Po-ta, had seen fit to call a ceasefire on the battle of the two slogans. While still affirming the validity of 'national defence literature', Ch'en acknowledged that 'the attitudes toward this slogan need not be unified' (thus imparting a slight rebuff to Chou Yang). Out of respect for Lu Hsun's stance, Ch'en paid an equal tribute to the other slogan. 'Mass literature of national revolutionary war', Ch'en stated in a tactical synthesis, should belong to 'the left wing' of national defence literature because it constituted 'an essential part as well as a major force of national defence literature'.[46]

[45] Ts'an-k'ao tzu-liao, 1.567–75.   [46] Ibid. 1.561–4. T. A. Hsia, 125.

The battle of the two slogans can be said to have formally come to an end in early October (shortly before Lu Hsun's death on 19 October 1936) when twenty writers, including Mao Tun, Lu Hsun, Kuo Mo-jo, Pa Chin and Lin Yutang (with Chou Yang's group conspicuously absent), signed a joint declaration calling for a unified front of all writers – old and new, left and right – for 'purposes of national salvation'. Neither slogan was mentioned, but the principle of creative freedom, which had been advocated forcefully by Lu Hsun, Mao Tun, Hu Feng and Feng Hsueh-feng, was finally affirmed.

LITERARY CREATIVITY AND SOCIAL CRISIS

The series of ideological debates brought much sound and fury to the literary scene of the early thirties, but they failed to stimulate much literary creativity. It seems that the most ideologically vociferous writers were often the least creative: Ch'ü Ch'iu-pai, Chou Yang, Feng Hsueh-feng, Liang Shih-ch'iu, Hu Ch'iu-yuan and other theoreticians had no creative output to their credit. Other ideological writers produced meagre work of low quality. Chiang Kuang-tz'u, for instance, achieved popular status by virtue of a best-selling novel, *Ch'ung-ch'u yun-wei ti yueh-liang* (The moon forces its way through the clouds), which must be counted as artistically one of the worst works of the period.[47] Even the energetic Lu Hsun sometimes expressed personal regret for not being able to write more lyrical pieces in the vein of his earlier stories and prose poetry.[48]

While the ideologues on the left often monopolized the spotlight, less ideological, but by no means uncommitted writers made far more significant contributions to the new literary legacy. Some of the best creative writers in the 1930s – Mao Tun, Lao She, Wu Tsu-hsiang, Chang T'ien-i, Pa Chin, Ts'ao Yü and Wen I-to – all had leftist leanings. But their leftism was mainly the expression of personal conscience and of an artistic sensitivity which was increasingly affected by their socio-political environment. A small minority of others – Li Chin-fa, Tai Wang-shu, Feng Chih – were mostly poets and not very political. Their works are often artistically more inventive than the leftist writers, though their impact remained marginal. It was mainly due to the efforts of these creative writers that the thirties witnessed the flowering of fiction (mainly the novel), poetry and drama. By the eve of the Japanese invasion, modern Chinese literature was on the verge of a true literary 'renaissance' as writers gradually established their mature identities as committed artists.

[47] The novel enjoyed six printings in the five-month period after it was published. See Tagore, 71–2. For an analysis of Chiang's life and works, see T. A. Hsia, 'The phenomenon of Chiang Kuang-tz'u', in his *Gate of darkness*, 55–100.

[48] Feng Hsueh-feng, *Hui-i Lu Hsun* (Reminiscence of Lu Hsun), 23.

But this surging creative potential was not fully realized: the war put a sudden end to the fertile experiments in modernistic poetry; it rechannelled the energies of novelists from their major literary projects. Only drama prospered as a means of wartime propaganda and, in Chungking and Japanese-occupied Shanghai, as escapist entertainment. In terms of artistic creativity, the true culprit in this period was not the Kuomintang (whose suppressive measures nurtured a writer's critical spirit quite conducive to creativity) nor the CCP (whose literary control policies under Chou Yang had little visible impact on creative writers) but the Japanese: almost overnight the literary milieu was destroyed by the invaders' bombs and cannon-fire in 1937.

The trauma of war experience in literature will be discussed in a moment, but first we must note the four burgeoning modes of literary creation: the essay, the novel, modern verse and spoken drama.

The essay (tsa-wen)

The immediate impact of ideological polemics on literature was the popularity of the *tsa-wen* – the 'miscellaneous essay' or, in Ch'ü Ch'iu-pai's foreign term, 'feuilleton'. For purposes of doctrinal debate as well as social criticism and cultural commentary, the *tsa-wen* proved to be a most effective form. In this genre, Lu Hsun was the undisputed master.

Lu Hsun began experimenting with the short essay form at the same time he started writing short stories. Published first in *New Youth* and later in *Yü-ssu*, his 'random thought' pieces combined a free-flowing prose (written in the vernacular but interlaced with classical terms and phrases) with flexibility of content. While most of his essays were social in thrust and satirical in tone, as most Lu Hsun scholars have noted,[49] his approach was by no means narrowly utilitarian. Especially in his essays written before 1930, the critical intelligence of a social commentator was often combined with the lyrical sensitivity of a personal essayist. Behind his didactic assault on the evils of Chinese culture and society lurked a highly subjective quest for the shadows of China's collective psyche. The interplay of prose and poetry, didacticism and lyricism, of a sharp cynical intellect and a tense emotional psyche, characterizes the best of Lu Hsun's creative work, including his *tsa-wen*. The formal differences of genres – essay, prose, poetry and short story – were not so clearly marked in Lu Hsun's mind as Western scholars might expect. The common denominator of Lu Hsun's work (except his translations) is the brevity of each piece

[49] For a detailed analysis of Lu Hsun's *tsa-wen* art, see David E. Pollard, 'Lu Xun's *Zawen*'.

in a lifetime's voluminous output. Perhaps his mind was cluttered with a chaotic array of thoughts and feelings which never took on a coherent, systematic form. Thus the *tsa-wen* served as both a communicative vehicle and a literary by-product of Lu Hsun's mode of creativity.

As Lu Hsun became more politicized in the early 1930s, the inner personal dimension of his essay writing also became submerged under public layers of polemical outcry. For Lu Hsun himself, this shift from lyricism to polemicism was necessitated by the demands of political commitment. But his followers and enemies had embraced the Lu Hsun *tsa-wen* style as a major canon, and a mass of imitations flooded the publishing scene. These lesser *tsa-wen* writers totally ignored the inner depth of Lu Hsun's prose in their efforts to emulate only the surface brilliance of his satire. The result was a corpus of crude, shrill and shallow essays devoid of lasting literary value. Thus Lu Hsun's inimitable *tsa-wen* left an ironic legacy: it procreated in later periods of modern Chinese literary history an over-cynical and unnecessarily satirical style of essay writing without, however, the kernel of intellectual sophistication.

If *tsa-wen* was defined by leftists as an essentially ideological weapon in the 1930s, some non-leftist writers rallied around the personal essay (*hsiao-p'in wen*) as an alternative form of prose writing. The major spokesmen were Lu Hsun's brother, Chou Tso-jen, and the group of writers published in Lin Yutang's three magazines. Chou's essay style owes a clear debt to the classical tradition, particularly the works of the Kung-an and Ching-ling schools in the seventeenth century, which emphasized essay writing as personal expression.[50] Chou cultivated this 'personal style' almost to perfection: his prose is terse yet unhurried, elegant yet not flowery, reflecting a balanced and temperate mentality at great odds with Lu Hsun's. Writing in a similar vein, Chu Tzu-ch'ing and Yü P'ing-po produced essays with a personal touch sometimes verging on sentimentality, as in Chu's famous essay about his father, 'Shadow' (*Pei-ying*). Both Chou Tso-jen and Yü P'ing-po were the major contributors to Lin Yutang's publications which, following the tradition of the personal essay, advocated apolitical humour written in an urbane leisurely tone. Lin argued for a purposefully apolitical stance perhaps as a gesture of protest against the over-politicization of literature. And as gems of stylized writing, some of the best specimens of the *hsiao-p'in wen* are much more flavourful than the crudely combative *tsa-wen*. But in spite of its popularity in the mid-1930s (in publishing circles the year 1934 was designated as the year of the 'personal essay'), the cause Chou Tso-jen

[50] For an analysis of Chou Tso-jen's essays, see David E. Pollard, *A Chinese look at literature: The literary values of Chou Tso-jen in relation to the tradition.*

and Lin Yutang championed became increasingly out of date. It was against the prevalent impact of the 'personal essay' that Lu Hsun wrote his famous article, 'The crisis of the personal essay', in 1933. He attacked the 'leisure' and 'humour' of his brother and former friend as petty 'window dressing', 'elegant toys' and 'decorations for the rich and the powerful'. In an age of crisis, in which not only the writer's own survival but the survival of his art were at stake, Lu Hsun saw the essay form also reaching a point of crisis: 'The living essay must be a dagger and a spear with which it, together with the readers, can battle through a bloody path towards life.'[51]

Between the shoddiness of the *tsa-wen* and the frivolity of the *hsiao-p'in-wen*, the essay in the 1930s all but forfeited its creative potential. The most vital form of prose writing which combined a mature style with social meaning was fiction, particularly the novel.

Fiction

The period from 1928 to 1937 was clearly a decade of growth for modern Chinese fiction. In his masterful survey, *A history of modern Chinese fiction*, Professor Hsia devotes a chapter to each of the six outstanding authors of this period – Mao Tun, Lao She, Shen Ts'ung-wen, Chang T'ien-i, Pa Chin and Wu Tsu-hsiang – as compared to only one (Lu Hsun) in the preceding period (1917–27). The attention given here clearly indicates that modern Chinese fiction reached maturity in the 1930s. While Lu Hsun towered over May Fourth literature with his short stories, five of the six fiction writers in the second decade published novels, and all continued to produce short stories.

Of these six writers, Mao Tun played an instrumental role in shaping the novel into a major genre. By the time Mao Tun singled out Yeh Shao-chun's *School-teacher Ni Huan-chih* (1928) for praise as one of the few good novels of the May Fourth period, he had himself completed a trilogy of novels, *Shih* (Eclipse). As C. T. Hsia comments: 'this work was of such scope and honesty that it cast into utter insignificance the few novels of the first period'.[52] Following *Eclipse*, Mao Tun published another outstanding novel, *Hung* (Rainbow) and in 1933 his *chef-d'oeuvre*, *Tzu-yeh* (Midnight), which established him as one of the two or three foremost novelists in modern Chinese literature. In these pioneering works, Mao Tun succeeded in painting a social fresco of epic proportions by

[51] *Lu Hsun ch'üan-chi*, 5.173.
[52] C. T. Hsia, *A history of modern Chinese fiction*, 2nd. ed., 141.

modernizing the late Ch'ing social novel with the techniques of European naturalism.[53]

Mao Tun was a most learned and conscientious practitioner of 'naturalism' in his meticulous gathering and deployment of material, his adoption of a macroscopic objective point of view, and his portrait of characters as victims of socio-economic forces. But he was not a master of its technique. Rather, naturalism served as an artistic means to realize his truly monumental vision of modern Chinese society. Despite his early membership in the Chinese Communist Party, Mao Tun's fictional vision is essentially tragic, for it is concerned mainly with the futility of life in a class society doomed to decline and extinction. *Eclipse* drew upon Mao Tun's personal experience and depicted petty-bourgeois intellectuals disillusioned with 'making revolution' yet searching for personal fulfilment. In *Rainbow* Mao Tun continued his portraiture of urban intellectuals through his consummate portrait of the heroine. The story of her life is 'by design an allegory of recent Chinese intellectual history' as it captures the initial phase of the May Fourth cultural revolution through 'the bankruptcy of individualism in the early twenties, and its degeneration into libertinism and irresponsibility' to a leftist rejection of romantic idealism in favour of Marxist materialism.[54] However, the last part of this novel is inferior to the first two parts, precisely because Mao Tun failed to blend an ideological belief with a sense of artistic truth. As Mao Tun mentioned many times in his polemical essays, he felt more at home with the bourgeoisie than with the proletariat and he was prepared to defend his realistic and tragic view of this decadent class as in some way meaningful to 'revolutionary literature'. Nowhere is this vision more powerfully presented than in *Midnight*. In this long novel of more than 500 pages, Mao Tun erected a massive edifice of urban bourgeois society in Shanghai, dissected its many components – bankers, landlords, stockbrokers, students, socialites – and depicted in detail the process of its inevitable crumbling. The workers were not prominently represented.

It seems that from *Eclipse* to *Midnight* Mao Tun had delineated the urban milieu in the process of a 'long night before a dawn' with all its ambiguous anguish. When he turned his attention to the Chinese countryside of the 1930s, as in his famous rural trilogy of short stories ('Spring silkworms', 'Autumn harvest' and 'Winter ruin'), he was likewise torn by a dilemma in which he attempted to see more hope in

[53] For analysis of Mao Tun's early fiction, see the articles by Yu-shih Ch'en, John Berninghausen, and Cyril Birch in Merle Goldman, ed. *Modern Chinese Literature in the May Fourth era*, 233–80, 385–406.

[54] C. T. Hsia, *A history*, 153.

a landscape of despair. As one might expect, the first story of the trilogy, 'Spring silkworms', is an artistic masterpiece which is not matched in excellence by its two sequels, in which political messages intrude rather visibly into a naturalistic depiction of rural misery.

Like Mao Tun, Shen Ts'ung-wen and Lao She also evinced a strong sense of urban pessimism in their works. Shen Ts'ung-wen satirized the urban hypocrisy in a pointed fantasy, *A-li-ssu Chung-kuo yu-chi* (Alice's travels in China), while Lao She wrote a less successful satire entitled *Mao-ch'eng chi* (The city of cats). Clearly, the sympathies of both novelists lay with their rural characters, whether in an urban or rural setting. Shen Ts'ung-wen's approach was more pastoral: he saw in his beloved fellow provincials of the southern countryside a robust, earthy, almost 'noble savage' quality and a 'life-giving stream of emotional integrity and instinctive honesty.'[55] This pastoralism takes on a special moral nobility when contrasted with the malaise and decay of the cities. Unlike the sombre depiction in Lu Hsun's and Mao Tun's stories, Shen Ts'ung-wen's works are always informed with a glowing lyricism. In spite of the suffering and misery contained in their subject matter, Shen's rural portraits – in such memorable works as the short stories 'Ching' (Quiet) and 'Hsiao Hsiao', and the novelettes *Pien-ch'eng* (Border town) and *Ch'ang-ho* (Long river) – impart an endearing love of life which sprang from his personal experience. His autobiography, *Ts'ung-wen tzu-chuan*, recounting his colourful and many-faceted early life prior to becoming a writer, reads in fact like a vivid picaresque novel.

Like Shen Ts'ung-wen, Lao She had a profound sense of personal commitment to the rural values of 'old China' – simplicity, decency, honesty, and the high regard for manual labour. In Lao She's life and art, the city of Peking occupied a central place as a self-contained world which comprised the very best elements of traditional China. But as conveyed in his most famous novel, *Lo-t'o Hsiang-tzu* (Camel Hsiang-tzu),[56] even this cherished world was in a sorry process of deterioration. The tragedy of Camel Hsiang-tzu, a basically rural character whose dream to own his own rickshaw is gradually shattered by the corruptive influences around him, signifies also, in a larger scale, the tragedy of old Peking as it was caught in the currents of rapid social change. The sights and sounds of Lao She's beloved city provide a source of needed sustenance for Hsiang-tzu, but the reader is also made aware that it, too, has been

---

[55] *Ibid.* 191.

[56] An English translation by Evan King (Robert Ward) was published under the title *Rickshaw boy* and became a bestseller in the United States. But Mr King supplied his own 'happy ending' to the novel. For two recent translations with the original tragic ending, see *Rickshaw*, tr. Jean M. James; *Camel Xiangzi*, tr. Shi Xiaoqing.

contaminated by the evils of the 'modernizing' forces. The process of the brutalization of life was regarded by Lao She, not without a sense of pained resignation, as inevitable: the 'small men' like Hsiang-tzu, who should be the true 'souls' of Peking, were victimized and corrupted by an increasingly intolerable environment caused not only by socio-economic changes but by the slackened moral fibre of the middle and upper classes. This is a theme which recurred in several of Lao She's early works: *Chao Tzu-yueh*, *Niu T'ien-tz'u chuan* (Biography of Niu T'ien-tz'u), and *Li-hun* (Divorce).

A sensitive and refined man with broad humanitarian sympathies (Hsiang-tzu's onetime employer, a professor who treats him kindly and who embraces the ideals of Robert Owen, is probably Lao She's capsule self-portrait), Lao She is not a narrowly political writer. His leftist leanings were confined to a saddened comment on the futility of individual effort which made collective action more and more urgent. But as Lao She's own sad fate testifies, the socialist reality after liberation proved also too much for him: he committed suicide or was killed in 1966, at the beginning of the chaotic Cultural Revolution. Lao She once wrote that he was 'a good teller of stories but not a first-rate novelist': 'my sentimentalism exceeds my desire for positive struggle; and my humour dilutes my sense of justice.'[57] Yet precisely because of his gentle humanity and a tragic vision touched, however, with wit and humour, Lao She has been warmly received by Chinese readers of all political persuasions. In spite of his Manchu background and his brief sojourn in London, Lao She has always been remembered as one of the most popular 'native' writers.[58]

The most popular novelist of the 1930s, particularly among young readers, was undoubtedly Pa Chin, whose *Chia* (Family) has been called the 'Bible of modern Chinese youth'.[59] The popularity of *Family*, and of Pa Chin, is a phenomenon that can be analysed only from a historical perspective, for Pa Chin is not an accomplished writer despite his voluminous output. What he lacks in artistic craftsmanship he more than makes up for by an effusive display of passion. The story of *Family*, a largely autobiographical account, is basically the story of 'new youth': the three Kao brothers clearly represent three dominant types of the young

---

[57] Quoted in Wang Yao, *Chung-kuo hsin wen-hsueh shih-kao* (A draft history of modern Chinese literature), 1.232–3.

[58] For studies of Lao She, see Cyril Birch, 'Lao She: the humourist in his humor', *CO* 8 (Oct.–Dec. 1961) 45–62; Zbigniew Slupski, *The evolution of a modern Chinese writer*; Ranbir Vohra, *Lao She and the Chinese revolution*; and Hu Chin-ch'uan, *Lao She ho t'a-ti tso-p'in* (Lao She and his works).

[59] For a study of Pa Chin, see Olga Lang, *Pa Chin and his writings: Chinese youth between the two revolutions*. *Chia* has enjoyed 23 printings since its publication (Li Mu, 202). See also its English version, *Family*, tr. Sidney Shapiro.

May Fourth intelligentsia in rebellion against the 'feudal' society. Published in 1933, after a decade of heady activism on behalf of the causes of the May Fourth movement, the novel's instant popularity was almost guaranteed. In a way, Pa Chin celebrated in words the agony and ecstasy of a whole generation that lived through the May Fourth euphoria. Basking in its afterglow, most of Pa Chin's novels of this period – the *Love* trilogy and the trilogy *Torrent*, of which *Family* formed the first part – became, in a sense, outmoded in spite of their popularity: the battles of anti-traditionalism and personal emancipation were already won and the leftism of the early thirties called for a different set of political convictions. While variations on love and revolution among urban intellectuals continued to be written (by Pa Chin, Chiang Kuang-tz'u, and many lesser writers), the focus of creative attention gradually shifted by the mid-1930s to subjects other than urban radical youth. Placed side by side with the major works of his contemporaries, Pa Chin's fiction of unbridled passion reads as rather embarrassingly jejune, deficient in both ideological and artistic sophistication. By the time Pa Chin was able to demonstrate his full maturity as a novelist with the publication of *Han-yeh* (Cold nights) in 1947, the whole tradition of individual creativity – the legacy of the 1920s and the 1930s – had all but come to an end.

Of the numerous short-story writers of the period, the two most brilliant are Chang T'ien-i and Wu Tsu-hsiang. Both of them were committed to the Communist cause without, however, yielding to the temptation to be ideological.

C. T. Hsia considers Chang as possessing 'a breadth of human truth uncommon in an age of humanitarian didacticism'. 'Few of his contemporaries,' Hsia adds, 'have grasped so clearheadedly and dispassionately his satiric and tragic view of man's fundamental perversity and his disposition for evil.'[60] To convey this human truth with 'taut realism', Chang is adroit in the use of earthy colloquial expressions and in the subtle manipulation of conflict as an artistic means of depicting class inequality. In his story, 'Twenty-one', for instance, Chang pinpoints the conflict between the soldiers and their officers. In 'Spring breeze',[61] his famous long story, Chang depicts an elementary school as a microcosm of class oppression. The irony is all the more compelling because this segment of Chinese society – the educational institutions – should have been the least corrupt. Yet in Chang's story, the teachers are cruel and narrow-minded and pupils from well-to-do families become the teachers' accomplices in their oppression of poor pupils.

[60] C. T. Hsia, 223.
[61] This story, together with Wu Tsu-hsiang's 'Fan village' and others, is included in C. T. Hsia, ed. *Twentieth-century Chinese stories*.

Chang's effortless portrait of snobbery and tension in this and other stories thus reveals an insight into human perversity which is ultimately attributed to the larger social environment. In this regard, he is joined by Wu Tsu-hsiang, another committed leftist writer. Wu's approach has little of Chang's comic or satirical touch, but it carries the darker weight of 'bold symbolism' and 'savage irony.'[62] In 'Kuan-kuan's tonic', for example, the weakling son of a landlord literally supports his life on the blood and milk of peasants. In 'The Fan village', the glaring disparity between wealth and poverty, snobbery and misery, is presented in a daring way as a fatal conflict between mother and daughter.[63] By depicting the mother as a penny-pinching miser who through long habituation to city life has assimilated her urban employer's exploitative ideology, Wu Tsu-hsiang makes the strongest dramatic statement that class antagonism exists even among blood relations. To accentuate his Marxist perspective, Wu builds up to the tragic climax of matricide and leaves the reader to make his own judgment: is the peasant woman's murder of her own mother justifiable? By forcing the reader to arrive at a positive verdict, Wu thus points to the crucial issue of dire economic need.

Wu Tsu-hsiang certainly did not resort to sensationalism for its own sake. The tragic intensity in the works of this 'foremost practitioner of peasant fiction among leftist writers'[64] underlines his strong sense of political commitment to the revolutionary cause. However, like Mao Tun and Chang T'ien-i, Wu Tsu-hsiang was not so much enthused with the revolutionary future as he was anguished by the pre-revolutionary reality of pain and suffering, especially among the rural masses. Wu Tsu-hsiang's works were representative of a new trend in fiction. The more conscientious leftist writers could no longer afford to pose as arm-chair philosophers of Marxist theory in Shanghai cafés. Although most of them still lived in the cities, their attention was turned increasingly to the countryside; more and more writers began to depict rural subjects. According to the tabulations of a Kuomintang scholar from Taiwan, of the three major themes of thirties fiction – the rural situation, the intellectuals, and anti-Japanese patriotism – the rural theme dominated the majority of works.[65] These findings clearly indicate that the immediate May Fourth legacy of subjective individualism – of concentrating on the personal feelings and thoughts of the urban intellectual – was given a social

[62] C. T. Hsia, A history, 282–3.
[63] For English translations of Wu Tsu-hsiang's stories and many other works published from 1919 to 1949, see Joseph S. M. Lau, C. T. Hsia and Leo Ou-fan Lee, eds. Modern Chinese stories and novellas, 1919–1949.
[64] C. T. Hsia, A history, 286.   [65] Li Mu, 201.

reorientation, as the scope of fiction was extended to the countryside and 'realism' attained an authentically rustic ring.

A new literary sub-genre was gradually emerging – 'regional literature', in which the author attempted to capture the earthy flavour and local colour (*hsiang-t'u*) of a particular rural region, often the author's native place. A large volume of creative output can be included in this category. In addition to Wu Tsu-hsiang's fiction, some of Chang T'ien-i's works, and the rural trilogy of Mao Tun (all of which used the Lower Yangtze countryside as their setting), we find such leading samples as Shen Ts'ung-wen's writings on south and south-western China (*Border Town* and his stories of the Miao people), Lao She's novels set in Peking (an urban milieu depicted in rural terms), and the short stories of Sha Ting (about north-western Szechwan), Ai Wu (about Yunnan), Yeh Tzu (the villages of south-western Hunan) and many others. In all of them, an intense love of the 'good earth' is combined with an acute awareness of socio-economic crisis. Since most writers actually came from the rural areas which they depicted in their fiction, rural hardship and suffering are made all the more poignant by their deep-seated devotion to their original milieu. In some cases, such as Shen Ts'ung-wen's, a nostalgia for the rural scene is evoked by the author's bitter discomfort and alienation in his urban dwelling.[66] In others, such as Mao Tun and Wu Tsu-hsiang, the countryside is almost purposefully depicted as the victim of urban evils; the rape of rural China by the economic forces of Western imperialism from the coastal cities provides a painful reminder of the need for revolutionary action. But whatever their motivations, the glaring gap between rural and urban China – this fundamental source of the socio-economic crisis in the 1930s – was painfully perceived and vividly portrayed by these literary intellectuals who were totally alienated from the KMT government. Whether satiric, idyllic, realistic or agitational, their literature of the countryside thus became almost ipso facto a literature of protest and dissent against a regime which did so little to ameliorate the people's livelihood.

The political significance of this new type of regional literature was given a dynamic thrust by the arrival in Shanghai of a group of refugee writers from the North-eastern provinces (Manchuria), which the Japanese had invaded in 1931. In the vortex of patriotism that soon devoured the entire nation, these young writers, who were the first witnesses of Japanese aggression, became famous almost overnight. Their works depicting the Manchurian countryside, ravaged by the alien overlords,

---

[66] For a detailed study of Shen Ts'ung-wen's view of western Hunan, see Jeffrey C. Kinkley, 'Shen Ts'ung-wen's vision of Republican China' (Harvard University, Ph.D. dissertation, 1977).

brought freshness and vitality to regional literature and all but replaced the urban-style 'proletarian literature' in popularity and distinction.

The leader of this group of Manchurian writers was Hsiao Chün, whose novel, *Pa-yueh ti hsiang-ts'un* (Village in August), had the distinction of being the first contemporary Chinese novel to be translated into English, in addition to being the first specimen of war fiction.[67] Published in 1934 under Lu Hsun's aegis, the novel owed its scanty artistic structure to Fadeyev's *The rout*. But as Lu Hsun commented in the preface: 'It is serious and tense. The emotions of the author, the lost skies, earth, the suffering people, and even the deserted grass, *kao-liang*, frogs, and mosquitos – all are muddled together, spreading in gory-red colour before the very eyes of the reader.'[68] The authenticity of feeling – the emotions of Hsiao Chün from his immediate experience – accounted for the work's instant popularity. But at the age of 26, Hsiao Chün was still a novice craftsman whose art was better developed in later works, such as his short story, 'Yang' (Goats), and his long novel, *Ti-san tai* (The third generation).

A much more talented writer than Hsiao Chün in the Manchurian group was his wife, Hsiao Hung. Her debut piece, a novelette entitled *Sheng-ssu-ch'ang* (The field of life and death), was also published in 1934 but was not as popular.[69] With her expert use of the dialects and idioms of the Manchurian region, Hsiao Hung succeeded in giving a loving portrait of peasant life as it revolved around seasonal changes and the major stages of the human life-cycle – birth, age, sickness and death. But this natural rhythm was interrupted by the Japanese soldiers, whose presence became an inhuman violation of this harmonious world of nature and man. In Hsiao Hung's other stories and sketches (particularly *Hulan-ho chuan* or Tales of Hulan River), the peasant life-cycle is personified by a gallery of memorable characters – school children, hunters, bandits, old peasant women, newly-married young girls, even Russians – who also embodied for her the primitive vitality of the Manchurian people. With a sensitivity to the smells and sounds of her land, this most talented but short-lived woman writer brought to her readers a lively sense of Manchuria, the loss of which was both a personal blow and a national tragedy.

Another Manchurian writer, a friend of the Hsiaos and potentially a

---

[67] T'ien Chun (Hsiao Chün), *Village in August*, tr. Evan King, with an introduction by Edgar Snow. For a study of Hsiao Chün, see Leo Ou-fan Lee, *The romantic generation of modern Chinese writers*, ch. 11.

[68] Quoted in Lee, *The romantic generation*, 228.

[69] For English translation see Hsiao Hung, *Two novels of Northeastern China: The field of life and death and Tales of the Hulan River*, tr. Howard Goldblatt and Ellen Yeung. For a study, see Howard Goldblatt, *Hsiao Hung*.

more ambitious novelist, is Tuan-mu Hung-liang, whose works have received neither commercial popularity nor scholarly attention until very recently.[70] Tuan-mu wrote his first novel, *K'o-erh-ch'in ch'i ts'ao-yuan* (The steppe of the Khorchin banner), in 1933 at the precocious age of twenty-one. But unlike the Hsiaos' works which received Lu Hsun's immediate sponsorship, the novel was not published until 1939. If Hsiao Hung painted the Manchurian landscape with the subtlety of a sketch artist, Tuan-mu Hung-liang approached his native region even more ambitiously by imbuing it with epic grandeur. The long novel is a chronicle of a landlord family from its earliest Chinese settlement to its patriotic awakening on the eve of the Japanese invasion. Written in majestic prose and borrowing from film techniques, this sprawling novel, with its archetypal characterization, could have achieved the stature of a national epic. But Tuan-mu was perhaps too impetuous and ambitious a young writer to cultivate the narrative skills of telling a good story. This manifest defect mars an otherwise magnificent novel – a grand masterpiece *manqué* that could have been a milestone in the development of the modern Chinese novel.

After *The steppe of the Khorchin banner*, Tuan-mu produced two other major novels, *Ta-ti ti hai* (The sea of earth) and *Ta-chiang* (The great river), as well as several short stories. In these works, he further demonstrated his versatility as a 'descriptive lyricist' – an 'ability to define landscape and physical sensation with lyrical exactitude'. Two chapters from *The great river* are praised by C. T. Hsia as 'showpieces of modern Chinese prose'.[71] Had it not been for the eight long years of the Sino-Japanese War, which consumed the energies of the entire nation and deprived modern Chinese writers of a stable milieu to develop their art, the talents of Tuan-mu and others would have advanced modern Chinese fiction to a new height.

Poetry

The early phase of modern Chinese poetry was characterized by a persistent effort to break away from the shackles of the traditional poetic mode. In their eagerness to experiment with new forms and to have free expression, the new poets often disregarded matters of poetic meaning. Hu Shih, K'ang Pai-ch'ing, Ping Hsin and other early May Fourth poets

---

[70] Professor C. T. Hsia is at work on a full-scale study of war fiction, of which two papers on Tuan-mu Hung-liang have been completed.
[71] C. T. Hsia, 'The Fiction of Tuan-mu Hung-liang', 56–61.

shared a common weakness: a simplicity of conception and a paucity of imagery.[72]

It was not until Hsu Chih-mo returned from England in 1922 that experimentation with Western – mainly English – poetic forms began in earnest.[73] Hsu's early poems, as collected in his *Chih-mo ti shih* (Chih-mo's poetry, 1925), were outbursts of 'effusive, unbridled emotions' encased in stilted imitative forms borrowed from English Romantic poetry. His poetic techniques became more refined in his subsequent collections – *Fei-leng-ts'ui ti i-yeh* (A night in Florence, 1927) and *Meng-hu chi* (Fierce tiger, 1928). While he achieved more freedom and inventiveness in poetic metre and rhyme, the predominantly 'foreign' sentiments inspired by Wordsworth, Shelley and Keats read as curiously unoriginal, especially for students of Western poetry. Hsu was at his best when conveying a pleasant exoticism in such heavily foreign-flavoured poems as 'Second farewell to Cambridge' and 'A night in Florence', or when the auditory elements were blended with the visual to achieve an eerie state, as in 'Sea rhymes' (a work inspired by Keats's 'La belle dame sans merci', which was later set to music by Chao Yuan-ren). But when in his later poems Hsu attempted to be more philosophical or to adapt foreign imagery to a Chinese milieu, the result was not as successful. Even in his longest 'philosophic' statement, 'Love's inspiration' (1930), one senses an ebullient poetic mind struggling, yet unable, to reach full maturity. Had Hsu not met sudden death in a plane crash in 1931, his achievements would no doubt have been greater.

Hsu's friend and colleague at the Crescent Moon Society, Wen I-to, was more visually inclined, perhaps due to his training in painting. Like Hsu, Wen was interested in formalistic experimentation: his early works were sometimes designed to startle his readers with striking metaphors and allusions. But Wen's progress from the self-indulgent romanticism of his first collection, *Hung-chu* (Red candles, 1923), to the mature artistry in his second collection *Ssu-shui* (Dead water, 1929) is more impressive than Hsu Chih-mo, though Wen's total poetic output was far less than Hsu's. The appearance of Wen's poem, 'Dead water', was something of a landmark because of its original and poetic vision of Chinese society:

> Here is a ditch of hopelessly dead water.
> No breeze can raise a single ripple on it.
> Might as well throw in rusty metal scraps
> or even pour left-over food and soup in it.

[72] See Julia C. Lin, *Modern Chinese poetry: an introduction*, ch. 1.
[73] For an analysis of Hsu's borrowing from English poetry, see Cyril Birch, 'English and Chinese metres in Hsu Chih-mo', *Asia Major*, N.S., 8.2. (1961) 258–93.

Perhaps the green on copper will become emeralds.
Perhaps on tin cans peach blossoms will bloom.
Then, let grease weave a layer of silky gauze,
and germs brew patches of colorful spume.

Let the dead water ferment into jade wine
covered with floating pearls of white scum.
Small pearls chuckle and become big pearls,
only to burst as gnats come to steal this rum.

And so this ditch of hopelessly dead water
may still claim a touch of something bright.
And if the frogs cannot bear the silence—
the dead water will croak its song of delight.

Here is a ditch of hopelessly dead water—
a region where beauty can never reside.
Might as well let the devil cultivate it—
and see what sort of world it can provide.[74]

Julia Lin has commented on the 'compact stanzaic pattern' of this poem
with its neat metrical sequence and end-stopped lines, which offers 'the
structural integrity Wen strives for'.[75] But more important than poetic
form is Wen's ability to compress immediate reality into a metaphorical
vision. The sombre imagery of this poem is a far cry from Hsu Chih-mo's
rosy idylls and Kuo Mo-jo's apocalyptic incantations. The symbolism of
decay and rebirth is vaguely reminiscent of Kuo's 'Nirva of the
phoenixes', but Wen's vision of China – as a ditch of dead water which
may ferment to splendour – has an intellectual depth which is lacking in
Kuo's fertile imagination. 'Dead water' is also more daringly 'modernistic'
in its use of visual metaphors laden with considerable ambiguity.[76]

This attempt to create an imagistic world which may not show a clear
correspondence with reality, to evoke and intimate rather than to state
directly, is a familiar trait of Western Symbolist poetry which, to some
extent, can also be found in traditional Chinese poetry. It is nevertheless
a far cry from early May Fourth poetry which aims, as Hu Shih argued,
to be simple, free, and easily understood. Whether or not modern Chinese
poetry made a corresponding 'progress' from romanticism to symbolism
as in Europe may be debatable,[77] but by the late twenties and early thirties
a more 'symbolist' tendency was clearly visible in the works of a small
number of poets.

[74] Translated by Kai-yu Hsu in his *Twentieth-century Chinese poetry: an anthology*, 65–6.
[75] Julia Lin, 82.
[76] For a study of the life and poetry of Wen I-to, see Kai-yu Hsu, *Wen I-to* and in Chinese *Hsin-shih
ti k'ai-lu jen – Wen I-to* (A pioneer of modern poetry – Wen I-to).
[77] For a detailed analysis of this issue, see the section on 'Impact of Foreign literature' in Leo Ou-fan
Lee, 'Literary trends 1: the quest for modernity, 1895–1927', *CHOC* 12.489–99.

One of the chief contributors to this trend was Li Chin-fa. While studying in France as a member of the Work-Study Programme in the early 1920s, Li began to write poetry. Chou Tso-jen noticed his originality and arranged to have two volumes of Li's poetry published in 1925 and 1927. Upon his return to China in 1925, Li was called a 'poet eccentric', his poetry curiously 'incomprehensible'. Criticized by many leftist and non-leftist writers but appreciated by a few (among them, Chou Tso-jen and Chu Tzu-ch'ing), Li naturally thought of himself as an 'avant-gardist' ahead of his time.[78]

Li's poetry does not claim to have any 'meaning' except as a series of fragmentary images and symbols which he makes no attempt to elucidate. Apparently indebted to Baudelaire, Verlaine and Mallarmé, whose works he read with avidity and introduced into China, Li Chin-fa seems enamoured of 'exotic' elements. In the opinion of Communist literary historians, these boldly sensual and sometimes grotesque images are but empty devices which veil Li's decadent, reactionary mentality.[79] But a modern Western scholar considers Li's poetry to be 'the most defiant departure from tradition, and at the same time the most daring innovation, in the course of modern Chinese poetry'.[80] A more balanced perspective might place Li as one of the few 'new rebels' who reacted strongly against the superficial romanticism or realism of early May Fourth poetry; he performed a second 'emancipation' which freed modern Chinese poetry, at least temporarily, from its obsessive concern with nature and society and pointed to the possibility of a surrealistic world of artistic symbols. He came close to creating an aesthetic vision so daringly new that, as in European surrealistic art, it could serve as an artistic statement of protest against the philistine status quo.

Li Chin-fa's pioneer efforts were taken up in the pages of a new journal, *Hsien-tai* (Contemporary, 1932–5) edited by Shih Chih-ts'un. The reigning poet of the *Hsien-tai* group, who professed to be politically neutral, was Tai Wang-shu. Likewise interested in French symbolism, Tai had inherited Li's penchant for impressionism and mysticism; he claimed that the purpose of poetry was to express that 'poetic mood', which he defined as an evocation of 'something between the self and the hidden self.'[81] But Tai's poems did not achieve the jarring effect of Li's dark, bizarre imagery. Instead, he seemed to carry on the aural values of Hsu Chih-mo's poetry; he shared with the Crescent Moon poets – particularly Ch'en Meng-chia

---

[78] See the fascinating interview of Li Chin-fa by the poet Ya Hsien in *Ch'uang shih-chi* (The epoch poetry quarterly), 30 (Jan. 1975) 5. See also Liu Hsin-huang, 687–8.

[79] Wang Yao, 1.201.

[80] Julia Lin, 153.

[81] Quoted in Wang Yao, 1.200.

and Fang Wei-te, after the untimely deaths of Hsu and Chu Hsiang – the emphasis on musicality, texture, and suggestive nuance. An example of Tai's 'softer' symbolism can be found in 'The alley in the rain' (1927), the poem which earned him the sobriquet, 'the poet of the rainy alley':

> She seems to be in this lonely alley,
> Holding an oilpaper umbrella
> Like me,
> Just like me,
> Silently walking back and forth,
> Cold, lonely, and melancholy.
>
> Silently she moves close;
> Moving close, she casts
> A glance like a sigh,
> She floats by
> Like a dream,
> Sad lingering, and faint.
>
> Drifting by in a dream,
> Like a spray of clove,
> She passes by my side:
> Farther, farther away she goes,
> To the broken hedge walls,
> To the end of the rainy valley.
>
> Holding an oilpaper umbrella, alone,
> Wandering in the long, long,
> Desolate alley in the rain,
> I hope to encounter
> The girl who holds her grief
> Like cloves.[82]

The effect of 'synesthesia' created in the poem, according to Julia Lin's analysis, produces 'an atmosphere permeated with effeminate charm, languorous grace, and mellifluous music that is worthy of his poetic guide, Paul Verlaine'.[83]

In the leftist scholarship of modern Chinese literature, the works of Li and Tai are viewed as an 'adverse current'; for they were against the mainstream of the thirties literature which continued to be preoccupied with the reality of life and society.[84] But new talents continued to emerge. Three students of Peking University – Pien Chih-lin, Li Kuang-t'ien and Ho Ch'i-fang – published a joint collection titled *Han-yuan chi* (The Han

---

[82] Quoted and translated in Julia Lin, 165–6. For a collection of Tai's poetry, see Ya Hsien, ed. *Tai Wang-shu chüan* (Collected works of Tai Wang-shu).   [83] Julia Lin, 166.

[84] Wang Yao, 1.201. However, since 1981, Tai's stature has been reassessed and his works republished in China.

garden) which contained some of the most original work of the period. Of the three, the most learned was probably Pien Chih-lin. A translator of Baudelaire, Mallarmé, and later an admirer of Yeats, Auden and T. S. Eliot, Pien Chih-lin has informed his own works with a meditative, sometimes metaphysical quality which is rare among modern Chinese poets. For this 'beauty of intelligence'[85] Pien's works are not easily understood by most Chinese critics who tend to prefer the more flamboyant and more proletarian Ho Ch'i-fang.

Ho Ch'i-fang's early poems were even more ornately romantic than Pien Chih-lin's. Likewise influenced by French symbolism, Ho believed that in poetry 'beauty is achieved primarily through the use of imagery or symbols' and that the ultimate goal of poetry is 'to release the imagination, to escape from reality into dreams and fantasy'.[86] But as Bonnie McDougall has shown, 'the political crisis which forced Ho Ch'i-fang home in the summer of 1933 brought an abrupt change in his work. The luxuriant imagery of his verse was toned down.'[87] In a group of poems written in 1936–7, Ho bade farewell to Western romantic works which had failed to sustain him. Instead, he discovered a new reality – the impoverished and dislocated peasants:

> 'I love those clouds, those drifting clouds...'
> I am the stranger in Baudelaire's prose poem,
> Mournfully craning his neck
> To look at the sky.
>
> I went to the countryside.
> The peasants were too honest and lost their land.
> Their households shrank to a bundle of tools.
> By day they seek casual work in the fields,
> At night they sleep on dry stone bridges.
>
> In the future I'll insist on expressing my opinions:
> I want a thatched roof,
> I do not love the clouds, I do not love the moon,
> I do not even love the many stars.[88]

'I have always recalled with gratitude,' Ho wrote, 'that small district in the Shantung peninsula where my thoughts of resistance ripened like a fruit. At least I clearly realized that a true individual had only two choices: either to commit suicide, or abandon his isolation and indifference and go to the masses, to join in the struggle ... from now on I will use my

[85] The phrase, made in English, is by Liu Hsi-wei, as quoted in Chang Man-i *et al. Hsien-tai Chung-kuo shih-hsuan, 1917–1949* (Modern Chinese poetry: an anthology, 1917–1949), 1.709.
[86] Bonnie S. McDougall, ed. and tr. *Paths in dreams: selected prose and poetry of Ho Ch'i-fang*, 223–4.
[87] *Ibid.* 228.   [88] *Ibid.* 126.

writing as a weapon in the struggle, as Lermontov once said, "Let my song become a whip".'[89]

In poetry, the modernist experiments came to a sudden halt in the mid-thirties, to be replaced by a simple, proletarian style. The young poet who embodied this new trend was Tsang K'o-chia, whose first collection of poetry, *Lo-yin* (Branded imprint), was hailed in 1934 as a major event by Wen I-to, Mao Tun and other writers. In their view, Tsang's poetry achieved more force by its very simplicity, its 'refusal to paint and decorate reality' through 'beautiful words'. Tsang explained the title of his first collection in two lines: 'The pain brands my heart / Reminding me, every minute, that this is life.'[90] Tsang K'o-chia was one of the harbingers of rural proletarian poetry – a trend which prospered during the war years in the works of Ho Ch'i-fang, Ai Ch'ing, T'ien Chien, and the later Kuo Mo-jo. A positive outlook on life through suffering, a poetic focus on the 'flesh-and-bone' figures of the Chinese countryside, and a more adroit use of the colloquial idiom for poetic effect, became their common hallmarks. By the beginning of the Sino-Japanese War, both poetry and fiction had converged on themes of immediate reality. And the urban tradition of symbolism and modernism disappeared from the Chinese mainland.[91]

Drama

The development of modern Chinese drama shows many parallels to that of modern Chinese poetry. Both began as Western-inspired new forms in conscious reaction against tradition. From its inception in 1907, when a small group of Chinese students organized the Spring Willow Society (Ch'un-liu she) in Japan and performed such translated plays as *La dame aux camélias* (*Ch'a-hua nü* or Lady of the camellias) by Dumas *fils* and Mrs Stowe's *Uncle Tom's cabin* (*Hei-nu yü-t'ien lu*) with an all-male cast, the amateur practitioners of this new genre called it 'new theatre', 'new drama' and later 'civilized drama' or 'modern drama' to distinguish it from traditional theatre. In 1927, T'ien Han, one of the early playwrights, adopted the term 'spoken drama' (*hua-chü*), to demarcate its important departure from the traditional-style Peking opera which is essentially a 'singing drama'.[92]

Like new poetry, the new drama formed an integral part of the Literary Revolution and, in fact, played a more prominent role as a medium of

[89] *Ibid.* 169.
[90] Wang Yao, 1.208–9; Kai-yu Hsu, *Chinese poetry*, 277.
[91] This modernistic tradition, however, has been revived and is now thriving in Taiwan and in urban China as 'obscure poetry'.
[92] John Y. H. Hu, *Ts'ao Yü*, 16.

propagating new ideas. Hu Shih's introduction of Ibsen in *New Youth*, followed by the Chinese translation of *A doll's house* and Hu Shih's Ibsenesque play, *Chung-shen ta-shih* (The great event in life), turned the new dramatic medium toward social reform. But in artistic quality, the new drama developed in the 1920s was even more crude than poetry, despite the considerable number of foreign plays translated into Chinese. The few plays then written were no more than literary exercises on the themes of social rebellion or personal frustration: Hu Shih's *Chung-shen ta-shih*, Kuo Mo-jo's trilogy, *San-ko p'an-ni ti nü-hsing* (Three rebellious women), Hung Shen's *Chao yen-wang* (Chao the King of Hell), and T'ien Han's *Hu-shang ti pei-chü* (Tragedy on the lake), *K'a-fei tien chih i-yeh* (A night at the café), and *Ming-yu chih ssu* (The death of a famous actor).

As a performing art, the new drama met with more difficulties than the written genres of poetry and fiction. Although a number of dramatic clubs or societies were organized in the 1920s, particularly the Popular Drama Society (Min-chung chü she, 1921) and South China Society (Nan-kuo she, 1922), they were 'amateurish' in both senses of the term, merely groups of writers and students who 'loved' the theatre (*ai-mei*) and had little or no professional knowledge of stagecraft. In spite of the efforts of T'ien Han, Ou-yang Yü-ch'ien, and especially Hung Shen (who had received practical training with Professor Baker's 47 Workshop at Harvard), there was no professional 'theatre' to speak of in the 1920s. A play seldom received more than one or two performances, often given in high school auditoriums or at other public functions as part of the festivities. The non-professional troupes lacked money and resources; sometimes their performances were stopped by school or local authorities as a source of bad influence on student morals. As late as 1930, according to an interesting account by Hsia Yen, the amateur group he belonged to gave a 'grand performance' of Remarque's *All quiet on the Western Front* in a rented Japanese-owned theatre in Shanghai with a movable stage, but the few 'actors' and 'actresses' had to perform several roles each besides serving, together with the director, as stage hands to change the sets and move the stage between acts.[93]

Not until the early 1930s did modern Chinese drama finally come of age in both writing and performance, due in large measure to the efforts of a single man.

Ts'ao Yü wrote his first play, *Lei-yü* (Thunderstorm), while a student at Tsing-hua university: published in 1934, it was performed in 1935 by

---

[93] T'ien Han, Ou-yang Yü-ch'ien *et al. Chung-kuo hua-chü yun-tung wu-shih-nien shih-liao chi, 1907–1957* (Historical materials on the modern Chinese drama movement of the last fifty years, 1907–1957), first collection, 151.

students at Futan University under the direction of Hung Shen and
Ou-yang Yü-ch'ien. In 1936, it was taken on tour by the Travelling
Dramatic Troupe and achieved unprecedented success.[94] Ts'ao Yü's next
play, *Jih-ch'u* (Sunrise, 1936), received a literary prize from the Shanghai
newspaper *Ta-kung-pao*. More plays followed as Ts'ao Yü gradually
developed his art in the wake of wide popularity – *Yuan-yeh* (The
wilderness, 1937), *Shui-pien* (Metamorphosis, 1940), *Pei-ching jen* (Peking
man, 1940), and *Ch'iao* (The bridge, 1945) – which established Ts'ao Yü
as the foremost playwright in modern China.

Of all his plays, *Thunderstorm* and *Sunrise* remain the most popular,
although *Peking man* may be artistically his best work. The popular success
of *Thunderstorm* is easily understandable, for its subject involves the crucial
May Fourth issue: the assertion of 'personal freedom and happiness under
the crippling weight of the traditional patriarchal society'.[95] Added to this
reigning theme of emancipation is a nascent socialist concern for the plight
of the workers under capitalist exploitation. But Ts'ao Yü was not content
to cast his first work in the simplistic mould of the early May Fourth 'social
problem' play. Rather, the message is conveyed in a complex plot of
passion and fate in the tradition of Greek tragedy, through which Ts'ao
Yü showed himself to be a most resourceful playwright, far more talented
than all his predecessors. The protagonist of the play, Chou Fan-yi, is a
woman, a possessed figure who has an incestuous passion for her stepson.
The sources of Ts'ao Yü's characterization, as Joseph Lau has convincingly
demonstrated, can be traced to Racine (*Phaedre*), Eugene O'Neill (Abbie
Putnam in *Desire under the elms*) and Ibsen (Mrs Alving in *Ghosts*).[96] It is
possible that Ts'ao Yü conceived of the play as a Chinese variation on
A doll's house (similar to the way in which Ibsen wrote *Ghosts* in order
to convince the audience that what befalls Mrs Alving in the end could
have been the fate of Nora if she had chosen to stay with her husband).
But Ts'ao Yü's attempt to explore the theme of incestuous passion as a
tragic protest against traditional family ethics was even more daring. Ts'ao
Yü deserved the popularity he received for this creative use of Western
dramatic sources.

In *Sunrise*, Ts'ao Yü's intention is more sociological. Like Mao Tun's
Midnight, Ts'ao Yü's play is designed as a scathing portrait of the passing
of the capitalist order. To heighten this theme, Ts'ao Yü took another
bold step. 'When I wrote *Sunrise*,' he recalled, 'I decided to abandon the
structure of *Thunderstorm* and not to concentrate on a few characters. I

---

[94] John Hu, 21–2.
[95] Joseph S. M. Lau, *Ts'ao Yü: the reluctant disciple of Chekhov and O'Neill, a study in literary influence*, 6.　　　　　　　　　　[96] *Ibid.* 10.

wanted to use the fragmentary method for *Sunrise*, in which a certain conception is expounded through slices of human life.'[97] The play presents a cluster of characters without any central protagonist. And to show the contrasting slices of life, Ts'ao Yü encompasses in four acts both the upper and lower classes. Act 3, which takes place in a brothel, invokes a poignant mood of debauchery and suffering, perhaps the most daringly conceived dramatic act in modern Chinese theatre.[98]

One of the crucial factors in Ts'ao Yü's success was his acute sense of drama. He was one of the two modern Chinese playwrights (the other being Hung Shen) who conceived of drama not only as literature but also as performance. His stage directions were elaborately prepared in order to achieve maximum tension. The brothel scene in *Sunrise* is presented on a split stage with two sets of action proceeding simultaneously. In *The wilderness*, tom-tom drums and mute visions are employed in the manner of O'Neill's *Emperor Jones* to create an atmosphere of psychological horror. And the conscious use of Greek tragedy conventions in *Thunderstorm* is another example of Ts'ao Yü's zealous endeavour to master stagecraft.

While clearly imitative of Western models in technique, Ts'ao Yü's plays are distinctly Chinese in content. His works dramatized the shared feelings and concerns of his generation. The themes of his plays, exemplified in *Thunderstorm* and *Sunrise*, are quite familiar: the tragedy of the old marriage system, the feudal family structure, the oppression of the lower classes, the corruption of urban capitalists, and the frustrations of young intellectuals. But Ts'ao Yü was able to bring to these themes the shattering force of emotional expression. In this he resembled Pa Chin, whose novel *Family* he adapted into a play. Like Pa Chin, Ts'ao Yü was very much at the mercy of his emotions. When writing *Thunderstorm*, he wrote: 'I was seized with a sudden passion so overwhelming that I could not but seek to release it.' He was likewise dominated, when writing *Sunrise*, by 'strong emotion from beginning to end'.[99] In fact, most of Ts'ao Yü's plays can be seen as enactments of his own emotions. They also betray the same defects one finds in Pa Chin's novels: undisciplined style, over-zealous use of hyperbolic language, and a tendency toward melodrama and sensationalism. But as a dramatist, Ts'ao Yü had an obvious advantage over Pa Chin in being able to convey his emotional truth through a live medium.

For all his sympathies with the downtrodden, Ts'ao Yü was not narrowly political. He was not interested in using the medium which he

---

[97] Quoted and translated in John Hu, 54.
[98] Because of its bold content, this act was often omitted in performance, much to Ts'ao Yü's chagrin.   [99] Joseph Lau, 6; John Hu, 24.

had so painstakingly developed merely as a propaganda vehicle. As an artist and social critic he was concerned only with his vision of the pervading gloom before 'sunrise' – the evils of gruesome reality on the eve of war and revolution. Like Lu Hsun and Mao Tun, he could offer neither positive remedies nor concrete vistas of the future. At the end of *Sunrise*, the heroine quotes from her dead poet-husband's novel: 'The sun is risen, and darkness is left behind. But the sun is not for us, and we shall be asleep.'[100]

These celebrated lines were prophetic. In 1936 China was indeed on the eve of a national cataclysm but the new 'dawn' did not bring much light to the lives of Ts'ao Yü's compatriots; rather, it ushered in a period of prolonged warfare and protracted revolution.

WAR AND REVOLUTION 1937–1949

The saga of 'national resistance'

When the Marco Polo Bridge incident on 7 July 1937 set off full-scale war between China and Japan, it also unleashed a crescendo of literary activities. An unprecedented unity among literary intellectuals replaced the factionalism of the early thirties. The debate over the 'two slogans', which had so divided the leftist literary ranks, disappeared almost overnight. All slogans were submerged under the resounding call to 'the war of resistance' (*k'ang-chan*). Organizations were formed spontaneously and anti-Japanese manifestos issued. Finally, in March 1938, shortly after the Japanese invasion of Shanghai in January, an overall All-China Resistance Association of Writers and Artists (Chung-kuo ch'üan-kuo wen-i chieh k'ang-ti hsieh-hui) was established in Hankow with Lao She as president and with branches soon springing up in a score of major cities.

This association initiated a series of activities to further the war effort. It organized writers into 'battlefront visiting teams', who made trips to military defence positions, fraternized with the troops, and wrote emotion-tinged reports. The association also set up a network of 'literary reporters' (*wen-i t'ung-hsun yuan*): inexperienced young writers, some in rural areas, were organized into local groups under the direction of the branch offices of the association. They met frequently to discuss themes assigned by the association and wrote reports on local literary activities

---

[100] Ts'ao Yü, *Jih ch'u* (Sunrise), 236. For an English translation of Ts'ao Yü's plays, see *Thunderstorm* and *Sunrise*, both translated by A. C. Barnes; *The wilderness*, tr. Christopher C. Rand and Joseph S. M. Lau.

which, together with samples of their creative writing, were forwarded to their superiors in the association for comments and corrections. In Kwangtung province, more than three hundred initial literary reports were organized in a matter of days; the Shanghai area boasted an equal number. Even in the rural regions of North China, membership supposedly reached five to six hundred. Most of these reporters were students, but some were shop clerks, workers, or minor functionaries in local governments.[101]

Aside from the writers' visiting teams and the literary reporters programme, the association also organized initially five propaganda teams (each consisting of sixteen members) and ten dramatic troupes (with thirty members each). Popular dramatic groups sprang up with such speed that by 1939, according to one account, there were 130,000 people engaged in dramatic performances.[102]

These organizations gave clear evidence that as a result of the war modern Chinese literature was losing its urban elitist character. Joining in the nationwide movement to resist aggression, the urban writers forsook their sheltered existence, whether willingly or not, and reached out to their compatriots in the countryside and on the battlefront. Two reigning slogans indicated the mood of patriotic commitment: 'Literature must go to the countryside! Literature must join the army!' 'Propaganda first, art second!' Some zealous writers even championed 'going to the front' and giving up literature altogether.

In 1938, Kuo Mo-jo was appointed to head the Third Section of the National Military Council's newly created Political Department in charge of propaganda. Thus, the writers' propaganda activities became formally sanctioned by the government and more of them were drawn into official ranks. But in spite of this initial gesture the Kuomintang was obviously preoccupied with military and administrative matters, thus leaving the field of propaganda almost entirely to Communists and their sympathizers.[103] The various propaganda units staffed mainly by writers and artists came to be, in fact, front organizations of the CCP, which deftly capitalized on the energies and emotions of this broadening mass of intelligentsia.

The Japanese occupation of the major coastal cities forced Chinese writers into the hinterland. From 1937 to 1939, Wuhan and Canton replaced Shanghai and Peking as new centres of literary activity. While some of the major journals in Shanghai folded, new ones, often hastily

---

[101] Lan Hai, *Chung-kuo k'ang-chan wen-i shih* (A history of Chinese literature during the war of resistance), 51–2.

[102] *Ibid.* 47. See also Liu Hsin-huang, 748.   [103] Liu Hsin-huang, 756.

and sloppily printed on primitive paper, mushroomed in smaller cities. The total volume of book production and sales in the war period actually increased. According to one widely cited source, sales of new books doubled from one or two thousand copies per printing in the prewar period to three or four thousand, sometimes even ten thousand.[104]

With the loss of Wuhan and Canton in 1939, literature penetrated further inland; Chungking, the wartime capital, 'hummed with literary activity almost as Peking did during the Literary Revolution twenty years ago'.[105] But the momentum of the first years of war did not persist. As the second United Front fell apart, the Nationalist government in Chungking returned to its repressive policies against leftist writers through censorship and arrests. Some of them made the exodus to Yenan; others, like Mao Tun, withdrew to Hong Kong, which prospered briefly as a centre of literary activity. On Christmas day, 1941, Hong Kong was captured by the Japanese, and Kweilin took its place for the congregation of writers. After Kweilin fell to the Japanese in 1944, Chungking became the last bastion of the 'great interior'.

The protracted war exacted a heavy toll – both physical and spiritual. Writers' living conditions deteriorated. Under rampant inflation, Chungking newspapers could offer their contributors one to two dollars (local currency) per thousand characters – roughly the same fee a printer received for typesetting the same number of characters.[106] Several young writers died of poverty and illness. Men as famous as Tsang K'o-chia and Lao She had to live on coarse rice, and meat was hard to come by even for Ting Ling. Wang Chi-chen notes that 'newspapers of the time carried frequent appeals on behalf of sick and undernourished writers'.[107] With no victory in sight, low morale, decay and paralysis set in. The militancy of early war literature subsided. Of about thirty plays produced in Chungking in 1942–3, only one third dealt directly with war themes; the rest were historical dramas and translations. Reprints of older works and translations of long Western novels became increasingly popular, as did erotic and pornographic works for those seeking escape from the grim realities of their lives.[108]

For the conscientious writer who had not migrated to Yenan, it was, as Shao Ch'üan-lin put it, like 'living in an endlessly long night, not knowing when the day would break'.[109] During the early years, the nation

[104] Lan Hai, 40.   [105] Chi-chen Wang, ed. *Stories of China at war*, v.

[106] Liu I-ch'ang, 'Ts'ung k'ang-chan shih-ch'i tso-chia sheng-huo chih k'un-k'u k'an she-hui tui tso-chia ti tse-jen' (The responsibility of society toward writers: a view based on the writers' impoverished lives during the war years), *Ming-pao yueh-k'an* (Ming-pao monthly), 13.6 (June 1978) 58–61.   [107] Chi-chen Wang, vi.

[108] Lan Hai, 60–1.   [109] *Ts'an-k'ao tzu-liao*, 2.279.

had been united to fight the invader from without. Now the enemy was mainly within, as this hilly city became a world of frustration and lethargy – a claustrophobic world hemmed in by the almost daily Japanese air raids, when thousands died of suffocation in poorly ventilated shelters. War-profiteering ran rampant, and deep-seated animosities between the native Szechwanese and the outsiders from 'down river' flared up time and again. It was also increasingly a world of Tai Li's secret police, of government arrests and assassinations in an effort to clamp down on dissent.

The fall of Kweilin in late 1944 finally roused some intellectuals to action. On 22 February 1945, a manifesto of Chungking cultural circles appeared in newspapers demanding an end to censorship, secret police activities, military infighting and war profiteering, and asking for guarantees of personal safety, freedom of speech, congregation, research, publication, and cultural activity generally. On 4 May, the Resistance Association at its seventh anniversary celebration declared May Fourth each year to be 'the day of art and literature' in order to resuscitate the May Fourth legacy of science and democracy.[110] But the government retaliated with some arrests and assassinations. In 1946, one of the most prominent spokesmen of this rising 'tide of democracy', the poet and scholar Wen I-to, was assassinated in Kunming. Wen's death, attributed to KMT agents, heightened the anti-government sentiments of the intelligentsia, which the CCP utilized again to its great advantage. The Sino-Japanese War had politicized the intellectuals and the CCP again became their champion.

The literature of 'patriotic gore'

War focused the attention of all writers on the exigencies of the national situation. Artistic experimentation for its own sake was immediately irrelevant. Literature was entirely oriented towards the realities of life – no longer fragments of individual experience but the collective experience of a whole nation. In the first years of the war, different forms of short reportage – reports, sketches, posters, speeches, poems and stories designed to be read aloud, and one-act plays to be performed in street corners and market places – all but replaced the longer forms of fiction as the most popular modes of literature.[111] These numerous pieces of journalistic or proto-journalistic literature, steeped as they were in what Edmund Wilson called 'patriotic gore', were written 'with more

[110] Lan Hai, 62.   [111] *Ibid.* 68–73.

sentiment than artistry; their topical interest and emotional appeal are quickly lost when read out of context.'[112]

While they lacked artistic qualities, they gained immeasurably in popularity. Reportage, in Chou Yang's view, was the 'major form of national resistance literature', because it served most effectively the immediate goal of 'educating the masses' to the realities of this 'national self-defensive struggle'.[113] The war had accelerated the process of popularization by bringing literature, however sloppy in quality, away from the urban ivory tower in Shanghai to the small towns and villages. This period witnessed the first large-scale effort of writers 'going to the people'. In order to appeal to the tastes of the rural populace, the erstwhile urban writers eagerly resorted to the use of folk themes, idioms, tunes, as well as such traditional popular forms as village operas, oral story-telling, and *ta-ku* (beating the drum while telling a story). Suddenly, the use of 'old forms' with 'new content' became a fad; Lao She was one of the most avid practitioners.

Some writers went in for collective authorship. A few days after the Marco Polo Bridge incident, some sixteen dramatists in Shanghai organized themselves to write a three-act play, *Pao-wei Lu-kou-ch'iao* (Defend the Marco Polo Bridge), which several theatrical troupes competed to have the rights to perform even before it was finished.[114] Reports of writers' teams visiting the battlefront were sometimes also written collectively.

In an article of 1939, Hu Feng detected five major weaknesses of war literature: (1) it gave merely neat propaganda formulas; (2) it tended to present all the trivial details without, however, attaining any depth of vision, thus losing rather than gaining a sense of reality; (3) in some cases it gave fantastic twists to real stories; (4) due to these defects, war literature had not produced either great heroic epics or works of vivid realism; (5) 'intellectual poverty' in turn begot artistic poverty, and the task of popularizing literature was yet to achieve success.[115] Hu Feng's criticism obviously showed his dissatisfaction with the lowering of artistic standards. Together with Mao Tun, he was opposed to the excessively politicized view that wartime literature should only depict the 'healthy' and 'bright' side of life. A critic of integrity should call upon writers, as Mao Tun put it, not only to portray 'the new brightness' but also to expose aspects of 'new darkness'.[116] Some critics in Chungking, however, opposed the erosion of literary quality by propaganda and argued, on the

[112] Julia Lin, 171.   [113] *Ts'an-k'ao tzu-liao*, 1.631, 638.
[114] Lan Hai, 43.
[115] Hu Feng, *Min-tsu chan-cheng yü wen-i hsing-ko* (The national war and the character of literature), 53–5.   [116] *Ts'an-k'ao tzu-liao*, 1.670–1.

contrary, that the two should be totally separated. Chu Kuang-ch'ien stressed the importance of 'dispassionate observation' and the autonomy of art. Shen Ts'ung-wen saw a clear distinction between writers, who should be artists, and cultural workers, who were propagandists. Writers, Shen argued, should not be mixed up with political tasks. Liang Shih-ch'iu, the erstwhile foe of the leftists, went one step further by promoting the cause of 'irrelevant' literature: 'There are many subjects in human life that we can write about; we should not restrict our works to those related to the war.'[117]

These pleas for literary quality went unanswered. C. T. Hsia has concluded that the fiction produced in the 'great interior' generally lacked 'excitement and distinction'; the number of good works was much smaller than that of the prewar decade. 'The stereotypes of guerrilla warfare and student romance and the ubiquitous note of patriotic propaganda mar most of the wartime novels.'[118]

Of the established writers, only Mao Tun and Pa Chin produced significant works. Mao Tun's two novels written before 1942 – Fu-shih (Putrefaction) and Shuang-yeh hung ssu erh-yueh hua (Maple leaves as red as February flowers) – were not overtly concerned with wartime. Maple leaves deals with a small-town situation in 1926. Putrefaction, on the other hand, is a strictly political novel which depicts the evils of Kuomintang secret police. A fictional interpretation of the infamous 'New Fourth Army' incident of 1941, the novel has been acclaimed by Communist critics as on a par with Midnight.[119]

Compared to Mao Tun, Pa Chin made steady progress during the war years. His two sequels to Family are better written: Ch'iu (Autumn), in particular, represents Pa Chin's emotional maturity. But his best work is surely Han-yeh (Cold nights), written near the end of the war and published in 1947, which established Pa Chin as 'a psychological realist of great distinction'. In his depiction of three ordinary characters – a man, his mother and his wife – living under the same roof in wartime Chungking and caught in the familial web of love and jealousy, Pa Chin succeeds in presenting 'not only a parable of China in her darkest hour of defeat and despair but a morality play about the insuperable difficulties facing Everyman walking the path of charity'.[120]

Another veteran, Lao She, wrote many propaganda plays and poems in the folk idiom, but could produce only one mediocre novel, Huo tsang

---

[117] Ibid. 691–5; Liu Shou-sung, 2.63–4.
[118] C. T. Hsia, A history, 317.
[119] Wang Yao, 2.87. The Japanese scholar Osaka Tokushi also gives it high praise for its inventive technique; see his Chūgoku shin bungaku undō shi, 2.245–7.
[120] C. T. Hsia, A history, 386.

(Cremation), which he hastily published in order to get money for food. His ambitious undertaking, a three-part novel entitled *Ssu-shih t'ung-t'ang* (Four generations under one roof), begun immediately after the war, was never fully completed and the first two parts, published in 1946, 'must be rated as a major disappointment'.[121]

Like reportage, poetry of the war period was written to serve only one purpose – to arouse patriotic sentiments against the enemy. It was often meant to be recited aloud or sung to a large audience. Thus, simple, prose-like language, folk idioms, realistic descriptions, and slogan-shouting became the common features characterizing a host of 'patriotic poets'. Two of the most avid practitioners were Tsang K'o-chia and T'ien Chien. Tsang spent five years in the front lines and wrote more than a dozen collections of poetry. 'I love peasants,' he once confessed. 'I feel close even to the scars on their bodies.'[122] Praised with equal fervour by Wen I-to as the 'drummer of our age', T'ien Chien had dropped his early idol, Mayakovsky, and began writing 'drumbeat verse' with short lines and quick vigorous rhythm deemed more suitable to the tempo of war. The following shoddy example of T'ien's drumbeat verse was seen by Wen as 'exploding with life's heat and energy':

> This Asian
> Soil
> Is dyed in
> Anger and
> Shame.
>
> O tillers of my fatherland!
> Leave those dirty ditches
> And run-down
> Villages!
> To the war,
> Drive away the imperialist
> Armies.
> With our stubborn will
> Let's start sowing
> Mankind's new birth![123]

The literary genre which proved more enduringly popular than poetry and reportage was spoken drama. The profusion of one-act plays in the early years of the war had established a new tradition of living theatre, of which audience response and participation was an integral part. Moreover, the Shanghai film industry in the early thirties had nurtured a first crop of

---

[121] *Ibid.* 369.
[122] *Hsien-tai Chung-kuo shih hsuan*, 2.912.
[123] Quoted and translated in Julia Lin, 191–2.

actors and actresses who now entered the theatrical profession. Numerous amateur troupes in various regions – composed mainly of teachers and students – also stood ready to perform new works from Chungking and Kweilin, the two centres of wartime drama in the great interior. Wu-chi Liu says, 'at one time ninety dramatic troupes from five south-western provinces assembled for a dramatic festival in Kweilin', and 'during two seasons of fog in Chungking, when the city was comparatively safe from air raids, more than thirty full-length plays were presented to capacity audiences'.[124]

As patriotic idealism waned after the initial years of the war, the theatre assumed the function of escapist entertainment. But it also allowed the playwrights and actors of the Communist-dominated theatre world 'to sidestep censorship regulations and still make oblique comments on contemporary events'.[125]

Sung Chih-ti's *Wu Ch'ung-ch'ing* (Foggy Chungking), which focused on war-profiteering businessmen and intellectual opportunists, Ch'en Pai-ch'en's *Sheng-kuan t'u* (A chart for official promotion) which satirized official corruption, and above all Ts'ao Yü's *Shui-pien* (Metamorphosis) which depicted the primitive conditions of a poorly managed military hospital, were all successful.[126] In these works of negative exposure the authors had returned to the familiar mentality of the thirties.

The flowering of modern drama during wartime was also a phenomenon in Japanese-occupied Shanghai. The ban on American films and Japanese control of the Chinese film industry led to a commercial boom in the new drama, which competed successfully with traditional theatre. Historical plays, comedies, and romantic 'soap operas' enjoyed unparalleled popularity partly because they were safe subjects for innocuous entertainment. Yao K'o wrote a well-structured historical play about the late Ch'ing empress dowager and the Kuang-hsu Emperor, *Ch'ing-kung yüan* (translated into English as *The malice of empire*)[127] which has been hailed as a landmark. A Ying (Ch'ien Hsing-ts'un), an erstwhile leftist turned literary historian, wrote a dozen plays, of which *Ming-mo yi-hen* (Sorrows of the fall of the Ming) was his *chef-d'oeuvre*. Yang Chiang, wife of Ch'ien Chung-shu and perhaps the most polished comedy writer, established her reputation with *Ch'eng-hsin ju-i* (As you desire) and *Nung-chen ch'eng-chia* (Truth into jest).

As Edward Gunn has argued, most of these plays bespeak a traditional trend which was also a subtle gesture to preserve notions of Chinese

[124] Wu-chi Liu, 'The modern period', in Herbert A. Giles, *A history of Chinese literature*, 479–80.
[125] C. T. Hsia, *A history*, 320.
[126] Wu-chi Liu, 481.
[127] See Yao Hsin-nung, tr. Jeremy Ingalls, *The malice of empire*.

culture against Japanese domination.[128] Chou Tso-jen, living in Peking in the style of a traditional recluse, suggested subtly in his essays that it was still the Chinese people, and not their Japanese rulers, who could best appreciate the humanity of their own tradition. Chang Ai-ling (Eileen Chang), whom C. T. Hsia regards as modern China's finest writer, used the family system as a central focus in stories like 'The golden cangue' to explore the impact of tradition on the modern psyche.[129] And finally, Ch'ien Chung-shu, in *Wei-ch'eng* (Fortress besieged), in a picaresque fashion dissected with learned wit and scathing satire a host of characters that 'in absurd postures of vanity and fraud' show an intelligentsia failing to grasp the essence of both traditional and modern cultures.[130] Thus some of the finest works of both drama and fiction were created in 'occupied' China.

Few committed writers in the 1930s foresaw any possible discrepancy between their creative vision and the socio-political goals they espoused. During the war period, however, several prominent writers, Lao She in particular, voluntarily gave up their individual visions in their patriotic zeal to serve their country. The result was an increasing emphasis on the significance of one's audience and so drama naturally became the most powerful literary medium. The issue of individual creativity became a serious political problem when such a vision came to be at odds with a prescribed collective vision which the individual author *also* fervently supported; when the modern Chinese writer could no longer claim, as he had done ever since the May Fourth period, that he was endowed with more sensitivity and compassion toward his fellow countrymen, which enabled him to achieve more profound insight into his society. The challenge to individual creativity in this sense never existed in occupied China, nor was it perceived by writers in the great interior. It was not until Mao Tse-tung delivered his Talks on Art and Literature at Yenan in 1942 that this challenge was brought forth, with all the intellectual force and political power at Mao's command, for the specific purpose of rectifying the thinking of the literary intellectuals and altering the very definition of literature.

---

[128] This information on wartime drama in Japanese-occupied Shanghai is entirely drawn from the pioneering research of Edward Gunn. See his *Unwelcome muse: Chinese literature in Shanghai and Peking, 1937–1945*, and his research paper, 'Chinese writers under Japanese occupation (1937–45)'.

[129] The novelette is included in C. T. Hsia, ed. *Chinese stories*, 138–91, and in Lau, Hsia and Lee, eds., 530–59.

[130] C. T. Hsia, *A history*, 445.

THE YENAN FORUM

Mao's convening of the famous Yenan Forum on Literature and Art in May 1942 was part of the newly initiated rectification campaign directed at all Communist cadres. Mao's ideological intent – to remould the minds of Yenan intellectuals – was evident. But as an intellectual himself, Mao was also interested in new literary trends since the May Fourth period. As his Talks revealed, he was well informed about literary debates in the early thirties and he may have kept up with some of the creative writings, particularly the works of Lu Hsun, produced in leftist literary circles. Thus the Yenan Talks can be read as Mao's own reassessment, following the footsteps of Ch'ü Ch'iu-pai, of modern Chinese literature from May Fourth to 1942. But at the same time, Mao was certainly aware of certain recent issues on the literary scene which required clarification and solution.

Earlier in 1938, in a speech at the CCP sixth plenum, entitled 'The position of the Chinese Communist Party in the national struggle', Mao called upon his fellow party members to 'make Marxism concretely Chinese', to abolish 'foreign-slanted pedantry and obscurantism', and to replace it with a 'fresh and vivid Chinese style and manner, of which the Chinese masses are fond'. Mao concluded by asserting that 'to separate international content from national forms is to betray one's ignorance of internationalism; we must weld the two closely together'.[131]

Mao's directive did not specifically touch on literature, but its relevance to the literary field was soon picked up by the Yenan cultural commissars – notably Ch'en Po-ta, Ai Ssu-ch'i and Chou Yang. The ensuing debate on 'national forms' in 1939–40 was extended to Chungking. Articles arising from the debate were filled with confusing arguments, because no one was exactly clear what Mao meant by 'national forms' and 'international content'; the heated diatribes therefore were really groping attempts by the authors concerned to find the true source of 'national forms'. One group, represented chiefly by Lin Ping, considered 'national forms' to be the same as traditional popular art forms enjoyed by the people. Following Ch'ü Ch'iu-pai, they attacked the May Fourth brand of new literature as 'foreign-slanted pedantry' and products of the urban bourgeoisie which must be rejected. Writers in the opposite camp, however, rallied to the defence of the 'May Fourth revolutionary tradition' by maintaining that the mainstream of the New Literature represented, in fact, the 'national form' or was moving in this direction. In the words of Hu Feng, its most articulate spokesman, 'national forms

[131] Quoted in *ibid.* 301–2.

represent in essence the direction of the May Fourth tradition of realism in its active development under new conditions'.[132] Moreover, Hu Feng considered this new tradition as a complete break with the old tradition, which was feudal and regressive. Arguing in a convoluted Marxist vein, Hu Feng admitted that foreign borrowings were, in fact, viable. To this extent Hu Feng directly challenged Mao's implicit denigration of Western influence. A third group, mainly of party commissars and Kuo Mo-jo, attempted to reconcile the two sides. Chou Yang argued that one should assimilate the 'superior elements' of traditional art forms, while the 'new forms' arising from New Literature should also be retained and further developed. On balance, however, Chou Yang's argument was closer to Hu Feng's than to Lin Ping's, for he concluded that 'the establishment of new national forms cannot depend merely on old forms but rather on a serious understanding of all aspects of the present life of our nation'[133] – in other words, realism.

Chou Yang's implicit agreement with Hu Feng behind his fence-sitting posture testifies to Hu Feng's prestige as a disciple of Lu Hsun and the leading leftist critic in Chungking, with whom Chou Yang could not afford to clash again (as he had done in the debate on the 'two slogans'). It is also likely that the issues raised by Mao's terms were barely comprehensible even to the commissars themselves. Himself a fairly informed student of Soviet literary theory, Chou Yang may have interpreted Mao's dictum as a call for further popularization and not an all-out critique of May Fourth literature. It was time for Mao himself to resolve all ambiguities.

The tentative tone in Chou Yang's pronouncements seems also to indicate that party bureaucrats like him were not in a commanding position over writers. Before the launching of the rectification campaign, the heroic self-image of Yenan intellectuals had not been challenged. For several writers who had migrated to this primitive mecca of revolution, the reality of life there fell far short of their preconceived ideas. In early 1942, Wang Shih-wei led the attack with a series of articles, in the style of Lu Hsun's essays and published in the *Liberation Daily* under the title of 'Wild lilies'. Ting Ling deplored the fate of women in Yenan in an article commemorating 8 March, Women's Day, and in a story, 'In the hospital'. Hsiao Chün soon followed suit with a scathing critique of higher-echelon party cadres.[134] Thus the confusion and discontent among many literary intellectuals in Yenan presented a potentially explosive

---

[132] Wang Yao, 2.26.
[133] *Ibid.* 2.23. See also Li Mu, 104.
[134] For an analysis of the dissenting writers in Yenan, see Merle Goldman, *Literary dissent in Communist China*, ch. 2.

situation which Mao had to deal with in a decisive fashion. Hence the convening of the Yenan Forum on 2 May 1942.

Mao gave two speeches at the forum: an introduction (on 2 May) and a long conclusion (23 May). In his introductory remarks, Mao confronted his audience of some two hundred writers and artists and unequivocally defined the objectives of the forum in the following way:

It is very good that since the outbreak of the war of resistance against Japan, more and more revolutionary writers and artists have been coming to Yenan and our other anti-Japanese base areas. But it does not necessarily follow that, having come to the base areas, they have already integrated themselves completely with the masses of the people here. The two must be completely integrated if we are to push ahead with our revolutionary work. The purpose of our meeting today is precisely to ensure that literature and art fit well into the whole revolutionary machine as a component part, that they operate as powerful weapons for uniting and educating the people and for attacking and destroying the enemy, and that they help the people fight the enemy with one heart and one mind.[135]

With this clearly articulated political purpose, Mao then proceeded to attack some erroneous tendencies in the behaviour of Yenan writers. He raised four problems, all intended for these recalcitrant writers: 'class stand', 'attitude', 'audience' and 'study'. The general theme is quite clear. Some of the Yenan 'comrades' had failed to adopt the class stand of the proletariat. They were unaware of the radically different situation in the base areas when they continued in their zeal to 'expose', rather than to 'praise' the new revolutionary reality. They persisted in this erroneous path because they failed to realize that their audience had changed; in the 1930s in Shanghai 'the audience for works of revolutionary literature and art consisted mainly of a section of the students, office workers, and shop assistants' – in other words, the petty-bourgeoisie – but the new audience in the base areas was composed of 'workers, peasants, soldiers, and revolutionary cadres'. In order to change their mistaken perceptions and behaviour, the writers and artists had to plunge seriously into 'the study of Marxism-Leninism and of society' – and, of course, the theories of Mao Tse-tung.

In his conclusion, Mao returned to these problems, elaborated upon their ramifications and, in some cases, provided specific solutions. In expounding his views, Mao also subjected the two vital legacies of modern Chinese literature – the May Fourth tradition and its extension in the 1930s – to a veiled, but nonetheless devastating critique.

In the rectification campaign, the two hallmarks of May Fourth

---

[135] Mao Tse-tung, 'Talks at the Yenan Forum on literature and art', in *Mao Tse-tung on literature and art*, 2. For a more scholarly translation, see Bonnie S. McDougall, *Mao Zedong's 'Talks at the Yan'an conference on literature and art': a translation of the 1943 text with commentary*.

literature – individualism and subjectivism – were transformed from positive to negative values, because these romantic traits had led, from a Maoist point of view, to their worst excesses: self-aggrandizement, elitism, and total disregard for the masses. The concepts of love and humanitarianism, so central to the romantic ethos of the 1920s, were singled out by Mao for specific disparagement: 'As for love, in a class society there can be only class love; but these comrades are seeking a love transcending classes, love in the abstract.... This shows that they have been very deeply influenced by the bourgeoisie. They should thoroughly rid themselves of this influence and modestly study Marxism-Leninism.' 'As for the so-called love of humanity, there has been no such all-inclusive love since humanity was divided into classes.... There will be love of all humanity when classes are eliminated, but not now. We cannot love enemies, we cannot love social evils, our aim is to destroy them. This is common sense; can it be that some of our writers and artists still do not understand this?'[136]

This kind of class analysis of love and humanitarianism had already been advanced by Lu Hsun and other leftist writers in their critique of Liang Shih-ch'iu. Mao incorporated it in his Talks and turned this Marxist 'common sense' into official canon. While he commended the leftist stance against 'bourgeois' and 'reactionary' writers in the 1930s, he was not generous in his assessment of its achievement. In Mao's view, even at its best (as in Lu Hsun's satirical *tsa-wen* and the fiction of social realism) the literature of the 1930s had expressed a sense of moral outrage on the part of the individual leftist writer. It had performed a 'critical' function in exposing the evils of the old society. In his glowing tribute to Lu Hsun, who symbolized this critical spirit, Mao also argued, albeit implicitly, that writers like Lu Hsün had already served their purpose, living as they did 'under the rule of the dark forces'. In the new revolutionary environment of Yenan, however, 'where democracy and freedom are granted in full to the revolutionary writers and artists and withheld only from the counter-revolutionaries, the style of the essay should not simply be like Lu Hsun's'.[137]

This is tantamount, in fact, to a censure of all Lu Hsun imitators, whether in spirit or in style, and a virtual announcement that the era of Lu Hsun – and of critical realism – was over. A new era had begun and a new kind of literature had to be created which would represent a radical break, both in content and form, from that of the 1920s and 1930s. Essentially, this literature should be a positive literature of the people and for the people; it should have, in other words, a clear peasant-

---

[136] Mao Tse-tung, 'Talks', 8.   [137] *Ibid.* 33–4.

worker-soldier focus in its content and it must fulfil the needs of the masses before it could educate them. The order of priorities since the May Fourth period was now reversed: instead of the personality and imagination of the author being reflected in his literary work and imparted to an adulatory audience, it was now the audience of peasants, workers and soldiers that provided the subject-matter of revolutionary literature and guided the creativity of the author.

Mao chose to formulate this audience-oriented view of literature and art in a pragmatic question – the 'crux of the matter' at the Yenan Forum: how could literature and art serve the masses? Mao enjoined Yenan writers to 'take the class stand of the proletariat' and to 'fuse their thoughts and feelings with those of the masses of workers, peasants, and soldiers' by living with them and learning from them. In addition to giving this pragmatic piece of advice, which applied to all cadres, Mao also tried to enter the realm of Marxist literary theory. His 'theoretical' arguments were presented dialectically as a series of interrelated contradictions: popularization vs. raising standards, motive vs. effect, political criterion vs. artistic criterion, political content vs. artistic form. While demanding 'the unity of politics and art, the unity of content and form, the unity of revolutionary political content and the highest possible perfection of artistic form[138] – a goal all Marxist theoreticians would heartily agree to – Mao spelled out only the political side in these dialectical polarities but left the aesthetic side unspecified, presumably for writers and artists themselves to solve.

As a new theory of Marxist aesthetics, the Yenan Talks left more lacunae than the works of Marx and Engels. As might be expected, there was considerable divergence of opinion on how to interpret this new orthodox canon and how to fill its gaps. The role of arbiters was assumed, however, by the party literary bureaucrats, whose views and criticism were resented by the creative writers. It was these literary bureaucrats – Ch'en Po-ta, Ai Ssu-ch'i, and especially Chou Yang – who in the name of implementing Mao's theoretical injunctions instituted 'literary control' and imposed the 'party line' on creative writers. The dissension between these two groups grew into large-scale ideological campaigns and purges in which a number of writers – Wang Shih-wei, Ting Ling, Hsiao Chün, Hu Feng, Feng Hsueh-feng – became victims to party discipline.[139]

The literary bureaucrats emphasized correctly the political thrust of Mao's Talks, for Mao did decide that of his dialectical polarities the political factors ultimately held sway over artistic factors. For instance,

[138] *Ibid.* 30.
[139] This is the theme of Merle Goldman's *Literary dissent*; see especially chs. 1–8.

on the important issue of popularization vs. raising standards, Mao
concluded that 'in present conditions' the former was 'the more pressing
task'. He also affirmed that 'all classes in all class societies invariably put
the political criterion first and artistic criterion second' and that the
socio-political effect of a piece of literary work was more important than
the author's original 'motive'. But the exact issues of aesthetics were
hardly touched upon. For instance, Mao chose to sidestep the problem,
which had been debated heatedly during the 'national form' controversy,
as to whether the existing traditional folk arts contained too many 'feudal'
elements. Presumably new content had to be instilled, but in what
'popular forms'? The widely practised approach of 'putting new wine
in old bottles' was also problematic, especially when applied to such forms
as the Peking opera. On a more sophisticated level, the issues of literary
technique and literary quality, which distinguish a piece of revolutionary
literature from revolutionary propaganda, were barely analysed in the
Yenan Talks. Mao intimated, perhaps in reaction against the exposure-
oriented realistic literature of the 1930s, that new works of literature and
art 'ought to be on a higher plane, more intense, more concentrated, more
typical, nearer the ideal, and therefore more universal than actual everyday
life'.[140] This vague generalization smacks of a rudimentary reformulation
of Soviet 'socialist realism'. Mao in fact called his new literature 'socialist
realism', which further revealed his indebtedness to the Soviet example.

In this regard, Mao's emphasis was certainly placed, as in the Soviet
case, more on 'socialism' than on 'realism' – to extol the typical and the
ideal, and to portray reality on a higher ideological plane. But Mao seems
to have contradicted his earlier injunction to abolish 'foreign-slanted
pedantry and obscurantism'. Although he was clearly influenced by the
familiar Soviet concepts of *partiinost* (party spirit), *ideinost* (ideology) and
narodnost (national character),[141] he did not openly acknowledge this
borrowing, nor did he confront the more relevant and pressing question:
whether the Soviet models could be effectively transplanted on to Chinese
soil.

It is evident that Mao had made a strong case for the political nature
of literature, but his venture into more strictly literary matters – especially
his attempt to evolve a Marxist view of literary criticism – betrayed the
shallowness of a layman. The most fundamental issue in Marxist
aesthetics – the problem of the integral relationship between form and
content – was never explored in depth. Bypassing any discussion of the
social origins of various literary forms, Mao concentrated on matters of

[140] Mao Tse-tung, 'Talks', 19.
[141] T. A. Hsia, 'Twenty years after the Yenan Forum', in his *Gate of darkness*, 255.

content. In so doing, he also imposed certain limitations on the themes and subject-matter of socialist realism. The peasant-worker-soldier nexus dictated a confining scope of such themes as land reform, struggles against landlordism, guerrilla warfare, and industrial construction. And the rigid manner in which the Maoist literary bureaucrats later carried out such specifications, leaving little room for writers to reinterpret the canon or to fill in its gaps, served only further to cripple creative efforts even to produce good socialist literature.

Yenan literature

The most pronounced feature of Yenan literary practice immediately after the Talks was its experimentation with native folk forms and idioms. According to Lu Ting-i, Mao's Talks prompted the emergence, in the order of popularity, of the following new types of literature and art: (1) folk dance and folk drama; (2) woodcuts in the 'national' style; (3) novels and stories in the traditional style of story-telling; (4) poetry in imitation of the folk-song rhythm and idiom.[142] All of them involved folk elements and apparently appealed, directly or indirectly, to the 'audio-visual' senses of the mass audience.

The best example – and the most prevalent – of this new folk culture was the *yang-ko* ('rice-sprout song'), a local song-and-dance which became immensely popular in the 'liberated' areas. Originally a ritual dance performed by villagers during the lunar new year, it was spotted by Yenan cadres for its propaganda potential. A certain Liu Chih-jen is said to have been the first to modernize this folk form by instilling revolutionary content and by combining it with other forms of popular theatre. Aside from the *yang-ko* dance, the '*yang-ko* opera' was invented, which fused *yang-ko* dance steps with local folk songs, modern costumes, and dramatic gestures and expressions borrowed from Peking opera. Both forms provided opportunities for mass participation, and reportedly everyone in Yenan was soon dancing the *yang-ko*. In 1943, a new *yang-ko* campaign was launched which resulted in the production of fifty-six new *yang-ko* operas.[143] The most famous of these was *Pai-mao nü* (The white-haired girl), a collaborative effort by the staff members of the Lu Hsun Academy of Arts and Literature in Yenan, who turned an apparently real story into a 'first-rate melodrama' about a servant girl who, exploited

---

[142] *Ibid.* 246. For a detailed analysis of the various forms of Yenan literature, see Kikuchi Saburō, *Chūgoku gendai bungaku shi* (History of contemporary Chinese literature), vol.2, chs. 2–5. See also Ting Miao, *P'ing Chung-kung wen-i tai-piao tso* (On representative works of Chinese Communist literature).

[143] Lan Hai, 77–8; Liu Shou-sung, 2.24.

and oppressed by a landlord family, escaped into the wilderness and became a ghost-like white-haired goddess.[144] At the end of the play, the heroine, rescued by the Red Army, took her revenge on the landlord in a climactic mass meeting. From its first performance in 1944, *The white-haired girl* reaped such public acclaim that it was later adapted into a Peking opera, a film and a revolutionary ballet.

The popularity of *The white-haired girl* and other *yang-ko* operas also led to the revamping of another popular form, the Peking opera. The successful experiment was an opera called *Pi shang Liang-shan* (Driven to join the Liangshan rebels). First performed in 1943, the work was taken from Mao's own favourite novel, *The water margin*, and told the story of Lin Ch'ung, a military officer who, pursued by government agents, finally abandoned his career and family and joined the rebels of Liangshan. The current relevance of this new opera – as it obviously referred to the many intellectuals who joined the Communist forces in Yenan – and its attention to the 'people' in history won high praise from no less an authority than Chairman Mao himself.[145]

But experiments of putting new content in old forms also encountered unsurmountable obstacles. The plots of Peking operas abound in emperors, kings, generals and ministers; it was often impossible to inject revolutionary content into such 'feudal' structures short of writing totally new plays. The coupling of new plots with old music and performance conventions created an utterly incongruous effect which in turn might lose audience interest.[146] The problem was further compounded when the oral traditions of folk culture were adopted in a written medium, as in the case of novels and stories written in the style of traditional story-telling. Lao She's experiments in the initial period of the war were artistically disastrous. In Yenan, Chao Shu-li, perhaps the most celebrated folk novelist to emerge in this period, made a similar attempt in his short stories, such as 'The rhymes of Li Yu-ts'ai' and 'Hsiao Erh-hei's marriage'. The former uses the oral tradition as an integral part of the story, as the hero effortlessly makes up rhymes satirizing local events, exposing corruption and praising land reform. The latter story incorporates an abundance of folk idioms, phrases and aphorisms in dialogue and narration. In both cases, the liveliness of the oral elements is ill-matched with the dry prose narrative. The earthy humour and healthy fun exhibited

---

[144] The play is included in Walter and Ruth Meserve, eds. *Modern drama from Communist China*, 105–80.
[145] Yih-jian Tai, 'The contemporary Chinese theater and Soviet influence' (Southern Illinois University, Ph.D. dissertation, 1974), 96–7.
[146] In the 1960s, the Peking opera – in whatever form or content – was rejected entirely in favour of Chiang Ch'ing's 'revolutionary operas'. After the Cultural Revolution, however, old folk forms, including the Peking opera, were revived.

in the oral parts would certainly provide good entertainment for the audience, if they could be rendered 'live' or performed on stage. Yet imprisoned in a written story, they serve rather to deflate the tension and suspense which could have been effected through a well-constructed plot or carefully written descriptive passages. Chao seemed to waver between the oral and written elements in his stories, but eventually he returned to the latter.[147]

Chao Shu-li's works were hailed by Chou Yang as 'a triumph of Mao Tse-tung's thoughts in the practice of creative writing'. Aside from them there was little fiction of note published immediately following the Yenan Talks, in sharp contrast to the profusion of *yang-ko* operas and folk ballads.[148] If this phenomenon could be taken as an accurate reflection of Mao's intentions, it seems that the new path opened by the Yenan Talks would lead modern Chinese literature away from the confines of its written conventions and re-establish direct 'audio-visual' contact with the mass audience. This drastic measure may have been Mao's response to the series of leftist debates to popularize and Latinize the Chinese language in the early thirties. In a culture in which the written word had always been sacrosanct as the only enduring medium of literature (even the oral traditions in classical China were subsequently transcribed in writing), this Maoist trend would indeed have constituted a second literary revolution. Judged from this perspective, the emergence of revolutionary operas under Chiang Ch'ing during the Cultural Revolution was definitely a logical extension of Mao's literary radicalism.

But Mao did not entirely succeed in dispensing with the written forms; the momentum of fictional writing, which began as a major leftist mode of literary expression in the early thirties, was carried forward in the period 1945–9 in a more proletarian direction by creative writers, notably Ting Ling, Chou Li-po and Ou-yang Shan, who seem to have turned for guidance to Soviet novels of socialist realism available in Chinese translations. As C. T. Hsia observes, 'they celebrated the transformation of land and people under Communism in the standard socialist-realist manner rather than in a manner suggestive of a return to "national forms".'[149] But the impact of the Yenan Talks is also noticeable. The result,

---

[147] In Chao's short novel, *Li-Chia-chuang ti pien-ch'ien* (Changes in the Li village), published in 1945, the oral elements were largely dispensed with. Yet in the opinion of C. T. Hsia, it remained 'the most readable of his works'. See Hsia, *A history*, 483.

[148] Wang Yao, 2.123. For a sample collection of stories and reportage written during the Yenan period (both before and after the Talks), see Ting Ling, *et al. Chieh-fang ch'ü tuan-p'ien ch'uang-tso hsuan* (Selected short works from the liberated areas). In poetry, aside from folk ballads, the volume of creation was even slimmer. Ho Ch'i-fang stopped writing poetry altogether in favour of prose reportage. See McDougall, *Paths*, 173.

[149] C. T. Hsia, *A history*, 472–3.

therefore, was at best a mixed blessing. The case of Ting Ling is a most illuminating example.

Ting Ling was probably the best example of the romantic writer turned leftist; she was also the most prestigious writer in Yenan. Some of her better stories, such as 'New convictions' (1939) and 'When I was in Hsia village' (1940), were written before the Yenan Forum.[150] Both stories deal with peasant resistance to Japanese aggression, and Ting Ling imbues her rural characters, especially the heroine of the latter story, with a mature nobility and humanism in the best tradition of leftist fiction of the 1930s. After the Yenan Forum, which was convened partly to criticize writers like Ting Ling, she was reportedly 'caught up in the high tide of learning from the rectification movement'.[151] Instead of fiction, she wrote only journalistic pieces – records of her field work in the midst of the rural masses. Finally in 1949 her long novel, *T'ai-yang chao-tsai Sang-kan ho shang* (The sun shines over the Sangkan River), was published and won the Stalin Second Prize for Literature in 1951.

Ting Ling had conceived of portraying the process of land reform in a fictional trilogy, of which *The Sangkan River* dealt only with the initial phase of 'struggle'. The second and third parts – on redivision of land and militarization of the peasantry – were never written. This grand design might have been Ting Ling's ultimate statement of her devotion to the Chinese Communist Party and to the cause of social revolution. Ironically, the very success of the first volume brought about her eventual purge for being, among other charges, a 'one-book' author.

As a novel, *The Sangkan River* stands as an ambitious experiment. It presents a series of vignettes and a mosaic of character portraits, all loosely connected, which bring a vivid sense of life to the rural locale which Ting Ling had come to know so well. At the mid-point of the novel, Ting Ling introduces her 'positive hero', the model Communist cadre Chang P'in, who crosses over from the other side of the river and gradually, but masterfully, sets in motion the mechanism of peasant organization which finally culminates in a mass struggle meeting. Apparently Ting Ling intended her new novel to be documentary fiction, a new literary genre that had become popular during the early war years. It was also meant to be 'socialist realism', in the Soviet manner, which encompasses reality 'collectively' and 'positively' so that the intended effect would be, as Mao stated, 'more typical, more ideal, and therefore more universal than actual everyday life'. Yet the weaknesses of the novel stem also from this

---

[150] A translation of the latter story can be found in Lau, Hsia and Lee, eds., 268–78.
[151] Wang Yao, 2.123. On Ting Ling's writing overall, see Yi-tsi Feuerwerker, *Ding Ling's fiction – ideology and narrative in modern Chinese literature*.

very observation of the Maoist formula. Her treatment of party cadres is flat, as compared to her depiction of peasant characters with whom she evinced a certain emotional affinity. And the message-ridden mass meeting near the end is curiously lacking in cathartic power. Again it is the more 'realistic' aspects of the novel, rather than the socialist aspects, which hold the reader's attention.

The relative merits and demerits of Ting Ling's novel reflect a fundamental change, as a result of the Yenan Talks, in the very definition of creative writing in China. The familiar Western yardsticks – 'imagination, aesthetic experience, and the workings of the creative mind' which T. A. Hsia valued so highly in his devastating summation of the Yenan legacy[152] – are no longer so crucial in the Maoist perspective. For the function of the writer is no longer that of a creator or originator but that of a human medium through whom experiences of the mass audience are recorded and then transmitted back to them. Since audience participation is encouraged in the very process of creating a literary work, the written text is no longer authentic: constant revisions become the rule rather than the exception. Above all, the demands of ideology and popularization render an individual point of view, either as an extension of the author's personality or as an artistic device, all but impossible. The 'literary' quality of a work is judged by the degree of its appeal to the audience, in addition to its correct political content. Unlike wartime drama, the combination of politics and popularization had a crippling effect on writers, for, in order to find the correct 'political content', they had to follow every shift and turn of the party's policies. In linking a literary work with specific political issues or movements, Mao had also divested it of any enduring worth, artistic or political: the very elements that made a piece of literature topical at one time diminished its validity once the historical situation had changed. From hindsight, Ting Ling's fate after 1949 seems rather 'typical' and inevitable. As Berninghausen and Huters have pointed out, 'if revolutionary literature is required merely to follow the development of the political dialectic, it loses its capacity for independent criticism[153] – and, one might add, its very source of creativity.

However, the stultifying impact of Mao's Yenan canon was not immediately apparent in the brief postwar period of 1945–9, when the CCP leadership was too preoccupied with the military conquest of the KMT regime to enforce strictly its literary policy. It was in this period that literary creativity in both Communist-dominated areas and in the newly recovered urban centres reached another height.

[152] T. A. Hsia, *Gate of darkness*, 168.   [153] Berninghausen and Huters, 10.

ON THE EVE OF REVOLUTION 1945–1949

When the eight-year war of resistance finally came to an end in 1945, the mood of euphoria and relief proved short-lived. For millions of Chinese who returned to their home provinces, the new reality confronting them was even more chaotic. The Nationalist government was caught unprepared by the sudden victory over the Japanese. Instead of reconstruction, corruption and inflation became more acute, which generated growing unrest. The familiar Chungking syndrome – demoralization on top and disillusionment below – was now extended to the entire country. The poet and essayist Chu Tzu-ch'ing summed up a pervasive mood in 1946:

As victory arrived, we took an easy breath, and we couldn't help but envision an era of peace and prosperity which might be realized in three or five years ... But the cheers for victory soon passed away like lightning to be replaced by volleys of muffled thunder. The change has been too swift, and the disillusionment has come too fast.[154]

As warfare was resumed between Nationalist and Communist troops, the nationwide desire for peace was expressed most articulately in demonstrations and 'hunger strikes' by students and teachers from universities and middle schools. Again this hope for peace was cleverly exploited by the CCP to focus on the Kuomintang, which procrastinated in a belated process of constitution making. Anti-government sentiment, nurtured during the last years of the war, became stronger. A growing majority of Chinese intellectuals looked to the CCP as the only party which could bring them freedom, democracy and a new China. Thus on the eve of the CCP's military victory in 1949, its ideological hold on the Chinese intelligentsia was virtually assured.

In this uneasy atmosphere of chaos and unrest the literary scene fell increasingly under Communist influence. As hordes of writers and artists returned from the interior or re-emerged from semi-seclusion under Japanese occupation, the eastern cities resumed their role as centres of literary activity. Magazines published in Chungking moved to Shanghai or Peking. New journals were founded, old ones revived. Books were reprinted on better quality paper. The All-China Resistance Association, renamed the National Association of Chinese Writers and Artists, sponsored a flurry of activities, including an elaborate commemoration of Lu Hsun's death at its tenth anniversary (1946) and the republication of his complete works.

[154] Quoted in Liu Hsin-huang, 767.

The reorganized association, though maintaining a semblance of the united front, was clearly dominated by Communists or Communist sympathizers. Leftist writers also dominated the literary supplements of major newspapers: some were established as exclusive forums for leftist authors (such as the supplement to *Wen-hui pao* in Shanghai); others were compelled to include a number of leftist works, because of their fame. The assassination of Wen I-to, the liberal voice of the 'Third Force', on 15 July 1946 further strengthened the Communist cause because it was widely believed to be the work of the Kuomintang secret police. And the appearance of a few significant non-Communist fictional works – Ch'ien Chung-shu's *Fortress besieged* (1947), Pa Chin's *Cold nights* (1947), and Shih T'o's *Marriage* (1947) – had no visible impact on the leftist literary scene; they served merely as 'isolated examples' of creative integrity, utterly impotent to oppose the rising tide of a new Communist literature.[155]

Even C. T. Hsia, an avowed anti-Communist, notes that the period 1945–9 witnessed heightened productivity among Communist-area authors, especially novelists.[156] Aside from Ting Ling's *The Sangkan River* (1949), such works appeared as Chou Li-po's *Pao-feng tsou-yü* (The hurricane, 1949), Chao Shu-li's *Li-chia chuang ti pien-ch'ien* (Changes in Li village, 1949) and Ou-yang Shan's *Kao Ch'ien-ta* (1946). In poetry, Li Chi's long poem, 'Wang Kuei and Li Hsiang-hsiang' (1945) successfully adopted the folk ballad form of northern Shensi to tell a familiar story of landlord tyranny and chequered romance. Following the triumph of *The white-haired girl*, another folk opera, *Liu Hu-lan*, reaped critical acclaim.[157]

Against the burst of creativity in Communist-controlled areas, the urban literary scene of this period was relatively arid. Most of the works published were reissues or reprints of popular fiction and poetry. In the area of translations, an impressive array of Western authors – Flaubert, Zola, Balzac, Tolstoy, Dostoevsky, Gorky, Chekhov, Ibsen, Romain Rolland, Dickens and Shakespeare, among many others – were represented in multi-volume series. According to one account, the most popular Western novel of this period was Margaret Mitchell's *Gone with the wind*, translated by the versatile Fu Tung-hua under the succinctly appropriate title of *P'iao*.[158]

---

[155] C. T. Hsia, *A history*, 501.

[156] *Ibid.* 472. Kikuchi Saburō discusses the flow and ebb of Communist and non-Communist literature in the framework of a north-south polarity. The postwar years thus witnessed the triumph of the 'literature of the north' (Yenan) and the collapse of 'southern literature' (Chungking and Shanghai). See his *Chūgoku gendai bungaku shi*, vol. 2, pts. 3–4.

[157] Liu Shou-sung, 2.262–4.

[158] Ts'ao Chü-jen, *Wen-t'an wu-shih nien hsu-chi* (Sequel to Fifty years on the literary scene), 126.

The major creative medium in the cities was the cinema, which replaced drama in popularity. The two genres had had a close relationship of cross-fertilization. From its very beginning, the Chinese film industry had drawn upon talent from the world of drama. During the war years, film personnel enlisted in the numerous theatrical troupes in the service of the nation. With the end of the war, drama had outlived its propaganda purpose; most of the amateur troupes were disbanded. The influx of American movies (banned during the Japanese occupation) gave added stimulus to the film industry. The postwar years were a golden age of modern Chinese cinema.[159]

The reasons for the artistic success of this new genre are not hard to find. First-rate talent from literary circles was employed by the film industry: Eileen Chang, Yang Han-sheng, T'ien Han, Ou-yang Yü-ch'ien and Ts'ao Yü wrote original screen plays; other dramatists (such as K'o Ling) became expert adaptors of literature into film. Some of the best plays written during the war years – particularly *Cheng-ch'i ko* (The song of righteousness, about the famous Ming loyalist, Wen T'ien-hsiang), and *Ch'ing-kung yüan* (The malice of empire) – were made into excellent films. Fictional works became another rich source for adaptation: in some cases, such as Lao She's novelette, *Wo che i pei-tzu* (This life of mine), the film version even surpassed the original. To promote the cause of this new art form, T'ien Han and Hung Shen assumed the editorship of special film supplements to two major Shanghai newspapers, *Ta-kung-pao* and *Hsin-wen pao*. Finally, the acting skills of Liu Ch'iung, Shih Hui, Pai Yang and Hu Tieh (most of whom had their first training in dramatic troupes) also reached a height of subtlety and sophistication.

The literary and dramatic aspects of this new genre outshone the purely cinematic. The quality of a film was often due more to its script and acting than to its visual technique (camera work, lighting, cutting, montage, etc.). Cinema could be viewed, therefore, as a creative extension of dramatic literature. The film medium appropriated from literature not only some of its personnel but also its typical 'obsessions'. One was the postwar chaos. The high-handed, irregular practices of the so-called 'confiscation tycoons' (*chieh-shou ta-yuan*) from Chungking, who made personal fortunes in the name of the Nationalist government by confiscating property owned by former collaborators with the Japanese, were bitterly criticized in

[159] Serious research on modern Chinese cinema as art and as social history has not been done. There has been only one study in English, Jay Leyda, *Dianying, an account of films and the film audience in China*; see particularly ch. 6. For Chinese sources, see Ch'eng Chi-hua, *et al. Chung-kuo tien ying fa-chan-shih* (A history of the development of Chinese cinema), 2.213–14. This two-volume book remains the most comprehensive on Chinese cinema to date. A preliminary catalogue of Chinese films from 1908 to 1949 has been completed by Steve Horowitz for the Chinese Cinema Project sponsored by the Chinese Culture Foundation of San Francisco.

Huan-hsiang jih-chi (Diary of returning home), directed by Yuan Chün (Chang Chün-hsiang). Many film-makers were obsessed with the inequalities of wealth and poverty in China's cities. In a light, satirical vein, *Chia-feng hsü-huang* (The make-believe couple), one of the most popular films of the period, tells the story of how a poor barber, camouflaged as a rich dandy, courts an equally poor woman pretending to be wealthy. Another renowned film, *Yeh tien* (Night lodging) was based on Gorky's 'The lower depths', but the setting was changed to the Shanghai slums. The films of this period were infused with an overpowering humanism which not only deeply moved the viewer but compelled him to draw political messages; invariably it was the lower classes that represented the residual core of humanity in a society torn with inequalities and devoid of justice.

What was to be done? The more moderate films advocated education (as in *Ai-lo chung-nien* or The sorrows and joys of middle age). But the radical ones blatantly called for collective action: at the end of one such film, the rickshaw pullers of the entire city rise to save the victimized hero. If films can truthfully indicate the social mood, the solutions seemed to revolve around reform or revolution – gradual reform through education and other humanitarian means or total revolution so that the oppressed would 'turn over' (*fan-shen*) and become their own masters. Out of sheer desperation, more and more film-makers – and presumably much of their audience – opted for the latter. In short, the better films of this period may have done more to propagate the need for revolution than any other artistic genre. As the popular medium that reached the largest urban audience, the film proved its effectiveness. It combined the best elements of modern Chinese fiction and drama: in some ways, it was more 'live' than fiction and more flexible than drama. That Mao Tse-tung never paid much attention to the political potential of this new medium is obviously due to its urban, rather than rural, origin. But as the most recent urban art form it yields some historical lessons.

The urban-rural dichotomy has been a dominant feature in the history of modern Chinese literature. From its late Ch'ing beginnings, modern Chinese literature was nurtured in the urban setting. As it grew into 'New Literature' during the May Fourth period, it also became the exalted mouthpiece of the urban intelligentsia. But the urban writer's aggravated feelings of social discontent led him to look beyond the city walls into the countryside. Rural and regional literature, the artistic product of the conscience-stricken urban writer, thus became the major form of creativity in the 1930s. But the best poetry written in this period remained urban-oriented, and it inevitably became a symbol of urban decadence in the eyes of the committed leftist writers.

However, the leftist writers were themselves urban products. The advocates of proletarian revolutionary literature in the late twenties and early thirties, echoing perhaps the urban-based Chinese Communist Party, focused their sympathies mainly on the urban proletariat, only to be exposed by Lu Hsun for the hypocrisy of their ideological stance. As Lu Hsun was politicized to join the left in the League of Left-wing Writers the urban orientation of their activities and pronouncements continued to be evident. But Lu Hsun regarded the urban milieu as the very bastion of the dark forces – depravity, corruption, and the oppressive atmosphere produced by the Kuomintang's 'White terror'. Living in their midst, he took upon himself the role of a revolutionary 'rear-guard' by engaging those dark forces in mortal combat while harbouring no illusions of victory for himself.

Lu Hsun never claimed to understand the Chinese countryside. Despite his enthusiasm for the Long March, he refused to write a novel about it for reasons of ignorance of the rural scene.[160] Even his early stories reveal not so much an affinity with his rural characters (as most of his worshippers have argued) but a sense of alienated compassion on the part of an urban intellectual. Besides, the Shao-hsing countryside for Lu Hsun was part of a traditional world – an 'iron house' of cultural backwardness which ought to be destroyed (though he could not foresee such a possibility).

With Lu Hsun's death in 1936 and the outbreak of war in 1937, modern Chinese literature entered its rural phase. The 'great interior' centred in Chungking had a certain rural ambience, and the patriotic ethos led most writers to embrace the rural population. This populism, plus repeated demands for popularization of literature, provided the logical setting for Mao Tse-tung's theory of art and literature in Yenan. Of the three central subjects in this new canon the peasants, rather than the workers or soldiers, received the major share of creative attention from Yenan authors, just as the peasantry formed the backbone of Mao's own revolutionary strategy.

After the Yenan Forum in 1942, and even during the height of Soviet influence in the 1950s, peasant literature far outshone stories about industrial workers. Such urban masterpieces as Eileen Chang's stories, Ch'ien Chung-shu's *Fortress besieged*, or Yang Chiang's sophisticated comedies remained isolated cases.

Thus the urban film ran counter to the rural orientation of Communist literature. As a popularized version of the literature of the 1930s it expressed discontent, the compulsion to expose, rather than to extol, social

---

[160] Feng Hsueh-feng, 93–4.

reality. Literary creativity in modern China has thrived in the worst of times: the last decade of the Ch'ing, the chaotic period of warlordism, the years of impending war with Japan, and the eve of the final victory of the Communist Revolution. As Lu Hsun once remarked, literature is never content with the status quo, while politics always seeks to preserve it.[161] But Mao's redefinition of politics (as the revolutionary ideology for change) and literature (as a revolutionary weapon) meant that in a post-revolutionary situation there could be only laudatory works, and discontent would cease to be a motive for literary creation. Instead of the essential divergence between literature and politics, the Maoist canon posited their convergence.

In the Maoist version of the new China, moreover, the discrepancy between urban and rural – either as fact or as idea – never existed. The success of the Communist Revolution stripped modern Chinese literature of its urban component. With the loss of the urban 'mentality', modern Chinese literature also lost its subjective *élan*, its individualistic vision, its creative *angst*, and its critical spirit, even though it gained through the rural mainstream a genuinely popular scope and a more 'positive' character. 'Obsession with China' was superseded by adulation of the motherland and its people. In the collective moralism of the socialist society, what C. T. Hsia perceived to be the 'moral burden'[162] of modern Chinese literature was missing.

---

[161] *Lu Hsun ch'üan-chi*, 7.470–1. See also Lee, 'Literature on the eve of revolution', 278–86.

[162] C. T. Hsia, 'Obsession with China: the moral burden of modern Chinese literature', in his *A history*, 533–61.

CHAPTER 10

JAPANESE AGGRESSION AND CHINA'S INTERNATIONAL POSITION 1931–1949

Starting in the 1930s as a lone victim of aggression, enjoying little systematic help from the world community, China ended the Second World War as a member of a victorious global coalition, endowed with the status of a major power, only to see its position undermined because of a civil war. To trace this development in some detail is to understand the close links between domestic and international affairs, between China as it was and as it might have been.

THE WORLD ECONOMIC CRISIS: CHINA'S MARGINALITY

Any discussion of China's international affairs during the 1930s must start from the world economic crisis which began in 1929. This crisis primarily affected the advanced industrial countries which had, after the World War, sought desperately to re-establish a prewar-type international order for trade, investment and other forms of economic transactions. The landmarks of the 1920s – the return to the gold standard at prewar parity in the United States, Britain and elsewhere; the containment of dangerous inflational spirals in Germany, France and Italy; compromise settlements of the debt and reparations question – had hardly concerned China. Its trade never amounted to more than a fraction of the total volume of international trade, and foreign investments in China were not significant beside those in Japan or in European countries. The United States, the major sustainer of the international economic system after the war, did not expand its trade or investment in China. American goods and capital found other, more attractive outlets, especially in Germany and Japan.

Ironically, the very insignificance of China in the world economic picture during the 1920s enabled it to weather the storm of the world depression. As an overwhelmingly agrarian and silver-monetized economy, China was not initially affected by the crisis among the industrial economies. Rapid fluctuations in prices of commodities, chronic unemployment and slow rates of growth were nothing new in China, and the traumatic impact of such capitalist difficulties as the run on gold, exchange instability, and the loss of jobs by millions of factory workers was not duplicated there. While the United States, Britain and other industrial countries lost all sense of order and equanimity, rushing to stop-gap measures and temporary arrangements to meet the crisis, China was able to carry on after 1929 pretty much as it had before. The volume of foreign trade remained stable between 1929 and 1930, and it increased by over 20 per cent between 1930 and 1931. When new tariff schedules were put into effect in 1929, a product of the Nationalist government's assertive foreign policy, customs receipts more than doubled. Moreover, after 1930 collecting import duties in gold instead of silver saved the government from the effects of the fluctuating price of silver in the world market. Although the price of silver in fact fell, its immediate effect was to reduce China's chronically unfavourable balance of payments and make China more attractive for foreign investors. All this created a sense of relative stability at the moment when the industrial countries were experiencing acute difficulties.[1]

For the European powers the domestic stability sustained by a framework of international cooperation, that had been generated by the Locarno treaties of 1925, began to crumble after 1929. Revisionists in Germany, both on the left and the right, resumed their assault on the postwar treaty structure, calling for a radical departure in external affairs. Instead of maintaining international cooperation, they asserted that Germany must now boldly chart its own course. Normally, such trends in Germany would have called for determined efforts on the part of Britain, France and others to retain the framework of postwar internationalism and to deal with the emerging crisis in close consultation and through the League of Nations. Unfortunately, international cooperation had been so identified with the system of economic relations which faced a serious crisis after 1929 that it was soon being discredited among revisionist groups in Europe. Internationalism represented the outlook of a leadership which was fast losing confidence and popularity.[2]

The situation was similar in Japan. There, too, the political and economic leadership had defined the country's external affairs in terms of coöperation among the capitalist, industrial countries of the West. Their faith in this approach was such that as late as 1930 the government took what proved to be an unwise step to return to the gold standard at prewar

[1] For the Chinese economy during the world economic crisis, see Arthur N. Young, *China's nation-building effort, 1927–1937: the financial and economic record*; Sherman Cochran, *Big business in China. Sino-foreign rivalry in the cigarette industry, 1890–1930*.

[2] Charles Maier, *Recasting bourgeois Europe: stabilization in France, Germany, and Italy in the decade after World War I*; Melvyn P. Leffler, *The elusive quest: America's pursuit of European stability and French security, 1919–1933*; Jon Jacobson, 'Is There a New International History of the 1920s?', *American Historical Review*, 88.3 (June 1983) 617–45.

parity. Japan was one of the last countries to do so, and the fact that by 1930 the impact of the worldwide depression was being felt did not endear the government to dissatisfied groups at both ends of the political spectrum. Because the United States had been the mainstay of postwar Japanese economic and diplomatic relations, the domestic crisis had obvious diplomatic implications. As late as 1929 Tsurumi Yūsuke, the intellectual spokesman for Japan's postwar internationalism, could write of the coming of the American age, when American values, concepts and goods would become the norm throughout the world.[3] It was precisely such a view that came to be attacked after the onset of the economic crisis. Japan's leaders in government, business, and academia seemed too American-oriented at a time when the United States was experiencing severe economic difficulties and its position in world trade was faltering. Critics to right and left steadily raised their voices against the establishment. That they were not above resorting to violence was demonstrated when Prime Minister Hamaguchi Osachi was stabbed to death at Tokyo station in November 1930. Four months later a conspiracy among junior army officers was uncovered, a conspiracy which contemplated a coup d'état to destroy party government and replace it with a military dictatorship.

While forces within Germany and Japan were thus reacting against the postwar system of international cooperation and weakening those who stood for that system, politics in China were moving in another direction. The Kuomintang under Chiang Kai-shek was at least nominally creating a national government for the first time in more than ten years. Opposition to Chiang's leadership was strong, as were groups and factions unwilling to submit to the Nanking government. Still, the latter enjoyed prestige and status as it won significant concessions from the powers in revising the unequal treaties, and established the basis for national reconstruction. Although warlords, Kuomintang dissidents, Communists and others continued to harass Chiang and his regime, it should be noted that there was no rigid line separating those in and out of power. Chiang was able to arrange temporary agreements to obtain collaboration of some potential rivals, and a number of officials and generals who had worked for other regimes were willing to be recruited into the new government.[4]

The two factors sketched above – China's relative insignificance in international economic relations, and its increasing domestic unity – provided the background of the country's troubles after 1931. On the eve of the Manchurian incident, Chiang Kai-shek's authority had been steadily

[3] Tsurumi Yūsuke, *Taiheiyō jidai* (The Pacific era).
[4] Lloyd E. Eastman, *The abortive revolution: China under Nationalist rule, 1927–1937*, ch. 1; James C. Thomson, *While China faced west*, chs. 1–2.

extended, having weathered serious challenges from some warlords and party dissidents. Economically, Chinese finances were much better off than those in many industrial countries. Trade revenue, it is true, was beginning to decline because of the drop in the price of silver. But it had the effect of increasing commercial and industrial activity for a while, and there was certainly nothing comparable to the dislocations that were affecting international monetary and trade transactions among the industrial powers. China, to be sure, needed loans and investments from abroad, and the economic crisis could be expected to make it difficult in the long run to borrow overseas. At the same time, the country could hope to regain control over foreign enterprises, and through reform of tariff, internal tax, currency and administrative systems, China could raise enough money for undertaking much needed reconstruction programmes. For all these reasons, there was a sense of optimism and determination when Chinese leaders, officials and publicists looked at world affairs as the fourth decade of the century began.

Precisely the opposite kinds of perception, expectation and calculation led the Japanese to undertake acts of aggression against China. From the point of view of revisionists in Japan – army officers, right-wing dissidents, some intellectuals, and generally those dissatisfied with the leadership – China was becoming more and more unified and stronger, while Japan was hopelessly groping for ways out of its domestic ills. Given such a perception, the conclusions reached by the architects of the Mukden incident – Ishihara Kanji, Itagaki Seishirō and others – were simple and straightforward. They would repudiate internationalism as the foundation of national policy and survival. They would also reject the possibility of China emerging as a unified and strong nation capable of challenging Japanese rights and interests. Internationalism, in any event, seemed to be crumbling all over the world, while at the same time China was vigorously asserting its sovereignty. The only workable solution, if Japan were to continue as a viable nation, appeared to be bold action to bring China under decisive Japanese control.

Whether there was a systematic programme, a 'conspiracy' as alleged during the post-1945 war crimes trials, for establishing domination over the whole of China is difficult to say. Certainly, there would have been no Manchurian crisis if the Japanese – civilian as well as military – had not tied their nation's destiny to some degree of control over China. The process had begun in the late nineteenth century, and generations of Japanese had come to accept such control as a matter of necessity. There were, however, many ingredients in this domination. One was military and strategic, concerned with Japanese power vis-à-vis other powers. It was believed that China would be important not as a military power in its own right, but as a base from which Japan could confront potential adversaries, in particular Russia. A second was geographic and economic, reflecting the existential conditions of a country lacking in natural resources and desperately dependent on foreign trade. China had, quite simply, been a major supplier of soy-beans, iron, cotton and other goods, and a market for one-fifth to one-fourth of total Japanese exports. A third ingredient was more psychological and cultural. It was believed that as an Asian country that had successfully transformed itself and put an end to Western domination, Japan had an obligation, even a right, to lead its neighbours, especially China, toward a similar path of change. Finally, perhaps more important than any of these factors, was the domestic ingredient: the perceived linkage between internal and external affairs in such a way that a call for an assertive foreign policy was but a reflection of a movement to rearrange domestic social and political priorities.

The revisionist assault took the form of a call for domestic reconstruction so as to facilitate a new departure in Japanese relations with China. It is no accident that conspiracies, assassinations, and attempts at coups d'état predated the Mukden incident of September 1931. It was to be an external counterpart of a domestic reconstructionist movement that would put an end to the domination by business, bureaucracy, and 'liberal' intellectuals. This did not mean, however, that the revisionists were visualizing a return to a pre-industrial past. With the exception of a few advocates of 'agrarianism', the conspirators and their supporters accepted the need for economic growth. In fact, they were committed to the idea of making use of Manchuria's space and resources for the nation's industrialization, increasing agricultural output, and general well-being. Japanese civilians in Manchuria, numbering 230,000 on the eve of the Mukden incident, were a symbol of Japan's economic aspirations as well as frustrations. They also came to embody what, in the conspirators' perception, was wrong with the national leadership that seemed to have neglected the interests of the brethren in Manchuria. Instead of paying heed to their plight, the government at home seemed complacent, thinking only of domestic stability and order as prerequisites for international order.[5]

The situation, however, was becoming more acute, as the Japanese in Manchuria were finding themselves targets of aroused Chinese patriotism. Already by 1931 Manchuria's external affairs had been placed under Nanking's control, a new transportation committee set up for the Three Eastern Provinces to plan for a unified system of railways and telecommunications, and Kuomintang branches established in the

    [5] Akira Iriye, *After imperialism: the search for a new order in the Far East, 1921–1931*.

provincial capitals of Manchuria.[6] More specifically, the Chinese were intent upon undermining the South Manchurian Railway by building their own railways, developing Hulutao port as a competitor for Dairen, and bringing about the gradual stoppage of Japanese mining and forestry industries by refusing to renew their concessions or forbidding native labourers to work for them. Korean settlers in Manchuria, by far the most numerous 'Japanese' in China, were encountering increasing difficulties in engaging in farm work. Chinese authorities forbade the native population to sell or rent land to foreigners, at the very moment when Korean farmers in Chientao were being compelled to migrate across the Yalu to escape from worsening economic conditions.

The Chinese-Japanese conflict over Manchuria, then, was a clash of forces between an industrial country going through severe economic difficulties and a predominantly agricultural society determined to regain and retain national rights. It was symbolic that direct confrontation was triggered by Chinese attacks upon Korean peasants in Manchuria. Koreans were victims of Japan's rapid industrialization, driven homeless and landless by the colonial regime. From the Japanese point of view, these Koreans were the most dispensable segment of the population, and yet their status in Manchuria was of concern to Japanese authorities looking to that region for alleviation of economic ills at home. In Chinese perspective, on the other hand, it was essential for their national reconstruction and domestic stability to prevent further foreign encroachment. Japan's economic troubles were its own business, and should not be solved at the expense of China's sovereignty. It was too bad, the Chinese would say, that Japanese business enterprises in Manchuria were suffering from falling revenues, that tens of thousands of Japanese were out of work, that the South Manchurian Railway was going through the severest crisis in its history. But these, from the Chinese point of view, were a result of the worldwide recession, not to be blamed upon China's rights recovery movement. The Japanese believed, however, that but for Chinese attacks on their vested rights they would not be suffering so much. Japanese hotels, restaurants, building contractors, and entertainment houses were all experiencing a sharp decline in business, and they were convinced that this was China's doing. If only Japan acted vigorously and resisted China's anti-Japanese movement, everything would go back to normal and Japanese rights would be secured.

In this way the world economic crisis provided the immediate context for the outbreak of the Manchurian incident. For the Japanese involved, Manchuria was not an integral part of China, but a region where Japanese,

[6] Usui Katsumi, *Manshū jihen* (The Manchurian incident), 11–12, 19–20.

Koreans, Manchurians, (Han) Chinese and other races should live and prosper together – under Japanese guidance. Japan, they were convinced, had the military power, capital and technology necessary for turning the area into a haven for economic development, security and stability. Manchuria under Japanese control would alleviate the suffering not only of Japanese at home, but also China's 'proletarian masses', in the words of a pamphlet issued in July 1931 by the Manshū Seinen Renmei (Manchurian youth association).[7] Above all, decisive action would contribute to Japanese glory, prestige and expansion, now vitally needed to provide the people with a sense of purpose and national pride.

It is evident that in such thinking there was little room for internationalist considerations. The Kwantung Army and its supporters in Manchuria equated the postwar international system with the civilian government's 'weak-kneed' diplomacy, intent on placating Chinese nationalists and settling difficult disputes through peaceful negotiation, within the framework of the Washington Conference treaties. Since the treaties dealt with questions relating also to the Western powers, observance of the Washington system had entailed Japan's willingness to cooperate with these powers in preserving peace and stability in East Asia. For Foreign Minister Shidehara Kijūrō, therefore, China had not been the most fundamental question facing Japan. Most crucial had been Japan's internationalist diplomacy: the foreign policy of cooperation with the United States, Great Britain, and other advanced industrial countries, which alone would ensure Japan's successful industrialization and peaceful economic expansion. China would of course be important as a market and a source of raw materials, but Chinese-Japanese relations would not be unique in themselves; they would be part of the overall system of international relations to which Japan was committed as a great power.

Thus the confrontation in Manchuria became part of the global development in which the subtle and precarious balance between international order and domestic order steadily eroded. 'Radicals' in Japan were no more committed to the preservation of domestic or international order than their counterparts elsewhere. They were determined to disregard all such considerations and act boldly to impose their own arrangements for internal political affairs and, as an integral part of this undertaking, for Japanese rule in Manchuria. The Mukden incident of 18 September 1931 was the first decisive step.

[7] *Ibid.* 24.

THE MANCHURIAN INCIDENT: JAPAN'S REVISIONIST MILITARISM 1931–1932

The incident consisted of premeditated attacks upon the South Manchurian Railway some eight kilometres north of the Mukden station. As worked out in detail a few days earlier, the plot entailed the use of explosives by officers of the Kwantung Army to destroy two to three feet of railway tracks. The explosion served as a signal for nearby detachments to mobilize. Around eleven o'clock at night, barely forty minutes after the incident, General Itagaki, the senior staff officer of the Kwantung Army, issued orders for an attack upon Chinese forces in the area. The commander of the Japanese army, General Honjō Shigeru, who was at its headquarters in Port Arthur, was notified of these developments close to midnight and gave them his approval. He had, however, conferred a few days earlier with Itagaki and other conspirators, and the news must have come as no surprise to him. In any event, he decided to seize this opportunity to carry out more extensive military action, and on 19 September he telegraphed the supreme command that the time was ripe for the Kwantung Army 'to act boldly and assume responsibility for law and order throughout Manchuria'.[8] Although he did not immediately have his way, as the cabinet and the supreme command initially hesitated to sanction the Kwantung Army's ambitious designs, it did not take long before the latter accomplished one military feat after another, so that within several weeks most of southern Manchuria had fallen under Japanese control.

Here was obviously a challenge to the civilian government in Tokyo and what it stood for, domestically and externally. Blind approval of the faits accomplis in Manchuria would not only destroy the basis of Japan's cooperative foreign policy, but would also undermine the structure of its domestic politics. Foreign Minister Shidehara clearly understood the nature of the challenge; he recognized that unless contained the military action on the continent would jeopardize Japan's relations with the United States and Britain, which he believed were now becoming more crucial than ever because of the global economic crisis, and would give rise to radical movements at home by legitimizing unilateral behaviour by military officers. Unfortunately, few of Shidehara's colleagues, civilian and military, were interested in preserving the tenuous linkage between domestic and international order. Instead of viewing the Mukden uprising in the context of internationalist diplomacy and of parliamentary politics, they tended to react to it in the bilateral framework of Chinese-Japanese

[8] *Ibid.* 41–5.

relations. With the Kwantung Army jealously guarding the secret of its own complicity, civilian officials, including Prime Minister Wakatsuki Reijirō, were inclined to see the Manchurian crisis as an inevitable product of China's assault on Japanese rights. In the end, Shidehara was powerless to persuade others that Japan must give top priority to maintaining good relations with the League and with the Washington powers. The resignation of the Wakatsuki cabinet in December put an end to this phase of Japanese diplomacy.[9] By ignoring the framework of the Washington treaties and instead attempting to solve serious disputes with China by force and through bilateral arrangements, the Japanese were demonstrating their readiness to discard the principle of international cooperation when this did not serve their purposes.

For the other powers, the question then was whether to continue to view Japan as a member of a community of nations, or to ostracize it as a violator of the internationalist principle. Either alternative entailed risks. If Japan were to continue to be regarded as a Washington power, they would have to acquiesce in Japanese action in Manchuria in order not to alienate the country. Or else they would have to put enough pressure upon Japan to bring it back to its senses and keep it as a responsible power. Either way, the powers would need the right combination of cajolery and pressure so as to maintain the Washington framework as the best alternative. There was a risk in such a strategy, in that too much cajolery might embolden Japan to further acts of aggression, whereas an excessively forceful reaction might drive the country to give up any notion of international cooperation. The other alternative, that of castigating Japan in the international community, at best would mean the loss of Japan as a Washington power, and at worst it would have little effect in altering the course of events in East Asia.

Other things being equal, it would have been reasonable to expect that the United States and Great Britain would work together to develop a consistent approach to the Manchurian crisis, and a solution on the basis of continued internationalism. It is a testimony to the latent strength of the Washington Conference system that the United States and Britain did try initially to cooperate in order to cope with the Manchurian situation in an international framework. The United States, in particular, was extremely active in late 1931, and one could well argue that these were the finest hours of postwar American internationalism. Britain was much less active, but it did go along half way with the American initiative.

America's initial response to the Mukden incident was to internationalize it. Given the conceptual framework which had conditioned diplomacy

9 *Ibid.* 47, 80–6.

in East Asia after the war, that was the most predictable response. What was not so predictable was the degree of commitment shown by President Herbert C. Hoover, Secretary of State Henry L. Stimson, and their aides in the State Department to the idea of international cooperation. There was little doubt in their minds that Japan was at fault; as Stimson recorded, the Kwantung Army was defying the Washington Conference order by resorting to rash action. It was imperative, therefore, to call upon the Japanese government to renounce such acts of aggression on the part of the military and agree to peaceful settlement of whatever dispute they had with China. Stimson's diplomatic initiatives for three months after 18 September were undertaken with such objectives in mind. He did not hesitate to work closely with the League of Nations to which the Chinese government had taken the case. The United States was never again to cooperate so actively with the international organization. Stimson sent an observer to the council meetings, kept in close touch with League officials, and actively pushed for some League action that would provide the basis for terminating the hostilities. The League's adoption of a resolution, calling upon China and Japan to desist from further fighting and return to the status quo, was in line with the United States government's desires. In November the League established a commission of inquiry to investigate the Manchurian situation and make recommendations. The United States supported this step, and General Frank McCoy was appointed as American representative on the commission, which was to be headed by Lord Lytton of Britain.[10]

American diplomacy during the Manchurian crisis has been viewed as either unnecessarily petulant or woefully ineffectual. In the end, of course, nothing that the United States did deterred the Japanese military. But the essential goal of the government in Washington was to maintain an international framework in settling local disputes. To internationalist groups both within and outside the government, here was a rare opportunity for the United States to play a role on behalf of internationalism, stressing the advanced countries' responsibility to 'act as agencies to police mankind and preserve a righteous peace', as Ellery S. Stowell, the diplomat-scholar, wrote in 1931. There was a certain exhilaration in preparing for America's active cooperation with the League of Nations. Japan was forfeiting its membership in the community of powers by acting unilaterally. In short, the main concern of American diplomacy was not China but the principles of internationalism.[11]

[10] Gary B. Ostrower, *Collective insecurity: The United States and the League of Nations during the early thirties.*

[11] Robert D. Schulzinger, *The making of the diplomatic mind: the training, outlook, and style of United States Foreign Service officers, 1908–1931.*

Great Britain, France and other nations went along with the American initiatives. Britain, as a major Asian power, was in basic agreement with the United States that the framework of international cooperation must be maintained. London was more ready, however, to concede Japan's rights in Manchuria as one aspect of such cooperation. British officials at home and in East Asia tended to agree that Japan had legitimate complaints about Chinese nationalism, and that it was more desirable to keep Japan as a cooperative member of the world community by offering it concessions than by condemning its acts outright.[12] Thus by late 1931 the United States, Britain and the League of Nations were interested in solving the Manchurian crisis within the framework of international collaboration and without alienating Japan. The latter would remain part of the international endeavours to settle the dispute. This was something less than the Chinese wanted, an immediate end to the fighting and a straightforward condemnation of Japan, forcing it to restore the status quo ante. But they, too, were sensitive to the subtle balance between domestic and international affairs. The Nanking government under Chiang Kai-shek had been steadily extending its authority to the rest of China and had launched various economic projects for modernization, but the crisis in Manchuria was forcing it to pay more attention to foreign issues. It could conceivably arouse Chinese patriotism and solidify its power by acting boldly in defiance of Japan. But too deep an involvement in a military struggle in Manchuria would drain resources away from economic rehabilitation at a time when floods and famine were widespread. Most important, Chiang Kai-shek was concerned lest foreign war encourage the Communists and other dissidents to emerge as champions of national liberation and undermine Nanking's authority. So long as the major powers, including Japan, were committed to an internationalist framework, it would suit Chinese purposes as the Nanking regime could continue to work for regaining sovereign rights. In this way, the Mukden incident invited China as well as Japan to make use of internationalist means.[13]

Japan spurned all these offers, actual and latent, to resume its role as an internationalist. After January 1932, when the Kwantung Army occupied Chinchow and the navy landed marines in Shanghai, Japanese unilateralism became unmistakably clear. In the meantime, the Kwantung Army pushed toward the independence of Manchuria, assisted by various Japanese organizations in the region which had spearheaded the movement for unilateral solutions to pending issues. The independence of Manchuria

---

[12] W. Roger Louis, *British strategy in the Far East, 1919–1939.*
[13] Usui, Katsumi, *Manshū jihen,* 68–73.

for all these groups had symbolic as well as strategic significance. It would preserve the area's rich resources and strategic location for Japanese military use. It would also symbolize the ideal of Asian unity under Japanese leadership. Apologists for expansion accepted Ishihara's vision of turning Manchuria into a region of peace and stability where Chinese, Japanese, and others – 'the five races' of East Asia – would live in harmony. This was presented as a more viable alternative to Western imperialism, Soviet communism, or Chinese nationalism, which had poisoned Chinese-Japanese relations and served only to perpetuate Western influence in the East.[14]

The independence of Manchuria, proclaimed in March 1932, was thus a landmark in postwar international relations. Japan was taking unilateral steps to look after its own interests and create a region of stability under its rule, presumably free from divisive and exploitative forces in the world. The civilian government, though not pleased with such developments, did virtually nothing to prevent them.[15] The new foreign minister, Uchida Yasuya, had succeeded Shidehara on the Kwantung Army's recommendation, and he did not hesitate to advocate the recognition of Manchukuo. It came on 15 September 1932, more than two weeks before the report of the League commission of inquiry. Nothing more clearly revealed Japan's defiance of international authority. The Lytton report contained many passages conciliatory to Japan, and its acceptance by Tokyo would not have been difficult if there had existed a forceful leadership interested in continued cooperation with the West. Such was no longer the case, and the report's publication infuriated Japanese officials and publicists. To abide by its recommendations would have entailed cooperating with the powers to define anew their rights and interests in China, agreeing to Manchuria's maintaining a semi-autonomous but not a completely independent existence, and promoting Manchuria's economic development in collaboration with China and other countries. Such a solution would have perpetuated the internationalist framework of East Asian diplomacy, something the Japanese military had by then become determined to escape from. Japan would go its own way, irrespective of how the powers responded.

The powers' responses also began to change. At one level, they continued to cooperate within the existing treaty frameworks and in the League of Nations. But as this approach began to appear less and less productive, the United States and Great Britain had to search for alternatives. America's decision was to couple internationalism with

[14] Mark R. Peattie, *Ishiwara Kanji and Japan's confrontation with the West.*
[15] Usui, Katsumi, *Manshū jihen*, 80–1.

unilateral steps to bring Japan back to the fold. As Stimson said in June 1932, 'a judicious mixture of the new League methods and "old diplomacy"... can, I feel convinced, alone achieve the practical results for which we are striving'.[16] The 'new League methods' would include continued cooperation with other countries to maintain the peace. One expression of this was Stimson's proposal to Great Britain in January that the two powers join together in condemning Japanese acts at Shanghai as violations of the nine-power treaty of 1922, hoping Japan would be compelled by such pressure to retreat. By 'old diplomacy' Stimson did not initially mean alliances or war plans, but the United States acting unilaterally to uphold the status quo. Such thinking was behind the Stimson doctrine, enunciated on 7 January 1932, declaring that the United States would not recognize 'any situation, treaty or agreement which may be brought about by means contrary to the covenants and obligations of the Pact of Paris', the 1928 Kellogg–Briand pact. This unilateral declaration without British cooperation indicated the subtle divergence that was becoming apparent between London and Washington. The United States was going beyond the ineffectual steps thus far taken, with a further initiative to compel Japan to honour the principles of international cooperation. While there was no hint that forceful American measures would be taken to implement the doctrine, that was the obvious implication. The Stimson statement served to pit the United States, as the defender of the existing international system, against Japan which was defying that system. Obviously, two such powers might collide violently.

THE COLLAPSE OF INTERNATIONALISM

Of these approaches – internationalism and unilateralism – the first was becoming more and more difficult to achieve. The assumption that Japan would back down and resume its responsible and peaceful position in the community of nations was daily being honoured in the breach. More troublesome was Britain's disinclination to persist in this approach beyond what it had done in 1931. While cooperation with the United States on the Manchurian and other questions was considered essential, London was reluctant to associate itself with Washington in too strong a condemnation of Japan. Foreign Secretary Sir John Simon stressed that Britain would continue to work through the League of Nations so that the Japanese would not view British diplomacy as tending to an Anglo-American alliance directed against them. As a member of the League, Japan would

---

[16] Christopher Thorne, *The limits of foreign policy: the West, the League, and the Far Eastern crisis of 1931–1933*, 110.

be more likely to cooperate if all action took place at Geneva. Japan, however, was already denouncing the Lytton commission. Thus British opposition to joint action with America amounted to a refusal to strengthen the existing internationalist framework.

This divergence between Washington and London was due to the global trend toward economic regionalism. The international economic system based on the gold standard and a free flow of goods and capital had begun to break down by the early 1930s, and in 1932 there were unmistakable signs pointing to its collapse. Japan in 1932 went off the gold standard which it had readopted only two years previously. In Manchuria it obviously intended to turn the region into an economic hinterland of the home country. While as yet there were no final plans for the economic development of Manchuria under Japanese control, the architects of the Mukden incident and their supporters had conceived of many projects about railway construction, salt and iron mining, textile manufacturing, and the like. The idea was to use Manchuria as part of the economic sphere of Japan where hundreds of thousands of Japanese would settle and engage in productive activities, in a symbiotic relationship with the homeland.[17]

Japan was not the only country promoting economic regionalism. Germany, even before the coming of the Nazis to power in 1933, was pursuing an autarkic economic policy, seeking a customs union with Austria and Czechoslovakia and adopting an inflationary monetary policy in order to promote its export trade. Britain was convening a conference of the Commonwealth countries in order to set up a system of trade preferences among them. The resulting Ottawa agreement (August 1932) did nothing to alleviate the spreading fear that the days of Britain's commitment to economic internationalism were over. France, too, was revising its tariffs upward, bringing about retaliatory trade restrictions from the United States. All in all, 1932 marked the definite beginning of the breakup of the world economy into nationalistic and regionalist sub-systems.[18] In these circumstances, talk of continued international cooperation sounded hollow unless accompanied by measures to check the trend toward autarky. London was therefore less concerned to maintain cooperation with the United States. The postwar framework of internationalism had not disappeared completely, but its economic foundation was being undermined. Only a determined effort on the part of the major powers would be able to revive the spirit of cooperation and maintain the peace.

[17] Manshikai, ed. *Manshū kaihatsu yonjūnenshi* (Forty years of Manchurian development), 1.114–26.
[18] Leffler, ch. 8; David E. Kaiser, *Economic diplomacy and the origins of the Second World War.*

These were the momentous questions that the powers had to face after 1933, the year which marked the coming to power of Franklin D. Roosevelt in Washington and Adolf Hitler in Berlin. Both these leaders, it should be stressed, *were* interested in some kind of cooperation, but no longer in the old framework of internationalism. Hitler's Germany wanted to do away with the restrictions of the Versailles treaty system and its stigma of defeat and injustice. This Hitler would try to accomplish through rearmament and a Central European regional economic system with restrictive trade and monetary policies. Hitler initiated little in all these respects, but he did redefine Germany's foreign relations by openly denouncing the Versailles system and substituting for it an alliance system, principally with Italy and Great Britain. Through cooperation with these countries, Germany was to safeguard its security, recover a place in the sun, and solidify its Central European economic sphere.[19]

Roosevelt's America was not unlike Hitler's Germany in its negative outlook on the postwar framework of peace set up by various treaty arrangements. The new president did not share his predecessor's commitment to the capitalist internationalist structure characterized by the gold standard and stable rates of exchange; despite expressions of support for international cooperation, Roosevelt concentrated on domestic recovery through unilateral actions without consulting other industrial nations. The sense that the capitalist countries had a shared world of foreign trade and investment activities was now less compelling. The United States would rather go its own way. To the extent that it looked outward it would stress Pan-American regionalism by means of negotiating reciprocal, bilateral trade agreements with other American republics.[20] Roosevelt's new administration evinced little interest in trying to restore the internationalism of the 1920s. The realities of 1933 seemed to doom any effort to re-establish the Versailles or the Washington system. Instead, American foreign policy, to the extent that it was being formulated anew in 1933, called for re-establishing international relations in such a way as to prevent war. For this the United States would be willing to deal directly with Japan in Asia or with Germany in Europe, even outside the League of Nations and other existing arrangements. This became still more necessary as these two powers withdrew from the League in 1933.

Nothing better illustrates American willingness to discard the old internationalism for a new than its response to Japan's withdrawal from the League of Nations. When the Japanese delegation, led by Matsuoka Yōsuke, walked out of the General Assembly on 24 February 1932, after

[19] Klaus Hildebrand, *The foreign policy of the Third Reich.*
[20] Robert Dallek, *Franklin D. Roosevelt and American foreign policy, 1932–1945,* 55–60.

it voted to accept the Lytton report, the Japanese government declared it was not abandoning efforts to cooperate to settle international disputes. This provided an opening for other powers to try to minimize the implications of the Japanese withdrawal; the American government in particular was eager to maintain contact with Japan to prevent the crisis from developing into a serious clash. The diplomats – Joseph C. Grew, Nelson T. Johnson, and Hugh Wilson – had come to the conclusion that Japan was in Manchuria to stay, and that a stable relationship with Japan must be based on recognition of this reality. The State Department generally agreed with this assessment and stressed the cardinal importance of avoiding a war with Japan. The best way to do that was to negotiate further with Japan for the protection of their mutual interests in Asia and the Pacific. The stress now would be on bilateral arrangements, to be broadened to include other countries, not upon close cooperation with the League or with Great Britain.

Britain, while still placing top priority upon the integrity of the League, was also ready to abandon cooperation with the United States. As Ray Atherton, the American diplomat in London, observed in March, the British government had 'reluctantly come to the conclusion that while Anglo-American aims may coincide in their general outlines, any policy of effective cooperation is practically unobtainable in view of conflicting interests'.[21] Britain too was groping for a new arrangement to preserve the structure of peace, and in Europe this was beginning to take the shape of bilateral arrangements with Germany. In East Asia, however, officials were divided between those who favoured similar ties to Japan to protect the traditional interests of commerce and security, and those who advocated closer relations with China in order to ensure to Britain the benefits of a future market. The Foreign Office on the whole took the first position, the Treasury the latter. This second view assumed that collaboration with Japan was not likely to bring long-range benefits to British commerce, only short-term advantages, while the China market was growing. Britain would do better to support China than to connive with Japan.[22] This debate in London made British policy toward Asia seem confused.

These were discouraging developments for China. Japan had seized Manchuria with impunity despite censure by the League. The internationalism of 1931 had dissipated, and the two major outside powers were not cooperating. Japan, in the meantime, appeared to be satisfied with its gains in Manchuria. The Tangku truce of 31 May 1933 separated

[21] Thorne, *Limits*, 346.
[22] Stephen Lyon Endicott, *Diplomacy and enterprise: British China policy, 1933–1937*, ch. 3.

the 'four eastern provinces' from the rest of China by establishing a demilitarized zone south of the Great Wall. By agreeing to such a truce, the Nationalist government was admitting the need for a temporary respite, and recognizing Japan's presence in Manchuria. China would now concentrate on diplomacy to regain her lost rights, and on economic reconstruction as a basis of national resistance.[23] For this a favourable international setting was more crucial than ever, but the realities were rather harsh. Leaders like T. V. Soong, H. H. Kung, and Wang Ch'ung-hui, who advocated continued resistance to Japanese ambitions, had counted upon the League of Nations and Anglo-American cooperation to induce Japan to back down. When neither alternative worked, they had to fall back upon more specifically bilateral negotiations with Britain, the United States and others for economic assistance and political support. When T. V. Soong visited London to attend the World Economic Conference, he talked with Treasury and Foreign Office officials about obtaining credits for Chinese reconstruction. No comparable consultation took place when Soong was in Washington, the only practical achievement being the negotiation for a wheat and cotton loan totalling US $50,000,000, to be secured on China's customs receipts.[24] This was but a one-time affair related as much to America's domestic needs to reduce surplus products as to China's requirements.

The other European powers were not as involved in Asian affairs. For them the overriding concern in 1933 was Hitler's Germany. Because Hitler's tactic was to cooperate with Italy and Britain, quite inevitably France and Russia came closer together, in the hope that reviving their traditional entente could check the rising German power. In such a situation, France had little interest in Asian policy, although some individuals, notably Jean Monnet, were active in League programmes for China's economic development. The Soviet Union wanted to avoid premature clashes with Japan in Manchuria while it was so isolated in world politics. The isolation had come from its revolutionary diplomacy throughout the 1920s, aimed at weakening capitalist systems, and also from Joseph Stalin's policy of constructing a 'socialism in one country'. At the very time when capitalist nations were experiencing unprecedented difficulties and reverting to self-centred policies, Russia, instead of abetting this tendency by assisting revolutionary forces throughout the world, was emerging as one of the status-quo powers. Under Stalin's leadership it began emphasizing old-fashioned diplomacy to preserve a global balance. Overtures were extended to the United States to establish

---

[23] Matsumoto Shigeharu, *Shanghai jidai* (The Shanghai years), 1.167–91.
[24] Endicott, 34–6.

normal diplomatic ties, and conversations started with France looking to a defensive pact. In the Manchurian crisis Russia ridiculed League efforts to restore the peace as too puny but otherwise did not provoke Japan in northern Manchuria. Moscow was so eager to conciliate Japan that it offered to negotiate the sale of the Chinese Eastern Railway. Behind such moves was the concern lest Russia become involved in a war with Japan while the other powers stood by. Moscow wanted to restructure international affairs and find its place in a new framework of world politics before Japan or Germany might attack the Soviet Union.[25]

Germany was not yet deeply involved in Asia. Hitler had expressed his contempt for Asians, above all Japanese, in his writings, and had no vision of an Asian policy. He welcomed Japan's withdrawal from the League as a further assault on the postwar structure of peace. From his point of view, a stronger Japan would be a welcome check on Russia. At the same time, he found much to like in Kuomintang China. Chiang Kai-shek was apparently trying to build a new China not along bourgeois liberal lines but on an authoritarian basis. It would need foreign capital and technology as well as military advisers, and Hitler believed Germany should supply them. If China should eventually come under German influence, it would obviously be more favourable than Japanese hegemony in Asia which could menace German economic opportunities. Such considerations led Germany to pursue a bifurcated policy in Asia, one strand looking toward an understanding with Japan against the Soviet Union, while the other sought close ties with China. But while Nazi Germany steadily became a factor in East Asian affairs at a time when the Anglo-American powers' involvement was diminishing, it was not clear how it would contribute to a new approach to the Chinese-Japanese crisis.[26]

JAPAN'S ATTEMPT TO GET REGIONAL COOPERATION 1933–1937

Two years after the Mukden incident, then, it was clear that while the Manchurian crisis might have given the powers an excellent opportunity to solidify the postwar international system, they had not grasped it. Japan was supreme in Manchuria, in defiance of that system. No Western power was strong or bold enough to challenge Japan even though all, including China, were looking for ways to prevent a more extensive war. But Japan's

---

[25] Nihon kokusai seiji gakkai, ed. *Taiheiyō sensō e no michi* (The road to the Pacific war).

[26] Eastman, *Abortive revolution*, ch. 4. John P. Fox, *Germany and the Far Eastern crisis, 1931–1938.* On the German nurture of Nationalist military and industrial power in the early 1930s, through advisers like Seeckt and Falkenhausen and through the National Resources Commission under Weng Wen-hao and others, see William C. Kirby, *Germany and Republican China.* Hitler's turn to Japan broke off this Sino-German cooperation.

foreign minister, Hirota Kōki, believed a new and stable international order could be defined on the basis of changed realities. Coming to the Foreign Ministry in September 1933, his diplomacy tried to restore a sense of cooperation among the powers in Asia, based on the recognition of Japan's position in Manchuria and its special rights and interests in China. By 'cooperation among Japan, Manchukuo and China' he meant that Japan was willing not to go beyond its conquest in Manchuria in return for China's recognition of it. On that basis, Japan would promote China proper's economic development, and China in turn would desist from anti-Japanese policies. Trade between the two countries would increase; their economic relations would become more and more interdependent. At the same time, Japan would 'cooperate' with the United States, Britain and others to maintain peace and stability in Asia and the Pacific, providing they recognized the new realities. Friendly relations among the industrial powers, in other words, could be restored if they understood that world peace depended upon recognition of Japan's special needs and interests on the Asian continent.[27]

There was much to be said for this idea of new international cooperation. It was similar to the one Germany was putting forward in Europe which the United States, Britain and others were finding it expedient to accept. These powers were willing to endorse German revisionism in order to keep Germany within some definable system of international affairs. They would keep in close touch with one another so as to prevent an incident from developing into a major war. Japan, in a sense, was asking the same thing for itself. It would press America and Britain to recognize the new situation as a price for its willingness to maintain the framework of big-power collaboration. This was a delicate policy, dependent on a subtle equilibrium of Japan's and the other powers' perceived interests. It would also depend upon the readiness of Japan's military to support Hirota's strategy, and upon the willingness of the Chinese leaders to accept the status quo.

Hirota was not without success in 1934. At least outwardly, the Japanese military endorsed the strategy of using peaceful and political means to consolidate Chinese-Japanese ties and promote Japanese interests in China. There were, to be sure, those in the Kwantung Army and the Boxer Protocol Force in Tientsin (the so-called Tientsin Army) who were already plotting to penetrate North China. The South Manchurian Railway, anxious to keep its monopoly in the economic development of Manchuria but coming, for that very reason, under

[27] Dorothy Borg and Shumpei Okamoto, eds. *Pearl Harbor as history: Japanese-American relations 1931–1941*, 135.

increasing attacks from non-business Japanese expansionists, was also interested in extending its operations south of the Great Wall. At this time, however, these moves were not crystallizing into a formidable scheme for Japanese control over North China. Certainly in Tokyo the government and military leaders were content with the achievements of 1931–3.[28]

The powers, on their part, were generally acquiescent in the Japanese position in Manchuria. They even showed some interest in investing money in economic development there. With Japan stressing cooperation anew, the confrontation between Japan and the Anglo-American powers was disappearing. There were irritants, to be sure, such as the Amō statement of 17 April 1934, in which the Foreign Ministry spokesman strongly rejected other countries' military aid to China as well as such economic and technical assistance as had political implications. The statement was ambiguous, and when Washington and London sought clarification, the Foreign Ministry immediately backed down, reiterating its adherence to international cooperation.[29] No amount of rhetoric, of course, could hide the fact that Japan perceived itself as the major East Asian power. However, it was ready to re-establish the framework of international cooperation on that basis. After all, this was the time when Ellery S. Stowell was lecturing to American foreign service officers that 'International law is the law of the strong States, made to preserve for strong States their possessions and also very carefully made so that it will not interfere with keen competition with their rivals.'[30] Japan was offering to remain such a 'strong state' and promising not to elbow its rivals out of Asia. In the same spirit, Foreign Minister Hirota was interested in renegotiating naval disarmament treaties so as to retain a sense of big-power cooperation. For him as for Tokyo's civilian leaders, success at naval talks, scheduled for 1935, would guarantee that the United States, Britain and Japan could continue to live with one another in face of the new realities. Unfortunately, the Japanese navy had a different idea. Sold on the concept of independent diplomacy backed by unrestricted naval armament, they resisted any moves toward international agreement, especially one with the United States, for reduction of forces.[31] Even the navy, however, did not see an immediate prospect of war. What it wanted was superiority in the western Pacific, which the government was trying to achieve through diplomacy. Although naval conflict with the United States was

[28] Nakamura Takafusa, 'Japan's economic thrust into North China, 1933–1938', in Akira Iriye, ed. *The Chinese and the Japanese: essays in political and cultural interactions.*

[29] Borg and Okamoto, 108–10.

[30] Schulzinger, 94.

[31] Stephen E. Pelz, *Race to Pearl Harbor: the failure of the Second London Naval Conference and the onset of World War II*, 56–63.

seen as a distinct possibility, the navy was more interested in reaching a compromise with the British in East Asia. The success of such a compromise would depend, of course, on the willingness of the United States and Great Britain to support it, and here one came back to the naval disarmament negotiations as a test case for possible cooperation among the three. The important thing is that at that time the three countries were still looking for ways to stabilize their relations in Asia and the Pacific, and they were ready at least to meet and talk.

In 1934 also the Nanking government made personnel changes as though it was prepared to discuss a settlement with Japan on the basis of the status quo. T. V. Soong, the outspoken opponent of Japanese aggression, when he returned from London in late 1933, had been replaced by H. H. Kung. Wang Ching-wei stayed on as foreign minister, and T'ang Yu-jen, a Japanese educated bureaucrat, was appointed vice foreign minister. Kao Tsung-wu, another graduate of a Japanese university, was recruited to become acting chief of the Foreign Ministry's Asian bureau. Underneath these officials, there were many who had been trained and educated in Japan. Unlike more famous diplomats such as Alfred Sze and Wellington Koo, who were almost totally Western-oriented, these officials had personal ties with Japanese diplomats, intellectuals and journalists. Matsumoto Shigeharu's memoirs, the best source for informal Chinese-Japanese relations during 1933–7, list not only Wang, T'ang, and Kao, but scores of businessmen, military officers, intellectuals, and others with whom he had contact at this time, most of whom, he reports, expressed a serious desire for accommodation with Japan. Their reasoning was manifold. For some the Communists, both Russian and Chinese, were China's major menace, and until this threat was eradicated peace must be maintained with Japan. Others were convinced of the need for China's economic rehabilitation and industrialization. While they knew they had to turn to the Western powers for capital and technology, they also believed such enterprises could never succeed if they excluded Japan. Most important, these Chinese sought to stop further acts of Japanese aggression by talking of cooperation between the two countries. By offering cooperation, they felt they would find enough Japanese support so that army extremists could be isolated and checked.[32]

This was the background of the talks Minister Ariyoshi Akira held in 1934 with Chinese officials, including Foreign Minister Wang Ching-wei. The atmosphere was so cordial that Wang issued only a perfunctory protest when the Amō statement was published. A series of negotiations was successfully consummated, covering such items as mail and railway

[32] Matsumoto Shigeharu, 2.104–26.

connections between Manchuria and China proper, tariff revision, and debt settlement. Toward the end of the year Japan expressed readiness to raise its legation in China to the status of embassy, symbolizing Japan's recognition of China's newly gained position as a major nation. Chinese and Japanese leaders were evidently coming to the view that the two countries could gain more through friendly cooperation than through mutual recrimination. They wanted to put an end to the extreme hostility of their relations after 1931. This would entail at least tacit recognition of the status quo, China accepting the existence of Manchukuo as a separate entity and Japan pledging not to undertake further territorial acquisitions southward. China would also promise to suppress anti-Japanese movements by students, journalists, politicians and warlords, in return for which Japan would assist its economic development.

China's readiness to compromise with Japan in 1934 in part reflected the international setting. The ostracism of Japan on which the Chinese had counted had not come about. The United States, pursuing a self-centred policy under the Silver Purchase Act, began buying up silver at a price above world market rates. The immediate result was a huge drainage of silver from other countries, notably China, causing severe shortages and monetary crises. Banks closed and shops went out of business.[33] Resentment of the United States mounted, matched by a belief that China might have to live with Japan. Britain stood ready to help put China's finances back in order, but it was unlikely to undertake large-scale projects without Japan's endorsement. For all these reasons, some Chinese felt that the time had come for Chinese-Japanese reconciliation.

Those who supported rapprochement were fond of citing Sun Yat-sen's Pan-Asian speech of 1924. The frequency with which the statement was cited was an index of Chinese interest in peaceful relations with Japan. Not surprisingly, then, 1935 opened with a speech by Wang Ching-wei duly referring to Sun's stress on Chinese-Japanese cooperation and pledging an honest effort to bring the two countries together. As if to put such a policy into practice, the nationalist government and the Kuomintang instituted stringent regulations to control anti-Japanese boycotts and demonstrations. Elevation of the Japanese legation to an embassy soon followed, with an elaborate ceremony in Nanking on 15 June.

Unfortunately for those struggling so hard to stabilize Chinese-Japanese relations, that ceremony marked the end of a brief period of attempted accommodation. The same year, 1935, saw another reversal in Japanese policy, prompted by the army's determination to penetrate south of the

[33] Eastman, *Abortive revolution*, 186–8.

Great Wall. Neither the Kwantung Army nor the Tientsin Army had stopped their machinations, but it was primarily General Doihara Kenji, head of the former's special affairs division, who critically undermined the incipient structure of Chinese-Japanese accommodation. According to him, the Chinese government's conciliatory gestures toward Japan were an expression of weakness, a temporary expedient, not a genuine interest in cooperation. On the contrary, Doihara argued, the Chinese leaders were still basically anti-Japanese, refusing to recognize Japan's special position in Manchuria. Under the circumstances, Japan should not be misled by the appearance of friendliness on the part of Chiang Kai-shek or Wang Ching-wei, but should seek to consolidate its gains through bold initiatives in North China, designed to eliminate anti-Japanese elements from the area. To this argument was added the reasoning that only by incorporating North China could Japan hope to establish a viable regional entity. The opportunity would be lost forever if Japan persisted in conciliating the Nationalists, who aimed at bringing the region more directly under their own control.[34]

For two years, from 1935 to the beginning of 1937, Doihara and his fellow conspirators succeeded in carrying out their schemes. Their goal was to 'separate North China' – to remove Kuomintang influences from the region and establish provisional regimes pledged to neutrality but controlled closely by Japanese forces. 'North China' was coming to include the provinces of Hopei, Shantung, Shansi, Chahar and Suiyuan. Japan would not only try to separate them administratively from the rest of China; it would also develop economic enterprises to integrate the region more closely with Manchuria. The Tientsin Army asked the South Manchurian Railway to send a team of researchers to undertake a detailed investigation of North China's mining resources, marketing conditions, and financial institutions. The result was a 72-volume study, written by 151 researchers, which became a basis of Japanese economic planning for North China.[35]

Such moves should have been forcefully suppressed by the Japanese government if the latter were to carry out its part of a bargain with the Nationalists. Only by firmly refusing to approve North China schemes could Tokyo have maintained its credibility and consolidated the framework of Chinese-Japanese conciliation. These separatist Japanese moves coincided with the coming to East Asia of the British economic mission led by Frederick Leith-Ross. The mission had the strong backing of the Treasury, where Chancellor of the Exchequer Neville Chamberlain

---

[34] Satō Kenryō, *Daitōa sensō kaikoroku* (Memoirs of the Pacific war), 45–52.
[35] See Nakamura Takafusa, 'Japan's economic thrust'.

and Under Secretary Warren Fisher were emerging as advocates of an assertive policy in Asia. They were convinced of the need as well as the feasibility of playing a prominent role in the reconstruction of Chinese finances, which would secure both Chinese goodwill and markets for British goods. At the same time, Britain would offer to cooperate with Japan, and Anglo-Japanese cooperation in China (specifically, China south of the Wall) would be the key to peace and stability in Asia, much like British-German cooperation which was being implemented through the naval agreement. If put into effect, the Leith-Ross scheme could have served further to keep Japanese diplomacy within an international framework.[36]

By rejecting the British offer to cooperate, the Japanese government showed a complete lack of flexibility and imagination. Now more than ever before such cooperation should have been welcomed, but this was the very thing the army expansionists were determined to oppose. International arrangements to rehabilitate China not only would restrict Japan's freedom of action, but also would strengthen the central government at Nanking. These very reasons might have convinced Foreign Minister Hirota to take a gamble and work with Leith-Ross, but he utterly failed to grasp the significance of the mission and did nothing to encourage it. Nor did he do much to oppose separatist moves by the army in China. He meekly accepted one fait accompli after another: the Umezu-Ho agreement (June 1935), the Doihara-Chin agreement (June 1935), the establishment of the East Hopei autonomous government (November 1935), and the machinations leading to the institution of the Hopei-Chahar provisional government (December 1935). These deals all aimed at removing Kuomintang personnel and influence from North China, clearly contrary to Japan's official policy of conciliating the Chiang–Wang leadership.[37] But Tokyo totally ignored this contradiction. 'Hirota's three principles', worked out by the Foreign, War, and Navy ministries in October, said nothing about Japan's peaceful intentions or desire for international cooperation. Instead, they called on China to 'put an end to her dependence on Europe and America' and agree to Japan's special position in Manchuria and North China. The Foreign Ministry under Hirota was meekly accepting the army's separatist designs in North China and its opposition to international cooperation. In November Hirota even told Ambassador Ariyoshi to encourage General Sung Che-yuan's movement for North China's autonomy.[38]

[36] Endicott, ch. 5.
[37] Nihon kokusai seiji gakkai, ed. *Taiheiyō sensō e no michi.*
[38] Matsumoto Shigeharu, *Shanghai.*

China's leaders could not remain conciliatory when the Japanese army was stripping the country of its northern provinces. The failure to stop Japan's aggression in North China inspired student organizations, suppressed by the Kuomintang after 1931, to defy the bans on demonstrations. On 9 December 1935 thousands of students marched in Peking carrying anti-Japanese slogans and calling on China's leaders to stop their internecine warfare and to unite the nation against Japanese imperialism. This movement coincided with the new Chinese Communist united front strategy, which Hatano Yoshihiro dates from November 1935.[39] The rising tide of nationalism was reflected in the fact that those leaders who had maintained a friendly attitude toward Japan – Wang Ching-wei, T'ang Yu-jen, Kao Tsung-wu and others – steadily lost their influence. An attack on Wang's life, followed closely by T'ang's assassination at the end of 1935, followed the trend of Chinese opinion.

Japanese diplomacy continued bankrupt in 1936, when Hirota became prime minister following the 26 February army revolt in Tokyo. His foreign minister was Arita Hachirō. Obviously, the promising beginnings of 1934 had been dissipated. Japan was once again the target of Chinese nationalism while Britain's fiscal reforms in China were earning the gratitude of the Nationalists. Elsewhere in the world a new structure of international relations seemed to be emerging: in August 1935 the Comintern had called for a united front against fascist aggressors, and a popular front was appearing in France. The French-Russian pact of May 1935 pitted the popular front against Germany, which in turn approached Italy for an Axis front. The two groupings came together during the Spanish Civil War (July 1936–9) when these four joined Great Britain in forming a non-intervention committee, which at least showed the European powers' interest in maintaining a consultative framework. Britain, the power in between, sought intra-European cooperation as a substitute for the League or Anglo-American cooperation, both of which had by then been discredited. Meanwhile the steady re-entry of the Soviet Union into the European community was especially ominous for Japan. For the first time since the First World War, Russia was willing to act with the capitalist countries. Possibly a European state system based on mutual consultation would leave each power free to engage in extra-European affairs. It was no accident that Britain, Russia and Germany all began actively to support Chiang Kai-shek. After the Leith-Ross reforms, China was attractive for foreign investment, and Chiang Kai-shek a viable leader.

Japan could not cope with these developments. The one achievement

[39] Hatano Yoshihiro, Kok-Kyō gassaku (The Kuomintang-Communist alliance), 180–92.

of 1936 was the Anti-Comintern Pact with Germany in November. It was typical of Japan's lack of perception to turn to Germany for cooperation before all efforts had been exhausted to see if working arrangements could be restored with Britain or the United States, the traditional partners in China. Japan had had virtually no prior experience working with Germany in Asia. The anti-Soviet pact, while attractive enough to civilian as well as military leaders in Tokyo, did nothing except encourage the Russians to strengthen China's defences. By urging a united front in China, the Soviet Union hoped to end the Nationalist-Communist warfare and turn the united country against Japanese ambitions. The Sian incident of December 1936 attested to the success of that strategy.

Japanese policy was getting nowhere. The Japanese army in North China had doubled its size, and was pushing for a Japan-Manchukuo-China economic bloc. But self-sufficiency was hard to attain. In 1936 Asia accounted for only 38.2 per cent of Japan's total imports and 50.9 per cent of total exports. More than 30 per cent of Japanese purchases came from the United States, which took more than 20 per cent of Japan's exports. The balance of payments deficit was more than 40 million yen, including a net deficit of 253 million yen in trade with the United States and 22 million yen with Britain. Japan had to reassess its China policy.

The key documents in this effort were 'Implementation of policy toward China' and 'Directives for a North China policy', both adopted on 16 April 1937 by the four ministers' conference (the foreign, finance, war and navy ministers). The documents stressed 'cultural and economic' means to bring about 'coexistence and coprosperity' between the two countries, and the need to 'view sympathetically' the Nanking government's effort to unify China. It was decided not to seek North China's autonomy or to promote separatist movements. Local regimes would not be supported so as to encourage disunity, but instead Japan would try to create an atmosphere of mutual trust throughout China. Eventually, the four ministers agreed, the East Hopei autonomous regime might have to be dismantled and the smuggling trade discontinued. Toward the Hopei-Chahar provisional government Japan should adopt an attitude of fairness in order to placate the people. The economic development of North China, a key ingredient of Japanese policy in the 1930s, should, according to the new directive, be carried out through the infusion of Japan's private capital as well as Chinese funds. Third powers' rights would be respected, and cooperation with Britain and the United States would be promoted.[40]

This was an amazing reversal of policy, a frank admission of the failure

[40] *Gendaishi shiryō: Nit-Chū sensō* (Documents on contemporary history: the Sino-Japanese War).

of the army's unscrupulous tactics of aggrandizement. Unfortunately, it came too late. The Chinese had thoroughly lost confidence in Japanese professions of mutual friendship; the Sian incident had unified the country as never before. Chiang Kai-shek's authority now depended on taking a strong stand against Japan. The international environment was also moving in China's favour. By the beginning of 1937 the worst phase of the global depression was over. The world's industrial output that year was to surpass the level of 1929 for the first time, and the volume of trade was also to regain its pre-1929 magnitude. Foreign economic questions no longer preoccupied the diplomacy of the industrial powers. In London, Paris, Moscow and other capitals there was serious concern with preventing war. Most important, President Franklin D. Roosevelt, whose foreign policy during 1933–7 had been nationalistic, uncooperative and inconsistent, was willing to go back to the Hoover-Stimson strategy of internationalizing regional disputes. Critical of the neutrality legislation, he was convinced that America once again must take a lead in world affairs. Roosevelt invited Neville Chamberlain, shortly after he became prime minister in June, to come to Washington to discuss world problems. Under-Secretary of State Sumner Welles, with Roosevelt's backing, called for an international conference to lay down basic principles for the guidance of all nations. While nothing came of these proposals, they indicated the beginning of America's return to the international arena.[41]

In Europe this revival of internationalism was to culminate in the Munich compromise of 1938 which, as Welles was to characterize it, seemed to establish 'a new world order based upon justice and upon law'. Just as in East Asia during 1931–2, the years 1937–8 were the heyday of a new internationalism which was sometimes called 'appeasement'. It was an expression of the major powers' interest in avoiding war, albeit at the expense of smaller countries. In Asia in 1937, however, there was much less inclination among the Western powers to appease Japan, that is, to cooperate with Japan to stabilize political relations. Japan had become more of an outsider than Germany, more obviously an aggressor. The Japanese government needed to take energetic steps if it was going to persuade other powers of its commitment to its new China policy. Restoring a sense of international cooperation in East Asia in fact was the cardinal objective of the ministry of Konoe Fumimaro who came to power on 4 June 1937. Hirota was reappointed foreign minister, and it was to have been their principal goal to put an end to Japan's diplomatic isolation. At that very juncture the Marco Polo Bridge incident destroyed any prospect for peace and stability in Asia.

The shooting outside Peiping on 7 July had not been premeditated,

[41] Arnold A. Offner, *American appeasement: United States foreign policy and Germany, 1933–1938*.

according to most accounts.[42] It certainly should have been contained, for the major powers were now far more capable of intervening in the war. Pretty soon Germany, Britain, the United States and the Soviet Union would be doing so, politically or militarily, thus compounding the Japanese sense of isolation. When some of these powers met at Brussels in November 1937 to discuss the incident, Japan's isolation and ostracism were all too clear.

POWER CONFIGURATIONS DURING THE SINO-JAPANESE WAR 1937–1941

The dual phenomena of the mid-1930s – Japan's diplomatic isolation and the West's renewed interest in China – became more pronounced after the outbreak of war in July 1937. In sharp contrast to the victories on the battlefield was the elusive problem of war aims. Japan was using the bulk of its forces (over one million soldiers) in the Chinese war, and at home national mobilization was decreed in April 1938, to gear the entire nation for victory. But it was not clear what the war was all about. It had erupted just when Japan's political and military leaders were on the point of reorienting their Asian policy to help restore some sense of stability by a degree of cooperation with the United States and Britain. Now all this was out of the question, yet there was neither clear recognition of why the war must be fought, nor a shared vision of what would result from it. The rhetoric of a new order was the most conspicuous rationalization that the Japanese were able to devise at this time. The stress of newness signalled their sense that there was no going back to the past. Instead, the war was to be an instrument for the transformation of Japan, Asia and even the world. Japan was carrying out a historical mission to 'change contemporary social and economic organization'.[43] Domestically, this meant reducing, even eradicating, Western influences – party politics, private profit, hedonism. The Japanese, declared Takada Yasuma, a noted sociologist, must learn to live frugally, identifying individual well-being with the welfare of the entire nation. They must subject self-interest to societal control. Externally, the concept of a new order rationalized the war which, as Takada said, 'China and Japan are fighting not for the sake of fighting', but for nobler ends (usually referred to as Asianism or an Asian new order), in order to strengthen Asia's collective self-defence against the West.[44]

---

[42] The most reliable recent account of the Marco Polo Bridge incident is Teradaira Tadasuke, *Rokōkyō jiken* (The Marco Polo Bridge incident).

[43] Hasegawa Tadashi, *Tairitsu-suru sensō-ron* (Competing theories of war), 164.

[44] Takada Yasuma, *Tōa minzoku-ron* (On East Asian nationalism), 69, 77.

This self-serving rationalization revealed how desperate the Japanese perceived their situation to be. To appeal to Chinese Pan-Asianism was to admit that the war could not be won on the battlefield. This appeal might have been more than a desperate rhetorical device if the Chinese had felt they were being ignored by the West and had therefore no alternative to a Japan-defined new Asian order. To be sure, some Chinese who had earlier been inclined to befriend the Japanese, notably Wang Ching-wei, still retained a vision of the two countries' close relationship. They persuaded themselves of the unlikelihood of China's obtaining much assistance from other countries. This was their biggest miscalculation, as well as Japan's. Far from the two countries continuing their war in isolation, they were to find it becoming more and more part of a global conflict, inevitably involving other nations.

Such a favourable development, from the Chinese point of view, was not at all fore-ordained. During most of 1935–7 the popular front put forward at the 1935 Comintern Congress was more an idea than a reality, not least because the Americans and British would not tie themselves to the Soviet Union, which might involve them in a premature conflict with the fascist countries. Moreover, Russia's own power was weakened by Stalin's purges. Just on the eve of the Marco Polo Bridge incident, for example, Marshal M. N. Tukhachevsky and his colleagues, the highest military commanders, were shot. Ironically, it was Germany more than anyone else that had the potential of coming to China's assistance. Because it had good relations with both China and Japan, the Chinese hoped in the early stages of the war that Germany would exert pressure to moderate Japan's military action.[45] The United States and Britain, in contrast, could not be counted upon at first. Both were still profoundly affected by a pacifist, isolationist sentiment. Their sympathy with China did not translate itself into effective policy.

All this was to change with dramatic suddenness. In late 1937 and early 1938, significant steps were taken to check Japan through cooperation among America, Britain and Russia, whereas Germany, the country that could have done the most to assist China, veered closer to Japan. The Sino-Japanese War induced the world's major powers to realign themselves. For one thing, it led the Soviet Union and the Anglo-American powers to take greater heed of each other and, if possible, to arrange a joint response to restrain Japan. The Soviet Union in many ways took the initiative. Though reluctant to enter into a purely bilateral relationship with China which could provoke Japan, Stalin nevertheless agreed to provide China with planes and tanks in return for Chiang

45 Fox, 232–3.

Kai-shek's pledge not to use them against the Soviets. (This was the tenor of the non-aggression pact the two countries signed in August 1937.) But this was to be part of a more general system of aid to China. Russian diplomats were eager to work through the League of Nations, which the Soviet Union had joined in 1934, and to approach the United States, Britain and others for joint sanction against Japan.[46] The Soviets were eager for a meeting of the Washington Conference signatories, and they sent a representative to the Brussels Conference, convened in November 1937. This was the first time that Russia participated in an international conference dealing with the Far East.

The Brussels Conference, though it did not produce the international resolve and commitment the Soviets had hoped for, clearly marked the point where Russia, together with America and Britain, sought to isolate Japan and bolster China as much as possible to 'reinforce international security', as Le journal de Moscou put it. Brussels' meagre results – the delegates merely reiterated the powers' interest in a settlement compatible with the nine-power treaty of 1922, and no sanctions against Japan were adopted – did not obscure the fact that it clearly internationalized the Sino-Japanese War, and was thus in line with President Roosevelt's quarantine speech of October 1937, in which he had called upon all peace-loving nations to isolate aggressive forces in the world. By the end of 1937, it was clear that Japan's international position was eroding, and China's being enhanced in inverse proportion.

The only setback for China, and Japan's principal gain, was Germany's decision to recognize Manchukuo. By the end of 1937 Hitler had decided to annex Austria and Czechoslovakia so as to create an enlarged and economically more viable empire, and prepare for the ultimate 'holy war' against the Soviet Union. But it was necessary to neutralize Great Britain in Asia by an entente with Japan, just as the Berlin-Rome Axis would check Britain in Europe. Japan's cooperation must be bought by Germany's withdrawing military advisers from China and recognizing Manchukuo. Hitler was willing to take these drastic steps because he anticipated a showdown with Britain, and because he was led to believe, by his pro-Japanese aides, that China was destined to lose the war. This gamble would cost Germany dearly.

At the beginning of 1938, the Chinese could feel much less isolated. The Brussels Conference had at least shown that most countries interested in the Far East were united in sympathy for China. The Soviet Union was delivering hundreds of planes and guns. Russian pilots were arriving

[46] Nathan Haslam, 'Soviet aid to China and Japan's place in Moscow's foreign policy, 1937–1939', in Ian Nish, ed. Some aspects of Soviet-Japanese relations in the 1930s, 39–40.

in Chungking. More important, the United States and Britain were showing signs, cautious to be sure, of working together in Asian matters – as when Captain Royal E. Ingersoll of the United States navy went to London in January 1938 to exchange information on joint strategy toward Japan.[47] Chungking now had the undoubted support of America, Britain and Russia. The Sino-Japanese War fitted into their global policies to a far greater extent than before. Whereas the Manchurian crisis had mobilized the powers to preserve the existing framework of international relations, which they were forced to abandon, this time the Western powers were determined to oppose Japan's and possibly Germany's attempt to redefine the structure of world affairs. China would play a major role in new conceptions that were being developed for organizing a global alliance against Germany and Japan. The emerging alliance had two components. One was a carryover from the earlier anti-fascist popular front promulgated by Russia. The other was a scheme for Anglo-American cooperation, resurrected after years of neglect. Both were designed to restrain the fascist nations, particularly Japan, but they had different connotations. The popular front was broader in scope, the Anglo-American arrangement was more narrow. Ideologically, the former retained left-wing connotations, although much diluted, whereas the latter was oriented toward liberal democratic principles. It was not clear whether two such contrasting alignments could in fact be combined to form an effective power bloc. But in any case China could be fitted into both of them quite nicely. China qualified as anti-fascist, while at the same time it could be received into the Anglo-American democratic coalition as an honorary member, so to speak. In the Asian context, at least, China united under Chiang Kai-shek appeared as democratic as could be expected in wartime. While few claimed then that China was fighting for democracy, it was entirely clear that its people were refusing to submit to fascist invaders who were committing acts of pillage and carnage like the 'rape of Nanking'. The heroic resistance of the Chinese drew American and British admiration throughout 1938.

Unfortunately for China, the nascent global coalition against Japan underwent additional changes in 1938 and 1939 because of developments in Europe. For most of those two years, the popular front and the Anglo-American coalition were joined by a third scheme designed to stabilize international, in particular European affairs. This was the appeasement strategy, an alternative to the Soviet-initiated popular front and to the exclusively democratic combination of the United States and Britain,

---

[47] Peter Lowe, *Great Britain and the origins of the Pacific war: a study of British policy in East Asia, 1939–1941*, 34–5.

although in fact all three were pursued simultaneously. To put it in perspective, appeasement was an effort to return to some sort of internationalism, political as well as economic, to prevent the world from becoming hopelessly divided. Even though it was well recognized that the post-1919 internationalist framework could not be resurrected in toto, it appeared possible to the exponents of this scheme at least to strive for an end to the economic and political division of the 1930s world and re-establish machinery for global interdependence. Just as economic forces had been the basis for the 1920s internationalism, so were they viewed as the key to the new attempt. The roots of the international tensions appeared to be economic, so that if stability were to return to the world stage it would be necessary to recreate conditions favourable for the industrialization, trade and economic growth of all countries, including even Germany, Japan and Italy. Here was the major difference between appeasement and the other alternatives. Appeasement would not mean much unless all principal countries joined together for economic reintegration. The fascist powers would have to be brought into the scheme; in fact, this was the justification for the diplomacy of appeasement. It assumed, of course, that the Germans, Japanese and Italians shared the same concern over the economic roots of conflict and an interest in working with other countries for a better international order.

Such an idea had been there in the early 1930s, but had not been vigorously pursued; the Western countries, too, had adopted nationalistic economic policies. Now, for the first time in the decade, an opportunity seemed ripe for one more effort. In most countries industrial output had regained the level of 1929, yet world trade was still less than half its value before the depression. If peace were to be securely founded, it seemed vital to push for an open world market to encourage trade and investment. If Germany and Japan could be persuaded to concentrate on those activities, rather than militaristic aggrandizement, then they too could be part of the new arrangement. The advocates of appeasement saw it as a far preferable alternative to the popular front or the Anglo-American coalition, both of which could be divisive rather than reintegrationist, since both had the potential of turning into a global military alliance against the fascist nations, and the appeasement alternative was a way of avoiding such confrontations. It gave priority to reintegrating the advanced nations of Germany, Italy and Japan over cooperating with Russia or China.

The Chinese, for that reason, were disheartened by the appeasement diplomacy pursued by the United States and Britain throughout 1938. To be sure, the diplomacy primarily concerned Europe, not Asia. The British government, uncertain of the wisdom of too close a link to America and still confident of working with Hitler, sought to appease him over Czechoslovakia in the Munich agreement of September. The United States hailed it as an important accomplishment that would help re-establish internationalism. Asia was not directly involved, and neither Britain nor America wanted to apply a similar strategy to Japan, which was far more explicitly aggressive than Germany. Lord Halifax, who master-minded the Munich appeasement together with Prime Minister Neville Chamberlain, commented in May, 'China is fighting the battle of all the law-abiding States and she is incidentally fighting our own battle in the Far East, for if Japan wins, our interests there are certainly doomed to extinction.'[48] This was no language of appeasement toward Japan. Though the British were wary of war with Japan, they were far more willing to aid China than Czechoslovakia. The Americans, likewise, while applauding Munich, left no doubt as to their preferred course in Asia. Negotiations were begun in the autumn of 1938 for a loan of US $25 million to China, a modest amount but the first formal American commitment. Shortly before the loan announcement, when the Japanese government issued its 'new order in Asia' statement, both Washington and London quickly denounced it. Although they did not act jointly, Britain made sure that its position would approximate America's, and that the Japanese would know this.[49] The Soviet Union, while cautious toward Japan, was increasingly confident of its position in the Far East, due in part to the continued resistance by the Chinese, and also to the reports by Richard Sorge's spy ring in Tokyo that Japan was not prepared to fight Russia.[50] The Soviet leadership was aware that in giving China the most substantial outside help at this time it did not risk isolation, and that there was a good chance of the Anglo-American powers stepping up international pressures on Japan, of which Soviet power would form a part.

If these were encouraging signs from the Chinese point of view, British and American appeasement in Europe could not but affect Asia. This became evident when Stalin, seeing Munich as evidence of the capitalist countries' willingness to patch up their differences with the Nazis, moved during the spring and summer of 1939 steadily away from the popular front and cooperation with the Anglo-Americans to an accommodation with Germany. This was only a temporary expedient in response to the apparent eagerness of the Western governments to reintegrate Germany and Italy while once again isolating Russia from the world community. Although such fears were exaggerated, appeasement and the popular front

[48] Ibid. 41–2.   [49] Ibid. 50–3.   [50] Haslam, 48–9.

were incompatible. When Stalin entered into a non-aggression pact with Hitler in August 1939, the implications were obvious; the popular front was dead, and the world's anti-fascist forces – individuals and groups – were thoroughly dismayed. What was going to replace it? Appeasement, too, had to be a casualty, for an agreement between Germany and Russia was certainly not what the British, French and American governments had envisaged when they promoted reintegrationism. The Anti-Comintern Pact, too, was dealt a blow; a fascist coalition against the Soviet Communist state made no sense when a member of it was openly consorting with Russia.

For China these were appalling developments. The Nazi-Soviet rapprochement destroyed hope of cooperation among Britain, America and Russia in world affairs. Moreover, with Germany openly defying the Munich agreement by absorbing Czechoslovakia and intent upon attacking Poland next, Britain and the United States were likely to be preoccupied with Europe, yet the United States was still far more reluctant than the European countries to resist Germany by force. The only glimmer of hope for the Chinese was the fact that the Nazi-Soviet pact enabled the Soviet Union to transfer a large number of troops to the Far East; the Nomonhan incident, involving skirmishes between Russian and Japanese forces along the Manchurian-Mongolian border in the summer of 1939, demonstrated the superiority of Russian fire-power.

By the time the Second World War broke out in September 1939, therefore, the promising beginnings of cooperation among Britain, the United States, the Soviet Union and China had been replaced by a more fluid situation. With German-Japanese relations strained, there was even a chance that Tokyo might also reorient its policy, especially in view of the abrogation of the treaty of commerce with the United States, which Washington had announced in July as a unilateral act to put pressure on Japan. It had the desired effect of shocking Tokyo's officials into scrambling for ways to ameliorate Japanese-American relations. In the autumn and winter of 1939, during the European 'phony war', Japan and the United States carried on talks to see if they could agree upon a common definition of the status quo. If successful, they might have built a new stability on the de facto presence of Japanese power in China. The Chinese would have been the more discouraged, if they had known that some in London, notably Parliamentary Under-Secretary R. A. Butler, were talking vaguely about resurrecting the Anglo-Japanese alliance as a way of containing the Far Eastern crisis.[51]

Yet a Far Eastern appeasement, which would have been a devastating

[51] Lowe, *Pacific war*, 106.

blow to Free China, was not to be. Both Britain and America would have been interested in reintegrating Japan into a cooperative scheme, but not on the terms the Japanese insisted upon. Despite its overtures to Washington and London at the time for improving their relations, Tokyo could not give up its commitments in China, for it could not restrain its military. Even while the government sought to improve relations with London and Washington, it had to proclaim the establishment of a puppet regime in Nanking under Wang Ching-wei, an act certainly calculated to frustrate any negotiations with the West. As a British diplomat wrote, 'Let us see how much genuine Chinese support her new regime in China can command before we take an attitude towards it. And above all let us see how Japan is going to satisfy the United States Government in the forthcoming struggle about the commercial treaty, without allowing a wedge to be driven between ourselves and the Americans.'[52]

As can be seen in such a quote, the European war tied Britain and the United States together. An Anglo-American partnership re-emerged, now shorn of connotations of Soviet participation, or of the appeasement of the fascist states. It would be a genuine bilateral alliance for the preservation of democracy. (President Roosevelt would term his country the arsenal of democracy.) Power and ideals were firmly joined; as Reinhold Niebuhr wrote in his *Christianity and power politics*, the cherished civilization of the democracies could not be saved without power, for to do nothing would merely encourage further aggression. Peace was no longer a viable alternative, certainly not a peace of inaction, under-armament, and appeasement of fascist states. Thus international affairs in 1940 saw the clear emergence of the Anglo-American alliance upon the demise of the popular front and appeasement. All that remained was to globalize it, to have it applied in Asia as well as Europe.

This was accomplished when the European and the East Asian wars merged as a result of the German spring offensive of 1940 in France. Almost instantaneously, it rekindled the Japanese leaders' interest in a German alliance. Germany's victories in Europe offered Japan a unique opportunity to seize areas south of China, cutting off outside help to Chungking while obtaining the region's rich resources. For Berlin, a Japanese alliance would immobilize the United States in Asia and prevent its intervention in Europe. Such logic inevitably produced the Axis alliance of September 1940. It also brought the two wars into proximity.

To be sure, Anglo-American concentration on defending Britain could mean a lower priority for Asia, but they would never sacrifice China in order to appease Japan, now that appeasement of Germany had been given

[52] *Ibid.* 124.

up, and Japan and Germany were closely linked. All this enhanced the importance of China once again, as before 1938. This time, of course, the Soviet Union was not part of the pro-China coalition. Indeed, toward the end of 1940, as it became clear that Hitler would repudiate the non-aggression pact and turn on him, Stalin sought to mend fences with Japan so as to avoid a two-front war. Slowly but unmistakably, the Soviet Union and Japan effected a rapprochement, signing their neutrality pact in April 1941. The Soviet Union now definitely abandoned the popular front in Asia as well as in Europe. Meanwhile the increasing American and British support of China was being reinforced by the Dutch in the East Indies. Although the Netherlands had fallen to the Nazis, the Dutch colonial regime maintained its semi-independent existence and stubbornly resisted the Japanese efforts to procure petroleum. Dutch officials consulted closely their American and British counterparts, and the three devised a joint approach to Japan. This created the so-called ABCD group – America, Britain, China and the Dutch East Indies – which, while by no means a well-defined entity, at least provided for joint action and put immense psychological pressure on the Japanese. For their dreaded isolation in Asia was becoming a reality, which their ties to Germany and Italy did little to counter. The Axis alliance could not help Japan cope with the 'ABCD encirclement'.

Thus China found itself once again a part of the globalized Anglo-American alliance to prevent the Axis domination of the world. China's position now seemed far more secure, its destiny bound up with that of America and Britain. The United States brought China into its global strategy specifically by providing aviation experts, 'volunteer' pilots and aircraft, organized as the Flying Tigers, to fight the Japanese air force in China. When Congress enacted the Lend-Lease bill, Washington immediately applied the programme of aid to China as well as to Britain. London stiffened its policy toward Japan, confident of American support. While the Anglo-American strategic talks (the so-called 'ABC' sessions) in the winter of 1940–1 reaffirmed the primacy of the European theatre, the participants also agreed to coordinate strategic action in the Pacific. Above all, as the American and British leaders pledged to preserve democracy in the world, China, too, became part of their fight for democracy. In other words, by becoming part of the global struggle for power, China could be assured of ultimate deliverance from Japan. No wonder, then, that the Japanese-American negotiations that took place in Washington intermittently throughout 1941 reached no conclusion. The talks reflected Japanese desperation and a tactic to divide America from China by asking Washington to press Chungking to settle the war.

But American officials, though they agreed to continue the talks, primarily to gain time for military preparation, had no thought of accepting Japanese control over China.

China's international position was further strengthened when, on 22 June 1941, Hitler's army attacked Stalin's. The Nazi invasion added Russia to the Anglo-American–Chinese coalition. The German-Russian war meant a reprieve for Britain on the western front, while forcing the Soviet Union to shift its forces away from Asia to defend European Russia. When Japan decided not to attack Russia from the rear, but instead remain neutral, the Chinese realized they could get much less help from the Russians than before. Yet Soviet re-entry into the war resurrected the popular front and merged it into the Anglo-American alliance. China would now be part of this comprehensive alliance, and of the victory that was expected to be the allies' sooner or later. As the London *Times* correspondent reported from Chungking, in the Chinese view 'the German attack on Russia has at last aligned the free peoples of the world, led by the ABC front, against the forces of aggression'. In contrast, Japan's position was expected to become 'more hazardous, beset by economic difficulties, uncertain of her friends, and tempted by moves which might easily bring her into open conflict with Russia, Britain, the Indies, and possibly the United States, when she has over 1,000,000 troops tied up in China'.[53] Such thinking reflected confidence that China had at last succeeded in isolating Japan, while itself becoming one of the key powers in the world.

The ideology of the global war became more clear after the German assault on the Soviet Union. The Anglo-American allies and the Soviet Communists were now all together in a common task of defeating the Axis. The popular front and the democratic alliance were fused. An American writer termed the new alliance a 'world democratic front', an apt phrase combining the two earlier conceptions.[54] No longer would American democracy be sufficient unto itself; it would become part of a global movement for freedom. This new internationalism was best expressed in the joint declaration by Franklin D. Roosevelt and Winston Churchill at the end of their meeting in the Atlantic in August 1941, the Atlantic Charter. The two leaders pledged not merely to coordinate their countries' military resources and strategies, but also to cooperate to bring about a more secure and just international order. The charter enumerated principles such as self-determination, economic interdependence, international cooperation, collective security and arms reduction. By subscribing

[53] F 10904/280/10, in FO 371/27670, Foreign Office Archives, Public Record Office (London).
[54] *New Republic*, 105.8 (25 Aug. 1941) 238.

to them, China would join the Anglo-American democracies and make the war against Japan part of the global struggle for democracy. The Japanese, in contrast, felt themselves ostracized. As *Asahi* commented, the Atlantic Charter signified America's readiness to enter the war on the side of Britain and Russia, and also revealed an effort to appeal to Europeans and Asians alike to join the United States and Britain in the name of the new principles and to isolate Germany, Italy and Japan.[55]

Japan was clearly put on the defensive, forced either to effect some rapprochement with the Anglo-American powers to detach them from China, or to give up all such attempts and consolidate its Asian empire. In fact Tokyo pursued both these courses simultaneously. On the one hand, the talks in Washington were resumed after the Atlantic Conference. Even when Prime Minister Konoe was replaced by General Tōjō Hideki, representing the army's belligerent stance, it was considered wise to continue the talks to see if the United States would be willing to resume trade with Japan, lessen its commitment to China, and avoid a showdown in the Pacific. Any such agreement would, of course, be a blow to China's leaders, who were extremely sensitive about the Washington conversations. London, too, did not want the United States to make concessions to Japan at the expense of China; they would merely embolden Japan and reduce the likelihood of American military involvement in the Pacific. Thus during September to December 1941 Chinese and British officials kept in close contact with one another, anxiously awaiting the outcome of the Washington talks. As the British ambassador reported from Chungking, there was 'widespread and growing anxiety lest [the] United States Government, with ourselves following them, mean to sell out the Chinese'. The British sought to reassure the Chinese that it was inconceivable 'that the United States should have any idea of selling China down the river'. All of them 'were fighting the same war, whether in Europe or the Pacific'.[56] The idea that there was a global democratic alliance and that China should never be sacrificed in the short-term interest of preserving peace with an aggressive Japan was one that both Chiang Kai-shek and Churchill communicated to Roosevelt in late November, when they got wind of a modus vivendi being worked out in Washington. The president accepted their argument and, for this and other reasons, rejected the modus vivendi proposal. He could not have done otherwise. The only agreement with Japan that would have been acceptable to Chungking and London would have been along the lines of the Hull note of 26 November, calling on the Japanese army to evacuate China as well

55 *Asahi*, 16 Aug. (evening), 1941.
56 F 8496/60/10 and F 9109/60/10, in FO 371/27615, Foreign Office Archives.

as Indo-China and advising the Japanese nation to go back to the internationalism of the 1920s. In other words, they must join the democracies, or else remain ostracized.

The Japanese were coming to the same conclusion. Unless they made drastic concessions to the United States, and therefore to China, they would have to face the continued and solid opposition of the Western powers and be prepared to defend what they had even at the risk of war. That was the reasoning behind the war plans they worked out in the autumn of 1941 even as they talked in Washington. On the assumption that the Washington negotiations would lead nowhere, Japan's military and civilian leaders decided to face the possibility of war with America and Britain, in addition to China, in the near future. The most effective way of conducting such warfare would be to establish an impregnable Asian empire with access to the rich resources of South-East Asia. At the same time, Japan's armed forces would strike at the American and British fleets, to purge the region of potential threats to the empire. The plans made in early September signalled Japan's resolve to take on the major powers of the world. Japan would defend its isolated position by establishing Asian hegemony.

At that late hour, war could have been avoided only by the Japanese agreeing to the terms offered by the United States, specifically by endorsing the Atlantic Charter, the Hull note, and related documents expressive of American internationalism. This would have amounted to accepting the idea that Japan remained a member of the international community as defined by the Anglo-American powers and would be guided by its rules, including the recognition of Chinese sovereignty and independence. While a few Japanese leaders were ready to seek a peace on those bases, for the Tōjō cabinet and the military such a course would have meant giving up everything they had striven for since 1931. Faced with the choice of either rejoining the Western powers or defying them, Japan opted for defiance. War came in December 1941.

The Pacific war merged the Sino-Japanese conflict and the Japanese-American struggle, making China a fully-fledged member of the grand alliance against the Axis nations. For the first time since 1931, the Chinese could feel they were truly part of a global coalition.

CHINA AND JAPAN IN THE SECOND WORLD WAR 1941–1945

At the beginning of the Pacific war, Japanese forces successfully occupied Hong Kong, Singapore, Malaya, Burma, and other areas in South-East Asia, to seal off China from the outside world. For two years, the only routes available for shipment of supplies would be either the air route over the eastern end of the Himalayas or the north-west overland route from Russia through Sinkiang. This isolation gave China less importance in the global military situation. Naval and air battles in the Pacific, or the deadly struggles for a beachhead in the South Seas, would prove more decisive than skirmishes in China. The situation gave rise to the view, almost from the beginning of the Pacific war, that the fate of China was largely in the hands of its Anglo-American allies, and that the Chinese knew this. Barely two weeks after Pearl Harbor, a top British official was commenting that 'the Chinese will sit back and let the United States and ourselves fight Japan'. Even so, he went on, China would claim to have played a major role in the defeat of the enemy and insist on a say at the postwar peace settlement.[57]

The anomaly that China's military role would decline while its status as a major power would remain became more obvious as the war went on. This was, of course, far from Chinese intentions. From the beginning, the Nationalist leadership insisted on joining the Allies as a full-fledged co-belligerent under a unified command. Chiang Kai-shek did not conceal his chagrin that he was being consulted less frequently on matters of strategy than Stalin, not to mention Churchill, who made regular trips to Washington to discuss military plans with Roosevelt. Apart from the formation, in January 1942, of the United Nations, a loose apparatus including all governments at war with the Axis (they issued a declaration subscribing to the principles of the Atlantic Charter), the main inter-allied cooperation in Asia was to set up the China–Burma–India theatre, but even here Chinese, British and American forces had their respective commanders, and there was little institutional coordination among them. The American general, Joseph Stilwell, was sent as Roosevelt's representative to Chungking to assume control over United States forces in the theatre and be Chiang's nominal chief of staff, but there was a notable lack of communication between him and Chiang Kai-shek. Nor were Chinese-British relations anything other than stormy. The British command in India and the Nationalist leadership constantly disagreed over military operations in Burma. There was, in short, no formal alliance between China, the United States, Britain, and other countries in Asia fighting against Japan.

This unsatisfactory situation did not prevent the Chinese from presenting their country as a key member of an international coalition, both during the war and in its aftermath. To them it was axiomatic that China, having alone stood up to the Japanese challenge for so long, had led the way

[57] F 14155/13469/10, in FO 371/27753, *ibid.*

to creating such a coalition, and that it should be perpetuated after victory as the framework for postwar international order. As a *Ta-kung-pao* editorial noted on the first anniversary of Pearl Harbor, in 1942, when China was weak and unprepared, Chiang Kai-shek had nevertheless resolved to resist Japanese aggression because he and his countrymen knew that in time their friends would join them. The American rejection of Japanese terms in November 1941 had clearly indicated that Roosevelt and Churchill would not sacrifice China. Thus China, America and Britain were 'natural and dependable allies', and should remain so for ever. Allied cooperation should continue in the future with one power – China – entrusted to watch over Japan. *Ta-kung-pao* editorials in January 1943 asserted that the wartime coalition should see to the independence of Korea and the retrocession of Taiwan, the Ryūkyūs (Liuchius) and Manchuria to China. The Chinese, 'with all their hearts and minds', wanted to join in the collective security of a newly constructed world order.[58] It would be necessary to eradicate Japanese militarism once and for all. But no permanent subjugation of Japan was envisaged. Chinese leaders distinguished the Japanese people from their military. Chinese opinion was divided as to the advisability of destroying the emperor system but, ultimately, it should be possible to reconstruct Japan as a peaceful, democratic nation. China, of course, would closely watch over such a transformation. A democratic Japan, therefore, would be possible only if there emerged a strong China.[59]

Realizing this self-confident vision would depend both on Chinese ability to make good their claims as a major world power and on the willingness of other countries to accept the idea. Before the Cairo meeting of November 1943 Chaing Kai-shek had not personally been invited to meet with the American or the British leader. Churchill had never disguised his scorn at the idea of China as a world power. He had, to be sure, strongly promoted the idea of Anglo-Chinese cooperation prior to Pearl Harbor, and continued to believe in China's strategic significance in pinning down Japanese forces. But he did not welcome the possibility that China might be a crucial part of a postwar world coalition. When Roosevelt insisted, at his meeting with Foreign Secretary Anthony Eden in March 1943, on 'the need to associate China with other world Powers in the solution of world problems', Churchill immediately retorted, 'It is quite untrue to say that China is a world power equal to Britain, the United States or Russia.' He vetoed a Foreign Office statement that 'in the solution of the wider problems of world reconstruction which will

58 *Ta-kung-pao* editorials, 7 and 8 Dec. 1942; 3 and 9 Jan. 1943.
59 *Ibid.* 29 Jan. 1943.

confront us... we look upon China as one of the four leading Powers who have the greatest contributions to make'. China's status as one of the major powers after the war would give it a say in all sorts of matters throughout the world. But, Churchill wrote,

> The idea that China is going to have a say in the affairs of Europe 'other than ceremonial', or that China should be rated for European purposes above France or Poland or whatever takes the place of Austria-Hungary, or above even the smallest but ancient, historic and glorious States like Holland, Belgium, Greece and Yugoslavia – has only to be stated to be dismissed.[60]

Despite such negative views, British authorities had joined the Americans in signing new treaties with the Nationalists at the beginning of 1943, formally relinquishing extraterritoriality in China, a symbolic gesture to counter Japanese propaganda about Anglo-American imperialism but also an important step in bolstering China's sovereignty. More important, Churchill had gone along with American proposals for a conference of the four powers' foreign ministers, convened in Moscow in October. In the American view, the conference was an initial step to ensuring that the four powers' united action, 'pledged for the prosecution of the war, will be continued for the organization and maintenance of peace and security'.[61] This idea, a product of wartime American perceptions, was best exemplified by the words of Roosevelt cited above, since American officials considered it axiomatic that China would sooner or later develop into a modern, industrialized, militarily strong power, paralleling Japan's growth after the middle of the nineteenth century. Japan had begun as a responsible member of the international community and then deviated. The same thing should not be allowed to happen in the case of China. The best assurance of retaining Chinese cooperation was to start associating China more fully with the other powers so it would not go its own way. Although such ideas impressed most British officials as American romanticism, the United States succeeded in holding the Moscow conference, where the foreign ministers of America, Britain, Russia and China put their signatures to a declaration pledging continued cooperation after the war. This was followed within two months by the meeting of Roosevelt, Churchill and Chiang Kai-shek in Cairo, truly the high point of wartime collaboration among the three leaders. Although the fourth, Stalin, did not come to Cairo, as he hesitated to attend a conference of heads of states that were at war with Japan, he met with Roosevelt and Churchill at Teheran (2–7 December 1943), immediately after the Cairo meeting, thus in effect formalizing the framework of

---

[60] PREM 4, 28/9 and 30/11, Prime Minister's Papers, Public Record Office.
[61] US Department of State, *Postwar foreign policy preparation, 1939–1945*, 553.

four-power collaboration. At Cairo, Roosevelt and Churchill endorsed territorial changes on which the Chinese had insisted, namely the retrocession of Taiwan and Manchuria to China, and the independence, 'in due course', of Korea. The Cairo declaration of 1 December, which mentioned these changes, was silent on the future status of the Ryūkyūs, indicating that the Chinese view that the islands should revert to them was not shared by the Americans and British. (Officials in Washington who had studied the question had concluded that the islands could, if thoroughly demilitarized, be retained by Japan.) The Chinese felt euphoric that at last their leader was receiving his due as one of the world's great statesmen, and that their country was being assured an extensive role in a postwar international partnership. A *Ta-kung-pao* editorial asserted that by reducing Japan to its position before Perry, the three powers were providing a fundamental solution to Far Eastern problems. The four powers would now 'seize the destiny of the Pacific Ocean in their hands'.[62] Unfortunately the Cairo Conference was the high point of Anglo-American–Chinese agreement in postwar collaboration, for it was followed by disappointment and disillusion. By early 1944 two significant, interrelated developments were making a smooth transition to postwar order all but impossible. One was the prospect of Soviet entry into the war against Japan, and the other was the worsening domestic situation in China.

Soviet entry into the Japanese war, which was confirmed at the Cairo and Teheran Conferences, was accepted as inevitable by the Chinese who, at the same time, sought to ensure that it would not diminish the importance of the China theatre. Chiang Kai-shek and the Nationalist leaders renewed their call for more military assistance from the Allies, in particular the United States. Their request for a billion dollar loan from America shortly after the Cairo Conference was to build up the armed strength of China the better to defend the country against an expected Japanese offensive, and also to strengthen China under the Nationalists in preparation for the coming of peace. Since a Soviet arms buildup in Asia now had to be accepted, it would be important to match Soviet power with Chinese, if China were to remain a partner of the international coalition after the war.

Unfortunately, the United States refused to act on the loan request. As Ambassador Clarence E. Gauss cabled from Chungking, the Moscow and Cairo Conferences had already indicated the Allies' willingness to consider China a great power, and there was now no need to provide the Chinese

[62] *Ta-kung-pao* editorials, 3 and 7 Dec. 1943.

with a huge loan to affirm that decision.[63] To make matters worse for Chiang Kai-shek, after Cairo President Roosevelt and other American officials began entertaining misgivings about his leadership. At Cairo General Stilwell and his political adviser, John Paton Davies, second secretary at the United States embassy in Chungking, met Roosevelt and conveyed critical views of Chiang. On 31 December Davies wrote to Harry Hopkins (for Roosevelt's attention) that the generalissimo was 'probably the only Chinese who shares the popular American misconception that Chiang Kai-shek is China'. He was in fact no national leader, but only the head of a faction. 'His philosophy is the unintegrated product of his limited intelligence, his Japanese military education, his former close contact with German military advisers, his alliance with the usurious banker-landlord class, and his reversion to the sterile moralisms of the Chinese classics.' It was wrong, Davies implied, to turn to such a man as the sole object of allied support. The real China – more democratic, energetic, and willing to fight the war in cooperation with the United Nations – was to be found outside the coterie of the Nationalist leadership, Davies asserted. He, and an increasing number of American officials, were turning their attention to the Communists in the north-west, who impressed them as more likely ingredients in a vigorous 'democratic coalition' that would deserve allied support. If China were to become part of a system of international cooperation, it appeared better not to deal solely with the Nationalists who, Gauss asserted, were drifting 'definitely away from...liberal principles for mutually beneficial world economy', but to work with the Communists among whom, another official noted, 'we will find our most reliable information and our most devoted support'.[64]

These contrasting perceptions of the Nationalists and the Communists were confirmed throughout 1944. That year the Japanese Ichigo offensive (see chapter 11) against Nationalist-held areas was a remarkable success. The Communists in North China, in contrast, added to areas under their control. When the United States, with Chiang's reluctant agreement, sent an observation mission to Yenan in July 1944, its members were enormously impressed with what they found. 'We have come into a different country and are meeting a different people,' reported John S. Service, a foreign service officer. He and his colleagues found Yenan filled with energy, a place where leaders and masses alike seemed dedicated to the task of fighting the enemy and building a new society. Mao Tse-tung

[63] Akira Iriye, *Power and culture: the Japanese-American war, 1941–1945*, 156.
[64] President's Secretary's file: China, Franklin D. Roosevelt Papers (Hyde Park).

told Service the Chinese Communists wanted to cooperate with the United States both in war and after the war. The Communists must be equipped with American arms and trained by American officers, and the United States must cease to deal only with Chungking but put pressure on the Nationalists to share power with other groups.[65]

The Chinese Communists were thus emerging as a factor in wartime and postwar cooperation between China and other great powers. Aid to a Nationalist-dominated China would exacerbate tensions within Chinese society and keep the country divided. But for power to be more evenly distributed and China to be militarily and politically less divided, there would have to be a coalition of the various factions and, most important, the unification of all armed forces – a colossal undertaking, especially if it were to be brought about without a civil war.

Both alternatives contained risks, and there was no assurance that either would work. Moreover, both possibilities threatened to involve the United States and other countries in Chinese domestic politics. Whether the Nationalists were to be singled out for continued support, or to be pressed to share power with other groups, the United States, and to a lesser extent Britain and the Soviet Union, would have a decisive influence. This was inevitable, given the idea of international cooperation including China. The only way foreign powers could avoid becoming involved in Chinese politics would be by giving up schemes for cooperation and by reverting to an earlier strategy of managing affairs among themselves, relegating China merely to the status of a passive observer. That, of course, would nullify everything that the country had achieved in international status through its struggle against Japan after 1931.

These were serious dilemmas, and it is not surprising that no clearcut alternative was pursued by the powers at this time. The United States, the most influential outside factor, in effect carried out three approaches simultaneously during 1944 and 1945. The first and most desirable approach, from Washington's point of view, was to encourage Chinese unification through peaceful means. The attempt took a dramatic form in July 1944 when President Roosevelt asked Chiang Kai-shek to appoint General Stilwell commander of all Chinese forces. A unified command would, it was hoped, pave the way to establishment of a coalition government including Communists and other dissidents, which in turn would ensure China's emergence after the war as a full-fledged partner on the international scene. Sino-American collaboration, as the Chungking embassy stressed, thus hinged on the Nationalists' willingness to effect

[65] Michael Schaller, *The US crusade in China, 1938–1945*, 183–7.

domestic reforms and share power, and Stilwell's appointment seemed to be the first necessary step in that direction.[66]

This scheme was nipped in the bud when Chiang Kai-shek, after some initial hesitation, resolutely refused Roosevelt's request to place Stilwell in command of the Chinese forces. The idea held Communist support, but for that very reason was unacceptable to Chiang. Rather than meekly relinquishing his power, he decided to fight, gambling on America's reluctance to face a showdown with its wartime ally. He was correct. Roosevelt backed down, and the Stilwell scheme never materialized. Instead, American policy, now under the influence of General Patrick J. Hurley, who was sent as a special envoy to Chungking to ease tensions, reverted to the support of the Nationalist regime as the sole government of China. This was the second approach. Although Hurley would work energetically to bring about a coalition government in China, he never deviated from his support of Chiang, thus steadily alienating the Communists from the United States.

The idea of promoting a unified China through peaceful means would not be given up by America, but it never again took as dramatic a form as it did during the Stilwell episode. His recall and replacement by General Albert Wedemeyer at the end of 1944 marked the end of an era, an erosion of the concept of close collaboration between China and the powers. Roosevelt was exasperated by what he took to be Chiang Kai-shek's inability to see the cardinal importance of strengthening China's military capabilities. After the Stilwell episode, the American press began harping on the theme that the Chinese would not unite to fight but would rather turn on one another. An inevitable consequence of such developments was the emergence of a third theme: the diminishing importance the United States gave to China as a partner not only in the war but also after victory. A good indication of this may be provided by Prime Minister Churchill's perception of what he took to be American infatuation with a vision of China as a great power. Whereas he wrote, in August 1944, 'that China is one of the world's four great Powers is an absolute farce', only a month later, in the wake of the Stilwell imbroglio, he was able to note, 'The American illusion about China is being dispelled.' This, he said, was because of China's internal rift and 'the grotesque Chinese military failure in spite of all that the Americans have done'.[67] In the British embassy in Washington, Isaiah Berlin remarked at about the same time, 'Chinese stock has never been lower in official circles ... China is getting the treatment which we were accorded after Tobruk. Our own

[66] Iriye, *Power*, 199.
[67] PREM 4, 30/11, Prime Minister's Papers.

position is enhanced by contrast'.[68] The war cabinet in London agreed, noting that 'partly as a result of the friction between China and the United States, the British position [has] been improved'.[69]

In the winter of 1944–5 the United States solidified its ties with both Britain and Russia to such an extent that the vaunted big-four cooperation was being reduced to big-three collaboration. The meeting of Roosevelt, Churchill and Stalin at Yalta in February 1945, as the Chinese correctly judged then and since, put an end to the concept of China's full partnership in world affairs. At Yalta Stalin once again promised to enter the war against Japan approximately three months after Germany's defeat; he also reiterated his terms, and the three leaders agreed that after the war Russia would regain south Sakhalin and the Kurile Islands, lease the naval base of Port Arthur, establish a predominant position in Dairen, which was to be internationalized, and retain preponderant interests in the railways in Manchuria over which a joint Chinese-Russian agency would be established. These concessions, made without consulting the Chinese, formalized the impending establishment of a powerful Soviet sphere of power in north-eastern Asia, and a corresponding decline of China's position. Both Churchill and Roosevelt saw the situation in this light; the Soviet Union would gain a position of influence in Asia just as it did in Europe, and these spheres, together with British and American spheres of their own, would define the postwar global status quo. Gone was the vision of postwar cooperation among four powers, including China. Instead, America, Russia and Britain – and increasingly it was becoming evident that the first two would set themselves apart as a pair of super-powers – would serve as the definers and guarantors of the world after the peace. Where such an arrangement put China was not clear. The Yalta conferees accepted the Nationalist regime as the legitimate government of China. Stalin agreed with Roosevelt that Chiang Kai-shek should remain the dominant figure in Chinese politics.[70]

Russia's interest was to deal with Chiang and have him recognize the Yalta concessions on Manchuria. Stalin could not, of course, ignore the Chinese Communists, but apparently he did not believe they would soon emerge as plausible contenders for power. Nor was he insistent on forming a coalition government in China. His primary concern was with seizing strategic areas in north-eastern Asia, and he judged that this could best be achieved through an arrangement with the United States. He promised Roosevelt that the Soviet Union would negotiate with the

[68] Isaiah Berlin, Washington despatches, 1941–1945, 448.
[69] FE (44), CAB 96/5, Cabinet Papers, Public Record Office.
[70] Schaller, 211.

Nationalists to formalize the Manchurian agreement. But this very solicitousness of Chungking was at the expense of Chinese sovereignty and great-power status. About the only indication that the three wartime leaders were willing to consider China a major partner was their continued endorsement of the country as a permanent member of the executive (security) council in the new United Nations Organization that was to be established. But France, too, was being added to the permanent membership, and it meant little in view of the concessions in Manchuria and of the disunity in China. Whereas the three powers issued a declaration on liberated Europe, calling on each liberated country to establish representative government, no such announcement was made with respect to China. Roosevelt, Stalin and Churchill were content to leave the Chinese to their own devices. Without a unified, representative government, China's pretensions as a great power might be suspect, but the three Western nations were neither encouraging the growth of such government nor bolstering those pretensions.

That was the state of the once-powerful democratic partnership in early 1945. China had been fully incorporated into the coalition of all anti-fascist nations, but this global democratic front was being over-shadowed by the growing hegemony of the United States and the Soviet Union in world affairs. China's international position would now depend as much on developments in American-Soviet relations as on the course of the anti-fascist war.

The six months between Yalta and Japan's surrender in August 1945, moreover, witnessed the resurgence of an internationalist strain in American policy that harked back to prewar days. Earlier that internationalism had taken the form of appeasement of Germany and Japan in order to induce them to rejoin the world's capitalist, industrial nations as part of an open international system. The strategy had been replaced by the global democratic alliance, but internationalist thinking had never been totally submerged; it remained sufficiently resilient to provide the ideological basis of such wartime enunciations as the Atlantic Charter and the United Nations declaration. Now, toward the end of the war, internationalist formulations were once again affecting American policy, for the United States must now clarify its approaches toward postwar Germany and Japan. Although American officials remained divided on the treatment of Germany, with respect to Japan there was a remarkable consensus. Defeated Japan, they reasoned, should be deprived of its war machinery and thoroughly controlled so as not to present another menace to peace; at the same time, however, a reconstructed Japan should be encouraged to develop peaceful, commercial transactions with other countries as a member of an open international community. With such a Japan the United States would re-establish partnership, as it had before the Japanese began in the 1930s to chart their own course.

Although not the predominant strain in American policy toward Asia in 1945, such conceptions were nevertheless important, for they had at least a modicum of influence in ending the war in the Pacific. This was reflected in America's willingness to consider terminating the hostilities short of Japan's unconditional surrender, and the assurances given the Japanese that the United States and its allies did not insist on their subjugation. As best exemplified in the Potsdam declaration, issued in late July after a conference between President Harry S. Truman, Prime Minister Clement Attlee and Stalin, the idea was to disarm and punish but not to enslave or destroy Japan, which would eventually be permitted to participate in world trade relations. Moreover, the Japanese people would be encouraged to establish 'a peacefully inclined and responsible government' of their own. The Japanese acceptance, on 14 August, of the Potsdam declaration meant, whatever the legal niceties, that Japan was once again going to be integrated into an internationalist order and emerge, at some future time, as a responsible member of that community.

CHINA'S POSTWAR ECLIPSE 1945–1949

Chinese foreign policy at the war's end had to cope with two trends: the resurgence of reintegrationism, that is, collaboration among advanced industrial, capitalist nations on the one hand, and, on the other, the erosion of the worldwide democratic alliance because of the growth of Soviet and American power. Either way, China's relative position would suffer. The picture became even more complicated in the spring and early summer of 1945 when, following the death of President Roosevelt in April and Germany's surrender in May, tensions became visible in American-Soviet relations. In a sense the tensions were between the Anglo-American democratic coalition and the Soviet-initiated popular front. The two had been merged, after 1941, into a global democratic front, but had never been totally united. At Yalta the two formulations had been combined into the three-power scheme for postwar settlement, but the three were not able to sustain a solid framework for joint action. With the Soviet Union intent upon establishing 'friendly' regimes in Eastern Europe and extending its sphere of influence thereto, the United States was torn between going along with these developments so as to continue the popular front component of the grand alliance or emphasizing the democratic alliance component with a view to ensuring representative government in liberated Europe.

There were many possibilities, but none of them put China at the centre of the stage. At the end of the war, China seemed to occupy a back seat in the drama of world politics and postwar economic development. For this state of affairs, events inside China, of course, were in large part to blame. For the Chinese were never able to establish a unified government through peaceful means. Civil war erupted as soon as Japan surrendered. China was thrown into chaos, as the Nationalists waged a desperate struggle to survive the Communists' challenge.

The theme of international cooperation and Chinese willingness to share the responsibility for world order was reiterated by Nationalist spokesmen and the press throughout the immediate postwar years. These themes fitted admirably into the Nationalists' domestic programme. The stress on international solidarity and cooperation implied that other powers would assist the Nationalist regime in its task of postwar reconstruction. Such cooperation would enhance the government's prestige. It was absolutely essential to preserve the framework of international cooperation, for otherwise dissident elements in the country might turn to foreigners for help, or foreign governments might adopt discordant policies toward China to the detriment of political unity within the country.[71]

The Communists meanwhile feared that big-power cooperation would primarily benefit the recognized government, now re-established at Nanking, which would seize the opportunity to stamp out dissidence. For this reason, it was necessary to emphasize, as Mao Tse-tung and others did in 1945, that international cooperation should aim at promoting a truly representative government in China. They pushed for the establishment of a coalition government, and welcomed the mediatory effects of General George C. Marshall, launched in December 1945 and lasting throughout 1946. At the same time, however, the Communists feared the possibility that the United States, Britain, and even the Soviet Union might acquiesce in Nationalist control of China, and believed it important to consolidate and expand their bases in Manchuria and North China even as they supported the theme of international cooperation.[72] In time, as Marshall's efforts at mediation got nowhere and the civil war intensified, the Communists came openly to denounce the idea of international cooperation as a mask to conceal America's imperialistic ambitions, and to accuse the Nationalists of having sacrificed national welfare to those ambitions. The Nationalists, on their part, would turn more and more exclusively to the United States for support against the Communists. In the process, the ideal of China's position as a partner in the world arena would be eclipsed by

---

[71] *Chung-yang jih-pao*, 12 Sept., 21 and 25 Nov., 1945.
[72] See Okabe's and Nakajima's essays in Yōnosuke Nagai and Akira Iriye, eds. *The origins of the Cold War in Asia*.

that of its position as a member of one or other of the power blocs which now divided the once cooperative alliance of the big powers.

The erosion of the theme of international cooperation or, to put it differently, the origins of the American-Soviet Cold War can best be understood if one recalls that the wartime collaboration had contained three elements: the popular front, the democratic alliance, and reintegrationism. The victory over Germany and Japan did much to undermine the rationale for the popular front, although national leaders continued to pay lip-service to its underlying principle of anti-fascist struggle. That formulation was now to be applied to the postwar peace settlement to ensure the eradication of Axis militarism. But it was not sufficient to cope with new postwar problems, such as atomic weapons and anti-colonialism. In these and related matters, there was a tendency to revert to the Anglo-American democratic alliance, with its emphasis on the common interests and orientations of the Western democracies. In both the United States and Britain, Anglo-American cooperation, rather than Anglo-American–Soviet collaboration, re-emerged as the most plausible framework for postwar policy. In the meantime, the theme of reintegrationism grew in influence now that reconstruction of war-devastated lands dominated the concerns of governments. Economic recovery necessitated massive help by the one country that had retained and even increased its wealth during the war, the United States; and American officials avidly formulated principles for regional integration and development, resumption and expansion of global trade, and restabilization of world finances. By the end of 1946, certain key themes had emerged: European economic union, Asian regional development, German and Japanese reintegration. In their emphasis on German and Japanese recovery and reintegration, these themes recalled the earlier policy of appeasement with the same emphasis on the development of a global network of advanced industrial countries freely exchanging goods and capital among themselves.

The Cold War, in such a context, meant the decline of the popular front and its overshadowing by the other two themes – Anglo-American cooperation and reintegrationism (appeasement). Clearly, to the extent that the popular front had been an anti-fascist conception, its decline and the re-emergence of appeasement were no accident. For, in a sense, the Cold War implied the replacement of the US-Soviet-British alliance by a new coalition among the United States, Britain, Germany and Japan.

Where such developments placed China was quite obvious. To be sure, the Cold War in the sense of American-Soviet antagonism did not initially make an impact on Asia. Both Chinese Nationalists and Communists were slow to apply that framework to their country. The Nationalists continued to stress the theme of global cooperation up to at least 1947, in the obvious belief that the framework of cooperation among America, Britain, Russia and China still provided the best assurance for Asian security and for Nationalist survival. One key to such cooperation, of course, was Soviet adherence to the 1945 treaty.[73] The Communists, for their part, had never reconciled themselves to that treaty which provided for Moscow's recognition of the Kuomintang regime as the legitimate government of China. Although they did not conceal their ideological affinity with the Soviet Union, they were not certain of the extent to which they would count on Russian support against the Nationalists. It would be unrealistic, then, to work out their strategy in the Chinese civil war on the assumption that Russia would become involved in China as part of the global confrontation with the United States. As Okabe Tatsumi has shown, the Communist leadership devised a theory of an intermediate zone, in between the two giant powers, which was pictured as struggling for freedom from American imperialism. It was this struggle, in Communist conception, rather than the Cold War, that provided the immediate setting for the Chinese civil war and justified the strategy of an all-out offensive against the forces of Chiang Kai-shek.[74]

Both Nationalists and Communists were right in assuming that the Cold War was not of immediate relevance to China or, for that matter, to Asia as a whole. American-Soviet rivalry and antagonism were most evident in such countries as Iran, Greece and Turkey – areas in which the United States was steadily replacing Britain as the main power in contention with Russia. After 1947, moreover, the recovery and collective defence of Western Europe became the main objectives of American policy, whereas the Soviet Union responded to these initiatives by consolidating its control over Eastern Europe. In such a situation Asia remained mostly in the background. The picture was complicated by the postwar waves of nationalism throughout the underdeveloped areas of the world, which manifested themselves most strikingly in Asia. But Asian nationalism was only remotely linked to Soviet strategy, nor could it be neatly fitted into the Anglo-American strategy of containment. As a perceptive report of the under-secretary's committee of the Foreign Office in London pointed out,

We are faced…with an intense nationalism which is prickly in its international relationships. Though the idea of pan-Asia, sponsored originally by the Japanese, creates the danger of a cleavage between East and West, there is, in fact, little

---

[73] *Chung-yang jih-pao*, 6 Sept. 1947.
[74] Okabe's essay in Nagai and Iriye, eds.

or no cohesion between Asiatic countries, and it is probably true to say that there is greater fear, distrust and even dislike between Asiatic neighbours than there is between Asiatic and Western nations. Nevertheless, Asiatic nationalism is abnormally sensitive to anything which savours of Western domination or direction... It is unfortunate that the countries of South East Asia and the Far East should be passing through this stage of their development at a time when the Soviet Union is seeking to obtain domination over the whole Eurasian continent.[75]

This situation made it extremely difficult for the United States and Britain to devise a workable strategy to check the Soviet Union jointly with Asian countries. Britain, in fact, reduced its commitments in the region by granting independence to India and Pakistan as early as 1947, signalling its decline as an Asian power. The United States hesitated to act for fear that it might be seen as an upholder of colonialism. It did little in South-East Asia other than encourage the European nations to concede more rights to the indigenous populations. In these circumstances there was little cohesion in British and American approaches to the Chinese civil war. The two never coordinated their action as closely there as they did in Europe or the Middle East; in fact, the United States acted virtually unilaterally in China, often to the annoyance of British officials.

By 1949, when the Communists established their government in Peking and their claim to represent the whole of China, America's 'total failure', as a British official put it, was obvious. It had neither prevented the Communist take-over nor prepared the ground for accepting the fait accompli. There was, in fact, no policy. Britain, in contrast, had already begun reorienting its approach and considering the recognition of the People's Republic. Officials in London and their representatives in Asia agreed, at a meeting held in November 1949, the 'British interests in China and in Hong Kong demand earliest possible de jure recognition of the Communist Government in China'. The Foreign Office informed the United States that 'The Nationalist Government were our former allies in the war and have been a useful friend in the United Nations. Today they are no longer representative of anything but their ruling clique and their control over the remaining metropolitan territories is tenuous.' Britain had to accept the facts and prepare, through recognition of the new regime, for the day when China and the Soviet Union would develop a rift.[76] Here, too, British strategy hinged not so much on Anglo-American cooperation against the Soviet Union, as in Europe, but on a willingness to look after its own interests in a possible framework of close ties with the Chinese. The Cold War as such was not immediately relevant.

[75] F 17397/1055/6109, in FO 371/76030, Foreign Office Papers.
[76] F 16589/1023/10, in FO 371/75819, ibid.

After the failure of the Marshall mission, the United States government continued to provide a modicum of support to Chiang Kai-shek. But this was more in response to domestic pressures within America, where some erstwhile advocates of the popular front (Max Eastman, Whittaker Chambers, Freda Utley, *et al.*) were emerging as Cold Warriors and accusing others (Alger Hiss, Owen Lattimore, *et al.*) of having been dupes or, worse, agents of Soviet communism. In order to nullify the criticism that it was not doing enough to combat communism, the Truman administration extended economic and military aid, totalling US $3.5 billion, to the Kuomintang regime. But the programme of assistance never implied a commitment to involve the United States in force on the side of the Nationalists. Neither the joint chiefs nor the National Security Council (established in 1947) were willing to spread national resources thin when it was considered to be of primary importance to concentrate on the defence of the status quo in Western Europe and parts of the Middle East.

The Soviet Union also remained extremely cautious about developments in China. As if to belie the picture of Moscow's collusion with the Chinese Communists, the USSR continued to deal with the Nationalists as the government of China, its ambassador travelling with them all the way to Canton when they were driven out of Nanking. Stalin was reluctant to support the Communists openly for fear that it might provoke the United States. He, no more than Truman or Attlee, was willing to extend the Cold War to China. If anything, the Soviet government sought to protect its interests in North-east China (Manchuria) by establishing ties with Kao Kang, chairman of the people's government in the area.[77]

What these developments meant was that China, which was to have played a leading role in Asian and even in world affairs after 1945, entered a period of eclipse. From 1945 to 1949 it remained outside the major drama of international politics centring around the Cold War confrontation between the United States and the Soviet Union. It was allied to neither, and the two super-powers did not wish to extend their struggle to this land torn by civil war. The Nationalist leaders, in the meantime, failed to capitalize on their victory over Japan. They got neither American-Soviet cooperation, nor an alliance with one of them against the other – possibilities that would have better ensured their position.

Rather, they were left to their own devices against the increasingly confident Communists, who took the offensive. Chiang Kai-shek and his followers in 1949 took the dream of China's big-power status with them to the island of Taiwan. It would be another twenty years before China,

[77] Nakajima's essay in Nagai and Iriye, eds.

under a different leadership, would re-emerge on the world arena in the role of leader of 'the third world'.

Japan, in contrast, was brought back into the international scene much sooner than its former enemies, or even the Japanese themselves, had anticipated. The Cold War by definition meant, as noted above, the discarding of the popular front for reintegrationism, and this was tantamount to restoring the framework of appeasement of Germany and Japan. In fact, for postwar US foreign policy, Germany and Japan, together with Britain and Western Europe, became the cornerstone of international stability, on the basis of which the Soviet Union and its associates were to be kept from disrupting the status quo. By 1949, American-Japanese ties were replacing the United States-Chinese connection as the key to Asian-Pacific affairs.

The story of China's international position from 1931 to 1949 indicates that Japanese aggression, and the ways in which other nations coped with it, served steadily to transform the country from being a weak victim of invasion into a world power, a partner in defining a stable framework of peace. But the story also reveals that it is more difficult to define a nation's position in peace than in war. In war, as Clausewitz noted long ago, to know who the enemy is defines national politics and policies. In peace, it is not easy to say who the potential enemies are. Having bequeathed an enhanced status of the country to their successors, the Nationalists also left with the Communists the task of defining the peacetime objectives of the country's foreign policy. In the long perspective of the twentieth century, which has been convulsed by wars and revolutions, it remains to be seen if national policies can be defined and strengthened without war. The Nationalists did not have the opportunity to answer that question. But it was not altogether their fault.

CHAPTER 11

NATIONALIST CHINA DURING THE SINO-JAPANESE WAR 1937–1945

It lasted eight years. Some fifteen to twenty million Chinese died as a direct or indirect result.[1] The devastation of property was incalculable. And after it was over the Nationalist government and army were exhausted and demoralized. Thus it inflicted a terrible toll on the Chinese people and contributed directly to the Communist victory in 1949. The war with Japan was surely the most momentous event in the history of the Republican era in China.

INITIAL CAMPAIGNS AND STRATEGY 1937–1939

The fighting began in darkness, not long before midnight on 7 July 1937. Since 1901, in accordance with the Boxer Protocol, the Japanese had stationed troops in North China between Tientsin and Peiping. And on that balmy summer night, a company of Japanese troops was conducting field manoeuvres near the Lu-kou-ch'iao (Marco Polo Bridge), fifteen kilometres from Peiping and site of a strategic rail junction that governed all traffic with South China. Suddenly, the Japanese claimed, they were fired upon by Chinese soldiers.[2] A quick check revealed that one of their

---

[1] Precise and reliable figures do not exist. Two official estimates: (1) Chiang Kai-shek in 1947 stated that the number of 'sacrifices' by the military and civilians was 'ten million' (*ch'ien-wan*) – clearly a loose approximation. *Kuo-chia tsung-tung-yuan* (National general mobilization), 4. (2) The officially sanctioned *Chiang tsung-t'ung mi-lu* (Secret records of President Chiang), 13. 199, records 3,311,419 military and over 8,420,000 non-combat 'casualties'. The number who died from war-related causes – starvation, deprivation of medicine, increased incidence of infectious diseases, military conscription, conscript labour, etc. – was doubtless very large. Ho Ping-ti's estimate of 15–20 million deaths seems credible (*Studies on the population of China, 1368–1953*, 252). Ch'en Ch'i-t'ien put the total deaths at 18,546,000, but did not indicate his source (*Wo-te hui-i* (My memoirs), 235). Chiang Kai-shek's son, Wego W. K. Chiang, more recently put the number of 'casualties' at 3.2 million for the military and 'some twenty-odd millions' for civilians ('Tribute to our beloved leader', Part II, *China Post* (Taipei), 29 Oct. 1977, 4).

[2] It has been stated that the initial shooting may not have been by soldiers from the Wan-p'ing garrison, but from a third party, possibly the Communists, who hoped thereby to involve the National government in a war with Japan. The charge is not, however, supported by firm evidence. See Hata Ikuhiko, *Nitchū sensō shi* (History of the Japanese-Chinese War), 181–3; Tetsuya Kataoka, *Resistance and revolution in China: the Communists and the second united front*, 54–5; Alvin D. Coox, 'Recourse to arms: the Sino-Japanese conflict, 1937–1945', in Alvin D. Coox and Hilary Conroy, eds. *China and Japan: a search for balance since World War I*, 299.

number was missing, whereupon they demanded entry to the nearby Chinese garrison town of Wan-p'ing to search for him. After the Chinese refused, they attempted unsuccessfully to storm the town. This was the initial clash of the war.

That the Japanese must ultimately bear the onus for the war is not in question; their record of aggression against China at least since the Twenty-one Demands in 1915, and especially since they seized Manchuria in 1931, was blatant. Yet precisely what happened at Lu-kou-ch'iao and why is still debated. The Chinese have generally contended that the Japanese purposely provoked the fighting. The Japanese goal was allegedly to detach North China from the authority of the Nanking government; by seizing control of the Lu-kou-ch'iao–Wan-p'ing area, they could control access to Peiping and thereby force General Sun Che-yuan, commander of the 29th Army and chairman of the Hopei-Chahar Political Council, to become a compliant puppet. Moreover, the argument continues, the Japanese had witnessed the growing unity of the Chinese and chose to establish their domination of the Chinese mainland now before the Nationalists became strong.

Evidence supporting this contention is not lacking. In September 1936, for example, the Japanese had taken advantage of a similar incident to occupy Feng-t'ai, which sat astride the railway from Peiping to Tientsin. Later the same year they had attempted in vain to purchase some 1,000 acres of land near Wan-p'ing for a barracks and airfield. Japanese military commanders had also become concerned during the spring of 1937 that Sung Che-yuan was falling more under the influence of Nanking, thus threatening their position in North China. And, for a week prior to the incident, Peiping had been in a state of tension: rumours announced that the Japanese would soon strike; the continuation of Japanese field exercises for a week at such a sensitive spot as Lu-kou-ch'iao was unusual and disturbing; pro-Japanese hoodlums were creating disturbances in Peiping, Tientsin and Pao-ting. Significantly, too, the Japanese on 9 July informed the Chinese that the supposedly missing soldier had reappeared, apparently never having been detained or molested by the Chinese.[3]

Japanese documents of the period suggest, however, that the Japanese neither planned nor desired the incident at Lu-kou-ch'iao. In 1937, the Tokyo government was pursuing a policy emphasizing industrial development as a means of strengthening the foundations of its military

[3] Wu Hsiang-hsiang, *Ti-erh-tz'u Chung-Jih chan-cheng shih* (The second Sino-Japanese War), hereafter *CJCC* 1.359–80; Li Yun-han, *Sung Che-yuan yü ch'i-ch'i k'ang-chan* (Sung Che-yuan and the 7 July war of resistance), 179–212; Li Yun-han, 'The origins of the war: background of the Lukouchiao incident, July 7, 1937', in Paul K. T. Sih, ed. *Nationalist China during the Sino-Japanese War, 1937–1945*, 18–27; T. A. Bisson, *Japan in China*, 1–39.

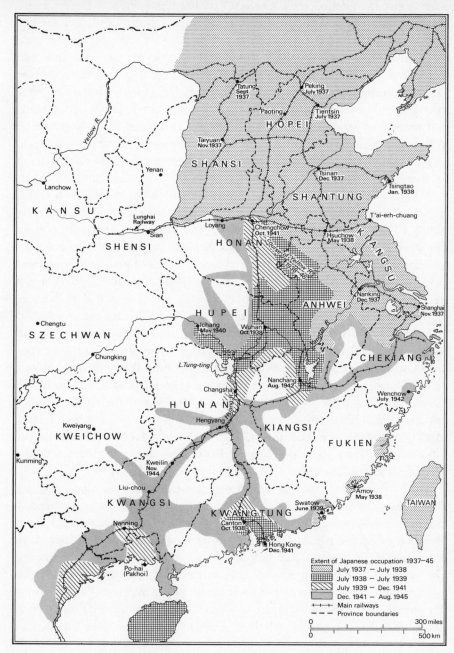

MAP 8. Japanese military occupation of China proper

forces, and the general staff as recently as June had again ordered its field commanders to avoid incidents that might provoke 'international trouble'. Officers of the Japanese army in North China were notorious, of course, for defying their superiors in Tokyo. Yet the size and deployment of the imperial forces in North China on 7 July suggests that the field commanders had made no preparations for the incident. They had only 5–7,000 men (Sung Che-yuan's 29th Army was approximately ten times that size), and most of these were engaged in manoeuvres in places where they were clearly not prepared to respond to the confrontation at Lu-kou-ch'iao. Thus only about 135 Japanese troops had been involved in the initial fighting.[4]

Whether or not the Japanese purposely provoked the Lu-kou-ch'iao fighting, the incident need not have led to a major war, for on 19 July Sung Che-yuan signed an agreement to withdraw his troops from Wan-p'ing and otherwise fully satisfied Japanese demands. But policy-makers in Nanking and Tokyo raised larger issues of principle, and these impelled the two nations into full-scale war. The National government recognized that any settlement concluded solely by regional authorities in Peiping bolstered Japanese claims that North China lay outside its sphere of authority. It consequently insisted on the preservation of full Chinese sovereignty in North China. It also advanced several (between two and four) army divisions from Central China into southern Hopei, near Pao-ting, posing a substantial threat to the Japanese forces in North China. The Japanese, on the other hand, predicated their China policy on the principle of excluding Nationalist authority from North China. And they were determined not to back down in the face of a Chinese show of strength. They therefore began reinforcing their own forces in the Peiping-Tientsin corridor.

On 25 July, the Japanese and Sung Che-yuan's forces again clashed. Three days later, the Japanese commander in North China announced 'a punitive expedition against the Chinese troops, who have been taking acts derogatory to the prestige of the Empire of Japan'.[5] Within four days, thousands of Chinese defenders lay dead, and the Japanese controlled the entire Peiping-Tientsin area. Meanwhile, the policies of the two governments were hardening. The Japanese prime minister, Prince Konoe Fumimaro, on 27 July proclaimed his determination to attain a 'fundamental solution of Sino-Japanese relations'.[6] And Chiang Kai-shek on 30 July

---

[4] Hata Ikuhiko, 162–83; Coox, 297–300; James B. Crowley, *Japan's quest for autonomy: national security and foreign policy, 1930–1938*, 310–28; Robert J. C. Butow, *Tojo and the coming of the war*, 91–5.

[5] Bisson, 28.

[6] Crowley, *Quest*, 338.

declared that 'the only course open to us now is to lead the masses of the nation, under a single national plan, to struggle to the last'.[7]

On 7 August, Chiang Kai-shek and his top advisers formally determined to wage an all-out war of resistance.[8] Chiang then made one of the greatest – and most debatable – gambles of his career. He decided to shift the major battleground of the war from North China to Shanghai. Shanghai, Nanking's strategists thought, was more suited for combat with the Japanese army than were the wide-open spaces of North China, because the constricted area of the city would nullify the Japanese superiority in tanks, artillery and logistic capabilities. An attack on the Japanese settlement in Shanghai would also divert Japanese attention from the north, enabling the Chinese there to strengthen their defences, especially of the key province of Shansi. Nanking also hoped for a political pay-off. Chinese public opinion would probably rally behind the government, as in 1932, if it took a firm stand at Shanghai. And a battle there, within a stone's throw of the large foreign community, would also draw the attention and sympathy – and possibly the intervention – of the Western powers.[9] Although pro-Nationalist writers still acclaim Chiang's gamble as a huge success, the losses probably far exceeded his worst expectations.

Chiang Kai-shek on 11 August had ordered the first three of his finest divisions – armed with German weapons and advised by General Alexander von Falkenhausen and his German staff – to take up positions inside the limits of greater Shanghai, though outside the foreign areas. The Japanese in their sector of the city (which comprised the Yangtzepoo and Hongkew sections of the International Settlement, and a salient $1\frac{1}{2}$ miles long by half a mile wide in the North Hongkew section of the Chinese city: see map 8) were caught by surprise, and they rushed in reinforcements. But when the fighting began on 13 August – there is still no agreement regarding which side started the shooting – the Chinese numbered about 80,000, the Japanese only 12,000. For a week the German-trained Chinese troops threatened to push the Japanese into the Whangpoo River. Thereafter, however, Japanese reinforcements landed on the banks of the Yangtze, on the northern edge of the city; the battle lines were now widened; and the Chinese forces had let their initial advantage slip from their grasp.

[7] Ibid. 339.

[8] Hsu Long-hsuen and Chang Ming-kai, comps. History of the Sino-Japanese War, 1937–1945, 1.357; Hsiang-hsiang Wu, 'Total strategy used by China and some major engagements in the Sino-Japanese War of 1935–1945', in Paul K. T. Sih, ed. Nationalist China, 52.

[9] Wu Hsiang-hsiang, 'Total strategy', 52–4; Ch'en Ch'eng, Pa-nien k'ang-chan ching-kuo kai-yao (Summary of experiences during the eight-year war of resistance), 9–10; Hsi-sheng Ch'i, Nationalist China at war, 41–9.

The fighting was devastating. Guns of Japanese warships, conveniently anchored in the Yangtze and Whangpoo Rivers, pounded Chinese positions at point-blank range. The Nanking government, determined not to retreat, poured in more troops. In three months of fighting, some 270,000 Chinese troops, fully 60 per cent of the Nationalist defenders and the nucleus of Chiang Kai-shek's modernized army, were killed or wounded.[10] Japanese casualties were over 40,000. Untold thousands of civilians were also slaughtered, and large portions of the city outside the Westerners' foreign concessions were destroyed.

In early November, the Japanese landed an amphibious force in Hangchow Bay, fifty miles south-west of Shanghai, and within a week this army threatened the rear of the city's defenders. The Chinese fell back toward Nanking. Their retreat was so disorganized, however, that they failed to stop at the carefully constructed concrete fortifications near Wusih on the Shanghai-Nanking railway, that had been built in imitation of the German Hindenburg Line. Nanking fell to the Japanese on 12–13 December 1937, after which the Japanese offensive slowed while their troops engaged in the most shameful episode of the war, the 'rape of Nanking'. During seven weeks of savagery, at least 42,000 Chinese were murdered in cold blood, many of them buried alive or set afire with kerosene. About 20,000 women were raped.[11] The Sino-Japanese War had begun.

Chiang Kai-shek had long attempted to avert hostilities. Since the Nationalists came to power in 1927, he had consistently favoured a conciliatory policy, despite Japan's numerous acts of interference and aggression. Convinced that China was too weak and divided to resist a strong foreign aggressor, he had acquiesced in the Japanese occupation of the four north-eastern provinces (Manchuria), concluded truces that had vitiated Nationalist influence in North China, and submitted to Japanese pressures to quash the anti-Japanese student movement. Beginning in late 1935, however, anti-Japanese sentiment had become so virulent that the National government felt constrained to harden its response to the Japanese. And, following the Sian incident of December 1936, Chiang gradually began readying for war. He had presumably purchased his release at Sian by promising verbally that he would resist future aggression. Thus, in February 1937 he removed his allegedly pro-Japanese foreign minister, Chang Ch'ün, and he began negotiating a rapprochement with his long-time enemies, the Communists. When the

[10] F. F. Liu, *A military history of Modern China, 1924–1949*, 198.

[11] F. F. Liu, 101 and 199; Lloyd E. Eastman, 'Facets of an ambivalent relationship; smuggling, puppets, and atrocities during the War, 1937–1945', in Akira Iriye, ed. *The Chinese and the Japanese: essays in political and cultural interactions*, 293–6.

fighting broke out at Lu-kou-ch'iao, therefore, Chiang had already determined to oppose further acts of Japanese aggression. All vocal parts of the nation stood behind him, more unified than in a generation.

Chiang Kai-shek's strategy was based on the principle of 'trading space for time'. Acutely sensitive to his army's inferiority to the Japanese, he had, even before the war, conceived the strategy of retreating into the remote hinterland of south-western China. 'Even if we lose fifteen ... of the eighteen provinces of China proper,' he told a gathering of political cadres in August 1935, 'with Szechwan, Kweichow and Yunnan provinces in our control we definitely will beat any enemy, and recover all the lost territory.'[12] Chiang Kai-shek's confidence was built on the realization that China's economy and society were still in a pre-modern, pre-industrial stage. He believed, therefore, that the nation's resistance could continue regardless of how many cities and factories fell to the enemy. Should the invading armies advance into China's virtually unlimited hinterland, they would be separated from their sources of supply and become exhausted. Occasionally, as at Shanghai, he did not adhere to the principle of trading space for time. In the long run, however, the strategy succeeded much as he had anticipated. The Japanese seized the urban centres of north and east China with relative ease and advanced rapidly in pronged attacks that followed the major roads and rail lines. These communications arteries did not, however, penetrate beyond the rising hills and mountains of west China, behind which the defending Chinese took cover. And the Japanese advance consequently faltered.

Unlike Chiang Kai-shek, the Japanese had no preconceived notion of the strategy or even the goals that they wished to pursue in China. During 1934–6, Foreign Minister Hirota Kōki had formulated three general desiderata for Japan in China: (1) suppression of anti-Japanese activities; (2) de facto recognition of Manchukuo and the creation of harmonious relations between that country, Japan and China; and (3) cooperation between China and Japan in the eradication of communism. But the precise meaning of Hirota's Three Principles was never clear. After the Lu-kou-ch'iao incident, Japanese policy-makers disagreed vehemently regarding their next moves. One segment of opinion, represented chiefly by the army general staff, argued against expansion in China proper. Japan's war potential was still limited, this group contended, and the opposition of the Chinese, who were now increasingly nationalistic and

[12] Wu Hsiang-hsiang, 'Total strategy', 48. In fact, Chiang had conceived the plan of establishing the national capital in Szechwan, in the event of war with Japan, as early as about 1932. See Chang Ch'i-yun, *Tang-shih kai-yao* (Survey history of the Kuomintang),2.914. On the Nationalists' strategic thinking generally, see Wu Hsiang-hsiang, 'Total strategy', 37–72; and Chiang Kai-shek's speeches in his *Resistance and reconstruction: messages during China's six years of war, 1937–1943*.

united, would be far more formidable than it had been in preceding years. Most Japanese leaders, civilian as well as military, however, did not comprehend the significance of the rising tide of Chinese nationalism. Remembering the ease with which they had seized Manchuria in 1931-2, they retained for the Chinese army a profound contempt. So optimistic were these proponents of war that they claimed it would be won within three months.[13]

Still, the Japanese expansionists during the early months of the war held very limited ambitions within China proper. This became evident when, on 5 November 1937, the Tokyo government proposed to settle the China 'incident' on terms similar to Hirota's Three Principles. The Chiang government did not agree to enter negotiations, however, until 2 December. By that time Shanghai had fallen, and the Nationalist armies were falling back toward Nanking in complete disarray. These easy victories whetted the Japanese appetite and the Tokyo government was no longer willing to negotiate on the basis of its November proposals. Instead, on 22 December it presented a new, harsher set of demands. These included de jure recognition of Manchukuo; demilitarization of North China and Inner Mongolia; payment of an indemnity; and – most ominous – creation of a 'special political structure' in North China which would work toward the realization of the co-prosperity of Japan, Manchukuo and China. The Chiang government did not respond to these demands, and Tokyo in January 1938 consequently announced its determination to 'annihilate' the National government.[14]

In none of the Japanese conditions for peace, now or later in the war, did they contemplate assuming direct administrative responsibilities within China proper. Japanese expansionists did, however, propose the effective subjugation of China, especially the five northern provinces, to the political will and economic needs of Japan. These were conditions that, in China's perfervid nationalistic atmosphere of 1937-8, Chiang Kai-shek could not accept, even if he wished. Chinese resistance did not collapse after the fall of Nanking, as the Japanese expansionists had complacently anticipated. Instead, the seat of the National government was moved to Chungking while Chiang, proclaiming a 'scorched-earth' policy, directed the resistance from Wuhan.

The Japanese thus made Wuhan their next objective. First, however, they endeavoured to unite their scattered armies by seizing control of the major railways linking North and Central China. In this they were

[13] Crowley, 230; Bisson, 53, 75, 124-5; Butow, 109; John Hunter Boyle, *China and Japan at war, 1937-1945: the politics of collaboration*, 53.
[14] Boyle, 68-82; Crowley, 354-78.

ultimately successful, although, as at Shanghai, they occasionally encountered heroic and brilliantly led forces of resistance. In early April 1938, for example, as the Japanese converged on the key transportation centre of Hsu-chou in northern Kiangsu, General Li Tsung-jen's forces enticed the attackers into a trap in the walled town of T'ai-erh-chuang. Li's troops inflicted heavy casualties – Chinese claimed that 30,000 Japanese were killed – and forced the Japanese remnants to retreat. This first major Chinese victory shattered the myth of Japanese invincibility. As happened too frequently, however, the Chinese did not pursue the defeated enemy, and their victory was thus ephemeral. Hsu-chou fell on 19 May. The Japanese commanders in North China and the Nanking area could now coordinate their movement in the forthcoming campaign against Wuhan.[15]

The Japanese received another notable setback in early June 1938, near Kaifeng. As they advanced westward along the Lunghai railway, the Chinese suddenly broke open the Yellow River dikes. Bursting out of its course, the river swept across the path of the approaching Japanese and continued across the plains of Honan, into Anhwei province and thence entered the sea south, rather than north, of the Shantung peninsula. The stratagem worked brilliantly. The invaders were temporarily halted, and the campaign against Wuhan was prolonged by perhaps three months. The decision to change the course of the Yellow River has, however, been bitterly criticized, and indeed the Nationalists for many years denied that they had purposely broken the dikes. For the flood had wrought even more devastation upon the Chinese populace than upon the Japanese. Some four to five thousand villages and eleven large towns had been caught in the flood waters and over two million persons were reportedly left homeless and destitute. Even seven years later, all that could be seen of some villages was the curving roof of a temple and top branches of leafless trees that poked through many feet of river silt.[16]

The determination evident at Shanghai, at T'ai-erh-chuang, and on the

---

[15] F. F. Liu, 200; Frank Dorn, *The Sino-Japanese War, 1937–41: From Marco Polo Bridge to Pearl Harbor*, 146–68; *China handbook*, henceforth *CHB*, *1937–1943: a comprehensive survey of major developments in China in six years of war*, 354–6.

[16] Dorn, 177–8; O. Edmund Clubb, *Twentieth century China*, 225; Laurance Tipton, *Chinese escapade*, 104. Estimates of the number of persons drowned by the waters released when the dikes broke ranged as high as 325,000 and even 440,000. (See Shih Ching-han, 'Huang-fan-ch'ü ti tsai-ch'ing ho hsin-sheng' (The disaster and rebirth of the Yellow River flood area), *Kuan-ch'a* (The observer), 3.3 (13 Sept. 1947), 22; and *China Weekly Review*, 105.12 (17 May 1947), 319.) Other sources state, however, that the loss of life on both the Chinese and Japanese sides was relatively light, because the Chinese residents had foreknowledge of the plan and because the flood waters advanced slowly. (See Frank Oliver, *Special undeclared war*, 209–10; and Archives of the United Nations Relief and Rehabilitation Administration, Monograph China 119, Box 2781, 'Honan regional office: history, as of 31 March 1947', 4.)

Yellow River were, however, atypical of the Nationalists' resistance during this initial phase of the war. Many Chinese commanders were hesitant and cowardly.[17] Most of them had enjoyed regional autonomy too long to risk their lives and power merely at Chiang Kai-shek's command. Governor Han Fu-chü, for example, ignominiously abandoned Shantung province to the Japanese, although he, in contrast to most, paid for his disregard of Chiang's orders with his life. He was executed in January 1938.

Although the Japanese suffered heavy losses in their long campaign to take Wuhan, their superiority in artillery, tanks and planes finally enabled them to seize the city on 25 October 1938. Only four days earlier, having met virtually no resistance, they had also taken Canton. Surely, Japanese strategists thought, the Chinese would now capitulate.

Some members of the Nationalist government had indeed felt revulsion against the horrible destruction of the war, evidenced for example in Chiang Kai-shek's scorched-earth policy which led, among other disasters, to the burning of Changsha in November 1938. Moreover, hopes for foreign intervention against Japan were bruised in September 1938, after England and France at Munich offered up Czechoslovakia to secure peace with Hitler. Only Soviet Russia provided aid to China, and it did so – some thought – merely to prolong the war and thus weaken the National government. The true beneficiaries of the war, it was therefore contended, were the Chinese Communists, who were using their respite from Nationalist annihilation campaigns to expand territorially.

The prime spokesman for those in the government who had misgivings about the policy of resistance was Wang Ching-wei. As vice director-general of the Kuomintang, he was nominally the second-ranking leader of the Nationalist movement. Although a charismatic politician with a sizeable following within the KMT, Wang wielded little influence within the Chiang Kai-shek-dominated government. Motivated perhaps equally, therefore, by overweening political ambition and despair of altering the strategy of resistance imposed upon the Chinese people, he defected from Chungking on 18 December 1938. Subsequently, in March 1940, he established a Reformed National government in Nanking, under the virtual dominance of the Japanese, as a rival to the government at Chungking.[18]

Chiang Kai-shek, on his part, appeared not to be dispirited. The

[17] Dorn, 167, 201; 205; Boyle, 139.

[18] Standard accounts of Wang Ching-wei's defection to the Japanese are: Boyle, cited above; Chu Tzu-chia (Chin Hsiung-pai), *Wang cheng-ch'üan ti k'ai-ch'ang yü shou-ch'ang* (The beginning and ending of the drama of the Wang regime); and Gerald Bunker, *The peace conspiracy: Wang Ching-wei and the China War, 1937–1941*.

abandonment of Wuhan, he optimistically proclaimed, 'marks a turning point in our struggle from the defensive to the offensive'.[19] Despite this seeming bravado, even the Japanese recognized that, by failing to knock out the Nationalist army at Wuhan, they had lost the chance of a rapid victory. Now the Nationalist forces had retreated into the rugged mountainous areas of the country, beyond the arteries of modern communication which had hitherto facilitated the Japanese advance. The Japanese high command envisioned victory not in three months but perhaps in three years.[20]

CHINA'S MOBILIZATION FOR WAR

For several years, despite repeated Japanese provocations, Chiang Kai-shek had postponed the inevitable, believing that he must first suppress the Communists and improve the quality of the army. Yet, in July 1937, Nationalist China remained woefully unprepared for war. During the next two years, therefore, there was a flurry of measures to put the nation on a war footing.

During the Nanking decade, Chiang had particularly stressed modernization of the armed forces. A corps of German advisers, most noted of whom were Generals Hans von Seeckt and Alexander von Falkenhausen, began training a modern officer corps. Substantial quantities of weapons and materiel, mostly of German manufacture, were imported for select units of the central army. The nucleus of an air force was established, and plans were conceived to equip the navy with German-built submarines, cruisers and torpedo boats.[21]

General von Seeckt had particularly emphasized to Chiang that a highly developed defence industry was essential for the maintenance of a modern army. Considering the manifest importance of such an industrial base, however, remarkably little had been accomplished. Not until 1935 was the National Resources Commission created for the purpose of developing heavy industry. The commission in 1936 inaugurated a three-year plan of industrial development, but it was very inadequately funded until after the war began.[22] In 1937, consequently, the nation's defence industry remained in its formative stages, and the army continued to rely heavily upon foreign sources for weapons and equipment. China's arsenals did produce substantial quantities of rifles and machine-guns, but

---

[19] Hollington K. Tong, *China and the world press*, 72.   [20] Butow, 135–6.

[21] F. F. Liu, 97; William C. Kirby, *Germany and Republican China*, 217–23; Jürgen Domes, *Vertagte Revolution*, 580–5.

[22] On the National Resources Commission, see above, ch. 3. This commission had been preceded by the National Defense Planning Committee, founded in 1932, which had been charged with surveying the military, industrial, cultural, etc. requirements of national defence. See *CJCC* 2.292.

virtually all heavy weapons, as well as trucks, petrol and radio equipment still had to be imported. About 300,000 troops had received German-type training, but only 80,000 of these were fully equipped with German weapons. The remainder of the approximately 1.7 million men in the Nationalist army were, by European and Japanese standards, badly trained, poorly equipped, and divided into numerous virtually independent and mutually jealous commands.[23]

Politically, too, China had begun mobilizing for the anticipated struggle with Japan, but progress had likewise been painfully slow. Following the Sian incident in December 1936 (see above, pp. 162-3), the Nationalists and Communists began negotiating a second united front. Chiang Kai-shek and Chou En-lai met five times during the first six months of the year, but the alliance had still not been consummated when the fighting erupted in July.[24]

In the spring of 1937, Chiang Kai-shek had also taken the unusual step of inviting more than 400 of the nation's leaders to a conference at the resort area of Lu-shan to exchange views on the nation's problems. Invited to the meeting were not only prominent Kuomintang members, but leaders of the minor political parties (such as the China Youth Party, the National Socialist Party, and the Third Party) and outstanding non-partisans from scholarly and professional organizations (such as Hu Shih, Fu Ssu-nien, and Chang Po-ling). The conference was actually not convened until 16 July, by which time fighting had begun. Though the government thus tried even prior to the war to align itself with the rising anti-Japanese sentiment, it still continued to incarcerate political prisoners such as Ch'en Tu-hsiu, and it prosecuted the so-called 'Seven Gentlemen', popular leaders of the anti-Japanese National Salvation Movement.

Once fighting began, however, the pace of war preparations quickened. The united front with the Communists was finally concluded. The leadership structure of the government was totally revamped. And, by no means least important, the vast migration of the government, people and materiel to the hinterland provinces of western China began. Both the structure and environment of Nationalist rule were consequently altered, although its essential character – a dictatorial regime dependent upon military force – remained unchanged.

To mobilize the country politically, the government attempted simultaneously to strengthen the centralized, authoritarian powers of Chiang Kai-shek and to broaden its base of popular support. As early as August

---

[23] Ibid. 1.324-6; F. F. Liu, 112, 153-5; Dorn, 6-10; Ch'en Ch'eng, table 9.
[24] See ch. 12 below (Van Slyke). On the meetings between Chiang and Chou, see US State Dept. 893.00/14154, 23 July 1937, encl., T. A. Bisson letter to Raymond Leslie Buell.

1937, Chiang was granted new and far-reaching powers. The unwieldy Central Political Council, which had been the party organ responsible for the general supervision and direction of the government, was replaced by a Supreme National Defence Conference (Kuo-fang tsui-kao hui-i) (in January 1939, it was reorganized as the Supreme National Defence Council – Kuo-fang tsui-kao wei-yuan hui). Chiang chaired this body, which was nominally the top organ of government. At the same time, and ultimately of greater significance, the Military Affairs Commission (Chün-shih wei-yuan hui), also chaired by Chiang, assumed control not only of the military, but of all administrative functions of government. Now, according to the commission's newly revised organization law, 'the chairman [of the Military Affairs Commission], in shouldering his full responsibility of national defence, shall have supreme command of the land, naval and air forces, *and shall direct the people of the entire nation*'.[25] With this mandate, Chiang Kai-shek established within the commission eight departments that were charged with the direction of political policies, heavy industries, light industries and commerce, international relations, and civilian defence, as well as military operations. The Executive Yuan and the various ministries of the National government remained in existence, but their duties were largely taken over by the Military Affairs Commission.[26]

Within five months, however, administration of the wartime state was in utter chaos. The jurisdiction of the Military Affairs Commission was so broad, its administration so complex and unwieldy, and its relations with other governmental bodies so unclear, that the government became engulfed in confusion. As a consequence, civilian administrative responsibilities were restored, at least formally, to the appropriate organs of the government and party. And the Military Affairs Commission was again charged solely with direction of military aspects of the war effort. Despite this reorganization, the commission throughout the war continued to be the effective centre of government. Chiang Kai-shek at various times held other high-ranking posts. He was, for example, chairman of the Supreme National Defence Council, president of the Executive Yuan (that is, premier of the government), chairman of the People's Political Council, and director-general of the Kuomintang. He preferred, however, to exercise his authority through the office of chairman of the Military Affairs Commission.

Within the commission, therefore, he created an Office of Councillors (Ts'an-shih-shih; directed by Wang Shih-chieh) which concerned itself

---

[25] *CHB, 1937–1943*, 321. Emphasis added.
[26] F. F. Liu, 116–18, 121–2; Chang Ch'i-yun, 3.1152; Ch'ien Tuan-sheng, *The government and politics of China*, 185–7.

with problems of economics, finance and governmental administration generally. Even in foreign policy, the Office of Councillors frequently spoke with greater authority than did the Ministry of Foreign Affairs. There was also the Office of Aides (Shih-ts'ung-shih) – better known as the generalissimo's personal secretariat. This office, staffed with such influential personages as Ch'en Kuo-fu and Ch'en Pu-lei, determined who met Chiang and what information reached his ears, as well as advising him on all appointments to official posts. The Military Affairs Commission also included a Bureau of Censorship and a Bureau of Investigation and Statistics (Chün-shih tiao-ch'a t'ung-chi chü), the latter being the much-feared secret police directed by General Tai Li. The commission was, consequently, the seat of an informal government that, throughout the war, held virtually unlimited authority over the formal offices of the National government.[27]

Within the Kuomintang, too, Chiang Kai-shek's personal leadership was acknowledged. For several years he had aspired to the position of *tsung-li* (director-general) of the party, the office through which Sun Yat-sen had wielded dictatorial control over the Nationalist movement after the party reorganization in 1924. After Sun's death, however, that title had been forever reserved for him, and the Kuomintang had thereafter been administered, formally at least, through a committee system. Chiang Kai-shek wished to resurrect the leadership principle, believing that he was due the honour and that the lack of a single leader had caused much of the party's divisiveness and instability since Sun's death. During the Nanking decade, powerful factions within the party, such as that centring around Hu Han-min in Kwangtung and Kwangsi, had been jealous of Chiang's growing powers. But in 1938 his popularity was at a peak. At the Extraordinary Congress of the KMT in Wuhan in March 1938, therefore, he was finally accorded the title of director-general. (In Chinese, the term was *tsung-ts'ai*, not *tsung-li*, a distinction without a difference.) His dominance of the party had already been virtually complete. Yet he was elated. 'I have struggled thirty years for the party and the nation,' he exulted, 'and only today have I received recognition from the entire party. Our party has been unstable for fifteen years, and only today is it stabilized.'[28] Following President Lin Sen's death in August 1943, Chiang also assumed the office of president. During the war, therefore, all supreme positions in the party, government and military became his.

Even as Chiang consolidated his dictatorship, he endeavoured to

[27] On organization of the government, see F. F. Liu, 116–17; Ch'ien Tuan-sheng, 185–7; *CHB*, *1937–1943*, 86, 322–3.
[28] Chang Ch'i-yun, 3.1214.

broaden its political base. In Wuhan in early 1938 the spirit of national unity pulsated with unprecedented and never again recaptured fervour. The Extraordinary Congress of the KMT called for the creation of both the People's Political Council (Kuo-min ts'an-cheng-hui), or PPC, and the Three-People's-Principles Youth Corps (San-min-chu-i ch'ing-nien t'uan). The PPC was a parliament-like body designed to provide a platform for popular participation in the affairs of the National government. It was initially made up of 200 members, selected in various ways designed to assure the participation of prominent persons not members of the KMT. As a result, the minor political parties and the Communists received about fifty seats; independents were granted seventy seats; Kuomintang members held no more than eighty seats. The new council was thus a remarkably representative and capable body that reflected the mood of national unity during the first year of the war.[29]

The PPC was not a fully-fledged parliament, however, for its powers were sharply limited. It could propose policies and criticize, but it could not enforce its decisions. Its powers were merely advisory. But as long as the spirit of cooperation pervaded the council, until about 1939, it was an influential organ of the government.

The Three-People's-Principles Youth Corps was a very different organization, designed to enlist the support of the nation's youth. All non-Kuomintang youth groups were now abolished – through the simple expedient of refusing them the required governmental registration – and young men and women were encouraged to flock to the leadership of Chiang Kai-shek. A second purpose of the Youth Corps, however, was to revitalize the Kuomintang. Chiang Kai-shek in 1938 continued to be bitterly disappointed with the KMT, which he felt was corrupt and ineffectual. 'Most party members,' he declared,

appear to be dejected, their living is lax, they lack enthusiasm and their work is lackadaisical. Moreover, like ordinary commoners, they indulge in ease and pleasure. They even struggle for power and for their own selfish concerns... Party members have therefore almost become a special class...and the masses...are not only cool toward the party but even become antagonistic toward it.[30]

Chiang hoped that the Youth Corps would imbue the Nationalist movement with a fresh idealism. 'The Kuomintang,' he stated, 'is the nation's arteries, but [members of] the Three-People's-Principles Youth Corps are new corpuscles within the arteries.'[31]

[29] On the People's Political Council, see Lawrence Nae-lih Shyu, 'The People's Political Council and China's wartime problems, 1937–1945'.

[30] Chang Ch'i-yun, 3.1226–7. On the political role of the Youth Corps, see Lloyd E. Eastman, *Seeds of destruction: Nationalist China in war and revolution 1937–1949*, 89–107.

[31] Chang Ch'i-yun, 4.1731.

Most dramatic of Nationalist China's several acts of wartime mobilization was the removal of population, government, schools and factories from the coastal areas to the interior. Prior to the war, the political, cultural and industrial centres of Chinese national life had been the cities in North China and in the coastal and riverine areas of Central and South China – in precisely the areas most easily overrun by the Japanese. Beyond those areas lay the vast provinces of the interior: Szechwan, Yunnan, Kweichow, Kwangsi, Hunan, Shensi, Sikang and Kansu.[32] Life in these provinces had changed little since the Ch'ing dynasty, but here the Nationalists made their wartime base.

Anticipating that the struggle with Japan would be a war of attrition, the National government immediately after the Lu-kou-ch'iao incident began removing key industrial enterprises to the interior. Military industries, such as aeroplane assembly plants and especially the arsenals in Nanking, Wuhan, Kwangtung and Shansi, constituted the bulk of the considerable industrial migration that began in August 1937. Private industrialists, too, were urged to move their factories out of the path of the Japanese. On 10 August, three days before fighting erupted at Shanghai, the government allocated money to the National Resources Commission to assist in transferring private factories from that city. War quickly overtook these preparations. The equipment of 146 factories, weighing 15,000 tons and accompanied by over 2,500 workers, was removed from Shanghai even as bullets were flying. The destination of most of these factories during this early stage of the war was Wuhan. Before much of the machinery could be uncrated and the factories resume production, however, Wuhan itself was endangered, and the flight to the interior resumed. Some factories were shipped by boat across Tung-t'ing Lake to Kwangsi or western Hunan; others went by rail to Sian and Pao-ch'i in Shensi. Many were put on junks and towed up the Yangtze. West of I-ch'ang, the river swirled through its narrow and steep-faced gorges, where boats often progressed upstream only when pulled by hundreds of straining, sweating trackers. Altogether, 639 private factories were removed to the unoccupied areas (of these, about three-fourths ultimately resumed production). Equipment from the two large but antiquated iron-and-steel plants at Wuhan, including the Hanyang Steel Works, represented a major part of this transshipment (37,000 tons). In addition, there was the machinery of 115 textile factories weighing 32,000 tons, and of 230 machine-making plants weighing nearly 19,000 tons. Joining these

---

[32] Because the Japanese armies generally succeeded in occupying only the cities, railway lines and coastal areas, sizeable parts of other provinces, such as Kwangtung, Fukien, Chekiang, Kiangsi, Hupei and Honan remained more or less under the jurisdiction of the National government.

factories in flight were 42,000 skilled workmen, 12,000 of whom came with the financial assistance of the government.[33]

The Nationalists have depicted this industrial migration as evidence of the heroic dedication of the Chinese people. Notable though the achievement was, its effect has been vastly exaggerated. The amount of machinery removed, totalling some 120,000 tons, was actually insignificant relative to both the existing industrial plant and Nationalist China's wartime needs. More important, if the government had planned this industrial migration in advance – as it might easily have done, because it had long anticipated the war – the operation might have been carried out far more safely and extensively. Actually, instead of standing as a monument to Chinese patriotism, the industrial migration betrayed a distressing degree of self-serving. When the arsenals were removed, for example, not only machinery, raw materials, and workers and their families were shipped, but everything owned by the workers, including house-doors and windows, was moved. And workers in the arsenals competed vigorously with each other for the limited means of transportation, sometimes even shooting at each other.[34] Private industrialists received lucrative inducements from the government. They were guaranteed profits of 5–10 per cent for a period of five to seven years, and were promised low-interest loans and free factory sites.[35] The large majority of industrialists, who were not given such attractive promises, preferred the amenities of Hong Kong or of the International Settlement in Shanghai to the rigours and uncertainties of the interior. Chinese financiers likewise ignored the government's appeals to transfer their investments to the interior. Billions of Chinese dollars lay idle in Hong Kong and Shanghai, or took flight to the United States. Thus, some Chinese evinced an exemplary spirit of national dedication and unity, but most industrialists and financiers felt little or no personal involvement in the cause of Chinese resistance, and showed little confidence in the government's war bonds. They did not allow patriotism to dull their business instincts.[36]

[33] 'Chan-shih hou-fang kung-yeh shih ju-ho chien-li-ti' (How the wartime industry in the rear was established), *Hsin-shih-chieh yueh-k'an* (New world monthly), 15 March 1944, 10–15; Li Tzu-hsiang, 'K'ang-chan i-lai Ssu-ch'uan chih kung-yeh' (Szechwan's industry during the war), *Ssu-ch'uan ching-chi chi-k'an* (Szechwan economics quarterly), hereafter *SCCC*, 1.1 (15 Dec. 1943), 27–33; Hsu Ti-hsin, 'K'ang-chan i-lai liang-ko chieh-tuan ti Chung-kuo ching-chi' (China's economy during the two stages of the war), *Li-lun yü hsien-shih* (Theory and reality), 1.4 (15 Feb. 1940), 34–44; *CHB, 1937–1943*, 436–9; Chang Kia-ngau, *The inflationary spiral: the experience in China, 1939–1950*, 211–18; Hubert Freyn, *Free China's New Deal*, 41–2.

[34] 'Chan-shih hou-fang kung-yeh shih ju-ho chien-li-ti', 12.

[35] *CHB, 1937–1943*, 438.

[36] Shih Hsi-min, 'K'ang-chan i-lai ti Chung-kuo kung-yeh' (Chinese industry during the war), *Li-lun yü hsien-shih*, 1.4 (15 Feb. 1940), 53–4; Lin Chi-yung, 'K'ang-chan ch'i-chung min-ying

Universities also joined the migration to the interior. Since they had been the fountainhead of opposition to Japanese imperialism, the Japanese army wreaked a special vengeance upon them. On 29 July 1937 Japanese planes bombed Nankai University in Tientsin. The next day, Japanese artillery pummelled the remains of the campus. Finally, using kerosene, they set flames to the ruins in order to complete the destruction of this anti-Japanese centre. Tsing-hua University in Peiping was first systematically stripped by Japanese looters, and then its buildings were converted into a barracks, hospital, bar, brothel and stables for the imperial army. Other universities, in Shanghai, Nanking, Wuhan and Canton, were repeatedly bombed.[37]

Students and professors became a part of the tide of refugees to the interior. By late 1939, only six of the universities, colleges and vocational schools originally in Japanese-occupied territory remained there. Of the rest, fully fifty-two educational institutions had fled into the interior, while twenty-five took refuge in the foreign concessions or Hong Kong. Those that joined the exodus to the west sometimes had to travel 2–3,000 miles before finding a wartime haven. Three of China's most noted universities (Tsing-hua, Peita and Nankai), for example, first fled to Changsha in Hunan, where they established a joint campus. By February 1938, however, the students and faculty had to move again, this time to Kunming, the capital of Yunnan. One group went by rail and ship by way of Canton and Hanoi. The second group, consisting of 257 students and eleven professors, trekked over a thousand miles, mostly on foot, to the new campus.

The war exacted a heavy toll on the educational establishment. Seventeen institutions had been forced to close; thousands of youths had their education halted. Some students, of course, stayed at home, but hundreds of others joined the Nationalist army or the Communist guerrillas, or participated in troop entertainment or nursing corps. For those who continued their studies, conditions in the refugee universities were often wretched. There were severe shortages of textbooks, library materials and scientific apparatus. Professors frequently had lost their lecture notes and other reference materials. Both students and professors, too, found living conditions harsh. Temples, ancestral halls or mud-and-wattle huts were

ch'ang-k'uang ch'ien-Ch'uan chien-shu' (Summary account of the move of privately-owned factories and mining to Szechwan during the war), *Ssu-ch'uan wen-hsien* (Records of Szechwan), 62 (1 Oct. 1967), 4–7; Freyn, *Free China's New Deal*, 42–3; Edgar Snow, *The battle for Asia*, 149; Barbara W. Tuchman, *Stilwell and the American experience in China, 1911–45*, 184.

37 On education during the war, see Hubert Freyn, *Chinese education in the war*; William P. Fenn, *The effect of the Japanese invasion on higher education in China*; John Israel, 'Southwest Associated University: survival as an ultimate value', and Ou Tsuin-chen', 'Education in wartime China', both in Paul K. T. Sih, ed. *Nationalist China*.

converted into classrooms and dormitories. Wooden crates served as desks; lighting was inadequate.

High morale, at least for a time, partially compensated for these material deprivations. Students felt they were defying the hated aggressor simply by continuing their education. Government authorities agreed that they were the nation's future leaders and could better serve the nation by preparing for the tasks of reconstructing the nation after the war than by serving in the army. Except for occasional air raids and other inconveniences, therefore, the educational system continued to operate on a business-as-usual basis. Moreover, because virtually all students received government financial aid and were exempt from military conscription, university enrolment grew from 42,000 students in 1936 to 79,000 in 1944.

The influx of several million refugees deeply affected the provinces of west China.[38] Hitherto they had been isolated, barely touched by the modernizing influences from the coastal areas. Many of the refugees, by contrast, were middle- and upper-class sophisticates accustomed to wealth, power, and modern amenities. They were often condescending to the more rustic natives, whose customs appeared quaint and whose language was virtually incomprehensible. They also resented the discriminatory prices and rents charged by local merchants and landlords. The local provincials, on the other hand, resented the airs and arrogance of the 'down-river people' (hsia-chiang jen). The new arrivals did indeed attempt to monopolize the major functions of government and to seize control of banking, trade and the economy generally. The most desirable jobs in government offices and factories were denied the natives, whom the down-river people regarded as lazy and unskilled. As the years passed, linguistic differences ceased to obstruct communication between natives and refugees, intermarriage became increasingly common, and the double standard of prices largely disappeared. Yet the natives' resentment against discrimination in jobs and social status never wholly dissipated as long as the war lasted.[39]

[38] Ta Ch'en, Population in modern China, 61. The precise number of immigrants to west China is impossible to determine. Chen estimated that 3,500,000 residents of the major cities of north and east China fled from the Japanese. These probably constituted the major portion of permanent refugees in the Nationalist areas. Chen estimated that an additional 10,750,000 fled from the less urbanized areas. Many of these doubtless were farmers, who fled their homes during periods of warfare, but subsequently returned. Some estimates of the number of refugees in west China go as high as 50 million. See Chang Kia-ngau, Inflationary spiral, 14, 25. This, however, is surely inaccurate. Theodore H. White, In search of history, 79, relates how an estimate of numbers of refugees could become grossly exaggerated.

[39] Ta Chen, 62–8; Kuo-heng Shih, China enters the machine age, a study of labor in Chinese war industry, 9–12 and passim.

DETERIORATION 1939–1945: THE MILITARY

After the fall of Wuhan and Canton in late October 1938, the character of the war and conditions in the Nationalist areas changed profoundly. The fighting progressively entered a stalemate. Especially after the Japanese attack on Pearl Harbor on 7 December 1941, Nationalist leaders anticipated that the Western Allies could defeat Japan without the necessity of further Chinese sacrifices. After all, they had fought Japan alone for four and a half years already. They consequently devoted less attention to combating the Japanese than to containing the Communists, whose growing power and territorial control augured badly for national unity and stability in the postwar period. Most of all, however, the Nationalist government at Chungking found itself caught in a seemingly irreversible process of deterioration – military, economic, social, and political – that left it by 1945 weak and demoralized.

When the Nationalists did not capitulate following their defeat at Wuhan in October 1938, the Japanese leaders realized that they had misjudged the Chinese powers of resistance and that the imperial army would merely exhaust itself if it continued to pursue the elusive defenders into the hinterlands. They therefore adopted a new strategy, stressing political means to secure control of China. First, they would consolidate control of the areas overrun since July 1937. They now effectively controlled only some 10 per cent of the territory in North and Central China – primarily the major cities and areas bordering the major railways and highways. They needed to eliminate many pockets of resistance and to harness the productive capabilities of the occupied areas to the economy of the homeland.[40]

Second, the Japanese determined to wear down the Nationalists until they collapsed from 'internal disintegration'.[41] They thus simultaneously tightened their economic blockade of the Nationalist areas and began a destructive air war. In the spring of 1939 they seized Nanchang in Kiangsi, cutting the important Chekiang-Hunan railway. In November they landed an amphibious force at Po-hai (Pakhoi) in western Kwangtung, and advanced a hundred miles to take Nanning, the capital of Kwangsi. This was a damaging blow to the Nationalists, for it severed the new railway line from Hanoi over which the Chinese were obtaining fully a third of their critically needed imports. Then, in September 1940 the Japanese occupied the northern part of French Indo-China, closing the important

[40] F. F. Liu, 202–3; Hata Ikuhiko, 296–7; Evans Fordyce Carlson, *The Chinese army: its organization and military efficiency*, 75; *CJCC* 2.573–4.
[41] Tetsuya Kataoka, 152.

rail line between Hanoi and Kunming. Thereafter the Nationalists were dependent for supplies from the outside world upon the newly opened but barely passable Burma Road, air transport from Hong Kong (which the Japanese were to occupy in December 1941), and the long caravan and truck route from Russia (see map).

The Japanese air raids struck indiscriminately at military and civilian targets. Their purpose was less to destroy military installations and factories than to demoralize the population. Virtually all cities in the Nationalist area, including Kweilin, Kunming and Sian, were hit. Chungking, however, suffered most severely. Bombed 268 times during 1939-41, much of the city was gutted, and many thousands died (4,400 were killed in just the first two days of heavy raids in May 1939).[42]

Yet neither the air raids nor the blockade broke the Chinese will to resist. Indeed, the perseverance of the Chungking population remained firm as long as the bombings continued, and wilted only after they ceased in late 1941. The blockade was less than a complete success, in part because the Nationalists in July 1939 had legalized, and thereafter actively promoted, the trade in most goods from areas held by the Japanese. The Japanese were at a loss to stop this trade. They were incapable of guarding every foot, or even every mile, of the more than 2,000 miles of border between occupied and unoccupied China. Many Japanese also actively colluded in this commerce, so that a sizeable but indeterminate part of Nationalist China's imports during the war came through this so-called smuggling trade.[43]

A momentous discussion by the Japanese cabinet in July 1940 also affected their operations in China. Perceiving that success in China would continue to elude them unless they obtained access to the rich natural resources of South-East Asia, and convinced that the Western powers were preoccupied with the war in Europe, the Japanese leaders agreed to broaden the scope of imperial expansion beyond the China theatre. They hoped, although without conviction, that they could attain their goals in the south by diplomacy. This decision inevitably altered the character of the China war and also led, within little more than a year, to the attack on Pearl Harbor.[44]

On the Chinese side, strategic and political considerations had persuaded the Nationalist leadership to wage a war of attrition. Chiang Kai-shek claimed that the Japanese were spreading their resources of men and

---

[42] *CJCC* 587-8.

[43] Yu-Kwei Cheng, *Foreign trade and industrial development of China: an historical and integrated analysis through 1948*, 148-9.

[44] Butow, 153; Boyle, 300; Fujiwara Akira, 'The role of the Japanese Army', in Dorothy Borg and Shumpei Okamoto, eds. *Pearl Harbor as history: Japanese-American relations, 1931-1941*, 191.

equipment too thin by advancing across the expanse of China. 'The longer our enemy struggles, the more he involves himself in difficulties; while the longer we struggle, the stronger and more determined we become.'[45] Chiang, like the Japanese, also wished to avoid decisive battles, because he anticipated that the Western Allies would ultimately be drawn into the struggle against Japan. Initially he looked to the Allies merely for material aid and for economic sanctions against Japan. But after Pearl Harbor – news of which was greeted joyously in Chungking – he expected that Great Britain and especially the United States, with its enormous technological resources, would assume the major burden of defeating Japan. By 1943, the American ambassador to China, Clarence E. Gauss, observed that 'The Chinese have persuaded themselves that [they] are too tired and too worn and too ill-equipped to make greater effort, especially when such effort may not be necessary; and that [they] can sit back, holding what they have against the Japanese, and concentrate their planning upon China's post-war political and economic problems.'[46]

The chief political problem that distracted the Nationalists' attention from the Japanese was the growing friction with the Chinese Communists. After the New Fourth Army incident in January 1941 (see p. 665) the united front had virtually ceased to exist. Influential Nationalist leaders – most notably the minister of war, Ho Ying-ch'in, and the party apparatchik, Ch'en Li-fu – at various times stridently advocated a final extermination campaign against the Communists. Chiang Kai-shek resisted these pressures, in large part because he feared that the Allies would cease aiding the Nationalist army if it became openly involved in civil war. Yet, since mid-1939, he had committed many of his best troops – at various times between 150,000 and 500,000 – to blockading the Communists' base in the north-west.[47]

Although both Nationalists and Japanese after late 1938 were content to wage a war of attrition, fighting by no means abated completely. Occasionally the Japanese launched an offensive to attain limited objectives. In June 1940, for example, they seized the important Yangtze River port of I-ch'ang in order to staunch the flow of goods between the rice-bowl provinces of Central China and Chungking and to obtain an air base closer to the Nationalist area. In the summer of 1942, after General James H. Doolittle's bombing of Tokyo, the Japanese struck into Chekiang and Kiangsi with 100,000 troops to destroy air bases that might

---

[45] Chiang Kai-shek, *Resistance and reconstruction*, 108.
[46] *FRUS, 1943, China*, 142.
[47] Charles F. Romanus and Riley Sunderland, *Stilwell's command problems*, 303; F. F. Liu, 205; L. P. Van Slyke, ed. *The Chinese Communist movement: a report of the United States War Department, July 1945*, 71–2.

be used in future raids against the home islands. Periodically, too, they launched attacks against the Nationalist lines, less to occupy new territory than to ravage the countryside, seize or destroy recent harvests, prevent the Nationalists from amassing potentially dangerous concentrations of troops, or train recent recruits in actual combat.[48] The casualties sustained in these years of so-called stalemate – particularly during the early period – were considerable. The Chinese admitted to suffering 340,000 dead in 1940; 145,000 in 1941; 88,000 in 1942; and 43,000 in 1943.[49] Yet the battle lines from 1939 to early 1944 were not significantly altered, and the strategic balance between the two enemies was little changed for nearly six years.

The Nationalist army during the latter half of the war numbered more than 3,500,000 men.[50] It was not, however, a united, national army, but a coalition of armies which differed in degrees of loyalty to the central government as well as in training, equipment, and military capabilities. At the heart of this heterogeneous assemblage was the 'Central Army' (Chung-yang-chün). In 1941, it comprised some thirty divisions (about 300,000 men) out of a total of over 300 divisions in the entire Nationalist army. As the war progressed, Chiang added to this force so that, by the end of the war, the Central Army counted about 650,000 men. Officers in the Central Army in 1937 were typically graduates of the Central Military Academy. There they had received an introduction to modern military techniques, often during the 1930s from German instructors. Political indoctrination had bulked large in their training; officers were intensely loyal to Chiang Kai-shek.[51]

Most of the Nationalist forces, however, were direct descendants of warlord armies, commanded by men who had risen to prominence independently of the central government. Their loyalties were therefore conditional and attenuated, and they were jealous and fearful of Chiang Kai-shek's growing power. Lung Yun, governor of Yunnan, for example, resisted central government encroachments upon his provincial power, and provided a refuge for intellectuals critical of the Chungking government. Governor Yen Hsi-shan, commander of the Second War

---

[48] Smythe to State, 'Significant military, political and economic developments in and with respect to China during 1940', US State Dept. 893.00/14662, 29 Jan. 1941, p. 7; F. F. Liu, 203–4; Theodore H. White and Annalee Jacoby, *Thunder out of China*, 62; Hsi-sheng Ch'i, *Nationalist China at war: military defeats and political collapse, 1937–1945*, 40–82.

[49] The official Chinese figure for total wartime casualties is 3,211,419, including 1,319,958 dead. *CHB, 1950*, 182.

[50] Ch'en Ch'eng, table 9. Probably no one, however, knew the exact size of the Nationalist army. Chang Kia-ngau (*Inflationary spiral*, 127) states that the army increased from 2.5 million men in 1940 to nearly 4.5 million in 1941. *CHB, 1937–1943*, 324, gives a figure of 6 million.

[51] Charles F. Romanus and Riley Sunderland, *Stilwell's mission to China*, 35; F. F. Liu, 112–13.

Zone in North China and vice chairman of the Military Council, ruled his native Shansi as an autonomous satrapy. He prohibited units of the Central Army from entering his war zone, and maintained his own political party (the Democratic Revolutionary Comrades' Association) as a counter to the Kuomintang. Indeed, since 1941, Yen had even maintained close and amiable relations with the Japanese. Other generals with provincial origins, such as Li Tsung-jen (Kwangsi), Hsueh Yueh (Kwangtung), Yü Hsueh-chung (Manchuria) and Fu Tso-i (Suiyuan) had lost their specifically regional bases, but retained command of armies that were loyal to them rather than to Chiang Kai-shek.[52]

The relationship between those non-Central Army commanders and the central government had been altered by the outbreak of war. Throughout the Nanking decade, the power of provincial militarists had been waning. Crucial to Chiang's growing power had been his control of a politically loyal and relatively proficient army. But the destruction of Chiang's best troops at Shanghai, including the bulk of his elite German-trained divisions, caused the military balance within the Nationalist forces to shift back toward the non-Central Army commanders. Chiang's political authority diminished proportionately.

Throughout the war, Chiang endeavoured to right the political and military balance between himself and the regional commanders by inserting KMT cadres into the provincial armies and by rebuilding his central forces with newly trained officers and modern equipment. These efforts excited the suspicions and animosity of the regional generals. They complained that the central government discriminated against them by sending their divisions into decimating combat with the Japanese while Chiang held his own forces safely in reserve. They were angered by inequitable allocations of fresh supplies, for Chiang distributed the bulk of new weapons and ammunition, including Lend-Lease equipment from the United States, to his own forces rather than to the less trustworthy provincial armies.[53]

Domestic politics, in short, underlay Chiang's conduct of the war, and he took advantage of it to enhance his central power. No modern state, of course – as Chiang's supporters have argued – could easily tolerate subversively independent attitudes among its military commanders. Yet the means that Chiang employed to enhance central government powers may not have been the most efficacious. In any event, the antipathies of the provincial militarists grew keener as the war progressed. In 1944, a coalition of the leading provincial militarists was actually plotting to

[52] Lloyd E. Eastman, 'Regional politics and the central government: Yunnan and Chungking', in Paul K. T. Sih, ed. *Nationalist China*, 329–55; Hsi-sheng Ch'i, 83–131.

[53] Romanus and Sunderland, *Stilwell's mission*, 34.

overthrow Chiang's government.[54] Meanwhile many non-Central Army commanders simply defected to the Japanese. Twelve of these generals defected in 1941; fifteen defected in 1942; and in 1943, the peak year, forty-two defected. Over 500,000 Chinese troops accompanied these defecting generals, and the Japanese employed the puppet armies to protect the occupied areas against Communist guerrillas.[55]

One of the deepest flaws in the Nationalist army, exacerbated during the war, was the poor quality of the officer corps. General Albert C. Wedemeyer, senior American officer in China after October 1944, characterized the Nationalist officers as 'incapable, inept, untrained, petty...altogether inefficient'.[56] This was also characteristic of the non-Central Army senior commanders, most of whom had gained distinction and position as a result less of their military skills than of their shrewdness in factional manoeuvring and timely shifts of loyalty. Even the senior officers who had graduated from the Central Military Academy, however, sorely lacked the qualities needed for military leadership. Most of them were graduates of the Whampoa Academy's first four classes during the 1920s, when the training had been rudimentary and had lasted just a few months. By the time they were promoted to command of divisions and armies as their rewards for loyalty to Chiang Kai-shek, their comprehension of military science and technology was frequently narrow and outdated. During the 1930s, these senior officers might have taken advantage of the advanced, German-influenced training in the staff college. By that time, however, they were of such high rank that they deemed it beneath their dignity to become students again.[57]

Some of the senior commanders, of course, transcended the system. Ch'en Ch'eng, Pai Ch'ung-hsi and Sun Li-jen, for example, stood above their peers as a result of their intelligence, incorruptibility and martial talents. Significantly, however, neither Pai Ch'ung-hsi nor Sun Li-jen were members of Chiang Kai-shek's inner circle. Chiang used their talents but kept them on taut leash, because they were not Central Army men and displayed an untoward independence of mind. Ch'en Ch'eng, who was a trusted associate of Chiang, nevertheless spent much of the war under a political cloud as a result of losing a factional quarrel with Ho Ying-ch'in, the pompous and modestly endowed minister of war.[58]

---

[54] See below, pp. 607–8.

[55] At the end of the war, the puppet armies numbered close to one million, because many troops were recruited within the occupied areas. Eastman, 'Ambivalent relationship', 284–92.

[56] Charles F. Romanus and Riley Sunderland, *Time runs out in CBI*, 233. Ellipsis in source. See also Albert C. Wedemeyer, *Wedemeyer reports!*, 325.   [57] F. F. Liu, 55–8, 81–9, 145–52.

[58] Donald G. Gillin, 'Problems of centralization in Republican China: the case of Ch'en Ch'eng and the Kuomintang', *JAS* 29.4 (Aug. 1970) 844–7; Wedemeyer, 325; Snow, 184–5; Romanus and Sunderland, *Time runs out*, 167.

When the war began, lower-ranking officers were generally more competent than their superiors. Between 1929 and 1937, the Central Military Academy had annually graduated an average of 3,000 cadets, and about 2,000 staff officers had received advanced training. The war, however, cut deeply into the junior officer corps. Ten thousand of them had been killed in the fighting around Shanghai and Nanking at the very outset. These losses were never fully recouped, because officer training during the war deteriorated greatly, both from lowered entrance requirements and from shortened courses of study. Indeed, the percentage of officers who were academy graduates in a typical infantry battalion declined from 80 per cent in 1937 to 20 per cent in 1945.[59] Because no army is better than its junior officers, these figures provide a rough index of the deterioration of the Nationalist army during the war.

That deterioration was most evident, however, at the lowest levels, among the enlisted men. China's wartime army was composed largely of conscripts. All males between eighteen and forty-five – with the exceptions of students, only sons, and hardship cases – were subject to the draft. According to law, they were to be selected equitably by drawing lots. In fact, men with money or influence evaded the draft, while the poor and powerless of the nation were pressganged into the ranks. Frequently conscription officers ignored even the formalities of a lottery. Some peasants were simply seized while working in the fields; others were arrested, and those who could not buy their way out were enrolled in the army.

Induction into military service was a horrible experience. Lacking vehicles for transport, the recruits often marched hundreds of miles to their assigned units – which were purposely remote from the recruits' homes, in order to lessen the temptation to desert. Frequently the recruits were tied together with ropes around their necks. At night they might be stripped of their clothing to prevent them from sneaking way. For food, they received only small quantities of rice, since the conscripting officers customarily 'squeezed' the rations for their own profit. For water, they might have to drink from puddles by the roadside – a common cause of diarrhoea. Soon, disease coursed through the conscripts' bodies. Medical treatment was unavailable, however, because the recruits were not regarded as part of the army until they had joined their assigned units.[60]

---

[59] F. F. Liu, 149.

[60] Milton E. Miles, *A different kind of war*, 348, Romanus and Sunderland, *Time runs out*, 369–70. John S. Service, *Lost chance in China: the World War II despatches of John S. Service*, 33–7; Ringwalt to Atcheson, 'The Chinese soldier', US State Dept. 893.22/50, 14 Aug. 1943, encl. p. 2. Langdon to State, 'Conscription campaign at Kunming: malpractices connected with conscription and treatment of soldiers', US State Dept. 893.2222/7–144, 1 July 1944, 2–3; F. F. Liu, 137; Chiang Meng-lin, 'Hsin-ch'ao' (New tide), *Chuan-chi wen-hsueh* (Biographical literature), 11.2 (Aug. 1967) 90.

The total number of such recruits who perished en route during the eight years of the war was probably well in excess of one million.[61]

Conscripts who reached their units had survived what was probably the worst period of their military service. Yet their prospects often remained bleak. In the Central Army units, food and clothing were generally adequate. But those so unfortunate as to be assigned to some of the provincial armies – such as those of Shensi and Kansu – were so miserable, John S. Service reported, 'as to almost beggar description'.[62]

Shortage of food, not of weapons, was the paramount problem reducing the fighting efficiency of the Nationalist army. When General Wedemeyer first took up his duties as Chiang's chief-of-staff in October 1944, he concerned himself primarily with problems of troop movements and disposition. Within a month, however, he realized that the soldiers were too weak to march and were incapable of fighting effectively, largely because they were half-starved. According to army regulations, each soldier was to be issued 24 oz of rice a day, a ration of salt, and a total monthly salary which, if spent entirely on food, would buy one pound of pork a month. A Chinese soldier could subsist nicely on these rations. In fact, however, he actually received only a fraction of the food and money allotted him, because his officers regularly 'squeezed' a substantial portion for themselves. As a consequence, most Nationalist soldiers suffered nutritional deficiencies. An American expert, who in 1944 examined 1,200 soldiers from widely different kinds of units, found that 57 per cent of the men displayed nutritional deficiencies that significantly affected their ability to function as soldiers.[63]

Primitive sanitary and medical practices similarly contributed to the enervation of the Nationalist army, and disease was therefore the soldiers'

---

[61] The precise number of mortalities among the conscripts will never be known. One official source acknowledges that 1,867,283 conscripts during the war were lost. (Information provided me in July 1978 by the director of the Ministry of Defence's Bureau of Military History, based on *K'ang-chan shih-liao ts'ung-pien ch'u-chi* (Collectanea of historical materials regarding the war of resistance, first collection), 295). Unfortunately, an analysis of this figure in terms of deaths and desertions is not given. Chiang Meng-lin, who was a strong supporter of the National government and a confidant of Chiang Kai-shek, estimated on the basis of secret documents that at least 14 million recruits died before they had reached their units. This figure is too large to be credible, and it is probably meant to be 1.4 million (see Chiang Meng-lin, 91). That the mortalities among conscripts were of this order of magnitude is also suggested in Hsu Fu-kuan, 'Shih shei chi-k'uei-le Chung-kuo she-hui fan-kung ti li-liang?' (Who is it that destroys the anti-Communist power of Chinese society?), *Min-chu p'ing-lun* (Democratic review), 1.7 (16 Sept. 1949), 6–7. Chiang Meng-lin, 90–1; Langdon to State, 'Conscription campaign', 3.

[62] *Lost chance*, 36. See also *Hu-pei-sheng-cheng-fu pao-kao*, 1942/4–10 (Report of the Hupei provincial government, April-October 1942), 113.

[63] Romanus and Sunderland, *Time runs out*, 65, 243. See also Gauss to State, 'The conditions of health of Chinese troops', US State Dept. 893.22/47, 14 Sept. 1942, encl. p. 2; and Gauss to State, 'Observations by a Chinese newspaper correspondent on conditions in the Lake district of Western Hupeh after the Hupeh battle in May, 1943', US State Dept. 740.0011 Pacific War/3559, 5 Nov. 1943, encl. pp. 4–5.

constant companion. Malaria was the most widespread and debilitating affliction. Dysentery, the incidence of which greatly increased during the war because of the deteriorating physical condition of the troops, was often ignored until cure was impossible. Then, able no longer even to eat, they soon died. Scabies, tropical skin ulcers, eye infections, tuberculosis, and venereal disease were also common.[64]

During the fighting in the south-west in 1945, American observers found that the 13th Army was unable to hike even a short distance 'without men falling out wholesale and many dying from utter starvation'.[65] Another American officer, Colonel David D. Barrett, reported seeing Nationalist soldiers 'topple over and die after marching less than a mile'.[66] A reporter for the highly regarded *Ta-kung-pao* ('L'Impartial') observed that 'where troops have passed, dead soldiers can be found by the roadside one after another'.[67] Units of the Nationalist army that were especially favoured or were trained by the United States – such as the Youth Army and the Chinese Expeditionary Forces trained in India – continued to be well fed and equipped. But they were exceptions.

There did exist an Army Medical Corps, but the medical treatment it provided was described by Dr Robert Lim (Lin K'o-sheng), chairman of the Chinese Red Cross medical Relief Corps, as 'pre-Nightingale'.[68] The formal structure of the medical corps – comprising first-aid teams, dressing stations, field hospitals and base hospitals – was unexceptionable, but it was undermined by inadequate and incompetent personnel, insufficient equipment and medicines, corruption and callousness.

There were only some 2,000 reasonably qualified doctors serving in the entire army – a ratio at best of about one qualified doctor for every 1,700 men, compared to about one doctor for every 150 men in the United States Army. An additional 28,000 medical officers served in the corps, but most of these had received no formal training, and had simply been promoted from stretcher-bearers, to dressers, to 'doctors'. The few really competent doctors tended to congregate in rear-area hospitals, out of reach of seriously wounded soldiers in the front lines. Because the stretcher units were often understaffed, and medical transport scarce, a wound in

64 White and Jacoby, 136–8; Gauss to State, 'The conditions of health of Chinese troops', encl. p. 2; Ringwalt to Atcheson, 'The Chinese soldier', encl. p. 3; Rice to Gauss, 'The health of Chinese troops observed at Lanchow', US State Dept. 893.22/52, 4 Dec. 1943, pp. 1–2.
65 Romanus and Sunderland, *Time runs out*, 245.
66 David D. Barrett, *Dixie Mission: the United States Army Observer Group in Yenan, 1944*, 60.
67 Gauss to State, 'Observations by a Chinese newspaper correspondent', encl. p. 5.
68 Gauss to State, 'The conditions of health of Chinese troops', encl. p. 2. On medical conditions in the army, see Lyle Stephenson Powell, *A surgeon in wartime China*; Robert Gillen Smith, 'History of the attempt of the United States Medical Department to improve the effectiveness of the Chinese Army Medical Service, 1941–1945'; F. F. Liu, 139–40; Szeming Sze, *China's health problems*, 44.

combat – even a minor wound – was often fatal. It could be a day before a wounded soldier received even preliminary first aid. Then he had to be hauled to dressing stations and hospitals in the rear. Rhodes Farmer, who saw wounded being transported to the rear in 1938, observed that 'gangrene was everywhere: maggots writhed in the wounds'.[69] With this kind of treatment, even minor wounds quickly became infected, and major injuries, such as a wound in the stomach or loss of a limb, were usually fatal. Few cripples were seen in wartime China.[70]

The Chinese soldier, ill fed, abused and scorned, inevitably lacked morale. This was indicated graphically by wholesale desertions. Most recruits, if they survived the march to their assigned units, had few thoughts other than to escape. Many succeeded. The 18th Division of the 18th Army, for example, was regarded as one of the better units, yet during 1942, stationed in the rear and not engaged in combat, 6,000 of its 11,000 men disappeared due to death or desertion. Ambassador Gauss commented that these statistics were not exceptional, and that similar attrition rates prevailed in all the military districts. Even the elite forces of Hu Tsung-nan – which, because they were used to contain the Communist forces in the north, were among the best trained, fed, and equipped soldiers in the army – reportedly required replacements in 1943 at the rate of 600 men per division of 10,000 men every month.[71] Official statistics lead to the conclusion that over eight million men, about one of every two soldiers, were unaccounted for and presumably either deserted or died from other than battle-related causes.[72]

[69] Rhodes Farmer, *Shanghai harvest: a diary of three years in the China war*, 136.

[70] Farmer, 137. Dorn, 65, writes that 'the Chinese usually shot their own seriously wounded as an act of mercy, since "they would only die anyway"'.

[71] Gauss to State, 'Observations by a Chinese newspaper correspondent', p. 3 and encl. p. 5.

[72] This conclusion is based on the fact that insignificant numbers of soldiers were released from the army during the war, and that, in addition to the nearly 1.8 million in the army in July 1937, 14,053,988 men were conscripted between 1937 and 1945, Yet the Nationalist army in August 1945 numbered (by Chinese count) only about 3.5 million or (by United States count) 2.7 million. Total casualties (including 1,761,335 wounded, some of whom doubtless returned to duty) were 3,211,419. An additional 500,000 or so defected to the Japanese. I have seen no figures on the number of prisoners taken by the Japanese, but the figure surely did not exceed another 500,000. Simple arithmetic suggests that at least 8 million, and perhaps as many as 9 million, men were unaccounted for. (This figure includes the 1,867,283 recruits that the government acknowledges were unaccounted for. See note 61 above.)

Sources: *CHB, 1950*, 182, 185. Figures on the size of the army are in Ch'en Ch'eng, Table 1; and Romanus and Sunderland, *Time runs out*, 382.

The above conclusion is drawn from the Nationalists' own data, but it is incompatible with their published figures for wartime desertions (598,107) and deaths due to illness (422,479). See Ch'en Ch'eng, table 10. This contradiction in the official data demonstrates the unreliability of Nationalist figures pertaining to the military. In fact, a former Nationalist general in Taiwan responded to my inquiries by asserting that the Chinese army had placed no value on mathematical exactness regarding casualties.

FOREIGN MILITARY AID

The Chinese army did not fight wholly alone, and the assistance – or lack of assistance – of its friends significantly affected the character of the Nationalists' struggle against the Japanese. From the beginning of the war, Chiang Kai-shek had placed large hopes upon foreign aid and intercession. The Western democracies did indeed sympathize with the Chinese struggle against arrant aggression, but their sympathy was only slowly translated into material assistance. Paradoxically, it was Soviet Russia that became the Nationalists' first and remarkably generous friend. Despite a decade of strained relations between Moscow and Nanking, the two governments shared a common interest in blocking Japanese expansion on the Asian mainland. Even before the Lu-kou-ch'iao incident, therefore, the Russians' policy toward the Nationalists had softened. They had encouraged the second united front. During the Sian incident, they had counselled Chiang Kai-shek's safe release. And, as early as September 1937 – without waiting for the conclusion of a formal aid agreement – they began sending materiel to the Nationalists. During 1937-9, the USSR supplied a total of about 1,000 planes, 2,000 'volunteer' pilots, 500 military advisers, and substantial stores of artillery, munitions and petrol. These were provided on the basis of three medium-term, low-interest (3 per cent) credits, totalling US $250 million. This flow of aid lessened after the war began in Europe in September 1939. Yet Soviet aid continued until Hitler's forces marched into Russia in 1941. Significantly, virtually none of the Russian aid was channelled to the Chinese Communists. According to T. F. Tsiang, China's ambassador to Russia, 'Moscow was more interested...in stirring up opposition to Japan in China than it was in spreading communism.'[73]

The Western democracies responded more slowly and uncertainly to China's pleas for aid. The French during the first year of the war loaned a meagre US $5 million for the construction of a railway from the Indo-China border to Nanning in Kwangsi. The United States bolstered China's dollar reserves, and hence purchasing-power on the international market, by buying up Chinese silver valued at US $157 million. Not until December 1938, however, nearly 1½ years after the outbreak of hostilities, did the United States and Britain grant rather modest credits to China in the amounts of US $25 million and £500,000 (US $2 million) respectively. Fearful of alienating the Japanese, moreover, the Americans and British specifically prohibited the Chinese from using these loans ω buy weapons or other war materiel. Beginning in 1940, Western aid

73 Arthur N. Young, *China and the helping hand, 1937-1945*, 18-21, 26, 54, 125-30.

gradually increased. The United States promised credits of $45 million in 1940 and $100 million in early 1941. In late 1941, too, the United States began sending armaments and other materiel to China under the terms of the recent Lend-Lease Act. The American Volunteer Group, an air contingent that became famous as the 'Flying Tigers', under the command of Claire L. Chennault, became operational in Burma in the latter part of 1941. After 4½ years of war, the total aid of the Western democracies approximately equalled that provided by Russia.[74]

After Pearl Harbor, America's interest in the war in China increased markedly. But relations between the two countries, now allies, were fraught with vexation. A basic cause of the strain was that the United States never provided the enormous infusions of military support and material aid that the Chinese thought was due them. After the Japanese severed the Burma Road in early 1942, the principal supply route to China was the treacherous flight from India, across the rugged foothills of the Himalayas, to Kunming in Yunnan. Partly because of America's shortage of planes, the supply of materiel over the 'Hump', as this route was known, was but a trifle compared with Chungking's expressed needs. Despite these transportation difficulties, China might have received significantly more aid, if it had not been for the Western Allies' policy of defeating Germany and Italy before concentrating against Japan. During 1941 and 1942, for example, the United States assigned to China only about 1.5 per cent of its total Lend-Lease aid and only 0.5 per cent in 1943 and 1944 – though the figure went up to 4 per cent in 1945.[75] The Nationalists were deeply aggrieved by the 'Europe first' policy.

Many of the complaints and misunderstandings that vexed Chinese-American relations after 1942 swirled around the figure of General Joseph W. Stilwell. Regarded at the time of Pearl Harbor as the most brilliant corps commander in the American army, Stilwell had initially been selected for the top combat assignment in North Africa. Because of his outstanding knowledge of China and the esteem which Chief-of-Staff

---

[74] *Ibid.* 207 and *passim.*
[75] Some figures indicating the amounts of supplies brought to China over the Hump route are (in number of tons):

1942			1943			1944			1945	
May	June	Sept.	Feb.	Apr.	June	Jan.	June	Dec.	Jan.	July
80	106	2,000	3,200	2,500	3,000	14,500	18,200	34,800	46,500	73,700

Sources: F. F. Liu, 157; Herbert Feis, *The China tangle: the American effort in China from Pearl Harbor to the Marshall mission,* 42, 67, 205. On Lend-Lease, see Young, *Helping hand,* 350, 399–402.

George C. Marshall held for him, however, he was named instead to what the secretary of war, Henry L. Stimson, subsequently termed 'the most difficult task assigned to any American in the entire war'.[76] Designated chief of Chiang Kai-shek's allied staff, as well as commander of the China-Burma-India theatre, Stilwell was specifically instructed to 'increase the effectiveness of United States assistance to the Chinese Government for the prosecution of the war and to assist in improving the combat efficiency of the Chinese Army'.[77] As the American theatre commander in China, Stilwell inevitably bore the brunt of Chinese dissatisfaction with Washington's priorities. He and Chiang initially fell out over the allied defeat in Burma. They represented different worlds and did not like each other. Stilwell was, among his other qualities, forthright to a fault, innocent of diplomacy, intolerant of posturing and bureaucratic rigmarole, and given to caustic sarcasm. Chiang Kai-shek, by contrast, tended to be vain, indirect, reserved, and acutely sensitive to differences of status. Soon Stilwell dismissed Chiang as 'an ignorant, arbitrary, stubborn man', and likened the National government to the dictatorship and gangsterism of Nazi Germany. Among friends, Stilwell disparagingly referred to Chiang as 'the peanut', and in mid-1944 he privately ruminated that 'The cure for China's trouble is the elimination of Chiang Kai-shek.' 'Why,' he asked, 'can't sudden death for once strike in the proper place.'[78] Chiang Kai-shek knew of Stilwell's attitude and slighting references to him, and in turn loathed the American. At least as early as October 1943 he tried to have Stilwell transferred from China. But Stilwell had the confidence of General Marshall and retained his post until October 1944.

Compounding their personal enmity was the fact that Chiang Kai-shek and Stilwell held fundamentally different objectives. Stilwell was concerned solely with the task of increasing China's military contribution to the war against Japan. To attain this goal, he began training Chinese troops flown over the Hump to India and proposed that the Nationalist army be fundamentally reorganized. The essential problem, he asserted, was not lack of equipment, but that the available equipment was not being used effectively. The army, he contended, 'is generally in desperate condition, underfed, unpaid, untrained, neglected, and rotten with corruption'.[79] As a remedy, he proposed that the size of the army be cut by half, inefficient commanders be purged, and an elite corps of first thirty, and ultimately one hundred, divisions be trained and equipped by the United States. He

[76] Tuchman, 232.
[77] Romanus and Sunderland, *Stilwell's mission*, 74.
[78] Joseph W. Stilwell, *The Stilwell papers*, ed. Theodore H. White, 115, 124, 215, 320, 321 and 322.
[79] Romanus and Sunderland, *Stilwell's mission*, 282.

also proposed that the American-trained Chinese divisions launch an offensive operation to retake Burma, because, as long as the Japanese controlled that country, China was dependent for foreign supplies upon the limited flow of goods over the Hump. Only by opening a land route through Burma, Stilwell thought, could sufficient materiel be imported to equip the Chinese army for a full-scale offensive against the Japanese in China.

Chiang Kai-shek placed a lower priority upon fighting the Japanese. In his view, the ultimate defeat of Japan, after the Allies had entered the war, was certain. The outcome of his struggle with the Communists was still undecided, however, and his primary concern was therefore to preserve and enhance his power and that of the National government. Stilwell's proposals to reorganize the army and to take the offensive against the Japanese were anathema to Chiang, because they threatened to upset the delicate balance of political forces that he had created. His best-equipped troops, for example, were commanded by men loyal to him, even though they were often militarily incompetent. If officers were to be assigned to posts solely on the basis of merit, as Stilwell was urging, military power would be placed in the hands of his potential political rivals. As a case in point, Stilwell held General Pai Ch'ung-hsi in high regard and would have liked to assign him a position of real authority in the Nationalist army. What Stilwell ignored, and what loomed foremost in Chiang's thinking, was that Pai Ch'ung-hsi was a former warlord in Kwangsi province with a long history of rebellion against the central government. In like manner, Stilwell in 1943 recommended that the Communist and Nationalist armies jointly launch a campaign against the Japanese in North China. To induce the Communists to participate in such an offensive, however, weapons and other materials would have to be supplied to them. Chiang, of course, could accept no scheme that would rearm or otherwise strengthen his bête noire.

More congenial to Chiang Kai-shek's purposes was Stilwell's nominal subordinate, General Claire L. Chennault. After Pearl Harbor Chennault had been reinducted into the United States army, and his 'Flying Tigers' were reorganized as the China Air Task Force (subsequently the 14th Air Force). Retaining his nearly religious faith in the efficacy of air power, Chennault in October 1942 asserted that with 105 fighter planes, 30 medium and 12 heavy bombers, he would 'accomplish the downfall of Japan...probably within six months, within one year at the outside'.[80] This fantastic plan was irresistible to Chiang Kai-shek, for it would make China a major theatre of the war – thus qualifying the National government

[80] Claire Lee Chennault, *Way of a fighter*, 214.

for larger quotas of material aid – without requiring large expenditures of her own resources. And the army reforms and active participation in the ground war, which Stilwell was demanding, would be unnecessary.

Stilwell, backed by General Marshall and secretary of War Henry L. Stimson in Washington, vehemently opposed the Chennault plan. Its crucial flaw, he argued, was that the Japanese would attack and destroy the American air bases as soon as the air strikes became effective. With the Chinese army in its current ineffectual condition, those air bases would be completely vulnerable. But Roosevelt sided with Chennault and Chiang Kai-shek, and Chennault's air offensive began. By November 1943, Japanese bases within China and their shipping along the China coast were sustaining significant losses. Japanese authorities, moreover, feared the Americans would use the air bases at Kweilin and Liu-chou to launch raids on the home islands, damaging their war industries. Stilwell's worst fears were then soon realized. For in April 1944, the Japanese launched the Ichigo (Operation Number One) offensive, their largest and most destructive campaign in China since 1938. It sliced through the Nationalists' defensive lines, posing a threat even to Kunming, a strategic key to all unoccupied China. This military threat coincided with an economic slump and mounting political discontent.

The success of the Ichigo campaign made China's military situation desperate. Seeking a solution to the crisis, Roosevelt on 19 September 1944 demanded that Chiang Kai-shek place Stilwell 'in unrestricted command of all your forces'.[81] Stilwell, after personally delivering the message, recorded in his diary: 'I handed this bundle of paprika to the Peanut and then sat back with a sigh. The harpoon hit the little bugger right in the solar plexus, and went right through him. It was a clean hit, but beyond turning green and losing the power of speech, he did not bat an eye.'[82] But Stilwell's exultation was brief. Chiang knew that, with Stilwell in command of the war effort, political power in China would slowly perhaps, but surely, slip from his grasp. This he could not accept and with indomitable insistence he persuaded Roosevelt to recall Stilwell. On 19 October 1944, General Albert C. Wedemeyer was named Chiang's chief-of-staff and commander of United States forces in China.

JAPAN'S ICHIGO OFFENSIVE 1944

Japan's Ichigo offensive inflicted a devastating defeat upon the Nationalists. It revealed to all Chinese and to the world how terribly the Nationalist

[81] Romanus and Sunderland, *Stilwell's command problems*, 443–6; Tuchman, 492–3.
[82] *Stilwell papers*, 333.

army and government had deteriorated during the preceding seven years of war. Japan's objective in this offensive was to seize or destroy the air bases in south-central China from which Chennault's 14th Air Force was launching its highly effective air attacks. To accomplish this, the Japanese in April 1944 first struck into Honan to gain full control of the Peiping-Hankow railway and so protect their rear. By late May they were ready. Moving southward from Hankow along the Hsiang River, the Japanese first invested Changsha, capital of Hunan province. Three times previously it had successfully resisted Japanese attacks, but this time the Chinese offered no firm defence, and the city fell on 18 June.

Ten days later the attack on Hengyang began. Here Hsueh Yueh's Cantonese forces, supported by Chennault's fighter planes and bombers, fought fiercely for six weeks. This was the single instance during the entire Ichigo offensive where Chinese forces staged a large-scale sustained resistance. Thereafter, however, Chinese defences collapsed. The Japanese pushed southward to the major air bases at Kweilin and Liuchow in Kwangsi. By November 1944 they had smashed Chennault's air bases, formed a pathway through Central China that connected Mukden with Hanoi, and then moved westward. They seemed unstoppable. Chinese armies were rushed into the breach, but – according to Wedemeyer – even well-equipped divisions 'melted away'. They 'appeared to lack spirit and simply would not hold ground'.[83] With the road to Chungking seemingly open to the invaders, Chiang Kai-shek bravely announced his determination to remain in Chungking and 'die if necessary' in its defence – a declaration that instilled slight confidence, for he had made similar vows at Nanking and Hankow before abandoning them.[84]

In early December, however, the Japanese army suddenly halted its advance. Why? At the time, the Japanese offensive had appeared irresistible and rumour-mongers charged that Chiang and the Japanese had struck an agreement that would spare Chungking. In fact, the Japanese had stopped moving westward because the objective of Ichigo, to destroy the American bomber bases, had been accomplished. Survival, and not destruction of the Chungking government, had by 1944 become the Japanese goal.

The Ichigo offensive had, however, inflicted terrible losses upon Nationalist China. Nearly 500,000 soldiers were dead or wounded; its territory was cut in half by the Japanese north-south corridor; fully a fourth of its factories were lost; sources of government revenue were

---

[83] Wedemeyer, 290 and 328.
[84] Wedemeyer, 293; Romanus and Sunderland, *Time runs out*, 166.

sharply reduced; and civilian casualties and property damage were enormous.[85]

Despite the manifest deterioration of the Nationalist army by 1944, assessments of its achievements during the war have varied widely. Ho Ying-ch'in, long-time minister of war, for example, has claimed that his forces fought 22 campaigns, 1,117 important engagements, and 38,931 small engagements against the Japanese. The Communists, he claimed, by contrast 'did not move a soldier against the enemy'. General Wedemeyer similarly insisted that 'the Nationalist Government of China, far from being reluctant to fight as pictured by Stilwell and some of his friends among the American correspondents, had shown amazing tenacity and endurance in resisting Japan', whereas 'no communist Chinese forces fought in any of the major engagements of the Sino-Japanese war'.[86]

It is assuredly true that, on a number of occasions, the Nationalist forces fought heroically against the Japanese. Three times at Changsha (once in 1939 and twice in 1941) the forces of General Hsueh Yueh resisted large-scale Japanese assaults. At Ch'ang-te, Hunan, in November–December 1943, the 57th Division of the Central Army fought with extreme determination, suffering casualties of fully 90 per cent. And in western Hupei in 1943, against one of Japan's so-called rice-bowl campaigns, the Chinese lost some 70–80,000 men as against 3–4,000 casualties for the Japanese.[87]

Critics of the Nationalists have tended to minimize these instances of heroism and combativeness. They claim, for example, that the brilliant defence of Hengyang in June–August 1944 was undertaken by a non-Central Army commander, Hsueh Yueh, despite obstructions of the Chungking government; and that, in the rare instances when the Nationalists took the offensive, it was because Chiang Kai-shek needed propaganda to convince Allied leaders that the China theatre warranted more material aid. The Communists, moreover, have ridiculed the Nationalist claims to belligerence against the Japanese, asserting that, until the Ichigo campaign, fully 84 per cent of the Japanese troops were concentrated against Communist forces and only 16 per cent against the Nationalists.[88] Stilwell,

[85] In Kwangsi, for example, losses in the war (most of which were sustained during the Ichigo campaign) were reportedly 110,000 persons killed, 160,000 wounded, 300,000 houses destroyed, 80,000 head of ploughing oxen killed. *Hsin-min-pao* (New people's press), 20 Mar. 1946, in *Chinese Press Review* (Chungking), hereafter *CPR*, 8 (21 Mar. 1946), 6.

[86] Ho Ying-ch'in, 'Chi-nien ch'i-ch'i k'ang-chan tsai po Chung-kung ti hsu-wei hsuan-ch'uan' (Commemorating the Sino-Japanese War and again refuting the Communists' false propaganda), *Tzu-yu chung* (Freedom's bell), 3.3 (20 Sept. 1972), 26; Wedemeyer, 279 and 284.

[87] Israel Epstein, *The unfinished revolution in China*, 311; Gauss to State, 'Observations by a Chinese newspaper correspondent', p. 1.

[88] Warren I. Cohen, 'Who fought the Japanese in Hunan? Some views of China's war effort', *JAS* 27.1 (Nov. 1967), 111–15; Dorn, 321–2; Epstein, *Unfinished revolution*, 312; Li I-yeh, *Chung-kuo*

before his dismissal in late 1944, also charged the top Nationalist commanders with 'colossal ignorance and indifference', and asserted that the Nationalist army under the existing leadership was totally incapable of making positive contributions against the Japanese.[89]

Whatever may be the final judgment on the issue, it remains a fact that the Nationalist forces persevered for eight long years against an enemy who possessed a vast technological superiority. The political, economic and human costs of this war of resistance were enormous. Yet they did not abandon the Allied war effort, and their forcing the Japanese to maintain an army of about one million men in China contributed significantly to the eventual victory. In the final analysis, however, the most important historical fact is that by the latter stage of the war, from about 1942, the greater part of the Nationalist army had so lost the will to fight that it had practically ceased to be capable of effective military operations. To this generalization there were exceptions. Stilwell's and Wedemeyer's programme to create a few high-quality Chinese divisions – trained, advised and equipped by Americans – had by 1945 finally begun to bear fruit. During April–June 1945, for instance, several of these divisions fought courageously and effectively in turning back a Japanese offensive in south-west Hunan. When the war ended, eight of these divisions had completed, and twenty-two more had begun, the thirteen-week schedule of training. The remainder of the 300-odd Chinese divisions, however, remained untouched.

The general deterioration of the Nationalist army during the war against Japan had momentous consequences. For the army was the foundation of Nationalist political power. When it began to crumble, it presaged the overthrow of Chiang Kai-shek and the National government. Chiang was seemingly powerless to reverse the process of disintegration. All attempts to reform the army – as General Stilwell learned to his dismay – quickly ran aground on the shoals of domestic politics. The army, for example, was too large, relative to available material resources, to be effective; yet proposals to reduce its size were impracticable because of the opposition of the regional commanders, who would lose their power if they lost their armies. Chiang's control of the governmental administration was also too tenuous to allow needed reforms. He had repeatedly ordered, for instance, that the conscription system be made more humane. But, because the system was dominated by local elites and corrupt officials who could not be controlled or disciplined, the terrors of the system remained.

jen-min tsen-yang ta-pai Jih-pen ti-kuo-chu-i (How the Chinese people defeated Japanese imperialism), 66.   [89] *Stilwell papers*, 157, 177, 316–19.

THE INFLATION DISASTER

The debility of the Nationalist government and army that was disclosed by the Ichigo offensive was the culmination of a long and complex process of deterioration. Of the many causes of that process, inflation was the most potent. Like leukaemic blood, the depreciated currency of the National government flowed through the body politic, enfeebling the entire organism – the army, government, economy, and society generally. Initially the rate of inflation had been rather moderate. Prices rose about 40 per cent during the first year of the war. By the latter half of 1941 and through 1944, prices more than doubled each year. Thereafter the rate of increase again spurted sharply upward.[90]

The fundamental cause of this inflation was monetary. That is, the volume of currency was vastly expanded, usually through the device of government borrowing from the four government banks, which met the demand by the wholesale printing of new money. Government expenditures increased immediately after the fighting began. During the first two years of the war, the government expended large sums in relocating and developing industries in the interior. Huge sums were devoted to new roads and railways in west China, to Indo-China, and through Burma. During this two-year period, the government's annual expenditures rose 33 per cent while its annual revenues declined 63 per cent. Prior to the war, the bulk of its revenue had been derived from the commercial and urban sectors of the economy – customs duties, salt taxes and commodity taxes contributed about 80 per cent. When the Japanese overran Shanghai and the other coastal cities, these sources of revenue were largely lost. About 75 per cent of the government's wartime expenditures were met by the creation of new paper currency (see table 10).

Although the growing volume of *fa-pi* had been, and perhaps always remained, the primary force fuelling the inflationary process, non-monetary factors accelerated the price increases. Chief among these were commodity shortages and declining confidence in the currency. The exigent demand for producer goods such as machinery, metals, electrical equipment, chemicals and fuels, and their short supply, placed them in the vanguard of the price increases. Prices of metals and metal products, for instance, increased 6.8 times during the first two war years, whereas the general price index merely doubled. Most producer goods had to be imported,

---

[90] The annual increase of retail prices was 49 per cent in 1938; 83 per cent in 1939; 124 per cent in 1940; 173 per cent in 1941; 235 per cent in 1942; 245 per cent in 1943; 231 per cent in 1944; and 251 per cent in January–August 1945. The major secondary sources on the inflation are Arthur N. Young, *China's wartime finance and inflation, 1937–1945*; Chang Kia-ngau, *Inflationary spiral*; and Shun-hsin Chou, *The Chinese inflation, 1937–1949*.

TABLE 10

Value of note issue in terms of prewar prices, 1937–45 (amount and value in millions of yuan)

End of the period	Amount of note issue of government banks	Average price index[a]	Value of issue in terms of prewar notes
1937, July	1,455	1.04	1,390
1938	2,305	1.76	1,310
1939	4,287	3.23	1,325
1940	7,867	7.24	1,085
1941	15,133	19.77	765
1942	34,360	66.2	520
1943	75,379	228	330
1944	189,461	755	250
1945, August	556,907	2,647	210
1945, December	1,031,932	2,491	415

[a] For December of each year, except for the months specified for 1937 and 1945.

Source: Arthur N. Young, *China's wartime finance and inflation, 1937–1945*, 304.

and Japan aggravated the shortages by clamping an economic blockade on the Nationalist areas.

The Japanese blockade, imposed in September 1937, was initially not effective, but progressively the noose tightened. After the loss of Canton and Hankow in October 1938, import prices jumped 72 per cent; they doubled again in the latter half of 1939 after the loss of the key supply link of Nanning in Kwangsi. Japan's war on Great Britain and the United States from December 1941 quickly eliminated Shanghai, Hong Kong and the Burma Road as sources of supply. A trickle of imports continued to flow over the long and expensive land route from the Soviet Union by way of Kansu and Sinkiang, and the air supply route over the Hump gradually grew in importance. Still, China's imports by 1944 had fallen to a mere 6 per cent of the prewar level.

During the first stage of inflation, 1937–9, ordinary Chinese were shielded from the worst effects because prices of consumer goods rose more slowly than those of producer goods. Most important, food prices rose only moderately – a modest 8.5 per cent in Chungking during the first two years of the war. The reason was that the Nationalist areas were favoured by excellent harvests in both 1938 and 1939 – 8 per cent above the prewar average in the fifteen provinces that now constituted unoccupied China. The prices of other daily necessities, like clothes and housing, rose more rapidly than food – the prices of clothing, for example, had approximately doubled by mid-1939. But most Chinese could defer purchases of new clothing. And the cost of housing, except in the cities where refugees congregated, did not rise sharply. As a consequence, most people during the first two years were able to absorb the effects of the inflation without extreme hardship.

During 1940, however, food prices began shooting upward, sharply affecting the people's livelihood and stimulating the entire inflationary process. Poor harvests were the initial cause of this change. In 1940 agricultural production fell 10 per cent below that of 1939, and declined an additional 13 per cent the next year. In July 1941, too, the government began collecting the land tax in grains rather than in money. This meant that less grain reached the free market, thus further upsetting the balance between supply and demand.

There were other non-monetary causes of the inflation. Domestic industrial production was generally unable to satisfy consumer demand. Such goods as cloth, medicines, paper and electric bulbs had been produced largely in the coastal cities that were now lost to the Japanese. Many small consumer-oriented factories were established in the interior during the war, but they were never able to meet more than a small fraction of the demand. Imports from the Japanese-occupied areas became an important source of consumer goods. Initially, both the Nationalists and the Japanese banned this trade. But in July 1939, with consumer demands inexorably mounting, the Chungking government legalized the trade in all but a few critical materials. Indeed, in 1943 it even created an official agency, directed by the powerful head of the military secret police, General Tai Li, to engage in and increase the trade in goods with the enemy-held areas. Still, neither this trade nor domestic production could satisfy the market. The Japanese, for their part, outlawed this trade throughout the war, but they too conspired in it.[91]

From 1940 onward, the most important non-monetary cause of the inflation was probably not commodity shortages, but lack of public confidence in the currency. In 1937–9 there was a strong tendency, especially among the rural population, to save *fa-pi*. This hoarding – a reaction against the customary shortage of money-income in the villages – had cushioned the impact of the inflation, for it reduced the volume of currency in circulation and thereby eased the demand for hard-to-obtain consumer goods. Following the poor rice harvest in the summer of 1940, however, farmers began hoarding grain rather than money. Speculators also bought up and stored large amounts of grain in anticipation of future

91 Eastman, 'Ambivalent relationship', 275–84.

price increases. Food prices in Chungking during 1940 and 1941 consequently shot up nearly 1,400 per cent. Industrial, transport, and other workers, as a result, demanded and received substantial wage boosts. This led to a spurt in consumer spending, which led, in turn, to further hoarding of goods. An inflationary spiral thus began, which was not effectively checked until after 1949.

Initially the Nationalist authorities had avoided creating large amounts of new currency by selling bonds and foreign-exchange reserves. Soon those alternatives were exhausted. Printing new money was irresistibly easier than controlling the budgetary deficit by creating new sources of tax revenue or holding down spending. Moreover, the authorities dismissed economists' warnings about the dangers of inflation, contending that it could not become a serious danger in an agrarian society like China. Only after prices started shooting upward in 1940 and 1941 did they gradually perceive that they must raise revenues and reduce expenditures if they would prevent the entire war effort from being undercut by the process of monetary depreciation.

In 1941–2 the government began seriously searching for new sources of revenue. The income tax was extended; a so-called consumption tax, in essence a revival of the old and much detested likin, was imposed on goods in transit; and the salt tax was increased, making it the most fruitful of the government's taxes. Another revenue-raising scheme was the creation in 1942 of state monopolies for the distribution of salt, sugar, tobacco and matches. These several measures were only marginally beneficial. The income and excess-profits taxes proved to be almost totally unenforceable, partly because of purposeful evasion. The consumption tax, although lucrative, created so many obstacles to trade that it was revoked in 1945. The inadequacy of all these revenue-raising schemes is revealed in the stark fact that less than 11 per cent of the government's wartime cash expenditures were covered by tax revenues.

The most far-reaching fiscal innovation was the land tax in kind. Since 1928, the agricultural land tax had been collected in money by the provincial governments. The central government therefore had to purchase rice for its mammoth army on the open market. But with rice prices shooting upward – the average price in June 1941 was over twenty times higher than on the eve of the war – the cost of maintaining the army had become insupportable. Beginning in July 1941, therefore, the central government took over the collection of the land tax from the provinces. It also assessed the tax not in money but in rice (or, in non-rice-producing areas, other foodstuffs such as wheat and barley; in rare cases, cotton was collected). The grain thus collected was, however, still insufficient to meet the needs of the army and civil servants. The government in July 1942 therefore instituted the practice of 'compulsory purchase' (in July 1943, this was changed to 'compulsory borrowing') of foodstuffs. That is, the taxpayer was now compelled to convey to the central government not only the land tax but an additional, and approximately equivalent, amount of grain for which he was subsequently to be reimbursed.

Through these measures, the central government obtained a sure source of foodgrains. It no longer had to expend *fa-pi* to buy expensive rice on the open market. This reduced one of the several pressures to print new money. The grain tax was, however, peculiarly susceptible to peculation, which deeply disgruntled the farmers and contributed to the moral deterioration of government. Chang Kia-ngau, an unusually objective high government official, was undoubtedly correct when he concluded that 'the long term political and social effects [of the tax in kind] to a large degree outweighed the immediate advantage of securing low cost food for the army'.[92]

Though the government was not notably successful in generating new sources of revenue, it did work manfully to limit spending. Realizing in 1940 that its open-handed encouragement of economic growth was generating a potentially dangerous inflationary trend, the government tightened its credit policies and cut back on the development of industry and communications. The most substantial savings, however, were made by clamping a lid on the wages of soldiers and government officials. Recognizing that the wages of government employees could keep pace with rising prices only if enormous sums of additional money were printed, the government did not substantially increase wages until 1944. The nominal purchasing power of officials' salaries decreased between 1937 and 1944 by about 85 per cent and of soldiers by about 94 per cent. In fact, of course, officials were supported partly through subsidized food and housing; and they also supported themselves in many cases by taking on more than one job and thus securing more than one salary. It must also be recognized that the area and population governed by the Nationalist regime during the war were both considerably smaller than pre-war. At any rate, annual government expenditures, measured in constant prices, in fact declined substantially over the course of the war. Although precision is impossible, government cash expenditures in 1944 *in real terms* had fallen to less than one-fourth of its prewar expenditures. The government was starving.

---

[92] Chang Kia-ngau, *Inflationary spiral*, 144. See also Young, *China's wartime finance*, 25-6. On the land tax generally, see Eastman, *Seeds of destruction*, 45-70.

Whether the government was wise to economize by holding down the wages of its employees is debatable. The low wages forced many, perhaps most, government officials and military officers to engage in peculation, to enrich themselves through unauthorized forms of trade with the occupied areas, or to obtain concurrent employment to the detriment of their efficiency in their government jobs. If, on the other hand, the government had pegged soldiers' and officials' pay to the rising cost-of-living, the government deficit would have grown enormously, thus adding to the inflationary pressures. The only economically acceptable means of holding down these government expenditures would have been to reduce the size of the army and bureaucracy. This would have reduced spending and probably would have increased efficiency. For political reasons, however, this measure was not adopted.

In 1942-4, the annual increase of prices had been about 237 per cent; from just January to August 1945, prices increased 251 per cent. On the monetary side, the government issued unprecedented amounts of new currency to meet a series of soaring new expenditures – the total number of *fa-pi* in circulation tripled between January and August 1945. One important cause of these rising expenditures was the growing presence of the United States in China. Its troop strength in China increased from 1,255 at the end of 1942, to 32,956 in January 1945, and to 60,369 in August 1945. These forces had to be supplied largely from the local economy, and at levels of consumption utterly beyond the ken of most Chinese. In mid-1944, H. H. Kung complained that 'in China your boys need six eggs a day, and now it is cut down to four eggs. But you eat a pound of beef a day...In order to supply the meat, we are feeding [you] our oxen, used for farm purposes... Soon there won't be any animals left to help the farmers farm their land.'[93] Indeed, one American soldier in China cost as much as 500 Chinese soldiers. In addition, the decision to build and operate four large air bases for the long-range B-29 bombers, and three fighter strips, all completed in June 1944, led to further huge expenditures. From November 1944 to May 1945, the monthly cost of the American presence increased from Y1 billion to Y20 billion. In retrospect, it is clear that the military benefits derived from the increased American role in China – and particularly of the B-29 operations, which staged a mere twenty raids during the war – were far outweighed by the fiscal damage inflicted upon China's weakened economy.[94]

The inflationary effect of Chinese expenditures for the American

---

[93] Young, *Helping hand* 291, 254-5. On United States troop strength in China, see Romanus and Sunderland, *Stilwell's mission*, 267; *Time runs out*, 258.

[94] Young, *China's wartime finance*, 272-3; Young, *Helping hand*, 290; Romanus and Sunderland, *Stilwell's command problems*, 115; FRUS, *1944*, 6.906-7.

military is suggested by the fact that they equalled fully 53 per cent of the new currency issues during the last 1½ years of the war. Still, the expenditures of the National government itself were also rising sharply, in large part as a result of reforms initiated upon the advice of the Americans. Thirty-nine divisions of the Chinese army, for example, were singled out for modernization, training, medical treatment and improved food. Salaries of government officials and teachers were boosted in late 1944 – although this only slightly eased their difficulties. At the same time, the expenditures and loans of the newly created War Production Board, even though only about 7 per cent of the government's total expenditures, also helped push prices ever upward during the first half of 1945. By the end of the war, the average retail price index was 2,600 times higher than in July 1937.

Not all segments of society were affected equally by the inflation. A narrow stratum of hoarders, speculators and corrupt officials acquired enormous wealth. Some groups, such as landlords and industrial workers, fared well in varying degrees and at different times. The majority of the population, however, was progressively reduced to, and even below, the bare subsistence level. Table 11 indicates changes in the purchasing power of several income groups in Nationalist China, although it does not precisely reflect their relative standards of living. The majority of farmers, for instance, fared much more poorly than the table suggests, because of poor harvests, increasing taxation and rents, and the burdens of military and labour conscription.[95] Government employees like soldiers, officials and professors, on the other hand, did not fare quite as badly as the table would indicate, because they received subsidies in such forms as cheap food and housing.

The ravages of inflation upon the standard of living of officials and soldiers affected the government's viability. As early as 1940, the purchasing power of officials' wages had declined to about one-fifth of prewar levels. By 1943, real wages were down to a tenth of what they had been in 1937. Although their plight was alleviated by monthly subsidies of rice, cooking oil and so on, officials were frequently living – in the words of Chang Kia-ngau – in 'abject poverty'.[96] Single men could scarcely survive on their salaries; officials with families became desperate, preoccupied with their personal situation. Some took second jobs; many became corrupt.

Corruption was very evident. High officials with gorgeously gowned ladies drove in chauffeured automobiles through the streets of fuel-short Chungking; they purchased perfumes, cigarettes, oranges, butter, and

[95] Eastman, *Seeds of destruction*, 66–70.
[96] Chang Kia-ngau, *Inflationary spiral*, 64.

TABLE 11

Indices of the purchasing power of monetary income of several income groups,
1937–45

	Professors[a]	Soldiers[b]	Civil servants[c] (Chungking)	Industrial[d] workers	Farmers[e]	Rural[c] workers (Szechwan)
1937	100	100	100	100	100	100
1938	95	95	77	124	87	111
1939	64	64	49	95	85	122
1940	25	29	21	76	96	63
1941	15	22	16	78	115	82
1942	12	10	11	75	101	75
1943	14	6	10	69	100	58
1944	11	—	—	41 (April)	81	—
1945	12	—	—	—	87	—

Sources: a. Indices for 1937–42 are from Wang Yin-yuan, 'Ssu-ch'uan chan-shih wu-chia yü ko-chi jen-min chih kou-mai-li' (Prices and purchasing power in wartime Szechwan), *Ssu-ch'uan ching-chi chi-k'an* (Szechwan economics quarterly), 1.3 (15 June 1944), 263; and those for 1943–5 are the June ratios (salaries/cost-of-living) in *Economic facts*, 22.177 (July 1943), 34.479 (July 1944), 46.701 (July 1945).
b. Wang Yin-yuan, 263.
c. Chang Kia-ngau, *The inflationary spiral*, 63.
d. Chang Kia-ngau, 63–4.
e. Chou Shun-hsin, *The Chinese inflation*, 243.

other luxuries smuggled from abroad; they dined at extravagant, multi-course banquets. Not all officials, of course, were corrupt. Some bravely suffered from malnutrition and saw the health of their families decline. Many, however, succumbed to temptation because it was easy to rationalize malfeasance when their superiors engaged in gross conspicuous consumption.

Inflation similarly ravaged the well-being of students and intellectuals. Books were few, scientific equipment sparse. Students lived in poorly lit, unheated dormitories, their beds crammed together like bunks in a ship. Faculty members frequently crowded in with the families of their colleagues. Meat and fat disappeared from their diets; some ate hardly two meals a day. Malnutrition in the academic community became almost universal. During the latter stage of the war, according to the *Ta-kung-pao*, both teachers and students were living 'on the verge of starvation', 'under the most miserable conditions imaginable'.[97] Health declined; malaria and tuberculosis were common. To supplement their meagre incomes, many faculty members taught at two or more universities, sold treasured books and art objects, or carved seals and wrote calligraphy for sale. The quality

[97] *Ta-kung-pao* (Chungking), 19 Mar. 1945, p. 2 (editorial); *ibid.* 13 Apr. 1945, p. 2 (editorial).

of their teaching suffered, and their disillusionment with the government rose.[98]

The government did endeavour to ease the economic plight of officials and professors who taught at government-run universities by providing special allowances, inexpensive housing, and various daily necessities at artificially low prices. Rice at one time was sold to government employees for Yo.10 a catty, while the price on the open market was Y5.00. But the government delayed granting meaningful salary increases, because these would have increased the budget. In 1943, government expenditures would have risen by 300 per cent if officials' real salaries had been raised to prewar levels. By 1944, discontent within the bureaucracy and army had swollen so greatly that wages were sharply increased – too little and too late, for by that time prices were rising uncontrollably. The demoralization of the bureaucracy and army continued until 1949.

THE INDUSTRIAL SECTOR

Free China's wartime industry developed upon minuscule foundations. When the war broke out, the area that was to become unoccupied China – comprising about three-fourths of the nation's territory – could boast of only about 6 per cent of the nation's factories, 7 per cent of the industrial workers, 4 per cent of the total capital invested in industry, and 4 per cent of the electrical capacity.[99] During the early years of the war, however, industry in the Nationalist area boomed. Consumer demand, especially from the government and army but also from the increased civilian population in the interior, created a nearly insatiable market for industrial products. Until 1940, food prices lagged far behind the prices of manufactured goods, so that wages remained low and profit margins were high. Until the Burma Road was shut down in March 1942, the purchase of critically needed machinery, spare parts, and imported raw materials, albeit difficult and exorbitantly expensive, was still possible.[100]

---

[98] Hollington K. Tong, ed. *China after seven years of war*, 112–13; Young, *China's wartime finance*, 323. Regarding the incidence of tuberculosis, a Communist source reported that X-ray examinations in 1945 revealed that fully 43 per cent of the faculty members at National Central University in Chungking – one of the most favoured universities – suffered from the disease, as did 15 per cent of the male students and 5.6 per cent of the female students. *Hsin-hua jih-pao*, 20 Feb. 1945, in *CPR* 47 (21 Feb. 1945) 3. This report doubtless needs corroboration.

[99] Li Tzu-hsiang, 'K'ang-chan i-lai', 23; *CJCC* 2.659. See also Chang Sheng-hsuan, 'San-shih-erh-nien Ssu-ch'uan kung-yeh chih hui-ku yü ch'ien-chan' (Perspectives on the past and future of Szechwan's economy in 1943), *SCCC* 1.2 (15 Mar. 1944), 258; and *CYB, 1937–1943*, 437.

[100] Chang Sheng-hsuan, 266. New textile-spinning equipment, for instance, was imported, increasing the number of spindles in the interior from just a few thousand before the war to about 230,000. Rockwood Q. P. Chin, 'The Chinese cotton industry under wartime inflation', *Pacific Affairs*, 16.1 (March 1943), 34, 37, 39.

TABLE 12

Factories* in unoccupied China

	1936 and before	1937	1938	1939	1940	1941	1942	1943	1944	Uncertain date of origin	Total
Number of plants established[a]	300	63	209	419	571	866	1,138	1,049	549	102	5,266
Capitalization of new plants in 1937 currency[a] (thousands of *yuan*)	117,950	22,166	86,583	120,914	59,031	45,719	9,896	14,486	3,419	7,317	487,481
Factories actually in operation	—	—	—	—	1,354[b]	—	2,123[c]	—	928[d]	—	—

* By official definition, a factory used power machinery and employed at least thirty workers.

Sources: a. Li Tzu-hsiang, 'Ssu-ch'uan chan-shih kung-yeh t'ung-chi', *Ssu-ch'uan ching-chi chi-k'an* 3.1 (1 Jan. 1946) 206.
b. Frank W. Price, *Wartime China as seen by Westerners*, 47. This figure *presumably* includes both government-owned and private factories.
c. *China Handbook, 1937–1943,* 433 and 441. This figure is approximate, being the sum of private factories in existence in May 1942, the factories created since 1936 by the National Resources Council (98), and the factories established by provincial governments by August 1942 (110).
d. *China Handbook, 1937–1945,* 363. This figure includes both government-owned and private factories.

These favourable factors led new factories to open in increasing numbers until 1943 (see table 12), and industrial output almost quadrupled between 1938 and 1943.

Despite this growth, industrial production did not remotely satisfy consumer demands. Although the population of wartime Nationalist China was approximately one-half that of the prewar period, the output of principal industrial products never exceeded 12 per cent of prewar levels. Cotton yarn, cotton cloth and wheat flour in 1944 were only 5.3 per cent, 8.8 per cent and 5.3 per cent, respectively, of their prewar figures.[101] In 1943–4, moreover, the industrial sector entered a profound crisis, and production fell off sharply during 1944. Table 13 shows the weak condition of industry during the latter half of the war. Capitalization of new factories had peaked in 1939. Thereafter, despite the increasing number of new plants, the total value of investment fell precipitously. The industrial boom had in fact ended by about 1940, but marginal operators, with limited experience and minimal financial resources, continued to open new plants in the vain expectation that the boom would resume.[102] Most of these small, marginal operations quickly folded. In 1944, only 928 factories were actually in operation in Nationalist China. They had suffered a mortality rate of 82 per cent.

Although output increased until 1943, the industrial sector in 1940 had begun to encounter obstacles that first caused the *rate* of growth to decline, and then produced the industrial crisis after September 1943.[103] The consequences of inflation were not all negative. During the eight years of war, for example, real wages of workers rose only during 1938; thereafter, to the benefit of employers, they declined.[104] But the inflation made investments in commerce and especially in speculative enterprises vastly more lucrative than investments in industry (see table 14). Hoarding of rice and other agricultural products became widespread. 'Smuggled' goods, both from occupied China and from abroad, brought huge returns that diverted capital from productive investments. It was sometimes more profitable just to hold commodities than to pay to have them processed. The price of raw cotton during 1940 and 1941, for example, rose at an average of 13 per cent a month, and investors made substantially larger profits simply by storing the cotton than by chancing long-term investment in mills that processed cotton. Thus most liquid capital – on

---

[101] Yu-Kwei Cheng, 109; Shun-hsin Chou, 94.
[102] Rockwood Q. P. Chin, 39.
[103] Liu Chi-ping, 'San-shih-san-nien Ssu-ch'uan chih shang-yeh' (The commercial economy of Szechwan in 1944), *SCCC* 2.2 (1 April 1945), 79; Li Tzu-hsiang, 'Wo-kuo chan-shih kung-yeh sheng-ch'an ti hui-ku yü ch'ien-chan' (The past and future of China's wartime industrial production), *SCCC* 2.3 (1 July 1945), 32.
[104] Shun-hsin Chou, 239–40.

TABLE 13

Indices of industrial production in Nationalist China, 1938–1945

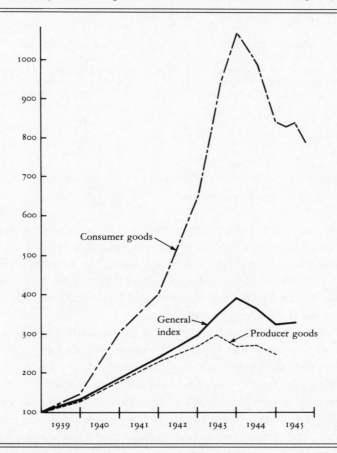

Source: a. Li Tzu-hsiang, 'Wo-kuo chan-shih kung-yeh sheng-ch'an te hui-ku yü ch'ien-chan', *Ssu-ch'uan ching-chi chi-k'an*, 2.3 (1 July 1945) 30.
b. Yu-Kwei Cheng, *Foreign trade and industrial development of China*, 110.
c. Chi-ming Hou, 'Economic development and public finance in China, 1937–1945', in Paul K. T. Sih, ed., *Nationalist China during the Sino-Japanese War, 1937–1945*, 214.
Note: There are discrepancies among these sources, although all are based upon data of the Chinese Ministry of Economics. Most significant, source *c* portrays no absolute decline in producer-goods production, but both sources *a* and *b* do indicate such a decline. The reason for the disparity may be that different commodities were included in computing the producer-goods index.

the order of 86 per cent in 1944 – had been channelled into commerce and speculation rather than production. Private modern and old-style banks increasingly withdrew from industrial investment, preferring to issue short-term commercial loans or to participate directly in hoarding and other forms of speculation. The government continued to provide

TABLE 14

Variations in real returns per individual from various types of activity,
Chungking
(1938 = 100)

Year	Agriculture	Manufactures	Retail	Speculation	US securities
1937	—	59	105	29	NA
1938	100	100	100	100	100
1939	61	106	111	297	180
1940	92	85	112	808	512
1941	109	71	119	550	1,373
1942	132	76	120	720	3,951
1943	124	69	124	263	10,260

Source: Chang Kia-ngau, *The inflationary spiral*, 60.

low-interest loans to private industry, but the value of these in constant currency was but a fraction of those provided in 1938–9. Industry consequently starved for want of working capital, an important cause of the industrial decline. Industrialists complained bitterly about the paucity of loans and the cumbrous procedures required. But those who did obtain government loans commonly used the money for speculation.[105]

Factors other than inflation aggravated the industrialists' difficulties. The tightening noose of the Japanese blockade, for example, cut off the infusions of machinery, parts, raw materials and fuels upon which China's industrial plant was heavily dependent. Much of the industrial equipment in the interior was already antiquated – machinery in the textile industry, for example, dated from the 1920s – and so its deterioration, without replacements and spare parts, was rapid. Many materials – such as high-alloy steels – were unavailable within China, and yet were crucial if production in several branches of industry was to continue.

Lack of skilled workers also hampered China's wartime industry. Locally recruited workers, recently off the farms, frequently lacked even a rudimentary acquaintance with machinery or labour discipline. Skilled

[105] Liu Min, 'San-shih-san-nien Ssu-ch'uan chih kung-yeh' (Szechwan's industry in 1944), *SCCC* 2.2 (1 April 1945), 35; Yung Lung-kuei, 'Chiu-chi chan-shih kung-yeh ti chi-pen t'u-ching' (Fundamental means of rescuing the wartime industry), *Chung-kuo kung-yeh* (Chinese industry), 25.8 (March 1944); Li Tzu-hsiang, 'Wo-kuo chan-shih', 36; Kuan Meng-chueh, 'Shan-hsi-sheng fang-chih-yeh chih wei-chi chi ch'i ch'u-lu' (The crisis of Shansi's textile industry and its solution), *Chung-kuo kung-yeh*, 19 (1 September 1943) 12; Juan Yu-ch'iu, 'Chin-jih hou-fang min-ying kung-yeh ti wei-chi' (The current crisis of private industry in the rear area), *Chung-kuo nung-min* (Chinese farmer), 3.1/2 (June 1943), 33; Fang Chih-p'ing *et al. Lun kuan-liao tzu-pen* (On bureaucratic capital), 36; P'an Tsu-yung, 'Hou-fang pan-ch'ang ti k'un-nan ho ch'i-wang' (Difficulties and hopes of factory management in the rear area), *Hsin-ching-chi* (New economy), 6.11 (1 March 1942), 237–9; Ch'en Po-ta, *Chung-kuo ssu-ta-chia-tsu* (China's four great families), 52.

industrial labourers, therefore, had to be recruited from cities on the coast. By 1940, however, only some 42,000 of these had followed the Nationalist government into the interior. Factory managers began poaching upon other factories in their quest for skilled employees. This competition drove up wages. It also contributed to a destructively high rate of labour turnover – in 1940, about 10 per cent a month for skilled workers and 18 per cent for unskilled. In May 1943, the monthly turnover for all workers was 23 per cent. This prodigious instability, together with the general shortage of skills and the deterioration of equipment, led to a rapid decline in worker efficiency. In textile mills, for example, it was judged to be about 60–85 per cent of prewar levels. An electrical worker estimated that the efficiency of his factory was only one-third what it had been in Shanghai.[106]

Paradoxically, some industries ran into a lack of consumer demand. The steady impoverishment of people limited their spending to only the most critical necessities. The market for textile goods became sluggish, despite the people's desperate need for new clothing, because their purchasing power had collapsed. Weakened demand also struck the manufacturers of producer goods. The iron industry, for example, had flourished prior to 1942 due to the construction of railways and air-raid shelters. When the government gave up such projects, the iron industry lapsed into the doldrums, injuring related sectors such as coal and coke. Demand for industrial machinery and military equipment remained high. But China's iron-and-steel manufacturers usually could not satisfy it, because they lacked the equipment, raw materials, and skilled labour required.[107]

To combat the inflation, the government had first tried as early as December 1938 to fix the prices of daily necessities. This quickly proved ineffective. Subsequently the government promulgated a rash of new regulations to eliminate speculation in commodities and to hold down the prices of food, industrial materials and rents. By October 1941, however, the Bank of China pronounced all these measures a 'complete failure'.[108]

The Nationalists' interest in price controls revived after the United

[106] Freyn, *Free China's New Deal*, 41; Kuo-heng Shih, 60–1, 134; *CHB, 1937–1945*, 385; Ta Chen, 55–6 and 122, table 58; Ch'en Ta, 'Chung-Kuo lao-kung chieh-chi yü tang-ch'ien ching-chi wei-chi' (China's working class and the current economic crisis), *She-hui chien-she* (Social reconstruction), 1.4 (1 Aug. 1948), 17; Li Tzu-hsiang, 'K'ang-chan i-lai', 43; Israel Epstein, *Notes on labor problems in Nationalist China*, 20–8.

[107] Liu Chi-ping, 79; Yung Lung-kuei, 8; T'ao Ta-yung, 'Lun tang-ch'ien ti kung-yeh chiu-chi' (Current means of rescuing industry), *Chung-kuo kung-yeh* (Chinese industry), 25.11 (Mar. 1944); Liu Min, 36–7.

[108] Chang Kia-ngau, *Inflationary spiral*, 344; Young, *China's wartime finance*, 144; *Ts'ai-cheng p'ing-lun* (Financial review), 5.1 (Jan. 1941), 25–37.

States adopted an anti-inflation law in October 1942, because they inferred that price controls were the mark of a modern nation at war. Financial and economic experts, such as Franklin Ho and Arthur Young, advised the Chungking leaders against price controls, on the grounds that they left the basic causes of inflation untouched and that the government lacked the administrative means to enforce them. They warned that the controls would be ignored and public confidence impaired. Disregarding these warnings, the government instituted on 15 January 1943 a new system of price controls. Black markets were banned and violators threatened with dire punishments, up to the death sentence. Also to control prices – and increase revenues – the state created monopolies of selected commodities. Beginning in 1942, it undertook to purchase such goods in bulk and sell them at low, fixed prices. These measures governed daily necessities (rice, salt, edible oil, sugar, fuel, etc.), industrial goods (iron, steel, cotton yarn, etc.), export items (tungsten, tin, tea, pig bristles, tung oil, etc.), and miscellaneous goods such as cotton, tobacco and matches.[109]

The government's several attempts to combat inflation with price controls were ineffective. China lacked the prerequisites: that is, firm territorial and political control, an efficient and honest bureaucracy, and a functioning system of transportation and communication. Outside a few major cities, the controls were largely inoperative. Controlled commodities fled those cities to other areas. Chungking several times faced severe rice shortages, because the price of rice was higher elsewhere. Even in major cities, actual market prices exceeded the official prices by an average of 14 per cent in 1943 and 67 per cent in 1945.[110]

The price controls sometimes had ruinous consequences for industry. In 1943, for instance, the official price of raw cotton was set so low that many farmers in Shensi – which provided most of unoccupied China's raw cotton – planted wheat instead and the mills in the Nationalist area reportedly had only enough cotton to operate for half a year. Not infrequently the cost of manufacturing a product exceeded its legal fixed price. In 1943, producing a ton of iron cost Y35,000; the government price of iron was Y30,000 a ton. In 1944 the cost of mining a ton of coal ranged from Y1,870 to Y5,000; the fixed market price of coal was Y1,200 a ton. A bale of cotton cost Y15,000 to produce; yet it could be sold for only Y12,000.[111]

Finally the Ichigo campaign in 1944–5 in Honan, Hupei, Hunan, Kweichow, Kwangsi and Kwangtung hit fully one-fourth of Nationalist

109 Chang Kia-ngau, *ibid.* 135–7, 345–9; Young, *China's wartime finance*, 35–6, 146–9.
110 Chang Kia-ngau, *ibid.* 345–6; Young, *ibid.* 149.
111 Kuan Meng-chueh, 7–9; Chang Kia-ngau, *Inflationary spiral*, 217; Liu Min, 37; Kan K'o-ch'ao, 'Chan-shih Ssu-ch'uan kung-yeh kai-kuan' (Survey of Szechwan's wartime economy), *SCCC* 1.2 (15 Mar. 1944), 72.

China's factories, accounting for 15 per cent or more of the total industrial capital. It also severed the remaining industrial plant of Nationalist China from its sources of supply (such as the raw cotton produced in Honan, Hunan and Hupei) and from market outlets, and destroyed investor confidence.

All these factors – inflation, lack of imports, shortage of skilled workers, withering consumer demand, obstructive price-control policies and military disaster – plunged Nationalist China's industry into a deep crisis. As one indication, arsenals in the autumn of 1944 were operating at only 55 per cent of capacity. Between 80 and 90 per cent of the iron-and-steel plants in Chungking closed between the spring of 1943 and early 1945; 50 of the 320 machine shops closed during 1944; about 185 of the 250 coal-mining units in the major coal-producing Chia-ling River area closed between 1943 and 1945.[112]

Unemployment had become a serious problem by March 1945. Mining production in 1944 was but a fraction of the 1942 levels (coal, 72 per cent; lead, 49 per cent; tungsten, 27 per cent; tin, 27 per cent; copper, 24 per cent; antimony, 6 per cent). Even cotton-handicraft production was in deep trouble by the end of 1944, largely from shortages of raw materials, transportation difficulties, and troublesome transit taxes. The industrial crisis was assuredly greater than the official production figures suggest (see table 13).[113]

The creation in November 1944 of the Chinese War Production Board, resulting in large government orders and infusions of new money, markedly stimulated some industries. Between November 1944 and May 1945, steel production increased by 52 per cent; pig iron, 46 per cent; coal, 35 per cent; and electric power, 8 per cent. Despite these increases, the general index of industrial production during the first three months of 1945 remained unchanged. Manifestly, the decline elsewhere in the industrial sector had not been impeded. The evidence is overwhelming that, on the eve of peace, Nationalist China's industry in particular, and the economy generally, were on the verge of collapse.[114]

War made the government the leading economic entrepreneur. Previously it had gained control of the banking sector, but it held only some 11 per cent of the capital in Chinese-owned industrial enterprises. By 1942, however, the Ministry of Economics reported that state-controlled

[112] Young, Helping hand, 335; Li Tzu-hsiang, 'Wo-kuo chan-shih', 28–9; Liu Min, 28–9.
[113] Ta-kung-pao (Chungking), (1 June 1945), p. 3; CHB, 1937–1945, 369; Shang-wu jih-pao, 9 Sept. 1945, in CPR 246 (12 Sept. 1945) 9; Chang Ta-ch'en, 'San-shih-san nien ti Ch'ung-ch'ing t'u-pu-yeh' (Chungking's handicraft textile industry in 1944), SCCC 2.2 (1 April 1945), 202.
[114] Chang Kia-ngau, Inflationary spiral, 67. See also Young, China's wartime finance, 141 and 316; Shang-wu jih-pao, 18 July 1945, in CPR 196 (22 July 1945) 1; Shang-wu jih-pao, 7 Aug. 1945, in CPR 217 (12 Aug. 1945) 1–4.

enterprises accounted for 17.5 per cent of the factories, 70 per cent of the capital, 32 per cent of the workers and 42 per cent of the horse-power in the Nationalist area.[115]

Three government agencies developed industry in the interior: the National Resources Commission (Tzu-yuan wei-yuan-hui), the Industrial and Mining Adjustment Administration (Kung-k'uang t'iao-cheng wei-yuan-hui) and the four government banks. The mandate of the National Resources Commission, created in 1935, was to 'develop, operate and control basic industries'. By December 1944 it operated 92 industrial units – 33 factories, 38 mines, and 21 electrical power plants. It also ran 11 industrial units conjointly with other agencies. The commission dominated the heavy and highly technical industries, in contrast to the private factories, which tended to be less mechanized and to produce light industrial goods.[116]

The initial responsibility of the Industrial and Mining Adjustment Administration, created just after the outbreak of the war, was to facilitate the removal of privately owned factories to the interior. From 1938 it also invested directly in industrial enterprises, frequently producing consumer goods in competition with private entrepreneurs – alcohol, textiles, paper and cement. In 1943 and 1944, its direct investments exceeded its loans to private industry by over 30 per cent. Sun Yat-sen had held that the government should limit its economic role to basic industries, but now it became a major participant in light industry as well.[117]

The four government banks were not 'government' banks in the usual sense, for private investors held substantial shares in three of them: the Bank of China, the Bank of Communications, and the Farmers' Bank. Like private commercial banks, all three, especially after 1940, increased their direct participation and ownership in industry and business. They did this to get tangible assets to protect the real value of their capital. This became, as Chang Kia-ngau observed, 'indistinguishable from speculation'.[118] Whatever their motives, the government banks, like the Industrial and Mining Adjustment Administration, became deeply enmeshed in the private industrial and commercial sectors.

Some critics, politically inspired, characterized the government's role in the economy as 'bureaucratic capitalism', through which officials were amassing private fortunes, squeezing out private entrepreneurs and impoverishing the common people. However, the growing economic role

[115] Parks Coble, Jr. *The Shanghai capitalists and the Nationalist government, 1927–1937*, 315–17; Ch'en Chen, ed. *Chung-kuo chin-tai kung-yeh tzu-liao* (Materials on the industry of modern China), 2.1422.
[116] *CHB, 1937–1943*, 431, 365; Ch'en Chen, 2.836–9, 853.　　　[117] *CHB, 1937–1943*, 438, 376.
[118] Chang Kia-ngau, *Inflationary spiral*, 189–90. See also *Ta-kung-pao* editorial, 13 Dec. 1941, cited in Ch'en Po-ta, 52.

of the National government might better be viewed as state capitalism, a rational response to the requirements of a modernizing agrarian society and to the unique economic demands of wartime. Few entrepreneurs, without government aid, could have relocated their factories or created large-scale new ones in the western provinces. Wartime China faced an especial need to rationalize the distribution of scarce resources, such as machinery, raw materials and power. It is not, therefore, the policy of state capitalism per se that can be criticized, but rather the implementation of that policy. Government enterprises were frequently inefficient, bureaucratic and corrupt, as was the government's administration elsewhere. Government-related factories, moreover, enjoyed numerous advantages – such as bank credit, raw materials, or trucks for transport – that were denied to private firms. Some companies, like the Chung-yuan Paper Mill, sought an official connection by voluntarily offering stock to the government. Failing this, private firms in large numbers foundered late in the war for want of working capital, raw materials or guaranteed markets,[119] while corrupt government officials became enormously wealthy. By the latter phase of the war, the government's economic entrepreneurship had become a political liability. In 1948 Mao Tse-tung elevated 'bureaucratic capitalism' to the level of feudalism and imperialism as a target of his New Democratic Revolution.[120]

POLITICAL DEBILITATION

An editorial in a Chengtu paper (the *Hua-hsi jih-pao*: West China daily) – never published, because it was quashed by the censor – trenchantly expressed the popular mood late in the war: 'Government officials are corrupt and laws are abused by them; the people's livelihood becomes daily more grievous and desperate. With the nation in hardship and the people in poverty, a small corrupt element is growing increasingly richer and living even more luxuriously. This rotten phenomenon, together with many other reactionary political factors, has lowered both the people's and the soldiers' morale nearly to the vanishing point.'[121]

Demoralization was a variable phenomenon, proceeding unevenly from

[119] Ch'en Chen, 2.1448–9; Chang Kia-ngau, *Inflationary spiral*, 188–90; An-min Chung, 'The development of modern manufacturing industry in China, 1928–1949', 227; Kan K'o-ch'ao, 72; Li Tzu-hsiang, 'Wo-kuo chan-shih', 34–7; Yen Hsi-ta, 'Ching-chi wei-chi yü kuan-liao tzu-pen' (The economic crisis and bureaucratic capital), *Ching-chi chou-pao* (Economics weekly), 4.6 (6 Feb. 1947) 9–11.

[120] 'On the question of the national bourgeoisie and the enlightened gentry', *Selected works of Mao Tse-tung*, 4.207–10.

[121] Penfield to Gauss, 'Censored editorial on PPC meeting', US State Dept. 893.00/9–1444, 14 Sept. 1944, encl. 1, p. 1.

place to place. In February 1939 it was reported that the martial spirit of the Hunanese was low, but morale in Kwangtung and Kwangsi was very high. In mid-1941, the people of Sikang appeared utterly indifferent while Chungking by contrast, despite – or, more probably, because of – three years of bombing, 'throbbed [to use the words of Theodore White] with the strength of a nation at war'.[122]

The demoralization of Nationalist China was largely due to the corrosive effects of inflation and the changing political and military aims of the government. After the United States and England joined the war and the Communist movement became a potent military and political force, Chiang Kai-shek and the Nationalist leaders became concerned less about surviving the Japanese onslaught than about the future of their own power. The government became conservative and repressive.

The People's Political Council, for example, had been a highly promising instrument for generating popular support. With its large number of non-KMT members, it epitomized the spirit of national unity. After 1940, however, many council members criticized the breakdown of the united front and the increase of censorship and repression. To maximize their political effectiveness, the minority party representatives in the council in March 1941 organized the Federation of Democratic Parties, a coalition of six minority parties and groups that had emerged during the 1920s and 1930s. These were typically formed of intellectuals, often foreign-educated, who resented the KMT dictatorship. There was, however, a broad ideological spread among them. The China Youth Party and the National Socialist Party were basically conservative, while the Third Party and members of the National Salvation Association were more radical. Because these minority parties hoped to dismantle the Kuomintang's one-party control of the government, however, they all spoke in the idiom of Western democracy. With the possible exception of the China Youth Party, which claimed about 30,000 members, none of them had a mass following. They were essentially congeries of intellectuals, highly elitist in outlook.[123]

Proclaiming itself a 'third force' – neither KMT nor CCP – the federation called for democratization, government by law, and freedom of speech, publication and assembly. It published the *Kuang-ming-pao*

[122] Peck to State, telegram, US State Dept. 893.00/14339, 28 Feb. 1939, pp. 1–3; Gauss to State, 'Transmitting copies of a report concerning some observations of a trip to Western Szechuan and Eastern Sikang', US State Dept. 893.00/14800, 18 Sept. 1941, encl. p. 8; White and Jacoby, 11, 19; Graham Peck, *Two kinds of time*, 56.

[123] *Chung-kuo ko hsiao-tang-p'ai hsien-k'uang* (Present state of the minority parties in China); 'Democracy vs. one-party-rule: the little parties organize', *Amerasia*, 7.3 (25 April 1943) 97–117; Melville T. Kennedy, Jr. 'The Chinese Democratic League', *Harvard papers on China*, 7 (1953) 136–75; Ch'ien Tuan-sheng, 351–62.

(Light) in Hong Kong and the *Min-hsien* (People's constitution) in Chungking and opened offices in major cities like Kunming, Chengtu and Kweilin. The federation spoke for intellectuals and professional people who identified with neither of the two major parties.[124]

Chungking had encouraged the PPC as long as it unreservedly supported government policies. When council members became captious and even formed a political party, however, it responded with customary ill grace. Publication of the federation's programme was suppressed by the censors, and its activities were constantly harassed by the secret police. In a government reorganization of the PPC in 1942, outspoken members of the federation lost their membership, and a reapportionment of the members assured the KMT of a dominant majority. In frustration, the Communists ceased attending meetings. Deprived of its popular and independent character, the PPC's deliberations thereafter had little impact upon government policy.[125]

The government's political style was illustrated in the National Spiritual Mobilization movement, inaugurated on 12 March 1939, the anniversary of Sun Yat-sen's death. Its objectives were to generate mass support for the government and mobilize the people for the war effort. The movement's methods, however, revealed the Nationalists' characteristic distrust of the masses. It encouraged people to swear to a 'Citizens Pact', all twelve articles of which were negatives – 'Not to act contrary to the Three People's Principles', 'Not to disobey laws and orders of the government', 'Not to participate in traitorous organizations', etc. Spiritual Mobilization – like the New Life movement of the 1930s – quickly foundered on bureaucratic inertia.[126]

Failing to mobilize the people and unwilling to permit them a meaningful role in politics, the National government remained an elitist regime, whose base of popular support eroded as the war dragged on. More and more it relied on force or the threat of force to maintain its political supremacy. Especially from 1939, as the United Front with the Communists broke down and popular discontent sharpened, the Nationalists unsheathed their weapons of repression. Wuhan in 1937–8 had seen considerable freedom of the press, but tight censorship was now reimposed. The Central News Agency invariably exaggerated victories and disguised defeats. Stories of corruption were expunged lest they

[124] Lyman P. Van Slyke, *Enemies and friends: the United Front in Chinese Communist history*, 169, 174–5.
[125] Lawrence Nae-lih Shyu, 'People's Political Council', 38–55.
[126] *China's spiritual mobilization: outline of the plan*; US State Dept. comment on telegram, Vincent to State, US State Dept. 893.00/14963, 13 Mar. 1943; *Kuo-min ching-shen tsung-tung-yuan yun-tung* (National spiritual mobilization movement), comp. San-min-chu-i ch'ing-nien-t'uan chung-yang t'uan-pu.

damage the war effort. Publishers were cowed by the heavy-handed pre-publication censorship, and China's wartime press was generally insipid. The Communists' *Hsin-hua jih-pao* (New China daily), published in Chungking as part of the United Front agreement, was the only newspaper that dared indicate, with symbols such as XXX, that the censors' blue pencils had reduced the original copy. Only in areas where Nationalist authority was attenuated, notably in Kweilin controlled by the Kwangsi clique (Li Chi-shen, Huang Hsu-ch'u *et al.*), and in Kunming where Lung Yun reigned, was the press able openly to express criticisms of the central government.[127]

After the New Fourth Army incident in January 1941, Communist activities were completely banned in Nationalist areas (except to a limited extent in Chungking), and known Communists were arrested. Communists, however, could take refuge in Yenan. It was individual liberals and members of the minority parties who most felt the sting of the Nationalists' political control. Ma Yin-ch'u, for example, a Kuomintang member and China's most noted economist, had criticized the large-scale war profiteering of government leaders. He was arrested in December 1940. Though freed in 1942, he was forbidden to publish on non-economic subjects and even to speak in public. Sa K'ung-liao, a well-known liberal journalist, was imprisoned in Kweilin in 1943. After the summer of 1940, many associated with the Chinese Industrial Cooperative Movement – nominally headed by H. H. Kung but tainted by radicalism because it related intimately with the common people – were arrested and some allegedly shot.[128]

Chungking's political controls fell particularly heavily upon the universities. The minister of education during most of the war (1938–44) was Ch'en Li-fu, leader of the CC clique and a fervent anti-Communist. On the pretext of eliminating invidious foreign influences (such as individualism, liberalism, and contempt for things Chinese) from the universities and raising their academic standards, Ch'en imposed rigid controls. His ministry published textbooks emphasizing China's traditions and KMT orthodoxy; it required courses in, inter alia, military training and the Three People's Principles; it provided syllabi for instructors; and it reduced student opportunities to take electives.[129] Ch'en Li-fu imposed a pervasive

[127] Lee-hsia Hsu Ting, *Government control of the press in modern China, 1900–1949*, 132–51.

[128] Hugh Deane, 'Political reaction in Kuomintang China', *Amerasia*, 5·5 (July 1941), 210–13; Lee-hsia Hsu Ting, 139–41; Gauss to State, US State Dept. 893.00/15319 (14 Mar. 1944), encl. (Memorandum by Graham Peck on unification of anti-Central Government elements), p. 6; Sa K'ung-liao, *Liang-nien ti cheng-chih-fan sheng-huo* (Two years in the life of a political prisoner), *passim*; Douglas Robertson Reynolds, 'The Chinese industrial cooperative movement and the political polarization of wartime China, 1938–1945', 306–8 and *passim*.

[129] Ou Tsuin-chen, 106–11; Jessie Gregory Lutz, *China and the Christian colleges, 1850–1950*, 386.

uniformity upon Chinese education, designed to assure Nationalist control over the nation's intellectuals and youth.

South-west Associated University (comprising Peita, Nankai and Tsing-hua Universities) in Kunming was favoured by the unusually high quality of its faculty members and by the political protection of Lung Yun. Most universities, however, succumbed to Ch'en Li-fu's pressures. The KMT secret police, which Ch'en controlled, devoted much of its attention to the academic community and cowed most professors. The Three-People's-Principles Youth Corps had cells on all campuses. Ardent members served as informers.[130]

The Nationalists' main instrument of political control, besides the KMT secret police and the Youth Corps, was the Military Commission's Bureau of Investigation and Statistics. Headed by one of Chiang Kai-shek's staunchest supporters, General Tai Li, this secret service expanded from 1,700 operatives in 1935 to 40–50,000 by the end of the war. Tai Li's responsibilities included military intelligence, under-cover operations in the Japanese-occupied areas, and political control of the army.[131] But his operatives also maintained surveillance of civilians, and ran most of Nationalist China's political prisons, at least ten in number, from which spread fearsome rumours of torture, doubtless not wholly unfounded. A primary purpose of the prisons was to 're-educate' persons with 'dangerous thoughts'. Inmates who responded positively to indoctrination were usually released after a year, but some were executed. Tai Li admitted to 130 executions between 1935 and 1945, although critics hinted at far larger numbers.[132] Tai Li's organization was the most feared in Nationalist China.

By 1944, political discontent was discernible at all levels of society. The depth of unrest in the rural areas may be exemplified by conditions in Honan. In 1940 and 1941, harvests there had been poor, and in 1942 the crop of spring wheat withered from drought. Although the farmers were in desperate need of food, officials relentlessly demanded full payment of the land taxes. Sometimes the farmers' entire harvests were seized, not even leaving seedgrain for the following year. Some farmers had to sell

[130] Lloyd E. Eastman, 'Regional politics', 340–1; Vincent to State, 'Meeting of Szechuan delegates of San Min Chu I Youth Corps', US State Dept. 893.408/1 (17 Mar. 1943); Langdon to Gauss, 'Activity among Chinese university students at Kunming', US State Dept. 893.42/8–3144 (31 Aug. 1944), p. 2.
[131] Tai Yü-nung hsien-sheng nien-p'u (Chronological biography of Tai Li), comp. Intelligence Section, Defence Ministry, 25; Ch'en Shao-hsiao, Hei-wang-lu (Record of the black net), 102–6; H. K. Tong, World press, 180–1.
[132] Li I-yeh, 51; Gauss to State, '"Labor camps" in China', US State Dept. 740.0011 Pacific War/3678 (24 Dec. 1943); Sa K'ung-liao, 41, and passim; Shang-jao chi-chung-ying (The Shang-jao concentration camp), 3, 23.

their work animals, furniture, and even their farms to satisfy the tax collectors. The result was wholesale famine in the winter of 1942–3, with many eating bark, roots and animal fodder. Cannibalism was reported. Some two or three million persons died in this tragedy; another three million took refuge outside the province. Subsequently hundreds of thousands of Honanese farmers were rounded up to transport grain in carts and wheelbarrows to collection centres, to find forage for the army's animals, to build roads, and to dig a huge 300-mile-long anti-tank trench which ultimately proved to be completely useless. Nearly a million persons were conscripted to erect dikes along the Yellow River. No pay for this labour was given to the farmers, who frequently had to provide even their own food. The depth of resentment became apparent in the spring of 1944. As Chinese soldiers retreated before Japan's Ichigo offensive, farmers ferociously attacked them. Armed with farm tools, knives and ancient guns, they disarmed 50,000 of their own soldiers, killing some – at times even burying them alive.[133]

In Hupei in 1943, a Chinese commander complained that 'the country folks...stealthily send pigs, beef, rice and wine across the line to the enemy. The country folks are willing to be ruled by the enemy, but do not wish to be free citizens under their own government.'[134] In almost every province in the Nationalist area, from Fukien and Kwangtung to Szechwan and Kansu, there were peasant uprisings, usually in protest against conscription and tax exactions. In the spring of 1943, for example, a peasant rebel force, numbering about 50,000 men, seized control of most of southern Kansu. In the autumn a band of 4,000 rose against the government in Fukien where, a United States official reported, 'the people are seething with unrest'.[135]

Active political disenchantment reverberated even inside the government. Sun Fo, son of Sun Yat-sen and the relatively liberal-minded president of the Legislative Yuan, in the spring of 1944 bitterly criticized

[133] White and Jacoby, 166–78; Service, Lost chance, 9–19; Chiang Shang-ch'ing, Cheng-hai mi-wen (Secrets of the political world), 157; US State Dept. 893.00/15251, encl. 1 ('Excerpts from informal report of December 26, 1943 from Secretary on detail at Sian'), pp. 1–2; Hal to Donovan, 'Recent events and trends in China', Office of Strategic Services XL2032 (4 Sept. 1944), 1–2; Rice to Atcheson, 'The conscription, treatment, training, and behaviour of Chinese Central Government troops in the Shantung-Kiangsu-Honan-Anhwei Border Area', Office of Strategic Services 116311, p. 2.

[134] Gauss to State, 'Observations by a Chinese newspaper correspondent', encl. p. 3.

[135] Hu-pei-sheng cheng-fu pao-kao, 1943/10–1944/9 (Report of the Hupei provincial government, October 1943 to September 1944), 132; Hu shang-chiang Tsung-nan nien-p'u (Chronological biography of General Hu Tsung-nan), 118–21; Wu Ting-ch'ang, Hua-hsi hsien-pi cheng-hsu-chi (Random notes at Hua-hsi), 2.194 and 199; Service, Lost chance, 21; Vincent to State 'Settlement of disturbances at Penghsien, Szechuan', US State Dept. 893.00/15022 (26 Apr. 1943); Atcheson to State, 'Conditions in Kweichow province: unrest in Free China', US State Dept. 893.00/15095 (27 July 1943); US State Dept. 893.00/15300, encl. ('General report on Fukien Province' by John C. Caldwell), p. 2.

the government for its dictatorial, inefficient and repressive tendencies. The Kuomintang, he charged, had adopted 'the attitude and habit of a ruling caste', out of touch with the people. Criticisms of the government were so thoroughly suppressed that 'the people dare not and cannot speak'. Nationalist China, he warned, was emulating its enemy, Nazi Germany.[136]

The Sixth Party Congress in May 1945 – the first KMT congress since early 1938 – became a sounding board for accumulated resentments. Broadly based elements in the party denounced the pervasive corruption, opportunism, inefficiency, disregard for the public welfare, and decline of morale in party, government and army.[137] No Communist propagandist could have uttered more mordant indictments.

A coalition of provincial militarists, in concert with radical leaders of the Federation of Democratic Parties, likewise mounted a challenge to the central government. The militarists – like Lung Yun in Yunnan, Yen Hsi-shan in Shansi, and P'an Wen-hua and Liu Wen-hui in Szechwan – were vestiges of the warlord era. Their local positions had been legitimized but they were convinced that Chiang Kai-shek was using the war to gain military supremacy over their own armies. An American official reported, in April 1943, 'a bitterness and antagonism that seethes beneath the surface' between National government and these provincial militarists.[138]

A common interest brought together these military commanders and the Federation of Democratic Parties. Yunnan had become a haven for minor-party members. There Governor Lung Yun employed several Federation leaders, including P'an Kuang-tan, P'an Ta-k'uei and Lo Lung-chi, as 'advisers'; he assisted federation members financially; and he sheltered them by restricting the activities of Chiang's secret police. Members of the federation, utterly disillusioned with the central government, were convinced that the Chungking regime was 'hopeless and ... doomed'. They deplored its increasingly dictatorial and repressive tendencies.[139] By 1943–4, moreover, they had become convinced that

[136] Gauss to State, 'Dr Sun Fo's views on democracy and planned economy', US State Dept. 893.00/15340 (14 Apr. 1944), encl. 1, p. 3; Gauss to State, 'Dr Sun Fo's speech criticizing the present objectives and methods of the San Min Chu I Youth Corps', US State Dept. 893.00/15366 (25 Apr. 1944), encl. pp. 2–4; Gauss to State, 'Dr Sun Fo's speech to the San Min Chu I Youth Corps' (7 June 1944), in *The Amerasia papers: a clue to the catastrophe of China*, 1.542.

[137] *Fu-hsing Chung-kuo Kuo-min-tang chien-i*; Office of Strategic Services doc. L57067, 25 May 1945, 1–4; *Hsin-kuan-ch'ang hsien-hsing chi* (The new 'Current state of the official arena'); Eastman, *Seeds of destruction*, 101–2, 109–24.

[138] Drumright to Vincent, 'Threatened clash Between Chengtu police and troops of Ching Pei Ssu Ling Pu', 26 Apr. 1943, US State Dept. 893.105/93, p. 2.

[139] Chang Wen-shih, *Yun-nan nei-mu* (The inside story in Yunnan), 16, 42; Langdon to State 'Future political developments in China: activities of the Federation of Chinese Democratic Parties at Kunming', US State Dept. 893.00/7–1444 (14 July 1944), p. 2.

Chiang himself was the source of the government's debilities. Clarence Gauss reported in July 1944 that even liberals who a year earlier had staunchly supported him 'see no hope for China under Chiang's leadership'.[140]

A group of intellectuals of the federation and provincial militarists incongruously became partners in a scheme to overthrow the central government. Convinced that Chungking was on the verge of collapse, the conspirators hoped to abstain from using military force. They concentrated instead on creating a successor Government of National Defence. To ratify these plans, a people's congress – comprising representatives from the Kuomintang (40 per cent), the Chinese Communist Party (20 per cent), the Federation of Democratic Parties (20 per cent), and other groups (20 per cent) – was scheduled to be held in Chengtu on about 10 October 1944. At the same time Lung Yun, P'an Wen-hua, Yü Han-mou and other military commanders agreed that they would put up no further resistance to the Japanese and let them destroy Chiang Kai-shek's armies.[141]

In the end, all this plotting bore no fruit. As the American consul in Kunming remarked, 'It would indeed be difficult to imagine a more heterogeneous group of feudal barons and radicals, idealists and practical politicians.'[142] They had not taken into account the political adroitness of Chiang Kai-shek to divide and conquer his rivals. Lung Yun, a key to the entire conspiracy, withdrew from the anti-Chiang movement in January 1945 in exchange for American Lend-Lease supplies sufficient to equip three of his Yunnan divisions. Then in a carefully staged military coup in October 1945, shortly after the Japanese surrender, Chiang stripped Lung Yun of his provincial posts and brought him to Chungking, where he was kept a virtual prisoner.

The anti-Chiang conspiracy, ill-conceived though it was, was symptomatic of the profound crisis that beset Nationalist China during the last year of the war. Economic production had decreased sharply, the inflation was out of control, the army was hapless before the Japanese, government was corrupt, and political disaffection suffused all levels of society. When the war ended on 14 August 1945, therefore, Nationalist China was demoralized and weak.

[140] FRUS, 1944, 492.
[141] Eastman, 'Regional politics', 346–7.
[142] Ringwalt to Gauss, 'Proposed Government of National Defense', US State Dept. 893.00/15420 (8 May 1944), p. 3.

CHAPTER 12

THE CHINESE COMMUNIST MOVEMENT DURING THE SINO-JAPANESE WAR 1937–1945

Chinese Communist leaders had long seen the war as inevitable because their experience and their ideology convinced them that Japanese expansion in China was fuelled by irreversible forces. 'The main characteristic of the present situation,' the CCP reiterated as a litany, 'is that Japanese imperialism wants to turn China into a colony.' The CCP also saw the war as necessary and, after the end of 1935, called for unified resistance at the earliest possible moment. Mao and his followers knew that in a Sino-Japanese war they could claim, as patriots, a legitimate, honourable, and self-defined role. Indeed, they intended to claim a leading role in moral terms. For them the only alternative would be a Sino-Japanese peace from which they would surely be excluded and which might be purchased at their expense. Every delay in resistance bought time which the KMT might use to continue campaigns against the CCP. Every delay prolonged the period in which Tokyo and Nanking might come to some further accommodation, possibly including joint anti-Communist action, as Japanese Foreign Minister Hirota had proposed in August 1936.

One need not impugn the CCP's sincerity to note that termination of civil war, a broad united front and resistance to Japan would also serve the party's interest. Its platform matched the mood of urban China – of students, intellectuals, large sections of the bourgeoisie, and many workers – far better than the Kuomintang's repressive call for 'unification before resistance'. So persuasive did the united front policy become among these groups, and even among some influential factions in the Kuomintang, that it weighed heavily in Chiang Kai-shek's decision, after his release on 25 December 1936, from two weeks' captivity in Sian, to call off the civil war and adopt a stronger posture toward Japan.

The author wishes to thank Ch'en Yung-fa and Gregor Benton for their careful and critical suggestions.

I. THE EARLY WAR YEARS 1937–1938

The agreements hammered out between representatives of the KMT and CCP in the months following the Sian incident were publicly proclaimed in August and September 1937, after the Shanghai fighting began on 13 August. These agreements formed the basis of KMT-CCP relations during the first years of the war and remained nominally in force throughout it. The CCP agreed (a) to strive for the realization of Sun Yat-sen's Three People's Principles (San-min chu-i); (b) to terminate its policies of armed revolt, sovietization, and forcible confiscation of landlords' land; (c) to abolish the present soviet government; and (d) to abolish the term 'Red Army' and place Communist troops under central government command. In return, the KMT allowed the CCP to set up liaison offices in several important cities, to publish the *New China Daily*, and to nominate representatives to its two principal advisory bodies. Civil rights were considerably extended, political prisoners were released, and a subsidy was initiated to help defray administrative and military expenses of the newly 'reintegrated' territories and armies.[1]

The outbreak of war thus transformed the political and military environment for all Chinese parties and forced the Chinese Communists into fundamental reconsideration of all important policies, of strategy and of tactics. The principal issues confronting Party Central during the first year and a half of the war – from the Marco Polo Bridge incident through the sixth plenum of the Central Committee in November 1938 – were the following:

1. The united front, and particularly the question of the CCP's relationship to the Kuomintang and the National government.
2. Military strategy and tactics, including coordination of operations with Nationalist and other units.
3. Leaders and leadership, especially Mao's efforts to strengthen his position vis-à-vis Chang Kuo-t'ao (who defected to the Nationalists in April 1938) and Wang Ming (pseudonym of Ch'en Shao-yü).

During these eighteen months, policy decisions and the disputes surrounding them rose to visibility in several important party meetings (see table 15). By early 1939 these issues had been clarified, if not fully resolved, and later developments in each of these areas can be traced from this

---

[1] The monthly subsidy, which lasted until 1940, was reported to be Ch. $100,000 for administrative expenses and Ch. $500,000 for the support of three authorized divisions in the newly renamed Eighth Route Army. See James P. Harrison, *The long march to power: a history of the Chinese Communist Party, 1921–72*, 279, and cited sources.

TABLE 15

Principal CCP meetings, July 1937–December 1938

Lo-ch'uan conference. Lo-ch'uan, Shensi, *c.* 20–25 August 1937. Major issues had to do with political and military reorganization as part of the national system; attitude toward the KMT; and united front policy.

Conference of party activists. Yenan, *c.* 12 November 1937. First meeting attended by Wang Ming, just returned from Moscow. Assessment of the military and political situation after the fall of Shanghai and Taiyuan.

Politburo meeting. Yenan, 9–13 December 1937. Most complete meeting of the Politburo since the fifth plenum (January 1934). Further debate over the KMT, united front, and military policies.

Politburo meeting. Yenan, 27 February–1 March 1938. Although relatively little is known of this meeting, views contradicting Mao's preferences seem to have prevailed: the positional defence of Wuhan, mobile warfare, and continued preparations for the Seventh Congress.

Sixth plenum (enlarged) of the Sixth CCP Central Committee. Yenan, 29 September–6 November 1938. The most comprehensive meeting of party leadership between the Sixth Congress in 1928 and the Seventh Congress in 1945. All outstanding issues were considered during this very protracted series of meetings, and a very large number of important documents were produced.

foundation. The frequency of such high-level policy meetings thereafter dropped sharply; even the rectification (*cheng-feng*) sessions in 1942 and the Seventh CCP Congress (April–June 1945) announced policy rather than debating it. This phenomenon undoubtedly reflected the consolidation of Maoist leadership, though by no means unanimity and full harmony within the party.

ATTITUDE TOWARD THE KUOMINTANG: THE UNITED FRONT

From the moment of its true adoption by the CCP in December 1935, the united front was conceived as a broad appeal to all those who would heed it and respond. To all those who did, the party was willing to make substantial concessions in both substance and spirit, so long as these did not compromise fundamental principles nor ultimate Communist control of the movement. In succeeding years, the scope of the united front steadily widened and its use became more sophisticated. As early as October 1939, Mao Tse-tung was identifying the united front, armed struggle and party-building as the three fundamental problems of the Chinese revolution, whose proper understanding was tantamount to correct leadership of the revolution as a whole. Even as it announced alliance with the KMT, the CCP asked,

Should the Anti-Japanese National United Front be confined to the Kuomintang and the Communist Party? No, it should be a united front of the whole nation, with the two parties only a small part of this united front...[It] is one of all parties and groups, of people in all walks of life and of all armed forces, a united front of all patriots – workers, peasants, businessmen, intellectuals, and soldiers.[2]

Disputes centred, rather, around the spirit of the relationship, whether the CCP would observe the limits set for it by the KMT and how fully it would obey the orders of its nominal superior. During the first years of the war, these disputes were coloured by factional struggle and by personality clashes, so that fact is difficult to separate from allegation. Publicly, CCP statements praised the leadership of Chiang Kai-shek and the KMT and pledged unstinting – but vague and unspecified – unity and cooperation. Suggestions, not criticisms, were offered, most of them having to do with further political democratization, popular mobilization and the like.

Mao Tse-tung's early position on the united front with the KMT appears fairly hard and aggressive, moderated by his absolute conviction that the Kuomintang had to be kept in the war. For Mao, the united front meant an absence of peace between China and Japan. Mao's quite consistent position, in both political and military affairs, was to remain independent and autonomous. He was willing to consider, for a time, Communist participation in a thoroughly reconstituted government ('the democratic republic') primarily to gain nationwide legality and enhanced influence. But, for the most part, he sought to keep the CCP separate, physically separate if possible, from the KMT. Other party leaders, including both Chang Kuo-t'ao and the recently returned Wang Ming, apparently questioned this line.

Some sources claim that in the November and December 1937 meetings Mao's line failed to carry the day. If so, Mao was probably laying out his general position rather than calling for an immediate hardening. In late 1937 the Nationalists' position was desperate, and it was no time to push them further: Shanghai was lost on 12 November, the awful carnage in Nanking took place the following month, and, most serious of all, Chiang was seriously considering a Japanese peace offer.

But as the new year turned and wore on, the peace crisis passed. The rape of Nanking strengthened Chinese will, and in January 1938 the Konoe cabinet issued its declaration of 'no dealing' (*aite ni sezu*) with Chiang Kai-shek. Whatever his preferences might have been, Chiang now had no choice but to fight on, and most of the nation, the CCP included, pronounced itself behind him. By summer, too, at the latest, it was clear that no last-ditch defence of the temporary Nationalist capital at Wuhan

---

[2] 'Kuo-kung liang-tang t'ung-i chan-hsien ch'eng-li hou Chung-kuo ke-ming ti p'o-ch'ieh jen-wu' (Urgent tasks of the Chinese revolution following the establishment of the KMT-CCP united front), *Mao Tse-tung chi* (Collected works of Mao Tse-tung), comp. Takeuchi Minoru *et al.*, hereafter *MTTC*, 5.266–7.

was anticipated. Government organs had begun functioning in Chungking as early as the previous December, and more were moving there all the time. While morale was high and a spirit of unity prevailed, Chiang vowed to continue his strategy of drawing the Japanese deeper into China, of scorched earth, of trading space for time.

These developments strengthened Mao's position. By the time of the sixth plenum, in the autumn of 1938, the official CCP position was fully to support Chiang Kai-shek and the two-party alliance. But in private Mao also approvingly quoted Liu Shao-ch'i as saying that if Wang Ming's slogan, 'everything through the united front', meant through Chiang Kai-shek and Yen Hsi-shan, then this was submission rather than unity. Mao proposed instead that the CCP observe agreements to which the KMT had already consented; that in some cases they should 'act first, report afterward'; in still other cases , 'act and don't report'. Finally, he said, 'There are still other things which, for the time being, we shall neither do nor report, for they are likely to jeopardize the whole situation. In short, we must not split the united front, but neither should we bind ourselves hand and foot.'[3]

MILITARY STRATEGY AND TACTICS

The Chinese Communist Party entered the war in command of approximately 30,000 men, a mix of the survivors of the various Long Marches, local forces already in being, and new recruits. In the reorganization of August and September 1937, they were designated collectively the Eighth Route Army (8RA) and were subdivided into three divisions: the 115th, 120th, and 129th commanded by Lin Piao, Ho Lung and Liu Po-ch'eng, respectively. (See below, pp. 622–4 for more on these units.)

Shortly after the war began, the National government also authorized the formation of a second Communist force, the New Fourth Army (N4A), to operate in Central China. The N4A was formed around a nucleus of those who had been left behind in Kiangsi and Fukien when the Long March began in 1934. Since that time, in ever dwindling numbers, they had survived precariously in separated groups against incessant Nationalist efforts to destroy them. Their initial authorized strength was 12,000 men, but it took several months to reach that level. The nominal commanding officer of the N4A was Yeh T'ing, an early Communist military leader who later left the party, but who somehow managed to remain on good terms with both Communists and Nationalists. Actual military and political control was vested in Hsiang Ying and Ch'en I.

[3] 'The question of independence and initiative with the united front', Mao Tse-tung, *Selected Works*, hereafter, Mao, *SW*, 2.215–16. Dated 5 Nov. 1938.

The first major issue posed by reorganization was whether or not to accept two Nationalist proposals: first, that they assign staff officers to the Eighth Route Army; and second, that Communist and non-Communist forces operate together in combat zones designated by the Nationalists. According to Chang Kuo-t'ao, a number of ranking party members (including Wang Ming, Chu Te and P'eng Te-huai) favoured these proposals. Although this is not well documented, they may have argued that acceptance would further consolidate the united front and would justify a claim that Nationalist forces share their weapons and other equipment. Some military leaders, probably represented by P'eng Te-huai, wanted to lessen Communist reliance on guerrilla warfare in favour of larger unit operations and more conventional tactics. Mao Tse-tung and others resisted these proposals, on the grounds that they would leave the 8RA too open to Nationalist surveillance, that coordinated operations would subordinate CCP units to non-Communist forces, and that the initiatives of time and place would be lost.

Mao foresaw a protracted war divided into three stages: (1) strategic offensive by Japan, (2) prolonged stalemate (this was the 'new stage' which Mao identified at the sixth plenum), and (3) strategic counter-attack, leading to ultimate victory. He was quite vague about the third stage, except that he anticipated it would be coordinated 'with an international situation favourable to us and unfavourable to the enemy'.[4] Meanwhile, Mao was acutely aware of the CCP's strategic weakness. Such a situation, he believed, called for guerrilla warfare and for the preservation and expansion of one's own forces.

But if, in Mao's words, the CCP was not only to 'hold the ground already won' but also to 'extend the ground already won', the only alternatives were either to expand in unoccupied China, at the expense of their supposed allies, or in occupied China, behind Japanese lines and at the expense of the enemy. And when Mao said 'ground', he meant it: territorial bases under stable Communist leadership.[5] The choice was an easy one. The former alternative led to shared influence, vulnerability, and possible conflict – all of which actually took place in CCP relations with Yen Hsi-shan in Shansi. But the latter alternative clearly served the interests of resistance, and, to the extent that KMT forces had been driven out of these occupied areas, the CCP could avoid conflict with its allies.

These principles are succinctly summed up, then explained more fully, in Mao's 'Problems of strategy in guerilla war against Japan'.[6] Complexities in the real world, of course, prevented such neat and clean distinctions as Mao was able to make in his writings. The CCP could not avoid contact

---

[4] *MTCC* 6.182, 'On the new stage', Oct. 1938.
[5] The term Mao chose for 'ground' was *chen-ti*, defined as 'a staging area for military operations or combat'.   [6] Mao, *SW* 2.82.

with other Chinese forces on the exterior line and in the rear: around the perimeter of Shen-Kan-Ning, in Shansi, and in the Lower Yangtze region. Nor were the occupied areas entirely devoid of Nationalist units; early in the war, especially, significant Nationalist forces remained behind Japanese lines. But there is no mistaking Mao Tse-tung's strategic import.

LEADERS AND LEADERSHIP

At the outbreak of the war, Mao Tse-tung's position in the Chinese Communist movement was that of *primus inter pares*. Veteran comrades were prepared to argue with him over basic policy, and at least two rivals directly challenged him. These were Chang Kuo-t'ao and Wang Ming. By the end of the sixth plenum, in late 1938, Mao was well on his way toward building that coalition which would carry him to undisputed leadership by 1942 or 1943.

Chang Kuo-t'ao had suffered mortal blows to his power during and just after the Long March. In August 1935, when his temporarily stronger forces linked up with those of Mao Tse-tung in north-western Szechwan, the two clashed over a wide range of issues, including questions of leadership, of army command, and of the destination of the Long March (see above, ch. 4, note 187). Chang contested the leading position Mao had assumed at the technically irregular Tsun-yi Conference (January 1935), which he and some other Politburo members had been unable to attend. Consequently, Chang led his reconstituted army westward into the high mountains of Sikang and Chinghai, while Mao struck north-west toward Shensi and the Pao-an/Yenan region, arriving there in October 1935. But Chang was unable to hold out in this inhospitable area and, in a series of marches and counter-marches, lost much of his army to fierce, pro-KMT Muslim forces in the Kansu corridor. Finally, in October 1936 – a full year later than his rival – he and his surviving followers reached Pao-an, where Mao had already done much to consolidate his position. Chang was given nominally high posts, specifically, the vice-chairmanship of the Shen-Kan-Ning Border Region government and a place on the preparatory committee for the Seventh CCP Congress, which was later postponed and not convened until 1945. But Chang knew his star had set, and he took advantage of a ceremonial visit to Sian in the spring of 1938 to flee to Wuhan, where he denounced Mao's united front line as seeking 'defeat for all' (i.e. of both the KMT and the Japanese) during the war. A few fruitless conversations took place in Wuhan between Chang and the CCP Liaison Group stationed there, but by the time of the sixth plenum, in autumn 1938, he had been read out of the party as a renegade.

Wang Ming was a more potent rival. Having returned to China in October 1937 with Stalin's blessings and probably the authority of the Comintern, he might have expected support from those who had been closely associated with him during his period of ascendancy (see above, chapter 4) in the CCP, the somewhat derisively labelled 'returned-students'. Highly educated and articulate, Wang had spent most of his adult life in the Soviet Union. He had an easy cosmopolitanism that contrasted with Mao's parochialism and quick temper, and he was far more at home than Mao in the realm of formal Marxist theory, where he condescended to his older Hunanese comrade. Indeed, in late 1937, he 'conveyed the instruction that Mao should be strengthened 'ideologically' because of his narrow empiricism and 'ignorance of Marxism-Leninism'.[7] The two men probably felt an almost instinctive antipathy for each other, so different were their temperaments and their styles.

Whatever the orientations of Wang's former colleagues, he did not now have a clear faction behind him. Chang Wen-t'ien (Lo Fu), secretary-general of the party, mediated a number of intra-party disputes early in the war in such a way as to allow Mao's policies to prevail in most of their essentials. Ch'in Pang-hsien (Po Ku) appears to have been guided by Chou En-lai, himself a one-time associate of Wang Ming who had thrown in his lot with Mao and his group. Nor did Wang have any appreciable base in either the party's armed forces or its territorial government. Returning to a China much changed during his absence, Wang retained mainly his international prestige, his Politburo membership, and his powers of persuasion. But these considerable assets proved inadequate to an open challenge – and, indeed, Wang apparently never attempted such a showdown with Mao.

Some portray Wang Ming as the exponent of a strategy that clashed with Mao's on two fundamental issues, raising in their wake many other related points of conflict.[8] The first issue had to do with the CCP's relationship to the KMT and the central government. The second issue involved an urban revolutionary strategy based on workers, intellectuals, students, and some sections of the bourgeoisie versus a rural revolution based on the peasantry. Of course, in-fighting for leadership and personal dislike added heat to these two issues. Except in the Soviet Union, the Maoist version has held sway: Wang Ming was ready to sacrifice CCP independence in virtual surrender to the KMT, and he was unsympathetic to rural revolution.

---

[7] Gregor Benton, 'The "Second Wang Ming line" (1935–1938)', *CQ* 61 (March 1975) 77.
[8] *Ibid.* Also Tetsuya Kataoka, *Resistance and revolution in China: the Communists and the second united front*, 72ff.

This simplistic account raises puzzling questions. If his views were as Mao described them, how could Wang Ming have sought to justify them within the CCP? It is unthinkable that he would describe *himself* as a capitulationist who cared little for the peasantry. In trying to reconstruct his position we can assume that Wang Ming invoked the authority of Stalin and the Comintern after his return to China. Stalin had long wanted a Chinese resistance centring around Chiang and the KMT, a policy that Mao and the CCP adopted only reluctantly and incompletely in mid-1936, six months after Stalin's position was clear. Although the CCP moved toward such a united front in the second half of 1936 (culminating in the Sian incident, 12-25 December) more for reasons of its own than because of outside promptings, Stalin's name and the authority of the Comintern remained formidable. Not even Mao wished openly to defy Moscow's will. Wang thus had a two-edged weapon: a delegated authority from Stalin and protection against purge, for any such move would have incurred Stalin's wrath. Wang could further argue that it was the united front with the KMT that had brought an end to civil war, and, in the face of Japanese invasion, had led the CCP to an honourable and legitimate role in national affairs. Now was the time to expand and legalize that role throughout the country, rather than to remain simply a regional guerrilla movement in backward provinces. This might be accomplished, Wang apparently thought, through a reorganized central government and military structure, in which Communists would be integrally and importantly included, in response to the needs of unity and national resistance. This would, of course, require the cooperation and consent of Chiang Kai-shek. The negotiations would be difficult, but Wang's statements were sufficiently general – or vague – to allow much room for manoeuvre. Wang also implied that a 'unified national defence government' might bring the CCP a share of the financial and military resources – perhaps even some of the Soviet aid – now virtually monopolized by the Nationalists. These possibilities were tempting to many senior party members and commanders who had long suffered great poverty of means.[9] Evidently Wang Ming felt that Japanese aggression, aroused patriotism within China, and international support (especially from the Soviet Union), would eventually move Chiang to further concessions, just as they had moved him toward the united front after Sian. If so, Wang's slogan, 'everything through the united front', did not imply capitulation to Chiang, but continued pressure upon him.

[9] At the December Politburo meeting, Chang Kuo-t'ao recalls Mao sighing ruefully, 'If so much [Russian aid] can be given to Chiang Kai-shek, why can't we get a small share.' *The rise of the Chinese Communist Party, 1928-1938: volume two of the autobiography of Chang Kuo-t'ao*, 566.

Wang was soon posted to Wuhan, which during the first six months of 1938 brimmed with dedication to the war effort. The spirit of the united front pervaded all social classes and political circles, and the apparent cordiality between Nationalists and Communists surprised many. Wang may have felt that this strengthened his hand. In any case, he continued to call for a 'democratic republic' well into the spring.[10] Thereafter, realizing that Chiang Kai-shek would not consent to such sweeping changes in the government and party he controlled, Wang Ming backed off: 'The National Government is the all-China government which needs to be strengthened, not reorganized.'[11] He also called for 'national defence divisions (*kuo-fang-shih*)', a similar scaling down of his former proposals for a unified national military structure. In Wuhan, Wang was apparently able to win Chou En-lai's partial support for his programme.

The fatal flaw in Wang Ming's united front efforts lay in their dependence on the consent of the suspicious Kuomintang government. But the only leverage he had was public opinion in the Kuomintang's own constituencies.[12] Wang Ming was no capitulationist but had painted himself into a corner, whereas Mao retained much greater freedom of action.

As to the second issue, whether the revolution should be based on the countryside or the cities, Wang Ming had never lived or worked among the peasantry. Though he grew up in a well-to-do rural Anhwei family, both his instincts and his theoretical bent were quite thoroughly urban. After his return to China in late 1937, Wang rarely referred to the peasantry, and none of his known writings addressed this subject so close to Mao Tse-tung's heart. Wang nowhere called for giving up the peasant movement, but he clearly felt that without a strong foothold in the cities and among the workers and other nationalistic elements (such as students, the national bourgeoisie), the movement would eventually lose its Marxist-Leninist thrust, and pursue backward, parochial, and essentially petty-bourgeois peasant concerns. Holding the cities was thus much more important to Wang Ming than to Mao Tse-tung, who preferred to trade space for time and who – like Chiang Kai-shek after the fall of Nanking – was unwilling to see Nationalist resistance crushed in fruitless positional warfare. Wang, on the other hand, called for a Madrid-like defence of Wuhan which would mobilize the populace. Here, of course, Wang's united front conceptions and his urban bias came together, for only with KMT cooperation or tolerance could such mobilization take place.

[10] *Chieh-fang pao* (Liberation), 36 (29 Apr. 1938), 1. The statement was written on 11 March 1938.
[11] 'The current situation and tasks in the War of Resistance', in Kuo Hua-lun (Warren Kuo), *Analytic history of the Chinese Communist Party*, 3.363.
[12] Kataoka Tetsuya, 75.

Wang Ming meanwhile had party work to do in Wuhan. He was head of the newly-formed United Front Work Department and of the regional Yangtze River Bureau, both directly responsible to the Central Committee. In addition, he was at least the nominal leader of the Communist delegations appointed to the People's Political Council and the Supreme National Defence Council, the advisory bodies organized as sounding boards by the National government in early 1938 to symbolize multi-party unity. From these various platforms, Wang Ming proclaimed, over the head of the government, the patriotic message that was so influential in keeping urban public opinion behind resistance to Japan. Patriotism and wholehearted devotion to the war effort were his keynotes, not Mao's exhortation to 'hold and extend the ground we have already won'.

Wang also undertook organizational activities independent of the Kuomintang, particularly with youth groups, and he sought to knit a wide variety of patriotic organizations into the 'Wuhan Defence Committee'. But in August 1938 the Wuhan Defence Committee was disbanded, along with the mass organizations associated with it, and *Hsin-hua jih-pao*, the CCP paper in Wuhan, was shut down for three days as a result of its protests. With Chiang Kai-shek's decisions not to attempt an all-out defence of Wuhan nor to allow independent popular mobilization, Wang's efforts to maintain a quasi-legal organized CCP base in urban China flickered out.

Compromised by these losses and separated from party centre, Wang's influence gradually declined during 1938. In September, the CI expressed its support for Mao's leadership. The sixth plenum (October–November) thus marked Wang's substantial eclipse, and a significant strengthening of Mao's leadership. Yet the convening of a Central Committee (enlarged) plenum, rather than the anticipated full Seventh Congress, which would have required the election of a new Central Committee and Politburo, suggests that Mao was not yet ready, or perhaps able, fully to assert his primacy throughout the party. Wang continued for a time to direct the United Front Work Department, and the Chinese Women's University, and to publish frequently in party organs. But he and his views were no longer a serious threat to Mao's 'proletarian leadership', and the final discrediting of 'returned-student' influence in the 1942 rectification (*cheng-feng*) campaign was anti-climactic. After 1940, little was heard from Wang Ming.

ORGANIZATIONAL STRUCTURE AND ACTIVITIES

Both the Chinese Communist Party and its principal armies – the Eighth Route and the New Fourth – expanded greatly during the Sino-Japanese

TABLE 16

Wartime expansion of the Chinese Communist Party

1937	40,000
1940	800,000
1941	763,447
1942	736,151
1944	853,420
1945 (Seventh Congress)	1,211,128

Source: John W. Lewis, *Leadership in Communist China*, 110.

War. The first three years of the war, until 1940, saw very rapid growth. The army grew five times larger, the party twenty (see tables 16 and 17). Nor do these figures tell the whole story, for they omit the auxiliaries of the regular armies (the militia and the self-defence forces), and also tens of thousands of activists, the political infrastructure, and the mass organizations under party influence. Needless to say, such pell-mell growth brought many serious problems, since quality, experience and training were often neglected in the rush to expand.

As the tables show, both the party and the armies shrank during the early 1940s, primarily as a result of Japanese and Nationalist efforts to restrict or destroy Communist influence. By imposing cruel necessities, these efforts forced the CCP to consolidate its forces, to emphasize quality over quantity, and to organize and mobilize more effectively. This period of constriction and consolidation continued until the last year of the war. Not until the twelve months from mid-1944 to mid-1945 was there a second period of growth. These three periods, 1937–8, 1939-43, and 1944–5 were the principal phases of the Communist movement during the Sino-Japanese War.

The movement acted through the interlocking structures of party, army and government. Each of these systems had its own organization and, in addition, interacted closely with the other two. Furthermore, each reached outward and downward into society at large, seeking to create the infrastructures and mass base upon which the movement ultimately depended. Finally, administration was further complicated by enormous regional variations and the dispersal of the movement over mountains and plains, across North and Central China, behind Japanese lines and in areas contested with the KMT. One major problem of the CCP during the war was how to maintain the coherence and thrust of the movement, steering a precarious course between the Scylla of rigid centralization – unattainable, in any case – and the Charybdis of degeneration into sheer

TABLE 17[13]

Wartime expansion of Eighth Route and New Fourth Armies

	Eighth Route Army	New Fourth Army	Total
1937	80,000	12,000	92,000
1938	156,700	25,000	181,000
1939	270,000	50,000	320,000
1940	400,000	100,000	500,000
1941	305,000	135,000*	440,000
1942	340,000	110,960	450,960
1943	339,000	125,892	464,892
1944	320,800	153,676	474,476
1945 (Apr.)	614,000	296,000	910,000

* Prior to the 4 January 1941 New Fourth Army incident. See also table 16.

localism, what the party terms 'mountain-topism' (*shan-t'ou chu-i*). Higher levels of party and army, more than regional governments, were the sinews holding the movement together from the centre in Yenan.

Party. In outline, Chinese Communist Party organization remained as it had always been, a hierarchical pyramid with the Politburo, the Standing Committee, and the Central Committee at its apex (see table 18). Policy decisions reached at this level, particularly by the Politburo or by its chairman, Mao Tse-tung, were channelled through the Secretariat, which set goals in general terms and also determined which agencies or departments should be responsible for pursuing the required tasks.

Two types of sub-structures handled the work of the party. The first were functional, task-oriented departments, responsible at the highest level directly to the Secretariat and the Politburo. The most important of these are listed, along with their directors, in table 18.

The second type of sub-structure was regional, corresponding to the areas in which the party was operating. These regional bureaus, like the Central Committee departments, were responsible to Party Central in Yenan. Downward in the chain of command, they supervised the work of branch bureaus (located mainly in the North China base areas), and lower-level committees and branches. At bureau level and below, task-oriented departments, like those at the central level, were replicated in simplified form.

Finally, the party maintained branches in government and army at all

[13] Harrison, *Long march*, 294. The figures for party and army should not be added together, since many army men were simultaneously party members. Perhaps one-third of the armed forces had some sort of party affiliation (full, probationary or prospective).

TABLE 18

Party organization during the Sino-Japanese War

Central Committee	
Political bureau	Mao Tse-tung, Chang Wen-t'ien, Ch'in Pang-hsien, Chou En-lai, Ch'en Yun and others
Secretariat	The above, plus Jen Pi-shih, Chu Te and K'ang Sheng (later, Liu Shao-ch'i and others)
Key Central Committee Departments	
Military Affairs	Mao Tse-tung
Organization	Ch'en Yün (later, P'eng Chen, about 1943-4)
Propaganda	K'ai Feng
United Front Work	Chou En-lai (Li Wei-han after about 1944)
Enemy Occupied Areas Work	Chou En-lai (concurrent, also K'ang Sheng, Liu Shao-ch'i and others)
Cadre Education	Liu Shao-ch'i (later, Li Wei-han)
Social Affairs	K'ang Sheng (later, Chou Hsing and Li K'o-nung)
Popular Movement	Ch'en Yun
Labour	Ch'en Yun (concurrent)
Women	Ts'ai Ch'ang
Youth	Feng Wen-pin
Press	Chang Wen-t'ien
Regional bureaus	North China, North-west China Yangtze (until 1938), South China, Central Plains (these two est. 1939), South-east China (the latter two merged in 1941 to form the Central China Bureau), and, after 1945, North-east China
Sub-bureaus (or branch bureaus)	Chin-Ch'a-Chi, Shangtung, Chin-Sui and South-eastern Shansi (part of Chin-Chi-Lu-Yü), South China
Lower-level committees	Province where applicable, county, town, district, and subdistrict

Source: Harrison, *Long march*, 293, and cited sources.

levels and in the mass organizations as well. The party thus served as a nerve system, connecting the various parts of the movement, transmitting and processing information, and issuing commands.

Military. The formal structure of the Eighth Route Army and the New Fourth Army, in North and Central China respectively, is shown in table 19. The 8RA and N4A, as the regular, full-time field forces, were the top layer of what came to be a three-layer military structure. These two armies were the best the Communists could put into the field, in training, leadership and equipment – though their equipment, at least, left much

TABLE 19

Organization of Eighth Route and New Fourth Armies

Eighth Route Army headquarters (Yenan)	
Commander	Chu Te
Deputy commander	P'eng Te-huai
Chief of staff	Yeh Chien-ying
Dir. Political Dept.	Wang Chia-hsiang (1937–8, Jen Pi-shih)
115th Division (former First Front Army; Chin-Ch'a-Chi base area)	
Commander	Lin Piao (wounded, late 1937)
Deputy commander	Nieh Jung-chen (acting CO from 1938 on)
Political officer	Lo Jung-huan
120th Division (former Second Front Army; Chin-Sui base area)	
Commander	Ho Lung
Deputy commander	Hsiao K'o
Political officer	Kuan Hsiang-ying
129th Division (former Fourth Front Army; Chin-Chi-Lu-Yü base area)	
Commander	Liu Po-ch'eng
Deputy commander	Hsü Hsiang-ch'ien
Political officer	Teng Hsiao-p'ing
New Fourth Army	
Commander	Yeh T'ing (after 1941, Ch'en I)
Deputy commander	Hsiang Ying (after 1941 Chang Yun-i)
Dir. Political Dept.	Yuan Kuo-p'ing (after 1941, Teng Tzu-hui)
Political officer	Hsiang Ying (after 1941, Liu Shao-ch'i)
Deputy political officer	Jao Shu-shih

Source: Harrison, *Long march*, 296.

to be desired.[14] Units of these two armies were available for assignment wherever needed, but each base had its own detachment. To avoid adverse Nationalist propaganda, the Communists never enlarged the top commands of the 8RA and N4A, but regiments, battalions and companies proliferated at lower levels. Actual operations were carried out by these smaller units; divisions never fought as intact units, and regiments did so only infrequently.

In the CCP base areas, two other types of forces came into being: local forces (*ti-fang chün*) and the militia (*min-ping*). Local forces, for the most part, also had full-time military responsibilities, but unlike 8RA and N4A, each remained permanently within its own territorial jurisdiction. The militia theoretically included the entire able-bodied population between the ages of 16 and 45 but, unlike the field or local forces, they were not 'divorced from production' (*t'o-li sheng-ch'an*), and were available for

[14] As late as 1944, the better units of the 8RA had about one-half as many rifles and carbines as total combat personnel, and even greater deficiencies in machine-guns and mortars. Artillery was almost completely missing. See Lyman P. Van Slyke, ed. *The Chinese Communist movement: a report of the United States War Department, July 1945*, 185.

part-time duty when needed. Meanwhile they carried on their regular occupations. Of course, deficiencies in training and equipment became increasingly pronounced as one descended through this military structure. The militia was armed mostly with broadswords and farm tools, their old-fashioned bird guns and rifles (*t'u-ch'iang*) having been appropriated for use by the field or local forces.

Although the creation of this military structure was a complex and difficult task, with wide variation in time and place, the Communists nevertheless gradually built up a linked hierarchy of military power reaching downward into local society. When an element of the 8RA or N4A entered an unfamiliar area, it could expect to work with auxiliaries who knew the terrain and the enemy's dispositions, and with a local population who provided logistic support, intelligence, guides and shelter. Each level was a recruiting ground for the level above, a source of training and replenishment of manpower. Indeed, most of the increases in the size of the 8RA and the N4A during the last year of the war (see above, table 17) came from wholesale redesignation of local forces.

Everywhere it went, the CCP sought to reduce traditional peasant resentment and mistrust of military service, which in folklore and bitter experience usually meant that a beloved son or husband and his badly needed labour were lost forever. But everyone was familiar with the idea of a young man working in the fields and coming to the defence of family and village when necessary. If some of these young men then moved on to full-time military service in the local forces or in the regular armies, the shock was not so great – particularly if their families were given certain tax breaks, help with their crops, and the prestige of having contributed to the Tzu-ti Chün ('the army of sons and brothers'). Indeed, enlisting a son was one way that wealthier rural families sought favour and immunity.

In public, the CCP spoke of their military forces as aroused Chinese citizens fighting against the Japanese invaders and their traitorous puppets. But in addition to this role, Communist-led forces at all levels performed many other tasks, among which were contesting for territorial control with various local rivals, enforcement of social and economic policies, security and police functions. The Communists also had to calculate how large a force 'divorced from production' each locality could support, since many party and government cadres also needed to be fed and housed through others' labour. Where ordinarily slender surpluses were further reduced by the impact of the war, economically non-productive personnel could easily become a crushing burden.

Coordination. One cannot, of course, gauge the effectiveness of an organization simply by its formal structure. Unlike the Ch'ing bureaucracy, where decision-making, implementation, and the up and down flow of communications have been substantially traced out, only certain aspects of the CCP system's functioning can be described. One frequently-used technique was rotation of key personnel from one post to another, or from one area to another, so that experience gained in the former could be brought to the latter. The outstanding example of this kind of trouble-shooting was provided by Liu Shao-ch'i, who spent the first six years of the war shuttling back and forth between Yenan and the base areas behind Japanese lines, first in North China, then in Central China, where his and Mao's theories of base-area construction were being successfully put into practice. Yet many other lower-ranking cadres were also moved about, as in 1939, when several thousand Eighth Route Army political workers arrived in Central China to beef up mass mobilization work in the New Fourth Army bases. But such rotation of personnel was always selective, never wholesale, thus ensuring continuity of leadership, familiarity with local conditions, and the maintenance of morale and discipline that come with loyalty to known leaders.

Party and army schools at various levels, based on the experience of the Kiangsi period, were another source of cadre training and indoctrination.[15] Some of these, such as Resist Japan University (K'ang-Jih ta-hsüeh) in Yenan, assigned its graduates wherever they were needed but, in addition, each major base area had its own branch of K'ang-ta and its network of cadre schools, short-term training classes, and so on. Meetings of all kinds – open and closed, large and small – became one of the hallmarks of the Communist movement. Attendance and partici-pation were virtually mandatory for party members, soldiers and activists, particularly to explain policy to the many illiterate cadres.

Printed materials were another important medium of communication and guidance. The CCP published two major newspapers for general readership, *Liberation Daily* (*Chieh-fang jih-pao*) in Yenan and the frequently censored *New China Daily* (*Hsin-hua jih-pao*) in the Nationalist capitals.[16] These and other open publications carried sanitized news reports from all over China, major international events, general statements by Communist leaders, certain documents, and propaganda. Again, each major base area published its own local newspapers and periodicals. More sensitive materials were circulated by courier in a variety of forms: secret periodicals, classified collections and reports, individual directives. Local

[15] Jane L. Price, *Cadres, commanders, and commissars: the training of Chinese Communist leadership, 1920–1945*, chs. 8–9.

[16] Until the summer of 1941, *Liberation* appeared at approximately ten-day intervals, in periodical form. It then shifted to daily newspaper publication.

levels often used such primitive methods as handwritten hectograph copy printed on very crude paper. Some information could be transmitted by wireless, but equipment was makeshift and scarce, with few personnel capable of operating and maintaining it. Transmitting Chinese characters by number code led to frequent errors, and of course could be intercepted.[17] Despite great difficulties and not infrequent failures, this communication system worked well enough to coordinate party, army and government efforts at various levels and in many locales.

JAPANESE INVASION AND CHINESE INITIAL RESPONSES

In July 1937 the Japanese military in China was represented most strongly by the Kwantung Army. Headquartered in the Manchurian city of Ch'ang-ch'un (Hsin-ching), its principal responsibility was to watch over Japanese interests in the puppet state of Manchukuo, but it also sought to create a pliable buffer zone in North China from which Nationalist influence could be excluded. Largely successful for a time, the Kwantung Army failed embarrassingly in late 1935, when it manoeuvred to detach five northern provinces (Hopei, Shantung, Shansi, Chahar and Suiyuan) from their connections with Nanking. This clumsy effort touched off the patriotic fire of student-led demonstrations in Peiping on 9 December 1935, a fire that soon spread to most major cities of China. In North China itself, a much smaller Garrison Army was headquartered at Tientsin under the terms of the Boxer Protocol. Its leading officers competed with the Kwantung Army for influence in northern Hopei, and their ambitions far outran the forces then at their command. It was a detachment of this Garrison Army, which totalled only about 6,000 men, that clashed at the Marco Polo Bridge on July 7 with Chinese patrols of Sung Che-yuan's much larger 29th Army.

Japanese motives in North China were economic as well as political and military. In order to link the North China economy with that of Manchukuo and the home islands, endless negotiations were taking place between Manchukuoan authorities (the Kwantung Army and the South Manchurian Railway Company), North China interests (the Tientsin Garrison Army and its economic creature, the Hsing-cheng kung-shu), and financial interests in Japan.[18] Each military command lobbied for itself

---

[17] Michael Lindsay, *The unknown war: north China, 1937–1945*, not paged. Lindsay recalls Mao's 'from masses win respect' being received, through code errors, as 'from fog win treasure'. For about a year, in 1941–2, the Japanese broke the CCP code and were able to read their transmissions.

[18] Takafusa Nakamura, 'Japan's economic thrust into North China, 1933–1938: formation of the North China Development Corporaton', in Akira Iriye, ed. *The Chinese and the Japanese: essays in political and cultural interactions*, 220–53.

with policy-makers in Tokyo, but frequently disregarded directives with which they were not in sympathy. The policy-makers in Tokyo, hardly more unified, were acutely aware of their limited control over commanders in the field. Indeed, the Japanese never found a way truly to unify their effort in China.

Shortly after 7 July, the Garrison Army was reinforced from the Kwantung Army and the home islands. Reorganized as the North China Area Army (NCAA), it soon reached a strength of about 200,000. Meanwhile, in Central China, the scene of the heaviest fighting during the first sixteen months of the war, Japanese forces totalling 250,000 were directed by what eventually became the Central China Expeditionary Army (CCEA).

In North China, the Garrison Army quickly occupied Peiping and Tientsin, then the beefed-up NCAA moved out along the spokes of the region's railway system, as shown in map 9. For the most part, the Japanese advance met light resistance. Sung Che-yuan's 29th Army, after an initial show of firmness, soon withdrew to the south. The governor of Shantung, General Han Fu-ch'ü, collapsed without a fight, opening the way across his province toward the crucial rail junction and gateway to Central China at Hsu-chou, in northern Kiangsu. (Shortly thereafter, Han was arrested and executed by Chiang Kai-shek.)

To the north-west and west, fighting was heavier. Elements of the Shansi army, under the overall command of the crafty warlord-governor Yen Hsi-shan, defended Niangtzukuan (Ladies' Pass) bravely for a time. North of Tatung, combined elements of the Shansi army and the CCP's 115th Division, commanded by Lin Piao, won a heartening but not strategically significant victory at Pinghsingkuan (Flat Pass) in late September 1937 (see below, pp. 639–40). Nevertheless, Shansi's capital, Taiyuan, fell on 9 November 1937, and the Japanese advance continued south-west along the T'ung-P'u railway line toward the great bend of the Yellow River. A year after the skirmish at the Marco Polo Bridge, the Japanese occupation of North China was approximately as shown in map 9.

This was, of course, no true occupation at all, but a network of points and lines. During its advance, the NCAA occasionally left the main communications corridors and fanned out across the countryside. Villages in their path were sometimes attacked but the NCAA made no effort to garrison the countryside, which was beyond their capacity. In North China alone, the major railway lines stretched for about 3,000 miles; simply protecting these lines and garrisoning the towns and cities along them spread thin their army of 200,000 or so. As a result, control over the deeper

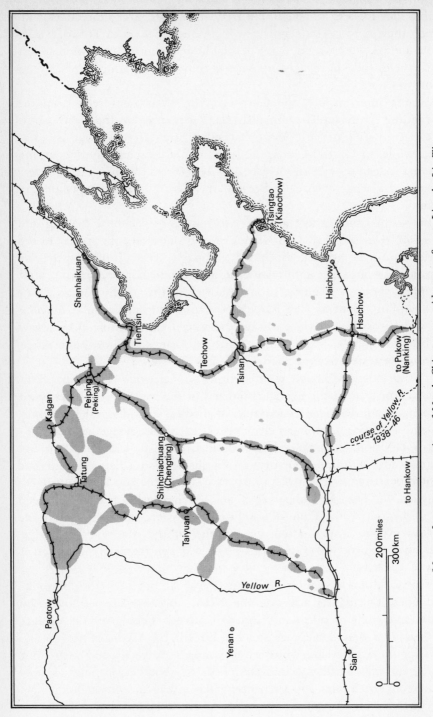

MAP 9. Japanese occupation of North China, to c. mid-1940s. *Source*: Lincoln Li, *The Japanese army in north China, 1937–1941: problems of political and economic control*, 8

Labels on map: Shanhaikuan, Tientsin, Tsingtao (Kiaochow), Haichow, Hsuchow, Techow, Tsinan, to Pukow (Nanking), course of Yellow R. 1938–46, Kalgan, Peiping (Peking), Tatung, Shihchiachuang (Chengting), to Hankow, Taiyuan, Paotow, Yellow R., Yenan, Sian

200 miles
300 km

TABLE 20

Major railway lines: North and Central China (c. 1942)

(distances include branches)

	miles
Peiping-Mukden, to Great Wall at Shanhai Kuan	289
Tientsin-Pukow (Tsin-Pu), to n. bank of Yangtze River	694
Peiping-Hankow (Ping-Han)	803
Peiping-Suiyuan (Ping-Sui), to Pao-t'ou	547
Tatung-Fenglingtu (T'ung-P'u), to n. bank of Yellow River[a]	420
Kiaochow-Tsinan (Kiao-Tsi)	288
Shihchiachuang-Taiyuan (Cheng-Tai)[a]	151
Techow-Shihchiachuang[b]	124
Haichow-Sian (Lung-Hai)	652
Nanking-Shanghai (Kiangnan)	109

[a] When the war began, the T'ung-P'u and Cheng-Tai lines were metre gauge rather than standard. The Japanese completed conversion of these lines to standard gauge in 1939.
[b] This link in the North China rail system was constructed by the Japanese between June and December 1940.
Source: Chang Kia-ngau, *China's struggle for railway development*, 86–7, 203, 205, 322–5.

countryside had to be left to Chinese collaborators. In a vague directive of December 1937, the NCAA put the burden on country-level police and unspecified local militia. But police were to number no more than two hundred per county, armed with pistols, and militia were to have only those weapons already in their possession or captured from opponents.[19] In time, a variety of more formally organized puppet organizations were charged with propaganda, rural administration, economic exploitation of conquered territories, and internal security, but the NCAA never trusted their Chinese collaborators – a characteristic, in various degrees, of the Japanese everywhere in China during the war.

In ordinary times, lightly armed police and local militias might have sufficed to maintain order outside the railway corridors. But these were not ordinary times. The Japanese invasion shattered local administration, and down to the county level the majority of magistrates and other functionaries left their posts. Below this level, local elites remained largely in place rather than abandoning their homes and property. As always in times of disorder, these local elites sought protection by enlarging or organizing quasi-military bands known by various names: *min-t'uan* (militia), *t'uan-lien* (trained bands), *lien-chuang-hui* (joint village associations), as well as secret societies such as the Big Swords or Red Spears. Ordinary peasants often cooperated with such groups. Bandit gangs were also a

[19] Lincoln Li, 203.

feature of chaotic times, a kind of predatory complement to the protective associations designed to keep them away.[20] Now, however, predators and protectors alike fed upon defeated Chinese armies for both men and weapons. Guns were often thrown down and left behind, while dispersing soldiers, fleeting from the railway zones, were ready for almost anything in return for food and shelter.

Although such spontaneous 'mobilization' did not in itself create resistance to the Japanese, there were also resisters on the local scene: students and teachers, especially from the larger cities, some Nationalist units, and local Communists. Students and teachers as vanguards of Chinese nationalism had touched off the National Salvation movement in December 1935. Even before the war began, many had left Peiping during summer vacation to return home or to seek safer haven in Yenan, Sian or Taiyuan. In Hopei alone during the first year of the war, the number of students and teachers at middle-school level or above dropped by 70 per cent, a combined total of 50,000.[21] Some of these dropped out or followed their universities into exile in Kuomintang-controlled Free China. But many others remained in the areas later to be incorporated into the Communist bases.

An often-cited example is that of Yang Hsiu-feng, a French-trained academic, born in 1898 in eastern Hopei. As an underground party member, he had been an active supporter of the National Salvation movement while teaching at the Hopei Provincial College of Law and Commerce in Tientsin. When the war broke out, Yang, his wife, and a few students escaped to southern Hopei, and linked up with certain Nationalist units and local leaders. But, after a falling out, Yang made contact with Communist elements in south-eastern Shansi, where a number of his former students were already active. Yang's invitation to the Communists led directly to their penetration of south Hopei, and he remained prominent in CCP affairs thereafter.

Not all Nationalist forces retreated. Some small units in North China either carried on independent resistance, or eventually became puppets under the Japanese, or affiliated with the CCP. Manchurian-born Lü Cheng-ts'ao chose the last course. A regimental commander separated from his Nationalist 53rd Army during its retreat south, he led his men east of the Peiping-Hankow railway line, into the plains of north-central Hopei. In late 1937, after his detachment had suffered considerable losses at the hands of the Japanese, Lü made contact with both local and recently-arrived Communists. With their help he organized a resistance

[20] Elizabeth J. Perry, *Rebels and revolutionaries in North China, 1845–1945*, 1–9 and ch. 6.
[21] Lincoln Li, 108.

base and, like Yang Hsiu-feng, rose in the Communist hierarchy to hold important posts after 1949.

More Communists were active in North China than has usually been realized. By 1935, anti-Communist suppression had put the party almost out of action, and many Communists and other activists were in jail in Peiping, Tsinan and Taiyuan. But in the spring of 1936, Liu Shao-ch'i took over the North China Bureau (NCB) of the CCP. Japanese pressure, the rising tide of nationalism, and united front policies brought increased tolerance, and by summer political prisoners were being quietly released. Recruitment was stepped up. Even before the war began, more than 5,000 party members were under the NCB's jurisdiction.[22]

When the war broke out a few months later, most of them were in their home towns, ready to try to organize local resistance and to welcome comrades from the Eighth Route Army. Their actions, the maraudings of bandit gangs and soldiers on the loose, and the efforts of local communities to ward off these predators – these constituted most of the 'spontaneous mobilization' created by the first shocks of the Japanese invasion. 'What evidence there is points overwhelmingly to the conclusion that the local resistance forces were not formed spontaneously and that the spontaneously organized forces were not formed for the purposes of resistance.'[23] In support of this conclusion, one finds very few examples of organized anti-Japanese activity of any kind in those zones – the cities and the railway corridors connecting them – where the Japanese invasion was most directly felt. The vast majority of the North China peasantry did not experience the Japanese presence until 1939, when the NCAA enlarged its pacification efforts beyond the railway zones. By this time, the principal North China base areas were already well established.

FORMATION OF BASE AREAS

Despite the importance of leadership struggles, high policy and ideology, it is nevertheless true that without the base areas the CCP would have been a structure without a foundation. In Mao's vivid phrase, these bases were 'the buttocks (*p'i-ku*) of the revolution', supporting its entire body. They provided haven for the party and the army, and from them came the resources of manpower, material, and popular support upon which the CCP's power ultimately depended.

[22] Po I-po, 'Liu Shao-ch'i t'ung-chih ti i-ko li-shih kung-chi' (An historic achievement of Comrade Liu Shao-ch'i), *Jen-min jih-pao* (People's daily) (5 May 1980) p. 2.
[23] Kathleen Hartford, 'Step-by-step: reform, resistance and revolution in the Chin-Ch'a-Chi border region, 1937–1945' (Stanford University, Ph.D. dissertation, 1980), 118–19.

1. *Shen-Kan-Ning* (an abbreviation for Shensi-Kansu-Ninghsia, i.e., the headquarters or 'Yenan area'). This was the nerve centre of the CCP, from the time of Mao's arrival at the end of the Long March in October 1935 until its capital, Yenan, was abandoned to the Nationalists in March 1947. As the only base in existence prior to the Sino-Japanese War, it produced the most voluminous and easily accessible materials on the CCP and was the CCP area most frequently visited by foreign observers, from Edgar Snow's trip in 1936 – out of which came *Red star over China* – to the journalists, foreign service officers, and military personnel of the US Military Observer Group ('Dixie Mission'; see below pp. 712–14) in late 1944 and 1945.

Shen-Kan-Ning (shown in map 10) was one of the most barren, chronically depressed, and sparsely populated regions in China. Despite its broad area (roughly the size of Ohio), it had only about 1.4 million inhabitants. Most were desperately poor, yet one estimate claimed that landlords and rich peasants comprised 12 per cent of the population and owned 46 per cent of the land. Agriculture was precarious, with a short growing season and scanty, unpredictable rainfall, which might nevertheless come in sudden cloudbursts to wash away crops and cut ravines in the defrosted loess slopes. Between 1928 and 1933, famine had stalked north-west China, including Shen-Kan-Ning (SKN); millions died and much land fell into disuse. Severe earthquakes might periodically collapse the dwellings tunnelled into loess cliffs. Along with the harshness of nature, the region had long been plagued by unrest, disorder and violence. It had never fully recovered from the terrible Muslim rebellions of the 1870s. Banditry and warlordism were endemic.

Several circumstances made Shen-Kan-Ning a special case, not representative of other base areas. (1) As the headquarters area of the CCP, most of it had passed through the agrarian revolution (confiscation of landlords' land) prior to the adoption of the milder united front land policy, so that local elite opposition was less than in other bases. (2) SKN was the only base beyond the furthest advance of Japanese armies. Although Yenan was bombed a few times, SKN was spared the problems of security and survival with which other base areas had to cope. (3) The military situation was simpler in SKN because central government and puppet forces were absent. (4) Where the bases behind Japanese lines were a mix of often scattered areas, variously consolidated, semi-consolidated, or guerrilla zones, SKN was almost entirely consolidated. (5) Because SKN was sparsely populated and backward, measures for improved livelihood could be more effective and more obvious than in other bases. Garrison units of the 8RA were freer too, to assist in these efforts.

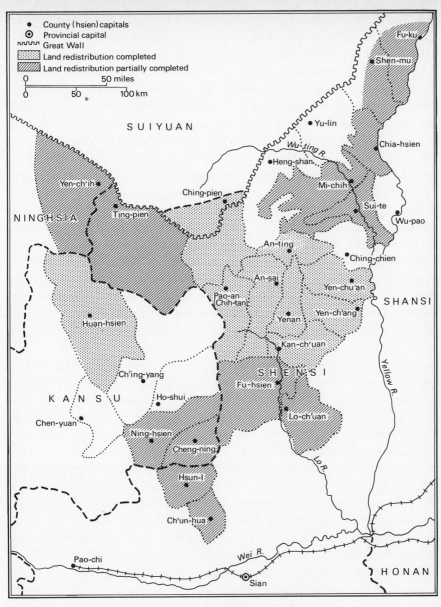

Legend:
- County (hsien) capitals
- Provincial capital
- Great Wall
- Land redistribution completed
- Land redistribution partially completed

0 ____ 50 miles
0 __ 50 __ 100 km

SUIYUAN

NINGHSIA

KANSU

SHENSI

SHANSI

HONAN

Fu-ku
Shen-mu
Yu-lin
Chia-hsien
Wu-ting R.
Heng-shan
Mi-chih
Sui-te
Wu-pao
Yen-ch'ih
Ching-pien
Ting-pien
An-ting
Ching-chien
An-sai
Yen-chu'an
Pao-an
Chih-tan
Yenan
Yen-ch'ang
Huan-hsien
Kan-ch'uan
Ch'ing-yang
SHENSI
Fu-hsien
Ho-shui
Lo-ch'uan
Chen-yuan
Lo R.
Ning-hsien
Cheng-ning
Hsun-I
Ch'un-hua
Pao-chi
Wei R.
Sian
Yellow R.

MAP 10. Shen-Kan-Ning: basic data

Territory and administration:
5 sub-regions
15 counties (*hsien*) in 1937, expanding to 29 by 1941
266 districts (*ch'ü*), 1,549 townships (*hsiang*) by 1941

Population and personnel:
Total population: *c.* 1.4 million
Armed forces in 1941: 8RA, 18,000; public security, 15,000; militia self-defence, 224,000
Party/government, 8,000

Sources: Mark Selden, *The Yenan way in revolutionary China*, 102. Basic data is taken from Selden and from Andrew Watson, *Mao Zedong and the political economy of the border region: a translation of Mao's 'Economic and financial problems'*, 12–15.

(6) The presence in SKN of Mao Tse-tung and the central party-government-military apparatus meant that policies could be carried out with close and continuous supervision from the highest levels.

Although the formal inauguration of the Shen-Kan-Ning Border Region government was announced on 6 September 1937, it had been in operation long before this time. Until the spring of 1937, it resembled the earlier Kiangsi soviet, with much responsibility vested in local military-administrative committees overseen by the party hierarchy. On the adoption of united front policies in 1937, confiscation of landlords' property was terminated, and a more participatory, 'new democratic' system was instituted – without, however, any relinquishing of ultimate party control. Assemblies were to be elected at each level, with administrative councils drawn from the assemblies to carry on the actual work of government. Although universal suffrage was proclaimed, the party could debar certain people from voting or being elected: traitors, criminals, enemy agents, defectives, and so on. KMT members could vote and run for the assemblies, but only as individuals, not as representatives of an organized political party. Furthermore, each administrative council had to be approved by and was responsible to the council at the next higher level. Party members were heavily represented in the assemblies; in councils, they usually constituted a majority. Significantly, the election process was soon terminated, and the Border Region assembly did not convene until January 1939, which meant that in name as in fact the entire structure was directed by the Border Region government, appointed by Party Central.

Chairman of the Border Region government from 1937 until well after the end of the war was one of the CCP's most respected 'elder statesmen', Lin Po-ch'ü (also known as Lin Tsu-han). Born in 1886, seven years before Mao Tse-tung, he had been an early member of Sun Yat-sen's T'ung-meng hui and of the Kuomintang. During the first united front in the 1920s, he worked for both the KMT and CCP. After 1927, he went to Moscow before returning to the Kiangsi soviet and participating in the Long March. By 1938, he was a member of the Party Central Committee.

In addition to this administrative apparatus, mass organizations – workers, women, youth – were called for and gradually began to appear at various levels, but they do not seem to have been very active during this period. Except for the militia, the military was virtually independent of these united front structures, being controlled directly by the Central Military Affairs Committee. Within two years or so, a very considerable bureaucracy was visible in Yenan and throughout Shen-Kan-Ning. Meanwhile, between 1937 and 1940 an estimated 100,000 people immigrated, mostly with the approval of the Border Region authorities.[24] Some were peasants displaced from other provinces, taking up land that had gone out of cultivation; some were veterans, disabled soldiers, and dependents. But perhaps one half came from the fallen cities of east and central China – students, teachers, journalists, writers, intellectuals of all types. In late 1938, 20,000 students were said to be awaiting permission to enter SKN.[25] Yet despite their idealism, the harshness of Yenan and the SKN base came as a shock to many. Some had difficulty adjusting not only to such spartan physical conditions, but also to a political environment in which individualism and critical independence of mind were not so valued as they had been in Peiping or Shanghai.

Although SKN remained very poor by any standard, the Border Region economy was quite stable during the first years of the war. It was a mixed economy, with some public ownership or monopoly, but with a large private sector operating under overall government supervision and price control. Except for land confiscated earlier, private ownership and cultivation were encouraged. Tenancy and hired labour were permitted, with rent ceilings and minimum wages stipulated but not always enforced. Economic burdens on the peasantry were quite light during this period. Most miscellaneous taxes had been abolished, and even the land tax had been so widely remitted that it bore on only a small proportion of the rural population. This was possible in part because of resources available from contributions and confiscation, in part because of the important Nationalist subsidy, and in part because of extensive trade with areas outside SKN.[26] These conditions were to change dramatically by 1940.

For Mao Tse-tung, the period from mid-1936 to mid-1939 was one of unusual security and release from day-to-day pressures, and he had more time now for study and reflection than at any time in the past. With the assistance of his idea man, Ch'en Po-ta, Mao wrote during these years many of his most penetrating and significant essays.[27] It is from this period that one begins to hear, with increasing frequency, of 'the thought of Mao Tse-tung' and 'the sinification of Marxism'. (See Schram, ch. 14, 844ff.)

2. *Shansi*. Shansi lay just across the Yellow River on the east of SKN;

---

[24] Peter Schran, *Guerrilla economy: the development of the Shensi-Kansu-Ninghsia Border Region, 1937-1945*, 99. Another 86,000 immigrants arrived between 1941 and 1945.

[25] John Israel and Donald W. Klein, *Rebels and bureaucrats: China's December 9ers*, 179.

[26] The importance of this subsidy has usually been overlooked. The total subsidy of Ch. $600,000 per month was equivalent in mid-1937 to US $180,000 (at an approximate exchange rate of 3.35 : 1) or US $2,150,000 per year. 'This sum sufficed in 1938 to meet more than the entire public expenditures of 1936. It thus appears that the alliance relieved the SKN border region government of all previous financial difficulties for a period of nearly two years.' Schran, 183.

[27] Raymond F. Wylie, *The emergence of Maoism: Mao Tse-tung, Ch'en Po-ta, and the search for Chinese theory, 1935-1945*, chs. 2–4.

its south-west corner extended to T'ung-kuan, gateway to Sian and Shensi province at the great eastward bend of the Yellow River. CCP forces going behind Japanese lines had to cross Shansi, through which communications also had to pass back and forth between Yenan and all the North China bases. Except for Shantung, all these bases were headquartered in the mountains of eastern Shansi.

Nowhere was the CCP's united front more effective than in Shansi, and this effort was well under way before the outbreak of the war. Above all, this meant dealing with the warlord-governor of the province, Yen Hsi-shan, and the CCP made him a united front target second only to Chiang Kai-shek. By instinct and temperament, Yen was clearly anti-Communist. But his instinct for survival was even stronger, and this had served him well in maintaining his hold over Shansi for more than two decades. Yen feared any penetration of his bailiwick, quite apart from its political colouration; by early 1937 he feared Chiang Kai-shek and the Japanese more than the Communists.[28] When Yen called for reinforcements to help counter a Communist invasion of south-west Shansi in the spring of 1936, Chiang and the central government began to move in on Shansi, and this continued during the manoeuvring touched off by the Sian incident of December 1936. The Japanese threat had been evident from the time of the North China autonomy movement in late 1935, if not earlier, and the fighting in Suiyuan just to the north, during November 1936, clearly indicated the Kwantung Army's intention to outflank Shansi and bring it into its political and economic sphere. Japanese agents were also intriguing within the province. Shansi's resources, especially the Ching-hsing coal mines, powerfully appealed to the Japanese expansionists.

Yen Hsi-shan was acutely aware that his Shansi house was not in order. His armies were not very effective, and his rule was tolerated rather than actively supported. In late 1935, he called for the creation of the 'Force for the Promotion of Justice', a mass organization designed to gain popular support by moderating the worst abuses of local elites and also to squeeze more money out of them for himself. By late summer 1936, Yen was ready to collaborate more actively with leftists, even with Communists. Yen's reassessment dovetailed with the CCP's united front line, which sought friends and allies – or at least acquiescent patrons – on the twin bases of anti-Japanese nationalism and some tolerance of the party's activities. In return the CCP was prepared, up to a point, to keep these activities from going beyond the bounds which would alienate the potential ally or patron. In this atmosphere, activist members of the Justice Force persuaded Yen to form the 'League for National Salvation through

28 Donald G. Gillin, *Warlord: Yen Hsi-shan in Shansi province, 1911-1949*, esp. chs. 9-12.

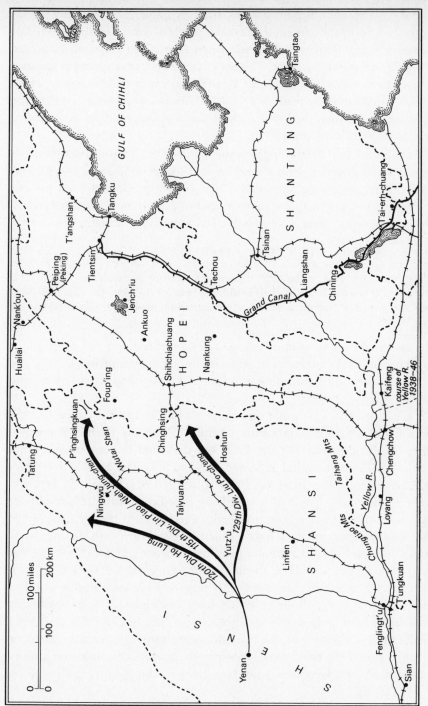

MAP 11. Eighth Route Army deployment, July–December 1937. *Source:* Johnson, *Peasant nationalism*

Sacrifice'. The Sacrifice League accordingly came into existence on 18 September 1936, the fifth anniversary of the Mukden incident, pledged to support the anti-Japanese national united front. Yen Hsi-shan is quoted as saying, at about this time, 'There *is* some risk in a united front, but if we don't collaborate with the CCP, what else can we do? For now, using the Communists is the only way, for otherwise we cannot hold off the Japanese and Chiang Kai-shek. I will use the Communists as a way of weakening the Communists.' [29]

Many individual Communists were active in the Sacrifice League from the start, along with patriotic teachers and students, liberals, and various others. Party members, such as Po I-po, recently released from prisons in Peiping or Taiyuan, set to work with a will, as a classified KMT intelligence report later acknowledged in hyperbolic terms:

Their 'loyalty' and 'hard work' far surpassed the ordinary. Furthermore, they often relinquished or would not assume positions of authority, but were quite willing to work without sparing themselves (seizing particularly on low-level work, for this is the heart of their policy). Their loyalty was like that of a dog; their docility like that of a sheep. Any lord who had such slaves would be delighted.[30]

The Sacrifice League spun off a large number of training and propaganda programmes in the military, in schools, among government officials, and in the countryside – spreading the united front message and recruiting for the party as it went.

Thus when the war broke out, there was no bar to the passage of the three main divisional commands of the 8RA across Shansi. Almost at once, the headquarters of the CCP North China Bureau moved from Peiping to Taiyuan, capital of Shansi, and Liu Shao-ch'i arrived to oversee CCP activities in the province. Prior to the fall of Taiyuan, as Japanese pressure mounted, Yen had allowed the Sacrifice League to step up the organization of military units and had turned over to them a quantity of light infantry equipment. This so-called 'New Army' – to distinguish it from what was left of the regular provincial forces, the 'Old Army' – was organized into four 'Dare-to-die columns' (*chueh-ssu tsung-tui*), each commanded by a party member who served simultaneously as political officer. Before long, about 70 of Shansi's 105 counties were headed by magistrates belonging to the Sacrifice League, and five of the seven larger administrative districts in the province were said by Communists to be in 'our hands'. All this was a promising beginning, but not much more than that. As Po I-po later told Jack Belden, the New Army's 'strong

[29] Po I-po, 3.
[30] Lyman P. Van Slyke, *Enemies and friends: the united front in Chinese Communist history*, 142.

point was its close relations with the people; its weak point, its lack of unity, central leadership, and military experience. Such a force, composed of students who hardly knew how to fire rifles, professors who knew nothing of tactics, and farmers who knew neither tactics nor politics, was in danger of disintegrating for lack of a directing head and of being wiped out for the lack of technique.[31]

But help was on the way in the form of the 115th, 120th, and 129th Divisions of the English Route Army, commanded by Lin Piao, Ho Lung and Liu Po-ch'eng, respectively. The North China base areas were thus born in the mountains of Shansi through the link-up of 8RA units with scattered pockets of anti-Japanese resistance behind enemy lines. As soon as possible, the Communists reached out into neighbouring provinces: Hopei, Honan, Suiyuan. Small detachments of the 115th and 129th Divisions were sent even further afield, into Shantung.

3. *Setting up the bases.* The movement of these three divisions was authorized by both Chiang Kai-shek and Yen Hsi-shan, who had been named commander of the Second War Zone. In the face of the Japanese offensive in Shansi, these units – and especially the 115th – collaborated with regular Shansi army detachments, but remained organizationally separate. From this collaboration came the first Chinese victory of the war, at Pinghsingkuan in north-eastern Shansi, on 25 September 1937. In the heavy but confused fighting in this region – most of it by elements of the Shansi army – Lin Piao set a careful ambush for the supply train at the rear of Itagaki's crack 5th Division. Caught by surprise in a narrow ravine, the Japanese were cut to pieces. Yet the Communists acquired only about 100 rifles and no prisoners; in a last-ditch measure, surviving Japanese soldiers destroyed their equipment and committed suicide.[32]

The experience of Pinghsingkuan may have helped persuade Mao and those who agreed with him of the unwisdom of conventional warfare against a superior enemy, in coordination with 'friendly armies'. In his battle report, Lin Piao – who probably sided with Mao in this debate – implicitly confirmed such a conclusion:

(1) Coordination by the friendly forces is in reality extremely bad. They decide on a plan for attack but are unable to follow through with it themselves... (7) The enemy soldiers have enormous fighting ability. We never encountered such a strong foe in the Northern Expedition or Soviet period. Their infantrymen are able to deploy themselves with individual initiative in combat situations. Although wounded, they refuse to give up arms ... (12) Our army's military skill

---

[31] Jack Belden, *China shakes the world*, 52.
[32] P'eng Te-huai, 'Kuan-yü hua-pei ken-chü-ti kung-tso ti pao-kao' (Report on work in the base areas of North China), in *Kung-fei huo-kuo shih-liao hui-pien* (Collected historical materials on the national disaster caused by the Communist bandits), 3.351.

and training still leave a great deal to be desired. In the past half year, our troops have had a chance to rest and regroup, and their discipline, morale, and regularization have progressed greatly; but in combat training we still have a long way to go.[33]

While the Japanese invasion of Shansi was still in progress, some elements of the 115th Division (about 2,000 men) under the command of Nieh Jung-chen took up positions in the north-eastern part of Shansi and in the adjacent mountainous regions of western Hopei. (Lin Piao was seriously wounded in January 1938 and returned to Yenan, then went to the USSR to recuperate.) The activities of Nieh Jung-chen in the Wu-t'ai/Fou-p'ing area marked the beginning of what was to become the Shansi-Chahar-Hopei Border Region – better known as Chin-Ch'a-Chi (CCC) after the ancient names of these provinces.

As early as November 1937, the hazy outlines of the CCC base area were beginning to take shape. Local 'mobilization committees' and other preliminary organizations were active in about thirty counties of north-east Shansi and west Hopei, twenty counties in central Hopei (east of the P'ing-Han line), and four counties in southern Chahar. Resistance groups did not yet fully control these counties, nor in many cases were they adjacent to each other. Little coordination yet existed among them.

Between 10 and 15 January 1938, the base area was formally established in a conference held at Fou-p'ing, a county town in the mountains of western Hopei. A total of 148 delegates from thirty-nine counties attended, representing some 28 'organizations' ranging from Mobilization Committees and the Salvation League through various military units to the Yellow Temple Lama Monks. It was very definitely a united front assembly, and it was fully guided by the CCP. The assembly adopted a series of resolutions endorsing anti-Japanese resistance, military mobilization, political organization and moderate economic reforms. It also endorsed the organizational structure of the CCC base, which was to guide the base for the next five years, since a full congress of the CCC base was not to meet again until January 1943. The Fou-p'ing delegates approved a nine-member administrative committee, headed by Sung Shao-wen, a Salvation League activist, concurrently magistrate of Wu-t'ai county.[34] Nieh Jung-chen was overall commander of the military district, which was separate from the civil-political hierarchy though interacting with it at all levels. This apparatus had overall jurisdiction over eleven Special Districts, the areas in which resistance organizers were most active. On

---

[33] Quoted in Kataoka Tetsuya, 64–5.

[34] Sung was a graduate of Peking University and had been imprisoned, 1933–4, for anti-Japanese agitation. See Hartford, 'Step-by-step', 84–9.

22 January 1938, Chiang Kai-shek and Yen Hsi-shan reluctantly approved the establishment of the Chin-Ch'a-Chi Border Region. Of all the bases established by the CCP behind Japanese lines, it was the only one to achieve formal central government recognition. Simultaneous with the development of CCC, Ho Lung's 120th Division was active in north-west Shansi – an area almost as poor and backward as SKN – in what was to become the Shansi-Suiyuan (Chin-Sui) base. Chin-Sui was important primarily as a strategic corridor linking the Yenan area with bases farther east, and as a shield partially protecting the north-east quadrant of SKN.

Liu Po-ch'eng moved his 129th Division into the T'ai-hang mountains of south-east Shansi, near its boundaries with Hopei and Honan. This region, together with a part of western Shantung, became the Chin-Chi-Lu-Yü base (CCLY). For most of the war, this was really two loosely integrated bases, one west of the Ping-Han railway line, the other to the east. Later to develop was the peninsular Shantung base, further from the main strength of the 8RA, where struggles between Communists, Japanese, puppets, local forces, and units affiliated with the central governments were very complex.

In Central China, certain differences from North China slowed the development of CCP influence. In the areas attacked most forcefully by Japan, especially the Yangtze delta and the Shanghai-Nanking axis, local administration often broke down, order disintegrated, and armed bands of all types quickly appeared, just as in the north. Here too, the Japanese paid scant attention at first to occupying the regions through which they passed. But elsewhere, Central China was somewhat less disrupted by the Japanese invasion. Local and provincial administrations continued to function, often in contact with Nationalist-controlled Free China. In those parts of Anhwei and Kiangsu north of the Yangtze River which had not been directly subject to Japanese attack, Nationalist armies remained, without retreating. South of the Yangtze in the Chiang-nan area, though most Nationalist forces retreated at first, some units were soon reintroduced and more followed. Many of these forces were either elements of the Central Armies or closely associated with Chiang Kai-shek, unlike the regional 'inferior brands' of military (*tsa-p'ai chün*) in the 8RA's areas. This region had been, after all, the core area of KMT power, the Nationalists were very sensitive about intrusions, and they were in a better position to thwart such efforts.

Although the New Fourth Army was smaller and for several years less effective than the Eighth Route Army, Mao Tse-tung and Liu Shao-ch'i were soon to call for aggressive base-building throughout this area, especially north of the Yangtze. Officially, the Nationalists assigned to the N4A the zone of operations shown on map 12. A monthly subsidy of about Ch. $130,000 was to be paid by the central government to help meet operating costs. North of the Yangtze, their theatre was part of the Nationalist Fifth War Zone, commanded by the formidable leader of the Kwangsi faction, Li Tsung-jen; south of the river was the Third War Zone, under General Ku Chu-t'ung, a close and trusted associate of Chiang Kai-shek. Until the sixth plenum, late in 1938, the N4A operated with rather little direct control from Yenan. Although some of the senior cadres in Hsiang Ying's headquarters – Yeh T'ing did not have much power – had been sent from Yenan, the N4A's political chain of command ran through the Yangtze River Bureau, then headed by Wang Ming. Initial military operations, almost entirely south of the river, involved getting the small N4A detachments in place, enlarging them by recruiting or absorbing miscellaneous armed bands, and carrying on such anti-Japanese activities as were within their limited power. Sometimes their ragtag appearance led local peasants to confuse them with the many bandit gangs ravaging the region; once or twice they were mistakenly welcomed as Japanese troops come to restore order. Their reception by local people – ordinary peasants and landlords alike – often depended more on their ability to disarm bandits than on their opposition to Japan.[35] Nowhere during the first year or so of the war did the Communists in Central China seek to seize administrative authority and establish the kind of bases that were beginning to take shape further north.

This situation began to change after the sixth plenum of late 1938. During 1939 the N4A expanded greatly, with the forces north of the Yangtze River becoming increasingly important, to some extent at the expense of those to the south. This military expansion was part of the increasing tension between Hsiang Ying on the one hand and Party Central on the other – Mao Tse-tung, Chou En-lai, and above all Liu Shao-ch'i. This expansion and emphasis on base-building of course brought the Central China Communists into increasingly bitter conflict with Nationalist authorities on central, provincial, and local levels.

At the sixth plenum, Liu Shao-ch'i became the highest party authority in Central China. This reflected both the decline of Wang Ming's influence and Mao's determination to achieve closer control and pursue the North China base-building policies in Central China.[36] Table 21 and map 12 show

---

35 Ch'en Yung-fa, 'The making of a revolution: the Communist movement in eastern and central China 1937–1945' (Stanford University, Ph.D. dissertation, 1980), 38–48.
36 The headquarters of the Central Plains Bureau was first located at Ch'ueh-shan on the P'ing-Han railway line, about half way between Chengchow and Wuhan. This was shortly after the fall of Wuhan, and the CCP may have reckoned that the Japanese would make a major push along the railway line through Hunan and Hopei, in which case the bureau would be well situated to direct operations. After it became clear that the Japanese were ignoring this section of the P'ing-Han line, the Central Plains Bureau moved eastward.

TABLE 21
New Fourth Army (late 1939)

Headquarters CO: Yeh T'ing. Vice CO/Political Officer: Hsiang Ying. Chief of Staff: Chang Yun-i. Head, Political Dept.: Yuan Kuo-p'ing. Vice-head: Teng Tzu-hui.

South Yangtze Command (formed July 1939)
  1st Detachment. CO: Ch'en I. Efforts to expand east and south of Lake T'ai during 1939 were not very successful. Most of these forces were transferred north of the Yangtze River, March–June 1940.
  2nd Detachment. CO: Chang Ting-ch'eng. In early 1939, Lo Ping-hui led part of these forces across the Yangtze to help form the 5th Detachment, placed under his command.
  3rd Detachment. CO: T'an Chen-lin.

North Yangtze Command (formed July 1939). CO: Chang Yun-i.
  4th Detachment. CO: Tai Chi-ying. Originally formed from Communist remnants surviving north of Wuhan in the Ta-pieh mountains of Hupei (near Huang-an), the old O-Yü-Wan soviet. Led by Kao Ching-t'ing, a former poor peasant butcher. Kao resisted N4A orders, discipline; refused collaboration with KMT forces. He reluctantly moved east to Lake Chao (Anhwei), was denounced as a 'tyrannical warlord', and was executed in April 1939 by order of Yeh T'ing after a public trial. Some elements of the 4th Det. were sent to help form the 5th Det. The 4th Det. served mainly as a training unit.
  5th Detachment. CO: Lo Ping-hui. Formed in spring 1939 at Lu-chiang, SW of Lake Chao; moved to Lai-an/Liu-ho area on the Kiangsu-Anhwei border, opposite Nanking, in July 1939. In late 1939, moved further east to the Lake Kao-yu/Grand Canal area in Kiangsu. 5th Det. saw much combat with both Nationalists and Japanese.
  6th Detachment. CO: P'eng Hsueh-feng. Formed in the summer of 1939 from elements sent south into Honan from the 8RA. Absorbed many local armed groups and stragglers from Nationalist armies. In early 1940, moved from eastern Honan (T'ai-k'ang/Huai-yang) eastward into northern Anhwei. 6th Det. was the main military and base-building force in northern Anhwei and northern Kiangsu.

Note: in recent years Kao Ching-t'ing has been posthumously rehabilitated; it is said he was traduced and wrongly executed in 1939.
Sources: from material in Ch'en Yung-fa, ch. 2, and Johnson, *Peasant nationalism*, 124–32.

the N4A's deployments during the first two years of the war – a general movement toward the east and north, further behind Japanese lines and away from the Nationalist rear areas. The most important of the other military forces affiliated with the N4A was the Honan-Hupei assault column led by Long March veteran Li Hsien-nien, which took up positions near those originally occupied by the 4th Detachment, north of Wuhan astride the P'ing-Han railway line. Li Hsien-nien's column was not made a formal part of the N4A until 1941, in the reorganization that followed the New Fourth Army incident. Much further east, and south of the Yangtze River, were two local semi-guerrilla groups, the Chiang-nan Anti-Japanese Patriotic Army and the Chiang-nan Assault Column led by Kuan Wen-wei. Kuan, a local CCP leader (from Tan-yang) who until 1937 had lost touch with the party, helped open up a corridor through which N4A elements could pass north of the river, across Yang-chung Island. Both these units and the 1st Detachment contested with the Chungking-affiliated Loyal National Salvation Army.

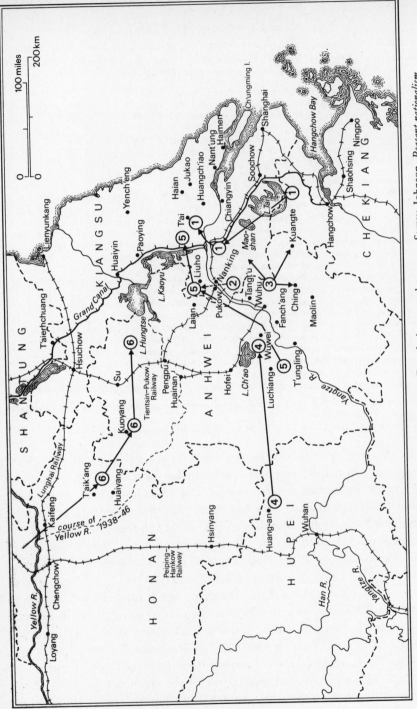

MAP 12. Disposition and movements of the New Fourth Army, to late 1940. *Source:* Johnson, *Peasant nationalism*

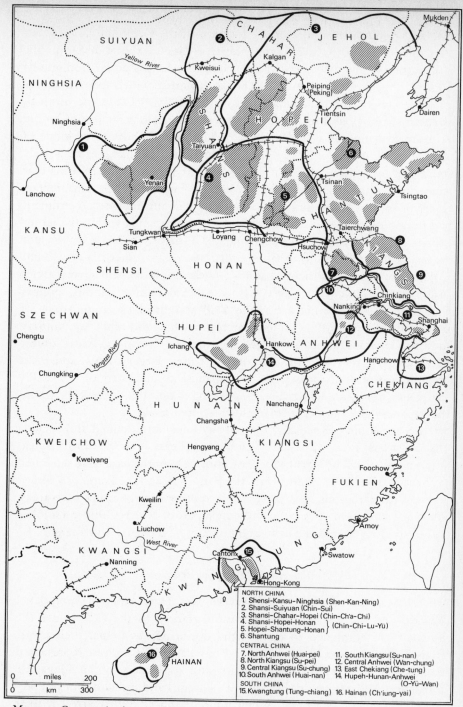

MAP 13. Communist bases as claimed overall (late 1944). *Source*: Van Slyke, *Chinese Communist movement*, xii–xiii. This map has been prepared from CCP sources dated August and October 1944.

Map 13 shows the approximate location of the Communist bases, but like most simplified CCP maps prepared late in the war for public consumption, this map shows large, contiguous areas under Communist control. This is quite misleading. The bases were in widely different stages of development and consolidation, from SKN and CCC in the north to the two shadowy and insubstantial guerrilla zones not far from Canton. A more realistic but still simplified picture would show three kinds of territories, all quite fluid. (1) Zones in which the CCP had created a fairly stable administration, able to function openly and institute reforms that were quite frankly less than revolutionary but nevertheless more far-reaching and deeply rooted in local society than any Chinese government had previously achieved. These core areas were islands within the larger expanse of bases shown on unclassified CCP maps. (2) More ambivalent regions, often referred to in Communist sources as 'guerrilla areas' and in Japanese sources as 'neutral zones'. These might contain several types of forces: Communists, KMT elements, local militia, bandits, puppet forces. In these guerrilla areas, the CCP sought allies on the basis of immediate sharing of common interests. They did only preliminary organizational work, and attempted only modest reform. (3) Areas subject in varying degrees to Japanese control. Cities, larger towns, and main communications corridors were the Japanese counterparts of the CCP's core areas, alongside which lay a fluctuating penumbra of territory where the Japanese and puppet forces held the upper hand.

In North China, especially, the railway lines both defined and divided the major base areas. Chin-Ch'a-Chi lay to the east of the Tatung-Taiyuan line, and north of the Cheng-Tai. The core areas of the base were separated from each other by the P'ing-Han, the P'ing-Sui, and the Peiping-Mukden lines. With variations, this pattern was repeated in the other base areas. The very confusion of map 14, showing a part of North China in October 1938, vividly conveys the actual complexity of the early war years.

Processes of Base Construction

The widespread disruption of government from county (*hsien*) level upward and the quasi-legal recognition granted to the CCP under the united front combined to open many opportunities to party elements. Eighth Route Army members and civilian CCP cadres represented themselves as a legitimate authority and as leaders of anti-Japanese resistance. Military and political control went hand in hand, but military affairs at first took priority. When units of the 8RA first arrived, their initial task was to link up with local Communists or 'progressives', then

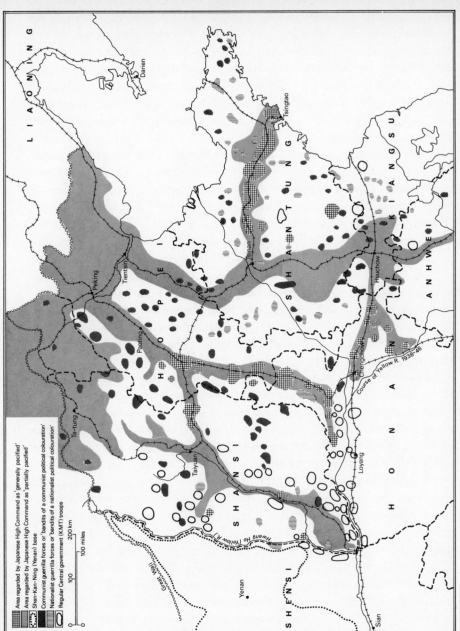

MAP 14. Military situation, North China, October 1938. *Source:* Bōeicho bōei kensujo senshi shitsu, *Hokushi no chiansen,* map folio

Legend:

▦ Area regarded by Japanese High Command as 'generally pacified'

⋰ Area regarded by Japanese High Command as 'partially pacified'

⋮ Shen-Kan-Ning (Yenan) base

● Communist guerrilla forces or 'bandits of a communist political colouration'

◆ Nationalist guerrilla forces or 'bandits of a nationalist political colouration'

○ Regular Central government (KMT) troops

Place names: LIAONING, Darren, HOPE[I], Peking, Tientsin, Paoting, Ta-tung, SHANSI, Taiyuan, Yenan, SHEN'SI, Sian, Great Wall, Hwang Ho (Yellow R.), Loyang, HONAN, Chengchow, Course of Yellow R. 1938-46, Hsuchow, ANHWEI, KIANGSU, SHANTUNG, Tsingtao, Tsinan

Scale: 0   100   200 km
0   100 miles

to make contact with the kaleidoscope of local forces and local communities in whose midst they found themselves. Contact with native activists provided manpower, information and access to the populace. As Po I-po noted, locals lacked leadership, organization, discipline, and experience that could all be provided by outsiders, but without the locals, outsiders were likely to be distrusted, tolerated perhaps but not really supported, and could not sink roots into local society. Nationalist forces never fully mastered this linkage.

In the mountainous Shansi-Hopei borderlands, the Salvation League, headed by Sung Shao-wen, was one of the first groups with which Nieh's units made contact. Across the P'ing-Han railway, on the plains of north-central Hopei, approaches were made to Lü Cheng-ts'ao. Liu Shao-ch'i estimated that after the war began in 1937 as many as 200 armed bands, with perhaps 30,000 participants, quickly sprang up.[37] According to Liu, they were fairly easy to win over – provided the 8RA treated them well, assisted in maintaining order, did not demand too much from them in manpower and ignored a certain amount of semi-bandit behaviour. Well-entrenched bandit groups and local protective associations posed more difficult problems. Dealing successfully with them was a long process, which might have to be repeated as the base areas expanded or were forced to move. Bandits and vagrants (*yu-min*) were both a threat to local order and a source of recruits to militia forces organized by the 8RA. Despite their unpopularity with local peasants, upon whom they frequently preyed 'as upon meat and fish', many vagrants were enlisted. P'eng Chen recalled that 'the overwhelming majority actively participated in the anti-Japanese movement. At this time, the masses were, in general, still waiting to see what would happen. Most of the vagrants, with no family obligations and scant attachment to the status quo, rose up first and together with a minority of revolutionary activists, formed a path-breaking vanguard.'[38] But P'eng and other party cadres also knew that they wanted mainly to keep their bellies filled, and that they would take whatever side delivered more. 'If it gives milk,' vagrants often said, 'then call it mother.' Liu Shao-ch'i directed local cadres to handle organized bandit groups in whatever manner seemed best: to ally with them and win them over, to recruit their men and leave their leaders isolated, or to attack and break them up. In core areas, bandit groups were to be brought to heel or offered the opportunity to leave. But, according

[37] Liu Shao-ch'i, 'Chien-ch'ih Hua-pei k'ang-chan chung ti wu-chuang pu-tui' (Firmly support armed groups taking part in the north China war of resistance), in Chieh-fang she, *K'ang-Jih min-tsu t'ung-i chan-hsien chih-nan* (Guide to the anti-Japanese national united front), 5.42.

[38] P'eng Chen, *Chung-kung 'Chin-Ch'a-Chi pien-ch'ü' chih ko-chung cheng-ts'e* (Various policies in the CCP's 'Chin-Ch'a-Chi Border Region'), 6b.

to Liu, 'if local bandits active in the enemy-occupied area are strong enough to wreck the enemy's order, and if the anti-Japanese forces are relatively weak there, then we should persuade and unite with the bandits'.[39] This kind of united front with lumpen elements added manpower and weapons, and gradually reduced disorder in the base areas.

Local associations were a more difficult problem than bandits, according to Liu Shao-ch'i, who noted their long history in China and the impetus added by wartime conditions. The Red Spears, the Heaven's Gate Society, and joint village associations (*lien-chuang-hui*) were all 'pure self-defence organizations sharing the goals of resisting exorbitant taxes and levies and harassment by army units or bandits'. Generally controlled by local elites and 'politically neutral', they could summon mass support because they appealed to the 'backward and narrow self-interests' of the peasantry while the secret societies added superstitious beliefs to other forms of influence. They were ready to fight all intruders, including anti-Japanese guerrilla forces. Moreover, if a small force settled in their vicinity, they often attacked it for its weapons, even if it posed no threat. The associations had no permanent military organization but could respond to a summons with 'a very large military force', so long as the action took place in their local area.

Liu Shao-ch'i summarized the approaches that had proved most effective. (1) Take no rash action. (2) Strictly observe discipline; make no demands and do not provoke them, but be very watchful. (3) Scrupulously avoid insulting their religious beliefs or their leaders; show respect. (4) When they are harassed by the Japanese or by puppets, help in driving them away. (5) Win their confidence and respect by exemplary behaviour and assist them in various ways. (6) Most important, carry on patient education, propaganda and persuasion in order to raise their national consciousness, to lead them into the anti-Japanese struggle, and to provide supplies voluntarily to guerrilla forces. (7) Seek to break up associations that serve the Japanese. (8) Do not help the associations to grow, especially in the base areas or in guerrilla zones. (9) In enemy-occupied territories, help push the associations' self-defence struggles in the direction of the anti-Japanese movement. Finally, Liu noted that sometimes superstition could be turned to advantage. Some secret societies believed that Chu Te, commander of the Eighth Route Army, must be descended from their patron deity and founder of the Ming dynasty, Chu Yuan-chang. Relations between these secret societies and local 8RA units were particularly good. In short, said Liu, 'in many regions of North China, the anti-Japanese united front in rural villages

[39] Liu Shao-ch'i, 'Chien-ch'ih', 45–6.

depends mainly on how our relations and work with the associations is handled'.[40]

Thus the intrusion of Communist influence behind Japanese lines did not in the first instance depend upon nationalism, socio-economic programmes or ideology. In fact, it was quite feasible for possessors of military power to live off the Chinese countryside with a different ideology, or with no ideology at all, as the following description of Sun Tien-ying makes clear:

One of his [Sun's] lieutenants said to me, 'The reason we have an army is so that everyone gets to eat,' the implication being that whether or not they fought was unimportant. From the beginning of the war to the end of the war, he manoeuvred between the Communists and the central government, even going over to the Japanese for a time... When the war broke out, he rounded up his former associates to fight Japan. The central government designated his force the New Fifth Army, with headquarters in Lin-hsien, Honan ... Because of connections with the secret societies (*pang-hui*), he had contacts everywhere, so of course it was easy to do business and manage things. Although Lin-hsien is a small, out-of-the-way place, even goods from Shanghai could be bought and enjoyed.[41]

Everywhere, the CCP viewed military and political control as the essential prior condition for all other work. The distinction between consolidated, semi-consolidated and guerrilla zones measured the different degrees of such control. At an early stage, the situation might be described as 'open', in the sense that individuals and groups in society had a variety of options which the CCP was unable to prevent them from exercising. In these circumstances, the united front recognized the party's relative weakness, and it relied mainly on persuasion, accommodation, infiltration and education.

At the other extreme was a 'closed' situation, in which the CCP was powerful enough to define the options and to shape both the incentives and the costs of choice in such a way as to produce the desired behaviour. If necessary the party could impose coercive sanctions, even violence, upon those who opposed it. As this control was achieved and deepened, a kind of political revolution took place, even without any change as yet in social and economic structure. The party and its followers were wresting power from the traditional rural power holders, but establishment of control was a gradual and uneven process, influenced by terrain, by local society, and by the presence of competing or hostile forces. Even in the most successful of the base areas, Chin-Ch'a-Chi, progress was difficult. The masses did not spontaneously rally to the Communist side.

40 *Ibid.* 48.
41 Ch'ü Chih-sheng, *K'ang-chan chi-li* (A personal account of the war of resistance), 37.

Of the middle peasants, poor peasants, and other 'impoverished masses', P'eng Chen wrote, 'While the base area was being created, their capacity for political and organizational independence did not really show up ... but after these same peasants actually engaged in a certain amount of struggle (when the initiative came from the top down), they gradually awakened and found the courage to resist.' Finally, in late 1941, he could say, 'With regard to the class relationships within this region, we hold a dominant position in military and political affairs; the basic masses have already turned over and achieved dominance. But economically, the landlord-bourgeois class is still definitely predominant.'[42]

One question that runs through much of the history of the Chinese Communist movement is whether or not conditions existed in certain areas that made them more susceptible than other areas to Communist penetration, organization and control. In particular, did conditions of poverty, exploitation and social dislocation create a riper situation for Communist activity than existed in more prosperous and socially integrated areas? The answer appears to be that 'there was no single pattern of Communist success or influence in China ... The expansion of Communist forces in any area during any period was likely to be better correlated with [prolonged] Communist presence in the vicinity than with any other social phenomenon.'[43] Indeed, Mao, Liu and other leaders never accepted the position that specific social and economic conditions made some areas suitable and others unsuitable for base area construction. On the contrary, Mao believed that in principle bases could be built anywhere that the party had an opportunity for sustained operation. For example in May 1938 he insisted that bases could be established on the plains, as well as in more difficult terrain.[44] When these leaders cite local conditions (tenancy, usury, etc.), they do so to provide concrete examples to be applied flexibly in other areas, not to suggest that it was *only* under such conditions that base construction was possible. Although tenancy rates in much of North China were rather low – and rent reduction policies therefore had limited appeal – Communist leaders argued that there were other problems, other forms of exploitation, that could serve in its stead. It was up to cadres at the local level to analyse social and economic conditions in their region and set to work in the spirit of general directives. The question of whether conditions in a particular area were bringing the peasants more exploitation and misery or remaining about the same, or even improving slightly, did

[42] P'eng Chen, 1a.
[43] Roy Hofheinz, Jr. 'The ecology of Chinese communist success: rural influence patterns, 1923–1945', in A. Doak Barnett, ed. *Chinese Communist politics in action*, 72, 77.
[44] Mao Tse-tung, 'Problems of strategy in guerrilla war against Japan', Mao, *SW*, 2.95.

not interest Communist leaders or local cadres. They were convinced there was enough misery and injustice everywhere in the countryside to fuel revolutionary change.

Still, the Communists did not succeed in creating base areas everywhere, nor were they always able to maintain bases once established. The most successful bases *were* located in poorer regions: in mountainous areas, in marshlands, and in other remote areas – in short, in traditional bandit lairs such as those used by Sung Chiang and his fellows in the picaresque novel *Shui-hu chuan*. And for the same reasons. Distant from centres of population and state control, often straddling provincial boundaries, these peripheral areas offered greater security and better opportunities for uninterrupted work than did densely populated plains nearer to large cities and major communication routes.[45] In short, geography (one might even say military geography) might be more important to the success of a particular base than its social and economic structure.

What enabled the Communists to survive and grow was the combination of military-political control and popular support, both expressed in interlocking organizational structures reaching down (at least in consolidated bases) to the village level. Control came first, but what the Communists did with that control marked the difference between them and their rivals. Political, economic and social changes accompanied the extension and deepening of control in a phased and mutually interactive way. Ideally, no reform should be undertaken until the party was confident of its ability to carry it out successfully. Conversely, every change should further enhance the control of the party and the 'basic masses'. If properly handled, therefore, each change strengthened both control and support and prepared the way for the next change.

When a particular reform (an election, a production compaign, a struggle meeting) was called for, it was usually understood that this referred to the consolidated and perhaps to the semi-consolidated regions, but not to guerrilla areas which were too 'open'. Furthermore, many policies were not carried out all at once, even in consolidated bases. Instead, they were first instituted in carefully prepared 'model districts' where intensive preliminary work and concentration of personnel made success likely. The spectacle of a particularly notorious landlord humiliated in public and deprived of some or all of his property then served as a powerful example elsewhere. Other landlords, not yet so painfully singled

45 G. William Skinner describes China as being made up of nine macro-regions, each of which contains a core area usually associated with river basins and plains. The peripheries are much poorer than the cores – indeed, they are 'exploited' by the cores for cheap labour, timber, natural resources, etc. Provincial boundaries often – but not always – follow peripheries and enclose cores. See G. William Skinner, ed. *The city in late imperial China*, 211–20.

out, were 'persuaded' to cooperate, especially when assured that their property would not be confiscated and that they would continue to receive their rents and interest, albeit on a reduced scale. More important, peasants were emboldened to define themselves in class terms, to overcome ingrained attitudes of fatalism, of passive resignation, and of community harmony – in short, to *act*. Each action made the next one easier, and burnt the bridges back to old ways. A tenant might for a time secretly pay his landlord the original, unreduced rent out of fear of retaliation or in the interest of community harmony. But once he had spoken out against him in a struggle meeting, he had probably passed the point of no return.

For the first time some peasants were beginning to think of themselves – often hesitantly or reluctantly – as political and social actors in their own right, rather than as the passive objects of action by others. The party's goal was a guided but also voluntary participation that it called 'democracy'. Alexis de Tocqueville was enunciating a general principle when he wrote, 'Patiently endured so long as it seemed beyond redress, a grievance comes to appear intolerable once the possibility of removing it crosses men's minds.'[46] P'eng Chen thus describes how the same tenants who once conspired to pay their full rent now came 'to settle scores' (*ch'ing-suan*) with landlords, refusing to pay any rent at all or demanding compensation. Poor peasants often roughed up landlords encountered on the roads or at market. 'In sum, everything was turned upside-down ... Corrections have now begun [mid-1940], and the struggle between the two sides is being held within a certain compass.'[47]

As control was being established, three sets of relationships provided the issues over which organization and mobilization might begin: (1) between landlord and tenant, focusing on rent; (2) between creditor and debtor, focusing on interest; and (3) between government and governed, focusing on taxes.[48] These issues were used to sharpen class struggle against 'feudal elements'. Step-by-step measures opened local society for deeper Communist penetration and broader organization, but at each step those being organized had to perceive actual benefit to themselves without

[46] Quoted in Arthur L. Stinchcombe, *Theoretical methods in social history*, 34. Note also Leon Trotsky: 'In reality the mere existence of privations is not enough to cause an insurrection; if it were, the masses would be always in revolt. It is necessary that the bankruptcy of the social regime, being conclusively revealed, should make these privations intolerable, and that new conditions and new ideas should open the prospect of a revolutionary way out. Then in the cause of the great aims conceived by them, those same masses will prove capable of enduring doubled and tripled privations.' In *ibid*. 33–4. Trotsky viewed spontaneous insurrection as an unlikely 'herd mutiny'.

[47] P'eng Chen, 4b.

[48] Ch'en Yung-fa, 175. The issues posed by these relationships were not limited to rent, interest and taxes. There were other elements as well (e.g. water rights, labour service, customary 'favours', *droit de siegneur*, etc.).

excessive risk, or else they might not respond. Concrete measures had to be found with immediate or near-term payoff, described in the vivid, earthy language to which peasants were accustomed – reserving the rhetoric of class struggle for a later date.

The first benefits brought to the local populace would depend on circumstance and had to be coordinated with the logistic needs of the CCP military and administrative personnel moving into the area. As P'eng Te-huai described it,

We provided for ourselves according to the principle of 'those with money contribute money, those with strength contribute strength'. Having set up a base area, we could collect national salvation grain levies where we had political power. Where we had not yet established base area political power, we relied on contributions, loans, requisitions, and confiscation of traitors' assets; we did not depend on the Kuomintang to issue rations or supplies.[49]

Although rent and interest reduction were stated policy, neither could be systematically carried out until control had been established to the consolidated areas of the more advanced bases. Rent reduction was described as fulfilling Sun Yat-sen's pledge to lower rents by 25 per cent (from an average rent-to-harvest ratio of 50 per cent down to 37·5 per cent) as part of the 'land to the tiller' programme which was an official but ignored element of Kuomintang ideology. This made it difficult for KMT supporters, including landlords, to criticize what the CCP was doing. From the outside, CCP rent policy looked quite moderate. Yet the complexity and variety of land relationships enabled the party to act with restraint or severity as the local situation and the mood of the cadres seemed to call for. Landlord obstructionism courted charges of damaging the cause of resistance and in effect collaborating with the enemy.[50] This could lead to severe sanctions, even confiscation of property. In any case, landlords' options were limited: 'Their land is in the rural areas and cannot be carried off into the cities.' P'eng Chen went on to write,

Generally, the enlightenment of landlords in the Chin-Ch'a-Chi Border Region took place after the basic masses had stood up, democratic rule had been firmly established, and their feudal dictatorship had been broken down. This proves that if peasants and landlords do not pass through the necessary struggles, the enlightenment of the landlords is not possible, nor is adjustment of landlord-peasant relationships.[51]

49 P'eng Te-huai, Tzu-shu, 227.
50 Landlords resisted both actively and passively. If they did not have armed manpower at their command, they might call in nearby militia (see above, ch. 6). They sometimes passed intelligence to Nationalists, puppets or Japanese agents. They used a combination of threats, cajolery and bribery to try to keep local peasants in line. More passively, they might appear to cooperate with the new regime. A common tactic was to enlist a son in the 8RA, or to become a local activist.
51 P'eng Chen, 3a.

Interest reduction was difficult to carry out, and might also be more radical than it looked if it involved cancellation of principal or accrued interest on past loans. These losses, combined with lowered rates on new loans, often persuaded potential lenders to hold their money in reserve. Shrinkage of rural credit caused hardship, since many poor peasants required loans to survive, particularly during the spring famine in north and north-central China, when the previous year's grain stores were running low and the harvest of winter crops in May and June was still some weeks off. Furthermore, not all lenders were rich merchants or landlords. Poor and middle peasants might have a little cash, too little to invest in land or commerce, which they loaned out for additional income. Families lacking labour power – widows or childless couples – might sell land they could not cultivate in order to have money to loan. Consequently interest reduction succeeded only when the base area government itself had sufficient resources to make credit available at the prescribed interest rate.

Taxes also could be changed only slowly. Unlike Shen-Kan-Ning, bases behind Japanese lines received no outside subsidies and, as P'eng Te-huai indicated, had to rely on their own efforts. During the first two years of the war, even Chin-Ch'a-Chi was able to make only modest structural changes in the tax system, by abolishing many but not all of the miscellaneous and surtaxes that had proliferated above and beyond the basic land tax in most parts of China during the first decades of the twentieth century, and by imposing a customs duty on trade with Japanese-occupied areas. Other reforms aimed at more effective collection of the land tax by registering 'black land' (*hei-t'ien*: land formerly untaxed because it was kept off the tax rolls), and by reducing corruption so that taxes collected actually wound up in official coffers. Remaining deficits were made up by internal loans and by other ad hoc measures.

In 1939, administrative control had advanced sufficiently to permit a more regularized tax system, the 'rational burden' (*ho-li fu-tan*) plan, to be instituted in the core areas of the CCC base. Under this plan, each county was assigned a tax quota which was in turn subdivided by township and village, according to estimated total assets and capacity to pay. The village quota was then divided among the resident families, according to a calculation intended to be steeply progressive. In addition, very wealthy families were separately assessed.[52] Rent and interest reductions were designed to make the tax system more effective by preventing landlords

[52] Michael Lindsay, 'The taxation system of the Shansi-Chahar-Hopei Border Region, 1938–1945', *CQ* (Apr.–June 1970) 2–3; Kataoka Tetsuya, 124–32. Regardless of class, desirable commercial, industrial or handicraft activities were not taxed, and taxes were remitted on lands newly opened or returned to cultivation.

and rich peasants from recouping their tax payments by passing them on to tenants and debtors. Clearly, this system could not work unless its authors had confidence in those who would have to carry it out at county and village levels. P'eng Chen's report notes that it was not until well into 1939 that CCC was able to certify or replace village heads, set up village representative councils, and create a unified administrative system – and even then only in consolidated areas.[53]

The rational burden tax system was used, somewhat later, in similar form in other bases, as was the second major change, a shift from money to grain as the main unit of fiscal calculation. In CCC, the government kept its main accounts in units of millet, or their equivalent. Salaries and tax quotas were thus separated from currency fluctuations. Cadres and other functionaries were on a supply system, and received only the most meagre pocket-money income. Troops or others travelling on official business were issued grain coupons (*liang-p'iao*), which they could exchange for grain anywhere within base area jurisdiction. When a village paid its tax quota, it could deliver either grain or coupons, or a mixture of the two. Since villages were responsible for transporting their tax grain to the collection depot, they preferred the convenience of the coupons.[54]

When Communist cadres and village leaders chose, they could impose confiscations, levies, contributions, and rational-burden taxes in such a way that particular individuals or categories of local residents experienced pronounced changes in their economic condition. This worked to the advantage of tenants, poor peasants, and middle peasants, and to the disadvantage of rich peasants and landlords, especially the latter. One scholar claimed that the 'tax and rent reduction program of the CCP was revolutionary. It amounted to confiscation by instalment.'[55]

Although this assessment may be correct for certain villages in the core areas of Chin-Ch'a-Chi, it overstates what happened elsewhere in CCC and in other bases. By its own admission, the CCP lacked the capacity to carry out these policies throughout the base areas. Even where such radical transformation was within their power, the Communists usually settled for somewhat less, so long as it deepened their control and helped mobilize peasant support. For one thing, landlords and rich peasants were the most productive and economically effective operators on the rural scene, if not through their own direct labour then because of their access to capital, draft animals, tools, know-how, and understanding of market conditions. Moreover the class demarcations the CCP used as shorthand represented only very crudely the more complex reality in which peasants

<hr />

[53] P'eng Chen, 9b.   [54] Lindsay, 'Taxation system', 3.   [55] Kataoka Tetsuya, 129–32.

perceived themselves.[56] Despite Communist concepts of class struggle and the reality of resentment of the rural poor toward those who took advantage of them, strong traditions of community solidarity, habits of social harmony, and fatalistic acceptance of things as they were discouraged radical action. Indiscriminate measures against those whom the Communists designated 'landlords', 'rich peasants', or more simply 'feudal elements' could well intimidate ordinary peasants, who might fear they would be next despite promises to the contrary. The literate and educated were also clustered in these petty rural elites, and if the party was to recruit local cadres capable of handling day-to-day administrative tasks, many would have to come from these groups. Finally, the Communists realized that news of harsh treatment would spread to other areas, making their penetration and united front with local elites more difficult.

By the second anniversary of the Marco Polo Bridge incident, the Chinese Communists were in an unprecedented position. Twice before the movement had grown rapidly and twice it had come face to face with extinction. Both times, in 1927 with the bloody breakup of the first united front and in 1934–5 with the hardships of the Long March, survivors had nursed the sparks of revolution and coaxed them back to life. Now, as a result of the war, the Communists were stronger and more widely spread, with armies, territories and followers scattered across North and Central China. Leadership was more unified than before, yet no longer was there a single dominant centre, such as Shanghai or the Kiangsi soviet, where the Communists might possibly be dealt a mortal blow.

Viewed from the perspectives of 1927 and 1935, the growth in CCP power was impressive. But in comparison with the strength of the Nationalists and their affiliates, or with the Japanese and puppet forces, and in comparison also with the vastness and social complexity of these new territories, this growth in CCP power appears much more limited. Would it be able to survive a third great challenge?

[56] The standard shorthand classification was as follows: *Landlord*: lived entirely on rents and other income; did not personally engage in labour. *Rich peasant*: engaged in agricultural or other labour, but had excess land to rent out. *Middle peasant*: self-sufficient owner-operator. Did not rent land either in or out. *Poor peasant*: owned some land, but not enough to support his family; rented land to make up the difference. *Tenant*: owned no land, but had recognized rights of cultivation (annual, long-term, or permanent) to land owned by others. Paid rent on all land cultivated. *Farm labourer*: hired labour, either as a regular hired hand or for a stipulated period of days, weeks, etc.

This scheme belied the enormous variety of land tenure arrangements, as the Communists well knew (see above, ch. 5). Some very poor peasants rented out all their land because age or ill-health prevented them from cultivating it. Tenants were occasionally landlords as well, owning no land in their own name, but living off sub-let rents. Consequently, in classifying peasants, local cadres also stressed income/consumption levels, life styles, and degree of cooperation with the party's policies.

II. THE MIDDLE YEARS 1939–1943

Transition to the second phase of the war began in early 1939, as the result of the stalemate foreseen by Mao at the sixth plenum in late 1938. Mao had predicted that during this protracted 'new stage' the forces of resistance (meaning principally, of course, Communist-led forces) would grow stronger. In reality the balance sheet was mixed. In Shantung and in Central China, new bases came into being, but in much of North China territory, manpower and population were lost to Japanese consolidation. Base area economies faced severe problems and the peasantry suffered more intensely than at any other time.

Stalemate had two dimensions. The first was growing Nationalist resentment over Communist expansion, which contrasted so strikingly with their own losses. While the Nationalists were being driven out of the regions of their greatest wealth and power in the central and lower Yangtze basin, losing the cream of their armies in the process, the CCP was seeping into the broad countryside behind Japanese lines, extending its influence over territory and gaining popular support.

The second dimension was the Japanese desire – and need – to consolidate the territories they had nominally conquered, and to derive economic benefit from them. After all, the rationale for the China incident was to use China's labour and resources to augment Japanese strength, not to drain its treasure away in China's vast territories.

'Why, oh why,' lamented a Japanese colonel, 'didn't we cut the China Incident short, after we had attained our initial objectives? It was senseless of us to get lured into the hinterland...All we ever ended up with was real estate, not popular support from those we "liberated"...We bogged down, deeper and ever deeper, in that endless morass of attrition.'[57] The Japanese authorities – still divided and competing among themselves – sought to improve their situation in several ways. A new peace offensive was aimed at Chiang Kai-shek simultaneously with efforts to set up a 'reformed' Nationalist government under Wang Ching-wei, who had fled Chungking in December 1938. More collaborators and puppets were recruited. Finally, the Japanese undertook forceful military, political and economic measures to establish territorial control and eliminate opposition.

[57] Quoted in Alvin D. Coox and Hilary Conroy, eds. *China and Japan: a search for balance since World War I*, 303.

'FRICTION' WITH THE NATIONALISTS

The Communists used the euphemism 'friction' (*mo-ts'a*) to describe their conflicts with the Nationalists during the middle years of the war. By 1939, what had appeared to many observers – perhaps erroneously – as an unexpectedly cordial entente began to fade. In early 1939, the KMT Central Committee adopted a series of measures to restrict the CCP.[58] Military clashes began in the summer and continued into the autumn and winter with growing frequency and intensity, most of them taking place in and around the North China bases. The Communists called the period between December 1939 and March 1940 'the first anti-Communist upsurge'. Of course, each side called the other the aggressor, and claimed self-defence against unwarranted attack. But strategically this north China 'upsurge' was a Nationalist effort to check the unauthorized expansion of the CCP beyond the areas assigned to them and to regain influence in areas already lost to the Communists or the Japanese. Chiang Kai-shek spoke as a traditionalist insisting on his legal rights, while the Communists insisted on their evolutionary right to question the moral value of the government's legal rights.

During 1939, the Nationalists began to blockade Shen-Kan-Ning all around its southern and western perimeter. Within a year, this blockade numbered nearly 400,000 troops, including some of the best remaining Central Armies under the overall command of Hu Tsung-nan. The blockade halted further Communist expansion, particularly in Kansu and Suiyuan, and it ended direct contact between SKN and Communists active in Sinkiang (Chinese Turkestan), adjacent to Soviet Central Asia. The Sinkiang Communists, including Mao Tse-tung's brother, were liquidated in 1942. Sharp fighting broke out on the Kansu-Shensi border and in the north-east corner of SKN along the Great Wall near Suite, as the blockading forces probed for soft spots. Elements of Ho Lung's 120th Division had to be called back from the Chin-sui base across the Yellow River to beef up SKN's regular garrison.

Economically, the blockade was even more serious. The central government's subsidy to the Border Region budget was cut off during 1939. Trade between the Border Region and other parts of China was brought to a near standstill, a serious blow to a region unable to supply itself with many basic commodities.

Nationalist and regional forces also sought to intrude their military and

---

[58] These were (a) 'Measures to restrict the activities of other parties', (b) 'Measures to deal with the Communist problem', and (c) 'Measures for guarding against Communist activities in Japanese-occupied areas'. See Van Slyke, *Enemies and friends*, 97.

administrative authority into Hopei, Shansi, Honan, and Shantung – regions now viewed by the CCP as their base areas. In opposing these efforts, the CCP predictably accused their rivals of harming the resistance and damaging the people's interests. The 'experts in dissension' were said to be working with the Japanese and their puppets. Noting the increasing collaboration of regional units with the Japanese, the CCP implied that this was a deliberate and cynical tactic called 'crooked-line patriotism' (*ch'ü-hsien chiu-kuo*) to preserve these units for future anti-Communist operations. Even so, the CCP sought to avoid an open rupture with the Nationalist government in Chungking. In public, the CCP consistently described these military clashes as initiated by local commanders exceeding orders from higher authority, even though they knew this was not the case. Chiang Kai-shek, of course, could not deny this fiction, and it appeared to justify a vigorous Communist response.

Mao Tse-tung enunciated the general policy for resisting these efforts: 'justification, expedience and restraint' (*yu-li, yu-li, yu chieh*).[59] The CCP should fight, in other words, when they could claim justification for doing so, and when they could gain an advantage. But they should not press the attack beyond the limits of Nationalist tolerance or to the detriment of their public image as selfless patriots. CCP forces should keep the initiative as fully as possible in their own hands, deciding when and whether to engage and when to break off.

The most spectacular episode of the 'first anti-Communist upsurge' was the rupture with Yen Hsi-shan in December 1939. All through the summer and autumn, tension in Shansi had been growing, as Yen and his conservative followers associated with the Old Army saw the Sacrifice League and the Dare-to-die Corps of the New Army amalgamate with Communist forces. When the base areas and the Japanese occupation took over most of his province, Yen was forced into exile at Ch'iu-lin, across the Yellow River in Shensi. In November, Yen ordered his Old Army to disarm the Dare-to-die forces with the help of central units sent by Hu Tsung-nan. Out of the bloody fighting that ensued, these elements one by one broke free of even nominal provincial control, and completed their linkup with Communist forces. More than 30,000 went over to the Communists. A KMT intelligence agent summed it up with rueful eloquence:

This is the way the Communists always work. At first they were full of sweet words, flattery, and obsequious distortions, in order to open things up and cover their actions ... But once they were fully fledged, and once the low-level base had been achieved, they turned at once and bit ... We guessed in our hearts that

[59] 'Current problems of tactics in the anti-Japanese united front', Mao, *SW* 2.427.

things might end like this, but we weren't aware of how fast events were moving
... nor did we believe this could happen at the very moment when the CCP's
calls for 'united front' and 'maintenance of unity for resistance' were filling the
skies.[60]

A month or so later, in February and March 1940, elements of the 8RA
beat back this so-called upsurge. Chang Yin-wu's forces were disarmed
and dispersed on the plains of north Hopei. To the south, Chu Huai-ping
and Shih Yu-san were pushed out of the base area, as was the KMT-
appointed provincial governor, Lu Chung-lin. Although a few non-
Communist forces remained in the area, the CCC and CCLY bases were
never again seriously threatened by forces affiliated with the central
government. In apparent confirmation of CCP charges, Shih Yu-san was
executed later that year by the central government for his collaboration
with the Japanese.

By late 1939, CCP central authorities asserted that 'the regions in which
we can now expand our armed forces are limited principally to Shantung
and Central China'.[61] In these two areas, the CCP was still trying to carve
out bases in which they could operate.

The situation in Shantung was confused. After the Japanese invasion,
most of the Nationalist-affiliated forces had remained in the province,
whereas Communist forces and bases were weaker and more widely
separated than further west. Not until late 1938 did significant 8RA units
from the 115th and 129th Divisions, under Hsü Hsiang-ch'ien and Lo
Jung-huan, enter the province to link up with the Shantung column and
local guerrillas, including the remnants of a large band that had recently
been decimated by the Japanese.[62] These actions led to clashes with both
the Japanese and various Nationalist-affiliated groups, both of which were
stronger than the Communists at this time. Until late 1940, CCP clashes
with these Nationalist forces were bloodier than those with the Japanese.

The CCP knew that their Chinese rivals were deeply suspicious of one
another, and that their attitudes toward the CCP varied widely. The main
Nationalist forces had not been closely affiliated with the central
government or Chiang Kai-shek, but were under independent, sometimes
disaffected regional commanders. Communist tactics were summed up in

[60] Quoted in Van Slyke, *Enemies and friends*, 142.
[61] 'Chung-yang kuan-yü tsai Shan-tung Hua-chung fa-chan wu-chuang chien-li ken-chü-ti ti chih-
shih' (Central directive concerning development of armed forces and establishment of base areas
in Shantung and Central China), 28 January 1940, *Chung-kung tang-shih ts'an-k'ao tzu-liao* (Reference
materials on the history of the CCP), 4.138.
[62] David Paulson, 'War and revolution in North China: the Shandong base area, 1937–1945'
(Stanford University, Ph.D. dissertation, 1982), 75–7. This was the column led by a subordinate
of Han Fu-ch'ü, Fan Chu-hsien, who led a growing number of resistance fighters, until he was
surrounded and defeated in November 1938. Fan was wounded and committed suicide to avoid
capture.

slogans: 'develop progressive forces, win over fence-sitters, isolate die-hards'; 'flatter top echelons, enlist the middle ranks, hit the rank and file'; and 'win over Yü Hsueh-chung, isolate Shen Hung-lieh, eliminate Ch'in Ch'i-jung.'[63] Unlike the other North China bases, however, the Communists were for several years unable to neutralize Nationalist forces in Shantung, and might not have been able to do so even then, had Japanese mop-up campaigns not weakened them.

By November 1940, Hsu Hsiang-ch'ien claimed considerable progress, but acknowledged that Shantung was not yet a consolidated base. CCP efforts were most successful along parts of the Shantung-Hopei border, around the Taishan massif in central Shantung, and near the tip of the peninsula, far to the east. Elsewhere, he said, 'progressive forces are still weak'. Regular 8RA troops numbered perhaps 70,000, far below the levels called for by party centre – 150,000 regulars and 1.5 to 2 million self-defence forces.[64] Virtually no systematic economic reforms had yet been instituted. The familiar confiscations, collections of national salvation grain, contributions and loans were used alongside the conventional tax system which was adjusted to favour the poorer peasants.

Communist expansion in Central China was even more fraught with danger of large-scale conflict with central government forces than was the case further north. Whereas in most of North China 'friction' resulted from rapid Communist expansion into a partial vacuum, in Central China the CCP's base-building efforts required that they displace an existing Nationalist military-administrative presence with close ties to Chiang Kai-shek and the Chungking government.

The burden of this expansion was carried primarily by the 6th Detachment (northern Anhwei and Kiangsu) and by the 5th Detachment, strongly reinforced by 15,000 to 20,000 8RA troops under Huang K'o-ch'eng. As Ch'en I's 1st Detachment crossed from south to north, through the corridor provided by Kuan Wen-wei's local forces, they too became actively engaged. This expansion, responding to directives from Mao and Liu which became increasingly urgent through the latter part of 1939 and into 1940, brought the N4A forces north of the river into ever more frequent and sharper conflict with Nationalist authorities in Anhwei and Kiangsu, especially with forces under the Kiangsu governor, Han Te-ch'in.

South of the river, however, Hsiang Ying did not directly challenge Chungking's commanders. Perhaps he had been influenced by Wang Ming, as Mao later charged, or perhaps he saw no alternative. His forces – the three detachments, plus the headquarters unit – were heavily outnumbered

[63] Paulson, *War and revolution*, 94.   [64] *Ibid.* 107.

by Ku Chu-t'ung's Nationalist units, to say nothing of the Japanese and their puppets. Despite Mao's insistence that bases could be built anywhere, the Shanghai-Hangchow-Nanking triangle was an exceptionally difficult environment. Hsiang Ying and his followers had survived with great tenacity and courage in the mountains of South China between 1934 and 1937, in the face of savage search-and-destroy missions that were not called off until the war broke out. It seems unlikely that those who could weather such experiences would suddenly become 'right-wing capitulationists'. More plausibly, Hsiang Ying's 'accommodations' and 'compromises' reflected the true balance of power in this region. By spring 1940, however, Mao was pressing Hsiang Ying even harder:

in all cases we can and should expand. The Central Committee has pointed out this policy of expansion to you time and again. To expand means to reach out into all enemy-occupied areas and not to be bound by the Kuomintang's restrictions but to go beyond the limits allowed by the Kuomintang, not to expect official appointments from them or depend on the higher-ups for financial support but instead to expand the armed forces freely and independently, set up base areas unhesitatingly, independently arouse the masses in those areas to action and build up united front organs of political powers under the leadership of the Communist Party.[65]

The contest between the Nationalists and the Communists involved more than struggles for control of territory behind Japanese lines. It also involved national-level politics, ideology and leadership. To the CCP, one worrisome development was the campaign, all during 1939, to increase Chiang Kai-shek's prestige and formal power. More titles were added to his list of top party, government and military posts. In early 1939, the Central Executive Committee named him 'director-general' of the Kuomintang, reminiscent of the title previously borne by Sun Yat-sen. Furthermore, during the summer and autumn of 1939, there was talk of constitutional rule. In November, the KMT announced plans to convene a constitutional assembly a year later. If Chiang could fulfil these long-awaited promises, he and his government might have a new legitimacy and greater popularity.

Mao Tse-tung and his colleagues could not let these moves go unchallenged. If the KMT was to have a paramount leader and authoritative spokesman, the CCP should have one also. It is no accident that his famous 'On the new democracy' was written in late 1939 and published the following January.[66] Its substance had been anticipated in earlier statements, but its timing and full development were influenced by the

---

[65] 'Freely expand the anti-Japanese forces and resist the onslaughts of the anti-communist die-hards', Mao, *SW*, 2.431.
[66] Mao, *SW*, 2.339–84. This version has undergone considerable editing. The original text, with later changes indicated, may be found in *MTTC* 7.147–206.

KMT constitutional movement. It was the CCP's entry in the competition, both a bid for support (away from the KMT) and a statement of the multiclass united front coalition the CCP desired to lead. The apparently temperate and moderate tone of 'On the new democracy' persuaded many Chinese that the CCP had either diluted its revolutionary objectives or had deferred them to a distant future. But here, as in so many other CCP statements, language was used on two levels of meaning. To those in Kuomintang-controlled areas, the text invited an interpretation according to the liberal values of Anglo-American democracy: popular participation, multi-party government, legally protected civil rights. But in the territories the CCP controlled, the same words had more authoritarian, class-based connotations. In classified inner-party documents not for public consumption the ambiguity was dropped, and one can see clearly the tough, patient and flexible commitment of the party not only to resistance but also to social control and social change.

During this same period, the Communists professed a deep concern over the danger of Nationalist capitulation to Japan, not only on the battlefields behind Japanese lines, but at the highest levels. To be sure, some of this was propaganda, but behind the propaganda was genuine worry. During late 1939 and early 1940, all politically aware Chinese knew that Japan was negotiating with the mercurial Wang Chang-wei, who had fled Chungking a year earlier. A 'reorganized national government' in Nanking was finally established in March 1940, the most formidable collaboration to date.

Less well known was that, at the same time, the Japanese were seeking an understanding with Chiang Kai-shek himself, through intermediaries in Hong Kong. 'Operation Kiri', as this effort to 'spread a feast for Chiang' was called, had elements of both high intrigue and low comedy. Chiang's reported interest in peace may have been a hoax designed to further discredit Wang Ching-wei, who was kept waiting in the wings until Operation Kiri had fallen through, but even if Chiang had no intention of coming to terms with the Japanese, the Communists could not be sure of the outcome of this multi-pronged peace offensive until after its failure.

Never had China been so isolated as she was by the middle of 1940. In Europe, the 'phony war' ended in the spring with the German blitz across the Low Countries. France was soon knocked out, and England seemed likely to fall. Japan took advantage of the situation to demand the severance of China's last tenuous links with the outside world: the Burma Road, trade with neutral Hong Kong, and the railway line from Hanoi to Kunming. Meanwhile Russia was engaged in a nasty and embarrassing war with Finland and was cutting back on its military aid to the

Nationalists. The United States was only gradually moving away from isolationism and clearly considered England more important than China. In Chungking and elsewhere in Free China, signs of war weariness, despair and demoralization were visible.

THE NEW FOURTH ARMY INCIDENT[67]

In these circumstances, Mao's call for aggressive expansion was either a bold gamble that Chiang would not capitulate to Japan or urgent preparation to be as well situated as possible, should a KMT-CCP split take place. In Central China, the scale and tempo of the fighting continued to grow, beginning in the last months of 1939, when Lo Ping-hui's 5th Detachment clashed with elements of Han Te-ch'in's Kiangsu army near Lake Kaoyu. In the months that followed, Kuan Wen-wei's forces ranged all along the left bank of the Yangtze and made frequent contact with Lo's troops farther north. Lo also began to receive some 8RA reinforcements, moving south via the territories held by the 6th Detachment. Clearly a major confrontation was shaping up in north and central Kiangsu.

Meanwhile, the South Yangtze Command was faring rather badly. Nationalist commanders Leng Hsin and Ku Chu-t'ung were so severely restricting its activities that Mao and Liu gradually abandoned the idea of trying to establish a consolidated base in this area. During the late spring and early summer, Ch'en I transferred most of his 1st and 2nd Detachments north of the Yangtze. In September, the 3rd Detachment followed, moving across the river to the vicinity of Lake Chao, where the 4th Detachment was stationed. This left only the Headquarters Detachment under Yeh T'ing and Hsiang Ying still south of the Yangtze, at Ching-hsien in southern Anhwei.

As the military situation moved toward a showdown, negotiations began in June 1940 between KMT and CCP representatives. At issue were Communist operating zones and the authorized size of the CCP-led armies. Proposals and acrimonious counter-proposals were exchanged without agreement. The KMT considered it a concession to allow the CCP free rein north of the pre-1938 course of the Yellow River, with the exception of southern Shansi, which was to remain the bailiwick of Yen Hsi-shan. In return, all 8RA and N4A units were to evacuate Central China. In essence, the KMT was offering the CCP what it already had in return for giving up what it might be about to get by force of arms. A series of deadlines was issued by Nationalist authorities, without clear indication of the consequences of their violation.

On the surface, the CCP appeared partly to comply. The movements

[67] This account is based largely on material contained in Ch'en Yung-fa, ch. 1, and on information supplied by Gregor Benton.

of Ch'en I and the South Yangtze Command might look like obedience, although actually they were responding to orders of their own superiors, not to those of the Nationalists. Hsiang Ying's continuing delays and evasions during the autumn and winter of 1940 remain somewhat puzzling. He may have felt, quite justifiably, that Mao had lost confidence in him and that he would lose his command as soon as he reached that north bank of the river. Moreover, Yenan's directives were sometimes ambiguous and contradictory. He may also have wanted to reach secure agreements with KMT commanders concerning evacuation routes and safe conduct out of the area.

For a time, Han Te-ch'in kept the bulk of his forces – an estimated 70,000 men, far outnumbering the N4A – in north Kiangsu, blocking the expansion of the 6th Detachment and further southward intrusions by 8RA troops. But by midsummer he realized he would have to counter the build-up of N4A forces in central Kiangsu or risk writing it off to the Communists. A confused sequence of engagements followed, culminating in a decisive battle in early October 1940, near the central Kiangsu town of Huang-ch'iao. Over four days, several main force units of Han's 89th Army were destroyed, and others dispersed. This was also the signal for the 6th Detachment to move more aggressively in the north. In the aftermath, one of Han's principal commanders entered collaboration with the CCP, another defected to Wang Ching-wei's Nanking government. Although Han Te-ch'in was able to retain a foothold in Kaingsu until 1943, his real power was broken. Not much was made of the battle of Huang-ch'iao in the Chinese press: the KMT did not want to publicize a disastrous defeat, and the Communists were content to remain silent about an episode that contradicted their professed united front policy.

Quite understandably, during the autumn, after Han Te-ch'in's defeat, KMT-CCP negotiations took a turn for the worse. In early December, Chiang Kai-shek personally ordered all N4A forces out of southern Anhwei and southern Kiangsu by 31 December; the entire 8RA was to be north of the Yellow River by the same deadline, to be joined a month later by the N4A. Discussions then ensued between Yeh T'ing and Ku Chu-t'ung's deputies concerning the route to be taken, safe conduct, and – incredibly – the money and supplies to be given to the N4A to assist it in moving.[68] On 25 December Mao Tse-tung ordered Hsiang Ying to evacuate at once, but not until 4 January 1941 did Yeh and Hsiang actually begin to move. Almost at once, Ku Chu-t'ung's forces harassed and dispersed the N4A's Headquarters Group, which included administrative personnel, wounded soldiers and dependents, as well as combat-ready

[68] Ch'en Yung-fa, 95–7.

troops. In an effort to regroup, they moved south-west to Mao-lin, where they were surrounded by Nationalists and during the next several days cut to pieces.

Losses were high on both sides. The CCP suffered an estimated 9,000 casualties. Hsiang Ying twice tried unsuccessfully to break out of the blockade on his own and was denounced as a deserter by Yeh T'ing, who took over full command of the doomed forces. Hsiang Ying finally made good his escape, only to be killed a couple of months later by one of his bodyguards, for the N4A's gold reserves which he had taken with him. To the very end Hsiang either failed or refused to seek refuge in Liu Shao-ch'i's domain north of the Yangtze. The unfortunate Yeh T'ing was arrested and spent the rest of the war in prison; finally released in 1946, he died a month later in a plane crash, along with several other ranking party members. On 17 January Chiang Kai-shek declared the New Fourth Army dissolved for insubordination. Direct contacts between Yenan and Chungking virtually ended, and CCP military liaison offices in a number of Nationalist-held cities were closed.

Such was the New Fourth Army incident, also called the South Anhwei incident. Clearly an act of retribution for the defeats inflicted on Han Te-ch'in in north and central Kiangsu, it ended any realistic chance for a consolidated Communist base south of the Yangtze. Still, in a strategic sense, these losses were more than compensated for by the gains achieved further north – and, in fact, a few months later the reorganized N4A began quietly to reintroduce some units into this region, where they carried on guerrilla activities without a secure territorial base.

In marked contrast to the silence surrounding the Huang-ch'iao fighting, the New Fourth Army incident was the subject of bitter and prolonged controversy. The CCP charged that this was a second 'anti-Communist upsurge', even more serious than the first. Presenting themselves as martyred patriots, they characterized their antagonists as those who

want to put an end to the War of Resistance by what they call Sino-Japanese cooperation in 'suppressing the Communists'. They want to substitute civil war for the war of resistance, capitulation for independence, a split for unity, and darkness for light ... People are telling each other the news and are horrified. Indeed, the situation has never been so critical as it is today.[69]

The Nationalist rejoinder, of course, was that provocations had been many and serious and that breaches of military discipline could not be tolerated, but reluctance to detail its own defeats at CCP hands forced it into vague generalities. The CCP had much the better of this propaganda battle and

[69] 'Order and statement on the southern Anhwei incident', Mao, *SW* 2.454.

the political capital that could be made of it. 'If it is politically valuable to be thought of as a national hero, it is even more valuable to be a national martyr ... No single event in the entire Sino-Japanese War did more to enhance the Communists' prestige vis-à-vis the Nationalists than the destruction of the New Fourth Army headquarters while it was "loyally following orders"'.[70]

Many concerned Chinese and other observers were indeed 'horrified' and feared the open resumption of civil war. Although civil war did not ensue, the events culminating in the New Fourth Army incident have been seen, with few exceptions, as marking the breakdown of the second united front. This view is wrong on two counts. First, the CCP saw the united front as a strategy to be flexibly applied to all political, military and social forces in China, from the top of the central government down to the smallest village. Relations with Chiang Kai-shek and the Kuomintang regime as a whole were important, but in no way constituted the whole of the united front. Even with respect to Chiang and the Nationalists, however, the customary interpretation is misguided. Throughout the war, a cardinal goal of the united front was to prevent peace between Japan and the Nationalists. Thus, when clashes between CCP forces and those of the central government on so large a scale as at Huang-ch'iao and Mao-lin could take place without leading to peace with Japan and full-scale resumption of civil war, this was not the end of the united front but its fundamental vindication.[71] If friction on such a scale could somehow be tolerated by Chiang Kai-shek, fears of his accommodation with Japan in the future were greatly eased.

Reorganization of the Communist political and military presence in Central China followed in the wake of the New Fourth Army incident. The Central Plains and South-east China Bureaus of the CCP were merged and renamed the Central China Bureau with Liu Shao-ch'i in charge, reflecting the importance of this area to Party Central. The New Fourth Army was also completely reorganized and substantially regularized. Ch'en I became its new acting commander (since Yeh T'ing was in prison), directing the seven divisions into which the force was now divided. Each of these divisions had a territorial responsibility, and in each region the CCP claimed the establishment of a base (see map 15 and table 22). Indeed, base area construction got under way in earnest only after the friction of 1940 and the New Fourth Army incident. In the years that followed, the operating zones of the First to Fourth Divisions contained expanding enclaves of consolidated territory, where military dominance was combined with open party activity, administrative control, development of mass

[70] Johnson, *Peasant nationalism*, 139–40.   [71] Kataoka Tetsuya, 226–8.

TABLE 22

The New Fourth Army after 18 February 1941

Headquarters

Acting Commander: Ch'en I
Vice Commander: Chang Yun-i
Political Commissar: Liu Shao-ch'i
Chief of Staff: Lai Ch'uan-chu
Chief, Political Department: Teng Tzu-hui

Division	Commander	Political Commissar	Previous designation	Operating area
First	Su Yü	Liu Yen	First Detachment	*Central Kiangsu military area*: the region bounded by the Yangtze on the south, the Grand Canal on the west, a line between Huaiyin and the coast on the north, and the Pacific Ocean on the east.
Second	Chang Yun-i (concurrently army vice-commander)	Lo Ping-hui	Fourth and Fifth Detachments	*South Huai military area*: the region bounded by the Yangtze and a line between Nanking and Hofei on the south, Hofei to Pengpu on the west, the Huai River on the north, and the Grand Canal on the east.
Third	Huang K'o-ch'eng	Huang K'o-ch'eng	Part of Eighth Route Army	*North Kiangsu military area*: the region north of Huaiyin and Founing, bounded on the west by the Grand Canal.
Fourth	P'eng Hsueh-feng	P'eng Hsueh-feng	Sixth Detachment	*North Huai military area*: the region bounded by the Huai River on the south, the Tientsin-Pukow railway on the west, a line between the Grand Canal and Hsuchou on the north, and the Grand Canal on the east.
Fifth	Li Hsien-nien	Li Hsien-nien	Honan-Hupeh Volunteer Column	*The Hupeh-Honan-Anhwei military area*: Li Hsien-nien's guerrilla area north of Hankow.
Sixth	T'an Chen-lin	T'an Chen-lin	Third Detachment	*South Kiangsu military area*: the region around Lake T'ai. T'an Chen-lin's unit, which had evacuated north of the river in September 1940, re-entered the mountainous Kiangsu-Chekiang border area in 1941.
Seventh	Chang Ting-ch'eng	Tseng Hsi-sheng	Second Detachment	*Central Anhwei military area*: both banks of the Yangtze westward to Susung, in Anhwei. This area contained the fewest regular forces (5,000) at the end of the war, owing undoubtedly to the presence of strong KMT forces and the area's strategic value to the Japanese.

Sources: Johnson, *Peasant nationalism*, 144–5, checked against material in Ch'en Yung-fa and Kataoka Tetsuya. Map 15, is derived from this table.

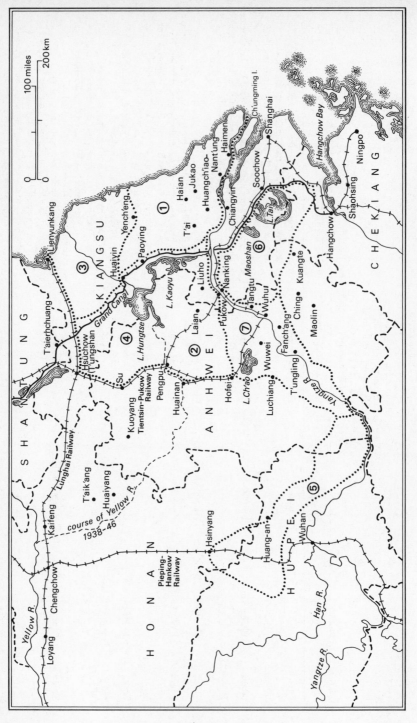

MAP 15. Disposition of New Fourth Army after the 'New Fourth Army incident'

organizations, local elections, and socio-economic reforms. The other three regions wavered between semi-consolidated and guerrilla status.

The worst of the KMT-CCP conflict was now over. When CCP documents speak of a third upsurge, in 1943, they refer to a frankly political effort. With the exception of Shantung, where a fairly strong Nationalist presence continued longer, the balance of power among Chinese forces behind Japanese lines had come by mid-1941 to favour the CCP. In succeeding years the preponderance became ever greater, until by the end of 1943 the Communists were virtually unchallenged by Chinese rivals. This thought may have been in Chiang Kai-shek's mind in September 1943 when he spoke to the KMT's Central Executive Committee: 'I am of the opinion that first of all we should clearly recognize that the Chinese Communist problem is a purely political problem and should be solved by political means...'[72] In most areas behind Japanese lines, the Nationalists no longer had the capacity to attempt any other sort of solution.

JAPANESE CONSOLIDATION

Simultaneously with the 'friction' between the KMT and the CCP, the Japanese were trying to control and exploit the territories they had nominally conquered. Treating friction and consolidation separately does some violence to the real complexity and difficulty of the problems the CCP faced in dealing with both at the same time. At times, the CCP was fighting a two-front war. But if the worst of KMT-CCP friction was over by 1941, the most serious and painful challenges of Japanese consolidation were still to come. The two chronologies must be superimposed if something approaching reality is to be recovered.

The Japanese knew that consolidation was an urgent task because most of the territory behind their army's furthest advances was largely out of their control. Some areas could be put in order by fairly straightforward means: restoring local administration and policy authority, repairing transportation and communication lines, enrolling Chinese personnel (usually untrustworthy, it turned out) as police or militia under puppet governments, registering the local population and requiring them to carry identity cards. In time-honoured Chinese fashion, techniques of collective security were widely used. One was the familiar *pao-chia* system in one form or another. A variant was the 'railway-cherishing village'. A village was assigned a nearby stretch of track; if residents failed to 'cherish' it,

[72] US Department of State, *United States relations with China, with special reference to the period 1944–1949*, 530. Hereafter *China white paper*.

TABLE 23

Damage to North China railways (Jan. 1938–Oct. 1940)

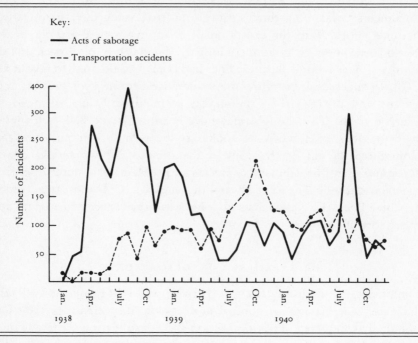

Source: Bōeicho senshi shitan, *Hokushi no chiansen*, 1.407.

they were held collectively responsible. Yet the laxity of early Japanese control in North China was vividly illustrated by three young foreigners during the summer of 1938. On vacation from teaching in Peiping, and curious to know what was going on, they loaded their bicycles on a southbound train, got off at the Paoting station, and pedalled west until they encountered 8RA detachments.[73]

Early in the war, commanders wanted to use mobile warfare, but Mao insisted on de-escalation and dispersal of the 8RA and N4A into small units as nuclei for combat, recruitment, political work, and base area construction. With this strategy, few engagements could be very dramatic or significant. Each skirmish had to be carefully planned, utilizing local intelligence and the element of surprise so that the detachment could hit and run before its limited ammunition was gone or enemy reinforcements could arrive. Small Japanese patrols and puppet units might be ambushed in order to obtain weapons and other material as well as inflict casualties. Active collaborators or Japanese-sponsored administrative personnel

[73] Lindsay, *Unknown war*, not paged.

might be assassinated. Above all, the Communists aimed to disrupt transportation: to mine roads, to cut down telegraph poles and steal the wire, to cut rail lines and sabotage rolling stock. Sometimes they carried off steel rails to get material for their primitive arsenals, or tried to cause a derailment. Destroying a bridge or a locomotive was a major accomplishment. Table 23 shows how effectively the Communists used these opportunities in North China.

Both the Communists and the Japanese knew that these tactics had little influence on the strategic balance but were effective at other levels. To the Japanese, these actions were like numerous small cuts – painful, bleeding, and possible sources of infection. Few areas in the countryside were safe. Japanese sources document the growing exasperation of field commanders as they tried to eliminate resistance, restore administration, collect taxes, and prepare for the more effective economic exploitation of conquered territory. Guerrilla warfare against the Japanese cannot be assessed in conventional terms of battles won, casualties inflicted, terrain occupied. It must also be evaluated politically and psychologically, as Mao frequently emphasized. Since the wartime legitimacy of the CCP depended on its patriotic claims, enough military action had to be undertaken to maintain credibility. Moreover, military success was crucial to gaining the support of the 'basic masses', persuading waverers to keep an open mind, and neutralizing opposition. 'It was not that people always chose the side that was winning, but that few would ever join a side they thought was losing.' As one experienced cadre observed,

Among the guerrilla units ... there is a saying that 'victory decides everything'. That is, no matter how hard it has been to recruit troops, supply the army, raise the masses' anti-Japanese fervor or win over the masses' sympathy, after a victory in battle, the masses fall all over themselves to send us flour, steamed bread, meat, and vegetables. The masses' pessimistic and defeatist psychology is broken down, and many new guerrilla soldiers swarm in.[74]

Later, when the Japanese began to extract a heavy price for each engagement, whether victorious or not, this attitude changed.

In North and Central China, Japan's earliest pacification sweeps posed few problems for the CCP. Initially, the Japanese made few distinctions among the various Chinese forces. They simply tried to mop up or disperse them, regardless of their character. They soon realized, however, that these sweeps were only making it easier for the CCP to expand. By the second half of 1939 the Japanese were being more discriminating. Chinese non-Communist forces stood aside while the Japanese hunted for

[74] Kathleen Hartford, 'Repression and Communist success: the case of Jin-Cha-Ji, 1938–1943' (unpubl. MS.) 370–1.

the 8RA, the N4A, and their local affiliates. The Japanese also made more positive appeals to the non-Communists. According to Japanese army statistics, during the eighteen months between mid-1939 and late 1940, about 70,000 men from more or less regular Nationalist units in North China alone went over to the Japanese. The Japanese also had informal 'understandings' with several regional commanders whose units totalled perhaps 300,000 men.[75] This was, of course, the 'crooked-line patriotism' against which the CCP so strongly inveighed.

When pacification efforts began in earnest in late 1939 and 1940, some differences became apparent in the strategies employed by Japanese armies in North and Central China. In North China, the approach was heavily military in its emphasis, political tactics being limited mainly to the enlistment of collaborators. Authorities in Central China did not hesitate to use military force, either, but they sought to supplement this force with more comprehensive political and economic solutions through the formation of tightly controlled 'model peace zones'. Although both strategies ultimately failed, they brought enormous difficulties to the Chinese Communists, until the Japanese were forced to ease off in 1943 because of the burdens of the Pacific War against the United States.

When the Communists survived Japanese consolidation and repression most observers attributed it to mass mobilization and popular support, tracing that support either to anti-Japanese nationalism aroused by the invaders' brutality or to socio-economic reforms and the 'mass line'. No doubt both these factors played some part, but careful examination of detailed intra-party documents shows that repression also demobilized peasant support and terrorized populations into apathy, grudging acquiescence, or active collaboration with the Japanese. And in a locale that had been reduced from consolidated to guerrilla status, the capacity and will were frequently lacking to administer complex reforms in systematic fashion. Passive and defensive survival strategies were at least as important in weathering these storms as what lay behind the heroic public images projected by the party.

Consolidation in North China

Systematic pacification in North China in late 1939 and 1940 worked outward from the areas held more or less firmly by the Japanese and puppets, into guerrilla and contested zones. The ultimate goal was to crush resistance or render it ineffective. The approach was first to sweep an area clear of anti-Japanese elements, then set up a series of inter-connected

[75] Kataoka Tetsuya, 200–6.

strong points capable of quickly reinforcing each other. This was to be followed by extension of puppet government to take increasing charge of civil administration and 'pacification maintenance', while Japanese forces repeated the first steps farther out in contested territory. Violence was employed selectively against individuals, groups or villages charged with acts of resistance. Selective violence aimed to deter active participation in Communist-led programmes, to deprive Communist forces of a population willing to harbour them, and to persuade informers to come forward. Such, at least, was the strategy. While it fell far short of achieving Japanese objectives, it was effective enough to cause the 8RA great concern.

In practice, the framework of this strategy was the main transport lines. Railways and roads, adequately fortified and protected, would separate resistance forces from one another and deprive them of mobility, one of their most effective weapons. These 'cage' (ch'iu-lung) tactics made it possible to enlarge pacified areas by nibbling outwards 'as a silkworm feeds on mulberry leaves' (ts'an-shih). In addition, this approach aimed at the more effective economic exploitation of North China. To this end, the Japanese worked hard to improve and extend both the railway and road networks. When the war began, both the Cheng-T'ai (Shihchiachuang-Taiyuan) and the T'ung-P'u (Tat'ung-T'ungkwan) lines in Shansi province were metre-gauge, incompatible with the standard-gauge lines of the rest of China – part of Yen Hsi-shan's scheme to prevent penetration of his province (see map 9 and table 14). By the end of 1939, the Japanese had used forced labour to convert both lines to standard gauge. One benefit was the greater ease with which high-quality anthracite coal could be moved from the Ching-hsing mines (on the Cheng-T'ai line) to industrial users in North China and Manchukuo. Of the newly constructed roads and railway lines, the most important was the Te-Shih line (from Te-chow in north-eastern Shantung to Shihchiachuang); its construction began in June 1940 and was completed in November, connecting the Tientsin-Pukow, Peiping-Hankow and Cheng-T'ai lines and thus facilitating troop movements and the transport of raw cotton. With the completion of the Te-Shih link, the Japanese had direct connections between the point of their furthest advance, at the elbow of the Yellow River, and all the major cities of North China, and beyond to Manchukuo. Communist sources began to speak of the 'transportation war', and to note with concern the moats and ditches, the blockhouses, and the frequent patrols protecting the lines.

Both militarily and economically, these measures weighed heavily on Communist-led forces in North China and on the populations under their control, particularly on the plains of central and eastern Hopei. One measure of their effectiveness was the rapid decline in 'acts of sabotage' against North China railways in 1939 and the first half of 1940 (see table 23; but 'transportation accidents' almost certainly includes covert sabotage). A cadre in Chin-Ch'a-Chi reported that, in mid-1940, 'The enemy has adopted a blockhouse policy, like that of the [Kiangsi soviet]. They are spread like a constellation. In central Hopei alone, there are about 500, separated by one to three miles.'[76] Normal trading patterns were disrupted as Japanese or puppets occupied administrative-commercial centres, and peasants were caught between regulations imposed by the Communists and those enforced by the other side. Finally, landlords, moneylenders, loafers, bandits – all those who felt abused by the new order in the base areas – could take advantage of pacification programmes to try to recover lost influence or simply gain revenge. Some turned informers. After 8RA and local units had been driven away, they might kill remaining cadres or activists and settle scores with their peasant supporters. Until the 'first anti-Communist upsurge' was defeated, local elites and other disaffected elements might also find Nationalist support. It was even possible for an armed band to operate for several months in consolidated regions of the CCC base, killing cadres as they went.[77] Of this period, P'eng Te-huai later recalled,

Under the enemy's brutal pressure, the masses in a few districts even wavered or capitulated. From March to July 1940, large areas of the North China bases were reduced to guerrilla regions. Before the Cage-bursting battle [i.e. 100 Regiments], we controlled only two county seats, P'ing-hsün in the T'ai-hang mountains and P'ien-kuan in north-west Shansi. Masses who had previously had only one set of obligations now had two [toward the anti-Japanese regime and toward the puppet regime].[78]

The situation in North China had not yet reached a crisis, but it was certainly serious. Some action was necessary to regain the initiative.

The Battle of the Hundred Regiments

On 20 August 1940, the Eighth Route Army launched its largest sustained offensive of the war on Japan. Screened from observation by the 'green curtain' of tall crops, and making the most of the element of surprise, a force of 22 regiments (about 40,000 men) attacked the transportation network of North China, singling out the rather lightly defended Cheng-T'ai line for particularly heavy assault. All the major railway lines

[76] *Ibid.* 206. Translation paraphrased.   [77] Hartford, 'Repression', 432–4.
[78] P'eng Te-huai, *Tzu-shu*, 235. If P'eng is correct, then the CCP did not control *any* county seats in the Chin-Ch'a-Chi base at this time.

and motor roads were brought under attack and repeatedly cut. Heavy damage was inflicted on roadbeds, bridges, switching yards, and associated installations. Facilities at the important Ching-hsing coal mines were destroyed and production halted for nearly a year. This first phase of the campaign, lasting about thee weeks, gave way to a second phase during which the main targets were the blockhouses and other strongpoints the Japanese had pushed out into contested areas. This shift corresponded to shifting vulnerabilities: while the Japanese were actively using the strongpoint system, the transportation network was less securely defended; conversely, when outlying detachments were pulled back to stem the attacks on railways and roads, the blockhouses were more attractive targets. Indeed, the campaign aimed to force the Japanese to give up their cage and silkworm strategy, pull back to well-defended garrisons and leave the countryside once again to the Communists. During this second phase of the campaign many more regiments entered the fray, until a total of 104 were involved. Years later, P'eng Te-huai, the commander responsible for the Hundred Regiments, said cryptically that they joined in 'spontaneously', without orders from his 8RA headquarters.[79] By early October, the second phase was drawing to a close, and a third was developing, during which reinforced Japanese columns sought to engage and destroy 8RA units. Several fierce counter-attacks punctuated the next two months, after which the Hundred Regiments campaign was considered at an end.

The background of the Hundred Regiments offensive – who authorized and planned it and for what reasons – still remains unclear. The Japanese response to this campaign was so ferocious that it looked in retrospect to have been a mistake, and some leaders, especially Mao, may have wished to disavow it. There are indirect hints in his writings during the succeeding months and years that he viewed it critically, and he may have had misgivings all along. It was not his sort of military strategy. Over twenty years later, during the Cultural Revolution, Red Guards charged that Mao had not even known of the plan in advance, due to the deliberate duplicity of P'eng Te-huai, who was then being denounced. Though this seems unlikely, it may have some substance. Writing in his own defence against these charges, P'eng stated that after 8RA headquarters, which was located not in Yenan but in Chin-Ch'a-Chi, had planned the operation, it sent mobilization orders downward to each regional command, and also notified the Central Military Affairs Commission, headed by Mao. In the original plan, the action was to begin in early September. But, writes P'eng,

[79] P'eng Te-huai, *Tzu-shu*, 237.

In order to prevent enemy discovery and to insure simultaneous surprise assaults, thereby inflicting an even greater blow to the enemy and the puppets, we began about ten days ahead of the original schedule, i.e. during the last week of August. So we did not wait for approval from the Military Affairs Commission (this was wrong), but went right into combat earlier than planned.[80]

There is also the question of the spontaneous action of over eighty regiments, unauthorized by 8RA headquarters, to say nothing of Yenan.

If P'eng Te-huai's account – written in 1970, shortly before his death – is accepted, then Mao and Party Central had no hand in conceiving or planning the Hundred Regiments campaign, and the 'grand strategy' motives for undertaking it disappear, except as they may have been considered by P'eng and his colleagues. One of these alleged motives was to counter any tendency toward capitulation on the part of Chiang Kai-shek and the Chungking regime: if the war heated up and the CCP threw itself into the fray, any accommodation between Chiang and the Japanese would look like cowardly surrender. Related to this explanation was the sensitivity of Communist leaders to the charge that they were simply using the war to expand their influence, avoiding the Japanese and leaving most of the real fighting to KMT armies. The Nationalists were giving much publicity to their claim that deliberate and cynical CCP policy was to devote 70 per cent of its efforts to expansion, 20 per cent to coping with the KMT, and only 10 per cent to opposing Japan.[81] A third suggested motive was to divert attention from the New Fourth Army's offensives against Nationalist forces in Central China, which were peaking at just about this time.

P'eng Te-huai acknowledged that the campaign was 'too protracted', but defended its importance in maintaining the CCP's anti-Japanese image in the wake of anti-friction conflicts, in demonstrating the failure of the cage and silkworm policy, in returning no fewer than twenty-six county seats to base control, and in keeping 'waverers' in line. Even if these reasons were less important than regional and tactical considerations in undertaking this campaign, there was no bar to using them for propaganda after the fact. Whatever misgivings Mao and Party Central may have had, they kept them to themselves. Mao radioed congratulations to P'eng on his smashing victory, and in public statements the Hundred Regiments were made the stuff of legends.

---

[80] *Ibid.* 236–7. P'eng also asserted that the military actions of the first anti-Communist upsurge were planned and executed on his orders alone without any prior knowledge or approval from Yenan. If so, Mao and his colleagues in Yenan must have felt great frustration at being unable to control senior commanders in both North China and Central China.

[81] This has become an article of faith in Nationalist histories. I have examined this issue in some detail and believe that no such policy was ever enunciated; in this sense the charge is a fabrication. But in some times and places, actual CCP behaviour approximated this division of effort. See Van Slyke, *Enemies and friends*, 159.

Mopping-up campaigns after the Hundred Regiments (1941–1943)

If the Hundred Regiments campaign aimed to defeat Japanese pacification efforts, it hardly succeeded. Shocked and stung by the 8RA's action, the North China Area Army redoubled its efforts to bring North China under control. Under General Tada and his successor, General Okamura Yasuji (July 1941–November 1944), the Japanese inflicted brutal and sustained violence on all the North China bases. Between 1941 and 1944, about 150,000 Japanese troops were assigned full-time to pacification duty, assisted by about 100,000 Chinese in units of widely varying description and effectiveness. The balance of the NCAA (150,000 to 200,000 men) was assigned to other tasks such as garrisoning major cities, and containing Nationalist forces. Communist regulars were estimated at about 250,000 in the base areas and 40,000 in SKN.

The Japanese and their Chinese auxiliaries invested even more than before in the construction of moats, ditches, palisades and blockhouses. Japanese sources claimed that by 1942 their forces had built 11,860 km of blockade line and 7,700 fortified posts, mostly in the Hopei plains and foothills of the Taihang mountains. A huge trench ran for 500 km along the west side of the P'ing-Han railway line, with a depopulated and constantly patrolled zone on either side. The 250 Japanese outposts established in southern Hopei by December 1940 were more than quadrupled by mid-1942. These were the principal measures for control over the plains areas, and by the end of 1941 all of the Communist bases in such terrain had been reduced to guerrilla status. Many main force units (such as those of Lü Cheng-ts'ao and Yang Hsiu-feng) were forced to move west into the mountains in order to survive.

What distinguished the new Tada-Okamura approach from earlier tactics were the much larger and more protracted search-and-destroy missions sent into the core areas of the mountain bases, and the substitution of indiscriminate, generalized violence for the selective repression employed prior to the Hundred Regiments' offensive. These were the infamous 'Three-all' mop-up campaigns: kill all, burn all, loot all. Frustrated by their continuing inability to distinguish ordinary peasants from Communists, the Japanese made war on all. After trying to seal off important consolidated regions of the base areas, the Japanese sent in very large detachments, seeking out Communist forces, civilian cadres and activists. But, in addition, they sought to destroy base facilities and stockpiles of war material, to disrupt agriculture by burning crops or interfering with planting and harvesting, and to carry off stores of grain. Entire villages were razed, and all living things found in them killed. Unlike the earlier mop-ups, which swept an area and then departed, these

TABLE 24

TABLE 24

Japanese campaigns and blockade system in Chin-Ch'a-Chi

Campaign began	Duration (months)	Troop strength	Targeted area
August 1941	2+	100,000	Pei-yueh
Early 1942	3+	40,000	East Hopei
May 1942	3+	50,000	Central Hopei
September 1943	3	40,000	Pei-yueh

Status of blockade system in Chin-Ch'a-Chi, December 1942

	Pei-yueh	Central Hopei	East Hopei	P'ing-pei	Total
Base points and forts	1,219	1,635	329	175	3,358
Highways (in *li*)	9,238	11,987	3,062	2,618	26,905
Blockade ditches (in *li*)	1,779	5,000	924	282	7,985
Blockade walls (in *li*)	395	502	N/A	N/A	897

Source: Hartford, 'Repression', 345, 347.

campaigns left troops in the targeted areas for considerable periods of time to 'comb' back and forth, and to establish at least temporary strongpoints in the more accessible areas of mountainous bases. The data in Table 24 show how extensive these operations were in Chin-Ch'a-Chi; similar campaigns were mounted against all the North China bases.

These mopping-up campaigns took a heavy and painful toll of the rural population through which they passed. Undoubtedly, those harsh tactics and the atrocities that so frequently accompanied them did indeed cause many peasants, rich and poor alike, to harbour deep hatred of the Japanese and commit themselves more fully to the Communist side. But inner-party sources also depict many instances in which this repression served even more effectively than earlier efforts to drive a wedge between the party and peasantry:

If we only stress concealment...we are bound to be divorced from the masses. The morale of the masses cannot be sustained for long either. On the other hand, if we only seek fleeting gratification in careless fighting, we may also invite still more cruel enemy suppression. That will also alienate the masses.[82]

Communist spokesmen acknowledged that, in the North China bases, population under party control fell from 44 million to 25 million, and the 8RA declined from 400,000 to 300,000.[83] Local sources paint an even

[82] Yang Ch'eng-wu, quoted in Kataoka Tetsuya, 280.
[83] Many of the 25 million were living in semi-consolidated or guerrilla areas; the population in consolidated areas declined even more sharply than these general figures would indicate. Only

grimmer picture. By 1942, 90 per cent of the plains bases were reduced to guerrilla status or outright enemy control. In the mountainous T'ai-yüeh district of the Chin-Chi-Lu-Yü base, a cadre admitted that 'not a single county was kept intact and the government offices of all its twelve counties were exiled in Chin-yuan'.[84] All twenty-six county seats occupied in the wake of the Hundred Regiments fighting were lost.

Although Japanese pacification was aimed mainly at the 8RA, this was not always the case. Nationalist forces with whom the Japanese had been unable to reach 'understandings' were attacked also, partly to free more forces for anti-Communist action, partly to keep pressure on Chiang Kai-shek, and partly to have more successes to report. The most significant of these actions took place during the spring of 1941 in southern Shansi, when over twenty divisions under General Wei Li-huang were pushed south of the Yellow River (the Battle of the Chung-t'iao Mountains, or the Chūgen campaign). Almost as important were later actions in Shantung against Yü Hsueh-chung and Shen Hung-lieh. These cleared additional areas for Communist penetration once Japanese and puppet forces withdrew; the consequences became fully evident when Japanese pressure on the Communists moderated during the last phase of the war.

Japanese consolidation in Central China

The China Expeditionary Army followed a different pattern from that pursued by the North China Area Army. Although the total forces available to the CEA were larger than those of the NCAA (c. 300,000 in Central China, and another 165,000 in the south), a smaller proportion was devoted to pacification, perhaps 50,000 to 75,000. Most of the remainder of the CEA was deployed opposite Nationalist units in Hupei, Hunan and Kiangsi. On the other hand, larger and presumably more effective puppet forces could be employed in the Lower Yangtze region because of its proximity to the Nanking regime of Wang Ching-wei.

Japanese and puppet forces concentrated on the area of greatest strategic importance to them: the Nanking-Shanghai-Hangchow triangle,

---

a part of 8RA losses was due to direct combat casualties. Other factors included reassignment of some regulars to service as guerrilla forces (to strengthen the latter, to merge more closely with the local population, to reduce burdens of troop support); elimination of inferior or disabled soldiers; and desertion. One CCP document from late 1939 (presumably Chin-Ch'a-Chi) gave two examples of desertion rates: 16·4 % in 'one main force unit', and 20·8 % in 'one newly established guerrilla unit'. Desertion was particularly serious when a unit was moved out of its home area; peasant-soldiers in the local forces often refused to leave. This was yet another motive for reducing some full-time soldiers to militia status.

84 Warren Kuo, *History*, 4.75.

together with the region just north of the Yangtze River and east of the Grand Canal. The Wuhan region, farther west, was also heavily pacified. These efforts and a strong Nationalist presence in Hupei prevented Li Hsien-nien and the N4A's 5th Division from setting up a fully consolidated base in the Ta-pieh Mountains until late in the war. But other areas in Kiangsu, Anhwei and Honan were deemed less significant from either a military or economic viewpoint. Japanese forces maintained control over major transportation routes in east-central China and over the major cities. Occasional sweeps were sent through remoter areas. These were rather easily evaded by N4A elements but inflicted serious damage on Chungking-affiliated forces.[85]

Not until the second half of 1941 did the Japanese begin serious pacification in the Yangtze delta, with the adoption by General Hata Shunroku of a plan to establish 'model peace zones'. This was a phased programme in which carefully defined areas were to be brought under ever tighter military, political and economic security. When one zone had reached a certain level of development, an adjacent area would be added. The first step was to carry out intense clearing operations in order to drive out all resistors and begin with a clean slate. Tight boundary controls were then enforced, using dense bamboo palisades or other defensive works. Within the zone, local police undertook careful population registration, and administrative personnel were assigned a comprehensive programme of 'self-government, self-defence, and economic self-improvement'. In the most developed of the model peace zones, Japanese troop density reached 1·3 per sq. km., three and a half times larger than in North China. Harsh coercion was applied as necessary. As a result, security within the model peace zones in the northern Yangtze delta became quite good. Tax revenues collected by agents of the Nanking regime went up sharply, as did compulsory labour service. Japanese soldiers and well-known local collaborators claimed, with relief, that they could come and go without fear of ambush.

Yet even at their most successful, these efforts were not a general solution to the problem of Chinese resistance, either Nationalist or Communist. The model peace zones required so much manpower and other resources that they were very limited in extent. By 1943, when such efforts no longer had high priority, only a few such zones were classified as having passed through all the planned phases, the remainder being stalled in one or another preliminary stage. The only such effort well to the north of the Yangtze was the late (February 1944) and almost completely futile creation of a new province, Huai-Hai, with its capital

<hr>

[85] Ch'en Yung-fa, 110–11.

at Lienyunkang. And even within the securest of the model peace zones, both the Communists and the Nationalists were able to maintain a continuing low-level presence.

Further reasons for the limited success and ultimate failure of the model peace zones were that many tasks had sooner or later to be turned over to the Chinese themselves, either Wang Ching-wei appointees or recruits from the local populace. Both were the constant despair of the Japanese: the former because of their incompetence, corruption and factional disputes; the latter because they would do only what they felt compelled to do or what was in their self-interest. In the end, the model peace zones bore witness to the short-term and territorially limited effectiveness of superior power. They also demonstrated that such a solution was no solution at all across the vast breadth and population of 'occupied China'.

CCP RESPONSES: SURVIVAL AND NEW POLICIES

The combined effects of friction and pacification confronted the Chinese Communist Party with its most serious and prolonged crises of the Sino-Japanese War. Ironically, these challenges were exacerbated because Communist military and political expansion early in the war had often stressed rapid growth at the expense of consolidation and deep penetration of the villages. At the same time, after three good years, adverse weather led to poor harvests in 1940 and 1941, adding to already serious economic problems. The CCP's responses to these challenges, begun in piecemeal fashion, were as many-sided as the problems themselves. Some existing policies were overhauled and adapted to new circumstances. Some new policies were continued long after the immediate difficulties had been overcome, while others were ad hoc, common sense measures to minimize losses or gain new support. In retrospect the new pattern can be seen as early as 1940. By 1942 it was in full swing. The Maoist leadership now saw it as an integral whole.

Inseparable from the urgent practical tasks of this arduous period was the definitive elevation of Mao Tse-tung as the supreme leader and ideological guiding centre of the CCP. Between 1942 and 1944, the last major elements were added to complete 'the thought of Mao Tse-tung', and the last remnants of opposition to his primacy were removed or silenced. From this time, at the latest, the movement bore the indelible stamp of his policies and personality. The experience of these years shaped the CCP. Like the Long March a decade earlier, the Yenan era took on an independent existence – part history, part myth – capable of influencing future events.

New policies in Shen-Kan-Ning

Economic problems. The principal economic changes in Shen-Kan-Ning during the middle years of the war have already been mentioned: the end of the Nationalist subsidy, the blockade, and poorer harvests than in the years immediately preceding. These changes had profound, widespread and enduring effects. They very nearly caused the economy of SKN to collapse. Looking back on this period, Mao wrote in 1945: 'When [the war] began we had food and clothing. But things got steadily worse until we were in great difficulty, running short of grain, short of cooking oil and salt, short of bedding and clothing, short of funds.'[86]

The Nationalists' eonomic warfare deprived SKN of its principal source of 'hard currency' and either cut off or greatly changed the terms of its trade with other regions of unoccupied China. The party, government and army bureaucracies together with large numbers of immigrants, made the Border Region's resources, insufficient even in normal times, all the more inadequate. The goal of the party, therefore, was to bring the region as close as possible to economic self-sufficiency. Although full autarky was impossible, considerable progress was eventually made. Meanwhile economic conditions deteriorated rapidly.

All sources agree on the severity of the problems. Deprived of its main source of Nationalist *yuan* currency, yet continuing to depend on external trade for cotton cloth and nearly all manufactured goods, SKN once again adopted its own Border Region currency so that *yuan* reserves could continue, so far as possible, to finance essential imports. After 1939, these circumstances fuelled an inflation even more rapid than that experienced in Chungking (see table 25). In all areas of the economy, 1941 was the year of deepest crisis.

Loss of revenue, rapidly worsening terms of external trade, and inflation forced the Communists to find new income. Confiscations and 'voluntary' contributions were no longer fruitful, because most landlords and other holders of wealth had already passed through the agrarian revolution, before the more moderate united front land policies came into effect. They now had nothing more to give. Reluctantly but inevitably, the party was forced to impose taxes on virtually the entire population of Shen-Kan-Ning. Taxes were of three general types: (1) grain levies, based on actual production rather than landholdings; (2) other taxes in kind, particularly of straw and wool; and (3) taxes in cash. These levies were most sharply felt by the middle and lower-middle peasants, who up

---

[86] Mao, *SW*, 3.328–9.

TABLE 25

Price indices, 1937–1945: 'Free China' and Yenan

	'Free China'	Yenan
1937	100	100
1938	145	143
1939	323	237
1940	724	500
1941	1,980	2,200
1942	6,620	9,900
1943	22,800	119,900
1944	75,500	564,700
1945	179,000	N/A

Sources: for 'Free China', Arthur N. Young, *China's Wartime finance and inflation, 1937–1945*, 152; for Yenan, see Schran, *Guerrilla economy*, 184.

until this time had paid few if any taxes. The poorest one-fifth or so of the peasantry (those with an annual per capita income of up to about one hundred pounds of grain) remained exempt from grain levies and other taxes in kind, but by 1941 grain tax levies had increased twenty times over those collected in 1938 – a burden that created considerable popular resentment. Thereafter, tax levels dropped off a bit until the substantial decline in 1945, which was probably caused by a poor harvest and reduction of public sector expenditures following the Japanese surrender (see table 26).

In 1941, this burden was very close to estimates of taxes collected by provincial authorities in the early 1930s, but it was much fairer, being imposed on a sharply progressive basis. To ease the tax load on poorer elements of the peasantry and to mitigate as much as possible their resentment, Party Central began in mid-1940 to issue more urgent calls for rent and interest reduction, hoping thereby partially to substitute one exaction for another.

Taxes in kind on straw and wool, earlier abolished by the Border Region government, were reimposed in 1941. The straw was badly needed as fodder for transport animals in both the civilian and military sectors, and wool deliveries helped meet the need for textiles.

Several types of cash taxes were either imposed for the first time, or raised to higher levels. Sales taxes on a wide range of commodities and services resembled the often condemned 'miscellaneous taxes and surcharges' of previous regimes, but they were calculated in such a way as to discourage unnecessary consumption of imported products and luxuries such as tobacco, liquor, and religious items. Various commercial taxes were also collected from the many small-scale private enterprises

TABLE 26
SKN grain tax levies, 1937-45
(in piculs: 1 picul = c. 330 lbs.)

	Grain produced	Grain collected	%
1937	1,260,000	10,000	0.8
1938	1,270,000	10,000	0.8
1939	1,370,000	50,000	3.6
1940	1,430,000	90,000	6.3
1941	1,470,000	200,000	13.6
1942	1,500,000	160,000	10.7
1943	1,600,000	180,000	11.3
1944	1,750,000	160,000	9.1
1945	1,600,000	125,000	7.8

Source: Schran, *Guerrilla economy*, 128,188.

still existing in SKN; in 1941 these brought in about 8 million SKN *yuan* (equivalent to 30,000 piculs of millet).

Since income from these taxes was insufficient, such expedients as deficit financing and increased corvée labour were also employed. But Mao warned that juggling finances and increasing demands on SKN's populace were no long-term solution:

All empty words are useless; we must give the people visible material wealth ... The primary aspect of our work is not to ask things of the people but to give things to the people. What can we give the people? Under present conditions in the Shen-Kan-Ning Border Region, we can organize, lead, and help the people to develop production and increase their material wealth. And on this basis we can step-by-step raise their political awareness and cultural level.[87]

It was above all in the production campaigns that the party and the region finally stemmed economic deterioration and achieved stability – albeit at a lowered level – once again. No campaign of the period received more attention; in December 1942, Mao published his own extensive yet unfinished essay on 'Economic and financial problems'. Although ideology lurks in the background, nearly all his proposals stand on their own. Many were commonsense, pragmatic measures that rural reformers had advocated for years, but had been unable to carry out. Space permits mention of only the most important areas in which production was significantly raised. Table 26 shows that between 1937 and 1944, grain production increased almost 40 per cent. Cotton production was nil at the beginning of the war and still negligible in 1939; by 1944, it had reached 3 million catties of lint and twice that in seed. Livestock also

[87] Watson, *Mao Zedong*, 232.

recorded impressive gains. Given the poor endowments of SKN and very modest new technological inputs, this was a remarkable achievement obtained by better and more varied organization, widened market incentives, and dramatic increases in cultivated land. Between 1937 and 1945, sown area almost doubled (from 8·6 to 15·2 million *mou*).[88]

The output of the weaving industry paralleled the production of raw cotton. A mere 7,370 bolts (*c.* 25 m² per bolt) in 1938, it doubled over each of the next two years, reached 45,000 bolts in 1942, then shot up to 105,000 bolts in 1943.[89] Natural resource extraction (salt, coal, a few primitive oil and gas wells), irrigation, expanded pasturage, and afforestation were all actively developed. By 1944, many problems still faced leaders and local cadres alike in Shen-Kan-Ning, but by that time the economic perils of the middle years of the war had been sufficiently overcome to permit relative security, renewed and deepened popular support or acceptance, and a tempered self-confidence.

Rectification. In the ideological and political realms, the most visible effort was the 'rectification campaign'.[90] It formally began on 1 February 1942, when more than one thousand party cadres assembled in Yenan to hear Mao Tse-tung address the opening of the CCP's Party School. Cadre education and concern for the party's ideological soundness had always been an important concern, as can be seen in the earlier writings of Mao, Liu Shao-ch'i and others. But the decision to launch this particular campaign was probably made at an 'enlarged session' of the Political Bureau, held in September 1941, which called for 'development of a party-wide ideological revolution' and elimination of 'factions which formerly existed and played an unwholesome role in the history of our party.'[91] Unfortunately, none of the documents of this very significant meeting are presently available and little is known about it.

The campaign was never formally declared to be over, but by the second half of 1944 its principal goals were apparently thought accomplished and it no longer made a major claim upon the time and attention of party members. Throughout, the rectification campaign was an intra-party exercise, limited to party members, none of whom could ignore the compelling force of Mao's addresses and statements delivered during the spring and summer of 1942. In Shen-Kan-Ning, no party member could

---

[88] Schran, 120.

[89] Schran, 146. Textile production data are broken down into various sectors (percentages for 1943): home industry (44%), state-owned enterprises (31%), capitalist enterprises (19%), Chinese Industrial Cooperatives (6%).

[90] 'Rectification' is the customary translation of *cheng-tun tso-feng. Cheng-tun* means to set things aright by a very thorough shaking up; *tso-feng* refers to all aspects of the way one does things, to one's 'work style'.

[91] Wylie, 166.

avoid the incessant small-group sessions in which rectification documents were struggled through to proper understanding and internalization. For the party as a whole, this was an arduous exercise in discipline and consensus-building.

The rapid expansion of the party during the first few years of the war had made for an extremely heterogeneous membership, the majority of which was organizationally inexperienced and new to Marxism-Leninism, to say nothing of the evolving body of Mao's thought. Intellectuals, students, illiterate peasants, hard-bitten Long March veterans, even some sons of landlords all joined the expanding party. Young men and women from middle-class families in Shanghai and Peking were thrown together with villagers who had never been further from home than the nearest market town and who instinctively distrusted all outsiders. It was no secret that numerous incompetents, opportunists, and spies had made it into the party. Mao's most recent rivals – Chang Kuo-t'ao and Wang Ming – still had sympathizers among mid-echelon cadres. If, from Mao's standpoint, the party was successfully to meet the challenges facing it and be prepared for the uncertainties of the future, these elements had to be purified, fused, and honed.

His own doctrines would lead the way, justified and undergirded by the principles of Marxism-Leninism. This was the 'sinification of Marxism', 'the creative application of Marxism-Leninism to the concrete realities of China'.[92] Coached by ideologues such as Ch'en Po-ta and assisted by such experienced and able colleagues as Liu Shao-ch'i, Chou En-lai and Ch'en Yun – among others – Mao Tse-tung now felt ready to claim both ideological and personal dominance over the Communist movement in China.

In his address to the Party School on 1 February 1942, Mao sounded the keynotes. After routine praise for the basically sound condition of the party, he defined its three principal defects as 'subjectivism, sectarianism, and party formalism'. He enlarged on all three in later pronouncements.[93] Mao gave these vague-sounding terms vivid, earthy meanings which are by no means easy to summarize. Subjectivism referred mainly to those who regarded abstract book-knowledge of Marxism-Leninism as a

92 See Stuart Schram, ch. 14 below. A functional analysis of Mao's ideology, drawing a distinction between 'thought' (ssu-hsiang) and 'theory' (li-lun), may be found in Franz Schurmann, Ideology and organization in Communist China, 2nd ed., 21ff. Schurmann argues that Chinese Communists distinguished between pure theory – the general and abstract principles of Marxism-Leninism, valid everywhere – and the creative application of these principles to concrete situations ('thought'). For the historical evolution of Mao's ideological/political primacy, see Wylie, The emergence of Maoism. Wylie disputes Schurmann's analysis.

93 MTTC 4.63. Many of the cheng-feng documents may be found in Boyd Compton, Mao's China: party reform documents, 1942-44.

talisman or panacea, but made no effort to apply its principles to actual problems. These half-baked intellectuals were like chefs who studied recipes but never cooked a dish, or those who 'merely take the arrow in hand, twist it back and forth, and say again and again in praise, "excellent arrow, excellent arrow" but are never willing to shoot it'. Instead,

Our comrades must understand that we do not study Marxism-Leninism because it is pleasing to the eye, or because it has some mystical value.... It is only extremely useful.... We must tell them honestly, 'Your dogma is useless', or, to use an impolite phrase, it is less useful than shit. Now, dogshit can fertilize a field, and man's can feed a dog, but dogma? It can't fertilize a field or feed a dog. What use is it?[94]

But if Mao's most scathing remarks were directed at dogmatic intellectuals who acted like the mandarins of old, subjectivism also had an opposite side: empiricism. This was the tendency to view each situation exclusively in its own terms and to rely only upon one's own experience, with no ideological guidance. Empiricism was more likely to be encountered in poorly educated peasant cadres whose horizons were narrow. In both cases, Mao called for the wedding of theory with practice.

Sectarianism was nearly as serious. Here Mao spoke of democratic-centralism, charging the sectarians (naming only Chang Kuo-t'ao, already read out of the party, but again implying Wang Ming) with forgetting centralism – the ultimate authority of the Central Committee, now clearly controlled by Mao and his followers. Sectarianism had seemingly prosaic dimensions as well, affecting the relations between local cadres and outsiders, between army and civilian cadres, between old and new cadres, and between party members and those outside the party. Sometimes individual units or localities put their interests ahead of the general good by 'not sending cadres on request, sending inferior men as cadres, exploiting one's neighbors and completely disregarding other organs, localities, and men. This reveals a complete loss of the spirit of communism.'[95] Although these problems sounded ordinary, they were both serious and quite intractable. Their effects might be ameliorated, but were never fully removed.

Mao then turned to the subject of 'party formalism', or *tang pa-ku*, devoting an entire address to this subject.[96] *Pa-ku* summoned up for Mao's listeners memories of the rigidly structured 'eight-legged' essays which had been the centrepiece of the old imperial civil service examination

[94] *MTTC* 8.75; Compton, 21–2. Such crudities have been expunged from Mao's *Selected works*.
[95] Compton, 27.
[96] 'Oppose party formalism' (8 Feb. 1942). Contained in Compton, 33–53. The short extracts below are drawn from this source (sometimes retranslated).

system. Although he spoke of *pa-ku* most directly in terms of the way in which many party members attempted to communicate with the masses (in literature, propaganda, directives, etc.), he clearly meant this rubric to cover all manifestations of dogmatic subjectivism and sectarianism: 'if we oppose subjectivism and sectarianism but do not at the same time eradicate party formalism, they still have a place to hide'. Once again using the language of the *lao-pai-hsing*, the ordinary peasant, Mao described – perhaps with deliberate irony – eight ways in which *pa-ku* formalism showed itself. It was wordy, windy and disgusting, 'like the lazy old woman's long, foul-smelling footbindings which should be thrown into the privy at once'. It was pretentious, abstract, insipid, cliché-ridden; worse, it made a false show of authority and aimed to intimidate the reader or hearer. It contained many foreign terms and constructions which had little meaning for the average person, but seemed very learned. It often lapsed into irresponsibility and pessimism, to the detriment of the people, the resistance, and the revolution. No one, Mao asserted, would understand or listen to a party that spoke in *pa-ku* style, much less want to follow it or join it.

Writers, intellectuals, former students and educated cadres generally were obviously the principal object of Mao's attack. They were, of course, more numerous in the Shen-Kan-Ning base than anywhere else, and many of them were becoming restive and dissatisfied. Just a few weeks after Mao's speeches before the Party School and the issuance of a central directive on cadre education, a number of prominent intellectuals loosed a barrage in the pages of *Liberation Daily*.[97] Ting Ling, the famous woman author, criticized the party's compromises in the area of sexual equality and the gap between noble ideals and shabby performance more generally. Others such as Ai Ch'ing and Hsiao Chün added their voices. Perhaps the most biting critique was contained in an essay entitled 'Wild lilies', by an obscure writer, Wang Shih-wei, who employed the satiric *tsa-wen* (informal essay) style made famous by Lu Hsun. Although none of these critics questioned the legitimacy of the party or the necessity for revolution, they felt that art had an existence apart from politics and they graphically portrayed the dark side of life in Yenan. By implication, they were asserting the autonomy of the individual and the role of the intellectual as social critic, just as they had – with party blessing – before the war in Kuomintang-controlled areas of China.

[97] Merle Goldman, *Literary dissent in Communist China*, 21ff. At this time the chief editor of *Liberation Daily* was Ch'in Pang-hsien (Po Ku), and one of his associates was Chang Wen-t'ien. Both had belonged to Wang Ming's faction in the early 1930s, though they had later moved much closer than he to the Maoist camp. Yet without their approval, the dissidents could not possibly have had their writings published in *Liberation Daily*. Ting Ling was the paper's cultural affairs editor.

What had been praiseworthy in Shanghai during the early 1930s, however, was unacceptable in Yenan a decade later. These intellectuals must have felt they were taking a risk, but they could hardly have anticipated the severity of the party's response. All of them were severely criticized and made to recant, though most were eventually rehabilitated. Wang Shih-wei, less prominent and more corrosive than most, was repeatedly attacked in mass meetings, discredited, jailed, and secretly executed in 1947.

If his February addresses and other party directives had failed properly to educate the intellectuals, Mao was ready to go further. He took these steps in May 1942, in the lengthy 'Talks at the Yenan Forum on art and literature'. Here he laid down, in explicit detail, the role of intellectuals under the leadership of the Chinese Communist Party. This statement remained authoritative throughout Mao's lifetime, and continues after his death to exert its influence. In brief, 'Talks' denies the independence and autonomy of the mind, apart from social class. One can only speak or write from a class standpoint; intellectuals are quite wrong to think that there is some objectively neutral ground upon which they can stand. Since this is so, art is one form of politics and the question then becomes *which* class it will represent. Revolutionary intellectuals must take their stand with the proletariat for otherwise they serve the bourgeoisie or other reactionary classes, even when they deny they are doing so. It follows that the ultimate arbiter and guide for literature and art is the Chinese Communist Party (led by Mao Tse-tung), since this is the vanguard, the concentrated will, of the working classes.

Mao thus turned the tables on the intellectuals: no longer independent critics, they were now the targets of criticism. So long as intellectuals were willing to play the role of handmaidens to the revolution, as defined by the CCP, they were needed and welcomed. There was no denying their creativity and their skills, but these talents were to be valued only within the limits set by the party. Socialist realism was to be the major mode of literature and art, given naturalistic Chinese forms that would be at once accessible to the masses and expressed in their own idiom, not that of Shanghai salons. This meant that intellectuals had to go among the peasants and workers, absorb their language and experience the harsh realities of their lives. Altogether, Mao was calling for the transformation of party intellectuals and of party members more generally.

By April 1942, the Central Committee had published a list of twenty-two documents to serve as the basis of cadre study and examination.[98] The

---

[98] See Compton, 6–7. The list contained six items by Mao; five Central Committee documents (probably authored in whole or in part by Mao); one each by Liu Shao-ch'i, Ch'en Yun and K'ang Sheng; a propaganda guide; an army report; three by Stalin; one by Lenin and Stalin; one by

means employed to inculcate their teachings included the now familiar small-group study and struggle sessions, usually involving 'criticism and self-criticism'. Straightforward instruction combined with peer pressure, self-examination and coercive persuasion were designed to build to ever higher levels of intensity until catharsis and commitment were achieved. Mao likened the process to the curing of a disease: 'The first step in reasoning [sic] is to give the patient a good jolt: yell at him, "You're sick!" so the patient will be frightened and break out all over in sweat; then you can treat him effectively.' Yet the object is to '"cure the disease, save the patient"...The whole purpose is to save people, not cure them to death.' 'Savage struggle' and 'merciless attack' should be unleashed on the enemy, but not on one's comrades.

Mao's apotheosis did not, of course, occur suddenly in the midst of the *cheng-feng* campaign. His own instincts for power, his success in building an influential and able coalition, and the proven effectiveness of his policies were the main causes of his gradual rise to unchallenged pre-eminence during the years after the Long March. As noted above (pages 663–4), the parallel rise in stature of Chiang Kai-shek also played a role. With the outbreak of the Pacific War in December 1941, Chiang instantly became a leader of world renown and the symbol of China's resistance to Japan. By late 1943, Chiang stood recognized at the Cairo Conference as one of the Big Four, and publication of his famous – or notorious – *China's destiny* a few months earlier was part of a bold effort to claim exclusive leadership domestically. Mao and the CCP vigorously disputed this claim.[99] Put crudely, if there was a cult of Chiang, there had also to be a cult of Mao; an anonymous 'Party Central' would not do.

Political and organizational issues. As we have already seen, political power in Communist-controlled areas was exercised at all levels through the interlocking structures of party, government, army and mass organizations. These structures were better developed in Shen-Kan-Ning than in the bases behind Japanese lines, and superimposed upon them was the apparatus of Party Central and the headquarters of the Eighth Route Army. These organizations were much more comprehensive and effective than those of imperial or Republican China. They were also democratic

---

Dimitrov (Comintern head); and the 'Conclusion' to the *History of the CPSU*. Four of the documents from the USSR were added later, as if by afterthought.

[99] Mao and his supporters (especially Ch'en Po-ta) took this challenge very seriously, probably using it to argue within the party that nothing should be done to hamstring Mao or compromise his image. As late as 1945 (at the Seventh CCP Congress), Mao acknowledged that 'it [the KMT] still has considerable influence and power.... We must lower the influence and position of the Kuomintang in the eyes of the masses and achieve the opposite with respect to ourselves.' See Wylie, 218–25.

in the specific sense that they enlisted – or required – broad participation by many elements of the populace, but not in the sense that the governed elected their ultimate leaders or determined policy. Yet the realities of political control and popular support fell well short of the standards set by the party itself and of the public image it tried to project. It was some of these shortcomings that intellectuals such as Ting Ling and Wang Shih-wei had dared to expose publicly, in a style unacceptable to the party. In its confidential materials, however, party leaders at various levels candidly acknowledged similar difficulties.

One problem was a growing bureaucracy and creeping routinization, an almost inevitable consequence of such rapid expansion not only in governing Shen-Kan-Ning itself, but also in directing an increasingly far-flung war effort in the base areas far from Yenan. Many cadres were 'withdrawn from production', a burden that bore heavily on a population facing economic distress in a backward region.[100]

A second problem lay in the fact that political structures did not fully penetrate the village (ts'un) level, but usually stopped at the next higher township (hsiang) level, with jurisdiction over a variable number of villages. Party Central was also concerned about the administrative 'distance' between county (hsien) and township (hsiang) levels.[101] Moreover, coordination of activity at each level was hampered by the emphasis on hierarchy. Despite the interlocking nature of the major organizational structures, each had its own vertical chain of command to which it primarily responded. Different units at the same level often had difficulty working with one another. This tendency was most pronounced in the party and the military, where 8RA cadres often looked down on their civilian counterparts. Low morale was a problem, if a survey published in April 1942 is typical: in the Central Finance Office (Chung ts'ai-t'ing), 61 per cent of party members surveyed reported themselves 'discontented' (pu-an-hsin) with their work assignment.[102]

[100] Only crude estimates are possible. Party membership is not directly useful, since many low-ranking party members did engage in production. In late 1941, there were about 8,000 officials who received grain stipends (Selden, 152). This figure apparently does not include upper-echelon party cadres nor the garrison forces of about 40,000, most of which, up to this time, were also non-producers. The total, therefore, may have reached 50,000. In a population of 1.4 million, probably no more than one-third were males between the ages of 15 and 45. Thus, perhaps as many as 10% of the able-bodied male population of SKN was withdrawn from production.

[101] Evasion at the village level is graphically portrayed in an officially celebrated short story, 'Li Yu-ts'ai's clapper-talk', by the folk-writer Chao Shu-li. The unlikely hero, an impoverished and illiterate farm labourer with a talent for satiric spoken rhymes (clapper-talk), uses pointed doggerel to expose village big-wigs who for years had hoodwinked party cadres on their tours of inspection from district headquarters.

[102] Chieh-fang jih-pao (3 April, 1942). The survey also revealed that 87% had joined the party after the outbreak of the war; 39% were illiterate. This is the only such 'public opinion survey' known to me.

Such difficulties were attacked in two closely related new policies which bore the unmistakeable stamp of Mao Tse-tung. Both began in December 1941, a few months before the rectification campaign. The first, called 'crack troops and simple administration' (*ching-ping chien-cheng*), aimed to cut back the civil and military bureaucracy. The second, '*Hsia-hsiang*' (to the villages), was designed to penetrate the villages more deeply, in part by transferring downward many cadres removed from higher levels. These policies combined to decentralize many political and economic tasks, thus providing a better balance between vertical command structures and lateral coordination at each level. In the process, many civil and military cadres were ordered back into production; for most, that meant to engage in farming, land reclamation, or primitive industry. Especially marked for transfer to basic levels were young intellectuals, both to be toughened by the harsh conditions of life among the peasants (a corrective to subjectivism, dogmatism and formalism), and to contribute their badly needed skills to the conduct of village affairs.

These campaigns were actively pushed during the winters of 1941, 1942 and 1943, when they could be timed to coincide with the slack agricultural season. Army units were directed to produce as much as possible of their own food and other supplies, in a modern form of the *t'un-t'ien* (garrison farm) system of medieval times. The model project for this was at Nan-ni-wan, about thirty miles south-east of Yenan, where the 359th Brigade of the 8RA was assigned full-time for several years to agricultural and rudimentary industrial development. By 1943, the brigade claimed it was supplying about 80 per cent of its own needs. Even Mao Tse-tung, an inveterate chain-smoker, cultivated a symbolic tobacco patch outside his cave in Yenan.

Although hard evidence is unavailable, these policies undoubtedly had some effect, particularly in organization and mobilization. 'Yet the failure to report accomplishments in the aggregate, the emphasis on exemplary achievements such as the Nanniwan project, and the [repeated] promulgation of the policy of "better troops and simpler administration"... suggest also that the progress may not have been so significant.' In early 1943, during the third round of 'simpler administration', a senior leader acknowledged that the number of full-time officials had grown from 7,900 in 1941 to 8,200.[103]

Given the general tone of these reforms in Shen-Kan-Ning and the emphasis on 'mass line' and 'from the masses, to the masses', it is

---

[103] The quotation is from Schran, 193. For personnel data, see Selden, 215–16. This leader (Lin Po-ch'ü, chairman of the SKN government) stated that 22,500 persons, exclusive of the military, were supported at public expense.

surprising that mass organizations as such seem to have played no prominent role. Our only data on such organizations in SKN come from 1938, when 30 per cent of the population (421,000 out of 1,400,000) was said to be enrolled in peasant associations; at the same time, about 25 per cent of women and 32 per cent of men were members of women's organizations and of the part-time militia, respectively. 'One suspects that these organizations for the most part lapsed into inactivity and that their functions were taken over principally by government and party.... In between...periods of intense activity [such as the 1942 rent-reduction campaign] their membership and organization existed largely on paper.'[104]

United front. Worsening relations with the Nationalists and the impact of Japanese consolidation brought more attention to united front work, not less. Beginning in mid-1940, CCP headquarters repeatedly issued confidential directives stressing the importance of such work in approaches to 'friendly armies', to all but the most pro-Japanese or anti-Communist organizations, and to all classes and strata of society. United Front Work Departments (UFWD) had been established in 1937 under the Central Committee, and at lower levels as well. The importance accorded this work is indicated by the fact that from late 1939 (when Wang Ming was transferred) until 1945 or 1946, Chou En-lai's principal responsibilities were as head of the central UFWD and the closely related Enemy Occupied Areas Work Department. He repeatedly called for the further extension and reinvigoration of UFWD at all levels, insisting upon its importance and implying that it had fallen seriously into neglect under his predecessor.[105]

The united front, thus, was not simply a tactical device but part of a general strategy of particular value in times of weakness or crisis. Each concrete problem, from local affairs to national policies, could be analysed as having three components: the party and its dedicated supporters, a large intermediate stratum (or strata), and 'die-hard' enemies. The goal was to isolate the 'die-hards' by gaining the support or neutrality of as many intermediate elements as possible. Isolated enemies might then be dealt with one by one. As early as October 1939, Mao had asserted that 'the united front, armed struggle, and party-building are the three fundamental questions for our party in the Chinese revolution. Having a correct grasp of these three questions and their interrelations is tantamount to giving correct leadership to the whole Chinese revolution.'[106] Applications of this strategy, however, were tactical and extremely flexible, aimed at

[104] Selden, 142–3.
[105] See Van Slyke, *Enemies and friends,* 116–21.
[106] Mao, 'Introducing *The Communist*', Mao, *SW,* 2.288.

carefully defined groups or organizations. Precisely because the united front served long-range revolutionary goals, it avoided ideological formulae, seeking in each case to find and exploit those individuals, issues, incentives or pressures that might further the party's cause:

In the past, the usual approach was toward making political contacts; very rarely was serious work done to make friends, even to the point of remaining aloof and uncooperative. Hereafter, we must use all possible social connections (family, fellow townsmen, classmates, colleagues, etc.) and customs (sending presents, celebrating festivals, sharing adversities, mutual aid, etc.), not only to form political friendships with people, but also to become personal friends with them so that they will be completely frank and open with us.[107]

In this spirit the CCP began in the spring of 1940 to publicize the 'three-thirds system' (*san-san chih*). According to this approach, popular organs of political power – but not the party or the army – should if possible be composed of one-third Communists, one-third non-party left-progressives, and one-third from 'the intermediate sections who are neither left nor right'. As Mao explained,

The non-party progressives must be allocated one-third of the places because they are linked with the broad masses of the petty-bourgeoisie. This will be of great importance in winning over the latter. Our aim in allocating one-third of the places to the intermediate sections is to win over the middle bourgeoisie and the enlightened gentry.... At the present time, we must not fail to take the strength of these elements into account and we must be circumspect in our relations with them.[108]

The policy thus aimed to make base area regimes more acceptable to the upper levels of the rural population, but it represented no relinquishment of Communist leadership. In practice, representation varied widely. Mao's directive itself had noted that 'the above figures for the allocation of places are not rigid quotas to be filled mechanically; they are in the nature of a rough proportion, which each locality must apply according to its specific circumstances'.

In Shen-Kan-Ning, the proportion of party members in popular organs after 1941 conformed fairly well to the one-third guideline for CCP members. In a few cases, elected party members withdrew, with public fanfare, from their assembly seats in order to conform more closely to the desired ratio. Border Region leaders felt that the policy was quite helpful in allaying the fears and enlisting the support of the middle and upper strata of the peasantry, who had been hardest hit by the steep

[107] From a directive of the Central Committee United Front Work Department, 2 Nov. 1940. See Van Slyke, *Enemies and friends*, 269.
[108] 'On the question of political power in the anti-Japanese base areas', Mao, *SW*, 2.418.

increases in taxes – even though poorer peasants had misgivings about former landlords and evil gentry worming their way back into positions of influence. This partly real, partly symbolic improvement of their political fortunes, combined with their share of production increases, kept these social strata well in line – particularly since they had few alternatives.

Altogether, then, the economic, ideological and organizational/political steps taken in Shen-Kan-Ning between 1940 and 1944 may not have fully measured up to the public image the CCP sought to project, nor the assessment sometimes made by outside observers. But they were impressively effective nevertheless, particularly when contrasted with the performance of the Nationalist regime during the same period.

New policies in bases behind Japanese lines

The North and Central China base areas behind Japanese lines faced crises not only more severe but somewhat different from those in Shen-Kan-Ning during the middle years of the war. For example, SKN did not have to cope with military attacks, nor was it forced to move from one area to another. SKN's administrative apparatus was much more fully developed than those in the base areas, and prewar socio-economic change had progressed much further. Because the CCP-controlled regions behind Japanese lines were so varied and the data concerning them so fragmentary, base-by-base treatment is impossible in the space available here. We are thus constrained to describe events and policies in rather general terms, illustrating them with examples from one or more bases. This will distort complex realities by making them appear more uniform than they actually were.

In the face of Japanese military pressure, all base area organs undertook a wide range of active and passive defence measures. Villagers, grain stores, animals and other possessions were evacuated to safer areas or went into hiding. Valuables were buried. Military units dispersed after planting primitive mines and booby traps, and merged with the peasantry, though this was scant protection when the Japanese tried to kill all who fell into their hands, or when they could be identified by collaborators or resentful local elites anxious to settle scores.

Many bases, especially those on the North China plain, literally went underground into what became an astonishing network of caves and tunnels, often on two or more levels and linking up a number of villages. Multiple hidden entrances, blind alleys, and subterranean ambush points frustrated Japanese pursuers. When the Japanese countered by trying to flood the tunnels or by pumping poison-gas into them, the Chinese responded with diversion channels and simple air locks.

Survival depended on the organized leadership of the party and the army, and on the tenacity of the peasantry. But where bases had to evacuate or reduce their operations to guerrilla status, the existence of other bases where they might take haven was also essential. Those left behind, whether cadres or ordinary peasants, were encouraged to take on 'white skins and red hearts', that is, to acquiesce when there was no other choice. Despite the ingenuity and courage with which the Chinese peasantry met these challenges, departure from a particular locale of most of the party-led apparatus and main force military units sometimes imposed too heavy a burden upon local self-defence forces. On occasions when they collapsed, villages reverted to the control of local elites who often took violent revenge. Meanwhile, in more secure settings, organized activity continued, as the exiles waited to restore or reactivate the infrastructures of their home districts. The network of bases across North and Central China provided the Communist-led movement with a resilience and capacity for recovery possessed by no other Chinese forces.

That the surviving core areas were able under these conditions to pursue their political, social and economic objectives at all was remarkable. Yet they did so quite actively, with varying degrees of success. Chin-Ch'a-Chi and some parts of Chin-Chi-Lu-Yü undertook the most extensive and effective reforms. The Central China bases, most of which came into sustained operation about two years later, were less advanced. Shantung lagged even further behind.

Economically, the shift from the first to the second phases of the war was less abrupt in these bases than in SKN because they had always operated under difficult conditions and without any outside subsidy. But they too had for a time depended upon contributions – 'those with strength give strength, those with money give money' – loans, and some confiscations. The shift to 'rational burden' and ultimately to a unified progressive tax system took place as political control and administrative machinery became more effective. In Chin-Ch'a-Chi, the rational burden system was adopted in 1939, and gave way to the unified progressive tax plan in 1941. In fact, however, several systems were operating at the same time, depending on whether the region in question was a consolidated core area, a recently established base, or a guerrilla zone. None of the other bases behind Japanese lines were able to adopt the unified tax system. While the land tax was the principal source of revenue, many of the older surtaxes had to be continued as a supplement, especially in partly

TABLE 27
Land tax as a percentage of total production

	Chin-Sui	Pei-yueh
1937	Bases not yet established	
1938	N/A	6.27
1939	N/A	7.12
1940	N/A	9.71
1941	24.6	14.98
1942	17.4	13.62
1943	19.61	10.07
1944	19.35	8.9
1945	21.0	N/A

Source: Li Ch'eng-jui, 'K'ang-Jih chan-cheng shih-ch'i chi-ko jen-min ken-chü-ti ti nung-yeh shiu-shou chih-tu yü nung-min fu-tan' (Agricultural tax systems and peasant burdens in people's revolutionary base areas during the anti-Japanese war), *Ching-chi yen-chiu* (Economic research), 2 (1956) 108–9.

consolidated or guerrilla areas. In contested areas, collection was not only difficult but limited by the fact that peasants there were doubly burdened – taxed by the Japanese or puppet regimes as well as by the Communists. If Communist data are accurate, the land-tax burden was much heavier in the Chin-Sui base than in SKN, and about the same in the consolidated Pei-yueh region of Chin-Ch'a-Chi (after 1941; before that it was considerably heavier). As in Shen-Kan-Ning, taxes peaked in 1941, then slowly declined. The per household burden was twice as heavy in consolidated areas as in other regions.

Like Shen-Kan-Ning, the bases behind Japanese lines sought to achieve economic self-sufficiency by issuing their own regional currency, establishing banks, and imposing taxes on trade in and out of the base. These taxes raised some revenue, but their principal purpose was to discourage trade:

Territorial autarky was the goal, but for opposite reasons [from SKN]. The Japanese were to be isolated in the cities, deprived of the foodstuffs and raw materials which the surrounding countryside produced. To this end, trade was to be prevented rather then promoted. In the extreme the base areas had to revert to subsistence economy to the greatest possible degree, against the will and the active intervention of the enemy.[109]

Such policies, of course, were difficult or impossible to enforce in contested areas. As in Shen-Kan-Ning, cooperatives, simple industries, handicrafts, and other productive activities were encouraged, and were for the most part untaxed.

[109] Schran, 251.

TABLE 28

Class composition in 35 villages, Chin-Ch'a-Chi

	1937		1943	
	% families	% land	% families	% land
Landlord	2.42	16.43	1.91	10.17
Rich peasant	4.50	21.93	7.88	19.56
Middle peasant	35.42	41.69	44.31	49.14
Poor peasant & farm labourer	47.53	19.10	40.95	20.12

Sources: Chao Kuo-chün, *Agrarian policy*, 64. See Hartford, *Step-by-step*, 169–228 *passim*, for efforts to calculate changing income differentials in core areas of Chin-Ch'a-Chi.

The extraction of taxes was accompanied, as we have seen, by rent and interest reduction. Once again, Chin-Ch'a-Chi took the lead, but as late as October 1943, a directive noted that 'in many areas rent reduction has not been realized', and urged cadres 'to organize the peasants to carry out the provision that rent must not exceed 37·5 per cent of the principal crops'.[110] The Central China bases were considerably later. In the Huai-pei base (northern Anhwei), only 9,000 tenant families had benefited by 1941. By 1943, the movement had accelerated, with some 43,000 families affected; in the following year, the number probably doubled, as the base expanded.[111] Finally, in the Shantung base, serious rent and interest reduction had hardly begun prior to the winter of 1943–4. Many cadres doubted the importance of the policy, since tenancy rates were not high; some considered this to be thankless and difficult work, much less attractive than military service; others, concerned about shaky political control, feared that a hard line would excessively alienate still-powerful local elites.[112]

Available evidence bears out P'eng Chen's observation that property relations in base areas underwent no great structural change during the war. Probably inequalities in income were reduced more than inequality of property ownership. All the tax systems bore heavily on the rich, and actual practice often exceeded the regulations, particularly under the rational burden tax system. If this was the situation in an advanced base, it is likely that other bases would show less change, not more.

Production campaigns were stressed, just as in Shen-Kan-Ning. Quanti-

[110] Chao Kuo-chün, *Agrarian policy of the Chinese Communist Party, 1921–1959*, 51.
[111] Ch'en Yung-fa, 234.
[112] Hsueh Mu-ch'iao, *K'ang-Jih chan-cheng shih-ch'i ho chieh-fang chan-cheng shih-ch'i Shan-tung chieh-fang-ch'ü ti ching-chi kung-tso* (Economic work in the Shantung liberated areas...), 52ff.

TABLE 29

Grain production, Pei-yueh region

	piculs
1940	1,860,000
1941	1,478,000
1942	1,552,000
1943	2,191,000
·1944	2,360,000

tative data are scarce, but in the Pei-yueh region of Chin-Ch'a-Chi, grain production declined rather sharply from the 1940 level until the upturn in 1943 and 1944 (table 29).[113] Production campaigns also had political motives. Benefits could not indefinitely be brought to the poorer peasantry at the expense of the wealthy without wholesale confiscation, which the united front and common sense precluded. Mobilization initially achieved on the basis of limited class struggle could, however, be continued through organization for production managed by peasant associations and labour exchange teams. Leading cadres often encouraged production campaigns in precisely these terms, as a sublimated form of class struggle and popular mobilization.[114]

While the CCP tried to increase the active participation of the populace, the other side of the coin was to weaken and isolate those who opposed the new order. In public statements these measures were almost always described as 'democratic', with emphasis on their moderation and consistency with *San-min chu-i*. In confidential reports and directives, however, this vocabulary was often replaced with that of class struggle and structural change. The two levels of discourse referred to the same phenomena. Despite the heavy admixture of propaganda in the former, the party did not see the two as contradictory, because of its definition of 'democracy' (if others read their own definitions into the term, that was their business) and because the explicit content of its policies did not at this time aim at revolutionary transformation. 'Superiority' (*yu-shih*) not 'dictatorship' (*chuan-cheng*) was the goal.

Through the innumerable details of the specific measures undertaken at various levels in different regions and bases, certain patterns can be discerned: imposition of military and political control from the top down, investigation and replacement where necessary of personnel within the

---

[113] Derived from data in Li Ch'eng-jui, 108–9. Some of the decline in 1941 and 1942 was probably due to fluctuations in the size of the base and to the mopping-up campaigns of those years.
[114] See Ch'en Yung-fa, 338ff.

existing administrative apparatus, further penetration of that apparatus by party cadres followed by structural and procedural changes. Alongside this takeover of the political machinery lay the military (regular units, local forces, self-defence corps or militia) and the mass organizations, especially peasant associations from which landlords and most rich peasants were excluded.

When these developments had reached a certain level of maturity, but not before, direct elections were held for a limited number of administrative posts and representative assemblies up to county level. Higher level assemblies – where they existed – were elected indirectly by those at the next lower level. Although assemblies nominally supervised administrative committees at the same level, the latter were clearly in charge, with the assemblies meeting rather infrequently as sounding boards and to approve action proposed or already taken. Despite occasional irregularities, the party carried out elections with procedural honesty. But the slate of nominees was carefully screened in advance, and few seats were contested. Instead, the election campaigns were designed to educate and involve the local population in the political process: guided participation was the hallmark of base area democracy. Election campaigns began in Chin-Ch'a-Chi in 1939, but not until 1943 was a full Border Region assembly convened – the only time it met during the course of the war. Sub-regional elections in Chin-Chi-Lu-Yü began a little later. Bases in Central China and Shantung initiated local elections considerably later, in 1942. Nowhere save in Shen-Kan-Ning and Chin-Ch'a-Chi were base-wide assemblies elected.

As in Shen-Kan-Ning, the three-thirds system was carried out in the base areas as part of renewed attention to the united front, despite the misgivings of poorer peasants. Like the united front as a whole, three-thirds was never intended to compromise party control and leadership but to make it more effective. But in the bases, three-thirds was less thoroughly implemented than in SKN. In thirteen *hsien* in the Wu-t'ai region (a part of Chin-Ch'a-Chi), a 1941 election resulted in seating between 34 and 75 per cent CCP members. As late as 1944, a Kiangsu district reported party electees as comprising 60–80 per cent, and made no mention of three-thirds. As P'eng Chen noted, three-thirds 'cannot be made a written regulation, because to fix the three-thirds system in legal terms would be in direct opposition to the principles of truly equal and universal suffrage', but he also observed that 'when we brought up and implemented the three-thirds system and strictly guaranteed the political rights of all anti-Japanese people, the landlords finally came to support and participate in the anti-Japanese regime'. A classified KMT intelligence report (April

1944) confirmed the frequent effectiveness of the CCP's united front: 'Gentry who in the past had been dissatisfied ... filled the skies with praise, feeling that the [CCP] government wasn't so bad after all, that it could recognize its own mistakes and ask for criticism....The Central Government has been away from them too long.'[115]

Although some local activists came forward spontaneously, recruitment of good village leaders from the right strata of the rural population was difficult. Some who came forward were unsuitable, or were later found to have been incompetent or corrupt. A small but significant minority were KMT agents, collaborators, or under the influence of local elites. Negative attitudes were deeply rooted: narrow conservatism, submissiveness and fatalism, lack of self-confidence, an aversion to contact with officials and government, a desire to remain inconspicuous, apprehension that one might excite envy or resentment from one's neighbours. Furthermore, poor peasants were usually illiterate and inexperienced in affairs larger than those involving their own families, and they might resent being pressed into troublesome but uncompensated service. To a degree that troubled higher levels, many of these feelings were also expressed by party members in the villages. Local cadres often reported these attitudes in the colourful and direct language of the peasants themselves. These images, therefore, must be placed alongside the more familiar portrayals of the dedicated and militant peasant, fighting to protect village and nation, working to build a new and better society. Rural China was a kaleidoscope of attitudes, interests and social groups to which no simple depiction does justice.

Organizational measures such as 'crack troops, simple administration' and 'to the villages' were applied in some bases but hardly mentioned in others. Not surprisingly, Chin-Ch'a-Chi pushed these policies in 1942 and 1943, including a substantial simplification of the Border Region government itself. But in most bases, bureaucratism in the Yenan sense seems not to have been perceived as a serious problem – indeed, lack of administrative personnel was quite often bemoaned (commandism, the practice of issuing arbitrary and inflexible orders, was widely deplored). Since the party was already and overwhelmingly in the villages, 'to the villages' had little meaning. Regular army units and local forces were so often engaged with military tasks that they had less opportunity than the SKN garrison to participate in production, though they helped out when they could.

Cadre education looked quite different in most bases than in Shen-Kan-Ning: it was simpler in ideological content and more oriented toward

[115] The data and quotations in this paragraphs are taken from Van Slyke, *Enemies and friends*, 150–3.

accomplishment of specific tasks like running local elections, carrying out rent reduction, organizing production, or military recruitment and training. In these bases, few party cadres had the time or educational background to engage in the study of documents or prolonged discussions of dogmatism, subjectivism and formalism. As a result, *cheng-feng* was mentioned less frequently than in SKN, and usually with different meaning. To rank and file members rectification meant mainly invigorating party branches, overcoming negative attitudes, regularization of work, and the constant, painful task of weeding out undesirables. Basic party doctrine and major writings were presented in simplified form, sometimes as dialogues or aphorisms easily memorized. Straight indoctrination and struggle sessions were employed more than 'criticism/self-criticism'. Good and bad models of party behaviour were held up for emulation or condemnation. Meetings were held as opportunity allowed. Training and other campaigns were timed to coincide with seasonal activities: rent and interest reduction campaigns peaked at the spring and autumn harvests, elections were usually held in the early winter after the harvest, army recruitment was easiest during the nearly annual 'spring famine'.

For better educated cadres, standards were somewhat higher. Usually these were 'outside' cadres working at district or regional levels. Liu Shao-chi'i, in particular, tried to transplant Yenan-style rectification to the bases over which he had jurisdiction through the Central China Bureau. The same corpus of documents was designated for study and criticism/self-criticism meetings were called. In 1942, Liu Shao-chi'i's approach to rectification 'had an impact, however, only among high cadres of the army and other organizations under close supervision of the regional party headquarters'.[116]

The middle years of the war imposed great pressures on the Chinese Communist Party. But where in 1927 and in 1934–5 the movement had narrowly avoided annihilation, the mid-war crises did not threaten the party's very existence. By 1940, under wartime conditions, the Communist movement had sufficient territorial reach and popular support to weather the storm. Yet this outcome was not inevitable, as the experience of Nationalist guerrillas showed. The CCP's base of popular support, reinforced and enhanced by organizational control and step-by-step reforms, was both genuine and incomplete. The party's mandate had to be continually renewed and extended. It had to call upon all its resources and experience, to face difficulties realistically, to recognize its short-comings, and above all to persist.

[116] Ch'en Yung-fa, 532ff.

III. THE LAST YEARS OF THE WAR 1944-1945

On the fifth anniversary of the war (7 September 1942), Mao Tse-tung wrote in a *Liberation Daily* editorial that 'the war of resistance has in fact entered the final stage of the struggle for victory'. Although he characterized the present period as 'the darkness before dawn' and foresaw 'great difficulties' ahead, he suggested that the Japanese might be defeated within two years.[117]

Mao was too sanguine in this prediction, but there were signs that the tide was turning against the Axis powers. The heroic Russian defence of Stalingrad, the highwater mark of the German offensives in the east, was followed closely by the Allied invasion of North Africa. In the Pacific, the battles of the Coral Sea (May) and Midway (June) clearly foreshadowed American command of the seas. In August, US Marines landed on the Solomon Islands to take the offensive against Japan.

On the battlefields of China in late 1942 and particularly in the Communist-controlled base areas, harbingers of victory were still a long way off. But over the following year, as 1943 wore on, the warmer winds of change were unmistakable. Even the Japanese high command in Tokyo – though the CCP could hardly have known it – had begun to plan on avoiding defeat rather than achieving victory. What the Communists could see, however, was the decline of intensive pacification efforts and the increasing withdrawal of Japanese forces from the deep countryside. Occasional quick sweeps, like those of the early period of the war, replaced and protracted mop-up campaigns of 1941 and 1942.

OPERATION ICHIGO AND ITS CONSEQUENCES

In fact, the Japanese were preparing for their greatest military offensive in China since 1937-8, Operation Ichigo.[118] The main aim of this campaign, which in one form or another had been stalled on the drawing-boards since 1941, was to open a north-south corridor all the way from Korea to Hanoi, thus providing an overland alternative to the sea lanes which had been swept virtually clear of Japanese vessels capable of bringing essential raw materials to the home islands. A secondary goal was to destroy the American airfields in south-east China.

Ichigo began in April 1944, with campaigns against Chengchow and

---

[117] Mao, *SW*, 3.99.

[118] This summary of Operation Ichigo draws heavily on Ch'i Hsi-sheng, *Nationalist China at war: military defeats and political collapse, 1937-1945*, 73-82.

Loyang, then swept south through Honan along the P'ing-Han railway. During the summer, the heaviest fighting took place south of the Yangtze River, in Hunan, as the Japanese sought to clear the railway line between Wuhan and Canton. Changsha fell to the invaders in June, Hengyang in August. By early winter, the north-south link-up had been achieved, and the Japanese advance was swinging westward to take the airfields at Kweilin, Liuchow and Nanning. To the north-west lay Kweiyang, beyond which stretched the road to Chungking. So serious did the threat appear that in December American and British civilians were evacuated from the wartime capital, and dire predictions of defeat or capitulation were rampant. In fact, however, the Japanese advance had spent itself and could go no further.

Japanese losses were dwarfed by the damage inflicted on the Nationalists. Chungking authorities acknowledged 300,000 casualties. Japanese forces were ordered to destroy the best units of the Nationalist central armies first, knowing that regional elements would then collapse. Logistical damage was also enormous: equipment for an estimated forty divisions and the loss of resources from newly-occupied territories, especially in Hunan, 'the land of fish and rice'.

Politically, too, Ichigo was a disaster for the Nationalists, as incompetence and corruption (despite some brave fighting in Hunan) were laid bare for nearly half a year, both in Chungking and on the battlefield. Nowhere was this more striking than in the opening phase of Ichigo, which coincided with the great Honan famine in the spring of 1944. Neither the Chungking government nor the civilian-military authorities in Honan had prepared for the famine, though its coming was clearly foreseen. Far from providing relief when the famine hit, the authorities collected taxes and other levies as usual. Profiteering was common. When Chinese forces fled in the face of Ichigo, long-suffering peasants disarmed and shot them, then welcomed the Japanese. Tens of thousands starved to death in Honan during the spring of 1944.[119] Although the second half of 1944 saw the successful culmination of the Allied campaign in Burma and the reopening of an overland route into south-west China, these victories, achieved under US tactical command and with the participation of US and British forces, did not compensate for the Nationalists' losses elsewhere or redeem their damaged prestige.

The strains of Operation Ichigo and closer scrutiny of Chinese politics by the United States provided greatly expanded opportunities for Communist work in the 'big rear area' – the regions controlled to one degree or another by the Nationalist government in Chungking. Until the

[119] Theodore White and Annalee Jacoby, *Thunder out of China*.

fall of Hankow in late 1938, the CCP had enjoyed considerable latitude for open and semi-open work. Thereafter, Nationalist censorship and repression again forced it underground, except for officially sanctioned liaison groups and journalists. At all times, of course, the CCP tried to infiltrate the Nationalist government organs and military units, a secret war fought by both sides with considerable success. But the situation was still so dangerous that instructions from Yenan were to lie low, maintain or improve one's cover, and await changes in the working environment.

As the Ichigo offensive rolled on south and south-west, dissident regional elements began talking quietly about the possible removal of Chiang Kai-shek. Yunnan province, under the independent warlord Lung Yun, was a haven for liberal intellectuals and disaffected political figures clustered around South-west Associated University in Kunming – which was also the China terminus of the Burma Road and the 'over the Hump' air transport route from India. In September 1944, when the currents of Ichigo, the Stilwell crisis, and anti-Nationalist dissidence all swirled together, a number of minor political parties and splinter groups came together to form the China Democratic League.[120] As in the wake of the New Fourth Army incident in early 1941, these figures sought to play moderating and mediating roles. Most believed in liberal values and democratic practices, and called for fundamental but non-violent reforms in the Nationalist government. Although the Democratic League lacked a popular base and was by no means a unified movement, league intellectuals – many of them Western-trained – nevertheless had an influence upon educated public opinion and foreign observers out of all proportion to their own limited numbers. Both as individuals and as members of the Democratic League, they seemed to speak, many believed, for all the right things: peace, justice, freedom, broader participation in government.

For the most part, the CCP was content to let the Democratic League speak in its own voice (though it did have operatives in the league). If the KMT undertook reform or granted concessions, the CCP and not the Democratic League would be their true beneficiary. On the other hand, when the Nationalists stonewalled or counter-attacked the league, they further compromised themselves as reactionary and drove more moderates toward the CCP. Neither the Democratic League's idea of a 'third force' nor darker talk of some sort of anti-Chiang coup produced any results. But both provided new opportunities for the CCP to improve its image at the expense of Chiang Kai-shek and the KMT.

[120] For the dissidents, see Ch'i Hsi-sheng, 113–17; for the Democratic League and its relations with the CCP, see Van Slyke, *Enemies and friends*, 168–84.

TABLE 30

Japanese and puppet forces in China, June 1944

	North China	Central China	South China	Total
Japanese	220,000	260,000	80,000	560,000
Puppets (not classified by geographical area)				
(1) enlisted from regular or regional Nationalist units			*c.* 480,000	
(2) enlisted by force from the peasantry or by integration of bandits, vagrants, etc.			*c.* 300,000	
(3) collaborating local militia and police			*c.* 200,000	
Sub-total			*c.* 1,000,000	
Total				1,560,000

Source: 'Chung-kung k'ang-chan i-pan ch'ing-k'uang ti chieh-shao' (Briefing on the general situation of the CCP in the war of resistance), *Chung-kung tang-shih ts'an-k'ao tzu-liao* (Reference materials on the history of the Chinese Communist Party), 5.226–8, 233. This was a briefing given on 22 June 1944 to the first group of Chinese and foreign journalists to visit Yenan.

POLITICAL AND MILITARY EXPANSION

The Japanese committed nearly 150,000 troops to the Honan phase of Ichigo, and over 350,000 to the Hunan-Kwangsi phase. Although the total number of Japanese troops in North and Central China did not markedly decline, the demands of Ichigo's second phase pulled many experienced officers and men out of these theatres, replacing them with garrison troops or with new recruits from the home islands. The Japanese also increased their reliance on puppet forces, to take up some of the military slack. According to Yeh Chien-ying, chief-of-staff in Yenan, the situation in June 1944 was as shown in table 30.

On the Communist side, the party and the army resumed their growth, but during the last phase of the war the pattern of expansion in the party differed from that in its armed forces. From approximately mid-1943 to the end of the conflict in mid-1945, the party expanded once again, though at a much slower pace than in the first years of the war. As noted above (table 16), the CCP grew by about 100,000 (*c.* 15 per cent) from mid-1943 to mid-1944. At the time of the Seventh CCP Congress (April 1945), Mao claimed a party membership of 1·2 million, an increase of 40 per cent over that of just a year earlier, and more than 60 per cent above the 1942 low. Thus, by the end of the war, nearly half the party's membership had less than two years' experience.

TABLE 31

(see also table 18)

Chinese Communist forces, 1944–1945

	8RA	N4A	Total
1944 (June)	320,000	153,676	474,476
1944 (October)	385,000*	185,000*	570,000
1945 (March)	513,000*	247,000*	760,000
1945 (April)	614,000*	296,000*	910,000

* Assuming same proportions as in June 1944.

Sources: this is a composite table. The June 1944 total is from the report cited in table 30, n. 139, by Yeh Chien-ying. October 1944 and March 1945 figures were published in *Chieh-fang jih-pao* (17 March 1945). The April figures are those claimed by Mao Tse-tung at the Seventh CCP Congress.

In contrast to the continuous expansion of the party, the army remained for several years almost constant in size, recruiting only a little more than enough to replace casualties. This situation changed abruptly during the second half of 1944. In less than one year, Communist authorities claimed a virtual doubling of their full-time armed forces (field forces plus local units).

This rapid growth partly responded to the opportunities for territorial expansion in 1944 and 1945, but also anticipated Japan's defeat, and the importance which the army would then have, both as an instrument of policy (taking over Japanese-held territory or contesting with the Nationalists), and as a bargaining chip (since the terms of any negotiated settlement would reflect the realities of power in being). Most of this growth came from rapid integration of regional forces into the field forces; the large numerical increases claimed for the 8RA and the N4A, therefore, derived more from reclassification than from new recruitment. Below these full-time forces were the part-time people's militia – about 1·5 million for North China and a half million for Central China. Members of the militia were quite useful as village security and policy auxiliaries and in local intelligence, short-distance courier service, supply transport, stretcher bearing, etc. But their training was rudimentary and virtually no weapons could be assigned to them. The militia was not expected to serve as a regular combat force, and it rarely did so.

Yeh Chien-ying reported a sharp increase in the number of military engagements from mid-1943 to mid-1944 over those of previous years; at the same time, however, the scale of the engagements was smaller, a greater proportion of engagements were against puppet forces, and the casualty ratio increasingly favoured the CCP. Between mid-1943 and mid-1944, Communist casualties numbered 29,000, less than half the 64,000 suffered between mid-1941 and mid-1942.[121]

In a recurrence of some of the controversies of the first months of the war, some military leaders argued for a rapid expansion and a shift from traditional guerrilla tactics to more conventional operations. Some high-level leaders apparently wanted to attack small and intermediate cities at once. During the spring of 1944, with Ichigo under way, the Eighth Route Army carried out probing operations in Hopei around the strategic Shihchiachuang rail junction and even briefly occupied the important city of Paoting. During this period, too, the plains bases were reactivated in both north and south Hopei. In principle, Mao agreed with a forward strategy and in positioning the party to take advantage of Japan's eventual defeat. In the spring of 1944, he urged his comrades to 'pay attention to work in the big cities and along the main lines of communication and raise the work in the cities to a position of equal importance with that in the base areas'. Yet he still counselled caution, flexibility, and a realistic assessment of the party's capacities:

Our party is not yet sufficiently strong, not yet sufficiently united or consolidated, and so cannot yet take on greater responsibility than we now carry. From now on, the problem is further to expand and consolidate our party, our army, and our base areas in the continued prosecution of the war of resistance; this is the first indispensable item in our ideological and material preparation for the gigantic work of the future.[122]

Mao also worried that his field commanders might act impetuously and without coordination or understanding of the full strategic picture. On several occasions he inveighed against precisely this sort of 'mountain-top-ism'; memories of the unauthorized Hundred Regiments offensive and of his inability to control Hsiang Ying must have come to mind.

There was no reason, however, to hold back in those areas where the CCP had first established its bases, and where the Nationalist presence had already been cleaned out. In these regions, the only questions were tactical – how much could be accomplished with the resources at hand, and how much Japanese or puppet opposition could be expected. Much more sensitive was the issue of opening extensive new base areas in regions still claimed by the KMT or only recently lost as a result of Operation Ichigo. Chu Te, Yeh Chien-ying and Ch'en I all indicated that much thought had been given to such expansion; they apparently found the prospects very appealing. In the upshot, although the CCP did move into some of these areas, it did so cautiously, selectively, and with a low profile.

During the last year of the war, the CCP rang the changes on political,

[121] *Chung-kung k'ang-chan i-pan ch'ing-k'uang ti chieh-shao*, 238.   [122] Mao, *SW* 3.171–2.

social and economic policies previously developed, doing so both with confidence born of success and with a realistic appreciation of the limitations of its influence and power. In newly 'liberated' areas, the CCP acted very much as it had in earlier waves of expansion, doing whatever was necessary to get an initial toehold, then extend its influence. In established bases, stress was placed on both production campaigns and class struggle. Most frequently, class struggle meant further extension of rent and interest reduction.

In many bases – including some core areas – rent and interest reduction had not been thoroughly carried out, or rural elites had tried to undo the reforms already imposed. Campaigns with names like 'investigate rent – reduce rent' (*ch'a-tsu chien-tsu*) were seen at all levels and in all areas. Many detailed and vivid documents reported shockingly poor performance. Cadres were regularly criticized for their lack of understanding and interest in mass work. Evasion and corruption were not uncommon. Peasant involvement was too often spotty and grudging.

How should one interpret these reports? On the one hand, they seem to have come from consolidated districts, where systematic surveys were possible. Yet it is in just such areas that one would have expected the reforms to have been most thorough and effective. This may suggest that in semi-consolidated or guerrilla zones, little if any rent or interest reduction had been accomplished. But, on the other hand, these reports are designed to spur the movement, to show that much remained to be done, and to highlight errors – in short, to serve as strongly negative examples. Yet even if one accepts the didactic purpose of these documents and discounts for exaggeration, the very need for them shows that full achievement of even these limited reforms was beyond the party's capacity. Furthermore, experience had shown that the imposition of more radical economic policies not only lowered production but often frightened and alienated many middle peasants, even though such policies were not aimed at them.

Although there was no weakening of the commitment to revolutionary change in the Chinese countryside, party leaders realized that premature, poorly-planned efforts to achieve it were doomed to failure and that abstract preaching had little persuasive power. 'Nationalism' and 'class struggle' had to be given palpable, concrete meaning on a daily basis before they could be understood and accepted by a peasantry unschooled in such vague notions. Mao's caution was not so much a lack of confidence as it was a realistic appraisal of the still limited capacities of the party and its military forces. And by 1944, a new actor was playing an important role on China's already crowded stage: the United States.

THE UNITED STATES AND THE CHINESE
COMMUNISTS

When the Japanese attacked Pearl Harbor (7 December 1941), the Sino-Japanese War merged with the Second World War. Through most of 1942, the United States was in retreat or on the defensive against Japan, and could provide little direct assistance to the struggle in China. Europe had priority over Asia, and before long the strategy of island-hopping across the Pacific took precedence over efforts to defeat Japan on the Asian mainland. The China-Burma-India (CBI) theatre, under command of General Joseph W. (Vinegar Joe) Stilwell, became a backwater of the war, important primarily to keep large numbers of Japanese troops tied down and as a site for Allied air bases. Like all other nations, the United States recognized the Nationalist regime, headed and symbolized by Chiang Kai-shek, as the legitimate government of China.

In order to keep Chiang in the struggle (he sometimes hinted – or threatened – that China was exhausted and might not be able to go on) and to compensate politically for the meagre military aid being sent to China, President Roosevelt urged that China be recognized as one of the Big Four and that the century-old 'unequal treaties' be abolished. Both were accomplished, over deep British misgiving, in 1943. The long-range goal of the United States was to help a 'unified, democratic, and friendly' China become the centre of postwar stability in Asia.

Under the confusing cross-currents of events was the strategic import of US involvement – that Japan would eventually be defeated mainly by the Americans. This was soon clearly understood by both Chiang Kai-shek and Mao Tse-tung. Neither leader had much incentive to undertake anti-Japanese combat for purely military reasons, if to do so would weaken forces needed later to cope with the domestic rival. Although Mao could not acknowledge it in such terms, this was the 'international situation favourable to us and unfavourable to the enemy' that he had predicted in his 1938 treatise, 'On the new stage'.

Direct contacts between Americans and the Chinese Communists in the early and middle years of the war were very limited. Between 1937 and early 1942, US embassy staff members met occasionally with members of the CCP liaison team in Wuhan and Chungking. These meetings took place more often after the US entry into the war, and sometimes involved both American military and foreign service officers. Despite increasingly insistent requests, the Nationalists declared all base areas out-of-bounds to foreigners. Only a few refugees, like Michael Lindsay or Clare and William Band, and sympathizers, like Agnes Smedley, reported on the

Communist regions. At last, when Vice-President Henry Wallace visited China in June 1944, during Operation Ichigo, embassy officials persuaded him to press their request to visit Yenan upon Chiang Kai-shek. As a concession to this representative of an obviously impatient President Roosevelt, Chiang reluctantly authorized the creation of a US Observer Group in Yenan. A press delegation left at once; by August the official group was in place and functioning. Thus the 'Dixie Mission' was born.[123] Headed by a colourful old China hand, Colonel David D. Barrett, the group included political as well as military observers, such men as John S. Service and John P. Davies whose reports and recommendations later became so controversial during the inflamed debates in the US about the 'loss of China'. Virtually all Western journalists on the China beat wrote dispatches and books about 'Red China'. Their experience recalled that of Edgar Snow in 1936. Now, as then, the Communists seemed unusually open, forthcoming, and concerned to get their story before the world.

The timing was significant. In 1944 and 1945 the CCP was resurgent, while Nationalist shortcomings were glaringly exposed by Operation Ichigo and by the final clash between Chiang Kai-shek and General Stilwell, resulting in the latter's recall. During the more difficult middle years of the war, when the CCP was wrestling with problems of survival and carrying on the rectification campaign, Nationalist recalcitrance had prevented US observers from seeing the Communists at first hand.

For Mao and the CCP, the United States was a wild card. To all appearances, the US was committed to Chiang Kai-shek and the Nationalists. But the United States was also committed to winning the war against Japan as quickly as possible and to a unified, democratic and peaceful China after the war. If the US perceived the Communists as a dedicated and effective anti-Japanese force – in welcome contrast to Nationalist performance during Ichigo – perhaps war material and financial backing might come their way. After all, to gain victory over Germany and Japan, the US was working with the widest variety of allies, regardless of their professed ideologies. But clearly the CCP could not present itself to the United States in a favourable light if it was openly fighting the Nationalists, taking advantage of their misfortunes during 1944.

Establishment of the Dixie Mission was limited recognition by the United States, and the Chinese Communist leaders seized the opportunity to offer assistance (to downed airmen, to prepare for an Allied landing in North China) and to widen the avenues of direct communication. Full recognition and military assistance were the maximum prizes to be won,

[123] John S. Service, Dixie's most famous member, speculated that this name came from the song lyric, 'Is it true what they say about Dixie?' Dixie was of course the rebel side.

but any friendly association with the US, any wedge between the US and the Nationalists, was desirable so long as it did not curtail CCP initiative and autonomy. Whether or not this was a principal motive, the CCP did in fact use restraint in areas where they might have come into conflict with the Nationalists, and moved forward with prudent speed where such action could demonstrate their effectiveness in the war against Japan.

The recall of Stilwell in October 1944 was a keen disappointment to the CCP, for it showed the continuing strength of Chiang Kai-shek's influence over American China policy. Meanwhile, changes in personnel – Wedemeyer for Stilwell as theatre commander and Patrick J. Hurley as Roosevelt's special representative (later ambassador) – seemed unpromising.[124] The Communists soon made their assessment of Hurley, who, as Roosevelt's personal envoy, seemed to have a special authority to speak for the United States. Hurley believed that the CCP was not really revolutionary; he had been told by Molotov himself that the Russians considered them synthetic communists and would agree not to meddle in Chinese domestic politics. Hurley was convinced that when the CCP realized they could expect no assistance from the USSR, they would be willing to make their peace with the Kuomintang. Conversely, the CCP would be more intransigent if it believed it might obtain recognition or support from either the Soviet Union or the United States. Hurley also felt confident that he could persuade Chiang Kai-shek to accept CCP participation in a multi-party government. More than once he likened the CCP to the Republican Party in the United States – both were opposition parties, each seeking a larger role in the country's political life.

Hurley's surprise visit to Yenan in early November led to the joint drafting of a five-point proposal more sweeping in its language – partly inspired by his fondness for the Gettysburg Address – than anything the CCP had previously entertained. But when Hurley returned to Chungking with this document, which he himself had signed, Chiang Kai-shek refused to consider it. Hurley, in essence, reversed his field and disavowed the proposals he had helped to draft. CCP disappointment over Stilwell's recall deepened into disillusion with Hurley and the United States.

The political positions of the two Chinese parties had, however, been considerably clarified. In brief, the Nationalists insisted that the CCP place itself under the civil and military authority of the Chinese government as

---

[124] Hurley apparently received only verbal instructions from FDR, and from the start operated independently of the Department of State, which he held in considerable contempt. He later claimed his mission was to prevent a Nationalist collapse, to sustain Chiang Kai-shek, to harmonize relations between the generalissimo and the American commander, to prevent economic collapse, to unify all military forces in China for the purpose of defeating Japan, and to promote internal unity in China. See below, ch. 13.

a precondition to discussing reform and reorganization. Since the Kuomintang was the government of China, it could not negotiate with the CCP as an equal any more than Lincoln could have negotiated a division of the United States with Jefferson Davis. The Communist position was the Nationalist's mirror image: satisfactory political and military reforms must come first as a precondition to participation in a restructured government. The CCP considered itself the political equal – and the moral superior – of the Kuomintang, and it had no intention of submitting its territories or its armed forces to outside control. The call for formation of a 'coalition government' (*lien-ho cheng-fu*) was first enunciated by the CCP in mid-September 1944. Thereafter, until well after the end of the war with Japan, coalition government remained the centrepiece of both the CCP's negotiating position and its propaganda campaigns, just as improvements in its political and military situation in the base areas were made with civil war in mind.

With the evidence of Stilwell's recall and Hurley's inconsistency, CCP leadership apparently gave up on the possibility of being recognized by the US as coequal with the Kuomintang in the Chinese political arena. By late 1944, Chou En-lai was refusing to return to Chungking – a clear statement that the CCP believed that negotiations with the KMT would be fruitless. His brief visit to Chungking in January 1945 confirmed that the impasse had grown more bitter than ever.

Yet, even then, the party did not entirely abandon hope of receiving military assistance from the United States. There had been recurrent discussion of landing US forces in North China as a step toward the invasion of Kyushu (tentatively scheduled for October 1945). The Communists apprised Wedemeyer of the location of coastal base areas both north and south of the Shantung peninsula. From October to December 1944, sporadic discussions ensued concerning the possibility of joint US-CCP military operations on a fairly large scale – apparently without Hurley's knowledge. Extravagant language was exchanged. American colonels suggested that full equipment for up to 25,000 guerrillas was not out of the question; at one point, Mao indicated a desire to visit Washington and a willingness to have his forces serve under American commanders: 'We will accept your help with gratitude any time, now or in the future. We would serve with all our hearts under an American General, with no strings or conditions attached.... If you land on the shores of China, we will be there to meet you, and to place ourselves under your command.'[125]

When Hurley heard of these conversations, he quickly put an end to

[125] Quoted in James B. Reardon-Anderson, *Yenan and the great powers*, 56.

them and demanded a full investigation, feeling that his own efforts at a political settlement had been undermined by persons on Wedemeyer's staff and in his own embassy. By February 1945, when Hurley and Wedemeyer returned to Washington for consultations related to the Yalta Conference, the CCP had apparently all but written off hopes of recognition and support from the United States. KMT-CCP negotiations were also, for the moment at least, dead.

THE SEVENTH CONGRESS

In organizational terms, the culminating event of the last phase of the war was the convening of the long-heralded, long-deferred Seventh National Congress of the Communist Party of China, the first such gathering since the dark days of the Sixth Congress, held in Moscow in 1928. As we have noted, plans for the Seventh Congress had been well under way by early 1938, until 'wartime pressures' led to its indefinite postponement, with the sixth plenum of late 1938 taking its place. Nor did a seventh plenum meet until immediately before the Seventh Congress, nearly six years later. In the interim Mao had built his coalition, weakened or removed his rivals, and developed his ideology as the guiding centre of the Chinese Communist movement. By 1944, at the latest, Mao Tse-tung had risen far above his former peers, and was now overwhelmingly the dominant leader of the CCP. If any of his comrades had misgivings about this apotheosis, they kept silent in public.[126]

The timing of the Seventh Congress was influenced by both international and domestic considerations. Internationally, the rapid march toward victory in both Europe and Asia required that the CCP set forth its strategic line in the clearest and most forceful terms. Domestically, the CCP's Seventh Congress was timed to meet simultaneously with the Kuomintang's Sixth National Congress, to pose an alternative to the KMT at every point, and to upstage Chungking. Once again, a thrust by one contender led to parry and counter-thrust by the other. This 'congress of solidarity and victory' – hailed as 'one of the most important events in the history of modern China' – met from 23 April to 11 June, 1945, a full fifty days. The major business before the congress was the following:

(1) Acknowledgment of Mao Tse-tung as the unquestioned leader of the Chinese Communist Party and the Chinese revolution, and parallel acknowledgment of 'the thought of Mao Tse-tung' as the guide to all analysis and action. This spirit, indeed, pervaded the entire congress. It

---

[126] It appears that the doughty P'eng Te-huai expressed some such misgivings at the seventh plenum. See Wylie, 262.

was clearly expressed in the 'Resolutions on certain questions in the history of our party', which had been formally adopted by the seventh plenum a few days earlier, although, judging from its placement in volume 3 of the *Selected works*, it may have been drafted as early as mid-1944. This was nothing less than 'the new Maoist version of party history that was to become the official orthodoxy...one momentous process – the emergence and struggles of Mao's correct line prior to 1935, and its initial triumph and gradual, victorious development since Tsunyi.'[127] This view of history was also incorporated into the new party constitution, which further stated: 'The Chinese Communist Party takes the thought of Mao Tse-tung – the unified thought of Marxist-Leninist theory and Chinese revolutionary practice – as the guide to all its work.' If these affirmations were not enough, the congress also heard self-criticisms from a number of returned-students, including Po Ku (Ch'in Pang-hsien), Lo Fu (Chang Wen-t'ien) and Wang Ming.

(2) Political and military reports, delivered by Mao and Chu Te respectively, in order to define in authoritative terms the party's line, present and future. Mao's political report was the lengthy and comprehensive 'On coalition government' (later substantially edited for inclusion in the *Selected works*). This treatise can be viewed as a continuation of 'On new democracy', since it sets forth the CCP's view of China's present situation and future prospects as explicit alternatives to those of the KMT. The coalition government for which Mao called was essentially the new democratic government described five years earlier, 'under the leadership of the working class'. Although unity was the keynote, it was hardly a unity the KMT could accept. Indeed, models for a nationwide coalition government already existed: 'In every one of the Liberated Areas... popularly elected governments, that is, local coalition governments, have been or are being set up.' Mao also claimed that the pledge to implement Sun Yat-sen's Three Principles of the People had been 'completely carried into effect in China's Liberated Areas'.[128]

Yet 'On coalition government' drew a careful line between minimum and maximum programmes, and sought to keep open as many options as possible. In this regard, Mao was providing justification for the policies he had already been following for about a year: to recognize that competition with the Kuomintang might be either political or military, or some mixture of the two. The overall tone of this report, however, was quite aggressive and challenging. Mao did not rule out negotiation and compromise, but this was not the prevailing tone.

(3) The adoption of a new party constitution, following a lengthy report

[127] Wylie, 261.   [128] Mao, *SW* 3.269-70.

by Liu Shao-ch'i during which he praised Mao in such fulsome terms – 'Our Comrade Mao Tse-tung is not only the greatest revolutionary and statesman in Chinese history, but also the greatest theoretician in Chinese history' – that some have guessed he may not have been entirely sincere. This constitution replaced the one adopted at the Sixth Congress in 1928 (and would remain in force until the Eighth Congress in 1956, when – significantly – all references to the 'thought of Mao Tse-tung' were deleted). The constitution of 1945, reflecting of course the preferences of Mao Tse-tung, differed from its predecessor in several ways.[129] Chief among these was the greater centralization of power both in the party as a whole, and at its apex, where for the first time there was created the post of chairman of the Central Committee, who was concurrently chairman of the Central Political Bureau and the Central Secretariat. The new constitution also gave greater representation to the rural areas, put more stress on intra-party democracy, and dropped all references to the Soviet Union and to the international revolutionary movement. The 1945 Constitution had a strongly home-grown flavour, much different from that of the Sixth Congress, seventeen years earlier.

(4) Election of the new Central Committee (44 regular and 33 alternate members) and the staffing of the higher echelons of the party. Precisely because there were so few surprises, those few stood out: Li Li-san ranked 15th, well above Chou En-lai (23rd); Ch'en Po-ta, Mao's ideological expert, was no higher than 3rd on the alternate list. Perhaps because of his collisions with Mao, P'eng Te-huai ranked low (33rd), much lower than his military responsibilities might have suggested; the same was true of Yeh Chien-ying (31st). Wang Ming and Po Ku were the last two names on the list.[130]

THE CHINESE COMMUNISTS AND THE SOVIET UNION

During the last phase of the war in China, the role played by the USSR was, for the most part, that of a brooding presence rather than an active participant. It was only with her declaration of war on 8 August 1945 – just six days before Japan's surrender – that the USSR suddenly and forcefully emerged from the shadows to centre stage in East Asia. This did not mean, however, that other actors in China could ignore her. On the contrary, the United States and the Chinese Nationalists as well as the Chinese

---

[129] This summary follows that presented in Conrad Brandt, et al. A documentary history of Chinese communism, 419–21.

[130] Ibid. 292. See also Donald W. Klein and Anne B. Clark, Biographic dictionary of Chinese communism, 1921–1965, App. 50, 1081–9.

Communists had to include the USSR in all their calculations. Until Japan's abrupt surrender, following the two thermonuclear attacks, official US policy was to get the Soviet Union into the war against Japan as soon as possible. This attitude underlay Roosevelt's approach to Stalin at the Yalta Conference (February 1945) and continued to affect Truman as late as the meetings at Potsdam in July. But rivalry and mutual suspicion were already gnawing away at the alliance.

Chiang Kai-shek's goal was to forestall recognition and support of the CCP by either the US or the USSR. Chiang's principal means for achieving this was to offer to Stalin concessions that only he could deliver, in return for the USSR's exclusive recognition of him and his government. Needless to say, this goal had to be pursued in Stalin's direction with the greatest discretion, and this was much on Chiang Kai-shek's mind during the visit of Vice-President Henry Wallace to China in June 1944. In conversations over three days, Chiang time and again complained of the CCP's duplicity and disobedience, and alleged that the Chinese Communists were subject to control from Moscow. He urged that 'Roosevelt act as an arbiter or "middleman" between China and the USSR'. In response to Wallace's urging that points of possible conflict between China and the USSR be resolved, Chiang promised to do 'anything that was not detrimental to the sovereignty of the Chinese government'. Roosevelt almost certainly believed he had wide latitude to explore Sino-Russian relations with Stalin. In a letter to Chiang, he wrote: 'I welcome the indication given me by Mr Wallace of your desire for improved relations between the USSR and China, and your suggestion that I use my good offices to arrange for a conference between Chinese and Russian representatives is being given serious thought.'[131] These thoughts were an important element in Roosevelt's secret conversations with Stalin at Yalta. In essence, Roosevelt was using concessions by China to induce Russia to enter the war against Japan, feeling justified that in doing so he was also contributing to the improvement of Sino-Russian relations which Chiang had indicated he wanted and would pay for. In return, Stalin and Molotov indicated to Hurley that they did not consider the Chinese Communists to be communists at all, that they were not supporting the CCP, and that they were ready to recognize and deal with Chiang Kai-shek on the basis of their understanding of the Yalta discussions.

Hurley informed Chiang Kai-shek of the Yalta Conference in mid-June, negotiations between China and the USSR began the following month, and the Sino-Soviet Treaty of Friendship and Alliance was signed on 14 August 1945, the very day of Japan's capitulation. Chiang got what he

---

[131] *China white paper*, 549–60.

wanted: a pledge of recognition and non-interference, and a promise to give moral support and military aid entirely to the 'National Government as the central government of China'. The price was high – an inflated understanding of the Yalta terms, plus several other loose ends – and led subsequently to bitter Nationalist denunciation of the US role in these events. Russia thus returned to a position more advanced than any she had held under the tsars prior to the Russo-Japanese War. Meanwhile, Russian forces quickly overran all of Manchuria and North Korea, most of the conquest being completed in the days following the Japanese surrender. On 19 August, Russian and Chinese Communist military units linked up for the first time in history.

Throughout the war, the CCP had either praised and defended the USSR or it had kept silent. But clearly Mao was playing an independent hand and had reason for deep displeasure with much that the Russians had done: exclusive aid to the Kuomintang early in the war, the Nazi-Soviet pact of 1939, the treaty of neutrality with Japan in 1941, continued and only occasionally critical recognition of Chiang Kai-shek. He probably suspected that Stalin did indeed harbour doubts about him as the first Chinese Communist leader to come to power without help or blessing from the Kremlin, about his policies, and above all about the CCP's prospects of success. In what was undoubtedly a deliberate decision by Mao, the CCP's Seventh Congress almost totally ignored the Soviet Union and Stalin.[132]

The CCP press in Yenan and Chungking had barely finished celebrating the Soviet entry into the conflict on 8 August when Japan surrendered and the Sino-Soviet treaty was announced. The joy of victory must have been tempered by the disappointment of the treaty. Although in public the CCP tried to put the best possible face on it, party leaders were hurt, angry and bewildered. One mid-level cadre must have spoken for many:

In order to maintain and stabilize the peace in the Far East, the Soviet Union has signed the Sino-Soviet Friendship Treaty. This is beneficial to the people of China and the world, but not to Japan and all other warmongers. At the same time, however, in order to carry out its duty under this treaty, the Soviet Union cannot directly aid us, and this imposes certain limitations upon us.... We do not understand actual Russian policy.[133]

Mao later recalled with bitterness, 'They did not permit China to make revolution: that was in 1945. Stalin wanted to prevent China from making revolution, saying that we should not have a civil war and should

---

[132] In the rather brief sections of 'On coalition government' devoted to the international situation, Mao referred to the USSR only as one of the three (or five) great nations jointly defeating the fascist powers. The USSR is accorded no leading role, and Stalin's name is not mentioned.
[133] Quoted in Reardon-Anderson, 103 (but retranslated).

cooperate with Chiang Kai-shek. Otherwise, the Chinese nation would perish.'[134]

PROSPECTS

The surrender of Japan was, of course, an event of great and joyful significance across China's war-torn land. It symbolized the end of the foreign aggression, and the hope of all Chinese that genuine peace might at last be achieved after seemingly endless pain and death. But Japanese surrender did not mean that the war was over in China, since the Japanese invasion was only one part of a complex, many-sided political and military conflict, all other aspects of which continued much as before. Even with the Japanese, shooting continued as Japanese troops responded to orders from the Nationalists to hold their positions and refuse surrender to Communist forces.

Thus Mao and his colleagues hardly had time to pause and congratulate themselves on the progress they had made since 1937. In 'The situation and our policy after the victory in the war of resistance against Japan' (13 August 1945), however, Mao took time to look both backward and forward. The past was portrayed in black and white; no shades of grey entered the description of the Kuomintang and its leaders, either prior to or during the Sino-Japanese War. According to Mao, the risk of civil war was very great, because Chiang Kai-shek and his foreign backers would try to seize a victory that rightly belonged to the people. Mao was hard-headed enough to see that the balance of power in China did not yet favour the CCP: 'That the fruits of victory should go to the people is one thing, but who will eventually get them...is another. Don't be too sure that the fruits of victory will fall into the hands of the people.' Some of these fruits – all the major cities and the eastern seaboard – would surely go to the KMT, others would be contested, and still others – the base areas and some Japanese-occupied countryside – would go to 'the people'. The only question was on what scale the struggle would be fought: 'Will an open and total civil war break out?... Given the general trend of the international and internal situation and the feelings of the people, is it possible, through our own struggles to localize the civil war or delay the outbreak of a country-wide civil war? There is this possibility.' It was in this spirit that Mao Tse-tung, Chou En-lai, and General Patrick Hurley flew from Yenan to Chungking on 28 August to discuss with Chiang Kai-shek the problems of peace, democracy and unity.

Finally, Mao Tse-tung stressed self-reliance. He identified the United States as a hostile imperialist power and insisted that no direct help from

[134] Stuart Schram, *Chairman Mao talks to the people*, 191.

the Soviet Union was needed: 'We are not alone...[in the world, but] we stress regeneration through our own efforts. Relying on the forces we ourselves organize, we can defeat all Chinese and foreign reactionaries.' Yet at the same time, 'Bells don't ring till you strike them...Only where the broom reaches can political influence produce its full effect. ...China has a vast territory, and it is up to us to sweep it clean inch by inch... We Marxists are revolutionary realists and never indulge in idle dreams.'

CHAPTER 13

THE KMT-CCP CONFLICT 1945–1949

NEGOTIATIONS AND AMERICAN INVOLVEMENT

By 1944 the American government had become increasingly anxious to quell the dissension that was undermining the anti-Japanese war effort in China, and forestall a possible civil war that might involve the Soviet Union on the side of the CCP once the Japanese surrendered. The negotiations between the KMT and CCP, broken off after the New Fourth Army incident in 1941, had been resumed by 1943. The Americans became actively involved with the arrival in China of Major General Patrick J. Hurley, President Roosevelt's personal representative to Chiang Kai-shek, in September 1944. Appointed US Ambassador a few months later, Hurley's mission was, among other things, 'to unify all the military forces in China for the purpose of defeating Japan'.

The Hurley mission: 1944–1945

Optimistic interludes to the contrary notwithstanding, the first year of Hurley's efforts to promote reconciliation between the leaders of China's 'two great military establishments' bore little fruit. The Communist position announced by Mao at the Seventh Party Congress in April 1945 called for an end to KMT one-party rule and the inauguration of a coalition government in which the CCP would share power. This proposal gained the enthusiastic support of the nascent peace movement in the KMT areas, where fears of renewed civil conflict were mounting as the fortunes of the Japanese aggressor declined. But it was not the sort of proposal that the KMT government was inclined to favour. Then on the day Japan surrendered, 14 August, Chiang Kai-shek invited Mao to journey to Chungking to discuss the outstanding issues between them. Mao eventually accepted, and Ambassador Hurley personally escorted him to the government's wartime capital from his own at Yenan. The ambassador continued to play his mediator's role in the subsequent negotiations.

Mao returned to Yenan on 11 October. General principles had been agreed upon, but the details of implementation had yet to be devised. Chou En-lai remained in Chungking to work toward that end. The general principles announced in their 10 October agreement, at the close of the talks between Chiang and Mao, included democratization, unification of military forces, and the recognition that the CCP and all political parties were equal before the law. The government agreed further to guarantee the freedoms of person, religion, speech, publication and assembly; agreed to release political prisoners; and agreed that only the police and law courts should be permitted to make arrests, conduct trials, and impose punishments.

According to the agreement, a political consultative conference representing all parties was to be convened to consider the reorganization of the government and approve a new constitution. The Communists agreed to a gradual reduction of their troop strength by divisions to match a proportional reduction of the government's armed forces. The Communists also agreed to withdraw from eight of their southernmost and weakest base areas.[1] The government had bowed to the Communist demand for an end to one-party KMT rule; the Communists had abandoned their demand for the immediate formation of a coalition government. In so doing, both sides were acknowledging the widespread desire for peace on the part of a war-weary public, and the political advantages to be gained from apparent deference to it.

A key issue on which not even superficial agreement could be reached, however, was that of the legality of the remaining ten Communist base areas and their governments. Chiang Kai-shek demanded that they be unified under the administrative authority of the central government; the Communists not surprisingly demurred. Even more crucial: while their leaders were thus engaged in talking peace, the Communist and government armies were engaged in a competitive race to take over Japanese-occupied territory north of the Yangtze. That territory included the strategic North-east provinces (Manchuria, as they were then known), where the Communists were rushing to create a new base area.

General Douglas MacArthur, Supreme Commander of the Allied Powers (SCAP), in his General Order Number One, authorized the Chinese government to accept the Japanese surrender in China proper, the island of Taiwan, and northern Indo-China. The forces of the Soviet Union were to do the same in Manchuria. But the government, from its wartime retreat in the south-west, was at a clear disadvantage in taking

---

[1] *China white paper*. 2.577-81; Mao Tse-tung, 'On the Chungking negotiations', *Selected works*, hereafter Mao, *SW*, 4.53-63.

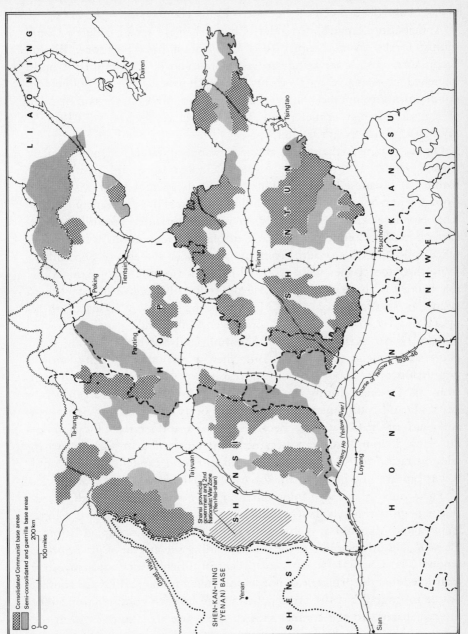

Consolidated Communist base areas
Semi-consolidated and guerrilla base areas

SHEN-KAN-NING
(YENAN) BASE

Yenan

Shansi provincial
government and 2nd
Nationalist War Zone
(Yen Hsi-shan)

Taiyuan

Great Wall

Ta-tung

Peking

Tientsin

Paoting

H O P E I

S H A N S I

S H E N S I

Sian

Loyang

Hwang Ho (Yellow River)

Course of Yellow R. 1938-46

H O N A N

A N H W E I

K I A N G S U

Hsuchow

Tsinan

Tsingtao

S H A N T U N G

L I A O N I N G

Dairen

200 km
100 miles

MAP 16. Zones under substantial Communist control in August 1945

over from the Japanese north of the Yangtze, since the Communists already controlled much of the North China countryside.

Anticipating Japan's surrender, Chiang Kai-shek had ordered Communist forces on 11 August 1945 to maintain their positions. But in accordance with conflicting orders from Yenan, Communist troops launched an offensive on all fronts against Japanese-held keypoints and communications lines to compel their surrender. Mao and the commander of the Communist armies, Chu Teh, cabled a rejection of Chiang's 11 August order five days later.

On 23 August, therefore, the commander-in-chief of government forces, General Ho Ying-ch'in, ordered General Okamura Yasuji, commander of Japanese forces in China, to defend Japanese positions against Communist troops if necessary, pending the arrival of government troops. The Japanese were also ordered to recover territory recently lost or surrendered to Communist forces, and offensive operations were undertaken following this order. From late August to the end of September, more than 100 clashes were reported between Communist forces on the one hand, and those of the Japanese and their collaborators on the other, acting as surrogate for the KMT government. As a result of these operations, the Communists lost some twenty cities and towns in Anhwei, Honan, Hopei, Kiangsu, Shansi, Shantung and Suiyuan.[2] Among their gains was Kalgan (Changchiak'ou), then a medium-sized city with a population of 150,000-200,000, and capital of Chahar province. Taken from the Japanese during the final week of August 1945, Kalgan was a key trade and communications centre for goods and traffic moving north and south of the Great Wall. Because of its size and strategic location not far from Peiping, Kalgan became something of a model in urban administration for the Communists and a second capital for them until it was captured by government forces one year later.

The United States also intervened on the government's behalf, transporting approximately half a million of its troops into North China, Taiwan and Manchuria. A force of 53,000 US marines occupied Peiping, Tientsin and other points in the north pending the arrival of government troops. The US War Department order authorizing such assistance had instructed that the principle of non-involvement in the KMT-CCP conflict not be infringed. Yet the order contained an implicit contradiction, since the two parties to the conflict viewed their race to take over from the Japanese as part of their mutual rivalry. The US thus compromised the principle of 'non-involvement' from the start in a manner that would

<hr />

[2] *Hsin-hua jih-pao* (*New China daily news*), Chungking, 17 and 20 Sept., 5, 6 and 22 Oct. 1945 (translated in *Chinese Press Review*, hereafter *CPR*, same dates except Oct. 23 for the last cited). Also *Foreign relations of the United States*, hereafter *FRUS*, *1945*, 7.567–68.

characterize the American role in China throughout the period. The Chinese Communists began at once to protest the American garrison duties and troop movements as US interference in China's domestic affairs.[3]

The presence of the Russians further complicated the clash of interests in China at the end of the Second World War. The Soviet Union entered the war against Japan on 9 August 1945, in accordance with the Yalta Agreements of 11 February 1945. Soviet troops had just begun entering Manchuria when the Japanese surrendered on 14 August, the same day that the Soviet and Chinese governments announced the conclusion of a treaty of friendship and alliance between their two countries. During the negotiations, Stalin had conveyed assurances to the Chinese representative, T. V. Soong, that Soviet forces would complete their withdrawal from the North-east within three months after a Japanese surrender.[4] The deadline for Soviet withdrawal was thus set for 15 November 1945.

The Chinese Communists were in a position to take maximum advantage of those three months during which the Russians occupied the cities and major lines of communications in the North-east, and no one controlled the countryside. During this time, while government forces were leap-frogging over and around them in American transport planes and ships, elements of the Communist Eighth Route and New Fourth Armies were entering Manchuria by junk from Shantung and overland on foot from several northern provinces. They were joined by a small force of North-eastern troops led by Chang Hsueh-szu, a son of the Manchurian warlord Chang Tso-lin, which had been cooperating with the Communists' guerrilla activities against the Japanese in North China. Another son, the popular Young Marshal, Chang Hsueh-liang, remained a hostage to the KMT-CCP united front under house arrest in KMT territory for his role in the 1936 Sian incident.

There is little evidence of direct Soviet military assistance to the Chinese Communists at this time. But large quantities of arms and equipment from the 700,000 surrendering Japanese troops in the North-east did find their way either directly or indirectly into Chinese Communist hands.[5] The soviets also adopted delaying tactics at a number of points to prevent the Americans from landing Government troops at North-east ports. Finally, Chou Pao-chung and remnants of his old Communist North-east anti-Japanese allied army, which had fled across the border into the Soviet Union, returned with Soviet forces in 1945. Other remnants of this army, which the Japanese had effectively destroyed by 1940, emerged

[3] FRUS, 1945, 7.576, 577.　　　　　　　　　[4] Ibid. 612.

[5] China white paper, 1.381. Most of the arms and equipment of the 1.2 million Japanese troops that surrendered elsewhere in China went to the government armies.

from prison and from underground at this time and began reorganizing at once in cooperation with the Communist forces arriving from North China.

By early November, the KMT government was aware that Soviet withdrawal on schedule would mean immediate occupation of much of the North-east by the Chinese Communists. Despite American assistance, the government had already lost the race to organize a military and civilian takeover operation for Manchuria. The Chinese government therefore negotiated with the Soviets who formally agreed both to extend their stay and to allow government troops to enter the region by the conventional routes. New dates were set for Soviet withdrawal, first early December and then early January. The date was extended twice more, by which time the Soviets had more than overstayed their welcome. They did not actually complete their evacuation from Manchuria until early May 1946.

Meanwhile, on 15 November, with some of his best troops transported from the south and deployed along the Great Wall, Chiang Kai-shek attacked Shanhaikuan, the gateway to Manchuria at the point where the Wall meets the sea. He then proceeded to fight his way into the North-east to take by force a region which had been controlled for fourteen years by the Japanese and before that by the family of the Old Marshal, Chang Tso-lin, but never by the KMT government. The still feeble Chinese Communist forces in the region were as yet no match for Chiang's American-equipped units. His strategy to take over the North-east, aided by the Americans and no longer obstructed by the Soviets, thereafter proceeded apace.

The Soviets took advantage of their delayed departure to augment their war booty, dismantling and removing with their departing forces tons of Manchuria's most modern Japanese industrial equipment.[6] With the action shifting increasingly to the battlefield, the continuing negotiations between the antagonists appeared pointless and Chou En-lai returned to Yenan in late November. Yet these economic and political costs paled beside the strategic military error, later admitted by Chiang himself, of transporting his best American-equipped troops directly to the North-east from their deployment area in Yunnan and Burma without first consolidating control of the territory in between. Whether these troops would have been more successful in the battle for North China than they were in the North-east must remain for ever an unanswered question. But some of Chiang Kai-shek's best divisions entered the North-east never to re-emerge. His decision to commit them to the takeover of that region was a blunder that would come to haunt the generalissimo, for it was in

6 *Ibid.* 2.596-604.

the North-east, with the failure of these troops to defeat the Communist forces there, that his cause was finally lost.[7]

Meanwhile, several more acts had yet to be played out on the diplomatic stage. Also in late November 1945 Hurley resigned as ambassador to China, damning certain American foreign service officers as he went for allegedly undermining his mediation effort by siding with the CCP. These charges would fester for years before culminating in the anti-Communist allegations of the McCarthy era.[8] But in December 1945, President Truman immediately appointed General George Marshall as his special envoy to take up the mediator's task cast aside by Hurley. The president instructed Marshall to work for a ceasefire between Communist and government forces, and for the peaceful unification of China through the convocation of a national representative conference as agreed upon by Mao and Chiang during their Chungking negotiations.

The Marshall mission: 1946

Marshall arrived in China on 23 December 1945. The US was just then completing delivery of equipment for 39 divisions of the government's armed forces and eight and a third wings for its air force, fulfilling agreements made before the Japanese surrender. Despite the obvious implications of the American supply operation completed within the context of the developing civil war in China, Marshall's peace mission produced immediate results.

Agreement was quickly reached on the convocation of a Political Consultative Conference (PCC) and a committee was formed to discuss a ceasefire. This was the 'Committee of Three', comprising General Marshall as chairman, General Chang Chün representing the government and Chou En-lai representing the CCP. A ceasefire agreement was announced on 10 January 1946, the day prior to the opening of the PCC. The agreement called for a general truce to go into effect from 13 January, and a halt to all troop movements in North China. The right of government forces to take over Manchuria and the former Japanese-occupied areas south of the Yangtze River was acknowledged by the

---

7 Chiang Kai-shek, *Soviet Russia in China: a summing-up at seventy*, 232–3. Li Tsung-jen later claimed that his advice against this troop deployment went unheeded (*The memoirs of Li Tsung-jen*, 435).

8 Hurley's first charges against the Foreign Service officers were made in his letter of resignation, reprinted in *China white paper*, 2.581–4; also, *FRUS, 1945*, 7.722–44. Among the many accounts now available of this inglorious episode are: O. Edmund Clubb, *The witness and I*; John Paton Davies, Jr. *Dragon by the tail*; Joseph W. Esherick, ed. *Lost chance in China*; E. J. Kahn, Jr. *The China hands*; Gary May, *China scapegoat*; John S. Service, *The Amerasia papers*; Ross Y. Koen, *The China lobby in American politics*; and Stanley D. Bachrack, *The Committee of One Million: 'China Lobby' politics, 1953–1971*. See also Kenneth W. Rea and John C. Brewer, eds. *The forgotten ambassador: the reports of John Leighton Stuart, 1946–1949*.

ceasefire agreement. An executive headquarters was set up in Peiping to supervise the ceasefire and began functioning at once. It was led by three commissioners representing the government, the CCP and the United States. Its truce teams were to be made up of equal numbers of government and CCP personnel, with the American role confined to that of assistance only.

The PCC met from 11 to 31 January 1946 for the declared purpose of seeking a peaceful solution to the KMT-CCP conflict. Great hopes were placed in this conference, if not by the two main antagonists, then at least by all other concerned parties. For a time it was the chief focus of popular attention and even after the hopes were shown to be illusory, the authority of the PCC agreements was invoked by the government to legitimize a number of its subsequent political actions.

The PCC participants, although not democratically elected, were acknowledged by all to be representative of the major and minor political groupings within the Chinese political arena. The participants comprised 38 delegates: eight from the KMT, seven from the CCP, five from the Youth Party, two from the Democratic League, two from the Democratic-Socialist Party, two from the National Salvation Association, one from the Vocational Education Association, one from the Rural Reconstruction Association, one from the Third Party, and nine non-partisans.

Agreement was reached on virtually all political and military issues outstanding between the KMT and the CCP. The agreements concerned: the reorganization of the national government; a political programme to end the period of KMT tutelage and establish constitutional government; revision of the 1936 Draft Constitution; membership of the proposed National Constitutional Assembly which would adopt the revised constitution; and reorganization of government and CCP armies under a unified command.

The PCC provided that a three-man military committee be formed to devise plans for implementing conference resolutions calling for general troop reductions and the integration of CCP forces into a unified national army. This group, the Military Sub-committee, was made up of General Chang Chih-chung for the government and Chou En-lai for the CCP, with Marshall serving as adviser. They announced agreement on 25 February, with plans for a massive troop reduction on both sides. This was to be accomplished within 18 months, at the end of which there would be roughly 840,000 government troops in 50 divisions, and 140,000 troops in 10 divisions on the Communist side, which would be integrated into the national army. Agreement was also reached on the disposition of these forces with the majority of the Communist divisions to be deployed in

North China, reflecting the area of their greatest strength and concentration.

Unfortunately, there was no superior authority capable of enforcing either the ceasefire or the military and political accords. Dependent only on the mutual trust and good faith of the adversaries themselves for implementation, the agreements came apart very quickly once the initial momentum, generated by the arrival in China of General Marshall and the convocation of the PCC, had passed. Perhaps the two main parties to the agreements were sincere in concluding them. From the hindsight of history, they appear rather to have been a cynical manoeuvre entered into by both rivals in order to pacify Chinese public opinion and the American ally, while buying time for the most advantageous possible deployment of their mutual armed forces. In fact, the truth may lie somewhere in between, since both Chiang Kai-shek and Chou En-lai subsequently indicated that genuine disagreement had existed within their respective parties at this time on the merits of working out a compromise accommodation between them.[9] The implication is that the two parties were perhaps still undecided in early 1946, and that the resolve to settle their differences through full-scale war emerged only with the progressive breakdown of the agreements reached at that time.

Right-wing elements within the KMT, opposed to the PCC resolution, were able to revise the party's position on a number of points at a meeting of KMT's Central Executive Committee in March 1946. The two most significant revisions placed curbs on provincial autonomy and provided for the continuation of presidential government, as opposed to the cabinet system approved by the PCC. Subsequently, the KMT also refused to grant the CCP and its political ally, the Democratic League, joint veto power in the 40-member State Council which was to be the highest organ of state power prior to the establishment of constitutional government.

The two parties therefore claimed that the KMT had violated both the letter and the spirit of the original PCC agreements, and refused to participate further in their implementation. The government, undeterred, proceeded unilaterally in accordance with the PCC agreements. The National Constitutional Assembly was convoked in November 1946 for the purpose of adopting the revised draft of the 1936 Constitution. The new constitution was promulgated on 1 January 1947; elections were held later in the year for delegates to the First National Assembly, which met during April 1948, to choose the nation's president and vice president.[10]

[9] Lyman P. Van Slyke, *Marshall's mission to China, December 1944–January 1947*, 1.353–4; and *FRUS, 1949*, 8.358.

[10] On the negotiations over the ceasefire agreements of 10 January see *FRUS, 1946*, 9.1–130. On the PCC and the breakdown of the agreements it produced: *ibid.* 131–77, 177–341; Van Slyke,

Meanwhile, troop reductions and the unification of the armies made even less headway than political reorganization. In this area, the Communists appeared the more intransigent, refusing even to provide the lists of their military units as required by the 25 February military reorganization accord. Blame for the disintegration of the ceasefire, however, seemed to fall about evenly on both sides. For example, General Marshall sought permission in late January to send an Executive Headquarters truce team to the Manchurian port of Yingkou, where clashes were reportedly taking place. The CCP approved but the government initially declined and then dithered over their authority. Truce teams did not actually enter Manchuria until early April, by which time hostilities were already well advanced. In Marshall's view, the government was not only responsible for refusing to honour the ceasefire in Manchuria and to allow truce teams to operate there, but also for numerous other violations of the ceasefire agreement both in South and North China.[11]

The Communists, for their part, had built up their strength so rapidly in the North-east that they were able to challenge the advancing government forces and did so repeatedly. Communist troop movements in Manchuria were technically not a violation of the agreements since the troop movement prohibition applied only to North China and not the North-east. But hostilities then occurred at many points. When the Russians finally began their withdrawal in mid-March, they apparently acted in coordination with Chinese Communist forces which were ready to move in behind them as they evacuated most of Manchuria's major cities, including Mukden (Shenyang), Changchun, Kirin, Harbin and Tsitsihar.

At Mukden, government troops were able to evict Chinese Communist forces within 24 hours. But at Changchun, units led by Chou Pao-chung engaged advance government forces and local militia for three days before entering the city on 18 April. Government forces succeeded in capturing Szupingkai on 19 May, but only after more than a month of fighting. After this defeat, the Communists then withdrew from Changchun and government units occupied that city on 23 May. In North China, the Communists also openly violated the terms of the truce with offensive troop movements in Shantung, along the Tientsin-Pukow railway, and in northern Kiangsu.[12]

Marshall's mission, 1.8-68; Carsun Chang, *The third force in China*, 142-222; and Ch'ien Tuan-sheng, *The government and politics of China*, 317-45, 375-81. The constitution adopted by the National Constitutional Assembly is translated in Appendix D of the latter volume. Conference resolutions and news releases concerning the March 1946 meeting of the KMT Central Executive Committee are in *China white paper*, 2. 610-21, 634-9.   [11] Van Slyke, *Marshall's mission*, 1.49-63.

[12] O. Edmund Clubb, *Twentieth-century China*, 267-71; Lionel Max Chassin, *The Communist conquest of China: a history of the civil war, 1945-1949*, 77-82.

With the ceasefire in disarray, Marshall temporarily withdrew as formal mediator but continued to act as an intermediary between the two sides. In this capacity, he succeeded in arranging a two-week truce for Manchuria commencing 7 June 1946. During that time negotiations were to be conducted, so as to bring about: (1) an end to the fighting in the North-east; (2) the resumption of rail communications in North China, where Communist forces were blocking the vital north-south railway links as well as the Tsinan-Tsingtao line, thus disrupting the northward movement of the government's military transport and southward-bound coal shipments for its industrial base in the Lower Yangtze valley; and (3) the implementation of the 25 February military reorganization agreement. Chiang Kai-shek declared that this would be the last time he would attempt to resolve his differences with the CCP at the conference table, and similar statements appeared in the KMT press.

Marshall resumed formal mediation and the truce was extended to the end of June, but agreement was not reached. The major stumbling block as the truce expired was the Communists' unwillingness to permit government administration of northern Kiangsu following the agreed withdrawal of CCP forces from that region. The Communist side insisted on the continuation of all existing local governments in areas of North China to be evacuated by their troops. By this time, however, the government's plans for a full-scale offensive against the Communist areas were already complete and the CCP was aware of them, making further negotiations a futile exercise.

The failure of the Marshall mission and its implications for US China policy

The Marshall mission was not formally terminated until 6 January 1947. But with the expiration of the truce period on 30 June, and in the absence of the agreements necessary to extend it, the failure of the American peace mission appeared inevitable. A new US ambassador, Dr J. Leighton Stuart, was named to fill the post which had remained vacant since Hurley's resignation. After his arrival in July, Stuart shared with Marshall the increasingly thankless task of mediation until the latter's recall to the US in early 1947. But the fate of their continuing effort had been sealed by the government's coordinated general offensive against the Communist-held areas, which began within days after the expiration of the June truce.

Shortly after the offensive began and apparently not yet aware of its import, the Americans tried one last time to salvage the negotiations. They proposed on 1 August the formation of a five-man negotiating committee with two government representatives, two for the CCP, and Ambassador

Stuart as chairman. Chiang Kai-shek demanded as a precondition wide-ranging Communist troop withdrawals – from virtually all of the areas that were the targets of his offensive. The Communists refused to agree until the status of the local governments in the areas from which they were to withdraw had been solved to their satisfaction. Military operations continued meanwhile and on 19 August, shortly after government forces bombed Yenan, the Communists declared a general mobilization for war throughout the areas under their authority.

With the government attack against the Communist-held city of Kalgan in progress, Marshall recommended to Washington in early October that he be recalled, arguing that the peace negotiations were now clearly being used as a cover for government military operations against the Communist areas. To forestall Marshall's resignation on these grounds, Chiang Kai-shek declared a short truce at Kalgan, which the CCP rejected as unsatisfactory. Chou En-lai, the Communists' chief negotiator throughout 1946, demanded instead a withdrawal of government forces to their positions at the time of the original 13 January truce in China proper, and of the 7 June truce in the North-east. The government declined and its forces captured Kalgan on 10 October.

The government then unilaterally convened the National Assembly. The CCP and the Democratic League refused to participate on the grounds that the KMT had not honoured the terms of the PCC resolutions on government reorganization. Chou En-lai returned to Yenan on 19 November, a gesture marking the formal withdrawal of the CCP from the mediation exercise. In early December, the Communists indicated their unwillingness to accept further American mediation and forwarded to Nanking their preconditions for resuming negotiations, namely, dissolution of the National Assembly and withdrawal of government forces to their January positions. These conditions were naturally unacceptable. Both sides had by now determined that they had more to gain on the battlefield than at the conference table.

As the year 1946 progressed, Marshall's role as mediator had grown increasingly difficult. Although it could not be foreseen at the time, his problems contained all the elements of the trauma that would overtake US China policy in the years to come. The hardening postures of the KMT and CCP toward each other in 1946 were paralleled by a growing resentment on both sides over the role being played by the US. The war party within the KMT – led by the CC clique of the brothers Ch'en Kuo-fu and Ch'en Li-fu – saw the American mediation effort as frustrating their plans to exterminate the Communists, the only solution to the problem in their eyes. This view would later be pursued with great vengeance by sympathizers in the United States.

Perhaps more significant was the general resentment within the KMT government generated by American demands for its reform. Prime Minister T. V. Soong noted, with reference to this gratuitous advice, that in the old days 'for one government to tell another it should do these things would mean war'.[13] Yet Chinese and American leaders both knew that the latter had no means of inducing the former to implement the wide-ranging political, economic and military reforms necessary to revive the government's sinking fortunes. Moreover, KMT leaders were also well aware that however dissatisfied the Americans might be with them, capitalist America would still support them in any showdown with the Communists.[14]

The Communist side was also aware of this basic fact of international political life. But their protestations highlighted the more immediate contradiction inherent in Marshall's position although, to be sure, the Communists did not choose to escalate the pressure on this point until even the pretence of possible success for the mediation effort could no longer be maintained. Nevertheless, Marshall had been placed in the awkward position of attempting to mediate a peace settlement while simultaneously representing a country that was the chief source of aid and support for one of the two parties to the dispute.

Only about half the arms and equipment promised to the KMT government under the 39 army divisions and air force supply programme had been delivered when Japan surrendered. The remainder was delivered later, when the enemy it would be used against was already clearly visible. The US had also aided the government in its race with the CCP to take over the former Japanese-occupied territories by transporting government troops into those areas. In some cases, US marines were even used to hold them in trust pending the government's arrival. On 25 February 1946, the same day the military reorganization agreement was announced, the US authorized the formation of a military advisory group in China to aid and assist the government in developing its armed forces. The group was set up in March. The Americans also contributed US $500 million to the China aid programme of the United Nations Relief and Rehabilitation Administration, the great bulk of which was delivered to the KMT areas. On 14 June 1946, the Lend-Lease 'Pipeline' Credit Agreement was concluded, whereby the US extended additional credit to the Chinese government for the purchase of civilian-type equipment and supplies contracted for during the Second World War but not yet delivered under

---

[13] John Robinson Beal, *Marshall in China*, 330.

[14] For a recent re-statement of this earlier belief, see Nancy Bernkopf Tucker, 'Nationalist China's decline and its impact on Sino-American relations, 1949–1950', in Dorothy Borg and Waldo Heinrichs, eds. *Uncertain years*, 153; and the same author's *Patterns in the dust*.

the wartime lend-lease programme. And in August, after the KMT offensive against the Communist areas had already begun, the Americans concluded yet another agreement authorizing the sale on credit of US $900 million worth of war surplus property to the KMT government for a net sum of $175 million. This 'civilian-type' property included small ships, vehicles, construction materials, air force supplies and materiel, and communications equipment. At the same time, negotiations were under way for a treaty of friendship, commerce and navigation between the US and Chinese governments.[15]

Such assistance may have been entirely legitimate for the recognized government of a major American ally. But within the context of Chinese domestic politics, Marshall's position as an impartial mediator between the rival parties was compromised from the start by his country's continuing strategic support for the KMT government. The Communists escalated their propaganda attacks against this relationship during the summer of 1946, accusing the US of strengthening the government's military power and thereby encouraging the KMT to seek a military solution to the conflict. Implicitly acknowledging the validity of this charge, the US placed an embargo on the shipment of arms and ammunition to China beginning in late July 1946. This was part of Marshall's declared 'efforts to influence China's governmental course of action and the determined stand and plans of political reactionaries, civil and military.'[16]

Nevertheless, the embargo, partially lifted in October and rescinded entirely in May 1947, exemplified the constraints built into Marshall's mission by his country's China policy. The ban came too late to have any restraining influence on the government's war plans or the course of the negotiations. It therefore did little to mollify the Communists. Indeed, any utility it might have had in this respect was almost immediately undermined by the August decision to sell $900 million worth of war surplus property to the government. Yet anti-Communist critics in the US would soon seize upon the embargo as an important issue in their attack on US China policy, claiming that the consequent shortage of munitions was a crucial factor in the defeat of the government's armies.

Hence the American mediation effort pleased virtually no one and accomplished little except to provide Marshall, soon to be named US secretary of state, with first-hand experience as to the futility of attempting to intervene in the Chinese civil war. Lacking the means to induce KMT

---

[15] *China white paper*, 1.225-9, 311-12; also *FRUS, 1945*, 7.527-721 *passim*; Tsou Tang, *America's failure in China, 1941-50*, 429-30.

[16] *FRUS, 1946*, 10.753.

compliance with any of its demands, the US still could not for reasons of its own domestic and international political concerns withdraw support completely from the KMT government in its struggle with the CCP. Thus neither could the gesture of the 1946 arms embargo induce the government to alter significantly its war plans or win any goodwill from the Communist side. Instead, the embargo's only lasting result was to heighten the resentment of the Chinese government ally and its supporters in the United States. Meanwhile, other forms of material aid and diplomatic support for that government continued as it embarked upon the course of all-out war. Perhaps the greatest failure of the Marshall mission was not that it had so little influence on the course of the civil war in China, but that the Americans should ever have assumed their mediation effort might actually do so. That erroneous assumption was part of a more deep-seated belief on the part of many in the United States, growing out of its Second World War role as the chief arbiter of Asia's fortunes, that in one way or another American policy-makers had the power and responsibility to determine the political fate of China.

THE DECLINE OF KMT RULE

The KMT government in August 1945 could claim authority over all the country's major cities, its entire industrial base, and more than three-quarters of a total population estimated at about 450 million. That government had not only won acclaim as the leader of Free China against the Japanese, but had also led China into the arena of world politics where it had come to be recognized as one of the great powers. Hence it was not surprising that Chiang Kai-shek and the government he led gambled on an all-or-nothing solution for their 'Communist problem' at the end of the Japanese war.

The government's armies numbered over 2.5 million men in 1945, more than double the Communist forces, and also enjoyed a clear superiority of arms, equipment and transport capability. Communist forces – with little fighting experience other than guerrilla warfare, with no air force, navy, nor anything comparable to the government's American-trained and equipped divisions – appeared to most observers to be no match for the Nationalists. Chiang and his generals, like the Americans who were supplying and training their armies, were impressed with modern fire-power and expected it to win in China as it had just done against Japan. That this did not happen was a surprise to almost everyone except perhaps the Communists. Before pursuing the course of the civil war of 1946–9, let us look at the contemporary process of decay within Nationalist China.

For the eventual Communist victory was founded upon the weaknesses of the old society and the political establishment which governed it.

Contemporary participants and observers did not need to subscribe to the CCP's theoretical explanations concerning feudalism, imperialism, landlord domination of the countryside, and the leading families' monopoly of the urban economy, to understand the gravity of the KMT's problems. These were clearly visible during the 1940s and were described repeatedly by diplomats and foreign correspondents, as well as an only partially-controlled Chinese press. 'Incompetent and corrupt' was the catchphrase used to describe the government's performance in virtually every sphere from the conduct of war to school administration. In March 1947 Professor Ch'u An-p'ing, founder and editor of *Kuan-ch'a* (The observer), the most popular journal of political commentary in KMT China during the late 1940s, summed up a widely held view:

The basis of the present regime's support has been the urban population: government employees and teachers, intellectuals, and business and industrial circles. At present, no one among these people has any positive feelings toward the Nanking regime. The KMT's tyrannical style of behaviour is causing deep hatred among liberal elements; as for civil servants and teachers, the skimpiness of their salaries since the end of the Anti-Japanese War has caused them to lose hope in the present political regime; the government officials by indulging in corrupt practices and creating every kind of obstruction have caused extreme dissatisfaction in business and industrial circles; and the violent rise in prices due to erroneous financial and monetary policies and the continuation of the civil war is causing sounds of resentment to be heard everywhere among the urban population.[17]

Takeover from the Japanese

After 1927, urban China was KMT territory and its heartland was the main coastal cities together with those along the Yangtze River valley. Most of that area came under Japanese occupation during the Second World War, while the KMT government retreated into the south-west. The beginning of popular urban disillusionment with the government came during the reassertion of its authority over the occupied territories after the Japanese surrender. By the end of 1945, virtually every sector of the population in the nation's major urban centres had acquired specific grievances for which the government's policies and the behaviour of its officials could be held directly responsible.

The hallmark of the period was the takeover process itself, referred to

---

[17] Ch'u An-p'ing, 'Chung-kuo ti cheng-chü' (China's political situation), *Kuan-ch'a*, 8 March 1947, p. 3.

in Chinese as *chieh-shou*. Civilian and military officials representing the government took control of all offices of the Japanese-sponsored administration and all properties, both public and private, owned by the Japanese and their collaborators. All assets were supposed to be either returned to their original owners if taken illegally, or handed over to new owners in accordance with officially established procedures. In the interim, factories were supposed to cease production; the movement of goods in or out of sealed warehouses was prohibited; and occupants of buildings were supposed to vacate them.

As the officials returned and the process unfolded, however, it became common to substitute one or more homophonous characters in writing the term *chieh-shou*, thus transforming its meaning into robbery or plunder. The takeover policies themselves were either ill-conceived or improperly implemented, and there were few institutional safeguards to inhibit abuse. As a result, the takeover process everywhere devolved into an unseemly scramble as the arriving officials raced each other to lay claim to enemy property. Everything was fair game: industrial machinery, public buildings, houses, vehicles, even furnishings and office equipment – all requisitioned for the use or profit of whoever was able to lay the first or at least the strongest claim to them. The carpet-bagging official from Chungking became the symbol of the period. According to popular saying he had but five concerns: gold bars, automobiles, houses, Japanese women, and face.[18]

Meanwhile, hundreds and thousands of workers suddenly found themselves unemployed due to the suspension of industrial production. Its cause was twofold, namely, the takeover process in the coastal areas, and the closure of wartime industries in the hinterland. Factory-owners and businessmen in Free China had expected to be compensated with enterprises taken over from the Japanese and their collaborators, since some had suffered considerable losses in following the government to the south-west during the war. Instead, the government ignored these political obligations, while letting its officials and others take over the industrial wealth of occupied China. But the economy in the recovered areas soon deteriorated to the point where it was often more profitable to dismantle and sell factory machinery, which many did, than to operate it. More than a year after the surrender, the Ministry of Economic Affairs admitted that only 852 of the estimated 2,411 factory units taken over from the Japanese and their collaborators had actually resumed operation.[19]

[18] Wang Chien-min, *Chung-kuo kung-ch'an-tang shih-kao* (A draft history of the Chinese Communist Party), 3.544.
[19] *Ho-p'ing jih-pao*, Shanghai, 13 Nov. 1946 (*CPR*, 27 Dec.).

By late 1946, there were many other reasons for the industrial depression; but it had begun with the disruption created by the bizarre behaviour of government officials racing to take over the wealth left by the Japanese.

These transgressions were compounded by the government's official attitude towards and treatment of the population in the former occupied areas. Initially the government was compromised after VJ Day by its need to rely on Japanese and Chinese puppet troops to maintain 'law and order', that is, it had to rely on the armed forces of the defeated enemy to prevent a Communist takeover of North China cities, and towns. The Japanese and their collaborators were permitted to function for an uncertain period as the Chinese government's political representatives. In the midst of the public outcry over the issue, regulations governing the punishment of collaborators were issued in late September 1946, but they contained a number of loopholes and were only selectively applied. Despite the arrest of several prominent collaborators, there was no systematic effort to settle all the claims and accusations before some impartial court or official body. Many who had served the Japanese in official capacities were entrusted with equally influential posts by the returning government.

While the government was compromising itself over the collaborator issue, however, its officials were returning clothed in self-righteousness inherited from the hardships they had suffered to sustain Free China's struggle in the hinterland. The official posture of condescension was particularly evident in the takeover of Taiwan and Manchuria. Both regions had long been under Japanese rule, Taiwan for half a century. The mutual hostility that developed between the Taiwanese and the takeover personnel from the mainland culminated in the bloodily suppressed rebellion of February 1947.[20] In the North-east, it was commonly said afterwards that a rebellion would have broken out there as well, except that everyone who wanted to rebel simply crossed over to the Communist side.

The issue was perhaps most explicitly stated in the government's policy of educational reconversion which formally stigmatized teachers and students. Special courses in KMT ideology were made mandatory for students by order of the Ministry of Education. Those who had graduated from colleges, universities and middle schools during the occupation were required to pass a written examination in order to retain their status as graduates. Teachers were also supposed to pass examinations designed to test their knowledge of and loyalty to the KMT. The resentment arose not so much over the courses themselves, since the underlying aim was generally supported and the examinations were not particularly rigorous.

[20] George H. Kerr, *Formosa betrayed*, passim.

Rather the issue was the stigma officially attached to the re-education process. In announcing it, the Ministry of Education asserted that all students who had attended schools in areas controlled by the collaborator government were assumed to have been corrupted, and until they were re-educated and their thoughts purged, they would be unfit for further education. As 'puppet students' they should be helped to 'wash off their ideological stains'.[21] But with the public scandal created by the venality of the newly-arrived officials from the south-west, local people initially on the defensive soon rose to question why such individuals should presume to sit in judgment on anyone.

Yet, despite its transgressions during this period, the KMT government suffered little more than a loss of prestige and public confidence. There were few calls for anything more drastic than the restoration of that confidence through the correction of the errors committed. Unfortunately for the government, most of the issues that aroused such disillusionment after the Japanese surrender were never satisfactorily resolved, becoming instead a prelude for what was to follow. Hence, what might have been forgotten as a temporary postwar lapse came to be recognized afterwards as the beginning of the end of popular urban support for the KMT government.

Economic incompetence: the policy of inflationary finance

Monetary inflation probably contributed more than any other single issue during the civil war years to the loss of urban public confidence in the KMT's ability to govern. The policy of inflationary finance began during the Anti-Japanese War when the government was cut off from the coastal and Yangtze River cities which had been its main base of financial support. By 1945, government income, not including bank credits, equalled only one-third of expenditures and the deficit was made up almost entirely by printing-press money. In the resulting inflation average prices rose over two thousand times between 1937 and August 1945. The gap between government income and expenditure continued throughout the civil war years, as did the principal means of bridging it, while the effects of the ensuing hyper-inflation played themselves out to their inevitable conclusion. Perhaps the most dangerous consequence of the decision to rely on printing press money was that it allowed those who made it to believe there was an easy solution to the nation's financial difficulties.

[21] *Chung-mei jih-pao*, Shanghai, 20 Nov. 1945 (*CPR*, 20 Nov.); also, *Shih-shih hsin-pao*, Chungking, 12 Sept. 1945 (*CPR*, 12 Sept.); *Chung-yang jih-pao*, Chungking, 12 Sept. 1945 and *Ta-kung-pao*, Chungking, 11 Sept. 1945 (both in *CPR*, 13 Sept.).

Government leaders not surprisingly opted to finance their war against the CCP in the same manner as that against the Japanese. The result was a government with neither the will nor the ability to do anything but watch over the deterioration of the nation's urban economy.

The inflation provided ready-made issues for a labour force suddenly freed, in August 1945, from the constraints of eight years of Japanese rule and ten years of KMT domination before that. After Japan's surrender the KMT was unable to re-create the network of organizational control with which it had contained the labour movement from 1927 to 1937. Now labour flouted the officially established procedures for the resolution of labour-management disputes. With its old strike-breaking tactics no longer effective, the government had no choice but to accept labour's demand for automatic wage adjustments corresponding to the rise in the cost of living. But this decision, announced in April 1946, not only accelerated the upward wage-price spiral; it also compromised the government's long-standing alliance with business and industry and roused the resentment of entrepreneurs, who felt the concession to labour was contributing to their own rising production costs. Meanwhile, official statistics demonstrated the KMT's inability to pacify labour. In 1936, just prior to the Japanese invasion, there had been 278 strikes and labour disputes recorded for the whole country. By comparison, in 1946 there was a total of 1,716 strikes and labour disputes recorded in Shanghai alone. In 1947 the number for that city reached 2,538.[22]

The government often charged that labour's aggressiveness was the work of professional Communist agitators. The labour movement, at least in Shanghai, did indeed appear to be well infiltrated.[23] But the issues were ready-made and available for exploitation by anyone. As the economy became disrupted by rampant inflation and the consequent contraction of business and industry, urban labour had no form of protection or unemployment benefits, and so refused, as did other sectors of the public on many occasions and in a variety of ways, to comply with the government's pleas for cooperation.

High wage payments were but one of many problems responsible for stifling industrial production. These included continuing increases in energy and transport costs: increasing trade and production taxes; high interest rates; and declining demand due to the reduction in real

---

[22] *China Weekly Review: monthly report*, 31 Jan. 1947, p. 13; *Ta-kung-pao*, Shanghai, 26 Feb. 1947 (*CPR*, 5 March); and *Lih pao*, Shanghai, 7 Jan. 1948 (*CPR*, 12 Jan.).

[23] See for example, Liu Ch'ang-sheng, *et al. Chung-kuo kung-ch'an-tang yü Shang-hai kung-jen: Shang-hai kung-jen yun-tung li-shih yen-chiu tzu-liao chih erh* (The Chinese Communist Party and the Shanghai workers: Shanghai labour movement historical research materials number two), *passim*.

purchasing power. By late 1947 these conditions had resulted in a general contraction of industrial output.

But in order to increase its income, the government allowed the continued existence of an irrational tax system which placed numerous and often exorbitant levies on legitimate business operations, while it left untouched the personal incomes of speculators and profiteers. The government's foreign trade policy also resulted in an unfavourable balance which harmed local producers. These conditions were only partially corrected by reforms in November 1946, aimed at encouraging exports and restricting imports.

The KMT government was vulnerable to the charge that instead of promoting economic development it encouraged bureaucratic capitalism, meaning the use of public office for personal enterprise and profit. Government officials and their associates used their connections to obtain foreign exchange, import commodities, and gain other advantages not readily available to the ordinary entrepreneur. One example was a scandalous government loan in 1946 to Shanghai rice merchants, who used it, apparently with official connivance, for speculative purposes, causing a further rise in the price of rice.[24] Meanwhile, when the government offered bonds for sale during the first half of 1947, capitalists were reluctant to buy. Similarly, some businessmen were said to have large sums of money which they refused to invest in their own enterprises because the profits would have been more uncertain than those which could be gained through speculation. The opportunities for speculation included buying, selling and hoarding commodities; speculating on the securities market; investing in gold and foreign currencies; and lending at black-market interest rates. The result was further cutbacks in production, collapsing enterprises and rising unemployment.

Emergency reforms of 1947 and 1948

The government launched two ambitious campaign-style reform programmes aimed, it was said, at the overall stabilization of the economy. The first was proclaimed on 16 February 1947, when all wages were frozen at their January levels, and ceilings placed on the prices of certain essential commodities, foremost among them rice, cotton and fuel. Trading in and hoarding of gold and foreign currencies by private persons was prohibited. Measures were also introduced to curb the flight of capital to Hong Kong. Yet the failure of the system of price controls was inevitable, first because

---

[24] *Hsin-wen pao*, 12 June 1946; *Shih-shih hsin-pao*, 14 June 1946; *Ta-kung-pao* 19 June 1946; and *Wen hui pao*, 9 July 1946, all Shanghai (all *CPR* for the same dates).

it was limited in scope, and second because it was not uniformly implemented, being rigorously enforced only in the cities of the Shanghai-Nanking area. Production costs therefore continued to rise, as did prices generally, while only the market prices of the essential commodities remained frozen. The price of rice in areas where it was grown soon reached levels higher than in the cities where it was to be sold. The continuous rise in the price of raw cotton made textile production unprofitable. Coal and edible oil were similarly affected. A rice shortage developed. A black market in US dollars was in existence by early April, and most of the essential commodities on the price control list emerged on the black market soon thereafter. The government was unable to provide the guaranteed allocation of these commodities to workers under the proposed factory ration scheme, and decided instead to pay subsidies corresponding to the value of the goods that would have been allocated to each worker. But the subsidies covered only the costs of essential commodities which were increasingly unavailable at the fixed prices, while those of everything else continued to rise. During the month of May, the wholesale price index for Shanghai rose 54 per cent, in comparison with a 19 per cent increase during the month prior to the start of the reform programme. Finally, under the combined pressures created by labour's demand that wages be unfrozen, the collapse of the rice market, and rice riots which spread to more than a dozen cities during late April and May, all of the emergency reform measures were formally abandoned.[25]

With this experience so recently concluded, the 19 August 1948 emergency reform programme was only a last gesture by desperate men foundering in the economic chaos they had themselves created. It was evident from the start that this new reform effort could not succeed because it contained the same flaws responsible for the failure of the 1947 programme. Yet government leaders declared, in August 1948, that this was their last chance; the reform programme had to succeed because they had no other means at their disposal with which to try to stabilize the economy and revive public confidence. When the programme was abandoned at the end of October, the only achievement anyone could think of was that it had allowed the government to confiscate US $170 million worth of gold, silver and foreign currencies from the public, in accordance with the regulation that all such holdings had to be exchanged for the new currency, the Gold Yuan. The most overtly indignant group in Shanghai, where the new programme had been most stringently enforced, was not the long-suffering middle class but business and

[25] Chang Kia-ngau, *The inflationary spiral: the experience in China, 1939–1950,* 72–3, 350–2.

industry – previously a major pillar of KMT support. Some three thousand businessmen, including some of Shanghai's most prominent, had been imprisoned at the start of the campaign. Later they denounced the 'quack doctors' who had used the four million people of Shanghai as 'specimens for an experiment' and demanded punishment for the officials who had devised it. Foremost among them was Chiang Kai-shek's son, Chiang Ching-kuo, who had been responsible for enforcing the reform measures in Shanghai.[26]

The assertion has nevertheless been made that the inflation also cost the government the support of the urban salaried middle class. The main groups making up this middle-income minority were the intellectuals, that is, college professors, school teachers, writers and journalists; and government employees. While this is too simple an explanation for their growing dissatisfaction with the KMT and the government it led, the soaring prices and depreciating currency did create a major burden for this sector of the population. Its impoverishment began during the Anti-Japanese War when inflation reduced their real incomes to between 6 and 12 per cent of their pre-1937 salaries. By 1946, according to one estimate made in Kunming, the real income of college teachers there had been reduced by 98 per cent.[27] And while it could at least decree that the wages of labour be pegged to the cost-of-living index, the government was not able to do the same for its own employees. These included the majority of college teachers whose pay scales as employees in state-financed institutions were comparable to those of other civil servants. The salaries of all public employees were revised upwards on the average of once quarterly. But these adjustments were never proportional to the rise in the cost of living. It was regularly claimed in the late 1940s that the real incomes of teachers and civil servants were not sufficient to maintain their basic livelihood in terms of food, clothing and shelter.

The new impoverishment of the intellectual community did, moreover, help to inspire the students' anti-war movement. Indeed, the professors themselves apparently precipitated the widespread Anti-Hunger Anti-Civil War demonstrations during the spring of 1947, which demanded among other things a reduction in military expenditures and an increase in the budget for education. Clearly, the hardships created by the use of printing-press money to finance the war effort provided one major issue for those opposed to that effort and helped to undermine support for it.

[26] *Ta-kung-pao*, Shanghai, and *Chung-hua shih-pao*, Shanghai, 2 Nov. 1948 (both in *CPR* of same date); Chang Kia-ngau, *Inflationary spiral*, 357–60; Lloyd E. Eastman, *Seeds of destruction*, 172–202.

[27] *Ta-kung-pao*, Shanghai, 30 Aug. 1946 (*CPR*, 31 Aug.); also Chang Kia-ngau, *Inflationary spiral*, 63–5; and Chou Shun-hsin, *The Chinese inflation, 1937–1949*, 244.

But, even so, the intellectuals as a group, like the civil servants, did not actually abandon the government until it was defeated militarily.

Political incompetence: the mismanagement of the peace movement

If their impoverishment was the main fact of economic life for China's intellectuals during the 1940s, their dominant political preoccupation was opposition to the civil war. The government refused to acknowledge the legitimacy of this protest, treating it instead as a contrivance of the Communist underground. Because of this misconception and the repression that followed therefrom, it was the government and not the CCP which ultimately had to bear the heavier burden of public censure for the military conflict.

Thus the student protest movement did not simply spring up full-blown but developed in the course of the students' demonstrations and the government's reaction to them. There were four major demonstrations which aroused nationwide attention. The December First movement (1945) was the smallest of these. The principal action was in Kunming where four young people were killed and several others seriously injured on 1 December 1945 by unknown assailants attempting to intimidate the anti-war protesters. As a result of this violent act, what had begun as a campus anti-war meeting at South-west Associated University came to be known as the first major protest of the period. In late December 1946 and January 1947, a series of anti-American demonstrations protested the alleged rape of a Peking University student by a US marine. The behaviour of the marines was only the immediate provocation. Beyond that the students queried why American military personnel were in China at all and whether they were not in fact participants in the civil war on the side of the government. The momentum generated over this issue grew into the Anti-Hunger Anti-Civil War movement which swept through universities and secondary schools in most major cities throughout the country during May and June 1947. This last big 'student tide', as they were called, merged with the Movement to Protest American Support of Japan between April and June 1948.

Despite local concerns and personalities that were often involved, the basic motivations of the national student protest were the same everywhere. The students' primary demands were an immediate end to the civil war; an end to US backing for the KMT in that war; and a shift in public expenditure from military to civilian priorities. The government responded initially by trying to divert the movement into other channels. Besides the informers and secret agents planted by the authorities in schools where students were most active, students sympathetic to the government, such as members of the KMT San-min-chu-i Youth Corps, were supposed to organize and lead student activities as loyal Nationalist supporters. Yet it was common knowledge that the brightest and most energetic student leaders in the country's best schools were all critical of the government and its war policy.

Nevertheless, government decision-makers remained constricted by their belief that if only the very few 'real' Communist agitators among the students could be eliminated, their movement could be controlled.[28] The consequent harsh tactics in turn further alienated the students. Their leaders, particularly officials of the university self-governing associations, were the chief targets of beatings, arrests and abduction by an assortment of law enforcement personnel. On the basis of tip-offs by informers, the arrest of student activists became a common occurrence. Blacklists of activists and suspected underground Communists were drawn up. These students, if not caught off campus, might be apprehended in night raids on school dormitories. Students arrested or abducted often simply 'disappeared'. Execution was the anticipated punishment for genuine Communist agents if their identity could be ascertained. Torture was also a common means of extracting information.

In this manner, what had begun as a manoeuvre to publicize the students' demands for a peaceful solution to the KMT-CCP conflict soon developed into a movement that challenged the authority of the KMT government. Of greatest significance in this respect were not the students who physically fled to the Communist side, for these seem to have been relatively few in number. More important was the wider resentment engendered by the government's attempts to subdue the protest movement. This probably did not transform the students into Communists or sympathizers. But it did intensify the students' opposition to the government and their refusal to support its war against the CCP.

The reasoning behind the students' demands was spelled out by the older generation of intellectuals in a steady stream of commentary criticizing the war and the disaster it was wreaking upon the nation. They assumed, as did most foreign observers, that the war was likely to continue indefinitely because neither side could defeat the other – the general view until about mid-1948. The costs of the war included the inflation that had completely disrupted the urban economy and the further impoverishment of the rural areas. Besides the printing press, the government's finance was also dependent upon a land tax, compulsory

---

[28] Ch'en Li-fu, head of the powerful CC clique within the KMT, expressed this view in an interview with Doak Barnett (Barnett, *China on the eve of Communist takeover*, 50).

purchase of grain at lower than market prices, and collection of grain on loan. These levies together with additional requisitions to support local needs, the abuses associated with conscription, and the disruptions caused by a poorly disciplined and underpaid army in the field, created in many areas an insupportable burden for the peasantry. The many wartime requisitions meant increased opportunities for graft on the part of local officials, while inflation increased the incentives. In describing conditions in the countryside, the term 'blood-sucking devil' was a favourite epithet of urban-based writers, and was used with reference to the local *hsiang*, *chen*, *pao* and *chia* officials. These constituted the basic levels of administration where, the critics argued, the war was actually creating the very conditions most favourable to the continued growth of the CCP.

The government's failure to win popular backing for its war against the CCP was also evident in the general inclination to blame it more than the CCP for the war. This was acknowledged at the time and a number of reasons were offered in explanation. First, the government, as the legitimate ruler of China, alone had the power to reform itself and end the war. Hence the anti-war petitioners in the KMT areas directed their effort against the government in the hope of compelling it so to act. Second, the Communists had won the balance of popular opinion during the peace negotiations of 1945-6. There was a general belief that they had been sincere, for example, at the Political Consultative Conference in January 1946, when they agreed to several compromises aimed at avoiding all-out war. The government lost credibility in this contest when the KMT Central Executive Committee unilaterally broke a number of conference agreements a few weeks later. Reinforcing this impression was the disruption of a meeting at Chiao-ch'ang-k'ou in Chungking on 10 February 1946, held to celebrate the successful conclusion of the Political Consultative Conference. This was followed by an attack on the offices of the CCP newspaper in Chungking a few days later. Both incidents were commonly thought to have been the work of thugs hired by elements within the KMT opposed to the conference agreements.[29]

Finally, the most important reason for directing anti-war sentiment primarily against the government was the general assumption that the strength of the CCP was being built upon the shortcomings of the KMT. The government was held responsible for not having remedied its defects during twenty years in power. Professor Ch'ien Tuan-sheng presented the

---

[29] For the commonly accepted view of who was responsible for the violent incident on 10 February, see John F. Melby, *The mandate of Heaven*, 88-9. For the KMT right-wing's version of the same incident, see Chung-kuo lao-kung yun-tung shih pien-tsuan wei-yuan-hui, ed. *Chung-kuo lao-kung yun-tung shih* (A history of the Chinese labour movement), 4.1585-7.

political version of this argument in an analysis of the relationship between KMT militarism and the CCP's armed opposition. He traced the military influence within the KMT back to Sun Yat-sen's alliances with warlords. What was then a marriage of convenience soon grew into a force within the KMT that could not easily be eliminated. When reorganized in 1924, the KMT tried to cut itself off from the warlords, but then proceeded to develop a military establishment of its own at the Whampoa Military Academy. In the late 1920s, after the Northern Expedition, the military period of KMT development should have ended; but in fact the period of political tutelage prescribed by Sun Yat-sen had no way to begin. Chiang Kai-shek the military leader had taken over political leadership as well. Chiang then began to fight the Communists, which made military control a continuing necessity. A mutually reinforcing relationship developed thereafter between the growing strength of the CCP and the expansion of Chiang's power within the KMT government. His Whampoa Academy men constituted the core of the military clique within the KMT. Because of their access to Chiang and their control of the army, they became the most important element within the KMT and the government. And once a military faction gained political power, concluded Ch'ien, opposition political parties also had no recourse except to arms. Hence the dominance of the military within the KMT and a government that was ultimately responsible for the civil war. He expressed a common sentiment in his demand that the military be removed from politics and brought under the control of a unified civilian government.[30]

Government responsibility for the war was asserted even more strongly by the economist, Professor Wu Ch'i-yuan. Unlike most of his colleagues, who tended to see the inflation as a consequence of the war, Professor Wu saw the war as a consequence of the government's economic policies. These had resulted in progressive economic deterioration and division of wealth. Middle-income groups, 'except for cliques of corrupt officials', had all seen their incomes eroded by the inflation. At the same time, the peasants were suffering all kinds of oppression, including 'depredations caused by soldiers, bandits, grain requisitions, conscription, and natural disasters'. 'With society in such a state,' queried Professor Wu, 'would there not be a civil war whether or not there was a CCP?'[31] But it was usually Ch'u An-p'ing, the editor of *Kuan-ch'a* (The observer), who

---

[30] Ch'ien Tuan-sheng, 'Chün-jen pa-hu ti Chung-kuo cheng-fu' (China's government usurped by military men), *Shih-tai p'i-p'ing*, Hong Kong, 16 June 1947, pp. 2–3. For a later scholarly treatment based on the same hypothesis, see, Ch'i Hsi-sheng, *Nationalist China at war: military defeats and political collapse, 1937–1945.*

[31] Wu Ch'i-yuan, 'Ts'ung ching-chi kuan-tien lun nei-chan wen-t'i' (Talking about civil war problems from an economic viewpoint), *Kuan-ch'a*, Shanghai, 7 Sept. 1946, pp. 3–4.

articulated popular sentiments most dramatically, as in his response to the American ex-diplomat William Bullitt's recommendation, in 1947, that more US aid be given to the KMT government:

Mr Bullitt advocates aid for this government because it is anti-Soviet and anti-Communist....Is it possible that Mr Bullitt has not considered under what circumstances the CCP has risen to the position it occupies today? In this writer's view, the corrupt control of the KMT is the major factor which has created the rising power of the CCP.... If, in the past twenty years, politics had not been so corrupt and incompetent, how could people have been made to feel that the future is so empty that they have turned and entrusted their hopes to the CCP?[32]

Like the students, however, the older generation did not appear to welcome a CCP-dominated government. Ch'u An-p'ing, for example, looked to the British Labour Party's victory in 1946 to prove that it was possible to realize socialism and democracy without going the way of Moscow. As for the CCP, what he feared was the kind of political life it seemed to espouse. He queried whether the CCP was not really anti-democratic and whether there was much difference between Communists and fascists in this respect. He and his colleagues expressed reservations about the CCP's attitudes toward the individual, toward censorship, toward intellectual and political freedom, and toward literature and art. These liberal intellectuals suggested that if the KMT's performance left much to be desired on all these counts, the CCP would undoubtedly be worse.[33] Nor was anyone willing to argue that the CCP's ultimate aim was anything but the realization of communism. However, they did not think the CCP would ever be able to achieve it by force of arms.

The perceived military stalemate was therefore thought to provide a basis for compromises on both sides, and for a coalition government wherein the two parties could each serve as a check upon the other. General Marshall had given up this cause as hopeless in 1946 but non-Communist non-KMT intellectuals in China continued for almost two more years to hope that it might somehow succeed. The end result for the KMT government was that even key groups within its own constituency refused to support its struggle with the CCP. In the absence of reforms that might have made the war seem worth while, KMT leaders had no means of reversing the popular conclusion that they were sacrificing the interests of the nation as a whole in order to perpetuate

---

[32] Ch'u An-p'ing, 'P'ing P'u-li-t'e ti p'ien-ssu ti pu-chien-k'ang ti fang Hua pao-kao' (A critique of Bullitt's biased unhealthy report on his visit to China), *Kuan-ch'a*, 25 Oct. 1947, p. 5.

[33] Ch'u An-p'ing, 'Chung-kuo ti cheng-chü', 6. Chang Tung-sun, 'Chui-shu wo-men nu-li chien-li "lien-ho cheng-fu" ti yung-i' (Reflections on our intention to strive to establish a 'coalition government'), *Kuan-ch'a*, 5 April 1947, p. 7; Chou Chung-ch'i, 'Lun ko-ming' (On revolution), *Kuan-ch'a*, 25 Jan. 1947, p. 10; Yü Ts'ai-yu 'T'an chin-t'ien ti hsueh-sheng' (Discussing today's students), *Kuan-ch'a*, 24 April 1948, p. 18.

themselves in power. Even so the great majority of students and intellectuals who had raised their voices so persistently in favour of peace and political reform did not actually abandon the government until its fate was sealed on the battlefield.

THE GROWTH OF COMMUNIST POWER

The political mandate extended to the CCP from urban China was thus ambivalent, coming not directly but as a vote of non-confidence for the KMT. The informed urban public was generally aware, however, that the true source of the CCP's growing power lay in its rural social and economic policies. And it was specifically land reform that was most often cited as the basis of the CCP's strength in the countryside, allowing it to 'put down roots' there while the government was doing nothing to meet that challenge.

Yet, contrary to popular assumptions created in large measure by the Communists' own propaganda, their appeal to the peasantry was not based solely on the issue of tenancy. During the Anti-Japanese War they had abandoned land reform in favour of the overtly more moderate rent and interest-rate reduction policy designed to facilitate a united front of all classes against the Japanese invader. In areas immediately threatened by the enemy, even rent reduction was temporarily deferred in deference to that objective. But the policy was evolving in more secure areas, albeit without formal public acknowledgement, until by 1945 it included an attack against a long list of other grievances. These included local tyrants, low wages, corruption, unpaid taxes, spies, bandits, thieves, and even loose women. The party had explicitly redefined the double reduction policy to mean the elimination of 'all the most flagrant exploitations', both political and economic, in the countryside. This was an important development in North China, the Communists' main area of expansion after 1937, because peasants there often owned the land they tilled and tenancy was not always a key issue.

Equally significant were the methods being used to implement the policy. The liquidation struggle, or the struggle to settle accounts of past exploitation, became an important instrument of the party's land policy after 1943, and remained so thereafter. On the basis of the peasants' claims, the amount of past exploitation for whatever reason was fixed and calculated in terms of cash, grain, or other property. The proceeds were collected from the exploiters and redistributed in different ways which became more direct and egalitarian over time. This method not only allowed the peasants to be schooled in all the many forms of exploitation by encouraging them to recall every past injustice; it also drew them directly into the struggle by forcing them to state their claims openly and directly against the power holders in the village. The positive economic appeal to the poor thus contained a complementary destructive force. Together they represented the full political significance of the CCP's land policy. It aimed to destroy not merely the economic superiority of the main 'struggle objects', that is, landlords and rich peasants, but also the political power structure which supported them and which they supported. This then made it possible for the Communists to replace that structure with one loyal to them and sustained by the active interest of the peasants mobilized in the struggle.

Closely associated with the struggle technique and equally significant both in terms of destructive potential and precedents set for the future was the mass movement method of implementing the party's land policy. The guiding principle was Mao's oft-quoted 1927 'Report on an investigation of the peasant movement in Hunan', and especially the concept that, 'in correcting wrongs, it is necessary to go to extremes or else the wrongs cannot be righted'. Applying this principle, Mao wrote in November 1945 that rent reduction had to come as a result of mass struggle, not as a favour from the government, and that in the struggle 'excesses' could not be avoided. But 'as long as it is really a conscious struggle of the broad masses, any excesses that have occurred can be corrected afterwards'.[34] Indeed, such excesses were not only not harmful but were positively beneficial in weakening the 'forces of feudalism'. Li Yü, chairman of the CCP-sponsored Shantung provincial government, placed the concept of excesses or leftism in its operational context in terms of the 'law of the mass movement'. In the initial phase of a movement, excesses could be dangerous since the masses were not yet sufficiently aroused to resist the enemy. Only after organizations had been basically established, cadres trained, activists discovered, and the peasants propagandized was the stage set for the second or struggle phase of the movement. During this phase, leftism and excesses could not be avoided. The cadres were to 'help the masses attack the landlords, smash the reactionary control of the landlord class in the countryside, and establish the superior power of the masses'. Landlord counter-attacks had to be resisted repeatedly until the landlords understood that they had no alternative but to acquiesce. This led to the third stage, when unity became the guiding principle. For leadership cadres, Li explained, the most serious error lay neither in being excessively right nor excessively left, but in misjudging

---

[34] Mao Tse-tung, 'Rent reduction and production are two important matters for the defence of the liberated areas', Mao, *SW* 4.72.

the point at which the limits of one phase had been reached and the next should begin within the context of the developing mass movement.[35] The party had discovered not only the issues that aroused the peasantry but also how to harness the destructive energies of the spontaneous peasant violence that regularly rose and fell in response to local grievances but with little lasting result.

The land policy and the class friction it generated could become the 'mother of all other work' in a village, however, only after certain military and political preconditions had been met in the area as a whole. The basic prerequisite, established during the Japanese war, for the successful implementation of rent reduction was the capacity to protect it against its enemies both military and political. The anti-Japanese resistance mobilized the manpower and the CCP provided the leadership necessary to establish those preconditions all across North China as the strength of the Japanese began to recede in 1943. Such military and political security on so large a scale was a condition the Chinese Communist movement had never enjoyed prior to the 1940s, and it grew directly out of the Communists' successful effort to build a resistance movement against the Japanese.

After 1945, the party's land policy could then become the key to the CCP's relationship with the 'basic masses' of North China and that policy was founded on a direct appeal to the poor and landless. In addition to the material incentives provided by the distribution of the 'struggle fruits', the Communists could also offer a solution for what the peasantry as a whole apparently perceived as its most immediate grievance: the corrupt and arbitrary use of political power and social position within the village community. In exploiting these issues – together with all the others associated with the ownership and use of land, unpaid labour and indebtedness – the CCP had found the formula for transforming the military-political movement it had mobilized to resist the Japanese into one that could build a new indigenous power structure, sustained by popular participation and support once the Japanese were defeated.[36]

The May Fourth Directive of 1946, which formally marked the shift from the reduction of rents and interest rates back to land reform, did not therefore represent that sharp a distinction between the two policies. The directive in fact only acknowledged a development that had been in process within the Communists' liberated areas for several years. In accordance with that development, the directive authorized several

[35] Li Yü, *Lun ch'ün-chung lu-hsien yü Shan-tung ch'ün-chung yun-tung* (On the mass line and the mass movement in Shantung).
[36] Suzanne Pepper, *Civil War in China: the political struggle, 1945–1949*, 229–77.

different methods of transferring wealth from those who had it to those who did not, including land sales and a land contribution scheme. But these were soon abandoned because they were carried out in the absence of any retribution against the exploiters and power holders. The more typical sequence being followed in 1946-7 was the settling accounts struggles followed by increasingly egalitarian efforts to redistribute the struggle fruits. This process culminated in the complete expropriation of the landlords, including their land, houses and all moveable property; and the more or less equal redivision of all village lands and other means of production – as formalized in the 1947 Agrarian Law.

Towards the end of 1946, not long after the start of the government's military offensives against the Communists' liberated areas, Mao summarized the role of land reform in the Communists' defence strategy. He asserted that the peasants had only stood firmly with the Communists against the attacking KMT forces where the May Fourth Directive had been carried out and the land problem solved 'radically and thoroughly'. The peasants, he claimed, took a 'wait-and-see attitude' wherever this had not been done or where land reform was neglected on the excuse of preoccupation with the war. He therefore directed that all areas, regardless of the military situation therein, should lead the peasants in implementing the May Fourth Directive.[37]

Other party documents also indicated clearly that the party regarded land reform as the basic condition for winning a genuine mass response to the army recruiting drives. In early 1947, in twelve counties along the Shantung-Honan border, 50,000 young men were reported to have rallied to the Communist colours in the immediate wake of land reform. It was claimed that a similar recruiting drive in the same area in 1946 prior to land reform had failed to develop into a 'large-scale mass movement'.[38]

Army recruiting was, of course, only the most direct and immediately essential of the military support tasks which the Communists' style of warfare made necessary. The reliance of the regular army on an extensive civilian support network in a 'peoples' war' style of fighting had developed during the Anti-Japanese War and continued after 1945, even though guerrilla warfare now played a less important role. This civilian support network included militia units, local defence corps, women's associations and village peasant associations.

---

[37] Mao Tse-tung, 'A three months' summary', Mao, *SW*, 4.116. The May Fourth Directive was not published, nor Liu Shao-ch'i's authorship acknowledged, until the early 1980s.

[38] Hsu Yün-pei, 'Ts'an chün yun-tung chien-pao' (A brief report on the army recruiting movement), in *I-chiu-ssu-ch'i-nien shang-pan-nien lai ch'ü tang wei kuan-yü t'u kai yun-tung ti chung-yao wen-chien* (Important documents on the land reform movement during the first half of 1947 from the (Hopei-Shantung-Honan) regional party committee), 69–74.

Militia units were organized, ideally several thousand men per county, to support the regular army by being responsible for sentry duty, garrisoning newly-occupied areas, diversionary activities and the like. The militia also protected local party and government organizations, guarded prisoners, suppressed local anti-Communist activities, exposed enemy agents, and kept communication lines open.

Local self-defence corps were organized at the village and district levels. Their main tasks were to transport supplies to the front, and transfer captured war materiel and the wounded to the rear. They organized military transport and stretcher teams in the villages to carry out this work. All able-bodied civilian men between the ages of 16 and 55 were obliged to participate in it as required by the army.

The women's associations maintained village sentry systems to keep watch on inter-village travellers; and also assisted with hospital work and handicraft production to support the war effort.

The village peasant associations were responsible for the army recruiting drives and, similarly, youth associations mobilized their members to join the army and perform rear-service work.

Finally, all civilians in the war zones were expected to obey the orders of military units and of the local political authorities in support of the war effort by repairing defence installations, digging trenches, aiding the wounded, and voluntarily reporting on the activities of enemy agents.[39]

While this was the ideal pattern, its realization depended on first carrying through the land reform process. And this was not as easy as the contemporary accounts issued by the New China News Agency were wont to imply. These portrayed the relationship between land reform and peasant participation on the side of the CCP in terms of material incentives and fear of landlord revenge.[40] Yet intra-party documents from the same period indicated that the causal relationship was not so direct nor the results so easily achieved. Instead, the peasants were often afraid to participate in the struggle because they feared the KMT might return and allow the struggle objects to take their revenge, which indeed many did. These fears were reinforced by the reality of the heavy losses suffered

[39] This outline of wartime support tasks is based on three proclamations issued for the liberated areas of Shantung immediately after the Japanese surrender: 'Shan-tung sheng jen-min tzu-wei tui chan-shih ch'in-wu tung-yuan pan-fa' (Wartime logistics mobilization methods of the Shantung people's self-defence corps), 17 Aug. 1945; 'Chan-shih jen-min chin-chi tung-yuan kao-yao' (Wartime emergency mobilization outline), 18 Aug. 1945; and 'Min-ping hsien ta-tui kung-tso kao-yao' (Work outline of the county militia brigades), all in *Shan-tung sheng cheng-fu chi Shan-tung chün-ch'ü kung-pu chih ko-chung t'iao-li kang-yao pan-fa hui-pien* (A compilation of various regulations, programmes and methods issued by the Shantung provincial government and the Shantung military region), 18–26, 40–2.

[40] For example, Hsinhua News Agency, Yenan, 9 Nov. 1946 (translated in *For your information*, 10 Nov. 1946); and Hsinhua News Agency, dispatched by Sidney Rittenberg for Agence France Presse, 5 Dec. 1946 (trans. in *FYI*, 6 Dec. 1946).

during the government's 1946–7 advances into the base areas. In addition, peasants were often reluctant to leave their families and newly-won plots of land to participate in the war. The reluctance of the peasants was, moreover, mirrored in a lack of resolve on the part of local cadres. For example, some military cadres entertained no genuine class hatred. They had entered the army primarily to resist the Japanese and protect their families. Many were themselves of landlord or rich peasant origin and had never thought of destroying feudalism, much less turning over their family property to the peasants. Since landlords had participated in the anti-Japanese resistance, some cadres even pitied them and sought to protect them. Many local civilian cadres also disliked army recruiting work. They had to try to overcome the peasants' initial reluctance to struggle against the landlords, born of the fear that the KMT would return; and then immediately ask the peasants to defend their new lands against the threat of the advancing KMT armies.[41]

As an antidote for these failings the party prescribed the mass line method of recruiting and outlined the procedure. At village mass meetings, activists should explain the importance of the recruiting campaign and encourage the peasants to express their reservations. All the mass organizations in the village were expected to participate in overcoming the peasants' doubts and the traditional notion that good men did not become soldiers. The peasants' associations would discuss and decide who should and should not volunteer; and the women's groups were called upon to mobilize their members to encourage the menfolk to do so. After the understanding of the villagers was thus developed, emulation campaigns could be launched using the example of progressive villages to influence the more backward. Individual villages should name model families and model peasant volunteers as an inspiration for others. If necessary at this stage, CCP members themselves should come forward and take the lead in joining the army.

In villages where land reform had not yet been thoroughly carried out, the recruiting campaign could develop simultaneously with the division of land and property. Not only would landlord property be distributed to the peasants but in addition, allegedly evil landlords might be imprisoned or even killed. Declared one report: 'It is necessary to destroy their feudal control.... Experience proves that only if the landlord's land

---

[41] *Sung Jen-ch'iung t'ung-chih liu-yüeh shih-wu-jih tsai chung-yang-chü tang hsiao kuan-yü cheng-chih kung-tso ti pao-kao* (Comrade Sung Jen-ch'iung's report on political work at the central Party School on 15 June), 1–2; and several reports compiled in *I-chiu-szu-ch'i-nien shang-pan-nien*, 69–70, 55, 63–4. The peasants' desire to remain on their newly-won plot of land is also highlighted in Chou Li-po's novel about land reform in the North-east: *Pao-feng tsou-yü* (The hurricane).

and grain are all distributed and he falls to the level of a middle peasant … will it be impossible for him to resume his old attitude in the village.'[42] Clearly, the provision of material benefits to the peasantry was not land reform's only objective. Equally important was the destructive force, both economic and political, that the movement generated. Hence one criticism, raised against the land contribution movement that was promoted for a time in some border regions in 1946, was that it accomplished the task of economic redistribution without struggle. As a result, it could not achieve the overthrow of the landlords, nor the political and psychological liberation of the peasants.[43] Mao declared, in October 1948, that during the preceding two years the party had 'mobilized some 1,600,000 of the peasants who obtained land to join the People's Liberation Army'.[44] The link between the benefits proffered and the support received, however, was the struggle movement. For it enabled the Communists to transform the nascent class consciousness, inspired by property redistribution, into the specific kinds of support necessary to fight the war. The key consideration was that the struggle movement with its many targets destroyed the political and economic domination of the rural ruling class.

The subsequent construction of a new village power structure was the final step in making land reform the 'mother of all other work'. Peasants who participated most actively in the multi-featured accusation movement provided new recruits for the CCP and new local leadership. Those who had received land and property became the backbone of the peasant associations and other village organizations. And this was the institutional structure, administered by the peasants themselves, that the Communists could then rely on to assume responsibility for collecting the grain tax, raising a local militia, organizing military transport teams, and exerting social pressure on reluctant volunteer recruits. These were the roots the party put down in the countryside, which could indeed guarantee the supplies of grain and manpower necessary to sustain the military struggle with the KMT government.[45] In this manner, the party was able to harness the destructive energies roused by both the Japanese invasion and the unequal distribution of wealth and power in the Chinese countryside. This achievement highlighted the KMT government's failure to respond

[42] Li Chen-yang, 'Chia-chi pien yu-chi ch'ü t'u kai ti chi-tien t'i-hui' (Understanding a few points about land reform in the Chiahsiang-Tsining guerrilla area), in *Kung-tso t'ung-hsün, 32: yu-chi chan-cheng chuan-hao*, supplement, 15.

[43] 'Kuan-ch'e kuan-hsing keng-che yu ch'i t'ien chi-ko chü-t'i wen-t'i ti chih-shih' (Directive on some concrete problems in the thorough implementation of land-to-the-tiller), in *I-chiu-szu-ch'i nien shang-pan-nien*, 14.

[44] Mao Tse-tung, 'On the September meeting', Mao, *SW*, 4.271.

[45] The classic eyewitness account of land reform during the civil war years is William Hinton, *Fanshen: a documentary of revolution in a Chinese village.*

similarly to the challenges provided by the Japanese and by the inertia of
the country's underlying agrarian foundations.

THE CIVIL WAR 1946-1949

In early November 1946 Chiang Kai-shek confided to Marshall that,
whereas previously the KMT government had been divided on the
question, agreement had recently been reached: force was the only means
of settling the conflict with the CCP.[46] That decision was based on a
persisting miscalculation not only of the Communists' weakness but also
of his own strength. During his year in China, Marshall had tried
repeatedly to warn Chiang about some of the dangers he faced. At one
point, Marshall had even admonished that the government's actions
'would probably lead to Communist control in China' since the 'chaotic
condition now developing would not only weaken the Kuomintang but
would also afford the Communists an excellent opportunity to undermine
the government'.[47]

In October 1946 Marshall appraised the Communists' military strategy,
pointing out to Chiang that although in retreat they were not surrendering.
While they were giving up their cities, the Communists were not losing
their armies and clearly had no intention of doing so since they refused
to stand and fight. With their main strength preserved, they were in a
position to create endless trouble for him militarily.[48] Finally, as he was
preparing to leave China, Marshall again advised Chiang that the
Communists were now so strong a military and political force that the
KMT government could probably not destroy them by military means.
To this Chiang replied that there would be no difficulty in solving the
Communist problem once their military forces were destroyed, which he
was confident could be accomplished within eight to ten months.[49]

His strategy was first to recapture cities and towns on all fronts and
to gain control of the major communications arteries north of the
Yangtze. From these strongpoints and railway corridors, government
forces would then move out into the Communists' liberated areas to
re-establish control over minor points and ultimately the countryside
itself. In accordance with this strategy, government forces launched their
July 1946 general offensive, which Communist historiography marks as
the start of the Third Revolutionary Civil War.

[46] Van Slyke, *Marshall's mission*, 1.353-4.
[47] *Ibid.* 196.
[48] *China white paper*, 1.202.
[49] Van Slyke, *Marshall's mission*, 1.407.

The first year, 1946–1947 : retreat

During the first year of the war from July 1946 to June 1947, government forces captured virtually all the cities and towns in the North-east with the exception of Harbin; recaptured the county towns of northern Kiangsu; occupied Kalgan and Yenan; gained control of large portions of Hopei and Jehol provinces; and cleared much of the Lunghai and Tsinan-Tsingtao railway lines. Thereafter, the fighting moved back and forth across all China's major railway systems north of the Yangtze. In addition to the east-west Lunghai line running from the sea in northern Kiangsu to Paochi near the Kansu-Shensi border, and the Tsinan-Tsingtao line transversing Shantung, these railways included the north-south Tientsin-Pukow (Tsin-Pu) and Peiping-Hankow (P'ing-Han) lines. In Manchuria, the railways that provided the main focal points for the fighting were the Peiping-Mukden line, the only one running from North China to the North-east provinces, and the railways linking the four major cities of Mukden, Szupingkai, Changchun and Kirin. As the fighting developed, the two main theatres of the war were Manchuria and east China, that is, northern Kiangsu and Shantung.

Communist forces were renamed the People's Liberation Army (PLA) in July 1946. They remained largely on the defensive before the government advance, following a policy of strategic withdrawal from the towns back to the countryside. In September, Mao Tse-tung outlined the strategy and tactics the PLA would follow. During the Anti-Japanese War, explained Mao, the dispersal of Communist forces into small units for guerrilla warfare had been primary and the concentration of forces for mobile war supplementary. With the changing conditions of the civil war, the position of the two would be reversed. However, the government's forces were on the offensive, stronger and better armed than those of the Communists. Hence the latter's time-honoured operational principle of 'concentrating a superior force to wipe out the enemy forces one by one' had to remain unchanged until the power balance could be reversed.

Complete annihilation and quick decision were the hallmarks of this kind of fighting. Annihilation of enemy units had become the PLA's main source of weapons and an important source of its manpower as well, since captured enemy soldiers were regularly integrated into the Communist armies. The objective of wiping out the enemy's forces was to destroy his ability to fight, not to win territory. The purpose of seeking a quick solution was to permit a swift escape with a minimum of casualties in the event that the enemy could not be destroyed. 'Using this method we shall

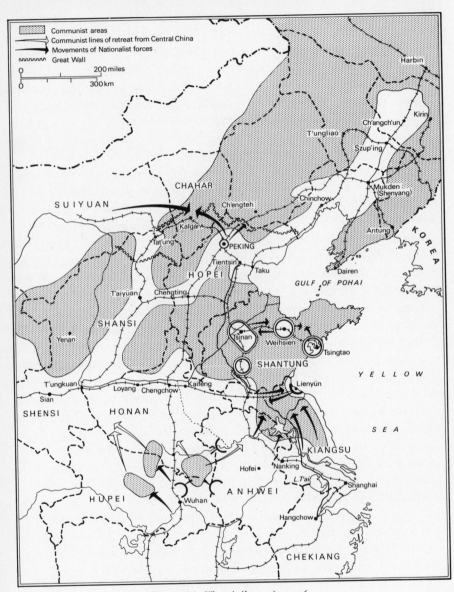

MAP 17(a). The civil war in 1946

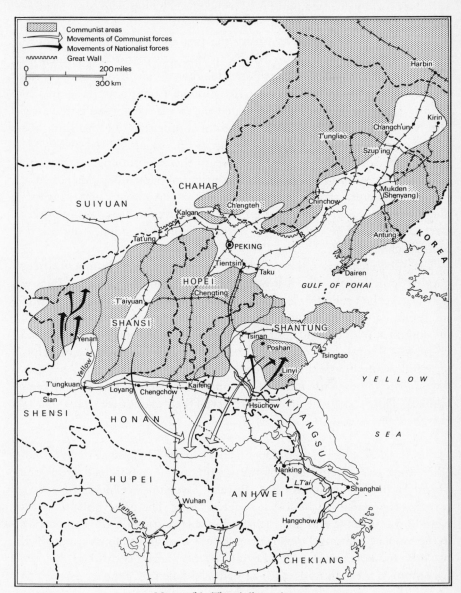

MAP 17(b). The civil war in 1947

win,' asserted Mao. 'Acting counter to it we shall lose.'[50] Here in summary form were the operational principles which would soon become famous.

The government offensive during the first week of July 1946 moved to surround Communist units led by Li Hsien-nien and Wang Chen on the Honan-Hupei border north of Hankow. They broke out of the encirclement and made their way back to the Communist base area in Shensi. The government had eliminated the threat they posed in the area, but the forces themselves survived to fight another day. In Shantung, the government declared the Tsinan-Tsingtao line to have been cleared of Communist forces on 17 July. But due to their continuing harassment, railway traffic still had not resumed by the end of September. Also in July, government units crossed the Yellow River and moved into southern Shansi. In the eastern part of the province, however, Communist forces were able to cut the railway line running from the capital, Taiyuan, to Shihchiachuang.[51]

The July offensive in northern Kiangsu began with government forces moving north from the Yangtze and east from the Tientsin-Pukow railway. At the time, the Communists controlled twenty-nine counties in the region. By the following spring, government forces had retaken all the county seats there and county governments were being re-established under KMT control. Everywhere, the Communists followed the principle of withdrawing before the advance of a superior force. The army regulars retreated together with most of the militia, the party cadres and their families. This strategy of survival preserved their main forces but at heavy cost.

Shansi-Hopei-Shantung-Honan. Documents captured by government armies when they had entered one of the Communists' major base areas, the Shansi-Hopei-Shantung-Honan Border Region (Chin-Chi-Lu-Yü), revealed the extent of the losses suffered there. The government's gains were both extensive and unanticipated in that region. Of the 64 counties in the Hopei-Shantung-Honan sub-region, for example, 49 were occupied by government forces. Of the 35 county seats controlled by the Communists there in mid-1946, 24 had also fallen by January 1947. The CCP had not expected this. They had to revise their plans and began preparing for a long-term guerrilla war. Party documents spelled out the strategy: the Communists' regular army units and militia would remain intact while the enemy's units were gradually being destroyed. With 80-90

---

[50] Mao Tse-tung, 'Concentrate a superior force to destroy the enemy forces one by one', Mao, *SW*, 4.103-7.   [51] *FRUS, 1946*, 10.231-3.

per cent of his forces on the attack, Chiang Kai-shek had no source of replacements. 'So long as we keep up our spirits and continue to destroy Chiang's forces coming into our territory,' noted one of the documents, 'then we will not only stop the enemy's offensive, but must also change from the defensive to the offensive and restore all of our lost area.'[52] The strategy was sound, but exhortations were not enough to keep spirits up during the bleak winter of 1946-7.

The principle of withdrawal as a tactic of guerrilla warfare should have included the evacuation of the local population as well as the military and political units, the objective being to save human life, village organization, and the grain stores. In 1946, however, the villages were not prepared for the reversion to guerrilla warfare conditions. As a result, cadres and defence forces fled and unarmed peasants paid with their lives and property while the village organizations were destroyed. As in northern Kiangsu, local KMT-sponsored governments were quickly set up to replace them. Following soon after came the return-to-the-village corps (hui hsiang t'uan). These were armed units led by landlords and others bent on re-establishing their position. They began settling accounts of their own, seizing back the land and grain that had been distributed by the Communists to the peasants. Reports of revenge and retaliation abounded.[53] The documents acknowledge that thousands of peasants were killed in this region. Destroyed with them during only a few months was an old Communist base area that had taken nearly a decade to build. In districts subsequently recaptured, returning Communist forces were cursed by the peasants for having failed to protect them. The peasants were unwilling to restore peasant associations, form new militia units, or even attend an open meeting, so little faith did they have in the staying power of the Communists in such areas.[54]

The plans for another long-term guerrilla war like that waged against the Japanese did not fully materialize, however, because by May 1947 the government's offensive had already begun to weaken. Its forces were now spread too thinly across a vast area, unable to occupy minor keypoints as the Japanese had been able to do at the height of their penetration of

[52] Ch'ü tang wei, 'Kuan-yü k'ai-chan ti-hou yu-chi chan yü chun-pei yu-chi chan te chih-shih' (Directive on developing and preparing guerilla warfare in the enemy's rear), 20 Nov. 1946, *Kung-tso t'ung-hsun, 32: yu-chi chan-cheng chuan-hao* (Work correspondence, no. 32: special issue on guerrilla warfare), 49-50; also, Ch'ü tang wei, 'Chi-lu-yü wu-ko yueh lai yu-chi chan-cheng te tsung-chieh yü mu-ch'ien jen-wu' (A summary of the past five months of guerrilla war in Hopei-Shantung-Honan and present tasks), 2 Feb. 1947, *Kung-tso t'ung-hsun, 32*, p. 37.

[53] For an eyewitness account of these incidents, see Jack Belden, *China shakes the world*, 213-74.

[54] 'Chi-lu-yü wu-ko yueh...', 42; Kuan-yü k'ai-chan ti-hou...', 48-52; and 'P'an Fu-sheng t'ung-chih tsai ti wei tsu-chih-pu chang lien-hsi hui shang te tsung-chieh fa-yen' (Statement by Comrade P'an Fu-sheng at a joint conference of organization department heads of the sub-district party committees), 8 March 1947, in *I-chiu-szu-ch'i-nien shang-pan-nien*, 38.

this same region. Meanwhile, the main forces of the Communists' regular army, still largely intact, had stopped retreating and had been able to launch a number of small counter-attacks. In Shantung, Communist forces were beginning to seize the initiative, and in Manchuria they were already engaging in limited offensives. The party was claiming that a total of ninety enemy brigades had been destroyed nationwide and that when the figure reached one hundred the military balance would favour the Communist side.[55]

In fact, the military balance did shift rapidly in 1947. US military analysts had predicted in September 1946 that the government offensive would bog down within a few months due to overly extended communications lines which would require ever more troops to defend. These same analysts, however, foresaw a protracted stalemate due to the superior training and equipment of the government forces: foreign observers 'generally agreed that the Communists cannot win either in attack or defence in a toe-to-toe slugging match with National Government forces'.[56]

No one anticipated the speed and skill with which Communist commanders would be able to transform their anti-Japanese guerrilla experience into campaigns of mobile warfare. The Communists were soon deploying larger units than they had used against the Japanese to harass and destroy their enemy's forces piecemeal while preserving and building their own strength. Losses were replaced by integrating militia units and captured enemy soldiers into the regular armies, and by large-scale military recruiting campaigns that accompanied land reform in the Communist areas in 1946-7. The development of Communist political power in the countryside that was an integral part of land reform also made possible the civilian support work necessary to sustain these military operations in areas that had not borne the brunt of the 1946 government offensive.

The North-east. The earliest successful application of this strategy occurred in Manchuria under the direction of Lin Piao, overall commander in the North-east. His forces had been pushed north of the Sungari River by the end of 1946, and government troops were poised for a spring offensive against their final objective, Harbin. But Lin then began a series of hit-and-run raids into government territory, which would allow him to seize the initiative in Manchuria by midsummer and culminate in decisive

---

[55] Chang Erh, 'Chiu-ko yueh yu-chi chan-cheng tsung-chieh yü chin-hou jen-wu' (A nine-month summary of the guerrilla war and future tasks), May 1947, *Kung-tso t'ung-hsun, 32*, 19.
[56] *FRUS, 1946*, 10.235-6.

victory two years later. His timing was appropriate for a strategy of surprise and feint, since the onset of the bitterly cold North-eastern winter was an unlikely season to initiate military manoeuvres. In November 1946, when Lin Piao's forces first launched a small diversionary attack across the frozen Sungari, the significance of their action was not apparent. After this brief foray southwards they quickly withdrew. An estimated force of 60,000 men crossed the river again on 6 January 1947. This time government troops suffered heavy casualties during at least one engagement and were able to take few prisoners before the intruders withdrew. Government commanders were therefore apprehensive as they anticipated a third drive, which occurred in mid-February. But it was over by the end of the month. Lin Piao's units withdrew quickly rather than meet a concentration of government forces, which this time refused to be trapped as they had been during the January operations.

The fourth Communist drive across the Sungari lasted from 7 to 18 March 1947. It inflicted heavy damage on one government division and captured large quantities of arms and ammunition before again retreating. The significance of these limited military excursions was now apparent: government forces had been weakened and, more important, their strategic plans for the North-east disrupted. The threat to Harbin was delayed and the Communists' position strengthened. Lin Piao then launched his fifth drive across the Sungari in May 1947, embarking on a well-coordinated campaign which marked the beginning of the end of the battle for Manchuria. A force of 400,000 men participated in the May-June operations with advances in central, southern and south-western Manchuria. The target of the main force was Szupingkai, midway between Manchuria's two main cities, Changchun and Mukden. During the five-week seige of Szupingkai, the attacking Communist troops suffered some 40,000 casualties and could not prevent the arrival of government reinforcements sent to relieve the Szupingkai garrison. After lifting the seige of the city on 30 June and withdrawing across the Sungari, Lin Piao personally accepted responsibility for the tactical errors that led to the government's defensive victory at Szupingkai.

Despite Lin's defeat, however, his North-east Field Army had gained the initiative and would retain it until final victory the following year. Government troops had been forced to abandon their outposts on the north bank of the Sungari and between the river and the Changchun-Kirin sector, advancing the front line some 150 miles south of its position six months previously. The government-held cities of Changchun, Kirin and Mukden were isolated by the destruction of their connecting railway lines, some of which were not restored until after the war. Government forces suffered losses in arms, supplies, manpower, and morale from which they also never recovered.[57]

As the Communists moved on to the offensive in the North-east and elsewhere, government armies lapsed into a strategy of static defence. Typically they would either withdraw too late from over-extended strongpoints which had ceased to have any strategic value; or they would remain inside them behind walls and trenches leaving the initiative to their adversary to lay seige or not as he chose. The cause of the government's developing Manchurian debacle, according to US military analysts at the time, was the initial over-extension of its forces and the ineptitude of their leadership, most notably that of their commander, General Tu Yü-ming. Yet the transfer of command in the North-east to General Ch'en Ch'eng in mid-1947, after the Communists' fifth offensive, and his removal in early 1948 after the sixth offensive, did little to retrieve the government's declining fortunes in the region. Its forces were still superior in equipment and training. But it was increasingly apparent that the Communists excelled in strategy and tactical application, as well as morale or fighting spirit and sense of common purpose.

The morale factor naturally had many roots. Besides the negative effects of corruption, incompetence, and losing strategies on the KMT side was, especially in the North-east, the issue of regionalism. A key goal of the government's takeover in the North-east after the Second World War was to prevent the re-emergence there of the semi-autonomous power base dominated by the family of the Old Marshal, Chang Tso-lin. Consequently the overwhelming majority of the troops sent to the area were units from elsewhere in China. The government partitioned the three North-east provinces into nine administrative divisions and filled virtually all the top posts therein with outsiders. The government's local allies tended to be landlords and others who had collaborated with the Japanese, since these were the only elements loyal neither to the Communists nor to the Young Marshal, Chang Hsueh-liang, son and heir apparent to Chang Tso-lin. Perhaps because of his continuing popularity, the Young Marshal was kept under house arrest for his role in kidnapping Chiang Kai-shek during the Sian incident and was removed to a more secure exile on Taiwan, although his release had been widely expected.

---

[57] This account of the early Sungari River offensives is based on the following accounts: *Civil war in China, 1945-50*, tr. Office of the Chief of Military History, US Dept. of the Army, 81-3; *Military campaigns in China, 1924-1950*, tr. W. W. Whitson, Patrick Yang and Paul Lai, 125-9; William W. Whitson and Huang Chen-hsia, *The Chinese high command: a history of Communist military politics, 1927-71*, 306-9; and *FRUS, 1947*, 7.26-7, 36-7, 49-50, 88-9, 130-1, 134-7, 157-9, 166-8, 171-3, 178-81, 192-3, 195-6, 198-9, 203, 208-12, 214-17, 240-1.

After the Japanese surrender, initial support for the KMT in the North-east appeared genuine according to contemporary accounts. But the 'southerners' soon wore out their welcome. Resentment created by their discriminatory takeover policies and the venality of their officials quickly produced a resurgence of regionalism. Regional loyalties might not have weighed so heavily had the government's record in the North-east been less open to criticism. People in the North-east, as in Taiwan, a region with an even longer history of Japanese rule, were often heard to comment that Japan had given them better government than the KMT. In particular, the government's effort against the Communists in the region could hardly have succeeded without the participation of local leaders. Yet so great was the KMT suspicion of them and the power they represented that it spurned even such aid as they were willing to offer. Li Tsung-jen in his *Memoirs* traces this error to Chiang Kai-shek himself, who remained 'prejudiced against native Manchurians'. Thus a locally formed North-east Mobilization Commission volunteered to organize a defence force to fight the Communists. But the offer was refused, although government commanders were never able to organize an effective local guerrilla force themselves. General Ma Chan-shen, a cavalry officer who had served under both the Old and Young Marshals, agreed to work with the government and was made a deputy commander of the North-east Command, but he was never given anything to do nor any troops to lead. Meanwhile, government commanders in the North-east were obliged to rely on 'outsiders' as their major source of troop replacements. Due to the failure of their recruiting drives in the North-east, government forces had to bring replacements for their lost and damaged divisions from areas inside China which could ill afford to lose them.[58]

The Communists took full advantage of the popular resentment these measures aroused. They avoided the central government's arrogant attitude toward the people of the North-east and used local talent wherever possible. Most of the surviving units from the old North-east army of Chang Tso-lin and Chang Hsueh-liang went over to the Communists, as did one of the latter's younger brothers, General Chang Hsueh-szu. The Communists welcomed them as allies and allowed them to retain their identity as a non-Communist force under the overall command of Lin Piao. As the Communist administered areas expanded, the North-east Field Army was able to replenish its regular units by recruiting locally; it organized an effective second-line force of local irregulars and mobilized more than a million civilian support workers to serve under its logistics command.

[58] Li Tsung-jen, 434; *FRUS, 1947*, 7.141–2, 144–5, 211–12, 232–5.

A contemporary writer summarized the Communists' successes:

It should be known that when the Chinese Communists pull up the railway tracks, or bury land mines, or explode bombs, it is not the Communists that are doing it; the common people are doing it for them. The Chinese Communists had no soldiers in the North-east; now they have the soldiers not wanted by the central government. The Chinese Communists had no guns; now they have the guns the central government managed so poorly and sent over to them, and sometimes even secretly sold to them. The Chinese Communists had no men of ability; now they have the talents the central government has abandoned.[59]

There could be few better examples of how poorly the KMT government was served by its habit of disregarding popular demands and sensibilities.

Shantung. The Communists' retreat in the important Kiangsu-Anhwei-Shantung sector was more difficult to reverse than that in Manchuria. Government forces were not as over-extended in this region, and the Communists lacked the safe sanctuary for retreat that Lin Piao enjoyed north of the Sungari. Nevertheless, the commander of Communist forces in east China, Ch'en Yi, used the same strategy and tactics to equal advantage. In Shantung, Communist troops under Hsu Shih-yu were defeated at Kao-mi in early October 1946, in a relatively large-scale action fought for control of the Tsinan-Tsingtao railway. This was reopened under government control and the Communists were reported to have suffered some 30,000 casualties before retreating northward. Then in early January 1947, Communist units retreating from northern Kiangsu joined with others from central Shantung to counter-attack their pursuers at Tsao-chuang in southern Shantung. Government forces were defeated with the loss of some 40,000 men and twenty-six tanks, with which the Communists began building an armoured column of their own. Ch'en Yi could not hold his newly-won positions, but evacuated his headquarters in Lin-yi county town in time to successfully ambush part of the force sent to surround him. The ensuing defeat of government forces in the vicinity of Lai-wu in February cost them another 30,000 men and control of the Tsinan-Tsingtao railway, which was again closed to through traffic.

The government's answer was a major campaign against Ch'en Yi's base in the I-meng Mountains during April and May 1947, using some twenty divisions, about 400,000 men, against an estimated 250,000 Communists. But government losses were again heavy, including 15,000 men claimed

---

[59] Ch'ien Pang-k'ai, 'Tung-pei yen-chung-hsing tsen-yang ts'u-ch'eng-ti?' (What has precipitated the grave situation in the North-east?), *Ch'ing-tao shih-pao* (Tsingtao times), 19 Feb. 1948, reprinted in *Kuan-ch'a* (The observer), Shanghai, 27 March 1948, p. 16.

to have been killed or wounded during the epic battle of Meng-liang-ku in south-central Shantung, from 14 to 16 May. The government's 74th Reorganized Division, veteran of many encounters with Communist forces in the region during the preceding year, was completely annihilated. With the majority of his troops dead on the battlefield, the division commander, Chang Ling-fu, and his staff committed suicide. Still outnumbered, however, Ch'en Yi was finally forced to withdraw from the field in July, leaving government forces to claim victory at the battle of Nan-ma in central Shantung. But the bulk of Ch'en's army was left to re-group and fight again.

KMT military historians subsequently provided a candid assessment of Communist strengths and government errors during the 1947 Shantung campaigns: government commanders failed to judge Ch'en Yi's intentions and so failed also to contain his forces as they retreated out of northern Kiangsu. Later, in the vicinity of Tsao-chuang, government forces crowded the road and moved too slowly, stopping to rest along the way. Ultimately they were trapped by their strategy of defending points and lines, while the Communists' main force remained essentially intact. With their front line too widely extended and without sufficient mobility, government forces were unable to prevent individual units from being isolated, surrounded, and crushed individually. They lacked experience in night fighting. Coordination was poor between ground, air, and artillery units. And the tank battalion was immobilized by rain and mud.

The adversary, by contrast, was lightly equipped and able to move rapidly into and about the battle area. The Communists' use of 'shifting forces' at Tsao-chuang was typical. They outmanoeuvred their opponents through swift troop movements from one point to another, sabotaging the government's communications and attacking its troop reinforcements in the process. When Ch'en Yi's main force withdrew form Lin-yi, it moved secretly at night along paths in the hills beside the main road. Air reconnaissance failed to detect this and government forces were consequently ambushed from trenches dug along the road. The defeat at Meng-liang-ku was also blamed on faulty intelligence and the failure of air reconnaissance. Thinking Ch'en Yi's main force had moved much further north, the 74th Division was thus surprised and encircled in a locality where sustained defence was impossible. Moreover, central Shantung had long been Communist territory and its manpower and materiel were thoroughly mobilized. The result was fast accurate intelligence and a well-organized supply system. By contrast, government communications were never secure, its troop replacements always arrived late, and supplies were insufficient. 'Compared with the Communists,' noted the military historian's account, 'all our intelligence, propaganda, counter-intelligence and security were inferior.'[60]

The second year, 1947–1948: counter-attack

At the end of summer, 1947, Mao evaluated the results of the first year of the war and spelled out plans for the second. Chiang Kai-shek had committed 218 of his total 248 regular brigades and had lost over 97 of them, or approximately 780,000 men by Mao's reckoning. Mao reported CCP losses as 300,000 men and large amounts of territory occupied by the advancing government forces. The main task for the second year would be to abandon the strategy of withdrawal and carry the fight directly into government territory. The secondary task was to begin taking back the areas lost during the preceding year and destroy the occupying forces.[61]

Central and North China. In the summer of 1947, the Communists launched the second phase of the war with a developing nationwide counter-offensive. Liu Po-cheng, the 'one-eyed general', commander of the Shansi-Hopei-Shantung-Honan Field Army, on 30 June dramatically led 50,000 men across the Yellow River in south-western Shantung, diverting government forces from their campaign against Ch'en Yi farther east. While Ch'en retreated into Shantung, Liu's forces marched across the Lunghai railway into Honan ending in a thrust 300 miles to the south, where he set up a new base area in the Ta-pieh Mountains on the Hupei-Honan-Anhwei border, the site of the old O-Yü-Wan soviet established in the 1920s.

In a related action in late August, a smaller force of 20,000 men from Liu's army led by Ch'en Keng crossed the Yellow River in southern Shansi, moving south into the Honan-Shensi-Hupei border area and then linking up with Liu's columns. A month later, Ch'en Yi led part of his East China Field Army back through south-western Shantung and into the Honan-Anhwei-Kiangsu Border Region where they could compensate for the movement of Liu's army out of the area. The Communists had thus pushed the war southward into government territory in Central China and opened up a new theatre of operations between the Yellow and Yangtze Rivers. These initiatives brought together the forces of Ch'en

---

[60] *Civil war in China*, 86–99; also, *Military campaigns*, 139–45; Whitson and Huang, 230–9; and *FRUS, 1947*, 7.27, 58–9, 68–9, 72–3, 171–2, 244.

[61] Mao Tse-tung, 'Strategy for the second year of the war of liberation', Mao, *SW*, 4.141–2.

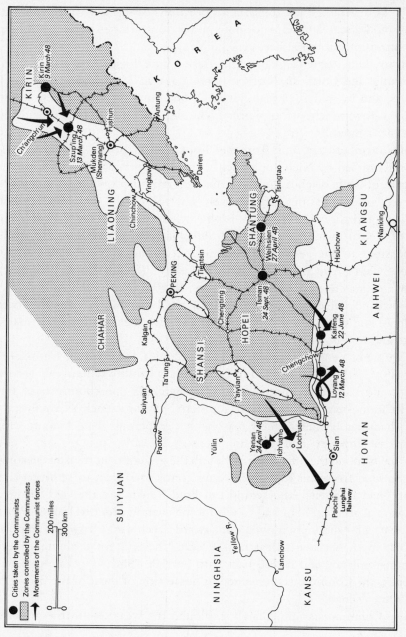

Legend:
- Cities taken by the Communists
- Zones controlled by the Communists
- Movements of the Communist forces

200 miles
300 km

KIRIN
Kirin
9 March 48
Ch'angch'un
Szup'ing
13 March 48
Mukden
(Shenyang)
Fushun
Antung
Dairen
Yingkow
Chinchow
LIAONING
KOREA
CHAHAR
Kalgan
Ta'tung
PEKING
Tientsin
Chengting
HOPEI
SHANSI
Taiyuan
SHANTUNG
Tsingtao
Weihsien
27 April 48
Tsinan
24 Sept 48
Chengchow
Kaifeng
22 June 48
Loyang
12 March 48
Hsüchow
KIANGSU
Nanking
ANHWEI
HONAN
Lochuan
Sian
Ichuan
Yenan
24 April 48
Paochi
Lunghai
Railway
Yülin
SUIYUAN
Paotow
Suiyuan
NINGHSIA
Lanchow
KANSU
Yellow R.

MAP 18. The CCP offensive, spring and summer 1948

Yi, Liu Po-ch'eng and Ch'en Keng, positioning them to coordinate some of the most strategically important operations of the war. In the interim they could attack all the major communications arteries in Central China and interrupt rail traffic between the Yangtze valley and the north.[62]

Meanwhile, other units of the East China Field Army in eastern Shantung and northern Kiangsu were fighting a succession of minor battles, and by mid-1948 had gained all Shantung province except a few isolated government strongpoints including the capital, Tsinan, and the port of Tsingtao.[63]

In November 1947, units from the Chin-Ch'a-Chi (Shansi-Chahar-Hopei) Field Army led by Nieh Jung-chen won an important victory with their capture of Shihchiachuang. With this key rail junction the Communists gained large quantities of materiel; control of the Peiping-Hankow railway; and the site for a new capital which they had lacked since the fall of Yenan in March 1947. The Shihchiachuang campaign also made it possible to merge the Communists' two main North China base areas – Chin-Ch'a-Chi and Chin-Chi-Lu-Yü (Shansi-Hopei-Shantung-Honan) – into one continuous territory. In addition, by the end of 1947 they had gained possession of most of the Inner Mongolian provinces of Jehol and Chahar, and all of Shansi and Hopei except for a few major cities and towns.

Capture of Yenan had provided a psychological boost for the Nationalist war effort, although it proved to be a military liability tying down troops that could have been more useful elsewhere. As one commentator put it, Hu Tsung-nan's removal from southern Shansi to attack Yenan in early 1947 had merely traded thirty reasonably prosperous Shansi counties for forty-five impoverished ones in Shensi.[64] In early spring 1948, P'eng Te-huai went on the offensive. Although the government transferred some 20,000 men from the Kaifeng-Loyang sector in Honan to reinforce Hu Tsung-nan in Shensi, they could not hold Yenan and the two changed hands in April 1948. Hu had to abandon Yenan in order to pursue P'eng Te-huai, who suddenly moved out toward Szechwan. P'eng was stopped in May by a decisive defeat near Paochi, the western terminus of the Lunghai railway, and forced back into northern Shensi. Yet despite this setback, the Communists remained in possession of most of the province including Yenan.

The Communists immediately exploited the weakness in the govern-

---

[62] Mao Tse-tung, 'On the great victory in the North-west', Mao, *SW* 4.215–16n; Whitson and Huang, 174–6; *FRUS, 1947*, 7.269–70.

[63] Mao, *SW* 4.217n.

[64] Li Tzu-ching, 'Chin-nan chieh-fang ch'ü ti tou-cheng ch'ing-hsing' (The struggle situation in the liberated districts of south Shansi), *Kuan-ch'a*, 6 March 1948, p. 15.

ment's Honan defences, created by the transfer of forces into Shensi, by moving against Loyang on the Lunghai railway. The city changed hands three times, ending in victory for Ch'en Keng's forces in early April 1948. CCP units were then in a position to capture Linfen, the last government stronghold in southern Shansi, in mid-May, linking up the Communist areas of Shansi with those of Liu Po-ch'eng's base in Central China. By the end of the month the armies of Ch'en Yi, Ch'en Keng and Liu Po-ch'eng, under the overall command of Ch'en Yi, had converged on Kaifeng in a coordinated operation that lasted for several weeks. They occupied the city, capital of Honan, in mid-June. Although Ch'en Yi's forces could not hold Kaifeng and were actually defeated in a subsequent battle nearby, the Loyang-Kaifeng campaigns were major turning points in the war. The Communist armies had demonstrated their ability to sustain the offensive on several fronts simultaneously, and to engage in large-scale positional battles in open country, the final step in moving from guerrilla operations to mobile warfare. And whereas previously the main fighting had been in Shantung and Manchuria, now the Loyang-Kaifeng operations, following close upon those at Shihchiachuang and Yenan, had created a major new battle zone in North China. These victories also made possible the expansion and unification of hitherto separate Communist border regions. The Shansi-Chahar-Hopei and the Shansi-Hopei-Shantung-Honan Border Regions were merged into the North China Liberated Area in May 1948. A unified North China People's government was established in August with its capital at Shihchiachuang.[65]

The North-east. One final turning point by mid-1948 was the reversal of the power balance in Manchuria. September 1947 brought the start of Lin Piao's sixth offensive across the Sungari, aimed this time to isolate completely the major cities of central and south Manchuria and cut land communications with North China by severing the Peiping-Mukden railway line. These goals were essentially achieved by the end of November.[66] Preliminary attacks heralding the onset of the seventh offensive began in mid-December. Command of Nationalist forces in the North-east passed from Ch'en Ch'eng to General Wei Li-huang. But Lin Piao was now strong enough to attack on three fronts simultaneously. At the start of his seventh offensive, Communist forces converged on Mukden from the north, west and south. When reinforcements were flown into the city from Changchun and Kirin, however, Lin immediately

---

[65] *Civil war in China*, 144–53; *Military campaigns*, 145–52; Chassin, *Communist conquest*, 168–77; Mao Tse-tung, 'A circular on the situation', Mao, *SW* 4.226n.
[66] *FRUS, 1947*, 7.257–8, 270–1, 287–8, 290, 298, 302, 306–8, 315–20, 356–8, 362–3, 373–80.

shifted his main operations northward in the direction of those two cities, besieging neighbouring Szupingkai for the third time in two years. The city surrendered on 13 March; the Nationalists had already abandoned Kirin a few days earlier. During the three months of fighting from mid-December to mid-March 1948, Lin Piao's forces captured a total of nineteen cities and towns.[67]

At this time, Chiang Kai-shek rejected the suggestion put forward by the head of the US Army Advisory Group, Major General David Barr, to take advantage of the reduced Communist pressure around Mukden and withdraw from the North-east while it was still possible.[68] Chiang thus lost his last chance to save what was left of the armies he had committed to the takeover of Manchuria. By mid-1948, the power balance there had shifted irreversibly against him. The Communists now claimed to have 700,000 regular troops in the region, plus 330,000 local or second-line forces, and 1.6 million civilian support workers. The government's increasingly demoralized troops numbered only about 450,000 with no effective second-line replacements.[69]

Nationwide, according to the government's estimates, the strength of its regular armies had been reduced by one-third by June 1948, in comparison with mid-1945. Government forces now numbered 2,180,000 men, only 980,000 of whom were armed. The Communist side had 1,560,000 regular troops and 700,000 irregulars, of whom an estimated 970,000 were armed. Heavy weapons numbered 21,000 on the government side as opposed to 22,800 with the Communists.[70] And as Mao had pointed out earlier, Communist gains were being made at the expense of the government's losses, since captured enemy materiel comprised the main source of arms and ammunition for the PLA, and surrendered government soldiers an important source of new recruits.

The third year, 1948–1949: victory

In March 1948, Mao was able to report that the government's armies retained the initiative in only two sectors, both in Central China, and were on the defensive everywhere else. He predicted that the CCP would probably establish a central people's government in 1949, by which time they would have captured one or two of China's largest cities and merged into one continuous area all of North-eastern China, North China,

---

67 Mao Tse-tung, 'On the great victory in the North-west', Mao, SW, 4.216n; Whitson and Huang, 310–11; Civil war in China, 121–4; FRUS, 1947, 7.403–4, 411–15; FRUS, 1948, 7.1–4, 8–9, 22–4, 26–7, 36–7, 58–9, 65–6, 86, 93–5, 97–9, 103–6, 115, 121–2, 127–8, 143–5, 152–3.

68 China white paper, 1.325.   69 Whitson and Huang, 312; FRUS, 1948, 7.340–3.

70 Chassin, Communist conquest, 177.

Shantung, north Kiangsu, Honan, Hupei, and Anhwei. He estimated the defeat of the KMT within three years.[71]

The Communists now had the men, weapons, organization and experience necessary to sustain large-scale positional engagements. These began with the successful siege of Tsinan, capital of Shantung, in September 1948. The Communists' spring operations had completely isolated the city and Ch'en Yi's troops campaigning in Honan had returned to Shantung by September. As in Manchuria earlier, Chiang Kai-shek's American advisers warned him that the situation of his troops at Tsinan was hopeless. But again Chiang refused to evacuate them. The attack on the city began on 16 September, and was over within ten days. The majority of the demoralized garrison had essentially refused to fight and some actually defected to the Communists, a sure sign that the tide was turning.[72]

The transformation from passive defence into defection and surrender that occurred at Tsinan was repeated several times over during the final year of the war, as the psychological effect of the government's accumulating defeats took hold. This undoubtedly helped speed up the timetable for destruction of the government's forces, which occurred in the course of three decisive campaigns fought between mid-September 1948 and the end of January 1949. These campaigns, planned as a coordinated general offensive against three major concentrations of government armies, were: the Liaohsi-Shenyang (Mukden) campaign, 12 September – 2 November, which ended in the complete defeat of the Nationalist armies in Manchuria; the Peiping-Tientsin campaign, 21 November – 31 January, which ended government resistance in North China; and the Huai-hai campaign, 6 November – 10 January, which removed the last major obstacle to the Communists' march southward to the Yangtze and beyond.

The Liaohsi-Shenyang campaign. This was Lin Piao's eighth and final offensive campaign in Manchuria, confirming his reputation among military historians and the Chinese public alike as one of China's great military leaders.[73] Considering the scale of operations, the end for the

[71] Mao Tse-tung, 'A circular on the situation', Mao, *SW* 4.219–26.

[72] *China white paper*, 1.319–20, 331–2; Mao Tse-tung, 'The concept of operations for the Huai-Hai Campaign', Mao, *SW*, 4.282n; *Civil war in China*, 156–7; *Military campaigns*, 158–60; *FRUS, 1948*, 7.464, 467–71, 478, 480–6.

[73] The reappraisal of Lin Piao's pre-1949 military career occurred in 1974–5, as part of the national campaign to criticize him following his death allegedly in a plane crash while trying to flee to the Soviet Union. If private conversations with ordinary Chinese are any indication, the military critique was the least convincing part of the propaganda campaign against him. For examples of that critique, see *Hsueh-hsi yü p'i-an* (Study and criticism), 9 (1974) 19–26, and 8 (1975) 18–22; *Hung-ch'i* (The red flag), 1 (1975) 39–44; *Li-shih yen-chiu* (Historical research), 1 (1975) 24–30.

government came almost as rapidly in the North-east as at Tsinan, albeit not quite so ingloriously. Lin Piao's troops numbered approximately 700,000 for this final Manchurian offensive against something under 500,000 on the government side. The three main targets were government troop concentrations at Chinchow, a key supply centre on the Peiping-Mukden railway, at Mukden itself, and at Changchun. The largest concentration was the Mukden garrison numbering 230,000 men.

The attack on Chinchow began on 12 September, although the objective was not immediately apparent due to diversionary operations against Changchun. Government troops in the vicinity of Chinchow were surrounded and isolated within two weeks. By the end of September the airfield was under attack and ammunition was already running low, making it necessary to supply the garrison by air drop. Despite heavy preliminary fighting at nearby points, most notably at Yi hsien, the Chinchow garrison was unable to withstand a sustained attack by Communist forces, two government divisions defected, and the city surrendered on 15 October.

A relief force of some 100,000 men sent out from Mukden in early October failed to break through in time to save Chinchow. Lin Piao's second major objective then became the annihilation of this force before it could return to Mukden. Feigning a march to the south-west, he instead moved his main force north-east from Chinchow. Again despite heavy fighting the relief column could not break out of the trap Lin had so swiftly laid, and surrendered on 28 October. With the Mukden garrison reduced by half its strength, the city capitulated on 2 November, after only minimal resistance. Meanwhile, at Changchun, both civilians and military had been reduced to near-starvation by Communist encirclement. The 60th Army, composed of troops from Yunnan known to be unreliable, defected to the Communists on 17 October. Other units soon surrendered there as well, ending all resistance.

Despite his earlier proven incompetence, General Tu Yü-ming rejoined the North-east command during the battle, while Chiang Kai-shek personally took over the direction of military operations from his command post in Peiping. It may never be possible to untangle the effects of the Communists' strengths as opposed to the government's weaknesses. But as the US consul-general at Mukden cabled on 27 October: 'Government military tactics North-east past week resemble comedy errors if consequences government were not so tragic'. By mid-November, exactly two years after Lin Piao had launched his first offensive across the Sungari, the last government garrisons in the North-east had either surrendered or were fleeing southward. The government had lost at least

400,000 troops including some of its best, together with all their arms and equipment during this final phase of the battle for the North-east.[74]

The Peiping-Tientsin campaign. Lin Piao's armies began their march southward immediately following their victory in Manchuria. The subsequent Peiping-Tientsin campaign brought a combined force of 890,000 regular Communist troops from the North China and North-east Field Armies under the overall command of Lin Piao, against some 600,000 troops led by one of the government's more capable commanders, Fu Tso-i. Lin Piao's main force moved rapidly south of the Great Wall and into the Peiping-Tientsin region, supported to the west by Nieh Jung-chen's North China Field Army already threatening Kalgan. Nieh's objective around Kalgan had been to discourage Fu from weakening his defence of Peiping by sending aid to the North-east. With that area now secure, the new objective was to prevent Fu from moving south to reinforce government troop concentrations in northern Kiangsu, target of the Communists' crucial Huai-Hai campaign, which began in early November. Communist strategy for the Peiping-Tientsin region therefore aimed at surrounding Fu Tso-i's forces at five points, dealing with each in turn so as to cut off their escape and prevent reinforcements from reaching them as well.

Within two weeks after the main troop movements out of Manchuria began on 21 November, Lin's forces had reached the outskirts of Tientsin and a major deployment area to the north-west of Tangshan. Within two more weeks they had consolidated their positions. The first major attack was at Fu's weakest point, Hsin-pao-an, north-west of Peiping, where the garrison was defeated by Nieh Jung-chen's forces on 22 December. Two days later Kalgan also surrendered. Meanwhile, the Communist encirclement of Peiping and Tientsin was being steadily strengthened. The Nationalist commander at Tientsin, determined to resist, flooded a large area outside the city to block the Communist advance. He then refused to surrender without a fight, but Communist forces prevailed after the 14–15 January battle of Tientsin. The nearby port of Tang-ku fell two days later, its 50,000-man garrison fleeing by sea. In this crisis, with escape routes blocked, all nearby troop concentrations defeated, and his 200,000 troops at Peiping now overwhelmingly outnumbered, Fu Tso-i negotiated a settlement. He agreed on 22 January to withdraw his forces from the city without fighting and to reorganize them into the PLA. Communist

---

[74] *Civil war in China*, 124–9; *Military campaigns*, 155–7; Mao Tse-tung, 'The concept of operations for the Liaohsi-Shenyang campaign', Mao, *SW* 4.261–6; Whitson and Huang, 312–19; *FRUS*, *1948*, 7.457–8, 463, 469–70, 474, 477–8, 486–7, 495, 501–4, 508–9, 520, 522–5, 527–32, 537–8, 548–9.

troops entered Peiping on 31 January. In the Peiping-Tientsin campaign the government had lost close to another half million troops, together with two of China's most important cities.[75]

The Huai-Hai campaign. The third decisive campaign of the civil war occurred concurrently with the Peiping-Tientsin operations. The famous 65-day battle of the Huai-Hai was fought between 6 November 1948 and 10 January 1949. The main battle zone was bounded on the north by the Lunghai line and on the south by the Huai River, hence the name Huai-Hai. Fighting centred around the city of Hsuchou, seat of the government's Bandit Suppression Headquarters, strategically positioned at the junction of the Lunghai and Tientsin-Pukow railways. The battle climaxed the collaboration of Ch'en Yi, Liu Po-ch'eng and Ch'en Keng, commanders of the PLA's East China and Central Plains Field Armies, who had been campaigning together in the region for more than a year.

The two sides were about evenly matched in terms of regular troop strength: each committed upwards of half a million men. But the Communists with their already well-developed civilian support network were able to mobilize an additional two million peasants for the massive logistical effort necessary to sustain their battlefield operations. The military and civilian support work actually extended into four provinces: Kiangsu, Shantung, Anhwei and Honan, and was coordinated by an ad hoc General Huai-Hai Front Committee headed by Teng Hsiao-p'ing. The main government commanders were Liu Chih, Tu Yü-ming and Huang Wei, with Liu Chih in overall command and Chiang Kai-shek personally overseeing operations as he had done during the final Manchurian campaign.

The Huai-Hai battle unfolded roughly although not precisely in accordance with a three-phase 'concept of operations' drafted by Mao Tse-tung and issued on 11 October 1948. The entire campaign was completed within two months as the plan directed. During the first phase, the objective was the annihilation of the army led by Huang Po-t'ao. This was accomplished by Ch'en Yi's forces in the vicinity of Nien-chuang on the Lunghai railway between Hsuchou and the Grand Canal in a battle which lasted two weeks as planned, between 6 and 22 November.

The second phase, 23 November – 15 December, entailed the destruction of government forces in the vicinity of Shuang-tui-chi, south of Hsuchou

---

[75] *Civil War in China*, 142–4; *Military campaigns*, 165–7; Mao Tse-tung, 'The concept of operations for the Peiping-Tientsin campaign', Mao, *SW*, 4.289–93; *FRUS, 1948*, 7.532–5, 557, 592, 638–40, 643–50, 663–73, 680–1, 691–3, 700–5, 723–5; *FRUS, 1949*, 8.19, 30–1, 36, 44, 46–59, 71–2, 75–7, 87–8, 98.

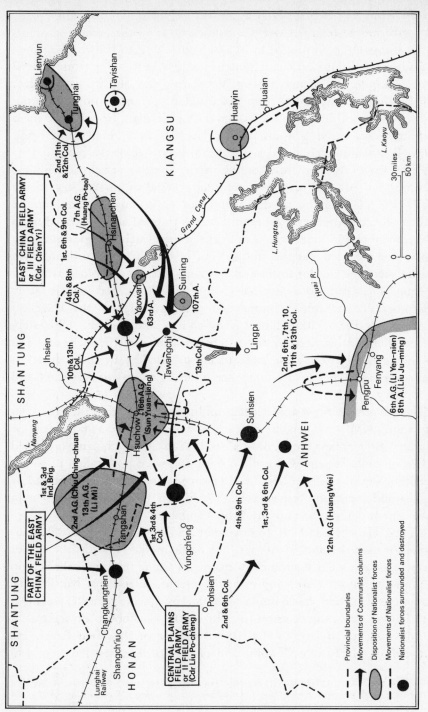

MAP 19. The battle of Huai-Hai, November 1948–January 1949

not far from the Tientsin-Pukow railway. The Communists anticipated that government reinforcements would come from the eastern terminus of the Lunghai line, brought in by sea from Tsingtao. Chiang Kai-shek instead ordered reinforcements under Huang Wei to come from Central China. Despite this change Huang Wei's army was quickly surrounded. Relief columns sent north from the Huai River area around Pengpu, Anhwei, were turned back by Communist guerrillas. Nor did the main reinforcements moving south from Hsuchou ever reach him, being themselves surrounded and destroyed in phase three of the campaign.

Phase three also was not fought in the locality anticipated by the Communists' original plan, but unfolded instead in an area just to the south-west of Hsuchou in the vicinity of Ch'en-kuan-chuang on the Anhwei-Kiangsu border. Communist forces trapped and destroyed three government armies here – the main force in the Hsuchou region totalling almost 300,000 men – as they moved out of the city in accordance with Chiang Kai-shek's order to reinforce Huang Wei. The advance army led by Sun Yuan-liang was encircled and virtually wiped out in early December. Tu Yü-ming commanded the remainder of the Hsuchou garrison together with Ch'iu Ch'ing-ch'üan and Li Mi. Ultimately surrounded and besieged by the combined armies of Ch'en Yi and Liu Po-ch'eng, Tu's forces were inadequately supplied by air and reduced to near starvation. They finally surrendered during an assault between 6 and 10 January.

The government lost another half million troops during the Huai-Hai campaign, with some 300,000 taken prisoner and the remainder dead or injured. Commanders Huang Po-t'ao and Ch'iu Ch'ing-ch'üan were killed in battle, while Huang Wei and Tu Yü-ming were both taken prisoner. Generals Sun Yuan-liang and Li Mi escaped the battlefield disguised as beggar and merchant respectively. The defeat removed the last main government defence line north of the Yangtze.[76]

Chiang Kai-shek and his commanders had no one but themselves to blame for their defeat at Huai-Hai. The battle marked not just the end of effective government resistance in mainland China, but the culmination of years of military errors and mismanagement, defects that had become characteristic of Nationalist military operations. Chiang himself is credited with having made the decision to fight on the Hsuchou plain instead of withdrawing as advised to the natural barrier of the Huai River. He furthermore placed overall command of the battle in the hands of Liu

[76] Whitson and Huang, 178–86, 240–3; Seymour Topping, *Journey between two Chinas*, 24–48; Mao Tse-tung, 'The concept of operations for the Huai-Hai campaign', Mao, *SW*, 4.279–82; *Civil war in China*, 157–60; *Military campaigns*, 161–4.

Chih and Tu Yü-ming, hardly his most capable generals. Finally, Chiang Kai-shek personally interfered with battle plans and issued operational orders while the fighting was in progress, as was his custom. With so much power concentrated in the hands of one man, responsibility for the failures could not but be concentrated there as well.

Despite the valour that many government units displayed on the battlefield, they found themselves once again outmanoeuvred by superior PLA strategy and tactics. The Communists as usual attacked weaker points, first at Nien-chuang and then Shuang-tui-chi, while the government's main forces remained unengaged at Hsuchou. When these finally moved out, they were as usual too late and too slow, their vehicles clogging the roads out of town. They were then pursued, surrounded and destroyed piecemeal at Ch'en-kuan-chuang in the time-honoured tradition of guerrilla warfare – except that this time the venue was an open battlefield containing a total of one million men.

Government commanders had never learned the lessons of speed and decisiveness that had been mastered by their adversaries. But government commanders also lacked an adequate understanding of mechanized warfare and the use of air power. Hence they were never able to gain the advantages they should have enjoyed from their absolute monopoly in both areas. Their defence was marred not only by disunity and indecision but by inadequate tactical planning, intelligence and logistical support as well. As a result they found themselves repeatedly surprised, hemmed in, and immobilized. During this and other battles, their performance seemed to confirm the judgment of one of the KMT's staunchest American supporters, William C. Bullitt, that 'There is not a single Government general who has the military training and technical skill to handle the over-all problems of logistics involved in meeting the attack of a Communist army of more than 2,000,000 men.'[77]

PLA commanders, by contrast, seemed able to adapt at will to changing battlefield situations. They were united, most immediately, by years of cooperation in applying a strategy that elevated flexibility in the field to the highest art of defensive warfare. They were then successful in applying these principles to increasingly large-scale offensive operations. In particular, their civilian support network was an indispensable feature of their success. Horse carts, wheelbarrows and carrying poles provided the chief means of conveyance on the Communists' supply lines, underscoring the old maxim that primitive things which work are better than modern

[77] 'Report by consultant William C. Bullitt to the Joint Committee on Foreign Economic Cooperation Concerning China', 80th Congress, 2nd session (24 December 1948), 12, quoted in Tsou Tang, 491.

things that don't. The Communists had crafted their war machine on the basis of the human and material resources most readily at hand. As a result, their civilian manpower network provided the logistical and intelligence support necessary to sustain their military operations, ultimately negating the initial advantages enjoyed by the government armies in numbers, training and materiel.

More generally, as the Communists moved onto the offensive in 1947, government commanders had lapsed into a strategy of passive defence from which they never freed themselves. They remained as if stunned once the enemy they had forced into retreat on all fronts in 1946 suddenly turned and began the counter-attack. The antiquated custom of withdrawing behind city walls continued to dominate government military thinking long after the Communists' battlefield performance had rendered such operational concepts obsolete. But when government forces did move out, they were regularly overwhelmed by their opponents' tactical superiority, further reinforcing their own defensive mentality.

The Communists' experience with fighting a stronger adversary during the Anti-Japanese War thus paid off handsomely after 1945. Government armies, for their part, had used the opportunity provided by the Japanese invasion neither to develop an effective guerrilla movement nor to master the art of modern warfare that Joseph Stilwell and others had tried to teach them. When the Japanese were removed from the scene and the two Chinese armies were left to face each other, government commanders could not match the performance of their enemy. By the latter half of 1948 this had developed into an effective integration of guerrilla tactics with mobile and positional warfare, allowing the Communists to orchestrate simultaneous coordinated offensives by a force of well over one million fighters.

Shortly after the fall of Tsinan in September 1948, Chiang Kai-shek had indicated that a thorough overhaul of military strategy, tactics, training and field organization was in order. In particular, the practice of holding strongpoints regardless of the cost would have to be abandoned.[78] Chiang had apparently at last grasped the nature of his military problems, but that understanding had come too late.

THE DEMISE OF THE KMT GOVERNMENT AND FAILURE OF AMERICAN POLICY

After the conclusion of the 1948-9 winter campaigns, all that followed was anti-climax. With its main forces destroyed, the demise of Chiang Kai-shek's government was a foregone conclusion. On 14 January 1949,

[78] *China white paper*, 1.332.

the Communists issued their conditions for peace, a harsh eight-point proposal very different from their negotiating posture in 1945–6. Now they were demanding, among other things, Chiang Kai-shek's punishment as a war criminal, the integration of his remaining armed forces into the PLA, and the abolition of the KMT government. Chiang declined to accept the conditions but on 21 January resigned the presidency. Vice-President General Li Tsung-jen succeeded him as acting president and opened formal peace negotiations. A government delegation led by Chang Chih-chung arrived in Peiping on 1 April, but was able to gain little beyond the eight-point conditions of 14 January, and a 20 April deadline for their acceptance. The KMT government rejected the conditions and the PLA began its advance across the Yangtze immediately the deadline had passed.

The PLA had used the intervening months to rest, regroup and reorganize. In early 1949, its field armies were renamed in preparation for their movement out of the regions where they had fought their major battles, P'eng Te-huai's North-west Field Army was redesignated the First Field Army; Liu Po-ch'eng's Central Plains Field Army was reorganized as the Second Field Army; Ch'en Yi's East China Field Army became the Third Field Army; and Lin Piao's North-east Field Army became the Fourth Field Army. Nieh Jung-chen's North China Field Army was formally deactivated later in the year.

On 21 April, the armies of Ch'en Yi and Liu Po-ch'eng moved together once more, crossing the Yangtze along a 300-mile front. Against minimal resistance they took the KMT capital, Nanking, on 24 April; Hangchow, capital of Chekiang, on 3 May; Nanchang, capital of Kiangsi, on 22 May; and Shanghai on 27 May. In mid-May, Lin Piao's army crossed the Yangtze in the vicinity of Wuhan, taking that city on 16–17 May. His progress was temporarily checked in southern Hunan, where a large force led by Pai Ch'ung-hsi blocked Lin's march southward from July to October. Both sides reported heavy casualties before Pai was finally forced to withdraw from the field in early October. Lin then proceeded more or less unobstructed, occupying Canton on 14 October and Kweilin on 22 November. It was late April 1950, however, before Lin's forces had finally eliminated all resistance in Kwangsi and Hainan Island.

In the north and north-west, the Shansi warlord, Yen Hsi-shan, held out in his capital, Taiyuan, until 24 April 1949, when the city surrendered to Nieh Jung-chen. Sian surrendered a month later to P'eng Te-huai, and Lanchou did the same at the end of August after the three main government commanders in the north-west refused to cooperate in the defence of Kansu.

The KMT government disintegrated as it retreated one step ahead of the advancing Communist armies. On 23 April, Acting President Li Tsung-jen fled Nanking for Canton, the new capital, where the government ministries had been relocating since the start of the year. Yet even the trauma of having lost the northern half of the country was not sufficient to galvanize a unified anti-Communist opposition among the KMT's cliques and factions. Chiang Kai-shek continued to manipulate military and political affairs first from his retirement home at Fenghua, Chekiang, and then from Taiwan, where he established a personal headquarters in July 1949. He resumed active control of KMT affairs about the same time. Earlier in the year he had successfully removed to Taiwan the Nationalist air force and navy, together with some of the best of the remaining army divisions loyal to him, and the government's US $300 million worth of gold, silver, and foreign exchange reserves.

Chiang's plan, which only gradually became apparent in 1949, was to abandon all the Chinese mainland and retreat to a fortress in Taiwan from which he could rebuild his own power. There he would await the inevitable onset of the Third World War between the United States and the Soviet Union which would, he thought, allow him to fight his way back under American aegis to the realm he had lost. During the half year of his retirement from public office, he worked with some determination to implement this plan. For example, he acted to undermine Li Tsung-jen's attempt to organize – together with his fellow Kwangsi clique member, General Pai Ch'ung-hsi – a credible defence south of the Yangtze. Fearing the challenge of his own plans and power should they succeed, Chiang refused to allocate the arms, ammunition and money needed by Pai Ch'ung-hsi in midsummer when his forces were blocking Lin Piao's advance in southern Hunan. Similar requests for assistance in the north-west were also denied, adding to the hopelessness of the disunited defence command in that region.[79]

By October, when Lin Piao's army occupied Canton, the KMT government had removed to its Second World War capital, Chungking. Chiang Kai-shek rejoined it there in mid-November. As the PLA's First and Second Field Armies moved through the south-west in the autumn of 1949, Chiang moved what remained of his government from Chungking to Chengtu, and then on to Taiwan on 9 December. Li Tsung-jen's plan to establish a separate resistance movement in South China never materialized. He was away from Chungking when Chiang arrived there and refused to return. Li proceeded to Hong Kong and then departed in early December for medical treatment and exile in the United States. Taiwan became the refuge for some two million KMT supporters, including half a million survivors of Chiang's armed forces.

[79] FRUS, 1949, 8.280–8, 290, 293–4, 327–8, 476–7, 489, 493, 552–3; Li Tsung-jen, Memoirs, 517–28.

While Chiang and the remnants of his government were flying from city to city in search of a final resting place, a new Political Consultative Conference was organized in Peiping. It met from 21 to 28 September, and was attended by 662 representatives from the CCP, the Democratic League, other democratic groups, labour, peasants, business and industry. Among other things, the conference adopted the Common Programme of the People's Republic of China and designated Peiping the official capital, formally changing its name back to Peking (Beijing) on 27 September. Four days later, on 1 October, Mao Tse-tung officially proclaimed the founding of the People's Republic.

For the United States, the dilemmas apparent in its China policy since 1944–5 had now overwhelmed it. America's KMT ally was defeated and the basis for any relationship with the new Communist government had been all but destroyed. The closest the United States ever officially came to an accommodation with the Chinese Communists was during 1946, when the mediation efforts of the Marshall Mission sought to bring the CCP into a coalition government. The distance between the CCP and the Americans grew with the failure of that effort and the escalation of military hostilities. The Americans continued their diplomatic and material support for the KMT and abandoned the idea of a coalition government that would include the CCP.

In reality, the United States had few options open to it in post-Second World War China. The global context of America's China policy grew increasingly important during these years when the Chinese civil war developed simultaneously with the expansion of Communist power in Europe. The first and most basic assumption of United States foreign policy was that Europe was its primary sphere of interest. Hence the dominant portion of United States aid and concern was channelled in that direction with the Truman Doctrine, aid to Greece and Turkey, and the Marshall Plan for Western Europe. The Cold War and consequent political pressures in the United States precluded any substantive tilt toward the Chinese Communists. The growing furore over the Hurley charges showed the constraints preventing that option. KMT leaders were correct in their estimate that, however unpalatable they might be to the United States, the latter had little choice but to support them. The same forces that precluded a tilt toward the CCP precluded also a complete withdrawal of support from the KMT.

But the weakness of the KMT government showed what a great effort would have been required to prop it up. General Marshall warned, after he became secretary of state, that the Chinese government was evidently incapable of eliminating the CCP as a political threat in China. Hence for any such effort to succeed, he advised the US Congress in 1948, 'it would be necessary for the US to underwrite the Chinese Government's military effort, on a wide and probably constantly increasing scale, as well as the Chinese economy. The US would have to be prepared virtually to take over the Chinese Government and administer its economic, military and governmental affairs.' That was so grandiose an undertaking that he felt compelled to advise against it. He recommended the only realistic alternative in his view, namely, a programme of limited economic aid.[80]

One final consideration was the estimate prevailing from about 1946, that while the KMT government could not eliminate the Communists as a political force in China, neither did the Communists have the strength to defeat the government militarily. Hence the American policy-makers' decision to let China simmer on the back burner, while the main thrust of the anti-Communist effort was directed toward Europe. In May 1947, therefore, the ten-month arms embargo imposed during the Marshall Mission was lifted. But the Nationalist requests in May and June for large-scale economic aid were rejected. Instead, President Truman sent General Wedemeyer, commander of United States forces in China at the end of the Second World War, back to China on a fact-finding mission. After one month in China during July and August 1947, Wedemeyer addressed an assembly of KMT dignitaries including Chiang Kai-shek himself. The general presented an uncompromising critique of the government they led, warning that their survival depended on drastic political and economic reforms. On returning to Washington, he nevertheless proposed an expansive economic and military aid programme for the KMT government, together with an international trusteeship for Manchuria to contain Communist influence there.[81] The KMT spurned Wedemeyer's demands for its reform while the Truman administration, fearing active involvement in the Chinese civil war, rejected the idea of sending to China the 10,000 officers required for his military aid proposals. The policy of limited assistance to the KMT government seemed the only realistic solution, albeit complicated by the demands of the China lobby on the one hand and economy-minded members of Congress on the other. But given the existing constraints, the basic decisions against wider intervention and for limited assistance were rationally made.

In the end, of course, the policy of limited assistance pleased no one and gained nothing. It was unable to delay disaster for the KMT government on the Chinese mainland. Yet it also earned the condemnation of the non-Communist anti-war movement there, as an American attempt

---

[80] *China white paper*, 1.382-3. The US policy of limited assistance to China is analysed in Tsou Tang, 349-493.

[81] *China white paper*, 2.758-814.

to promote its own interests by disregarding those of China through continuing support for the unregenerate Chiang Kai-shek. But it was not the policy itself that was at fault, so much as the erroneous estimates on which it was based with respect to the Chinese Communists and the underlying assumptions which led to those estimates. For the policy was founded on the mistaken calculation of the Communists' chances of victory. The prevailing view was, as Marshall advised Congress in 1948, only that the government could not defeat the Communists, not that they might actually defeat the government. The American public was never prepared for the latter contingency. Nor did American policy-makers ever appear to contemplate that China could be governed by any party other than the KMT, or the KMT led by anyone other than Chiang Kai-shek. After the military campaigns of late 1948, when even Chiang Kai-shek had accepted the inevitable, American diplomats turned to the idea of north-south partition as a possible solution. The anticipated scenario for the civil war in China was thus protracted stalemate of one form or another.

The weaknesses of the KMT government were readily apparent to all observers; only the strength of the Communists was not. The voices of the American foreign service officers, who tried to explain this towards the end of the Second World War, were silenced after the Hurley affair, and there were no United States diplomatic observers in the Communist areas during the subsequent civil war years. Meanwhile, the antipathy towards the presumed threat seemed to preclude even the serious contemplation of it, relegating that exercise to the forbidden zone of subversive activity. The most basic failure of the Americans, therefore, was to deny themselves the ability to consider on any terms other than their own the nature of the Communist-led Chinese revolution. Hence they could not estimate that the Communists might prevail, much less grasp the reasons why. Consequently, they also had no real understanding of the changes in the KMT government that would have been required before it could defeat its enemy; or of the time that would have been required to realize such reforms even had there been the will to do so; and no understanding as to how the United States could inspire such a will when it was otherwise clearly lacking. The tones of desperation that crept into American diplomatic despatches in late 1948 and early 1949, as they assessed stop-gap remedies for the ever more 'rapidly deteriorating situation', attest to the lack of understanding on all those counts. This failure led in turn to years of painful and inconclusive recriminations over the 'loss of China' and the responsibility of individual Americans for it, as though China was theirs to lose.

In later years, however, it eventually became acceptable to contemplate the event more dispassionately. Much speculation then arose about 'what might have been', as various attempts of Chinese Communist leaders during the 1940s to establish official contacts with the United States became more widely known. These included Mao's statements to the Dixie Mission in 1944; the invitation to American Ambassador J. Leighton Stuart to visit Peiping in the summer of 1949; and Chou En-lai's extraordinary approach to the Americans at this same time, using the Australian journalist, Michael Keon, as intermediary.[82] The United States failed to respond positively to any of these overtures from the Chinese Communists. Yet whether there could have been anything more than a communications channel between them seems doubtful, however rational the larger possibilities might have been in hypothetical terms. Preoccupied as they were with the expanding power of the Soviet Union and their irreducible fear of communism, American makers of policy and public opinion were in no mood to experiment with more flexible and selective approaches toward the new Chinese government during the McCarthy era of the early 1950s. Nor did the Chinese Communists expend undue effort to hold themselves apart from the mounting Cold War tensions of the period. The strident anti-American themes of the official CCP pronouncements that pursued Stuart out of China in August 1949 were matched by the uncompromising anti-Communist tones which dominated contemporary American diplomatic reports and public opinion in general. Together these Chinese and American postures indicated differences so great that they would require more than two decades to surmount.

[82] On the Dixie Mission, see Esherick, ed. *Lost chance*; on the Peiping invitation: Topping, 81–90; Shaw Yu-ming, 'John Leighton Stuart and US-Chinese Communist rapprochement in 1949', *CQ* 89 (March 1982) 74–96; *FRUS, 1949*, 8.766–70, 779, 784–5, 791; on Chou En-lai's approach to the Americans and a similar one to the British: *ibid.* 357–60, 372–3, 388, 389, 397–9, 496–8, 779–80; and Edwin W. Martin, 'The Chou demarche', *Foreign Service Journal* (November 1981), 13–16, 32.

CHAPTER 14

MAO TSE-TUNG'S THOUGHT
TO 1949

Mao Tse-tung's thought, as it had found expression prior to the
establishment of the Chinese People's Republic, was at once the synthesis
of his experience down to 1949, and the matrix out of which many of
his later policies were to grow. This chapter seeks to document and
interpret the development of Mao's thought during the first three decades
of his active political life. It also tries to prepare the reader better to
understand what came after the conquest of power. While stressing those
concerns which were uppermost in Mao's own mind in the earlier years,
it also devotes attention to ideas of which the implications were fully
spelled out only in the 1950s and 1960s.

As will be abundantly clear from earlier chapters, the period from 1912
(when Mao, at the age of $18\frac{1}{2}$, returned to his studies after half a year as
a soldier in the revolutionary army) to 1949 (when he became the titular
and effective ruler of a united China) was one of ceaseless and far-reaching
political, social and cultural change. Mao lived, in effect, through several
distinct eras in the history of his country during the first half-century of
his life, and the experience which shaped his perception of China's
problems, and his ideas of what to do about them, therefore varied
radically not only from decade to decade, but in many cases from year
to year. The present effort to bring some order and clarity to the very
complex record of Mao's thought and action adopts an approach partly
chronological and partly thematic. It begins by looking at the development
of Mao Tse-tung's political conceptions from early manhood down to
1927, when he first embarked on a revolutionary struggle of a distinctive
stamp in the countryside.

FROM THE STUDENT MOVEMENT TO THE PEASANT MOVEMENT
1917-1927

In terms both of age and of experience, Mao Tse-tung was a member of
the May Fourth generation. An avid reader of *New Youth* (*Hsin ch'ing-nien*)
from the time of its first appearance in 1915, he served his apprenticeship

in political organization and in the study of politics under the influence of the 'new thought' tide, and his career as a revolutionary effectively began in the wake of the May Fourth demonstrations.

Although he had many strongly marked individual traits, Mao shared certain attributes characteristic of this group as a whole. One of the most important was that it was a transitional generation. Of course all generations are 'transitional', since the world is constantly changing, but Mao's life and that of his contemporaries spanned not merely different phases but different eras in China's development. The process of adaptation to the Western impact had begun in the mid-nineteenth century and was to continue into the mid-twentieth century and beyond, but the May Fourth period marked a great climacteric after which nothing would ever be the same again. In a word, the members of the May Fourth generation were aware of the certainties regarding the enduring superiority of the Chinese Way which had comforted their elders, but they were never able to share this simple faith. Some of them, including Mao, soon espoused Westernizing ideologies to which they remained committed for the rest of their lives, but most remained deeply marked both by faith in the intrinsic capacities of the Chinese people, and by the traditional modes of thought which they had repudiated. Thus they were fated to live in circumstances of permanent political and cultural ambiguity and instability.

Mao Tse-tung's political views prior to his early twenties are known only from odd fragments of contemporary documentation, and from his own recollections and those of others many years afterwards.[1] He first emerges clearly into our field of vision with an article written when he was approximately 23, and published in the April 1917 issue of *New Youth*.

Although this, Mao's first article, was written long before he was exposed to any significant Marxist influences, it reveals many personality traits, and many strands of thought, which can be followed through subsequently. The overriding concern – one might almost say obsession – which penetrates the whole article is anxiety lest the Chinese people should suffer the catastrophe of *wang-kuo*, that is, of losing their state and

---

[1] The fullest account of Mao's life and thought in the early years is to be found in the biography of the young Mao by Li Jui, first published in 1957 under the title *Mao Tse-tung t'ung-chih ti ch'u-ch'i ko-ming huo-tung*. This version has been translated into English by Anthony W. Sariti as *The early revolutionary activities of Comrade Mao Tse-tung*, ed. James C. Hsiung, with introduction by Stuart R. Schram. Li Jui has now published a very substantially revised and expanded second edition, *Mao Tse-tung ti tsao-ch'i ko-ming huo-tung*. This version incorporates a considerable amount of new material, including a whole chapter on Mao's thought before and after the May Fourth period, originally published in *Li-shih yen-chiu*, hereafter *LSYC*, 1 (1979) 33–51. It should henceforth be regarded as the standard. In some cases, for the convenience of non-Sinologist readers, I also cite the translation.

becoming 'slaves without a country'. This theme, so widespread in China in the late nineteenth and early twentieth centuries, is vigorously stated in the opening sentences:

Our nation is wanting in strength. The military spirit has not been encouraged. The physical condition of the population deteriorates daily. This is an extremely disturbing phenomenon....If this state continues, our weakness will increase further....If our bodies are not strong, we will be afraid as soon as we see enemy soldiers, and then how can we attain our goals and make ourselves respected?[2]

Mao thus evoked at one stroke two basic themes of his thought and action throughout the whole of his subsequent career: nationalism, or patriotism, and admiration for the martial spirit. But if he is clearly preoccupied here with what might loosely be called nationalist goals, was his nationalism at this time conservative or revolutionary? An obvious touchstone for deciding this point is whether or not he saw the aim of *fu-ch'iang* (increasing the wealth and power of the state) as in any way tied to a social and cultural revolution perceived as a necessary precondition for strengthening the nation. In fact, the article shows us a Mao concerned with China's fate, but almost totally uninterested in reform, let alone revolution.

Of the twenty-odd textual quotations, or explicit allusions to particular passages from classical writings contained in the article, there are a dozen to the Confucian canon; one to the Confucian 'realist' Hsun-tzu, a precursor of the Legalists, and two to the Sung idealist interpreter of Confucianism, Chu Hsi, as well as one to his late Ming critic, Yen Yuan. There are also three references to Mao's favourite Taoist classic, the *Chuang-tzu*. The range of his knowledge at this time was clearly very wide, for he refers in passing to obscure biographical details regarding a number of minor writers of various periods. (It is all the more noteworthy that eleven out of twelve references to the Confucian classics should be to the basic core of the *Four books*).

And yet, though there are no explicit references to social change, nor even any suggestion that it is necessary, the article does contain many traces of modern and non-conformist thinking, of both Chinese and

---

[2] 'Erh-shih-pa hua sheng' (Mao Tse-tung), 'T'i-yü chih yen-chiu' (A study of physical education), *New Youth*, 3.2 (April 1917) (separately paginated) 1; translated in S. Schram, *The political thought of Mao Tse-tung*, hereafter *PTMT*, 153. This book contains only extracts from Mao's 1917 article. I have also published a complete translation in my monograph *Mao Ze-dong. Une étude de l'éducation physique*. In 1975, M. Henri Day translated the whole text into English in his Stockholm thesis *Máo Zédōng 1917–1927: documents*, 21–31. This very valuable work, which contains translations of all of Mao's writings included in volume 1 of the Tokyo edition of the Chinese text (Takeuchi Minoru, ed. *Mao Tse-tung chi*, hereafter *MTTC*), together with provocative and original, though occasionally unconvincing commentaries, is an important contribution to our knowledge of the young Mao and his thought.

Western origin. To begin with, there is the emphasis on the value of the martial spirit, expressed in the opening sentences quoted above, and summed up in the statement: 'The principal aim of physical education is military heroism.'[3] To justify this view, Mao hails the example of many heroes of ancient times, and quotes from Yen Yuan, who had denounced Chu Hsi for 'emphasizing civil affairs and neglecting military affairs' (*chung-wen ch'ing wu*), thus creating a harmful tradition contrary to the teachings of Confucius.[4]

The dual matrix out of which Mao's thinking at this time had evolved is explicitly evoked in a letter he wrote in 1916, at about the time when he was working on the article for *New Youth*:

In ancient times, what were called the three great virtues of knowledge, benevolence, and courage were promoted simultaneously. Today's educationalists are of the view that we should combine virtue, knowledge, and [a sound] body. But in reality, virtue and knowledge depend on nothing outside the body, and knowledge, benevolence, and [a sound] body are of no use without courage.[5]

Thus Mao not only underscored at the outset the crucial importance of the body, i.e., of material reality, but also exalted the ancient Chinese virtue of courage (*yung*). Mao did not of course derive this strain in his thought primarily from books. Like many other Chinese in the early twentieth century, he developed his ideas in response to circumstances similar to those which prevailed at the end of the Ming, when the unity and integrity of the Chinese nation was threatened as a result of military weakness.

If this enthusiasm for things military remained a permanent trait of Mao's thinking, an even more basic theme of the 1917 article, and one which revealed more unmistakably modern influences, was that of the importance of self-awareness (*tzu-chueh*) and individual initiative (*tzu-tung*). He put the point forcefully in the opening paragraph of his article: 'Strength depends on drill, and drill depends on self-awareness....If we wish to make physical education effective we must influence people's subjective attitudes and stimulate them to become conscious of physical education.'[6]

The source for the idea that the key to effective action lies in first transforming the hearts of men lies, of course, partly in the Confucian tradition. But the main inspiration for passages such as this is to be found

---

[3] *Ibid.* 5; PTMT 157.

[4] Yen Yuan, 'Ts'un hsueh', book 2 in Yen Yuan, *Ssu ts'un pien*, 63.

[5] 'Kei Li Chin-hsi ti hsin' (Letter to Li Chin-hsi), *MTTC, pu chüan*, 1, 17–18. Li Chin-hsi was a former teacher at the Normal School in Changsha who had moved to Peking. (See Li Jui, 28 for a brief biography.) The contemporary 'educationalists' referred to by Mao who spoke of virtue, knowledge and a sound body included in particular, as Benjamin Schwartz has pointed out, Herbert Spencer, whom Mao had certainly read in Yen Fu's translation.

[6] Mao Tse-tung, 'T'i-yü', 1; PTMT 153.

no doubt in the eclectic, and yet basically Westernizing ideas Mao had absorbed from his reading of *New Youth* and from the lessons of his ethics teacher and future father-in-law, Yang Ch'ang-chi.

Yang, who was a disciple of Chu Hsi as well as of Kant and Samuel Smiles, taught a moral philosophy which combined the emphasis of Western liberalism on self-reliance and individual responsibility with a strong sense of man's duty to society.[7] To this end, he had compiled a volume of extracts from the Confucian *Analects*, with accompanying commentaries, to illustrate his own interpretation of 'self-cultivation'. The first chapter of this book took its title from the concept of 'establishing the will' (*li chih*), and contains the statement: 'If one has an unbreakable will, there is nothing that cannot be accomplished.'[8]

Like Yang Ch'ang-chi, Mao laid particular stress on the role of the will. 'Physical education,' he wrote in his 1917 article, 'strengthens the will....*The will is the antecedent of a man's career*.'[9] This belief in the importance of the will and of subjective forces was a central and characteristic element of his outlook. In a letter he wrote to Miyazaki Toten in March 1917, with the aim of inviting him to give a speech at the First Normal School in memory of Huang Hsing, Mao described himself as a student who had 'to some extent established [his] will (*p'o li chih-ch'i*)'.[10]

But at the same time, in very Chinese fashion, he regarded an authentic will as impossible without understanding or enlightenment. In a letter of 23 August 1917 he wrote: 'truly to establish the will is not so easy; one must first study philosophy and ethics, in order to establish a standard for one's own words and actions, and set this up as a goal for the future'. But it was not merely a matter of subjective attitudes; action and commitment were required:

Then one must choose a cause compatible with this goal, and devote all one's efforts to pursuing it; only if one achieves this goal, is it possible to speak of having [a firm] will. Only such a will is a true will, not the will which consists in blind obedience....A simple inclination to seek the good, the true or the beautiful is nothing but an impulse of passion, and not an authentic will....If, for a decade, one does not obtain the truth, then for a decade, one will be without a will...[11]

[7] Edgar Snow, *Red star over China*, 143.
[8] Li Jui, *Mao Tse-tung tsao-ch'i*, 30; translation, 18.
[9] Mao Tse-tung, 'T'i-yü', 5–6; *PTMT* 157–8.
[10] Or, as Jerome Ch'en translates, 'disciplined [his] aspirations' (*Mao papers*, 3). Text in *MTTC* 1.33. For the circumstances in which this letter was written, see Day, *Máo Zédōng*, 18–20.
[11] In one Cultural Revolution collection (*Tzu-liao hsüan-pien*, 10–11) this is identified as having been written to Yang Huai-chung (Yang Ch'ang-chi) himself, but it was in fact addressed to Li Chin-hsi. For the full text, see *MTTC, pu chüan*, 1, 19–23; the passage quoted here is on pp. 20–1.

Some idea of Mao's overall political position at this time is furnished by the fact that he says only three people in China have had, in recent years, ideas about how to rule the country as a whole (*chih t'ien-hsia*): Yuan Shih-k'ai, Sun Yat-sen and K'ang Yu-wei. Of these, only K'ang really had something like basic principles (*pen-yuan*), and even his ideas were mainly rhetoric. The sole figure of the modern age he truly admired, wrote Mao, was Tseng Kuo-fan, whom he called (as in the *New Youth* article) by his posthumous title, Tseng Wen-cheng.[12]

Despite this, the pattern of Mao's thinking of 1917 was by no means purely traditional. The goal he wished to pursue was, of course, the strengthening and renewal of China. The realm (*t'ien-hsia*), he wrote, was vast, the organization of society complicated, and the knowledge of the people limited. In order to get things moving, it was necessary to move people's hearts. The first requirement for this was to have some great basic principles (*ta pen-yüan*). At present the reformers were beginning with details, such as assemblies, constitutions, presidents, cabinets, military affairs, industry, education and so on. The value of all this should not be under-estimated, but all these partial measures would be ineffectual if they were not founded in principle. Such principles should embrace the truth about the universe, and about man as a part of the universe. And, Mao went on:

Today, if we appeal (*hao-chao*) to the hearts of all under heaven on the basis of great principles can any of them fail to be moved? And if all the hearts in the realm are moved, is there anything which cannot be achieved? And…how, then, can the state fail to be rich, powerful, and happy?

In Mao's view, the place to start was with philosophy and ethics, and with changing the thinking (*ssu-hsiang*) of the whole country. China's thinking, he wrote, was extremely old, and her morals extremely bad. Thought ruled men's hearts, and morals ruled their actions; thus both must be changed.[13]

But though Mao saw China's ancient and rigid thought-patterns as an obstacle to progress, he did not propose wholesale Westernization as a remedy. Commenting on the view, attributed by Yang Ch'ang-chi to 'a certain Japanese', that Eastern thought entirely failed to 'correspond to real life', Mao observed: 'In my opinion, Western thought is not necessarily all correct either; very many parts of it should be transformed at the same time as Oriental thought.'[14]

---

[12] *Ibid.* 19–20.   [13] *Ibid.* 20.

[14] *Ibid.* 20–1. In his view that China, too, had something to contribute to the world, Mao was following the basic orientation of his teacher, Yang Ch'ang-chi, who had taken the style 'Huai-chung' (literally, 'yearning for China') during his long period of study abroad, to express his patriotic sentiments. On this, see Li Rui, 'Hsueh-sheng shih-tai ti Mao Tse-tung' (Mao Tse-tung during his student years), *Shih-tai ti pao-kao* 12 (December 1983); reprinted in *Hsin-hua wen-chai* 1984 1.178.

Having said this, however, Mao embarks on a notably untraditional discussion of the importance, in the enterprise of uniting the hearts of the people on the basis of thought and morals, of the little people (*hsiao-jen*), as compared to the 'superior men' (*chün-tzu*). To be sure, it is the latter who have a high level of knowledge and virtue, but they exist only on the basis of political institutions and economic activities mainly established by ordinary people, the mass of whom constitute the source of the 'superior men' (*hsiao-jen lei chün-tzu*). Thus, the 'superior men' must not only be benevolent toward the little people, but must educate and transform them in order to attain the goal of 'great harmony' (*ta-t'ung*). Already at this time Mao proposed to set up a private school (*ssu-shu*), combining traditional and modern methods, to prepare people for study abroad.[15]

As for the theme of practice, which was to play so large a part in Mao's subsequent thinking, he asserted in his 1917 article that hitherto there had been all too much talk about physical education: 'The important thing is not words, but putting them into practice.'[16] Mao's stress on linking theory and practice has often been traced back to Wang Yang-ming, but this is mere speculation; there is not the slightest mention of Wang in any of Mao's known writings, and no evidence that he was influenced by him. More relevant, in any case, to Mao's development during the May Fourth period are the Westernizing ideas he assimilated in 1917-18.

Mao's thinking evolved very rapidly during his last two years at the First Normal School in Changsha. Perhaps the most important single element which makes its appearance at this time is an explicit and strongly-marked individualism. For example, in marginal annotations to a textbook on ethics by the German neo-Kantian, Friedrich Paulsen, Mao wrote:

The goal of the human race lies in the realization of the self, and that is all. What I mean by the realization of the self consists in developing our physical and mental capacities to the highest degree....Wherever there is repression of the individual, wherever there is a violation of individuality, there can be no greater crime. That is why our country's 'three bonds' must go, and why they constitute, with the churches, capitalists, and autocracy, the four evil demons of the realm....[17]

Like older and more eminent intellectuals of the time, such as Ch'en Tu-hsiu, Li Ta-chao or Lu Hsun, Mao had seized on the notion of the absolute value of the individual as a weapon to 'break out of the nets' of the old culture and the old society. He was by no means unaware of the social framework necessary to the realization of the individual,

[15] *MTTC*, *pu chüan*, 1, 22–3.
[16] Mao Tse-tung, 'T'i-yü', 7; translated in *Mao Ze-dong. Une étude de l'éducation physique*, 52; and Day, 27.
[17] Quoted by Li Jui, 110. The full text of Mao's annotations on Paulsen has been reproduced in *MTTC*, *pu chüan*, 9, 19–47.

describing how groups were formed from individuals, societies were formed from groups, and states were formed from societies. In this complex interrelationship between the individual and the state, or civil society (*kuo-min*), Mao stressed that the individual was primary; Paulsen's contrary emphasis reflected, he said, the influence of 'statism' in Germany.[18]

A dialectical approach to the relations between opposites is, indeed, one of the hallmarks of Mao's thought from this time forward. Among the pairs which he treated as in some sense identical were concept and reality, finite and infinite, high and low, *yin* and *yang*, as well as two which would be criticized by the Soviets decades later: life and death, and male and female. Man he saw as the unity of matter and spirit, and morality as arising from the interaction of conscience and desire. (The view that moral law had been laid down by a command of the spirits he stigmatized as a 'slave mentality'.) Moreover, because matter was indestructible, man and society were likewise indestructible, though constantly changing and renewing themselves through reform and revolution. For this reason, he no longer feared, as he had done, that China would perish; she would survive by reform of the political system, and transformation of the nature of the people. Such reform was possible only under the guidance of new knowledge, and knowledge would be effective if it was first built into belief, and then applied. 'Knowledge, belief, and action,' he wrote, 'are the three steps in our intellectual activity.' The medium of action could only be 'various social and political organizations'.[19]

Thus the stress of the April 1917 article on practice was strongly reasserted, and a new theme, that of organizing for reform, emerged. Both of these were to be central to the very important essay entitled 'The great union of the popular masses', which Mao published in July and August 1919.

The most startling passage of Mao's 1919 article[20] is no doubt that contrasting Marx and Kropotkin:

As to the actions which should be undertaken once we have united, there is one extremely violent party, which uses the method 'Do unto others as they do unto you' to struggle desperately to the end with the aristocrats and capitalists. The leader of this party is a man named Marx who was born in Germany. There is another party more moderate than that of Marx. It does not expect rapid results,

---

[18] *MTTC, pu-chüan*, 9, 21, 40–1.

[19] *Ibid.*, 28–34, 37–9, 42, 45–6. Most but not all of these passages are included in Li Jui, 114–16; translation, 40.

[20] I have published a full translation in *The China Quarterly*, hereafter *CQ*, together with an analysis. Mao Tse-tung, 'The great union of the popular masses', followed by S. Schram, 'From the "Great union of the popular masses" to the "Great alliance"', *CQ* 49 (Jan.–March 1972) 76–105. See also Day, 85–100. The Chinese text is available in *MTTC* 1.57–69.

but begins by understanding the common people. Men should all have a morality of mutual aid, and work voluntarily....The ideas of this party are broader and more far-reaching. They want to unite the whole globe into a single country, unite the human race into a single family.... The leader of this party is a man called Kropotkin, who was born in Russia.[21]

Quoting this passage verbatim, Li Jui comments that, although at this time Mao could not clearly distinguish between Marxism and anarchism, 'The great union of the popular masses' and other articles he wrote for the journal he edited in Hunan, the *Hsiang River Review* (*Hsiang-chiang p'ing-lun*), already displayed glimmerings of class analysis, and constituted the earliest building blocks of the future great edifice of Mao Tse-tung's Thought.[22] But while Mao was unquestionably, in the summer of 1919, learning rapidly about the theory and practice of revolution, it is very difficult to find in his writings of the period serious elements of Marxist analysis. Concepts such as class struggle, dialectics, or the materialist view of history are not even mentioned, and the very term 'class' is used only once, and then in a totally un-Marxist sense (the 'classes' of the wise and the ignorant, the rich and the poor, and the strong and the weak).[23] If the article has a discernible philosophical bias, this is to be found neither in Marx nor in Kropotkin, but in the ideas of Western liberals as transmitted – and transmuted – by certain Chinese writers of the late nineteenth and early twentieth century. Among these were Yen Fu and Liang Ch'i-ch'ao, the Hunanese revolutionary thinker and martyr T'an Ssu-t'ung, as well as Mao's teacher Yang Ch'ang-chi, all of whom developed in one way or another the view that spontaneous action by members of society, unfettered by the old hierarchical bonds, would maximize the energy of society as a whole.

Another important influence on Mao's thought during the May Fourth period was that of Hu Shih. It has often been pointed out that Mao's articles of 1919 were enthusiastically hailed following their publication by the Peking journal *Weekly Review* (*Mei-chou p'ing-lun*). Summarizing the contents of the first few issues of Mao's *Hsiang River Review* one commentator said: 'The strong point of *Hsiang River Review* lies in discussion. The long article "The great union of the popular masses" published in the second, third and fourth issues...exhibits exceedingly

---

[21] *CQ* 49. 78–9. Understandably, this paragraph was not included in the extracts from this article reproduced in 1957 by Li Jui, since it would hardly have supported the view he put forward there to the effect that 'The great union of the popular masses' was 'one of the most important writings' in which Mao 'began to combine a Marxist-Leninist viewpoint with the reality of the Chinese revolution'. (*Ibid.* 1st ed., 106; translation, 115.) As noted below, his approach in the revised edition of 1980 is radically different.

[22] *Ibid.* 213.   [23] *CQ* 49. 77–8.

far-reaching vision, and exceedingly well-chosen and effective arguments. Truly it is one of the important articles which have appeared recently.'[24] The author of these words was in fact none other than Hu Shih himself.

This appears less surprising when we note that, in his editorial for the first issue of the *Hsiang River Review*, Mao said, after enumerating the progress in various domains which had been achieved by humanity since the Renaissance (for example, from a dead classical literature for the aristocracy to a modern, living literature for the common people, and from the politics of dictatorship to the politics of parliamentarianism), that in the field of thought or philosophy (*ssu-hsiang*) 'we have moved forward to pragmatism'.[25] I do not mean to suggest, in noting this point, that Mao was a disciple of Hu Shih or John Dewey. His favourable evaluation of pragmatism in 1919 did reflect, however, an attitude he was to maintain *almost* until the end of his life, to the effect that one should not spin theories without linking them to concrete experience.

If Mao's ideas in 1919, like those of older and more learned men at the time, were a mosaic of many influences, his article 'The great union of the popular masses' had one remarkable peculiarity: it represented one of the few attempts to put forward a general programme on the basis of concrete experience of the revolutionary mass movements of the May Fourth period. It is true that Mao's hierarchy of social categories in the total picture as he saw it was quite un-Marxist: he attributed maximum importance to the student movement, and relatively little to the peasants, not to mention the workers. He also, characteristically, devotes considerable attention to women, and to school teachers. Looked at as a whole, his vision of the revolutionary alliance he is striving to create is not unlike that of the 'New Left' in the United States and elsewhere in the 1960s. The central theme of the articles is that China's renewal will come above all from the rebellion of young people, and especially of students, against the old order. The instrument and motive force of change lies in democratic organizations spontaneously building up from the grass roots.

The goal of the whole process will be, in Mao's view (and here he

---

[24] *Mei-chou p'ing-lun*, 36 (24 August 1919), 4.

[25] *MTTC* 1.53–4, translated in Day, 81. (For the reasons for translating *shih-yen chu-i* as 'pragmatism' see Day, 83, n. 2.) Hu Shih's influence on Mao at this time (which had earlier been acknowledged by Mao himself in his autobiography as told to Edgar Snow) was, of course, unmentionable in China until recently. (For some brief but pithy observations on the subject by a Western scholar, see Day, 47–8.) It is a reflection of the remarkable revolution which has taken place since 1978 in the climate of intellectual enquiry in China that an article published in 1980 should not only call attention to Hu's praise of Mao and to Mao's regard for pragmatism as the 'leading ideology' (*chih-tao ssu-hsiang*) of the time, but should explicitly state that in 1919 differences of principle had not yet emerged between them. See Wang Shu-pai and Chang Shen-heng, 'Ch'ing-nien Mao Tse-tung shih-chieh-kuan ti chuan-pien' (The transformation in the world view of the young Mao Tse-tung), *LSYC* 5 (1980) 83.

reveals himself as a true disciple of Yen Fu), not merely the liberation of the individual from the shackles of the old society, but also, and by that very fact, the strengthening and renewal of the Chinese nation as a whole. In a supremely eloquent peroration, Mao addressed his compatriots thus:

in every domain we demand liberation. Ideological liberation, political liberation, economic liberation, liberation [in the relations between] men and women, educational liberation, are all going to burst from the deep inferno where they have been confined, and demand to look at the blue sky. Our Chinese people possesses great inherent capacities! The more profound the oppression, the greater its resistance; since [this] has been accumulating for a long time, it will surely burst forth quickly. I venture to make a singular assertion: one day, the reform of the Chinese people will be more profound than that of any other people, and the society of the Chinese people will be more radiant than that of any other people. The great union of the Chinese people will be achieved earlier than that of any other place or people. Gentlemen! Gentlemen! We must all exert ourselves! We must all advance with the utmost strength! Our golden age, our age of glory and splendour, lies before us![26]

There is more than one echo here of Mao's 1917 article, in the emphasis on persistent efforts and a firm resolve as the keys to national resurgence. In the intervening two years, he had learned much, both from books and from experience, about the way to tap and mobilize the energies which he perceived to be latent in the Chinese people. He had, however, a great deal still to learn before he could even begin to devise a complete and effective strategy for making revolution in a country such as China.

Although Mao showed little understanding of Marxism at this time, his imagination had been caught by the victory of the Russian Revolution. He listed the establishment of a soviet government of workers and peasants first among the worldwide exploits of what he called the 'army of the red flag', and went on to mention the Hungarian Revolution, and the wave of strikes in America and in various European countries.[27] Other articles by Mao in the *Hsiang River Review* evoke themes which were later to become classic in his thought, such as the need of politicians to 'wash their brains' and 'go to the factories to work and the countryside to cultivate the land, together with the common people' (*p'ing min*), or the idea that 'the true liberation of humanity' would come on the day when thousands and tens of thousands of people in America shouted together in the face of injustice and the despotism of the trusts, 'This must not be!' (*pu-hsu*). But Mao also expressed very strong support for the Germans, who are presented as an oppressed people dictated to by the Entente.[28]

[26] *CQ* 49.87.   [27] *CQ* 49.84.

[28] On going to the factories, see [Mao] Tse-tung, 'Cha-tan pao-chü' (A brutal bomb attack), *Hsiang River Review*, 1 (14 July 1919), 3. On shouting in unison, Tse-tung, 'Pu-hsu shih-yeh chuan-chih'

The idea of China as a proletarian nation, which should show solidarity with other oppressed peoples, was of course commonly put forward in the years immediately after the May Fourth period by Li Ta-chao, Ts'ai Ho-sen and others. Mao, too, was naturally drawn in this direction.

A phase in Mao's subsequent apprenticeship, which provides a highly suggestive complement to his analysis, in 1919, of the role of grass-roots organizations in social change, was his participation in the Hunanese autonomy movement in the following year. This hitherto obscure episode has only recently been illuminated by the publication of important documents.[29] The record of this episode throws a revealing light not only on Mao's intense Hunanese patriotism, but on his attitude to political work generally. In an article published on 26 September 1920, Mao wrote:

> In any matter whatsoever, if there is a 'theory', but no 'movement' to carry it through, the aim of this theory cannot be realized....I believe that there are two kinds of real movements: one involves getting inside of things (*ju yü ch'i chung*) to engage in concrete construction; the other is set up outside, in order to promote [the cause].

Both types of movement, he added, were and would remain important and necessary. At the same time, he stressed that an effective movement must have its origin in the 'people' (*min*). 'If this present Hunanese autonomist movement were to be successfully established, but if its source were to reside not in the "people", but outside the "people", then I venture to assert that such a movement could not last long.'[30]

As for the broader context in which these statements were made, Mao and the co-authors of the proposal of 7 October 1920 for a constitutional convention summed up their views about the relation between political developments at the provincial and national levels as follows:

> The self-government law the Hunanese need now is like that of an American state constitution....China is now divided into many pieces, and we do not know when a national constitution will be produced; in fact, we are afraid that first

(No to the despotism of industry and commerce), *ibid*. 1.3. On the oppression of Germany see (among many articles, some by other authors) Tse-tung, 'Wei Te ju hu ti Fa-lan' (France fears Germany as if it were a tiger), *ibid*. 3 (28 July 1919), 2. Giorgio Mantici has published a complete Italian translation of the available issues of the *Hsiang River Review* under the title *Pensieri del fiume Xiang*. The articles just mentioned appear on 76–8 and 164–5. I wish to thank Mr Mantici for kindly giving me a copy of the Chinese text of these materials. All of these texts have now been published in *MTTC*, *pu chüan*, 1.

29 These materials – four articles by Mao, and a proposal for a constitutional convention drafted jointly with two others, were discovered by Angus McDonald in the course of research on his doctoral dissertation 'The urban origins of rural revolution' (University of California, Berkeley, 1974), also published in book form under the same title. McDonald has published the Chinese texts in *Hōgaku kenkyū*, 46.2 (1972) 99–107, with a commentary in Japanese, and has also discussed them in English in *Rōnin* (Tokyo), 14 (December 1973), 37–47, and in *CQ* 68 (December 1976), 751–77.   30 *MTTC*, *pu chüan*, 1.229–30.

every province will have to produce its own constitution, and only later will we have a national constitution. This is just like the route from separation to unification followed by America and [Bismarckian] Germany.[31]

This dimension of Mao's 1920 writings reflects the circumstances of the times, and by no means corresponds to his long-term view, which consistently stressed, from 1917 to the end of his life, the importance of national unity and a strong state. In other respects, however, the ideas put forward in the passages quoted above are altogether typical of Mao Tse-tung's political approach throughout his subsequent career as a revolutionary. On the one hand he called for 'getting inside things' to engage in concrete construction, by which he meant obviously that revolutionaries, or reformers, should immerse themselves in social reality. But at the same time, he perceived the need for a movement set up outside, in order to promote the cause. In other words, although political activists should respond to the objective demands of the 'people', and should immerse themselves in the people, in order to mobilize them, another organization, standing outside the people, was also required. It could be said that the Leninist-type Communist Party which Mao joined in the following year was precisely such an organization which did not allow itself to be confounded with the masses but stood outside them. But at the same time Mao never hesitated, throughout his political career, to enter boldly into things, and to participate in concrete organizational work.

The other question raised by Mao's writings during the Hunanese autonomist movement concerns the 'people' on whose behalf these activities were to be carried out, and from whom the initial impulse and inspiration for the movement were to come. By putting the term in quotation marks, Mao himself underscored its ambiguity. Were these the 'popular masses' (*min-chung*) of his 1919 article? Or were they the 'Chinese people' or 'Chinese nation' (*Chung-hua min-tsu*), who were never far from the centre of his concerns? It is perhaps a characteristic trait of Mao's thought that these two entities are indissolubly linked. He was never, at any time after 1918 or 1919, a nationalist solely, or primarily, interested in China's 'wealth and power'. But neither was he a 'proletarian' revolutionary like M. N. Roy, who never thought in terms of the nation.

In the course of the year 1920, Mao Tse-tung's attitude toward the problem of learning from the West how to transform Chinese society underwent a significant change. This shift is symbolized by the changing views regarding the narrower problem of study abroad expressed by Mao Tse-tung in a letter of 14 March 1920 to Chou Shih-chao, and another of 25 November 1920 to Hsiang Ching-yü. In the first, he declared that,

[31] *Ibid.* 242.

although a lot of people had a kind of superstitious reverence for the benefits of foreign study, in fact only a very few of the tens or hundreds of thousands of Chinese who had gone abroad had really learned anything of value. In any case, he wrote, the two currents of Eastern and Western culture each occupied half the world, and Eastern culture 'could be said to be Chinese culture' (*k'o-i shuo chiu shih Chung-kuo wen-ming*); he would master that first, before proceeding abroad, though he was not opposed in principle to all study abroad.[32]

Half a year later, Mao wrote, on the contrary, to Hsiang Ching-yü in France complaining that there was very little progressive education for women (or for men either) in Hunan, and urging her to lure as many women comrades as possible abroad, adding: 'One more person lured [abroad] is one more person saved (*yin i jen, chi to chiu i jen*).'[33]

The shift in Mao's basic attitude toward ideologies of Western origin was not so dramatic as suggested by these contrasting passages. One of his reasons, in March, for preferring to remain in China was, according to his letter to Chou Shih-chao, that a person could absorb foreign knowledge more rapidly by reading translations. His ideological orientation remained unsettled, however, as he said himself: 'To be frank, among all the ideologies and doctrines, I have at present still not found any relatively clear concept.' Mao's aim was to put together such a 'clear concept' (*ming-liao kai-nien*) from the essence of culture Chinese and Western, ancient and modern. In his plans for creating a 'new life' in Changsha within three years or so, Mao said that the individual was primary, and the group secondary. He went out of his way to stress his links with Hu Shih, and even noted that Hu had coined the name 'Self-Study University' (*tzu-hsiu ta-hsueh*) for an institution Mao proposed to set up in Changsha. But in this university, said Mao, 'we will live a communist life' (*kung-ch'an ti sheng-huo*), and he also declared that 'Russia is the number one civilized country in the world'.[34]

By the end of November 1920, Mao still advocated, in his letter to Hsiang Ching-yü, that Hunan should set itself up as an independent country (*tzu li wei kuo*), in order to detach itself from the backward northern provinces, and 'join hands directly with the nations of the world endowed with consciousness'. But at the same time he expressed great disillusionment with the absence of ideals and of far-sighted plans even among the educated elite of Hunan, and with the corruption of political

[32] *Hsin-min hsueh-hui tzu-liao*, hereafter HMHHTL (*Materials on the New People's Study Society*), 62–5. (*Chung-kuo hsien-tai ko-ming-shih tzu-liao ts'ung-k'an*). Reprinted in *MTTC, pu chüan*, 1.191–4.
[33] HMHHTL 75–6. *MTTC, pu chüan*, 1.261–2.
[34] HMHHTL 63–5. *MTTC, pu chüan*, 1.192–4.

circles, which made reform wholly illusory. It was necessary, he said, to 'open a new road'.[35]

An important influence in Mao's search for such a road was the group of Hunanese students, members of the New People's Study Society, then studying in France, and above all his intimate friend (who was also Hsiang Ching-yü's lover), Ts'ai Ho-sen. This was, incidentally, the case not only in the explicitly political realm, but in the attitude of iconoclasm and rebellion against established customs which was so prominent a feature of the May Fourth era and its aftermath. Having learned, in a letter of May 1920 from Ts'ai, that he and Ching-yü had established 'a kind of union based on love', Mao responded with enthusiasm, denouncing all those who lived under the institution of marriage as the 'rape brigade' (ch'iang-chien t'uan), and swearing that he would never be one of them.[36]

A year earlier, in the context of his campaign against arranged marriages, following the suicide of a young girl in Changsha forced by her father to marry against her will,[37] Mao had called rather for the reform (kai-ko) of the marriage system, to replace 'capitalist' marriages by love matches. Already in 1919 he had concluded that among the various human desires, for food, sex, amusement, fame, and power, hunger and sexual desire were the most important. Then he had written that members of the older generation were interested only in food, and hence in exploiting their daughters-in-law as slaves, and not, like the young, in love and sexual desire, which involved 'not only the satisfaction of the biological urge of fleshly desire, but the satisfaction of spiritual desires, and desires for social intercourse of a high order'. Thus they were the natural allies of capitalism against the fulfilment of the desires of young people.[38] Now he had decided that marriage as such was the 'foundation of capitalism', because it involved the prohibition of 'that most reasonable thing, free love' (chin-chih tsui ho-li ti tzu-yu lien-ai).[39]

Just as the strongly patriotic Li Ta-chao went in 1920 through an internationalist phase, in which he proclaimed that all the members of humanity were brothers,[40] Mao Tse-tung, as he embraced Ts'ai Ho-sen's

---

[35] HMHHTL 75–6. MTTC, pu chüan, 1.261.
[36] HMHHTL 127 (Ts'ai's letter of 28 May 1920) and 121 (Mao's letter of 25 November 1920 to Lo Hsueh-tsan). The latter is also in MTTC, pu chüan, 1.275–7.
[37] Mao wrote in all nine articles on this theme. For a brief summary, see Li Jui, translation, 119–21. Extracts are translated in PTMT 334–7. For the full texts of all nine articles, published in the Changsha Ta-kung-pao between 16 and 28 November 1919, see MTTC, pu chüan, 1.143–72.
[38] See, especially, 'Lien-ai wen-t'i – shao-nien-jen yü lao-nien-jen' (The question of love – young people and old people), ibid. 161–3. Also 'Kai-ko hun-chih wen-t'i' (The problem of the reform of the marriage system), ibid. 149.   [39] Ibid. 276.
[40] Li Ta-chao, 'Ya-hsi-ya ch'ing-nien ti kuan-ming yun-tung' (The luminous Asiatic youth movement), Li Ta-chao hsuan-chi, 327–9; extracts in H. Carrère d'Encausse and S. Schram, Marxism and Asia, 208–10.

vision of a revolution like that of the Russians, also accepted Ts'ai's view that all socialism must necessarily be internationalist, and should not have a 'patriotic colouration'. Those born in China should work primarily (though not exclusively) in 'this place, China', because that was where they could work most effectively, and because China, being both 'more puerile and more corrupt' than other places in the world, was most in need of change, but this did not mean that they should love only China and not other places. But in the same letter of 1 December to Ts'ai Ho-sen, and in discussions at a meeting of the New People's Study Society in Changsha on 1–3 January 1921, Mao insisted that the goal of the society should be formulated as 'transforming China and the world'. Others argued that, since China was part of the world, it was not necessary to mention it separately. For Mao it was important.[41]

As for the goals of political change, and the methods to be used in pursuing them, Mao replied on 1 December to several communications he had received from Ts'ai Ho-sen, Hsiao Hsü-tung (Siao Yü) and others detailing their own views and the debates among members of the society in France about these matters. Ts'ai and Hsiao had formed, with Mao, during their years at the Normal School in Hunan, a trio who called themselves the 'three worthies' (san-ko hao-chieh), but following their exposure to Western influences they had moved in opposite directions, Ts'ai toward Bolshevism and Hsiao toward a more moderate vision of revolution vaguely anarchist in character. Mao agreed unequivocally with Ts'ai's view that China's road must be the Russian road. But at the same time, in the process of refuting the arguments of Hsiao, and of Bertrand Russell, who had just been lecturing in Changsha along similar lines, in favour of non-violent revolution, without dictatorship, he showed only the vaguest understanding of Marxist categories. Thus he divided the world's total population of one and a half billion into 500 million 'capitalists' (tzu pen chia) and a billion 'proletarians' (wu-ch'an chieh-chi).[42]

Plainly, Mao's usage here reflects an understanding of the term wu-ch'an chieh-chi closer to its literal meaning of 'propertyless class' than to the Marxist concept of the urban, or even of the urban and rural proletariat. In the course of the next few years he came to know better intellectually, though it is a moot point whether, in terms of instinctive reactions, the Chinese expression did not continue to signify for him something more like 'the wretched of the earth'.

---

[41] HMHHTL 146, and 15–41, especially 20–3.

[42] HMHHTL 144–52; MTTC, pu chüan, 1, 289–96; extracts translated in PTMT 196–8 (there misdated, following the then available source, November 1920). For the letters of August 1920 from Ts'ai and Hsiao, see HMHHTL 128–43. The problem of Ts'ai's influence on Mao at this time is discussed by R. Scalapino in 'The evolution of a young revolutionary – Mao Zedong in 1919–1921', JAS 42.1 (Nov. 1982) 29–61.

Nevertheless, although his understanding of Marxist categories was as yet somewhat uncertain, Mao was definitely moving, during the winter of 1920–1, toward an interpretation of politics more in harmony with that of Lenin. Above all, he had grasped a Leninist axiom which was to remain at the centre of his thinking for the rest of his life, namely the decisive importance of political power. Replying on 21 January 1921 to a letter of 16 September 1920 from Ts'ai, declaring that the only method for China was 'that of the proletarian dictatorship as applied now in Russia',[43] Mao wrote:

The materialist view of history is our party's philosophical basis....In the past, I had not studied the problem, but at present I do not believe that the principles of anarchism can be substantiated.

The political organization of a factory (the management of production, distribution etc. in the factory) differs from the political organization of a country or of the world only in size, and not in nature [chih yu ta-hsiao pu t'ung, mei yu hsing-chih pu-t'ung]. The view of syndicalism [kung-t'uan chu-i] according to which the political organization of a country and the political organization of a factory are different in nature, and the claim that these are two different matters which should be in the hands of different kinds of people...only proves that they are confused and do not understand the principles of things. Moreover, if we do not obtain political power, we cannot promote [fa-tung] revolution, we cannot maintain the revolution, and we cannot carry the revolution to completion....What you say in your letter [to the effect that China needs a proletarian dictatorship exactly like that in Russia] is extremely correct, there is not a single word with which I disagree.[44]

Mao Tse-tung's experience during the six years after the First Congress of the Chinese Communist Party in July 1921 falls neatly into three segments. During the first two years he was engaged in organizing the labour movement in Hunan, and this could be called his workers' period. Thereafter, in 1923 and 1924, he served as a member of the Chinese Communist Party's Central Committee, and of the Shanghai Executive Bureau of the Kuomintang, in Canton and Shanghai, and this could be called his period as an 'organization man'. Finally, as everyone knows, he devoted himself in 1925–7 largely to organizing the peasant movement, and this could be called his peasant period.

The most striking thing about the first of these periods is that it appears, on the basis of all the available primary and secondary sources, to have been, in comparison with what came before and after, intellectually sterile. In any case, Mao's writings from this workers' period are few in number,

43 HMHHTL 153–62.
44 HMHHTL 162–3. This and the previous letter, as well as Ts'ai's letters of 28 May and 13 August, and Mao's letter of 1 December 1920 to Ts'ai and Hsiao, are reproduced in a more widely available openly published source: Ts'ai Ho-sen wen-chi (Collected writings of Ts'ai Ho-sen), 37–40, 49–73. Mao's letters of December 1920 and January 1921 to Ts'ai are the first two items in Mao Tse-tung shu-hsin hsuan-chi (Selected letters of Mao Tse-tung), 1–16.

and largely lacking in the fire and eloquence which, on other occasions, he showed himself so capable of manifesting. To be sure, Mao, like everyone else in the party, was overwhelmingly busy with organizational tasks during these first two years. The main explanation lies, however, in the fact that Mao himself had never really lived the life of a worker, as he had lived both the life of a peasant and the life of a student and city-based intellectual. He had, to be sure, organized a night-school for workers when he was a student at the Normal School in Changsha, and befriended individual workers on many occasions. His instinctive understanding of their problems was not, however, quite the same. Thus, although Mao's work in organizing strikes in a variety of industries undoubtedly influenced his intellectual and political development in the long run, at the time the harvest was meagre.

It is suggestive that the only item by Mao dating from the period mid-1921 to mid-1923 available in complete form outside China until very recently (thanks to the fortuitous circumstance that a widely-circulated magazine reprinted it in 1923) belongs in fact rather to the tail end of Mao's May Fourth period activities. It is the 'Declaration on the inauguration of the Hunan Self-Study University' which Mao wrote in August 1921 when he finally set up that intriguing institution.[45]

This text places, as Mao had done since 1917, the emphasis on individual initiative and self-expression in the learning process; it also echoes the articles Mao had written a year earlier on the mission of the Hunanese. But though Mao denounces vigorously the fact that 'learning is monopolized by a small "scholar clique" and becomes widely separated from the society of the ordinary man, thus giving rise to that strange phenomenon of the intellectual class enslaving the class of ordinary people', he shows as vague an understanding of what is meant by the 'so-called proletariat' as he had in his letter to Ts'ai of the previous December.

The writings of Mao's 'workers' period' relating specifically to the workers' movement are few and far between. Li Jui, whose biography of the young Mao is the principal source for texts of this period, is able to find only one item worthy of quoting at any length. This dates from December 1922, a time when Mao was engaged in leading the strike of the Changsha printing workers, and constitutes his reply to an attack by the editor of the Changsha *Ta-kung-pao* on the workers for getting involved in politics and lending themselves to other people's experiments. In a few characteristic sentences, Mao wrote:

What we workers need is knowledge; that is entirely correct. We workers are more than willing that people with knowledge should come forward and be our

45 MTTC, 1.81–4; Day, *Máo Zédōng*, 140–3. This appeared in *Tung-fang tsa-chih*, 20.6 (1 March 1923).

real friends....Sir, you must never again stand on the sidelines....We acknowledge as good friends only those who are capable of sacrificing their own positions, and of enduring hunger and hardship in order to work on behalf of the interests of us workers, who constitute the great majority [of society]....Please, take off your long robe in a hurry![46]

We find here once again the recurrent theme that those who seek to reform society (as the *Ta-kung-pao* editor claimed he also wanted to do) should 'enter into the midst of things', and not remain on the sidelines as observers, or believe themselves superior to ordinary people. There is nothing here, however, about the role of the working class in the revolution, not to mention working-class hegemony. The *Ta-kung-pao* was not, perhaps, the place to put forward such ideas, but Li Jui is not able to cite anything at all from Mao's period as a labour organizer on this theme.

The explanation may well lie in the line of the Chinese Communist Party at the time. In 1922 the Comintern envoy Maring (Sneevliet) had pushed his Chinese comrades into the singular organizational form for a united front with the Nationalists known as the 'bloc within', under which the Chinese Communists joined the Kuomintang as individuals. This idea was originally put forward in March 1922 by Maring on the basis of his experience in the Dutch East Indies, where left-wing socialists had cooperated in a similar way with Sarekat Islam, a nationalist organization with (as the name implies) a pronounced religious colouration. Ch'en Tu-hsiu and a majority of the other leading members of the Chinese Communist Party having rejected this idea out of hand, Maring travelled to Moscow, put his case to the Executive Committee of the International, and obtained a formal mandate from the Comintern endorsing his policy. Armed with this, he was able, following his return to China in August 1922, to ram the 'bloc within' down the throats of his reluctant Chinese comrades.[47]

This pattern of collaboration has been the object of intense controversy

[46] Li Jui, 428–30; translation, 251–2. The editors of the supplement to the Tokyo edition of Mao's works, who have cast their net very widely indeed, have also come up with only two or three very brief texts, in addition to this one, relating to the workers' movement. See *MTTC, pu-chüan*, 2.89–107.

[47] He lied, therefore, when he told Harold Isaacs that he had persuaded the Chinese to accept the proposal simply on the basis of his personal authority, and had 'no document in his hand' from Moscow to back him up. (*CQ* 45 (January–March 1971) 106.) The essential facts are conveniently outlined by Dov Bing, 'Sneevliet and the early years of the CCP', in *CQ* 48 (Oct.–Dec. 1971) 677–97; see also his reply, in *CQ* 54, to criticisms published in *CQ* 53. His view, which I have summarized in the text, is shared by both Soviet and Chinese scholars. See, on the one hand, V. I. Glunin, 'The Comintern and the rise of the communist movement in China (1920–1927)', in R. A. Ulyanovsky, ed. *The Comintern and the East*, 280–344, esp. 289–93. For a recent Chinese account, see Hsiao Sheng and Chiang Hua-hsuan, 'Ti-i-tz'u Kuo-Kung ho-tso t'ung-i chan-hsien ti hsing-ch'eng' (The formation of the first Kuomintang-Communist United Front), *LSYC*, 2 (1981), 51–68, esp. 58.

ever since its inception. So far as is known, Mao Tse-tung played no significant part either in devising it, or in securing its adoption. He was, however, one of the first to participate actively in implementing it. In the summer of 1922, Mao was involved in the organization of the Socialist Youth League in Hunan, and wrote to the Central Committee of the league in his capacity as secretary of the Changsha branch. Fifteen months later, in September 1923, he was already active in establishing Kuomintang organizations in the same localities, and wrote to the Central Office of the Kuomintang asking that he be formally appointed a member of the Preparatory Committee for this purpose, in order to facilitate contacts on all sides.[48]

From that time onwards, Mao Tse-tung was to play an important role in 'united front work'. Broadly speaking, once Ch'en Tu-hsiu and the other Chinese Communist leaders had accepted the 'bloc within', there was a tendency on their part to conclude that this implied accepting the leadership of the Nationalists, as the 'party of the bourgeoisie', at least for the time being. Such was Ch'en's position in 1923, and Mao for his part went very far in that direction during his period as an 'organization man'.

This is clearly apparent in the article entitled 'The foreign powers, the militarists, and the revolution' which Mao published in April 1923, on the eve of the crucial Third Congress, which formally adopted the 'bloc within'. Within China, he declared, only three factions (*p'ai*) were to be found: the revolutionary democratic faction, the non-revolutionary democratic faction (*fei ko-ming ti min-chu p'ai*), and the reactionary faction. Regarding the first of these, he wrote: 'The main body (*chu-t'i*) of the revolutionary faction is, of course, the Kuomintang; the newly-arisen (*hsin-hsing*) Communist faction (*kung-ch'an p'ai*) is cooperating with the Kuomintang.'

The non-revolutionary democratic faction included on the one hand the Research Clique and the 'faction of the newly-arisen intellectual class' (*hsin-hsing ti chih-shih chieh-chi p'ai*) of Hu Shih, Huang Yen-p'ei and others; and on the other hand the newly-arisen merchant faction. The reactionaries were, of course, the three main cliques of militarists.

The division of the totality of social forces into three was, and would remain, highly characteristic of Mao's approach to politics and to revolution. Another trait very much in evidence here is what might be called the dialectics of disorder and oppression, on which Mao had laid

---

[48] See his letter of 20 June 1922, 'Chih Shih Fu-liang ping She-hui-chu-i ch'ing-nien-t'uan chung-yang' (To Shih Fu-liang and the Central Committee of the Socialist Youth League), and his letter of 28 September 1923, 'Chih Lin Po-ch'ü, P'eng Su-min' (To Lin Po-chü and P'eng Su-min), *Selected letters*, 21–4.

great stress in his 1919 article 'The great union of the popular masses'. Because of the power of the militarists, and because the union of China under a democratic government would be contrary to the interests of the imperialists, there can be, Mao argues, neither peace nor unity for another eight or ten years. But the more reactionary and confused the political situation, the more this will stimulate the revolutionary sentiments and organizational capacity of the people of the whole country, so that in the end democracy and national independence will triumph over the militarists.[49]

The merchants, who were to have a share in the victory of the democratic forces, revolutionary and non-revolutionary, were featured more prominently in an article of July 1923 entitled 'The Peking coup d'état and the merchants', which has been the subject of considerable controversy. In this text, Mao stated in part:

The present political problem in China is none other than the problem of a national revolution [kuo-min ko-ming]. To use the strength of the citizens [kuo-min, literally the people of the country] to overthrow the militarists, and also to overthrow the foreign imperialists with whom the militarists are in collusion to accomplish their treasonable acts, is the historic mission of the Chinese people. This revolution is the task of the people as a whole, and the merchants, workers, peasants, students and teachers should all come forward to take on the responsibility for a portion of the revolutionary work. Both historical necessity and present realities prescribe, however, that the work for which the merchants must take responsibility in the national revolution is both more urgent and more important than the work that the rest of the people should take upon themselves....

The broader the organization of merchants, the greater will be their...ability to lead the people of the whole country, and the more rapid the success of the revolution![50]

It has been suggested that Mao's July 1923 article is not about the role of the merchants in the Chinese revolution at all, but rather about the nature of the tasks in the present 'bourgeois-democratic' stage of the revolution.[51] This view not only flies in the face of the evidence, but completely fails to note the epoch-making shift in Mao's outlook between 1923 and 1925–6, from an urban-oriented perspective to one turned toward the countryside. In another passage of his July 1923 article, Mao wrote:

[49] 'Wai li, chün-fa yü ko-ming' (The foreign powers, the militarists, and the revolution), *MTCC*, *pu-chüan*, 2.109–111.
[50] *The Guide Weekly*, 31/32 (11 July 1923), 233–4; translated in *PTMT* 106–9.
[51] Lynda Shaffer, 'Mao Ze-dong and the October 1922 Changsha construction workers' strike', *Modern China*, 4 (Oct. 1978) 380, 416–71. The same argument is repeated in L. Shaffer, *Mao and the workers: the Hunan labor movement, 1920–1923*, 1–2, 222–3.

We know that the politics of semi-colonial China is characterized by the fact that the militarists and foreign powers have banded together to impose a twofold oppression on the people of the whole country. The people of the whole country obviously suffer profoundly under this kind of twofold oppression. Nevertheless, it must be acknowledged that the merchants are the ones who feel these sufferings most acutely and most urgently.

In other words, Mao regarded the merchants, and more broadly the city-dwellers directly exposed to imperialist oppression, as most capable of playing a leading role in the national revolution because they suffered the most. This whole sociological analysis was turned right around three years later, after Mao had discovered the revolutionary potential inherent in the peasantry. Before we consider these developments, another persistent trait in Mao's July 1923 article deserves to be noted. The conclusion reads as follows:

Everyone must believe that the only way to save both himself and the nation [*kuo-chia*] is through the national revolution [*kuo-min ko-ming*]....Circumstances call upon us to perform an historic task....To open a new era by revolutionary methods, and to build a new nation – such is the historic mission of the Chinese people [*Chung-hua min-tsu*]. We must never forget it!

Here once again, we can see how clearly people in the political sense (*kuo-min* or citizens) and people in the biological sense (*min-tsu* or nation) were linked in Mao Tse-tung's thought.

Few substantial texts by Mao are available outside China for the period of nearly two and a half years from the appearance of this and two briefer articles in the Chinese Communist Party organ *Hsiang-tao* (The guide) until Mao took up the editorship of the Kuomintang organ *Cheng-chih chou-pao* (The political weekly) in December 1925. He spoke briefly at the First KMT Congress in January 1924, and drafted some resolutions for submission to the KMT Central Executive Committee (of which he was a member) in February 1924. Even in this formal context, some of Mao's utterances illustrate the persistent traits of his work style and political strategy. Thus, at the first KMT Congress, he opposed a proposal for setting up a 'research department' on the grounds that this would have as its consequence 'the separation of research from application – something which our party, as a revolutionary party, cannot do'.[52]

Following his sojourn in Shanghai as a member of the Shanghai Executive Bureau of the KMT, Mao returned in early 1925 to Hunan for a rest, and began his practical apprenticeship in organizing the peasants. He came back to Canton in the autumn of 1925 to take de facto charge

---

[52] *Chung-kuo Kuo-min-tang ch'üan-kuo tai-piao ta-hui hui-i-lu* (Minutes of the National Congress of the Kuomintang of China), 47.

of the Kuomintang Propaganda Department, edit *Cheng-chih chou-pao*, begin lecturing at the Peasant Movement Training Institute (which he was to head from May to October 1926), and participate in the Second Congress of the KMT. By this time he had come to hold the view, from which he was never afterwards to waver, that the centre of gravity of China's revolution lay with the peasants in the countryside.

Enumerating the weak points of Kuomintang propaganda in his report on the subject to the Second Congress in January 1926, Mao noted: 'We have concentrated too much on the cities and ignored the peasants.'[53] To some extent, this shift in Mao's outlook merely reflected the changing pattern of the revolution itself: the increasing militancy of the peasantry, and the activity of P'eng P'ai and many others, as well as of Mao, in mobilizing the peasants. Only by tapping this potential, Mao had concluded, would the revolutionary party (or parties) be able to create the force necessary to the achievement of their anti-imperialist goals – which Mao continued to proclaim in all his writings of the 'peasant period', 1925–7. But though the Chinese Communist Party, or a substantial fraction of it, turned its attention to the peasantry in the mid-1920s, the case of Mao Tse-tung is unique, not only in the obvious sense that he subsequently assumed the leadership of a revolution which effectively encircled the cities from the countryside, but because he formulated as early as 1926 theoretical propositions foreshadowing the future course of the Chinese revolution.

The emergence of Mao's ideas regarding a peasant-based revolution has probably been the subject of more discussion than any other single topic in the history of the Chinese Communist movement. Many historical and theoretical questions have been clarified in the course of this scholarly debate, but some points have until very recently remained obscure for lack of adequate documentation. In his interviews of 1936 with Edgar Snow, Mao declared that he had become aware of the revolutionary potential to be found in the Chinese peasantry only after the May Thirtieth incident of 1925 and the subsequent upsurge of patriotic sentiment in the countryside as well as in the city. The available evidence tends to confirm Mao's statement, and indeed suggests that he truly shifted his attention to the problem of rural revolution only toward the end of 1925. In order to bring out the over-arching continuity in Mao's thinking, despite such shifts of focus, however, it is appropriate to say a few words about his attitude toward the peasantry on the eve of the foundation of the Chinese Communist Party, before analysing the ideas he put forward in 1926–7.

In the latter part of 1919, Mao had drawn up an extensive plan for

[53] Day, 232; *MTTC* 1.151.

promoting 'new villages' along the lines earlier advocated in Japan, and a chapter from this was published in Changsha in December. Apart from the 'new village' slogan itself, this article called for young Chinese to follow the example of Russian youth in entering the villages to preach socialism.[54] In both these respects, the ideas advocated by Mao on this occasion reflected Li Ta-chao's influence.[55] Other elements, however, such as the discussion of the concept of 'work and study' in the United States, of which 'our Chinese students in America have taken advantage' seem to come rather from Dewey and Hu Shih.

More important, however, than these intellectual influences was Mao's own experience of peasant life, upon which he drew in developing his ideas in the early 1920s. In a lecture of September 1922, at the Self-Study University, Mao expounded views on the class structure of the Chinese countryside contained in an article published in a party organ in December 1920. Although Mao most probably had not written this article, he implicitly endorsed the analysis put forward there by taking it as his text. Refuting those who said that the life of the Chinese peasants was not so very hard, and the distribution of land not so very unequal, Mao divided the 'classes making up the peasantry' into four categories:

1. Those who own a lot of land but do not till it themselves (either employing people to till it, or renting it out for cultivation) and sit at home collecting rent. Such people do not really count as peasants, and where I come from we call them local moneybags [t'u ts'ai-chu].
2. Those who till their own land and are able to keep their whole family on the produce. They may also rent other people's land and till it, in addition to their own. These are the middle peasants.
3. Those who do have a bit of land, but are quite unable to keep their whole family on what it produces, and who thus have no alternative but to rely on tilling other people's land and being allotted a measure of what is produced in order to support themselves. These can be called lower [hsia-chi] peasants.
4. There are the paupers [ch'iung kuang-tan], who have not even a piece of land big enough to stick a needle into it, and rely exclusively on other people's land to keep body and soul together. These are the poorest of all the peasants.

The third and fourth categories, said Mao, made up the overwhelming majority of the peasantry, and moreover those in the third category were constantly being obliged by debt to sell their land to the 'rural money-bags' or the middle peasants, and descend into the fourth category.[56]

---

54 Mao Tse-tung, 'Hsüeh-sheng chih kung-tso' (The work of the students), *Hunan chiao-yü* (Hunan education), 1.2 (Dec. 1919), quoted in Wang Shu-pai and Chang Shen-heng, *LSYC* 5 (1980) 59–60.

55 See Maurice Meisner, *Li Ta-chao and the origins of Chinese Marxism*, esp. 55–6 and 80–9.

56 'Kao Chung-kuo ti nung-min' (Address to China's peasants) was originally published in *Kung-ch'an-tang* 3 (23 December 1920); it is reproduced in *I-ta ch'ien-hou* (Before and after the First Congress), 207–14. The fact that Mao gave a lecture using this text is noted in Li Jui, 455. The attribution of authorship to Mao in *Tzu-liao hsuan-pien*, 24, appears to be wrong.

Although the analysis is far more rudimentary, one can detect a faint resemblance between the text I have just summarized and Mao's two articles of January and February 1926, analysing respectively the class structure of the Chinese countryside and of Chinese society as a whole.[57] When, after analysing class relations in the countryside, and discussing the exploitation of the tenants by extortionate rents, and the tendency toward the concentration of land ownership, Mao went on to draw the political consequences, he adopted a categorically egalitarian position. 'We members of the human race,' he declares, 'are all equal as we come from our mother's womb; all of us should, in the same way, have food to eat and clothes to wear, and we should all work in the same way.' Formerly, everyone had used the land in common; the private property which allowed a minority to live in idleness, eating meat and wearing satin, was based on nothing else but the theft of what should rightfully belong to the peasants, and the peasants should arise and take it back. As soon as they arose, communism (which meant food and work for all) would come to their aid.[58] No doubt this rhetoric was designed to appeal to the peasants' mentality, but it also reflected the fact that, even in 1922, neither Mao nor the Chinese Communist Party as a whole had a coherent and realistic strategy for rural revolution. Four years later Mao had gone a long way toward the elaboration of such a strategy.

The general level of Mao's understanding of Marxist theory in 1925–6 was by no means high. Toward the beginning of his article of February 1926, he declared: 'In any country, wherever it be under the heavens, there are three categories of people; upper, middle, and lower.'[59] In this general framework, he classified the big landlords as part of the big bourgeoisie, and the small landlords as part of the bourgeoisie, and defined sub-groups in classes, both urban and rural, as much by their levels of wealth or poverty as by their relation to the means of production. In thus stressing whether or not peasant households could 'make ends meet', rather than the more orthodox Marxist criteria of land ownership or the hiring of labourers as the standard for defining strata in Chinese rural society, Mao adopted a framework quite different from that employed in 1923 by Ch'en Tu-hsiu.[60]

---

[57] 'Analysis of the various classes of the Chinese peasantry and their attitudes toward revolution' (January 1926) and 'Analysis of all the classes in Chinese society' (February 1926), in *MTTC* 1.153–73; extracts from the article on the peasantry analogous to the passages quoted above are translated in *PTMT* 241–6.   [58] *I-ta ch'ien-hou*, 212–14.

[59] Mao Tse-tung, 'Chung-kuo she-hui ko chieh-chi ti fen-hsi' (Analysis of all the classes in Chinese society), *MTTC* 1, 161–74. The sentence quoted is translated in *PTMT* 211.

[60] I have compared Mao's analysis of class relations in the countryside and that of Ch'en Tu-hsiu in my article 'Mao Zedong and the role of the various classes in the Chinese revolution 1923–1927', in *Chūgoku no seiji to keizai* (The polity and economy of China – The late Professor Yuji Muramatsu commemoration volume), 227–39.

It is therefore entirely wrong to argue[61] that Mao's categories and those of Ch'en were basically the same. But it is true that the main difference between the two men, and Mao's essential originality, lay elsewhere, namely in his resolve to make rural revolution on the basis of his own experience, and in his propensity to interpret, or even mould analysis to fit tactical goals.

Mao's analysis of social forces in China in their attitudes toward revolution in fact took shape in late 1925. One of five articles he contributed to the first five issues of *Cheng-chih chou-pao* under the pseudonym 'Tzu Jen' outlined essentially the same scheme he was to use in early 1926, minus the division of the peasant proprietors and other 'petty bourgeois' elements into those with a surplus, those who could just make ends meet, and those who did not have enough to live on.[62] In this piece, published in January, but corresponding probably to the substance of a speech he delivered in October 1925 to the First Kwangtung Provincial Congress of the KMT, Mao discussed, basically in the same terms he was to use in his famous article 'Analysis of all the classes in Chinese society' of February 1926, the implications of social divisions for political behaviour, and more particularly for factionalism within the Kuomintang. Here the apparently unorthodox division of society into 'upper', 'middle' and 'lower' came into its own, for having put the upper classes (big bourgeoisie and big landlords) firmly in the camp of the counter-revolution, and the lower classes (petty-bourgeoisie, semi-proletariat, urban and rural, and proletariat) in the camp of revolution, Mao proceeded to consider how the 'bourgeoisie' (national bourgeois and small landlords) would be pulled asunder and forced to choose, in the wake of the polarization which had developed following the emergence of the 'Western Hills' faction. As he did in 1926, and was consistently to do thereafter, Mao placed the overwhelming majority of the Chinese people (395 out of 400 million) on the side of revolution, leaving only one million hard-core reactionaries,

---

61 As Philip Huang has done in his article 'Mao Tse-tung and the middle peasants, 1925–1928', *Modern China*, 1.3 (July 1975), 279–80.

62 These articles were first attributed to Mao Tse-tung by John Fitzgerald in his article 'Mao in mufti: newly identified works by Mao Zedong', *The Australian Journal of Chinese Affairs*, 9 (January 1983) 1–16. Fitzgerald's arguments are altogether convincing in themselves, but the fact of Mao's authorship was also confirmed by Hu Hua, head of the Department of Party History of People's University, in a conversation with me on 10 September 1982. For a complete translation of Mao's article entitled 'The reasons underlying the secession of the GMD rightist faction and its ramifications for the future of the revolution', *Cheng-chih chou-pao*, 4 (10 January 1926) 10–12, see Fitzgerald, 9–15. Mao had, in fact, taken the name Tzu-jen as an alternative style as early as 1910, when he was a student at the Tungshan Higher Primary School. He did so out of respect for Liang Ch'i-ch'ao, whose influence on Mao at that time has already been noted. Liang's honorific name being Liang Jen-kung, 'Tzu-jen' had the meaning 'son of Jen'. See Li Jui, 'Hsueh-sheng shih-tai ti Mao Tse-tung', 176.

corresponding to the 'upper' category, and four million of those wavering people in the middle, who were torn both ways.[63]

As for the problem of leadership, Mao, in early 1926, while stressing the numerical importance of the peasantry and the degree of privation – and therefore of sympathy for the revolution – prevailing in the countryside, also characterized the urban proletariat as the 'main force' in the revolution.[64] Thus, even though the concept of 'proletarian hegemony' was inserted in this text only in 1951, he did recognize in early 1926 the Marxist axiom that the workers would play the central role in the revolutionary process. In September 1926 he allowed himself to be carried away by enthusiasm for the revolutionary forces which had been unleashed in the countryside to such a point that he turned the axiom of working-class leadership explicitly on its head.[65]

Mao's article, 'The national revolution and the peasant movement', published at this time, begins with the statement: 'The peasant question is the central [chung-hsin] question in the national revolution.' This in itself was not at all remarkable, for the upsurge of revolutionary activity in the country, since the middle of 1925, had forced itself on the attention even of the most urban-oriented, to such an extent that a bow in the direction of the peasant movement had become a cliché automatically included in almost every utterance of a Communist and/or Kuomintang spokesman. Mao's argument demonstrating the importance of the peasantry in terms of the structure of Chinese society was, on the other hand, very remarkable indeed. 'The greatest adversary of revolution in an economically backward semi-colony,' he wrote, 'is the feudal-patriarchal class [the landlord class] in the villages.' It was on this 'feudal landlord class' that the foreign imperialists relied to support their exploitation of the peasantry; the warlords were merely the chieftains of this class. Thus, as the example of Hai-feng showed, the domination of the imperialists and the warlords could be overthrown only by mobilizing the peasantry to destroy the foundations of their rule. 'The Chinese revolution,' he wrote, 'has only this form, and no other.'[66]

Not only did Mao Tse-tung assert the importance of the rural forces

---

[63] For the argument to the effect that the article by Tzu Jen corresponded to Mao's speech of 1 October see Fitzgerald, 5 and 9. The identical figures used in this article and in that of February 1926 for various categories of the population are clearly presented in the table in Fitzgerald, 4. The parallel passages in the two articles stressing that 395 millions support the revolution are translated in Fitzgerald, 14–15, and *PTMT* 213–14.

[64] Mao Tse-tung, 'Analysis of all the classes', *MTTC* 1.170; *PTMT* 247.

[65] Mao Tse-tung, 'Kuo-min ko-ming yü nung-min yun-tung' (The national revolution and the peasant movement), *MTTC* 1.175–9; for a more detailed discussion, with extracts in translation, see my article 'Mao Zedong and the role of the various classes'.

[66] *MTTC* 1.175–6.

of reaction in the old society, and of the rural revolutionary forces in overthrowing them – he went on to argue against the importance of the cities:

There are those who say that the rampant savagery exercised by the compradors in the cities is altogether comparable to the rampant savagery of the landlord class in the countryside, and that the two should be put on the same plane. It is true that there is rampant savagery, but it is not true that it is of the same order. In the whole country, the areas where the compradors are concentrated include only a certain number of places such as Hong Kong, Canton, Shanghai, Hankow, Tientsin, Dairen, etc., on the sea coast and the rivers. It is not comparable to the domain of the landlord class, which extends to every province, every *hsien*, and every village of the whole country. In political terms, the various warlords, big and small, are all the chieftains chosen by the landlord class....This gang of feudal landlord chieftains...use the comprador class in the cities in order to dally with the imperialists; both in name and in fact the warlords are the hosts, and the comprador class are their followers. Financially, 90 per cent of the hundreds of millions of dollars the warlord governments spend each year is taken directly, or indirectly, from the peasants who live under the domination of the landlord class...Hence, although we are aware that the workers, students, and big and small merchants in the cities should arise and strike fiercely at the comprador class, and directly resist imperialism, and although we know that the progressive working class, especially, is the leader of all the revolutionary classes, yet if the peasants do not arise and fight in the villages, to overthrow the privileges of the feudal-patriarchal landlord class, the power of the warlords and of imperialism can never be hurled down root and branch.

Despite the ritual reference to the 'leading role' of the working class, the implication of this passage is clearly that the real centre of power of the old society is to be found in the countryside, and the real blows must therefore be struck in the countryside. This is spelled out explicitly, in startlingly bald terms, in the concluding paragraph of the article:

The peasant movement in China is a movement of class struggle which combines political and economic struggle. Its peculiarities are manifested especially in the political aspect. In this respect it is somewhat different in nature from the workers' movement in the cities. At present, the political objectives of the urban working class are merely to seek complete freedom of assembly and of association; this class does not yet seek to destroy immediately the political position of the bourgeoisie. As for the peasants in the countryside, on the other hand, as soon as they arise they run into the political power of those village bullies, bad gentry, and landlords who have been crushing the peasants for several thousand years...and if they do not overthrow this political power which is crushing them, there can be no status for the peasants. This is a very important peculiarity of the peasant movement in China today.[67]

In other words, the workers ('at present' – but for how long?) are merely

[67] *Ibid.* 176–7.

reformists, pursuing limited benefits for themselves; they are animated, it could be said, by 'trade union consciousness'. The peasants, on the other hand, not only occupy a decisive position in society, so that they cannot achieve their aims without overthrowing the whole edifice of the old order; they are aware of the situation, and are deliberately waging a broad struggle, political as well as economic.

Never afterwards was Mao to go so far in explicitly putting the peasants in the place of the workers as the conscious vanguard of the revolution. His Hunan peasant report of February 1927 attributed to the poor peasants the leading role in the struggle in the countryside; it did not downgrade the importance of the cities, and of the classes based in the cities, in the same graphic terms, though there are indications suggesting that he had not abandoned his position of the previous September. The famous phrase attributing 70 per cent of the achievements of the revolution to date to the peasants[68] might be interpreted as relating to force rather than to leadership, and as merely describing a temporary condition. Another passage summarizes in capsule form the analysis developed in the September article to the effect that the 'patriarchal feudal class of local tyrants, evil gentry and lawless landlords has formed the basis of autocratic government for thousands of years and is the cornerstone of imperialism, warlordism, and corrupt officialdom', and adds: 'To overthrow these feudal forces is the real objective of the national revolution.'[69]

That the peasantry, though it is an important revolutionary force, must follow the leadership either of the workers or of the bourgeoisie, and cannot play an autonomous political role, is one of the most basic political axioms of Marxism, going back to Marx himself. Mao's theoretical contribution, during the ensuing half century, consisted not in replacing this axiom by its opposite, but in weaving together the principle of working-class leadership and his conviction that the fate of the Chinese revolution ultimately depended on what happened in the countryside.

In September 1926 Mao said, in effect, that the peasants could not emancipate themselves without emancipating the whole of Chinese society. He seemed to be investing them with a mission not unlike that which Marx attributed to the urban proletariat in the capitalist societies of the West. At the same time, as we have seen, he recognized that the workers were the 'leaders of all the revolutionary classes'. These two statements can be reconciled if we take the one as relating to the form of the revolutionary struggle in the immediate future, and the other as defining the long-term pattern of events, though the synthesis implied by such an interpretation would attribute to the peasants a degree of initiative scarcely

[68] *MTTC* 1.211–12; *PTMT* 252.   [69] Mao, *SW* 1.27.

compatible with Marxist orthodoxy. In any case, if this was Mao's understanding of the matter, the second half of his approach to the peasant problem would come into play only after the conquest of power, in fixing the pattern for the revolutionary transformation of society. And before that moment arrived, both Mao and the Chinese Communist movement had a long road to travel.

PARTY, ARMY AND MASSES 1927–1937

As noted in the previous section of this chapter, Mao Tse-tung, though he played no part in devising the singular organizational framework of the 'bloc within', worked forcefully to implement it from 1923 onwards. Manifestly, he was able to work effectively in such a context because he attached primary importance to national unification and China's struggle to throw off the domination of the imperialists, and accepted that, for the moment, the Kuomintang and its army were the best instrument for achieving this.

Mao therefore did his utmost, in particular during the eight-month period from October 1925 to May 1926, when he effectively ran the Propaganda Department of the Kuomintang Central Executive Committee, to consolidate the overwhelming majority of the Nationalist Party and its supporters on positions which were radical, but in no sense Communist or Marxist. Indeed, he devoted a large part of his introductory editorial for the Kuomintang organ *The Political Weekly* (*Cheng-chih chou-pao*) to refuting the accusations that Kwangtung was being 'communized'. The true goals of the revolution, he wrote, were 'to liberate the Chinese nation...to bring about the rule of the people...to see that the people attain economic prosperity'.[70] In other words, the goal was to implement the 'Three People's Principles'.

In his article of January 1926, 'The reasons underlying the secession of the KMT rightist faction and its ramifications for the future of the revolution', Mao argued that the emergence of a new rightist faction was not the result of the machinations of the KMT left, but the natural outcome of the interaction between the development of the revolution and the class basis of the KMT. 'The real force for revolution,' he wrote, was the alliance of petty-bourgeoisie, semi-proletariat, and proletariat. Landlord and big-bourgeois elements who had supported the anti-Manchu Revolution of 1911 could not accept the demand for 'people's rights' and 'people's livelihood'. 'Hence, as the revolution has developed and the

---

[70] *MTTC* 1.109–11; translated in Day, 205–6.

KMT has progressed, the old and the new rightist factions have split off one by one like bamboo shoots from their stem.'[71]

At this time, in early 1926, as I noted above in discussing Mao's approach to peasant revolution, he still believed that 395 million of China's 400 million people were on the side of the revolution. Thus he was able to accept Stalin's view that the Kuomintang was the only vehicle for reaching the vast masses, particularly in the countryside.

Following his investigation of the peasant movement in Hunan in early 1927, Mao's views on this and other matters changed fundamentally. He expressed his new insights more forthrightly in a separate report, dated 16 February 1927, to the Central Committee of the Chinese Communist Party than he did in the well-known document openly published at the time. Dividing the course of events in the countryside into three periods – that of organizing the peasant associations, that of the rural revolution, and that of setting up a united front – he stressed very strongly that a genuine revolutionary catharsis was indispensable between the first and third stages. The united front would not produce the desired results unless it was preceded by a period of 'fierce struggle to overthrow the power and prestige of the feudal landlords'. To be sure, he said that conflicts which arose in the countryside should, insofar as possible, be dealt with through the KMT apparatus rather than directly by the Communist Party under its own banner, but Mao clearly saw this as a temporary tactic. The masses, he said, were moving toward the left, and were eager for another revolution; the Communist Party must not shrink back from leading them in that direction.[72] Later in 1927, in any case, having lost all hope that Chiang Kai-shek or even the so-called 'Left Kuomintang' would support action by the peasants which went dead against their own class interests, Mao Tse-tung was one of the very first to call for a radical break with these former allies, and for the raising of the red flag in the countryside.

The twenty-two years from the Autumn Harvest uprising to the proclamation of the Chinese People's Republic were spent by Mao Tse-tung almost wholly in a rural environment, and witnessed the emergence and triumph of a strategy of 'surrounding the cities from the countryside'. In this sense, they marked the continuation and fulfilment of his earlier ideas regarding the role of the peasants in the revolution. But they were also years of unremitting military struggle, and to that extent constituted a fundamental rupture with the past. Mao Tse-tung had, of course, known

[71] *MTTC, pu chüan*, 2; translated in Fitzgerald, 9–15.
[72] 'Shih-ch'a Hunan nung-yun kei chung-yang ti pao-kao' (Report to the Central Committee on an inspection of the peasant movement in Hunan), *MTTC, pu-chüan*, 2.255–7.

intermittent fighting throughout the greater part of his life, and had been a soldier at the age of 18. He had also shown a keen insight, in 1925–7, into the political opportunities offered by the civil war between the Kuomintang and the northern warlords. It was, however, quite another matter for the Communists to organize their own independent armed forces, and to rely on these as a primary instrument in the revolutionary struggle.

The imprint of this dimension of Mao's experience on his theoretical contributions, beginning in 1927, was many-faceted. To begin with, he developed progressively more elaborate conceptions of the strategy and tactics of guerrilla warfare, which must be regarded as an integral part of his thought as a whole. The matrix of guerrilla warfare which shaped the Chinese Communist movement in Ching-kang-shan, Kiangsi and Yenan days did not, however, merely incite Mao to write about military problems; it also influenced deeply both his ideas as to how revolutionary leadership should be organized, and the spirit which pervaded his outlook. The last point, though very important, should not be exaggerated. Mao's stress on the role of armed force in the Chinese revolution did not make of him, as Wittfogel and others have argued, a thug or fascist who delighted in naked military force for its own sake. It did, however, unquestionably strengthen the emphasis on courage, firmness of heart, and the martial spirit which is visible in his first published article, and never left him until the end of his life.

Of more lasting significance were the patterns of organization and political work adopted by the Chinese Communists at the time, and to some extent conserved by them later, even when circumstances had changed. In a word, a guerrilla army mobilizing peasant masses is a thing quite different from a Communist Party mobilizing the urban workers, and neither the relation between the revolutionary elite and its supporters, nor the ideology which defines and justifies the nature of the whole enterprise, can be entirely the same.

The contrast between the Chinese revolution and its Russian and European predecessors was not, of course, so stark as the preceding one-sentence summary suggests. Even in Kiangsi, if not on the Ching-kang-shan, there was some small-scale industry and therefore some workers; and throughout the whole period 1927–49, there existed a Chinese Communist Party to which the Red Army was theoretically subordinate. Therefore, it was not a question of the army leading the peasants, but of party and army leading 'masses', rural and urban. The fact remains that, throughout the greater part of these twenty-two years, the party existed in significant measure as a soul or parasite in the body of the army. Even to the extent that the Chinese Communist Party appeared on the stage as an actor in its own right, it owed its very survival to the protecting shield of the Red Army, rather than to the solidity of its working-class basis. And though neither party nor army could have endured without the support of a large proportion of the population, the relation of such a Communist movement to the people was different from any which had been known before.

As Mao himself pointed out in later years, the differences between the patterns of the Chinese and Soviet revolutions lay not merely in the fact that the Chinese Communists had engaged in armed struggle, and armed struggle in the countryside. They also flowed from the exercise, by Mao and his comrades, of effective political control over varying but often considerable areas and populations, long before the actual conquest of power. Because of this the Chinese Communist movement stood in a threefold relationship to the people: that of a revolutionary army, seeking to draw from the 'ocean' of the masses the sustenance necessary to the conduct of its operations; that of the 'vanguard party', seeking to guide the proletariat in the accomplishment of its historical mission; and that of government, or state within a state, in which capacity it established with the population under its control a complex network of interactions on many levels.

Mao Tse-tung was one of those most closely attuned to the singular realities of the Chinese revolution, and these various dimensions of the relationship between leaders and masses all find expression in his thought. The over-arching concept which, in principle, infused all of these relationships was that of the 'mass line'.

The mass-line approach to leadership represents a very important element in the political and ideological heritage of the Chinese Communist Party, which sets off Chinese communism from that of the Soviet Union. Although it was fully elaborated by Mao in theoretical terms only in the early 1940s, the key concepts and methods emerged progressively during the previous decade and a half, when the sheer necessity of survival required that the Chinese Communists establish the closest kind of relationship with the populations among whom they worked.

To work with the people did not, however, mean for Mao to lose oneself in them, in some great orgy of populist spontaneity. Nor should the Yenan heritage be romanticized, or sentimentalized, to make of Mao a believer in some kind of 'extended democracy' with overtones of anarchism. The classic directive of 1 June 1943 itself, in which Mao first formulated systematically his ideas on the mass line, reflected, to be sure, his concern that policy-makers should listen to those below and learn from experience at the grass roots. His injunction to 'link the nucleus of leadership closely with the broad masses', and to 'sum up the experience of mass struggles' was seriously meant. But in the end the aim was to take the 'scattered and unsystematic ideas of the masses', turn them into 'concentrated and systematic ideas', and then 'go to the masses and propagate and explain these ideas *until the masses embrace them as their own* (*hua wei ch'ün-chung ti i-chien*)...'[73]

In other words, the people were to be made to interiorize ideas which they were quite incapable of elaborating for themselves. There is a remarkable parallel between this last phrase and Lenin's view that class consciousness could only be imported into the proletariat from outside. And yet there were significant differences between Mao's approach to leadership and that of Lenin, as well as in the revolutions they led. Let us now look at the development of Mao's ideas regarding these matters, from 1927 onwards, beginning first with the role of the army.

In August 1927, when the Central Committee criticized his strategy for the Autumn Harvest uprising, accusing him of attaching undue importance to military force, lacking faith in the strength of the masses, and turning this action into a 'mere military adventure', he replied bluntly that the Central Committee was practising 'a contradictory policy consisting in neglecting military affairs and at the same time desiring an armed insurrection of the popular masses'.[74] In fact, Mao had already answered such criticisms in his remarks at the 7 August emergency conference, where he said:

In the past, we criticized Sun Yat-sen for running a purely military movement, and we did just the opposite, not engaging in any military movement but concentrating on the mass movement....Now we have begun to pay attention to this, but we have not grasped the issue resolutely. For example, the Autumn Harvest uprising will be impossible without attention to military matters, and the present meeting must attach due importance to this question....We must be aware that political power grows out of the barrel of a gun.

This appears to be the first occasion on which Mao used this famous aphorism. He repeated it ten days later at a meeting of the Hunan Provincial Party Committee, adding that in the existing circumstances 60 per cent of the party's energies should be devoted to the military movement.[75] Only armies, Mao was persuaded, or in any case organized

---

[73] *PTMT* 316–17. (Italics added.)

[74] For the text of letters dated 20 and 30 August 1927, and presumed to have been written by Mao, see *MTTC* 2.11–14. Extracts from this correspondence are translated and its implications analysed in my article, 'On the nature of Mao Tse-tung's "deviation" in 1927', *CQ* 27 (April-June 1964), 55–66.

[75] *MTTC, pu-chüan*, 2.297–8, 299–300.

and disciplined guerrilla units, could fight armies; the masses could not fight the white armies bare-handed.

For a moment, in the autumn of 1927, the Central Committee, in the context of the chiliastic vision of uninterrupted revolution which had seized the Ch'ü Ch'iu-pai leadership, was persuaded that they could, but these hopes and illusions soon evaporated. For his part, Mao never wavered, after the Autumn Harvest uprising, from the conviction that a Red Army was indispensable to the survival of the revolution.

Until the collapse of the Li Li-san line in the late summer of 1930, Mao Tse-tung was inclined to believe that the central role of the army was merely a temporary phenomenon; thereafter, he came to see the encirclement of the cities from the countryside as the long-term pattern of the Chinese revolution. (I shall return subsequently to the strategic aspect of Mao's thinking.) But despite these changes in his ideas regarding the time-scale of the revolution, his view of the relations between the army and the masses, so long as the form of the struggle was primarily military, remained constant. In essence, they were summed up in the metaphor of the fish and the ocean, which he put forward in the 1930s. Clearly, this formulation does not underestimate the importance of the population, for without the 'ocean' of mass sympathy and support, the 'fish' of the revolutionary army would die helplessly. The Communists must therefore cultivate carefully the sources of popular support, so that the ocean which sustains them does not dry up. But, at the same time, Mao's metaphor makes perfectly clear that the military struggle will be waged by the Red Army on behalf of the masses, and not by the masses themselves.

A detailed analysis of the evolution of Mao Tse-tung's thought in all its aspects from the 1920s to the 1940s would overlap to a great extent with the chronological accounts of chapters 3 and 10. What follows is a succinct summary of the main traits of Mao's ideas regarding the aims and tactics of the revolution, by broad periods.

As early as 1920, in the Ching-kang-shan, Mao discovered the importance not only (as already noted) of regularly constituted guerrilla units, but of base areas, in which the Red Army could rest and recuperate, and where it could develop the contacts with the population without which its campaigns would become mere military adventures. Mao did not, however, at that stage, have a clear idea of the relation between the actions in which he was engaging in a remote mountainous area, and the nationwide 'revolutionary high tide' which not only Li Li-san, but Mao himself, was confidently expecting. In his report of 25 November 1928 on the struggles in the Ching-kang-shan, Mao declared that the activities of his forces did not amount to an insurrection, but merely to 'contending for the country' (*ta chiang-shan*), and would remain so as long as there was no revolutionary high tide in the country as a whole. But very rapidly the idea began to germinate in his mind that the rapid expansion of the territory held by the Red Army could significantly contribute to the rising of the tide. Thus, replying on 5 April 1929 to a letter from the Central Committee advising him and Chu Te to scale down their efforts to small-scale guerrilla activities aimed at arousing the masses, Mao replied that the assessment of the situation on which this advice was founded was excessively pessimistic. It was perfectly feasible, taking advantage of the conflict between Chiang Kai-shek and the Kwangsi clique, to conquer all of Kiangsi, as well as western Fukien and western Chekiang, within one year. At the same time, bases for proletarian struggle could be created in Shanghai, Wusih, Hangchow, Foochow and other places, to lead the struggle in these three provinces.[76]

For its part, the Comintern, though it frequently could not make up its mind as to how fast the high tide was approaching, and consequently whether it should tell the Chinese Communists to advance or consolidate their positions, had a perfectly clear and coherent theoretical position on these matters. In essence, Moscow's view was that the activities of the Red Army and the establishment of base areas in the countryside were important, but could lead to the victory of the revolution only if these activities were carried out side by side with effective work in the cities, to make the urban proletariat once more a force to be reckoned with. Thus, in February 1928, the Executive Committee of the International declared in a Resolution:

In leading spontaneous [*sic*] demonstrations by peasant partisans in the different provinces, the party must bear in mind that these demonstrations can become a starting point for a victorious national uprising only on condition that they are linked with the new upsurge of the tide of revolution in the proletarian centres. Here too, the party must see its main task as the organization of general and coordinated demonstrations in the country and in the *towns, in a number of* neighbouring provinces, and of other uprisings on a *wide* scale.[77]

A Comintern letter of December 1929 gave a decisive impetus to Li Li-san's plans for immediate revolutionary action, by telling the Chinese Communist Party that a new upsurge was beginning, and steps must therefore be taken to set up a peasants' and workers' dictatorship as soon as the tide had risen high enough. The Comintern further explained: 'One distinctive characteristic of the national crisis and the revolutionary upsurge in China is the peasant war.' But although the movement in the

---

[76] For the relevant passage from the report of November 1928, see *MTTC* 2.59. Mao's letter of 5 April 1929 is now available in *MTTC*, *pu-chüan*, 3.37–45.

[77] Translated in Carrère d'Encausse and Schram, 243. (Italics in Russian original.)

countryside (in which the Comintern lumped together the soviets under Mao's leadership and the activities of traditionalistic organizations such as the 'Red Spears') was 'in the process of becoming one of the courses along which the mighty upsurge of the all-Chinese revolution will continue to develop', the 'truest and most substantial indication of the swelling upsurge' was 'the animation of the workers' movement, which has emerged from its depressed state following the heavy defeat of 1927'.[78]

In other words, guerrilla warfare in the countryside was a legitimate and valuable part of the revolutionary effort, under Chinese conditions, but the more conventional and less exotic activities of the workers in the cities were not only more fundamental, but in the last instance would be more decisive. For his part, Li Li-san was initially far more sceptical than the Comintern regarding the significance of anything which took place in the countryside. In early 1930, however, as he began to lay his plans for a great offensive the following summer, it struck him that the Red Army could provide an extremely useful auxiliary force to distract the attention of the Kuomintang from the workers' movement, and ultimately to permit victory through a two-pronged attack from the cities and from the countryside.

On the issue of the relative weight of the cities and the countryside in the Chinese revolution, Mao Tse-tung and Li Li-san stood at opposite extremes, with Moscow occupying a centrist position. On the two other points, of the time-scale of the revolution and of the central role of China in the world revolution, Mao and Li stood in many respects close to one another, and in opposition to Moscow.

The divergences between Li Li-san and Moscow about the immanence of the revolutionary high tide are somewhat obscured by the fact that communications between China and the Soviet Union were poor, so that letters often took several months to reach their destination. As a result, the two protagonists were often responding to positions which had long since been abandoned. To take only one example, the Comintern letter of June 1930 (commonly dated 23 July in Chinese sources because that is when it was received in Shanghai) was drafted in Moscow in May in response to what was known there of decisions adopted by the Chinese Communist Party in February.[79] Even if the sequence of argument and

---

[78] Ibid. 243–4.
[79] These matters have been clarified by recent Soviet publications, which, though strongly biased in their interpretations, are probably accurate regarding many such factual details, drawn from the Comintern archives. Perhaps the most conveniently available of these is A. M. Grigoriev, 'The Comintern and the revolutionary movement in China under the slogan of the soviets (1927–1931)', in Ulyanovsky, ed., 345–88. The correct date of the June 1930 directive was given in Soviet publications of the 1930s, and there is no excuse whatsoever for continuing to refer to it as the '23 July directive'.

counter-argument is thus obscured, however, this does not prevent us from grasping the broad differences in perspective between Stalin and Li Li-san, though it does complicate the historian's task of assigning responsibility for specific decisions, and in particular for costly blunders, during the first half of 1930. (For these matters see above, chapter 3.)

Thus in June 1930, the Comintern, while noting that there was still not an objective revolutionary situation in the whole country, because the 'waves of the workers' movement and the peasants' movement' had still not merged into one, predicted that the revolutionary situation would shortly encompass 'if not the whole of Chinese territory, then at least the territory of a number of key provinces'.[80] None the less, though the Comintern expected the decisive battles in China to take place in the near future, they did not agree with Li Li-san that the time for an offensive had already come. Moscow therefore explicitly refused to sanction Li's decision to order an attack on Wuhan, Changsha, etc. and for co-ordinated uprisings in those cities, arguing that both the Red Army and the workers' movement should first be further strengthened.[81]

For his part, Mao Tse-tung was initially reluctant to throw his forces against such Kuomintang strongpoints, thus risking both the future of the revolution and the foundations of his own power. To this extent he was in agreement with Moscow. But by early 1930, he had in fact become extremely sanguine regarding the prospects for rapid victory. In a letter of January 1930 to Lin Piao, he criticized Lin for his undue pessimism about the coming of the high tide, and declared that though the time limit of one year he himself had set in April 1929 for the conquest of all of Kiangsi had been 'mechanical', such an achievement was not far off.[82]

Mao Tse-tung's attitude toward the Li Li-san line in 1930 has recently been the subject of a wide-ranging debate among Chinese scholars, enjoying access to the relevant sources. Although some of these authors still adhere to the view laid down in the resolution of 1945 on party history according to which Mao never agreed with Li's plan to attack the cities, and only implemented it because discipline required obedience to orders, others argue that Mao Tse-tung was won over to this strategy by the spring of 1930, and some even go so far as to suggest that from early 1930 he followed it spontaneously and enthusiastically. In any case, there is clear evidence that as late as October 1930 Mao Tse-tung continued to profess a radical line. A resolution adopted in Chi-an on 7 October, when Mao's forces were holding the town, noted the existence of 'a revolutionary situation in the whole world, in the whole country, in all

---

[80] Carrère d'Encausse and Schram, 244.   [81] Grigoriev, 369–73.
[82] MTTC 2.139.

provinces', and concluded: 'In the course of this revolutionary "high tide"...soviet power must undoubtedly burst upon the scene in the whole country and in the whole world.' And a letter by Mao dated 19 October called for the rejection of pessimism, and for an immediate attack on Nanchang and Chiu-chiang to annihilate the enemy, in the context of the existing 'high tide'.[83]

If there is still room for some disagreement as to the extent of Mao's chiliastic expectation of an immediate and all-encompassing revolutionary tide in the autumn of 1930, since some of the above statements might be interpreted as telling the Central Committee what he thought it wanted to hear, there can be no argument at all about Mao's conviction that the Chinese revolution was a central and decisive factor in the world revolution. And in this respect, he was altogether in agreement with Li Li-san, and aligned with Li against Moscow.[84]

On one point in particular Mao's agreement with Li was complete: they both held that foreigners did not, and could not, understand the Chinese revolution. At the 'trial' to which he was summoned in Moscow in the winter of 1930–1, Li Li-san was quoted by a Comintern inquisitor as saying: 'The Chinese revolution has so many peculiarities that the International has great difficulty in understanding it, and hardly understands it at all, and hence cannot in reality lead the Chinese Communist Party.' In consequence, he was denounced by Manuilsky as an 'extreme localist'. For his part, Mao declared, three decades afterwards:

Speaking generally, it is we Chinese who have achieved understanding of the objective world of China, not the comrades concerned with Chinese questions in the Communist International. These comrades of the Communist International simply did not understand...Chinese society, the Chinese nation, or the Chinese revolution. For a long time even we did not have a clear understanding of the objective world of China, still less the foreign comrades![85]

On another and crucial aspect of this matter, however, Mao Tse-tung did

83 For articles illustrating a range of views on this issue, see the contributions to the authoritative inner-party journal *Tang-shih yen-chiu* (Research on party history) by Lin Yun-hui, 'Lueh lun Mao Tse-tung t'ung-chih tui Li-san lu-hsien ti jen-shih ho ti-chih' (A brief account of Comrade Mao Tse-tung's understanding of and resistance to the Li-san line), *TSYC* 4 (1980) 51–9; T'ien Yuan, 'Tsai lun Mao Tse-tung t'ung-chih tui Li-san lu-hsien ti jen-shih ho ti-chih' (More on Comrade Mao Tse-tung's understanding of and resistance to the Li-san line), *TSYC* 1 (1981) 65–71; and Ling Yü, 'Mao Tse-tang t'ung-chih ho Li-san lu-hsien ti kuan-hsi t'ao-lun tsung-shu' (A summary of the discussion regarding Comrade Mao Tse-tung's relationship to the Li-san line), *TSYC* 3 (1982) 78–80. The resolution of 7 October 1930 is quoted in an article by Ch'ü Ch'iu-pai in *Shih-hua* (True words) (Shanghai) 2 (9 December 1930), 3–4. For Mao's letter of 19 October, see 'Kei Hsiang tung t'e-wei hsin' (Letter to the East Hunan Special Committee), *MTTC, pu-chüan,* 3.157–8.
84 For a brief summary of some of Li's statements about China's role in the world revolution, see S. Schram, *Mao Tse-tung,* 148–9.
85 Talk of 30 January 1962, in S. Schram, *Mao Tse-tung unrehearsed,* 172. (See also the official version, translated in *Peking Review* 27 (1978) 14.)

not take the same line as Li Li-san. Li set out quite explicitly to provoke Japanese and other imperialist intervention in North-east China, and thereby to unleash a 'world revolutionary war' into which the Soviet Union would be drawn whether she liked it or not.[86] With such a strategic vision Mao could not possibly agree, for it implied that the fate of the Chinese revolution would ultimately be decided outside China, and not in the first instance by the Chinese themselves. He was, of course, acutely conscious of the weight of the foreign imperialist presence in China, and of the importance of the international factor in the Chinese revolution. It was, however, a corollary of the shift in his sociological perspective, between 1923 and 1926, analysed above, that since the main foundations of the old reactionary order were to be found in landlord domination in the countryside, and not in the influence of the imperialists and their urban allies, victory in the Chinese revolution could only be achieved by mobilizing the workers, peasants and other exploited classes throughout the length and breadth of the land to destroy this 'feudal power' of the landlords and their political agents.

Whatever Mao's position in the summer of 1930, there is no doubt that the retreat from Changsha in September 1930 marked a crucial turning point in his thinking toward a relatively long-term strategy of encircling the cities from the countryside. In such a context, the military tactics he had been developing since he had ascended the Ching-kang-shan and joined forces there with Chu Te, in 1928, became an explicit and integral part of Mao's political thought.

According to Mao's own statement, it was in 1931, by the time Chiang Kai-shek's third 'encirclement and annihilation' campaign had been defeated, that 'a complete set of operational principles for the Red Army' took shape.[87] The earliest known text by Mao himself in which these principles were expounded is a short book entitled *Guerrilla war*, dated 1934.[88] This may well have been his first systematic formulation of the strategic ideas he was to put forward in debates at the Tsun-yi Conference, which marked a decisive stage both in the emergence of a new military line, and in opening the road to Mao's rise to supreme power in the party eight years later.[89] In December 1936, Mao delivered a series of lectures entitled *Problems of strategy in China's revolutionary war*, reviewing in detail

[86] Li's 'plot' to involve the Soviet Union in a war for the sake of the Chinese revolution naturally excites great indignation on the part of the Soviet authors; see, for example, Grigoriev, 365–7.

[87] Mao, *SW* 1.213.

[88] For a summary of a portion of this work, see Ch'en Po-chün, 'Lun k'ang-Jih yu-chi chan-cheng ti chi-pen chan-shu: hsi-chi' (On the basic tactic of the anti-Japanese guerrilla war: the surprise attack), *Chieh-fang*, 28 (11 Jan. 1938) 14–19.

[89] The Tsun-yi Conference is dealt with in chapter 4. For the latest and most authoritative collection of sources, see *Tsun-yi hui-i wen-hsien* (Documents on the Tsun-yi Conference).

the lessons of the five encirclement campaigns, and restating his case against his critics. Finally, in 1938, he wrote two works regarding the application of guerrilla tactics in the special circumstances of the Anti-Japanese War: *Questions of strategy in the Anti-Japanese guerrilla war*, and *On protracted war*. A third book, *Basic tactics*, was attributed to him in some editions.[90]

Military tactics is a specialized domain, which cannot be dealt with here at length. What follows therefore tries to view the matter from the interface between war and politics. Mao himself summed up the whole question when he wrote: 'Our strategy is "pit one against ten", and our tactics are "pit ten against one"; these contrary and yet complementary propositions constitute one of our principles for gaining mastery over the enemy.'[91]

The meaning of this aphorism is, of course, as Mao explained at length in the remainder of the passage, that while the Red Army at that time was greatly inferior in numbers and equipment to the Kuomintang and other white forces in the country as a whole, and even in each separate theatre of operations, it should fight only when it enjoyed overwhelming superiority on the battlefield. Such a tactical advantage should be obtained by concentrating the greater part of one's own forces against isolated white units, and thus 'destroying the enemy one by one'. And this, in turn, while it depended partly on skill in using troops, was very largely the result of superior intelligence, obtained by the Red Army thanks to its intimate links with the population.

The methods of the Communists for mobilizing the peasantry and thereby obtaining not only information regarding the adversary's movements but other advantages, such as voluntary service by the masses as porters or auxiliary troops, were different from anything envisaged by China's ancient military strategist Sun Tzu, yet Mao's strictly tactical principles were strikingly similar to those of Sun Tzu, who wrote:

By discovering the enemy's dispositions and remaining invisible ourselves, we can keep our forces concentrated while...the enemy must be split up into fractions. Hence there will be a whole pitted against separate parts of the whole, which means that we shall be many in collected mass to the enemy's separate few [literally, 'ten against one']....And if we are thus able to attack an inferior force with a superior one, our opponents will be in dire straits.[92]

[90] Some of the editions of this book have Mao's name on the title page, others do not, and his authorship is doubtful. Although it appears in a bibliography of Mao's works published by the PLA (Chung-kuo jen-min chieh-fang chün cheng-chih hsueh-yuan hsun-lien pu t'u-shu tzu-liao kuan, *Mao Tse-tung chu-tso, yen-lun, wen-tien mu-lu* (Peking), Feb. 1961, 28), the weight of the evidence at present is against attributing it to Mao. In the introduction to my English translation (*Basic tactics*), I have sketched an interpretation of the stages in the elaboration of Mao's military tactics.　　　　[91] Mao, *SW* 1.237.

[92] Sun Tzu, *The art of war*, Giles' trans., Ch. VI, par. 13.

Mao himself, questioned in his later years about what he had learned from the Chinese classics, was generally whimsical and frequently contradictory in his replies. In one of his most balanced statements, he said in 1968 that he had read the *Romance of the three kingdoms* before he began to fight in 1927, and that he had taken a look at Sun Tzu before writing his own works on military tactics in 1936–8.[93] There is no doubt, in any case, that he very frequently quoted, in these writings, both from Sun Tzu and from historical works, as well as from novels such as the *Romance of the three kingdoms* and *Water margin*.

How did Mao Tse-tung contrive to justify in theoretical terms the view that a Communist Party of uncertain composition, operating primarily through the instrumentality of the army, in a highly ambiguous social context, could yet constitute the vanguard of the proletariat? A crucial issue here is the role of the subjective factors in defining man's class nature, and the possibility of modifying a person's objective essence by changing his thinking. We have seen that Mao's emphasis on the importance of subjective attitudes goes back to 1917. One of the most striking formulations of the period under consideration here is to be found in his report of 28 November 1928 on the struggle on the Ching-kang-shan. Discussing the problem raised by the fact that the greater part of his small Red Army was made up not of workers, or even of proper peasants, but of rural vagabonds or *éléments déclassés*, Mao said:

The contingent of *éléments déclassés* should be replaced by peasants and workers, but these are not available now. On the one hand, when fighting is going on every day, the *éléments déclassés* are after all especially good fighters. Moreover, casualties are mounting high. Consequently, not only can we not diminish the *éléments déclassés* now in our ranks, but it is even difficult to find more for reinforcements. In these circumstances, the only method is to intensify political training, so as to effect a qualitative change in these elements.[94]

In his letter of January 1930 to Lin Piao, Mao criticized Lin for 'over-estimating the importance of objective forces and underestimating the importance of subjective forces'.[95] By 'objective forces' Mao meant in particular the white armies, which were outside the Communists' direct control, whereas 'subjective forces' referred to the Red Army, which they perceived from inside, and whose motivation and strategy they therefore understood. But it is plain that he was also talking about objective factors in the broader sense of objective historical circumstances, and subjective factors in the sense of the human capacity to influence those circumstances by 'conscious action'.

[93] Dialogue with Red Guards, 28 July 1968, in *Miscellany of Mao Tse-tung thought*, 476 (JPRS no. 61269). Chinese in *Mao Tse-tung ssu-hsiang wan-sui* (1969), 694.
[94] *MTTC* 2.36–7; *PTMT* 268–9.   [95] *MTTC* 2.130.

This element in Mao's thinking had been, as I suggested earlier, reinforced by the context of military struggle in which he developed his ideas and undertook to make revolution from 1927 onwards. Mao saw war as the highest manifestation of 'conscious action' and the supreme test of the human spirit. He put the point in a passage which he liked so much that he repeated it in almost identical words in 1936 and in 1938:

Conscious activity is a distinctive characteristic of man, especially of man at war. This characteristic is manifested in all of man's acts, but nowhere more strongly than in war. Victory or defeat in a war is decided on the one hand by the military, political, economic, and geographical conditions, by the character of the war, and by international support on both sides. But it is not decided by these alone; these alone constitute only the possibility of victory or defeat; they do not in themselves decide the issue. To decide the issue, subjective efforts must be added, efforts in directing and waging the war, i.e. conscious activity in war.

People who direct a war cannot strive for victories beyond the limit allowed by the objective conditions, but within that limit they can and must strive actively for victory. The stage of action for these directors of war must be built upon objective conditions, but on this stage, they can direct the performance of many living dramas, full of sound and colour, of power and grandeur...[96]

This passage eloquently expresses what I have called Mao Tse-tung's 'military romanticism', born out of the experience of many years of bitter struggle for survival. It would, however, be a gross over-simplification to interpret Mao's faith in the limitless capacities of man, and especially of the Chinese people, solely in terms of his romantic temperament, or of his life of combat. His emphasis on subject factors corresponded also, as I have already suggested, to the necessities of revolution in a transitional society made up of many disparate elements.

It is this aspect of Chinese reality which provides the link between the military and political dimensions of Mao's thought and experience. Just as the outcome of a battle can rarely be predicted with certainty, but depends in part, as Mao stressed in the passage just quoted, on subjective factors such as the courage of the soldiers and the tactical skill of the commanders, so the terms of the political combat appeared less clearly defined in China than in Western Europe or even in the former Russian empire. Although the Chinese Communist Party and the Kuomintang might be regarded loosely as the representatives respectively of the workers and of the capitalists, the socio-economic weight of the peasants in the former, and of the landlords in the latter, was in fact greater. Moreover, the picture was significantly modified by the impact of the foreign presence. Marx and Engels, with reference to the Polish question, and Lenin, with reference to the colonies in the twentieth century, had

[96] *MTTC* 6.98–9, 284–5.

already established the principle that the behaviour of classes within a given society might be modified by a reaction of solidarity against the foreign oppressor. Mao Tse-tung, for his part, did not merely accept this as a theoretical possibility; he was persuaded, from the early 1930s onward, that an alliance for the pursuit of national goals could be effectively realized, and that its establishment depended in large part on the success of the Communists in modifying the subjective attitudes of other strata of Chinese society, apart from the workers and their immediate allies the peasantry.

This concern with national unity as the condition of national salvation, though it marked Mao's thought and policies to a greater or lesser degree from beginning to end, by no means signified that he had become a mere nationalist. Even in the late 1930s, as he concluded and implemented a new alliance with Chiang Kai-shek, Mao made crystal clear that the Chinese Communist Party had no intention of abandoning its maximum programme. And in the late 1920s and early 1930s, social revolution was the main focus of his thought and action. Nor did he approach it solely in terms of moral values and psychological transformation. Though he believed that objective social realities could be modified by changes in consciousness, he also saw participation in revolutionary action as one of the most effective means for changing men's thinking. Indeed, an acute awareness of the interaction between the subjective and the objective, and the deliberate manipulation of this dialectic was one of the hallmarks of Mao Tse-tung's thought, and one of the secrets of his political success.

The concept of revolutionary struggle as an instrument for promoting cultural revolution was formulated by Mao as early as 1927, in his Hunan peasant report, where he wrote: 'The abolition of the clan system, of superstitions, and of one-sided notions of chastity will follow as a natural consequence of victory in the political and economic struggles. ... The idols should be removed by the peasants themselves...'[97]

Throughout the ensuing two decades, the countryside remained the main theatre of Mao's experiments both in social and in cultural revolution. The heart of his activity in this domain was, of course, land reform. That topic is not discussed here, because agrarian policy has been dealt with at length in chapter 5. One episode, which offers particularly striking illustration of Mao's faith in the technique of changing attitudes through revolutionary struggle, was the 'land verification movement' of 1933–4. Mao may not have launched this, but he did place his stamp on it in 1933. The ostensible economic goal of this campaign, which was to determine whether or not land reform had been properly carried out, in fact merely provided the framework within which to pursue essentially political aims. Given the inherited prestige of the landlords and rich peasants, and the fact that they had the advantage of literacy and facility in speech, Mao was convinced that whatever changes were made in the formal property structure, these formerly privileged elements would succeed in one way or another in worming their way back into positions of authority in the peasant associations. The only way to prevent such a disguised return to the old order of things was constantly to stir up the peasantry at the grass roots and encourage poor peasants to engage in struggle against their former exploiters, in order to develop their self-confidence and allow the conviction to take root that henceforth they were the masters of society.

Exactly similar aims were pursued during the land reforms which accompanied and followed the civil war and the conquest of power in the late 1940s. The mass meetings, at which the peasants were encouraged to 'speak their bitterness' against the landlords for their previous oppression, followed in some cases by the execution of the worst offenders, were designed not only to break the spirit of the gentry, but above all to allow the peasants to rid themselves of their inferiority complex and stand up as men at last. Thus Mao undertook to carry out a cultural revolution in the sense of a change in attitudes toward authority, and used revolutionary struggle as an instrument toward this end. But while this method of work was prominent in his line from the 1920s to the 1940s and after, the political context within which he applied these techniques changed significantly over the years.

A crucial aspect of the tactical situation during the period of the Kiangsi Soviet Republic was the contradiction between military and political imperatives. In order to obtain maximum support from the population, Mao Tse-tung and Chu Te had practised in earlier years the principle of 'luring the enemy deep' into the heart of the base area, where land reform had been carried out and the sympathy for the Red Army was therefore warmest. These tactics meant, however, that the faithful supporters of the Communist forces were frequently exposed to the perils and losses of war, and this undermined the credibility of the Chinese Soviet Republic to constitute a veritable state within a state, since it could not protect its own citizens. In a sense, the 'forward and offensive strategy' constituted a response to this dilemma – a response which consisted in putting the political imperative of defending the prestige and integrity of the soviet republic ahead of realistic evaluation of the military possibilities. It ended in disaster, but that does not necessarily mean that Mao's earlier tactics would have worked in 1934. In any case, it was only the rapidly accelerating Japanese advance into China, and the consequent threat to China's very survival as an independent nation, which effectively allowed the Communists to break out of the dilemma in which they found themselves. Moreover, it was only in the new circumstances which took shape in 1935–7 that Mao, who had had little of any theoretical interest to say for several years, once more began to speak out in confident tones. No doubt the fact that he was again in a strong position in the party, whereas in 1933–4 he had been reduced to little more than a figurehead, had something to do with his new eloquence. But the phenomenon also resulted, unquestionably, from the fact that a war for national liberation was something about which he had a great deal to say. Even in the early 1930s, Mao's statements about the relation between the internal and external enemies of the revolution were suggestive of what was to come.

The evolution which brought Communists and Kuomintang, and the old enemies Mao Tse-tung and Chiang Kai-shek, once more into an alliance was very much against the grain of both parties. What was the theoretical justification which Mao put forward for the second united front?

In September 1931, when the Japanese action in Manchuria first brought to the fore the issue of resistance to foreign aggression, the position of the Chinese Communist Party regarding collaboration with the bourgeoisie was basically similar to that of the Comintern, summed up in the slogan of 'class against class'. Nevertheless, although this was understood to mean in principle the struggle for hegemony between the proletariat and the bourgeoisie, Mao's sociological vision of the concrete struggle remained that which he had entertained in 1926. A letter of 25 September 1931, signed by Mao and others, to 'our brothers the soldiers of the White Army', after calling on them to kill their reactionary superior officers and unite with the workers, peasants, and toiling masses to overthrow the 'fucking Kuomintang government', continued:

confiscate the land of the landlord class and distribute it among the poor peasants; confiscate the food and the houses of the wealthy and distribute them among the poor; let the workers do only eight hours of work a day; then, organize yourselves to run your own affairs. In this way, you will have created a government of workers, peasants, and soldiers, that is, a soviet government.[98]

Clearly, for Mao the countryside was where the Chinese revolution principally was at. In this text, the 'Kuomintang militarists' were treated as the 'running dogs of imperialism', as well as the creatures of the landlord class, just as in Mao's writings of the 1920s, but the domestic reactionary role of the Kuomintang in 'exploiting and butchering the

98 MTTC 3.14; PTMT 219.

masses' was still given the greatest prominence. To the extent that Mao's attack focused on the problem of resistance to Japanese aggression, his position was the mirror image of Chiang Kai-shek's 'unify before resisting'. Since 'only the Red Army' could 'overthrow imperialism and really defend the people', it was necessary first to deal with the domestic enemy, in order to make possible effective action against the foreign invader.

In April 1932, in the wake of the Japanese aggression against Shanghai in January of that year, the Chinese Soviet government declared war on Japan, thus bringing questions of foreign affairs closer to the centre of its political strategy. A change in Mao's outlook regarding collaboration with other political forces was signalled by a declaration of 17 January 1933, which offered, on certain conditions (cessation of attacks on the soviet regions, granting of democratic rights, and arming of the masses against Japan), to conclude an agreement with 'any armed force', that is, with any dissident commander prepared to deal with the Communists.[99] Although this position still remained within the framework of the 'united front from below' laid down in the line of the Comintern, that is to say, an alliance with the supporters of other political movements rather than with their leaders, the willingness to deal with high-ranking officers of the Kuomintang (though not with Chiang Kai-shek himself) marked a significant step toward the 'united front from above' which was to be set up in 1937.

In the proclamation on the northward march of the Red Army to fight Japan, which he signed on 15 July 1934 together with Chu Te, Mao called once again for a 'national revolutionary war', and an alliance with those willing to wage such a war, while striving to overthrow the 'band of traitors of the Kuomintang'.[100] Nevertheless, while Mao Tse-tung gave high place to nationalism as an idea and a political force, he was markedly more reticent than the Soviet leaders about going all the way to a second united front, and the declaration of 1 August 1935 calling for such a front was in fact issued from Moscow on behalf of the Chinese Communist Party by Wang Ming, in the context of the Seventh Comintern Congress.

For their part, Mao and his comrades found it far more distasteful than did Stalin to embrace once again Chiang Kai-shek, whom they knew as the butcher of their friends and perceived as a traitor to the revolution. By the end of 1935, as his forces regrouped in December in Wayaobao, Mao was prepared to cooperate not only with the 'national bourgeoisie' but with those sectors of the capitalist class who were linked to European

[99] *Su-wei-ai Chung-kuo*, 91–4; MTTC 3.183–5.   [100] MTTC 4.363–7; PTMT 220–2.

and American imperialism, and were therefore inclined to oppose 'Japanese imperialism and its running dogs'. With their support, the 'workers' and peasants' republic' would be changed into a 'government of national defence'. But Chiang Kai-shek, as the 'chieftain' of the 'camp of traitors to the nation', and the representative of the evil gentry, warlords and compradors, was specifically excluded from the proposed united front.[101]

By April 1936, however, Chang Hsueh-liang had met with Chou En-lai, and had urged the Communists to stop fighting Chiang and concentrate on the Japanese, promising to use his influence with Chiang to persuade him to accept such a truce. On 5 May 1936, a telegram was accordingly addressed directly to the Military Affairs Council in Nanking, and this was subsequently characterized by Mao as marking the 'abandonment of the anti-Chiang Kai-shek slogan'.[102] Henceforth, Mao was in regular contact with Chang Hsueh-liang, Yang Hu-ch'eng and other political and military leaders about the possibility of cooperation against Japan,[103] writing in particular to Chang on 5 October 1936 expressing his desire for an 'agreement between the Kuomintang and the Communist Party to resist Japan and save the country'. On 1 December 1936, Mao signed, together with eighteen other senior Communist political and military leaders, a letter to Chiang himself, expressing the hope that he would change his ways, so posterity would remember him not as the man responsible for China's ruin, but as 'the hero who saved the country and the people'.[104]

All of these gestures, which were based on political realism, did not mean that the feelings of the Communists toward Chiang had changed fundamentally. When he was taken prisoner by Chang Hsueh-liang and Yang Hu-ch'eng in Sian on 12 December, there was an instinctive reaction on the part of Communist cadres, high and low, that it would be very agreeable to put him on trial for his crimes against the revolution, but there is no evidence that such a policy was seriously considered by Mao and others at the top level. On the contrary, Mao Tse-tung wrote to Yen Hsi-shan on 22 December 1936 assuring him that 'we do not in the least wish to take revenge on Nanking'.[105] Mao's frequently reported rage on receipt of a peremptory telegram from Moscow ordering him not to kill Chiang was therefore provoked not by frustration at being deprived

---

[101] Report of 27 December 1935, Mao, *SW* 1.153–78. The term used in the *Selected works* is 'people's government'; I am assuming that Mao originally spoke in 1935, like the Central Committee resolution of two days earlier (*MTTC* 5.26–8), of a government of national defence.

[102] Mao, *SW* 1.264, 279–80.

[103] See the numerous letters from the second half of 1936 in *Selected letters*, 30–97.

[104] *Ibid.* 78–9, 87–90.   [105] *Ibid.* 95–7.

of his victim, but by Stalin's doubts about his loyalty, or his common sense.[106]

In any case, once embarked on a policy of cooperation with the Kuomintang, the Chinese Communists, and Mao in particular, showed themselves inclined to throw themselves into it with a will. The reason was, manifestly, that for them the salvation of the Chinese nation was not merely, as for Lenin, the basis for tactical manoeuvres; it was a value in itself.

Mao could not, of course, call for a change of such importance without justifying it, both for himself and for his followers, in terms of the stage currently reached by the Chinese revolution, and the tasks which could accordingly be pursued at that time. He began to sketch out his ideas on this theme in his speech of 27 December 1935 just mentioned; they were fully elaborated and given their definitive formulation only in 1939–40. But before continuing this discussion of Mao's political thought, which reached a notably higher level of maturity and complexity during the Yenan period, it is necessary to give some account of the emergence, in 1937, of philosophical ideas which were to occupy an increasingly central place in his thinking as a whole.

NATIONAL CONTRADICTIONS AND SOCIAL CONTRADICTIONS 1937–1940

While Mao Tse-tung had occasionally touched on philosophical questions in his writings of the 1920s and 1930s, it was in the winter of 1936–7 that he first undertook the serious study of Marxist philosophy. Edgar Snow has recorded how Mao interrupted the interviews, which were to form the basis for his autobiography, in order to devour a pile of Soviet works on philosophy in Chinese translation which had just reached the Communist capital of Pao-an. Having read these, Mao proceeded almost immediately to deliver a series of lectures on dialectical materialism, of which the works now known as 'On practice' and 'On contradiction' were originally the concluding sections.[107]

Only 'On practice' and 'On contradiction' have, of course, been

[106] For details regarding the sequence of events, and further references, see above, ch. 12 by Lyman Van Slyke. The above interpretation is based on interviews with Hu Hua and Li Hsin, respectively on 10 and 23 September 1982 in Peking.

[107] 'Pien-cheng-fa wei-wu-lun (chiang-shou t'i-kang)' (Dialectical materialism – lecture notes) in K'ang-chan ta-hsueh, 6 to 8 (April to June 1938). This portion of the text includes chapter 1, and the first six sections of chapter 2. It is not known whether or not the remainder of the work was serialized in K'ang-chan ta-hsueh. Sections 7 to 10 of chapter 2 were included in a version circulated during the Cultural Revolution (Mao Chu-hsi wen-hsuan), and the whole of the first two chapters, less section 11 of chapter 2 (corresponding to 'On practice'), was reproduced in MTTC 6.265–305. Subsequently, two editions of the work containing the original version of

officially published in China since 1949, respectively in 1950 and 1952. The contemporary evidence that Mao did in fact deliver a course of lectures on dialectical materialism in 1937 is, however, conclusive and irrefutable.[108] It is therefore of some moment that, when asked about the matter by Edgar Snow in 1965, Mao denied authorship of *On dialectical materialism*.[109] It is true that he generally preferred people to read his works only in editions revised and approved by himself, but he did not always go to the trouble of explicitly repudiating items no longer thought suitable.

The reasons for Mao's sensitivity in this case are not far to seek. A reputation as a Marxist theoretician and philosopher has been regarded, since Lenin's day, as one of the indispensable qualifications for leadership within the Communist movement. It was no doubt with the aim of establishing his credentials in this respect (as Stalin had sought to do before him) that Mao had originally delivered these lectures. His rivals in the party, with whom he was to have an ongoing trial of strength during the next five or six years, were all schooled in Moscow, and he thus felt himself vulnerable to the charge that he was nothing but a leader of peasant guerrillas, with no grasp of Marxist theory and no capacity for dealing with abstract categories. It soon became apparent, however, that Mao's lectures on dialectical materialism did not effectively serve their purpose. In very large part, they amounted (especially in the early sections) to unashamed plagiarism of his Soviet sources, and where Mao had expressed himself in his own words, the result was often very crude.[110]

'On practice' have come to light, and one of these also contains chapter 3, corresponding to 'On contradiction'. The complete text appears in *MTTC, pu-chüan*, 5.187–280. For a translation of selected passages and a detailed analysis both of the form and of the content of the original version of 'On contradiction', see Nick Knight, 'Mao Zedong's *On contradiction* and *On practice*: pre-liberation texts', *CQ* 84 (December 1980), 641–68. Mr Knight has also published a complete translation: *Mao Zedong's 'On contradiction'. An annotated translation of the pre-liberation text.*

[108] It suffices to mention three points, any of which would be sufficient in itself. The first is that, as already indicated, a considerable portion of the text was published at the time in *K'ang-chan ta-hsueh*. The second is the reference to this work by Chang Ju-hsin, then (with Ch'en Po-ta) one of those most actively engaged in building up Mao as a theoretician, in an article published in *Chieh-fang jih-pao* (18 and 19 February 1942), where he characterized it as the most important source on Mao's methodology and dialectics. Finally, almost the whole text of the work, broken up into fragments by theme, is reproduced in an authorized compilation on Mao's philosophical thought: 'Pei-ching ta-hsueh che-hsueh hsi', *Mao Tse-tung che-hsueh ssu-hsiang (chai-lu)*, 11–14, 19–21, 49–51, 53–5, 64–9, 97–9 and *passim.*

[109] As originally published in *The New Republic*, this disclaimer was strong, but Mao carefully edged away from a flat statement that he had never given any such lectures; when the interview was re-published as an appendix to *The long revolution*, it was 'improved' to make of it a categorical denial of authorship. A comment by Snow (*The long revolution*, 194–5) suggests that this may have been done at the request of the Chinese authorities, or of Mao himself.

[110] On Mao's plagiarism, see the note in my article 'Mao Tse-tung and the theory of the permanent revolution, 1958–1969', *CQ* 46 (April–June 1971), 223–4; also K. A. Wittfogel, 'Some remarks

In the context of the view (explicitly stated in 1981, but implicit since 1978 or 1979) that Mao Tse-tung was a man subject to human error, and that 'Mao Tse-tung thought' was not his creation alone, both the fact that Mao did indeed lecture on dialectical materialism in 1937, and his debt to other authors, especially to Ai Ssu-ch'i, have now been officially placed on record in China.[111]

I shall not analyse here Mao's lectures as a whole, but this episode does provide valuable background for evaluating the two essays that did become an integral part of 'Mao Tse-tung thought'. The first point to be made is that the portions of the lectures corresponding to 'On practice' and 'On contradiction' are notably more original and more interesting than the earlier part of the work. Moreover, while epistemology was often dealt with at some length in writings and translations from Soviet works to which Mao was exposed in 1936–7, and often came (like 'On practice') relatively near the end of one-volume surveys of Marxist philosophy, the prominence given by Mao to the subject of contradictions was without parallel in any of his potential sources. Most of these had a section on the unity and struggle of opposites, the negation of the negation and related topics, but it was generally short, and in no case was it placed, as in Mao's lectures, at the end, thus making it the culmination and synthesis of the whole course.

Many reasons could no doubt be given for the prominence Mao attached to contradictions. Two of them flow naturally from the interpretation of his thought already sketched in this chapter. On the one hand, his understanding of dialectics was strongly marked by Taoism and other currents in traditional Chinese thought. On the other, he was, as I have stressed throughout, acutely aware of the complex and ambiguous character of Chinese society (in other words, of the contradictions within it), and sought to incorporate these insights into his revolutionary tactics. The first of these characteristics might be seen by some as a flaw in his understanding of dialectics; the second might well be construed as an

on Mao's handling of concepts and problems of dialectics', *Studies in Soviet thought*, 3.4 (Dec. 1963), 251–77.

[111] See the materials in *Chung-kuo che-hsueh*, 1.1–44, including Mao's extensive reading notes on Ai's *Che-hsueh yü sheng-huo* (Philosophy and life) dated September 1937, a letter of early 1938 from Mao to Ai about a point in this work, and an article (Kuo Hua-jo, 'Mao chu-hsi k'ang-chan ch'u-ch'i kuang-hui ti che-hsueh huo-tung' (Chairman Mao's brilliant philosophical activity during the early period of the anti-Japanese war)) discussing the variants between the original versions of 'On practice' and 'On contradiction' and those in Mao, *SW*. Other writings by Ai which Mao certainly read included his translation of an article by Mitin from the Great Soviet Encyclopedia, *Hsin che-hsueh ta-kang* (Outline of the new philosophy) (Tu-shu sheng-huo ch'u-pan-she, 1936), from which he cribbed many passages, and *Ta-chung che-hsueh* (Philosophy for the masses), which a reader of *K'ang-chan ta-hsueh* (8, 187) showed an embarrassing tendency to confuse with Mao's lectures.

advantage. The ensuing brief discussion of Mao's 'On contradiction' deals first with the one and then with the other of these two points.

Some idea of the importance attached by Mao to contradictions can be gained from the fact that chapter 3 ('Materialist dialectics') of his lecture notes runs to 53 out of a total of 110 pages of the Dairen edition of *Dialectical materialism*. The portion of this chapter (beginning on p. 64) which corresponds fairly closely to 'On contradiction' runs to approximately 25,000 characters, as compared to about 22,000 for the *Selected works* version. While there are significant differences between the two texts, the correspondence is sufficiently close to dispose once and for all of the theory, put forward by Arthur Cohen and others, according to which Mao could not possibly have written such a substantial work in 1937.[112] There remains, however, the problem of why this portion of the lectures was so much superior to the earlier sections. In essence, the answer lies, I think, in the fact that Mao was dealing not only with notions which appealed to him, but with their concrete application to the circumstances of the Chinese revolution. The first chapter of *Dialectical materialism* was, on the other hand, in large part simply a summary of the history of philosophy in Greece and the West, as perceived by Soviet authors. Here Mao could only copy his sources, and was in no position to add anything of himself.

As for the substance of 'On contradiction', the problem of the unorthodox character of Mao's dialectics became acute only after 1949, partly as a result of polemics with the Soviets, and to this extent does not fall within our scope here. In a word, it is commonly held that Soviet journals (which had praised 'On practice' in 1950) took no notice of 'On contradiction' two years later because they objected to the implied challenge to Stalin's theoretical primacy. There is no doubt whatever that this was indeed a factor, but it is altogether possible that the Soviets also found Mao's understanding of dialectics strange and heretical.

On many occasions in the 1950s Mao complained that the *Concise*

---

[112] It is true, of course, that this text was published nearly a decade later. On the other hand, editions of Mao's writings which appeared in 1946-7 do not commonly show extensive rewriting. Moreover, this version has been placed in circulation by the Soviets, who would surely not wish to contribute to any misunderstanding which might enhance Mao Tse-tung's reputation for theoretical maturity during the Yenan period. In other words, if it had been rewritten, as Cohen argues, to take account of Stalin's works of the late 1930s, Soviet specialists would certainly have pointed this out. For Cohen's argument (now invalidated), see A. Cohen, *The communism of Mao Tse-tung*, 14–28.

Confirmation both of Mao's authorship of the lecture notes on dialectical materialism, and of the fact that the 1946 Ta-lien edition was simply a reprint of what had been reproduced in mimeographed form in Yenan in 1937, without editorial changes, has been provided recently from an extremely authoritative source. See the article by Kung Yü-chih, Deputy Director of the Research Centre on Party Literature under the Central Committee, '"Shih-chieh lun" san t'i' (Three points regarding 'On practice'), in *Lun Mao Tse-tung che-hsüeh ssu-hsiang* (On Mao Tse-tung's philosophical thought), 66–86, especially 66–72.

philosophical dictionary made a speciality of criticizing his view of contradictions, and on one occasion he noted that he was speaking of the fourth edition of this work (published in Moscow in 1953) which reflected, he said, Stalin's views. The Soviet complaint was that the transformation of birth into death was 'metaphysical', and that the transformation of war into peace was wrong.[113] A case can be made regarding the para-traditional character of Mao's dialectics in his old age, when (in 1964) he abandoned two of the three basic axioms of Marxist and Hegelian dialectics, including the negation of the negation.[114] And while his outlook in 1937 was more derivative, and therefore on the whole more orthodox in Marxist terms, it could be argued that he was already leaning in the direction he was to follow a quarter of a century later. Perhaps the clearest pointer is to be found in the statement that 'the law of the unity of opposites' is 'the fundamental law of thought',[115] which seems to place this axiom in a higher category than the other two principles (the negation of the negation, and the transformation of quantity into quality) Mao subsequently rejected.[116]

The original version of Mao's lecture notes contains an allusion to the fact that Lenin regarded the unity of opposites as the 'kernel of dialectics',[117] and in 1957 Mao cited the relevant fragment explicitly: 'In brief, dialectics can be defined as the doctrine of the unity of opposites. This grasps the kernel of dialectics, but it requires explanations and development.'[118] This remark of Lenin's occurs, however, in rough reading notes on Hegel's *Logic*, and the passage summarizing Hegel's ideas to which it refers mentions both the negation of the negation, and the transformation of quantity into quality.[119]

To pursue this problem further would not only require detailed discussion of developments in Mao's thought after 1949, but would take us too far from the mainly political concerns of this chapter toward the consideration of strictly philosophical issues. Mao's analysis of Chinese society, and the theoretical conclusions he drew from it, lie on the other

---

[113] Mao, *SW* 5.368; Schram, *Mao unrehearsed*, 109 (speech of 20 March 1958).

[114] I have examined this problem in my essay 'The Marxist' in Dick Wilson, ed. *Mao Tse-tung in the scales of history*, 60–4. See also F. Wakeman, *History and will*, 297–9, 310, 323–6, etc.

[115] Mao, *SW* 1.345.

[116] This point was noted by Wang Jo-shui in a conversation of 7 May 1982 in Peking, though Mr Wang did not agree that Mao's emphasis on the unity and struggle of opposites reflected traditional influences. Steve Chin has interpreted Mao's stress on the unity of opposites as a new theoretical development going well beyond Marx and Engels. (Steve S. K. Chin, *The thought of Mao Tse-tung*, 60–4.) The preface to a 1946 edition of the lectures points out that the sections on the other two laws are 'missing'. *MTTC, pu-chüan*, 5.279. Note also Mao's disagreement with Ai Ssu-ch'i's view that mere differences (such as between pen, ink and table) do not necessarily constitute contradictions: *Chung-kuo che-hsueh*, 1.29.

[117] Knight, trans., 39.   [118] Mao, *SW* 5.366.

[119] V. I. Lenin, 'Conspectus of Hegel's *Science of logic*', *Collected works* 38, 222–3.

hand at the centre of our concerns, and can serve as a convenient transition from philosophy to other aspects of Mao's thought. It has often been argued, and up to a point the claim is accepted even by Cohen, that Mao's most notable contribution to the science of dialectics lay in his elaboration of the concepts 'principal contradiction' and 'principal aspect of the principal contradiction'. I should like to suggest, to begin with, that Mao's use of these categories can be linked directly to his subtle understanding of Chinese reality. A Marxist revolutionary in a society of the type observed by Marx himself, which was perceived as increasingly polarized into capitalists and proletarians, should have been in no doubt as to which were the basic contradictions between classes, or between the productive forces and the mode of production. In broad terms, this pattern was expected to remain more or less the same until the conflict was resolved by revolution. In China, on the other hand, where neither the internal situation nor relations with foreign powers were stable or predictable, it was not merely an intriguing intellectual problem, but a pressing tactical necessity, to determine which factor, or contradiction, was crucial or dominant at a given time.

It is interesting to note that one of the earliest Soviet writings translated in China, a volume published in Shanghai in 1933, devoted a section to the 'leading' (*chu-tao*) aspect of contradictions, but stated that this was in general always *the same*: for example, in the contradictions between base and superstructure, the base was always dominant.[120] This is one of the points in Mao's essay which Cohen finds most significant; he draws attention to the passage which reads:

Some people think that...in the contradiction between the productive forces and the relations of production, the productive forces are the leading aspect; in the contradiction between theory and practice, practice is the leading aspect; in the contradiction between the economic foundation and its superstructure, the economic foundation is the leading aspect, and that there is no change in their respective positions.... True, the productive forces, practice, and the economic foundation generally manifest themselves as the leading and decisive factors...But there are times (*yu shih*) when such aspects as the relations of production, theory and the superstructure in turn manifest themselves as the leading or decisive factors; this must also be admitted. When the productive forces cannot be developed unless the relations of production are changed, the change in the relations of production plays the leading and decisive role.... When the superstructure – politics, culture, and so on – hinders the development of the economic foundation, political and cultural reforms become the leading and decisive factors...[121]

[120] Li Ta and others (translators), *Pien-cheng-fa wei-wu-lun chiao-ch'eng* (by Hsi-lo-k'e-fu (Shirokov), and others), 295.

[121] *Pien-cheng wei-wu-lun*, 93; *MTTC, pu-chüan*, 5.264. There are some variants in this passage, but with

Cohen makes of this passage one of the key links in his argument that Mao did not write 'On contradiction' in 1937; Mao could not possibly, he says, have gone against Marxist 'determinism' in this fashion until Stalin had shown him the way, with his writings of 1938 and 1950. The facts speak otherwise. It would seem that Mao derived his 'voluntarism' directly from the study of Lenin (to whom the term was, after all, first applied), and also from his own personality, and the experience of the Chinese revolution. Indeed, it could be argued that the original text of 'On contradiction' puts even more emphasis on subjective factors.

The most important variant here is the replacement of the expression 'there are times' by 'in certain circumstances'. The implication of this formulation, inserted in the *Selected works*, would appear to be that such circumstances, or the totality of the necessary preconditions, will be present only for limited periods, at times of crisis or revolution. The looser 'at times' might be taken, on the other hand, to suggest that this reversal of roles between basis and superstructure might last for a significant period. This conclusion is reinforced by the sentence which follows immediately the passage just quoted (in both versions, original and rewritten): 'The creation and advocacy of revolutionary theory plays the principal and decisive role in those times of which Lenin said, "Without revolutionary theory there can be no revolutionary movement".'[122] Since Lenin saw this axiom as applicable to the whole historical period in which the proletarian revolution was to be planned, organized and carried out, Mao's use of it here can well be interpreted to mean that, while generally speaking the superstructure does not play the leading and decisive role in historical change, one of those 'times' when it does will occur, in fact, in China during a large part of the twentieth century.

One final point about Mao as a philosopher concerns his debt to Stalin. The current version of 'On contradiction' has a long and fulsome passage about Stalin's analysis of the peculiarities of the Russian Revolution as a 'model in understanding the particularity and universality of contradiction'.[123] This turns out to have been completely absent from the original version, where Mao illustrates his point rather by the exegesis of a quotation from Su Tung-p'o, who is said to have thoroughly understood the relation between the universal and the relative.[124]

the exception of the replacement of *chu-tao* (leading) by *chu-yao* (principal), Mao made no fundamental changes in 1952 in those portions which I have actually quoted here. (The translation is from *PTMT* 199; see also Nick Knight, trans., 28 and notes.) Mao's criticism may have been directed against the work cited in the previous note, though in 1941 he recommended Shirokov's book for study by cadres (*Selected letters*, 189).

[122] Knight, trans., 28.
[123] Mao, *SW* 1.229–30.
[124] *Pien-cheng wei-wu-lun*, 86; *MTTC*, *pu-chüan*, 5.258; Knight, trans., 24, and 146. The passage in

Chapter 2 of *Dialectical materialism* contains the statement that, because the 'dialectical materialist currents developing in China today do not result from taking over and reforming our own philosophical heritage, but from the study of Marxism-Leninism', we must 'liquidate the philosophical heritage of ancient China', which reflected the 'backwardness of China's social development'.[125] Plainly, this statement was the product of a momentary feeling of intimidation on Mao's first exposure to Marxist dialectics. It was entirely superseded by his call, in October 1938, for the 'sinification of Marxism', and did not represent a consistent position even in 1937.

If we look now concretely at Mao Tse-tung's analysis of strategic and tactical problems in the late 1930s, a fundamental issue is that of the relation between the Chinese Communist Party and the 'general staff of the world proletariat' in Moscow. Mao's view of this matter was absolutely clear. He summed it up in 1936 when, replying to a question from Edgar Snow as to whether, in the event of a Communist victory, there would be 'some kind of actual merger of governments' between Soviet China and Soviet Russia, he declared: 'We are certainly not fighting for an emancipated China in order to turn the country over to Moscow!' And he continued, spelling out the basis for this rejoinder:

The Chinese Communist Party is only one party in China, and in its victory it will have to speak for the whole nation. It cannot speak for the Russian people, or rule for the Third International, but only in the interests of the Chinese masses. Only where the interests of the Chinese masses coincide with the interests of the Russian masses can it be said to be 'obeying the will' of Moscow. But of course this basis of common benefit will be tremendously broadened once the masses of China are in democratic power and socially and economically emancipated, like their brothers in Russia.[126]

This passage shows that Mao, in 1936, felt the bond of solidarity uniting all the world's Communist Parties. But it also makes plain that for him solidarity did not mean subservience. Other things being equal, an 'emancipated China' – that is, a China ruled by the Communist Party – would have more intimate ties with the Soviet Union than with other countries. But if things were *not* equal – if Moscow did not show the respect for China's interests which Mao regarded as normal and

question is from Su's famous poem 'The red cliff', and reads as follows: 'If we regard this question as one of impermanence, then the universe cannot last for the twinkling of an eye. If, on the other hand, we consider it from the aspect of permanence, then you and I, together with all matter, are imperishable' (Cyril Drummond Le Gros Clark, *The prose-poetry of Su Tung-p'o*, 128).

[125] *MTTC* 6.275; *PTMT* 186.

[126] Originally published in the *Shanghai Evening Post and Mercury*, 3–5 Feb. 1936; reproduced from Edgar Snow's manuscript in *PTMT* 419.

appropriate – China's policy, under his guidance, might take a different direction.

There were those in the Chinese Communist Party in the 1930s who did not adopt the same independent attitude, just as there were those in later years who were prepared to be more flexible than Mao in dealings with Moscow. The history of the struggle between Mao Tse-tung and the so-called 'internationalist' (i.e. pro-Soviet) faction in the Chinese Communist Party from 1935 to 1945 is a long and complicated story, which has been told elsewhere in this volume. Here our concern is not with power relations between Moscow and the Chinese Communist Party, or its various factions, but rather with the nature and significance of the theories by which Mao asserted his independence from Soviet tutelage. And among the concepts Mao put forward in the late 1930s, the boldest and most unequivocal symbol of his belief in the uniqueness of the Chinese revolution, and the need for the Chinese to solve their own problems in their own way, was that of the 'sinification of Marxism'.

This slogan was in fact used by the Chinese Communists only for a relatively short period, which began in 1938, when Mao first made the term his own, and reached its culmination in 1945 when, at the Seventh Congress of the Chinese Communist Party, Liu Shao-ch'i hailed Mao's gigantic achievements in creating theories which were 'thoroughly Marxist, and at the same time thoroughly Chinese'. But if the term itself was relatively ephemeral, the concerns it expresses were present before 1938, and have not only survived but grown in importance since the establishment of the Chinese People's Republic.

Mao Tse-tung's reasons for putting forward this idea are not difficult to understand. The concept of sinification symbolized the affirmation of China's national dignity in the face of the patronizing and domineering attitude of the Comintern; it was therefore valuable not only as a weapon in the inner-party struggle, but as a slogan for appealing to non-Communist opinion at a time of national crisis. But it also reflected a genuine conviction on Mao's part that in the last analysis an ideology of Western origin would not work in the Chinese context, unless it were adapted to the mentality and conditions of the Chinese people.

Exactly what sinification meant to Mao in 1938 is a more complex question. To call for the 'nationalization' of Marxism (as Liu Shao-ch'i put it in 1945),[127] not only in China but in other non-European countries, implies the adaptation of Marxist theories to national reality at many different levels, from language and culture to the economic and social structure of largely pre-capitalist agrarian societies. Moreover, the

[127] Carrère d'Encausse and Schram, 260.

question also arises as to which 'Marxism', or what elements of Marxism, are to be sinified.

The intermingling of the various dimensions of the problem is evoked in Mao Tse-tung's classic statement regarding sinification, in October 1938, when he said in part:

Today's China is an outgrowth of historic China. We are Marxist historicists; we must not mutilate history. From Confucius to Sun Yat-sen we must sum it up critically, and we must constitute ourselves the heirs to this precious legacy. Conversely, the assimilation of this legacy itself becomes a method that aids considerably in guiding the present great movement. A Communist is a Marxist internationalist, but Marxism must take on a national form before it can be of any practical effect. There is no such thing as abstract Marxism, but only concrete Marxism. What we call concrete Marxism is Marxism that has taken on a national form, that is, Marxism applied to the concrete struggle in the concrete conditions prevailing in China, and not Marxism abstractly used. If a Chinese Communist, who is a part of the great Chinese people, bound to his people by his very flesh and blood, talks of Marxism apart from Chinese peculiarities, this Marxism is merely an empty abstraction. Consequently, the sinification of Marxism – that is to say, making certain that in all of its manifestations it is imbued with Chinese characteristics, using it according to Chinese peculiarities – becomes a problem that must be understood and solved by the whole party without delay. We must put an end to writing eight-legged essays on foreign models; there must be less repeating of empty and abstract refrains; we must discard our dogmatism and replace it by a new and vital Chinese style and manner, pleasing to the eye and to the ear of the Chinese common people.[128]

The simplest and least controversial aspect of Mao's conception of sinification is that dealt with in the last sentence of this quotation. Obviously, if Marxism is to have any impact in a non-European country, it must be presented to the people of that country in language which is not only intelligible to them but vivid and meaningful in the light of their mentality and traditions, rather than in jargon literally translated from another language and another culture. But such sinification of the form of Marxism, though indispensable in Mao's view, was only the outward manifestation of a more fundamental enterprise, aiming to transform the very substance of Marxism in order to adapt it to Chinese conditions.

In seeking to clarify the issues involved here, let us look first of all at the meaning of Mao Tse-tung's statement: 'There is no such thing as abstract Marxism, but only concrete Marxism.' In the light of his other writings in Yenan days, and of his words and actions in later years, the ideas underlying this assertion could be spelled out roughly as follows. The theory of scientific socialism was first expounded by Marx. Certain aspects of his writings – for example, his analysis of capitalism, and of

[128] *MTTC* 6.260–1; *PTMT* 172–3.

the transition from capitalism to socialism, and the basic axioms of dialectics – are of universal validity, but the theory as a whole reflects both its origins in the nineteenth century, and Marx's specifically European mentality and experience. When we talk, therefore (like Stalin and everyone else from Lenin on down), about applying the universally valid principles of Marxism to Chinese conditions, it is the timeless kernel of these theories which we should seek to grasp and adapt to our needs.

And what is that timeless kernel? Mao himself, in the report of October 1938 already quoted, declared: 'We must not study the letter of Marxism and Leninism, but the standpoint and methodology of its creators, with which they observed and solved problems.'[129] In February 1942 he called upon his comrades of the Chinese Communist Party to 'take the standpoint, viewpoint and methods of Marxism-Leninism, apply them to China, and create a theory from the conscientious study of the realities of the Chinese revolution and Chinese history'.[130]

These formulations raise two problems. What did Mao mean by 'standpoint', 'viewpoint', and 'methods'? And what was the relation between such attitudes or principles derived from Marxism, and the 'method' which, he said, could emerge from the assimilation of the precious legacy of China's past?

As for the first point, the current Chinese interpretation is that Mao was talking about adopting the standpoint of the proletariat, the viewpoint of historical materialism, and the method of dialectics. But if Mao was indeed referring to aspects of Marxism as broadly defined as these, does it not follow that, in his view, the theories of Marx himself constituted in fact 'German Marxism', just as the ideas of Lenin were characterized by his critics in the early twentieth century as 'Russian Marxism'? In other words, by 'abstract Marxism' Mao meant 'absolute Marxism', or Marxist theory unconditionally valid in all countries and at all times. And when he said that such Marxism 'did not exist', he meant that Marx's own writings did not have the status of a higher-level general theory, but were merely one concrete incarnation of the standpoint, viewpoint and methods which he had devised, in no way superior to the application of the same principles by Stalin, or by Mao himself.

For Mao it was not, however, merely a question of applying Marxism to China; he also proposed, as we have seen, to enrich it with elements drawn from China's experience. Nor were the 'Chinese peculiarities' with which Mao proposed to imbue his Marxism merely the economic traits China shared with other Asian countries. They were also the 'precious qualities' which, as he put it in 1938, had been exhibited 'in the history

[129] *PTMT* 171.   [130] *MTTC* 8.75; *PTMT* 179–80.

of our great people over several millennia', and had been shaped both by historical experience and by the genius of the Chinese people.[131]

The view that China today bears the imprint of the past is in no way remarkable. Marxists, at least those of the Leninist persuasion, have long agreed that social customs and forms of political organization, though they change in the wake of modifications in the economic infrastructure of society and as a result of the class struggles these engender, are themselves a variable in the historical equation. But the question must be raised whether, in Mao's view, cultural realities were basically determined by levels of technology and 'modes of production', or whether the 'national peculiarities' he stressed constituted for him an independent, or partially independent, variable.

In my opinion, there is very little doubt that for Mao Tse-tung culture, both in the narrow and in the broad sense, constituted a partially autonomous dimension of human experience. One may applaud or deplore this attitude on his part, and there are those who do both, often with considerable heat. We cannot, however, ignore this aspect of his thought without distorting our perception of the man and his ideas.

Precisely how central this theme was to Mao Tse-tung's whole vision of revolution in China is indicated by the extraordinary statement, in the passage quoted earlier from his report of October 1938, that the assimilation of the Chinese heritage 'itself becomes a method that aids considerably in guiding the present great movement'. The preceding injunction to 'sum up critically' the experience of the past does not carry the same implications, for in it the active and guiding role appears to rest with the 'viewpoint and methodology' of Marx and Lenin, which is to be used to sort out the wheat from the chaff in the record of Chinese history. The suggestion that a deeper knowledge of the past will not merely widen the revolutionaries' understanding of their own society, but will actually provide an instrument for leading the revolution is something else again, and opens vistas without precedent in the history of Marxism down to 1938.

What was the nature of this method, which Mao said could be distilled from the experience of 'historic China', and what elements in the past were to be drawn upon in producing it? He did not spell this out explicitly, but there are hints in his writings of the Yenan period that he was thinking about a domain which could be loosely defined as that of the art of

131 *MTTC* 6.260; *PTMT* 172. Ray Wylie has discussed the problem of the 'sinification of Marxism' and its significance from a parallel but somewhat different perspective, placing greater emphasis on the philosophical issue of the relation between the universal and the particular and its implications for the originality of 'Mao Tse-tung thought': Ray Wylie, *The emergence of Maoism: Mao Tse-tung, Ch'en Po-ta, and the search for Chinese theory, 1935–1945*, 55–8, 88–95 and *passim*.

statecraft.[132] Thus, in another section of the report of October 1938 in which he first put forward the idea of sinification, Mao dealt with the problem of making proper use of cadres – which, he said, had been referred to in the past as 'employing people in the administration' (*yung-jen hsing-cheng*). He went on to discuss the continuity between the present and the past in the following terms:

Throughout our national history there have been two sharply contrasting lines on the subject of the use of cadres, reflecting the opposition between the depraved and the upright, one being to 'appoint people on their merit', and the other being 'to appoint people by favouritism'. The former was the policy of sagacious rulers and worthy ministers in making appointments; the latter was that of despots and traitors. Today, when we talk about making use of cadres, it is from a revolutionary standpoint, fundamentally different from that of ancient times, and yet there is no getting away from this standard of 'appointing people on their merit'. It was utterly wrong in the past, and is still utterly wrong today, to be guided by personal likes and dislikes, to reward fawning flatterers and to punish the honest and forthright.[133]

Here Mao was clearly indicating that in his view there were standards of political conduct which remained valid for Communist revolutionaries in the present, even though they were originally evolved in the context of a pre-capitalist and bureaucratic society.

Rather more surprisingly, Mao Tse-tung also found positive elements in Confucian philosophy. Commenting in 1939 on an article by Ch'en Po-ta on this theme, Mao indicated that he was basically in agreement, but that, in criticizing Confucius' doctrine of the rectification of names as 'idealist', Ch'en had failed to note that, from the epistemological standpoint, it contained important elements of truth, because of its emphasis on the link between theory and practice. He also saw Chu Hsi's interpretation of Confucius' theory of the mean as parallel to the Communists' principle of struggle on two fronts, against left and right deviations. Not going far enough (*pu chi*), he said, stood for rightism; going too far (*kuo*) stood for leftism.[134]

Appeals of this kind to the national past were, of course, singularly appropriate at a time when Mao Tse-tung was concerned to address himself to the widest possible spectrum of opinion, in order to promote the establishment of a new united front. They must also be taken seriously, however, as an expression of the substance of his thinking. Before turning to the analysis of Mao's ideas specifically about the alliance with bourgeois nationalists against Japanese aggression, let us explore further his

---

[132] On this tradition, see *CHOC* 11, 145–7.
[133] Mao, *SW* 2.202, supplemented by *MTCC* 6.250–1.
[134] 'Chih Chang Wen-t'ien' (To Chang Wen-t'ien), 20 Feb. 1939, *Selected letters*, 144–8.

interpretation of Chinese history, especially in the nineteenth and twentieth centuries, for it is this context which served to define the current stage of the Chinese revolution as he saw it, and accordingly the tactics appropriate at such a time.

The most systematic statement of Mao's views regarding Chinese history in general dating from the Yenan period is to be found in the first chapter of *The Chinese Revolution and the Chinese Communist Party*. (Strictly speaking, this text was not drafted by Mao himself, who wrote only the second chapter of the work, but Mao did choose to include it in his *Selected works*, and thereby took responsibility for the contents.) The details of this wide-ranging discussion fall for the most part outside the scope of this chapter, but certain points should be noted.

To begin with, Mao here places the transition from slave-holding society to feudalism at the beginning of the Chou dynasty, or roughly in the eleventh century BC. The relevant passage reads as follows:

[China's] feudal society, beginning with the Chou and Ch'in dynasties, lasted about 3,000 years...
It was the feudal landlord state which protected this system of feudal exploitation. While the feudal state was torn apart into rival principalities under the Chou, it became an autocratic and centralized feudal state after Ch'in Shih-huang unified China, though a degree of feudal separatism remained...[135]

Thus the Ch'in dynasty was seen as marked simply by a change in the form of the state, and not by a transition from one mode of production to another.[136]

The notion of an 'autocratic and centralized feudal state', which may appear to Western readers to be a contradiction in terms, was the formula arrived at by Mao and his comrades, after the debates of the 1920s and 1930s about the nature of traditional society, in order to assert simultaneously the 'feudal' (and hence universal) character of Chinese society and its uniqueness. At the same time, there remained in the original version of this text of 1939 traces of the notion of China as an 'Asiatic' society, which had in principle been repudiated. Thus, Mao asserted that Chinese society prior to the Opium War had been completely stagnant for centuries, and was only prodded into motion by the impact of the West.[137]

---

[135] Mao, *SW* 2.307–8; *MTTC* 7.100–1.
[136] Although there was ongoing scholarly controversy on this point, it did not become a burning political issue until the *p'i-Lin p'i-K'ung* campaign of 1973–4. The views put forward at that time were in flat contradiction with those Mao had espoused in 1939.
[137] In 1952, he would insert into *SW* the thesis, more agreeable to national pride, that changes were already at work which would have led to the birth of capitalism in China even without foreign intervention (Mao, *SW* 2.307–9; *MTTC* 7.100–3).

Two other points in Mao's survey of Chinese history are worthy of special emphasis. We have seen that, in 1919, Mao Tse-tung had boldly made what he called a 'singular assertion': 'one day, the reform of the Chinese people will be more profound than that of any other people, and the society of the Chinese people will be more radiant than that of any other people'. Twenty years later, the same faith in the exceptional capacities of his compatriots found expression in passages such as this:

In the many-thousand-year history of the Chinese people, many national heroes and revolutionary leaders have emerged. China has also given birth to many revolutionary strategists, statesmen, men of letters and thinkers. So the Chinese people [*min-tsu*] is also a people with a glorious revolutionary tradition and a splendid historical heritage.[138]

Secondly, Mao continued, as he had done since 1926, to give particular emphasis to the role of the peasantry. Not only were the 'hundreds of peasant revolts' throughout Chinese history characterized as the decisive cause of each and every dynastic change, but these 'peasant revolts and peasant wars', on a 'gigantic scale...without parallel in world history' were said to form the only 'real motive force of China's historical evolution'. At the same time, however, Mao stressed the limitations on such actions by the peasants alone, in a 'feudal' society, as far as their capacity to promote the development of the productive forces or change the mode of production was concerned. On this point, he wrote:

each peasant revolt and peasant war dealt a blow to the existing feudal regime; thus to some extent it changed the productive relations of society and to some extent furthered the development of the productive forces of society. However, since neither new productive forces nor new modes of production nor a new class force nor an advanced political party existed in those days, and the peasant wars and revolts consequently lacked the leadership of an advanced class and an advanced political party, such as the correct leadership given by the proletariat and the Communist Party today, the peasant revolutions invariably failed, and the peasants were utilized...by the landlords and the nobility as a tool for bringing about dynastic changes. Thus, although some social progress was made after each peasant revolutionary struggle, the feudal economic relations and feudal political system remained basically unchanged.[139]

When and how, in Mao's view, did a situation arise in which the proletariat and the Communist Party could exercise 'correct leadership' over the Chinese revolution? As he saw it, this process took place in two stages. First, the 'feudal' relations of production which had existed until the

[138] Mao, *SW* 2.306; *MTTC* 7.99.
[139] Mao, *SW* 2.308–9; *MTTC* 7.102. Here, and elsewhere in *SW*, Mao replaced the term he had originally used for peasant uprisings, *pao-tung* (revolt, armed rebellion), with *ch'i-i* (righteous uprising). The nuance lies, of course, in the fact that *pao-tung* suggests something more sporadic and less directly linked as a precursor to the rural revolution led by the Communists.

nineteenth century were partly broken down, and the position of the old ruling class undermined by the impact of the West and the ensuing development of capitalism, and of an embryonic bourgeoisie. At this stage, the landlord class, backed by the imperialists, still constituted the ruling class of Chinese society, but the bourgeois elements were the natural leaders of the revolutionary challenge to the existing order. Then, in a second stage, conditions became ripe for the proletariat to assert its hegemony over the revolution.

In Mao's interpretation, this transition took place roughly at the time of the May Fourth movement; the periods of bourgeois and proletarian hegemony he referred to respectively as the 'democratic' or 'old democratic' revolution and the 'New Democratic' revolution. Before discussing his periodization of modern Chinese history, let us consider what precisely he meant by 'New Democracy', for this concept was not only important in its day, but has continuing relevance to China's later problems.

Since 'New Democracy' was intended to be a category of Marxist-Leninist analysis, it is necessary to remind ourselves briefly of the doctrinal background. Marx had considered that, as a matter of course, the capitalist stage in the development of society would be characterized by the domination of the bourgeoisie, just as the feudal stage had been marked by the domination of the nobility. The bourgeois-democratic revolution which constituted the decisive phase in the transition from feudalism to capitalism would likewise be the task of the bourgeoisie. As for the proletariat, it would support the bourgeoisie in the democratic revolution, meanwhile prodding it forward to satisfy in so far as possible the immediate demands of the workers, until the time came to put an end to the capitalist system by a socialist revolution led by the proletariat.

The writings of Marx and Engels regarding revolution in pre-capitalist societies, especially those which had felt the impact of Western colonialism, are fascinating and suggestive, but at the same time fragmentary and contradictory. In any case, it is impossible (whatever attempts may have been made) to extract from them a clear tactical line for the guidance of Asian revolutionaries. At the time of the 1905 Revolution, first Trotsky and then Lenin put forward the view that, in such backward lands, the 'bourgeois-democratic revolution' could take place under the hegemony of the proletariat, that is, in a political context dominated by the Communist Party. This idea, subsequently elaborated by Stalin, Mao and many others, has been an axiom of Marxism, as interpreted by the Soviets and their disciples, ever since.

Thus, the class nature of a given historical stage was effectively dissociated from the class character of the actors in such a stage. The proletarian dictatorship, or some precursor or variant of it, can, it has been postulated for three-quarters of a century, preside over a 'bourgeois' revolution which will constitute the functional equivalent of the capitalist stage in the development of Western societies.

To return now to the nature and significance of Mao Tse-tung's ideas regarding this stage, which he baptized 'New Democratic', it is of interest to note not only how he defined its content, but when he postulated that it had begun. For it was in this context that Mao undertook to justify the new alliance with the Nationalists, in terms of the evolving balance of forces, and the aims of the revolution at that time.

In some passages Mao dated the transition from 'old' to 'new' democracy in 1919 precisely, and for purposes of convenience the dividing-line between 'modern' and 'contemporary' Chinese history has been fixed since Yenan days at the time of the May Fourth movement. Mao was, however, naturally aware that decisive changes such as this do not occur overnight, and for the most part he situated the emergence of 'New Democracy' more loosely in the period from the outbreak of the First World War to the foundation of the Chinese Communist Party (that is, in the 'May Fourth period' as commonly and broadly defined). In *On new democracy*, Mao wrote in January 1940: 'A change...occurred in China's bourgeois-democratic revolution after the outbreak of the first imperialist world war in 1914 and the founding of a socialist state on one-sixth of the globe as a result of the Russian October Revolution of 1917.'[140]

The reasons here given or suggested for the change in the nature of China's revolution include the weakening and discrediting of Western 'bourgeois' democracy, the emergency of an alternative model in the new Soviet republic, and also the possibility of material and moral assistance from the Soviets. It was partly for this last reason that Mao, following Stalin (who himself was following Lenin), declared China's New-Democratic revolution to be an integral part of the proletarian-socialist world revolution. On this theme, he wrote:

In an era in which the world capitalist front has collapsed in one corner of the globe... and has fully revealed its decadence everywhere else, in an era in which the remaining capitalist portions cannot survive without relying more than ever on the colonies and semi-colonies... in such an era, a revolution in any colony or semi-colony that is directed against imperialism... no longer comes within the old category of the bourgeois-democratic world revolution, but within the new category...

[140] Mao, *SW* 2.343; *MTTC* 7.153.

Although during its first stage or first step, such a revolution in a colonial and semi-colonial country is still fundamentally bourgeois-democratic in its social character, and although its objective demand is still fundamentally to clear the path for the development of capitalism, it is no longer a revolution of the old type, led *entirely* by the bourgeoisie, with the aim of establishing a capitalist society and a state under bourgeois dictatorship. It is rather a revolution of the new type, *with the participation of the proletariat in the leadership*, or led by the proletariat, and having as its aim, in the first stage, the establishment of a new-democratic society and a state under the joint dictatorship of all the revolutionary classes...[141]

This passage speaks of a 'joint dictatorship', and the words in italics (which Mao removed in 1952) imply that the proletariat might not even enjoy primacy among the various dictators. Indeed, in the original version of *On new democracy* Mao went so far as to state explicitly that, if the Chinese bourgeoisie should prove itself capable of leading the people in 'driving out Japanese imperialism and introducing democratic government', they (i.e., the Kuomintang) would continue to enjoy the people's confidence.[142] It was plain, however, that this was merely a rhetorical gesture to Chiang Kai-shek, and that Mao fully intended his own party to exercise hegemony on behalf of the proletariat within the 'joint dictatorship of all the revolutionary classes'. In *The Chinese Revolution and the Chinese Communist Party*, addressed directly to party members rather than to a non-party audience of intellectuals (as was *On new democracy*), Mao said bluntly, 'Unless the proletariat participates in it and leads it, the Chinese revolution cannot... succeed.'[143] And on the eve of victory in June 1949, he put the same view more categorically still: 'Why did forty years of revolution under Sun Yat-sen end in failure? Because in the epoch of imperialism the bourgeoisie cannot lead any genuine revolution to victory.'[144]

In sum, though he expressed it with varying degrees of frankness, Mao's view from the time he first began to use the term 'New Democracy' in 1939 was that in China, after 1919 or thereabouts, leadership of the revolution rightfully belonged to the proletariat. How could he claim such a role for a class which, in the second decade of the twentieth century, was only beginning to develop, and for a party which counted, until the alliance with the Nationalists in 1923–7, only a handful of members? Apart from the fact that the Communists, as already noted, enjoyed external support and sympathy from the Soviet Union, Mao argued as follows:

As distinct social classes, the Chinese bourgeoisie and proletariat are new-born and never existed before in Chinese history.... They are twins born of China's

---

[141] Carrère d'Encausse and Schram, 252; *MTTC* 7.153–4. (The words in italics have been removed in Mao, *SW*.) [142] Carrère d'Encausse and Schram, 254; *MTTC* 7.162.
[143] Mao, *SW* 2.325; *MTTC* 7.126. [144] Mao, *SW* 4.422; *MTTC* 10.305.

old (feudal) society, at once linked to each other and antagonistic to each other. However, the Chinese proletariat emerged and grew simultaneously not only with the Chinese national bourgeoisie but also with the enterprises directly operated by the imperialists in China. Hence, a very large section of the Chinese proletariat is older and more experienced than the Chinese bourgeoisie, and is therefore a greater and more broadly-based social force'.[145]

This is an ingenious argument, and not without substance. Nevertheless, Mao's assertion of proletarian hegemony from 1917–21 onwards must be read not as a statement of fact about the strength of the opposing political forces, but as an assertion that, from this time forward, it was appropriate, and not wholly unrealistic, for the Communists to *strive* for leadership over the national revolution.

If such was indeed Mao's intimate conviction, even though he did not always state this openly, was it not meaningless or hypocritical to talk about a 'united front' at all? Or, to put it differently, would not such an alliance necessarily assume the character of a 'united front from below', that is, of an attempt to mobilize the rank and file of the Kuomintang against its leadership? Not necessarily, especially if we interpret Mao's periodization, as I have done above, in the sense that, in the late 1930s, it had long been legitimate for the Communists to seek to assert their hegemony. For what was legitimate might not, at any given time, be expedient, or politically 'correct'. If the external threat from Japan to China's very existence as an independent state, and therefore to the possibility of political change within the country, became so grave that the struggle against Japan replaced the struggle against Chiang Kai-shek as the Communists' number one policy goal, and if the Kuomintang was not only militarily and politically stronger than the Communists but willing to fight Japan, then it might be appropriate to accept, for a time, Kuomintang predominance in such a struggle.

As noted above, Mao had accepted by December 1935 the need for a new united front, and he had agreed, by late 1936, that Chiang Kai-shek must be the titular leader of such an alliance. It was in October 1938, in his report to the sixth plenum of the Central Committee, that Mao went farthest in recognizing the leading role of the Kuomintang, not only during the Anti-Japanese War, but in the phase of national reconstruction which would follow it. In a paragraph entitled 'The Kuomintang has a brilliant future' he declared:

The Kuomintang and the Communist Party are the foundation of the Anti-Japanese United Front, but of these two it is the Kuomintang that occupies first place....In the course of its glorious history, the Kuomintang has been responsible for the

[145] Mao, *SW* 2.310; *MTTC* 7.104–5.

overthrow of the Ch'ing, the establishment of the Republic, opposition to Yuan Shih-k'ai...and the great revolution of 1926–7. Today it is once more leading the great anti-Japanese war. It enjoys the historic heritage of the Three People's Principles; it has had two great leaders in succession – Mr Sun Yat-sen and Mr Chiang Kai-shek....All this should not be underestimated by our compatriots and constitutes the result of China's historical development.

In carrying out the anti-Japanese war, and in organizing the Anti-Japanese United Front, the Kuomintang occupies the position of leader and backbone [*chi-kan*]...Under the single great condition that it support to the end the war of resistance and the United Front, one can foresee a brilliant future for the Kuomintang...[146]

Although this report expressed the softest line ever taken by Mao Tse-tung toward Chiang Kai-shek and the Kuomintang, it was by no means the blank cheque it might at first glance appear. The 'single great condition' alone, stated in the last sentence of the preceding quotation, limited severely the scope of Mao's concessions to Chiang. To the extent that he regarded Chiang and the Kuomintang as, in the long run, congenitally incapable of supporting unflinchingly the united front and the war against Japan, Mao looked forward to the time when his acceptance of Chiang's leadership would necessarily lapse. Moreover, though the original 1938 text of this report did not speak, as do the rewritten extracts in the *Selected works*, of leadership by the Communists, it did refer to 'the way in which the Communists should become conscious of their own role and strengthen themselves, in order to be in a position to assume their great responsibilities in the national war'. And these responsibilities he defined succinctly by saying that the Communists 'should exercise the role of vanguard and model in every domain'.[147] Quite obviously, if the Kuomintang should falter in its leadership, its place would be taken by those who had already established themselves as 'vanguard and model'.

Finally, Mao's proposal, in his report of October 1938, that the 'bloc within' should be resuscitated, and that Communists should once more join the Kuomintang as individuals, was a two-edged and ambiguous one. For though he offered in advance to give Chiang Kai-shek a complete list of all such Communists with dual party membership, thus satisfying one of the conditions which Chiang had laid down following the 'reorganization' of May 1926, he also sought to persuade Chiang to turn the Kuomintang into a 'national league'. The aim of this second proposal was all too obviously to weaken the Leninist stranglehold which had made it impossible, in 1926–7, for the Communists to manipulate the

[146] *MTTC* 6.198; *PTMT* 228–9.
[147] *MTTC* 6.243–4; *PTMT* 229.

Kuomintang from within. It is therefore not surprising that Chiang saw this as a 'Trojan horse' manoeuvre, and rejected it.[148]

In a little over a year, Mao's position evolved, as we have already seen, from recognition that the Kuomintang must take 'first place' in the united front to the assertion of Communist leadership as an accomplished fact. In *On new democracy* (January 1940) this bald claim was covered with a rhetorical fig leaf; in *The Chinese Revolution and the Chinese Communist Party* (December 1939) it was quite unambiguous.[149] *The Chinese Revolution and the Chinese Communist Party*, though written chiefly for a Communist audience, was openly sold. In his Introduction to the inner-party periodical *The Communist* (October 1939), Mao did not even raise the question of who should exercise hegemony; he simply assumed that leadership belonged to the Communists, and proceeded to discuss how they should go about exercising it.

Apart from the question of leadership, two directly related points merit discussion here: Mao's views regarding the role of various classes in the revolution, and about the nature of the political movement or regime which should represent the revolutionary forces.

In essence, Mao's view regarding the class forces supporting the revolution at the time of the Anti-Japanese War was simple and consistent. He saw them as composed of Stalin's four-class bloc of the 1920s, with the addition of a certain portion of the 'comprador bourgeoisie' tied to powers whose interests were in conflict with those of Japan. Understandably, the line enclosing possible allies was drawn most tightly in the Introduction to *The Communist*, and most loosely in *On new democracy*. In the former, the peasantry is characterized as a 'firm' ally of the proletariat, and the urban petty-bourgeoisie as a 'reliable' ally. As for the national bourgeoisie, it will take part in the struggle 'against imperialism and the feudal warlords' at 'certain times and to a certain extent', because it suffers from foreign oppression, but it will also 'vacillate and defect' on occasion 'because of its economic and political flabbiness'. The bourgeoisie or big bourgeoisie, even when it joins the united front against the enemy, 'continues to be most reactionary', opposes the development of the proletarian party, and ultimately plans to capitulate to the enemy and split the united front.[150]

The original version of *On new democracy* exhibits one curious anomaly:

---

[148] On this episode, see chapter above by Lyman Van Slyke, as well as S. Schram, *Mao Tse-tung*, 202–3. For the text of Mao's proposal, see *MTTC* 6.228–9.

[149] *MTTC* 7.129; *PTMT* 230–1.

[150] Mao, *SW* 2.228–89; *MTTC* 7.228–9. The passage (paragraph 3) putting a slightly more optimistic view of the (comprador) bourgeoisie was added in *SW* and does not appear at all in the 1939 text.

it refers throughout to a three-class, rather than a four-class bloc. The difference is one of form rather than substance, but it is not without interest. It results from lumping together the peasantry (which has always been regarded by Marxists as petty-bourgeois in nature) with the urban petty-bourgeoisie, and calling the resulting category '*the*' petty-bourgeoisie, instead of counting the peasants as a separate class. Thus we read, for example, that in 1927–36, as a result of the 'going over of the Chinese bourgeoisie to the counter-revolutionary camp...only two of the three classes originally composing the revolutionary camp remained...': the proletariat and the petty-bourgeoisie (including the peasantry, the revolutionary intellectuals, and other sections of the petty-bourgeoisie).[151]

With the coming of the Anti-Japanese War, continued Mao, the Chinese revolution, 'pursuing its zig-zag course', had again arrived at a united front of three classes. But this time, he added,

the scope is much broader. Among the upper classes, it includes all the rulers; among the middle classes, it includes the petty-bourgeoisie in its totality; among the lower classes, it includes the totality of the proletarians. All classes and strata of the country have become allies, and are resolutely resisting Japanese imperialism.[152]

It is quite clear that the swallowing-up of the peasantry in the catch-all category of the 'petty-bourgeoisie' served to attenuate the emphasis on the unique character of China's revolution, and especially on one of its original traits: guerrilla warfare in the countryside. In his Introduction to *The Communist*, Mao made of these aspects of China's experience one of the main themes of his analysis:

since China is a semi-colonial and semi-feudal country, since her political, economic and cultural development is uneven, since her economy is predominantly semi-feudal and since her territory is vast, it follows that the character of the Chinese revolution in its present stage is bourgeois-democratic, that its principal targets are imperialism and the feudal forces, and that its basic motive forces are the proletariat, the peasantry, and the urban petty-bourgeoisie, with the national bourgeoisie etc. taking part at certain times and to a certain extent; it also follows [*sic*] that the principal form of struggle in the Chinese revolution is armed struggle.

It is not quite clear why the last conclusion should follow from the facts enumerated by Mao Tse-tung in this sentence, but it is obviously a valid

---

[151] *MTTC* 7.196; Carrère d'Encausse and Schram, 256–7. There is an intriguing prefiguration of this three-class analysis in Mao's reply of November 1925 to a survey by the Young China Association (*MTTC*, *pu-chüan*, 2.127), in which he declared that though he was a Communist and a partisan of a 'proletarian social revolution', a single class was not in a position in China, to overthrow the internal and external forces of reaction, so the 'national revolution' must be carried out by the proletariat, the petty-bourgeoisie, and the left wing of the middle class (*chung-ch'an chieh-chi*).   [152] *MTTC* 7.197–8; Carrère d'Encausse and Schram, 257.

one. 'Indeed,' Mao goes on, 'the history of our party may be called a history of armed struggle. Comrade Stalin has said, "In China the armed people are fighting armed counter-revolution. That is one of the specific features of the Chinese revolution." This is perfectly true.' The quotation from Stalin represents a particularly cynical instance of citing out of context; when Stalin made this statement in December 1926 the 'armed people' he was talking about were represented by Chiang Kai-shek, in whose fidelity to the cause he still had full confidence, and Mao knew this very well. Still, once again, the point was well taken: 'armed struggle in China', added Mao, 'is, in essence, peasant war and the party's relations with the peasantry and its close relation with the peasant war are one and the same thing'.[153]

In this text, Mao Tse-tung characterizes the united front, armed struggle, and party-building as the Chinese Communist Party's three 'magic weapons'. We have already spoken in this chapter of the place of armed struggle in Mao's strategy. As for the united front, his essential message in the Introduction to *The Communist* is that it should be marked by both unity and struggle. The precise form such unity should take is not discussed, but as we have already seen Mao laid down in the other two basic texts of this same period that the vehicle for cooperation should be the 'joint dictatorship of all the revolutionary classes'. In *The Chinese Revolution and the Chinese Communist Party* he also referred to it as the 'joint revolutionary-democratic dictatorship of several revolutionary classes over the imperialists and reactionary traitors'.[154] The term 'revolutionary-democratic dictatorship' was obviously modelled on Lenin's 'revolutionary-democratic dictatorship of the workers and peasants', a slogan first coined at the time of the 1905 Revolution and often reiterated thereafter. Mao's dictators were, of course, more numerous than Lenin's; the difference he explained, as we have already seen, by the special conditions of a country under foreign domination.

The third of Mao's 'magic weapons', party-building, meant in fact something far more sweeping and significant than would at first glance appear. It implied defining a correct doctrine, and unifying and rectifying the party on the basis of that doctrine. A passage somewhat modified in the *Selected works* noted that, if in the past the Chinese Communist Party had been unsuccessful in its pursuit of consolidation and 'bolshevization', this was because its members had not adequately linked Marxism to the concrete practice of the Chinese revolution, and did not have an adequate knowledge of Chinese history and of Chinese society.[155]

[153] Mao, *SW* 2.286–7; *MTTC* 7.72.   [154] *MTTC* 7.129; *PTMT* 230.
[155] Mao, *SW* 2.292–3; *MTTC* 7.79–80.

This meant, quite plainly, that they did not yet have the benefit of the 'sinified Marxism' which Mao Tse-tung was then engaged in elaborating, precisely in the works we have been discussing. In other words, the 'party-building' for which Mao called in October 1939 was destined to take the form of the great rectification or *cheng-feng* campaign which, in 1942–3, definitively established his ideological predominance in the party.

THE TRIUMPH OF MAO TSE-TUNG'S THOUGHT 1941–1949

When Mao had first put forward the slogan of adapting Marxism to Chinese conditions, his main concern, as I have already suggested, was to shape the approach of the Chinese Communist Party to fit the political and cultural circumstances of the time. The next main phase in the development of his ideas on this theme, in 1941–3, was much more directly linked to Mao's struggle with his rivals in the party, and the views he propagated were explicitly designed to serve his interests in that struggle.

The same was true of other aspects of Mao's thought. If the philosophical core of his thinking had taken shape as early as 1937 with the theory of contradictions, in a wide range of other domains, from economic work to literature and from administrative principles to the interpretation of the Marxist heritage, the definitive formulation of Mao's ideas prior to 1949 dates from the early 1940s. And in all of these areas the links between ideology and political in-fighting are palpable and direct.

This chapter focuses, of course, primarily on ideas rather than on historical fact. The following succinct chronology brings out clearly, however, the concrete significance of certain theoretical statements:

5 May 1941. Mao makes a speech to a cadre meeting in Yenan criticizing 'scholars of Marxism-Leninism' who 'can only repeat quotes from Marx, Engels, Lenin and Stalin from memory, but about their own ancestors…have to apologize and say they've forgotten'.

1 July 1941. Adoption of Central Committee resolution on 'strengthening the party spirit', stressing the importance of discipline and of absolute subordination of cadres at all levels to higher authority.

13 July 1941. Sun Yeh-fang writes a letter to Liu Shao-ch'i (using the pen name Sung Liang), referring to the two opposing deviations of slighting theoretical study and scholasticism, and asking for some 'Chinese examples' of the correct relation between theory and practice. Liu replies the same day stressing the difficulties of sinifying Marxism, and blaming the lack of progress thus far partly on the fact that few Chinese Communist Party members can read Marx in the original.

23 January 1942. Mao orders army cadres to study his Ku-t'ien Resolution of December 1929 until they are thoroughly familiar with it.

1 February and 8 February 1942. Mao delivers his two keynote speeches on rectification. In the second of these, he complains that his 1938 call for 'sinification' has not been heeded.

May 1942. Mao delivers two talks to the Yenan Forum on Literature and Art, but these are not published for nearly a year and a half.

December 1942. Mao delivers a report *On economic and financial problems*.

20 March 1943. Mao elected chairman of the Politburo of the Chinese Communist Party, and chairman of the three-man Secretariat, with the right to outvote the two other members.

April 1943. Movement to investigate cadres pressed forward vigorously in Yenan – in fact, a harsh purge of dissident or anti-Maoist elements in the party, under the control of K'ang Sheng.

26 May 1943. Mao, commenting on the dissolution of the Comintern, declares that, although Moscow has not intervened in the affairs of the Chinese Communist Party since the Seventh Comintern Congress of August 1935, the Chinese Communists have done their work very well.

1 June 1943. Resolution, drafted by Mao, on methods of leadership puts forward the classic formulation of the 'mass line'.

6 July 1943. Liu Shao-ch'i publishes the article 'Liquidate Menshevik thought in the party', hailing Mao as a true Bolshevik and denouncing the 'International faction' as Mensheviks in disguise.

19 October 1943. Mao's 'Yenan Talks' finally published in *Chieh-fang jih-pao*.

April 1945. Apotheosis – Mao's thought written into the party constitution as the guide to all the party's work, and Mao hailed by Liu Shao-ch'i for his earth-shaking contributions in 'sinifying' or 'nationalizing' Marxism.[156]

These facts have, of course, been selected and arranged to suggest that the establishment of Mao Tse-tung's absolute predominance in the party was, from the outset, a primary goal of the rectification campaign of 1942–3. Though they may sharpen and oversimplify the picture to some extent, I do not believe that they distort the broad outline.

[156] Most of these events are well known, and since the main stuff of this chapter is ideas rather than facts, I shall not footnote them all in detail. Liu Shao-ch'i's article 'Liquidate Menshevik thought', and the Central Committee resolution of 1 July 1941 are translated by Boyd Compton, *Mao's China: party reform documents, 1942–44*. The 1 June 1943 resolution and Mao's speeches (except *Economic and financial problems*) are to be found in Mao, *SW* and many other sources, including the Compton volume. Liu's letter to 'Comrade Sung Liang' has long been known to exist. See my discussion of it in 'The party in Chinese Communist ideology', in J. W. Lewis, ed. *Party leadership and revolutionary power in China*, 177.

It has now been reprinted, and Sung Liang identified as Sun Yeh-fang (*Hung-ch'i* 7 (1980) 2–4), but Sun's original letter is not included in this version. For the latter, see Liu Shao-ch'i, *Lun tang* (On the party), 345–6. For key passages from Liu's report of April 1945 (which has recently been reprinted in China), see Carrère d'Encausse and Schram, 259–61. Regarding Mao's formal position in the party from March 1943, see *Tang-shih yen-chiu*, 2 (1980), 77–8.

To be sure, Mao wrote, with real or feigned modesty, in April 1943, when the rectification campaign had basically achieved its objectives, that his thought, which was a form of Marxism-Leninism, was not in his own opinion fully mature and thought out, and did not constitute a system. It was, he said, still not in the stage where it should be preached or advocated (*ku-ch'ui*), except perhaps for a few pieces contained in the documents studied during the campaign.[157] The fact remains, however, that it was quite clearly regarded, from 1943 onwards, and especially from 1945, as the definitive exemplar of the adaptation of Marxism-Leninism to Chinese conditions, and the summing-up and culmination both of Marxism and of Chinese culture.[158]

If we accept that Mao, after his humiliation at the hands of the '28 Bolsheviks' in 1932–4, and a long hard struggle, from 1935 to 1943, to establish his own political and ideological authority, at length achieved this goal in the course of the rectification campaign, what sort of political and economic system did he establish at that time in the Yenan base area, and what were the principles underlying it? It has been repeatedly argued that the essence of the Yenan heritage lies in an intimate relationship between the party and the masses. There is much truth in this, but the matter should not be looked at too one-sidedly.

In the second section of this chapter, I evoked the classic directive of 1 June 1943 on the 'mass line', and argued that this was an ambiguous concept, which pointed in two directions: toward Leninist elitism, and toward the genuine involvement of people in their own affairs.

To suggest that ordinary people may be a source of ideas from which correct policies are elaborated, and that they can in turn understand these policies, rather than blindly applying them, marked a very great rupture with one of the central themes of traditional Chinese thought. According to the *Analects*: 'The people may be made to follow a path of action, but they may not be made to understand it.'[159] This is one of the Confucian prejudices that Mao strove for half a century to break down. As already emphasized, he did not, however, cast doubt in so doing on the Leninist axiom that class consciousness can only be imported into the working class from outside, and more broadly that the Communist Party must provide ideological guidance to society as a whole.

---

[157] 'Chih Ho K'ai-feng' (To Ho K'ai-feng), 22 April 1943, *Selected letters*, 212–13.

[158] On this point, Ray Wylie (273–4) is, in my opinion, right, and Franz Schurmann wrong, about the interpretation of Liu Shao-ch'i's report to the Seventh Congress, and of the party statutes adopted on that occasion. Whether or not, in the early 1950s, the Chinese adopted a distinction between 'pure' and 'practical' ideology is quite another question, which I shall not take up here.

[159] *Confucian analects*, 8, ch. 9, in James Legge, *The Chinese classics*, 1.211.

Within the broad limits defined by Mao's insistence both on a measure of initiative and involvement from below, and on firm centralized guidance from above, there is room for an infinite variety of formulations and shades of emphasis. From Yenan days onwards, Mao Tse-tung rang the changes on these themes. Consistently, however, at least until the Cultural Revolution, he regarded centralized leadership as in the last analysis even more important than democracy.

Mao's ideas about methods of work and patterns of organization had taken shape progressively during a decade and a half of military and political struggle in the countryside, from the Autumn Harvest uprising to the rectification campaign. Now, in the early 1940s, the lessons of this experience were summed up, systematized, and applied to economic work as well as to guerrilla tactics.

A key slogan of this time was 'centralized leadership and dispersed operation' (*chi-chung ling-tao, fen-san ching-ying*). Such an approach was particularly appropriate in circumstances where only a relatively small proportion of the total area controlled by the Communists was located in the main Yenan base area, and the technical level of the economy was so low that rigorously centralized planning of inputs and outputs was neither possible nor desirable. Even in these circumstances, however, the accent was by no means on continued and unmitigated dispersion of responsibility and effort. Mao Tse-tung made this point quite unequivocally in his report of December 1942, *Economic and financial problems*.[160] Asking the rhetorical question why the self-sufficient industry of the Border Region should be run in such a dispersed fashion, Mao replied:

The main reason is that the labour force is divided among the various branches of the party, government and army. If it were centralized, we would destroy their activism. For example, we encouraged 359 Brigade to set up the Ta-kuang Textile Mill and did not order it to combine with a government mill because most of the several hundred employees at the mill were selected from the officers and men of 359 Brigade. They work to produce the bedding and clothing requirements of the Brigade and their enthusiasm is high. If we centralized, we would destroy this enthusiasm.... Adopting the policy of 'dispersed operation' is correct and ideas aimed at centralizing everything are wrong. However, enterprises of the same kind carried out within the same area should be centralized as much as possible. Unlimited dispersal is not profitable. At present we are already carrying out...centralization of this kind....Perhaps this process of dispersal at first and centralization later cannot be avoided...[161]

---

[160] Only the first part of this very long work appears in the current canon of Mao, *SW*. The passages quoted below are from part 7, 'On developing a self-sufficient industry', *MTTC* 8.263–4.

[161] The translation is that of Andrew Watson, *Mao Zedong and the political economy of the border region*, 149–50.

Later in the same section, listing the economic measures which should be pursued in 1943, Mao placed second (immediately after increased capital investment) that of 'establishing a unified leadership for the whole of self-supporting industry, overcoming the serious anarchy which exists now'.[162] In order to achieve this result, he called for the establishment of a 'unified plan', drawn up under the 'unified leadership' of the Finance and Economy Office (*Ts'ai-ching pan-shih-ch'u*), but at the same time he specified that agriculture, industry and commerce should not be 'put entirely in the hands of one single official organization for the whole Border Region'. Instead, the unified plan should be 'handed over to the party, government and army systems for separate implementation'. Nevertheless, Mao's final conclusion was that the problem of unified leadership was 'the central problem in advancing self-supporting industry during 1943'.[163]

The sentence just quoted poses explicitly the problem of the relation between party, state and army, which remained a central and often controversial issue after 1949. A key concept, introduced in Yenan, conveys the essence of the party's unifying and guiding role as conceived at that time. The term is *i-yuan-hua* – literally 'to make one', 'to make monolithic'. It has sometimes been translated 'to coordinate', but that is probably too weak a rendering; 'to unify', which has also been used, is unsatisfactory because it seems best to reserve this English term as the equivalent for *t'ung-i*, just as 'centralized' is best kept for translating *chi-chung*. The English equivalent which I propose to use is 'integrate', but this question of translation is less important than the concerns which underlay the adoption of the Chinese expression in the early 1940s. Because this concept has hitherto received far less attention than democratic centralism or the mass line, I shall give a number of illustrations of its use, before summing up my understanding of its significance.

The *locus classicus* of this term seems to be found in the Resolution of the Politburo dated 1 September 1942, 'On the unification of party leadership in the anti-Japanese bases, and adjusting the relations between various organizations'.[164]

This resolution asserts explicitly and forcefully the link between party-government and party-army relations on the one hand, and the

[162] Watson, *Mao Zedong*, 160.
[163] *MTTC* 8.265, 273; Watson, *Mao Zedong*, 151, 160–1.
[164] This is one of the documents studied in the course of the rectification campaign, and an English translation can be found in Boyd Compton, *Mao's China*, 161–75. Authorship of the resolution has not been officially attributed to Mao, but the Chinese text is included in the Tokyo *MTTC*, 8.155–63.

hierarchical structure of each individual organization on the other. Paragraph 8 of the resolution begins as follows:

The integration [*i-yuan-hua*] of party leadership is [to be] expressed on the one hand in the mutual relations between party, governmental, and mass organizations at the same level; on the other hand, it is [to be] expressed in the relations between upper and lower levels. In this [latter respect], strict adherence to the principle of obedience of lower to higher echelons and obedience of the entire party to the central committee is of decisive significance in unifying party leadership...[165]

A somewhat clearer definition and explanation of the meaning of the elusive term *i-yuan-hua* is to be found in the decision of 1 June 1943, drafted by Mao Tse-tung, from which I quoted earlier the well-known paragraph on the 'mass line'. In an immediately following passage (paragraph 7) of this directive, Mao declares:

In relaying to subordinate units any task... a higher organization should in all cases go through the leader of the lower organization concerned, so that he may assume responsibility, thus achieving the goal of combining division of labour with unified leadership [*i-yuan-hua*]. A department at a higher level should not go solely to its counterpart at the lower level (for instance, a higher department concerned with organization, propaganda or counter-espionage should not go solely to the corresponding department at the lower level), leaving the person in overall charge of the lower organization (such as the secretary, the chairman, the director or the school principal) in ignorance or without responsibility. Both the person in overall charge and the person with specific responsibility should be informed and given responsibility. This *i-yuan-hua* method, combining division of labour with unified leadership, makes it possible, through the person with overall responsibility, to mobilize a large number of cadres...to carry out a particular task, and thus to overcome shortages of cadres in individual departments and turn a good number of people into cadres for one's own work. This, too, is a way of combining the leadership with the masses...[166]

It will have been seen (as well as such things can be seen in translation) that *i-yuan-hua* is twice used as an appositive for 'combining division of labour with unified leadership'. The sense, plainly, is that the necessary division of labour between various organs can exist without posing a threat to the unity of the movement only on condition that the whole system be penetrated and controlled by a unifying force in the shape of the party. To convey this function, the English equivalent 'to integrate' seems most appropriate.

The use of the term *i-yuan-hua*, with its strong verbal force, reflects the perception, on the part of the Chinese Communist leadership, of the situation that prevailed in the early 1940s in the base areas, which were

---

[165] Compton, 171–2; translation modified on the basis of the Chinese text in *MTTC* 8.161.
[166] *SW* 3.120–1; revised on the basis of *MTTC* 9.29, to take account of changes (which are not particularly extensive) in the official Chinese text as compared to the 1943 version.

fragmented, often isolated, and exposed to enemy attack. In such circumstances, the various agencies of political, economic, and administrative control could scarcely be effectively integrated. They stressed, therefore, the necessity of *making* things monolithic (*i-yuan-hua*), because excessive dispersal in fact prevailed.

One might assume that, once the Chinese Communists had established their authority throughout the whole of the country and set up the People's Republic of China, dispersionism would no longer be a threat. In fact, for many complex historical and practical reasons, the problems of fragmentation and of divided authority by no means evaporated in 1949, and the concept of 'integrated leadership' therefore did not become irrelevant, even though the whole context did, of course, change radically with the conquest of power.

CONCLUSION: TOWARD A PEOPLE'S DEMOCRATIC MODERNIZING AUTOCRACY?

As indicated in the third section of this chapter, Mao had already in 1939–40 characterized the regime to be established after the war as a 'joint dictatorship of several revolutionary classes', and had made it fairly clear that this dictatorship was to be under the effective control of the proletariat, or of its 'vanguard', the Chinese Communist Party. When the prospect of a 'coalition government' with the Kuomintang, which Mao had envisaged as a useful tactical expedient in 1944–5, finally evaporated in 1946, and was replaced by open civil war, there was no longer any reason for maintaining the slightest ambiguity about the party's immediate political goals. Mao therefore spelled out, on 30 June 1949, in an article written to commemorate the 28th anniversary of the foundation of the Chinese Communist Party, the precise nature of the 'people's democratic dictatorship' which he proposed to establish three months later.

As for the class nature of the new state, Mao defined the locus of authority in terms of what has often been called a concentric-circle metaphor. The 'people' who were to exercise the dictatorship would be composed of the working class, the peasantry, the urban petty-bourgeoisie and the 'national bourgeoisie'. Of these four classes, the workers would enjoy hegemony, and the peasants constituted their most reliable allies. The petty-bourgeoisie were to be largely followers, while the national bourgeoisie had a dual nature: they were part of the people, but at the same time exploiters. Consequently, those elements among them who behaved badly could be re-classified as not of 'the people', and find themselves on the receiving end of the dictatorship, the objects rather than the subjects of revolutionary change.

Mao made no mystery at all of the form of the state which was to represent these four classes. Replying to imaginary critics who complained that the Communists were 'autocrats', he declared:

My dear sirs, you are right, that is just what we are. All the experience the Chinese people have accumulated through several decades teaches us to enforce the people's democratic dictatorship – which one could also call people's democratic autocracy [*tu-ts'ai*], the two terms mean the same thing – that is, to deprive the reactionaries of the right to speak and let the people alone have that right...

Don't you want to abolish state power? Yes, we do, but not right now; we cannot do it yet. Why? Because imperialism still exists, because domestic reaction still exists, because classes still exist in our country. Our present task is to strengthen the people's state apparatus – mainly the people's army, the people's police, and the people's courts – in order to consolidate the national defence and protect the people's interests. Given this condition, China can develop steadily, under the leadership of the working class and the Communist Party, from an agricultural into an industrial country, and from a new-democratic into a socialist and communist society, abolish classes and realize the Great Harmony [*ta-t'ung*].

In this task of guiding the development of China 'from an agricultural into an industrial country', Mao said that 'the education of the peasantry' was 'the serious problem'. For, he added: 'The peasant economy is scattered, and the socialization of agriculture, judging by the Soviet Union's experience, will require a long time and painstaking work.'[167]

These brief quotations evoke several crucial dimensions of the problem of carrying out a Marxist revolution in China after 1949. On the one hand, Mao's theory of the 'people's democratic dictatorship' was the lineal descendant of Lenin's 'revolutionary-democratic dictatorship of the workers and peasants', and of Stalin's 'four-class bloc', and Mao himself freely acknowledged this ideological debt, and went out of his way to stress the relevance of Soviet experience. Indeed, however unorthodox his road to power, as soon as victory was plainly within his grasp Mao had announced his intention of doing things henceforth in the orthodox way. 'From 1927 to the present,' he declared in March 1949, 'the centre of gravity of our work has been in the villages – gathering strength in the village in order to surround the cities, and then taking the cities. The period for this method of work has now ended. The period of "from the city to the villages" and of the city leading the village has now begun. The centre of gravity of the party's work has shifted from the village to the city.'[168] Hence Mao's statement: 'the serious problem is the education of the peasantry', in other words, the bringing of modern knowledge, and the resources of the modern industrial sector, from the cities to the countryside. Hence the stress, in 1949, on working-class leadership of the

[167] Mao, *SW* 4.418–19.   [168] Mao, *SW* 4.363.

'people's dictatorship'. Hence the attempt, which was to be made in the early 1950s, to draw large numbers of real flesh-and-blood workers into the Chinese Communist Party, in order to 'improve' its class composition.

And yet, despite all this, and despite Mao's explicit statement, in 1962, that during these early years there had been no alternative to 'copying from the Soviets',[169] his article of 30 June 1949 itself contained, as already suggested, elements that point in a significantly different direction. Thus the old-fashioned term 'autocracy' (*tu-ts'ai*) was used as a synonym for dictatorship (*chuan-cheng*), *ta-t'ung* or 'Great Harmony' was used as an equivalent for communism, and the unique character of China's revolutionary experience was repeatedly underscored.

The question of whether or not the Chinese revolution after 1949 followed a course which could be characterized as 'orthodox' in Marxist terms, and of when, how, and why it diverged from the Soviet model is not a proper topic for discussion here, since it will be taken up in two further volumes of the *Cambridge History of China*. What does seem appropriate, in summing up the record of Mao's development as a theorist of revolution during the period ending in 1949, is to consider which of the trends that were to emerge during the first three decades of the People's Republic were already implicit in his thinking prior to the conquest of power, if people had only had the wit to read the signs of the times.

One domain where, in my opinion, this is not the case is that of the political economy of development. There are, of course, those who argue that 'Maoist economics' was born in Yenan, if not before. While it is certainly true that there are significant hints of Mao's future economic thinking to be found in the experience of the Yenan base areas (as summed up in 'Economic and financial problems'), these beginnings were too one-sided to justify the conclusion that the ideas of the Great Leap Forward of 1958 were in any sense implicit in them. They involved only peasant self-help and not the complex multi-faceted organization which characterized the communes; only a stress on indigenous methods, and not large-scale inputs or modern technology. In a word, there was no 'walking on two legs' combining the large and the small, the modern and the traditional in Yenan, and no idea of 'walking on two legs' in Mao's writings of the period. As already noted, Mao proposed in 1949 to transform China 'from an agricultural into an industrial country' through a process of modernization and economic development. And the rural population, though it would participate actively in this process, was to have no say as to the ultimate destination: it would have to accept 're-education', and the resulting change in its mentality and way of life.

[169] Schram, *Mao unrehearsed*, 178 (speech of 30 January 1962).

Thus, if one can distinguish a certain existential continuity between the self-sufficient economy of Yenan and the new policies adopted under the slogan of self-reliance (*tzu-li keng-sheng*) a decade and a half later, there was no intellectual continuity in terms of detailed policy formulations, and certainly no unbroken chain of development in Mao's own thinking, since he explicitly repudiated in 1949 many of the rudimentary ideas he had put forward in the early 1940s. There was, to be sure, as already noted, substantial continuity in the philosophical core of Mao Tse-tung's thought, from 1937 to the early 1960s at least. But if Mao's theory of contradictions was ultimately incompatible with the logic of the Soviet model of economic development, Mao himself did not discover this until the period of the Great Leap.

The one domain in which there was almost total continuity in Mao's approach from the 1930s to the 1970s was that of patterns and methods for the exercise of political authority. Moreover, in this case it should have been possible, I would argue, to discern in Mao's speeches and writings prior to 1949 the signs of many things to come.

Mao said in 1949 that the new regime he was about to set up could be called a 'people's democratic autocracy' just as well as a 'people's democratic dictatorship'. Too much should not be made of this terminological difference, for *tu-ts'ai* was sometimes used in years past, when Marxist expressions did not yet all have standard equivalents in Chinese, as a translation for 'dictatorship'. None the less, to the extent that it carries an aura of old-fashioned Chinese-style autocracy, this term in fact sums up rather well the essence of Mao's approach to political leadership.

On the one hand, he promoted grass-roots participatory democracy on a larger scale than any other revolutionary leader of modern times. In this respect he served the Chinese people well, and helped to prepare them for the next stage in their political development. But at the same time he regarded the promotion of democracy as feasible only within the framework of a 'strong state'. In this he was, in my opinion, correct. Unfortunately, his idea of a strong state was something very like an autocracy, in which he, as the historic leader of the Chinese revolution, remained in the last analysis the arbiter as to what political tendencies were legitimate, and which were not.

As stressed in the third section of this chapter, Mao sought to promote, in the period from 1939 onwards, a 'new democratic' revolution in China which would be a kind of functional equivalent of the capitalist stage in the development of European society. On the one hand, this meant, of course, modernization and industrialization, in order to create the economic foundation on which socialism could ultimately be established. But he was also bent on completing the work of China's abortive capitalist stage in another sense, by continuing the attack on the old Confucian values launched at the time of the May Fourth movement. Indeed, he actually wrote, in August 1944, in a letter calling for emancipation from the old family system: 'There are those who say we neglect or repress individuality [*ko-hsing*]; this is wrong. If the individuality which has been fettered is not liberated, there will be no democracy, and no socialism'.[170] One must none the less ask whether this goal was compatible with Mao's outlook as a whole.

Behind this, and the other questions I have just posed, lurk the fundamental issues raised by the process of cross-cultural borrowing which has been under way in China since the beginning of this century, and has still not led to any clear-cut result. The violent rejection of traditional Chinese values in favour of ideas of Western origin which had characterized, on the whole, the May Fourth period, had been succeeded in the 1930s, in the context of the Anti-Japanese War, by a reaffirmation of the dignity of Chinese culture. In the case of Chiang-Kai-shek and the Kuomintang, this swing of the pendulum had led virtually to the negation of the whole May Fourth spirit, and the assertion that Confucianism provided the answer to all the world's problems. Mao Tse-tung, as an adherent of that most radical of Westernizing philosophies, Marxism-Leninism, could not go to such an extreme, but there is none the less a certain parallelism between the trends in Kuomintang ideology which led to the writing of *China's destiny*, and Mao's call for 'sinification'.

In the late 1940s, as nationwide victory approached, Mao Tse-tung began to emphasize more strongly, as noted above, explicitly Marxist concerns such as the need for leadership by the cities and by the working class, and the central role of industrialization in transforming both Chinese society and Chinese culture. But could 'feudal' culture truly be abolished, and could a party truly undergo reform and acquire a more democratic work style, under the guidance of an 'autocrat', albeit a benevolent one? Could a 'people's democratic autocracy', such as Mao Tse-tung set up in 1949, truly carry out modernization, if this included by implication profound changes in the traditional political culture? Or would the form of such a regime ultimately vitiate or distort the content? That is the question which can be clearly seen to hang over Mao's political creed, at his moment of triumph in 1949.

[170] 'Chih Ch'in Pang-hsien' (To Ch'in Pang-hsien), 31 August 1944, *Selected letters*, 239.

BIBLIOGRAPHICAL ESSAYS

I. INTRODUCTION: GENERAL AND SUPPLEMENTAL

In the growing flood of publication on modern Chinese history, especially from the PRC, research aids and documentary materials seem to be increasing even faster than historical studies that make use of them. The following items are in addition to items cited in volumes 10, 11 and 12 of this series, which describe in some detail archives and publications, particularly in Taiwan.

Research aids

The Institute of Historical Research, Chinese Academy of Social Sciences (Peking), comp. *1900–1975 ch'i-shih-liu nien shih-hsüeh shu-mu* (Bibliography of books on history published during the 76 years 1900–1975), lists by subject more than 9,000 titles by Chinese authors and includes an author index. Fudan University (Shanghai), Department of History, comp. *Chung-kuo chin-tai shih lun-chu mu-lu, 1949–1979* (Catalogue of publications during 1949–1979 on modern Chinese history), arranges more than 10,000 articles and 1,200 books under some eighty topics. Chinese Historical Association, comp. *Chung-kuo li-shih-hsüeh nien-chien* (Yearbook of Chinese historiography), summarizes each year's publications and other activities; the volume titled *1979* appeared in 1981; the volume labelled *1981* deals with 1980 and was published in 1982; while the volume titled *1982* covers 1981. We have last seen *1984*, published in October of that year. The Association also publishes the quarterly *Shih-hsüeh ch'ing-pao* (History newsletter), which began to appear in this public form in 1982. The bibliographies, summaries of current research, and substantive discussions in these two publications are most useful; so also are the bibliographies on 'modern history' which appear regularly in the quarterly journal of the Institute of Modern History, Chinese Academy of Social Sciences, '*Jin dai shi yan jiu*' (Studies in modern history).

Edited jointly by the First Historical Archives in Peking (Ming and Ch'ing documents) and the Second Historical Archives in Nanking (Republican era documents), the journal '*Lishi dang'an*' (Historical archives quarterly), 1981– , publishes scholarly studies, documents, and articles about the collections of these

We are indebted to Professor Noriko Kamachi, University of Michigan, Dearborn, for bibliographical assistance concerning Japanese publications throughout these essays and to Professor Gilbert Rozman, Princeton University, for advice on Soviet studies.

two national archives and other historical archives in the PRC. The First Historical Archives publishes the documentary series *Ch'ing-tai tang-an shih-liao ts'ung-pien* (Historical materials from the Ch'ing archives), while the Second Archives issues *Chung-hua Min-kuo shih tang-an tzu-liao hui-pien* (Archival materials on the history of the Republic of China). The series *Chung-kuo chin-tai ch'i-k'an p'ien-mu hui-lu* (Collected tables of contents of modern Chinese periodicals), edited by the Shanghai Library, begins with 1857 and will eventually include detailed listings for some 11,000 issues of 495 periodicals up to 1918.

Volume 8 in the series *Chung-kuo li-shih ti-t'u chi* (A collection of historical maps) – now at long last publicly available – contains good provincial maps for the Ch'ing period with prefectural boundaries and county capitals shown. *Chung-kuo chin-tai shih tz'u-tien* (A dictionary of modern Chinese history), compiled by historians in Shanghai, is useful for the period 1840–1919. Ch'en Kung-lu, *Chung-kuo chin-tai shih tzu-liao kai-shu* (An outline of sources for modern Chinese history), his lectures at Nanking University in the 1950s, introduces the principal types of historical sources and in doing so provides a fine window on the outlook of many contemporary Chinese historians. A detailed description of the Ch'ing governmental structure is available in Chang Te-tse, *Ch'ing-tai kuo-chia chi-kuan k'ao-lueh* (A study of Ch'ing government organs). Ch'ien Shih-fu's four-volume *Ch'ing-tai chih-kuan nien-piao* (Tables of Ch'ing officials) provides a year-by-year listing of the incumbents of all of the principal metropolitan and provincial offices over two and a half centuries.

Economic and social history

This has long been a favourite topic of Japanese scholars. Shigeta Atsushi, *Shindai shakai keizaishi kenkyū* (Studies of the socio-economic history of the Ch'ing period) looks mostly at gentry power and landlords in Hunan province, while Okuzaki Hiroshi, *Chūgoku kyōshin jinushi no kenkyū* (Studies of gentry-landlords in China) examines closely a landlord family in Chekiang. Kojima Shinji, *Taihei Tengoku kakumei no rekishi to shisō* (History and ideology of the Taiping revolution) is a collection of his studies. The 1911 Revolution is reviewed in Onogawa Hidemi and Shimada Kenji, eds. *Shingai kakumei no kenkyū* (Studies of the 1911 Revolution) which includes thirteen pieces by the new generation of the 'Kyoto school' of Japanese scholarship. Nakamura Tadashi, *Shingai kakumei shi kenkyū* (Studies of the 1911 Revolution) collects his essays over the years on this topic. Note also 'Shingai kakumei nanajushūnen kinen Tōkyō kokusai gakujutsu kaigi' (Papers from the International Conference on the 1911 Revolution held in Tokyo to commemorate its 70th anniversary).

Economic trends and foreign economic interests in Republican China are treated in Shima Ichirō, *Chūgoku minzoku kōgyō no tenkai* (Development of Chinese national industries), and Takamura Naosuke, *Kindai Nihon mengyō to Chūgoku* (The modern Japanese cotton industry and China). A Kyoto University research group (Hazama Naoki *et al.*) has produced the collection *Go-shi undō no kenkyū* (Studies of the May Fourth movement). On Japanese scholarship on modern China in general, in addition to bibliographies noted in *CHOC* 12.827, which survey publications down to 1969, note especially Joshua A. Fogel's translations in *Ch'ing-shih wen-t'i* of bibliographic surveys in *Shigaku zasshi*.

Articles on social and economic history are published in many of the new or revived post-Cultural Revolution academic journals in the PRC. Especially note '*Zhongguoshi yanjiu*' (Studies in Chinese history) published by the Institute of Historical Research in Peking, and '*Zhongguo shehui jingjishi yanjiu*' (Studies in Chinese social and economic history) published by Amoy University. Note also the new *Li-shih hsueh-pao* (Bulletin of historical research) published by the National Taiwan Normal University. On recent PRC scholarship see also Albert Feuerwerker, ed. *Chinese social and economic history from the Song to 1900.*

Four collections of articles contain the major publications on 'capitalist sprouts': People's University, Department of History, comp. *Chung-kuo tzu-pen chu-i meng-ya wen-t'i t'ao-lun chi* (Collected debates on the question of the 'sprouts of capitalism' in China) reprints 33 items. Nanking University, Department of History, comp., ...*hsü-pien* (Continuation [of the preceding title]) contains 20 items. *Ibid.*, *Ming Ch'ing tzu-pen chu-i meng-ya yen-chiu lun-wen chi* (Collected research essays on capitalist sprouts in the Ming and Ch'ing dynasties) contains 25 items and a list of 218 articles published 1949–79. *Ibid.*, *Chung-kuo tzu-pen chu-i meng-ya wen-t'i lun-wen chi* (Essays on capitalist sprouts in China) contains 18 articles and a bibliography. Huang I-p'ing, comp. *Chung-kuo chin-tai ching-chi shih lun-wen hsuan-chi* (A collection of studies on Chinese modern economic history) is a good selection of articles originally published 1949–66 on the Chinese economy in the nineteenth and twentieth centuries, and it concludes with a 110-page bibliography of more than 1,000 pre-Cultural Revolution studies on this period.

Recent publications of source materials on the society and economy of the Ming and Ch'ing periods include: Shanghai Museum, comp. *Shang-hai pei-k'e tzu-liao hsuan-chi* (A collection of Shanghai inscriptions) containing the transcribed texts of 245 stone carvings; Li Hua, comp. *Ming Ch'ing i-lai Pei-ching kung-shang hui-kuan pei-k'e hsuan-pien* (A collection of inscriptions of Peking guilds since the Ming and Ch'ing periods), texts of 90 carvings; Soochow History Museum, Departments of History of Kiangsu Teachers College and Nanking University, comps. *Ming Ch'ing Su-chou kung-shang-yeh pei-k'e chi* (A collection of inscriptions of Soochow guilds in the Ming and Ch'ing periods), texts of 258 stone carvings – this is mainly the work of Professor Hung Huan-ch'un of Nanking University; and First Historical Archives and Institute of Historical Research, Academy of Social Sciences, comps. *Ch'ing-tai ti-tsu po-hsueh hsing-t'ai* (Forms of land rent exploitation in the Ch'ing period), which prints 399 documents for the Ch'ien-lung reign from the archives of the Board of Punishments.

A new collection of essays by Professor Fu I-ling of Amoy (Hsia-men) University reprints 29 items published over three decades beginning in the 1940s: *Ming Ch'ing she-hui ching-chi shih lun-wen chi* (Collected essays on Ming and Ch'ing social and economic history). Two recent studies of Ming and Ch'ing rural society are: Ho Ling-hsiu *et al.*, *Feng-chien kuei-tsu ta-ti-chu ti tien-hsing – K'ung-fu yen-chiu* (A model feudal noble great landlord – studies of the Confucian family estates); and Yeh Hsien-en, *Ming Ch'ing Hui-chou nung-ts'un she-hui yü tien-p'u chih* (Hui-chou rural society in the Ming and Ch'ing and the system of semi-free field servants).

To date, four studies have been published by the Institute of Modern History Academia Sinica, Taipei, Taiwan, from its ambitious project on the modernization of China, 1860–1916. Each provincial study carries the series title *Chung-kuo hsien-tai hua ti ch'ü-yü yen-chiu* (A regional study of modernization in China), and a volume title giving the name of the province: Su Yun-feng, *Hu-pei sheng, 1860–1916* (Hupei province); Chang Yü-fa, *Shan-tung sheng, 1860–1916* (Shantung province); Li Kuo-ch'i, *Min-Che-T'ai ti-chü, 1860–1916* (Fukien, Chekiang, and Taiwan); and Chang P'eng-yuan, *Hu-nan sheng, 1860–1916* (Hunan province).

Recent publications on late-Ch'ing and Republican modern-type industry and other enterprises by PRC scholars include: Chang Kuo-hui, *Yang-wu yun-tung yü Chung-kuo chin-tai ch'i-yeh* (The westernization movement and China's modern industry); Shanghai Academy of Social Sciences, Economic Research Institute, comp. *Jung-chia ch'i-yeh shih-liao* (Historical materials on the Jung family enterprises); *ibid.*, *Liu Hung-sheng ch'i-yeh shih-liao* (Historical materials on the enterprise of Liu Hung-sheng); and four volumes to date from the previously unpublished papers of Sheng Hsuan-huai held by the Shanghai Library: Ch'en Hsu-lu, Ku T'ing-lung, and Wang Hsi, eds. *Sheng Hsuan-huai tang-an tzu-liao hsuan-chi* (Select papers from the Sheng Hsuan-huai archives).

In the late 1950s, Premier Chou En-lai urged non-Communists to write memoirs of their experiences prior to 1949. The result has been a huge outpouring of memoir literature by former warlords, Kuomintang officials, Nationalist army commanders, educators, and others. The first volume of this genre was *Wen-shih tzu-liao hsuan-chi* (Selected literary-historical materials), published in 1960 by the national headquarters of the Chinese People's Political Consultative Conference (Chung-kuo jen-min cheng-chih hsieh-shang hui-i). Subsequently, branch offices of the PPCC in each province, major cities, and even in several hsien, began publishing regional versions of *Wen-shih tzu-liao*. For an index to *Wen-shih tzu-liao* volumes published between 1960 and 1981 see *Wu-shih-erh-chung wen-shih tzu-liao p'ien-mu fen-lei so-yin* (A topical index to 52 series of *Wen-shih tzu-liao*).

Recent research on social history

Documents on the labour movement recently published in the PRC include: Kwangtung Academy of Social Sciences, History Research Office, comp. *Sheng-Kang ta pa-kung tzu-liao* (Materials on the great Canton-Hong Kong strike); and Museum of the Chinese Revolution, comp. *Pei-fang ti-ch'ü kung-jen yun-tung tzu-liao hsuan-pien 1921–1923* (Selected materials on the local workers' movement in North China 1921–1923). New scholarship has greatly added to the treatment in Jean Chesneaux, *The Chinese labor movement, 1919–1927*. Ming-kou Chan, 'Labor and empire: the Chinese labor movement in the Canton delta, 1895–1927'; Gail Hershatter, 'Flying hammers, walking chisels: the workers of Santiaoshi'; Emily

Honig, 'Women cotton mill workers in Shanghai, 1912–1949' and 'The contract labor system and women workers: pre-liberation cotton mills of Shanghai'; Lynda Shaffer, *Mao and the workers: the Hunan labor movement, 1920–1923*; David Strand and Richard Weiner, 'Social movements and political discourse in 1920s Peking: analysis of the tramway riot of October 22, 1929', all increase our knowledge of the Chinese proletariat. Angus McDonald, Jr. *The urban origins of rural revolution*, also has information on the Hunan labour movement. Ming K. Chan, *Historiography of the Chinese labour movement, 1895–1949*, is a bibliographical guide.

Two histories of 'economic thought' – very broadly defined – are reasonably comprehensive: Chao Ching and I Meng-hung, *Chung-kuo chin-tai ching-chi ssu-hsiang shih* (History of modern Chinese economic thought); and Hou Hou-chi and Wu Ch'i-ching, *Chung-kuo chin-tai ching-chi ssu-hsiang shih-kao* (Draft history of modern Chinese economic thought), the first volume covering 1840–64. Meanwhile American historians' theories and discussions of Western influence on China are critically surveyed by Paul A. Cohen, *Discovering history in China*.

Social history has been materially assisted by the three massive volumes of G. W. Skinner *et al.*, *Modern Chinese society: an analytical bibliography* (1973). American historians of rural Chinese society have also drawn upon theoretical frameworks developed in the study of other peasant societies. G. William Skinner, 'Chinese peasants and the closed community: an open and shut case', suggests cyclical variations in the degree of contact between villagers and society outside. Others have used the work of Eric Wolf, *Peasant wars of the twentieth century*, James Scott, *The moral economy of the peasant*, Samuel Popkin, *The rational peasant: the political economy of rural society in Vietnam*, and Eric Hobsbawm, *Primitive rebels*. Some issues relevant to adapting the Wolf-Scott conception of 'moral economy' to Chinese circumstances are brought out in James M. Polachek, 'The moral economy of the Kiangsi soviet, (1928–1934)', and other articles in 'Peasant strategies in Asian societies: moral and rational economic approaches – a symposium', *JAS* 52.4 (Aug. 1983) 753–868.

Many publications of the last decade fell into one of these four categories: interlocking regional analysis and spatial studies that may be combined with cultural anthropology or demographic theory; studies of the upper classes; studies of rural society and peasant rebellion; and works on the urban proletariat. In this rapidly developing field, works cited as dissertations may be expected soon to appear as books.

Regional analysis is represented in different ways by Gilbert Rozman, *Urban networks in Ch'ing China and Tokugawa Japan* and by the articles of Skinner and others in G. William Skinner, ed. *The city in late imperial China* and Mark Elvin and G. William Skinner, eds. *The Chinese city between two worlds*. Approaches derived from Skinner's theories of marketing systems have also been used in detailed studies by historians in Taipei, e.g. Li Kuo-ch'i and Chu Hung, 'Ch'ing-tai Chin-hua-fu te shih-chen chieh-kou chi ch'i yen-pien' (The structure and progressive changes of market towns in Chin-hua prefecture during the Ch'ing). G. William Skinner, 'Mobility strategies in late imperial China', combines regional analysis with family studies. The issue of urbanization is explored further in Susan Mann, 'Urbanization and historical change in China'. Three examples of the growing number of local studies are James Cole, 'Shaohsing: studies in Ch'ing social history'; William Rowe, *Hankow: commerce and society in a Chinese city, 1876–1889*; and Randall Stross, 'A hard row to hoe: the political economy of Chinese agriculture in Western Jiangsu, 1911–1937'. Liu Yao, 'Tai-p'ing t'ien-kuo shih-pai hou Chiang-nan nung-ts'un ching-chi pien-hua ti tsai t'an-t'ao' (Another inquiry into economic changes in agricultural villages of Kiangnan after the defeat of the Taipings) looks at the effects of commercialization from a Marxist perspective.

Social historians have also turned to cultural anthropology for insights. James Watson's 'Chinese kinship reconsidered: anthropological perspectives on historical research' is a comprehensive guide to anthropological literature on kinship, especially lineages. Basic anthropological approaches are represented by articles in Maurice Freedman, ed. *Family and kinship in Chinese society*, and Arthur Wolf, ed. *Religion and ritual in Chinese society*. A new effort to apply principles of cultural anthropology in the light of socio-economic circumstances is exemplified by Stevan Harrell, *Ploughshare village: culture and context in Taiwan*. Rubie S. Watson's 'Class differences and affinal relations in South China' combines study of kin and class structures. Patricia Ebrey and James Watson, *Kinship organization in late imperial China*, pioneers an organized approach to historical anthropology.

A new phase of demographic studies takes off from Ho Ping-ti, *Studies on the population of China, 1368–1953*, but uses methodologies developed in the study of European demographic history. James Lee, 'Food supply and population growth in Southwest China' and James Lee and Robert Eng, 'Population and family history in eighteenth-century Manchuria: Daoyi, 1774–1798' illustrate this trend. Wang Shu-huai, 'Ch'ing-mo Min-ch'u Chiang-su sheng ti jen-k'ou fa-chan' (Population growth in Kiangsu province in the late Ch'ing and early Republic) is a detailed study of demographic changes in that province. Fu Chu-fu, 'Jen k'ou yin-su tui Chung-kuo she-hui ching-chi chieh-kou ti hsing-ch'eng ho fa-chan so ch'an-sheng ti chung-ta ying-hsiang' (The great effects of population factors on the formation and development of the Chinese social and economic structure); and Chou Yuan-ho, 'Ch'ing-tai jen-k'ou yen-chiu' (Research on Ch'ing dynasty population) represent work being done on population in the People's Republic of China. Pierre-Étienne Will, *Bureaucratie et famine en Chine au 18e siècle*; all the articles in 'Food, famine and the Chinese state – a symposium', in *JAS* 41.4 (Aug. 1982); and James Lee, Pierre-Étienne Will and R. Bin Wong eds. *State granaries and food supply in Ch'ing China, 1650–1850*, break new ground in the study of food supply, government policy, and demography.

In the United States much of the work on the upper classes has focused on elites rather than on the traditional Chinese divisions of merchants and gentry or the more fragmented upper-class divisions of the Republican period. Representative works include Keith Schoppa, 'The composition and functions of the local elite in Szechuan' and Mary Backus Rankin, 'Rural-urban continuities:

leading families of two Chekiang market towns'. Keith Schoppa, *Chinese elites and political change*, analyses elite organizational development in Chekiang province within core and peripheral zones. Studies of elite institutions other than kinship are still underdeveloped, but Richard J. Smith, *China's cultural heritage*, analyses the pervasive use of ritual and the sense of order. Basic works on guilds remain Ho Ping-ti, *Chung-kuo hui-kuan shih-lun* (An historical study of Landsmannschaften in China) and Negishi Tadashi, *Shanhai no girodo* (The guilds of Shanghai). Gary G. Hamilton, 'Regional associations and the Chinese city: a comparative perspective', compares such Chinese associations with those in developing societies of Asia, Africa and Latin America. Wang Shih-hsin, 'Wo kuo shou-kung-yeh hang-hui ti ch'an-sheng, hsing-chih chi ch'i tso-yung' (The origin, nature and functions of handicraft guilds in China) is an informative study of Ch'ing guilds.

The more familiar Chinese class divisions have also received attention. On the bourgeoisie see the bibliographical notes of Marie-Claire Bergère in *CHOC* 12, ch. 12. Japanese historians, in particular, have continued to study gentry society, defined in terms both of degree-status and of landholding. The annual bibliographical essays on 'Ming Ch'ing studies in Japan' and 'Japanese studies of post-Opium War in China' in May issues of *Shigaku zasshi* are good guides to this work, as well as to other Japanese research on social history. As noted above, essays for 1978–82 have been translated into English by Joshua Fogel in *Ch'ing-shih wen-t'i*, 4.3, 4.6–10, and 5.1.

Historical research on social classes by historians in the PRC follows Marxist patterns of closely integrating social and economic history in stages of historical development. Much of Ch'ing social history is linked to the issue of sprouts of capitalism noted above. Ching Chun-chien, 'Lun Ch'ing-tai she-hui ti teng-chi chieh-kou' (On the class structure of Ch'ing dynasty society) is an excellent theoretical summary. Among the detailed studies of upper classes by American historians, Frank Lojewski, 'The Soochow bursaries: rent management during the late Ch'ing' suggests some new perspectives on Muramatsu Yūji's still magisterial study of landlord bursaries, summarized in English as 'A documentary history of Chinese landlordism in late Ch'ing and early republican Kiangnan'. James Polachek, 'Gentry hegemony: Soochow in the T'ung-chih Restoration' looks at upper gentry society of Kiangnan. The well-known works of Chang Chung-li (*The Chinese gentry* and *The income of the Chinese gentry*) and Ho Ping-ti, *The ladder of success in imperial China*, are still essential starting points in studying the gentry. An interesting and more recent article is Wang Ssu-chih, 'Tsung-tsu chih-tu ch'ien-lun' (A brief discussion of the lineage system). For insight into the complexity of personal connections among the scholar class see James Polachek, 'The inner Opium War', manuscript awaiting publication; and Luke S. K. Kwong, *A mosaic of the Hundred Days: personalities, politics and ideas of 1898*.

Still more research has been directed toward rural society and peasant rebellions, for which Hsiao Kung-chuan, *Rural China: imperial control in the nineteenth century*, remains an important basis. The voluminous Japanese literature on land relationships is surveyed in Linda Grove and Joseph Esherick, 'From feudalism to capitalism: Japanese scholarship on the transformation of Chinese rural society'. Philip C. C. Huang, *The peasant economy and social change in North China*, is a major study of North China rural society and economy. Frederic Wakeman, Jr. 'Rebellion and revolution: the study of popular movements in Chinese history'; and Kwang-ching Liu, 'World view and peasant rebellion: reflections on post-Mao historiography', are two comprehensive guides to the literature on peasant rebellions. The latter concentrates on Chinese historical writing after 1978, while James P. Harrison, *The Communists and Chinese peasant rebellions: a study in the rewriting of Chinese history*, remains a standard survey of Chinese Marxist historiography of the 1950s and 1960s. Additional perspectives are suggested in Joseph Esherick, 'Some introductory remarks' to 'Peasant rebellions in China, symposium', in *Modern China*, 9.3 (July 1983). Joseph Esherick (Chou Hsi-jui), 'Lun I-ho-ch'üan yun-tung ti she-hui ch'eng-yin' (On the social causes of the Boxer movement) reinterprets the Boxer Rebellion. Elizabeth Perry, 'Social banditry revisited: the case of Bai Lang, a Chinese brigand', suggests new perspectives on 'White Wolf's' rising in the early Republic.

Articles in Jean Chesneaux, ed. *Popular movements and secret societies in China: 1840–1950*, are guides to this important aspect of illegal rural organization. Historians in China appear to have paid somewhat more attention to rebellions than to secret societies *per se*, but the latter have received their share of attention. Ts'ai Shao-ch'ing, 'Ko-lao hui yü 1891 Ch'ang-chiang liu-yü ti fan-yang-chiao tou-cheng' (The Ko-lao hui and the 1891 struggle against foreign missionaries in the Yangtze basin); and Hu Chu-sheng, 'Ch'ing-pang shih ch'u-t'an' (A preliminary inquiry into the history of the Green Gang) are examples.

Popular sects have attracted even more attention. Daniel Overmyer, *Folk Buddhist religion: dissenting sects in late traditional China*; Overmyer, 'Alternatives: popular religious sects in Chinese society'; and Stevan Harrell and Elizabeth J. Perry, 'Syncretic sects in Chinese society: an introduction', provide general frameworks. Susan Naquin, *Millenarian rebellion in China: the Eight Trigrams uprising of 1813*, is a case study of an important early nineteenth-century rising. Studies of other individual sects appear in the articles of the symposium on 'Syncretic sects in Chinese society', in *Modern China*, 8.3 (July 1982) and 8.4 (October 1982). Philip A. Kuhn, 'Origins of the Taiping Vision: cross-cultural dimensions of a Chinese rebellion', puts Taiping millenarianism in a Sino-Western framework. Rudolph G. Wagner's *Reenacting the Heavenly vision: the role of religion in the Taiping Rebellion* is a revolutionary analysis of the content and influence of Hung Hsiu-ch'uan's religion.

Recent works have underlined the variety and complexity of rural social patterns; many have focused on areas of unrest where social relationships did not necessarily conform to those within more stable, prosperous agricultural cores. Elizabeth Perry, *Rebels and revolutionaries in north China: 1845–1945*, uses ecological principles and anthropological concepts of social strategy to analyse a century of disorder in an impoverished part of the North China plain; and Harry J. Lamley, 'Hsieh-tou: the pathology of violence in southeastern China', examines endemic unrest in Kwangtung province. Guy Alitto's 'Rural elites in transition: China's cultural crisis and the problem of legitimacy' looks at the world of separatist, militarist rural leaders during the Republic. R. G. Tiedemann, 'The persistence of banditry: incidents in border districts of the North China plain'; and Philip Billingsley, 'Bandits, bosses, and bare sticks: beneath the surface of local control in early Republican China', provide additional information on social disorder in North China during the Republic.

David Faure, 'Local political disturbances in Kiangsu province, China, 1870–1911' examines causes of social unrest in the very different environment of the urbanized Lower Yangtze. Roxanne Prazniak, in 'Community and protest in rural China: tax resistance and county-village politics on the eve of the 1911 Revolution', looks at new social strains arising during the last Ch'ing decade. Arthur Rosenbaum, 'Gentry power and the Changsha rice riot of 1910' is a detailed study of a major urban riot – which is also analysed in a different way in Joseph Esherick, *Reform and revolution in China: the 1911 Revolution in Hunan and Hubei.*

There are, of course, many other works that do not fit the above categories. A variety of republican studies is presented in Joshua A. Fogel and William T. Rowe, eds. *Perspectives on a changing China: essays in honor of Professor C. Martin Wilbur.* Women's history has also received attention. A good introduction is Margery Wolf and Roxane Witke, eds. *Women in Chinese society. One day in China, May 21, 1936,* Sherman Cochran and Andrew Hsieh, trans., is an abridgement of a kaleidoscopic collection of personal accounts (with a 'progressive' orientation, to be sure) of that day published in Shanghai, 1936. Its variety is an introduction to the kind of material that still awaits research in the newspapers and periodicals from the 1870s onwards.

Soviet studies of late Ch'ing and Republican China

In a less imperfect world, historians of China in all countries would contribute to a shared, though diverse, understanding of modern Chinese history. In such a world market-place of ideas, general agreement would be less likely than general argument, but written history would stand to gain a greater command both of verifiable fact and of theoretical interpretation. In recent years contact and exchange among historians of China have increased rapidly between the three major sinological areas of China, Japan and the Atlantic community, but less rapidly with the fourth major area, the Soviet Union. This is due to several factors. Few China specialists outside the USSR read Russian. Few Russian China specialists are sent abroad, nor are their publications made easily available. Research topics, like researchers, are judged and restricted in the USSR by political criteria. Nevertheless an increasing flow of historical scholarship has been produced in Russian since 1960, much of it bearing on subjects of interest to non-Soviet historians of China. As Professor Gilbert Rozman of Princeton says in *Soviet studies of pre-modern China: assessments of recent scholarship*, 'Studies of Chinese history and literature by Soviet authors are surprisingly numerous, broad in coverage, and often distinctive in choice of topic or original in interpretation.' Both he and Professor Don C. Price of the University of California at Davis discuss in the above volume a variety of Soviet works on the late Ch'ing and early Republic. Topics include early Cantonese nationalism, the Taiping, Nien and Boxer movements, imperialism and reform in the 1890s, Sun Yat-sen, the constitutional movement and revolutionary thought, and the 1911 Revolution. On socio-economic change there are substantial works dealing with cities, craft guilds, early capitalism and agrarian relations; also peasant rebellions, the revolution of 1925–7, CCP policies toward the peasantry in the 1920s, and state capitalism under the KMT government. The breadth of current research interest is indicated in the hundred or so published reports from the annual conference on *Obshchestvo i gosudarstvo v Kitae* (Society and state in China) distributed in a limited edition, usually in three volumes, and edited by L. P. Deliusin of the Chinese Studies Department, Institute of Oriental Studies, Moscow. In short, Soviet sinologists, even though secluded from contact, work on many of the same issues, using the same sources, as China historians elsewhere.

2 AND 10. CHINA'S FOREIGN RELATIONS, 1911–1949

The best introduction to modern Japanese expansion and aggression in China is provided by Marius Jansen's survey *Japan and China: from war to peace, 1894–1972*. For Japanese involvement in Chinese domestic affairs in the early Republican period, see the same author's *The Japanese and Sun Yat-sen*. Additional information, based primarily on Chinese sources, can be obtained from the essays by Ernest P. Young and Madeleine Chi in Akira Iriye, ed. *The Chinese and the Japanese: essays in political and cultural interactions*. Among Japanese-language studies, the most useful are Kurihara Ken, *Tai-Man-Mō seisakushi no ichimen* (An aspect of Japanese policies toward Manchuria and Mongolia); Usui Katsumi, *Nihon to Chūgoku* (Japan and China); Tsunoda Jun, *Manshū mondai to kokubō hōshin* (The Manchurian question and national defence); and Horikawa Takeo, *Kyokutō kokusai seijishi josetsu: Nijūikkajō yōkyū no kenkyū* (International relations in the Far East: a study of the Twenty-one Demands).

The early Republican period has also been a subject of study by historians of Western diplomacy. See, for instance, Peter Lowe, *Great Britain and Japan, 1911–1915*; and James Reed, *The missionary mind and American East Asia policy, 1911–1915*. This latter puts American policy toward the Republic in the context of the rise of missionary influences on foreign policy. The role of missionaries both at home and in China is a fascinating historical phenomenon, and excellent monographs have explored it, among them Valentine Rabe, *The home base of American China missions, 1880–1920*; and Jane Hunter, *The gospel of gentility: American women missionaries in turn-of-the-century China*.

The period of turmoil, from the Twenty-one Demands to the Versailles conference, has been treated by numerous writers, but mostly in terms of Chinese politics and intellectual movements. The best treatment of the country's foreign relations is still Madeleine Chi, *China diplomacy, 1914–1918*. For the Shantung question that triggered the May Fourth movement, see Russell Fifield, *Woodrow Wilson and the Far East*; Noel H. Pugach, *Paul S. Reinsch*; and Ian Nish, *Alliance in decline*.

The 1920s has been one of the best studied periods in Chinese foreign affairs. One can start with Dorothy Borg, *American policy and the Chinese revolution, 1925–1928*, whose pioneering contributions have been amplified by such other works as Paul Varg, *Missionaries, Chinese, and diplomats*; Warren I. Cohen, *The Chinese connection: Roger S. Greene, Thomas W. Lamont, George E. Sokolsky and American-East Asian relations*; and Robert Allbert Dayer, *Bankers and diplomats in China, 1917–1925*. International relations in Asia following the Washington Conference continue to be a subject of lively discussion. The best study of the conference is Roger Dingman, *Power in the Pacific*. For a broad conceptual presentation, see Akira Iriye, *After imperialism: the search for a new order in the Far East, 1921–1931*. Japanese policy toward China during the 1920s is well studied in a number of monographs, including Nobuya Bamba, *Japanese diplomacy in a dilemma*; William Morton, *Tanaka Giichi and Japan's China policy*; several essays in Hosoya Chihiro and Saitō Makoto, *Washington taisei to Nichi-Bei kankei* (The Washington conference system and Japanese-American relations); and the articles by Asada Sadao, Uno Shigeaki, and Ōhata Tokushirō in Akira Iriye and Aruga Tadashi, *Senkanki no Nihon gaikō* (Japanese diplomacy between the wars).

The collapse of the 'Washington system' in the period of the world economic crisis is well treated by Christopher Thorne, *The limits of foreign policy: the West, the League and the Far Eastern crisis of 1931–1933*. The Far Eastern crisis itself has been explored by Sadako Ogata, *Defiance in Manchuria*; Usui Katsumi, *Manshū jihen* (The Manchurian incident); James B. Crowley, *Japan's quest for autonomy*; and Shimada Toshihiko, *Manshū jihen* (The Manchurian incident). See also James C. Thomson, Jr. *While China faced West: American reformers in Nationalist China, 1928–1937*, for an excellent treatment of the turmoil which provided the frustrating setting for American efforts to help China.

Japanese aggression in China during 1931–45 is given dramatic treatment by Saburō Ienaga, *The Pacific war*, in which a noted Japanese historian writes of the events in a self-critical, remorseful mood. Many of his contemporaries, as well as younger writers, have collaborated in publishing Tsunoda Jun, ed. *Taiheiyō senso e no michi* (The road to the Pacific war). This latter, a seven-volume collection of articles by some of Japan's leading historians, was published in 1962–3 and still retains a freshness produced by the uncovering of archival documents as well as bold conceptualizations. Some of these volumes have been translated into English, the most recent being James W. Morley, ed. *The China quagmire: Japan's expansion on the Asian continent, 1933–1941*; and *ibid. Japan's road to the Pacific War:*

Japan erupts. The London Naval Conference and the Manchurian incident 1928–1932.
The best English-language studies of the ideology of Japanese expansionism in
the 1930s are Mark Peattie, *Ishiwara Kanji*; and Miles Fletcher, *The search for a
new order: intellectuals and fascism in prewar Japan.*

There are authoritative studies of the response of the Western powers to the
Chinese-Japanese conflict. For the United States, see Dorothy Borg, *The United
States and the Far Eastern crisis of 1933–1938*; for Germany, John P. Fox, *Germany
and the Far Eastern crisis, 1931–1938*; for Britain, Anne Trotter, *Britain and East
Asia, 1933–1937*; Stephen Lyon Endicott, *Diplomacy and enterprise: British China
policy, 1933–1937*, and William Roger Louis, *British strategy in the Far East,
1919–1939*. Anglo-American diplomacy in Asia on the eve of Pearl Harbor has
been a subject of lively debate for a generation. A key issue has been the role
of China in causing the crisis and eventual war between Japan and the United
States. Recent monographs such as Peter Lowe, *Great Britain and the origins of
the Pacific war*; and David Reynolds, *The creation of the Anglo-American alliance*,
offer detailed analyses. Also worthy of mention in this connection are several
essays contained in two multinational collaborative volumes: Dorothy Borg and
Shumpei Okamoto, eds. *Pearl Harbor as history*; and Ian Nish, ed. *Anglo-Japanese
alienation, 1919–1952.*

Unfortunately, there are few monographs dealing with China's own foreign
policy in the 1930s. This in part reflects the paucity of documentation, but also
the scholars' predominant interest in examining Chinese domestic politics, in
particular Nationalist-Communist relations. The anomaly of studying Chinese
foreign affairs mostly through Japanese and Western sources will someday be
rectified. In the meantime, one has to do with what few studies have been
published, such as Wu Tien-wei, *The Sian Incident*; and the essays by Susan Han
Marsh, Lloyd Eastman, and Akira Iriye in Iriye, ed. *The Chinese and the Japanese.*
For a listing of recent Japanese articles examining Chinese responses to Japan's
aggression, see Japan Association of International Affairs, ed. *Sengo Nihon no
kokusai seijigaku* (International studies in postwar Japan).

Wartime China's diplomatic affairs have again tended to be dealt with in terms
of the foreign policies of the major powers. Among the most recent are
Christopher Thorne, *Allies of a kind: the United States, Britain, and the war against
Japan, 1941–1945*; Michael Schaller, *The US crusade in China, 1938–1945*; and Akira
Iriye, *Power and culture: the Japanese-American war, 1941–1945.*

American-Chinese relations during and after the war constitute a special
category in itself in view of the growing importance of the United States in China's
politics and economy, and also because of the China controversy in postwar
American politics. The pioneering study of this subject, Tang Tsou's *America's
failure in China*, has now been supplemented, though not altogether superseded,
by others that have made use of archival documents not available to Tsou. See,
for instance, Russell D. Buhite, *Patrick J. Hurley and American foreign policy*;
Kenneth Chern, *Dilemma in China: America's policy debate, 1945*; Paul A. Varg,
The closing of the door: Sino-American relations, 1936–1946; Wilma Fairbank,
America's cultural experiment in China, and Gary May, *China scapegoat, the diplomatic*

ordeal of John Carter Vincent. Postwar American strategy toward China has been fully explored by the essays in Dorothy Borg and Waldo Heinrichs, eds. *Uncertain years: Chinese-American relations, 1947–1950*; Robert Blum, *Drawing the line: the origins of the American containment policy in East Asia*; Nancy Bernkopf Tucker, *Patterns in the dust: Chinese-American relations and the recognition controversy, 1949–1950*; and William Whitney Stueck, Jr. *The road to confrontation: American policy toward China and Korea, 1947–1950.* All these studies need to be put in the larger context of postwar Asian international affairs. Helpful in this regard are such works as Yōnosuke Nagai and Akira Iriye, eds. *The origins of the cold war in Asia*; Donald F. Lach and Edmund S. Wehrle, *International politics in East Asia since World War II*; Akira Iriye, *The cold war in Asia*; and Nakajima Mineo, *Chū-so tairitsu to gendai* (The Sino-Soviet confrontation).

3. NATIONALIST CHINA DURING THE NANKING DECADE, 1927–1937

Until the mid-1960s, the history of the Nanking decade was little studied. Since then, however, it has become one of the most popular and exciting periods of historical inquiry, partly because interpretations of the period have been highly controversial. In 1970, Paul K. T. Sih edited a symposium on *The strenuous decade: China's nation-building efforts 1927–1937*, written mainly by persons with pro-Kuomintang sympathies. The general import of that work, which examined political, economic and educational aspects of the Nanking decade, was that the Nationalist government created a firm foundation for national strength. If the war with Japan had not broken out in 1937, Sih and his fellow authors suggest, China would have become a modern and prosperous nation. Jürgen Domes, in his massive *Vertagte Revolution: die Politik der Kuomintang in China, 1923–1937*, published in 1969, generally shared the optimism of the Sih interpretation. Domes nonetheless also candidly noted that the Nationalists quickly lost their revolutionary momentum after gaining power, failed to win mass support, and lacked the capacity to carry out land reform. These seemingly self-contradictory interpretations aside, Domes's work is the most encyclopaedic study available of the institutions and policies of the Kuomintang during the Nanking decade.

The favourable assessments of the Nationalists by Sih and Domes were soon challenged by two books that stressed the shortcomings in the institutions and programmes of the Nationalists. The first of these was Hung-mao Tien's *Government and politics in Kuomintang China, 1927–1937.* Tien examined the institutional and administrative structures of the Nationalists and concluded that, at least by 1937, they were organizationally too weak to create a strong and integrated nation. Lloyd E. Eastman, in *The abortive revolution: China under Nationalist rule, 1927–1937*, particularly stressed that the Nationalists lost their revolutionary drive after coming to power in 1927; he sought to provide evidence for that thesis by examining a series of political and economic phenomena during the ensuing ten years.

Other works focus more narrowly on particular aspects of the Nanking decade.

Ch'ien Tuan-sheng examined the political institutions of the period as part of his two magisterial books: *Min-kuo cheng-chih shih* (The history of governmental institutions under the republic), and *The government and politics of China*. The most detailed examination of the history of the Nationalist Party during this period is that of Chang Ch'i-yun's 5-volume *Tang-shih kai-yao* (Survey of party history), although allowances must be made for the author's pro-Kuomintang bias. There is still no biography of Chiang Kai-shek dealing with this period that can be recommended unqualifiedly, although the following may prove of interest: Hollington K. Tong, *Chiang Kai-shek*, and Brian Crozier, *The man who lost China: the first full biography of Chiang Kai-shek*.

The first in the spate of books that have been published since the mid-1960s on the Nanking decade was John Israel's *Student nationalism in China*, which examined the patriotic response of China's students to Japanese aggression throughout the 1930s. Japan's aggression, per se, is described in T. A. Bisson's still useful *Japan in China*; in Chou K'ai-ch'ing, *K'ang-chan i-ch'ien chih Chung-Jih kuan-hsi* (Sino-Japanese relations before the war of resistance); and in Hata Ikuhiko, *Nitchū sensō shi* (History of the Japanese-Chinese War). Japan's policy toward China, as perceived through the Japanese political process, is the subject of James B. Crowley, *Japan's quest for autonomy: national security and foreign policy, 1930–1938* and *The China quagmire: Japan's expansion on the Asian continent, 1933–1941* edited by James William Morley. This latter work consists of translations from a major, 8-volume Japanese study, *Taiheiyō sensō e no michi: kaisen gaikō shi* (The road to the Pacific war: a diplomatic history of the prewar years). The Sian incident, which was important in the events leading up to the outbreak of war with Japan in 1937, has recently been re-examined in Tien-wei Wu, *The Sian Incident: a pivotal point in modern Chinese history*.

Military aspects of the period are usefully adumbrated in F. F. Liu's *A military history of modern China*. The Nationalists relied heavily upon Germany in their efforts to modernize the army, and William C. Kirby has analysed this important link in *Germany and Republican China*.

In view of the generally retarded development of Chinese economic history, it is surprising that the economy of the Nanking decade has received more attention than most aspects of the period. Two classic accounts written in the 1930s provide an overall background: John Lossing Buck, *Land utilization in China* and R. H. Tawney, *Land and labour in China*. Valuable statistical analyses are in Liu Ta-chung, *China's national income, 1931–1936: an exploratory study*, and (in collaboration with Kung-chia Yeh) *The economy of the Chinese mainland: national income and economic development, 1933–1959*. Arthur N. Young, who served as financial adviser to the Nationalist government from 1929 to 1947, concentrates on monetary questions, but also provides sharp insights into the economy generally, in *China's nation-building effort, 1927–1937: The financial and economic record*. Banking and money markets are examined in Frank M. Tamagna, *Banking and finance in China*. Also useful regarding the development of the modern sectors are Yu-Kwei Cheng, *Foreign trade and industrial development in China*; and John K. Chang, *Industrial development in pre-Communist China: a quantitative analysis*.

The increasing sophistication of studies on the period is evidenced in the growing number of works, several still unpublished, that focus on local and regional aspects of China under Nationalist rule. The first of these was Parks M. Coble's *The Shanghai capitalists and the Nationalist government, 1927–1937*, which stresses the tension between the Nationalists and the entrepreneurial strata in Shanghai. Coble's interpretation is challenged in Richard Clarence Bush, *The politics of cotton textiles in Kuomintang China*. The Nationalists' relations with provincial elites are examined in two doctoral dissertations: Noel Ray Miner, 'Chekiang: the Nationalists' effort in agrarian reform and construction, 1927–1937'; and Bradley Kent Geisert, 'Power and society: the Kuomintang and local elites in Kiangsu province, China, 1924–1937'. In a similar study with a provincial focus, William Wei has assessed Nationalist political, economic and military efforts in 'The Kuomintang in Kiangsi: the suppression of the Communist bases, 1930–1934'. Several comparable studies of the Nanking decade are currently in advanced stages of preparation.

Primary sources pertaining to the Nanking decade tend to be diffuse and widely dispersed. Readers will find further references in the bibliographies of Domes, Hung-mao Tien, Eastman, and other works mentioned above, as well as in other essays in this volume.

4. THE COMMUNIST MOVEMENT 1927–1937

Since basic works on the early CCP are noted in *CHOC* 12.850–2, we try to avoid repetition here. On the early period the most important single source of archival materials is the Ch'en Ch'eng Documents on microfilm which are easily available to scholars in this field outside the People's Republic of China. They contain not only mimeographed government decrees and party resolutions, but also many periodicals, e.g. *Hung-se Chung-hua* (Red China), the official organ of the Soviet government, *Hung-hsing* (Red star) of the army, *Hung-ch'i* (Red flag), *Tou-cheng* (Struggle), *Pu-erh-sai-wei-k'e* (The Bolshevik), and *Shih-hua* (Honest words) of the party and youth corps – all being necessary reading for researchers. The CI official organ, *International Press Correspondence*, 1925–1935, continues to be essential.

Chronologically, this period opened with the Ch'ü Ch'iu-pai leadership from summer 1927 to summer 1928. In English the only monograph on Ch'ü's policies and their implementation is Hsiao Tso-liang, *Chinese communism in 1927: city vs. countryside*, whereas in Chinese the story is far more complex, touching all the issues of the history of the party. In the famous resolutions on party history adopted on 20 April 1945, although Ch'ü's leadership was not called a 'line' (*lu-hsien*), it was nevertheless described as 'leftist', 'adventuristic', 'commandistic' and 'factionalistic', and in the same breath also 'extremely democratic'. This confused assessment evolved into an unambiguous condemnation in the Cultural Revolution period and finally into further uncertainty in 1980. Up to now, no serious attempt has been made to write a monograph on his leadership. The Li Li-san period is dealt with competently in R. C. Thornton, *The Comintern and the*

Chinese Communists, 1928–1931. Li also was severely criticized in the 1945 resolutions, yet scholarly monographs in Chinese on both Ch'ü and Li are still lacking.

As to the land revolution and the creation of soviets, Hsiao Tso-liang's two early compilations – *Power relations within the Chinese communist movement, 1930–1934* and *The land revolution in China, 1930–1934* – remain unsurpassed. In the late 1960s and early 1970s, scholarly interest in political institutions and issues resulted in three well-researched works – J. Rue, *Mao Tse-tung in opposition, 1927–1935*, I. J. Kim, *The politics of Chinese Communism*, and T. Lötviet, *Chinese communism, 1931–1934*. For a fuller treatment of the Kiangsi soviet see Ts'ao Po-i, *Chiang-hsi Su-wei-ai chih chien-li chi ch'i peng-k'uei* (The establishment and collapse of the Kiangsi soviet). The role of the Soviet Union in these and succeeding years is surveyed in Charles B. McLane, *Soviet policy and the Chinese communists, 1931–1946*. Yet another perspective, very critical of Mao Tse-tung, is provided by the last of the Comintern advisers to serve in China: Otto Braun, *A Comintern agent in China 1932–1939*. Documentary compilations on this period include *Kung-fei chung-yao tzu-liao hui-pien* (Essential materials concerning the Communist bandits) by the Sixth Section of the KMT Central Committee, in two volumes, and Liu P'ei-shan, *Chung-kuo Kung-ch'an-tang tsai Chiang-hsi ti-ch'ü ling-tao ko-ming tou-cheng ti li-shih tzu-liao* (Historical materials on the revolutionary struggles led by the CCP in Kiangsi).

The Long March immediately followed the destruction of the central China soviets. Here Dick Wilson has given his readers *The Long March, 1935* and G. Walter and C. H. Hu, *Ils étaient cent mille (la Longue Marche, 1934–1935)*. Accounts of the Long March in Chinese, too numerous to mention here, unfortunately are mostly reminiscences spiced with anecdotes, not serious history. The world knows very little of the strategic and tactical decisions, the organization, the logistics and supplies of this epic event. Likewise, it knows very little of the organization and training, logistics and supplies, rewards and punishments, and many other aspects of the Red Army. J. Gittings, *The role of the Chinese Red Army* and S. B. Griffith, *The Chinese People's Liberation Army* should be read together with two Chinese works, *Chiao-fei chan-shih* (History of the war to suppress the bandits) compiled by the History Bureau of the Ministry of Defence, Taipei, in six volumes; and General Hsueh Yueh, *Chiao-fei chi-shih* (A factual account of the campaigns against the bandits), which are far more detailed. S. B. Griffith's *Mao Tse-tung on guerrilla warfare* may be read in conjunction with W. Laqueur, *Guerrilla, a historical and critical study* (notably chapter 6).

Works and biographies of Mao Tse-tung are surveyed in the last essay below. Biographical materials on CCP leaders are voluminous but scattered in Chinese sources, while biographic works in English still suffer from superficiality. The life history of Chu Te is told by A. Smedley in *The great road* and those of several other CCP leaders by Nym Wales in sketches in her *Red dust*.

In recent years, Western scholars have been paying deeper attention to the socio-economic roots of the Chinese Communist movement. Jean Chesneaux's

The Chinese labor movement, 1919–1927 is a monumental pioneer work, followed by Peter Schran, *Guerrilla economy* and A. McDonald, *The urban origins of rural revolution*. More recent are P. C. Huang *et al.*, *Chinese communists and rural society, 1927–1934* and J. M. Polachek, 'The moral economy of the Kiangsi soviet (1928–1934)', which represent a new trend in the study of China's social unrest. Three series of articles in *Kuo-wen chou-pao* in 1933, 1934 and 1935 by Ch'eng Ch'ang-sheng, Ch'i Ch'i-sheng and Hsün-shih, respectively, are all concerned with socio-economic aspects of the Communist movement.

Wang Fan-hsi, *Chinese revolutionary: memoirs 1919–1949*, throws light on the political socialization of a Chinese Communist (a Trotskyist) and on party life in general. It serves as a companion volume to Sheng Yueh, *Sun Yat-sen University in Moscow and the Chinese Revolution: a personal account*.

Since 1977, Chinese historians' revisions of party history have stressed verification of facts, along with political events and personalities, putting their main effort into compilation and description. An interpretive essay like Tang Pao-lin, 'Shih-lun Ch'en Tu-hsiu yü T'o-p'ai ti kuan-hsi' (Exploring Ch'en Tu-hsiu's relations with the Trotskyists), *Li-shih yen-chiu*, 1981, no. 6, is rare. One new trend is to divert attention during the land revolution period from the central soviet in Kiangsi to the other soviets, as in *O-Yü-Wan su-ch'ü ko-ming-shih tzu-liao hsuan-pien* (Selected documents of the revolutionary history of the O-Yü-Wan soviet), vol. 1, compiled by the party historians of the Central China Teachers' College; and *Ch'uan-Shan ko-ming ken-chü-ti li-shih wen-hsien hsuan-pien* (Selected historical documents of the Szechwan-Shensi revolutionary base area) in two volumes. There is also a spate of books on Chou En-lai, Ho Lung and others, even including a hitherto little-known founder of the CCP, Pao Hui-seng. Both these trends help to redress an imbalance in party historiography – people other than Mao, or the Kiangsi soviet, or the First Front Army also contributed to the Communist movement. Here Hu Hua's multi-volume biographies, *Chung-kung tang-shih jen-wu-chuan* (Biographies of eminent members of the CCP), which began to appear in Sian in 1981 are particularly noteworthy. Hu Hua has revised his *Chung-kuo ko-ming-shih chiang-i* (Lectures on the history of the Chinese revolution) in two volumes; no other general history of the period of the new democratic revolution has emerged to replace it. The problem is surveyed by Arif Dirlik, *Revolution and history: origins of Marxist historiography in China, 1919–1937*.

5. THE AGRARIAN SYSTEM

In the 1920s and 1930s many wrote about China's deteriorating agrarian circumstances. A review of some of this literature and an attempt to classify much of it under various paradigms can be found in Ramon H. Myers, *The Chinese peasant economy: agricultural development in Hopei and Shantung, 1890–1949*, chapter 2. This study also contains an extensive bibliography related to North China agriculture in the twentieth century. Amano Motonosuke, *Chūgoku nōgyō no sho mondai* (Problems of Chinese agriculture) contains the most comprehensive bibliography of pre-1952 studies of Chinese agrarian conditions. The best recent survey of Japanese scholarship for this period is by Masatoshi Tanaka in *Ajia Keizai* (Asian economics), 19.1–2 (Jan.–Feb. 1978) 41–51. Post-1953 Japanese studies can be found in Noriko Kamachi, John K. Fairbank and Chūzō Ichiko, eds. *Japanese studies of modern China since 1953*, 368–93. And of course consult the three volumes of G. William Skinner *et al.*, eds. *Modern Chinese society: an analytical bibliography*.

The two major sources for reliable crop statistics for the Republican years are J. L. Buck, *Land utilization in China*, and Chang Hsin-i's crop statistical survey made in 1929–31. The former was based on a sample of 16,786 farms located in 168 counties of 22 provinces. The latter was reported in various issues of the government journal *T'ung-chi yueh-pao* (Statistical monthly); note especially the summary report in the Jan.–Feb. 1932 issue.

The best survey of land tenure was undertaken by the Nanking government's Land Commission (T'u-ti wei-yuan-hui) set up on 2 August 1934. It employed over 3,000 persons from government departments and universities to carry out its research and survey work in 22 provinces. The survey selected at least 20 per cent of the counties in each province, from which 20 per cent of the rural households were surveyed according to household land, income, expenditures etc. The full particulars of the survey, except summary tables of general findings, were never published because of the outbreak of war with Japan. The preliminary report published in Nanking in 1937 is *Ch'üan-kuo tiao-ch'a pao-kao* (Draft report of the land survey of China).

The South Manchurian Railway Company's Research Department (Chōsabu) had branches in different cities of China where its officials launched hundreds of village surveys and travel trips for collecting information on Chinese rural economic, social and political conditions. Many of these reports can be found in John Young, *The research activities of the South Manchurian Railway Company, 1907–1945. Mantetsu chōsa geppō*, a journal issued by the South Manchurian Railway Company from 1919 until late 1944, contains a remarkable number of original and unique surveys of villages and countryside conditions during those decades, and is one of the best sources on the agrarian society of the Republican era. *Chōsa geppō* is another Japanese journal that began in 1939 and continued until late 1944.

For the still little-known wartime period (1937–45) consult the valuable collection of primary data gathered and published in the journal *Economic Facts* by the Department of Agricultural Economics of the University of Nanking, Chengtu, September 1936 to January 1946, nos. 1–53. This monthly journal of economic statistics issued by the Chungking wartime government provides a wealth of information virtually untapped by researchers studying the rural economy of China and its society under wartime conditions. It includes surveys on such topics as grain marketing, crop-production costs, allocation of labour and capital by farm size, land-use patterns, transportation costs, and living standards of various social classes, as well as many otherwise unobtainable articles by John Lossing Buck.

The contractual aspect of Chinese rural society has been examined by Fu-mei Chang Chen and Ramon H. Myers in a series of articles published in *Ch'ing-shih wen-t'i*, 3.5 (Nov. 1976) and 3.10 (Nov. 1978). Roughly fifty contracts were translated by these authors to show the great variety of resource exchange between households over the course of their life cycle. Robert Ash's *Land tenure in pre-revolutionary China: Kiangsu province in the 1920s and 1930s* is a useful sketch of land tenure and rural income changes in the 1930s. This study paints the deteriorating rural conditions in this province when world depression and domestic monetary deflation had struck hard at the fabric of the rural economy.

By an imaginative analysis of the National Land Commission 1937 survey report, Charles Robert Roll, Jr. estimated income distribution for 1.7 million households in 16 provinces (*The distribution of rural incomes in China: a comparison of the 1930s and 1950s*). He also estimated income distribution in 1952 and found that the inequality in the income structure was about one-third lower than that of 1937 as a result of Communist land-distribution programmes. Among the factors to which Roll attributed the very unequal income distribution in the 1930s were unequal landholdings and the flexibility of labour allocation between farming and other income-earning pursuits. In regions where households could allocate more labour to non-farming activities, however, income was more evenly distributed.

Pre-1949 agriculture considered by region is studied in the last major work by Japan's leading scholar of China's agriculture: Amano Motonosuke, *Chūgoku nōgyō no chiiki teki tenkai* (Regional development of Chinese agriculture). For rural Manchuria consult Nakagane Katsugi, *Kyū Manshū nōson shakai keizai kōzō no bunseki* (Analysis of the socio-economic structure of villages in traditional Manchuria). And North China is depicted in great detail, based on surveys made in 1944, by Imahori Seiji, *Chūgoku hōken shakai no kōzō – sono rekishi to kakumei zenya no genjitsu* (The structure of China's feudal society – its history and condition on the eve of the Communist revolution).

A newly available primary source for China's agrarian situation is the 200-volume set of essays (including field notes) at the Central Political Institute in Nanking, written during the 1930s by master's degree students who conducted field work on a variety of rural administration and village problems. Edited by Hsiao Cheng, these were published in Taiwan by Ch'eng-wen Publishers in 1977 in a series titled *Min-kuo erh-shih nien-tai Chung-kuo ta-lu t'u-ti wen-t'i tzu-liao* (Materials on the land question on the China mainland during the 1930s). See also the valuable index compiled by the Land Management Institute in Taipei, *Min-kuo 20–30 nien-tai Chung-kuo ching-chi nung-yeh t'u-ti shui-li wen-t'i tzu-liao* (Materials on China's economic, agrarian, land and water control problems in the 1930s and 1940s), based on newspaper clippings.

6. PEASANT MOVEMENTS

Although Ssu-yü Teng, *Protest and crime in China: a bibliography of secret associations, popular uprisings, peasant rebellions* covers all periods of Chinese history, a sizeable proportion of its nearly 4,000 entries deals with events in the first half of the twentieth century. The PRC's Second Historical Archives in Nanking contain a few files relating to local peasant struggles, besides those footnoted in chapter 6 (n. 12 and 23). See especially files 1/2/999: 'Chiang-su An-hui Hu-nan teng-sheng nung-min k'ang-tsu tou-cheng' (Peasant resistance to rents in Kiangsu, Anhwei and Hunan provinces, 1929–1941) and 1/2/1000: 'Su Wan Hsiang teng sheng nung-min k'ang-tsu tou-cheng' (Peasant resistance to rents in Kiangsu, Anhwei and Hunan provinces, November 1929 – January 1930). While much more voluminous than 1/2/1000, file 1/2/999 contains almost no information on riots or other violent collective actions. It is, however, very informative on disputes, complaints or requests (such as tenants asking officials to prevent landlords from raising the land rent, or complaining that the military has taken back land rented out to them). The United States Archives offer less detailed reports, but rather more numerous mentions of peasant disturbances, especially in the vicinity of consular posts. Particularly rewarding are the monthly consular reports (Department of State: 893.00 PR), as well as headings 893.43 (Secret Societies), 893.48 (Calamities, Famine conditions), 893.108 (Crime, Banditry). Precious bits of information are also scattered among the vast body of materials under 893.00 (Political Affairs) and 893.00B (Bolshevism).

Extracts of otherwise not easily available reports by Chinese newspapers and periodicals can be found in the two compilations by Chang Yu-i, *Chung-kuo chin-tai nung-yeh shih tzu-liao, ti-san chi* (Materials on China's modern agricultural history, third collection, 1927–1937) (see pp. 1012–1033) and Feng Ho-fa, *Chung-kuo nung-ts'un ching-chi tzu-liao* (Materials on the Chinese rural economy), as well as in *Ti-i-tz'u kuo-nei ko-ming chan-cheng shih-ch'i ti nung-min yun-tung* (The peasant movement during the first revolutionary civil war period). Somewhat more detailed accounts of peasant riots occasionally appear in *Chung-kuo nung-ts'un* (The Chinese village), a Shanghai monthly which shares with the three above compilations a left-wing bias, as well as in *Tung-fang tsa-chih* (Eastern miscellany). Two useful surveys are: Ts'ai Shu-pang, 'Chin shih-nien lai Chung-kuo tien-nung feng-ch'ao ti yen-chiu' (Research on tenant riots in China during the past ten years) and Tzu-ming, 'I-chiu-san-ssu nien Chung-kuo nung-ts'un chung ti ko-chung sao-tung feng-ch'ao i-lan-piao' (List of the various categories of disturbances stirred up in Chinese villages in 1934). Most of these materials are in the nature of newspaper reporting. They usually provide very crude data, if any, on the number of participants in every incident recorded, almost none concerning the social status and positions of the leaders, or the social composition of the rank and file. Access to provincial or hsien-level archives including police reports or judiciary records would, one hopes, allow the research to proceed much further. One file in the Nanking archives (2/2/1130) records lawsuits brought against landlords or local tyrants or ruffians in Chekiang, Fukien and Hunan from December 1930 to October 1933, but none of these cases apparently involves a riot or even a minor disturbance.

In the West, as opposed to China (on Maoist and post-Mao Chinese historiogaphy, see James P. Harrison, *The Communists and Chinese peasant rebellions* and K. C. Liu, 'World view and peasant rebellion'), the study of spontaneous (*tzu-fa*) local peasant agitation is a recent development. But the field is rapidly growing, a fact attested by many issues of *Modern China*, the single most useful periodical on the subject in any Western language. One approach emphasizes the social consciousness of the peasantry and the revolutionary potential of its spontaneous struggles: it is shared by many contributors to, and the editor (Jean Chesneaux) of, the collective volume *Popular movements and secret societies in China, 1840–1950*. A recent study by Ralph Thaxton, *China turned rightside up*, likewise concludes that the Chinese peasants turned towards revolution before, and independently of, their mobilization by the Communists. At variance with the above views are those expressed by Elizabeth Perry in *Rebels and revolutionaries in North China, 1845–1945* and by Lucien Bianco in Claude Aubert *et al. Regards froids sur la Chine*, as well as in articles quoted in chapter 6. For a stimulating symposium on the debate opened by James C. Scott (*The moral economy of the peasant*) and Samuel I. Popkin (*The rational peasant*), see 'Peasant strategies in Asian societies: moral and rational economic approaches' (*JAS* 42.4). Finally, three monographs devote substantial developments to a famous bandit chieftain (Pai Lang) and a no less famous secret society, both active in Northern China during the early Republican period: Philip Billingsley, 'Banditry in China, 1911 to 1928, with particular reference to Henan province'; Tai Hsuan-chih, *Hung-ch'iang-hui* (The Red Spear Society); Roman Slawinski, *La Société des Piques Rouges et le mouvement paysan en Chine en 1926–1927*.

A pioneer study on the Hai-Lu-feng soviet is that of Shinkichi Etō, 'Hai-lu-feng: the first Chinese soviet government'. More details can be found in Roy Hofheinz, *The broken wave*. The definitive in-depth study of P'eng P'ai's revolutionary career and the Hai-Lu-feng soviet is: Fernando Galbiati, 'P'eng P'ai, the leader of the first soviet: Hai-lu-feng, Kwangtung, China (1896–1929)'. This monumental three-volume thesis will be published in a condensed form by Stanford University Press. P'eng P'ai's own report ('Hai-feng nung-min yun-tung', The peasant movement in Hai-feng) is both graphic and lucid. His many insights into the problems and techniques of peasant organization are available in the translation by Donald Holoch, *Seeds of peasant revolution*. The sources and studies relating to later developments (1928–49) can be found in the bibliographical essays for chapters 4, 12 and 13. Let us only recall here two seminal works: Chalmers Johnson, *Peasant nationalism and Communist power* and William Hinton, *Fanshen: a documentary of revolution in a Chinese village*. Few 'China books' have been so much discussed and criticized by so many authors (including myself) over the last two decades as was *Peasant nationalism*, but it is the privilege of truly original works to provoke infinite debate. Most recent scholarship stresses the economic over the national factors in the Communist mobilization of peasants. That that mobilization was no easy job is eloquently illustrated by Hinton's *Fanshen*, a richly documented, first-hand account of revolution in a North Chinese village. It exhibits, in spite of the author's obvious sympathies, the superb ambivalence of a classic work.

7. THE DEVELOPMENT OF LOCAL GOVERNMENT

The archival basis for the study of twentieth-century local government is not yet established. The background in Ch'ing administration will one day be studied through the archives of Shun-t'ien prefecture (Chihli). More than 12,000 items cover the official system, civil administration, constitutional reform, judicial system, finance and currency, and ten other subjects, spanning the period from the 1720s to 1911. This rich source, held by the First Historical Archives in Peking, awaits cataloguing and preservation, and access to it is uncertain. Of the Pa county (Pa-hsien) archives in Szechwan, no general description is available, though researchers have begun to use them. The Ch'ing archives of Tan-shui subprefecture and Hsin-chu county held by National Taiwan University have been described by David C. Buxbaum, 'Some aspects of civil procedure and practice at the trial level in Tanshui and Hsinchu from 1789 to 1895', *JAS* 30.2 (Feb. 1971) 255-79. The modern evolution of local administration is beginning to be researchable at the Second Historical Archives, Nanking, which holds materials from 1911 to 1949, but access to that collection is still limited. Both the First and Second Archives have begun extensive publication of holdings on certain topics. For example, the local self-government component of late Ch'ing constitutionalism may be studied in *Ch'ing-mo ch'ou-pei li-hsien tang-an shih-liao* (Archival materials on the late Ch'ing constitutional movement), a publication of the First Historical Archives.

The normative basis for local government since the late Ch'ing is found in compilations such as *Ta-Ch'ing Kuang-hsu hsin fa-ling* (New laws of the Kuang-hsu period) and similar volumes listed under the 3.2 heading in J. K. Fairbank and K. C. Liu, *Modern China*. The problem is to discover how far these rules were applied in practice. For this purpose, gazettes (*kung-pao*) of government organizations, particularly of provincial administrations, show how governments reacted to concrete local situations. Publications such as *Chiang-su sheng cheng-fu kung-pao* (Gazette of the Kiangsu Provincial Government) are described in P. K. Yü *et al.*, eds. *Research materials on twentieth-century China: an annotated list of CCRM publications*, 71ff. Government year books (*nien-chien*) can often serve the same purpose.

Extensive surveys of local society contain rich information on how local governments operated. Japanese local fieldwork studies are introduced in John Young, *The research activities of the South Manchurian Railway Company, 1907-1945*. Probably the best first-hand source is the village-by-village study of certain areas in Hopei and Shantung from the early 1940s, Chūgoku nōson kankō chōsa kankōkai, ed. *Chūgoku nōson kankō chōsa* (Investigations of Chinese village customs). In addition to interview transcripts, there is primary material on local government since the late Ch'ing. The political side of these materials has been studied by Prasenjit Duara, 'Power in rural society: North China Villages, 1900–1940'. Japanese studies of this subject are also extensively explored in Duara's work. A compendium of field reports prepared under the Land Administration Academy (Ti-cheng hsueh-yuan) of the Central Political Institute (Chung-yang cheng-chih hsueh-hsiao) during the 1930s includes much information on local government: *Min-kuo erh-shih nien-tai Chung-kuo ta-lu t'u-ti wen-t'i tzu-liao* (Materials on land problems in mainland China during the 1930s).

The major collaborative research project on regional studies of China's modernization at the Institute of Modern History, Taiwan (mentioned above) reveals much of the context in which local administration evolved in the late Ch'ing and early Republic. Also consult articles in this institute's *Chung-yang yen-chiu-yuan Chin-tai-shih yen-chiu-so chi-k'an* (Bulletin of the Institute of Modern History, Academia Sinica), vol. 6 (1977) by Chang Yü-fa, 'Ch'ing-mo min-ch'u ti Shan-tung ti-fang tzu-chih' (Shantung local self-government in the late Ch'ing and early Republic), and Wang Shu-huai, 'Ch'ing-mo Chiang-su ti-fang tzu-chih feng-ch'ao' (Riots against local self-government in Kiangsu during the late Ch'ing period).

Study of the politicization of local elites should begin with Chang P'eng-yuan, *Li-hsien-p'ai yü Hsin-hai ko-ming* (The constitutionalists and the 1911 Revolution), and R. Keith Schoppa, *Chinese elites and political change: Zhejiang Province in the early twentieth century*. The local self-government movement as a whole is treated by Philip A. Kuhn, 'Local self-government under the Republic: problems of control, autonomy, and mobilization', in Frederick Wakeman Jr and Carolyn Grant, eds. *Conflict and control in late imperial China*. How local elites interacted with government throughout the modern period is addressed in *Select papers from the Center for Far Eastern Studies*, University of Chicago, 3 and 4 (1978–9). See in particular articles by Guy S. Alitto, Susan Mann Jones, and Philip A. Kuhn (as listed in the bibliography). An influential study of the imperial background is Wada Sei, *Chūgoku chihō jichi hattatsu shi* (Development of Chinese local self-government), a reprint of the 1939 edition which, however, contains an important new bibliography by Yamane Yukio. Hsiao Kung-ch'uan's *Rural China: imperial control in the nineteenth century* and Ch'ü T'ung-tsu's *Local government in China under the Ch'ing* are still valuable introductions to the Ch'ing background.

The local systems of regional regimes left many volumes of material, most of it programmatic and self-congratulatory. Yet much can be read between the lines of such collections as Shan-hsi ts'un-cheng-ch'u, comp. *Shan-hsi ts'un-cheng hui-pien* (Collected materials on Shansi village government), which contains documents flowing from province to county during the period 1916–27. On Kwangsi, see Diana Lary, *Region and nation: the Kwangsi clique in Chinese politics, 1925–1937*.

The Kuomintang's local administration and its background are introduced in Ch'en Po-hsin, *Chung-kuo ti ti-fang chih-tu chi ch'i kai-ko* (China's local system and its reform); and Ch'ien Tuan-sheng *et al.*, *Min-kuo cheng-chih shih* (The history of governmental institutions under the republic). County administration is treated by Ch'eng Fang, *Chung-kuo hsien-cheng kai-lun* (Chinese county government), which cites and summarizes much of the existing literature up to 1939; and Shih Yang-ch'eng's comprehensive work of 1946 does the same for provincial government: *Chung-kuo sheng hsing-cheng chih-tu* (Chinese provincial administration). The background in the early Republic is surveyed by Baba Kuwatarō, 'Shina chihō gyōsei seido no kenkyū' (The local government system of China), *Shina kenkyū* (Research on China) 1927.12, 81–317. A revealing institutional study is Odoric Y. K. Wou, 'The district magistrate profession in the early Republican period: occupational recruitment, training and mobility', *Modern Asian Studies* 8.2 (April 1974) 217–45. Tung Hsiu-chia summarizes the Kuomintang's putative system for local self-rule in *Chung-kuo ti-fang tzu-chih wen-t'i* (The problem of China's local self-government). The highly touted 'new county system' is treated by a prominent Kuomintang programmatist, Li Tsung-huang, *Hsin-hsien-chih chih li-lun yü shih-chi* (The theory and practice of the new county system).

On the local politics of the rural reconstruction movement, the basic work is Guy S. Alitto, *The last Confucian: Liang Shu-ming and the Chinese dilemma of modernity*. The rich Chinese literature in this field can be approached through the bibliography of this work, as well as through P. K. Yü's *Research materials on twentieth-century China*, cited above. Charles W. Hayford has studied the Ting-hsien case in 'Rural reconstruction in China: Y. C. James Yen and the Mass Education Movement'.

8. THE GROWTH OF THE ACADEMIC COMMUNITY 1912–1949

The academic community embraced individuals and institutions whose histories are recorded in a varied complex of literature that touches upon intellectual currents, political trends, and other aspects of the socio-cultural environment. Here we can only cite basic materials for the present chapter, devoted to higher education.

Government archives in Peking, Nanking and Taipei, as well as in Tokyo, London, Paris and Washington, DC, remain comparatively unexplored in this field. The Rockefeller Foundation Archive at Tarrytown, New York, offers data on American assistance, especially in medical and other sciences.

Published documentation is extensive. Shu Hsin-ch'eng's early four volumes, *Chin-tai Chung-kuo chiao-yü shih-liao* (Source materials on modern Chinese education), documented the transition from 1898 to the inauguration of party education in 1928. Shu Hsin-ch'eng's three volumes published posthumously in 1962, *Chung-kuo chin-tai chiao-yü shih tzu-liao* (Source materials on the history of modern Chinese education), is a quite different work with documents spanning the period 1852–1922. Taga Akigorō's four volumes of 1976, *Kindai Chūgoku kyōikushi shiryō* (Historical materials on the history of education in modern China) reproduces many thousands of pages of sources from late Ch'ing to 1948, making it the most extensive single collection. A week-by-week chronology to 1933 is provided by Ting Chih-p'in, *Chung-kuo chin ch'i-shih-nien lai chiao-yü chi-shih* (Events in Chinese education during the past 70 years). Wang Yun-wu, *Shang-wu yin-shu-kuan yü hsin-chiao-yü nien-p'u* (A chronology of the Commercial Press and the New Education) provides data and documentation from 1897 to 1972 (after 1949 concerning Taiwan). Extensive data are also compiled in Lin Tzu-hsun, *Chung-kuo liu-hsueh chiao-yü shih* (A history of Chinese students studying abroad).

Among journals, *Chiao-yü tsa-chih* (Chinese educational review) was published by the Commercial Press in Shanghai from 1909, and *Chung-hua chiao-yü chieh* (Chung Hua educational review) by the Chung-hua Book Company from 1912. *Hsin-chiao-yü* (The new education) edited at first by Chiang Monlin (Meng-ling) was published from 1919 under the sponsorship of the Kiangsu Education Association (Chiang-su sheng chiao-yü kung-chin she).

For a concise early survey up to 1930 see Wang Feng-chieh, *Chung-kuo chiao-yü, shih ta-kang* (An outline history of Chinese education). For the years after 1930 a number of surveys were published under diverse auspices: among them were Ts'ai Yuan-p'ei *et al. Wan-Ch'ing san-shih-wu-nien lai chih Chung-kuo chiao-yü (1897–1931)* (Chinese education in the 35 years since late Ch'ing (1897–1931)). *K'ang-chan ch'ien shih-nien chih Chung-kuo* (China in the decade before the war) contains several chapters on academic institutional development; P'an Kung-chan, ed. *Wu-shih-nien lai ti Chung-kuo* (China in the last 50 years) includes chapters by leading academic figures. Chuang Tse-hsuan, ed. 'K'ang-chan shih-nien lai ti Chung-kuo hsueh-hsiao chiao-yü tsung chien-t'ao' (General assessment of Chinese education in the ten years since the [beginning of the] war of resistance) was a special issue of *Chung-hua chiao-yü chieh*, new series 1.1 (1947). Official figures on the educational establishment include three volumes issued by the Ministry of Education, Office of Statistics, *Erh-shih-i [erh, san] nien-tu ch'üan-kuo kao-teng chiao-yü t'ung-chi* (Statistics of higher education in China for the academic year 1932–3 [1933–4, 1934–5]). Two educational year books were published: *Ti-i-tz'u Chung-kuo chiao-yü nien-chien* (The first China education year book), 6 vols in 1934 with a preface by Wang Shih-chieh as minister of education; and *Ti-erh-tz'u...* (The second year book) in 1948 with a preface by Chu Chia-hua.

Since 1981 a series has been under publication in Taipei with the general designation *Hsueh-fu chi-wen* (Records and reminiscences of academic institutions), which consists of single-volume histories of leading universities. Among the first volumes to appear are, for example, *Kuo-li Pei-ching ta-hsueh* (National Peking University), *Kuo-li Ch'ing-hua ta-hsueh* (National Tsing-hua University), *Kuo-li Wu-han ta-hsueh* (National Wuhan University), *Kuo-li Hsi-nan lien-ho ta-hsueh* (National South-west Associated University), *Ssu-li Yen-ching ta-hsueh* (Yenching University). Contents include a variety of materials, from formal chronological accounts, contemporary articles and reports and public speeches, to commemorative papers and personal reminiscences, much of it anecdotal. The monthly journal *Chuan-chi wen-hsueh* (Biographical literature) and its press in Taipei have published a Biographical Literature Series (BLS) on personalities of the Republican period, including many in the academic community: Wang Wen-t'ien, *Chang*

Po-ling yü Nan-k'ai ta-hsueh (Chang Po-ling and Nankai University), BLS no. 26, 1968; Liang Shih-ch'iu, *T'an Wen I-to* (About Wen I-to), BLS no. 3, 1967; Lo Chia-lun, *Shih-che ju-ssu chi* (Recollections of those who are gone), BLS no. 14, 1967; *Ts'ai Yuan-p'ei tzu-shu* (Autobiography of Ts'ai Yuan-p'ei), BLS no. 22, 1978: Hu Shih *et al. Ting Wen-chiang che-ko jen* (Ting Wen-chiang as a person), BLS no. 21, 1979; Yang Liang-kuang, *Tsao-ch'i san-shih-nien ti chiao-hsueh sheng-huo* (My life as an educator: the first 30 years), BLS no. 98, 1980.

On the special contribution of Ts'ai Yuan-p'ei to modern Chinese academic life, see T'ao Ying-hui, *Ts'ai Yuan-p'ei nien-p'u* (A chronological biography of Ts'ai Yuan-p'ei), and two detailed articles in the *Bulletin of the Institute of Modern History*, Academia Sinica, Taipei, no. 5, 1976, and no. 7, 1978. In addition to the widely known *Ts'ai Yuan-p'ei ch'üan-chi* (Collected works), there is a separate volume that concentrates on Ts'ai's pronouncements on educational matters, Kao P'ing-shu, ed. *Ts'ai Yuan-p'ei chiao-yü wen-hsuan*, published in 1980. Some alumni magazines contain useful historical data, such as *Ch'ing-hua hsiao-yu t'ung-hsun* (Alumni gazette) of Tsing-hua University. First-hand accounts of academic personalities in English include Chiang Monlin, *Tides from the West*.

The story of the Christian colleges in China and their interaction with the Chinese environment is told in Jessie G. Lutz, *China and the Christian colleges, 1850–1950*; see also Anthony C. Li, *The History of privately controlled higher education in the Republic of China*. The histories of individual colleges have been issued by the United Board of Christian Higher Education of Asia; although uneven in quality, these works serve the dual purpose of providing an outline of Christian educational endeavour in China since the nineteenth century, based mainly on mission archives and private papers, and revealing the divergent attitudes prevalent among the Christian educators and their chroniclers. The volumes include: Charles Hodge Corbett, *Shantung Christian University* (1955); Clarence Day, *Hangchow University* (1955); Dwight W. Edwards, *Yenching University* (1959); Mary Lamberton, *St John's University, Shanghai, 1879–1951* (1955); Mrs Lawrence Thurston and Ruth M. Chester, *Ginling College* (1955); L. Ethel Wallace, *Hwa Nan College: the women's college of South China* (1956); and Lewis C. Walmsley, *West China Union University* (1974). See also Reuben Holden, *Yale in China: the mainland, 1901–1951*. For recent analyses of the Western – especially American – impact on the development of higher education and scientific research in China see *American science and modern China 1876–1936* by Peter Buck, and Philip West, *Yenching University and Sino-Western relations 1916–1952*.

The whole area of Japanese influence on Chinese culture and education was most fully opened up by the great pioneer Sanetō Keishū, whose early works of 1939–45 (see items 6.8.1 to 6.8.5 in J. K. Fairbank *et al. Japanese studies of modern China*) reached their climax in his *Chūgokujin Nihon ryūgakushi* (A history of Chinese students in Japan) of 1960. For a Chinese version see Huang Fu-ch'ing, *Ch'ing-mo liu-Jih hsueh-sheng* (Chinese students in Japan in the late Ch'ing period). The Sanetō collection in Tokyo remains a major resource for this field, without a counterpart in any other country. Y. C. Wang, *Chinese intellectuals and the West,*

1872–1949 is an introductory survey; but in general the personal memoirs of Chinese who studied abroad remain an untapped resource. Sally Borthwick, *Education and social change in China*, lists some 50 volumes of such memoirs on pp. 200–1.

The most useful starting points among recent publications, in addition to Philip West, *Yenching University and Sino-Western relations, 1916–1952*, include the detailed Tsing-hua history from Peking, *Ch'ing-hua ta-hsueh-hsiao shih-kao*, completed 1965, published 1981 (of which John Israel has published selected portions) and Jerome Grieder's survey, *Intellectuals and the state in modern China: a narrative history*, of 1981.

9. LITERARY TRENDS: THE ROAD TO REVOLUTION 1927–1949

The general state of the study of modern Chinese literature was discussed in the bibliographical essay for the chapter 'Literary trends I: the quest for modernity' in *CHOC* 12. The present essay provides additional information which was not available when that chapter and the present one were written.

Since the downfall of the 'gang of four' in 1976, a resurgence of intellectual activity has brought forth a rich harvest of scholarship on modern Chinese literature. (In the Chinese way of chronological division, the 'modern period', *hsien-tai*, refers to 1917–1949, which is followed by the 'contemporary period', *tang-tai*, from 1949 to the present.) Among the mushrooming journals, at least half a dozen are devoted to literary resources and studies of the *hsien-tai* period, of which the most notable include: *Hsin wen-hsueh shih-liao* (Historical materials on new literature), featuring the memoirs of Mao Tun and other significant sources; *Chung-kuo hsien-tai wen-hsueh yen-chiu ts'ung-k'an* (Collection of modern Chinese literature studies); and *Chung-kao hsien-tai wen-i tzu-liao ts'ung-k'an* (Collected materials on modern Chinese literature and art). In addition, several journals are concerned exclusively with Lu Hsun studies (the year 1981 marked the centenary of Lu Hsun's birth). A massive dictionary of Chinese writers, *Chung-kuo wen-hsueh-chia tz'u-tien*, is being issued by the Foreign Languages Institute: the first volume of the *hsien-tai* section, published in 1978 in draft form, contains biographies of 405 writers; volume 2, published in 1982, is bulkier with 582 biographies. The standard literary histories cited in this chapter, including those by Li Ho-lin, Wang Yao and Liu Shou-sung, have been reissued, and a number of new textbooks have been published.

A new national archives centre for the study of modern Chinese literature is being established; future archives will be housed in a sixteenth-century longevity temple in the vicinity of Beijing. According to information provided in *Chinese Literature* (February 1983), the collection 'will include manuscripts, letters, diaries, photos, portraits, reference films, recordings and video tapes of modern writers, theorists, translators and literary activists since the 1919 May Fourth Movement, along with their works in various editions, journals and other important materials' (p. 137). Perhaps the most ambitious undertaking, which has already begun, is the compendious series *Chung-kuo hsien-tai wen-hsueh shih tzu-liao hui-pien* (Collected materials on the history of modern Chinese literature), which will consist of materials on literary movements, societies, controversies, as well as on writers and their works, plus indexes to individual writings and articles in newspapers and journals. This massive project represents a collaborative effort of scholars from a dozen leading universities under the supervision of the Institute of Literature of the Academy of Social Sciences. When publication is completed (projected for 1985), this new compendium, numbering perhaps hundreds of volumes, will become the most valuable repository for students and researchers of the field, both Chinese and Western.

This sheer quantity of Chinese scholarship is, however, not necessarily matched by interpretive quality. Although post-1976 works evince less Maoist ideology, the basic Marxist-Leninist framework, made vulgarly schematic by successive ideological campaigns over the past thirty years, is not abandoned. Most recent textbooks still tend to emphasize the literary debates of the 1930s and the significance of party leadership in the League of Left-wing Writers and, of course, in the Yenan literary scene. Accordingly, leftist literary trends and works receive more extensive coverage than non-leftist writers or artistically interesting works, especially those published in wartime Chungking and in Japanese-occupied Shanghai. Among writers of the *hsien-tai* period, Lu Hsun remains a towering giant occupying a politically deified position, although a small number of studies (such as a refreshing biography by Liu Tsai-fu and Lin Fei, *Lu Hsun chuan*) have attempted to portray him in more human proportions.

Most recent textbooks on the history of modern Chinese literature tend to give prominence to six major writers, ranked in the following order: (1) Lu Hsun, (2) Kuo Mo-jo, (3) Mao Tun, (4) Pa Chin, (5) Lao She, and (6) Ts'ao Yü. Those who are valued highly in C. T. Hsia's *A history of modern Chinese fiction* – Chang T'ien-i, Wu Tsu-hsiang, Shen Ts'ung-wen, Ch'ien Chung-shu, and Eileen Chang – seem obscured in Chinese literary histories. The modernistic trend in poetry, which flowered briefly in the early 1930s, hardly received any attention in previous Chinese studies and is only beginning to attract scholarly interest in China, partly as a result of the recent controversy centred around the young practitioners of 'obscure poetry' (*meng-lung shih*).

In contrast, poetry and the works of such non-leftist writers as Hsu Chih-mo and Yü Ta-fu remain the only part of the larger legacy of May Fourth literature which is allowed to be read in Taiwan, whereas most other writers, including Lu Hsun, are banned for being 'Communists'. A rather daring scholarly series, *Chung-kuo hsien-tai wen-hsueh yen-chiu ts'ung-k'an* (Collection of modern Chinese literature studies), edited by Chou Chin and numbering about thirty volumes, represents an initial effort to circumvent the official ban, although the intellectual quality of the individual volumes is uneven.

Much remains to be done, therefore, in advancing the study of modern Chinese literature as *literature* in the context of social and cultural history, rather than mainly as a reflection of political ideology and policy. This challenge is being met by a growing number of Western scholars who have been able in recent years to have direct personal contacts with the writers they were studying. Among recent studies (published or about to be published) which have benefited from such an experience, the most notable include: Yi-tsi Feuerwerker, *Ding Ling's fiction – ideology and narrative in modern Chinese literature*; Ko Hao-wen (Howard Goldblatt), *Hsiao Hung p'ing-chuan* (A critical biography of Hsiao Hung, expanded and revised from the author's English monograph, *Hsiao Hung*); Jeffrey Kinkley's forthcoming book on Shen Ts'ung-wen (revised from his dissertation at Harvard, 'Shen Ts'ung-wen's vision of Republican China'); and Theodore Huters, *Qian Zhongshu*. These scholars have either interviewed their subjects in person, or done research at the actual locations of the subject's life, or both. Following in their wake, a number of graduate students from American universities have done research or interviewing in China on such figures as Wu Tsu-hsiang, Lao She, Hsiao Chun, Ai Wu, and Ting Ling and on such generic topics as autobiographical literature and symbolist poetry.

The general area of concentration among Western scholars remains, however, the literature of the 1930s. This is understandable, owing to the productivity and artistic maturity of the writers of this period despite the pressing socio-political circumstances. On the other hand, literary polemics and the activities of the League of Left-wing Writers have not been extensively studied by Western scholars, with the notable exceptions of Paul Pickowicz, *Marxist literary thought in China: the influence of Ch'ü Ch'iu-pai* and a recent dissertation on the league by Anthony Kane: 'The League of left-wing writers and Chinese literacy policy'. The period of the 1940s, in which modern Chinese literature was embroiled in war and revolution, has received scant attention in Western scholarship. The wartime writings of Mao Tun and Pa Chin await further research and translation. Mao Tun's novels, such as *Shih* (Eclipse) and *Fu-shih* (Putrefaction), have not been rendered into English; Pa Chin's best novel, *Han-yeh* (Cold nights), has only recently been translated by Nathan Mao. Wartime drama in Chungking is a crucial subject yet to be explored. And the literary scene in Japanese-occupied Shanghai receives its first scholarly treatment in Edward Gunn's masterful book, *Unwelcome muse*. The Yenan scene has been studied by David Holm, who has written articles on the Yang-ke movement and on Lu Hsun's legacy in Yenan. Mao Tse-tung's famous Talks on art and literature received a new and careful English translation by Bonnie McDougall, based on the earlier 1943 text. The post-war film industry, briefly discussed in this chapter, is being researched by Paul Pickowicz, Paul Clark and others as a source for social history; its artistic and literary merits remain to be assessed. (Jan Leyda's book on modern Chinese cinema, *Dianying*, is seriously flawed.) In short, the entire period offers a rich territory for continuing scholarly exploration.

The growth of a new field can be gauged also by collective scholarly activities such as workshops and conferences. Since the ground-breaking workshop and conference at Harvard in 1974, which resulted in a significant book, *Modern Chinese literature in the May Fourth era* (edited by Merle Goldman), half a dozen international gatherings have been held, of which three are directly relevant to the period covered in this chapter. The first of these conferences was a colloquium held in Paris in June 1980, organized by Robert Ruhlmann. The conference volume, published in 1982 under the title of *La littérature chinoise de la guerre de résistance contre le Japon (de 1937 à 1945)*, contains twenty-nine papers by European, American, and Chinese scholars and writers, with special *hommages* paid to Ting Ling and Ai Ch'ing (the latter attended in person). The second international conference, devoted entirely to 'Lu Hsun and his legacy', was held as Asilomar, California, in August 1981. Now in preparation under the editorship of Leo Ou-fan Lee is a volume which includes a dozen papers assessing the broad-ranging impact of Lu Hsun on modern Chinese literature, politics, and thought as well as his reception in world literature. The most recent academic gathering was a workshop on 'Critical approaches to modern Chinese short stories', held in Honolulu in December 1982. Some twenty scholars discussed the viability of employing Western critical theories for the analysis of specific Chinese short stories from the early May Fourth period to the present. The workshop marked the first sustained exploration of the intrinsic structures of selected stories as *literary texts*, not as historical documents or biographical data of their authors.

One may also consult the bibliographical essays contained in Winston L. Y. Yang and Nathan K. Mao, eds. *Modern Chinese fiction: a guide to its study and appreciation*; and Donald Gibbs and Yun-chen Li, eds. *A bibliography of studies and translations of modern Chinese literature, 1918–1942*.

The most comprehensive sampling in English of modern Chinese fiction is Joseph S. M. Lau, C. T. Hsia, and Leo Ou-fan Lee, eds. *Modern Chinese stories and novellas, 1919–1949;* of modern Chinese poetry, Kai-yu Hsu, *Twentieth-century Chinese poetry*; and of modern drama, Edward Gunn, ed. *Twentieth-century Chinese drama: an anthology..*

For Chapter 10, see bibliographical essay 2 and 10, above.

11. NATIONALIST CHINA DURING THE SINO-JAPANESE WAR, 1937–1945

Despite its drama and manifest importance, the period of the war against Japan remains an undeveloped segment of China's modern history. Perhaps the best general portrayal of the Nationalists during the war is still that of two American journalists who were in China at the time: Theodore H. White and Annalee Jacoby, *Thunder out of China*. This work was highly critical of the Nationalists, but its general assessment is being corroborated by more recent scholarly studies. The most comprehensive study of the period is the two-volume work by modern China's most prolific historian, Wu Hsiang-hsiang, entitled *Ti-erh-tz'u Chung-Jih chang-cheng shih* (History of the second Sino-Japanese War). Although useful for its presentation of data, Wu's study is remarkably weak in critical interpretation or analysis. A work that is analytically stronger and has valuable information about the Nationalists' war effort, treating especially the effects of military factionalism and political demoralization, is Hsi-sheng Ch'i, *Nationalist China at war: military defeats and political collapse, 1937–45*. Lloyd E. Eastman also views the Nationalists in a critical light in *Seeds of destruction: Nationalist China in war and revolution, 1937–1949*. For a symposium volume whose essays are mixed both in quality and in their assessments of the Nationalists see Paul K. T. Sih, ed. *Nationalist China during the Sino-Japanese War, 1937–1945*. Some of the shrewdest analyses of the Nationalists were made on the spot by a US foreign-service officer, John S. Service, whose wartime reports have been compiled and edited by Joseph W. Esherick in *Lost chance in China*. Another American, Graham Peck, viewed wartime China from the vantage point of the common man; his *Two kinds of time* is a rare and delightful work, filled with ironic humour and empathy for China's ordinary folk.

On military aspects of the war, F. F. Liu's *A military history of modern China* provides a good survey. Dick Wilson's *When tigers fight: the story of the Sino-Japanese War, 1937-1945* is a general, popular account. An official Nationalist version of the war, with rather detailed descriptions of the battles, is Hsu Long-hsuen and Chang Ming-kai, *History of the Sino-Japanese War, 1937–1945*; this work is a synopsis of a 101-volume study in Chinese edited by Hu P'u-yü and published by the Nationalist Ministry of Defence, *K'ang-Jih chan-shih* (Military history of the anti-Japanese war). Several shorter Chinese-language military histories are available, including Ho Ying-ch'in, *Pa-nien k'ang-chan chih ching-kuo* (Experiences in the eight-year war of resistance), and *Chung-Jih chan-cheng shih-lueh* (Historical survey of the Sino-Japanese War) prepared by the Historical Bureau of the Ministry of Defence.

The United States military role in the China war is given near-definitive treatment in a three-volume history by Charles F. Romanus and Riley Sunderland, written under the auspices of the US Department of the Army's Office of the Chief of Military History. The titles of these volumes, which thoroughly research the English-language documentation, are: *Stilwell's mission to China*; *Stilwell's command problems*; and *Time runs out in CBI*. General Joseph W. Stilwell, the key American military officer in China during the war, is the subject of Barbara W. Tuchman's Pulitzer Prize-winning biography, *Stilwell and the American experience in China, 1911–45*. Studies that examine the American role in China in a broader, political context are Tang Tsou, *America's failure in China, 1941–50* and, more recent, Michael Schaller, *The US crusade in China, 1938–1945*. Works on the Japanese side of the war are noted above in the essay for chapters 2 and 10.

The domestic political history of Nationalist China during the war has received scant scholarly attention. Political institutions are examined in three works of the 1940s – Paul M. A. Linebarger, *The China of Chiang K'ai-shek: a political study*; Ch'ien Tuan-sheng, *The government and politics of China*; and, with a broader focus but less detail, Lawrence K. Rosinger, *China's crisis*.

Economic aspects of the war, and especially the inflation, receive skilled treatment in three studies: Chang Kia-ngau, *The inflationary spiral: the experience in China, 1939–1950*, Shun-hsin Chou, *The Chinese inflation, 1937–1949*, and Arthur N. Young, *China's wartime finance and inflation, 1937–1945*. Young, who was financial adviser to the Nationalist government, has also written a splendid history of the American economic involvement with wartime Nationalist China, *China and the helping hand, 1937–1945*, which provides much information on the Chinese economy generally. Yu-Kwei Cheng, *Foreign trade and industrial development of China: an historical and integrated analysis through 1948*, is a succinct and solidly documented study of the modern sector of the economy.

Japan's economic policies in the areas it controlled and the reactions they provoked are examined in Asada Kyōji, *Nihon Teikokushugika no Chūgoku – Chūgoku senryō chiiki keizai no kenkyū* (China under Japanese imperialism; studies of the economy of occupied China). Huge gaps in our understanding of the war period remain. The cultural and social aspects, for example, have barely been touched, and detailed studies of local history, which offer such great promise for elucidating the Nanking decade, have not begun on the Nationalist area during the 1940s.

12. THE CCP DURING THE WAR AGAINST JAPAN, 1937–1945

This essay tries not to duplicate citations already made in chapter 4 above or in the essays in *CHOC* 12. It also tries to avoid the writings and biographical studies of Mao Tse-tung that are discussed in chapter 14 below.

There are no large-scale collections of documents covering the entire period between 1921 and 1949. Brandt, Schwartz and Fairbank, *A documentary history of Chinese communism*, was a very early reconnaissance (1952), though still a useful introduction. Much the same is true of Chao Kuo-chün, *Agrarian policy of the Chinese Communist Party, 1921–1959*. By the 1960s Hsueh Chün-tu, ed. *The Chinese communist movement* (vol. 1. *1921–1937*; vol. 2. *1937–1949*) provided a general entrée to Chinese-language materials, based on the excellent collection of the Hoover Institution at Stanford University. Also useful is Edward J. M. Rhoads et al., eds. *The Chinese Red Army, 1927–1963; an annotated bibliography*.

Documentary and other materials on 'party history' (*tang-shih*) have been published in China at a gradually increasing rate. Because of the many sensitivities of this subject, however, publication has lagged behind that in most conventional academic fields, and some of it is limited to 'internal circulation' (*nei-pu fa-hsing*). One regular periodical devoted entirely to party history is *Tang-shih yen-chiu* (Research on party history). Two series, published at irregular intervals, are *Ko-ming hui-i lu* (The revolution remembered), and *Tang-shih yen-chiu tzu-liao* (Research materials on party history). An eight-volume collection of documents which spans the three decades under review here is *Chung-kung tang-shih ts'an-k'ao tzu-liao* (Reference materials on the history of the CCP). Of similar scope is the three-volume *Chung-kung tang-shih chiao-hsueh ts'an-k'ao tzu-liao* (Reference materials for instruction in the history of the CCP).

The evolution of the second united front is covered in Van Slyke, *Enemies and friends, the united front in Chinese Communist history*. The most dramatic and crucial event in this evolution – the Sian incident – was reported contemporaneously in James Bertram, *First act in China: the story of the Sian mutiny*. The most comprehensive account is Wu Tien-wei, *The Sian Incident: a pivotal point in modern Chinese history* (see also his survey of new materials on the Sian incident in *Modern China*, 10.1 (Jan. 1984).

Efforts to theorize about this first great peasant revolution of the twentieth century began with Chalmers Johnson's seminal *Peasant nationalism and communist power: the emergence of revolutionary China, 1937–1945*. Reacting against Johnson's argument that CCP victory was based primarily on a war-induced nationalist mobilization rather than on a revolutionary imperative within modern Chinese society was Mark Selden, *The Yenan way in revolutionary China*, a work which drew general conclusions from examination of the headquarters territorial base, Shen-Kan-Ning. A third effort to explain CCP success during the war was that of Tetsuya Kataoka, *Resistance and revolution in China: the communists and the second united front*; Kataoka argued that the CCP imposed a 'frame of steel' around cellular and apolitical organizational networks long present in rural China, while in urban China, the imperatives of nationalism prevented Chiang Kai-shek from either vigorous anti-Communist operations or peace with Japan. These early formulations can be considered at best only partially valid, and hence unsatisfactory as general explanations. Several studies of Communist base areas provide historical perspectives: Stephen Averill, 'The shed people and the opening of the Yangzi highlands' and 'Revolution in the highlands: the rise of the Communist movement in Jiangxi province'; Robert Marks, 'Peasant society and peasant uprisings in South China: social change in Haifeng County, 1630–1930'; and Linda Grove, 'Rural society in revolution: the Gaoyang district, 1910–1947'. Ph.D. dissertations on the history of specific base areas behind Japanese lines include Kathleen Hartford and Carl Dorris for Chin-Ch'a-Chi, Ch'en Yung-fa and Gregor Benton for the Central China bases, and David Paulson for the Shantung base. Supplementing Selden for the Shen-Kan-Ning base are Peter Schran, *Guerrilla economy: the development of the Shensi-Kansu-Ninghsia Border Region, 1937–1945*, and Andrew Watson's translation of Mao's 'Economic and financial problems' (1942). The many observer accounts of the war in and around the Communist base areas are clustered in the first few years of the war and once again during its last two years. The difficult middle years went almost unobserved by Westerners except for the writings of Michael Lindsay, especially *The unknown war: north China, 1937–1945*. Out of the extensive publications in China on this period we can cite in this space only examples such as *P'eng Te-huai tzu-shu* (Autobiography of P'eng Te-huai) and Hsueh Mu-ch'iao, *Shan-tung chieh-fang-ch'ü ti ching-chi kung-tso* (Economic work in the Shantung liberated area). The August 1984 international conference on the anti-Japanese base areas will produce further publication.

For a description and guide to the holdings of the Bureau of Investigation in

Taiwan see Donovan, Dorris and Sullivan, *Chinese communist materials at the Bureau of Investigation Archives, Taiwan*. The official Japanese military history, *Hokushi no chiansen* (North China war of pacification), 2 vols., is filled with valuable data. Annual volumes of *Foreign relations of the United States* contain much more information about the CCP, particularly in its relations with the Nationalist government and the Kuomintang. The perspective in James B. Reardon-Anderson, *Yenan and the Great Powers: the origins of Chinese Communist foreign policy, 1944–1946*, is carried through to 1949 by a number of the essays in Dorothy Borg and Waldo Heinrichs, eds. *Uncertain years: Chinese-American relations, 1947–1950*.

13. THE KMT-CCP CONFLICT 1945–1949

The two preceding essays on the Nationalist government and the Communist movement respectively have described major Chinese sources thus far available for research on the post-Second World War and civil war period. One may confidently expect further documents and studies to emerge from the archives in Nanking, Taipei and elsewhere.

A selection of studies on various aspects of pre-1949 military history has been translated into English under the auspices of the Office of the Chief of Military History, US Department of the Army. These studies were originally written in Taiwan, based on materials available in military archives there. The selection is available on microfilm from the US Library of Congress under the title 'Chinese military studies and materials in English translation'.

Also available on microfilm from the Library of Congress are the US Consular press translations series for the 1945–9 period. The series covers the press of several KMT cities and radio broadcasts from Communist-held territory, but contains few items from Communist news publications of the period. The two most important of these were *Chieh-fang jih-pao* (Liberation daily) and *Ch'ün-chung* (The masses). Nor are news magazines adequately covered by the press translations series. The best English-language periodical of the period was the *China Weekly Review*. The leading Chinese journal of news and commentary was the Shanghai publication, *Kuan-ch'a* (The observer), also regarded during the period as one of the few popularly available sources of information on the progress of the war, due to the journal's authoritative military contacts. The above sources, together with the US State Department's *Foreign relations of the US* series, reflect the paucity of information available in KMT cities, both about the Communists and about the war itself, a fact of contemporary history which may escape latter-day historians as they probe the extensive archival sources now available on both subjects.

On American China policy in the 1940s there is already a vast literature, as indicated in essay 2/10 above. For an historical approach to the 'loss of China' issue, one illuminating recent study is Michael H. Hunt, *The making of a special relationship: the United States and China to 1914*, which puts Christian missions to China, Chinese anti-missionary incidents, the Chinese-exclusion movements in the United States and Sino-American diplomatic relations into a common framework. The basic narrative for the American war effort in China in the 1940s is the three-volume official history of the China-Burma-India theatre by Charles Romanus and Riley Sunderland. The most popular background reading on the period is Barbara Tuchman's *Stilwell and the American experience in China, 1911–45*. For a 60-page bibliography of American manuscript collections, government archives, published documentation, intelligence reports, dissertations, oral histories, articles and books, see Nancy Bernkopf Tucker, *Patterns in the dust: Chinese-American relations and the recognition controversy, 1949–1950*.

14. MAO TSE-TUNG'S THOUGHT TO 1949

Under this special topic we try to avoid repeating items cited under sections 4 and 12 above. The documentation available on this protean subject, especially the full texts of Mao's writings, has at least tripled in quantity since the early 1970s. The flood of new historical information gives us a deeper perspective on Mao's ideas. Though his policies post-1949 have been called most into question, several earlier issues have also arisen. For example, the date of Mao Tse-tung's effective conversion to Marxism, his attitudes toward the Li Li-san line in 1930 and toward the Fukien rebels in 1933 have been the object of an extremely lively debate among Chinese scholars, especially in internal publications such as *Tang-shih yen-chiu* (Research on party history). The main change regarding Mao's intellectual development down to 1949 lies, however, in the availability of new materials.

Before the early 1970s, the sources available on Mao's thought prior to the establishment of the Chinese People's Republic consisted essentially of the four volumes of the *Selected works* (in Chinese, English, and various other languages), plus those writings published in books or periodicals from the 1920s to the 1940s which could be found in libraries outside China. Although a fair proportion of items in the second category were available somewhere, they were so scattered among widely separated centres that the cost in time and money of using them systematically was very nearly prohibitive. The first great breakthrough took place in 1970–1, when the 10-volume edition of Mao's writings from 1917 to 1949 was published in Tokyo: *Mao Tse-tung chi* (Collected writings of Mao Tse-tung). Unfortunately, the press run of this edition was very small, and it was thus not widely available outside the major Sinological libraries. However, Professor Minoru Takeuchi and those associated with him in this enterprise have not only been able to reissue the original ten volumes, with minor corrections, under a new imprint, but have embarked on the publication of a number of supplementary volumes containing entirely new materials (*Mao Tse-tung chi, pu chüan*). Six volumes had been published under this title by October 1984, and further volumes were scheduled to appear at two-monthly intervals. In the end, there will be a total of eight supplementary volumes, instead of the five originally announced, plus a chronological volume; the complete set will thus comprise 19 volumes.

At the same time, the Chinese themselves have begun to publish a number of Mao's writings, especially from his pre-Marxist period, but including also important items from the years 1921–49. Some of these items are to be found in internal (*nei-pu*) collections such as *I-ta ch'ien-hou* (Before and after the First Congress) and *Hsin-min hsueh-hui tzu-liao* (Materials on the New People's Study Society). There are, however, many extremely interesting and previously unknown texts in the collection of Mao's letters published on his 90th birthday, *Mao Tse-tung shu-hsin hsuan-chi* (Selected letters of Mao Tse-tung), and in other volumes on particular themes published, or to be published, under the auspices of the agency responsible for the compilation of the writings of leaders such as Mao Tse-tung, Liu Shao-ch'i, Chou En-lai, Chu Te, Teng Hsiao-p'ing, and Ch'en Yun: the Chung-kung chung-yang wen-hsien yen-chiu-shih (Research Centre on party literature under the Central Committee of the Chinese Communist Party).

These circumstances make all the existing works on Mao (including even the most recent) at least partially out of date. Despite the lacunae in the documentation, however, a number of authors have formulated basic issues in thought-provoking fashion, and sketched out hypotheses which will be of great value in guiding future research. The following is a brief, selective list of some significant contributions.

Of the works dealing in systematic fashion with all, or a substantial portion of, the period down to 1949, the most recent, thoughtful, and balanced is that of Brantly Womack, *The foundations of Mao Zedong's political thought, 1917–1935*. Although this book stops in 1935, and fails to use some key sources on the years 1917–21, it is nonetheless the best available introduction to Mao's thought during his formative years. John Bryan Starr's *Continuing the revolution: the political thought of Mao* is marred by the author's tendency to treat everything Mao wrote from the 1920s to the 1970s as a single corpus, from which quotations can be selected at random to illustrate various aspects of his thought conceived in largely a-historical terms. It contains, however, thoughtful comments, and a useful compilation of materials. Another book covering the whole of Mao's pre-1949 intellectual development, as well as his ideas after 1949, is that of James Chieh Hsiung, *Ideology and practice. The evolution of Chinese communism*, an interesting and original interpretation, even though the view of *ssu-hsiang* or thought (as in Mao Tse-tung thought) as a type of intellectual activity different in kind from the systematic doctrines ('isms' or *chu-i*) common in the West (such as Marxism), in keeping with traditional Chinese patterns is controversial. (The Chinese, for their part, insist that Mao's thought *does* constitute a system.) Hsiung's study is assuredly one of the best in the field. S. Schram's *The political thought of Mao Tse-tung* and *Mao Zedong: a preliminary reassessment* both deal to a substantial extent with Mao's thought before 1949, but are both somewhat out of date as regards documentation.

Regarding the earliest years, the best single contribution is Li Jui, *Mao Tse-tung ti tsao-ch'i ko-ming huo-tung* (The early revolutionary activities of Mao Tse-tung), which devotes several chapters to Mao's thoughts from 1915 to 1927. Other works are Frederick Wakeman's *History and will: philosophical perspectives of Mao Tse-tung's thought*, mainly devoted to the pre-Marxist period, though it also touches on the Cultural Revolution; and Giorgio Mantici, *Pensieri del fiume Xiang* (Thoughts of the Hsiang River), a complete translation of the periodical edited by Mao in 1919, the *Hsiang River Review*. Benjamin Schwartz's *Chinese communism and the rise of Mao* also offers profound and subtle insights, despite the limitations imposed by a documentary basis thirty years out of date. Finally, Ray Wylie's *The emergence of Maoism* is the best available work on Mao's thought during the Yenan period. It is thoughtful and well-documented, and focuses squarely on the problem of the relation between the development of Mao's thought and the matrix of political struggle within which it took shape.

BIBLIOGRAPHY

CHINESE AND JAPANESE PUBLISHERS

Cheng-chung 正中 (Taipei)
Chuan-chi wen-hsueh 傳記文學 (Taipei)
Chung-hua (CH) 中華 (major cities)
Chung-kuo she-hui k'o-hsueh ch'u-pan-she 中國社會科學出版社 (Peking)
Commercial Press (CP) 商務印書館 (major cities)
Jen-min 人民 (Shanghai and other cities)
San-lien (Sheng-huo, Tu-shu, Hsin-chih 生活，讀書，新知）三聯書店
  (Peking, Shanghai)
Tokyo Daigaku Shuppankai 東京大学出版会
Wen-hai 文海 (Taipei)

An inbuilt ambiguity haunts any bibliography of Chinese writings: entries that are immediately intelligible to the reader of English, like *Central Daily News* or *Liberation Daily*, are not directly clued to the Chinese characters in which the originals are written (*Chung-yang jih-pao*, *Chieh-fang jih-pao*). Yet on the other hand an entry like *Chin-tai shih yen-chiu-so*, though more accurate in the esoteric script of romanization, may be translated variously as Modern History Institute or Institute of Modern History. In this situation we have put romanized accuracy ahead of English-translated intelligibility, but with occasional cross-references.

Another problem is that large compilations of documents are usually edited by committees, departments or other institutional organs, so that listing such works by compiler or editor would confront the reader with many words but little information. In such cases we prefer to list by title. Compilers and editors are then cited in the body of the entry.

WORKS CITED

Abe Yoshinori 阿部良忠, trans. 'Anki tochi chōsa nikki' 安徽土地調査日記 (A diary of land investigation in Anhwei), part 2, in SMR: *Mantetsu chōsa geppō*, 19.1 (Jan. 1939) 118–36
Abend, Hallett *et al. Can China survive?* New York: Ives Washburn, 1936
Academia Sinica. See Chung-yang yen-chiu yuan

Academy of Social Sciences. See Chung-kuo she-hui k'o-hsueh yuan

Ai Ssu-ch'i 艾思奇. *Ta-chung che-hsueh* 大衆哲學 (Philosophy for the masses). Shanghai: Tu-shu sheng-huo, 1936

Ai Ssu-ch'i. *Che-hsueh yü sheng-huo* 哲學與生活 (Philosophy and life). Shanghai: Tu-shu sheng-huo, 1937

Alitto, Guy S. 'Rural elites in transition: China's cultural crisis and the problem of legitimacy', in Susan Mann Jones, ed. *Select papers from the Center for Far Eastern Studies*, University of Chicago, 3 (1978–9) 218–75

Alitto, Guy S. *The last Confucian: Liang Shu-ming and the Chinese dilemma of modernity*. Berkeley: University of California Press, 1978

Altman, Albert A. and Schiffrin, Harold Z. 'Sun Yat-sen and the Japanese: 1914–16'. *Modern Asian Studies*, 6.4 (Oct. 1972) 385–400

Amano Motonosuke 天野元之助. *Shina nōgyō keizai ron* 支那農業經濟論 (On the Chinese agricultural economy). Tokyo: Kaizōsha 改造社, vol. 1, 1940 and vol. 2, 1942

Amano Motonosuke. *Shina nōson zakki* 支那農村襍記 (Miscellaneous notes on Chinese villages). Tokyo: Seikatsusha 生活社, 1942

Amano Motonosuke. *Chūgoku nōgyō no shomondai* 中國農業の諸問題 (Problems of Chinese agriculture). 2 vols. Tokyo: Gihōdo 技報堂, 1952

Amano Motonosuke. *Chūgoku nōgyō shi kenkyū* 中國農業史研究 (A study of the history of Chinese agriculture). Tokyo: Ochanomizu, 御茶の水, 1962

Amano Motonosuke. *Chūgoku nōgyō no chiiki teki tenkai* 中国農業の地域的展開 (Regional development of Chinese agriculture). Ryūkei shosha 龍溪書舍, 1979

Amerasia: a monthly analysis of America and Asia. New York: Amerasia, Inc. 11 vols. March 1937 – July 1947. Superseded *China Today* (subtitle varies). Ed. by P. Jaffe and others

The Amerasia papers: a clue to the catastrophe of China. 2 vols. Prepared by the Subcommittee to Investigate the Administration of the Internal Security Act and Other Internal Security Laws of the Committee on the Judiciary, United States Senate. Washington, DC: US Government Printing Office, 1970

Amoy University. See Hsia-men ta-hsueh

Arkush, R. David. *Fei Xiaotong and sociology in revolutionary China*. Cambridge, Mass.: Council on East Asian Studies, Harvard University, 1981

Asada Kyōji 浅田喬二. *Nihon Teikokushugika no Chūgoku—Chūgoku senryō chiiki keizai no kenkyū* 日本帝国主義下の中国—中国占領地域経済の研究 (China under Japanese imperialism: studies of the economy of occupied China). Tokyo: Rakuyū shobō 楽游書房, 1981

Ash, Robert. *Land tenure in pre-revolutionary China: Kiangsu province in the 1920s and 1930s*. London: Contemporary China Institute, School of Oriental and African Studies, University of London, 1976

Atwell, William. 'Notes on silver, foreign trade, and the late Ming economy'. *CSWT* 3.8 (Dec. 1977) 1–33

Aubert, Claude, Bianco, Lucien, Cadart, Claude, and Domenach, Jean-Luc.

Regards froids sur la Chine. Paris: Editions du Seuil, 1976

Australian Journal of Chinese Affairs. Semi-annual. Canberra: Australian National University, Contemporary China Centre. 1979–

Averill, Stephen C. 'Revolution in the highlands: the rise of the Communist movement in Jiangxi province'. Cornell University, Ph.D. dissertation, 1982

Averill, Stephen C. 'The shed people and the opening of the Yangzi highlands'. *Modern China*, 9.1 (Jan. 1983) 84–126

Baba Kuwatarō 馬場鍬太郎. 'Shina chihō gyōsei seido no kenkyū' 支那地方行政制度の研究 (The local government system of China). *Shina kenkyū* 支那研究 (Research on China), 1927.12, 81–317

Bachrack, Stanley D. *The Committee of One Million: 'China Lobby' politics, 1953–1971*. New York: Columbia University Press, 1976

Baker, John Earl. 'Fighting China's famines'. Unpublished manuscript, 1943

Balazs, Étienne. *Chinese civilization and bureaucracy: variations on a theme*, trans. by H. M. Wright. New Haven and London: Yale University Press, 1964

Bamba, Nobuya. *Japanese diplomacy in a dilemma: new light on Japan's China policy, 1924–1929*. Vancouver: University of British Columbia Press; Kyoto: Minerva Press, 1972

Barnett, A. Doak. *China on the eve of Communist takeover*. New York: Praeger, 1963

Barnett, A. Doak, ed. *Chinese Communist politics in action*. Seattle: University of Washington Press, 1969

Barrett, David D. *Dixie Mission: the United States Army Observer Group in Yenan, 1944*. Berkeley: Center for Chinese Studies, University of California, 1970

Bartlett, Beatrice S. 'The vermillion brush: the Grand Council communications system and central government decision-making in mid-Ch'ing China'. Yale University, Ph.D. dissertation, 1980

Bastid, Marianne. 'La diplomatie française et la révolution chinoise de 1911'. *Revue d'histoire moderne et contemporaine*, 16 (April-June 1969) 221–45

Bastid-Bruguière, Marianne. 'Currents of social change'. *CHOC* 11.535–602

BDRC. See Boorman. *Biographical dictionary of Republican China*

Beal, John Robinson. *Marshall in China*. Garden City, New York: Doubleday, 1970

Beattie, Hilary J. 'The alternative to resistance: the case of T'ung-ch'eng, Anhwei', in Jonathan D. Spence and John E. Wills, Jr., eds. *From Ming to Ch'ing*, 239–76

Becker, C. H., Falski, M., Langevin, P. and Tawney, R. H. *The reorganisation of education in China*. Paris: League of Nations, 1932

Bedeski, Robert E. *State-building in modern China: the Kuomintang in the prewar period*. Berkeley: University of California Press, 1981

Belden, Jack. *China shakes the world*. New York: Harper, 1949

Benton, Gregor. 'The "second Wang Ming line" (1935–38)'. *CQ* 61 (March

1975) 61–94

Benton, Gregor. 'The origins and early growth of the New Fourth Army'. Unpublished manuscript

Bercé, Yves-Marie. *Croquants et nu-pieds*. Paris: Gallimard/Julliard, 1974

Bercé, Yves-Marie. *Histoire des Croquants: étude des soulèvements populaires au XVIIème siècle dans le sud-ouest de la France*. 2 vols. Geneva: Droz, 1974

Bergère, Marie-Claire. 'The Chinese bourgeoisie, 1911–37'. *CHOC* 12.721–825, 856–8

Bergère, Marie-Claire. ' "The other China": Shanghai from 1919 to 1949', in Christopher Howe, ed. *Shanghai*, 1–34

Bergson, Abram. *The economics of Soviet planning*. New Haven: Yale University Press, 1961

Berkley, Gerald W. 'Peasant mobilisation in China, 1924–26'. Unpublished paper, Washington and Southeast Regional Seminar on China, March 1979

Berlin, Isaiah. *Washington despatches, 1941–45: weekly political reports from the British Embassy*, ed. by H. G. Nicholas. Chicago: University of Chicago Press, 1981

Bernard, Léon. 'French society and popular uprisings under Louis XIV'. *French Historical Studies*, 3.4 (1964) 454–74. New York: Kraus Reprint Corporation, 1966

Berninghausen, John. 'The central contradiction in Mao Dun's earliest fiction', in Merle Goldman, ed. *Modern Chinese literature in the May Fourth era*, 233–60

Berninghausen, John and Huters, Ted, eds. *Revolutionary literature in China: an anthology*. White Plains, NY: M. E. Sharpe, 1977. First published in *Bulletin of Concerned Asian Scholars*, 8.1–2 (1976)

Berton, Robert A. See Chang Kuo-t'ao

Bertram, James M. *First act in China: the story of the Sian mutiny*. New York: Viking, 1938. Also published as *Crisis in China: the story of the Sian mutiny*. London: Macmillan, 1937

Bianco, Lucien. 'Les paysans et la révolution: Chine 1919–49'. *Politique étrangère* (Paris), 2 (1968) 117–41

Bianco, Lucien. 'La mauvaise administration provinciale en Chine (Anhui, 1931)'. *Revue d'histoire moderne et contemporaine* (Paris), 16 (April-June 1969) 300–18

Bianco, Lucien. *Origins of the Chinese Revolution, 1915–49*. Stanford: Stanford University Press, 1971

Bianco, Lucien. 'Secret societies and peasant self-defense, 1921–1933', in Jean Chesneaux, ed. *Popular movements and secret societies in China, 1840–1950*, 213–24

Bianco, Lucien. 'Peasants and revolution: the case of China'. *The Journal of Peasant Studies*, 2.3 (April 1975) 313–35

Biggerstaff, Knight. *The earliest modern government schools in China*. Ithaca:

Cornell University Press, 1961

Billingsley, Philip Richard. 'Banditry in China, 1911 to 1928, with particular reference to Henan province'. University of Leeds, Ph.D. dissertation, 1974

Billingsley, Philip R. 'Bandits, bosses, and bare sticks: beneath the surface of local control in early Republican China'. *Modern China*, 7.3 (July 1981) 235–88

Bing, Dov. 'Sneevliet and the early years of the CCP'. *CQ* 48 (Oct.-Dec. 1971) 677–97

Biographical literature. See *Chuan-chi wen-hsueh*

Birch, Cyril. 'English and Chinese meters in Hsu Chih-mo'. *Asia Major*, NS 8.2 (1961) 258–93

Birch, Cyril. 'Lao She: the humourist in his humour'. *CQ* 8 (Oct.-Dec. 1961) 45–62

Birch, Cyril. 'Change and continuity in modern Chinese fiction', in Merle Goldman, ed. *Modern Chinese literature in the May Fourth era*, 385–406

Bisson, Thomas Arthur. *Japan in China*. New York: Macmillan, 1938

Blok, Anton. 'The peasant and brigand: social banditry reconsidered'. *Comparative Studies in Society and History*, 14.4 (Sept. 1972) 495–504

Blum, Robert M. *Drawing the line: the origin of the American containment policy in East Asia*. New York: Norton, 1982

Bōeicho bōei kensujo senshi shitsu 防衛庁防衛研修所戰史室. *Hokushi no chiansen* 北支の治安戰 (Pacification war in North China). 2 vols., map folios. Tokyo: Asagumo shimbunsha 朝雲新聞社, 1968

Boorman, Howard L. and Howard, Richard C., eds. *Biographical dictionary of Republican China*. New York: Columbia University Press, 4 vols. 1967–71 and index volume (vol. 5) 1979

Borg, Dorothy. *American policy and the Chinese revolution, 1925–1928*. New York: Institute of Pacific Relations and Macmillan, 1947

Borg, Dorothy. *The United States and the Far Eastern crisis of 1933–1938*. Cambridge, Mass.: Harvard University Press, 1964

Borg, Dorothy and Heinrichs, Waldo, eds. *Uncertain years: Chinese-American relations, 1947–1950*. New York: Columbia University Press, 1980

Borg, Dorothy and Okamoto, Shumpei, eds. *Pearl Harbor as history: Japanese-American relations 1931–1941*. New York: Columbia University Press, 1973

Borg, Dorothy. See Cohen, Warren I.

Borthwick, Sally. *Education and social change in China: the beginnings of the modern era*. Stanford: Hoover Institution Press, 1983

Bowers, John Z., M.D. *Western medicine in a Chinese palace: Peking Union Medical College, 1917–1951*. New York: Josiah Macy, Jr. Foundation, 1972

Boyle, John Hunter. *China and Japan at war, 1937–1945: the politics of collaboration*. Stanford: Stanford University Press, 1972

Brandt, Conrad. *Stalin's failure in China 1924–1927*. Cambridge, Mass.:

Harvard University Press, 1958

Brandt, Conrad, Schwartz, Benjamin and Fairbank, John K. *A documentary history of Chinese communism*. Cambridge, Mass.: Harvard University Press; London: Allen & Unwin, 1952

Brandt, Vincent S. R. 'Landlord-tenant relations in Republican China'. *Papers on China*, 17 (1963) 192–234

Braun, Otto. *A Comintern agent in China 1932–1939*, trans. by Jeanne Moore. Intro. by Dick Wilson. Stanford: Stanford University Press, 1982. First published in German in 1975 as *Chinesische Aufzeichnungen (1932–1939)*. Berlin: Deitz Verlag (GDR)

Braun, Otto. See Heinzig, D.

Brown, Edward J. *Russian literature since the revolution*. New York: Collier, 1963; rev. edn., 1969

Brown, William A. See Shirendev, B.

Brunnert, H. S., and Hagelstrom, V. V., rev. by N. T. Kolessoff, trans. from Russian by A. Beltchenko and E. E. Moran. *Present day political organization of China*. Shanghai: Kelly & Walsh, 1912

Buck, David D. 'Educational modernization in Tsinan, 1899–1937', in Mark Elvin and G. William Skinner, eds. *The Chinese city between two worlds*, 171–212

Buck, David D. *Urban change in China: politics and development in Tsinan, Shantung, 1890–1949*. Madison: University of Wisconsin Press, 1978

Buck, John Lossing. *Chinese farm economy*. Nanking: University of Nanking, 1930.

Buck, John Lossing. *Land utilization in China: a study of 16,786 farms in 168 localities, and 38,256 farm families in twenty-two provinces in China, 1929–1933*. 3 vols. Nanking: University of Nanking; Chicago: University of Chicago Press, 1937; 2nd printing, New York: Paragon Book Reprint Corp., 1964

Buck, John Lossing, *et al*. *There is another China*. New York: King's Crown Press, 1948. (Ann Arbor: University Microfilms International, 1980).

Buck, Peter. *American science and modern China 1876–1936*. Cambridge: Cambridge University Press, 1980

Buckley, Thomas H. *The United States and the Washington Conference, 1921–1922*. Knoxville: University of Tennessee, 1970

Buhite, Russell D. *Patrick J. Hurley and American foreign policy*. Ithaca: Cornell University Press, 1973

Bulletin of Concerned Asian Scholars. New York City and other places. May 1968–

Bulletin of the Institute of Modern History, Academia Sinica. See *Chung-yang yen-chiu-yuan Chin-tai-shih yen-chiu-so chi-k'an*

Bulletin of the School of Oriental and African Studies. London: University of London, 1940–

Bullock, Mary Brown. *An American transplant: the Rockefeller Foundation and Peking Union Medical College*. Berkeley: University of California Press, 1980

Bunker, Gerald E. *The peace conspiracy: Wang Ching-wei and the China War, 1937–1941*. Cambridge, Mass.: Harvard University Press, 1972

Burgess, John S. See Gamble, Sidney D.

Bush, Richard Clarence, III. 'Industry and politics in Kuomintang China: the Nationalist regime and Lower Yangtze Chinese cotton mill owners, 1927–1937'. Columbia University, Ph.D. dissertation, 1978

Bush, Richard C. *The politics of cotton textiles in Kuomintang China, 1927–1937*. New York: Garland Publishers, 1982

Butow, Robert J. C. *Tojo and the coming of the war*. Princeton: Princeton University Press, 1961

Buxbaum, David C. 'Some aspects of civil procedure and practice at the trial level in Tanshui and Hsinchu from 1789 to 1895'. *JAS* 30.2 (Feb. 1971) 255–79

Caillard, Duval and Guillet, Gricourt. *À travers la Normandie des XVIIème et XVIIIème siècles*. Caen: Cahier des Annales de Normandie no. 3, 1963

Cambridge history of China. Cambridge: Cambridge University Press. Vol. 3, *Sui and T'ang China 589–906, part 1*, ed. by Denis Twitchett, 1979; vol. 10, *Late Ch'ing 1800–1911, part 1*, ed. by John K. Fairbank, 1978; vol. 11, *Late Ch'ing 1800–1911, part 2*, ed. by John K. Fairbank and Kwang-Ching Liu, 1980; vol. 12, *Republican China 1912–1949, part 1*, ed. by John K. Fairbank, 1983

Carlson, Evans Fordyce. *The Chinese army: its organization and military efficiency*. New York: Institute of Pacific Relations, 1940

Carrère d'Encausse, H. and Schram, S. *Marxism and Asia*. London: Allen Lane, The Penguin Press, 1969

CASS. Chinese Academy of Social Sciences

Cavendish, Patrick. 'The "New China" of the Kuomintang', in Jack Gray, ed. *Modern China's search for a political form*, 138–86

CCP. Chinese Communist Party

CEC. Central Executive Committee

Chan, Adrian. 'Development and nature of Chinese communism to 1925'. Australian National University, Ph.D. thesis, 1974

Chan, F. Gilbert, ed. *China at the crossroads: Nationalists and Communists, 1927–1949*. Boulder, Colo.: Westview Press, 1980

Chan, Gilbert 陳福霖. 'Sheng Shih-ts'ai's reform programs in Sinkiang: idealism or opportunism?'. *Bulletin of the IMH*, 12.365–84

Chan, F. Gilbert and Etzold, Thomas H., eds. *China in the 1920s: nationalism and revolution*. New York and London: New Viewpoints, 1976

Chan, Lau Kit-ching. 'The Lincheng incident—a case study of British policy in China between the Washington Conference (1921–22) and the first Nationalist revolution (1925–28)'. *Journal of Oriental Studies*, 10.2 (July 1972) 172–86

Chan, Ming K. 陳明銶. *Historiography of the Chinese labor movement, 1895–1949: a critical survey and bibliography of selected Chinese source materials at the Hoover Institution*. Stanford: Hoover Institution Press, 1981

Chan, Ming-kou. 'Labor and empire: the Chinese labor movement in the Canton Delta, 1895–1927'. Stanford University, Ph.D. dissertation, 1975

'Chan-shih hou-fang kung-yeh shih ju-ho chien-li-ti' 戰時後方工業是如何建立的 (How the wartime industry in the rear was established). *Hsin-shih-chieh yueh-k'an* 新世界月刊, 15 March 1944, 10–15

Chan, Wellington K. K. 'Government, merchants and industry to 1911'. *CHOC* 11.416–62

Chang, Carsun (Chang Chün-mai) 張君勱. *The third force in China*. New York: Bookman, 1952

Chang Ch'i-chün 張起鈞. 'Hsi-nan-lien-ta chi-yao' 西南聯大紀要 (Essential facts concerning the South-west Associated University), in *Kuo-li Hsi-nan lien-ho ta-hsueh* 國立西南聯合大學 (The National South-west Associated University), a volume in the *Hsueh-fu chi-wen* 學府紀聞 series. Taipei: Nan-ching 南京, 1981

Chang Ch'i-yun 張其昀. *Tang-shih kai-yao* 黨史概要 (Survey of party history). 5 vols. Taipei: Chung-yang wen-wu 中央文物, 1951

Chang Chih-i. See Fei Hsiao-t'ung

Chang Ch'ih-chang 張熾章. *Chi-luan wen-ts'un* 季鸞文存 (Collected essays of Chi-luan [Chang Ch'ih-chang]). Taipei: Wen-hsing shu-tien 文星書店, 1962

Chang Ching-lu 張靜廬, ed. *Chung-kuo hsien-tai ch'u-pan shih-liao* 中國現代出版史料 (Historical materials on contemporary Chinese publications). *Chia-pien* 甲編 (Part I), 1954; *I-pien* 乙編 (Part II), 1955; *Ping-pien* 丙編 (Part III), 1956; *Ting-pien* 丁編 (Part IV), 2 vols. 1959. Peking: Chung-hua

Chang Ching-lu, ed. *Chung-kuo chin-tai ch'u-pan shih-liao* 中國近代出版史料 (Materials on the history of publication in modern China). 2 vols. Ch'ün-lien 群聯, 1953–4

Chang Chung-li 張仲禮. *The Chinese gentry*. Seattle: University of Washington Press, 1955

Chang Chung-li. *The income of the Chinese gentry*. Seattle: University of Washington Press, 1962

Chang, Hao 張灝. 'Intellectual change and the reform movement, 1890–8'. *CHOC* 11.274–338

Chang Hsin-i 張心一. *Chung-kuo liang-shih wen-t'i* 中國糧食問題 (China's foodgrain problem). Shanghai: International Committee of the IPR of China, 1932

Chang Jo-ku 張若谷, ed. *Ma Hsiang-po hsien-sheng nien-p'u* 馬相伯先生年譜 (A chronological biography of Ma Hsiang-po [Ma Liang]). Changsha: CP, 1939

Chang, John K. 'Industrial development of Mainland China, 1912–1949'. *Journal of Economic History*, 27.1 (March 1967) 56–81

Chang, John K. *Industrial development in pre-Communist China: a quantitative analysis*. Chicago: Aldine, 1969

Chang Jyh-er Kinzelbach. 'La condition paysanne d'après la littérature chinoise contemporaine, 1919–1942'. École des Hautes Études en Sciences Sociales, Paris, unpublished dissertation, 1976

Chang Kia-ngau 張嘉璈. *China's struggle for railway development*. New York: John Day, 1943

Chang Kia-ngau. *The inflationary spiral: the experience in China, 1939–1950*. Cambridge, Mass.: MIT Press, 1958

Chang Kuo-hui 張國輝. *Yang-wu yun-tung yü Chung-kuo chin-tai ch'i-yeh* 洋務運動與中國近代企業 (The westernization movement and China's modern industry). Peking: Chung-kuo she-hui k'o-hsueh ch'u-pan-she, 1979

Chang Kuo-p'ing 張國平. *Pai Ch'ung-hsi chiang-chün chuan* 白崇禧將軍傳 (A biography of General Pai Ch'ung-hsi). Canton, 1938

Chang Kuo-t'ao 張國燾. *Wo-ti hui-i* 我的回憶 (My recollections). *Ming-pao yueh-k'an* (Ming-pao monthly), Hong Kong, 1.3–6.2 (March 1966 – Feb. 1971). Reissued in three volumes, Hong Kong, 1973. Trans. under the title *The rise of the Chinese Communist Party* by R. A. Berton

Chang Kuo-t'ao. *The rise of the Chinese Communist Party, 1928–1938. Volume two of the autobiography of Chang Kuo-t'ao*, trans. by R. A. Berton. Lawrence, Kansas: University of Kansas Press, 1972

Chang Kuo-t'ao, Liu Ning 柳寧 *et al. I-ko kung-jen ti kung-chuang chi ch'i-t'a* 一個工人的供狀及其他 (A working man's confession and other essays), n.p., n.d.

Chang, Kwang-chih 張光直. *The archaeology of ancient China*. 3rd ed. New Haven and London: Yale University Press, 1977

Chang Man-i 張曼儀 *et al. Hsien-tai Chung-kuo shih-hsuan, 1917–1949* 現代中國詩選, 1917–1949 (Modern Chinese poetry: an anthology, 1917–1949). 2 vols. Hong Kong: Hong Kong University Press and the Chinese University of Hong Kong Publications Office, 1974

Chang P'ei-kang 張培剛. 'Min-kuo erh-shih-san nien ti Chung-kuo nung-yeh ching-chi' 民國二十三年的中國農業經濟 (China's agricultural economy in 1934). *Tung-fang tsa-chih* 32.13 (1 July 1935) 133–45

Chang P'eng-yuan 張朋園. *Liang Ch'i-ch'ao yü Ch'ing-chi ko-ming* 梁啓超與清季革命 (Liang Ch'i-ch'ao and the late Ch'ing revolution). Taipei: Chung-yang yen-chiu yuan chin-tai-shih yen-chiu-so, 1964

Chang P'eng-yuan. *Li-hsien p'ai yü Hsin-hai ko-ming* 立憲派與辛亥革命 (The Constitutionalists and the 1911 Revolution). Taipei: Chung-kuo hsueh-shu chu-tso chiang-chu wei-yuan hui, 1969

Chang P'eng-yuan. 'Political participation and political elites in early Republican China: the parliament of 1913–1914'. *JAS* 37.2 (Feb. 1978) 293–313

Chang P'eng-yuan. 'Provincial assemblies: the emergence of political participation 1909–1914'. *Bulletin of the Institute of Modern History*, Academia

Sinica, 12 (June 1983) 273–99

Chang P'eng-yuan. *Chung-kuo hsien-tai-hua ti ch'ü-yü yen-chiu: Hu-nan sheng, 1860–1916* 中國現代化的區域研究：湖南省, 1860–1916 (Modernization in China, 1860–1916: a regional study of social, political and economic change in Hunan province). Taipei: Institute of Modern History, 1983

Chang Pi-lai 張畢來. 'I-chiu-erh-san nien "Chung-kuo ch'ing-nien" chi-ko tso-che ti wen-hsueh chu-chang' 一九二三年「中國青年」幾個作者的文學主張 (The literary views of some authors from *Chinese Youth* in 1923), in Li Ho-lin *et al.*, *Chung-kuo hsin wen-hsueh...*, 36–49

Chang Po-ling 張伯苓. 'Ssu-shih-nien Nan-k'ai hsueh-hsiao chih hui-ku' 四十年南開學校之回顧 (Retrospect of Nankai after forty years 1944), in Wang Wen-t'ien *et al.*, *Chang Po-ling yü Nan-k'ai* (Chang Po-ling and Nankai), 81–107. Taipei: Chuan-chi wen-hsueh, 1968

Chang Sheng-hsuan 張聖軒. 'San-shih-erh-nien Ssu-ch'uan kung-yeh chih hui-ku yü ch'ien-chan' 三十二年四川工業之回顧與前瞻 (Perspectives on the past and future of Szechwan's economy in 1943). *Ssu-ch'uan ching-chi chi-k'an*, 1.2 (15 March 1944) 258–70

Chang Ta-ch'en 張大琛. 'San-shih-san-nien ti Ch'ung-ch'ing t'u-pu-yeh' 三十三年的重慶土布業 (Chungking's handicraft textile industry in 1944). *Ssu-ch'uan ching-chi chi-k'an*, 2.2 (1 April 1945) 202–4

Chang Te-tse 張德澤. *Ch'ing-tai kuo-chia chi-kuan k'ao-lueh* 清代國家機關考略 (A study of Ch'ing government organs). Peking: Chung-kuo Jen-min Ta-hsueh ch'u-pan-she 中國人民大學出版社, 1981

Chang T'ien-i 張天翼. 'Ch'ou-hen' 仇恨 (Hatred), in *Chang T'ien-i hsuan-chi* 張天翼選集 (Chang T'ien-i's selected work), 40–69. Peking: K'ai-ming shu-tien 開明書店, 1951

Chang Tung-sun 張東蓀. 'Chui-shu wo-men nu-li chien-li "lien-ho cheng-fu" ti yung-i' 追述我們努力建立「聯合政府」的用意 (Reflections on our intention to strive to establish a 'coalition government'). *Kuan-ch'a*, 5 April 1947, pp. 5–7

Chang Wen-shih 張文實. *Yun-nan nei-mu* 雲南內幕 (The inside story in Yunnan). Kunming: K'un-ming kuan-ch'a, 1949

Chang Yu-i 章有義, comp. *Chung-kuo chin-tai nung-yeh shih tzu-liao, ti-san chi, 1927–1937* 中國近代農業史資料，第三輯, 1927–1937 (Historical materials on modern China's agriculture, third collection, 1927–1937). Peking: San-lien, 1957. See also Li Wen-chih

Chang Yü-fa 張玉法. *Ch'ing-chi ti li-hsien t'uan-t'i* 清季的立憲團體 (Constitutionalist groups of the late Ch'ing period). Taipei: IMH, Academia Sinica, 1971

Chang Yü-fa. 'Ch'ing-mo min-ch'u ti Shan-tung ti-fang tzu-chih' 清末民初的山東地方自治 (Local self-government of Shantung in late Ch'ing and early Republican China). *Chung-yang yen-chiu-yuan Chin-tai-shih yen-chiu-so chi-k'an* 6 (June 1977) 159–84

Chang Yü-fa. *Chung-kuo hsien-tai-hua ti ch'ü-yü yen-chiu: Shan-tung sheng, 1860–*

1916 中國現代化的區域研究：山東省, 1860–1916 (Modernization in China, 1860–1916: a regional study of social, political and economic change in Shantung province). Vol. I. Taipei: IMH, 1982

Chao Ching 趙靖 and I Meng-hung 易夢虹. *Chung-kuo chin-tai ching-chi ssu-hsiang shih* 中國近代經濟思想史 (History of modern Chinese economic thought). 2 vols. Rev. ed. Peking: Chung-hua, 1980

Chao Ju-heng 趙如珩. *Ti-fang tzu-chih chih li-lun yü shih-chi* 地方自治之理論與實際 (Theory and practice of local self-government). Shanghai: Hua-t'ung shu-chü 華通書局, 1933

Chao, Kang 趙岡. *The development of cotton textile production in China.* Cambridge, Mass.: Council on East Asian Studies, Harvard University, 1977

Chao, Kang. 'New data on land ownership patterns in Ming-Ch'ing China— a research note'. *JAS* 40.4 (Aug. 1981) 719–34

Chao Kuo-chün. *Agrarian policy of the Chinese Communist Party, 1921–1959.* New Delhi: Asia Publishing House, 1960

Chao Shu-li 趙樹理. *Li-chia-chuang ti pien-ch'ien* 李家莊的變遷 (Changes in the Li village). Shansi: Hua-pei hsin-hua shu-tien 華北新華書店, 1946

Chapman, H. Owen. *The Chinese revolution, 1926–1927.* London: Constable, 1928

Chassin, Lionel M. *The Communist conquest of China: a history of the civil war, 1945–1949.* Cambridge: Harvard University Press, 1965

CHB. See *China handbook*

'Che-chiang erh-wan nung-min pao-tung' 浙江二萬農民暴動 (The uprising of twenty thousand peasants in Chekiang). 1933. Manuscript of three pages. Hoover Institution, no. 4398.29/3314

'Che-chiang ko-hsien ch'eng-ch'ing ch'ü-hsiao shih-hsing erh-wu chien-tsu i-mien chiu-fen' 浙江各縣呈請取消施行二五減租以免糾紛 (Petitions from various hsiens of Chekiang requesting that the 25 per cent rent reduction be no longer applied in order to avoid conflicts.) (Nov. 1931 – June 1934.) Second Historical Archives, Nanking, no. 2/2/1129

'Che-chiang ko-ti nung-min k'ang-tsu tou-cheng' 浙江各地農民抗租鬥爭 (Peasant resistance to rents in various localities in Chekiang) (1927–1930). Second Historical Archives, Nanking, no. 1/2/1001 and 1/2/1002

Chen, Fu-mei Chang 陳張富美 and Myers, Ramon H. 'Customary law and the economic growth of China during the Ch'ing period'. *CSWT* 3.5 (Nov. 1976) 1–32; 3.10 (Dec. 1978) 4–27

Chen-hai hsien-chih 鎮海縣志 (Chen-hai county gazetteer), 1931

Chen-p'ing hsien tzu-chih kai-k'uang 鎮平縣自治概況 (Local self-government in Chen-p'ing county). Chen-p'ing, 1933

Ch'en Chen 陳真 and Yao Lo 姚洛. *Chung-kuo chin-tai kung-yeh shih tzu-liao* 中國近代工業史資料 (Source materials on the history of modern industry in China). 4 collections (*chi* 輯) totalling 6 vols. Peking: San-lien, 1957–61

Ch'en Chen-han 陳振漢. 'Cheng-fu yin-hang hsueh-shu chi-kuan yü fu-hsing nung-ts'un' 政府銀行學術機關與復興農村 (Government, banks, academic institutions, and revival of the villages). *Kuo-wen chou-pao*, 10.46 (20 Nov. 1933), articles pp. 1–8

Ch'en Ch'eng 陳誠. *Pa-nien k'ang-chan ching-kuo kai-yao* 八年抗戰經過概要 (Summary of experiences during the eight-year war of resistance). n.p.: Kuo-fang-pu shih-liao-chü 國防部史料局, n.d.

Ch'en Cheng-mo 陳正謨. *Ko-sheng nung-kung ku-yung hsi-kuan chi hsu-kung chuang-k'uang* 各省農工僱傭習慣及需供狀況 (Hiring practices in agriculture and industry and the supply of and demand for labour in various provinces). Nanking: Chung-shan wen-hua chiao-yü kuan 中山文化教育館, 1935

Ch'en Ch'i-t'ien 陳啓天. *Wo-ti hui-i* 我的回憶 (My memoirs)

Ch'en Chih-mai 陳之邁. *Chung-kuo cheng-fu* 中國政府 (The Chinese government). 3 vols. 2nd edn. Shanghai: CP, 1946

Ch'en Chih-mai. 'Chan-shih li-fa wen-t'i' 戰時立法問題 (Problems of wartime legislation). *Hsin-ching-chi*, 2.3 (16 July 1949) 76–70

Ch'en Chih-mai. 'Ch'iu-hsueh yü chih-hsueh [of Tsiang T'ing-fu]' 求學與治學 (Study and research [of Tsiang T'ing-fu]), in *Chiang T'ing-fu ti chih-shih yü sheng-p'ing* 蔣廷黻的治事與生平 (The life and deeds of Tsiang T'ing-fu). Taipei: Chuan-chi wen-hsueh, 1967

Ch'en Han-seng 陳翰笙. 'Kantō nōson no seisan kankei to seisanryoku' 廣東農村の生産關係と生産力 (Production relationships and production power in Kwangtung villages). *Mantetsu chōsa geppō* 滿鐵調查月報, 15.6 (June 1935) 167–86

Ch'en Hsueh-chao 陳學昭. *Man-tsou chieh-fang-ch'ü* 漫走解放區 (Wanderings in the liberated areas). Shanghai: Shang-hai ch'u-pan kung-ssu 上海出版公司, 1950

Ch'en, Jerome 陳志讓. *Mao and the Chinese revolution.* London: Oxford University Press, 1965

Ch'en, Jerome. 'Resolutions of the Tsunyi conference'. *CQ* 40 (Oct.-Dec. 1969) 1–38

Ch'en, Jerome. *Mao papers.* London: Oxford University Press, 1970

Ch'en, Jerome. 'Ideology and history'. Report on the visit of the North American delegation on socialism and revolution to the People's Republic of China, June-July 1980, xeroxed for circulation, 1980

Ch'en, Jerome. 'The Chinese communist movement to 1927'. *CHOC* 12.505–26

Ch'en Kung-lu 陳恭祿. *Chung-kuo chin-tai shih tzu-liao kai-shu* 中國代近史資料概述 (An outline of sources for modern Chinese history). Peking: Chung-hua, 1982

Ch'en Kung-po 陳公博. *Han-feng chi* 寒風集 (Cold wind). Shanghai: Ti-fang hsing-cheng-she 地方行政社, 1944

Ch'en Kung-po. *The Communist movement in China: an essay written in 1924.* Ed. with an introduction by C. Martin Wilbur. New York: Columbia University Press, 1960

Ch'en Kung-po. *K'u-hsiao lu: Ch'en Kung-po hui-i* 苦笑錄：陳公博回憶 (Record of tears and laughter: the memoirs of Ch'en Kung-po), ed. Li O 李鍔 *et al.* Hong Kong: Hong Kong University, Centre of Asian Studies, 1979

Ch'en Kuo-fu 陳果夫. *Su-cheng hui-i* 蘇政回憶 (Memories of governing Kiangsu). Taipei: Cheng-chung, 1951

Ch'en Li-fu 陳立夫. *Four years of Chinese education (1937–1941)* Chungking: China Information Committee, 1941. Ann Arbor: University Microfilms International, 1980

Ch'en Neng-chih 陳能志. 'Chan-ch'ien shih-nien Chung-kuo ta-hsueh chiao-yü ching-fei wen-t'i' 戰前十年中國大學教育經費問題 (Problems of financing Chinese higher education in the decade before the war, 1927–1937). *Li-shih hsueh-pao* (Bulletin of historical research), 11 (June 1983). Taipei: National Taiwan Normal University: Institute of History and the Department of History

Ch'en-pao 晨報 (The morning post). Peking. 15 Aug. 1916–

Ch'en Po-chün 陳伯鈞. 'Lun k'ang-Jih yu-chi chan-cheng ti chi-pen chan-shu: hsi-chi' 論抗日游擊戰爭的基本戰術—襲擊 (On the basic tactic of the anti-Japanese guerrilla war: the surprise attack). *Chieh-fang* 解放, 28 (11 Jan. 1938) 14–19

Ch'en Po-hsin 陳伯心. *Chung-kuo ti ti-fang chih-tu chi chi'i kai-ko* 中國的地方制度及其改革 (China's local system and its reform). Changsha: CP, 1939

Ch'en Po-ta 陳伯達. *Chung-kuo ssu-ta-chia-tsu* 中國四大家族 (China's four great families). Hong Kong: Chung-kuo 中國, 1947

Ch'en Po-ta. *Kuan-yü shih-nien nei-chan* 關於十年內戰 (On the 10 years of civil war). Peking: Jen-min, 1953

Ch'en Shao-hsiao 陳少校. *Hei-wang-lu* 黑網錄 (Record of the black net). Hong Kong: Chih-ch'eng 致誠, 1966

Ch'en Shao-yü 陳紹禹. *Ch'en Shao-yü (Wang Ming) chiu-kuo yen-lun hsuan-chi* 陳紹禹（王明）救國言論選集 (Selected statements of Ch'en Shao-yü (Wang Ming) on national salvation). Hankow: Chung-kuo ch'u-pan-she 中國出版社, 1938

Ch'en Shao-yü. See Wang Ming

Ch'en, Ta 陳達. *Population in modern China.* Chicago: University of Chicago Press, 1946

Ch'en Ta. 'Chung-kuo lao-kung chieh-chi yü tang-ch'ien ching-chi wei-chi' 中國勞工階級與當前經濟危機 (China's working class and the current economic crisis). *She-hui chien-she* 社會建設, 1.4 (1 Aug. 1948) 17–19

Ch'en Teng-yuan 陳登原. *Chung-kuo t'ien-fu shih* 中國田賦史 (A history of land tax in China). Shanghai: CP, 1936; Repr. Taipei: CP, 1966

Ch'en Tu-hsiu 陳獨秀. *Wen-ts'un* 文存 (Collected essays). 4 vols. Shanghai: Ya-tung 亞東, 1922

Ch'en Tu-hsiu. 'Kao ch'üan-tang t'ung-chih-shu' 告全黨同志書 (Letter to all the comrades of the party). 10.12.1929. Mimeographed

Ch'en Tu-hsiu. *Pien-shu-chuang* 辯述狀 (My defence). n.p. 20 Feb. 1933.

Mimeographed

Ch'en Tun-cheng 陳敦正. *Tung-luan ti hui-i* 動亂的回憶 (Memoirs of upheaval). Taipei: Yuan-hsia 元霞, 1979

Ch'en Yu-shih. 'Mao Dun and the use of political allegory in fiction: a case study of his "Autumn in Kuling" ', in Merle Goldman, ed. *Modern Chinese literature in the May Fourth era*, 261–80

Ch'en Yung-fa 陳永發. 'The making of a revolution: the Communist movement in eastern and central China, 1937–1945'. 2 vols. Stanford University, Ph.D. dissertation, 1980

Chen, Yu-Kwei. *Foreign trade and industrial development of China: an historical and integrated analysis through 1948*. Washington, DC: University Press of Washington, 1956

Cheng-chih chou-pao 政治週報 (Political weekly). Peking, 1924–

Ch'eng Chi-hua 程季華 *et al*. *Chung-kuo tien-ying fa-chan-shih* 中國電影發展史 (A history of the development of Chinese cinema). 2 vols. Peking: Chung-kuo tien-ying 中國電影, 1963

Ch'eng Fang 程方. *Chung-kuo hsien-cheng kai-lun* 中國縣政概論 (An introduction to county government in China). 2 vols. Changsha: CP, 1939

Ch'eng Mao-hsing 程懋型. *Chiao-fei ti-fang hsing-cheng chih-tu* 剿匪地方行政制度 (Governmental system of the bandit-suppression areas). Shanghai: CH, 1936

Ch'eng Yuan-chen 程元斟. 'Ko-hsin yun-tung chih-hsu ch'eng-kung pu-hsu shih-pai' 革新運動只許成功不許失敗 (The renovation movement can only succeed and must not fail). *Ko-hsin chou-k'an* (Renovation weekly), 1.5 (24 Aug. 1946) 3–5

Chennault, Claire Lee. *Way of a fighter*. New York: G. P. Putnam Sons, 1949

Chern, Kenneth S. *Dilemma in China: America's policy debate, 1945*. Hamden, Conn.: Archon Books, 1980

Chesneaux, Jean. *The Chinese labor movement, 1919–1927*, trans. by H. M. Wright. Stanford: Stanford University Press, 1968

Chesneaux, Jean, ed. *Popular movements and secret societies in China, 1840–1950*. Stanford: Stanford University Press, 1972

Chi, Madeleine. *China diplomacy, 1914–1918*. Cambridge, Mass.: East Asian Research Center, Harvard University, 1970

Chi, Madeleine. 'Ts'ao Ju-lin (1876–1966): his Japanese connections', in Akira Iriye, ed. *The Chinese and the Japanese*, 140–60

Ch'i Hsi-sheng 齊錫生. *Nationalist China at war: military defeats and political collapse, 1937–1945*. Ann Arbor: University of Michigan Press, 1982

Ch'i-shih-liu nien shih-hsueh shu-mu 1900–1975 七十六年史學書目, 1900–1975 (Bibliography of books on history published during the 76 years 1900–1975), comp. Chung-kuo she-hui k'o-hsueh-yuan, Li-shih yen-chiu so tzu-liao-shih 中國社會科學院歷史研究所資料室 Peking: Chung-kuo she-hui k'o-hsueh ch'u-pan-she, 1981

Ch'i Shu-fen 漆樹芬. *Ching-chi ch'in-lueh hsia chih Chung-kuo* 經濟侵略下之中國 (China under economic aggression). Shanghai: Ku-chün tsa-chih 孤軍雜誌, 1925

Ch'i-wu lao-jen 栖梧老人. 'Chung-kuo Kung-ch'an-tang ch'eng-li ch'ien-hou ti chien-wen' 中國共產黨成立前後的見聞 (My impressions before and after the founding of the Chinese Communist Party). *Hsin kuan-ch'a* 新觀察 (New observer), Peking, 13 (1 July 1957) 16–18

Chia-ting hsien hsu-chih 嘉定縣續志 (Chia-ting county gazetteer), rev. edn, 1920

Chiang Chieh-shih. See Chiang Kai-shek

Chiang Chung-cheng (Chiang Kai-shek). *Soviet Russia in China: a summing-up at seventy*. New York: Farrar, Straus and Cudahy, 1957

Chiang Kai-shek 蔣介石. *Resistance and reconstruction: messages during China's six years of war, 1937–1943*. New York: Harper, 1943

Chiang Kai-shek. *Chiang tsung-t'ung yen-lun hui-pien* 蔣總統言論彙編 (President Chiang's collected speeches). 24 vols. Taipei: Cheng-chung, 1956

Chiang Kai-shek. 'Tzu-shu yen-chiu ko-ming che-hsueh ching-kuo ti chieh-tuan' 自述研究革命哲學經過的階段 (Stages traversed in studying revolutionary philosophy), in Chiang Kai-shek, *Chiang-tsung-t'ung yen-lun hui-pien*, 10.48–60

Chiang Kai-shek. *Chiang-tsung-t'ung ssu-hsiang yen-lun chi* 蔣總統思想言論集 (Collection of President Chiang's thoughts and speeches). 30 vols. Taipei: Chung-yang wen-wu 中央文物, 1966

(Chiang Kai-shek). *Chiang tsung-t'ung mi-lu* 蔣總統祕錄 (Secret records of President Chiang). 15 vols. Taipei: Chung-yang jih-pao 中央日報, 1974–8

Chiang Monlin 蔣夢麟 (Meng-lin). *Tides from the West*. New Haven: Yale University Press, 1947; Taipei reprint: China Academy, 1974

Chiang Mu-liang 蔣牧良. 'Chi-ch'eng-ssu-kung' 集成四公 *Wen-chi yueh-k'an*, 2.1 (1 Dec. 1936) 44–54

Chiang Shang-ch'ing 江上清. *Cheng-hai mi-wen* 政海祕聞 (Secrets of the political world). Hong Kong: Chih-ch'eng 致誠, 1966

'Chiang-su An-hui Hu-nan teng-sheng nung-min k'ang-tsu tou-cheng' 江蘇安徽湖南等省農民抗租鬪爭 (Peasant resistance to rents in Kiangsu, Anhwei and Hunan provinces, 1929–1941). Second Historical Archives, Nanking, no. 1/2/999

'Chiang-su Chiang-tu hsien nung-min fan-tui ch'ing-ch'a t'ien-fu yun-tung' 江蘇江都縣農民反對清查田賦運動 (The movement of opposition to fiscal inquiry by the peasants of Chiang-tu hsien, Kiangsu). Second Historical Archives, Nanking, no. 2/2/973

Chiang Yung-chen 江勇振. 'The Yenching Sociology Department: from social service to social engineering, 1919–1945'. Unpublished paper, 1984

Chiang Yung-ching 蔣永敬. *Pao-lo-t'ing yü Wu-han cheng-ch'üan* 鮑羅廷與武漢政權 (Borodin and the Wuhan regime). Taipei: Chung-kuo hsueh-shu chu-tso chiang-chu wei-yuan-hui 中國學術著作獎助委員會, 1963

Chiao-fei chan-shih 剿匪戰史 (History of the war to suppress the bandits), ed. by History Bureau, Ministry of Defence, Republic of China, Taipei. 6 vols., 1962

Chiao-yü kung-pao 教育公報 (Educational gazette). Peking, May 1916–

Chiao-yü pu 教育部 (Ministry of Education). *Ta-hsueh ling* 大學令 (Ordinance on colleges and universities). Ministry of Education, 1912

Chiao-yü-pu kao-teng chiao-yü-ssu 教育部高等教育司, comp. *Ch'üan-kuo kao-teng chiao-yü t'ung-chi* 全國高等教育統計 (Statistics of national higher education, August 1928 to July 1931). Nanking, 1931–3

Chiao-yü tsa-chih 教育雜誌 (Chinese educational review). Shanghai: CP, January 1909–

Chiao-yü tsa-chih 教育雜誌 (The journal of education). Special issue. *K'ang-chan i-lai ti kao-teng chiao-yü* 抗戰以來的高等教育 (Higher education since the beginning of the War of Resistance). 31.1 (10 Jan. 1941). Hong Kong: CP

Ch'iao Ch'i-ming 喬啓明. *Chiang-su K'un-shan Nan-t'ung An-hui Su-hsien nung-tien chih-tu chih pi-chiao i-chi kai-liang nung-tien wen-t'i chih chien-i* 江蘇崑山南通安徽宿縣農佃制度之比較以及改良農佃問題之建議 (A comparison of the farm tenancy system of K'un-shan and Nan-t'ung in Kiangsu and Su-hsien in Anhwei, and a proposal on the question of the reform of farm tenancy). Nanking: Chin-ling ta-hsueh nung-lin ts'ung-k'an 金陵大學農林叢刊 (Nanking University, agriculture and forestry series), 1926

Chieh-fang jih-pao 解放日報 (Liberation daily news). Yenan, 1941–; Shanghai, 1949–

Chieh-fang pao 解放報 (Liberation). Published at approximately weekly intervals in Yenan by the CCP Central Committee, from May 1937 to July 1941; thereafter became *Liberation Daily*.

Chieh-fang she 解放社, comp. *K'ang-Jih min-tsu t'ung-i chan-hsien chih-nan* 抗日民族統一戰綫指南 (Guide to the anti-Japanese national united front). Yenan: 1938–40

Ch'ien Chung-shu 錢鍾書. *Fortress besieged*, trans. by Jeanne Kelly and Nathan K. Mao. Bloomington and London: Indiana University Press, 1979

Ch'ien Chung-shu. See Huters, Theodore

Ch'ien I-shih 錢亦石. *Chung-kuo wai-chiao shih* 中國外交史 (History of Chinese foreign policy). Shanghai: Sheng-huo shu-tien, 1947

Ch'ien Pang-k'ai 錢邦楷. 'Tung-pei yen-chung-hsing tsen-yang ts'u-ch'eng-ti?' 東北嚴重性怎樣促成的？ (What has precipitated the grave situation in the Northeast?). *Ch'ing-tao shih-pao* 青島時報 (Tsingtao times), 19 Feb. 1948, reprinted in *Kuan-ch'a*, 27 March 1948, pp. 16, 14

Ch'ien Shih-fu 錢實甫. *Ch'ing-tai chih-kuan nien-piao* 清代職官年表 (Tables of Ch'ing officials). 4 vols. Peking: CH, 1980

Ch'ien T'ang 錢塘. *Ko-ming ti nü-hsing* 革命的女性 (Revolutionary women). Shanghai: Kuang-wen she 廣文社, 1949

Ch'ien Tuan-sheng 錢端升. *Min-kuo cheng-chih shih* 民國政制史 (The history of governmental institutions under the republic). 2 vols. in one. Shanghai: CP, 1939

Ch'ien Tuan-sheng. 'Chün-jen pa-hu ti Chung-kuo cheng-fu' 軍人跋扈的中國政府 (China's government usurped by military men). *Shih-tai p'i-p'ing*, 時代批評 (Modern critic). Hong Kong, 16 June 1947, 2–3

Ch'ien Tuan-sheng. *The government and politics of China*. Cambridge, Mass.: Harvard University Press, 1950, reprinted 1961

Chin Fan 金帆. *Tsai Hung-chün ch'ang-cheng ti tao-lu shang* 在紅軍長征的道路上 (On the route of the Red Army's Long March). Peking: Chung-kuo ch'ing-nien ch'u-pan-she 中國青年出版社, 1957

Chin, Rockwood O. P. 'The Chinese cotton industry under wartime inflation'. *Pacific Affairs*, 16.1 (March 1943) 33–46

Chin, Steve S. K. *The thought of Mao Tse-tung*. Hong Kong: University of Hong Kong, Centre of Asian Studies, 1979

Chin-tai-shih tzu-liao 近代史資料 (Source materials of modern history), ed. by Institute of Historical Research, Academy of Sciences, Peking, 1954–

Chin-tai-shih yen-chiu ('*Jin dai shi yan jiu*') 近代史研究 (Studies in modern history), ed. by Chung-kuo she-hui k'o-hsueh-yuan Chin-tai-shih yen-chiu-so 中國社會科學院近代史研究所 (Modern history institute of CASS). Peking: Chung-kuo she-hui k'o-hsueh ch'u-pan-she, 1979–

China. Inspectorate General of Customs. *Returns of trade and trade reports published by order of the Inspectorate General of Customs*. Shanghai, 1865–. Statistical returns and trade reports published together from 1882

China. Inspectorate General of Customs. *Decennial reports on the trade, navigation, industries, etc. of the ports open to foreign commerce in China and Korea and on the condition and development of the treaty port provinces*, compiled for the decades 1881–1891, 1892–1901, 1902–1911, 1912–1921, 1922–1931 (subtitles vary); published by the Inspectorate General, Shanghai, usually two years after the end of the decade in question

China. The Maritime Customs. *Treaties, conventions, etc. between China and foreign states*. 2 vols. Shanghai: Statistical Department of the Inspectorate General of Customs, 1917

China handbook 1937–1943: a comprehensive survey of major developments in China in six years of war, comp. Chinese Ministry of Information. New York: Macmillan, 1943. *China handbook, 1937–1944: . . . in seven years . . .* Chungking: Chinese Ministry of Information, 1944. *China handbook, 1937–1945* (*Chan-shih Chung-hua chih* 戰時中華誌), new edition with 1946 supplement. New York: Macmillan, 1947. *China handbook, 1950*, comp. China Handbook Editorial Board. New York: Rockport Press, Inc., 1950

China Quarterly. Quarterly. London, 1960–. 1960 to Dec. 1976 published by Congress for Cultural Freedom; from Dec. 1976 by the Contemporary China Institute of the School of Oriental and African Studies, University of London

China Weekly Review. Shanghai, 1917–

China white paper. See United States Department of State, *United States relations with China*

The China year book, ed. by H. G. W. Woodhead. London: George Routledge & Sons, Ltd., 1912–21; Tientsin: The Tientsin Press, 1921–30; Shanghai: The North China Daily News & Herald, Ltd., 1931–9

China's spiritual mobilization: outline of the plan. Chungking: The China Information Committee, 1939

Chinese Academy of Social Sciences: Chung-kuo she-hui k'o-hsueh yuan 中國社會科學院

Chinese Economic Journal. Peking. Monthly, Jan. 1927–

Chinese Economic Monthly. Peking. Incorporated in *Chinese Economic Journal* from Jan. 1927

Chinese Literature. Monthly. Peking: Foreign Languages Press, Autumn 1951–

Chinese Press Review, comp. by United States Consulates. Chungking, 1942–5; Shanghai, 1946–9

Chinese Recorder. Shanghai, 1867–1941

Chinese Republican Studies Newsletter. Semi-annual 1975–83. From 9.2 (Feb. 1984) became *Republican China*

Ching-chi chou-pao 經濟週報 (Economics weekly). Shanghai, Nov. 1945–

Ching-chi yen-chiu 經濟研究 (Economic research). Peking, April 1955–

Ching Chun-chien 經君健. 'Lun Ch'ing-tai she-hui ti teng-chi chieh-kou' 論清代社會的等級結構 (On the class structure of Ch'ing dynasty society). *Ching-chi yen-chiu so chi-k'an* 經濟研究所集刊 (Bulletin of the institute of economic research), 3 (1981) 1–65

Ching Su 景甦 and Lo Lun 羅崙. *Ch'ing-tai Shan-tung ching-ying ti-chu ti she-hui hsing-chih* 清代山東經營地主底社會性質 (Landlord and labour in late imperial China: case studies from Shantung). Chinan: Jen-min, 1959

Ching Yuan-shan 經元善. *Chü-i ch'u-chi* 居易初集 (A first collection of Chü-i). 3 vols. Shanghai, 1902

Ch'ing-hua ta-hsueh hsiao-shih pien-hsieh-tsu 清華大學校史編寫組, comp. *Ching-hua ta-hsueh hsiao-shih-kao* 清華大學校史稿 (Draft history of Tsing-hua University). Peking: Chung-hua, 1981

Ch'ing-mo ch'ou-pei li-hsien tang-an shih-liao 清末籌備立憲檔案史料 (Archival materials concerning the preparation for constitutionalism in the late Ch'ing), comp. Ku-kung po-wu-yuan, Ming-Ch'ing tang-an pu 故宮博物院, 明清檔案部 Peking: CH, 1979

Ch'ing-shih lun-ts'ung 清史論叢 (Essays on Ch'ing history). Peking: CH, 1979–

Ch'ing-shih wen-t'i 清史問題 (Ch'ing history problems). Journal of the Society for Ch'ing Studies, founded by Mary C. Wright and Jonathan Spence; irregular, then semi-annual, April 1965–

Ch'ing-tai chih-kuan nien piao. See Ch'ien Shih-fu

Ch'ing-tai tang-an shih-liao ts'ung-pien 清代檔案史料叢編 (Historical materials from the Ch'ing archives), issued by the First Historical Archives (Chung-kuo ti-i li-shih tang-an-kuan 中國第一歷史檔案館). Peking: CH, 1978–

Ch'ing-tai ti-tsu po-hsueh hsing-t'ai 清代地租剝削形態 (Forms of land rent exploitation in the Ch'ing period). 2 vols. comp. Chung-kuo ti-i li-shih tang-an-kuan and Chung-kuo she-hui k'o-hsueh-yuan li-shih yen-chiu-so (Institute of history, CASS) Peking: CH, 1982

Ch'ing-tao shih-pao 青島時報 (Tsingtao times). Tsingtao, May 1932–

Ch'iu Ch'ang-wei 邱昌渭. *Kuang-hsi hsien-cheng* 廣西縣政 (County government in Kwangsi). Kweilin: Kuei-lin wen-hua kung-ying she 桂林文化供應社, 1941

Ch'iu Yü-lin. 'Ching-shih ta-hsueh-t'ang yen-ko lueh' 京師大學堂沿革略 (A brief history of Peking University), in Ch'iu Yü-lin, comp. *Ch'ing-tai i-wen* 清代軼聞 (Informal records of the Ch'ing period), chüan 5.1–7. n.p. Reprint, Taipei: Hua-wen shu-chü 華文書局, 1969

CHOC. See *The Cambridge history of China.*

Chou Ch'eng 周成. *Shan-hsi ti-fang tzu-chih kang-yao* 山西地方自治綱要 (An outline of Shansi local self-government), in Chou Ch'eng, comp. *Ti-fang tzu-chih chiang-i* 地方自治講義 (Lectures on local self-government). Shanghai: T'ai-tung shu-chü 泰東書局, 1925

Chou Chin 周錦, ed. *Chung-kuo hsien-tai wen-hsueh yen-chiu ts'ung-k'an* 中國現代文學研究叢刊 (Series of studies on modern Chinese literature). 30 vols. Taipei: Ch'eng-wen 成文, 1980

Chou Chung-ch'i 周鍾岐. 'Lun ko-ming' 論革命 (On revolution). *Kuan-ch'a,* 25 Jan. 1947, pp. 6–10

Chou En-lai 周恩來. 'Mu-ch'ien tang ti tsu-chih wen-t'i' 目前黨的組織問題 (Current problems of the organization of the party). n.p. May, 1929. Mimeographed

Chou En-lai. 'Shao-shan pao-kao' 少山報告 (Report by Shao-shan). n.p.: 1931. Mimeographed

Chou, Eric. See Crozier, Brian

Chou K'ai-ch'ing 周開慶. *K'ang-chan i-ch'ien chih Chung-Jih kuan-hsi* 抗戰以前之中日關係 (Sino-Japanese relations before the war of resistance). Taipei: Tzu-yu 自由, 1962

Chou Li-po 周立波. *The hurricane (Pao-feng tsou-yü* 暴風驟雨). Peking: Foreign Languages Press, 1955

Chou Pang-tao 周邦道. *Chin-tai chiao-yü hsien-chin chuan-lueh* 近代教育先進傳略 (Biographical sketches of early leaders of modern education in China). Taipei: Publications Division, University of Chinese Culture, 1981

Chou Shun-hsin 周舜莘. *The Chinese inflation, 1937–1949.* New York: Columbia University Press, 1963, reprinted 1969

Chou Yang 周揚. 'Kuan-yü kuo-fang wen-hsueh' 關於國防文學 (Concerning national defence literature), in Lin Ts'ung, 林淙, ed. *Hsien chieh-tuan ti wen-*

hsueh lun-chan 現階段的文學論戰, 31–8

Chou Yuan-ho 周源和. 'Ch'ing-tai jen-k'ou yen-chiu' 清代人口研究 (Research on Ch'ing dynasty population). *Chung-kuo she-hui k'o-hsueh* 中國社會科學 (Social sciences in China), 2 (1982) 161–88

Chow, Yung-teh 周榮德. *Social mobility in China; status careers among the gentry in a Chinese community.* New York: Atherton Press, 1966

Christie, Clive. 'Great Britain, China and the status of Tibet, 1914–21'. *Modern Asian Studies*, 10.4 (Oct. 1976) 481–508

Chu Chia-hua 朱家驊. 'K'ang-chan ti-pa-nien chih chiao-yü' 抗戰第八年之教育 (Chinese education in the eighth year of the war), in Wang Yü-chün 王聿均 and Sun Pin 孫斌, *Chu Chia-hua hsien-sheng yen-lun chi* 朱家驊先生言論集 (Dissertations of Dr Chu Chia-hua), 171–3. Taipei: IMH, 1977

Chu Pao-chin. *V. K. Wellington Koo: a case study of China's diplomat and diplomacy of nationalism, 1912–1966.* Hong Kong: Chinese University Press, 1981

Chu, Samuel C. 朱昌峻. *Reformer in modern China: Chang Chien, 1853–1926.* New York: Columbia University Press, 1965

Chu Tzu-chia 朱子家 (Chin Hsiung-pai 金雄白). *Wang cheng-ch'üan ti k'ai-ch'ang yü shou-ch'ang* 汪政權的開場與收場 (The beginning and ending of the drama of the Wang regime). 6 vols. Hong Kong: Wu Hsing-chi shu-pao-she 吳興記書報社, 1974

Ch'u An-p'ing 儲安平. 'Chung-kuo ti cheng-chü' 中國的政局 (China's political situation). *Kuan-ch'a*, 8 March 1947, pp. 3–8

Ch'u An-p'ing. 'P'ing P'u-li-t'e ti p'ien-ssu ti pu-chien-k'ang ti fang Hua pao-kao' 評蒲立特的偏私的不健康的訪華報告 (A critique of Bullitt's biased unhealthy report on his visit to China). *Kuan-ch'a*, 25 Oct. 1947, pp. 3–5

Ch'ü Chih-sheng 曲直生. *K'ang-chan chi-li* 抗戰紀歷 (A personal account of the war of resistance). Taipei, Chung-hua, 1965

Ch'ü Ch'iu-pai 瞿秋白. 'Chi-an ti ch'ü-te he sang-shih' 吉安的取得和喪失 (The conquest and loss of Chi-an). *Shih hua* 實話 (True words) (Shanghai), 2 (9 Dec. 1930) 3–4

Ch'ü Ch'iu-pai. 'Chung-kuo hsien-chuang yü Kung-ch'an-tang ti jen-wu' 中國現狀與共產黨的任務 (The present situation in China and the tasks of the CCP), report at the November conference, in Hu Hua, *Chung-kuo hsin-min-chu chu-i . . . tzu-liao*, 220–2

Ch'ü T'ung-tsu 瞿同祖. *Local government in China under the Ch'ing.* Cambridge, Mass.: Harvard University Press, 1962

Chuan-chi wen-hsueh 傳記文學 (Biographical literature). Monthly. Taipei, 1962–

Chuan, Han-sheng 全漢昇 and Kraus, Richard A. *Mid-Ch'ing rice markets and trade; an essay in price history.* Cambridge, Mass.: East Asian Research Center, Harvard University, 1975

Ch'uan Shan ko-ming ken-chü-ti li-shih wen-hsien hsuan-pien 川陝革命根據地歷史文獻選編 (Selected historical documents of the Szechwan-Shensi revolutionary base area). 2 vols. Chengtu: Ssu-ch'uan Jen-min, 1979

Ch'üan-kuo tiao-ch'a pao-kao 全國調查報告 (Draft report of the land survey of China). Nanking: 1937

Chuang Tse-hsuan 莊澤宣. 'K'ang-chan shih-nien-lai Chung-kuo hsueh-hsiao chiao-yü tsung-chien-t'ao' 抗戰十年來中國學校教育總檢討 (General assessment of Chinese formal education in the ten years since the [beginning of the] war of resistance). *Chung-hua chiao-yü-chieh* (Chinese education), NS, 1.1 (15 Jan. 1947)

Chuang Yü 莊俞 and Ho Sheng-nai 賀聖鼐, eds. *Tsui-chin san-shih-wu-nien chih Chung-kuo chiao-yü* 最近三十五年之中國教育 (Chinese education in the last thirty-five years). Shanghai: CP, 1931

Ch'uang shih-chi 創世紀. (The epoch poetry quarterly). Taipei. October 1954–

Chūgoku no seiji to keizai: ko Muramatsu Yūji kyōju tsuitō ronbunshū 中国の政治と経済：故村松祐次教授追悼論文集 (The polity and economy of China—the late Professor Yūji Muramatsu commemorative volume). Tokyo: Tōyō Keizai Shinpō sha 東洋経済新報社, 1975

Chūgoku nōson kankō chōsa kankōkai 中國農村慣行調查刊行會 comp. *Chūgoku nōson kankō chōsa* 中國農村慣行調查 (A survey of traditional customs in Chinese villages). 6 vols. Tokyo: Iwanami shoten 岩波書店, 1952

Ch'un-ch'iu 春秋 (Spring and autumn). Taipei. July 1964–

Ch'ün-chung 群衆 (The masses). Chungking: 1938 (vol. 2)–

Ch'ün-yun chih-shih hui-pien 群運指示匯編 (A compilation of mass movement directives). n.p.: Chung-kung Chi-Lu-Yü pien-ch'ü tang wei 中共冀魯豫邊區黨委, Sept. 1945

Chung, An-min. 'The development of modern manufacturing industry in China, 1928–1949'. University of Pennsylvania, Ph.D. dissertation, 1953

Chung-hua chiao-yü chieh 中華教育界 (Chung Hua educational review). Special issues. 'Chan-hou liang-nien lai Chung-kuo chiao-yü ch'üan-mao' 戰後兩年來中國教育全貌 (The state of Chinese education two years after the war). NS 2.1, 2 (15 Jan. 1948; 15 Feb. 1948). Shanghai: CH

Chung-hua min-kuo k'ai-kuo wu-shih-nien wen-hsien pien-tsuan wei-yuan-hui 中華民國開國五十年文獻編纂委員會 (Editorial committee for the fiftieth year of the founding of the Republic of China), ed. *Kung-fei huo-kuo shih-liao hui-pien* 共匪禍國史料彙編 (A collection of historical materials on the national disaster caused by the Communist bandits). 3 vols. Taipei: Cheng-chung, 1964

Chung-hua min-kuo shih tang-an tzu-liao hui-pien 中華民國史檔案資料匯編 (Archival materials on the history of the Republic of China) issued by Chung-kuo ti-erh li-shih tang-an-kuan 中國第二歷史檔案館 (Second Historical Archives). Kiangsu: Jen-min, 1979–

Chung-hua min-kuo t'ung-chi t'i-yao. See Kuo-min cheng-fu chu-chi-ch'u

Chung-Jih chan-cheng shih-lueh 中日戰爭史略 (Sketch history of the Sino-Japanese War). Taipei: Cheng-chung, 1968

Chung-kung k'ang-chan i-pan ch'ing-k'uang ti chieh-shao 中共抗戰一般情况的介紹

(A briefing on the Chinese Communist war activities). Photocopy with English title. Chieh-fang-she 解放社, comp. n.p., 1944

Chung-kung tang-shih ts'an-k'ao tzu-liao 中共黨史參考資料 (Reference materials on the history of the CCP). Chung-kung chung-yang tang-hsiao tang-shih chiao-yen-shih 中共中央黨校黨史教研室 (Party history research office of the CCP central party school), ed. Nei-pu fa-hsing 內部發行 (internal use only). 10 vols. Peking: Jen-min, 1979

Chung-kung ti cheng-chih kung-tso 中共的政治工作 (The political work of the Chinese Communist Party), Kiangsu Provincial Committee, n.d.

Chung-kuo che-hsueh 中國哲學 (Chinese philosophy). Peking, August 1979–

Chung-kuo chin-tai ch'i-k'an p'ien-mu hui-lu 中國近代期刊篇目彙録 (Collected tables of contents of modern Chinese periodicals), ed. by Shang-hai t'u-shu-kuan 上海圖書館. Shanghai: Jen-min, 1965–

Chung-kuo chin-tai ching-chi shih yen-chiu chi-k'an 中國近代經濟史研究集刊 (Studies in modern economic history of China). Quarterly. Peking, 1932–

Chung-kuo chin-tai shih lun-chu mu-lu, 1949–1979 中國近代史論著目録, 1949–1979 (Catalogue of publications during 1949–1979 on modern Chinese history), comp. by Fu-tan ta-hsueh li-shih-hsi tzu-liao-shih 復旦大學歷史系資料室. Shanghai: Jen-min, 1980

Chung-kuo chin-tai shih tz'u-tien 中國近代史詞典 (A dictionary of modern Chinese history), comp. by Ch'en Hsu-lu 陳旭麓 *et al.* Shanghai: Shang-hai tz'u-shu ch'u-pan-she 上海辭書出版社, 1982

Chung-kuo chin-tai ssu-hsiang-shih tzu-liao 中國近代思想史資料 (Materials of modern Chinese intellectual history). See also Shih Chün. Tokyo: Daian, 1968

Chung-kuo ching-chi 中國經濟 (Chinese economy). Nanking, April 1933–

Chung-kuo ch'ing-nien 中國青年 (Chinese youth), ed. by Yun Tai-ying 惲代英 *et al.* Shanghai, 20 Oct. 1923–1927

Chung-kuo hsien-tai wen-hsueh shih ts'an-k'ao tzu-liao 中國現代文學史參考資料 (Research materials on the history of modern Chinese literature), ed. by Pei-ching shih-fan ta-hsueh Chung-wen hsi hsien-tai wen-hsueh chiao-hsueh kai-ko hsiao-tsu 北京師範大學中文系現代文學教學改革小組 (Peking Normal University, Chinese Literature Department, Contemporary literature teaching reform group). 3 vols. Peking: Kao-teng chiao-yü 高等教育, 1959

Chung-kuo hsien-tai wen-hsueh shih tzu-liao hui-pien 中國現代文學史資料滙編 (Collected materials on the history of modern Chinese literature), an over-all title for several hundred volumes of source materials on individual writers and general literary history published by several publishers since about 1981, subdivided into at least two sub-series each under an editorial committee, under the overall supervision of the Institute of Literature of the Chinese Academy of Social Sciences, Peking

Chung-kuo hsien-tai wen-hsueh yen-chiu ts'ung-k'an 中國現代文學研究叢刊 (Collection of modern Chinese literature studies). Peking: Pei-ching ch'u-pan-she

北京出版社, 1979–

Chung-kuo hsien-tai wen-i tzu-liao ts'ung-k'an 中國現代文藝資料叢刊 (Collected materials on modern Chinese literature and art). Shanghai: Shang-hai wen-i 上海文藝, 1979

Chung-kuo hsien-tai wen-i tzu-liao ts'ung-k'an ti-i chi 中國現代文藝資料叢刊第一輯 (Sources of modern Chinese literature, first series), ed. by Shang-hai wen-i ch'u-pan-she pien-chi pu 上海文藝出版社編輯部 (Editorial department of *Shanghai literature*). Shanghai: Shang-hai wen-i, 1962

Chung-kuo jen-min chieh-fang chün cheng-chih hsueh-yuan hsun-lien pu t'u-shu tzu-liao kuan 中國人民解放軍政治學院訓練部圖書資料館, *Mao Tse-tung chu-tso, yen-lun, wen-tien mu-lu* 毛澤東著作言論文電目錄 (A list of Mao Tse-tung's works, utterances, and telegrams). Peking, February 1961

Chung-kuo jen-min ta-hsueh Chung-kuo li-shih chiao-yen shih 中國人民大學中國歷史教研室, *Chung-kuo tzu-pen chu-i meng-ya wen-t'i t'ao-lun chi* 中國資本主義萌芽問題討論集 (Collected articles on the question of capitalist sprouts in China). 2 vols. Peking: San-lien, 1957

Chung-kuo jih-pao 中國日報 (China daily). Nanking, 1934–

Chung-kuo ko hsiao-tang-p'ai hsien-k'uang 中國各小黨派現況 (Present state of the minority parties in China). n.p., 1946

Chung-kuo ko-ming po-wu-kuan 中國革命博物館 (Museum of the Chinese Revolution), comp. *Pei-fang ti-ch'ü kung-jen yun-tung tzu-liao hsuan-pien 1921–1923* 北方地區工人運動資料選編, 1921–1923 (Selected materials on the local workers' movement in North China 1921–1923). Peking: Pei-ching ch'u-pan-she 北京出版社, 1981

Chung-kuo ko-ming po-wu-kuan tang-shih yen-chiu-shih 中國革命博物館黨史研究室 (Party history research office, Chinese revolutionary museum), ed. *Tang-shih yen-chiu tzu-liao* 黨史研究資料 (Research materials on party history). Ch'eng-tu: Jen-min, 1980

Chung-kuo k'o-hsueh yuan Shang-hai ching-chi yen-chiu so 中國科學院上海經濟研究所, comp. *Shang-hai chieh-fang ch'ien-hou wu-chia tzu-liao hui-pien (1921–1957)* 上海解放前後物價資料 (1921年–1957年) (Collected materials on prices before and after the liberation of Shanghai, 1921–57). Shanghai: Jen-min, 1958

Chung-kuo Kung-ch'an-tang tsai Chiang-hsi ti-ch'ü ling-tao ko-ming tou-cheng ti li-shih tzu-liao 中國共產黨在江西地區領導革命鬥爭的歷史資料 (Historical materials concerning the revolutionary struggles led by the CCP in Kiangsi). ed. by Kiangsi Jen-min ch'u-pan-she, Kiangsi, 1958. See Liu P'ei-shan

Chung-kuo kung-yeh 中國工業 (Chinese industry). Nanking, Nov. 1932–; Kweilin, Jan. 1942–

Chung-kuo kuo-min cheng-fu Chün-shih wei-yuan-hui wei-yuan-chang Nan-ch'ang hsing-ying 中國國民政府軍事委員會委員長南昌行營 (Head-quarters of the Chairman of the National Government Military Commission), comp. *Ko-sheng kao-chi hsing-cheng jen-yuan feng-chao Nan-ch'ang chi-hui chi-lu* 各省高級行政人員奉召南昌集會紀錄 (Record of the meeting of high provincial administrators held at Nanchang). Nanchang, 1934

Chung-kuo Kuo-min-tang ch'üan-kuo tai-piao ta-hui hui-i-lu 中國國民黨全國代表大會會議錄 (Minutes of the National Congress of the Kuomintang of China). Reprinted, Washington, DC, Center for Chinese Research Materials, 1971

Chung-kuo lao-kung yun-tung shih pien-tsuan wei-yuan-hui 中國勞工運動史編纂委員會, ed. *Chung-kuo lao-kung yun-tung shih* 中國勞工運動史 (A history of the Chinese labour movement). 5 vols. Taipei: Chung-kuo lao-kung fu-li ch'u-pan-she 中國勞工福利出版社, 1959

Chung-kuo li-shih-hsueh nien-chien 1979 中國歷史學年鑑 1979 (1979 year book of Chinese historiography), comp. by Chung-kuo li-shih-hsueh nien-chien pien-chi-tsu 中國歷史學年鑑編輯組. Peking: Jen-min, 1981; ... *1981*. Peking: Jen-min, 1981; ... *1982*, comp. by Chung-kuo shih-hsueh-hui Chung-kuo li-shih-hsueh nien-chien pien-chi-pu 中國史學會《中國歷史學年鑑》編輯部. Peking: Jen-min, 1982

Chung-kuo li-shih ti-t'u chi, ti-pa-ts'e 中國歷史地圖集, 第八冊 (Collection of Chinese historical maps, vol. 8), ed. by Chung-kuo li-shih ti-t'u chi pien-chi-tsu 中國歷史地圖集編輯組. Shanghai: Chung-hua ti-t'u hsueh-she 中華地圖學社, 1975

Chung-kuo nung-min 中國農民 (The Chinese farmer). Canton: Farmers' Bureau of the Central Executive Committee of the Kuomintang of China, Jan. 1926–; also Chungking, Feb. 1942–. Photolithographic reprint edn. of Canton pub., Tokyo: Daian, 1964.

Chung-kuo nung-ts'un 中國農村 (The Chinese village). Shanghai, Oct. 1934–

Chung-kuo she-hui k'o-hsueh-yuan: Chinese Academy of Social Sciences (CASS), Beijing (Peking), many institutes and branches

Chung-kuo she-hui k'o-hsueh-yuan Li-shih yen-chiu so 中國社會科學院歷史研究所, ed. *Chung-kuo shih yen-chiu* ('Zhongguoshi yanjiu') 中國史研究 (Studies in Chinese history). Peking, 1979–

Chung-kuo tzu-pen chu-i meng-ya wen-t'i lun-wen-chi 中國資本主義萌芽問題論文集 (Essays on capitalist sprouts in China), comp. by Ming-Ch'ing History Study Section, Department of History, Nanking University. Nanking: Chiang-su Jen-min, 1983

Chung-kuo tzu-pen chu-i meng-ya wen-t'i t'ao-lun chi 中國資本主義萌芽討論集 (Collected debates on the question of the 'sprouts of capitalism' in China), comp. Chung-kuo jen-min ta-hsueh Chung-kuo li-shih chiao-yen shih 中國人民大學中國歷史教研室 (Chinese People's University, Chinese History Department). 2 vols. Peking: San-lien, 1957 ... *Hsü-pien* 續編 (... Continuation [of the preceding item]). Peking: San-lien, 1960

Chung-kuo wen-hsueh chia tz'u-tien 中國文學家辭典 (Dictionary of Chinese writers), ed. by Pei-ching yü-yen hsueh-yuan Chung-kuo wen-hsueh chia tz'u-tien pien-wei hui 北京語言學院中國文學家辭典編委會. *Hsien-tai* 現代 period, vol. 1. Peking: Pei-ching yü-yen hsueh-yuan, 1978; vol. 2. Ch'eng-tu: Szechwan Jen-min, 1982

Chung-yang jih-pao 中央日報 (Central daily news). Nanking, 1928–

Chung-yang kao ch'üan-tang t'ung-chih shu 中央告全黨同志書 (Letter from the centre to all comrades). n.p.: 11 Nov. 1928. Mimeographed

'Chung-yang kuan-yü tsai Shan-tung Hua-chung fa-chan wu-chuang chien-li ken-chü-ti ti chih-shih' 中央關於在山東華中發展武裝建立根據地的指示 (Central directive concerning development of armed forces and establishment of base areas in Shantung and Central China), 28 January 1940.

Chung-yang nung-yeh-pu chi-hua ssu 中央農業部計劃司, comp. *Liang-nien-lai ti Chung-kuo nung-ts'un ching-chi tiao-ch'a hui-pien* 兩年來的中國農村經濟調查彙編 (A collection of surveys on the Chinese farm economy in the past two years). Shanghai: CH, 1952

Chung-yang pan-yueh-k'an 中央半月刊 (Central semi-monthly). Nanking, 1928–

Chung-yang t'ung-hsin 中央通信 (Central newsletter). Organ of the Central Committee of the Chinese Communist Party, Aug. 1927–

Chung-yang yen-chiu yuan: Academia Sinica, Nanking, Taipei, several institutes

Chung-yang yen-chiu-yuan Chin-tai-shih yen-chiu-so chi-k'an 中央研究院近代史研究所集刊 (Bulletin of the Institute of Modern History, Academia Sinica). Taipei, Aug. 1969–

CI. Communist International, Comintern

Civil war in China, 1945–50. Taiwan: translated and prepared at the field level under the auspices of the Office of the Chief of Military History, (US) Dept. of the Army; Library of Congress microfilm 51461

CJCC: see Wu Hsiang-hsiang, *Ti-erh-tz'u Chung-Jih chan-cheng shih*

CKNT: see *Chung-kuo nung-ts'un*

Clopton, Robert W. and Ou Tsuin-chen, trans. and ed. *John Dewey, lectures in China, 1919–1920.* Honolulu: East-West Center, 1973

Clubb, O. Edmund. *Twentieth century China.* New York: Columbia University Press, 1964; 3rd edn. 1978

Clubb, O. Edmund. *The witness and I.* New York: Columbia University Press, 1974

Coble, Parks M. *The Shanghai capitalists and the Nationalist government, 1927–1937.* Cambridge, Mass.: Council on East Asian Studies, Harvard University, 1980

Cochran, Sherman. *Big business in China: Sino-foreign rivalry in the cigarette industry, 1890–1930.* Cambridge, Mass.: Harvard University Press, 1980

Cochran, Sherman and Hsieh, Andrew, trans. *One day in China, May 21, 1936.* New Haven: Yale University Press, 1983

Cohen, A. *The communism of Mao Tse-tung.* Chicago: University of Chicago Press, 1964

Cohen, Paul A. *Between tradition and modernity: Wang T'ao and reform in late Ch'ing China.* Cambridge, Mass.: Harvard University Press, 1974

Cohen, Paul A. 'Christian missions and their impact to 1900'. *CHOC* 10.543–90

Cohen, Paul A. *Discovering history in China: American historical writing on the recent Chinese past.* New York: Columbia University Press, 1984

Cohen, Paul A. and Schrecker, John E., eds. *Reform in nineteenth-century China.* Cambridge, Mass.: East Asian Research Center, Harvard University, 1976

Cohen, Warren I. "Who fought the Japanese in Hunan? Some views of China's war effort'. *JAS* 27.1 (Nov. 1967) 111–15

Cohen, Warren I. *The Chinese connection: Roger S. Greene, Thomas W. Lamont, George E. Sokolsky and American–East Asian relations.* New York: Columbia University Press, 1978

Cohen, Warren I., ed. *New frontiers in American–East Asian relations: essays presented to Dorothy Borg.* New York: Columbia University Press, 1983

Cole, James. 'Shaohsing: studies in Ch'ing social history'. Stanford University, Ph.D. dissertation, 1975

Cole, James. 'The Shaoxing connection: a vertical administrative clique in late Qing China'. *Modern China*, 6.3 (July 1980) 317–26

Cole, James. *The people versus the Taipings: Bao Lisheng's 'Righteous Army of Dongan'.* Berkeley: Institute of East Asian Studies, University of California, 1981

Comintern and the East, The. Moscow, 1979. English edn. of *Komintern i vostok.* See Ulyanovsky, R. A.

Committee on Survey of Chinese Students in American Colleges and Universities, comp. *A survey of Chinese students in American universities and colleges in the past one hundred years.* New York, 1954

Comparative Studies in Society and History. Quarterly. Cambridge, England and New York: Cambridge University Press, 1959–

Compton, Boyd. *Mao's China: party reform documents, 1942–44.* Seattle: University of Washington Press, 1952

Congrès international des sciences historiques, XIIIème. *Enquête sur les mouvements paysans dans le monde contemporain, rapport général.* Moscow: Editions 'Nauka', 1970

Coox, Alvin D. 'Recourse to arms: the Sino-Japanese conflict, 1937–1945', in Alvin D. Coox and Hilary Conroy, eds. *China and Japan.*

Coox, Alvin D. and Conroy, Hilary, eds. *China and Japan: a search for balance since World War I.* Santa Barbara: Clio Press, 1978

Corbett, Charles Hodge. *Shantung Christian University (Cheeloo).* New York: United Board for Christian Colleges in China, 1955

CP. Commercial Press

CPR. See *Chinese Press Review*

CQ. See *The China Quarterly*

Creel, Herrlee G. *The origins of statecraft in China*, vol. 1, *The Western Chou empire.* Chicago: University of Chicago Press, 1970

Croly, Herbert. *Willard Straight.* New York: Macmillan, 1924

Crowley, James Buckley. *Japan's China policy, 1931–1938: a study of the role of the military in the determination of foreign policy.* Ann Arbor: University

Microfilms, 1960

Crowley, James B. *Japan's quest for autonomy: national security and foreign policy, 1930–1938.* Princeton: Princeton University Press, 1966

Crowley, James B., vol. ed. *Modern East Asia: essays in interpretation* (under the general editorship of John Morton Blum). New York: Harcourt, Brace & World, 1970

Crozier, Brian. *The man who lost China: the first full biography of Chiang Kai-shek.* With the collaboration of Eric Chou. New York: Scribner, 1976

CSWT. See *Ch'ing-shih wen-t'i*

CWR. See *China Weekly Review*

CYB. See *China year book, The*

Dallek, Robert. *Franklin D. Roosevelt and American foreign policy, 1932–1945.* New York: Oxford University Press, 1979

Davies, John Paton, Jr. *Dragon by the tail: American, British, Japanese, and Russian encounters with China and one another.* London: Robson, 1974

Day, Clarence Burton. *Hangchow University: a brief history.* New York: United Board for Christian Colleges in China, 1955

Day, M. Henri. *Máo Zédōng 1917–1927: documents.* Skriftserien för Orientaliska Studier no. 14. Stockholm, 1975

Dayer, Robert Allbert. *Bankers and diplomants in China, 1919–1925: the Anglo-American relationship.* London, Totowa, NJ: F. Cass, 1981

Deane, Hugh. 'Political reaction in Kuomintang China'. *Amerasia*, 5.5 (July 1941) 209–14

DeBary, W. Theodore. 'Chinese despotism and the Confucian ideal: a seventeenth century view', in John K. Fairbank, ed. *Chinese thought and institutions*, 163–203

Degras, Jane. *The Communist International 1919–1943: documents.* 3 vols. London: Oxford University Press for Royal Institute of International Affairs, 1956, 1960, 1965

Deliusin, L. P., ed. *Obshchestvo gosudarstvo v Kitae* (Society and state in China). Moscow: Nauka, annual, 1970–

Deliusin, L. P. See Grigoriev, A. M.

Dernberger, Robert F. 'The role of the foreigner in China's economic development, 1840–1949', in Dwight H. Perkins, ed. *China's modern economy in historical perspective*, 19–47

Deyon, Pierre and Jacquart, Jean, eds. *Les hésitations de la croissance 1580–1730*, vol. 2 of *Histoire economique et sociale du monde*, under the direction of Pierre Léon. Paris: Armand Colin, 1978

Dingman, Roger. *Power in the Pacific: the origins of naval arms limitation, 1914–1922.* Chicago: University of Chicago Press, 1976

Dirlik, Arif. 'Mass movements and the left Kuomintang'. *Modern China*, 1.1 (Jan. 1975) 46–74

Dirlik, Arif. 'The ideological foundations of the New Life Movement: a study in counterrevolution'. *JAS* 34.4 (Aug. 1975) 945–80

Dirlik, Arif. *Revolution and history: origins of Marxist historiography in China, 1919–1937*. Berkeley: University of California Press, 1978

Dirlik, Arif. 'Chinese historians and the Marxist concept of capitalism: a critical examination'. *Modern China*, 8.1 (Jan. 1982) 105–32

Domes, Jürgen. *Vertagte Revolution: die Politik der Kuomintang in China, 1923–1937*. Berlin: Walter de Gruyter & Co., 1969

Donovan, Peter, Dorris, Carl E. and Sullivan, Lawrence R. *Chinese communist materials at the Bureau of Investigation Archives, Taiwan*. Ann Arbor: University of Michigan, Center for Chinese Studies, 1976

Dorn, Frank. *The Sino-Japanese War, 1937–41: from Marco Polo Bridge to Pearl Harbor*. New York: Macmillan, 1974

Dorris, Carl E. 'People's war in north China: resistance in the Shansi-Chahar-Hopeh border region, 1938–1945'. University of Kansas, Ph.D. dissertation, 1975

Dorris, Carl E. 'Peasant mobilization in North China and the origins of Yenan Communism'. *CQ* 68 (Dec. 1976) 697–719

Duara, Prasenjit. 'Power in rural society: North China villages, 1900–1940'. Harvard University, Ph.D. dissertation, 1983

Duiker, William J. *Ts'ai Yuan-p'ei, educator of modern China*. University Park: Pennsylvania State University Press, 1977

Eastman, Lloyd E. '*Ch'ing-i* and Chinese policy formation during the nineteenth century'. *JAS* 24.4 (Aug. 1965) 595–611

Eastman, Lloyd E. 'Fascism in Kuomintang China: the Blue Shirts'. *CQ* 49 (Jan.-March 1972) 1–31

Eastman, Lloyd E. *The abortive revolution: China under Nationalist rule, 1927–1937*. Cambridge, Mass.: Harvard University Press, 1974

Eastman, Lloyd E. 'Regional politics and the central government: Yunnan and Chungking', in Paul K. T. Sih, ed. *Nationalist China during the Sino-Japanese War, 1937–1945*, 329–62

Eastman, Lloyd E. 'Facets of an ambivalent relationship: smuggling, puppets and atrocities during the war, 1937–1945', in Akira Iriye, ed. *The Chinese and the Japanese*, 275–303

Eastman, Lloyd E. 'Peasants, taxes, and Nationalist rule, 1937–1945'. Unpublished paper, Conference on Republican China, Taipei, 1981

Eastman, Lloyd E. *Seeds of destruction: Nationalist China in war and revolution 1937–1949*. Stanford: Stanford University Press, 1984

Ebrey, Patricia and Watson, James. 'Kinship organization in late imperial China', forthcoming

Edwards, Dwight W. *Yenching University*. New York: United Board for Christian Higher Education in Asia, with a section by Y. P. Mei on Yenching in Chengtu, 1959

Eihara Masao 老原正雄, trans. *Shina ryokō nikki* 支那旅行日記 (Diary of travel in China). (Translation of Ferdinand von Richthofen, *Tagebücher aus China*.) 2 vols. Tokyo: Keiō shuppansha 慶應出版社, 1944

Elman, Benjamin. 'The unravelling of Neo-Confucianism: the Lower Yangtze academic community in late imperial China'. University of Pennsylvania, Ph.D. dissertation, 1980

Elman, Benjamin. *From philosophy to philology: intellectual and social aspects of change in late Imperial China*. Cambridge, Mass.: Council on East Asian Studies, Harvard University, 1984

Elvin, Mark. *The pattern of the Chinese past*. Stanford: Stanford University Press, 1973

Elvin, Mark. 'The administration of Shanghai, 1905–1914', in Mark Elvin and G. William Skinner, eds. *The Chinese city between two worlds*, 239–69

Elvin, Mark. 'Market towns and waterways: the county of Shang-hai from 1480 to 1910', in G. William Skinner, ed. *The city in late imperial China*, 441–73

Elvin, Mark and Skinner, G. William, eds. *The Chinese city between two worlds*. Stanford: Stanford University Press, 1974

d'Encausse, Hélène and Schram, Stuart R., eds. *Marxism and Asia*. London: Allen Lane, Penguin Press, 1969

Endicott, Stephen Lyon. *Diplomacy and enterprise: British China policy, 1933–1937*. Manchester: Manchester University Press; Vancouver, University of British Columbia Press, 1975

Eng, Robert. 'Imperialism and the Chinese economy: the Canton and Shanghai silk industry, 1861–1932'. University of California, Ph.D. dissertation, 1978

Epstein, Israel. *The unfinished revolution in China*. Boston: Little, Brown, 1947

Epstein, Israel. *Notes on labor problems in Nationalist China*. New York: Institute of Pacific Relations, 1949

'Erh-shih-pa hua sheng' 二十八畫生 [Mao Tse-tung]. 'T'i-yü chih yen-chiu' 體育之研究 (A study of physical education). *Hsin ch'ing-nien*, 3.2 (April 1917) 1–11 (sep. pag.)

Esherick, Joseph W., ed. *Lost chance in China: the World War II despatches of John S. Service*. New York: Random House, 1974

Esherick, Joseph W. *Reform and revolution in China: the 1911 Revolution in Hunan and Hubei*. Berkeley: University of California Press, 1976

Esherick, Joseph W. 'Number games: a note on land distribution in prerevolutionary China'. *Modern China*, 7.4 (Oct. 1981) 387–411

Esherick, Joseph (Chou Hsi-jui 周錫瑞). 'Lun I-ho-ch'üan yun-tung ti she-hui ch'eng-yin' 論義和拳運動的社會成因 (On the social causes of the Boxer movement). *Wen shih che* 文史哲 (Literature, history, and philosophy), 1 (1981) 22–31

Esherick, Joseph W. 'Symposium on peasant rebellions: some introductory comments'. *Modern China*, 9.3 (July 1983) 275–84

Esherick, Joseph W. *See* Grove, Linda

Esthus, Raymond A. *Theodore Roosevelt and Japan*. Seattle: University of Washington Press, 1966

Etō, Shinkichi 衛藤瀋吉. 'Hai-lu-feng—the first Chinese soviet government'. Pt I. *CQ* 8 (Oct.-Dec. 1961) 161–83; pt II, *CQ* 9 (Jan.-Mar. 1962) 149–81

Etō, Shinkichi. *Higashi-Ajia seijishi kenkyū* 東アジア政治史研究 (A study of East Asian political history). Tokyo: University of Tokyo Press, 1968

Etō, Shinkichi. *See* Miyazaki Tōten

Eudin, Xenia Joukoff and North, Robert C. *Soviet Russia and the East, 1920–1927; a documentary survey*. Stanford: Stanford University Press, 1957

Ewing, Thomas E. *Between the hammer and the anvil? Chinese and Russian policies in Outer Mongolia 1911–1921*. Bloomington: Indiana University Uralic and Altaic Series, vol. 138, 1980

Fairbank, John K. *Trade and diplomacy on the China coast: the opening of the treaty ports, 1842–1854*. Cambridge, Mass.: Harvard University Press, 1953

Fairbank, John K., ed. *Chinese thought and institutions*. Chicago: University of Chicago Press, 1957

Fairbank, John King, ed. *The Chinese world order: traditional China's foreign relations*. Cambridge, Mass.: Harvard University Press, 1968

Fairbank, John King. *Chinabound: a fifty-year memoir*. New York: Harper & Row, 1982

Fairbank, John K., ed. See *Cambridge history of China*.

Fairbank, John King and Liu, Kwang-Ching. *Modern China: a bibliographical guide to Chinese works, 1898–1937*. Harvard-Yenching Institute Studies, 1. Cambridge, Mass.: Harvard University Press, 1950; corrected reprint, 1961

Fairbank, John K. and Teng, Ssu-yü. *Ch'ing administration: three Studies*. Cambridge, Mass.: Harvard University Press, 1960

Fairbank, John King, Banno Masataka 坂野正高 and Yamamoto Sumiko 山本澄子, eds. *Japanese studies of modern China: a bibliographical guide to historical and social-science research on the 19th and 20th centuries*. Harvard-Yenching Institute Studies, 26. Tuttle, 1955; reissued Cambridge, Mass.: Harvard University Press, 1971

Fairbank, John King, Bruner, Katherine Frost and Matheson, Elizabeth MacLeod, eds. *The I.G. in Peking: letters of Robert Hart, Chinese Maritime Customs, 1868–1907*, with an intro. by L. K. Little. 2 vols. Cambridge, Mass.: Belknap Press of Harvard University Press, 1975

Fairbank, Wilma. 'Chinese educational needs and programs of US-located agencies to meet them: a report to UNESCO'. Unpublished Manuscript, 1948

Fairbank, Wilma C. *America's cultural experiment in China, 1942–1949*. Washington, DC: US Department of State, Bureau of Educational and Cultural Affairs, 1976. Department of State Publication 8839

Fairbank, Wilma C. *See* Liang Ssu-ch'eng

Fan Ch'ang-chiang 范長江. 'Chi-o-hsien shang ti jen' 饑餓線上的人 (People on the line of hunger). *Han-hsueh yueh-k'an* 汗血月刊 (Sweat and blood monthly), 9.4 (July 1937) 116–36

Fan-Chiang yun-tung shih 反蔣運動史 (History of the anti-Chiang movement), ed. by Chung-kuo ch'ing-nien chün-jen she 中國青年軍人社. Canton: 1934

Fang Chih 方治. 'Min-tsu wen-hua yü min-tsu ssu-hsiang' 民族文化與民族思想 (National culture and national thought). *Wen-hua chien-she* 文化建設 (Cultural reconstruction), 1.2 (10 Nov. 1934) 15–20

Fang Chih-ch'un 方志純. *Kan tung-pei Su-wei-ai ch'uang-li ti li-shih* 贛東北蘇維埃創立的歷史 (A history of the foundation of the Northeast Kiangsi Soviet). Peking: Jen-min, 1980

Fang Chih-p'ing 方治平 *et al. Lun kuan-liao tzu-pen* 論官僚資本 (On bureaucratic capital). Canton: Tsung-ho 綜合, 1946

Fang Hsien-t'ing 方顯廷, ed. *Chung-kuo ching-chi yen-chiu* 中國經濟研究 (Studies of the Chinese economy). 2 vols. Changsha: CP, 1938. See also Fong, H. D.

Farmer, Rhodes. *Shanghai harvest: a diary of three years in the China War.* London: Museum Press, 1945

Faure, David. 'Local political disturbances in Kiangsu province, China, 1870–1911'. Princeton University, Ph.D. dissertation, 1976

Faure, David. 'The rural economy of Kiangsu province, 1870–1911'. *Journal of the Institute of Chinese Studies,* Chinese University of Hong Kong, 9.2 (1978) 365–472

Fei Hsiao-t'ung 費孝通. *Peasant life in China: a field study of country life in the Yangtze valley.* Preface by Bronislaw Malinowski. New York: Dutton, 1939; London: G. Routledge, 1939; Kegan Paul, 1943; New York: Oxford University Press, 1946; London: Routledge & Kegan Paul, 1962; New York: AMS Press, 1976

Fei Hsiao-t'ung and Chang Chih-i 張之毅. *Earthbound China: a study of rural economy in Yunnan.* Chicago: University of Chicago Press, 1945; London: Routledge, 1949. Revised English edn prepared in collaboration with Paul Cooper and Margaret Park Redfield

Fei Hsiao-t'ung. *China's gentry: essays in rural-urban relations.* Chicago: University of Chicago Press, 1953. (Revised by Margaret Park Redfield with six life histories of Chinese gentry families collected by Yung-teh Chow: intro. by Robert Redfield: University of Chicago Press, 1980.)

Fei Hsiao-tung. See Arkush, David.

Feigon, Lee. *Chen Duxiu: founder of the Chinese Communist Party.* Princeton: Princeton University Press, 1983

Feis, Herbert. *The China tangle: the American effort in China from Pearl Harbor to the Marshall mission.* Princeton: Princeton University Press, 1953

Feng Ho-fa 馮和法, ed. *Chung-kuo nung-ts'un ching-chi tzu-liao* 中國農村經濟資料 (Materials on the Chinese rural economy). 2 vols. Shanghai: Li-ming shu-chü 黎明書局, 1933 and 1935

Feng Hsueh-feng 馮雪峯. *Hui-i Lu Hsun* 回憶魯迅 (Reminiscence of Lu

Hsun). Peking: Jen-min wen-hsueh 人民文學, 1952

Feng Yü-hsiang 馮玉祥. *Wo so-jen-shih-ti Chiang Chieh-shih* 我所認識的蔣介石 (The Chiang Kai-shek I know). Hong Kong: Wen-hua kung-ying-she 文化供應社, 1949

Fenn, William P. *The effect of the Japanese invasion on higher education in China.* Kowloon: China Institute of Pacific Relations, 1940

Fenn, William Purviance. *Christian higher education in changing China 1880–1950.* Grand Rapids, Michigan: Wm. B. Eerdmans, 1976

Ferguson, Mary E. *China Medical Board and Peking Union Medical College: a chronicle of fruitful collaboration, 1914–1951.* New York: China Medical Board of New York, 1970

Feuerwerker, Albert. *China's early industrialization, Sheng Hsuan-huai 1844–1916 and mandarin enterprise.* Cambridge, Mass.: Harvard University Press, 1958

Feuerwerker, Albert (Fei Wei-k'ai 費維愷). 'Lun erh-shih shih-chi ch'u-nien Chung-kuo she-hui wei-chi' 論二十世紀初年中國社會危機 (On the social crisis in early twentieth-century China), in Ts'ai Shang-ssu 蔡尚思, ed., *Lun Ch'ing-mo Min-ch'u Chung-kuo she-hui* 論清末民初中國社會 (Chinese society in the late Ch'ing and early Republic), 101–35

Feuerwerker, Albert, ed. *Chinese social and economic history from the Song to 1900: report of the American delegation to a Sino-American symposium, Beijing, 26 October – 1 November 1980.* Ann Arbor: Center for Chinese Studies, University of Michigan, 1982

Feuerwerker, Albert. 'Economic trends, 1912–49'. *CHOC* 12.28–127

Feuerwerker, Albert. 'The foreign presence in China'. *CHOC* 12.128–207

Feuerwerker, Yi-tsi Mei 梅儀慈. *Ding Ling's fiction—ideology and narrative in modern Chinese literature.* Cambridge, Mass.: Harvard University Press, 1983

Fewsmith, Joseph. *Party, state, and local elites in Republican China: merchant organizations and politics in Shanghai, 1890–1930.* Honolulu: University of Hawaii Press, 1984

Fifield, Russell H. *Woodrow Wilson and the Far East: the diplomacy of the Shantung question.* New York: Crowell, 1952; Hamden, Conn.: Archon Books, 1965

Fincher, John H. *Chinese democracy: the self-government movement in local, provincial and national politics, 1905–1914.* London: Croom Helm, 1981; Canberra, Australian National University Press, 1983

First Historical Archives, Peking. Chung-kuo ti-i li-shih tang-an-kuan 中國第一歷史檔案館

Fitzgerald, John. 'Mao in mufti: newly identified works by Mao Zedong'. *Australian Journal of Chinese Affairs*, 9 (Jan. 1983) 1–16

Fletcher, Joseph. 'Ch'ing Inner Asia c. 1800'. *CHOC* 10.35–106

Fletcher, Joseph. 'The heyday of the Ch'ing order in Mongolia, Sinkiang and Tibet'. *CHOC* 10.351–408

Fletcher, William Miles. *The search for a new order: intellectuals and fascism in prewar Japan*. Chapel Hill: University of North Carolina Press, 1982

Fogel, Joshua A. and Rowe, William T., eds. *Perspectives on a changing China: essays in honor of Professor C. Martin Wilbur*. Boulder, Colo.: Westview Press, 1979

Fogel, Joshua A. English translations published in *Ch'ing-shih wen-t'i* (*CSWT*) of Japanese bibliographical surveys of Japanese studies of modern China published in *Shigaku zasshi* (*SZ*) in two series as follows:
(1) 'Ming-Ch'ing studies in Japan: 1979', from *SZ* 89.5 (May 1980) 205–11 in *CSWT* 4.6 (Dec. 1981) 111–29; *ibid.* '. . . 1980' from *SZ* 90.5 (May 1981) 203–10 in *CSWT* 4.9 (June 1983) 77–102; *ibid.* '. . . 1981' from *SZ* 91.5 (May 1982) 212–19 in *CSWT* 4.9 (June 1983) 77–102
(2) 'Japanese studies of post-Opium War China: 1979', from *SZ* 89.5 (May 1980) 212–19 in *CSWT* 4.7 (June 1982) 91–113; *ibid.* '. . . 1980' from *SZ* 90.5 (May 1981) 210–19 in *CSWT* 4.9 (June 1983) 47–76; *ibid.* '. . . 1981' from *SZ* 91.5 (May 1982) 219–26 in *CSWT* 4.10 (Dec. 1983) 111–39

Fogel, Joshua A. *Politics and sinology: the case of Naitō Konan (1866–1934)*. Cambridge, Mass.: Council on East Asian Studies, Harvard University, 1984

Folsom, Kenneth. *Friends, guests and colleagues: the Mu-fu system in the late Ch'ing period*. Berkeley: University of California Press, 1968

Fong, H. D. (Fang Hsien-t'ing 方顯廷). *Reminiscences of a Chinese economist at 70*. South Seas Society Monographs, no. 17. Singapore: South Seas Press, 1975

'Food, famine and the Chinese state—a symposium'. *JAS* 41.4 (Aug. 1982) 685–801

Foreign Relations of the United States. See US Department of State

Foreign Service Journal. 11 issues per year. 1924 – (from 1924–1951 was called *American Foreign Service Journal* and *American Consular Bulletin*). Washington, DC: American Foreign Service Association

Fox, John P. *Germany and the Far Eastern crisis, 1931–1938: a study in diplomacy and ideology*. Oxford: Clarendon Press; New York: Oxford University Press, 1982

Freedman, Maurice, ed. *Family and kinship in Chinese society*. Stanford: Stanford University Press, 1970

Freedman, Maurice. 'On the sociological study of Chinese religion', in Arthur P. Wolf, ed. *Religion and ritual in Chinese society*, 19–42

Freedman, Maurice. *The study of Chinese society: essays*, selected and introduced by G. William Skinner. Stanford: Stanford University Press, 1979

Freyn, Hubert. *Prelude to war: the Chinese student rebellion of 1935–1936*. Shanghai: China Journal Publishing Co., 1939; Westport, Conn: Hyperion Reprint Service, 1977

Freyn, Hubert. *Chinese education in the war*. Shanghai: Kelly & Walsh, 1940

Freyn, Hubert. *Free China's New Deal*. New York: Macmillan, 1943

Friedman, Edward. *Backward toward revolution: the Chinese Revolutionary Party*.

Berkeley: University of California Press, 1974

FRUS. See US Department of State, *Foreign Relations of the United States.*

Fu Chu-fu 傅築夫. 'Jen-k'ou yin-su tui Chung-kuo she-hui ching-chi chieh-kou ti hsing-ch'eng ho fa-chan so ch'an-sheng ti chung-ta ying-hsiang' 人口因素對中國社會經濟結構的形成和發展所産生的重大影響 (The great effects of population factors on the formation and development of the Chinese social and economic structure), *Chung-kuo she-hui ching-chi shih yen-chiu* 中國社會經濟史研究 (Research in Chinese social and economic history), 3 (1982) 1–14

Fu-hsing Chung-kuo Kuo-min-tang chien-i: Hsin-sheng tsa-chih-she chih liu-tz'u ch'üan-kuo tai-piao ta-hui tai-piao i-chien shu 復興中國國民黨建議：新生雜誌社致六次全國代表大會代表意見書 (A proposal to revive the Kuomintang: a recommendation from the New Life Magazine to representatives in the Sixth Party Congress). n.p.: [1945]

Fu I-ling 傅衣凌. *Ming Ch'ing she-hui ching-chi shih lun-wen chi* 明清社會經濟史論文集 (Collected essays on Ming and Ch'ing social and economic history). n.p.: Jen-min, 1982

Fujiwara, Akira. 'The role of the Japanese Army', trans. by Shumpei Okamoto in Dorothy Borg and Shumpei Okamoto, eds. *Pearl Harbor as history: Japanese–American relations, 1931–1941,* 189–95

Fung, Edmund S. K. *The military dimension of the Chinese revolution: the New Army and its role in the Revolution of 1911.* Vancouver, BC: University of British Columbia Press, 1980

Furth, Charlotte. *Ting Wen-chiang: science and China's new culture.* Cambridge, Mass.: Harvard University Press, 1970

Furth, Charlotte. 'Intellectual change: from the reform movement to the May Fourth movement, 1895–1920'. *CHOC* 12.322–405

Furushima Kazuo 古島和雄. 'Kyū Chūgoku ni okeru tochi shoyū to sono seikaku' 旧中国における土地所有とその性格 (Land ownership and its characteristics in traditional China), in Yamamoto Hideo and Nomo Kiyoshi, comps. *Chūgoku nōson kakumei no tenkai*

Gaillard, Duval, and Guillot, Orincourt. *À travers la Normandie des XVIIème et XVIIIème siècles.* Caen: Cahiers des Annales de Normandie, no. 3, 1963

Galbiati, Fernando. 'P'eng P'ai, the leader of the first soviet: Hai-lu-feng, Kwangtung, China (1896–1929)'. 3 vols. University of Oxford, Ph.D. dissertation, 1981

Gamble, Sidney D. *Ting Hsien: a North China rural community.* Foreword by Y. C. James Yen. Field work directed by Franklin Ching-han Lee. New York: International Secretariat, Institute of Pacific Relations, 1954; reprinted Stanford: Stanford University Press, 1968

Gamble, Sidney D. and Burgess, J. S. *Peking: a social survey.* New York: Doran, 1921

Garrett, Shirley S. 'The chambers of commerce and the YMCA', in Mark

Elvin and G. William Skinner, eds. *The Chinese city between two worlds*, 213–38

Gasster, Michael. 'The republican revolutionary movement'. *CHOC* 11.463–534

Geisert, Bradley Kent. 'Power and society: the Kuomintang and local elites in Kiangsu province, China, 1924–1937'. University of Virginia, Ph.D. dissertation, 1979

Geisert, Bradley. 'Toward a pluralistic model of KMT rule'. *Chinese Republican Studies Newsletter*, 7.2 (Feb. 1982) 1–10

Gendaishi shiryō: Nit-Chū sensō 現代史資料：日中戦争 (Documents on contemporary history: the Sino-Japanese War). 5 vols. Tokyo: Misuzu shobō みすず書房, 1964–6

Gewurtz, Margo S. 'Social reality and educational reform: the case of the Chinese Vocational Educational Association 1917–1927'. *Modern China*, 4.2 (April 1978) 157–80

Gibbs, Donald A. and Li, Yun-chen, eds. *A bibliography of studies and translations of modern Chinese literature, 1918–1942*. Cambridge, Mass.: East Asian Research Center, Harvard University, 1975

Giles, Herbert A., ed. *A history of Chinese literature*. Reprint, New York: Frederick Ungar, 1967; 1st edn, 1901

Gillin, Donald G. *Warlord: Yen Hsi-shan in Shansi province, 1911–1949*. Princeton: Princeton University Press, 1967

Gillin, Donald G. 'Problems of centralization in Republican China: the case of Ch'en Ch'eng and the Kuomintang'. *JAS* 29.4 (Aug. 1970) 835–50

Gittings, John. *The role of the Chinese Red Army*. Royal Institute of International Affairs. London: Oxford University Press, 1967

Glunin, V. I. 'The Comintern and the rise of the communist movement in China (1920–1927)', in R. A. Ulyanovsky, ed. *The Comintern and the East*, 280–344

Goldblatt, Howard. *Hsiao Hung*. New York and Boston: Twayne, 1976

Goldblatt, Howard. *See* Ko Hao-wen

Goldman, Merle. *Literary dissent in Communist China*. Cambridge, Mass.: Harvard University Press, 1967

Goldman, Merle, ed. *Modern Chinese literature in the May Fourth era*. Cambridge, Mass.: Harvard University Press, 1977

Gray, Jack, ed. *Modern China's search for a political form*. London: Oxford University Press, 1969

Grieder, Jerome B. *Hu Shih and the Chinese renaissance*. Cambridge, Mass.: Harvard University Press, 1970

Grieder, Jerome B. *Intellectuals and the state in modern China: a narrative history*. New York: Free Press; London: Collier Macmillan, 1981

Griffith, Samuel B., trans. *Mao Tse-tung on guerrilla warfare*. New York: Praeger, 1961. Published also as Mao Tse-tung and Che Guevarra, *Guerrilla warfare*. London: Cassell, 1964

Griffith, Samuel B. *The Chinese People's Liberation Army*. New York: McGraw-Hill, 1967

Grigoriev, A. M. 'The Comintern and the revolutionary movement in China under the slogan of the soviets (1927–1931)', in R. A. Ulyanovsky, ed. *The Comintern and the East*, 345–88. Evidently a translation of L. P. Deliusin, ed. *Komintern i vostok*

Grimm, Tilemann. 'Academies and urban systems in Kwangtung', in G. William Skinner, ed. *The city in late imperial China*, 475–98

Grove, Linda. 'Rural society in revolution: the Gaoyang district, 1910–1947'. University of California, Berkeley, Ph.D. dissertation, 1975

Grove, Linda. 'Creating a northern soviet'. *Modern China*, 1.3 (July 1975) 243–70

Grove, Linda and Esherick, Joseph. 'From feudalism to capitalism: Japanese scholarship on the transformation of Chinese rural society'. *Modern China*, 6.4 (Oct. 1980) 397–438

The guide weekly. See *Hsiang-tao chou-pao*

Guillermaz, Jacques. *A history of the Chinese Communist Party, 1921–1949*. London: Methuen; New York: Random House, 1972. Trans. by Anne Destenay of *Histoire du parti communiste chinois 1921–49*. Paris: Payot, 1968

Gunn, Edward Mansfield, Jr. 'Chinese writers under Japanese occupation (1937–45)'. Report on research in progress, Columbia University, Sept. 1976

Gunn, Edward Mansfield, Jr. 'Chinese literature in Shanghai and Peking (1937–45)'. Columbia University, Ph.D. dissertation, 1978

Gunn, Edward M., Jr. *Unwelcome muse: Chinese literature in Shanghai and Peking, 1937–1945*. New York: Columbia University Press, 1980

Gunn, Edward M., Jr., ed. *Twentieth-century Chinese drama: an anthology*. Bloomington: Indiana University Press, 1983

Hall, J. C. S. *The Yunnan provincial faction, 1927–1937*. Canberra: Australian National University, 1976

Hamilton, Gary G. 'Regional associations and the Chinese city: a comparative perspective'. *Comparative Studies in Society and History*, 21.3 (July 1979) 346–61

Hao, Yen-p'ing 郝延平 and Wang, Erh-min 王爾敏. 'Changing Chinese views of Western relations, 1840–95'. *CHOC* 11.142–201

Harrell, Stevan. *Ploughshare village: culture and context in Taiwan*. Seattle: University of Washington Press, 1982

Harrell, Stevan and Perry, Elizabeth J. 'Syncretic sects in Chinese society: an introduction'. *Modern China*, 8.3 (July 1982) 283–303

Harrison, James P. 'The Li Li-san line and the CCP in 1930'. *CQ* Part I, 14 (Apr.-June 1963), 178–94; Part II, 15 (July-Sept. 1963) 140–59

Harrison, James P. *The Communists and Chinese peasant rebellions: a study in the rewriting of Chinese history*. New York: Atheneum, 1969

Harrison, James Pinckney. *The long march to power: a history of the Chinese Communist Party, 1921–72.* New York: Praeger, 1972

Hartford, Kathleen. 'Repression and Communist success: the case of Jin-Cha-Ji, 1938–1943'. Unpublished manuscript

Hartford, Kathleen. 'Step-by-step: reform, resistance and revolution in the Chin-Ch'a-Chi border region, 1937–1945'. Stanford University, Ph.D. dissertation, 1980

Harvard Journal of Asiatic Studies. Cambridge, Mass.: Harvard-Yenching Institute, 1936–

Haslam, Nathan. 'Soviet aid to China and Japan's place in Moscow's foreign policy, 1937–1939', in Ian Nish, ed. *Some aspects of Soviet–Japanese relations in the 1930s.*

Hata Ikuhiko 秦郁彦. *Nitchū sensō shi* 日中戦争史 (History of the Japanese–Chinese war). Rev. edn, Tokyo: Kawade shobō shinsha 河出書房新社, 1971

Hatano Ken'ichi 波多野乾一, comp. *Gendai Shina no kiroku* 現代支那之記録 (Records of contemporary China). Monthly. Peking: 1924–1932. 23 reels.

Hatano Yoshihiro 波多野善大. *Kok-Kyō gassaku* 国共合作 (The Kuomintang-Communist alliance). Tokyo: Chūō Kōronsha 中央公論社, 1973

Hay, Stephen N. *Asian ideas of east and west: Tagore and his critics in Japan, China, and India.* Cambridge, Mass.: Harvard University Press, 1970

Hayes, James W. 'Old ways of life in Kowloon: the Cheng Sha Wan villages'. *Journal of Oriental Studies*, 8.1 (Jan. 1970) 154–88

Hayford, Charles. 'Rural reconstruction in China: Y. C. James Yen and the Mass Education Movement'. Harvard University, Ph.D. dissertation, 1973

Hazama Naoki 狭間直樹, Kataoka Kazutada 片岡一忠 and Fujimoto Hiroo 藤本博生. *Go-shi undō no kenkyū* 五四運動の研究 (Studies of the May Fourth movement). Tokyo: Dōhōsha Shuppan 同朋舎出版, 1982

HC. See Mao Tse-tung, *Hsuan-chi*

HCPP. See *Hung-ch'i p'iao-p'iao*

Heinlein, Joseph H., Jr. 'Political warfare: the Chinese Nationalist model'. American University, Ph.D. dissertation, 1974

Heinzig, D. 'The Otto Braun memoirs and Mao's rise to power'. *CQ* 46 (April-June, 1971) 274–88

Heliot, P. 'La guerre dite de Lustucru et les privilèges du Boulonnais'. *Revue du Nord* (Lille), 21 (1935) 265–318

Hershatter, Gail. 'Flying hammers, walking chisels: the workers of Santiaoshi'. *Modern China*, 9.4 (Oct. 1983) 387–420

HHLY. See *Hsing-huo liao-yuan*, also Liu Po-ch'eng for *HHLY* Hong Kong

Higashi Norimasa 東則正, comp. *Chūbu Shina keizai chōsa* 中部支那經濟調査 (Research on the economy of Central China). Tokyo: Fuzambō 富山房, vol. 1, 1915

Hildebrand, Klaus, trans. by Anthony Fothergill. *The foreign policy of the*

Third Reich. Berkeley: University of California Press, 1973

Hinton, William. *Fanshen: a documentary of revolution in a Chinese village.* New York: Random House, 1968

HJAS. See *Harvard Journal of Asiatic Studies*

HMHHTL. See *Hsin-min hsueh-hui tzu-liao*

Ho Ch'ang-kung 何長工. *Ch'in-kung chien-hsueh sheng-huo hui-i* 勤工儉學生活回憶 (Memoirs of the work-study programme). Peking: Kung-jen ch'u-pan-she 工人出版社, 1958

Ho Ch'i-fang. See McDougall, Bonnie S.

Ho, Franklin L. 'The reminiscences of Ho Lien 何廉 (Franklin L. Ho)', as told to Crystal Lorch, postscript dated July 1966. Unpublished manuscript in Special Collections Library, Butler Library, Columbia University. See also Ho Lien

Ho, Franklin L. 'First attempts to transform Chinese agriculture, 1927–1937: comments', in Paul K. T. Sih, ed. *The strenuous decade: China's nation-building efforts, 1927–1937,* 233–36

Ho Kan-chih 何幹之. *Chung-kuo hsien-tai ko-ming shih* 中國現代革命史 (A history of the modern Chinese revolution). Peking: Pei-ching kao-teng chiao-yü ch'u-pan-she 北京高等教育出版社, 1958, 2 vols; Hong Kong: San-lien, 1958. English edn, Peking: Foreign Languages Press, 1960

Ho Lien. 'The reminiscences of Ho Lien (Franklin L. Ho)'. Chinese Oral History Project, Columbia University, 1975. (Microfilming Corporation of America)

Ho Ling-hsiu 何齡修 *et al.*, comps. *Feng-chien kuei-tsu ta-ti-chu ti tien-hsing—K'ung-fu yen-chiu* 封建貴族大地主的典型—孔府研究 (A model feudal noble great landlord—studies of the Confucian family estates). Peking: Chung-kuo she-hui k'o-hsueh ch'u-pan-she, 1981

Ho Meng-hsiung 何孟雄. 'Ho Meng-hsiung i-chien-shu' 何孟雄意見書 (Ho Meng-hsiung's letters), 1, 1930 (mimeographed)

Ho Ping-sung 何炳松. 'San-shih-wu-nien lai Chung-kuo chih ta-hsueh chiao-yü' 三十五年來中國之大學教育 (Chinese higher education in the past 35 years), in Ts'ai Yuan-p'ei *et al. Wan-Ch'ing san-shih-wu-nien lai chih Chung-kuo chiao-yü, 1897–1931*

Ho Ping-ti 何炳棣. *Studies on the population of China, 1368–1953.* Cambridge, Mass.: Harvard University Press, 1959

Ho Ping-ti. *The ladder of success in imperial China: aspects of social mobility, 1368–1911.* New York: Columbia University Press, 1962

Ho Ping-ti. *Chung-kuo hui-kuan shih-lun* 中國會館史論 (A historical survey of Landsmannshaften in China). Taipei: Hsueh-sheng 學生, 1966

Ho Ping-ti and Tsou Tang 鄒讜, eds. *China in crisis.* 3 vols. Chicago: University of Chicago Press, 1968

Ho Ping-ti. 'Salient aspects of China's heritage', in Ping-ti Ho and Tang Tsou, eds. *China's heritage and the communist political system,* vol. 1 of *China in crisis*

Ho Ying-ch'in 何應欽. 'Chin-hou chih Chung-kuo Kuo-min-tang' 今後之中國國民黨 (The Chinese Kuomintang from now on). *Chung-yang pan-yueh-k'an*, 2 (Oct. 1927) 99–103

Ho Ying-ch'in. 'Chi-nien ch'i-ch'i k'ang-chan tsai po Chung-kung ti hsu-wei hsuan-ch'uan' 紀念七七抗戰再駁中共的虛偽宣傳 (Commemorating the Sino-Japanese War and again refuting the Communists' false propaganda). Part II. *Tzu-yu chung*, 3.3 (20 Sept. 1972), 26–30

Ho Ying-ch'in. *Pa-nien k'ang-chan chih ching-kuo* 八年抗戰之經過 (Experiences in the eight-year war of resistance). Taipei: Wen-hai, 1972

Hobsbawm, Eric. *Primitive rebels*. New York: Norton, 1965

Hofheinz, Roy, Jr. 'Peasant movement and rural revolution: Chinese Communists in the countryside, 1923–1927'. Harvard University, Ph.D. dissertation, 1966

Hofheinz, Roy. 'The Autumn Harvest uprising'. *CQ* 32 (Oct.–Dec. 1967) 37–87

Hofheinz, Roy, Jr. 'The ecology of Chinese communist success: rural influence patterns, 1923–1945', in A. Doak Barnett, ed. *Chinese Communist politics in action*, 3–77

Hofheinz, Roy, Jr. *The broken wave: the Chinese communist peasant movement, 1922–1928*. Cambridge, Mass.: Harvard University Press, 1977

Hōgaku kenkyū. See McDonald, A.

Hogan, Michael J. *Informal entente: the private structure of cooperation in Anglo-American economic diplomacy, 1918–1928*. Columbia: University of Missouri Press, 1977

Hokushi no chiansen. See Bōeicho senshishitsu

Holden, Reuben Andrus. *Yale in China: the mainland, 1901–1951*. New Haven: The Yale in China Association, 1964

Holland, W. L. and Mitchell, Kate L., eds., assisted by Harriet Moore and Richard Pyke. *Problems of the Pacific, 1936. Aims and results of social and economic policies in Pacific countries: proceedings of the sixth conference of the Institute of Pacific relations, Yosemite National Park, California, 15–29 August 1936*. Chicago: University of Chicago Press, 1937

Holoch, Donald, trans. *Seeds of peasant revolution: report on the Haifeng peasant movement by P'eng P'ai*. Ithaca: Cornell University China–Japan Program, 1973

Honig, Emily. 'Women cotton mill workers in Shanghai, 1912–1949'. Stanford University, Ph.D. dissertation, 1982

Honig, Emily. 'The contract labor system and women workers: pre-liberation cotton mills of Shanghai'. *Modern China*, 9.4 (Oct. 1983) 421–54

Horikawa Takeo 堀川武夫. *Kyokutō kokusai seijishi josetsu—21 kajō yōkyū no kenkyū* 極東国際政治史序説―二十一箇条要求の研究 (Introduction to the history of Far Eastern international politics: a study of the Twenty-One Demands). Tokyo: Yūhikaku 有斐閣, 1958

Hosoya Chihiro 細谷千博 and Saitō Makoto 斎藤真. *Washington taisei to*

Nichi-Bei kankei ワシントン体制と日米関係 (The Washington conference system and Japanese–American relations). Tokyo: Tokyo Daigaku Shuppankai, 1978

Hou, Chi-ming 侯繼明. *Foreign investment and economic development in China, 1840–1937.* Cambridge, Mass.: Harvard University Press, 1965

Hou, Chi-ming and Yu, Tzong-shien 于宗先, eds. *Modern Chinese economic history: proceedings of the Conference of Modern Chinese Economic History, Academia Sinica, Taipei, Taiwan, Republic of China, August 26–29, 1977.* Taipei: Institute of Economics, Academia Sinica; Seattle: distributed by University of Washington Press, 1979

Hou Chien 侯健. *Ts'ung wen-hsueh ko-ming tao ko-ming wen-hsueh* 從文學革命到革命文學 (From literary revolution to revolutionary literature). Taipei: Chung-wai wen-hsueh 中外文學, 1974

Hou Hou-chi 侯厚吉 and Wu Ch'i-ching 吳其敬, eds. *Chung-kuo chin-tai ching-chi ssu-hsiang shih-kao* 中國近代經濟思想史稿 (Draft history of modern Chinese economic thought). Harbin: Jen-min, 1982

Howe, Christopher, ed. *Shanghai: revolution and development in an Asian metropolis.* Cambridge: Cambridge University Press, 1981

Hsi-lo-k'e-fu 西洛可夫 [Shirokov] *et al.*, trans. by Li Ta 李達 *et al. Pien-cheng-fa wei-wu-lun chiao-ch'eng* 辯證法唯物論教程 (Course of instruction in dialectical materialism). Shanghai: Pi-keng-t'ang shu-tien 筆耕堂書店, 15 May 1933

Hsia, C. T. 夏志清 'Obsession with China: the moral burden of modern Chinese literature', in C. T. Hsia, *A history of modern Chinese fiction*, 533–54

Hsia, C. T. *A history of modern Chinese fiction.* New Haven: Yale University Press, 2nd edn, 1971

Hsia, C. T., ed. *Twentieth-century Chinese stories.* New York: Columbia University Press, 1971

Hsia, C. T. 'The fiction of Tuan-mu Hung-liang'. Paper delivered at the Dedham conference on modern Chinese literature (Aug. 1974)

Hsia-men ta-hsueh li-shih-hsi 厦門大學歷史系, ed. *Chung-kuo she-hui ching-chi shih yen-chiu* ('Zhongguo shehui jingjishi yanjiu') 中國社會經濟史研究 (Studies in Chinese social and economic history). Amoy, 1982–

Hsia, Tsi-an 夏濟安. *The gate of darkness: studies on the leftist literary movement in China.* Seattle: University of Washington Press, 1968

Hsiang-chiang p'ing-lun 湘江評論 (Hsiang River review). Changsha, 14 July 1919–

Hsiang-ning hsien-chih 鄉寧縣志 (Hsiang-ning county gazetteer), 1917

Hsiang-pao lei-tsuan 湘報類纂 (Classified compilation of articles from the *Hsiang-pao*). Shanghai: Chung-hua pien-i yin-shu kuan 中華編譯印書館, 1902; Taipei reprint: Ta-t'ung 大通, 1968

Hsiang River review. See *Hsiang-chiang p'ing-lun*

Hsiang-tao 嚮導 (The guide) also *Hsiang-tao chou-pao* 嚮導週報 (The guide weekly), official organ of the Central Committee, CCP, ed. Ch'en Tu-hsiu *et al.* 13 Sept. 1922–18 July 1927

Hsiao Ch'ao-jan 蕭超然 *et al. Pei-ching ta-hsueh-hsiao-shih, 1898–1949* 北京大學校史, 1898–1949 (A history of Peking University, 1898–1949). Shanghai: Shang-hai chiao-yü ch'u-pan-she 上海教育出版社, 1981

Hsiao Cheng 蕭錚, ed. *Min-kuo erh-shih nien-tai Chung-kuo ta-lu t'u-ti wen-t'i tzu-liao* 民國二十年代中國大陸土地問題資料 (Materials on land problems in mainland China during the 1930s). 200 vols. Taipei: Ch'eng-wen 成文, 1977

Hsiao Cheng. *T'u-ti kai-ko wu-shih-nien: Hsiao Cheng hui-i-lu* 土地改革五十年: 蕭錚回憶錄 (Fifty years of land reform: the memoirs of Hsiao Cheng). Taipei: Chung-kuo t'u-ti kai-ko yen-chiu-so 中國土地改革研究所, 1980

Hsiao Hsin-i. 'Économie et société rurale du Sichuan (Szechwan) de 1927 à 1945'. École Pratique des Hautes Études, Paris. Ph.D. dissertation, 1972

Hsiao Hung 蕭紅. *Two novels of northeastern China: The field of life and death and Tales of Hulan River*, trans. by Howard Goldblatt and Ellen Yeung. Bloomington: Indiana University Press, 1979

Hsiao Kung-chuan 蕭公權. *Rural China: imperial control in the nineteenth century*. Seattle: University of Washington Press, 1960

Hsiao Liang-lin, *China's foreign trade statistics 1864–1949*. Cambridge, Mass.: Harvard University Press, 1974

Hsiao Sheng 蕭牲 and Chiang Hua-hsuan 姜華宣. 'Ti-i-tz'u Kuo-Kung ho-tso t'ung-i chan-hsien ti hsing-ch'eng' 第一次國共合作統一戰線的形成 (The formation of the first Kuomintang-Communist united front). *Li-shih yen-chiu* 歷史研究, 2 (1981) 51–68

Hisao Tso-liang. *Power relations within the Chinese communist movement, 1930–1934*. Seattle: University of Washington Press, 1961

Hsiao Tso-liang. *The land revolution in China, 1930–1934: a study of documents*. Seattle: University of Washington Press, 1969

Hsiao Tso-liang. *Chinese communism in 1927: city vs. countryside*. Hong Kong: The Chinese University of Hong Kong, 1970

Hsieh Chen-min 謝振民. *Chung-hua min-kuo li-fa-shih* 中華民國立法史 (History of legislation in the Republic of China). Nanking: Cheng-chung, 1948

Hsieh, Winston 謝文孫. 'Peasant insurrection and the marketing hierarchy in the Canton delta, 1911', in Mark Elvin and G. William Skinner, eds. *The Chinese city between two worlds*, 119–41.

Hsieh, Winston. 'Guild capitalism in village China; the legacy of rural entrepreneurship in the Canton delta, 1875–1925'. Paper presented at the Columbia University Seminar on Modern China, November 1982

Hsien-tai 現代 (Contemporary). Shanghai: Hsien-tai shu-chü, 1932–35

Hsin che-hsueh ta-kang. See Mi-ting

Hsin chiao-yü 新教育 (The new education). Shanghai: Feb. 1919–Oct. 1925

Hsin-ching-chi 新經濟 (New economics). Chungking, 1938–

Hsin-ch'ing-nien 新青年 (The new youth), ed. Ch'en Tu-hsiu *et al.* Original name, *Ch'ing-nien tsa-chih* 青年雜誌 (Youth magazine), Shanghai, 15 Sept. 1915–15 Feb. 1916; *La Jeunesse, New Youth*, Peking, 1 Sept. 1916–1 May 1920; Shanghai, 1 Sept. 1920–1 April 1921; Canton, 1 May 1921–1 July 1922. *New Youth Quarterly* (official organ of the CCP), Canton, 15 June 1923–25 July 1926

Hsin-ch'uang-tsao 新創造 (New creation). Shanghai, 1932–

Hsin-hai ko-ming hui-i lu 辛亥革命回憶錄 (Reminiscences of the 1911 Revolution). Comp. by the Research Committee on Historical Sources, Chinese People's Political Consultative Conference. Peking: CH, 1961– (five volumes seen)

Hsin Hu-nan pao 新湖南報. *Hu-nan nung-ts'un ch'ing-k'uang tiao-ch'a* 湖南農村情況調查 (A survey of village conditions in Hunan). Hankow: Hsin-hua shu-tien 新華書店, 1950

Hsin hua jih-pao 新華日報 (New China daily news). Hankow, 1938–; Chungking, 1942–

Hsin kuan-ch'ang hsien-hsing chi 新官場現形記 (A new 'current situation in officialdom'). n.p.: 1946

Hsin-min hsueh-hui tzu-liao 新民學會資料 (Materials on the New People's Study Society), ed. by Chung-kuo ko-ming po-wu kuan 中國革命博物館. Hu-nan sheng po-wu kuan 湖南省博物館 (Chung-kuo hsien-tai ko-ming shih tzu-liao ts'ung-k'an 中國現代革命史資料叢刊) Peking: Jen-min, 1980

Hsin-shih-chieh yueh-k'an 新世界月刊 (New world monthly). Chungking, July 1932–

Hsin wen-hsueh shih-liao 新文學史料 (Historical materials on new literature). Peking: Jen-min wen-hsueh ch'u-pan-she 人民文學出版社, 1978–

Hsin-wen t'ien-ti 新聞天地 (News world). Hong Kong. Jan. 1945–

Hsing-cheng-yuan nung-ts'un fu-hsing wei-yuan-hui 行政院農村復興委員會, comp. *Chung-kuo nung-ts'un tiao-ch'a tzu-liao wu-chung: Chiang-su sheng nung-ts'un tiao-ch'a* 中國農村調查資料五種：江蘇省農村調查 (Five examples of Chinese village survey materials: Kiangsu province village surveys). Taipei: vol. 1–4, 1971

Hsing-cheng-yuan nung-ts'un fu-hsing wei-yuan-hui, comp. *Shan-hsi sheng nung-ts'un tiao-ch'a* 陝西省農村調查 (A survey of villages in Shensi province). Taipei: Hsueh-hai ch'u-pan-she 學海出版社, 1971

Hsing-huo liao-yuan 星火燎原 (A single spark can start a prairie fire). ed. by The People's Liberation Army. 10 vols. Peking: Jen-min wen-hsueh ch'u-pan-she 人民文學出版社, 1958–63

Hsiung, James Chieh 熊玠. *Ideology and practice. The evolution of Chinese communism*. New York: Praeger, 1970

Hsu, Francis L. K. 許烺光. *Under the ancestors' shadow: Chinese culture and personality*. New York: Columbia University Press, 1948; 2nd ed. with subtitle *kinship, personality, and social mobility in village China*, Garden City, NY: Anchor Books, 1967; 3rd edn, *Kinship, personality, and social mobility in China*, Stanford: Stanford University Press, 1971

Hsu Fu-kuan 徐復觀. 'Shih shui chi k'uei-le Chung-kuo she-hui fan-kung ti li-liang?' 是誰擊潰了中國社會反共的力量 (Who is it that destroys the anti-Communist power of Chinese society?) *Min-chu p'ing-lun* 民主評論, 1.7 (16 Sept. 1949) 5–7

Hsu, Kai-yu 許芥昱, trans. and ed. *Twentieth-century Chinese poetry; an anthology.* Garden City, NY: Doubleday, 1963; New York: Anchor, 1964; Ithaca: Cornell University Press, 1970

Hsu, Kai-yu. *Wen I-to.* Boston: Twayne, 1981

Hsu, Chieh-yu (Hsu Kai-yu) 許芥昱, *Hsin-shih ti k'ai-lu jen—Wen I-to* 新詩的開路人一聞一多 (A trail blazer of the new poetry—Wen I-to). Hong Kong, 1982

Hsu, King-i. 'Agrarian policies of the Chinese Soviet Republic, 1931–1934'. Indiana University, Ph.D. dissertation, 1971

Hsu Long-hsueh and Chang Ming-kai, comps. *History of the Sino–Japanese War, 1937–1945,* trans. by Wen Ha-hsiung. Taipei: Chung Wu Publishing Co., 1971

Hsu Ti-hsin 許滌新. 'K'ang-chan i-lai liang-ko chieh-tuan ti Chung-kuo ching-chi' 抗戰以來兩個階段底中國經濟 (China's economy during the two stages of the war). *Li-lun yü hsien-shih,* 1.4 (15 Feb. 1940) 33–46

Hsu Ti-hsin. *Kuan-liao tzu-pen lun* 官僚資本論 (On bureaucratic capital). Hong Kong: Nan-yang 南洋, 1947

Hsu Ying-lien 許鶯連 *et al. Ch'üan-kuo hsiang-ts'un chien-she yun-tung kai-k'uang* 全國鄉村建設運動概況 (General account of the nation-wide rural reconstruction movement). 2 vols. Tsou-p'ing: Shan-tung hsiang-ts'un chien-she yen-chiu-yuan 山東鄉村建設研究院, 1935

Hsu Yun-pei 徐運北. 'Ts'an chün yun-tung chien-pao' 參軍運動簡報 (A brief report on the army recruiting movement), in *I-chiu-ssu-ch'i-nien shang-pan-nien lai ch'ü tang wei kuan-yü t'u kai yun-tung ti chung-yao wen-chien* 一九四七年上半年來區黨委關於土改運動的重要文件 (Regional party commission's important documents concerning land reform movement since the first half of 1947), 69–77. Chi-Lu-Yü ch'ü-tang-wei 冀魯豫區黨委, June 1947

Hsueh Chün-tu 薛君度, comp. *The Chinese communist movement,* vol. 1. *1921–1937;* vol. 2. *1937–1949.* Stanford: Hoover Institution, 1960, 1962

Hsueh, Chün-tu. *Huang Hsing and the Chinese revolution.* Stanford: Stanford University Press, 1961

Hsueh-fu chi-wen 學府紀聞 (Records and reminiscences of academic institutions). 21 vols. Taipei: Nan-ching 南京, 1981

Hsueh-hsi yü p'i-p'an 學習與批判 (Study and criticism). Shanghai, Sept. 1973–

Hsueh Mu-ch'iao 薛暮橋. *K'ang-Jih chan-cheng shih-ch'i ho chieh-fang chan-cheng shih-ch'i Shan-tung chieh-fang-ch'ü ti ching-chi kung-tso* 抗日戰爭時期和解放戰爭時期山東解放區的經濟工作 (Economic work in the Shantung liberated areas during the anti-Japanese and civil wars). Peking: Jen-min jih-pao she 人民日報社, 1979

Hsueh Yueh 薛岳. *Chiao-fei chi-shih* 剿匪紀實 (A factual account of the campaigns against the bandits). Taipei, 1962

Hu, Chi-hsi. 'Hua Fu, the fifth encirclement campaign and the Tsunyi conference'. *CQ* 43 (July-Sept. 1970) 31–46

Hu, Chi-hsi. *L'Armée rouge et l'ascension de Mao*. Paris: Éditions de l'École des Hautes Études en Sciences Sociales, 1982

Hu Chin-ch'üan 胡金銓. *Lao She ho t'a-ti tso-p'in* 老舍和他的作品 (Lao She and his works). Hong Kong: Wen-hua·Sheng-huo ch'u-pan-she 文化·生活出版社, 1977

Hu Chu-sheng 胡珠生. 'Ch'ing-pang shih ch'u-t'an' 青幫史初探 (A preliminary inquiry into the history of the Green Gang). *Li-shih hsueh* 歷史學 (Historical studies), 3 (1979) 102–20

Hu Feng 胡風. *Min-tsu chan-cheng yü wen-i hsing-ko* 民族戰爭與文藝性格 (The national war and the character of literature). Chungking: Hsi-wang she 希望社, 1946

Hu Hua 胡華. *Chung-kuo hsin-min-chu chu-i ko-ming-shih ts'an-k'ao tzu-liao* 中國新民主主義革命史參考資料 (Historical materials on the Chinese new democratic revolution). Peking; Shanghai: CP, 1951

Hu Hua. *Chung-kuo ko-ming-shih chiang-i* 中國革命史講義 (Lectures on the history of the Chinese Revolution). Revised edn. 2 vols. Peking: Chinese People's University, 1979

Hu Hua. *Chung-kung tang-shih jen-wu-chuan* 中共黨史人物傳 (Biographies of eminent members of the CCP). Sian: Jen-min, 1981 (six volumes published up to 1982)

Hu, John Y. H. 胡耀恆. *Ts'ao Yü*. New York: Twayne, 1972

Hu-pei-sheng-cheng-fu pao-kao, 1942/4-10 湖北省政府報告, 1942/4-10 (Report of the Hupei provincial government, April-October, 1942). n.p: n.d.

Hu-pei-sheng-cheng-fu pao-kao, 1943/10-1944/9 湖北省政府報告 1943/10-1944/9 (Report of the Hupei provincial government, October 1943 to September 1944). n.p.: n.d.

Hu shang-chiang Tsung-nan nien-p'u 胡上將宗南年譜 (Chronological biography of General Hu Tsung-nan). Taipei: Wen-hai 文海, n.d.

Hu Sheng 胡繩. *Imperialism and Chinese politics, 1840–1925*. Peking: Foreign Languages Press, 1955 (first published in Chinese, 1948); Arlington, Va: University Publications of America, 1975

Hu Shih 胡適. *China, too, is fighting to defend a way of life*. Address, Washington, DC, March 1942. (Ann Arbor: University Microfilms International, 1980)

Hu Shih, *et al*. *Ting Wen-chiang che-ko jen* 丁文江這個人 (Ting Wen-chiang as a person). Taipei: Chuan-chi wen-hsueh, 1967

Hu Shih. 'Chang Po-ling, educator', in J. L. Buck *et al*. *There is another China*, 4–14

Hu Shih. 'Chin-jih chiao-hui chiao-yü ti nan-kuan' 今日教會教育的難關 (Difficulties facing Christian education today), in Hu Shih, *Hu Shih wen-ts'un*, 3. 728–36

Hu Shih. *Hu Shih wen-ts'un* 胡適文存 (Collected writings of Hu Shih), first to fourth series. Taipei: Yuan-tung t'u-shu kung-ssu 遠東圖書公司, 1953

Hu Shih. *Hu Shih liu-hsueh jih-chi* 胡適留學日記 (Diaries of Hu Shih as a student abroad). Taipei: CP, 1959

Hua Kang 華崗. *Chung-kuo min-tsu chieh-fang yun-tung-shih* 中國民族解放運動史 (A history of the Chinese liberation movement). 2 vols. Shanghai: Tu-shu, 1947

Hua-tzu jih-pao 華字日報 (The Chinese mail). Hong Kong, 1864–

Huang, Chen-hsia. See Whitson, William

Huang, Chien-chung 黃建中. 'Shih-nien-lai ti Chung-kuo kao-teng chiao-yü' 十年來的中國高等教育 (Higher education in China in the past ten years), in *K'ang-chan ch'ien shih-nien chih Chung-kuo*, 503–30

Huang Fu-ch'ing 黃福慶. *Ch'ing-mo liu-Jih hsueh-sheng* 清末留日學生 (Chinese students in Japan in the late Ch'ing period). Taipei: IMH, 1975

Huang Fu-ch'ing. *Chin-tai Jih-pen tsai Hua wen-hua chi she-hui shih-yeh chih yen-chiu* 近代日本在華文化及社會事業之研究 (Japanese social and cultural enterprises in China 1898–1945). Taipei: IMH, 1982

Huang I-p'ing 黃逸平, comp. *Chung-kuo chin-tai ching-chi shih lun-wen hsuan-chi* 中國近代經濟史論文選集 (A collection of studies on Chinese modern economic history). 5 vols. Shanghai: Shang-hai shih-fan ta-hsueh Li-shih-hsi 上海師範大學歷史系, 1979

Huang, Philip C. C. 黃宗智. 'Mao Tse-tung and the middle peasants, 1925–1928'. *Modern China*, 1.3 (July 1975) 271–96

Huang, Philip C. C. 'Intellectuals, Lumpenproletarians, workers, and peasants in the Communist movement: the case of Xingguo county, 1927–1934', in Philip C. C. Huang *et al. Chinese Communists and rural society, 1927–1934*

Huang, Philip C. C. *The peasant economy and social change in North China.* Stanford: Stanford University Press, 1985

Huang, Philip C. C., Bell, Lynda Schaefer and Walker, Kathy Lemons. *Chinese Communists and rural society, 1927–1934.* Berkeley: Center for Chinese Studies, University of California, 1978

Huang Tsun-hsien 黃遵憲. 'Speech to the Southern Study Society' in *Hsiang-pao lei-tsuan* 湘報類纂, 307–11

Huang Yen-p'ei 黃炎培 and P'ang Sung 龐淞, comps. *Chung-kuo shang-chan shih-pai shih* 中國商戰失敗史 (The history of China's commercial struggles and failures). Hong Kong, 1966. Republished in 1966 by Lung Men Press as *Chung-kuo ssu-shih-nien hai-kuan shang-wu t'ung-chi t'u-piao: (1876–1915)* 中國四十年海關商務統計圖表 1876–1915 (Statistical tables of China's 40 years of Maritime Customs and commercial affairs)

Hueneman, Ralph William. *The dragon and the iron horse: the economics of railroads in China 1876–1937.* Cambridge, Mass.: Council on East Asian Studies, Harvard University, 1984

Hummel, Arthur W., ed. *Eminent Chinese of the Ch'ing period, 1644–1912.* 2 vols. Washington, DC: United States Government Printing Office,

1943–4; Taipei: Ch'eng Wen, 1967

Hummel, Arthur W., trans. and ed. *The autobiography of a Chinese historian: being the preface to a symposium on ancient Chinese history* (*Ku Shih Pien*) [by Ku Chieh-kang]. Leiden: E. J. Brill, 1931; Taipei: Ch'eng-wen reprint, 1966

Hu-nan li-shih tzu-liao 湖南歷史資料 (Historical materials on Hunan), ed. by Hunan Historical Materials Editorial Commission. Changsha, 1959

Hung-ch'i 紅旗 (The red flag). Official organ of the centre of the CCP, Nov. 1928–1933

Hung-ch'i 紅旗 (The red flag). Peking, 1967–

Hung-ch'i p'iao-p'iao 紅旗飄飄 (Red flag flying). 16 vols. Peking: Chung-kuo ch'ing-nien ch'u-pan-she 中國青年出版社, 1957–61

Hung-hsing 紅星 (The red star), ed. by the General Political Department of the Red Army, 1932–4

Hung Jui (Shui)-chien 洪瑞堅. 'Su-chou k'ang-tsu feng-ch'ao ti ch'ien-yin hou-kuo' 蘇州抗租風潮的前因後果 (Causes and results of the tenant riots in Soochow). *Ti-cheng yueh-k'an* 地政月刊 (Land administration monthly), 4.10 (Oct. 1936) 1547–62

(Hung Shui-chien?). 'Su-chou ti nung-ch'ao' 蘇州的農潮 (The peasant riots in Soochow). *Chung-kuo nung-ts'un* 中國農村 2.9 (June 1936) 6–8

Hung-se Chung-hua 紅色中華 (Red China). Official organ of the Soviet Republic of China, 11 Dec. 1931–12 Dec. 1936

Hung-se feng-pao 紅色風暴 (The red tempest). 13 vols. Nanch'ang: Jen-min, 1958–62

Hung-se wen-hsien 紅色文獻 (Red documents) Yenan, 1938

Hunt, Michael. 'The American remission of the Boxer indemnity: a reappraisal'. *JAS* 31.3 (May 1972) 539–59

Hunt, Michael. *Frontier defense and the Open Door: Manchuria in Chinese–American relations, 1895–1911.* New Haven: Yale University Press, 1973

Hunt, Michael. *The making of a special relationship: the United States and China to 1914.* New York: Columbia University Press, 1983

Hunter, Jane. *The gospel of gentility: American women missionaries in turn-of-the-century China.* New Haven: Yale University Press, 1984

Huntington, Samuel P. *Political order in changing societies.* New Haven: Yale University Press, 1968

Huters, Theodore. *Qian Zhongshu.* New York: Twayne, 1982

I-chiu-ssu-ch'i nien shang-pan-nien lai ch'ü-tang-wei kuan-yü t'u-k'ai yun-tung ti chung-yao wen-chien 一九四七年上半年來區黨委關於土改運動的重要文件 (Important documents on the land reform movement during the first half of 1947 from the regional party committee). n. p.: Chi-Lu-Yü ch'ü tang wei 冀魯豫區黨委, June 1947

I-erh-chiu hui-i-lu 一二九回憶録 (Memoirs of December 9th). Peking: Chung-kuo ch'ing-nien ch'u-pan-she 中國青年出版社, 1961

I-ho t'uan 義和團 (The Boxers). Chung-kuo shih-hsueh hui 中國史學會 (Chinese Historical Association), ed. 4 vols. Shanghai: Jen-min, 1957

I Songgyu 李成珪. 'Shantung in the Shun-chih reign: the establishment of local control and the gentry response', trans. Joshua A. Fogel. *CSWT* 4.4 (Dec. 1980) 1–34, 4.5 (June 1981) 1–31

I-ta ch'ien-hou 一大前后 (Before and after the First Congress), ed. Chung-kuo she-hui-k'o-hsueh yuan hsien-tai shih yen-chiu-shih 中國社會科學院現代史研究室 and Chung-kuo ko-ming po-wu-kuan tang-shih yen-chiu-shih 中國革命博物館黨史研究室 (Chung-kuo hsien-tai ko-ming shih tzu-liao ts'ung-k'an 中國現代革命史資料叢刊) Peking: Jen-min, 1980

Ichiko, Chūzō 市古宙三. 'The role of the gentry: an hypothesis', in Mary Clabaugh Wright, ed. *China in revolution: the first phase, 1900–1913*, 297–313

Ichiko, Chūzō. 'Political and institutional reform, 1901–11'. *CHOC* 11.375–415

Ienaga, Saburō 家永三郎. *The Pacific War: World War II and the Japanese, 1931–1945*, trans. of *Taiheiyō sensō* 太平洋戦争. New York: Pantheon Books, 1978

Ikei Masaru. 'Japan's response to the Chinese Revolution of 1911'. *JAS* 25.2 (Feb. 1966) 213–27

Imahori Seiji 今堀誠二. *Pepin shimin no jichi kōsei* 北平市民の自治構成 (The self-government organizations of Peiping burghers). Tokyo: Bunkyūdō 文求堂, 1947

Imahori Seiji 今堀誠二. *Chūgoku hōken shakai no kōzō—sono rekishi to kakumei zenya no genjitsu* 中国封建社会の構造：その歴史と革命前夜の現実 (The structure of China's feudal society—its history and condition on the eve of the Communist revolution). Tokyo: Nihon Gakujutsu Shinkōkai 日本学術振興会, 1978

IMH: Institute of Modern History, Academia Sinica, Nankang, Taipei

Imprecor. See *International Press Correspondence*

Inaba Iwakichi 稲葉岩吉. *Tai-Shi ikkagon* 対支一家言 (A personal account of China). Tokyo: Nihon Hyōron sha 日本評論社 1921

Ingalls, Jeremy. See Yao Hsin-nung

Institute of Historical Research, Peking. See Chung-kuo she-hui k'o-hsueh yuan Li-shih yen- chiu so

Institute of Modern History, Academia Sinica, Taipei (IMH). See Chung-yang yen-chiu-yuan chin-tai-shih yen-chiu-so

Institute of Pacific Relations, comp. *Agrarian China*. Intro. by R. H. Tawney. Chicago: University of Chicago Press, 1939

Institute of Pacific Relations, Hearings before the subcommittee to investigate the administration of the Internal Security Act and other internal security laws of the Committee on the Judiciary. United States Senate, 82nd Congress. 14 vols. 1951–2

International Affairs. London: Royal Institute of International Affairs. Quarterly. 1922–

International Press Correspondence. Organ of the Executive Committee of the Communist International. English edn, 1925–35

Irie Keishirō. 入江啓四郎. *Shina henkyō to Ei-Ro no kakuchiku* 支那辺疆と英露の角逐 (Chinese frontiers and the Anglo-Russian power struggle). Japan:

Nauka-sha ナウカ社, 1935

Iriye, Akira 入江昭. *After imperialism: the search for a new order in the Far East, 1921–1931*. Cambridge, Mass.: Harvard University Press, 1965

Iriye, Akira. *Pacific estrangement: Japanese and American expansion, 1897–1911*. Cambridge, Mass.: Harvard University Press, 1972

Iriye, Akira. *The cold war in Asia: a historical introduction*. Englewood Cliffs, NJ: Prentice-Hall, 1974.

Iriye, Akira. 'Toward a new cultural order: the Hsin-min Hui', in Akira Iriye, ed. *The Chinese and the Japanese*, 254–74

Iriye, Akira, ed. *The Chinese and the Japanese: essays in political and cultural interactions*. Princeton: Princeton University Press, 1980

Iriye, Akira. *Power and culture: the Japanese-American war, 1941–1945*. Cambridge, Mass.: Harvard University Press, 1981

Isaacs, Harold R. *The tragedy of the Chinese revolution*. 2nd rev. edn, Stanford: Stanford University Press, 1961

Israel, John. *Student nationalism in China, 1927–1937*. Stanford: Published for the Hoover Institution, Stanford University Press, 1966

Israel, John. 'Southwest Associated University: survival as an ultimate value', in Paul K. T. Sih, ed. *Nationalist China during the Sino-Japanese War, 1937–1945*, 131–54

Israel, John, trans. *Draft history of Qinghua University*, a volume in the series *Chinese education: a journal of translations*, ed. by M. E. Sharpe, Autumn-winter 1982–3

Israel, John and Klein, Donald. *Rebels and bureaucrats: China's December 9ers*. Berkeley: University of California, 1976

[Iwai Eiichi 岩井英一]. *Ranisha ni kansuru chōsa* 藍衣社ニ関スル調査 (An investigation of the Blue Shirts). Issued by the Research Division of the Foreign Ministry, Tokyo, 1937

Iwase Suteichi 岩佐捨一. 'Hoku-Man nōson ni okeru daikazoku bunke no ichi jirei' 北滿農村に於ける大家族分家の一事例 (An example of equal division of property in a large family farm of a north Manchuria village). *Mantetsu chōsa geppō* 滿鐵調查月報 20.12 (Dec. 1940) 66–95

Jacobson, Jon. 'Is there a new international history of the 1920s?' *American Historical Review*, 88.3 (June 1983) 617–45

Jacquart, Jean. 'Les paysanneries à l'épreuve', in Pierre Deyon and Jean Jacquart, eds. *Les hésitations de la croissance 1580–1730*, 345–494.

Jansen, Marius B. *The Japanese and Sun Yat-sen*. Cambridge, Mass.: Harvard University Press, 1954

Jansen, Marius B. *Japan and China: from war to peace, 1894–1972*. Chicago: Rand McNally, 1975

Jansen, Marius B. 'Japan and the Chinese Revolution of 1911'. *CHOC* 11. 339–74

Jansen, Marius B. See Miyazaki Tōten

Japan. Ministry of Foreign Affairs (Gaimushō) 外務省. *Nihon gaikō bunsho*

日本外交文書 (Documents on Japanese foreign relations). Tokyo: Nihon Kokusai Rengō Kyōkai 日本国際連合協会, 1936

Japan. Ministry of Foreign Affairs (Gaimushō). *Nihon gaikō nempyō narabi ni shuyō bunsho* 日本外交年表竝主要文書 (Important documents and chronological tables of Japanese diplomacy). 2 vols. Nihon Kokusai Rengō Kyōkai, 1955; Tokyo: Hara Shobō, 1965

JAS. See *Journal of Asian Studies*

Jen, Hung-chün 任鴻雋. 'Wu-shih tzu-shu' 五十自述 (Autobiography at fifty). Unpublished manuscript, 1938

Jen, Hung-chün. 'Wu-shih-nien lai ti k'o-hsueh' 五十年來的科學 (Science in the past 50 years), in P'an Kung-chan, ed. *Wu-shih-nien lai ti Chung-kuo* (China in the past 50 years). Chungking: Sheng-li 勝利, 1945

Jen Hung-chün (H. C. Zen). *A summary report of the activities of the China Foundation for the Promotion of Education and Culture,1925–1945*. n.p., Dec. 1946

Jen-min jih-pao 人民日報 (People's daily). Peking, 1949–

Jen Pi-shih 任弼時. Changsha: Jen-min,1979

Jitsugyōbu, Rinji sangyō chōsakyoku 實業部, 臨時產業調查局, comp. *Nōgyō keiei zokuhen* 農業經營續篇 (A supplementary study of agricultural management). Ch'ang-ch'un: Manshū tosho kabushiki kaisha 滿洲圖書株式會社, 1936

JMJP. See *Jen-min jih-pao*

Johnson, Chalmers A. *Peasant nationalism and communist power: the emergence of revolutionary China,1937–1945*. Stanford: Stanford University Press, 1962; 2nd rev. edn 1966

Johnson, Chalmers. *Revolutionary change*. 1st edn, Little, Brown, 1966; 2nd edn Stanford: Stanford University Press, 1982

Jones, Susan Mann. 'Finance in Ningpo: the "ch'ien-chuang", 1750–1880', in W. E. Willmott, ed. *Economic organization in Chinese society*, 47–78

Jones, Susan Mann. 'The Ningpo *pang* and financial power at Shanghai', in Mark Elvin and G. William Skinner, eds. *The Chinese city between two worlds*, 73–96

Jones, Susan Mann and Kuhn, Philip A. 'Dynastic decline and the roots of rebellion'. *CHOC* 10.107–62

Jones, Susan Mann. 'The organization of trade at the county level: brokerage and tax farming in the Republican period'. *Select papers from the Center for Far Eastern Studies*, University of Chicago, 3 (1978–9) 70–99

Jones, Susan Mann. 'Misunderstanding the Chinese economy—a review article'. *JAS* 40.3 (May 1981) 539–58

Jones, Susan Mann. See also Mann, Susan

Jordan, Donald A. *The Northern Expedition: China's national revolution of 1926–1928*. Honolulu: University Press of Hawaii, 1976

Journal of Asian Studies, 1956–. Quarterly. (*Far Eastern Quarterly* 1941–56)

Journal of Oriental Studies. Hong Kong, Jan. 1954–. (Pub. by Hong Kong University Press for the Institute of Oriental Studies)

JPRS: Joint Publications Research Service. Pub. by US Government

Juan Yu-ch'iu 阮有秋. 'Chin-jih hou-fang min-ying kung-yeh ti wei-chi' 今日後方民營工業的危機 (The current crisis of private industry in the rear area). *Chung-kuo nung-min*, 3.1/2 (June 1943) 33–5

Jung-chia ch'i-yeh shih-liao 榮家企業史料 (Historical materials on the Jung family enterprises), ed. by Shang-hai she-hui k'o-hsueh-yuan ching-chi yen-chiu-so 上海社會科學院經濟研究所. 2 vols. Shanghai: Jen-min, 1980

Kahn, E. J., Jr. *The China hands: America's Foreign Service Officers and what befell them*. New York: Viking Press, 1975

Kaiser, David E. *Economic diplomacy and the origins of the Second World War: Germany, Britain, France, and Eastern Europe, 1930–1939*. Princeton: Princeton University Press, 1980

Kajima Morinosuke. *The diplomacy of Japan 1894–1922*, vol. 2, *Anglo-Japanese alliance and Russo-Japanese War*, trans. from *Nihon gaiko shi*. 3 vols. Tokyo: Kajima Institute of International Peace, Kajima Publishing Co., 1976–80

Kamachi, Noriko 蒲地典子, Fairbank, John K. and Ichiko Chūzō 市古宙三, eds. *Japanese studies of modern China since 1953: a bibliographical guide to historical and social-science research on the nineteenth and twentieth centuries, supplementary volume for 1953–1969*. Cambridge, Mass.: East Asian Research Center, Harvard University, 1975

Kan K'o-ch'ao 淦克超. 'Chan-shih Ssu-ch'uan kung-yeh kai-kuan' 戰時四川工業概觀 (Survey of Szechwan's wartime economy). *Ssu-ch'uan ching-chi chi-k'an*, 1.2 (15 March 1944) 64–72

Kane, Anthony James. 'The League of Left-wing Writers and Chinese literary policy'. University of Michigan, Ph.D. dissertation, 1982

K'ang-chan ch'ien shih-nien chih Chung-kuo 抗戰前十年之中國 (China in the decade before the war), comp. by Chung-kuo wen-hua chien-she hsieh-hui 中國文化建設協會, 1937. Hong Kong: Lung-men reprint, 1965

K'ang-chan ta-hsueh 抗戰大學. Organ of the Anti-Japanese Military-Political University, Yenan, 1937–

K'ang-Jih chan-cheng shih-ch'i chieh-fang-ch'ü kai-k'uang 抗日戰爭時期解放區概況 (The liberated areas during the anti-Japanese war). Peking: Jen-min, 1953

K'ang-Jih min-tsu t'ung-i chan-hsien chih-nan 抗日民族統一戰線指南 (Guide to the anti-Japanese national united front). 10 vols. Yenan, 1937–40

Kao P'ing-shu 高平叔, ed. *Ts'ai Yuan-p'ei chiao-yü wen-hsuan* 蔡元培教育文選 (Selected papers of Ts'ai Yuan-p'ei on education). Peking: Jen-min chiao-yü ch'u-pan-she 人民教育出版社, 1980

Kao T'ing-tzu 高廷梓. *Chung-kuo ching-chi chien-she* 中國經濟建設 (Chinese economic reconstruction). Shanghai: CP, 1937

Kapp, Robert A. *Szechwan and the Chinese Republic: provincial militarism and central power 1911–1938*. New Haven: Yale University Press, 1973

Kataoka Tetsuya. *Resistance and revolution in China: the Communists and the second united front*. Berkeley: University of California Press, 1974

Kawachi Jūzō 河地重造. 'Chūgoku no jinushi keizai' 中國の地主經濟 (The

landlord economy of China). *Keizai nempō* 經濟年報, 18 (1965) 48–124

Keenan, Barry. *The Dewey experiment in China: educational reform and political power in the early republic.* Cambridge, Mass.: Council on East Asian Studies, Harvard University, 1977

Kelley, Allen C. 'Demand patterns, demographic changes and economic growth'. *The Quarterly Journal of Economics*, 83.1 (Feb. 1969) 110–26

Kelley, David E. 'Temples and tribute fleets: the Luo sect and boatmen's associations in the eighteenth century'. *Modern China*, 8.3 (July 1982) 361–91

Kennedy, Melville T., Jr. 'The Chinese Democratic League'. *Harvard papers on China*, 7 (1953) 136–75

Kennedy, Thomas. *Arms of Kiangnan: modernization of the Chinese ordnance industry 1860–1895.* Boulder: Westview Press, 1978

Kerr, George H. *Formosa betrayed.* London: Eyre & Spottiswoode, 1966

Kikuchi Saburō 菊池三郎. *Chūgoku gendai bungaku shi* 中國現代文學史 (History of contemporary Chinese literature). 2 vols. Tokyo: Aoki 青木 1953

Kim, Ilpyong J. *The politics of Chinese Communism: Kiangsi under Soviet rule.* Berkeley: University of California Press, 1974

Kindai Chūgoku kenkyū 近代中國研究 (Studies on modern China), ed. by Kindai Chūgoku Kenkyū Iinkai 近代中國研究委員會 (The Seminar on Modern China) series. Tokyo: Tōyō Bunko 東洋文庫, 1958–

King, Evan. *See* Lao She

King, F. H. *Farmers of forty centuries: or, permanent agriculture in China, Korea and Japan.* Madison, Wis.: Mrs F. H. King, 1911; 2nd edn, London: Cape, 1927; edition ed. by J. P. Bruce, N.Y.: Harcourt, Brace, 1927

King, Wunsz. *China at the Washington Conference, 1921–1922.* New York: St John's University Press, 1963

Kinkley, Jeffrey C. 'Shen Ts'ung-wen's vision of Republican China'. Harvard University, Ph.D. dissertation, 1977

Kirby, William Corbin. 'Foreign models and Chinese modernization: Germany and Republican China, 1921–1937'. Harvard University, Ph.D. dissertation, 1981

Kirby, William Corbin. *Germany and Republican China.* Stanford: Stanford University Press, 1984

Kitaoka Shinichi 北岡伸一. *Nihon rikugun to tairiku seisaku* 日本陸軍と大陸政策 (The Japanese army and the continental policy). Tokyo: University of Tokyo Press, 1978

Klein, Donald W. and Clark, Anne B. *Biographic dictionary of Chinese communism, 1921–1965.* 2 vols. Cambridge, Mass.: Harvard University Press, 1971

KMT. Kuomintang

KMWH. See *Ko-ming wen-hsien*

Knight, Nick. 'Mao Zedong's *On contradiction* and *On practice*: pre-liberation texts'. *CQ* 84 (Dec. 1980) 641–68

Knight, Nick. *Mao Zedong's On Contradiction. An annotated translation of the pre-liberation text.* Nathan, Queensland: Griffith University, 1981

Ko Ching-chung 葛敬中. 'Wu-shih-nien lai Chung-kuo nung-yehshih' 五十年來中國農業史 (The last fifty years of Chinese agriculture), in *Wan-ch'ing wu-shih-nien lai chih Chung-kuo* 晚清五十年來之中國 (The last fifty years of China during the late Ch'ing period). Shanghai: Shang- hai shen-pao kuan 上海申報館, 1922

Ko Hao-wen 葛浩文 (Howard Goldblatt). *Hsiao Hung p'ing-chuan* 蕭紅評傳 (A critical biography of Hsiao Hung), trans. by Cheng Chi-tsung 鄭繼宗. Taipei: Shih-pao ch'u-pan kung-ssu 時報出版公司, 1980

Ko-ming hui-i lu 革命回憶錄 (The revolution remembered). Peking, 1980–

Ko-ming wen-hsien 革命文獻 (Documents of the revolution), comp. by Lo Chia-lun 羅家倫 *et al.* Taipei: Central Executive Committee of the Chung-kuo Kuomintang, many volumes, 1953–

Ko-ming yü chan-cheng 革命與戰爭 (Revolution and war) n.p., Aug. 1932–

Ko-sheng kao-chi hsing-cheng jen-yuan feng-chao Nan-ch'ang chi-hui chi-lu. See Chung-kuo kuo-min cheng-fu Chün-shih . . .

K'o Shu-p'ing 柯樹屏. 'Wang Hsueh-t'ing hsien-sheng tsai chiao-chang jen-nei chih chiao-yü ts'o-shih' 王雪艇先生在教長任內之教育措施 (Educational measures taken by Wang Hsueh-t'ing [Shih-chieh] as Minister of Education). *Chuan-chi wen-hsueh* (Biographical literature), 239 (April 1982) 125–31

Koen, Ross Y. *The China lobby in American politics.* New York: Harper & Row, 1974

Kojima Shinji 小島晋治. *Taihei Tengoku kakumei no rekishi to shisō* 太平天国革命の歴史と思想 (History and ideology of the Taiping revolution). Tokyo: Kembun Shuppan 研文出版, 1978

Kokuryūkai 黒龍会, ed. *Tōa senkaku shishi kiden* 東亜先覚志士記伝 (Biographical sketches of pioneer patriots in East Asia). 3 vols. Tokyo: Kokuryūkai Shuppanbu 黒龍会出版部, 1933–6. Reprinted in *Meiji hyakunenshi sōsho* 明治百年史叢書 (Historical materials of the century since the Meiji Restoration). Vols. 22–24. Tokyo: Hara Shobō 原書房, 1966

Korostovetz, Ivan J. *Von Cinggis Khan zur Sowjetrepublik.* Berlin: Walter de Gruyter, 1926

Kozawa Shigeichi. See under SMR

Kraus, Richard A. See Chuan Han-sheng

Ku Chieh-kang. See Hummel, Arthur W.

Kuan-ch'a 觀察 (The observer). Shanghai, 1947–

Kuan-ch'a chi-che 觀察記者. (The observer's correspondent). 'Ts'ung chan-chü k'an cheng-chü' 從戰局看政局 (Looking at political conditions from the military situation). *Kuan-ch'a.* Shanghai, 28 Feb. 1948, pp. 14–16

Kuan-ch'a chi-che. (The observer's correspondent). 'T'u-ti kai-ko, ti-tao chan' 土地改革, 地道戰 (Land reform, tunnel warfare). *Kuan-ch'a,* 3 April 1948, p. 14

Kuan Meng-chueh 關夢覺. 'Shan-hsi-sheng fang-chih-yeh chih wei-chi chi ch'i ch'u-lu' 陝西省紡織業之危機及其出路 (The crisis of Shensi's textile industry and its solution). *Chung-kuo kung-yeh* 中國工業, 19 (1 Sept. 1943) 6–13

Kuang-hsi min-t'uan kai-yao 廣西民團概要 (A general view of the Kwangsi militia). Issued by the militia office of the Fourth Army Headquarters, n.p., n.d., probably 1935

Kuhn, Philip. *Rebellion and its enemies in late imperial China: militarization and social structure, 1796–1864.* Cambridge, Mass.: Harvard University Press, 1970

Kuhn, Philip A. 'Local self-government under the Republic: problems of control, autonomy, and mobilization', in Frederic Wakeman, Jr. and Carolyn Grant, eds. *Conflict and control in late imperial China*, 257–98

Kuhn, Philip A. 'Origins of the Taiping vision: cross-cultural dimensions of a Chinese rebellion'. *Comparative Studies in Society and History*, 19.3 (July 1977) 350–66

Kuhn, Philip A. 'The Taiping Rebellion'. *CHOC* 10.264–317

Kuhn, Philip A. 'Local taxation and finance in Republican China'. *Select papers from the Center for Far Eastern Studies*, University of Chicago, 3 (1978–9) 100–36

Kuhn, Philip A. 'Late Ch'ing views of the polity'. *Select papers from the Center for Far Eastern Studies*, University of Chicago, 4 (1979–80) 1–18

Kumashiro Yukio 熊代幸雄. 'Kahoku ni okeru nōka no bunke to tochi no ugoki' 華北に於ける農家の分家と土地の動き (Peasant household division of land and land transfer in North China), in *Nōken hōkoku chōhen* 農研報告 長編 (Extended reports of rural investigation), 167–266. Peking: Kokuritsu Pekin daigaku fusetsu nōson keizai kenkyūjo 國立北京大學附設農村經濟 研究所, 1943

Kung-ch'an kuo-chi chih-hsing-wei-yuan-hui chih Chung-kung chung-yang wei-yuan-hui hsin 共產國際執行委員會致中共中央委員會信 (ECCI to CCP). n.p., 8 Feb. 1929. Mimeographed

Kung-ch'an-tang 共產黨 (The Communist Party). Shanghai, Nov. 1920–

Kung-ch'an tang-jen 共產黨人 (The Communist). No data

Kung Ch'u 龔楚. *Wo yü Hung-chün* 我與紅軍 (The Red Army and I). Hong Kong: Nan-feng ch'u-pan-she 南風出版社, 1954

Kung-fei chung-yao tzu-liao hui-pien 共匪重要資料彙編 (Essential materials concerning the communist bandits). 10 vols. *(ts'e)*; also a two-volume edition, Taipei: Chung-yang wen-wu 中央文物, 1952

Kung-fei huo-kuo shih-liao hui-pien 共匪禍國史料彙編 (Collected historical materials on the national disaster caused by the communist bandits). Chi-chi-mi 極機密 (top secret). 3 vols. Taipei: Chung-hua min-kuo k'ai-kuo wu-shih-nien wen-hsien pien-tsuan wei-yuan-hui 中華民國開國五十年文 獻編纂委員會, 1964

Kung-tso t'ung-hsun, 32: yu-chi chan-cheng chuan-hao 工作通訊, 32: 游擊戰爭專號 (Work correspondence, number 32: special issue on guerrilla warfare).

n.p.: Chi-Lu-Yü ch'ü tang wei min-yun pu 冀魯豫區黨委民運部, June 1947

Kung Yü-chih 龔育之. " 'Shih-chien lun' san t'i" 「實踐論」三題 (Three points regarding 'On practice'), in *Lun Mao Tse-tung che-hsueh ssu-hsiang* 論毛澤東哲學思想 Peking: People's Publishing House, 1983, pp. 66–86

K'ung Hsueh-hsiung 孔雪雄. *Chung-kuo chin-jih chih nung-ts'un yun-tung* 中國今日之農村運動 (The rural movement in contemporary China). Nanking: Chung-shan wen-hua chiao-yü kuan 中山文化教育館, 1935

K'ung Ling-ching 孔另境. *Wu-sa wai-chiao-shih* 五卅外交史 (Diplomatic relations of the May Thirtieth movement). Shanghai: Yung-hsiang yin-shu-kuan 永祥印書館, 1948

Kuo-chia tsung-tung-yuan 國家總動員 (National mobilization). n.p.: Hsing-cheng-yuan hsin-wen-chü 行政院新聞局, 1947

Kuo-fang nien-chien 國防年鑑 (National defence year book). Hsu Kao-yang 許高陽, ed. Hong Kong: Chung-kuo shih-hsueh yen-chiu hui 中國史學研究會, 1969

Kuo, Heng-yü. *Die Komintern und die Chinesische Revolution: die Einheitsfront zwischen der K P Chinas und der Kuomintang 1924–1927*. Paderborn: Ferdinand Schöningh, 1979

Kuo Hua-jo 郭化若. 'Mao chu-hsi k'ang-chan ch'u-ch'i kuang-hui ti che-hsueh huo-tung' 毛主席抗戰初期光輝的哲學活動 (Chairman Mao's brilliant philosophical activity early in the War of Resistance) *Chung-kuo che-hsueh* 中國哲學, 1 (1979) 31–7

Kuo Hua-lun 郭華倫 (Warren Kuo). *Chung-kung shih-lun* 中共史論 (An analytical history of the CCP). 4 vols. Taipei: Kuo-chi kuan-hsi yen-chiu-so 國際關係研究所, 1969

Kuo-li Hsi-nan lien-ho ta-hsueh 國立西南聯合大學 (National South-west Associated University), a volume in the *Hsueh-fu chi-wen* 學府紀聞 series. Taipei: Nan-ching 南京, 1981

Kuo-min cheng-fu chu-chi-ch'u t'ung-chi-chü 國民政府主計處統計局, comp. *Chung-hua min-kuo t'ung-chi t'i-yao* 中華民國統計提要 (Statistic abstract for the Republic of China). Nanking, 1947; reprint, Taipei: Hsueh-hai 學海, 1971

Kuo-min cheng-fu chün-shih wei-yuan-hui wei-yuan-chang hsing-ying. Hu-pei ti-fang cheng-wu yen-chiu-hui tiao-ch'a-t'uan 國民政府軍事委員會委員長行營湖北地方政務研究會調查團, comp. *Tiao-ch'a hsiang-ts'un chien-she chi-yao* 調查鄉村建設紀要 (Record of rural reconstruction investigations). Wuchang, 1935

Kuo-min ching-shen tsung-tung-yuan yun-tung 國民精神總動員運動 (National spiritual mobilization movement), comp. by San-min-chu-i ch'ing-nien-t'uan chung-yang t'uan-pu 三民主義青年團中央團部. n.p. 1944

Kuo, Thomas C. *Ch'en Tu-hsiu (1879–1942) and the Chinese communist movement.* South Orange, NJ: Seton Hall University Press, 1975

Kuo, Warren (Kuo Hua-lun). *Analytical history of the Chinese Communist Party.*

4 vols. Taipei: Institute of International Relations, 1966–71

Kuo-wen chou-pao 國聞週報. (Kuowen weekly, illustrated). Tientsin Kuowen Weekly Association, 1924–37

Kurihara Ken 栗原健, ed. and comp. *Tai Man-Mō sei sakushi no ichimen, Nichi-Ro sengo yori Taishōki ni itaru* 対満蒙政策史の一面—日露戦後より大正期にいたる (An aspect of Japanese policies toward Manchuria and Mongolia, from the end of the Russo-Japanese war to the Taishō period). Tokyo: Hara Shobō 原書房, Meiji hyakunenshi sōsho 明治百年史叢書, 1966

Kwok, D. W. Y. 郭穎頤. *Scientism in Chinese thought 1900–1950*. New Haven and London: Yale University Press, 1965

Kwong, Luke S. K. *A mosaic of the Hundred Days: personalities, politics and ideas of 1898*. Cambridge, Mass.: Council on East Asian Studies, Harvard University, 1984

Lach, Donald F. and Wehrle, Edmund S. *International politics in East Asia since World War II*. New York: Praeger, 1975

Lamb, Alastair. *The China–India border: the origins of the disputed boundaries*. London: Oxford University Press, 1964

Lamberton, Mary. *St John's University Shanghai, 1879–1951*. New York: United Board for Christian Colleges in China, 1955

Lamley, Harry J. '*Hsieh-tou*: the pathology of violence in southeastern China'. *CSWT* 3.7 (Nov. 1977) 1–39

Lan Hai 藍海. *Chung-kuo k'ang-chan wen-i shih* 中國抗戰文藝史 (A history of Chinese literature during the war of resistance). Shanghai: Hsien-tai 現代, 1947

Lang, Olga. *Pa Chin and his writings: Chinese youth between the two revolutions*. Cambridge, Mass.: Harvard University Press, 1967

Langer, William L. *The diplomacy of imperialism, 1890–1902*. 2 vols. New York: A. A. Knopf, 1935; 2nd edn., 1951

Lao She 老舍 (Shu Ch'ing-ch'un 舒慶春, She Yu 舍予). *Rickshaw boy*, by Lau Shaw, trans. from the Chinese by Evan King (Robert Ward). New York: Reynal and Hitchcock, 1945

Lao She. *Rickshaw: the novel Lo-t'o Hsiang-tzu*, trans. by Jean M. James. Honolulu: University of Hawaii, 1979

Lao She. *Camel Xiangzi*, trans. Shi Xiaoqing. Bloomington: Indiana University Press; Peking: Foreign Languages Press, 1981

Lao She. See Hu Chin-ch'üan

Laqueur, Walter. *Guerrilla, a historical and critical study*. Boston: Little, Brown, 1976

Lary, Diana. *Region and nation: the Kwangsi clique in Chinese politics, 1925–1937*. London: Cambridge University Press, 1974

Lary, Diana. 'Warlord studies'. *Modern China*, 6.4 (Oct. 1980) 439–70

Lattimore, Owen. *Inner Asian frontiers of China*. New York: American Geographical Society, 1940; 2nd edn, 1951

Lattimore, Owen. *Nomads and commissars: Mongolia revisited*. New York:

Oxford University Press, 1962

Lau, Joseph S. M. 劉紹銘. *Ts'ao Yü: the reluctant disciple of Chekhov and O'Neill, a study in literary influence.* Hong Kong: Hong Kong University Press, 1970

Lau, Joseph S. M., Hsia, C. T. and Lee, Leo Ou-fan, eds. *Modern Chinese stories and novellas, 1919–1949.* New York: Columbia University Press, 1981

League of Nations, Council Committee on Technical Cooperation between the League of Nations and China. Report of the technical agent of the council on his mission in China from the date of his appointment until April 1st, 1934

League of Nations report. *The reorganization of education in China.* See Becker, C. H. *et al.*

Lee, James. 'Food supply and population growth in Southwest China, 1250–1850'. *JAS* 41.4 (Aug. 1982) 711–46

Lee, James and Eng, Robert. 'Population and family history in eighteenth century Manchuria: Daoyi, 1774–1798'. *CSWT* 5.1 (June 1984) 1–55

Lee, James, Will, Pierre-Étienne and Wong, R. Bin, eds. *State granaries and food supply in Ch'ing China, 1650–1850.* Ann Arbor: Center for Chinese Studies, University of Michigan. Forthcoming

Lee, Leo Ou-fan 李歐梵. *The romantic generation of modern Chinese writers.* Cambridge, Mass.: Harvard University Press, 1973

Lee, Leo Ou-fan. 'Literature on the eve of revolution: reflections on Lu Xun's leftist years, 1927–1936'. *Modern China*, 2.3 (July 1976) 277–91

Lee, Leo Ou-fan. 'Literary trends I: the quest for modernity, 1895–1927'. *CHOC* 12.451–504

Lee, Leo Ou-fan, ed. *Lu Hsun and his legacy.* Berkeley: University of California Press, 1985

Lee, Robert H. G. *The Manchurian frontier in Ch'ing history.* Cambridge, Mass.: Harvard University Press, 1970

Leffler, Melvyn P. *The elusive quest: America's pursuit of European stability and French security, 1919–1933.* Chapel Hill, NC: University of North Carolina Press, 1979

Legge, James. *The Chinese classics.* 5 vols. Reprinted Hong Kong: Hong Kong University Press, 1960

Le Gros Clark, Cyril Drummond. *The prose-poetry of Su Tung-p'o.* Shanghai: Kelly & Walsh, 1935

Lei Hsiao-ts'en 雷嘯岑. *San-shih-nien tung-luan Chung-kuo* 三十年動亂中國 (Thirty years of China in turmoil). Hong Kong: Ya-chou 亞洲, 1955

Lenin, N. *et al. Lieh-ning Ssu-ta-lin lun Chung-kuo* 列寧斯大林論中國 (Lenin and Stalin on China). Peking: Jen-min, 1963

Lenin, V. I. 'Conspectus of Hegel's *Science of logic*'. *Collected works*, 38.85–238. Moscow: Foreign Languages Publishing House, 1961

Leong, Sow-theng. *Sino-Soviet diplomatic relations, 1917–1926.* Honolulu: University of Hawaii Press, 1976

Levenson, Joseph. *Revolution and cosmopolitanism: the Western stage and the*

Chinese stages. Berkeley, Los Angeles, London: University of California Press, 1971

Lewis, Charlton M. 'Some notes on the Ko-lao Hui in late Ch'ing China', in Jean Chesneaux, ed. *Popular movements and secret societies in China, 1840–1950*, 97–112

Lewis, John Wilson, ed. *Leadership in Communist China*. Ithaca: Cornell University Press, 1963

Lewis, John Wilson, ed. *Party leadership and revolutionary power in China*. Cambridge: Cambridge University Press, 1970

Leyda, Jay. *Dianying: an account of films and the film audience in China*. Cambridge, Mass.: MIT Press, 1972

Li Ang (Chu P'ei-wo, Chu Hsin-fan) 李昂(朱佩我, 朱新繁) *Hung-se wu-t'ai* 紅色舞台 (The red stage). Chungking, 1942; Peking, 1946

Li, Anthony C. *The history of privately controlled higher education in the Republic of China*. Washington, DC: Catholic University of America Press, 1954; Westport, Conn.: Greenwood Press reprint, 1977

Li Ch'ang 李昌. 'Hui-i min-hsien tui' 回憶民先隊 (Reminiscences of the National Salvation Vanguard), in Li Ch'ang *et al. I-erh-chiu hui-i-lu* 一二九回憶錄 (Memoirs of December 9), 3–34. Peking: Chung-kuo ch'ing-nien ch'u-pan-she 中國青年出版社, 1961

Li Ch'eng-jui 李承瑞. 'K'ang-Jih chan-cheng shih-ch'i chi-ko jen-min ken-chü-ti ti nung-yeh shui-shou chih-tu yü nung-min fu-tan' 抗日戰爭時期幾個人民根據地的農業稅收制度與農民負擔 (Agricultural tax systems and peasant burdens in people's revolutionary base areas during the anti-Japanese war). *Ching-chi yen-chiu* 經濟研究 (Economic research), 2 (1956) 100–15

Li Chi 李濟. *Anyang*. Seattle: University of Washington Press, 1977

Li Chin-fa 李金髮. Interview with Li Chin-fa by Ya Hsien 瘂弦. *Ch'uang-shih-chi* 創世紀 (The epoch poetry quarterly), 39 (Jan. 1975) 5

Li Chung-hsiang 李鍾湘. 'Kuo-li Hsi-nan lien-ho ta-hsueh shih-mo-chi' 國立西南聯合大學始末記 (History of the National South-west Associated University), part 1, in *Chuan-chi wen-hsueh* (Biographical literature), 231 (August 1981) 72–7

Li Ho-lin 李何林. *Chin erh-shih-nien Chung-kuo wen-i ssu-ch'ao lun* 近二十年中國文藝思潮論 (Chinese literary trends in the recent twenty years). Shanghai: Sheng-huo, 1947

Li Ho-lin *et al. Chung-kuo hsin wen-hsueh shih yen-chiu* 中國新文學史研究 (Studies on the history of new Chinese literature). Peking: Hsin chien-she tsa-chih she 新建設雜誌社, 1951

Li Ho-lin, ed. *Chung-kuo wen-i lun-chan* 中國文藝論戰 (Literary debates in China). Hong Kong: Hua-hsia 華夏, 1957

Li Hua 李華, comp. *Ming Ch'ing i-lai Pei-ching kung-shang hui-kuan pei-k'e hsuan-pien* 明清以來北京工商會館碑刻選編 (A collection of inscriptions of Peking gilds since the Ming and the Ch'ing periods). Peking: Wen-wu

文物, 1980

Li I-yeh 李一葉. *Chung-kuo jen-min tsen-yang ta-pai Jih-pen ti-kuo-chu-i* 中國人民怎樣打敗日本帝國主義 (How the Chinese people defeated Japanese imperialism). Peking: K'ai-ming, 開明, 1951

Li Jui 李鋭. *Mao Tse-tung t'ung-chih ti ch'u-ch'i ko-ming huo-tung* 毛澤東同志的初期革命活動 (The early revolutionary activities of Comrade Mao Tse-tung). Peking: Chung-kuo ch'ing-nien ch'u-pan-she, 1957

Li Jui. *The early revolutionary activities of Comrade Mao Tse-tung*, trans. by Anthony W. Sariti, ed. by James C. Hsiung, intro. by Stuart R. Schram. White Plains, NY: M. E. Sharpe, 1977. (Trans. of Li Jui, 1957)

Li Jui. *Mao Tse-tung ti tsao-ch'i ko-ming huo-tung* 毛澤東的早期革命活動 Changsha: Hu-nan Jen-min, 1980; rev. edn of Li Jui, 1957

Li Jui. *Mao Tse-tung ti ch'u-ch'i ko-ming huo-tung* 毛澤東的初期革命活動 (The early revolutionary activities of Mao Tse-tung). rev. edn, Peking: Jen-min, 1980

Li Jui 李鋭. 'Hsueh-sheng shih-tai ti Mao Tse-tung' 學生時代的毛澤東 (Mao Tse-tung during his student period). *Hsin-hua wen-chai* 新華文摘 I (1984) 175–81

Li Kuo-ch'i. *Chung-kuo hsien-tai-hua ti ch'ü-yü yen-chiu: Min-Che-T'ai ti-ch'ü, 1860–1916* 中國現代化的區域研究：閩浙臺地區, 1860–1916 (Modernization in China, 1860–1916: a regional study of social, political and economic change in Fukien, Chekiang and Taiwan). Taipei: IMH, 1982

Li Kuo-ch'i 李國祁 and Chu Hung 朱鴻. 'Ch'ing-tai Chin-hua-fu ti shih-chen chieh-kou chi ch'i yen-pien' 清代金華府的市鎮結構及其演變 (The structure and progressive changes in markets and towns in Chin-hua prefecture during the Ch'ing). *Li-shih hsueh-pao* (Bulletin of historical research), 7 (May 1979) 113–87

Li Li-san 李立三. *Fan-t'o* 反托 (Anti-Trotsky). n.p., n.d. Mimeographed

Li, Lillian M. *China's silk trade: traditional industry in the modern world, 1842–1937*. Cambridge, Mass.: Council on East Asian Studies, Harvard University, 1981

Li, Lillian M. 'Introduction' to 'Food, famine, and the Chinese state—a symposium'. *JAS* 41.4 (Aug. 1982) 687–708

Li, Lincoln. *The Japanese army in north China, 1937–1941: problems of political and economic control*. Tokyo: Oxford University Press, 1975

Li-lun yü hsien-shih 理論與現實 (Theory and reality) Shanghai, 1939–

Li Mu 李牧. *San-shih nien-tai wen-i lun* 三十年代文藝論 (On the literature and arts of the 1930s). Taipei: Li-ming 黎明, 1973

Li pao 立報. Hong Kong

Li-shih hsueh-pao 歷史學報 (Bulletin of historical research). Taipei: National Taiwan Normal University, Jan. 1973–

Li-shih tang-an ('Lishi dang'an') 歷史檔案 (Historical archives quarterly), ed. by First and Second Historical Archives, Chung-kuo ti-i li-shih tang-an-kuan 中國第一歷史檔案館, Chung-kuo ti-erh li-shih tang-an-kuan 中國第

二歷史檔案館. Peking, 1981–

Li-shih yen-chiu 歷史研究 (Historical research). Monthly. Peking, 1954–66, 1975–

Li Ta. 'Ko-hsin yun-tung ti ta ching-shen' 革新運動的大精神 (The great spirit of the renovation movement). *Ko-hsin chou-k'an* 革新週刊, 1.6 (31 Aug. 1946) 5

Li Ta-chao 李大釗. *Shou-ch'ang wen-chi* 守常文集 (Collected essays of Li Ta-chao). Shanghai: Jen-min, 1952

Li Ta-chao. *Li Ta-chao hsuan-chi* 李大釗選集 (Selected works of Li Ta-chao). Peking: Jen-min, 1962

Li Ta-chao. 'Ya-hsi-ya ch'ing-nien ti kuang-ming yun-tung' 亞細亞青年的光明運動 (The luminous Asiatic youth movement), in Li Ta-chao, *Li Ta-chao hsuan-chi*, 327–9

Li Tsung-huang 李宗黃. *Hsin-hsien-chih chih li-lun yü shih-chi* 新縣制之理論與實際 (The theory and practice of the new county system). Chungking: CH, 1944

Li Tsung-jen 李宗仁 and Tong Te-kong 唐德剛. *The memoirs of Li Tsung-jen.* Boulder, Colo.: Westview Press, 1979

Li Tzu-ching 李子静. 'Chin-nan chieh-fang ch'ü ti tou-cheng ch'ing-hsing' 晉南解放區的鬥爭情形 (The struggle situation in the liberated districts of south Shansi). *Kuan-ch'a*, 6 March 1948, p. 15

Li Tzu-hsiang 李紫翔. 'K'ang-chan i-lai Ssu-ch'uan chih kung-yeh' 抗戰以來四川之工業 (Szechwan's industry during the war). *Ssu-ch'uan ching-chi chi-k'an*, 1.1 (15 Dec. 1943) 17–43

Li Tzu-hsiang. 'Wo-kuo chan-shih kung-yeh sheng-ch'an ti hui-ku yü ch'ien-chan' 我國戰時工業生產的回顧與前瞻 (The past and future of China's wartime industrial production). *SCCC* 2.3 (1 July 1945) 26–41

Li Wen-chih 李文治, comp. *Chung-kuo chin-tai nung-yeh-shih tzu-liao* 中國近代農業史資料 (Historical materials on modern China's agriculture), vol. 1. Peking: San-lien, 1957. See also Chang Yu-i

Li Yü 黎玉. *Lun ch'ün-chung lu-hsien yü Shan-tung ch'ün-chung yun-tung* 論群眾路綫與山東群眾運動 (On the mass line and the mass movement in Shantung). n.p.: Chung-kung Chiao-tung-ch'ü tang wei 中共膠東區黨委, February 1946

Li Yun-han 李雲漢. *Ts'ung jung-Kung tao ch'ing-tang* 從容共到清黨 (From the admission of the Communists to the purification of the Kuomintang). 2 vols. Taipei: Chung-kuo hsueh-shu chu-tso chiang-chu wei-yuan-hui 中國學術著作獎助委員會, 1966

Li Yun-han. *Sung Che-yuan yü ch'i-ch'i k'ang-chan* 宋哲元與七七抗戰 (Sung Che-yuan and the 7 July war of resistance). Taipei: Chuan-chi wen-hsueh, 1973

Li Yun-han. 'The origins of the war: background of the Lukouchiao Incident, July 7, 1937', in Paul K. T. Sih, ed. *Nationalist China during the Sino-Japanese War, 1937–1945,* 3–32

Liang Ch'i-ch'ao 梁啓超 *et al. Wan-ch'ing wu-shih-nien lai chih Chung-kuo, 1872–*

1921 晚清五十年來之中國, 1872–1921 (China during the last fifty years, 1872–1921). Shanghai: Shun-pao kuan 申報館, 1923; Hong Kong reprint: Lung-men 龍門, 1968

Liang Shih-ch'iu 梁實秋. *T'an Wen I-to* 談聞一多 (About Wen I-to). Biographical Literature series no. 3. Taipei: Chuan-chi wen-hsueh, 1967

Liang Shih-ch'iu. 'Ch'ing-hua ch'i-shih' 清華七十 (Tsinghua University at seventy), in *Chuan-chi wei-hsueh* (Biographical literature), no. 231 (August 1981), 82–8

Liang Shu-ming 梁漱溟. 'Pei-yu so-chien chi-lueh' 北遊所見紀略 (An account of what I observed on my northward journey), in *Chung-kuo min-tsu tzu-chiu yun-tung chih tsui-hou chueh-wu* 中國民族自救運動之最後覺悟 (The final realization about the Chinese people's self-help movement), 257–88

Liang Ssu-ch'eng 梁思成, ed. and introd. by Wilma C. Fairbank. *A pictorial history of Chinese architecture: a study of the development of its structural system and the evolution of its types*. Cambridge, Mass.: MIT Press, 1984

Lieberthal, Kenneth G. *Revolution and tradition in Tientsin, 1949–1952*. Stanford: Stanford University Press, 1980

Lilley, Charles Ronald. 'Tsiang T'ing-fu: between two worlds, 1895–1935'. University of Maryland, Ph.D. dissertation, 1979. (Ann Arbor: University Microfilms International, 1980)

Lin Chen 林真. *Chung-kuo nei-mu* 中國內幕 (China's inside story). Shanghai: Hsin-wen tsa-chih 新聞雜誌, 1948

Lin Chi-yung 林繼庸. 'K'ang-chan ch'i-chung min-ying ch'ang-k'uang ch'ien-Ch'uan chien-shu' 抗戰期中民營廠礦遷川簡述 (Summary account of the move of privately-owned factories and mines to Szechwan during the war). *Ssu-ch'uan wen-hsien*, 62 (1 Oct. 1967) 3–9

Lin, Julia C. *Modern Chinese poetry: an introduction*. Seattle: University of Washington Press, 1972

Lin Sung-ho 林頌河. 'T'ung-chi shu-tzu hsia ti Pei-p'ing' 統計數字下的北平 (Peking: a statistical survey). *She-hui k'o-hsueh tsa-chih*, 2.3 (Sept. 1931) 376–419

Lin Ts'ung 林淙, ed. *Hsien chieh-tuan ti wen-hsueh lun-chan* 現階段的文學論戰 (Current literary debates). Shanghai: Kuang-ming 光明, 1936

Lin Tzu-hsun (Tze-Hsiun Lin) 林子勛 *Chung-kuo liu-hsueh chiao-yü shih* 中國留學教育史 (History of Chinese students studying abroad). Taipei: Hua-kang 華岡, 1976

Lin Wen-ch'ing po-shih tan-sheng pai-nien chi-nien k'an 林文慶博士誕生百年紀念刊, *Lin Wen-ch'ing chuan* 林文慶傳 (Life of Lim Boon Keng). n.p., n.d.

Lin Yueh-hwa (Yao-hua) 林耀華. *The golden wing; a sociological study of Chinese familism*. New York: Oxford University Press, 1947; London: Kegan Paul, Trench, Trubner, 1948

Lin Yun-hui 林蘊暉. 'Lueh lun Mao Tse-tung t'ung-chih tui Li-san lu-hsien ti jen-shih ho ti-chih' 略論毛澤東同志對立三路綫的認識和抵制 (A brief account of Mao Tse-tung's understanding of, and resistance to, the Li-san line). *TSYC* 4 (1980) 51–9

Linden, Allen B. 'Politics and education in Nationalist China: the case of the University Council, 1927–1928'. *JAS* 27.4 (Aug. 1968) 763–76

Lindsay, Michael. 'The taxation system of the Shansi-Chahar-Hopei Border Region, 1938–1945'. *CQ* 42 (April–June 1970) 1–15

Lindsay, Michael. *The unknown war: north China, 1937–1945*. London: Bergstrom & Boyle, 1975

Linebarger, Paul M. A. *The China of Chiang K'ai-shek: a political study*. Boston: World Peace Foundation, 1941; repr. Westport, Conn.: Greenwood Press, 1973

Ling Yü 凌宇. "Mao Tse-tung t'ung-chih ho Li-san lu-hsien ti kuan-hsi t'ao-lun tsung-shu" 毛澤東同志和立三路綫的關係討論綜述 (A summary of the discussion regarding Comrade Mao Tse-tung's relationship to the Li-san line). TSYC, 3 (1982) 78–80

Link, Arthur S. *Wilson*. Vol. 3. *The struggle for neutrality, 1914–1915*. Princeton: Princeton University Press, 1960; (*Wilson*. 5 vols. Princeton: Princeton University Press, 1947–65)

Link, Perry. *Mandarin ducks and butterflies: popular fiction in early twentieth-century Chinese cities*. Berkeley: University of California Press, 1981

Lippit, Victor D. 'The development of underdevelopment in China', in Victor Lippit *et al.* 'Symposium on China's economic history'. *Modern China*, 4.3 (July 1978); see pp. 251–328

Liu Ch'ang-sheng 劉長勝 *et al. Chung-kuo kung-ch'an-tang yü Shang-hai kung-jen: Shang-hai kung-jen yun-tung li-shih yen-chiu tzu-liao chih erh* 中國共産黨與上海工人：上海工人運動歷史研究資料之二 (The Chinese Communist Party and the Shanghai workers: Shanghai labour movement historical research materials number two). Shanghai: Lao-tung ch'u-pan-she 勞動出版社, August 1951

Liu Chen-tung 劉振東. 'Chung-kuo ch'u-lu wen-t'i' 中國出路問題 (The question of China's way out). *Kuo-wen chou-pao*, 10.24 (19 June 1933) 1–6 (sep. pag.)

Liu Chi-ping 劉吉丙. 'San-shih-san-nien Ssu-ch'uan chih shang-yeh' 三十三年四川之商業 (The commercial economy of Szechwan in 1944). *Ssu-ch'uan ching-chi chi-k'an*, 2.2 (1 April 1945) 75–81

Liu, F. F. *A military history of modern China, 1924–1949*. Princeton: Princeton University Press, 1956

Liu Hsin-huang 劉心皇. *Hsien-tai Chung-kuo wen-hsüeh shih-hua* 現代中國文學史話 (Discourse on the history of modern Chinese literature). Taipei: Cheng-chung, 1971

Liu Hung-sheng ch'i-yeh shih-liao 劉鴻生企業史料 (Historical materials on the enterprises of Liu Hung-sheng), ed. by Shang-hai she-hui k'e-hsüeh-yuan Ching-chi yen-chiu so 上海社會科學院經濟研究所. 3 vols. Shanghai: Jen-min, 1981

Liu I-ch'ang 劉以鬯. 'Ts'ung k'ang-chan shih-ch'i tso-chia sheng-huo chih k'un-k'u k'an she-hui tui tso-chia ti tse-jen' 從抗戰時期作家生活之困苦看社會對作家的責任 (The responsibility of society toward writers; a view based on the writers' impoverished lives during the war years). *Ming-pao yueh-k'an* (Ming-pao monthly), 13.6 (June 1978) 58–61

Liu, James T. C. 劉子健. 'An early Sung reformer: Fan Chung-yen', in John K. Fairbank, ed. *Chinese thought and institutions*, 105–31

Liu, Kwang-Ching 劉廣京. 'World view and peasant rebellion: reflections on post-Mao historiography'. *JAS* 40.2 (Feb. 1981) 295–326

Liu Min 劉敏. 'San-shih-san-nien Ssu-ch'uan chih kung-yeh' 三十三年四川之工業 (Szechwan's industry in 1944). *SCCC* 2.2 (1 April 1945) 27–43

Liu Ning. See Chang Kuo-t'ao

Liu P'ei-shan 劉培善. 'Hui-i Hsiang-Kan pien-ch'ü ti san-nien yu-chi chan-cheng' 回憶湘贛邊區的三年游擊戰爭 (Recollections of three years' guerrilla warfare in the Hunan-Kiangsi border region), in *Chung-kuo Kung-ch'an-tang tsai Chiang-hsi ti-ch'ü ling-tao ko-ming tou-cheng ti li-shih tzu-liao* 中國共產黨在江西地區領導革命鬥爭的歷史資料 (Historical materials concerning the revolutionary struggles led by the CCP in Kiangsi). Chiang-hsi jen-min, 1958

Liu Po-ch'eng 劉伯承, *et al*. *Hsing-huo liao-yuan* 星火燎原 (A single spark can start a prairie fire). Hong Kong: San-lien, 1960. See also *Hsing-huo liao-yuan*

Liu Shan-shu 劉善述. *Tzu-chih ts'ai-cheng lun* 自治財政論 (On local self-government finance). Shanghai: Cheng-chung shu-chü 正中書局, 1947

Liu Shao-ch'i 劉少奇. 'Lun kung-k'ai kung-tso yü mi-mi kung-tso' 論公開工作與秘密工作 (On open work and secret work). *Kung-ch'an tang-jen* (The Communist). Yenan, 1939. Manuscript. Copy in the Hoover Institution

Liu Shao-ch'i. 'Chien-ch'ih Hua-pei k'ang-chan chung ti wu-chuang pu-tui' 堅持華北抗戰中的武裝部隊 (Firmly support armed groups taking part in the north China war of resistance), in *K'ang-Jih min-tsu t'ung-i chan-hsien chih-nan* 抗日民族統一戰線指南 (Guide to the anti-Japanese national united front). 5. 39–54

Liu Shao-ch'i. *Lun tang* 論黨 (On the party). Dairen: Ta-chung shu-tien 大眾書店, 1947

Liu Shih-shun 劉師舜. 'I-chiu-erh-ling chi tsai-hsiao shih-tai chih Ch'ing-hua' 一九二〇級在校時代之清華 (Tsing-hua University in the days of the class of 1920). *Ch'ing-hua hsiao-yu t'ung-hsun* 清華校友通訊 (Tsing-hua Alumni/ae Gazette). NS 71, special anniversary issue. Hsinchu: 1981

Liu Shou-sung 劉綬松. *Chung-kuo hsin wen-hsueh shih ch'u-kao* 中國新文學史初稿 (A preliminary draft history of modern Chinese literature). 2 vols. Peking: Tso-chia ch'u-pan-she 作家出版社, 1956

Liu Ta-chung 劉大中. *China's national income, 1931–1936: an exploratory study*. Washington, DC: Brookings Institution, 1946

Liu Ta-chung 劉大中 and Yeh Kung-chia 葉孔嘉. *The economy of the Chinese mainland: national income and economic development, 1933–1959*. Princeton: Princeton University Press, 1965

Liu Tsai-fu 劉再復 and Lin Fei 林非. *Lu Hsun chuan* 魯迅傳 (Biography of Lu Hsun). Peking: Chung-kuo she-hui k'o-hsueh ch'u-pan-she 中國社會科學出版社, 1981

Liu Ts'ui-jung 劉翠溶. *Trade on the Han River and its impact on economic development, 1800–1911*. Taipei: Academia Sinica, Institute of Economics, 1980

Liu Wu-chi 柳無忌. 'The modern period', in Herbert A. Giles, ed. *A history of Chinese literature*, 445–500

Liu Yao 劉耀. 'T'ai-p'ing t'ien-kuo shih-pai hou Chiang-nan nung-ts'un ching-chi pien-hua ti tsai t'an-t'ao' 太平天國失敗后江南農村經濟變化的再探討 (Another inquiry into economic changes in agricultural villages of Kiangnan after the defeat of the Taipings). *Li-shih yen-chiu* (Historical research), 3 (1982) 105–20

Lo Chia-lun 羅家倫. 'Chiang Meng-lin hsien-sheng chuan-lueh' 蔣夢麟先生傳略 (Brief biography of Chiang Meng-lin) in his *Shih-che ju-ssu-chi*, 89–102

Lo Chia-lun. *Shih-che ju-ssu-chi* 逝者如斯集 (Recollections of those who are gone). Biographical Literature Series no. 14. Taipei: Chuan-chi wen-hsueh, 1967

Lo Chia-lun. 'Hsueh-shu tu-li yü hsin Ch'ing-hua' 學術獨立與新清華 (The independence of scholarship and the new Tsing-hua), in his *Shih-che ju-ssu-chi*, 7–15

Lo Chia-lun. 'Ts'ai Yuan-p'ei hsien-sheng yü Pei-ching ta-hsueh' 蔡元培先生與北京大學 (Mr Ts'ai Yuan-p'ei and Peking University), in his *Shih-che ju-ssu-chi*, 52–67

Lo Chia-lun. 'Wo so jen-shih ti Tai Chi-t'ao hsien-sheng' 我所認識的戴季陶先生 (The Tai Ch'i-t'ao I knew), in his *Shih-che ju-ssu-chi*, 144–50

Lo Chia-lun. See *Ko-ming wen-hsien*

Lo-fu (Chang Wen-t'ien) 洛甫 (張聞天) *et al. Ch'ing-nien hsueh-hsi wen-t'i* 青年學習問題 (Problems of young people's study). Shanghai: Hua-hsia shu-tien 華夏書店, 1949

Lojewski, Frank A. 'The Soochow bursaries: rent management during the late Ch'ing'. *CSWT* 4.3 (June 1980) 43–65

The Long March, eyewitness accounts. Peking: Foreign Languages Press, 1963

Lötveit, Trygve. *Chinese communism, 1931–1934: experience in civil government* Lund, Sweden: Studentlitteratur, 1973; Copenhagen: Scandinavian Institute of Asian Studies Monograph Series, no. 16, 1973

Louis, William Roger. *British strategy in the Far East, 1919–1939*. Oxford: Clarendon Press, 1971

Lowe, Peter. *Great Britain and Japan, 1911–1915: a study of British Far Eastern policy*. London: Macmillan; New York: St Martin's Press, 1969

Lowe, Peter. *Great Britain and the origins of the Pacific war: a study of British policy in East Asia, 1937–1941*. Oxford: Clarendon Press, 1977

LSYC. See *Li-shih yen-chiu*

Lu-ch'eng hsien-chih 潞城縣志 (Lu-ch'eng county gazetteer), 1885

Lu Hsun 魯迅. *Lu Hsun ch'üan-chi* 魯迅全集 (Complete works of Lu Hsun). 20 vols. Peking: Jen-min wen-hsueh ch'u-pan-she 人民文學出版社, 1973

Lu Hsun. *See* Feng Hsueh-feng; Hsia, Tsi-an; Lee, Leo Ou-fan; Lyell, W. A., Jr.; Mills, Harriet C.; Pollard, David E.; Yang, Gladys, among others

Lubot, Eugene. *Liberalism in an illiberal age: New Culture liberals in Republican China, 1919–1937.* Westport, Conn. and London: Greenwood Press, 1982

Lutz, Jessie Gregory. *China and the Christian colleges, 1850–1950.* Ithaca: Cornell University Press, 1971

Lutz, Jessie G. 'Chinese nationalism and the anti-Christian campaigns of the 1920s'. *Modern Asian Studies,* 10.3 (July 1976) 395–416

Lutz, Jessie Gregory. 'Nationalism, Chinese politics, and Christian missions'. Unpublished manuscript, 1984

Lyell, William A., Jr. *Lu Hsun's vision of reality.* Berkeley: University of California Press, 1976

Ma, Amy Fei-man. 'Local self-government and the local populace in Ch'uan-sha, 1911'. *Select papers from the Center for Far Eastern Studies,* University of Chicago, 1 (1975–6) 47–84

Ma Li-yuan 馬黎元. 'Chan-shih Hua-pei nung-tso-wu sheng-ch'an chi ti-wei tui liang-shih chih lueh-to' 戰時華北農作物生產及敵偽對糧食之掠奪 (Agricultural production and pillaging of foodstuffs by the Japanese and their puppets in North China during the war). *She-hui k'o-hsueh tsa-chih,* 10.1 (June 1948) 62–81

MacKinnon, Stephen. 'The Peiyang Army, Yuan Shih-k'ai, and the origins of modern Chinese warlordism'. *JAS* 32 (May 1972) 405–23

MacKinnon, Stephen R. *Power and politics in late imperial China: Yuan Shih-kai in Beijing and Tianjin, 1901–1908.* Berkeley: University of California Press, 1980

MacMurray, John von Antwerp, comp. and ed. *Treaties and agreements with and concerning China, 1894–1919; a collection of state papers, private agreements, and other documents, in reference to the rights and obligations of the Chinese government in relation to foreign powers, and in reference to the interrelation of those powers in respect to China during the period from the Sino-Japanese war to the conclusion of the world war of 1914–1919.* 2 vols. New York: Oxford University Press, 1921

MacNair, Harley F., ed. *Voices from unoccupied China.* Chicago: University of Chicago Press, 1944

Maier, Charles. *Recasting bourgeois Europe: stabilization in France, Germany, and Italy in the decade after World War I.* Princeton: Princeton University Press, 1975

Makino Tatsumi 牧野巽. *Shina kazoku kenkyū* 支那家族研究 (Studies of the Chinese family). Tokyo: Seikatsusha 生活社, 1944

Mallory, Walter H., with a foreword by Dr John H. Finley. *China: land of famine.* New York: American Geographical Society, 1926

Malraux, A. *Anti-memoirs*, trans. by T. Kilmartin. New York: Holt, Rinehart
& Winston, 1968

Mancall, Mark. *Russia and China: their diplomatic relations to 1728*. Cambridge,
Mass.: Harvard University Press, 1971

Mann, Susan. Review of G. Rozman, ed. *The modernization of China*. *JAS* 42.1
(Nov. 1982) 146–53

Mann, Susan. 'Urbanization and historical change in China'. *Modern China*,
10.1 (Jan. 1984) 79–115

Mann, Susan. See also Jones, Susan Mann

Manshikai 滿史会, ed. *Manshū kaihatsu yonjūnenshi* 滿州開発四十年史 (History
of forty years of Manchurian development). 3 vols. Tokyo: Manshū
kaihatsu yonjūnenshi kankōkai 滿州開発四十年史刊行会, 1964–5

Mantetsu. See SMR

Mantici, Giorgio. *Pensieri de fiume Xiang*. Roma: Editori Riuniti, 1981

Mao Tse-tung 毛澤東. *Selected works*. 4 vols. Peking: Foreign Languages
Press, 1961–5

Mao Tse-tung. *Hsuan-chi* 選集 (Selected works). Chinese ed. Peking, 1966

Mao Tse-tung. *Mao Tse-tung chi* 毛澤東集 (Collected writings of Mao Tse-
tung), ed. by Takeuchi Minoru 竹内実. 10 vols. Tokyo: Hokubōsha
北望社, 1970–2

[Mao Tse-tung.] *Mao Tse-tung chi, pu chüan*, 1 毛澤東集補卷 (... supplementary volumes, 1). Tokyo: Sōsōsha 蒼蒼社, 26 Dec. 1983. Six volumes
out of nine projected were issued up to October 1984

[Mao Tse-tung.] *Mao Tse-tung shu-hsin hsuan-chi* 毛澤東書信選集 (Selected
letters of Mao Tse-tung). Peking: Jen-min, 1983

[Mao] Tse-tung. 'Pu-hsu shih-yeh chuan-chih' 不許實業專制 (No to the
despotism of industry and commerce). *Hsiang River Review*, 1 (14 July
1919) 3

[Mao] Tse-tung. 'Cha-tan pao-chü' 炸彈暴舉 (A brutal bomb attack). *Hsiang
River Review*, 1 (14 July 1919) 3

[Mao] Tse-tung. 'Wei Te ju hu ti Fa-lan' 畏德如虎的法蘭 (France fears
Germany as if it were a tiger). *Hsiang River Review*, 3 (28 July 1919) 2

Mao Tse-tung. 'Min-chung ti ta lien-ho' 民衆的大聯合 (The great union of
the popular masses). *Hsiang River Review*, 2–4 (July–Aug. 1919). Trans. by
S. Schram in *CQ* 49 (Jan.–Mar. 1972) 76–87

Mao Tse-tung. 'Hsueh-sheng chih kung-tso' 學生之工作 (The work of the
students). *Hu-nan chiao-yü* 湖南教育 (Hunan education). 1.2 (Dec. 1919)

[Mao] Tse-tung. 'Pei-ching cheng-pien yü shang-jen' 北京政變與商人 (The
Peking coup d'état and the merchants). *The guide weekly*, 31/32 (11 July
1923) 233–4

Mao Tse-tung. 'Pien-cheng-fa wei-wu-lun (chiang-shou t'i-kang)' 辯証法唯
物論(講授提綱) (Dialectical materialism—lecture notes). *K'ang-chan ta-
hsueh* 抗戰大學 (organ of the Anti-Japanese Military-Political University),
6 to 8 (April to June, 1938) 123–5, 147–50, 184–7

Mao Tse-tung. *Chi-ch'u chan-shu* 基礎戰術 (Basic tactics). Hankow: Tzu-ch'iang ch'u-pan she 自強出版社, 1938

Mao Tse-tung. *Pien-cheng wei-wu-lun* 辯証唯物論 (Dialectical materialism). Dairen: Ta-chung shu-tien 大衆書店, n.d. [*c.* 1946]

Mao Tse-tung. *Ching-chi wen-t'i yü ts'ai-cheng wen-t'i* 經濟問題與財政問題 (Economic and financial problems). Hong Kong: Hsin-min-chu ch'u-pan-she 新民主出版社, 1949

Mao Tse-tung. *Basic tactics,* ed. and trans. by Stuart R. Schram. New York: Praeger, 1966. Trans. of *Chi-ch'u chan-shu*

Mao Tse-tung. 'Chung-kuo nung-min ko chieh-chi ti fen-hsi chi ch'i tui ko-ming ti t'ai-tu' 中國農民各階級的分析及其對革命的態度 (Analysis of all the classes of the Chinese peasantry, and their attitudes toward revolution). *Mao Tse-tung chi,* 1 153–9

Mao Tse-tung. 'Chung-kuo she-hui ko chieh-chi ti fen-hsi' 中國社會各階級的分析 (Analysis of all the classes in Chinese society). *Mao Tse-tung chi,* 1. 161–74

Mao Tse-tung. 'Kuo-min ko-ming yü nung-min yun-tung' 國民革命與農民運動 (The national revolution and the peasant movement). *Mao Tse-tung chi,* 1. 175–9

Mao Tse-tung. 'Kao Chung-kuo ti nung-min' 告中國的農民 (Address to the Chinese peasants). *Tzu-liao hsuan-pien* 資料選編, 24

Mao Tse-tung. *Mao Tse-tung on literature and art.* Peking: Foreign Languages Press, 1967

Mao Tse-tung. 'Talks at the Yenan Forum on literature and art', in Mao Tse-tung, *Mao Tse-tung on literature and art*

Mao Tse-tung. *Mao Tse-tung ssu-hsiang wan-sui* 毛澤東思想萬歲 (Long live the thought of Mao Tse-tung). Red Guard publication. 2 vols. 1967, 1969

Mao Tse-tung (?). Dialogue with Red Guards, 28 July 1968. JPRS 61269, 476 (Joint Publications Research Service, Washington, D.C.)

Mao Tse-tung (?). Dialogue with Red Guards, 28 July 1968. *Mao Tse-tung ssu-hsiang wan-sui* 1969, p. 694

Mao Tse-tung. 'Kai-ko hun-chih wen-t'i' 改革婚制問題 (Problems concerning the reform of marriage customs). *MTTC, pu chüan,* 1.149

Mao Tse-tung. 'Lien-ai wen-t'i – shao-nien-jen yü lao-nien-jen' 戀愛問題—少年人與老年人 (Problems of being in love – the youth and the elderly). *MTTC, pu-chüan,* 1.161–3

Mao Tse-tung. 'Wai li, chün-fa yü ko-ming' 外力軍閥與革命 (The foreign powers, the militarists, and the revolution). *MTTC, pu-chüan,* 2.109–11

Mao Tse-tung. 'Shih-ch'a Hu-nan nung-yün kei Chung-yang ti pao-kao' 視察湖南農運給中央的報告 (Report to the Central Committee on an Inspection of the Peasant Movement in Hunan). *MMTC, pu-chüan,* 2.255–7

Mao Tse-tung. 'Kei Hsiang-tung t'e-wei ti hsin' 給湘東特委的信 (Letter to the East Hunan Special Committee). *MTTC, pu-chüan,* 3.157–8

Mao Tse-tung. See Tzu Jen.

Mao Chu-hsi wen-hsuan 毛主席文選 (Selected essays by Chairman Mao). n.p., n.d.

Mao Tse-tung and Guevara, Che. *Guerrilla warfare.* Section by Mao trans. by Samuel B. Griffith. London: Cassell, 1964

Mao Zedong. *Une étude de l'éducation physique*, ed. and trans. by Stuart R. Schram. Paris: Mouton, 1962

Marks, Robert B. 'Peasant society and peasant uprisings in South China: social change in Haifeng County, 1630–1930'. University of Wisconsin, Ph.D. dissertation, 1978

Marks, Robert B. 'Social change in Haifeng county on the eve of the Haifeng peasant movement, 1870–1920'. Paper prepared for the Workshop on Chinese Communist Rural Bases, Harvard University, 1978

Márquez, Gabriel García. *Cent ans de solitude* (One hundred years of solitude). Paris: Éditions du Seuil, 1968

Marsh, Susan Han. 'Chou Fo-hai: the making of a collaborator', in Akira Iriye, ed. *The Chinese and the Japanese*, 304–27

Martin, Edwin W. 'The Chou demarche'. *Foreign Service Journal*, Nov. 1981, 13–16, 32

Marx, Karl. *Le Dix-huit Brumaire de Louis Bonaparte.* Paris: Éditions Sociales, 1976

Masuko Teisuke 益子逞輔. *Chūbu Shina* 中部支那 (Central China). Taipei: Taiwan Nichi Nichi Shimpōsha 台灣日日新報社, 1912

Matsumoto Shigeharu 松本重治. *Shanghai jidai* 上海時代 (The Shanghai years). 3 vols. Tokyo: Chūō Kōronsha 中央公論社, 1974–5

May, Gary, with intro. by John K. Fairbank. *China scapegoat: the diplomatic ordeal of John Carter Vincent.* Washington, DC: New Republic Books, 1979

McCord, Edward A. 'Recent progress in warlord studies in the People's Republic of China'. *Republican China*, 9.2 (Feb. 1984) 40–7

McCormack, Gavan. *Chang Tso-lin in Northeast China, 1911–1928: China, Japan and the Manchurian idea.* Stanford: Stanford University Press, 1977

McDonald, Angus. *Hōgaku kenkyū* 法学研究 46.2 (1972) 99–107

McDonald, Angus. *Rōnin* 浪人 (Tokyo), 14 (Dec. 1973) 37–47

McDonald, Angus W., Jr. 'Mao Tse-tung and the Hunan self-government movement, 1920: an introduction and five translations'. *CQ* 68 (Dec. 1976) 751–77

McDonald, Angus W., Jr. *The urban origins of rural revolution: elites and masses in Hunan province, China, 1911–1927.* Berkeley: University of California Press, 1978

McDonald, Angus W., Jr. 'Wallerstein's world economy: how seriously should we take it?' *JAS* 38.3 (May 1979) 535–40

McDougall, Bonnie S., trans. and ed. *Paths in dreams: selected prose and poetry of Ho Ch'i-fang.* Queensland, Australia: University of Queensland Press, 1976

McDougall, Bonnie S. *Mao Zedong's 'Talks at the Yan'an conference on literature and art': a translation of the 1943 text with commentary*. Ann Arbor: Center for Chinese Studies, University of Michigan, 1980

McElderry, Andrea Lee. *Shanghai old-style banks (ch'ien-chuang), 1800–1935: a traditional institution in a changing society*. Ann Arbor: Center for Chinese Studies, University of Michigan, 1976

McLane, Charles B. *Soviet policy and the Chinese communists, 1931–1946*. New York: Columbia University Press, 1958

Mei-chou p'ing-lun 每週評論 (Weekly review), ed. Li Ta-chao *et al.* Peking, 22 Dec. 1918–31 Aug. 1919

Mei Yi-pao 梅貽寶. *Ta-hsueh chiao-yü wu-shih-nien – pa-shih tzu-chuan* 大學教育五十年—八十自傳 (University education over fifty years – an autobiography at 80). Taipei: Lien-ching 聯經, 1982

Meisner, Maurice. *Li Ta-chao and the origins of Chinese Marxism*. Cambridge, Mass.: Harvard University Press, 1967

Melby, John F. *The mandate of Heaven*. Toronto: University of Toronto Press, 1968

Meliksetov, A. V. *Sotsial'no-ekonomicheskaia politika Gomin'dana v Kitae, 1927–1949* (Kuomintang social-economic policy in China, 1927–1949). Moscow: Glavnaia redaktsiia vostochnoi literatury, Nauka, 1977

Meng Kuang-yu 孟光宇 and Kuo Han-ming 郭漢鳴. *Szu-ch'uan tsu-tien wen-t'i* 四川租佃問題 (The tenant problem in Szechwan). Chungking: CP, 1944

Meserve, Walter, and Meserve, Ruth, eds. *Modern drama from Communist China*. New York: New York University Press, 1970

Metzger, Thomas. 'The organizational capabilities of the Ch'ing state in the field of commerce: the Liang-Huai salt monopoly, 1740–1840', in W. E. Willmott, ed. *Economic organization in Chinese society*, 9–46

Metzger, Thomas. 'On the historical roots of economic modernization in China: the increasing differentiation of the economy from the polity during late Ming and early Ch'ing times', in Chi-ming Hou and Tzong-shien Yu, eds., *Modern Chinese economic history*, 3–14

Mi Ti-kang 米廸剛. 'Yü chih Chung-kuo she-hui kai-liang chu-i' 余之中國社會改良主義 (My proposals for reforming Chinese society), in *Chai-ch'eng ts'un-chih*, Appendices, 25–91

Mi-ting 米定 (M. Mitin) and others, trans. by Ai Ssu-ch'i 艾思奇 and others. *Hsin-che-hsueh ta-kang* 新哲學大綱 (Outline of the new philosophy). Shanghai: Tu-shu sheng-huo ch'u-pan-she, 1936

Miao Ch'u-huang 繆楚黃. 'Chung-kuo kung-nung hung-chün ch'ang-cheng kai-shu 中國工農紅軍長征概述 (A brief account of the Long March of the Workers' and Peasants' Red Army of China). *Li-shih yen-chiu* (Historical research), 2 (1954) 85–96

Miao Ch'u-huang. *Chung-kuo Kung-ch'an-tang chien-yao li-shih* 中國共產黨簡要歷史 (A brief history of the CCP). Peking: Hsueh-hsi tsa-chih-she 學習雜誌社 1957

Michael, Franz. 'Regionalism in nineteenth-century China', intro. to Stanley

Spector, *Li Hung-chang and the Huai army.*

Migdal, Joel S. *Peasants, politics and revolution: pressures towards political and social changes in the Third World.* Princeton: Princeton University Press, 1974

Miles, Milton E. *A different kind of war: the little-known story of the combined guerrilla forces created in China by the US Navy and the Chinese during World War II.* Garden City, NY: Doubleday, 1967

Military campaigns in China, 1924–1950. See Ministry of National Defence

Mills, Harriet C. 'Lu Hsun: 1927–1936, the years on the left'. Columbia University, Ph.D. dissertation, 1963

Min-chu p'ing-lun 民主評論 (Democratic review) Hong Kong, July 1949–

Min-kuo 20–30 nien-tai Chung-kuo ching-chi nung-yeh t'u-ti shui-li wen-t'i tzu-liao 民國二〇三〇年代中國經濟農業土地水利問題資料 (Materials on China's economic, agrarian, land and water control problems in the 1930s and 1940s). An index compiled by the Land Management Institute in Taipei

Min Tu-ki 閔斗基. 'Ch'ŏngdae ponggŏllon ǔi kǔndaejŏk pyŏnmo' 清代封建論의近代의變貌 (The modern transformation of traditional political feudalism in the Ch'ing period), *Chungguk kǔndaesa yŏn'gu* 中國近代史研究 (Studies in modern Chinese history). Seoul: Il Cho kak 一潮閣, 1973

Miner, Noel Ray. 'Chekiang: the Nationalists' effort in agrarian reform and construction, 1927–1937'. Stanford University, Ph.D. dissertation, 1973

Miner, Noel Ray. 'Agrarian reform in Nationalist China: the case of rent reduction in Chekiang, 1927–1937', in F. Gilbert Chan, ed. *China at the crossroads: Nationalists and Communists, 1927–1949,* 69–89

Ming Ch'ing Su-chou kung-shang-yeh pei-k'e chi 明清蘇州工商業碑刻集 (A collection of inscriptions of Soochow guilds in the Ming and Ch'ing periods), comp. by Su-chou li-shih po-wu-kuan 蘇州歷史博物館, Chiang-su shih-fan hsueh-yuan li-shih-hsi 江蘇師範學院歷史系, Nan-ching ta-hsueh Ming Ch'ing shih yen-chiu shih 南京大學明清史研究室. Kiangsu: Jen-min, 1981

Ming Ch'ing tzu-pen-chu-i meng-ya yen-chiu lun-wen chi 明清資本主義萌芽研究論文集 (Collected research essays on capitalist sprouts in the Ming and Ch'ing dynasties), ed. by Nan-ching ta-hsueh li-shih hsi 南京大學歷史系 Shanghai: Jen-min, 1981

Ming-pao yueh-k'an 明報月刊 (Ming-pao monthly). Hong Kong, 1966–

Ministry of Education, Office of Statistics, comp. *Erh-shih-san nien-tu ch'üan-kuo kao-teng chiao-yü t'ung-chi* 二十三年度全國高等教育統計 (Statistics of higher education in China for the academic year 1934–5). Shanghai: CP, 1936

Ministry of National Defence, War History Bureau. *Military campaigns in China, 1924–1950,* trans. by W. W. Whitson, Patrick Yang and Paul Lai. Taipei, 1966

Mitin. See Mi-ting

Miyazaki Tōten 宮崎滔天. *My thirty three years dream: the autobiography of Miyazaki Tōten,* trans. and introd. by S. Etō and M.B. Jansen. Princeton:

Princeton University Press, 1982

Modern Asian Studies. Quarterly. Cambridge, England and New York: Cambridge University Press. 1967–.

Modern China: an international quarterly. Beverly Hills, Calif: Sage Publications. 1975–

Monroe, Paul. *China: a nation in evolution*. New York: Macmillan, 1928

Moore, Barrington, Jr. *Social origins of dictatorship and democracy: land and peasant in the making of the modern world*. Boston: Beacon Press, 1966

Morita Akira 森田明. *Shindai suirishi kenkyū* 清代水利史研究 (Studies in the history of water management during the Ch'ing period). Tokyo: Akishobō 亞紀書房, 1974

Morley, James William. *The Japanese thrust into Siberia, 1918*. New York: Columbia University Press, 1957

Morley, James William, ed. *The fateful choice: Japan's advance into Southeast Asia, 1939–1941: selected translations from Taiheiyō sensō e no michi, kaisen gaikō shi*. New York: Columbia University Press, 1980

Morley, James William, ed. *The China quagmire: Japan's expansion on the Asian continent, 1933–1941*. New York: Columbia University Press, 1983

Morley, James W., ed. *Japan's road to the Pacific War: Japan erupts. The London Naval Conference and the Manchurian Incident 1928–1932: selected translations from Taiheiyō sensō e no michi: kaisen gaikō shi*. Fourth vol. in a 5-vol. series. New York: Columbia University Press, 1984

Morse, Hosea Ballou. *The trade and administration of China*. 3rd rev. edn. Shanghai: Kelly & Walsh, 1921

Morton, William F. *Tanaka Giichi and Japan's China policy*. New York: St Martin's Press, 1980

Mote, F. W. *Intellectual foundations of China*. New York: Knopf, 1971

Moulder, Frances. *Japan, China and the modern world economy*. Cambridge: Cambridge University Press, 1977

Mousnier, Roland. *Fureurs paysannes; les paysans dans les révoltes du XVIIème siècle (France, Russie, Chine)*. Paris: Calmann-Lévy, 1967

MTTC. See *Mao Tse-tung chi*

MTTC, pu chüan, See *Mao Tse-tung chi, pu chüan*

Muhse, Albert C. 'Trade organization and trade control in China'. *American Economic Review*, 6.2 (June 1916) 309–23

Munro, Donald J. *The concept of man in early China*. Stanford: Stanford University Press, 1969

Munro, Donald J. *The concept of man in contemporary China*. Ann Arbor: University of Michigan Press, 1977

Muramatsu Yūji 村松祐次. See *Chūgoku no seiji to keizai*

Muramatsu Yūji. 'A documentary study of Chinese landlordism in late Ch'ing and early republican Kiangnan'. *Bulletin of the School of Oriental and African Studies*, 29.3 (Oct. 1966) 566–99

Muramatsu Yūji. *Kindai Kōnan no sosan* 近代江南の租棧 (Bursaries in the Lower

Yangtze area in modern times). Tokyo: Tokyo Daigaku shuppankai, 1970

Murphey, Rhoads. *The fading of the Maoist vision: city and country in China's development*. New York, London, Toronto: Methuen, 1980

Murphy, George G. S. *Soviet Mongolia: a study of the oldest political satellite*. Berkeley and Los Angeles: University of California Press, 1966

Murray, Dian. 'Mid-Ch'ing piracy: an analysis of organizational attributes'. *CSWT* 4.8 (Dec. 1982) 1–29

Museum of the Chinese Revolution. *See* Chung-kuo ko-ming po-wu-kuan

Myers, Ramon H. 'Cotton textile handicraft and the development of the cotton textile industry in modern China'. *Economic History Review*, 18.3 (1965) 614–32

Myers, Ramon H. *The Chinese peasant economy: agricultural development in Hopei and Shantung, 1890–1949*. Cambridge, Mass.: Harvard University Press, 1970

Myers, Ramon H. 'The commercialization of agriculture in modern China', in W. E. Willmott, ed. *Economic organization in Chinese society*, 173–191

Myers, Ramon H. 'Transformation and continuity in Chinese economic and social history'. *JAS* 33.2 (Feb. 1974) 265–77

Myers, Ramon H. 'Cooperation in traditional agriculture and its implications for team farming in the People's Republic of China'. in Dwight Perkins, ed. *China's modern economy in historical perspective*, 261–78

Myers, Ramon. 'Socioeconomic change in villages of Manchuria during the Ch'ing and Republican periods: some preliminary findings'. *Modern Asian Studies*, 10.4 (1976) 591–620

Myers, Ramon. *The Chinese economy: past and present*. Belmont, Calif.: Wadsworth, 1980

Myers, Ramon H. 'Economic organization and cooperation in modern China: irrigation management in Hsiang-t'ai county, Hopei province', in *Chūgoku no seiji to keizai* (The polity and economy of China—the late Professor Yūji Muramatsu commemoration volume), 189–212

Nagai, Yōnosuke and Iriye, Akira, eds. *The origins of the cold war in Asia*. New York: Columbia University Press, 1977

Nakagane Katsugi. *Kyū Manshū nōson shakai keizai kōzō no bunseki* 舊満洲農村社会経済構造の分析 (Analysis of the socio-economic structure of villages in traditional Manchuria). No data.

Nakajima Masao 中島正郎, ed. *Taishi kaiko roku* 対支回顧録 (Memoirs concerning China). 2 vols. Tokyo: Dai Nihon Kyōka Tosho, 1936

Nakajima Masao, ed. *Zoku Taishi kaiko roku* 續対支回顧録 (Memoirs concerning China, supplement). 2 vols. Tokyo: Dai Nihon Kyōka Tosho, 1941

Nakajima, Mineo 中嶋嶺雄. 'The Sino-Soviet confrontation in historical perspective', in Yōnosuke Nagai and Akira Iriye, eds. *The origins of the cold war in Asia*, 203–23

Nakajima Mineo. *Chū-So tairitsu to gendai: sengo Ajia no sai kōsatsu* 中ソ対立

と現代：戦後アジアの再考察 (The Sino-Soviet confrontation and the present day: a reexamination of postwar Asia). Tokyo: Chūō Kōronsha 中央公論社, 1978

Nakami Tatsuo 中見立夫. '1913 nen no Ro-Chū sengen: Chūkaminkoku no seiritsu to Mongoru mondai' 1913年の露中宣言—中華民国の成立とモンゴル問題 (Russo-Chinese Declaration of 1913: establishment of the Republic of China and the Mongol problem), *Kokusai seiji* 国際政治 (International politics), 66 (Nov. 1980).

Nakamura Tadashi 中村義. *Shingai kakumei shi kenkyū* 辛亥革命史研究 (Studies of the 1911 Revolution). Tokyo: Miraisha 未来社, 1979

Nakamura Takafusa 中村隆英. 'Go-sanjū jiken to zaikabō' 五・三十事件と在華紡 (The May 30 incident and the Japanese cotton industry in China), *Kindai Chūgoku kenkyū* 近代中國研究 (Studies on modern China), 6 (1964) 99–169

Nakamura Takafusa. 'Japan's economic thrust into North China, 1933–1938: formation of the North China Development Corporation', in Akira Iriye, ed. *The Chinese and the Japanese*, 220–53

'Nan-ch'ang ta-shih chi' 南昌大事記 (Important events at Nanchang). *Chin-tai-shih tzu-liao* 近代史資料, 4 (1957) 130

Nan-hsun chih 南潯志 (Gazetteer of Nan-hsun). Chou Ch'ing-yun 周慶雲, comp. 1922

Nan-k'ai ta-hsueh ching-chi yen-chiu so 南開大學經濟研究所 (Nankai Institute of Economics), ed. *1913–1952 nien Nan-k'ai chih-shu tzu-liao hui-pien* 1913–1952年南開指數資料彙編 (Nankai price indexes 1913–1952) Peking: T'ung-chi ch'u-pan-she 統計出版社, 1958

Nance, W. B. *Soochow University*. New York: United Board for Christian Colleges in China, 1956

Nankai Social and Economic Quarterly. Tientsin, 1928– (vol. 5–9, 1932–7; suspended 1937–9; resumed 1940)

Naquin, Susan. *Millenarian rebellion in China: the Eight Trigrams uprising of 1813*. New Haven: Yale University Press, 1976

Naquin, Susan. *Shantung rebellion: the Wang Lun uprising of 1774*. New Haven: Yale University Press, 1981

Naquin, Susan. 'Connections between rebellions: sect family networks in Qing China'. *Modern China*, 8.3 (July 1982) 337–60

Nathan, Andrew J. 'A factionalism model for CCP politics'. *CQ* 53 (Jan.–March 1973) 34–66

Negishi Benji 根岸勉治. *Minami Shina nōgyō keizai ron* 南支那農業經濟論 (Essays on South China's agricultural economy). Taipei: Noda shobō 野田書房, 1940

Negishi Tadashi 根岸佶. *Shanhai no girudo* 上海のギルド (The guilds of Shanghai). Tokyo: Nihon Hyōronsha 日本評論社, 1951

Nei-cheng nien-chien pien-tsuan wei-yuan-hui 內政年鑑編纂委員會. comp. *Nei-cheng nien-chien* 內政年鑑 (Ministry of Interior year book). Shanghai:

CP, 1936

Neu, Charles E. *An uncertain friendship. Theodore Roosevelt and Japan, 1906–1909.* Cambridge, Mass.: Harvard University Press, 1967

Nihon kokusai seiji gakkai 日本国際政治学会, ed. *Taiheiyō sensō e no michi* 太平洋戦争への道 (The road to the Pacific war). 8 vols. Tokyo: Asahi shimbunsha 朝日新聞社, 1962–3

Niida Noboru 仁井田陞. *Chūgoku no nōson kazoku* 中國の農村家族 (The Chinese rural family). Tokyo: Tokyo Daigaku shuppankai, 1954

Nish, Ian H. *The Anglo-Japanese alliance: the diplomacy of two island empires, 1894–1907.* London: University of London Press, 1966

Nish, Ian H. *Alliance in decline: a study in Anglo-Japanese relations 1908–1923.* London: Athlone Press, 1972

Nish, Ian, ed. *Anglo-Japanese alienation,1919–1952: papers of the Anglo-Japanese Conference on the History of the Second World War.* Cambridge, New York: Cambridge University Press, 1982.

Nish, Ian, ed. *Some aspects of Soviet-Japanese relations in the 1930s*

North China Herald. Weekly. Shanghai, 1850–

North, Robert C. *Moscow and Chinese communists.* Stanford: Stanford University Press, 1952; 2nd edn, 1963

North, Robert C. *Kuomintang and Chinese Communist elites.* Stanford: Stanford University Press, 1952

North, Robert C. See Eudin, Xenia

NTCC. See Feng Ho-fa, ed. *Chung-kuo nung-ts'un ching-chi tzu-liao*

NYTL. See Chang Yu-i, comp. *Chung-kuo chin-tai nung-yeh shih tzu-liao, ti-san chi, 1927–1937*

O-Yü-Wan su-ch'ü ko-ming-shih tzu-liao hsuan-pien 鄂豫皖蘇區革命史資料選編 (Selected documents of the revolutionary history of the O-Yü-Wan soviet). Vol. 1, compiled by the party historians of the Central China Teachers' College

Ocko, Jonathan K. *Bureaucratic reform in provincial China: Ting Jih-ch'ang in Restoration Kiangsu, 1867–1870.* Cambridge, Mass.: Council on East Asian Studies, 1983

Offner, Arnold A. *American appeasement: United States foreign policy and Germany, 1933–1938.* Cambridge, Mass.: Belknap Press, 1969

Ogata, Sadako N. *Defiance in Manchuria: the making of Japanese foreign policy, 1931–1932.* Berkeley: University of California Press, 1964.

Okamoto, Shumpei. *The Japanese oligarchy and the Russo-Japanese War.* New York: Columbia University Press, 1970. See also Borg, Dorothy

Okuzaki Hiroshi 奧崎裕司. *Chūgoku kyōshin jinushi no kenkyū* 中国郷紳地主の研究 (Studies of gentry-landlords in China). Tokyo: kyūko Shoin 汲古書院, 1978

Oliver, Frank. *Special undeclared war.* London: Jonathan Cape, 1939

Onogawa Hidemi 小野川秀美 and Shimada Kenji 島田虔次. *Shingai kakumei no kenkyū* 辛亥革命の研究 (Studies of the 1911 Revolution). Tokyo:

Chikuma Shobō 筑摩書房, 1978

Orb, Richard A. 'Chihli academies and other schools in the late Ch'ing: an institutional survey', in Paul A. Cohen and John E. Schrecker, eds. *Reform in nineteenth-century China*, 231–40

Osaka Tokushi 尾坂徳司. *Chūgoku shin bungaku undō shi* 中国新文学運動史 (History of the new literature movement of China). 2 vols. Tokyo: Hosei daigaku 法政大学, 1965

Ostrower, Gary B. *Collective insecurity: the United States and the League of Nations during the early thirties*. Lewisburg, Pa.: Bucknell University Press, 1979

Otte, Friederich. 'Correlation of harvests with importation of cereals in China'. *Chinese Economic Journal*, 15.4 (Oct. 1934) 338–414

Ou Tsuin-chen. 'Education in wartime China', in Paul K. T. Sih, ed. *Nationalist China during the Sino-Japanese War, 1937–1945*, 89–123

Ou Tsuin-chen. See Clopton, Robert W.

Ou Yuan-huai 歐元懷. 'K'ang-chan shih-nien lai ti Chung-kuo ta-hsueh chiao-yü' 抗戰十年來的中國大學教育 (Higher education in China in the decade since the [beginning of the] war), *Chung-hua chiao-yü chieh* (Chinese education), NS, 1.1 (15 Jan. 1947) 7–15

Overmyer, Daniel L. *Folk Buddhist religion: dissenting sects in late traditional China*. Cambridge, Mass.: Harvard University Press, 1976

Overmyer, Daniel L. 'Alternatives: popular religious sects in Chinese society'. *Modern China*, 7.2 (April 1981) 153–90

Paauw, Douglas S. 'The Kuomintang and economic stagnation, 1928–1937'. *JAS* 16.2 (Feb. 1957) 213–220

Pa Chin 巴金. *Cold nights: a novel*. trans. by Nathan K. Mao and Liu Ts'un-yan. Hong Kong: Chinese University Press; Seattle: University of Washington Press, 1978. Trans. of *Han-yeh*

P'an Kung-chan 潘公展, ed. *Wu-shih-nien lai ti Chung-kuo* 五十年來的中國 (China in the past 50 years). Chungking: Sheng-li, 1945; Taipei reprint, 1976

P'an Tsu-yung 潘祖永. 'Hou-fang pan-ch'ang ti k'un-nan ho ch'i-wang' 後方辦廠的困難和期望 (Difficulties and hopes of factory management in the rear area). *Hsin-ching-chi*, 6.11 (1 Mar. 1942)

P'ang Sung. See Huang Yen-p'ei

Papers on China. Annual. Vols. 1–24 (1947–71). East Asian Research Center, Harvard University

Paulson, David. 'Leadership and spontaneity: recent approaches to communist base area studies'. *Chinese Republican Studies Newsletter*, 7.1 (Oct. 1981) 13–18

Paulson, David. 'War and revolution in North China: the Shandong base area, 1937–1945'. Stanford University, Ph.D. dissertation, 1982

'Peasant rebellions in China, symposium'. *Modern China*, 9.3 (July 1983), entire volume; articles by Joseph W. Esherick, Jack L. Dull, William G.

Crowell, and Elizabeth J. Perry

'Peasant strategies in Asian societies: moral and rational economic approaches—a symposium'. *JAS* 42.4 (Aug. 1983) 753–868

Peattie, Mark R. *Ishiwara Kanji and Japan's confrontation with the West.* Princeton: Princeton University Press, 1975

Peck, Graham. *Two kinds of time: a personal story of China's crash into revolution.* Boston: Houghton Mifflin, 1950; first half reprinted 1968

Pei-ching ta-hsueh che-hsueh hsi 北京大學哲學系. *Mao Tse-tung che-hsueh ssu-hsiang (chai-lu)* 毛澤東哲學思想(摘錄) (Mao Tse-tung's philosophical thought—abstract). [Peking]: 1960

Pei-ching ta-hsueh yueh-k'an 北京大學月刊 (Peking University monthly). Peking, 1919–

Pei-fang ti-ch'ü kung-jen yun-tung tzu-liao hsuan-pien, 1921–1923 北方地區工人運動資料選編, 1921–1923 (Selected materials on the local workers' movement in North China 1921–1923). Chung-kuo ko-ming po-wu-kuan 中國革命博物館 (Museum of the Chinese Revolution), comp. Peking: Pei-ching ch'u-pan-she 北京出版社, 1981

Pei-p'ing she-hui tiao-ch'a so. See *Ti-erh-tz'u Chung-kuo* . . .

Peking Review. Peking. Weekly. March 4, 1958–

Pelz, Stephen E. *Race to Pearl Harbor: the failure of the Second London Naval Conference and the onset of World War II.* Cambridge, Mass.: Harvard University Press, 1974

P'eng Chen 彭真. *Chung-kung 'Chin-Ch'a-Chi pien-ch'ü' chih ko-chung cheng-ts'e* 中共「晉察冀邊區」之各種政策 (Various policies in the CCP's 'Chin-Ch'a-Chi Border Region'). n.p.: T'ung-i ch'u-pan-she 統一出版社, 28 Jan. 1938. Manuscript in Hoover Institution, Stanford University

P'eng P'ai 彭湃. 'Hai-feng nung-min yun-tung' 海豐農民運動 (The peasant movement in Hai-feng), in *Ti-i-tz'u kuo-nei ko-ming chan-cheng shih-ch'i ti nung-min yun-tung* 第一次國內革命戰爭時期的農民運動 (The peasant movement during the first revolutionary civil war period), 40–138. Peking: Jen-min, 1953

P'eng Shu-chih 彭述之. 'Jang li-shih ti wen-chien tso-cheng' 讓歷史的文件作証 (Let historical documents be my witness). *Ming-pao yueh-k'an*, 30 (June 1968) 13–22

P'eng Te-huai 彭德懷. *P'eng Te-huai tzu-shu* 彭德懷自述 (The autobiography of P'eng Te-huai). Shantung: Jen-min, 1981

P'eng Te-huai. 'Kuan-yü hua-pei ken-chü-ti kung-tso ti pao-kao' 關於華北根據地工作的報告 (Report on work in the base areas of North China), in *Kung-fei huo-kuo shih-liao hui-pien* (Collected historical materials on the national disaster caused by the Communist bandits), 3.346–406

P'eng Tse-i 彭澤益 ed. *Chung-kuo chin-tai shou-kung-yeh shih tzu-liao,* 中國近代手工業史資料, 1840–1949 (Source materials on the history of handicraft industry in modern China, 1840–1949). 4 vols. Peking: San-lien, 1957

People's University. See Chung-kuo jen-min ta-hsueh

Pepper, Suzanne. *Civil war in China: the political struggle 1945–1949*. Berkeley: University of California Press, 1978

Perdue, Peter. 'Official goals and local interests: water control in the Dongting Lake region during the Ming and Qing periods'. *JAS* 51.4 (Aug. 1982) 747–66

Perkins, Dwight H., with the assistance of Yeh-chien Wang, Kuo-ying Wang Hsiao [and] Yung-ming Su. *Agricultural development in China, 1368–1968*. Chicago: Aldine, 1969

Perkins, Dwight H., ed. *China's modern economy in historical perspective*. Stanford: Stanford University Press, 1975

Perry, Elizabeth J. *Rebels and revolutionaries in North China, 1845–1945*. Stanford: Stanford University Press, 1980

Perry, Elizabeth J. and Harrell, Stevan, eds. 'Symposium: syncretic sects in Chinese society, Part I'. *Modern China*, 8.3 (July 1982), entire; articles by Stevan Harrell, Elizabeth J. Perry, Richard Shek, Susan Naquin and David E. Kelley; Part II, 8.4 (Oct. 1982) 435–83; articles by David K. Jordan and Robert P. Weller

Perry, Elizabeth. 'Social banditry revisited: the case of Bai Lang, a Chinese brigand'. *Modern China*, 9.3 (July 1983) 355–82

Pickowicz, Paul G. 'Ch'ü Ch'iu-pai and the Chinese Marxist conception of revolutionary popular literature and art'. *CQ* 70 (June 1977) 296–314

Pickowicz, Paul G. *Marxist literary thought in China: the influence of Ch'ü Ch'iu-pai*. Berkeley: University of California Press, 1981

PLA. People's Liberation Army

PLA unit history. Taiwan. Translated and prepared at the field level under the auspices of the Office of the Chief of Military History, (US) Department of the Army

Po I-po 薄一波. 'Liu Shao-ch'i t'ung-chih ti i-ko li-shih kung-chi' 劉少奇同志的一個歷史功績 (An historic achievement of Comrade Liu Shao-ch'i). *JMJP* 5 May 1980

Polachek, James. 'Gentry hegemony: Soochow in the T'ung-chih Restoration', in Frederic Wakeman, Jr. and Carolyn Grant, eds. *Conflict and control in late imperial China*, 211–56

Polachek, James M. 'The moral economy of the Kiangsi soviet (1928–1934)'. *JAS* 42.4 (Aug. 1983) 805–29

Polachek, James. *The inner opium war*. Cambridge, Mass.: Council on East Asian Studies, Harvard University. Forthcoming

Pollard, David E. *A Chinese look at literature: the literary values of Chou Tso-jen in relation to the tradition*. Berkeley: University of California Press, 1973

Pollard, David E. 'Lu Xun's *Zawen*', paper prepared for the Conference on Lu Xun and His Legacy, Asilomar, California, 22–28 Aug. 1981

Popkin, Samuel I. *The rational peasant: the political economy of rural society in Vietnam*. Berkeley: University of California Press, 1979

Potter, Jack. 'Land and lineage in traditional China', in Maurice Freedman, ed. *Family and kinship in Chinese society*, 121–38

Powell, Lyle Stephenson. *A surgeon in wartime China*. Lawrence, Kansas: University of Kansas Press, 1946

Prazniak, Roxanne. 'Community and protest in rural China: tax resistance and county-village politics on the eve of the 1911 revolution'. University of California, Davis, Ph.D. dissertation, 1981

Prévert, Jacques. *Paroles*. Paris: Éditions Gallimard, 1949

Price, Don. C. *Russia and the roots of the Chinese Revolution, 1896–1911*. Cambridge, Mass.: Harvard University Press, 1974

Price, Frank W. Preface to *Wartime China as seen by Westerners*. Chungking: The China Publishing Co. Preface dated 1942

Price, Jane L. *Cadres, commanders, and commissars: the training of the Chinese communist leadership, 1920–1945*. Boulder, Colo.: Westview Press, 1976

PTMT. See Schram, Stuart, *The political thought of Mao Tse-tung*

Pu-erh-sai-wei-k'e 布爾塞維克 (The bolshevik). Official organ of the CCP center. Shanghai, Oct. 1927–

Pugach, Noel H. *Paul S. Reinsch, open door diplomat in action*. Millwood, NY: KTO Press, 1979

Pusey, James Reeve. *China and Charles Darwin*. Cambridge, Mass.: Council on East Asian Studies, Harvard University, 1983

Pye, Lucian W. *The dynamics of factions and consensus in Chinese politics: a model and some propositions*. Report prepared for the United States Air Force. Santa Monica: Rand Corporation, July 1980

Qian Zhongshu. See Ch'ien Chung-shu

Rabe, Valentin H. *The home base of American China missions, 1880–1920*. Cambridge, Mass.: Council on East Asian Studies, Harvard University, 1978

'Ranisha no soshiki to hanman kōnichi katsudō no jitsurei' 藍衣社の組織と反滿抗日活動の實例 (The organization of the Blue Shirts and examples of anti-Manchukuo, anti-Japanese activities), in *Ranisha ni kansuru shirō* 藍衣社に関する資料 (Materials on the Blue Shirts). n.p.: [1935?]

Rankin, Mary. *Early Chinese revolutionaries: radical intellectuals in Shanghai and Chekiang, 1902–1911*. Cambridge, Mass.: Harvard University Press, 1971

Rankin, Mary Backus. 'Rural-urban continuities: leading families of two Chekiang market towns'. *CSWT* 3.7 (Nov. 1977) 67–104

Rankin, Mary Backus. ' "Public opinion" and political power: *qingyi* in late nineteenth-century China'. *JAS* 51.3 (May 1982) 453–84

Rankin, Mary. 'Elite activism and political transformation in China: Zhejiang province 1865–1911'. Forthcoming

Rawski, Evelyn Sakakida. *Education and popular literacy in Ch'ing China*. Ann Arbor: University of Michigan Press, 1979

Rawski, Thomas. *China's republican economy: an introduction*. Toronto: University of Toronto – York University Joint Centre on Modern East Asia, 1978

Rea, Kenneth W. and Brewer, John C., eds. *The forgotten ambassador: the reports of John Leighton Stuart, 1946–1949*. Boulder, Colo.: Westview Press, 1977

Reardon-Anderson, James B. *Yenan and the Great Powers: the origins of Chinese Communist foreign policy, 1944–1946*. New York: Columbia University Press, 1980

Red China. See *Hung-se Chung-hua*

Red Flag. See *Hung-ch'i*

Red Star. See *Hung-hsing*

Reed, James. *The missionary mind and American East Asia policy, 1911–1915*. Cambridge, Mass.: Council on East Asian Studies, Harvard University, 1983

Reinsch, Paul S. *An American diplomat in China*. Garden City, NY and Toronto: Doubleday, Page, 1922

Reinsch, Paul S. See Pugach, Noel H.

Reischauer, Edwin O. and Fairbank, John K. *East Asia: the great tradition*. Boston: Houghton Mifflin, 1960

Republican China. Vol. 1.1 to 9.1 (1975–83) was *Chinese Republican Studies Newsletter*. New title began with vol. 9, part 2, Feb. 1984

Reynolds, Bruce. 'Weft: the technological sanctuary of Chinese handspun yarn'. *CSWT* 3.2 (Dec. 1974) 1–19

Reynolds, David. *The creation of the Anglo-American alliance, 1937–41: a study in competitive co-operation*. London: Europa Publications, 1981

Reynolds, Douglas Robertson. 'The Chinese industrial cooperative movement and the political polarization of wartime China, 1938–1945'. Columbia University, Ph.D. dissertation, 1975

Reynolds, Virginia. 'Social movements: an analysis of leadership in China 1895–1927'. Pennsylvania State University, Ph.D. dissertation, 1983

Rhoads, Edward J. M. *et al.*, eds. *The Chinese Red Army, 1927–1963: an annotated bibliography*. Cambridge, Mass.: East Asian Research Center, Harvard University, 1964

Rhoads, Edward J. M. *China's republican revolution: the case of Kwangtung, 1895–1913*. Cambridge, Mass.: Harvard University Press, 1975

Richardson, H. E. *A short history of Tibet*. New York: Dutton, 1962

Riskin, Carl. 'Surplus and stagnation in modern China', in Dwight H. Perkins, ed. *China's modern economy in historical perspective*, 49–84

Riskin, Carl. 'Discussion and comments', in Victor Lippit *et al.*, 'Symposium on China's economic history'.

Roll, Charles Robert, Jr. *The distribution of rural incomes in China: a comparison of the 1930s and 1950s*. New York: Garland, 1980

Romanus, Charles F. and Sunderland, Riley. Vol. 1. *Stilwell's mission to China*. Washington, DC: Office of the Chief of Military History, Dept. of the Army, 1953; vol. 2. *Stilwell's command problems*, same pub., 1956; vol. 3. *Time runs out in CBI*, same pub., 1959

Rōnin 浪人 (English-language periodical; title in characters and romanization). Tokyo, founded *c.* 1970

Rosenbaum, Arthur L. 'Gentry power and the Changsha rice riot of 1910'. *JAS* 34.3 (May 1975) 689–715

Rosinger, Lawrence K. *China's crisis.* New York: Alfred A. Knopf, 1945

Rossabi, Morris. *China and Inner Asia: from 1368 to the present day.* New York: Pica Press, 1975

Rossabi, Morris, ed. *China among equals: the Middle Kingdom and its neighbors 10th–14th centuries.* Berkeley: University of California Press, 1984

Rowe, William T. 'Rebellion and its enemies in a late Ch'ing city: the Hankow plot of 1883'. *Select papers from the Center for Far Eastern Studies, University of Chicago,* 4 (1979) 71–111

Rowe, William T. 'Review article: recent writing in the People's Republic on early Ch'ing economic history'. *CSWT* 4.7 (June 1982) 73–90

Rowe, William T. *Hankow: commerce and society in a Chinese city 1796–1889.* Stanford: Stanford University Press, 1984

Rozman, Gilbert. *Urban networks in Ch'ing China and Tokugawa Japan.* Princeton: Princeton University Press, 1973

Rozman, Gilbert, ed. *The modernization of China.* New York: Free Press, 1982

Rozman, Gilbert. *Soviet studies of pre-modern China: assessments of recent scholarship.* Ann Arbor: Center for Chinese Studies, University of Michigan, 1984

Rue, John E, with the assistance of S. R. Rue. *Mao Tse-tung in opposition, 1927–1935.* Stanford: Published for the Hoover Institution on War, Revolution and Peace by Stanford University Press, 1966

Ruhlmann, Robert. *La littérature chinoise au temps de la guerre de résistance contre le Japan (de 1937 à 1945).* Paris: Éditions de la Fondation Singer-Polignac, 1982

Sa K'ung-liao 薩空了. *Liang-nien ti cheng-chih-fan sheng-huo* 兩年的政治犯生活 (Two years in the life of a political prisoner). Hong Kong: Ch'un-feng 春風, 1947

Sanetō Keishū 實藤惠秀. *Chūgokujin Nihon ryūgaku shi* 中国人日本留学史 (A history of Chinese students in Japan). Tokyo: Kuroshio shuppan くろしお出版, 1960; revised edition, Chūka gakkai, 1970

Satō Kenryō 佐藤賢了. *Daitōa sensō kaikoroku* 大東亜戦争回顧録 (Memoirs of the Pacific War). Tokyo: Tokuma Shoten 徳間書店, 1966

Scalapino, Robert A. 'The evolution of a young revolutionary—Mao Zedong in 1919–1921'. *JAS* 42.1 (Nov. 1982) 29–61

Scalapino, Robert A. and Yu, George. *Modern China and its revolutionary process.* Vol. I: *Recurrent challenges to the traditional order, 1850–1920.* Berkeley and Los Angeles: University of California Press, 1985

SCCC. See Ssu-ch'uan ching-chi chi-k'an

Schaller, Michael. *The U.S. crusade in China, 1938–1945.* New York: Columbia University Press, 1979

Schiffrin, Harold Z. *Sun Yat-sen: reluctant revolutionary*. Toronto: Little, Brown, 1980

Schneider, Laurence A. *Ku Chieh-kang and China's new history; nationalism and the quest for alternative traditions*. Berkeley: University of California Press, 1971

Schoppa, R. Keith. 'The composition and functions of the local elite in Szechuan, 1851–1874'. *CSWT* 2.10 (Nov. 1973) 7–23

Schoppa, R. Keith. *Chinese elites and political change: Zhejiang province in the early twentieth century*. Cambridge, Mass.: Harvard University Press, 1981

Schram, Stuart R. 'On the nature of Mao Tse-tung's "deviation" in 1927'. *CQ* 27 (April-June 1964) 55–66

Schram, Stuart. *Mao Tse-tung*. Harmondsworth, Eng., Baltimore, Md.: Penguin Books, 1967, 1974

Schram, Stuart R. *The political thought of Mao Tse-tung*. Rev. edn, New York: Praeger, 1969

Schram, Stuart R. 'The party in Chinese Communist ideology', in J. W. Lewis, ed. *Party leadership and revolutionary power in China*, 170–202

Schram, Stuart R. 'Mao Tse-tung and the theory of the permanent revolution, 1958–1969'. *CQ* 46 (April-June 1971) 221–44

Schram, Stuart. 'From the "Great Union of the Popular Masses" to the "Great Alliance" '. *CQ* 49 (Jan.-March 1972) 76–105

Schram, Stuart R., ed. *Authority, participation, and cultural change in China: essays by a European study group*. Cambridge: Cambridge University Press, 1973

Schram, Stuart R., ed. *Mao Tse-tung unrehearsed: talks and letters, 1956–71*, trans. John Chinnery and Tieyun. Harmondsworth: Penguin, 1974; American edn, *Chairman Mao talks to the people: talks and letters: 1956–1971*. New York: Pantheon Books, 1974

Schram, Stuart R. 'Mao Zedong and the role of the various classes in the Chinese revolution, 1923–1927', in *Chūgoku no seiji to keizai* (The polity and economy of China—the late Professor Yūji Muramatsu commemoration volume), 227–39

Schram, Stuart R. *Mao Zedong: a preliminary reassessment*. Hong Kong: The Chinese University Press, 1983

Schran, Peter. *Guerrilla economy: the development of the Shensi-Kansu-Ninghsia Border Region, 1937–1945*. Albany: State University of New York Press, 1976

Schrecker, John E. *Imperialism and Chinese nationalism: Germany in Shantung*. Cambridge, Mass.: Harvard University Press, 1971

Schrecker, John E. See Cohen, Paul A.

Schulzinger, Robert D. *The making of the diplomatic mind: the training, outlook, and style of United States Foreign Service officers, 1908–1931*. Middletown, Conn.: Wesleyan University Press, 1975

Schurmann, Franz. *Ideology and organization in Communist China*. 2nd edn.

Berkeley: University of California Press, 1968

Schwartz, Benjamin I. *Chinese communism and the rise of Mao*. Cambridge, Mass.: Harvard University Press, 1951

Schwartz, Benjamin. *In search of wealth and power; Yen Fu and the West*. Cambridge, Mass.: Harvard University Press, 1964

Schwartz, Benjamin I. 'Themes in intellectual history: May Fourth and after'. *CHOC* 12.406–51

Scott, James C. *The moral economy of the peasant: rebellion and subsistence in Southeast Asia*. New Haven: Yale University Press, 1976

Scott, Roderick. *Fukien Christian University: a historical sketch*. New York: United Board for Christian Colleges in China, 1954

Second Historical Archives (Chung-kuo ti-erh li-shih tang-an kuan) 中國第二歷史檔案館, Nanking

Selden, Mark. *The Yenan way in revolutionary China*. Cambridge, Mass.: Harvard University Press, 1971

Select papers from the Center for Far Eastern Studies, University of Chicago. Chicago: University of Chicago Press. Vol. 1 (1975–6); vol. 2 (1977–8); vol. 3 (1978–9); vol. 4 (1979–80)

Sengo Nihon no kokusai seijigaku 戦後日本の国際政治学 (International studies in postwar Japan), ed. by Japan Association of International Affairs. Tokyo: Nihon kokusai seiji gakkai 日本国際政治学会, 1979

Service, John S. *The Amerasia papers: some problems in the history of US–China relations*. Berkeley: University of California Press, 1971

Service, John S. *Lost chance in China: the World War II despatches of John S. Service*, ed. by Joseph W. Esherick. New York: Random House, 1974

Shaffer, Lynda. 'Mao Ze-dong and the October 1922 Changsha construction workers' strike'. *Modern China*, 4 (Oct. 1978) 379–418

Shaffer, Lynda. *Mao and the workers: the Hunan labor movement, 1920–1923*. Armonk, NY: M. E. Sharpe, 1982

Shan-hsi ts'un-cheng hui-pien 山西村政彙編 (Collected materials on Shansi village government). 4 vols. comp. by Shan-hsi ts'un-cheng ch'u 山西村政處, n.p., 1928. Taipei reprint: Wen-hai, 1973

Shan-tung sheng cheng-fu chi Shan-tung chün-ch'ü kung-pu chih ko-chung t'iao-li kang-yao pan-fa hui-pien 山東省政府及山東軍區公佈之各種條例綱要辦法滙編 (A compilation of various regulations, programmes, and methods issued by the Shantung provincial government and the Shantung military region). n.p.: Chiao-tung ch'ü hsing-cheng kung-shu 膠東區行政公署, 1945

Shand, R. T. 'The development of trade and specialization in a primitive economy'. *The Economic Record*, 41 (June 1965) 193–206

Shang-hai ch'ien-chuang shih-liao 上海錢莊史料 (Material for the history of the *ch'ien-chuang* banks of Shanghai), comp. by Chung-kuo jen-min yin-hang Shang-hai-shih fen-hang 中國人民銀行上海市分行 (The Shanghai branch of the Chinese People's Bank). Shanghai: Jen-min, 1960

Shanghai Museum. See Shang-hai po-wu kuan

Shang-hai po-wu kuan t'u-shu tzu-liao shih 上海博物館圖書資料室. *Shang-hai pei-k'e tzu-liao hsuan-chi* 上海碑刻資料選輯 (A collection of Shanghai inscriptions). Shanghai: Jen-min, 1980

Shang-jao chi-chung-ying 上饒集中營 (The Shang-jao concentration camp). Rev. edn. Shanghai: Hua-tung jen-min, 1952

Shang-yü hsien-chih chiao hsu 上虞縣志校續 (Revised gazetteer of Shang-yü district), comp. by Hsu Chih-ching 徐志靖, 1898

Shaw Yu-ming 邵玉銘. 'John Leighton Stuart and US-Chinese Communist rapprochement in 1949: was there another "lost chance in China"?' *CQ* 89 (March 1982) 74–96

She-hui chien-she 社會建設 (Social reconstruction). Nanking, 1948–

She-hui hsin-wen 社會新聞 (The social mercury). Shanghai, Oct. 1932–July 1937

She-hui k'o-hsueh tsa-chih 社會科學雜誌 (Quarterly review of social sciences). Peking. 1930–

Shek, Richard. 'Millenarianism without rebellion: the Huangtian Dao in North China'. *Modern China*, 8.3 (July 1982) 305–37

Shen-pao ('Shun Pao') 申報. Daily, Shanghai, 1872–1949

Shen, T. H. 沈宗瀚. *Agricultural resources of China*. Ithaca: Cornell University Press, 1951

Shen Tsung-han. *Shen Tsung-han tzu-shu* 沈宗瀚自述 (Shen Tsung-han's memoirs). Taipei: Chuan-chi wen-hsueh, 1975

Sheng Hsuan-huai tang-an tzu-liao hsuan-chi 盛宣懷檔案資料選輯 (Select papers from the Sheng Hsuan-huai archives), ed. by Ch'en Hsu-lu 陳旭麓, Ku T'ing-lung 顧廷龍 and Wang Hsi 汪熙. 4 vols. to date. Shanghai: Jen-min, 1979–

Sheng-Kang ta pa-kung tzu-liao 省港大罷工資料 (Materials on the great Canton-Hong Kong strike). Kuang-tung che-hsueh she-hui k'o-hsueh yen-chiu so li-shih yen-chiu shih 廣東哲學社會科學研究所歷史研究室 Kuang-tung jen-min, 1980

Sheng Li-yü 盛里予. *Chung-kuo jen-min chieh-fang-chün san-shih-nien shih-hua* 中國人民解放軍三十年史話 (An informal history of the 30 years of the People's Liberation Army of China). Tientsin: Jen-min, 1959

Sheng, Yueh. *Sun Yat-sen University in Moscow and the Chinese Revolution: a personal account*. Lawrence, Kan.: Center for East Asian Studies, University of Kansas, 1971

Sheridan, James. *China in disintegration: the republican era in Chinese history, 1912–1949*. New York: The Free Press, 1975

Shiba Yoshinobu 斯波義信. 'Ningpo and its hinterland', in G. William Skinner, ed. *The city in late imperial China*, 391–440

Shigaku zasshi 史學雜誌 (Journal of historical studies). Dec. 1888–. Until 1893 published as *Shigakkai zasshi* 史學會雜誌 (Journal of the Historical Association)

Shigaku zasshi. Bibliographic essays on modern Chinese history in May issues

1978–81. See Fogel, Joshua A.

Shigemitsu, Mamoru. 重光葵 *Japan and her destiny*, trans. by O. White. London: Hutchinson, 1958

Shigeta Atsushi 重田徳. *Shindai shakai keizaishi kenkyū* 清代社会経済史研究 (Studies of the socio-economic history of the Ch'ing period). Tokyo: Iwanami shoten 岩波書店, 1975

Shih Ching-han 史鏡涵. 'Huang-fan-ch'ü ti tsai-ch'ing ho hsin-sheng' 黃泛區的災情和新生 (The disaster and rebirth of the Yellow River flood area). *Kuan-ch'a*, 3.3 (13 Sept. 1947), pp. 22–3

Shih Chün 石峻. *Chung-kuo chin-tai ssu-hsiang-shih tzu-liao – wu-ssu shih-ch'i chu-yao lun-wen-hsuan* 中國近代思想史資料 – 五四時期主要論文選 (Materials on modern Chinese intellectual history—selected important essays of the May Fourth period). Tokyo: Daian 大安, 1968

Shih Hsi-min 石西民. 'K'ang-chan i-lai ti Chung-kuo kung-yeh' 抗戰以來的 中國工業 (Chinese industry during the war). *Li-lun yü hsien-shih*, 1.4 (15 Feb. 1940) 48–55

Shih-hsueh ch'ing-pao 史學情報 (History newsletter), comp. by Chung-kuo shih-hsueh-hui Chung-kuo li-shih-hsueh nien-chien pien-chi-pu 中國史學 會中國歷史學年鑑編輯部 Peking: Jen-min, 1982–

Shih-hua 實話 (Honest words). Official organ of the central bureau of the Central Soviet, 30 Oct. 1930–7 Feb. 1931

Shih Kuo-heng 史國衡. *China enters the machine age: a study of labor in Chinese war industry*, ed. and trans. by Hsiao-tung Fei and Francis L. K. Hsu. Cambridge, Mass.: Harvard University Press, 1944

Shih-pao 時報 (The eastern times). Shanghai, 1904–

Shih-shih hsin-pao 時事新報 (The China times). Shanghai, 1924–

Shih-tai p'i-p'ing 時代批評 (Modern critic). Hong Kong, Jan. 1939–

Shih Yang-ch'eng 施養成. *Chung-kuo sheng hsing-cheng chih-tu* 中國省行政制度 (Chinese provincial administration). Shanghai: CP, 1947

Shima Ichirō 島一郎. *Chūgoku minzoku kōgyō no tenkai* 中国民族工業の展開 (Development of Chinese national industries). Tokyo: Mineruva Shobō ミネルヴァ書房, 1978

Shimada Toshihiko 島田俊彦, ed., *Manshū jihen* 満州事変 (The Manchurian incident). Tokyo: Misuzu Shobō みすず書房, 1964

Shina keizai zensho 支那經濟全書 (China economic series), vols. 1–4. Ōsaka: Maruzen 丸善, 1907; vols. 5–12, Tokyo: Tōa Dōbunkai 東亞同文會, 1908; each volume *c*. 700–1000 pp., illus.

'Shingai kakumei nanajushūnen kinen Tōkyō kokusai gakujutsu kaigi' 辛亥 革命七十周年紀念東京国際学術会議 (Papers from the International Con- ference on the 1911 Revolution held in Tokyo to commemorate its 70th anniversary)

Shirendev, B. and Sanjdorj, M. *History of the Mongolian People's Republic.* Vol. 3. *The contemporary period.* Ulan Bator, 1969; trans. by William A. Brown and Urgunge Onon, Cambridge, Mass.: Harvard University Press,

1976

Shu Ch'ing-ch'un. See Lao She

Shu Hsin-ch'eng 舒新城, ed. *Chin-tai Chung-kuo chiao-yü shih-liao* 近代中國教育史料 (Source materials on modern Chinese education). 4 vols. Shanghai: Chung-hua, 1928

Shu Hsin-ch'eng 舒新城, ed. *Chung-kuo chin-tai chiao-yü-shih tzu-liao* 中國近代教育史資料 (Source materials on modern Chinese education). 3 vols. Peking: Jen-min chiao-yü ch'u-pan-she 人民教育出版社 1962

Shu-wen 淑文. 'Ch'en Li-fu t'an CC' 陳立夫談CC (Ch'en Li-fu chats about the CC). *Hsin-wen t'ien-ti*, 20 (1 Feb. 1937) 13

Shue, Vivienne. *Peasant China in transition: the dynamics of development toward socialism, 1949–1956.* Berkeley: University of California Press, 1980

Shyu, Lawrence Nae-lih. 'The People's Political Council and China's wartime problems, 1937–1945'. Columbia University, Ph.D. dissertation, 1972

Shyu, Lawrence N. 'China's "wartime parliament": the People's Political Council, 1938–1945', in Paul K. T. Sih, ed. *Nationalist China during the Sino-Japanese War, 1937–1945*, 273–313

Sih, Paul K. T. 薛光前, ed. *The strenuous decade: China's nation-building efforts 1927–1937.* Jamaica, NY: St John's University Press, 1970

Sih, Paul K. T., ed. *Nationalist China during the Sino-Japanese War, 1937–1945.* Hicksville, NY: Exposition Press, 1977

Skinner, G. William. 'Marketing and social structure in rural China'. Part I, *JAS* 26.1 (Nov. 1964) 3–44. (Part II and III in subsequent issues)

Skinner, G. William. 'Chinese peasants and the closed community: an open and shut case'. *Comparative Studies in Society and History*, 13.3 (July 1971) 270–81

Skinner, G. William. 'Mobility strategies in late imperial China', in Carol Smith, ed. *Regional analysis*, vol. 1, *Economic systems*, 327–61. New York: Academic Press, 1976

Skinner, G. William, ed. *The city in late imperial China.* Stanford: Stanford University Press, 1977

Skinner, G. William, *et al.*, eds. *Modern Chinese society: an analytical bibliography.* 3 vols. Stanford: Stanford University Press, 1973

Skinner, G. William. See Elvin, Mark

Slawinski, Roman. *La Société des Piques Rouges et le mouvement paysan en Chein en 1926–1927.* Varsovie: Wydawnictwa Uniwersytetu Warszawskiego, 1975

Slupski, Zbigniew. *The evolution of a modern Chinese writer; an analysis of Lao She's fiction with biographical and bibliographical appendices.* Prague: Oriental Institute, 1966

Smedley, Agnes. *The great road: the life and times of Chu Teh.* New York: Monthly Review Press, 1956; London, 1958

Smith, Arthur H. *Village life in China: a study in sociology.* London: Oliphant, Anderson and Ferrier, 1899

Smith, Richard J. *Mercenaries and mandarins: the Ever-Victorious Army in nineteenth century China.* New York: KTO Press, 1978

Smith, Richard J. *China's cultural heritage: the Ch'ing dynasty, 1644–1912.* Boulder, Colo.: Westview Press, 1983

Smith, Robert Gillen. 'History of the attempt of the United States Medical Department to improve the effectiveness of the Chinese Army Medical Service, 1941–1945'. Columbia University, Ph.D. dissertation, 1950

SMR. South Manchurian Railway Co.

SMR: Hoku-shi keizai chōsajo, chōsabu 北支經濟調查所調查部, comp. *Hoku-shi nōson gaikyō chōsa hōkoku* 北支農村概況調查報告 (Research report on village conditions in North China). Dairen: South Manchurian Railway Co., vol. 2, 1939

SMR: Hoku-shi keizai chōsajo, comp. *Nōka keizai chōsa hōkoku, Shōwa jūninendo, Hojunken Sensochin Beishoson* 農家經濟調查報告, 昭和12年度, 豐潤縣宣莊鎮米廠村 (An investigation report of the farm economy for 1937: Mi-ch'ang village, Hsuan-chuang chen, Feng-jun county). Dairen: 1939

SMR: Kozawa Shigeichi 小澤茂一. *Shina no dōran to Santō nōson* 支那の擾乱と山東農村 (Shantung villages and the upheaval in China). Dairen: South Manchurian Railway Co., 1930

SMR: *Mantetsu chōsa geppō* 滿鐵調查月報 (SMR research monthly). Dairen, 1919–44

SMR: Mantetsu Shanhai jimusho chōsashitsu. *Kōsōshō Shōkōken nōson jittai chōsa hōkokusho* 江蘇省松江縣農村實態調查報告書 (Research report of village conditions in Sung-chiang county, Kiangsu). Shanghai: 1941

SMR: Mantetsu taiheiyō mondai chōsa jumbikai 滿鐵太平洋問題調查準備會, comp. *Nōka no keiei narabini keizai jōtai yori mitaru Manshū nōka to Chūbu Shina nōka no taishō* 農家の經營並に經濟狀態より見たる滿洲農家と中部支那農家の對照 (A comparison of Manchurian and central China farms as seen from the economic and managerial aspects of the family farm). Dairen: South Manchurian Railway Co., 1931

SMR: Minami Manshū tetsudō kabushiki kaisha 南滿洲鐵道株式會社, *Hoku-shi nōson gaikyō chōsa hōkoku* 北支農村概況調查報告 (Research report on village conditions in North China). Tokyo: Nihon Hyōronsha 日本評論社, 1940

SMR, Hsinking Branch Office: Research Division. Minami Manshū tetsudō kabushiki kaisha, chōsashitsu 南滿洲鐵道株式會社調查室, *Toshi no bōchō ni tomonau ichi nōson no ugoki* 都市ノ膨脹ニトモナウ一農村ノ動キ (Change in a village under the influence of urban growth). Ch'ang-ch'un: South Manchurian Railway Co., 1940

SMR, Shanghai Research Section: Mantetsu Shanhai jimusho chōsashitsu 滿鐵上海事務所調查室. *Chū-shi ni okeru nōson no shakai jijō* 中支ニ於ケル農村ノ社會事情 (Social conditions in villages of central China). Shanghai: 1939

SMR: Shanhai jimusho. *Shina shōhin sōsho:goma* 支那商品叢書：胡麻 (Chinese commercial product series: sesame). Shanghai: South Manchurian Railway Co., 1938

Snow, Edgar. Interview with Mao Tse-tung. *Shanghai Evening Post and Mercury*, 3–5 Feb. 1936

Snow, Edgar. *Red star over China*. London: Gollancz, 1937; New York: Random House, 1938; 1st rev. and enlgd. edn, Grove Press, 1968

Snow, Edgar. *The battle for Asia*. New York: Random House, 1941

Snow, Edgar. *Random notes on Red China, 1936–1945*. Cambridge, Mass.: East Asian Research Center, Harvard University, 1957

Snow, Edgar. *The long revolution*. London: Hutchinson, 1973

Songgyu, I. 'Shantung in the Shun-chih reign: the establishment of local control and the gentry response'. *CSWT* 4.4 (Dec. 1980) 19–27; 4.5 (June 1981) 13–23

Spector, Stanley. *Li Hung-chang and the Huai army*. Seattle: University of Washington Press, 1964

Spence, Jonathan. *Ts'ao Yin and the K'ang-hsi Emperor: bondservant and master*. New Haven: Yale University Press, 1966

Spence, Jonathan. *The Gate of Heavenly Peace: the Chinese and their revolution 1895–1980*. New York: Viking Press, 1981

Spence, Jonathan D. and Wills, John E., Jr., eds. *From Ming to Ch'ing: conquest, region, and continuity in seventeenth-century China*. New Haven: Yale University Press, 1979

Ssu-ch'uan ching-chi chi-k'an 四川經濟季刊 (Szechwan economic quarterly). Chungking, 1943–

Ssu-ch'uan wen-hsien 四川文獻 (Records of Szechwan). Taipei, 1962–

Ssu-i lu: Yuan Shou-ho hsien-sheng chi-nien ts'e 思憶錄：袁守和先生紀念冊 (Memorial volume on Mr Yuan Shou-ho [T. L. Yuan]). Taipei: CP, 1968. The English-language portion of this bilingual volume was entitled *T. L. Yuan: a tribute*

Ssu-ma Hsien-tao 司馬仙島. *Pei-fa hou chih ko-p'ai ssu-ch'ao* 北伐後之各派思潮 (The doctrines of the various cliques after the Northern Expedition). Peiping: Ying-shan-she 鷹山社, 1930

Starr, John Bryan. *Continuing the revolution: the political thought of Mao*. Princeton: Princeton University Press, 1979

Stilwell, Joseph. See Romanus, Charles A.; Tuchman, Barbara

Stilwell papers, The. Arr. and ed. by Theodore H. White. New York: Schocken Books, 1948

Stinchcombe, Arthur L. *Theoretical methods in social history*. New York: Academic Press, 1978

Storry, Richard (George Richard). *Japan and the decline of the West in Asia, 1894–1943*. London: Macmillan, 1979

Strand, David and Weiner, Richard. 'Social movements and political discourse in 1920s Peking: analysis of the tramway riot of October 22, 1929'. *Select papers from the Center for Far Eastern Studies*, University of Chicago, 3 (1978–9) 137–80

Stross, Randall. 'A hard row to hoe: the political economy of Chinese agriculture in Western Jiangsu, 1911–1937'. Stanford University, Ph.D. dissertation, 1982

Stuart, John Leighton. See Rea, Kenneth W.

Stueck, William Whitney, Jr. *The road to confrontation: American policy toward China and Korea, 1947–1950.* Chapel Hill: University of North Carolina Press, 1981

Su-chou ti nung-ch'ao 蘇州的農潮 (The peasant riots in Soochow). *Chung-kuo nung-ts'un*, 2.6 (June 1936) 6–8

Su Wan Hsiang teng-sheng nung-min k'ang-tsu tou-cheng 蘇皖湘等省農民抗租鬥爭 (Peasant resistance to rents in Kiangsu, Anhwei and Hunan provinces, Nov. 1929–Jan. 1930). Second Historical Archives, Nanking, no. 1/2/1000

Su-wei-ai Chung-kuo 蘇維埃中國 (Soviet China). Moscow: Izdatel'stvo Inostrannyky Rabochikh (Foreign Workers' Publishing House), 1934.

Su Wen 蘇汶, ed. *Wen-i tzu-yu lun-pien chi* 文藝自由論辯集 (Debates on the freedom of literature and art). Shanghai: Hsien-tai 現代, 1933

Su Yun-feng 蘇雲峯. *Chung-kuo hsien-tai-hua ti ch'ü-yü yen-chiu: Hu-pei sheng, 1860–1916* 中國現代化的區域研究：湖北省, 1860–1916 (Modernization in China, 1860–1916: a regional study of social, political and economic change in Hupeh province). Taipei: IMH, 1981

Sun, E-tu Zen 孫任以都. 'Sericulture and silk production in Ch'ing China', in W. E. Willmott, ed. *Economic organization in Chinese society*, 79–108

Sun Fo (Sun K'o) 孫科 *et al. T'ao Chiang yen-lun-chi* 討蔣言論集 (Anti-Chiang messages). Canton, 1931

Sun Yat-sen 孫逸仙. *Fundamentals of national reconstruction (Chien-kuo ta-kang* 建國大綱) (with Chinese text). Taipei: China Cultural Service, 1953

Sung Jen-ch'iung t'ung-chih liu-yueh shih-wu-jih tsai chung-yang-chü tang-hsiao kuan-yü cheng-chih kung-tso ti pao-kao 宋任窮同志6月15日在中央局黨校關於政治工作的報告 (Comrade Sung Jen-ch'iung's report on political work at the Central Party School on 15 June). n.p.: Chin-Chi-Lu-Yü chün-ch'ü cheng-chih pu 晉冀魯豫軍區政治部 December 1947

Suzuki, Takeo 鈴木武雄, ed. *Nishihara shakkan shiryō kenkyū* 西原借款資料研究 (Studies of materials on the Nishihara Loans). Tokyo: Tokyo Daigaku Shuppankai, 1972

SW. See Mao Tse-tung, *Selected works*

Swen, W. Y. 'Types of farming, costs of production, and annual labor distribution in Weihsien County, Shantung, China'. *Chinese Economic Journal*, 3.2 (Aug. 1928) 653

'Syncretic sects in Chinese society', symposium in *Modern China*, 8.3 (July 1982) entire and 8.4 (Oct. 1982) 435–84

Sze, Szeming. *China's health problems.* Washington, DC: Chinese Medical Association, 1944

Ta-Ch'ing Kuang-hsu hsin fa-ling 大清光緒新法令 (New laws of the Kuang-hsu period). Shanghai: CP, 1910

Ta-kung-pao 大公報 ('L'Impartial'). Tientsin, 1929–; Hankow, 1938–; Chungking, 1938–; Hong Kong, 1938–

Taeuber, Irene. 'Migrants and cities in Japan, Taiwan, and Northeast China', in Mark Elvin and G. William Skinner, eds. *The Chinese city between two worlds*, 359–84

Taga Akigorō 多賀秋五郎. *Kindai Chūgoku kyōikushi shiryō* 近代中國教育史資料 (Source material on modern Chinese education). 5 vols. Tokyo: Nihon gakujutsu shinkōkai 日本学術振興会, 1976

Tagore, Amitendranath. *Literary debates in modern China, 1918–1937*. Tokyo: Centre for East Asian Cultural Studies, 1967

Tai Hsuan-chih 戴玄之. *Hung-ch'iang-hui* 紅槍會 (The Red Spear Society). Taipei: Shih-huo ch'u-pan-she 食貨出版社, 1973

Tai Li. See *Tai Yü-nung*

Tai-Shi kōrōsha denki hensankai 対支功勞者傳記編纂会 (Commission for the compilation of biographical memoirs of those who rendered services regarding China), comp. *Tai-Shi kaikoroku* 対支回顧録 (A record looking back on China). 2 vols. Tokyo: Tai-Shi kōrōsha denki hensankai, 1936

Tai Wen 戴聞. *Chiang-chou huo an* 江洲火案 (The case of the Chiang-chou fire). Nanking: Chiang-su jen-min, 1957. (Hoover Institution on War, Revolution and Peace, no. 4393.8/4574)

Tai Yih-jian. 'The contemporary Chinese theater and Soviet influence'. Southern Illinois University, Ph.D. dissertation, 1974

Tai Yü-nung hsien-sheng nien-p'u 戴雨農先生年譜 (Chronological biography of Tai Li), comp. by Intelligence Section, Defence Ministry. Taipei, 1966

Taiheiyō sensō e no michi. See Nihon kokusai . . .

T'ai-ku hsien-chih 太谷縣志. (T'ai-ku county gazetteer), 1931

Takada Yasuma 高田保馬. *Tōa minzoku-ron* 東亞民族論 (On East Asian nationalism). Tokyo: Iwanami 岩波, 1939

Takamura Naosuke 高村直助. *Kindai Nihon mengyō to Chūgoku* 近代日本綿業と中国 (The modern Japanese cotton industry and China). Tokyo: Tokyo Daigaku Shuppankai, 1982

Takeuchi Minoru 竹内實, ed. *Mao Tse-tung chi* 毛澤東集 (Collected writings of Mao Tse-tung). 10 vols. Tokyo: Hokubōsha 北望社, 1970–72. See also *Mao Tse-tung chi*

Tamagna, Frank M. *Banking and finance in China*. New York: Institute of Pacific Relations, 1942

Tamura Kōsaku 田村幸策. *Saikin Shina gaikō shi* 最近支那外交史 (History of China's recent foreign relations). 2 vols. Tokyo: Gaikō Jihōsha 外交時報社, 1938–9

Tamura Kōsaku. *Daitōa gaikōshi kenkyū* 大東亜外交史研究 (Study of diplomatic history of Greater East Asia). 2 vols. Tokyo: Dainippon Shuppan 大日本出版, 1942

Tanaka Masatoshi 田中正俊. 'Chūgoku – keizai shi' 中国—経済史 (China – economic history) *Ajia Keizai* アジア経済 (Asian economics), 19.1–2

(Jan–Feb. 1978), 41–51

Tang, Peter S. H. *Russian and Soviet policy in Manchuria and Outer Mongolia 1911–1931*. Durham, NC: Duke University Press, 1959

Tang-shih ts'an-k'ao tzu-liao 黨史參考資料 (Reference material on the history of the party), ed. by Mongolia–Suiyuan Bureau, department of propaganda, Suiyuan, n.d.

Tang-shih yen-chiu 黨史研究. (Research on party history). Peking, People's Publishing House (for the Central Party School), 1980–

Tang-shih yen-chiu tzu-liao 黨史研究資料 (Research materials on party history). Periodical. 'Internal use only'. This item is composed of primary documents, while *Tang-shih yen-chiu* (Research on party history) contains secondary scholarship, essays, reminiscences, etc. Both are published by the Central Committee, CCP

Tang ti kai-tsao 黨的改造 (Reconstruction of the party). n.d.

T'ang Chih-chün 湯志鈞. *Wu-hsu pien-fa shih lun-ts'ung* 戊戌變法史論叢 (Collected essays on the 1898 Reform Movement). Hankow: Jen-min, 1957

T'ang Leang-Li. *The inner history of the Chinese Revolution*. London: Routledge, 1930

Tang Leang-li. *Suppressing communist bandits in China*. Shanghai, 1934

Tani Hisao 谷寿夫. *Kimitsu Nichi Ro senshi* 機密日露戰史 (Secret history of the Russo-Japanese War). Tokyo: Hara Shobō 原書房, 1961

T'ao Chiang yen-lun-chi. See Sun Fo

T'ao Hsing-chih 陶行知. *T'ao Hsing-chih chiao-yü wen-hsuan* 陶行知教育文選 (Selected essays on education by T'ao Hsing-chih). Peking: Chiao-yü k'o-hsueh ch'u-pan-she 教育科學出版社, 1981

T'ao Hsing-chih. *Hsing-chih shu-hsin chi* 行知書信集 (Collected letters of [T'ao] Hsing-chih). Anhwei: Jen-min, 1981

T'ao Ta-yung 陶大鏞. 'Lun tang-ch'ien ti kung-yeh chiu-chi' 論當前的工業救濟 (Current means of rescuing industry). *Chung-kuo kung-yeh*, 25 (Mar. 1944) 10–12

T'ao Ying-hui 陶英惠. *Ts'ai Yuan-p'ei nien-p'u* (*shang*) 蔡元培年譜（上）(A biographical chronology of Ts'ai Yuan-p'ei), Part I. Taipei: IMH monograph no. 36, Academia Sinica, 1976

T'ao Ying-hui. 'Ts'ai Yuan-p'ei yü Pei-ching ta-hsueh, 1917–1923' 蔡元培與北京大學 (1917–1923) (Ts'ai Yuan-p'ei and National Peking University 1917–1923). *Bulletin of the Institute of Modern History*, 5 (1976) 263–312

T'ao Ying-hui. 'Ts'ai Yuan-p'ei yü Chung-yang yen-chiu yuan 1927–1940' 蔡元培與中央研究院(1927–1940) (Ts'ai Yuan-p'ei and Academia Sinica 1927–1940). *Bulletin of the Institute of Modern History*, 7 (1978) 1–50

Tawney, R. H. *Land and labour in China*. New York: Harcourt Brace, 1932

Tawney, R. H. See Becker, C. H.

Teng, Ssu-yü 鄧嗣禹. *Protest and crime in China: a bibliography of secret associations, popular uprisings, peasant rebellions*. New York and London: Garland,

1981

Teradaira Tadasuke 寺平忠輔. *Rokōkyō jiken* 蘆溝橋事件 (The Marco Polo bridge incident). Tokyo: Yomiuri shimbunsha 讀売新聞社, 1970

TFTC. See *Tung-fang tsa-chih*

Thaxton, Ralph. *China turned rightside up: revolutionary legitimacy in the peasant world*. New Haven: Yale University Press, 1983

There is another China. Essays by J. L. Buck, Roger Greene, Hu Shih *et al*. New York: King's Crown Press, 1948

Thompson, E. P. 'The moral economy of the English crowd in the eighteenth century'. *Past and Present*, 50 (Feb. 1971) 76–136

Thomson, James C., Jr. *While China faced West: American reformers in Nationalist China, 1928–1937*. Cambridge, Mass.: Harvard University Press, 1969

Thorne, Christopher. *The limits of foreign policy: the West, the League and the Far Eastern crisis of 1931–1933*. London: Hamilton, 1972

Thorne, Christopher. *Allies of a kind: the United States, Britain, and the war against Japan, 1941–1945*. New York: Oxford University Press, 1978

Thornton, Richard C. *The Comintern and the Chinese Communists, 1928–1931*. Seattle: University of Washington Press, 1969

Thurston, Mrs Lawrence and Chester, Ruth M. *Ginling College*. New York: United Board for Christian Colleges in China, 1955

Ti-cheng yueh-k'an 地政月刊 (Land administration monthly). Nanking, Jan. 1933–

Ti-erh-tz'u Chung-kuo chiao-yü nien-chien 第二次中國教育年鑑 (The second China education year book). Shanghai: CP, 1948

Ti-erh-tz'u Chung-kuo lao-tung nien-chien 第二次中國勞動年鑑 (Second year book of Chinese labour), ed. by Pei-p'ing she-hui tiao-ch'a so 北平社會調查所 (Peiping Social Survey Institute), 1930

Ti-erh-tz'u kuo-nei ko-ming chan-cheng shih-ch'i shih-shih lun-ts'ung 第二次國內革命戰爭時期史事論叢 (Discourses on the history of the second revolutionary war period), ed. by Shih-hsueh shuang-chou-k'an she 史學雙週刊社, Peking: San-lien, 1956

Ti-i-tz'u ch'üan-kuo tai-piao ta-hui hsuan-yen 第一次全國代表大會宣言 (Manifesto of the First National Congress), KMT Department of Organization, n.p., 1927

Ti-i-tz'u Chung-kuo chiao yü nien-chien 第一次中國教育年鑑 (The first China education year book), comp. by the Ministry of Education. Shanghai: K'ai-ming shu-tien 開明書店, 1934

Ti-i-tz'u kuo-nei ko-ming chan-cheng shih-ch'i ti kung-jen yun-tung 第一次國內革命戰爭時期的工人運動 (The labour movement during the first revolutionary civil war period), ed. by Chung-kuo hsien-tai-shih tzu-liao ts'ung-k'an Peking: Jen-min, 1954

Ti-i-tz'u kuo-nei ko-ming chan-cheng shih-ch'i ti nung-min yun-tung 第一次國內革命戰爭時期的農民運動 (The peasant movement during the first revolutionary civil war period). Peking: Jen-min, 1953

Tiao-ch'a Che-chiang ching-chi so t'ung-chi-k'o 調查浙江經濟所統計課. *Che-chiang Chien-te hsien ching-chi tiao-ch'a* 浙江建德縣經濟調查 (Survey of the economy of Chien-te county, Chekiang). Hangchow: Chien-she wei-yuan-hui 建設委員會, 1931

Tiedemann, R. G. 'The persistence of banditry: incidents in border districts of the North China plain'. *Modern China*, 8.4 (Oct. 1982) 395–433

Tien Hung-mao 田弘茂. *Government and politics in Kuomintang China, 1927–1937.* Stanford: Stanford University Press, 1972

T'ien Chun 田軍 (Hsiao Chün 蕭軍). *Village in August*, trans. by Evan King, intr. by Edgar Snow. New York: Smith & Durrell, 1942

T'ien Han 田漢, Ou-yang Yü-ch'ien 歐陽予倩 *et al. Chung-kuo hua-chü yun-tung wu-shih-nien shih-liao chi, 1907–1957* 中國話劇運動五十年史料集, 1907–1957 (Historical materials on the modern Chinese drama movement of the last fifty years, 1907–1957). Peking: Chung-kuo hsi-chü 中國戲劇, 1957

T'ien Yuan 田園. 'Tsai lun Mao Tse-tung t'ung-chih tui Li-san lu-hsien ti jen-shih ho ti-chih' 再論毛澤東同志對立三路綫的認識和抵制 (More on Comrade Mao Tse-tung's understanding of and resistance to the Li-san line). *TSYC* 1 (1981) 65–71

Ting Chih-p'in 丁致聘. *Chung-kuo chin ch'i-shih-nien lai chiao-yü chi-shih* 中國近七十年來教育記事 (Events in Chinese education during the past seventy years). National Bureau of Compilation and Translation, 1935. Taipei: CP reprint, 1961

Ting I 丁易. 'Chung-kuo tso-i tso-chia lien-meng ti ch'eng-li chi ch'i ho fan-tung cheng-chih ti tou-cheng' 中國左翼作家聯盟的成立及其和反動政治的鬥爭 (The founding of the League of Left-wing Writers and its struggle against reactionary political forces), in Chang Ching-lu, ed. *Chung-kuo hsien-tai ch'u-pan-shih-liao. I-pien*, 35–49

Ting, Lee-hsia Hsu. *Government control of the press in modern China, 1900–1949.* Cambridge, Mass.: East Asian Research Center, Harvard University, 1974

Ting Ling 丁玲 *et al. Chieh-fang ch'ü tuan-p'ien ch'uang-tso hsuan* 解放區短篇創作選 (Selected short works from the liberated areas). 2 vols. n.p., 1947

Ting Miao 丁淼. *P'ing Chung-kung wen-i tai-piao tso* 評中共文藝代表作 (On representative works of Chinese Communist literature). Hong Kong: Hsin-shih-chi ch'u-pan-she 新世紀出版社, 1953

Tipton, Laurence. *Chinese escapade.* London: Macmillan, 1949

Tōa dōbun kai hensan kyoku 東亞同文會編纂局 *Shina keizai zensho* 支那經濟全書 (A compendium on the Chinese economy). Tokyo: Tōa dōbun kai, vol. 7, 1910

Tōa kenkyūjo 東亞研究所. *Shina seishi no sekai teki chii* 支那製絲の世界的地位 (The world status of Chinese silk-reeling). Tokyo: Tōa kenkyūjo, 1942

Tōa kenkyūjo. *Keizai ni kansuru Shina kankō chōsa hōkokusho: toku ni Hoku-Shi ni okeru kosaku seido* 經濟に關する支那慣行調查報告書——特に北支に於ける小作制度 (An investigative report of old customs in China concerning the economy: the tenant system in North China). Tokyo, 1943

Tong, Hollington K. (Tung Hsien-kuang 董顯光), ed. *China after seven years of war*. New York: Macmillan, 1945

Tong, Hollington K. *China and the world press*. Nanking, Feb. 1948

Tong, Hollington K. *Chiang Kai-shek, soldier and statesman: authorized biography.* 2 vols. Shanghai: The China Publishing Co. 1st edn, Nov. 1937. *Chiang Kai-shek.* Rev. edn, Taipei: China Pub. Co., 1953

Tong, Hollington. *Chiang Tsung-t'ung chuan* 蔣總統傳 (A biography of President Chiang). 3 vols. Taipei: Chung-hua wen-hua 中華文化, 1954

Tong Te-kong. See Li Tsung-jen

Topping, Seymour. *Journey between two Chinas*. New York: Harper & Row, 1972

Torbert, Preston M. *The Ch'ing Imperial Household Department: a study of its organization and principal functions, 1662–1796.* Cambridge, Mass.: Council on East Asian Studies, Harvard University, 1977

Tou-cheng 鬥爭 (The struggle). Official organ of the Central Committee of the CCP, *c.* 1928?–1934?

Trotter, Ann. *Britain and East Asia, 1933–1937.* London, New York: Cambridge University Press, 1975

Tsai, David. 'Party government relations in Kiangsu province, 1927–1932'. *Select papers from the Center for Far Eastern Studies*, University of Chicago, 1 (1975–6) 85–118

Tsai, Jung-fang. 'The predicament of the compradore ideologists: He Qi (Ho Kai, 1859–1914) and Hu Liyuan (1847–1916)'. *Modern China*, 7.2 (April 1981) 191–225

Ts'ai-cheng p'ing-lun 財政評論 (Financial review) Hong Kong, 1939–

Ts'ai-cheng-pu cheng-li ti-fang chüan-shui wei-yuan-hui 財政部整理地方捐稅委員會 (Committee for the reorganization of local taxes of the Ministry of Finance). *T'u-ti ch'en-pao tiao-ch'a pao-kao chih i: An-hui sheng Tang-t'u hsien t'u-ti ch'en-pao kai-lueh* 土地陳報調查報告之一：安徽省當塗縣土地陳報概略 (First report on the inquiry into land-registration: summary of the registration of land in Tang-t'u hsien, Anhwei). Nanking, 1935 (?)

Ts'ai-cheng-pu cheng-li ti-fang chüan-shui wei-yuan-hui. *T'u-ti ch'en-pao tiao-ch'a pao-kao chih erh: Chiang-su sheng Hsiao-hsien t'u-ti ch'en-pao kai-lueh* 土地陳報調查報告之二：江蘇省蕭縣土地陳報概略 (Second report on the inquiry into land-registration: summary of the registration of land in Hsiao hsien, Kiangsu). Nanking, 1935 (?)

Ts'ai-cheng-pu cheng-li ti-fang chüan-shui wei-yuan-hui. *T'u-ti ch'en-pao tiao-ch'a pao-kao chih san: Chiang-su sheng Chiang-tu hsien t'u-ti ch'en-pao kai-lueh* 土地陳報調查報告之三：江蘇省江都縣土地陳報概略 (Third report on the inquiry into land-registration: summary of the registration of land in Chiang-tu hsien, Kiangsu). Nanking, 1935 (?)

Ts'ai-cheng shuo-ming shu 財政説明書 (Explanatory accounts of fiscal administration), published by province. Ching-chi hsueh-hui 經濟學會, comp. Peking: Ts'ai-cheng pu 財政部, 1915

Ts'ai Ho-sen wen-chi 蔡和森文集 (Collected writings of Ts'ai Ho-sen). Peking: Jen-min, 1980

Ts'ai Shang-ssu 蔡尚思, ed. *Lun Ch'ing-mo Min-ch'u Chung-kuo she-hui* 論清末民初中國社會 (Chinese society in the late Ch'ing and early Republic). Shanghai: Fu-tan ta-hsueh 復旦大學, 1982

Ts'ai Shao-ch'ing 蔡少卿. 'Ko-lao hui yü 1891 nien Ch'ang-chiang liu-yü ti fan-yang-chiao tou-cheng' 哥老會與1891年長江流域的反洋教鬥爭 (The Ko-lao hui and the struggle against foreign missionaries in the Yangtze basin during 1891). *She-hui k'o-hsueh yen-chiu* 社會科學研究 (Social science research), 5 (1982)

Ts'ai Shu-pang 蔡樹邦. 'Chin shih-nien lai Chung-kuo tien-nung feng-ch'ao ti yen-chiu' 近十年來中國佃農風潮的研究 (Research on tenant riots in China during the past ten years). *Tung-fang tsa-chih*, 30.10 (16 May 1933) 26–38

Ts'ai T'ing-k'ai 蔡廷鍇. *Ts'ai T'ing-k'ai tzu-chuan* 蔡廷鍇自傳 (Ts'ai T'ing-k'ai's autobiography). 2 vols. Hong Kong: Tzu-yu hsun-k'an-she 自由旬刊社, 1946

Ts'ai Wu-chi 蔡無忌. 'Min-yuan lai wo-kuo chih nung-yeh' 民元來我國之農業 (Agriculture in our country since the outset of the Republican period), in Chu Ssu-huang 朱斯煌, ed. *Min-kuo ching-chi shih* 民國經濟史 (An economic history of the Republican period). 2 vols. Shanghai: Yin-hang hsueh-hui 銀行學會, 1948

Ts'ai Yuan-p'ei 蔡元培 *et al. Wan-Ch'ing san-shih-wu-nien lai chih Chung-kuo chiao-yü, 1897–1931* 晚清三十五年來之中國教育 (Chinese education in the 35 years since late Ch'ing 1897–1931). Shanghai: Commercial Press, 1931; Hong Kong: Lung-men reprint, 1969. See also Chuang Yü

Ts'ai Yuan-p'ei. 'San-shih-wu-nien lai Chung-kuo chih hsin-wen-hua' 三十五年來中國之新文化 (New Culture in China during the past thirty-five years), in Ts'ai Yuan-p'ei *et al., Wan-Ch'ing...*

Ts'ai Yuan-p'ei. *Ts'ai Yuan-p'ei ch'üan-chi* 蔡元培全集 (Collected works of Ts'ai Yuan-p'ei). Taipei: CP, 1968

Ts'ai Yuan-p'ei. *Ts'ai Yuan-p'ei tzu-shu* 蔡元培自述 (Autobiography of Ts'ai Yuan-p'ei). Taipei: Chuan-chi wen-hsueh, 1978

Ts'an-k'ao tzu-liao. See *Chung-kuo hsien-tai wen-hsueh shih ts'an-k'ao tzu-liao*

Tsang K'o-chia 臧克家. *Hsien-tai Chung-kuo shih-hsuan* 現代中國詩選 (Contemporary Chinese poetry), no data

Tsang K'o-chia. *Lo-yin* 烙印 (Branded imprint). Shanghai: K'ai-ming shu-chü 開明書局 1948 (1934)

Ts'ao Chü-jen 曹聚仁. *Wen-t'an wu-shih nien hsu-chi* 文壇五十年續集 (Sequel to Fifty years on the literary scene). Hong Kong: Hsin wen-hua 新文化, 1969

Ts'ao Po-i 曹伯一. *Chiang-hsi su-wei-ai chih chien-li chi ch'i peng-k'uei* 江西蘇維埃之建立及其崩潰 (The establishment and collapse of the Kiangsi soviet). Taipei: Cheng-chih ta-hsueh 政治大學, 1969

Ts'ao Yü 曹禺. *Jih-ch'u* 日出 (Sunrise). Shanghai: Wen-hua sheng-huo 文化生活, 1936

Ts'ao Yü. *Thunderstorm*, trans. by A. C. Barnes. Peking, 1958

Ts'ao Yü. *Sunrise*, trans. by A. C. Barnes. Peking: Foreign Languages Press, 1960

Ts'ao Yü. *The wilderness*, trans. by Christopher C. Rand and Joseph S. M. Lau. Hong Kong and Bloomington: Foreign Languages Press, 1980

Tsiang, T. F. 蔣廷黻 'The present situation in China'. *International Affairs* (14 July 1935)

Tsiang, T. F. See Chiang T'ing-fu

Tsiang, T'ing-fu. See Lilley, Charles Ronald

Tso-lien shih-ch'i wu-ch'an chieh-chi ko-ming wen-hsueh 左聯時期無產階級革命文學 (Proletarian revolutionary literature in the period of the Left-wing League), ed. by Nan-ching ta-hsueh Chung-wen hsi 南京大學中文系 (Department of Chinese, Nanking University). Nanking: Chiang-su wen-i 江蘇文藝, 1960

Tsou Lu 鄒魯. *Hui-ku-lu* 回顧錄 (Reminiscences). 2 vols. Shanghai, 1943; Taipei: Wen-hai, 1971

Tsou Tang 鄒讜. *America's failure in China, 1941–50*. Chicago University Press, 1963

Tsun-yi hui-i wen-hsien 遵義會議文獻 (Documents of the Tsun-yi Conference). Peking: Jen-min, 1985

Tsung Yuan-han 宗源翰. *I-ch'ing kuan wen-kuo chi* 頤情館聞過集 (Illustrious collection from the I-ch'ing Hall). 1877

Tsunoda Jun 角田順. *Manshū mondai to kokubō hōshin: Meiji kōki ni okeru kokubōkankyō no hendō* 満州問題と国防方針—明治後期における国防環境の変動 (The Manchurian problem and defence policies – change of defence conditions in the late Meiji era). Tokyo: Hara Shobō 原書房, 1967

Tsunoda Jun, ed., *Taiheiyō sensō e no michi* (The road to the Pacific war). See: Nihon kokusai seiji gakkai, ed., *Taiheiyō sensō* . . .

Tsurumi Yūsuke 鶴見祐輔. *Taiheiyo jidai* 太平洋時代 (The Pacific Era). Tokyo: Shinjiyūshugi kyōkai 新自由主義協会, 1929

Tsurumi Yūsuke 鶴見祐輔. *Gotō Shimpei* 後藤新平 (A biography of Gotō Shimpei). 4 vols. Tokyo: Gotō Shimpei Haku denki hensankai 後藤新平伯傳記編纂會, 1937–38

TSYC. See *Tang-shih yen-chiu*

Tu-li p'ing-lun 獨立評論 (Independent critic). Peking, May, 1932–

T'u-ti cheng-ts'e chung-yao wen-chien hui-pien 土地政策重要文件匯編 (A collection of important documents on land policy). n.p.: Chung-kung Chin-Ch'a-Chi chung-yang-chü hsuan-ch'uan pu 中共晉察冀中央局宣傳部, 1946

Tuchman, Barbara W. *Stilwell and the American experience in China, 1911–45*. New York: Macmillan, 1970

Tucker, Nancy Bernkopf. 'Nationalist China's decline and its impact on Sino-American relations, 1949–1950', in Dorothy Borg and Waldo Heinrichs, eds. *Uncertain years: Chinese-American relations, 1947–1950*, 131–71

Tucker, Nancy Bernkopf. *Patterns in the dust: Chinese-American relations and the recognition controversy, 1949–1950*. New York: Columbia University Press, 1983

Tung-fang tsa-chih 東方雜誌 (Eastern miscellany). Shanghai, 1904–48

Tung Hsiu-chia 董修甲. *Chung-kuo ti-fang tzu-chih wen-t'i* 中國地方自治問題 (The problem of China's local self-government). Shanghai: CP, 1937

Tung Shih-chin 董時進. 'K'ang-chan i-lai Ssu-ch'uan chih nung-yeh' 抗戰以來四川之農業 (Agriculture in Szechwan since the beginning of the war of resistance), in *Ssu-ch'uan ching-chi chi-k'an*, 1.1 (15 Feb. 1943) 48–52

T'ung-chi yueh-pao 統計月報 (Statistical monthly). Nanking, 1929–

T'ung-hsiang hsien-chih 桐鄉縣志 (Gazetteer of T'ung-hsiang county), comp. by Yen Ch'en 嚴辰, 1881

Tzu Jen 子任 [Mao Tse-tung]. 'Kuo-min-tang yu-p'ai fen-li ti yuan-yin chi ch'i tui-yü ko-ming ch'ien-t'u ti ying-hsiang' 國民黨右派分離的原因及其對於革命前途的影響 (The reasons underlying the secession of the KMT rightist faction and its implications for the future of the revolution). *Cheng-chih chou-pao*, 4 (10 Jan. 1926) 10–13

Tzu-liao hsuan-pien 資料選編. [Peking]: January 1967

Tzu-ming 自鳴 (pseud.). 'I-chiu-san-ssu nien Chung-kuo nung-ts'un chung ti ko-chung sao-tung feng-ch'ao i-lan-piao' 一九三四年中國農村中的各種騷動風潮一覽表 (List of the various disturbances stirred up in Chinese villages in 1934). *Chung-hua jih-pao* 中華日報 (China daily), 27 Feb.; 6, 13, 20, 27 March; 18, 25 April, 1935

Tzu-yu chung 自由鐘 (Freedom's bell). Berkeley, March 1965–

Uchida Tomoo 內田智雄. *Chūgoku nōson no bunke seido* 中國農村の分家制度 (The system of family division in rural China). Tokyo: Tokyo Daigaku shuppankai 1956

Ulyanovsky, R. A., ed. *The Comintern and the East*. Moscow: Progress Publishers, 1979

United States Department of State. *United States relations with China, with special reference to the period 1944–1949*. Washington, DC, 1949. Reissued with intro. and index by Lyman Van Slyke as *China white paper*. 2 vols. Stanford: Stanford University Press, 1967

United States Department of State. *Conference on the Limitation of Armament, Washington, November 12, 1921–February 6, 1922*. Washington, DC: Government Printing Office, 1922

United States Department of State. *Postwar foreign policy preparation, 1939–1945*

United States Department of State. *Foreign relations of the United States*. Various subtitles: *1945, the Far East, China*, vol. 7, pub. 8442 (1969); *1946, the Far East, China*, vol. 9, pub. 8561 (1972); *1946, the Far East, China*, vol. 10, pub. 8562 (1972); *1947, the Far East, China*, vol. 7, pub. 8613 (1972); *1948, the Far East, China*, vol. 7, pub. 8678 (1973); *1948, the Far East, China*, vol. 8, pub. 8583 (1973); *1949, the Far East, China*, vol. 8, pub. 8886 (1978); *1949, the Far East, China*, vol. 9, pub. 8774 (1974). All published Washington, DC: US Government Printing Office

United States War Department. See Van Slyke, Lyman

United States War Department, Military Intelligence Division. 'The Chinese Communist movement', 1945, in *Institute of Pacific Relations, hearings before the subcommittee to investigate the administration of the Internal Security Act and other internal security laws of the Committee on the Judiciary*. United States Senate, 82nd Congress, 1951–2

USDS. United States, Department of State Archives

Usui Katsumi 臼井勝美. *Nihon to Chūgoku – Taishō jidai* 日本と中国―大正時代 (Japan and China – the Taishō era). Tokyo: Hara shobō 原書房, 1972

Usui Katsumi. *Manshū jihen* 満州事変 (The Manchurian incident). Tokyo: Chūō Kōronsha 中央公論社, 1974

Van Slyke, Lyman P. *Enemies and friends: the united front in Chinese Communist history*. Stanford: Stanford University Press, 1967

Van Slyke, Lyman P., ed. *The Chinese Communist movement: a report of the United States War Department, July 1945*. Report prepared by the Military Intelligence Division. 'Originally published in 1952...as an appendix to official transcript of the 1951 Senate hearings on the Institute of Pacific Relations.' Stanford: Stanford University Press, 1968

Van Slyke, Lyman P., ed. *Marshall's mission to China, December 1945–January 1947: the report and appended documents*. 2 vols. Arlington, Va.: University Publications of America, 1976

Varg, Paul A. *Missionaries, Chinese, and diplomats: the American Protestant missionary movement in China, 1890–1952*. Princeton: Princeton University Press, 1958

Varg, Paul A. *The closing of the door: Sino-American relations, 1936–1946*. East Lansing: Michigan State University Press, 1973

Vilar, Pierre. *La Catalogne dans l'Espagne moderne: recherches sur les fondements économiques des structures nationales*. 3 vols. Paris: SEVPEN, 1962

Vilar, Pierre. 'Mouvements paysans en Amérique latine', in XIIIème Congrès international des Sciences Historiques, *Enquête sur les mouvements paysans dans le monde contemporain, rapport général*, 76–96. Moscow: Éditions 'Nauka', 1970

Vincent, John Carter. See May, Gary

Vogel, Ezra. 'From friendship to comradeship'. *CQ* 21 (Jan. – Mar. 1965) 46–60

Vohra, Ranbir. *Lao She and the Chinese revolution*. Cambridge, Mass.: East Asian Research Center, Harvard University, 1974

von Richthofen, Ferdinand Paul Wilhelm. *Tagebücher aus China*. See Eihara Masao, trans., *Shina ryokō nikki*.

Wada Sei 和田清. *Chūgoku chihō jichi hattatsu shi* 中國地方自治發達史 (History of the development of local self-government in China). Tokyo: Kyūko shoin 汲古書院, 1975, a reprint of 1939 edn with new bibliography by Yamane Yukio 山根幸夫

Wagner, Rudolph G. *Reenacting the Heavenly vision: the role of religion in the Taiping Rebellion.* Berkeley: Center for Chinese Studies, University of California, 1984

Wakeman, Frederic, Jr. *History and will: philosophical perspectives of Mao Tse-tung's thought.* Berkeley: University of California Press, 1973

Wakeman, Frederic, Jr. *The fall of imperial China.* New York: The Free Press, 1975

Wakeman, Frederic, Jr. 'Rebellion and revolution: the study of popular movements in Chinese history'. *JAS* 36.2 (Feb. 1977) 201–37

Wakeman, Frederic, Jr. and Grant, Carolyn, eds. *Conflict and control in late imperial China.* Berkeley and Los Angeles: University of California Press, 1975

Wales, Nym (Snow, Helen Foster). *Red dust.* Stanford: Stanford University Press, 1952

Wallace, L. Ethel. *Hwa Nan College: the women's college of South China.* New York: United Board for Christian Colleges in China, 1956

Wallerstein, Immanuel. *The modern world-system: capitalist agriculture and the origins of the European world-economy in the sixteenth century.* New York: Academic Press, 1974

Walmsley, Lewis C. *West China Union University.* New York: United Board for Christian Higher Education in Asia, 1974

Walter, Georges and Hu Chi-Hsi. *Ils étaient cent mille: la Longue Marche, 1934–1935.* Paris: J. C. Lattes, 1982

Wan-hsien hsin-chih 完縣新志 (Wan county gazetteer) new edn, 1934

Wang Cheng. 'The Kuomintang: a sociological study of demoralization'. Stanford University, Ph.D. dissertation, 1953

Wang Chi-chen 王際真, ed. *Stories of China at war.* New York: Columbia University Press, 1947

Wang Chien-min 王健民. *Chung-kuo kung-ch'an-tang shih-kao* 中國共產黨史稿 (A draft history of the Chinese Communist Party). 3 vols. Taipei: Wang Chien-min, 1965

Wang, Erh-min. See Hao, Yen-p'ing

Wang Erh-min 王爾敏. *Chung-kuo chin-tai ssu-hsiang shih-lun* 中國近代思想史論 (On the history of modern Chinese thought). Taipei: Hua-shih ch'u-pan-she 華世出版社, 1977

Wang Fan-hsi 王凡西. *Chinese revolutionary: memoirs, 1919–1949,* trans. and with an intro. by Gregor Benton. Oxford, New York: Oxford University Press, 1980

Wang Feng-chieh 王鳳喈. *Chung-kuo chiao-yü-shih ta-kang* 中國教育史大綱 (An outline history of Chinese education). 2nd ed. Shanghai: CP, 1930

Wang Gungwu 王賡武. 'Early Ming relations with Southeast Asia: a background essay', in John K. Fairbank, ed. *The Chinese world order,* 34–62

Wang Hsi 汪熙. 'Lun wan-Ch'ing ti kuan-tu shang-pan' 論晚清的官督商辦 (On the system of official supervision and merchant management during the late Ch'ing). *Li-shih hsueh* (Historical study), 1 (1979) 95–124

Wang I-chün 王聿均. *Chung-Su wai-chiao ti hsu-mu – ts'ung Yu-lin tao Yueh-fei* 中蘇外交的序幕—從優林到越飛 (Prelude to Sino-Soviet foreign relations – from Yourin to Joffe). Taipei: IMH, 1963

Wang I-chün and Sun Pin 孫斌, eds. *Chu Chia-hua hsien-sheng yen-lun chi* 朱家驊先生言論集 (Dissertations of Dr Chu Chia-hua). *Shih-liao ts'ung-k'an* 史料叢刊 (Historical materials collection) no. 3. IMH, 1977

Wang Ming 王明 (Ch'en Shao-yü 陳紹禹). 'Chung-kuo hsien-chuang yü Chung-kung jen-wu' 中國現狀與中共任務 (The present situation of China and the tasks of the CCP). Speeches at the 13th plenum of the ECCI, Moscow, 1934

Wang Ming (Ch'en Shao-yü). *Wang Ming hsuan-chi* 王明選集 (Selected works). 4 vols. Tokyo: Kyūko shoin 汲古書院, 1973

Wang Ming. *Mao's betrayal*, trans. by Vic Schneierson. Moscow: Progress Publishers, 1979

Wang Shih-chieh. See K'o Shu-p'ing

Wang Shih-chieh 王世杰. *Education in China*. Shanghai: China United Press, 1935 (Ann Arbor: University Microfilms International, 1980)

Wang Shih-hsin 汪士信. 'Wo kuo shou-kung-yeh hang-hui ti ch'an-sheng, hsing-chih chi ch'i tso-yung' 我國手工業行會的產生性質及其作用 (The origin, nature and functions of handicraft guilds in China). *Ching-chi yen-chiu-so chi-k'an* 經濟研究所集刊 (Bulletin of the Institute of Economic Research), 2 (1981) 213–47

Wang Shu-huai 王樹槐. 'Ch'ing-mo Chiang-su ti-fang tzu-chih feng-ch'ao' 清末江蘇地方自治風潮 (Riots against local self-government in Kiangsu during the late Ch'ing period). *Chung-yung yen-chiu-yuan Chin-tai-shih yen-chiu-so chi-k'an*, 6 (June 1977) 313–27

Wang Shu-huai. 'Ch'ing-mo Min-ch'u Chiang-su sheng ti jen-k'ou fa-chan' 清末民初江蘇省的人口發展 (Population growth in Kiangsu province in the late Ch'ing and early Republic). *Li-shih hsueh-pao* (Bulletin of historical research), 7 (May 1979) 327–62

Wang Shu-huai. *Chung-kuo hsien-tai-hua ti ch'ü-yü yen-chiu: Chiang-su sheng, 1860–1916* 中國現代化的區域研究：江蘇省, 1860–1916 (Modernization in China, 1860–1916: a regional study of social, political and economic change in Kiangsu province). Taipei: IMH, 1984

Wang Shu-pai 汪澍白 and Chang Shen-heng 張慎恒. 'Ch'ing-nien Mao Tse-tung shih-chieh-kuan ti chuan-pien' 青年毛澤東世界觀的轉變 (The transformation in the world view of the young Mao Tse-tung). *LSYC* 5 (1980) 47–64

Wang Ssu-chih 王思治. 'Tsung-tsu chih-tu ch'ien-lun' 宗族制度淺論 (A brief discussion of the lineage system). *Ch'ing-shih lun-ts'ung*, 4 (1982) 152–78

Wang Tseng-ping 王增炳 and Yü Kang 余綱. *Ch'en Chia-keng hsing-hsueh chi* 陳嘉庚興學記 (Tan Kah Kee's promotion of learning). Fu-chien chiao-yü ch'u-pan-she 福建教育出版社, 1981

Wang Wen-t'ien 王文田 and others. *Chang Po-ling yü Nan-k'ai* 張伯苓與南開 (Chang Po-ling and Nankai). Taipei: Biographical Literature series no. 26, 1968

Wang Yao 王瑤. *Chung-kuo hsin wen-hsueh shih-kao* 中國新文學史稿 (A draft history of modern Chinese literature). 2 vols. Shanghai: Hsin-wen-i ch'u-pan-she 新文藝出版社, 1953

Wang Yeh-chien 王業鍵. *Land taxation in imperial China, 1750–1911*. Cambridge, Mass.: Harvard University Press, 1973

Wang, Y. C. (Yi Chu) 汪一駒. *Chinese intellectuals and the West, 1872–1949*. Chapel Hill: University of North Carolina Press, 1966

Wang Yin-yuan 王銀元. 'Ssu-ch'uan chan-shih nung-kung wen-t'i' 四川戰時農工問題 (The problem of farm labour during wartime in Szechwan). *Ssu-ch'uan ching-chi chi-k'an*, 2.3 (June 1944)

Wang Yin-yuan 汪蔭元. 'Ssu-ch'uan chan-shih wu-chia yü ko-chi jen-min chih kou-mai-li' 四川戰時物價與各級人民之購買力 (Prices and purchasing power in wartime Szechwan). *SCCC* 1.3 (15 June 1944) 262–5

Wang Yun-wu 王雲五. *T'an wang-shih* 談往事 (Reminiscences). Biographical Literature series no. 1, Taipei, 1970

Wang Yun-wu. *Shang-wu yin-shu-kuan yü hsin chiao-yü nien-p'u* 商務印書館與新教育年譜 (A chronology of the Commercial Press and the New Education). Taipei: Taiwan CP, 1973

Wartime China as seen by Westerners. See Price, Frank W.

Watson, Andrew, ed. *Mao Zedong and the political economy of the Border Region: a translation of Mao's 'Economic and financial problems'*. Cambridge: Cambridge University Press, 1980

Watson, James. 'Chinese kinship reconsidered: anthropological perspectives on historical research'. *CQ* 92 (Dec. 1982) 589–627

Watson, Rubie S. 'Class differences and affinal relations in South China'. *Man*, 16.4 (Dec. 1981) 593–615

Wedemeyer, Albert C. *Wedemeyer reports!* New York: Henry Holt, 1958

Wei Ch'ing-yuan 韋慶遠 and Wu Ch'i-yen 吳奇衍, 'Ch'ing-tai chu-ming huang-shang Fan-shih ti hsing-shuai' 清代著名皇商范氏的興衰 (The rise and fall of the Fan: a famous Ch'ing imperial merchant family). *Li-shih yen-chiu* (Historical research), 3 (1981) 127–44

Wei, William. 'The Kuomintang in Kiangsi: the suppression of the Communist bases, 1930–1934'. University of Michigan, Ph.D. dissertation, 1978

Weiss, Robert N. 'Flexibility in provincial government on the eve of the Taiping rebellion'. *CSWT* 4.3 (June 1980) 1–43

Wen-chi yueh-k'an 文季月刊 (Wen-chi monthly). Shanghai, June 1936–

Wen-hua chien-she 文化建設 (Cultural reconstruction). Shanghai, Oct. 1934–

Wen hui pao 文匯報. Shanghai, 1946–

Wen shih che 文史哲 (Literature, history and philosophy). Tsingtao, 1952–

Wen-shih tzu-liao hsuan-chi 文史資料選輯 (Selected literary-historical materials), published by the Chung-kuo jen-min cheng-chih hsieh-shang hui-i 中國人

民政治協商會議, Chinese People's Political Consultative Conference. Peking: 1960

West, Philip. *Yenching University and Sino-Western relations, 1916–1952.* Cambridge, Mass.: Harvard University Press, 1976

White, John Albert. *The diplomacy of the Russo-Japanese War.* Princeton: Princeton University Press, 1964

White, Theodore H. *In search of history.* New York: Harper and Row, 1979

White, Theodore H. See *Stilwell papers, The*

White, Theodore H. and Jacoby, Annalee. *Thunder out of China.* New York: William Sloane Associates, 1946

Whiting, Allen S. *Soviet policies in China, 1917–1924.* New York: Columbia University Press, 1954

Whitson, William W. with Hung Chen-hsia. *The Chinese high command: a history of Communist military politics, 1927–1971.* New York: Macmillan, 1973

Wiens, Mi Chu 居蜜. 'Lord and peasant: the sixteenth to the eighteenth century'. *Modern China,* 6.1 (Jan. 1980) 3–40

Wilber, C. K., ed. *The political economy of development and underdevelopment.* New York: Random House, 1973

Wilbur, C. Martin, and How, Julie Lien-ying, eds. *Documents on communism, nationalism, and Soviet advisers in China, 1918–1927: papers seized in the 1927 Peking raid.* New York: Columbia University Press, 1956; London: Octagon Books, 1972

Wilbur, C. Martin. 'The ashes of defeat'. *CQ* 18 (April–June 1964) 3–54

Wilbur, C. Martin. *Sun Yat-sen: frustrated patriot.* New York: Columbia University Press, 1976

Wilbur, C. Martin. 'The Nationalist Revolution: from Canton to Nanking, 1923–28'. *CHOC* 12.527–720

Wilbur, C. Martin. See Fogel, Joshua A.

Will, Pierre-Étienne. *Bureaucratie et famine en Chine au 18e siècle.* Paris: Mouton, 1980

Willmott, W. E., ed. *Economic organization in Chinese society.* Stanford: Stanford University Press, 1972

Willmott, W. E. ' "Review" of *The development of underdevelopment in China'.* *JAS* 41.1 (Nov. 1981) 113–15

Wilson, Dick. *The Long March, 1935: the epic of Chinese communism's survival.* New York: Viking Press; London: Hamilton, 1971

Wilson, Dick, ed. *Mao Tse-tung in the scales of history.* Cambridge: Cambridge University Press, 1977

Wilson, Dick. *When tigers fight: the story of the Sino-Japanese war, 1937–1945.* New York: Viking Press, 1982

Witke, Roxane. 'Transformation of attitudes toward women during the May Fourth era of modern China'. University of California, Berkeley, Ph.D. dissertation, 1970

Wittfogel, Karl A. 'The legend of "Maoism" '. *CQ* 1 (Jan.–March 1960) 72–86; 2 (April–June 1960) 16–34

Wittfogel, K. A. 'Some remarks on Mao's handling of concepts and problems of dialectics'. *Studies in Soviet thought,* 3.4 (Dec. 1963) 251–77

Wo I 我一. 'Lin-shih chiao-yü-hui jih-chi' 臨時教育會日記 (Diary of the Provisional Educational Conference), in Shu Hsin-ch'eng, *Chung-kuo chin-tai chiao-yü-shih tzu-liao,* 1.296–310.

Wolf, Arthur. 'Gods, ghosts and ancestors', in Arthur Wolf, ed. *Religion and ritual in Chinese society,* 131–82

Wolf, Arthur, ed. *Religion and ritual in Chinese society.* Stanford: Stanford University Press, 1974

Wolf, Eric R. *Peasant wars of the twentieth century.* New York: Harper & Row, 1969

Wolf, Margery. *Women and the family in rural Taiwan.* Stanford: Stanford University Press, 1972

Wolf, Margery and Witke, Roxane, eds. *Women in Chinese society.* Stanford: Stanford University Press, 1975

Womack, Brantly. *The foundations of Mao Tse-tung's political thought, 1917–1935.* Honolulu: The University Press of Hawaii, 1982

Wong, R. Bin. 'Food riots in the Qing dynasty'. *JAS* 41.4 (Aug. 1982) 767–88

Wong, R. Bin and Perdue, Peter C. 'Famine's foes in Ch'ing China'. *HJAS* 43.1 (June 1983) 291–332

Woodhead, H. G. W. See *China year book*

Wou, Odoric Y. K. 吳應銑 'The district magistrate profession in the early republican period: occupational recruitment, training and mobility'. *Modern Asian Studies,* 8.2 (April 1974) 217–45

Wright, Arthur. 'Introduction' in Étienne Balazs, *Chinese civilization and bureaucracy: variations on a theme*

Wright, Mary Clabaugh, ed. and intro. *China in revolution: the first phase, 1900–1913.* New Haven: Yale University Press, 1968. Note 'Introduction', 1–63

Wu Ch'i-yuan 伍啓元 *Yu chan-shih ching-chi tao p'ing-shih ching-chi* 由戰時經濟到平時經濟 (From a war economy to a peace economy). Shanghai: Ta-tung 大東, 1946

Wu Ch'i-yuan. 'Ts'ung ching-chi kuan-tien lun nei-chan wen-t'i' 從經濟觀點論內戰問題 (Talking about civil war problems from an economic viewpoint). *Kuan-ch'a,* 7 Sept. 1946, pp. 3–4

Wu-Ch'ing chen-chih 烏青鎮志 (Gazetteer of Wu and Ch'ing towns). 1936

Wu Hsiang-hsiang 吳相湘. *Ti-erh-tz'u Chung-Jih chan-cheng shih* 第二次中日戰爭史 (The second Sino-Japanese War). 2 vols. Taipei: Tsung-ho yueh-k'an 綜合月刊, 1973

Wu Hsiang-hsiang. 'Total strategy used by China and some major engagements in the Sino-Japanese War of 1935–1945', in Paul K. T. Sih, ed.

Nationalist China during the Sino-Japanese War, 1937–1945, 37–80

Wu Hsiang-hsiang. *Yen Yang-ch'u chuan* 晏陽初傳 (Biography of Yen Yang-ch'u). Taipei: Shih-pao Publishing Co., 1981

Wu Hwa-pao 吳華寶. 'Agricultural economy of Yung-loh Tien in Shensi province'. *Nankai Social and Economic Quarterly,* 9.1 (April 1936) 164–76

Wu-shih-erh chung wen-shih tzu-liao p'ien-mu fen-lei so-yin 五十二種文史資料篇目分類索引 (A topical index to 52 series of *Wen-shih tzu-liao*), comp. by the History Department of Futan University, Shanghai, 1982

Wu-shih-nien lai ti Chung-kuo. See P'an Kung-chan

Wu, Silas H. L. 吳秀良 *Communication and imperial control in China. Evolution of the palace memorial system, 1693–1735.* Cambridge, Mass.: Harvard University Press, 1970

Wu-ssu shih-ch'i ch'i-k'an chieh-shao 五四時期期刊介紹 (An introduction to the periodicals of the May Fourth period), ed. by the CCP Centre. 3 vols. Peking: Jen-min, 1958–9

Wu Ta-k'un 吳大琨. 'Tsui-chin Su-chou ti nung-min nao-huang feng-ch'ao' 最近蘇州的農民鬧荒風潮 (The recent disturbances among Soochow peasants due to poor harvests). *TFTC* 32.2 (16 Jan. 1935) 83–4

Wu Ta-yeh 吳大業. 'Shih-chieh ching-chi shuai-lo chung chih Chung-kuo' 世界經濟衰落中之中國 (China during world economic collapse), in Fang Hsien-t'ing, ed. *Chung-kuo ching-chi yen-chiu* (Studies of the Chinese economy). See 1.45–56

Wu, Tien-wei. *The Sian Incident: a pivotal point in modern Chinese history.* Ann Arbor: Center for Chinese Studies, University of Michigan, 1976

Wu Tien-wei. 'New materials on the Sian incident: a bibliographic review'. *Modern China,* 10.1 (Jan. 1984) 115–41

Wu Ting-ch'ang 吳鼎昌. *Hua-hsi hsien-pi cheng-hsu-chi* 花谿閒筆正續集 (Random notes at Hua-hsi). 2 vols. Taipei: Wen-hai 文海, n.d.

Wylie, Raymond F. *The emergence of Maoism: Mao Tse-tung, Ch'en Po-ta, and the search for Chinese theory, 1935–1945.* Stanford: Stanford University Press, 1980

Ya Hsien 瘂弦, ed. *Tai Wang-shu chüan* 戴望舒卷 (Collected works of Tai Wang-shu). Taipei: Hung-fan 洪範, 1970

Yamamoto Hideo 山本秀夫 and Noma Kiyoshi 野間清, comps. *Chūgoku nōson kakumei no tenkai* 中国農村革命の展開 (The development of the Chinese agrarian revolution). Tokyo: Ajia keizai shuppankai アジア経済出版会, 1972

Yamamoto Sumiko 山本澄子. *Chūgoku Kirisuto kyōshi kenkyū* 中国キリスト教史研究 (Studies on the history of Christianity in China). Tokyo: Tokyo Daigaku shuppankai, 1972

Yang, C. K. 楊慶堃 *The Chinese family in the Communist revolution.* Cambridge, Mass.: MIT Press, 1959

Yang, C. K. *A Chinese village in early Communist transition.* Cambridge, Mass.: MIT Press, 1959

Yang, C. K. *Religion in Chinese society*. Berkeley, Los Angeles: University of California Press, 1961

Yang, C. K. 'Some preliminary statistical patterns of mass actions in nine-teenth-century China', in Frederic Wakeman Jr. and Carolyn Grant, eds. *Conflict and control in late imperial China*, 174–210

Yang, Gladys, ed. and trans. *Silent China: selected writings of Lu Xun*. Oxford: Oxford University Press, 1973

Yang Liang-kung 楊亮功. *Tsao-ch'i san-shih-nien ti chiao-hsueh sheng-huo* 早期三十年的教學生活 (My life as an educator: the first 30 years). Biographical Literature Series no. 98. Taipei: Chuan-chi wen-hsueh, 1980

Yang, Martin M. C. 楊懋春 *Chinese social structure: a historical study*. Taipei: The National Book Co., 1969

Yang, Winston L. Y. and Mao, Nathan K., eds. *Modern Chinese fiction: a guide to its study and appreciation*. Boston: G. K. Hall, 1981

Yao Hsin-nung 姚莘農. *The malice of empire*, trans. of *Ch'ing kung yüan* 清宮怨 and intro. by Jeremy Ingalls. Berkeley: University of California Press, 1970

Yeh Hsien-en 葉顯恩. *Ming Ch'ing Hui-chou nung-ts'un she-hui yü tien-p'u chih* 明清徽州農村社會與佃僕制 (Hui-chou rural society in the Ming and Ch'ing and the system of semi-free field servants). An-hui: Jen-min, 1983

Yeh Wen-hsin 葉文心. 'The alienated academy: higher education in Republican China'. University of California, Berkeley, Ph.D. dissertation, 1984

Yen Chung-p'ing 嚴中平 *et al.*, comps. *Chung-kuo chin-tai ching-chi-shih t'ung-chi tzu-liao hsuan-chi* 中國近代經濟史統計資料選輯 (Selected statistical materials on the economic history of modern China). Peking: K'o-hsueh ch'u-pan-she 科學出版社, 1955

Yen Hsi-ta 彥悉達. 'Ching-chi wei-chi yü kuan-liao tzu-pen' 經濟危機與官僚資本 (The economic crisis and bureaucratic capital). *Ching-chi chou-pao* 經濟週報 4.6 (6 Feb. 1947) 9–11

Yen Yuan 顏元. 'Ts'un hsueh' 存學, pp. 40–106 in Yen Yuan, *Ssu ts'un pien* 四存編. Peking: Ku-chi ch'u-pan-she, 古籍出版社, 1957

Yin Chung-ts'ai 尹仲材, ed. *Chai-ch'eng ts'un chih* 翟城村志 (Gazetteer of Chai-ch'eng village). 1925. Taipei reprint, 1968

Yip, Ka-che. 'Nationalism and revolution: the nature and causes of student activism in the 1920s', in F. Gilbert Chan and Thomas H. Etzold, eds. *China in the 1920s: nationalism and revolution*, 94–107

Yip, Ka-che. *Religion, nationalism and Chinese students: the anti-Christian movement of 1922–1927*. Bellingham: Center for East Asian Studies, Western Washington University, 1980

Young, Arthur N. *China and the helping hand, 1937–1945*. Cambridge, Mass.: Harvard University Press, 1963

Young, Arthur N. *China's wartime finance and inflation, 1937–1945*. Cambridge, Mass.: Harvard University Press, 1965

Young, Arthur N. *China's nation-building effort, 1927–1937: the financial and economic record.* Stanford: Hoover Institution Press, 1971

Young, Ernest P. *The presidency of Yuan Shih-k'ai: liberalism and dictatorship in early Republican China.* Ann Arbor: University of Michigan Press, 1977

Young, Ernest P. 'Chinese leaders and Japanese aid in the early Republic', in Akira Iriye, ed. *The Chinese and the Japanese*, 124–39

Young, Ernest P. 'Politics in the aftermath of revolution: the era of Yuan Shih-k'ai, 1912–16'. *CHOC* 12.208–55

Young, John. *The research activities of the South Manchurian Railway Company, 1907–1945: a history and bibliography.* New York: East Asian Institute, Columbia University, 1966

Yu, George T. *Party politics in Republican China: the Kuomintang, 1912–1924.* Berkeley: University of California Press, 1966

Yü Ch'ang-lin 喻長霖. 'Ching-shih ta-hsueh-t'ang yen-ko lueh' 京師大學堂沿革略 (Brief history of Peking University), in Shu Hsin-ch'ing, *Chung-kuo chin-tai chiao-yü-shih tzu-liao*, 159–62

Yü Chi-nan 于吉楠. *Chang Kuo-t'ao ho 'Wo-ti hui-i'* 張國燾和《我的回憶》 (Chang Kuo-t'ao and My Recollections). Chengtu: Jen-min, 1982

Yü-O-Wan-Kan ssu-sheng chih tsu-tien chih-tu 豫鄂皖贛四省之租佃制度 (The tenant system in the four provinces of Honan, Hupei, Anhwei and Kiangsi). Nanking: Chin-ling ta-hsueh 金陵大學, 1936

Yü, P. K. 余秉權, in collaboration with Knezevic, Ingeborg, Cheng, James and Chi, Ping-feng, eds. *Research materials on twentieth-century China: an annotated list of CCRM publications.* Washington, DC: Center for Chinese Research Materials, Association of Research Libraries, 1975

Yü Ts'ai-yu 余才友. 'T'an chin-t'ien ti hsueh-sheng' 談今天的學生 (Discussing today's students). *Kuan-ch'a*, 24 April 1948, pp. 17–18

Yuan, Cheng. *T. L. Yuan: a tribute.* See *Ssu-i lu*

Yuan T'ung-li. See *Ssu-i lu: Yuan Shou-ho hsien-sheng chi-nien ts'e* 思憶錄: 袁守和先生紀念冊 (Memorial volume on Mr Yuan Shou-ho [T. L. Yuan]). Taipei: CP, 1968

Yung Lung-kuei 勇龍桂. 'Chiu-chi chan-shih kung-yeh ti chi-pen t'u-ching' 救濟戰時工業的基本途徑 (Fundamental means of rescuing the wartime industry). *Chung-kuo kung-yeh*, 25 (Mar. 1944) 8–9

Zelin, Madeline. '*Huo-hao kuei-kung*: rationalizing fiscal reform and its limitations in eighteenth-century China'. University of California, Berkeley, Ph.D. dissertation, 1979

Zen, H. C. See Jen, Hung-chün

CONVERSION TABLE

Pinyin to Wade-Giles

Pinyin	Wade-Giles	Pinyin	Wade-Giles	Pinyin	Wade-Giles	Pinyin	Wade-Giles
a	a	chu	ch'u	er	erh	hou	hou
ai	ai	chuai	ch'uai			hu	hu
an	an	chuan	ch'uan	fa	fa	hua	hua
ang	ang	chuang	ch'uang	fan	fan	huan	huan
ao	ao	chui	ch'ui	fang	fang	huang	huang
		chun	ch'un	fei	fei	hui	hui
ba	pa	chuo	ch'o	fen	fen	hun	hun
bai	pai	ci	tz'u	feng	feng	huo	huo
ban	pan	cong	ts'ung	fo	fo		
bang	pang	cou	ts'ou	fou	fou	ji	chi
bao	pao	cu	ts'u	fu	fu	jia	chia
bei	pei	cuan	ts'uan			jian	chien
ben	pen	cui	ts'ui	ga	ka	jiang	chiang
beng	peng	cun	ts'un	gai	kai	jiao	chiao
bi	pi	cuo	ts'o	gan	kan	jie	chieh
bian	pien			gang	kang	jin	chin
biao	piao	da	ta	gao	kao	jing	ching
bie	pieh	dai	tai	ge	ke, ko	jiong	chiung
bin	pin	dan	tan	gei	kei	jiu	chiu
bing	ping	dang	tang	gen	ken	ju	chü
bo	po	dao	tao	geng	keng	juan	chüan
bu	pu	de	te	gong	kung	jue	chüeh
		dei	tei	gou	kou	jun	chün
ca	ts'a	deng	teng	gu	ku		
cai	ts'ai	di	ti	gua	kua	ka	k'a
can	ts'an	dian	tien	guai	kuai	kai	k'ai
cang	ts'ang	diao	tiao	guan	kuan	kan	k'an
cao	ts'ao	die	tieh	guang	kuang	kang	k'ang
ce	ts'e	ding	ting	gui	kuei	kao	k'ao
cen	ts'en	diu	tiu	gun	kun	ke	k'o
ceng	ts'eng	dong	tung	guo	kuo	ken	k'en
cha	ch'a	dou	tou			keng	k'eng
chai	ch'ai	du	tu	ha	ha	kong	k'ung
chan	ch'an	duan	tuan	hai	hai	kou	k'ou
chang	ch'ang	dui	tui	han	han	ku	k'u
chao	ch'ao	dun	tun	hang	hang	kua	k'ua
che	ch'e	duo	to	hao	hao	kuai	k'uai
chen	ch'en			he	ho, he	kuan	k'uan
cheng	ch'eng	e	o	hei	hei	kuang	k'uang
chi	ch'ih	ei	ei	hen	hen	kui	k'uei
chong	ch'ung	en	en	heng	heng	kun	k'un
chou	ch'ou	eng	eng	hong	hung	kuo	k'uo

Pinyin	Wade-Giles	Pinyin	Wade-Giles	Pinyin	Wade-Giles	Pinyin	Wade-Giles
la	la	ni	ni	re	je	ti	t'i
lai	lai	nian	nien	ren	jen	tian	t'ien
lan	lan	niang	niang	reng	jeng	tiao	t'iao
lang	lang	niao	niao	ri	jih	tie	t'ieh
lao	lao	nie	nieh	rong	jung	ting	t'ing
le	le	nin	nin	rou	jou	tong	t'ung
lei	lei	ning	ning	ru	ju	tou	t'ou
leng	leng	niu	niu	ruan	juan	tu	t'u
li	li	nong	nung	rui	jui	tuan	t'uan
lia	lia	nou	nou	run	jun	tui	t'ui
lian	lien	nu	nu	ruo	jo	tun	t'un
liang	liang	nü	nü			tuo	t'o
liao	liao	nuan	nuan	sa	sa		
lie	lieh	nüe	nueh	sai	sai	wa	wa
lin	lin	nuo	no	san	san	wai	wai
ling	ling			sang	sang	wan	wan
liu	liu	o	o	sao	sao	wang	wang
lo	lo	ou	ou	se	se	wei	wei
long	lung			sen	sen	wen	wen
lou	lou	pa	p'a	seng	seng	weng	weng
lu	lu	pai	p'ai	sha	sha	wo	wo
luan	luan	pan	p'an	shai	shai	wu	wu
lun	lun	pang	p'ang	shan	shan		
luo	lo	pao	p'ao	shang	shang	xi	hsi
lü	lü	pei	p'ei	shao	shao	xia	hsia
lüe	lueh	pen	p'en	she	she	xian	hsien
		peng	p'eng	shei	shei	xiang	hsiang
ma	ma	pi	p'i	shen	shen	xiao	hsiao
mai	mai	pian	p'ien	sheng	sheng	xie	hsieh
man	man	piao	p'iao	shi	shih	xin	hsin
mang	mang	pie	p'ieh	shou	shou	xing	hsing
mao	mao	pin	p'in	shu	shu	xiong	hsiung
mei	mei	ping	p'ing	shua	shua	xiu	hsiu
men	men	po	p'o	shuai	shuai	xu	hsu
meng	meng	pou	p'ou	shuan	shuan	xuan	hsuan
mi	mi	pu	p'u	shuang	shuang	xue	hsueh
mian	mien			shui	shui	xun	hsun
miao	miao	qi	ch'i	shun	shun		
mie	mieh	qia	ch'ia	shuo	shuo	ya	ya
min	min	qian	ch'ien	si	szu, ssu	yan	yen
ming	ming	qiang	ch'iang	song	sung	yang	yang
miu	miu	qiao	ch'iao	sou	sou	yao	yao
mo	mo	qie	ch'ieh	su	su	ye	yeh
mou	mou	qin	ch'in	suan	suan	yi	i
mu	mu	qing	ch'ing	sui	sui	yin	yin
		qiong	ch'iung	sun	sun	ying	ying
na	na	qiu	ch'iu	suo	so	yong	yung
nai	nai	qu	ch'ü			you	yu
nan	nan	quan	ch'üan	ta	t'a	yu	yü
nang	nang	que	ch'üeh	tai	t'ai	yuan	yuan
nao	nao	qun	ch'ün	tan	t'an	yue	yueh
ne	ne			tang	t'ang	yun	yun
nei	nei	ran	jan	tao	t'ao		
nen	nen	rang	jang	te	t'e	za	tsa
neng	neng	rao	jao	teng	t'eng	zai	tsai

Pinyin	Wade-Giles	Pinyin	Wade-Giles	Pinyin	Wade-Giles	Pinyin	Wade-Giles
zan	tsan	zhan	chan	zhou	chou	zi	tzu
zang	tsang	zhang	chang	zhu	chu	zong	tsung
zao	tsao	zhao	chao	zhua	chua	zou	tsou
ze	tse	zhe	che	zhuai	chuai	zu	tsu
zei	tsei	zhei	chei	zhuan	chuan	zuan	tsuan
zen	tsen	zhen	chen	zhuang	chuang	zui	tsui
zeng	tseng	zheng	cheng	zhui	chui	zun	tsun
zha	cha	zhi	chih	zhun	chun	zuo	tso
zhai	chai	zhong	chung	zhuo	cho		

GLOSSARY-INDEX

For some names cited in Western-language sources we have been unable to ascertain the Chinese characters, not for want of trying. Characters for some well-known names, such as those of provinces, have on the other hand been deemed unnecessary in this glossary.

CONTENTS OF VOLUME 12